ENNSYLVANIA

40   50 MI

80 KM

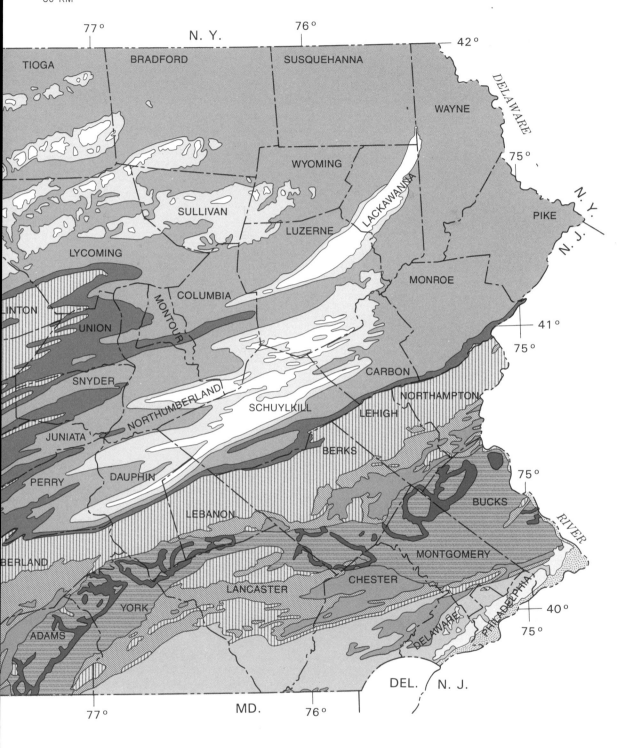

77°   N. Y.   76°   42°

TIOGA   BRADFORD   SUSQUEHANNA

WAYNE   DELAWARE

75°

WYOMING   N. Y.   N. J.

SULLIVAN   LACKAWANNA   PIKE

LYCOMING   LUZERNE   MONROE

LINTON   COLUMBIA   41°

MONTOUR   75°

UNION

SNYDER   CARBON

NORTHUMBERLAND   SCHUYLKILL   NORTHAMPTON

JUNIATA   LEHIGH

PERRY   BERKS   75°

DAUPHIN   BUCKS

LEBANON   RIVER

BERLAND   MONTGOMERY

LANCASTER   CHESTER

YORK   PHILADELPHIA   40°

ADAMS   DELAWARE   75°

DEL.   N. J.

77°   MD.   76°

 VONIAN
stone, gray shale,
e, limestone, and

 SILURIAN
Red and gray sandstone,
conglomerate, shale, and
limestone.

 ORDOVICIAN
Shale, limestone, dolomite,
and sandstone.

 CAMBRIAN
Limestone, dolomite, sandstone, shale, quartzite, and
phyllite.

 LOWER PALEOZOIC
Metamorphic rocks (meta-
sedimentary and meta-
igneous); schist, gneiss,
quartzite, serpentine, slate,
and marble.

 PRECAMBRIAN
Gneiss, granite, anortho-
site, metadiabase, meta-
basalt, metarhyolite, and
marble.

DATE	ISSUED TO

THE GEOLOGY
OF
PENNSYLVANIA

THE GEOLOGY

COMMONWEALTH OF PENNSYLVANIA
Mark Schweiker, Governor
DEPARTMENT OF
CONSERVATION AND NATURAL RESOURCES
John C. Oliver, Secretary
BUREAU OF TOPOGRAPHIC AND GEOLOGIC SURVEY
Jay B. Parrish, Director

OF PENNSYLVANIA

Edited by
Charles H. Shultz
Department of Geology
Slippery Rock University

Published by

**PENNSYLVANIA
GEOLOGICAL SURVEY**
Harrisburg

**PITTSBURGH
GEOLOGICAL SOCIETY**
Pittsburgh

1999

Reprinted 2002

FRONT COVER: Vista southeastward from Hyner View, Hyner Run State Park, Clinton County, showing accordant ridges in the Appalachian Plateaus province. The West Branch Susquehanna River flows 1,300 feet below the overlook. Photograph by G. Jeffrey Hoch, 1991.

BACK COVER: View looking northeastward over part of the Ridge and Valley province in Huntingdon County. Flooded meanders of Raystown Lake on the Raystown Branch Juniata River are in the foreground, and Terrace Mountain, the northwest flank of the Broad Top synclinorium, is in the upper right. Photograph by G. Jeffrey Hoch, 1991.

Printed in the Commonwealth of Pennsylvania, United States of America, on acid-free, recycled paper.

ISBN 0–8182–0227–0

Additional copies of this publication may be purchased from the State Bookstore, Commonwealth Keystone Building, 400 North Street, Harrisburg, PA 17120–0053, telephone 717–787–5109.

Composed in Agfa CG Times using Quark Xpress, v 3.32.

Technical editing, drafting, typesetting, and layout were done by staff of the Pennsylvania Bureau of Topographic and Geologic Survey, Department of Conservation and Natural Resources. The production supervisor was Christine E. Miles. The technical editors were Caron E. O'Neil, Christine E. Miles, Anne B. Lutz, and John H. Barnes. The drafters were James H. Dolimpio and John G. Kuchinski. Typesetting was by the editorial staff. Layout was by Christine E. Miles with assistance from the editorial staff. General design guidelines were by the Pittsburgh Geological Society; design of 16-page full-color section was by G. Jeffrey Hoch.

Second printing on Finch Casablanca Opaque paper by Pemcor, Inc., Lancaster, Pa. Bound by Bindery Associates, Inc., Lancaster, Pa.

Library of Congress Cataloging-in-Publication Data

The geology of Pennsylvania / edited by Charles H. Shultz.
        p.   cm. -- (Special publication ; 1)
    Includes bibliographical references (p.   -   ) and index.
    ISBN 0-8182-0227-0 (hardcover : acid-free paper)
    1. Geology--Pennsylvania.   I. Shultz, Charles H. (Charles High),
1936-   . II. Geological Survey of Pennsylvania.   III. Pittsburgh
Geological Society.   IV. Series: Special publication (Geological
Survey of Pennsylvania) ; 1.
    QE157.G413 1999   98-28890
    557.48--dc21   CIP

FOREWORD

More than 160 years ago, the first geologic map devoted to a single state of the United States was published in Philadelphia, then the seat of the developing science of geology in the United States. Since then, geology has contributed greatly to Pennsylvania's economy and growth through the investigation and development of Pennsylvania's bounteous natural earth resources.

The Geology of Pennsylvania was conceived, organized, and managed by the Pittsburgh Geological Society and was written by professional geologists in the state and federal governments, Pennsylvania colleges and universities, and Pennsylvania private industry. It is jointly published by the Department of Conservation and Natural Resources' Bureau of Topographic and Geologic Survey and the Pittsburgh Geological Society.

This work includes practical applications and guidance for developing water, energy, and other resources; and for protecting Pennsylvanians and their property from hazards such as landslides, flooding, and land subsidence. It is also a valuable reference for students and geologic practitioners alike. On behalf of all Pennsylvanians, I commend the editor, authors, and the Pittsburgh Geological Society for their efforts in producing this valuable reference book for the benefit of all Pennsylvania citizens.

John C. Oliver
Secretary
Department of Conservation and
Natural Resources

FOREWORD

In 1858, Henry Rogers, the first state geologist of Pennsylvania, summarized the geology of Pennsylvania in two very large volumes accompanied by wall-sized geologic maps and plates. Although Rogers was the credited author, the 1858 edition of *The Geology of Pennsylvania* was the product of a group of scientists. Likewise, this second summary, published 140 years later, is a group effort.

The Pittsburgh Geological Society, organizers of the present volume, did not have to select and train geologists as did Rogers. Nor did they follow Rogers' 1858 format, which was to include all that was known about the Commonwealth's geology in one publication and to prepare a bedrock map of the state. A new bedrock map was not prepared because the Bureau of Topographic and Geologic Survey had published one in 1980.

In contrast to the first *The Geology of Pennsylvania*, in which all style and controversy were resolved by one author, the new volume comprises the writing styles, understanding, and opinions of many authors. The effort of compression of current geological understanding into a small space was not easy for all authors.

A thorough reading of each chapter was conducted by reviewers recruited by the Pittsburgh Geological Society. In addition, all chapters and introductory material were reviewed by staff of the Survey. The latter reviewers were additionally assigned the task of ensuring that factual errors were absent, insofar as they knew them, and that the writing was directed to the intended audience. However, each author had freedom to express personal ideas, subject to reviewers' suggestions for improvement or clarification. Thus, there is variation in interpretation and concepts expressed in groups of chapters.

The Geology of Pennsylvania project was planned by the Pittsburgh Geological Society to be a product of the community of geologists knowledgeable about Pennsylvania. The Survey, as part of that community, supported the project from its inception. When a commercial publisher could not be found, the Survey agreed to become the publisher and marketer of the volume through its official publication procedures. Survey support was also provided through writing individual chapters. Credit for the project is thus due first to the Pittsburgh Geological Society as originator and organizer, and secondarily to the individual authors, who were the creative force.

Many authors deserve special appreciation for prompt manuscript preparation and revision. Special recognition is due to the editor, Charles H. Shultz, and *The Geology of Pennsylvania* Committee, who persevered to the completion.

We do not disclaim anything printed herein. As individual geologists, we may not agree with all interpretations and conclusions, but that is the nature of our science. Rather, we agree that much geologic research is yet to be done as our scientific capabilities improve. Indeed, we of the Survey have benefited greatly from this project, because it allows us to better perform our role of assisting the public and other government agencies by providing geologic information and advice. The Survey staff could not have prepared this volume by ourselves; we are too few in number. And, no one geologist of the Survey is competent, as was Henry Rogers, to summarize all now known about our state's complex geology.

This edition of *The Geology of Pennsylvania* will be supplemented in part or in whole, as was the 1858 edition, through additional research and resolution of differing opinions. The dynamic nature of our earth and our science demands no less. Until supplemented, this volume will be a constant and valuable reference for all geologists, especially those new to Pennsylvania who must learn about our complex geology in order to apply the information in resolving environmental and resource issues for public benefit.

Donald M. Hoskins
Ninth State Geologist

FOREWORD

In the history of any professional society, there are monumental achievements that stand out far and above the year-to-year functions and events of that society. For the past several years, *The Geology of Pennsylvania* Committee has been working feverishly toward the completion of this volume. The Pittsburgh Geological Society is proud to have been responsible for the inception of this idea and of having so many of its members involved in the committee's manuscript contributions. The society is equally proud of its partner in publication, the Bureau of Topographic and Geologic Survey, many of whose geologists were authors or reviewers, or contributors to the volume in other important ways.

Founded in 1945 by foresighted geological leaders of this area, the Pittsburgh Geological Society has always strived to serve its membership in ways that would strengthen its professionalism, stimulate geological thought, and disseminate geological knowledge. Just as Pennsylvania is rich in diverse cultures, arts, and medicine, it is equally endowed with a strong history of industry directly related to the abundant natural resources found in the variety of rock types of the state. Coal, oil, natural gas, glass sands, ores, and many other resources are important factors in the economic prosperity of this region. The interpretation and understanding of what these rocks tell us has, in part, led to the strong role of geology in Pennsylvania's industries, universities, and government.

In addition to the abundant mineral wealth of the state, the growth of Pennsylvania has been heavily dependent on the expertise of geologists for the construction of highways, dams, and urban structures. A geologist's understanding of near-surface conditions is necessary to protect the environment from hazardous materials fluid migration into our groundwater systems.

Increasingly, geology is being viewed as an integral body of knowledge with which everyone should have at least a general familiarity. The emphasis by schools, geological surveys, and local geological societies, such as the Pittsburgh Geological Society, is to educate and inform the public concerning the importance of this science to the future health and well-being of all Pennsylvanians.

This volume, therefore, represents the first comprehensive attempt to summarize, in detail, the geology of Pennsylvania. Many thousands of geologists and nongeologists alike will benefit from the exhaustive contents of *The Geology of Pennsylvania*. Congratulations to all involved in this outstanding achievement.

Robert M. Burger
President, 1997–98
Pittsburgh Geological Society

PREFACE AND ACKNOWLEDGMENTS

The purpose of this book was to bring together, under one cover from widely scattered and diverse sources, everything we thought we knew about the geology of Pennsylvania in the 1980's. In short, coverage was to be current and encyclopedic. That, it turns out, was a very slippery goal. It has taken more than 15 years to produce this book. Geologic research in Pennsylvania is an active endeavor. Consequently, what was written in 1985 may no longer be completely valid at the time of this printing. This is the nature of a dynamic field of inquiry.

The book is written with the professional geologist in mind, but it is also written for one who is unfamiliar with Pennsylvania's geology and geography. To the extent possible, it is written in straightforward English with a minimum of specialized nomenclature. The intent is that the volume will serve a broad audience, including, among others, college students, secondary-school science teachers, and interested nongeologists in industry, commerce, and government. Time will measure the success of our efforts.

Each chapter is a well-illustrated and brief summary of the essentials of the topic with references to the pertinent literature. Almost all chapters end with a summary of some unresolved problems plus a list of recommended reading that the reader may pursue for further details. As an aid to readers, it is highly recommended that reference be made to two important publications of the Bureau of Topographic and Geologic Survey. These are Map 1, *Geologic Map of Pennsylvania* (Berg and others, 1980), and General Geology Report 75, *Stratigraphic Correlation Chart of Pennsylvania* (Berg and others, 1993).

This project was conceived by Reginald ("Pete") Briggs. He convinced the Pittsburgh Geological Society to adopt and develop his dream. The first halting and naive steps began in 1983 with the formation of the ad hoc *The Geology of Pennsylvania* Committee, with Briggs as its leader. The first task of the Committee was to find an editor, and from tough competition in the summer of 1983, Charles H. Shultz was selected. The makeup of the Committee changed somewhat with passing years, but carrying the project through to its successful conclusion were Helen L. Delano, Jane L. Freedman, Paul W. Garrett, Jr., Stephen G. McGuire, and Donald W. Watson, in addition to Shultz and Briggs. This was a thoughtful and cohesive working group, altogether excellent, without whose unwavering dedication the project might well have become unravelled. Thomas W. Angerman acted with the Committee in fund raising. Also associated for limited times were Susan M. Carulli, Patrick M. Findle, and Michael Forth.

Early on, Arthur A. Socolow, then State Geologist and Director of the Bureau of Topographic and Geologic Survey (now retired), agreed to copublish the volume with the Society. His successor, Donald M. Hoskins, has strongly supported our efforts and encouraged us to proceed. We sincerely thank them both. By virtue of this relationship, Christine E. Miles, Chief of the Survey's Geologic and Geographic Information Services Division, became an associate of the Committee, and her efforts also are sincerely acknowledged.

Any endeavor of this magnitude requires the help, cooperation, and contributions of hundreds of individuals. Managing, directing, and coordinating such a large group was a giant task, taking much longer than originally anticipated, and now has consumed more than a decade. Contributions have been made by 90 authors, who are about equally distributed among academia, industry, and government, the latter equally split between state and federal. Others involved include reviewers, assistant editors, secretaries, financial contributors, photographers, students in the Department of Geology at Slippery Rock University, the Committee and other members of the Pittsburgh Geological Society, and the staff of the Bureau of Topographic and Geologic Survey. All have volunteered their time, expertise, effort, or money, dedicated to fulfillment of this dream and toward excellence in presentation of the current thought on the geology of the Commonwealth of Pennsylvania. While of inadequate compensation, we sincerely thank all persons who have helped in the creation of this volume.

The individual writers are recognized at the beginning of each writing unit, but think for a moment of all the secretaries, illustrators, photographers, and others who helped make each manuscript a reality. In many cases, the institutions, corporations, government agencies, and others who employ the writers have allowed regular working time as well as other resources to be used toward this effort. We thank them collectively for their support.

Of the 95 professionals who volunteered their time to serve as reviewers, we wish to recognize six individuals in particular who performed in outstanding fashion. In all cases, they agreed to do multiple reviews (up to 10 in one case), and provided particularly insightful, effective, and helpful critiques. They are Mary Rose Cassa, Jack B. Epstein, John A. Harper, Carla A. Kertis, David B. MacLachlan, and Robert C. Smith, II. Others who have served are as follows:

Thomas B. Alexander; Roddy V. Amenta; John A. Ames; Thomas H. Anderson; John H. Barnes; Robert L. Bates; Robert M. Beall; Thomas M. Berg; Samuel W. Berkheiser, Jr.; Edward C. Beutner; George K. Biemesderfer; Michael Bikerman; William A. Bragonier; William R. Brice; Reginald P. Briggs; Patricia F. Buis; Kent O. Bushnell.

William F. Chapman; Emery T. Cleaves; Craig B. Clemmens; Edward Cotter; Charles S. Cubbison; Helen L. Delano; Joseph W. Denardo; Maurice Deul; Wallace de Witt; Clifford H. Dodge; Jack D. Donahue; Nancy T. Duerring; Mark Evans; Rodger T. Faill; Carol Faul; John L. Fauth; John W. Felbinger; Patrick M. Findle; Michael Forth; Jane L. Freedman.

G. Robert Ganis; Paul W. Garrett, Jr.; Ernest F. Giovannitti; Albert D. Glover; Richard E. Gray; Mary Ann Gross; Samuel S. Harrison; Dennis S. Hodge; Donald T. Hoff; Carl Hoover; Donald M. Hoskins; Jon D. Inners; Uldis Kaktins; James F. Knight; William E. Kochanov; Edwin F. Koppe.

Christopher D. Laughrey; Wayne S. Leeper; Leonard J. Lentz; Edward G. Lidiak; Keith R. Lucas; Sherwood S. Lutz; Peter T. Lyttle; Antonette K. Markowski; Mark A. McConaughy; Thomas A. McElroy; Robert Metzger;

Michael E. Moore; Ronald M. Morosky; Judith E. Neelan; Michael O'Driscoll; Caron E. O'Neil.

Donald Partridge; James G. Phillips; John S. Pomeroy; Garry L. Price; Nicholas M. Ratcliffe; John Rodgers; Charles K. Scharnberger; Arthur P. Schultz; William D. Sevon; James R. Shaulis; Viktoras W. Skema; Arthur A. Socolow; Glenn H. Thompson, Jr.; Daniel Threlfall; David W. Valentino; Matthew E. Vavro; Frank J. Vento.

Donald W. Watson; Eugene G. Williams; J. Peter Wilshusen; Charles R. Wood; Donald L. Woodrow; Dawna Yannacci.

In addition to writing and reviewing, others have provided valuable services essential to the success of the project. In particular, the editor recognizes the word-processing skills and cogent advice provided by Sharon G. Isacco, secretary to the Department of Geology at Slippery Rock University. She typed many hundreds of letters, photocopied thousands of pages, and in general was indispensable to whatever success the editor has achieved. Thomas M. Berg, former Chief of the Geologic Mapping Division of the Bureau of Topographic and Geologic Survey (State Geologist of Ohio since March 1989) was a constant source of advice and encouragement, especially during the dark early days of the project. He provided excellent liaison between the Survey and the Pittsburgh Geological Society, and made numerous positive suggestions toward the solution of seemingly insolvable problems. On the financial side, Pauline F. Silsley, of Geomega, Inc., set up and maintained standard account books for the project. She typed the many requests for donations, meeting agendas, periodic reports of progress, and other project-related items that were sent out by the managing editor, and she did myriad other tasks that made the job easier for him throughout the life of the project. When early arrangements for indexing the volume fell through, Sandra Topping was called on late to do this work. Working under pressure, she did a first-rate job on the index, and we thank her for the excellent result. Others who served include Carol Barrette, computer designer of the project's descriptive pamphlet; Robert M. Burger, graphic designer; Charles S. Cubbison, editorial assistant; G. Jeffrey Hoch, graphic designer and photographer; and Barbara Jordan, clerk and typist.

Including the work of authors, reviewers, the Committee, the others cited, and ourselves, we estimate that the time spent in preparing the book approaches 25,000 hours, most of this time voluntary. This number does not include the many, many hours expended by Christine E. Miles and her staff at the Bureau of Topographic and Geologic Survey.

The staff of the Geologic and Geographic Information Services Division of the Survey deserve special recognition for providing the extensive technical editing, drafting, typesetting, layout, and related services necessary to transform the manuscript to a printed book. We especially thank the division chief and production supervisor, Christine E. Miles, for her perseverance in bringing the job to completion, despite many delays and obstacles, and for dedicating many hundreds of hours of her own time to the production effort. We also thank Caron E. O'Neil, senior geologist/editor, who, with Miles, edited much of the text and whose efforts resulted in many improvements to the publication. Assisting Miles and O'Neil was Anne B. Lutz, a geologist/

editor who joined the division midway through the project and who provided valuable editorial support, particularly in typesetting and proofreading. Others who deserve mention are John H. Barnes, a Bureau geologist who worked in the division during the early part of the project and who did preliminary editing and proofreading of several writing units; Lara K. Homsey, student intern, who ably assisted the editorial staff on a variety of tasks; and Connie A. Zimmerman and Jody R. Zipperer, clerk typists in the Bureau, who collectively spent several months in the very early part of the project typing into a word-processing system the many parts of the manuscript that were not received in digital form. The layout of the book was done by Miles, following general design recommendations of Shultz. The typesetting was done by Miles, Lutz, and O'Neil. The preparation of the camera-ready illustrations for the volume was a monumental task, requiring the editing and drafting of more than 2,200 separate pieces of artwork. Editing, typesetting, and layout of the illustrations, including specification of line weights, type styles and sizes, and color separations, was done by O'Neil and Miles, and O'Neil painstakingly proofread most of the drafted artwork. The expert drafting of all of the illustrations (except for the stratigraphic correlation chart inside the back cover) was done by James H. Dolimpio, cartographic drafter, and John G. Kuchinski, cartographic supervisor. The work of the division editors and drafters is an outstanding achievement that is, perhaps, made more significant considering that the Survey (like most of the authors who contributed to the volume) had very limited digital capabilities at the time the manuscript was received. Although up-to-date electronic-publishing hardware, software, and peripherals were acquired midway in the project and were used to produce galley/page proofs, computer-aided-drafting capabilities were not available in time to be used to prepare the illustrations, so almost all of the camera-ready artwork was produced by manual methods. Regardless of the method of production, the project, in terms of scope and work effort, is unequaled by any other publication in the history of the Fourth Pennsylvania Survey, and we extend our gratitude to the Survey and to the Department of Conservation and Natural Resources for committing staff time and resources to the completion of the book.

Many people, companies, societies, and institutions made donations in support of *The Geology of Pennsylvania* project for two principal purposes: to make possible the inclusion of multicolor illustrations and, most importantly, to keep the price to purchasers as low as possible, thus making the volume more generally available. Because of their generosity in contributing slightly more than $50,000, both of these goals have been achieved, and these benefactors have our heartfelt thanks.

In particular, we wish to thank The Consolidated Natural Gas Company Foundation for making a very substantial grant, then issuing a challenge offering a second, equal grant if we achieved a large portion of our overall funding goal.

Our thanks go equally to Mr. and Mrs. Robert E. Eberly, Sr., who matched the Foundation's extraordinary generosity, not only allowing us to meet the challenge but enabling us to exceed the larger overall goal.

Great generosity also was shown by The Sun Exploration and Production Company, ARCO Oil and Gas Company, Equitable Gas Company, Fairman

Drilling Company, S. W. Jack Drilling Company, Paul G. Benedum, Jr., PPG Industries Foundation, and Thomas W. Angerman.

We cannot say enough for the support of all the other companies and individuals who gave in lesser amounts, some of whom, we are sure, gave more than they should have, considering the depression in the mineral industries and the profession that coincided with our period of need. Our sincerest thanks are extended to the following:

John A. Ames; Donald D. Anderson; Zena H. Andrews; Gert Aron; Baker Engineers; Gary D. Ball; Lajos J. Balogh; Edith Baum; George K. Biemesderfer; Stephen D. Bill; Barbara Bloomfield; Richard Borkowski; P. N. Bossart and Associates; William A. Bragonier; Duane D. Braun; Tracy V. Buckwalter; Kent Bushnell; Marilyn Bushnell.

William F. Chapman; Raymond F. Cicero; John A. Comet; Maria Luisa Crawford; William A. Crawford; Ellie Cyr; Helen L. Delano; Maurice Deul; Doran and Associates; Nancy T. Duerring; Barbara J. Dunst; Brian J. Dunst; Earth, Inc.; Earth Science Consultants; Craig A. Eckert; Samuel P. English; Environmental Resources Management.

Marshall Fausold; John W. Felbinger; Harry F. Ferguson and Associates, Ltd.; Walter E. Fike; Patrick M. Findle; Jane L. Freedman; Donald D. Funnell; John T. Galey; Paul W. Garrett, Jr.; Joanne E. Garvin; Gearhart Industries; Geomega, Inc.; Geotechnical Services, Inc.; Richard E. Goings; John V. Goodman; Carlyle Gray and Associates; Richard E. Gray; Mary Ann Gross; Irving G. Grossman.

Haddad and Brooks, Inc.; Hanley and Bird; Ihor Havryluk; Donald T. Hoff; B. F. Howell, Jr.; James R. Huber; IESCO; Jacqueline H. Jansky; John Jansky; Robert L. John; William M. Jordan; Teresa Kaktins; Uldis Kaktins; Richard L. Kanaskie; Matthew H. Kenealy, III; Carla A. Kertis; William R. Kohl, Jr.; Timothy J. Kuntz.

Laura L. Langer; Loren R. Lasky; W. S. Leeper and Associates; Lehigh Portland Cement Company; Earl H. Linn; Keith R. Lucas; William S. Lytle; Philip L. Martin; John P. McCullough; Joseph M. McGuckin; Mary K. McGuire; Stephen G. McGuire; Noel N. Moebs; Momenee-King Associates; John S. Moore; Richard Murdy; Timothy M. Murin.

NUS Corporation; Nancy E. Neff; Joseph O'Rourke; John F. O'Neill; Pennsylvania Power and Light Company; Pennzoil Exploration; Salvatrice Perry; Douglas C. Peters; Pittsburgh Testing Laboratories; Noel Potter, Jr.; Frank Preston.

Mary S. Robison; Rochester and Pittsburgh Coal Company; SMC Martin; SRW Associates; Henry A. Salver; W. J. Santamour; Charles K. Scharnberger; Joseph Schwietering; Charles H. Shultz; Fred H. Sturm; Systems Supplies, Inc.

Tatlock Exploration, Inc.; Lee A. Thomas; Turm Oil Company; Eugene W. Vaskov; David J. Watson; Suzanne D. Weedman; Ned E. Wehler; James M. Wigal; Eugene G. Williams; Charles R. Wood; John C. Wright, Jr.; Charles W. Yost.

It is also a real pleasure to recount the support given most generously by our sister societies in Pennsylvania, the Pennsylvania Section of the American Institute of Professional Geologists, the Philadelphia Geological Society, the

Pittsburgh Association of Petroleum Geologists, and the Harrisburg Area Geological Society, as well as the Eastern Section of the American Association of Petroleum Geologists. Our thanks to the members of these organizations, some of whom are among the authors of this volume, for making the donations possible. We also thank Franklin and Marshall College and the Geoscience Department of Indiana University of Pennsylvania and their faculties for gifts to the project.

We express our gratitude to the Pittsburgh Geological Society, whose membership authorized the substantial seed money that made it possible to get the project under way, tiding it over the hungry early days. It is fair to say that without this support, *The Geology of Pennsylvania* would have remained a dream.

Last, but by no means least, we sincerely thank Slippery Rock University for use of University facilities and equipment such as word processors, a desk-top-publishing system, photocopiers, and meeting rooms with associated food services. We also thank the University for support of the project through indirect contributions of goods and services worth thousands of dollars. These include some release time and a summer sabbatical leave for the editor, secretarial services, the cost of student aides, computer time, printing, office supplies, and many hundreds of long-distance phone calls and mailings. The Chester Engineers and other organizations also provided in-kind services on more modest scales.

In summary, this volume is not just the production of the labors of the authors, reviewers, editor, *The Geology of Pennsylvania* Committee, and the Bureau of Topographic and Geologic Survey. Rather, it owes its existence to the support of many institutions and organizations, as well as to the broad mineral-industry and geological communities of Pennsylvania at large.

Charles H. Shultz
Editor
The Geology of Pennsylvania

Department of Geology
Slippery Rock University
Slippery Rock, PA 16057

Reginald P. Briggs
Managing Editor
The Geology of Pennsylvania Project

Geomega, Inc.
P. O. Box 12933
Pittsburgh, PA 15241

CONTENTS

Pulpit rocks on Warrior Ridge in Huntingdon County, composed of the Lower Devonian Ridgeley Sandstone. This lithograph by George Lehman (original in color) was used by Henry Darwin Rogers as the frontispiece in volume 1 of his 1858 two-volume work *The Geology of Pennsylvania*. At this location on September 26, 1986, a plaque was dedicated commemorating the 150th anniversary of the Pennsylvania Geological Survey. The site is included in the National Park Service registry of sites that are historically significant in the development of geology. Photograph by Clifford H. Dodge.

Part I

INTRODUCTION

This is the second work that has the title *The Geology of Pennsylvania*. The first was the monumental—two volumes, 1,631 pages—final report of the First Pennsylvania Geological Survey published in 1858 by Henry Darwin Rogers, the first State Geologist of Pennsylvania. His monograph was not the first publication on Pennsylvania geology, however. It followed reports on geological observations, principally related to the search for mineral resources, that began before the Revolutionary War. This long history of geological investigation is recounted in Chapter 1. It includes the work of the four state surveys, the involvement of the U.S. Geological Survey, and the contributions of academic and industrial geologists.

Chapter 2 sets the stage for what is to follow by providing an overall summary of this volume. The reader will note a significant emphasis on practical geology (natural resources, hazards, and environmental problems), for geology has long been an important factor in the economic well-being of the Commonwealth, its cultural development, and the safety of its citizens.

The content of this book is thus based on more than two centuries of geological observations. It is not the final word. Geological research in Pennsylvania is a dynamic and active pursuit, producing a continuing stream of new ideas, theories, and perspectives. The rate of progress is such that we probably will not have to wait another 135 years for a third version of *The Geology of Pennsylvania*.

—Charles H. Shultz

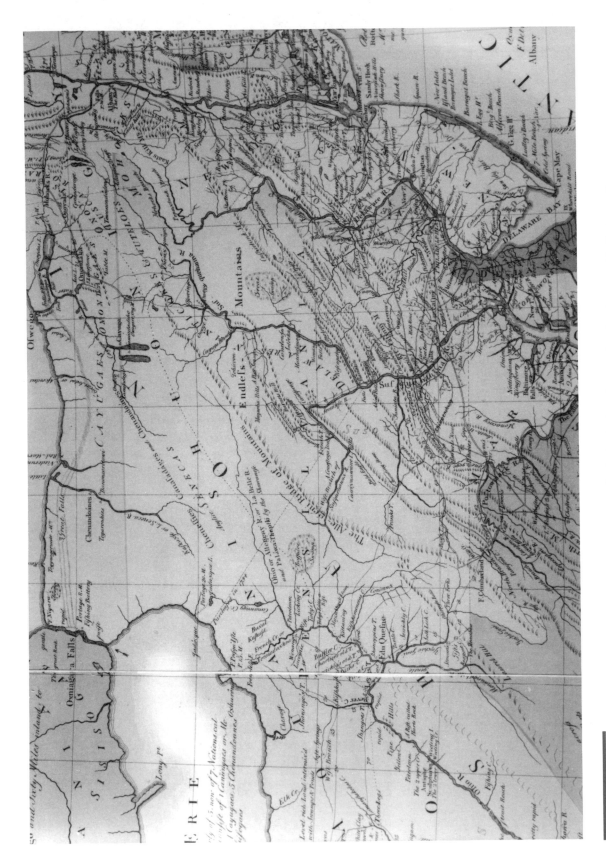

Figure 1–1. A portion of Lewis Evans' *A General Map of the British Colonies in America…*, showing topographic features of Pennsylvania (Evans, 1755).

CHAPTER 1   HISTORY OF GEOLOGICAL INVESTIGATIONS IN PENNSYLVANIA

DONALD M. HOSKINS
Bureau of Topographic and Geologic Survey
Department of Conservation and Natural
  Resources
P. O. Box 8453
Harrisburg, PA 17105

WILLIAM M. JORDAN
Department of Earth Sciences
Millersville University
Millersville, PA 17551

THE COLONIAL TO EARLY FEDERAL PERIODS, 1681 TO 1832

License to explore Pennsylvania for minerals was granted by William Penn as early as 1692, a decade after its founding in 1681. The first geological descriptions of Pennsylvania were extremely general because they were by-products of travelers' accounts. Prior to the American Revolution, a Welsh surveyor, Lewis Evans, and a Swedish botanist, Peter Kalm, traveled independently and widely in Pennsylvania, subsequently reporting their geological observations (Fergusson, 1981). *A Map of Pensilvania, New-Jersey, New-York, and the Three Delaware Counties*, based on Evans' cartographic data, was published in 1749 and expanded in 1755 (Figure 1–1) to include New England and Ohio. Evans (1755) subdivided the area west of the Hudson River into five "Stages," which were in reality topographic provinces, that he designated as "Lower Plains," "Uplands," "Piemont" (French for Piedmont, meaning "foot of the mountains"), "Endless Mountains," and "Upper Plains." Peter Kalm's *Travels into North America*, published in English in 1770–71, contains about 10 percent geological descriptions of Pennsylvania (Fergusson, 1981). The first known written geological observation at a specific locale is Thomas Hutchins' (1786) description of the falls of the Youghiogheny in Fayette County.

Johann David Schopf, a naturalist trained in Germany, traveled extensively in Pennsylvania and adjacent states during 1783 and 1784, publishing his observations in reports issued in Erlangen, Germany, in 1787 and 1788. In these, Schopf subdivided the terrain of eastern North America into many geological and physiographic units with remarkable geologic accuracy. As an example, he recognized and described the Fall Line.

Schopf's work unfortunately was "lost" as an influence on subsequent investigations of Pennsylvania geology. Constantin Volney, a French natural philosopher who traveled in the eastern United States from 1795 to 1798, knew nothing of Schopf. Volney's 1804 report contains descriptions of the Blue Ridge and Reading Prong. Unlike Schopf's report, it contains erroneous accounts of basalt in the Alleghenies, but builds only upon the work of Evans and Kalm. European printed editions of Volney's work contain the first colored geologic map of the United States.

William Maclure is considered the "father" of American geology (Merrill, 1924). Maclure, a wealthy Scot, prepared the first widely distributed colored geologic map of eastern North America, which appeared in his *Observations on the Geology of the United States* in 1809 (revised in 1817). Maclure's map shows the rocks of Pennsylvania divided, following the then-accepted Wernerian concept that all rocks were deposited in a primeval ocean, into "Primitive," "Transition," "Secondary," and "Alluvial" units. J. P. Lesley provided a summary of these early investigations in his 1876 *Historical Sketch of Geological Explorations in Pennsylvania and Other States*.

William Darby was another "lost" influence on systematic geological field observations in Pennsylvania that began in earnest in the 1830's and at first were accomplished mainly by official government surveys. Darby, born near Harrisburg, was a self-trained surveyor and geographer who wrote the first known geological essay prepared specifically to describe a state (Hoskins, 1986). To accompany this essay, Darby prepared a new version of a topographic map of Pennsylvania, which was then used as a base map for the earliest known geological map of Pennsylvania (see color section, Figure 9). Topographic maps of this era showed relative elevations of areas by means of schematic sketches rather than contours. Published in his own magazine (Darby, 1824), which failed after two issues, Darby's maps and essay were based on his own extensive travels in Pennsylvania. Although his geologic classification was derived from the map of William Maclure, Darby improved on Maclure's map by showing the geologic units on a more detailed base map and by actually mapping and describing the geologic contact between the shales and limestones in Pennsylvania's Great Valley.

THE GEOLOGICAL SOCIETY OF PENNSYLVANIA, 1832 TO 1836

Important to the development of geology in Pennsylvania was the 1832 formation of the Geological Society of Pennsylvania. This society and the subsequent state geological survey that was organized in Pennsylvania are traced to an 1824 meeting called by Philadelphia lawyer Peter A. Browne to propose a statewide geologic and mineralogic survey. The Society published many geological reports in its own *Transactions* in 1834 and 1835 in a manner similar to other Philadelphia-based scientific associations.

A primary purpose of the Society was to urge the establishment of a state-supported geological survey (Millbrooke, 1976, 1977). The Society's efforts were successful by March 1836, when legislation was passed authorizing the creation of the First Geological Survey. Henry D. Rogers, a member of the Society, was chosen to head the Survey. With the passage of the legislation, the Society ceased to function.

THE PERIOD OF THE FIRST GEOLOGICAL SURVEY OF PENNSYLVANIA, 1836 TO 1858

Economic forces during the early nineteenth century moved many state legislatures toward the establishment of geological surveys, the first in North Carolina in 1823. Henry D. Rogers (Figure 1–2), then Professor of Geology at the University of Pennsylvania and State Geologist of New Jersey, was chosen as Pennsylvania's first State Geologist in 1836.

Rogers began his work in Pennsylvania with an annual appropriation of $6,400 and the requirement that the survey be completed in five years. The selection of assistant geologists proved a major problem. Few individuals from whom he could choose had prior geologic instruction or experience. James Booth

Figure 1–2. Henry Darwin Rogers, State Geologist of Pennsylvania from 1836 to 1858. Photograph courtesy of The Historical Society of Pennsylvania, from an engraving by L. S. Punderson taken from a daguerreotype, Simon Gratz collection.

and John Frazer, both educated in geology, were assistant geologists during the first year but left after one field season because of Rogers' imperious demands (Hoskins, 1987a). In 1840, twelve persons were employed as geologists or chemists.

The completion of the Survey's tasks (Figure 1–3) was hampered by the huge size of the state, lack of adequate base maps, and underfunding. The Pennsylvania Legislature failed to renew appropriations in 1842 because of the Commonwealth's insolvency. As a result, the corps, now reduced to six persons, disbanded.

It was just two years prior to 1842 that one of the preeminent scientific societies of our nation, the American Association for the Advancement of Science (AAAS), was formed. In 1840, the AAAS began as the Association of American Geologists. Urged on by the members of the many young state surveys formed in the 1830's, geologists and other scientists met that year in the rooms of the Franklin Institute in Philadelphia to share and compare their findings. Nine of the 18 geologists present were from Pennsylvania (Anonymous, 1840). Six of these were, or had been, members of the First Geological Survey of Pennsylvania.

In 1851–52, the Rogers Survey was revived, and a smaller corps of geologists and draftsmen was hired for further work on the planned final report. The new corps concentrated on revising the geology of the anthracite area and making revisions to the planned multicolored state geological map.

Rogers had early adopted a policy of describing the results of each year's work in general terms only. Annual reports were issued in each of the years 1836 through 1841, but Rogers chose (unfortunately, in retrospect) to reserve the major scientific results for

Figure 1–3. Geological field camp, Somerset County, in 1839. Painted by William van Starkenborg in 1858, the scene is attributed to George Lehman, artist of the First Survey, and may have been based on one of the seven unpublished watercolors he is reported to have painted. Reproduction of a part of the original oil painting at the State Museum of Pennsylvania, Harrisburg.

presentation in a culminating final report. His monumental report (two volumes totaling 1,631 pages, with 23 full-page plates, 18 folded sheets of sections, 778 text figures, and a monographic chapter on fossil plants by the Swiss paleobotanist Leo Lesquereux) entitled *The Geology of Pennsylvania: A Government Survey with a General View of the Geology of the United States*, was a scientific and technical masterpiece for its day. The value of Rogers' report was diminished because it did not appear until 1858, sixteen years after the close of the major part of the actual field surveys in 1842. The final report was published first in Edinburgh, Scotland, where Rogers had gone to escape the many problems caused him by the Pennsylvania Legislature (Hoskins, 1987a). Rogers finished his career as Regius Professor of Geology in Glasgow, Scotland, where he died in 1866.

The Rogers Survey left a large practical and theoretical geological legacy. In fact, Rogers and first-year assistants Booth and Frazer were able to determine the basic stratigraphy of the "Folded Appalachians" in 1836, based on reconnaissance studies along Yellow Creek, near the Broad Top coal field. For their stratigraphic nomenclature (Table 1–1), Henry D. Rogers and his brother William B. Rogers, then State Geologist of Virginia, together developed a numerical system which evolved into a complex series of Latin-derived names designating time. The latter classification never gained the acceptance elsewhere as did the geographically based New York stratigraphic system of Lardner Vanuxem and James Hall, members of the New York Survey.

J. Peter Lesley, a geological field assistant on the First Survey and draftsman of many of the illustrations and maps, worked with Rogers until the spring of 1852, when personal differences caused them to sever their relationship (Ames, 1909). In 1856, Lesley independently wrote and published the useful and very well received *Manual of Coal and Its Topography*. This work clearly illustrates the topographic relief and geomorphic expression of major structural features related to the occurrence of coal in Pennsylvania. Because Lesley's *Manual* predates Rogers' *The Geology of Pennsylvania* by two years, and because Lesley did not feel properly credited for his work on the First Survey, animosity further developed between the two men (Jordan and Pierce, 1981). Lesley and other parties were legally enjoined in 1857 from publishing a geological map of Pennsylvania and were accused of piracy of the information by Rogers (Anonymous, 1859).

Table 1–1. *Nomenclature of the Paleozoic Rocks in Pennsylvania*

Formations of 1837	Formations of 1858		Equivalent modern formations
I	Primal	= dawn	Antietam to Pleasant Hill
II	Auroral	= daybreak	Warrior to Benner
III	Matinal	= morning	Nealmont to Reedsville
IV	Levant	= sunrise	Bald Eagle to Tuscarora
	Surgent	= ascending day	Rose Hill to Bloomsburg
V	Scalent	= high morning	Wills Creek to Tonoloway
VI	Premeridian	= forenoon	Keyser to Corriganville
VII	Meridian	= high noon	Mandata to Ridgeley
	Postmeridian	= afternoon	Needmore to Selinsgrove
VIII	Cadent	= waning day	Marcellus to Harrell
	Vergent	= descending day	Brallier to Lock Haven
IX	Ponent	= sunset	Catskill
X	Vespertine	= evening	Pocono
XI	Umbral	= dusk	Mauch Chunk
XII + XIII	Seral	= nightfall	Pottsville and "coal measures"

[1]Modified from Gertsner (1979, p. 183).

THE INTERVAL BETWEEN SURVEYS, 1858 TO 1874

The American Philosophical Society (APS), chartered in 1740, served as a forum for geology for many years, especially in the period between Surveys when J. P. Lesley was its Secretary-Librarian. Similarly, the Academy of Natural Sciences of Philadelphia, founded in 1812, and the Franklin Institute, founded in 1825, were publishers of geological investigations in Pennsylvania during this period. In addition to Lesley's many papers on coal, oil, and iron that were published by APS, he was very active in Pennsylvania as a consulting geologist and produced many privately printed reports for energy and mineral exploration companies. He also prepared a new summary geologic map with essays on geology and topography, published in Walling and Gray's (1872) *New Topographical Atlas of the State of Pennsylvania*.

Among others who investigated Pennsylvania's geology during this interval and published in the journals of the Philadelphia societies were Edward D. Cope and Joseph Leidy on vertebrate fossils (both wrote on Pennsylvania bone cave discoveries). In addition, Isaac Lea discovered a new mineral, later discredited, which he named "lesleyite" for J. P. Lesley; Frederick A. Genth published a treatise on corundum with descriptions of its associated minerals at the famous Chester County and Delaware County localities, and Benjamin S. Lyman discovered and traced the Carboniferous conglomerate (Pottsville) in Sullivan County. Many others, such as Albert R. Leeds, Henry G. Lewis, and Theodore Rand, sought out and published descriptions of many new mineral occurrences.

The mineral-based prosperity that followed the Civil War eventually brought authorization, in 1874, for the Second Pennsylvania Geological Survey. It was urged on the state by business in general and interests in the booming coal and oil regions in particular (Pierce and Jordan, 1982).

THE SECOND GEOLOGICAL SURVEY OF PENNSYLVANIA, 1874 TO 1889

The new organization was headed by J. Peter Lesley (Figure 1–4), by then Professor of Geology at the University of Pennsylvania and very well known throughout the mineral industry of Pennsylvania. The state was initially divided into five working districts, and 24 individuals were employed in the first year alone. The Second Survey was done on a grand scale; appropriations and expenditures through completion of the last of its publications in 1895 totaled more than $1.5 million, a very large sum for the times. Eventu-

Figure 1–4. J. Peter Lesley, State Geologist of Pennsylvania from 1874 to 1889. Photograph from Smithsonian Institution Archives.

ally, more than 86 persons in addition to Lesley were employed. Most notable for their geological accomplishments while with the Survey, and during their later careers, were Charles A. Ashburner, John F. Carll, T. Sterry Hunt, Leo Lesquereux, John J. Stevenson, and Israel C. White. Lesquereux, in addition to Lesley, had also been a member of Rogers' First Survey. In 1881, Ashburner was designated Geologist-in-Charge of a special Anthracite Survey that brought worldwide acclaim to the organization, and in 1885 he became First Assistant Geologist (Dodge, 1981).

Results of Survey activities were published as soon as possible, an overreaction, perhaps, to the extraordinary delay in making public the major conclusions of the First Survey. As a consequence, many of its reports are essentially voluminous compilations of descriptive field data. However, they were described by Merrill (1924) as "the most remarkable series of reports ever issued by any survey." Lesley provided illuminating prefaces and commentary on each.

Because of its mandate, Second Survey publications are strongly oriented toward economic matters and, except in special instances, such as Lesquereux's work with plant fossils, little paleontology was done. Noteworthy, however, were the pioneering work in petroleum geology by John F. Carll and the specialized investigation of anthracite geology and its mining methods under the direction of Charles A. Ashburner, which incorporated the first major use of structure-contour mapping. The extensive use of maps and illustrations, particularly the multicolored county and topical geologic maps and the many topographic contour maps, are a hallmark of the Second Survey. Their quality was unsurpassed at that time by the maps of other state surveys or the newly formed U.S. Geological Survey (USGS) (Dodge, 1987).

Due to ill health, Lesley completed only the first two volumes of his *Final Summary Report,* published in 1892; the third volume was finished by others in 1895, well after the official 1889 termination of the Second Geological Survey. Of the 124 reports issued by the Second Survey, notable is the 1885 *Geologic Hand Atlas* of colored geologic maps of all counties, designed for laymen's use. These were combined into a new geologic map of the state by A. DW. Smith and issued in 1893 in the *Atlas* to Lesley's *Final Summary Report.*

THE THIRD GEOLOGICAL SURVEY, 1899 TO 1919

The First and Second Surveys had been hampered, as both Rogers and Lesley repeatedly pointed out, by the lack of adequate topographic base maps. In 1899, the Commonwealth authorized a topographic and geological survey of the state to be operated and funded in cooperation with the USGS, which had begun a national program of topographic and geologic mapping. This joint effort constituted the initial phase of the Third Geological Survey of Pennsylvania and was supervised by an unpaid three-man commission. In the 10 years under this arrangement, half of the state was mapped topographically at a scale of 1:62,500, and during the same period, 37 of these 15-minute quadrangles were mapped geologically, either cooperatively or by the USGS alone. Eighteen of these were published by the USGS as part of a large-format, multimap Folio series between 1902 and 1909. Marius R. Campbell of the USGS, the author of three Folios, was the supervisor of field work until 1904, at which time George H. Ashley, later the first State Geologist of the Fourth Survey, assumed this responsibility (Sevon, 1987b). Other USGS geologists who made significant contributions toward understanding the geology of Pennsylvania during this time included Frederick G. Clapp, George B. Richardson, and Ralph W. Stone. Stone was later a member of the Fourth Survey and succeeded Ashley as State Geologist for a short time. Of special note was Charles Butts, who prepared USGS reports on the geology of southwestern and northern Pennsylvania as well as the complex folded belt of central Pennsylvania. Butts' beautiful Hollidaysburg-Huntingdon Folio was mapped in 1908 but was not printed until 1945.

The editor of the USGS Folios was George W. Stose, who held this position for 44 years, starting in 1897. Throughout his career with the USGS, Stose produced many reports on the geology of Pennsylvania, including several Folios, beginning with the 1909 report on the Mercersburg and Chambersburg quadrangles. Stose also authored or coauthored many geological Atlases and County Reports issued later by the Fourth Pennsylvania Geological Survey. With Anna Jonas, coauthor of many of these quadrangle reports, and, after 1938, his wife, Stose proposed novel ideas about the structural origin of the Reading Hills and recognized the presence of the Taconic sequence in Pennsylvania.

In 1909, the legislature authorized the organization of a "Topographic and Geological Survey" with staff salaries and publishing costs to be paid by the state. Richard R. Hice was appointed State Geologist under this arrangement. Cooperative topographic mapping with the USGS continued, but geologic

mapping was done independently with "so far as possible, college professors and advanced students who are residents...employed in the work" (Hayes, 1911). No funds were provided after 1914. Through 1914, eighteen reports were published. In the same period, nine additional USGS geologic Folios were issued. The Third Survey is the only one not to have published a new statewide geologic map.

One of the lasting benefits of the Third Survey was "the successful implementation of the cooperative Federal and State topographic mapping program which [continues] today" (Sevon, 1987b).

THE FOURTH GEOLOGICAL SURVEY, 1919 TO PRESENT

The present Topographic and Geologic Survey, the Fourth Survey, was established late in 1919 as a bureau within the Department of Internal Affairs. George H. Ashley (Figure 1–5), the first State Geologist of the Fourth Survey, was former Chief of the USGS section dealing with the eastern coal fields. During that time, he investigated the coal resources of Clearfield County, a task that he continued intermittently for many decades while directing the Fourth Survey (Hoskins, 1981). Ashley (1920, p. 7) noted "the reason why the Third Survey was replaced was because the Commission had no office at the State Capitol for giving information...it did not receive the support needed and was abolished." As with the Second Survey, the Fourth Survey has put heavy emphasis on the dissemination of geologic information to the public. Its 1920 work began with four geolo-

Figure 1–5. George Hall Ashley, State Geologist of Pennsylvania from 1919 to 1946. Photograph from Pennsylvania Geological Survey files.

gists in addition to Ashley, and 13 cooperating academics. Major emphasis was placed on continuing the cooperative topographic mapping program.

Cooperation with the Water Resources Division of the USGS began in 1925; a new publication series of Water Resource Reports resulted from this cooperation. It joined the already established Atlas, County, Mineral Resource, Information Circular, Progress Report, and General Geology series of reports.

The subsequent work of the Survey is detailed in "Miscellaneous Papers" issued under Ashley's name in 1923, 1931, 1934, and in 1944 in commemoration of the Survey's twenty-fifth anniversary. Faill's (1987) summary history of the Fourth Survey details the many accomplishments of Ashley and the State Geologists who followed his retirement in 1946 after 27 years of effort. Since then, Ralph W. Stone, Stanley H. Cathcart, Carlyle Gray, and Arthur A. Socolow have served as State Geologists. Socolow retired in 1986 and was succeeded by Donald M. Hoskins.

GEOLOGIC INVESTIGATIONS AT ACADEMIC INSTITUTIONS

Geology was taught as early as 1830 at Dickinson College, in 1835 at the University of Pennsylvania under Henry Rogers, in 1837 at Lafayette College, where Peter Browne became Professor, and in 1864 at the Western University of Pennsylvania, now the University of Pittsburgh. Lehigh University began teaching geology in its School of Mining in 1866. The Department of Geology and Zoology was created in 1882 at the Pennsylvania State College (now the Pennsylvania State University).

Many are the professors of Pennsylvania colleges and universities who have devoted their lives to their students. A notable example is Paul D. Krynine, of the Pennsylvania State University, who, while a major contributor to geologic research in Pennsylvania in his specialty of sedimentary petrology, is most fondly remembered for his untiring devotion to his students. In addition to Krynine, many other academicians were noted for preparing highly qualified graduate geologists while also being active field investigators in Pennsylvania. The careers of a sample of six are briefly described below; each made major contributions in unraveling Pennsylvania's complex geology. Their work stands as examples that could be repeated for other academic colleagues such as Charles H. Behre, Jr., Norman K. Flint, Jacob L.

Freedman, Benjamin F. Howell, Benjamin L. Miller, Frank M. Swartz, Edgar T. Wherry, Bradford Willard, and Herbert P. Woodward.

Joseph Barrell (1869–1919), during his teaching years at Lehigh University (1893–97 and 1900–03), collected data on the continental deposits of northeastern Pennsylvania. The culmination of his career came with the publication in 1913 by the *American Journal of Science* of his masterpiece paper "The Upper Devonian Delta of the Appalachian Geosyncline."

Florence Bascom (1862–1945) (Figure 1–6), the pioneer woman geologist in the United States, established the Geology Department of Bryn Mawr College in 1895. In addition to educating other young women such as Anna Jonas and Eleanora Bliss, both later well-known Pennsylvania geologists, Miss Bascom received the first doctorate given to a woman at Johns Hopkins University. Her brilliant disserta-

Figure 1–6. Florence Bascom, founder of the Bryn Mawr College Geology Department, recipient of the first doctorate awarded to a woman from Johns Hopkins University, and first woman geologist at the U.S. Geological Survey. Photograph courtesy of the Bryn Mawr College Archives.

tion on the petrography of the volcanic rocks of Pennsylvania's South Mountain began a career of mapping and investigations in southeastern Pennsylvania that produced many important geological discoveries. Florence Bascom was also the first woman geologist at the USGS and the coauthor of several Folios.

Ernst Cloos (1899–1974), Professor at Johns Hopkins University, contributed much to the understanding of Pennsylvania's geology through his focus on extensive field work and structural data collection in southern counties. In 1941, with student Anna

Hietanen, he authored the Geological Society of America's Special Paper 35, entitled *Geology of the "Martic Overthrust" and the Glenarm Series in Pennsylvania and Maryland*. This monograph was a major turning point in understanding fundamental problems of the Appalachian geosyncline. Moreover, as consultant to the Thomasville Stone and Lime Company of York County, he developed the concept of obtaining this commodity from large underground mines. He was a frequent participant and leader in annual meetings of the Field Conference of Pennsylvania Geologists, exemplifying his belief that the best place to observe geology was in the field. He demonstrated the value of careful field observations, particularly in detailed studies of small areas.

Charles R. Fettke (1888–1959), a graduate of Columbia University in 1914, spent the following 43 years as Professor at Carnegie Institute of Technology in Pittsburgh. During his decades of teaching, he was also a cooperating geologist with the Third and Fourth Geological Surveys. Fettke's work on the glass sands of Pennsylvania, eventually published as Report XII, was begun as state funds ceased for the Third Survey. Fettke continued at his own expense. With support of the newly organized Fourth Survey, he began the work on the oil sands of the Bradford oil field, the first "giant" field of the oil industry, culminating in the classic report, *The Bradford Oil Field, Pennsylvania and New York* (Fettke, 1938), published as Mineral Resource Report 21 of the Fourth Survey. Fettke was also a pioneer researcher in the study of well cuttings and demonstrated their usefulness in evaluating oil reservoirs.

Not all Pennsylvania investigators were academicians or Survey geologists. Samuel G. Gordon (1897–1952) was a 1911–12 student of Edgar T. Wherry, the discoverer of carnotite in the eastern United States, at the free classes offered by the Wagner Free Institute of Science. In 1913, Gordon began a long association as curator of minerals at the Academy of Natural Sciences of Philadelphia. He is best known for *The Mineralogy of Pennsylvania* (Gordon, 1922), which he completed at age 24, and which remains a standard reference work on Pennsylvania minerals.

Some scientists distinguished themselves in more than one field of research. Dean B. McLaughlin (1901–65) was a world-renowned astronomer, specializing in the planet Mars. In Pennsylvania, he became interested in the Mesozoic-age Newark Series while teaching at Swarthmore College. During summer vacations from teaching at the University of Michigan, McLaughlin conducted detailed mapping of these rocks and interpreted their notable conglomerates as alluvial-fan deposits.

THE FIELD CONFERENCE OF PENNSYLVANIA GEOLOGISTS

As academic programs in geology became better developed and it became desirable to view geology in its natural classroom, at the field outcrop, a new organization came into being. C. A. Bonine, Professor of Geology at The Pennsylvania State College, desiring that he "might become better acquainted with the other geologists located in or working in Pennsylvania" (Whitcomb, 1961, p. ii), invited geologists from the Pennsylvania Geological Survey, other academic institutions in Pennsylvania, and private industry to come to State College in the spring of 1931 (Figure 1–7).

Designated the Field Conference of Pennsylvania Geologists, the organization formalized its structure in 1932 (Field Conference of Pennsylvania Geologists, 1985). During the period from 1931 to 1995, it conducted 59 conferences consisting of two- and three-day field trips. Conferences have included visits to new and classic exposures of geology in Pennsylvania to consider and reconsider, by active discussion, the many interpretations offered by geologists engaged in mapping and other geologic investigations.

FUTURE HISTORY

Future historians will have the pleasure and the difficult task of evaluating the work of academic, government, and private-industry geologists to determine which were the important and substantive contributions to the geology of Pennsylvania. Some examples of work that remains open to such evaluation are as follows:

1. Was the 1934 stratigraphic and paleontologic work in northwestern Pennsylvania by Kenneth E. Caster, who introduced the term "magnafacies," a major new understanding of the interrelationships of rocks in an area where marine and nonmarine rocks interfinger?

2. Bradford Willard's 1939 report *The Devonian of Pennsylvania* was at one time considered the best reference on Devonian rocks in Pennsylvania, but has been largely replaced by modern stratigraphic interpretations resulting from detailed mapping by the Fourth Survey. Does Willard's report represent an outdated approach to stratigraphy?

Figure 1–7. Participants in the First Field Conference of Pennsylvania Geologists. Present at this 1931 conference were many academicians, including Frank M. Swartz (S), Benjamin L. Miller (M), Bradford Willard (W), and possibly Anna J. Stose (A?). Photograph from Pennsylvania Geological Survey files.

3. Was Carlyle Gray's 1954 description of recumbent folding in the Lebanon Valley in a short Pennsylvania Academy of Science paper the first recognition of nappe structures of alpine nature, and did it lead to a new way of mapping and understanding mineral resources of Pennsylvania?
4. Was Vinton Gwinn's 1964 exposition on deep structures, published by the Geological Society of America, simply an extension of thrust-fault tectonics understood elsewhere, or was it a major new contribution for Pennsylvania and the Appalachians?

Many are the journeymen geologists who have made careful and accurate observations in Pennsylvania. Each has built on the knowledge obtained by others. But which few of these have made substantive new contributions will be the judgment of the future. Is it even possible that a few of the chapters in this volume will be regarded by future historians as substantive syntheses that led to new ways of understanding Pennsylvania's complex geology?

RECOMMENDED FOR FURTHER READING

Drake, E. T., and Jordan, W. M. (1985), *Geologists and ideas: a history of North American geology*, Geological Society of America Centennial Special Volume 1, 525 p.
Rabbitt, M. C. (1979), *Minerals, lands and geology for the common defense and general welfare, Volume 1, Before 1879*, U.S. Geological Survey, 331 p.
_____ (1980), *Minerals, lands and geology for the common defense and general welfare, Volume 2, 1879–1904*, U.S. Geological Survey, 407 p.
_____ (1986), *Minerals, lands and geology for the common defense and general welfare, Volume 3, 1904–1939*, U.S. Geological Survey, 479 p.
Schneer, C. J. (1979), *Two hundred years of geology in America*, The University Press of New England, 385 p.

Figure 2–1. Oblique aerial view looking north-northwest through the Delaware Water Gap in Kittatinny Mountain. Pennsylvania is on the left; New Jersey and Interstate Route 80 are on the right. The hogback ridge is supported by the Lower Silurian Shawangunk Formation, which is dominantly siliceous sandstone and conglomerate. In the distance is the Glaciated Low Plateau section of the Appalachian Plateaus province. Photograph by Grant Heilman, © Grant Heilman Photography, Inc.

CHAPTER 2   OVERVIEW

CHARLES H. SHULTZ
Department of Geology
Slippery Rock University
Slippery Rock, PA 16057

PROLOGUE

The geology of Pennsylvania is perhaps unsurpassed in diversity by that of any other state in the Union. It includes a number of firsts in the history of geological investigations and the exploitation of natural resources. Pennsylvania was one of the first colonies in which Europeans produced clay for pottery and bricks, sand for glassmaking, and ores for iron manufacture. It is the birthplace of the commercial petroleum industry in the United States. The first geologic map of an entire state was the geologic map of Pennsylvania produced by Darby in the 1820's (Darby, 1824; see color section, Figure 9).

Numerous aspects of Pennsylvania geology are noteworthy. Many basic geologic concepts were developed and nurtured in this state. For instance, the Devonian Catskill delta is the classic model for orogenic control of sedimentary facies. The structure and physiography of the Appalachian Mountain section in the center of the state are particularly renowned. It is the archetypal folded foreland mountain chain. The geosynclinal theory and the concept of thin-skinned deformation associated with orogenic belts were established with reference to this section. It was here that William Morris Davis gathered data for his theories of landscape evolution and peneplanation. The accordance of ridge summits in the Appalachian Mountain section, in addition to the trellis drainage pattern, the transverse character of major rivers, and the formation of water and wind gaps, has engaged geomorphologists for more than a century.

Pennsylvania's geology has played important roles in our nation's history. Iron ore produced at Cornwall, Lebanon County, was an essential cornerstone for the Revolutionary War. The geology around Gettysburg, Adams County, determined the approaches to the town and the battle lines taken by both the Union and Confederate armies, and perhaps, to a large extent, even dictated the outcome of the most famous battle of the Civil War.

The overview that follows is a synthesis of notable points developed in this volume. It is designed to arouse your curiosity and perhaps spark your interest in doing scientific research to solve the host of geologic problems that still puzzle us. Documentation for statements made here can be found in the individual chapters, and readers are encouraged to consult maps and illustrations within other chapters or the color section.

FACE OF THE LAND AND ITS RIVERS

The landscapes of Pennsylvania are as varied as the geology that lies below. The origin and age of these landscapes are controversial and are closely tied to the origin of major trunk rivers.

The state is divided into seven physiographic provinces (see map B, p. 342). Three of these occupy most of the state. Listed from southeast to northwest, and in order of increasing area, they are the Piedmont, the Ridge and Valley, and the Appalachian Plateaus provinces. Each is subdivided into two or more sections. The other four provinces or sections within them (South Mountain section of the Blue Ridge province, Reading Prong section of the New England province, Coastal Plain province, and Central Lowlands province) occupy smaller areas in Pennsylvania and are described in later chapters. In concentric fashion, provincial boundaries generally follow the curving structural grain characteristic of Pennsylvania.

The Piedmont is a land of gentle hills with a few hundred feet of relief and elevations of 300 to 700 feet. It incorporates the youngest (Early Jurassic) and the oldest (Middle Proterozoic) indurated bedrock in the state. The southern Piedmont is underlain by complexly deformed Cambrian and Ordovician metasedimentary and carbonate rocks punctuated by uplifted and arched blocks of Precambrian gneisses. A northern section, the Gettysburg-Newark Lowland section, has radically contrasting bedrock. Here, Upper Triassic red mudstones and sandstones form lowlands, and coarse conglomerates plus Lower Jurassic diabase underlie highlands up to 1,300 feet in elevation.

The Ridge and Valley province is areally almost three times as large as the Piedmont. The Great Valley section, along the southeastern perimeter, has elevations and relief similar to the Piedmont but is underlain by mostly unmetamorphosed Cambrian and Ordovician strata. The Appalachian Mountain section, to the northwest, is characterized by long, linear ridges of resistant quartzitic sandstones rising 1,000 to 1,200 feet above intervening valleys underlain by mudrocks and carbonates. Rocks range in age from Cambrian to Pennsylvanian and were folded during the Permian Alleghanian orogeny. Erosion of the plunging folds created canoe-shaped and zigzag landscape patterns. A trellis drainage pattern is evident, and major trunk rivers cut across structure, forming prominent water gaps through resistant ridges (see Figure 2–1 and color section, Figure 1).

The Allegheny Front forms the northwest boundary of the Ridge and Valley and separates it from the Appalachian Plateaus province, which includes about 60 percent of the state. The Appalachian Plateaus province has the highest general elevations (greater than 1,200 feet), the highest point (Mount Davis, 3,213 feet, in Somerset County), and the greatest general relief (400 to 1,800 feet) in the state. Bedrock in the west is mainly subhorizontal coal-bearing Pennsylvanian strata; Devonian and Mississippian rocks predominate in the center and east. The northeastern and northwestern parts of the province have been glaciated.

Pennsylvania has about 45,000 miles of streams. Approximately 65 percent of the state's area drains to the Atlantic Ocean through the Susquehanna, Delaware, and Potomac Rivers. The Susquehanna basin alone occupies 46 percent of the state. The western third of Pennsylvania largely drains to the Gulf of Mexico through the Monongahela, Allegheny, and Ohio Rivers. Drainage divides, the origin and migration of which are controversial, do not correspond to physiographic boundaries. The general patterns of the rivers in the eastern part of the state, particularly the Susquehanna, are thought to have great antiquity, perhaps dating to the mid-Paleozoic. The directions of flow of many rivers have been reversed during this long history.

BEDROCK AND SURFICIAL MATERIALS

The geographic area called Pennsylvania is situated on the North American lithospheric plate. It is presently located from about 40 to 42 degrees north latitude, and its northern and southern borders are parallel to latitude lines. This was not always so. Based on the theory of plate tectonics, as well as biogeographic, paleoclimatic, and paleomagnetic data, geologists are convinced that, over long periods of time, continents have changed their relative positions, or drifted. In the late Precambrian (Grenville time),

North America, or Laurentia, may have been part of a single supercontinent called Proto-Pangea. By Late Cambrian time (550–540 Ma), Laurentia had become one of four landmasses isolated in a world ocean. At this time, the area comprising Pennsylvania was located at 15 to 20 degrees south latitude, and its present northern and southern borders had azimuths of about N20°W. In other words, the present east-west southern border was then to the west and oriented nearly north-south. Throughout the Paleozoic Era, Laurentia gradually drifted northward while rotating in a counterclockwise sense so that, by the end of the Permian Period, Pennsylvania was on or just south of the equator, and its east-west borders were oriented about N80°–85°W. During the Mesozoic Era, the area of Pennsylvania moved north of the equator and continued its gradual counterclockwise rotation. In the Triassic Period, it was at 5 to 10 degrees north latitude, and in the Jurassic, it was at about 24 degrees north latitude. By the end of the Cretaceous or by early Tertiary time (about 60 Ma), the area of Pennsylvania had attained its present position and orientation. To avoid confusion in the discussion that follows, modern compass directions are used, but the reader is alerted that these directions are strictly valid only for the last 60 million years.

The great range of rocks of almost every conceivable type in Pennsylvania is largely a result of long-continued plate-tectonic activity, chiefly along the eastern margin of Laurentia. The convergence of continent-bearing plates creates suture zones and orogenic belts with associated igneous and metamorphic activity. The loading of cratons with imbricate thrust sheets creates foreland basins that fill with thick wedges of detritus eroded from mountain ranges. The divergence of plates along rift zones triggers igneous activity and forms basins, which may become oceanic in scale.

At depth, Pennsylvania is underlain everywhere by Precambrian rock of Grenville age (about 1,000 Ma). In the northwest (Erie County), this basement is about 5,000 feet below sea level and, with a few interruptions, slopes gently southeastward to about 30,000 feet below sea level northwest of South Mountain and the Reading Prong. Allochthonous masses of Precambrian rocks are exposed in the Reading Prong and the Piedmont Upland.

Paleozoic sedimentary or metasedimentary rock underlies most, and perhaps all, of the state. Pennsylvanian strata are dominant in western Pennsylvania, and Cambrian and Ordovician strata are dominant in the southeast. Rocks of the Devonian System have the largest area of outcrop (about 35 percent) in the state. Mesozoic rocks are downfaulted into Paleozoic rocks in the Gettysburg-Newark Lowland section of the Piedmont province.

Several hundred feet of Cretaceous and Tertiary sand, gravel, and clay occur in the Philadelphia area, in the Atlantic Coastal Plain province. These are largely nonmarine channel fills deposited in an upper-delta-plain environment. Glacial drift, deposited during four major ice advances, occurs as surficial deposits in the northwestern and northeastern parts of the state. Pleistocene outwash occurs along some rivers, and Holocene alluvium is present along major stream courses. Colluvium is widespread on steeper slopes, and moderate to thick soils, partly saprolitic in the southeast, blanket much of the state.

The general character and distribution of late Precambrian (Eocambrian) and Paleozoic rocks is closely tied to the tectonic framework. The Appalachian cycle of sedimentation began about 750 Ma with the rifting of Laurentia to form the Iapetus (proto-Atlantic) Ocean. Bimodal basalt-rhyolite volcanism was initiated, and the deposition of detrital sediment occurred in rift basins, continuing unabated across the Precambrian-Paleozoic time boundary until a passive continental-margin environment evolved. The ocean continued to transgress across Pennsylvania but did not reach the present northwestern corner until early Middle Cambrian. The continental margin changed from passive to dynamic in the Late Ordovician as the Taconic plate convergence began, forming orogenic highlands in the southeast. This event cut off the state from the open ocean and created the Appalachian foreland basin and its epicontinental sea. The orogenic highlands, rejuvenated during the Acadian orogeny (Late Devonian), controlled the distribution of sediment through the remainder of the Appalachian cycle. As the highlands were eroded, the epicontinental sea transgressed eastward. With uplift, sediment prograded westward, forcing the sea to retreat. The sea was forced out of Pennsylvania for the last time during deposition of the Upper Pennsylvanian Conemaugh Group.

The general sedimentation pattern for most Paleozoic systems from the Late Ordovician Taconic orogeny to the end of the Permian is characterized by the deposition of coarse-grained continental sediments in the east and finer grained or chemically precipitated marine sediments westward. The foreland basin was asymmetric, with the axis of maximum subsidence biased eastward, close to the orogenic highlands. Thus, each system of rocks is crudely wedge shaped, gradually becoming thicker and coarser southeastward across the state, and probably abruptly thinning against the orogenic-highland source region.

Grenvillian Precambrian rocks, consisting of gneisses, migmatites, granulites, and anorthosites, were metamorphosed to upper amphibolite and granulite facies during the Grenville orogeny. The late Precambrian Catoctin Formation is composed of metabasalts and metarhyolites. It is overlain by metamorphosed siliciclastic rocks of the Eocambrian to Cambrian Chilhowee Series.

Rocks of the Cambrian System, which could possibly have been up to 15,000 feet thick, consist of basal sandstones overlain by very thick carbonate-bank deposits. Partly contemporaneous is the metasedimentary Glenarm Supergroup that was probably deposited in a separate deep-water basin to the southeast of the carbonate bank and had a provenance even farther to the southeast. Relationships among the Glenarm Supergroup, the Chilhowee Series, and "normal" Cambrian sedimentary rocks are unclear because of metamorphic overprints and tectonic juxtaposition.

Miogeoclinal carbonate-bank conditions along a passive continental margin continued into the Early Ordovician. Platform limestones of the Middle and Late Ordovician gave way to fine-grained clastics of the Martinsburg Formation as downflexing of the foreland basin was initiated by the start of the Taconic orogeny. In the Late Ordovician, siliciclastics up to 15,000 feet thick, derived from the growing orogenic highlands, built the Queenston delta into the basin.

Effects of the Taconic orogeny persisted into the Early Silurian, when quartzitic sandstones and conglomerates were deposited. As the Taconic Mountains were worn down during the Late Silurian, the sea transgressed eastward, depositing shales, carbonates, and evaporites.

Marine shelf conditions continued into the Early Devonian. Units deposited during this time include the Keyser Limestone, the Ridgeley Sandstone (important for natural gas), and the Huntersville Chert. The Onondaga Formation and the Hamilton Group were deposited in basinal marine environments during the Middle Devonian, after which a second major influx of detrital sediment was introduced into the basin from orogenic highlands created during the Acadian orogeny. This, of course, was the famous Upper Devonian Catskill delta, over 9,000 feet thick, that built westward into the foreland sea.

The Devonian-Mississippian boundary occurs within a series of transitional beds up to 2,400 feet thick. The Lower Mississippian is represented by braided-river deposits, and the upper part of the system is represented by red beds and tongues of marine limestone that occur mainly in the southwestern part of the state.

The Pennsylvanian System is crudely cyclic. It is a series of mostly detrital rocks up to 4,400 feet thick and includes subordinate coal and limestone. These rocks were deposited in alluvial-plain, delta-plain, swamp, and lacustrine environments. Formation boundaries are based on interval and sequence, because mudrocks and shales are the dominant lithologies and key beds with great lateral persistence are uncommon. In general, however, coarse clastics are common in the Pottsville Formation at the base of the system, and most commercial coals are in the Middle and Upper Pennsylvanian Allegheny Formation and Monongahela Group in the bituminous fields and the Llewellyn Formation in the anthracite fields. Up to eight thin marine zones are recognized in the lower part of the Pennsylvanian stratigraphic section.

The Permian System in the Dunkard basin in southwestern Pennsylvania is only 1,100 feet thick because erosion has removed the upper part of the original section. Lithologies are very similar to those of the Pennsylvanian, indicating a continuation of similar depositional environments.

The youngest indurated bedrock in the state occurs in two half-graben basins of the Gettysburg-Newark Lowland section. The Newark Supergroup, mostly fluvial in origin, consists of 6,800 feet of red arkosic sandstones overlain by the lacustrine Lockatong Formation (3,800 feet) and, above that, 21,000 feet of red mudstones and sandstones. In the "Narrow Neck" between the basins is 9,100 feet of Hammer Creek conglomerate. Early Jurassic diabase sheets, up to 2,000 feet thick, and a series of dikes oriented approximately north-south intrude the sedimentary rocks. Igneous rocks make up about 20 percent of the basin fill.

STRUCTURAL GEOLOGY AND TECTONICS

Most of the deformational structures observed in Pennsylvania were created during four orogenies (Grenville, Taconic, Acadian, and Alleghanian) and two continental-rifting events. Rifting in the late Precambrian (about 750 Ma) created the Iapetus Ocean and the Rome trough (in western Pennsylvania) and started the Appalachian cycle of deformation and sedimentation. In the Late Triassic (about 230 Ma), rifting created the Gettysburg-Newark basin, which was associated with the creation of the modern Atlantic Ocean.

In southeastern Pennsylvania, particularly in the Piedmont Upland section, structures are very complex and developed during several periods of deformation. In contrast, sedimentary strata in the Appalachian Plateaus province are largely undeformed. Between these extremes are two structural fronts where incremental changes in structural style and intensity occur. The Allegheny Front separates the Appalachian Plateaus province, where maximum structural relief is only a few thousand feet, from the Appalachian Mountain section of the Ridge and Valley province, where structural relief exceeds 20,000 feet. The Blue Mountain Front separates the Appalachian Mountain section from the Great Valley section. Northwest of this front, the main structures are kink folds created by flexural slip. The structural mode is more complex in the Great Valley. West of the Susquehanna River, structures in the Cumberland Valley subsection are mainly large, overturned anticlinoria and synclinoria created by shear. In the Lebanon-Lehigh Valley subsection to the east, the structures are great thrust-bounded recumbent folds (nappes) cored with Precambrian rocks.

The late Precambrian Grenville orogeny caused complex deformation, including primary flow foliation and lineation and the development of gneissic structure and recumbent isoclinal folds. Large-scale structures are poorly known, but on seismic-reflection profiles, low-angle faults have been detected in the basement complex beneath the Appalachian Plateaus.

The effects of the Late Ordovician Taconic orogeny are most apparent in southeastern Pennsylvania, southeast of a line from eastern Adams County in south-central Pennsylvania northeast to Harrisburg, and then east along the Blue Mountain Front to the Delaware River. The principal structure in this area is a series of at least four overlapping recumbent folds, which form the Reading Prong nappe megasystem. The Hamburg klippe was emplaced in the Late Ordovician Martinsburg basin shortly before encroachment of the nappes. Far to the west, southeast-dipping monoclinal flexures developed.

The Late Devonian Acadian orogeny produced only minor structures in the state. These include upfaulted blocks of Precambrian rocks and a vertical fracture cleavage in the rocks of the Piedmont. Ex-

tension in the Plateaus mobilized rock salt of the Silurian Salina Group along Taconic monoclines, creating small anticlinal structures.

The Appalachian cycle climaxed during the Permian with the Alleghanian orogeny. The fundamental tectonic element of that orogeny is the nonemergent décollement in the Upper Cambrian section that allowed tectonic transport to the northwest of all rock units in the southeastern half of the state. All structures here are probably rootless and lie, in theory, above relatively undisturbed Cambrian strata. Taconic nappes were advanced along bounding thrust faults. The South Mountain anticlinorium developed above a high-angle splay fault from the floor décollement, forming a rootless duplex structure. Each major anticline in the Appalachian Mountain section developed in a similar manner. The great curving arc of the Pennsylvania salient and the north-south oriented Juniata culmination developed at this time. The Allegheny Front marks the location where the décollement climbed stratigraphically into the Silurian Salina Group. Splays from this higher plane formed the anticlines that are particularly striking in the Allegheny Mountain section but have lesser amplitudes elsewhere in the Plateau.

A hypothetical late Alleghanian structure is the Anthracite thrust sheet. It may have been over 4 miles thick, overriding previously folded rocks of the Appalachian Mountain section. It possibly provided heat to create anthracite and, through very rapid subsequent erosion, may have been a source of a great molassic sheet that, in theory, inundated all of Pennsylvania. As rivers eroded through the thrust slab and the molasse from Late Permian to Middle Triassic time, they would have been superimposed as antecedent streams across the folded rocks beneath.

Crustal stretching in the Late Triassic initiated rifting, producing the two half-graben basins of the Gettysburg-Newark Lowland. Basin fill shows homoclinal dips of 15 to 30 degrees to the northwest into southeast-dipping listric normal faults along the north border of the lowland. These faults possibly are reactivated Alleghanian thrust faults.

Though Precambrian basement was not involved in the thin-skinned tectonic deformation in the Ridge and Valley province, gravity anomalies, surficial lineaments, kimberlite dikes, and some mapped faults are interpreted as indicators of fundamental fractures in the continental crust, which is about 25 miles thick. Thus, the Precambrian basement may be broken into semi-independent blocks. Jostling of these blocks under various imposed stress fields may have affected some aspects of Pennsylvania's geology throughout the Phanerozoic.

NATURAL RESOURCES AND ECONOMIC GEOLOGY

From the beginning, man has used geological resources. The time of the first arrival of *Homo sapiens* in Pennsylvania is unknown, but 16,500 years before present, Native Americans (paleo-Indian culture) occupied the Meadowcroft rockshelter in Washington County (southwestern Pennsylvania), the oldest such site known to exist in the state. In the millennia between then and the arrival of Europeans, the Native Americans used flint for projectile points, clay for pots, and rivers for transportation.

Water is probably our most important natural resource. The state is blessed with a humid continental climate and an average annual precipitation of about 42 inches. In addition to 45,000 miles of surface streams, Pennsylvania has 2,300 reservoirs, 76 lakes greater than 20 acres in area, and numerous wetlands in glaciated areas. Surface water is used for commercial transportation, water supplies, recreation, air conditioning, and power generation. The use of groundwater exceeds one billion gallons per day and is growing rapidly.

Soil may rank second in importance as a resource. Pennsylvania soils are considered to be youthful because they are weakly to moderately developed, owing to Pleistocene climatic and erosional effects. An understanding of soils is necessary for intelligent use of the land, for the construction of foundations, landfills, and septic systems, and for agriculture.

Pennsylvania also has a rich heritage of mineral exploitation, which is very important to the industrial base and economy of Pennsylvania. In 1990, nonfuel–mineral production was valued at $1,030 million. Petroleum and natural gas contributed about $477 million and coal about $2,130 million.

Pennsylvania led the nation in the production of iron ore from the mid-1700's to about 1860. It was a center of world nickel production in the 1800's and had significant zinc production for more than 100 years. Chromite was mined from the serpentinite belt in southern Lancaster and Chester Counties in the nineteenth century. The last metal production (zinc) was in 1983. Future prospects are not bright under current economic conditions and environmental constraints.

Cornwall-type magnetite deposits are the most significant metalliferous deposits in the state. They are hydrothermal deposits occurring where Jurassic diabase sheets come in contact with carbonate rocks. The Cornwall mines in Lebanon County were the oldest continuously active (1742–1973) mines in North America until they were flooded during tropical storm Agnes in 1972. At least 155 million tons of magnetite ore was produced from Cornwall-type deposits, and significant by-product copper, cobalt, gold, and silver were derived from associated sulfides. Other significant kinds of iron deposits, exploited mainly in the middle and latter nineteenth century, were residual limonite, Clinton-type oolitic hematite, Pennsylvanian siderite, and hematite/magnetite from crystalline rocks.

The most important zinc deposit was the Friedensville Mine, Lehigh County. This mine yielded more than 820,000 tons of zinc from a sphalerite ore assaying 6.5 percent zinc. There were dozens of other important zinc-lead mines or prospects, most notably in Lancaster, Chester, and Montgomery Counties.

The extraction of nonmetallic, or industrial, minerals is a very active and large industry in Pennsylvania. Most important by volume and dollar value are construction aggregates for concrete and railroad ballast. Eighty percent is crushed rock (mainly limestone) derived from quarries largely in southeastern Pennsylvania, and the balance is alluvial sand and gravel, glacial gravel, or slag. In 1990, Pennsylvania led the nation in the production of crushed stone (95.8 million tons; $502 million).

Lower Paleozoic carbonate rocks are quarried extensively for use in the manufacture of portland cement ($286 million, 1990) and for lime used by the steel industry ($93 million, 1990). Dolostone is used in the manufacture of refractories, and pulverized carbonates are used in agriculture and as fillers, whiting, and extenders. Rapid growth in the use of carbonate products is taking place in the environmental field for the removal of sulfur dioxide from flue-stack gases, neutralization of acidic mine waters, and sewage treatment.

Other important industrial minerals are dimension stone (slate, flagstone, and diabase); clays and shale for portland cement, bricks, pottery, and refractories; quartz sand for glass, abrasives, filters, and related products; and metabasalt for roofing granules. Others that were produced in the past but are no longer competitive include talc, asbestos, graphite, barite, feldspars, and phosphate rock.

The extraction of fossil fuels (coal, petroleum, and natural gas) generates the greatest dollar value of all mineral resources in Pennsylvania. For instance, in 1990, the value of bituminous coal produced was $1,992 million, and the value of anthracite produced was $138 million. Commercially important Pennsylvanian coal underlies perhaps one fifth of the state's area of 45,333 square miles. The Main Bituminous coal field occupies much of the Appalachian Plateaus province in western Pennsylvania. Ten economically significant coal beds (discontinuous sheets or multiple-bed complexes) are exploited. The Pittsburgh coal bed is the single most important unit. Extraction of the coals is about equally divided between underground methods and surface strip mining. The recoverable bituminous coal in beds greater than 2 feet thick is estimated at 32 billion tons.

Anthracite is mined in the structurally complex eastern end of the Appalachian Mountain section. The coal is mined from four distinct synclinorial fields, mainly from the lower part of the Pennsylvanian Llewellyn Formation. About 40 coal beds, generally somewhat thicker than those in the bituminous area, have been identified. Underground mining was the main extractive method when significant mining started in the 1820's, but open-pit mining expanded in the 1970's, and by the early 1990's, nearly all production was by stripping. About 5,500 million tons has been mined, and the estimated reserve recoverable by conventional methods is 1,505 million tons.

The production of hydrocarbons is mostly confined to the Appalachian Plateaus province. Oil production peaked in the early 1890's at 32 million barrels per year; 2.6 million barrels was produced in 1990. Pennsylvania-grade crude is a paraffinic oil that has excellent lubricating qualities and thus commands premium prices. Most oil is from Upper Devonian reservoirs consisting of nearshore-marine, fine-grained sandstones that have low porosity and permeability and require stimulation to improve flow rates.

Gas has been produced from many stratigraphic intervals, but the most productive has been the Devonian Ridgeley (Oriskany) Sandstone and overlying Huntersville (Onondaga) Chert. Cumulative production from this interval is more than 1,200 billion cubic feet, mainly from fracture porosity in faulted anticlines. Total recoverable natural gas from all intervals, including speculative resources, may exceed 19,000 billion cubic feet.

GEOLOGIC HAZARDS AND ENVIRONMENTAL PROBLEMS

Most destruction, injury, or death from geology-related hazards in the Commonwealth have to do with imprudent siting of roads and structures based on ignorance, indifference, or false economy. One

invites trouble if construction is sited in the bottom of a narrow valley, on a floodplain, on a steep slope underlain by ancient landslide debris, on nonengineered fill, above solution cavities in carbonate rock, above an underground mine, on a rapidly eroding wave-cut cliff, or on radioactive rocks. These points may be obvious to geologists, but flying into the face of natural laws and processes by stepping into potentially hazardous situations without much forethought seems to be a common human propensity.

Flooding is a statewide problem. Major tropical storms in summer or autumn can affect large sections of the state, especially in the east. For example, in 1972, tropical storm Agnes dumped 8 to 12 inches of rain in 60 hours on the Susquehanna River drainage basin. Abnormal winter storms combined with snowmelt, such as occurred in February 1936, can also create great floods. Serious local floods can result from ice jams, dam failures, or severe thunderstorms. Because they contain large areas of impervious surfaces, urban locales are particularly susceptible to flash flooding from large thunderstorms. This is especially true if slopes are steep and valleys narrow, as is common in the Appalachian Plateaus, particularly in the Pittsburgh and Johnstown regions.

Landsliding is another common hazard, especially in the Appalachian Plateaus and the Appalachian Mountain section. Typical types of landsliding are rockfalls or topples, slumps, soil slides, failure of poorly constructed fills, and flows of surficial materials, especially after major precipitation events.

Another problem is surface subsidence in areas of lower Paleozoic carbonate rocks in the southeastern third of the state, particularly after heavy rain of long duration. Improperly designed drainage associated with construction is commonly involved. Surface subsidence above underground mines is a significant problem in the Main Bituminous coal field of western Pennsylvania, as well as in the anthracite fields. Apparently, there is no depth for a mine at which the surface can be considered safe. More insidious is the fact that subsidence might not occur until more than 100 years after mining has ceased.

Earthquakes are uncommon in Pennsylvania, but 113 with a Modified Mercalli intensity of IV or better have been reported since 1724; 35 of these have caused light damage. Southeastern Pennsylvania has the most activity, especially near Lancaster and Philadelphia, where earthquakes with a Mercalli intensity of III to VI are fairly common.

A widespread hazard that first gained recognition in the late 1980's is the presence of elevated values of radon gas in houses. A flurry of research and media attention was initiated in 1984 when a house in the Reading Prong was found to have radon concentrations three orders of magnitude above the limits set by the U.S. Environmental Protection Agency (EPA). There are some houses all across the state that exceed EPA guidelines, but the problem seems to be most acute in an area from the center of the state toward the southeastern corner. Heat-flow anomalies may be, and aeroradioactivity maps are, useful in identifying broad groups of rocks that have anomalously high radioactivity, and, therefore, potentially higher radon concentrations. However, there are so many site-specific variables for potential radon risks that heat flow and aeroradioactivity cannot be relied upon to predict safe or hazardous areas.

From the paleo-Indians at Meadowcroft rockshelter to the residents of modern metropolitan areas, people have always had a propensity to dispose of that which was not wanted by tossing it over the closest hillside, dumping it into a hole in the ground, or pouring it into a local creek. Old, heavily industrialized states like Pennsylvania have developed serious threats to water quality after decades of abuse and indifference. Runoff from agricultural lands, accidental spills, improper sewage disposal, leachate from poorly "designed" landfills containing all kinds of waste, unlined lagoons containing hazardous and toxic sludges, and pollutants resulting from extractive industries (particularly acidic water from coal mining, and hydrocarbons and saltwater from oil production) have all contributed to the problem. Stringent state and federal laws now provide protection, but we are left with a legacy of past abuses requiring expensive and time-consuming remediation.

Surface mining, particularly coal mining, has degraded the aesthetic appeal of broad areas of Pennsylvania. Serious problems include crumbling highwalls, massive waste piles, erosion, siltation, and drainage of acidic water. The Appalachian Plateaus and the Anthracite region are pockmarked with abandoned surface mines. Today, strict laws involving permitting and bonding require erosion control and simultaneous reclamation as active strip mining proceeds. Federal and state programs have attempted to address the problem of abandoned mines.

AESTHETICS

The diversity of geology in Pennsylvania has resulted in attractive landscapes and features of outstanding beauty, some of which are shown in the color section of this volume. More than 500 documented geological sites are described in the Penn-

sylvania Geological Survey's two-part report *Outstanding Scenic Geological Features of Pennsylvania* (Geyer and Bolles, 1979 and 1987). Among these are the Hickory Run Boulder Field (Carbon County), Delaware Water Gap (Monroe County), Conemaugh Gorge (Cambria County), Pine Creek Gorge, called the "Grand Canyon of Pennsylvania" (Tioga County), Hyner View (Clinton County), Ohiopyle Falls (Fayette County), and Presque Isle (Erie County). In addition, there are many geological sites of historic significance, including Hopewell Furnace National Historic Site (Berks County), Drake Well Museum (Venango County), Horseshoe Curve (Blair County), Gettysburg National Military Park (Adams County), and Cornwall Iron Furnace (Lebanon County).

There are hundreds of named springs across the Commonwealth. Some that serve as local water supplies have also been developed as aesthetic attractions. The largest in the state is Enchanted Spring in Lycoming County, which produces 18,000 gallons per minute. The biggest waterfall among the hundreds known is Bushkill Falls ("Niagara of Pennsylvania") in Pike County. The upper part plunges 75 feet, and the lower part plunges 50 feet. The highest waterfall (200 feet) in Pennsylvania is Darbytown Falls in Wayne County. The hundreds of overlooks that provide grand vistas are especially common in the Appalachian Plateaus and the Appalachian Mountain section.

The beauty of the geology of Pennsylvania, of course, is not confined to the surface. Nearly 1,000 caves have been identified in Pennsylvania. Most are small solution caves in lower Paleozoic limestones of the Appalachian Mountain section. Caves are subterranean wildernesses that can be aesthetically pleasing, especially if they contain speleothems. There are 10 commercial caves open to the public in Pennsylvania.

CONCLUSION

This summary of the geology of Pennsylvania, detailed in the individual chapters, may leave the reader feeling that we now largely understand the geology of the state. After more than a century of investigation, some aspects of the geology, notably economic geology, are indeed fairly well known and understood. In other aspects, such as the deep tectonic framework, we are, in a sense, just getting started. Thus, the present volume is really an interim progress report. One of its primary purposes is to document and emphasize holes in the geological fabric that require further research.

What follows, with no ranking implied, is a sampling of unsolved problems or geological mysteries worthy of investigation. No claim is made that all significant problems are included, because the list is not comprehensive. Neither is it suggested that the problems noted are the most important ones. The intent of the list is to impress the reader with the broad range of problems remaining to be solved. It is hoped that this list and other problems noted at the end of each chapter will stimulate readers to pursue some of these topics and add to the geological knowledge of Pennsylvania.

1. How will we ensure the competitiveness of our extractive mineral industries and yet protect the environment?

2. Where is the Precambrian-Cambrian boundary in southeastern Pennsylvania?

3. What is the real age of the Glenarm Supergroup, and what is its relationship to the Chilhowee Series and "normal" Cambrian and Ordovician strata? In what tectono-depositional site was the Glenarm created? Does the origin of the "Martic Line" hold a partial answer to this question?

4. What is the relative influence of external and internal processes in the control of repetitive lithologies in the Pennsylvanian System?

5. To what extent was Cenozoic tectonism (uplift and warping) involved in the entrench-ment of major streams in southeastern Pennsylvania and in the Pittsburgh region?

6. Is there actually an "Eastern Overthrust Belt" and unmetamorphosed Cambrian strata beneath all rocks in southeastern Pennsylvania? Is there natural gas below the décollement?

7. What really caused drainage reversal in the Late Triassic?

8. Did the Anthracite thrust sheet exist along with a subsequent thick blanket of molassic sediment?

9. Are the parent rocks (protoliths) of Grenville gneisses in the Reading Prong and Piedmont Upland similar? Can these rocks be correlated; did they have the same tectonic and thermal history? If not, do they represent juxtaposed exotic terranes? If so, when did this happen?

10. Why is there a structural sag between the Reading Prong and South Mountain in northern Lancaster County? Why did these two external massifs have such different tectonic histories? Why did the area of the Paleozoic structural sag become structurally high ("Narrow Neck") during development of the Mesozoic basins? Is there cause and effect implied?

Vertical contact between the Upper Ordovician Juniata Formation (left, darker gray) and the Lower Silurian Tuscarora Formation (right, lighter gray) in the Juniata River water gap through Evitts Mountain along U.S. Route 30 just east of Bedford, Bedford County, in the Appalachian Mountain section of the Ridge and Valley physiographic province. Highway guardrail serves as scale.

Part II

STRATIGRAPHY AND
SEDIMENTARY TECTONICS

Rocks are the basic documents, or sources of fact, in any field of geologic inquiry. The interpretation of their sequence, physical properties, and lateral distribution provides an understanding of the succession of geological events that created what is observed today. These parameters can also be used as a guide to locate economically valuable mineral resources and to identify potential geologic hazards. In Part II of this volume, Precambrian to Jurassic bedrock and Upper Cretaceous to Holocene sediments are described, and interpretations of their characteristics are discussed. For convenience, the approach is systemic, beginning with the oldest, the Precambrian, and ending with the youngest, the Quaternary. This may seem somewhat artificial because there is commonly no easily discernible physical break between consecutive systems, although unconformities do occur locally and are widespread in some cases.

The bulk of Part II is about Paleozoic and Mesozoic sedimentary or metasedimentary rocks, but Precambrian crystalline rocks and Jurassic diabase and kimberlite intrusions are described as well. The depositional history of each system is explained along with its relationship to tectonic activity, which exerted a strong influence on lithology, facies changes, and depositional environment. Parts of Pennsylvania's stratigraphic sequence need more investigation because much is deeply buried or poorly exposed. As more research is carried out and new ideas develop, changes in our understanding of the stratigraphy will inevitably occur. New formations will be defined. Older stratigraphic concepts and names will be formally abandoned or will simply fall into disuse. New correlations will be discerned, and some formations may be subdivided into members or elevated to group status.

As an aid in understanding these chapters, it is strongly recommended that the reader consult General Geology Report 75, *Stratigraphic Correlation Chart of Pennsylvania* (Berg and others, 1986), published by the Pennsylvania Geological Survey.

—Charles H. Shultz

Migmatized amphibolite gneiss showing plunging and overturned isoclinal folds. This is part of the Grenville basement complex, identified as the Baltimore Gneiss. The location is the Glen Mills quarry on the east end of the Avondale anticline in Delaware County, 18 miles west-southwest of Philadelphia.

CHAPTER 3

PRECAMBRIAN AND LOWER PALEOZOIC METAMORPHIC AND IGNEOUS ROCKS

There are two fundamentally different groups of Precambrian rocks in Pennsylvania. One group is the basement complex, which is of Middle Proterozoic, Grenville age (circa 1,000 Ma). The second group is of Late Proterozoic age (circa 900 to 570 Ma) and marks the beginning of the Appalachian cycle. Structurally complex Grenville rocks are exposed in the Reading Prong section of the New England physiographic province and form distinct anticlinoria in the Piedmont Upland section of the Piedmont physiographic province. The Reading Prong occurrences, and probably those of the Piedmont, are allochthonous and constitute the deformed cores of large nappes. The only autochthonous basement complex that has been sampled is in northwestern Pennsylvania, where five wells penetrated the Precambrian. Late Proterozoic rocks (Catoctin Formation and Chilhowee Series) are exposed principally in the South Mountain section of the Blue Ridge province and in a series of small outliers (Pigeon Hills-Hellam Hills-Chickies Rock trend) in York and Lancaster Counties.

Associated with Grenville rocks in the eastern Piedmont are the metasedimentary Glenarm Supergroup, numerous ultramafite bodies, and the Wilmington Complex. Embedded within the Glenarm are other ultramafites (State Line district) and the Springfield Granodiorite. The Glenarm, once considered to be entirely Precambrian, is now believed to range in age from Eocambrian to Late Ordovician. Lower grade Glenarm rocks in the western Piedmont are described in Chapter 4. The relationship between the Chilhowee Series and the Glenarm Supergroup is enigmatic because of structural complexity, Taconic (Late Ordovician) regional metamorphism, and a lack of fossils.

—Charles H. Shultz

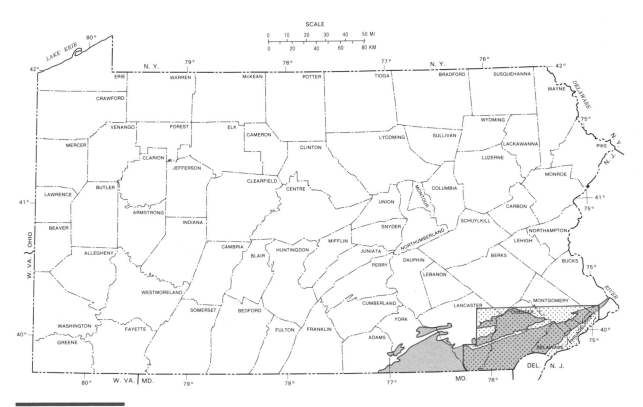

Figure 3A-1. Location of the Piedmont Upland section (color) in Pennsylvania (from Berg and others, 1989). The stippled area indicates the region shown in Figure 3A-2.

CHAPTER 3A

PRECAMBRIAN AND LOWER PALEOZOIC—SELECTED METAMORPHIC AND IGNEOUS ROCKS OF THE PIEDMONT UPLAND

MARIA LUISA CRAWFORD
Department of Geology
Bryn Mawr College
Bryn Mawr, PA 19010

WILLIAM A. CRAWFORD
Department of Geology
Bryn Mawr College
Bryn Mawr, PA 19010

ALICE L. HOERSCH
Department of Geology and Physics
LaSalle University
Philadelphia, PA 19141

MARY EMMA WAGNER
Department of Geology
University of Pennsylvania
Philadelphia, PA 19104

INTRODUCTION

The Piedmont Upland section of the Piedmont province in southeastern Pennsylvania (Figure 3A-1) is underlain by complexly deformed, metamorphosed igneous units, lesser amounts of metasedimentary Precambrian rocks, and a late Precambrian to early Paleozoic metasedimentary sequence with associated igneous bodies (Figure 3A-2 and Berg and others, 1980). Regional deformation and metamorphism occurred during two distinct tectonic episodes: one, the Grenville orogeny, at about 1,000 Ma and the second, the Taconic orogeny, at about 440 Ma (Sutter and others, 1980). Most of the pre-Grenville Precambrian rocks show the superimposed effects of both tectonic events; the late Precambrian to early Paleozoic sequence shows only the effects of the Late Ordovician Taconic orogeny.

The Piedmont Upland section is divided by the authors into two subsections: the Northern Upland consists of Mine Ridge and the Honey Brook Upland; and the Southern Upland includes the areas underlain by the Baltimore Gneiss, Wilmington Complex, Glenarm Supergroup, and Springfield granodiorite gneiss. These two subsections are separated in the eastern half of the Piedmont province by the Chester and Whitemarsh Valleys of the Piedmont Lowland section (Figure 3A-2).

NORTHERN UPLAND

The Honey Brook Upland (Figure 3A-2) is underlain by rocks metamorphosed to the granulite and amphibolite facies (Figure 3A-3) during the Grenville orogeny (Sutter and others, 1980). Work by Crawford and Hoersch (1984) in the Honey Brook Upland

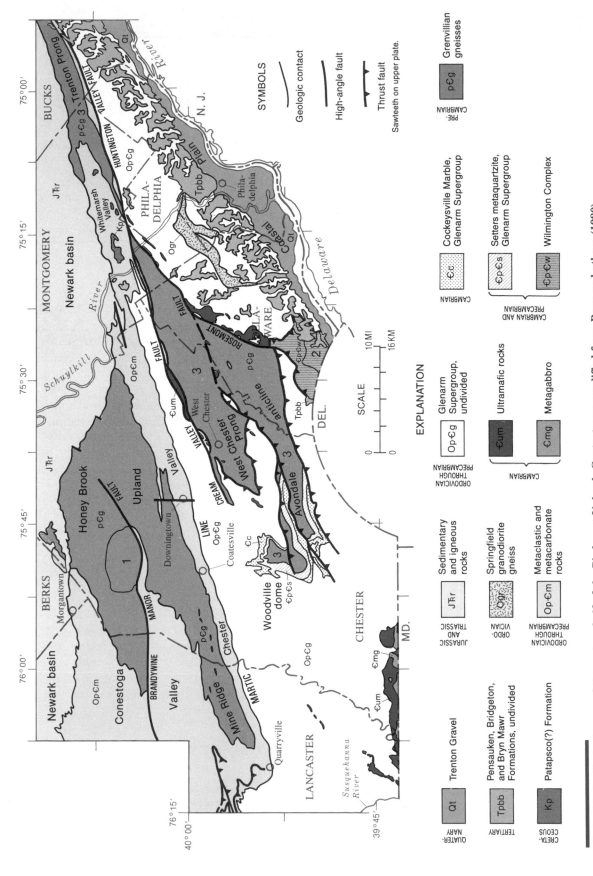

Figure 3A–2. Geologic map of the eastern half of the Piedmont Upland. Contacts are modified from Berg and others (1980). Geologic features identified by number are Honey Brook anorthosite (1), Arden pluton (2), and Baltimore Gneiss (3).

showed that most granulite-facies rocks lie north of the Brandywine Manor fault (Figure 3A–2), and many upper-amphibolite-facies rocks lie south of the fault. The mineral assemblages characteristic of these facies of regional metamorphism and their approximate conditions of formation are given in Table 3A–1. The Brandywine Manor fault dies out in the eastern part of the Honey Brook Upland, and the boundary between the two facies is gradational in this area. The granulite-facies rocks consist of felsic and intermediate charnockitic gneisses, mafic granulite gneisses, and meta-anorthosites (Figure 3A–4) (Crawford and Hoersch, 1984). The mafic granulite gneisses originally may have been basalts. Parents of the amphibolite-facies rocks, which include banded amphibolite (Figure 3A–5), intermediate to felsic gneisses (Figure 3A–6), and marble, were volcanic rocks of a basalt-andesite-rhyolite series, associated volcaniclastic and clastic sediments, and minor carbonate units (Crawford and Hoersch, 1984).

Some of the felsic gneisses of both metamorphic grades and all of the marbles contain graphite (Miller, 1912b). Carbon-isotope analyses by Crawford and Valley (1990) indicated that graphite formation in these gneisses and in the marble resulted from metamorphism of organic-rich muds and carbonates accompanied by fluid flow associated with the development of migmatites. The equilibrium fractionation of carbon isotopes between coexisting calcite and graphite in the marbles provides the means to calculate temperatures of metamorphism. Granulite-facies rocks record temperatures averaging 748°C, whereas the temperatures of amphibolite-facies rocks average 690°C.

Mine Ridge extends southwest from the southern part of the Honey Brook Upland (Figure 3A–2). It is underlain by intimately mixed felsic and mafic schists and gneisses that were metamorphosed to the lower amphibolite facies (defined by the presence of minerals listed in Table 3A–1). Hoersch and Crawford (1988) suggested that these schists and gneisses were originally igneous rocks of basaltic composition and sediments high in alumina and silica.

The Honey Brook Upland and Mine Ridge both contain small, elongated ultramafic bodies (some wholly or partially serpentinized), the trends of which generally parallel the foliation, bedding-plane, and fault-plane attitudes of enclosing gneisses.

Figure 3A–3. Amphibolite-facies gneisses cut by pegmatite dikes, Pa. Route 82 north of Coatesville, Chester County.

Table 3A–1. *Essential Minerals and Conditions of Formation of Metamorphic Facies in the Piedmont Upland*

Granulite facies: >700°C; >5 kilobars (>1,292°F; >72,500 psi)
    Charnockitic and other quartzo-feldspathic rocks:
        quartz-microperthite-hypersthene-plagioclase-garnet±
        hornblende±biotite
    Metabasaltic rocks:
        plagioclase-hypersthene-augite-quartz-garnet±hornblende
    Meta-argillites:
        quartz-perthite-garnet-plagioclase-sillimanite±cordierite

Upper amphibolite facies: 550–700°C; >5 kilobars (1,022–1,292°F; >72,500 psi)
    Quartzo-feldspathic rocks:
        quartz-plagioclase-potassium feldspar-biotite-hornblende-
        muscovite
    Metabasaltic rocks:
        plagioclase-hornblende±biotite±quartz±clinopyroxene
    Meta-argillites:
        quartz-plagioclase-muscovite-biotite-garnet-staurolite-
        kyanite

Lower amphibolite facies: 450–550°C; ~5 kilobars (842–1,022°F; 72,500 psi)
    Quartzo-feldspathic rocks:
        quartz-plagioclase-microcline-muscovite-biotite
    Metabasaltic rocks:
        hornblende-plagioclase-garnet±quartz±biotite±epidote
    Meta-argillites:
        quartz-plagioclase-muscovite-biotite-garnet±staurolite

Greenschist facies: 350–450°C; 4–5 kilobars (662–842°F; 58,000–72,500 psi)
    Quartzo-feldspathic rocks:
        quartz-albite-muscovite-chlorite
    Metabasaltic rocks:
        chlorite-actinolite-albite-biotite-epidote±quartz±calcite
    Meta-argillite:
        quartz-albite-muscovite-chlorite-biotite-garnet±chloritoid

Figure 3A–4. Meta-anorthosite, Honey Brook Upland, abandoned railroad parallel to Pa. Route 282 south of Glenmoore, Chester County. The rock is dominantly plagioclase with minor garnet (dark spots on either side of hammer handle).

Figure 3A–5. Banded amphibolite-facies gneiss, Honey Brook Upland, Little Conestoga Road west of Marsh Creek Lake, Chester County.

Figure 3A–6. Felsic gneiss, Mine Ridge, eastbound lane of U.S. Route 30 bypass west of Coatesville, Chester County.

All crystalline rocks of the Northern Upland are, to one degree or another, overprinted by lower-greenschist mineral assemblages (defined by blue-green amphibole rims around hornblende, uralitization of pyroxene, and saussuritization of plagioclase). This metamorphic overprinting probably formed during the Taconic orogeny, at which time the overlying lower Paleozoic units were metamorphosed to the greenschist facies.

Both the Honey Brook Upland and Mine Ridge are crosscut by diabase dikes (Figure 3A–7), some of which are metamorphosed to the greenschist facies but still preserve their igneous ophitic texture. Because the dikes do not cut the Cambrian-Ordovician sedimentary rocks, they are probably late Precambrian in age. Unmetamorphosed dikes, the trends of which parallel those of known Mesozoic-age dikes to the north, also occur in the area.

CHESTER AND WHITEMARSH VALLEYS

South of Mine Ridge and the Honey Brook Upland are the Chester and Whitemarsh Valleys. The Whitemarsh Valley is a narrow syncline of Cambrian to Precambrian metaquartzite, phyllites, and marble. The northern limb of this syncline continues to the west as the Chester Valley. The metasediments are the eastward extension of lower Paleozoic and Precambrian units exposed in the Conestoga Valley (Figure 3A–2), metamorphosed to the chlorite and biotite grades of the greenschist facies. These rocks unconformably overlie the Precambrian rocks that are exposed in the Northern Upland to the north of Chester Valley and the Trenton Prong to the east of the Whitemarsh Valley. The nature of their contact with rocks of the Glenarm Supergroup to the south and west (the Martic Line) has been a subject of debate for many years but is presently considered by most to be a stratigraphic boundary (see Chapter 16). The stratigraphy of these units is described in Chapter 4.

SOUTHERN UPLAND

Within the Southern Upland, south of the Chester and Whitemarsh Valleys, five distinct units are recognized: (1) Precambrian gneisses (Baltimore Gneiss), (2) gneisses and meta-

plutonic rocks of the Wilmington Complex, (3) metasedimentary and metavolcanic rocks and intrusive igneous bodies of the Glenarm Supergroup, (4) metamorphosed ultramafic rocks associated mostly with rocks of the Glenarm Supergroup, and (5) the Springfield granite/granodiorite gneiss.

The Baltimore Gneiss, the oldest unit in the Southern Upland, was metamorphosed during the Grenville orogeny. It occurs in four different blocks: the Trenton Prong, the West Chester Prong, the Avondale anticline, and the Woodville dome (Figure 3A–2). In the latter two blocks, the Baltimore Gneiss is unconformably overlain by the Setters metaquartzite and Cockeysville Marble, the lowermost members of the Glenarm Supergroup. In the Trenton Prong, the gneiss is unconformably overlain by the late Precambrian(?) Chickies Formation (see Chapter 4 for further discussion of the Chickies). Elsewhere, thrust faults and steeply dipping faults and shear zones separate the Baltimore Gneiss from the Wissahickon Formation, and the Wissahickon from the Octoraro Formation.

In the West Chester Prong, the Baltimore Gneiss includes various lithologically distinct units. Most common are coarse-grained rocks of approximately quartz-monzonitic composition and medium-grained gneisses of gabbroic composition. There are scattered occurrences of garnet and/or sillimanite metaquartzites, a few of which also contain spinel. These rocks were all metamorphosed to the granulite facies during the Grenville orogeny, resulting in two-pyroxene (hypersthene and augite) assemblages in most of the

Figure 3A–7. Massive charnockite of the Honey Brook Upland cut by a diabase dike (center of photograph), south of Pa. Route 401, 0.6 mile west of Union School, Chester County.

gneisses, many of which also contain garnet. As in the Northern Upland, these Grenville rocks are cut by diabase dikes. Both the granulite-facies gneisses of Grenville age and the undeformed diabase dikes are overprinted by a high-pressure amphibolite-facies metamorphism of Taconic age (Wagner and Crawford, 1975). This is the same metamorphic event that produced greenschist-facies assemblages in the Northern Upland and in the Chester and Whitemarsh Valleys. The mineral assemblages in both the gneisses and the diabase dikes were partially recrystallized during this metamorphism, although original textures are preserved in many of the rocks. Garnet coronas formed around all the mafic minerals wherever they were in contact with plagioclase (Figures 3A–8 and 3A–9). In the aluminous metaquartzites, sillimanite inverted to kyanite.

The poorly exposed amphibolite-facies gneisses of the Trenton Prong, the Woodville dome, and part of the Avondale anticline are dominantly felsic. In the eastern Avondale anticline, there are also intermediate to mafic rocks. The amphibolite-facies gneisses differ from those of the granulite facies in the absence of orthopyroxene and the scarcity of garnet. Few of the amphibolite-facies gneisses show evidence of being metamorphosed more than once; hence, they may be younger than the rocks of the granulite facies.

The Wilmington Complex (Ward, 1959) is probably the next younger unit in the Southern Upland. It consists of mafic and felsic two-pyroxene gneisses metamorphosed to the granulite facies. The Wilmington is intruded by gabbroic igneous rocks and a calc-alkaline norite-charnockite pluton, the Arden pluton (number 2 on Figure 3A–2) (Wagner and Srogi, 1987), dated at 502 ± 20 Ma by Foland and Muessig (1978). Rare aluminum-rich rocks contain garnet, cordierite, and sillimanite; some also have spinel and/or corundum. The gneisses show evidence of only one episode of metamorphism, considered to be of Taconic age (Grauert and Wagner, 1975), in contrast to the two distinct episodes recorded by the Grenville-age gneisses.

The Glenarm Supergroup is a thick sequence of metasediments, probably deposited between latest Precambrian and Late Ordovician time. From the base up, the Glenarm Supergroup includes the feldspathic and micaceous Setters metaquartzite; the impure calcit-

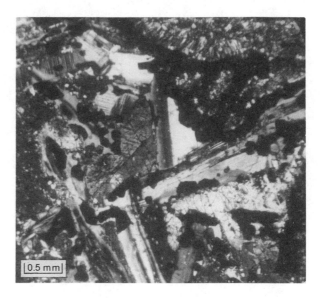

Figure 3A–8. Photomicrograph of metamorphosed diabase cutting Baltimore Gneiss showing a relict ophitic texture with garnet (black) growing between plagioclase laths and pyroxene grains. Crossed polars.

ic and dolomitic Cockeysville Marble; meta-argillitic and quartzitic schists and gneisses of the Wissahickon Formation and phyllites of the Octoraro Formation (Figure 3A–10); metaquartzites and metasiltstones of the Peters Creek Formation; the Cardiff quartz-pebble metaconglomerate; and the Peach Bottom Slate. Fur-

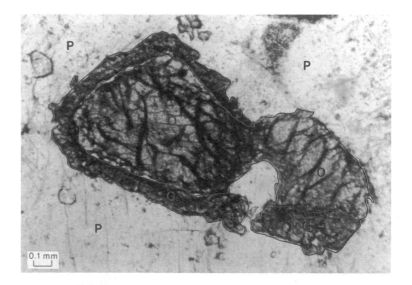

Figure 3A–9. Photomicrograph of mineral textures in polymetamorphic Baltimore Gneiss of the Southern Upland showing a garnet corona (G) around orthopyroxene (O), both of which are surrounded by plagioclase (P).

ther details on these Glenarm units are supplied in Chapter 4. Amphibolites of basaltic composition interlayered with schists of the Wissahickon Formation occur south of the Avondale anticline, south of the Trenton Prong, and in the westernmost Wissahickon, east of Hanover, York County. These probably represent metamorphosed basalt flows or diabase sills.

West of Philadelphia, the Springfield porphyroblastic granodiorite and augen gneiss (Figure 3A–2) intrudes and is surrounded by high-grade Wissahickon Formation schist (Postel, 1940). The northern and western margins of the augen gneiss are strongly sheared; elsewhere, crosscutting igneous contact relationships occur. Although it has not been dated, field relations suggest that the granodiorite intruded during the regional metamorphism of the host rocks.

The metamorphism of the Glenarm Supergroup, presumably Taconic, is greenschist facies in the west and northwest and amphibolite facies in the southeast. Quartz-albite-muscovite-chlorite assemblages characterize the greenschist-facies Octoraro Formation that lies north and west of the West Chester Prong-Woodville dome culmination. The most aluminous units contain chloritoid and paragonite. Around the west end of Mine Ridge and around the Woodville dome, higher grade garnetiferous schists crop out at the crests of postmetamorphic antiforms (Chapter 16). South of the Rosemont and Huntington Valley faults, the Wissahickon Formation was metamorphosed to the amphibolite facies (Figure 3A–11).

Figure 3A–10. Outcrop of phyllites of the Octoraro Formation, Montgomery Avenue near Gulph Mills, Montgomery County.

Figure 3A–11. Outcrop of upper-amphibolite-facies schist of the Wissahickon Formation, Springton Reservoir, Montgomery County.

In this area, the Wissahickon can be subdivided into rocks of garnet, staurolite, kyanite, and sillimanite (Figure 3A–12) grade (Weiss, 1949; Wyckoff, 1952). In general, the metamorphic grade in these rocks increases southward. The highest grade occurs near the Wilmington Complex and south of the Avondale anticline. Here, sillimanite-orthoclase-biotite-garnet assemblages are most common and are overprinted in some localities by kyanite-staurolite assemblages (Figure 3A–13). In localities near the Wilmington Complex, the Wissahickon contains cordierite-orthoclase assemblages.

Large ultramafic bodies, mainly serpentinites, occur along the state line between Pennsylvania and Maryland (Figure 3A–2). These ultramafic rocks are bordered just to the south by metagabbros. They are part of a large, layered intrusion, the Baltimore Mafic Complex, thought to be tectonically emplaced (Crowley, 1976). The Baltimore Mafic Complex is considered to be an ophiolite by some (Morgan, 1977), but

Figure 3A–12. Outcrop of sillimanite-grade gneiss of the Wissahickon Formation, Kelly Drive near Strawberry Mansion Bridge, Philadelphia County.

Figure 3A–13. Photomicrograph of Wissahickon schist showing staurolite (ST) growing over sillimanite (SI) needles. B indicates biotite.

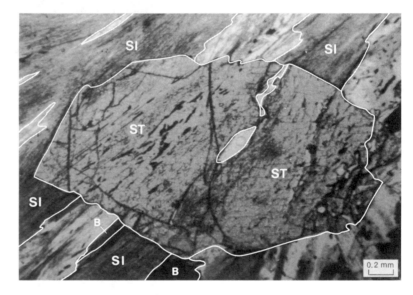

Figure 3A–14. Outcrop of serpentinite adjacent to the Rosemont fault, Lafayette Road, Montgomery County. Structures in the rock are due to movement along the fault.

this interpretation has been disputed (Shaw and Wasserburg, 1984; Sinha and Hanan, 1987). Additional, smaller ultramafic bodies are enclosed in schists of the Wissahickon Formation or occur between the Wissahickon Formation and Precambrian gneisses (Figure 3A–14) where the Setters metaquartzite and Cockeysville Marble are missing. Around the margins of the West Chester Prong, the ultramafic rocks are serpentinites (Figure 3A–2). Coarse-grained pyroxenites and mafic norites, all metamorphosed to varying degrees (Roberts, 1969), occur at the eastern end of the Avondale anticline. Some of the ultramafic bodies are entirely surrounded by Precambrian rocks.

PROBLEMS AND FUTURE RESEARCH

The geological relations in the Piedmont are complex and are not fully understood because of poor exposure and the lack of good age determinations for the individual rock units, their deformation, and their metamorphism. The Precambrian rocks and their metasedimentary cover in the Piedmont Upland are in some ways similar to, and in other ways different from, the units in the Reading Prong described in Chapter 3B. An important aim for future work should be to coordinate the geological history of the interior basement massifs and cover rocks and that of the exterior massifs, especially those of the Reading Prong.

Temperatures and pressures of metamorphism in the Piedmont Upland are imperfectly known, and more information is required to determine pressure-temperature-time paths for these rocks in order to understand the history of tectonic burial and subsequent uplift.

RECOMMENDED FOR FURTHER READING

Bascom, F. (1905), *Piedmont district of Pennsylvania*, Geological Society of America Bulletin, v. 16, p. 289–328.

Bascom, F., Clark, W. B., Darton, N. H., and others (1909), *Philadelphia folio, Pennsylvania-New Jersey-Delaware*, U.S. Geological Survey Geologic Atlas of the U.S., Folio 162, 23 p.

Bascom, F., Darton, N. H., Kümmel, H. B., and others (1909), *Trenton folio, New Jersey-Pennsylvania*, U.S. Geological Survey Geologic Atlas of the U.S., Folio 167, 24 p.

Bascom, F., and Miller, B. L. (1920), *Elkton-Wilmington folio, Maryland-Delaware-New Jersey-Pennsylvania*, U.S. Geological Survey Geologic Atlas of the U.S., Folio 211, 22 p.

Bascom, F., and Stose, G. W. (1932), *Coatesville-West Chester folio, Pennsylvania-Delaware*, U.S. Geological Survey Geologic Atlas of the U.S., Folio 223, 15 p.

———— (1938), *Geology and mineral resources of the Honeybrook and Phoenixville quadrangles, Pennsylvania*, U.S. Geological Survey Bulletin 891, 145 p.

Cameron, E. N., and Weis, P. L. (1960), *Strategic graphite—A survey*, U.S. Geological Survey Bulletin 1082-E, p. 201–322.

Crawford, M. L., and Crawford, W. A. (1980), *Metamorphic and tectonic history of the Pennsylvania Piedmont*, Journal of the Geological Society of London, v. 137, p. 311–320.

Crawford, W. A., Robelen, P. G., and Kalmbach, J. H. (1971), *The Honey Brook anorthosite*, American Journal of Science, v. 271, p. 333–349.

Knopf, E. B., and Jonas, A. I. (1929), *Geology of the McCalls Ferry-Quarryville district, Pennsylvania*, U.S. Geological Survey Bulletin 799, 156 p.

Smith, I. F. (1922), *Genesis of anorthosites of Piedmont Pennsylvania*, The Pan-American Geologist, v. 38, p. 29–50.

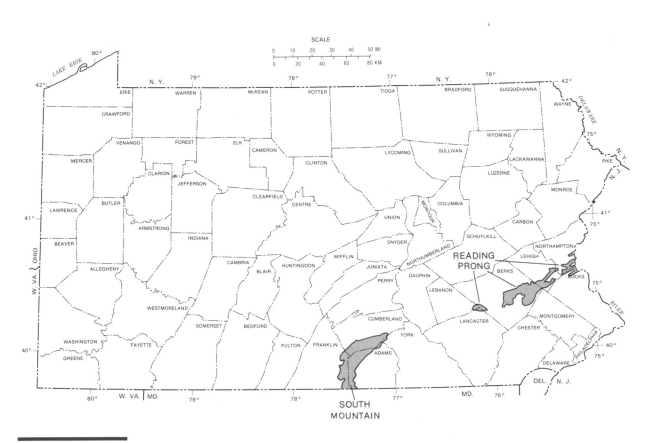

Figure 3B–1. Location of South Mountain and the Reading Prong (from Berg and others, 1989).

36

CHAPTER 3B   PRECAMBRIAN AND LOWER PALEOZOIC METAMORPHIC AND IGNEOUS ROCKS— SOUTH MOUNTAIN AND READING PRONG

AVERY ALA DRAKE, JR.
U.S. Geological Survey
928 National Center
Reston, VA 20192

INTRODUCTION

South Mountain is an upland that constitutes the northern extremity of the Appalachian Blue Ridge, a tectonic and physiographic province that extends from northwestern Georgia to near Dillsburg in York County (Figure 3B–1). The Reading Prong, another upland (Figure 28–2), is part of a prominent physiographic and geologic province that extends from east of the Hudson River to west of Reading in Berks County (Figure 3B–1). Both of these uplands are bounded on the southeast by the Newark-Gettysburg basin and on the northwest by the Great Valley.

These two uplands occur along the margin between the internal metamorphic zone and the foreland of the Appalachian orogen and have been termed external basement massifs by Drake and others (1988). Throughout most of its length, the Blue Ridge has a core of Middle Proterozoic crystalline rocks. These rocks, however, plunge out in central Maryland and are present only in the subsurface in Pennsylvania. Middle Proterozoic rocks form the core of the Reading Prong throughout its length. The Middle Proterozoic rocks that crop out in South Mountain in Maryland differ from those of the Reading Prong. In Pennsylvania, South Mountain is underlain by a thick sequence of metamorphosed Late Proterozoic volcanic rocks and Late Proterozoic and Cambrian sedimentary rocks, whereas only a few questionable volcanic rocks crop out within the Reading Prong. The sedimentary sequence is very thin. The stratigraphies of the two massifs are given in Figure 3B–2.

Petrographic and petrochemical data pertaining to the rocks described herein can be found in Stose (1932), Fauth (1968, 1978), and Rankin (1976) for South Mountain, and Aaron (1969) and Drake (1969,

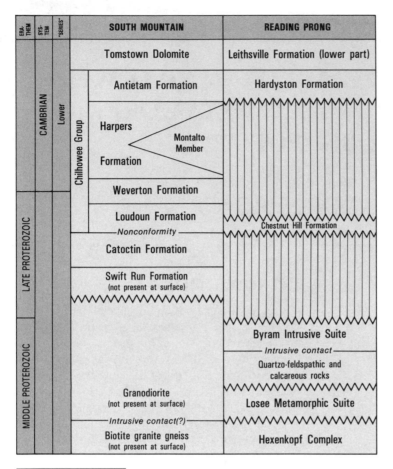

ERA-THEM	SYS-TEM	"SERIES"	SOUTH MOUNTAIN	READING PRONG
CAMBRIAN		Lower	Tomstown Dolomite	Leithsville Formation (lower part)
			Antietam Formation	Hardyston Formation
			Harpers Formation / Montalto Member	
			Weverton Formation	
LATE PROTEROZOIC			Loudoun Formation	
			—Nonconformity—	Chestnut Hill Formation
			Catoctin Formation	
			Swift Run Formation (not present at surface)	
MIDDLE PROTEROZOIC				Byram Intrusive Suite
				—Intrusive contact—
				Quartzo-feldspathic and calcareous rocks
			Granodiorite (not present at surface)	Losee Metamorphic Suite
			—Intrusive contact(?)—	
			Biotite granite gneiss (not present at surface)	Hexenkopf Complex

(Chilhowee Group spans Antietam, Harpers, Weverton, Loudoun Formations in South Mountain column)

Figure 3B–2. Stratigraphic nomenclature for South Mountain and the Reading Prong.

1984) for the Reading Prong. The stratigraphic nomenclature is based on that of the Pennsylvania Geological Survey (modified from Berg and others, 1983).

MIDDLE PROTEROZOIC ROCKS

The Middle Proterozoic basement rocks in the Maryland part of South Mountain include few, if any, unambiguous metamorphosed sedimentary rocks. The bulk appear to be metamorphosed and foliated granitoids (Rankin and others 1983; Drake, 1984). This is in marked contrast with the Reading Prong, in which about half of the Middle Proterozoic rocks are metasedimentary or metavolcanic (Drake, 1984).

South Mountain

Middle Proterozoic basement rocks in the core of South Mountain plunge beneath the surface about 20 miles south of the Pennsylvania-Maryland border. Stose and Stose (1946) recognized two major

rock types in the Maryland outcrop, biotite granite gneiss and granodiorite. The biotite granite gneiss appears to be the older rock and to be monzogranite. This unit contains some relict layers of biotite schist, which may represent an older metasedimentary rock. The granodiorite, a foliated granitoid, contains hornblende as the primary mafic mineral. These rocks have been through a Paleozoic greenschist metamorphism with their cover, presumably at chlorite grade based on the wholesale chloritization of garnet in the gneisses exposed along the Potomac River.

These rocks do not resemble those in the Reading Prong, nor do they resemble the Baltimore Gneiss. They are, however, similar to many rocks in the Grenville terrane of Quebec.

Reading Prong

The Middle Proterozoic rocks of the Reading Prong (Figure 3B–3) are known primarily from the work of Buckwalter (1959, 1962) and Drake (1969, 1984). The oldest rocks constitute the Hexenkopf Complex (Yh on Figure 3B–3) that underlies a small area 5 miles east of Bethlehem, Northampton County. Although quite heterogeneous, the complex consists of three general rock types, hornblende-augite-quartz-andesine gneiss (Figure 3B–4), epidote-augite-hornblende-plagioclase gneiss, and quartz-garnet-augite granofels. The first rock type constitutes about 60 percent of the complex and is thought to be a severely altered and metamorphosed mafic diorite or gabbro. The second rock type forms about 25 percent of the complex and is thought to be a metamorphosed and altered pyroxenite. The granofels constitutes about 15 percent of the complex and lies across the contact between the other rock types. It is thought to be a metamorphosed and altered impure chert above a mafic to ultramafic igneous body. The Hexenkopf Complex may be part of an ophiolite suite.

The Hexenkopf Complex is overlain by a highly sodic sequence of rocks called the Losee Metamorphic Suite (Yl on Figure 3B–3). The Losee, which is quite abundant in New Jersey, occurs in only three small bodies in Northampton County (Figure 3B–3) and in an even smaller body south of Allentown (not shown on Figure 3B–3). The rocks consist largely of sodic plagioclase and quartz and, in most cases, con-

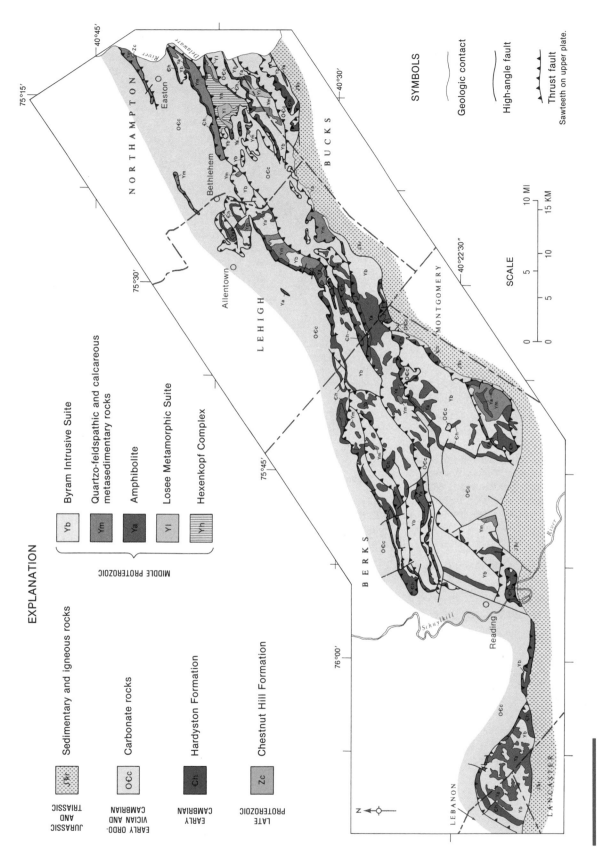

EXPLANATION

Sedimentary and igneous rocks — JTr — JURASSIC AND TRIASSIC

Carbonate rocks — OCc — EARLY ORDOVICIAN AND CAMBRIAN

Hardyston Formation — Ch — EARLY CAMBRIAN

Chestnut Hill Formation — Zc — LATE PROTEROZOIC

MIDDLE PROTEROZOIC

Yb — Byram Intrusive Suite

Ym — Quartzo-feldspathic and calcareous metasedimentary rocks

Ya — Amphibolite

Yl — Losee Metamorphic Suite

Yh — Hexenkopf Complex

SYMBOLS

—— Geologic contact

—— High-angle fault

⊥⊥⊥ Thrust fault
Sawteeth on upper plate.

SCALE

0   5   10   15 KM

0   5   10 MI

Figure 3B-3. Generalized geologic map of the Reading Prong (modified from Berg and others, 1980, and Lyttle and Epstein, 1987).

Figure 3B–4. Hornblende-augite-quartz-andesine gneiss of the Hexenkopf Complex on Gaffney Hill, Nazareth 7.5-minute quadrangle. Note the granitic veining (light-colored streaks and blotches) and the ductile deformation under the hammer. The hammer is 16.75 inches long. Photograph by J. M. Aaron.

Figure 3B–5. Within the Losee Metamorphic Suite, hornblende-bearing oligoclase-quartz gneiss (near hammer) grades into albite-oligoclase granite (lower right) and albite pegmatite (upper part of photograph). Note the large crystals of sodic hornblende in the pegmatite. The outcrop is on Elephant Rock, Easton 7.5-minute quadrangle. The hammer is 12.75 inches long.

tain only minor amounts of mafic minerals (Drake, 1969, 1984). Parts of the suite are well layered and foliated, other parts are poorly foliated granofels, and still other parts are granitoids or pegmatites (Figure 3B–5). Most contacts with metasedimentary rocks are conformable, but locally some contacts are slightly discordant.

The origin of the Losee Metamorphic Suite has been somewhat controversial. The phases are quite similar petrographically and chemically (Drake, 1969, 1984), and direct observation in the field shows that the granitic and pegmatitic phases have been generated within the oligoclase-quartz gneiss by anatexis at about the present level of erosion. The very high $Na_2O:K_2O$ ratios and the very high normative albite (Drake, 1969, 1984) have led to the interpretation that the Losee is quartz keratophyre (sodic felsite).

At places, the oligoclase-quartz gneiss of the Losee contains sparse to moderate amounts of inter-layered amphibolite. This amphibolite is more sodic

than the other amphibolites in the Reading Prong and is interpreted to be spilite (soda-rich basalt). The Losee, then, is interpreted to be a metamorphosed volcanic pile of quartz keratophyre and interlayered spilitic basalt.

Amphibolite (Ya on Figure 3B–3), the Pochuck Gneiss of previous workers, is associated with all the other rock units. It includes amphibolite, pyroxene amphibolite, and two-pyroxene amphibolite (Drake, 1969, 1984). The origins of these rocks are difficult to determine because of the lack of primary features and extensive migmatization. Some appear to have had a metasedimentary parentage, but others appear to be metamorphosed basalt because of their apparent relict pillow structure (Figure 3B–6).

The Losee Metamorphic Suite is overlain by a sequence of quartzo-feldspathic and calcareous metasedimentary rocks (Ym on Figure 3B–3) that are most abundant in the eastern part of the Reading Prong in Pennsylvania. The calcareous rocks are not abundant. Dolomite marble crops out at the northern edge of the Prong near the Delaware River, where it is metasomatically metamorphosed to serpentinite-talc rock and tremolite rock. This is the so-called Franklin Marble of other workers, but geologic mapping at the scale of 1:24,000 shows that these rocks are not continuous with the calcite marbles of the Franklin-

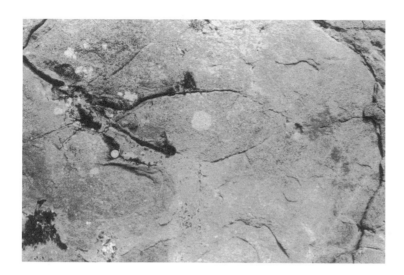

Figure 3B–6. Probable relict pillows in amphibolite in the Hamburg Mountains, New Jersey. The pillow below the coin has what appears to be a metamorphosed rind. The coin is 0.75 inch in diameter.

Sterling district in New Jersey (A. A. Drake, Jr., and R. A. Volkert, unpublished data). Only small bodies of marble interlayered with quartzo-feldspathic gneiss are known to occur elsewhere in the Prong.

Quartzo-feldspathic gneiss is common in eastern Pennsylvania and was included in the Byram Gneiss of earlier workers. Two types of gneiss are recognized, biotite-quartz-feldspar gneiss and potassic-feldspar gneiss. Biotite-quartz-feldspar gneiss is highly variable in both composition and texture but is characterized by conspicuous biotite and prominent compositional layering (Figure 3B–7). The unit is migmatized by alaskite (leucogranite) of the Byram Intrusive Suite at many places.

Potassic-feldspar gneiss (Figure 3B–8) is characterized by its high content of potassic feldspar and quartz and a paucity of plagioclase. Much of the unit is heterogeneous, and some phases approach quartzite in composition. It is quite siliceous and has high $K_2O:Na_2O$ ratios, thereby differing from the biotite-quartz-feldspar gneiss. In some places, the unit is granitic in appearance and forms small sheets, veins, lenses, and blotches within rocks of apparent metasedimentary aspect (Figure 3B–9). This has led some workers to interpret the entire unit to be an igneous rock. However, the general heterogeneity and the high silica and potash content support a metasedimentary origin. The granitic phases are thought to have resulted from local anatexis.

The Byram Intrusive Suite (Yb on Figure 3B–3) is a sequence of granitoid rocks consisting of quartz, potassic feldspar, oligoclase, and various amounts of mafic minerals. It is common throughout the Reading Prong and occurs in regionally conformable sheets, pods, and refolded bodies. Although regionally conformable, these granitic bodies locally cut across structures in the older rocks. Three mappable end members are microperthite alaskite, hornblende granite, and biotite granite. The Byram rocks have a primary flow foliation and lineation and, at many places, a secondary metamorphic foliation. Only the most deformed phases are gneissic. Most of the Byram rocks are syenogranites, some are monzogranites, and a few are alkali-feldspar granites. Chemically, the Byram rocks have a composition that would allow melting at a relatively low temperature. The determination of the origin of such rocks is always a problem (Drake, 1984). It is clear that the Byram rocks were mobile in most cases. Byram alaskite occurs in veins in both amphibolite and biotite-quartz-feldspar gneiss, forming migmatites. In some places, hornblende and biotite granites appear to result from the almost complete assimilation of amphibolite and biotite-quartz-feldspar gneiss by alaskite. The Byram is probably an anatectite that originated at a depth beneath the current level of erosion. Hornblende granite of the Byram Intrusive Suite

Figure 3B–7. Polydeformed, migmatitic, biotite-quartz-feldspar gneiss on Chestnut Hill, Easton 7.5-minute quadrangle. The light-colored material is alaskite (leucogranite) of the Byram Intrusive Suite. The pocketknife is 3.5 inches long.

Figure 3B–8. Well-layered potassic-feldspar gneiss near Steel City, Nazareth 7.5-minute quadrangle. Note the thin anatectic granite seams along the layering and foliation. The hammer is 16.75 inches long. Photograph by J. M. Aaron.

has a U-Pb age of about 1090 Ma (Drake and others, 1991).

The metamorphic history of the Reading Prong in Pennsylvania is not clear because of poor expo-

sure and because the composition of the rocks is not conducive to such studies. The more aluminous parts of the potassic feldspar gneiss contain sillimanite and no muscovite, and hypersthene-bearing rocks occur sporadically. This suggests metamorphism to at least upper amphibolite facies and, more likely, hornblende-granulite facies. The rocks later experienced a low greenschist-facies metamorphism during the Paleozoic, as have pelitic rocks in the sedimentary cover up to and including the Ordovician Martinsburg Formation.

The Hexenkopf Complex and the Losee Metamorphic Suite constitute a basement of oceanic rocks upon which a continental-margin sequence of calcareous and quartzo-feldspathic rocks was deposited (Drake, 1984). It is here suggested that the metasedimentary rocks were deposited in a rift basin outboard of a continental margin, much like those of Late Proterozoic and Early Cambrian age that were deposited in the rift basin outboard of the North American craton. If this is so, mafic volcanic rocks, now amphibolites, would be expected in the metasedimentary pile.

The Middle Proterozoic rocks of the Reading Prong are very much like those of the Adirondack Mountains of New York and probably the Honey Brook Upland to the south, in the Piedmont of Chester County. They have certain similarities to the external basement massifs of the northern Appalachians. They differ, however, from those of the Blue Ridge-South Mountain anticlinorium and the internal basement massifs of the central and southern Appalachians.

UPPER PROTEROZOIC AND LOWER CAMBRIAN ROCKS

South Mountain (Figure 3B–10) contains a rift-related sequence of Late Proterozoic volcanic rocks that is about 2,500 feet thick, and a 4,300-foot-thick sequence of Late Proterozoic and Lower Cambrian alluvial and clastic marine sedimentary rocks. The Reading Prong, on the other hand, contains only a very sparse amount of Late Proterozoic rocks, some of which may have a volcanic origin.

Figure 3B–9. Polydeformed, granitic-appearing, potassic-feldspar gneiss on Chestnut Hill, Easton 7.5-minute quadrangle. The more granitic parts have the composition of alkali-feldspar granite. The pocketknife (upper center) is 3.5 inches long.

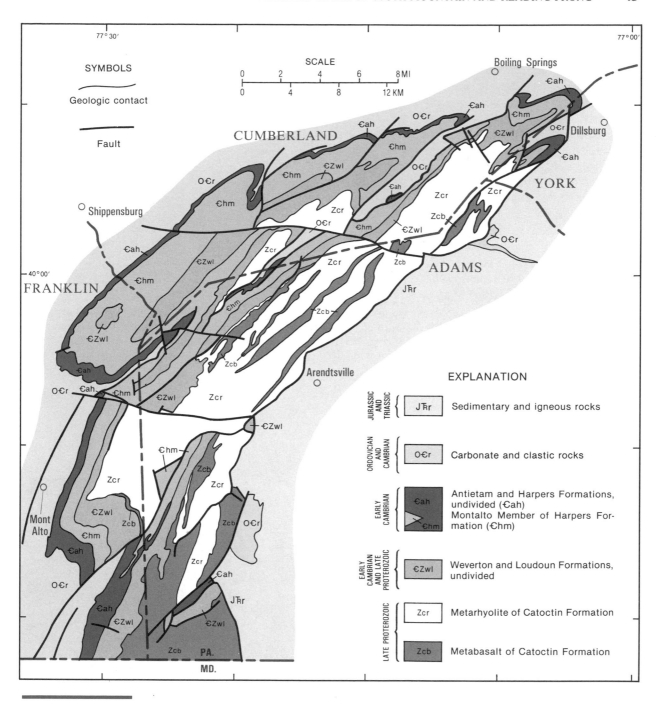

Figure 3B–10. Generalized geologic map of South Mountain (simplified from Berg and others, 1980).

Many of the metamorphosed diabase dikes that cut Middle Proterozoic rocks are probably of Late Proterozoic age. The Lower Cambrian clastic sequence in the Reading Prong is also quite thin (60 to 600 feet).

South Mountain

The Middle Proterozoic basement rocks of the Blue Ridge-South Mountain anticlinorium (not ex-

posed in Pennsylvania) are overlain by the Swift Run Formation, a sequence of tuffaceous slates, detrital quartzite, and, locally, some marble (Stose and Stose, 1946). The Swift Run, which does not crop out in Pennsylvania, is of Late Proterozoic age and is the precursor of the overlying sequence of volcanic rocks called the Catoctin Formation. In Pennsylvania, the Catoctin consists of both metabasalt (Zcb on Figure 3B–10) and metarhyolite (Zcr on Figure 3B–10) (Stose,

1932; Fauth, 1968, 1978). Catoctin metabasalt includes lava flows (Figure 3B–11) and tuffaceous beds. Much of the metabasalt is uniformly aphanitic to fine grained, although both amygdaloidal and porphyritic phases are known, as is some volcanic breccia. Although thoroughly metamorphosed to the greenschist facies, relict pyroxene and basaltic texture can be seen in places. The metabasalt is predominantly composed of albite, chlorite, epidote, and iron oxides. Basaltic tuff has been altered to actinolite-chlorite phyllite. The metabasalt commonly contains large, irregular bodies and veins of epidosite that have been shown by Reed and Morgan (1971) to result from greenschist metamorphism. Where well exposed in Virginia, the Catoctin has the features of a subaerial plateau basalt, such as columnar joints, thin breccia zones between flows, and flows of large areal extent (Reed, 1955). Chemically, the basalts are tholeiites (Reed, 1955; Reed and Morgan, 1971; Rankin, 1976).

Metarhyolite (Figure 3B–12) typically is a holocrystalline rock containing moderately abundant phenocrysts of albite and quartz. In most rocks, albite phenocrysts are more abundant than quartz phenocrysts (Fauth, 1978). Other metarhyolite is vitreous and phenocryst-poor. Some of the metarhyolite is flow-banded, but Fauth (1978) thought that most is not. The metarhyolite is high in alkalies; soda and potash total about 8 percent. The eruption of the rhyolitic rocks was subaerial, as indicated by well-formed columnar joints (Fauth, 1978). Most of the rocks were probably originally glassy, or partly glassy, and were interpreted by Fauth (1978) to represent both ash-fall tuffs and glassy lava flows.

The stratigraphic relationship of the metarhyolite to the metabasalt is uncertain, but on the basis of detailed field work, Fauth (1978) thought that these rock types occur in alternating layers (Figure 3B–13). Stose and Stose (1946) suggested that the Swift Run Formation that lies between Middle Proterozoic rocks and metabasalt in Maryland may be the distal end of a metarhyolite

Figure 3B–11. Rubbly-weathering metabasalt of the Catoctin Formation south of Pa. Route 16, near the Adams-Franklin County line, Iron Springs 7.5-minute quadrangle. The hammer is 16.75 inches long. Photograph by J. L. Fauth.

Figure 3B–12. Vitreous metarhyolite of the Catoctin Formation (left of pencil) intruded by a dike of metabasalt on the north side of Pa. Route 16, near the eastern border of the Iron Springs 7.5-minute quadrangle. The pencil is about 6 inches long. Photograph by J. L. Fauth.

layer. If this is so, early volcanic activity was rhyolitic at the north end of the Blue Ridge-South Mountain anticlinorium.

The Catoctin has been dated at about 820 Ma (Rankin and others, 1969). This age seems too old to many geologists, and Rankin (personal communi-

Figure 3B–13. Eighteen-inch layer or dike of metabasalt within vitreous metarhyolite in an outcrop at a Pennsylvania Department of Transportation supply area, Iron Springs 7.5-minute quadrangle. The hammer head is on the lower contact. The hammer is 16.75 inches long. Photograph by J. L. Fauth.

cation, 1984) has since suggested that 700 Ma may be a more realistic age. More recently, Badger and Sinha (1988) dated the Catoctin in central Virginia as 570 ± 36 Ma on the basis of an Rb-Sr isochron. The bimodal volcanic suite of South Mountain is characteristic of rift environments and is interpreted by Rankin (1976) to be the result of a rift event related to the opening of the Iapetus Ocean, which may date from about 700 Ma. Badger and Sinha (1988) suggested that the above data can be interpreted to indicate either a two-stage event or a very long episode of continental rifting.

The Catoctin is overlain by rocks of the Chilhowee Group (Figures 3B–2 and 3B–10); the contact appears to be nonconformable. The Chilhowee consists of, from oldest to youngest, the Loudoun, Weverton, Harpers, and Antietam Formations. Only the uppermost Antietam contains Early Cambrian fossils. All of these formations contain mineral assemblages consistent with the greenschist facies of regional metamorphism. The age of the Chilhowee has been a major problem in Appalachian geology, and any assignment was largely arbitrary. The Pennsylvania Geological Survey (Berg and others, 1983) considers the Loudoun, Weverton, and Harpers Formations to be Late Proterozoic and the Antietam to be Early Cambrian. The U.S. Geological Survey has traditionally considered the Antietam to be Early

Cambrian and the older units to be Early Cambrian(?). More recently, Simpson and Sundberg (1987) found Early Cambrian marine fossils about 600 feet above the base of the Unicoi Formation in southwestern Virginia. The Unicoi is the southern Appalachian equivalent of the Weverton Formation, so it would appear that the Weverton should be considered Late Proterozoic to Early Cambrian, the Loudoun Formation Late Proterozoic, and the Harpers Formation Early Cambrian. The Chilhowee has been interpreted to be an upwardly transitional (terrestrial to coastal to shallow) marine assemblage (Schwab, 1972).

The Loudoun Formation (200 feet thick) contains varicolored phyllite interbedded with laminated, very fine grained graywacke at the base and an upper unit of polymict conglomerate (Figure 3B–14). The Weverton Formation, having a minimum thickness of 900 feet, is conglomeratic at the base and consists largely of laminated and crossbedded quartzose graywacke (Figure 3B–15) containing some quartzite and phyllite. Both the Loudoun and Weverton are quite immature and probably represent waning rift-facies sedimentation. The Harpers Formation (2,500 feet in minimum thickness) consists of fine-grained graywacke and a lesser quantity of phyllite (Figure 3B–16). A massive quartzite, the Montalto Member, appears in southern Pennsylvania and becomes more prominent in the northeast, where South Mountain plunges out beneath the Great Valley (Figure 3B–10). The Antietam Formation (700 feet thick) is a quartzite (Figure 3B–17) that contains some fossiliferous friable sandstone at the top. The Montalto Member seems to be a lower tongue of this facies. The Antietam passes upward into the Tomstown Formation (see Chapter 4).

The thick Chilhowee sequence suggests rift-related sedimentation. This, combined with the peralkaline volcanism, led Rankin (1976) to suggest that the South Mountain area, his South Mountain salient, is the site of the failed arm of a tripartite rift system. This would appear to be a good interpretation.

Reading Prong

A poorly exposed sequence of arkose (Figure 3B–18), ferruginous quartzite, quartzite conglomerate, metarhyolite, and metasaprolite occurs along the northern border of the Reading Prong near the Delaware River. These rocks, the Chestnut Hill For-

Figure 3B–14. Conglomerate member of the Loudoun Formation, here containing a lens of quartzose phyllite, on the southeast slope of Piney Mountain, Arendtsville 7.5-minute quadrangle. The notebook is 8.5 inches long. Photograph by J. L. Fauth.

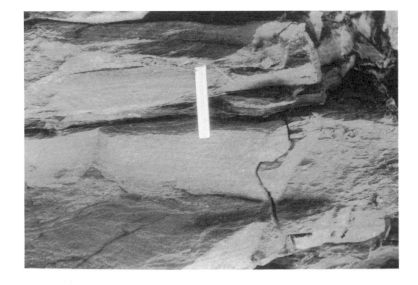

Figure 3B–15. Quartzose graywacke of the Weverton Formation on Wildcat Hill, Caledonia Park 7.5-minute quadrangle. The scale is 6 inches long. Photograph by J. L. Fauth.

Figure 3B–16. Quartzose phyllite and fine-grained graywacke of the Harpers Formation along the Old Tapeworm Railroad, Iron Springs 7.5-minute quadrangle. The field of view is about 30 feet across. Photograph by J. L. Fauth.

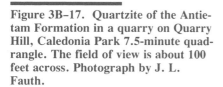

Figure 3B–17. Quartzite of the Antietam Formation in a quarry on Quarry Hill, Caledonia Park 7.5-minute quadrangle. The field of view is about 100 feet across. Photograph by J. L. Fauth.

mation (Zc on Figure 3B–3), contain biotite and have had a more complicated geologic history than the lower Paleozoic cover sequence. They are, therefore, thought to be of Late Proterozoic age. Their relations to the Lower Cambrian Hardyston Formation cannot be determined because their contact is not exposed. The rocks in the Chestnut Hill Formation are of the type commonly deposited in rift environments. Perhaps there was a minor event here related to the major rifting to the west and south.

Metamorphosed diabase dikes (not shown on Figure 3B–3) cut the Middle Proterozoic rocks of the Reading Prong. These dikes are fairly abundant in western Lehigh County and Berks County but are sparse farther east. Some of these dikes are clearly of Proterozoic age, as they do not cross contacts of gneiss with the overlying Cambrian Hardyston Formation. At least two dikes, however, are reported to intrude the Hardyston (Buckwalter, 1959) and have been interpreted to be Ordovician. Thus, it appears that there are dikes of two ages. The probable Late Proterozoic dikes can be related to the opening of the Iapetus Ocean, as can similar dikes in the Lincoln Mountain massifs of Vermont and in the Blue Ridge of Virginia and North Carolina. The origin of the post-Hardyston dikes is uncertain.

The Hardyston Formation is the basal Paleozoic unit in the Reading Prong (Ch on Figure 3B–3). It ranges in thickness from about 600 feet near Reading (Buckwalter, 1962) to 60 feet at the Delaware River (Drake, 1969). The Hardyston commonly has arkosic conglomerate (Figure 3B–19) at the base and passes upward into arkosic sandstone, orthoquartzite (Figure 3B–20), carbonate-cemented sandstone (Figure 3B–21), silty shale, and jasper. Arkosic conglom-

erate and arkose, however, occur at different stratigraphic positions, suggesting intraformational unconformities. At places where the Hardyston grades upward into the Leithsville Formation, it contains fossil fragments of Early Cambrian age. The more pelitic parts of the unit contain the mineral assemblage albite-muscovite-chlorite-quartz, indicating metamorphism to the lower greenschist facies. The Hardyston is commonly taken to be time equivalent to the Antietam Quartzite (Berg and others, 1983), but it is uncertain as to how much time is represented by its deposition.

Figure 3B–18. Conglomeratic arkose of the Chestnut Hill Formation along the Delaware River, Easton 7.5-minute quadrangle. The coin is 0.8 inch in diameter.

Figure 3B–19. Arkosic conglomerate of the Hardyston Formation from the Springtown klippe about 0.75 mile east of Springtown, Hellertown 7.5-minute quadrangle. Photograph by J. M. Aaron.

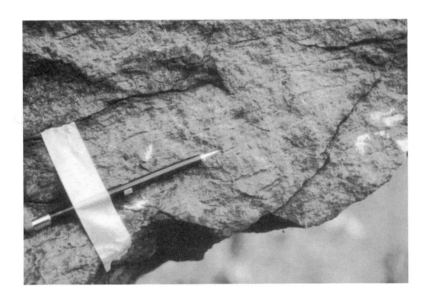

Figure 3B–20. Orthoquartzite of the Hardyston Formation from the Springtown klippe about 0.71 mile from Springtown, Hellertown 7.5-minute quadrangle. The pencil points to a *Skolithos* tube. Bedding is not visible in this view but is probably normal to the tubes. The pencil is 6 inches long. Photograph by J. M. Aaron.

Figure 3B–21. Carbonate-cemented sandstone of the Hardyston Formation from Morgan Hill, Easton 7.5-minute quadrangle. The pocketknife is 3.5 inches long.

Aaron (1969) interpreted the immature lower part of the formation to have had an alluvial origin, whereas the upper orthoquartzite part resulted from marine transgression. Perhaps the Hardyston represents the feather edge of the rift-drift facies transition so well marked by the Chilhowee Group to the southwest.

PROBLEMS AND FUTURE RESEARCH

South Mountain and the Reading Prong, except for two small areas in the East Greenville and Milford Square 7.5-minute quadrangles, have been mapped at the scale of 1:24,000. This work provides a framework for more fundamental studies. A current subject of major interest to Appalachian geologists is the rift event that led to the opening of the Iapetus (proto-Atlantic) Ocean. It is suggested that an integrated study be made of the whole-rock, trace-element, and isotope chemistry of the Catoctin flows in South Mountain, similar to the work done in central Virginia by Badger and Sinha (1988). Data from South Mountain, which is at the northern limit of the Blue Ridge tectonic province and contains rhyolite that is lacking in Virginia, would expand the model of Badger and Sinha (1988) and further contribute to our knowledge of the Appalachian rift event and the chemical evolution of lavas in general. In conjunction with this study, zircons from the Catoctin Formation should be dated using modern techniques to give us a better time fix for the rifting.

It is also suggested that a detailed sedimentologic study, in the manner of Simpson and Eriksson (1989), be made of the Chilhowee Group of South Mountain. This study would provide important information on the transition from rift to passive-margin sedimentation in this part of the central Appalachians and enhance our knowledge of the opening of the Iapetus Ocean.

The Grenville province of Canada has been interpreted to consist of an autochthon, a parautochthon, and an eastern collage of accreted terranes (Moore, 1986). The Grenvillian (Middle Proterozoic) rocks of the Appalachians all constitute accreted terranes. A major scientific plum would be to characterize these Middle Proterozoic rocks and separate them into the individual terranes. A beginning attempt at this was made by Drake (1984) for the Reading Prong. His work needs to be supplemented by minor-element, strontium-isotope, and stable-isotope chemistry. Zir-

cons should be collected from rocks of the Losee Metamorphic Suite and dated by modern U-Pb techniques. This work would date the Grenvillian basement.

An attempt should be made to determine, by petrochemical characterization, whether there are actually two generations of metadiabase dikes in the Reading Prong. This will be difficult because of the lack of suitable material, but any results would be extremely useful in furthering our knowledge of the tectonic history of the Reading Prong.

A sedimentologic study, similar to that proposed for the Chilhowee Group, should be made of the Hardyston Formation in the Reading Prong in order to compare the depositional environments of the two units and to gain a complete picture of the transition from rift to passive-margin sedimentation in Pennsylvania.

Finally, the pre-Mesozoic rocks in the East Greenville and Milford Square 7.5-minute quadrangles should be mapped. This will be a frustrating endeavor because of the extreme paucity of outcrop.

RECOMMENDED FOR FURTHER READING

Bascom, F. (1896), *The ancient volcanic rocks of South Mountain, Pennsylvania,* U.S. Geological Survey Bulletin 136, 124 p.

———— (1897), *Aporhyolite of South Mountain, Pennsylvania,* Geological Society of America Bulletin, v. 8, p. 393–396.

Bayley, W. S. (1941), *Pre-Cambrian geology and mineral resources of the Delaware Water Gap and Easton quadrangles, New Jersey and Pennsylvania,* U.S. Geological Survey Bulletin 920, 98 p.

Buckwalter, T. V., Jr. (1958), *Granitization in the Reading Hills, Berks County, Pennsylvania,* Pennsylvania Academy of Science Proceedings, v. 32, p. 133–138.

Fraser, D. M. (1937), *Basic rocks in the eastern Pennsylvania highlands,* American Geophysical Union Transactions, Annual Meeting, 18th, pt. 1, p. 249–254.

Freedman, Jacob (1967), *Geology of a portion of the Mount Holly Springs quadrangle, Adams and Cumberland Counties, Pennsylvania,* Pennsylvania Geological Survey, 4th ser., Progress Report 169, 66 p.

Jonas, A. I. (1917), *Pre-Cambrian and Triassic diabase in eastern Pennsylvania,* American Museum of Natural History Bulletin, v. 37, p. 173–181.

Montgomery, Arthur (1955), *Paragenesis of the serpentine-talc deposits near Easton, Pa.,* Pennsylvania Academy of Science Proceedings, v. 29, p. 203–215.

Stose, G. W. (1908), *The Cambro-Ordovician limestones of the Appalachian Valley in southern Pennsylvania,* Journal of Geology, v. 16, p. 698–714.

Wherry, E. T. (1918), *Pre-Cambrian sedimentary rocks in the highlands of eastern Pennsylvania,* Geological Society of America Bulletin, v. 29, p. 375–392.

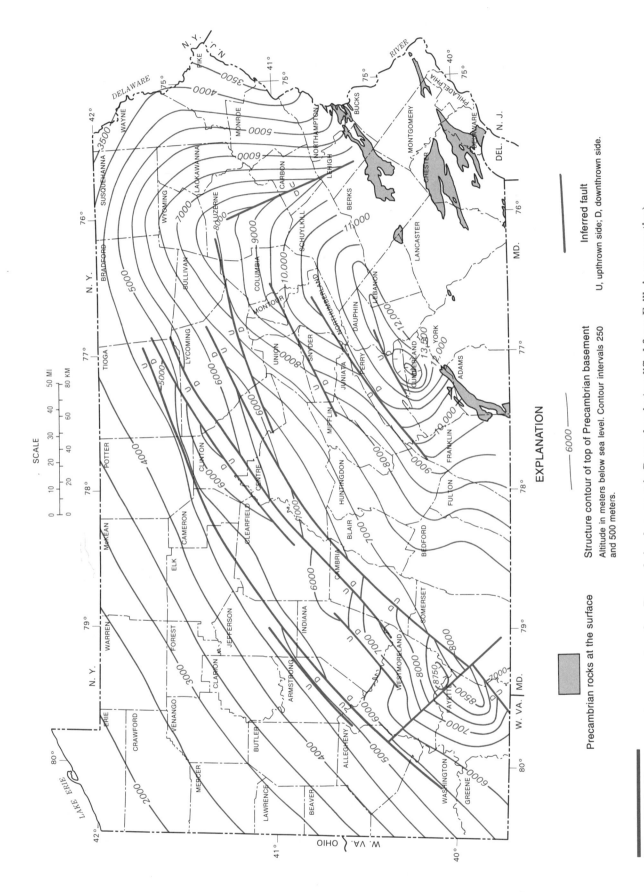

Figure 3C–1. Structure contours on subsurface Precambrian basement in Pennsylvania (modified from Faill, in preparation), and areas where Precambrian rocks (see Chapters 3A and 3B) are exposed (modified from Berg and others, 1980, and Pennsylvania Geological Survey, 1990).

EXPLANATION

Precambrian rocks at the surface

Structure contour of top of Precambrian basement
Altitude in meters below sea level. Contour intervals 250 and 500 meters.

Inferred fault
U, upthrown side; D, downthrown side.

CHAPTER 3C PRECAMBRIAN AND LOWER PALEOZOIC METAMORPHIC AND IGNEOUS ROCKS— IN THE SUBSURFACE

TIMOTHY E. SAYLOR
Chemistry and Earth Sciences Division
Buchart-Horn, Inc.
P. O. Box 15040
York, PA 17405

INTRODUCTION

Precambrian crystalline rocks underlie all of Pennsylvania but are exposed only in the Reading Prong, the Blue Ridge, and the Piedmont Upland (Figure 3C-1). The limited amount of detailed information on the subsurface comes from five deep exploratory oil and gas wells in northwestern Pennsylvania that penetrate basement rocks (Figure 3C-2). Seismic surveys have provided a basis for some speculation elsewhere. A summary report of the logs and petrologic description of the cuttings or cores from four deep wells that penetrate the Precambrian basement, three in Pennsylvania and one in Ohio, was published by the Pennsylvania Geological Survey (Saylor, 1968). Lytle and others (1965) provided detailed logs for the Kardosh well, located in Crawford County in northwestern Pennsylvania. Penetrations of the basement complex in Ohio, New York, and West Virginia have been described in some detail by Bass (1959), McCormick (1961), and Wickstrom and others (1985).

In 1985, the Ohio Division of Geological Survey drilled a well to a depth of 2,870 feet in Liberty Township, Seneca County, in northwestern Ohio (Figure 3C-2). The Precambrian basement was penetrated at a depth of 2,811.5 feet, where a dark-green to black gabbro was encountered (Wickstrom and others, 1985).

GEOLOGIC SETTING OF THE PRECAMBRIAN IN THE SUBSURFACE

A thick wedge-shaped sequence of Paleozoic sedimentary rocks underlies the Appalachian Plateaus province of Pennsylvania and covers the Pre-

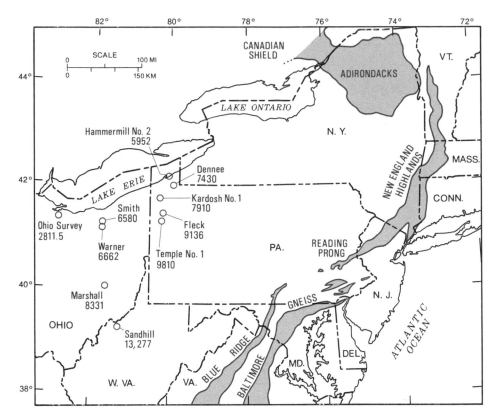

Figure 3C–2. Locations of wells that have penetrated Precambrian basement, and the approximate locations of Precambrian outcrop in Pennsylvania and adjacent areas (modified from Saylor, 1968). The depth to Precambrian basement is given in feet.

cambrian basement from the folded Appalachians westward across Pennsylvania, western New York, western West Virginia, and eastern Ohio. In Pennsylvania, the Appalachian Plateaus province is characterized by nearly horizontal bedding with very gentle folds, the axes of which are approximately parallel to the fold axes of the Ridge and Valley province to the southeast. The extent to which this structure reflects any influence of the basement complex is uncertain (see Chapter 20). Speculation has been considerable since about 1978, but it has been unsubstantiated by fact.

Basement involvement in the structural deformation of the Appalachian Plateaus and the Ridge and Valley provinces has been a source of much controversy and speculation over the years. Rowlands and Kanes (1972) reported that the basement underlying the Broad Top synclinorium in south-central Pennsylvania was comprised of a series of structural highs and lows with possible normal and reverse faulting. However, these suspected faults are not readily traced in seismic profiles of the overlying Middle and Upper Cambrian units. It was the opinion of Rowlands and Kanes that this suggested limited basement involvement.

The character of the Precambrian basement can only be estimated from seismic records and from drill logs and samples from the relatively few deep wells that have penetrated the basement (Figure 3C–2). Data from deep wells in eastern Ohio indicate that the apparent basement surface parallels known subsurface trends; that is, it is a regular, gently sloping surface, dipping eastward and forming the western margin of the Appalachian miogeosyncline (Bass, 1960). Despite a predominant east to southeast dip of the basement surface in Pennsylvania (Figures 3C–1 and 3C–3), there is evidence of significant basement warping and faulting, of which the Rome trough is a prime example (see also Chapter 20). Extensive normal faulting is indicated from seismic-refraction surveys (see Figure 20–4). Shumaker (1976) pointed out that basement deformation began much earlier than the deformation above detachment zones that occurred throughout the central Appalachian basin. The earliest deformation in Pennsylvania appears to have been in Precambrian time and related to the Grenville deformation.

Seismic-reflection data suggest depths to basement in the Broad Top synclinorium of 26,000 to 30,000 feet and a generally eastward-dipping base-

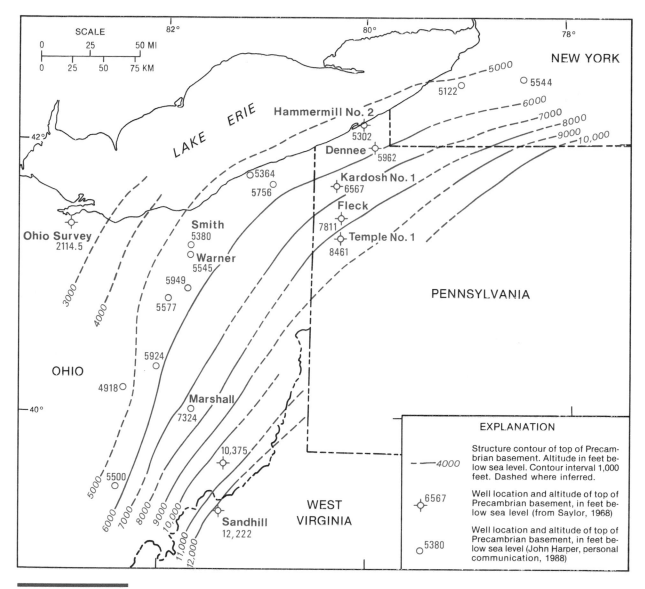

Figure 3C–3. Structure contours on the surface of the Precambrian basement in western Pennsylvania and adjacent areas (modified from Saylor, 1968).

ment surface (Rowlands and Kanes, 1972). This is comparable with trends established to the west and north by Sears (1964).

BASEMENT LITHOLOGY

The basement sections of three deep wells in Pennsylvania have been described in detail, based on examination of thin sections from a core and drill cuttings and a review of drill logs (Saylor, 1968). Samples from three other basement wells in eastern Ohio (McCormick, 1961) and one in northern West

Virginia (Bass, 1959) have also been described. A summary of the basement lithology and well data for these deep wells is included in Table 3C–1. Representative lithologic logs for the Temple No. 1 well in Pennsylvania, the Smith well in Ohio, and the Sandhill well in West Virginia are shown in Figure 3C–4.

Precambrian basement lithologies in eastern Ohio and western Pennsylvania are an extension of the Canadian Grenville belt. The most common lithologies reported are granites, biotite schists, gneisses, and weakly foliated biotite granites. Minor lithologies include basalt, amphibolite, dolomitic marbles, and syenite.

Table 3C–1. *Summary of Data for Wells Penetrating the Precambrian Basement in Pennsylvania, Ohio, and West Virginia*

Well and well location	Type of sample	Depth of logged interval (feet)	Depth to basement (feet)	Altitude of basement (feet)	Lithology
PENNSYLVANIA					
Hammermill No. 2 City of Erie, Erie Co.	3.5-inch section of drill core	5,952	5,952	–5,302	Contact between gray granitic schist and dark-green biotite phyllite or schist.
Kardosh No. 1 Summerhill Twp., Crawford Co.	Well cuttings	7,910–8,030	7,910	–6,567	Granite gneiss and quartz-biotite gneiss.
Temple No. 1 Lake Twp., Mercer Co.	Well cuttings	9,811–9,900	9,810	–8,461	Biotite granite, quartz-biotite gneiss, hornblende-bearing quartz-biotite gneiss, and quartzite.
Dennee Venango Twp., Erie Co.	Well cuttings	7,430–7,654	7,430	–5,962	Coarse-grained granite.
Fleck Sandy Creek Twp., Mercer Co.	Well cuttings	9,136–9,160	9,136	–7,811	Chloritic schist and granite grading into gneiss. All lithologies weathered.
OHIO					
Smith Hinckley Twp., Medina Co.	Core	6,678–6,680; 6,685	6,580	–5,380	Granite gneiss and marble. Granite gneiss has red potassium feldspar and chlorite bands grading to alternating microcline and greenish saussuritized plagioclase.
Warner Granger Twp., Medina Co.	Well cuttings	6,640–6,720	6,662	–5,545	Granite gneiss with alternating foliae of feldspar-muscovite-quartz and biotite-quartz.
Marshall Adams Twp., Guernsey Co.	Well cuttings	8,325–8,602	8,331	–7,324	Granite gneiss and amphibolite.
Ohio Geological Survey Liberty Twp., Seneca Co.	Well cuttings and core	2,811.5–2,870	2,811.5	–2,114.5	Dark-green to black gabbro with minor mineral-filled fractures.
WEST VIRGINIA					
Sandhill Wood Co.	Core	12,314–13,331	13,277	–12,222	"Granite wash," granodioritic to tonalitic gneiss, and amphibolite.

All the lithologies are metamorphosed to the greenschist or amphibolite facies (Bass, 1959, 1960; Saylor, 1968). Saylor (1968) reported that the granitic rocks in West Virginia range from granodiorite to tonalite, and Wickstrom and others (1985) reported that the Precambrian basement in northwestern Ohio is gabbro.

Perhaps the most detailed information to date is that from a 3.5-inch core from the Hammermill No. 2 well in Erie County, Pa. (Figure 3C–3). The principal lithologies are biotite gneiss, strongly foliated biotite schist, and weakly foliated granite largely lacking dark minerals (Saylor, 1968; Lapham, 1975).

The mineral composition of the biotite gneiss is variable and was described as a banded porphyritic and porphyroblastic biotite gneiss having metamorphism in the biotite grade of the greenschist facies

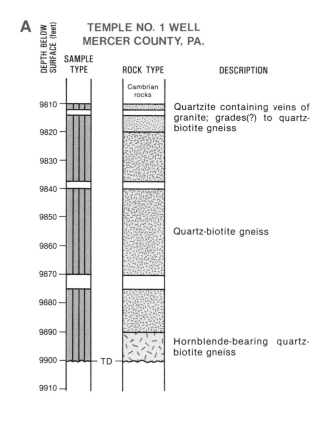

A

TEMPLE NO. 1 WELL
MERCER COUNTY, PA.

DEPTH BELOW SURFACE (feet)

SAMPLE TYPE   ROCK TYPE   DESCRIPTION

Cambrian rocks

9810 — Quartzite containing veins of granite; grades(?) to quartz-biotite gneiss

9820

9830

9840 — Quartz-biotite gneiss

9850

9860

9870

9880

9890 — Hornblende-bearing quartz-biotite gneiss

9900 — TD

9910

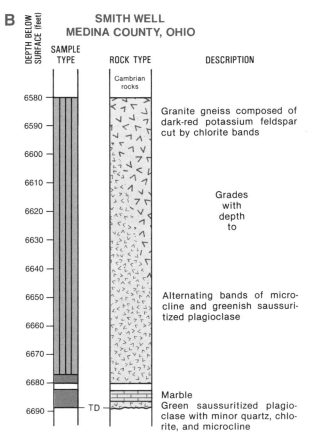

B

SMITH WELL
MEDINA COUNTY, OHIO

DEPTH BELOW SURFACE (feet)

SAMPLE TYPE   ROCK TYPE   DESCRIPTION

Cambrian rocks

6580 — Granite gneiss composed of dark-red potassium feldspar cut by chlorite bands

6590

6600

6610

6620 — Grades with depth to

6630

6640

6650 — Alternating bands of microcline and greenish saussuritized plagioclase

6660

6670

6680

6690 — TD — Marble
Green saussuritized plagioclase with minor quartz, chlorite, and microcline

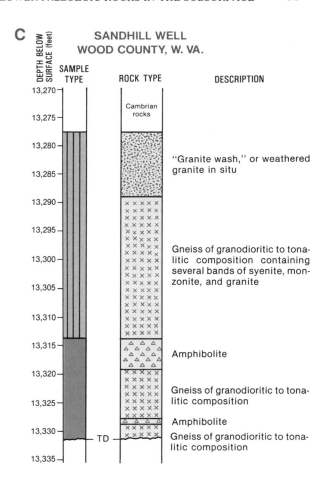

C

SANDHILL WELL
WOOD COUNTY, W. VA.

DEPTH BELOW SURFACE (feet)

SAMPLE TYPE   ROCK TYPE   DESCRIPTION

13,270

13,275   Cambrian rocks

13,280

13,285 — "Granite wash," or weathered granite in situ

13,290

13,295

13,300 — Gneiss of granodioritic to tonalitic composition containing several bands of syenite, monzonite, and granite

13,305

13,310

13,315 — Amphibolite

13,320

13,325 — Gneiss of granodioritic to tonalitic composition

13,330 — Amphibolite
TD — Gneiss of granodioritic to tonalitic composition

13,335

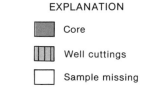

EXPLANATION

Core

Well cuttings

Sample missing

Figure 3C-4. Lithologic logs of three wells that penetrated Precambrian basement (logs A, B, and C modified from Saylor, 1968, p. 13, 17, and 19, respectively). See Figure 3C-2 for locations.

(Lapham, 1975). Although the original character of the rock was all but destroyed by processes of metamorphism and replacement, Lapham interpreted the original lithology to have been rhyolitic or intermediate in composition.

The granite, likewise, is variable in texture and mineralogy. Lapham (1975) concluded that the granite, as well as similar bands and pods occurring above the gneiss/granite contact, is a hybrid rock formed during successive stages of crystallization, recrystallization, and replacement, plus deformation of the rock fabric. Injection of microcline granite into the biotite gneiss was followed by a late-stage mobilization of a more quartz-rich and pegmatitic fraction, originating perhaps from the microcline granite magma. Minor fracturing and slip folding accompanied this late-stage mobilization. Finally, sericitization affected all of the lithologies below the overlying Cambrian(?) quartzite (Lapham, 1975).

Compositional trends of the Precambrian basement are difficult to determine from only a small number of wells. In the northwestern part of Pennsylvania, quartz-biotite gneiss containing granitic bands and pods, biotite schist, and quite possibly quartzite are predominant. Farther west, in eastern Ohio, granite gneiss and some amphibolite predominate. Amphibolite appears to increase in prevalence southward with a concomitant decrease in granite gneiss (Bass, 1960). In northwestern West Virginia, only the Sandhill well (Figures 3C-2 and 3C-4) has penetrated the basement, and little meaningful comparison can be made. Granite gneiss of variable petrography and some amphibolite are present (Saylor, 1968); however, neither is similar to the lithologies reported in eastern Ohio.

As with the lithologies, the extent and grade of metamorphism of the Precambrian basement are uncertain. In much of western Pennsylvania, a lack of calcium ($\pm$alumina) may have retarded the development of diagnostic mineral assemblages and may have aided retrograde metamorphic equilibration (Saylor, 1968). Greenschist facies is prevalent, however, in northwestern Pennsylvania (Lapham, 1975). In Ohio, mineralogic evidence indicates that some lithologies reached hornblende-amphibolite facies (Bass, 1960), and in West Virginia, diagnostic mineral assemblages indicate that, at the least, amphibolite facies was reached.

RADIOMETRIC AGES

Radiometric age determinations for the Precambrian basement complex in Pennsylvania are limited to one whole-rock potassium-argon (K-Ar) date and two rubidium-strontium (Rb-Sr) dates on samples from the Hammermill No. 2 well in Erie County (Figure 3C-2). Rb-Sr dates have also been determined for samples from several wells in central and western Ohio and the Sandhill well in Wood County, W. Va. (Figure 3C-2). A summary of the dates is presented in Table 3C-2.

Lapham (1975) discussed, in some detail, the apparent discrepancy between the K-Ar and the Rb-Sr ages determined for samples from the Hammermill No. 2 well (Table 3C-2). He believed that the K-Ar date is correct and represents the time of sericitization, which was the last thermal event to affect these rocks. The much younger Rb-Sr date resulted from the loss of radiogenic strontium through some unknown process. Lapham (1975) speculated that

Table 3C-2. *Radiometric Age Measurements for Basement Rocks in Selected Deep Wells in Pennsylvania, Ohio, and West Virginia*

Well and well location	Rock type	Date type	Apparent age (Ma)	Reference
Hammermill No. 2 Erie Co., Pa.	Biotite schist	Whole rock, K-Ar	908±9	Lapham (1975)
	Biotite schist	Whole rock, Rb-Sr	544±15	
	Granite	Whole rock, Rb-Sr	633±19	
Wells in central and western Ohio	Granite and rhyolite to amphibolite and tonalite	Whole rock, Rb-Sr	920 to 950; possibly 980	Tilton and others (1960)
Sandhill Wood Co., W. Va.	Granite gneiss	Biotite, Rb-Sr	870±10	Tilton and others (1960)

regional metamorphism converted volcanic rocks to biotite schist about 1,100 Ma. Injection of granite about 1,000 Ma partially reset the K-Ar and Rb-Sr clocks, and further adjustment occurred during late-stage sericitization. The dates from 908 to 980 Ma for the wells listed in Table 3C-2 are within the accepted range (900 to 1,100 Ma) for the Grenville orogeny.

It is quite obvious from work done by Lapham that the geologic history of the Precambrian basement, at least in northwestern Pennsylvania, is far more complex than had been previously recognized. It would also be reasonable to conclude that such a complex history applies to most, if not all, of the Precambrian basement in western Pennsylvania, eastern Ohio, northwestern West Virginia, and western New York.

PROBLEMS AND FUTURE RESEARCH

Investigation and research efforts into the Precambrian in the subsurface have been limited by the relatively small number of wells that have penetrated the basement complex; physical evidence, in the form of cores or well cuttings, has been sparse. Remote evidence, in the form of geophysical data, has also been limited because of its proprietary nature.

Oil and gas exploration will continue to be the primary source of new information. Some consideration should be given to a central repository for the storage of samples and geophysical data. Because of the scarcity of evidence and the proprietary classification of much of the information generated by oil and gas exploration companies, consideration should be given to developing an agreement between the repository agency and the exploration companies that would allow review of data for research purposes but that would maintain confidentiality.

Future research should continue to be directed toward developing a more detailed understanding of the physical characteristics of the subsurface Precambrian basement and of basement involvement in post-Grenvillian deformation events. The effort should, by necessity, consist of filling in gaps by employing new information as it becomes available, and by extrapolation from existing information.

RECOMMENDED FOR FURTHER READING

Lapham, D. M. (1975), *Interpretation of K-Ar and Rb-Sr isotopic dates from a Precambrian basement core, Erie County, Pennsylvania*, Pennsylvania Geological Survey, 4th ser., Information Circular 79, 26 p.

Lapham, D. M., and Root, S. I. (1971), *Summary of isotopic age determinations in Pennsylvania*, Pennsylvania Geological Survey, 4th ser., Information Circular 70, 29 p.

Rowlands, David, and Kanes, W. H. (1972), *The structural geology of a portion of the Broadtop synclinorium, Maryland and south-central Pennsylvania*, in Lessing, Peter, and others, eds., *Appalachian structures—origin, evolution, and possible potential for new exploration frontiers*, West Virginia University and West Virginia Geological and Economic Survey, p. 204–205.

Saylor, T. E. (1968), *The Precambrian in the subsurface of northwestern Pennsylvania and adjoining areas*, Pennsylvania Geological Survey, 4th ser., Information Circular 62, 25 p.

Sears, C. E. (1964), *Geophysics and Appalachian structure* [abs.], Geological Society of America Special Paper 76, p. 257.

Shumaker, R. C. (1976), *A digest of Appalachian structural geology*, in *Proceedings of the Seventh Annual Appalachian Petroleum Geology Symposium—Devonian shale—production and potential*, West Virginia Geological and Economic Survey, West Virginia University Department of Geology and Geography, and U.S. Energy Research and Development Administration, p. 75–78.

Wickstrom, L. H., Botoman, George, and Stith, D. A. (1985), *Report on a continuously cored hole drilled into the Precambrian in Seneca County, northwestern Ohio*, Ohio Division of Geological Survey Information Circular 51, 1 sheet.

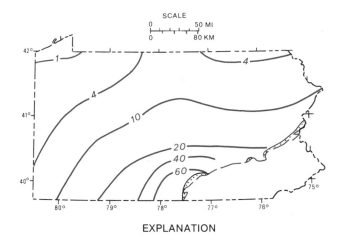

Figure 4–1. Isopach map of the Lower
Cambrian clastic sequence (modified from
Colton, G. W., *The Appalachian basin—its
depositional sequences and their geologic
relationships,* in Fisher, G. W., and others,
eds., *Studies of Appalachian geology: central
and southern,* Figure 11, p. 21, copyright
© 1970 by Interscience Publishers). Reprinted
by permission of John Wiley & Sons, Inc.

Figure 4–2. Isopach map of the Cambrian-
Ordovician carbonate sequence (modified
from Colton, G. W., *The Appalachian basin—
its depositional sequences and their geologic
relationships,* in Fisher, G. W., and others,
eds., *Studies of Appalachian geology: central
and southern,* Figure 13, p. 24, copyright
© 1970 by Interscience Publishers). Reprinted
by permission of John Wiley & Sons, Inc.

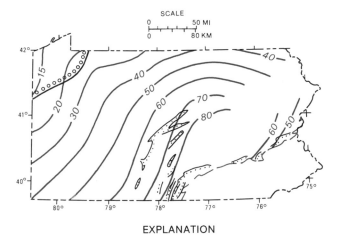

CHAPTER 4

EOCAMBRIAN, CAMBRIAN, AND TRANSITION TO ORDOVICIAN

MARVIN E. KAUFFMAN
P. O. Box 833
Red Lodge, MT 59068

INTRODUCTION

During latest Precambrian and Early Cambrian time, a great thickness of clastic sediments was deposited on an older Precambrian complex of igneous and metamorphic rocks. Later, from the Middle Cambrian into the Early Ordovician, a carbonate bank extended along the shelf edge in Pennsylvania, and deeper water sediments accumulated to the east and southeast. Stratigraphic and petrologic summaries of sections across Pennsylvania indicate the varied sedimentologic and tectonic settings and some of the problems that will require future research.

TECTONIC SETTING

North America was unusually stable during the latest Precambrian to earliest Paleozoic, and marine waters slowly transgressed across the continent during this time. In Pennsylvania, this transgression resulted in the deposition of a wedge of terrigenous sediments (Chilhowee Group) along the continental margin during much of the latest Precambrian and nearly continuously into Early Cambrian time (Figure 4–1). These rest unconformably on older sediments and volcanics, and their deposition was followed by that of several thousand feet of shelf carbonates (Figure 4–2). Part of the region from eastern Pennsylvania to western Massachusetts was positive during most of the Early Cambrian and was not covered by the sea until Middle Cambrian time.

Several nearly contemporaneous lithofacies developed in depositional belts that paralleled the margin of the Cambrian craton (Palmer, 1962, 1971). Nearest the craton was an inner detrital belt consisting of coarse clastics eroded from the cratonic mainland to the west and northwest (Goodwin and Anderson, 1974). Beyond this was a carbonate belt consisting principally of clean carbonate sediments with oolites and algal stromatolites, suggesting clear shallow water on shelf-edge banks. Seaward of these banks was an outer detrital belt consisting of two lithofacies. Deposition immediately adjacent to the carbonate bank resulted in the formation of black shales and thin argillaceous limestones. Sporadic lenses of angular carbonate blocks occur in this lithofacies and appear to be chaotic slumps fallen from the shelf edge (Rodgers, 1968). Farther offshore, graywackes, shales, and interbedded volcanic rocks formed (Figure 4-3). Many of these rocks are intensely folded and metamorphosed, and they are generally less understood than those of the other belts. Northwestward thrusting of these rocks has superimposed them on the nearer shore facies (see Chapter 18).

ENVIRONMENTS OF DEPOSITION

Interpretation of the environments of deposition for the Eocambrian to Early Ordovician units in Pennsylvania varies in difficulty, depending upon the degree of metamorphism, amount of exposure, and detail to which each unit has been studied.

Fossils are rare to absent in most of the Chilhowee Group, except for burrows of *Skolithos* and *Monocraterion*. Because this group lies unconformably on top of basement rocks, and because it grades conformably upward into units containing a typical Early Cambrian fauna, it commonly is considered to be late Precambrian or Eocambrian in age. This group typically has a basal conglomeratic member, the Hellam Member, which is locally absent. The Hellam is overlain by a vitreous, white, quartz-rich sandstone member (Chickies Formation) containing *Skolithos* tubes. This sandstone member is represented in other areas by the Weverton Formation, the Hardyston Formation, and the Montalto Member of the Harpers Formation (Figure 4-4). Slaty beds are common in parts of the Chickies Formation, especially in York County. Goodwin and Anderson (1974) considered the Chickies Formation to be a tidal-zone accumulation.

The Early Cambrian seas transgressed in a generally northwesterly direction. The sandy coastal deposits are represented by the Eocambrian Chickies Formation in southeastern Pennsylvania, the Eocambrian Weverton Formation and Montalto Member of the Harpers Formation in south-central Pennsylvania, and the late Middle Cambrian Potsdam Sandstone in western Pennsylvania.

Other clastic units within the Chilhowee do not lend themselves as easily to environmental interpretation. The Harpers Formation commonly consists of phyllite and has few, if any, sedimentary structures. The phyllite may represent a lagoonal deposit associated with the tidal-zone deposits of the Chickies and related formations.

The Antietam Formation has an irregular outcrop pattern throughout southeastern Pennsylvania. This outcrop pattern commonly has been interpreted as fault controlled (Bascom and Stose, 1938, and others). Kauffman and Frey (1979) suggested that it could partly reflect the original depositional pattern. They postulated that the Antietam was a barrier island because of its discontinuous and lenticular outcrop pattern in some areas, its low-angle cross-lamination, its pattern of grain-size distribution, and the presence of storm deposits, and because it interfingers with lagoonal sediments of the Harpers Formation.

Carbonate shelf deposits, which lay to the east of the inner detrital belt, onlapped the craton toward the northwest in a manner similar to the transgression of beach sands in the Chilhowee Group as the continental margin subsided. A deeper, partially euxinic basin to the southeast may have been bordered on its southeast during parts of its existence by a landmass (Africa?) or a volcanic island complex that shed clastics and volcanic-rich sediments in a westerly direction into the basin.

The Conestoga Formation in the Lancaster County region may be a deeper water facies, east of and correlative with part of the carbonate bank formations (Figure 4-3). In addition, the Conestoga may be correlated with part of the Glenarm Supergroup, including the Cockeysville Marble, in part, and a portion of the Wissahickon Formation (Figure 4-4).

The Kinzers Formation has yielded a rich assemblage of Early Cambrian fauna, including various species of brachiopods, molluscs, echinoderms, and especially trilobites, such as *Olenellus*, *Paedeumias*, and *Wanneria*. Fossils of Middle Cambrian age, especially *Ogygopsis klotzi*, have been reported from black shales that were thought to be in the upper part of the Kinzers (Campbell, 1971) but that have more recently been interpreted as the Long's Park Tongue of the deeper water Conestoga.

The Cambrian carbonate sequence, with its cyclic pattern of deposition, mud cracks, dolomites, and algal-laminated bedding, probably represents a shallow-water carbonate bank or shelf that was subjected to periodic episodes of near-drying conditions.

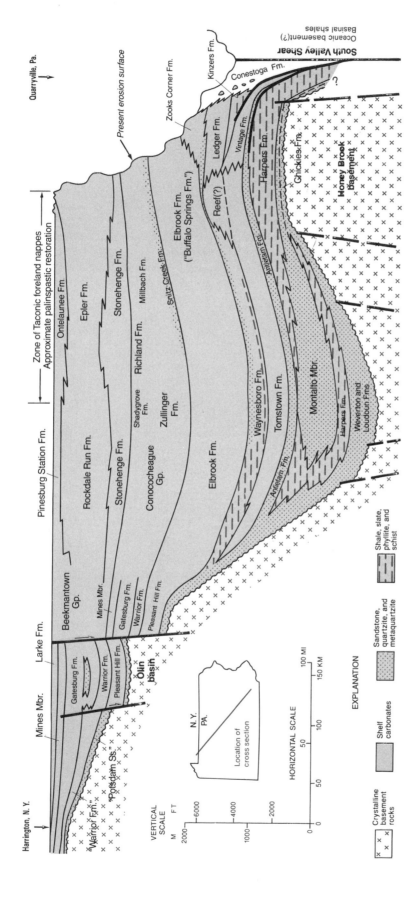

Figure 4–3. Generalized reconstruction of Eocambrian to Lower Ordovician formations. Cross section is not palinspastically restored for Alleghanian shortening east of the Allegheny Front and displacement along Alleghanian décollements in the area of the Taconic nappe zone. Eastern half is modified from MacLachlan (1994, Figure 1, p. 9). Western half is modified from Rankin, D. W., and others (1989), *Pre-orogenic terranes*, in Hatcher, R. D., Jr., and others, eds., *The Appalachian-Ouachita orogen in the United States*, The Geology of North America, v. F–2, Figure 12, p. 51. Western half is modified with permission of the publisher, the Geological Society of America, Boulder, Colorado USA. Copyright © 1989 Geological Society of America.

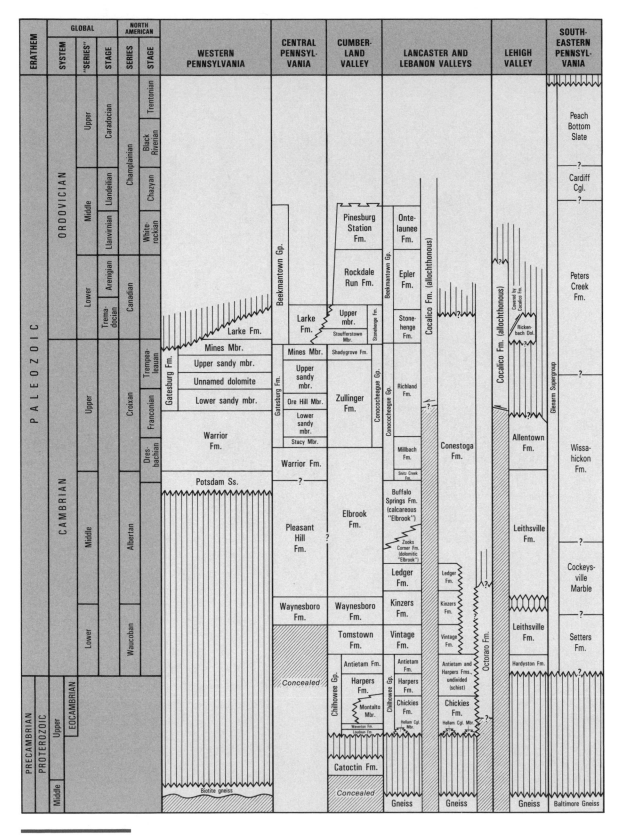

Figure 4–4. Correlation of Eocambrian to Lower Ordovician formations (modified from Berg, McInerney, and others, 1986).

EOCAMBRIAN TO EARLY ORDOVICIAN STRATIGRAPHY

The Eocambrian to Early Ordovician units crop out in southeastern and central Pennsylvania (Figure 4–5). The stratigraphy varies across the state and will be discussed in four parts: (1) Lancaster-Lebanon Valley and Piedmont sequence; (2) Cumberland Valley and South Mountain sequence; (3) Lehigh Valley sequence; and (4) stratigraphy of central and western Pennsylvania.

LANCASTER-LEBANON VALLEY AND PIEDMONT SEQUENCE

What has been called "basement complex" is, in fact, a variety of igneous and metamorphic rocks that have undergone a complex history of tectonic and metamorphic events. Rocks included as basement are biotite gneiss, banded gneiss, migmatite, veined gneiss, augen gneiss, and granitic gneiss.

The Setters Formation unconformably overlies basement rocks of the Baltimore Gneiss along the Pennsylvania-Maryland border in southeastern Pennsylvania (Figure 4–4). The rocks of the Setters Formation are commonly feldspathic mica schist, mica gneiss, feldspathic metaquartzite, and micaceous metaquartzite. The Setters varies in thickness from 0 feet to as much as 700 feet. Where the Setters is missing, the overlying Cockeysville Marble rests directly on basement rocks. The variation in thickness of the Setters is probably a result of deposition on an irregular surface, causing the formation to be thinner over highs and thicker in topographic lows.

The Cockeysville Marble overlies the Setters Formation in most of northern Maryland and southeastern Pennsylvania. It is very coarse grained and varies in lithology from metadolomite, calc-schist, and calcite marble to minor amounts of calc-gneiss and calc-silicate marble. Near the top is a phlogopitic marble member that is everywhere in contact with the overlying Wissahickon Formation. The Cockeysville ranges from 0 feet to nearly 5,000 feet in thickness.

The Wissahickon Formation is a thick sequence of metamorphosed pelitic (formerly clay-rich) and arenaceous rocks that overlies the Cockeysville Marble with slight unconformity. It is a well-foliated, fine-grained mica schist to quartz-rich schist (called "Octoraro" Schist in parts of Lancaster and Chester Counties). The thickness of the Wissahickon is unknown. It is probably several miles thick. The eastern

Wissahickon is almost entirely fine-grained chlorite-muscovite schist that is coarser grained in the upper part.

A quartzose schist above the Wissahickon commonly has been designated the Peters Creek Formation. This unit differs from the Wissahickon in having a much higher proportion of quartz. It contains metagraywackes and pebbly micaceous metaquartzites.

Overlying the Peters Creek Formation is several feet of quartz-pebble beds called the Cardiff Conglomerate. It is overlain by the Peach Bottom Slate, primarily a fine-grained slate containing graphite, albitic plagioclase, chloritoid, and traces of andalusite. Formerly thought to be Precambrian in age, these two formations are now assigned to the Ordovician (Figure 4–4).

In the Lancaster Valley, Chilhowee Group clastics rest unconformably on basement rocks. This part of the Chilhowee Group is assigned to the Eocambrian and will here be discussed with other rocks belonging to the Cambrian System (Figure 4–4).

The Chickies Formation is commonly the lowest unit in the Chilhowee Group. At its base is the Hellam Conglomerate Member, which contains quartz and quartzite pebbles (Figure 4–6), clear-blue quartz grains, and pink feldspar fragments; there are thin interbeds of sericitic metaquartzite. This member is locally absent and ranges up to 150 feet in thickness. The principal lithology of the Chickies Formation is thick-bedded, light-colored, vitreous metaquartzite (Figures 4–7 and 4–8), in which the quartz grains, where large enough to be observed, appear to be clear white or blue. The upper part of this member is thin-bedded and schistose, and has sericite partings and interbedded thin black slate. These upper beds, which have been extensively quarried, commonly disintegrate into fine, white siliceous clay and clayey sand.

Overlying the Chickies Formation is a poorly defined unit, consisting primarily of nonresistant grayish-green quartzose phyllite and dark-gray micaceous slate, called the Harpers Formation. In southeastern Pennsylvania, it crops out rarely because it weathers readily, owing to well-developed cleavage. The Harpers Formation and the overlying Antietam Formation are commonly mapped as a single unit because of their poor exposures.

Conformably overlying the Harpers, and grading up from it, is the Antietam Formation, consisting of well-bedded, light-gray, rusty-weathering quartzose sandstones, sericitic quartz schist, and biotite-bearing quartz phyllite. The Early Cambrian trilobite *Olenellus* has been found in the Antietam. This is the earliest well-dated Cambrian stratigraphic unit

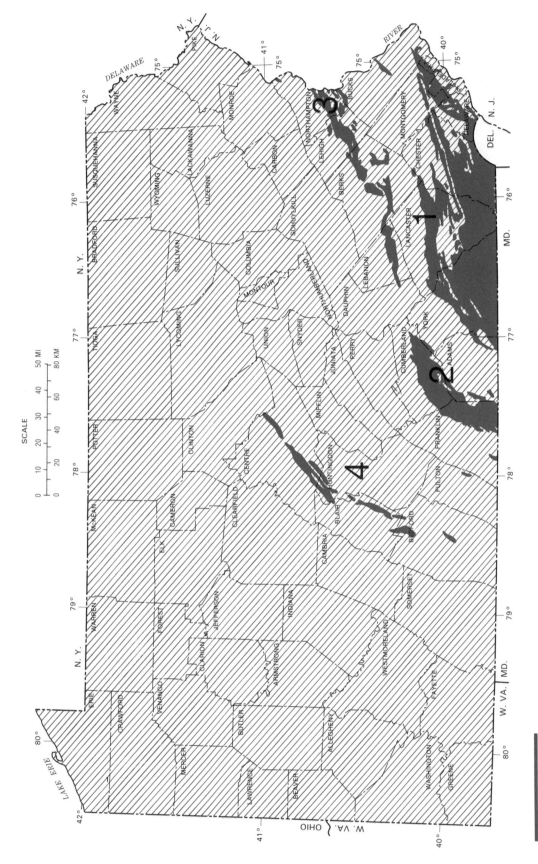

Figure 4-5. Map of areas containing Eocambrian to Lower Ordovician formations in Pennsylvania. Areas of outcrop are indicated by the solid color (from Pennsylvania Geological Survey, 1990). The diagonal line pattern denotes areas containing the same units in the subsurface. The locations of units discussed in the text are as follows: (1) Lancaster-Lebanon Valley and Piedmont; (2) Cumberland Valley and South Mountain; (3) Lehigh Valley; and (4) central and western Pennsylvania.

Figure 4–6. Quartz-pebble conglomerate beds of the Hellam Conglomerate Member of the Chickies Formation, Chimney Rock, York County. Photograph by A. R. Geyer.

in the region. Thus, the sedimentary units conformable below the Antietam are commonly called Eocambrian to distinguish them from the true Cambrian. The upper part of the Antietam is characterized by well-laminated, calcareous metaquartzite with rust-colored iron oxide pockets and molds of fossils. The formation varies in thickness from 0 feet to as much as 300 feet. It commonly forms elongate, discontinuous topographic highs along its strike. These ridges are, in places, terminated and offset by faults. In other places, the discontinuous nature may be caused by variations in its original depositional thickness.

The beginning of a tremendous thickness of carbonate rocks is marked by the Vintage Formation, a thick-bedded to massive, finely crystalline, gray dolomite. It commonly contains fine, wavy, siliceous or argillaceous laminae. Some beds appear knotty or mottled (Figure 4–9), having lighter and darker siliceous and calcareous masses in a finely crystalline dolomite matrix. These beds commonly weather to pinnacle surfaces. The crystal faces cause "sparkling" reflections on some surfaces. Locally, other lithologies are interbedded with the typical dolomites, including white, pinkish-gray, and medium-gray limestones and some finely crystalline marbles.

Overlying the Vintage Formation is a unit containing shale, limestone, and dolomite called the Kinzers Formation. The lower part is dominantly medium- to dark-gray shale (Figure 4–10) with rusty partings. The upper part is dominantly limestone.

Overlying the Kinzers Formation are light-gray dolomite beds of the Ledger Formation. The Ledger is

Figure 4–7. Chickies Rock, an anticline of massive-bedded metaquartzite layers, 3 miles north of Columbia, Lancaster County, along the east bank of the Susquehanna River.

Figure 4–8. Chickies Formation at the top of Chickies Rock, the type locality (same location as Figure 4–7). Bedding dips gently to the right; fracture cleavage dips steeply to the left. Identifiable figures include R. M. Foose, standing in the center foreground, and A. R. Geyer, head bent over, second from the left. Photograph from the archives of the Department of Geology, Franklin and Marshall College, Lancaster, Lancaster County.

Figure 4–9. Mottled beds of the Vintage Formation, weathering to a pinnacle surface, in a borrow pit along Pa. Routes 272 and 283, 2 miles northwest of Lancaster, Lancaster County.

dominated by massive-bedded, medium- to coarsely crystalline, sparkling dolomite (Figure 4–11). In fresh exposures, the rock commonly exhibits dark mottling. Near the middle of the formation, oolitic (Figure 4–12), siliceous, or cherty beds occur. This formation weathers to a dark, deep-red, granular clay soil, commonly containing residual, fine quartz grains and fine crystals of dolomite.

Conformably overlying and interbedded with the Ledger Formation is the Zooks Corner Formation. The dominant lithology is thin- to thick-bedded, medium-gray, very finely crystalline dolomite. The dolomite may be locally white to dark gray and silty or sandy. There are sporadic occurrences of dolomitic sandstones. Some siliceous and argillaceous laminae occur throughout the formation. Primary sedimentary structures include small-scale cross-lamination, ripple marks, graded bedding, mud cracks, and some rip-up clasts. Within the formation are some limestones, commonly with thin dolomite laminae. Near the base are white, light-gray, and pink to rust-colored dolomites. The Zooks Corner Formation is approximately 1,600 feet thick at its type locality in Lancaster County.

The interbedded limestone and dolomite sequence that is gradational with the underlying Zooks Corner Formation has been designated the Buffalo Springs Formation. The usage followed here coincides with that of Geyer and others (1963) and Berg, McInerney, and others (1986), who considered the formation to be Middle Cambrian. It is composed of white to very light pinkish gray to dark-gray limestones, which

Figure 4–10. Outcrop of shale of the lower Kinzers Formation, 2 miles northwest of Lancaster, Lancaster County, in the northeast quadrant of the interchange of Pa. Routes 72 and 283. The 10-foot-high outcrop shows steeply dipping bedding at depth and downhill creep toward the right, in the upper part of the exposure. Photograph by W. H. Bolles.

Figure 4–11. Outcrop of the Ledger Formation, 6 feet high (note the hammer in the right center of the photograph), composed of well-jointed, massive dolomite, from a railroad cut near Longs Park, on the northwest edge of Lancaster, Lancaster County. Bedding is obscure but is nearly horizontal.

weather light gray, interbedded with light-pinkish-gray to yellowish-gray and dark-gray dolomites, which weather to a yellowish-gray or buff color (Figure 4–13). The limestones contain local oolite lenses and some dolomite laminae. The dolomites contain argillaceous, silty, or sandy beds, algal mats, mud cracks, ripple marks (Figure 4–14), cross-laminations, and local rip-up clast conglomerates. Stromatolites occur in both the limestone and dolomite beds (Figure 4–15) (Meisler and Becher, 1968). The formation varies in thickness from about 1,500 feet up to 3,800 feet.

The Conococheague Group contains a variety of carbonate lithologies and can be variously subdivided into different formations in different parts of the region. Three formations, the Snitz Creek, Millbach, and Richland, persist over a wide area and are useful for mapping. The Snitz Creek is a sandy dolomite that commonly is light to dark gray and finely crystalline. It may be argillaceous, silty, or sandy. Some sporadic layers of dolomitic quartz sandstone occur within this formation. These beds are more resistant and commonly form a significant topographic rise above the surrounding carbonates. They weather to a very sandy soil. The Snitz Creek Formation grades upward into the Millbach Formation, which is dominated by limestones containing some chert beds, lenses, and stringers. Interbedded limestones and dolomites overlying the Millbach constitute the Richland Formation. The proportion of limestone to dolomite varies considerably in the Richland Formation. It is estimated to be 70 percent limestone and 30 percent dolomite in the Conestoga Valley section, whereas dolomite apparently dominates in the Lebanon area.

The Conestoga Formation occurs in contact with rocks as old as the Antietam Formation and as young as the Beekmantown Group. Rodgers (1968) considered it to be the deeper water equivalent of these shelf units. It includes gray, finely to coarsely crystalline limestone, argillaceous limestone, some graphitic to micaceous laminae, and some angular carbonate clasts in a calcareous matrix (Figure 4–16). The clasts range in size from pebbles to boulders up to 5 feet across. Jonas and Stose (1930) considered the clasts to be part of a basal conglomerate, but they have been found in a number of positions within the formation and have been interpreted as lenses or tongues of a shelf-edge breccia by Rodgers (1968). Some coarsely crystalline, silty, and sandy

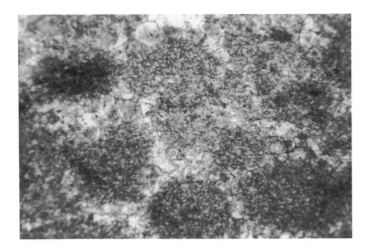

Figure 4–12. Photomicrograph showing relict ooids in recrystallized dolomite from the Ledger Formation along the railroad tracks 0.5 mile west of the Armstrong plant in the northern part of Lancaster, Lancaster County. Individual ooids are approximately 0.7 mm in diameter; the entire view is 2.5 mm wide. Cross-polarized light.

Figure 4–13. Tight isoclinal folds in the Buffalo Springs Formation along the Cornwall-area railroad tracks north of Rexmont, Lebanon County. Fold axes are nearly horizontal. Competent dolomite beds (white) show brittle-type fracture. Incompetent limestone beds (light gray) show flowage. Note the field notebook for scale. Photograph by A. R. Geyer.

limestones occur within the Conestoga, as do some beds of dark-gray dolomite. Because of intensive folding (Figure 4–17) and the absence of clear stratigraphic units within the Conestoga, its true thickness is in doubt. It must be at least 1,000 feet thick and could be considerably thicker.

CUMBERLAND VALLEY AND SOUTH MOUNTAIN SEQUENCE

The oldest exposed rocks in the Cumberland Valley are those of the Late Proterozoic Catoctin Formation, altered rhyolitic flows that are finely laminated in red to purple colors and altered basalt composed of chlorite and epidote (MacLachlan and Root, 1966). Overlying the Catoctin is the Loudoun Formation, consisting of sericitic slate and purplegray, poorly consolidated and poorly sorted, arkosic sandstone and conglomerate. It, in turn, is overlain by the Weverton Formation, which contains more than 1,000 feet of coarse, gray feldspathic sandstone and white quartzose sandstone. The Weverton has a quartz-pebble conglomerate at its base.

Dark-greenish-gray phyllite and schist make up the Harpers Formation in this area. The Montalto Member is a prominent, massive, hard, white to gray metaquartzite that occurs near the middle of the Harpers in the southern part of South Mountain and in contact with the Weverton in the northern half of South Mountain. This member contains *Skolithos* tubes and megaripples, and averages several hundred feet in thickness, except in the Shippensburg area, where it is 1,000 feet or greater. The total thickness for the Harpers Formation in this region ranges up to 2,750 feet.

Conformably overlying the Harpers Formation is the Antietam Formation, a metaquartzite, the color of which ranges from gray through blue gray to white. Some beds are very pure quartzose sandstones with many *Skolithos* tubes. The Antietam commonly weathers to brownish tan. It varies from 500 to 800 feet in thickness.

Undifferentiated massive dolomitic limestone marks the lower part of the Tomstown Formation. A mottled silty dolomite in the middle part of the formation is overlain by dolomitic limestone and limestone in the upper part. Thin shaly interbeds occur throughout the formation, which is estimated at 1,000 to 2,000 feet in total thickness.

The Waynesboro Formation consists of 1,000 feet or more of interbedded red to purple shale and sandstone in the lower and upper parts, and some beds of dolomite and blue, impure limestone in the

Figure 4–14. Ripple-marked (left side of photograph) and mud-cracked (center) silty limestones and dolomites in the Buffalo Springs Formation, 1 mile east of Morgantown, Berks County. The outcrop is 6 feet high (see person to right). The view is perpendicular to bedding.

middle part. The Waynesboro Formation is considered to be an upper Lower Cambrian to lower Middle Cambrian unit.

The Middle to Upper Cambrian Elbrook Formation is estimated to be greater than 3,000 feet in thickness. It consists of pure, dark limestone at the base, ridge-forming, medium-gray limestone and dolomite in the middle, and light-colored calcareous shale and argillaceous to silty limestone at the top.

The Conococheague Group consists of the Zullinger and Shadygrove Formations, and is considered to be primarily an Upper Cambrian unit. The Zullinger contains interbanded and interlaminated limestone and dolomite, thin- to thick-bedded stromatolitic limestone, and several thin, local quartz-sandstone beds. It is over 2,500 feet thick. The Shadygrove Formation contains pure, light-colored limestone that includes some stromatolites, and abundant pinkish limestones and cream-colored cherts. It averages 650 feet in thickness.

The Ordovician Beekmantown Group conformably overlies the Shadygrove Formation. The basal formation is the Stone-

Figure 4–15. Stromatolites in the Buffalo Springs Formation (same location as Figure 4–14).

henge, which includes in its lower part the Stoufferstown Member, a coarse, conglomeratic limestone containing dark-gray, siliceous laminae. This member forms prominent ridges. The upper member of the Stonehenge Formation is an unnamed stromatolitic, fine-grained limestone. Together, these members total about 1,000 feet in thickness.

The Rockdale Run Formation is the middle formation of the Beekmantown Group. Over 2,500 feet thick, it is mostly limestone with some dolomite interbeds. Nearly 500 feet of pinkish, marbly limestone and chert occurs near the base of the Rockdale Run. Some stromatolites and chert occur in the middle of the formation.

The Pinesburg Station Formation marks the top of the Beekmantown Group and is probably Middle Ordovician. It contains about 450 feet of light-colored,

Figure 4–16. Angular limestone clasts in a granular, crystalline, carbonate matrix within the Conestoga Formation, 3 miles west of Lancaster, Lancaster County.

Figure 4–17. Tightly folded Conestoga Formation along the east side of Pa. Route 272, 5 miles south of Lancaster, Lancaster County. Note the hammer for scale. Photograph by W. H. Bolles.

thick-bedded, finely laminated dolomite, and some limestone.

LEHIGH VALLEY SEQUENCE

Unconformably overlying basement rocks in the Lehigh Valley region of eastern Pennsylvania is the Hardyston Formation. The thickness of this resistant unit is variable, reaching a maximum of nearly 800 feet. The formation consists of a variety of lithic types: conglomerate and arkose (especially abundant near the lower contact), feldspathic sandstone, siliceous sandstone, silty shale, and some local jasper pebbles. The Hardyston has discontinuous lenticular beds of iron-stained quartz-pebble conglomerate, coarse, poorly sorted arkose, and some well-developed *Skolithos* tubes (Figure 4–18).

Conformably overlying the Hardyston Formation is a thick, poorly exposed carbonate sequence called the Leithsville Formation. It is composed of interbedded gray, fine- to coarse-grained dolomite and calcitic dolomite, light-gray to tan phyllite, calcareous phyllite, and thin stringers of quartz and sand-sized dolomite. Some thick beds of quartz sandstone are present. The formation ranges up to 1,000 feet in thickness. Cyclic bedding occurs within the Leithsville, which has repetitions of beds of thin quartz-bearing or sand-sized dolomite, some phyllite, local dark-gray chert, large oolites, rip-up clasts, ripple marks, and some graded bedding.

Conformably overlying the Leithsville Formation is the Allentown Formation. It is a gray, fine- to medium-grained, highly recrystallized dolomite that weathers to alternating light and dark beds. Bedding varies from finely laminated to thick bedded. Sedimentary features are common, including local disconformities, ripple marks, mud cracks, cross-laminations, graded beds, and load casts. Oolites are very abundant, forming well-sorted beds and lenses up to 2 feet thick. Several types of stromatolites also occur throughout the Allentown Formation. In most places, these are followed by supratidal dolomites with desiccation cracks. Cyclic units range from 5 feet to about 30 feet in thickness. The lower member of the cycle commonly has an irregular bottom contact and contains flat-pebble conglomerate beds and some oolites. This grades upward into thinly interbedded limestone and dolomite, which is followed by stromatolitic dolomite and mud-cracked dolomite. The entire formation is nearly 1,700 feet thick. Its upper contact with the Ordovician Rickenbach Dolomite is commonly picked at the top of the last shallow-water dolomite and the start of rocks having a higher calcite content (Drake, 1969, p. 84).

STRATIGRAPHY OF CENTRAL AND WESTERN PENNSYLVANIA

The subsurface stratigraphy of Cambrian units in western Pennsylvania is similar to that in the central part of the state (Wilson, 1952; Wagner, 1966b; Colton, 1970). Lying on the Precambrian basement complex in western and northwestern Pennsylvania (but cropping out only in New York) is the Potsdam Sandstone, a basal sandstone, varying from a feather edge to as much as 100 feet in thickness. It is a pink to red arkosic sandstone containing granules and pebbles of quartz and, rarely, gneiss and other lithic fragments.

The general thinning of the Cambrian section toward the continental interior is interrupted locally by a pronounced thickening into the Rome Trough in southwestern Pennsylvania (see Chapter 20).

The oldest formation exposed in central Pennsylvania is the Waynesboro Formation, which is of

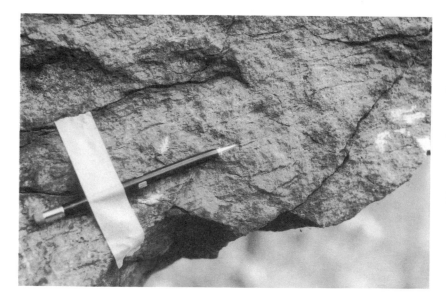

Figure 4–18. *Skolithos* tubes in siliceous sandstone of the Hardyston Formation in the Lehigh Valley. The pencil points to a well-developed tube emerging from the plane of the outcrop. Bedding is obscure and is oriented nearly vertical in the photograph. Photograph by J. M. Aaron.

Early to Middle Cambrian age. This unit is characterized by coarse- to medium-grained brown sandstone interbedded with red and green shales. In the south-central part of the state, the Waynesboro is underlain by clastics of the Chilhowee Group.

Overlying the Waynesboro is the Pleasant Hill Formation. The lower part of the Pleasant Hill is characterized by thinly layered, argillaceous, sandy, and micaceous limestone and some calcareous shale. The upper part is thick-bedded, fine-grained, dark-gray limestone (Butts, 1945). Some sandy, silty, and shaly limestone layers persist into the upper part locally. Middle Cambrian fossils have been collected from the upper part of this formation. Wilson (1952) considered the Pleasant Hill Formation to be of early Middle Cambrian age.

In western Pennsylvania, the Potsdam is overlain by the Warrior Formation. In central Pennsylvania, several units have been differentiated between the basal Cambrian section and the Warrior Formation. The Warrior Formation has a variety of rock types. The most common is a dark, argillaceous or platy, fine-grained limestone, which is characterized by oolites, stromatolites, and a variety of fossils. Interbedded with this limestone is dark, finely crystalline, silty dolomite. The proportion of limestone to dolomite varies from place to place. There appears to be a cyclic character to much of this formation. The upper and lower contacts of the Warrior appear to be conformable. The formation varies from about 400 feet in northwestern Pennsylvania to as much as 1,340 feet in north-central Pennsylvania.

The Gatesburg Formation consists of five mappable members, two thick interbedded sandstone and dolomite units and three thinner dolomites with little or no sandstone (Figure 4–4). These members include the Stacey Member, a dark, crystalline, massive dolomite; the Lower sandy member, a sandy dolomite and quartzose sandstone; the Ore Hill Member, a nonsandy carbonate sequence; the Upper sandy member, consisting of some limestone beds in central Pennsylvania and dolomite and sandstone in western parts of the state; and the Mines Member, a unit of dolomite having local chert, some siliceous oolite (Figure 4–19), and little or no sandstone.

The Cambrian-Ordovician contact is commonly placed at the upper boundary of the Gatesburg Formation (Mines Member). This appears to be a conformable contact with the overlying Larke Formation and its lateral equivalent, the Stonehenge Formation of the Beekmantown Group. Some workers place the Cambrian-Ordovician boundary within the Larke and Stonehenge Formations, making the lowest parts of each of these formations latest Cambrian in age (Figure 4–4).

PROBLEMS AND FUTURE RESEARCH

The nature of the Precambrian-Cambrian boundary continues to be an unresolved problem. Detailed mapping of the units near the boundary must be integrated with a regional analysis of past and current work.

The age, environment of deposition, and sedimentary tectonic history of units within the Glenarm Supergroup have not yet been resolved. Support can

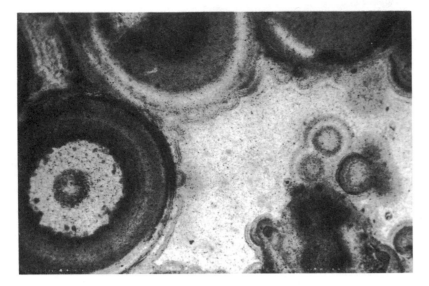

A

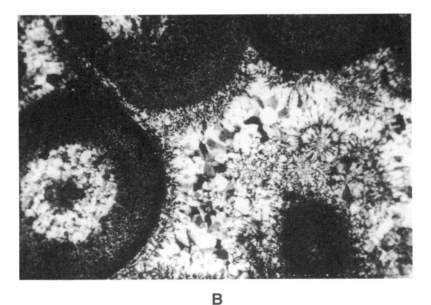

B

Figure 4–19. Photomicrographs of the oolitic Mines Dolomite Member of the Gatesburg Formation from near State College, Centre County. The width of view is 2.5 mm. A, plane-polarized light; B, cross-polarized light. Original carbonate ooids are completely replaced by very fine grained chert and overgrown by chalcedonic quartz (fibrous). The void space between ooids, perhaps originally occupied by calcite cement, is now occupied by coarse chert.

be found for both a Precambrian age and an early Paleozoic age. Continuation of mapping projects may produce paleontological, sedimentologic, and lithologic information to help solve these problems.

The nature of the outcrop pattern of the Antietam Formation has not been fully resolved. Whether the elongate topographic ridges are the result of primary deposition as shoestring sands or are tectonically controlled can only be resolved by further detailed mapping in critical areas.

The stratigraphic relationship of the Kinzers Formation to adjacent units has been a subject of much discussion. It has been determined that the shale member does not occur toward the north and/or northwest. Whether this is the result of stratigraphic pinchout, tectonic control, or lateral facies changes can only be determined by additional mapping.

The age of the Kinzers Formation has long been considered to be Early Cambrian because of the excellent *Olenellus* fauna found in Lancaster County (Jonas and Stose, 1930; Stose and Stose, 1944). More recently, Campbell (1971) reported the occurrence of a Middle Cambrian fauna, characterized by *Ogygopsis klotzi*, in black shales in the upper part of the Kinzers Formation. It has been suggested that the upper shale is another part of the Conestoga-like lithology intertonguing into the carbonate-shelf bank (Long's Park Tongue) (Kauffman and Campbell, 1969). The Kinzers Formation probably should be restricted to the Early Cambrian rather than extended up into the Middle Cambrian (Figure 4–4). The details of the black shale tongues can only be determined by further mapping and petrologic study of the shales.

Much has been written about the Conestoga Formation and its relationship to other Cambrian-Ordovician rocks in southeastern Pennsylvania. Jonas and Stose (1930) considered the Conestoga to be unconformable on at least the Ledger, Kinzers, and Vintage Formations. Others mapping in this region have described it as being in contact, perhaps, with rocks as old as the Antietam and as young as the Elbrook and even the Conococheague (Wise, 1970). Whether this contact is unconformable or intertonguing can only be determined by further detailed mapping and petrologic studies of the Conestoga and the units immediately adjacent to it.

RECOMMENDED FOR FURTHER READING

Agron, S. L. (1950), *Structure and petrology of the Peach Bottom Slate, Pennsylvania and Maryland, and its environment,* Geological Society of America Bulletin, v. 61, p. 1265–1306.

Drake, A. A., Jr. (1969), *Precambrian and lower Paleozoic geology of the Delaware Valley, New Jersey-Pennsylvania,* in Subitzky, Seymour, ed., *Geology of selected areas in New Jersey and eastern Pennsylvania and guidebook of excursions,* New Brunswick, N. J., Rutgers University Press, p. 51–131.

Fauth, J. L. (1978), *Geology and mineral resources of the Iron Springs area, Adams and Franklin Counties, Pennsylvania,* Pennsylvania Geological Survey, 4th ser., Atlas 129c, 72 p.

Gohn, G. S. (1978), *Revised ages of Cambrian and Ordovician formations of the Conestoga Valley near York and Lancaster, southeastern Pennsylvania,* in Sohl, N. F., and Wright, W. B., *Changes in stratigraphic nomenclature by the U.S. Geological Survey, 1977,* U.S. Geological Survey Bulletin 1457–A, p. A94–A97.

Higgins, M. W. (1972), *Age, origin, regional relations, and nomenclature of the Glenarm Series, central Appalachian Piedmont: a reinterpretation,* Geological Society of America Bulletin, v. 83, p. 989–1026.

MacLachlan, D. B. (1967), *Structure and stratigraphy of the limestones and dolomites of Dauphin County, Pennsylvania,* Pennsylvania Geological Survey, 4th ser., General Geology Report 44, 168 p.

Sando, W. J. (1957), *Beekmantown Group (Lower Ordovician) of Maryland,* Geological Society of America Memoir 68, 161 p.

Wagner, W. R. (1976), *Growth faults in Cambrian and Lower Ordovician rocks of western Pennsylvania,* AAPG Bulletin, v. 60, p. 414–427.

Wise, D. U., and Kauffman, M. E., eds. (1960), *Some tectonic and structural problems of the Appalachian Piedmont along the Susquehanna River,* Annual Field Conference of Pennsylvania Geologists, 25th, Lancaster, Pa., Guidebook, 103 p.

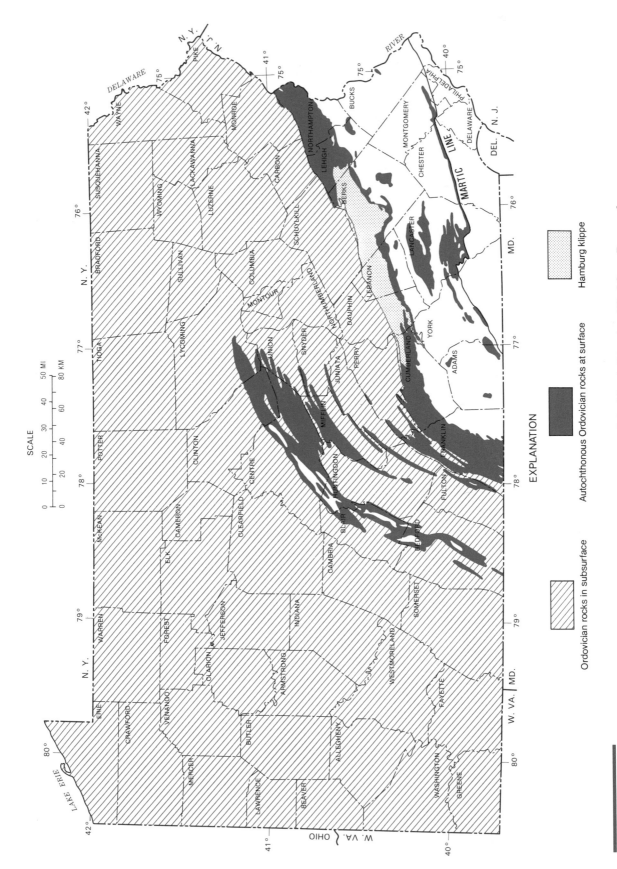

Figure 5-1. Distribution of Ordovician sedimentary rocks in Pennsylvania west of the Martic Line (modified from Berg and others, 1980, and Pennsylvania Geological Survey, 1990).

EXPLANATION

Ordovician rocks in subsurface

Autochthonous Ordovician rocks at surface

Hamburg klippe

SCALE

0   10   20   30   40   50 MI

0   20   40   60   80 KM

CHAPTER 5   ORDOVICIAN

ALLAN M. THOMPSON
Department of Geology
University of Delaware
Newark, DE 19716

INTRODUCTION

This chapter contains a summary of lithologic, facies, and temporal relationships of sedimentary rocks of Ordovician age in Pennsylvania west and northwest of the Martic Line (Figure 5–1).

Ordovician sedimentary rocks occur only in the subsurface of northern and western Pennsylvania (Fettke, 1961; Wagner, 1966b) and crop out in central and southeastern Pennsylvania (Figure 5–1). In central and south-central Pennsylvania, the Ridge and Valley belt contains a nearly complete Ordovician section. The Great Valley contains predominantly Lower and Middle Ordovician strata. The east-central part of the Great Valley contains allochthonous Cambrian to Middle Ordovician rocks of the Hamburg klippe; these rocks have been compared to the Taconian allochthons of eastern New York and western New England (Rodgers, 1970; Lash and others, 1984). The Piedmont Lowland contains carbonates and shale of Early and possibly Middle Ordovician age (Gohn, 1978).

Possibly coeval rocks of the Glenarm Supergroup, which occur southeast of the Martic Line (Figure 5–1), are penetratively deformed and variably metamorphosed (see Chapters 3A and 4). Some were assigned Early Ordovician ages by Berg, McInerney, and others (1986), but the evidence is equivocal. These rocks could be deep-water sedimentary and volcanic accumulations, and could have formed away from early Paleozoic North America (Williams and Hatcher, 1983).

CONTROLS ON ORDOVICIAN STRATIGRAPHY

During Ordovician time, what is now Pennsylvania constituted a small part of the eastern edge of the proto-North American, or Laurentian, craton. The character of the rocks was influenced by sedimentologic and tectonic processes in the Appalachian basin, a large, elongate depocenter that lay along the southeastern margin of the craton throughout Paleozoic time (in the sense used by Colton, 1970). The

Appalachian basin is a polygenetic feature. From latest Precambrian through Middle Ordovician time, it was an eastward-thickening, miogeoclinal basin that received primarily carbonate-platform-facies and carbonate-bank-facies sediments (Figure 5–2). The platform terminated seaward at a continental slope, beyond which lay deep-basin-floor sediments. The platform prograded eastward through Cambrian and Early Ordovician time. The basin axis lies along the present eastern edge of the outcrop belt, and the maximum thickness of the carbonate sediments occurs in east-central Pennsylvania. The bank and its facies define the traditional Appalachian miogeosyncline (Champlain belt of Kay, 1951), which was a

passive continental margin along the western edge of the proto-Atlantic, or Iapetus, Ocean in early Paleozoic time (Thompson and Sevon, 1982).

The craton margin was uplifted during the Taconian orogeny, beginning in Middle Ordovician time. With the onset of tectonism, the Appalachian basin evolved from a miogeoclinal carbonate platform to an exogeosynclinal foreland molasse basin. From Middle Ordovician through Late Silurian time, this basin received considerable amounts of the east-derived, terrigenous detritus that constitutes the Taconian clastic wedge (Figure 5–3).

The axis of maximum thickness for post-Middle Ordovician deposits in the foreland basin lies near the

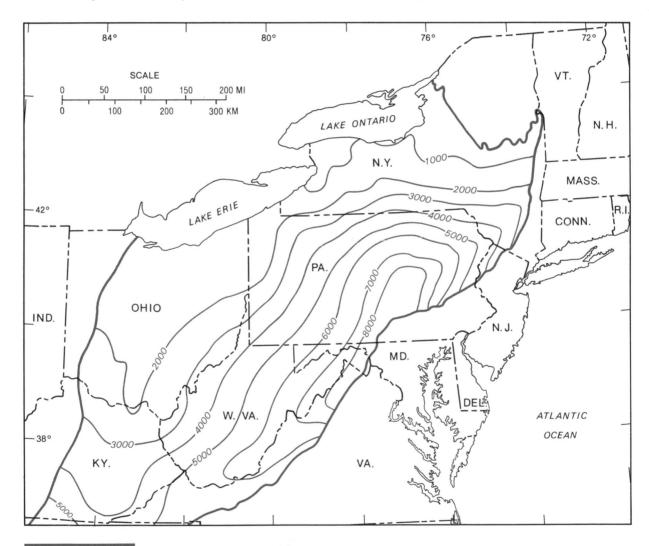

Figure 5–2. Isopach map of Upper Cambrian and Lower and Middle Ordovician rocks of the dolomite-limestone and limestone associations (modified from Colton, G. W., *The Appalachian basin—its depositional sequences and their geologic relationships*, in Fisher, G. W., and others, eds., *Studies of Appalachian geology: central and southern*, Figure 13, p. 24, copyright © 1970 by Interscience Publishers, reprinted by permission of John Wiley & Sons, Inc.). In southeastern Pennsylvania, the dolomite-limestone association includes 2,700 feet of Cambrian-age rocks. Contour interval is 1,000 feet. The heavy colored line represents the boundary of Colton's study area.

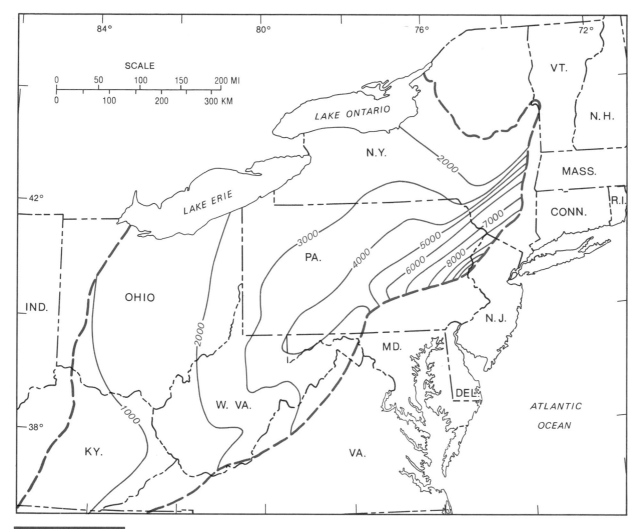

Figure 5–3. Isopach map of Upper Ordovician and Lower Silurian rocks of the siliciclastic association that constitute the Taconian clastic wedge (modified from Colton, G. W., *The Appalachian basin—its depositional sequences and their geologic relationships,* in Fisher, G. W., and others, eds., *Studies of Appalachian geology: central and southern,* Figures 16 and 18, p. 27 and 30, copyright © 1970 by Interscience Publishers, reprinted by permission of John Wiley & Sons, Inc.). Contour interval is 1,000 feet. The dashed line indicates the approximate boundary of Colton's study area.

present eastern limit of exposure (Figure 5–3). The axes of both carbonate-platform and foreland-basin sequences in the Appalachian basin nearly coincide, and the basin is, thus, sharply asymmetrical in cross section, essentially without an eastern side (Colton, 1970).

The major phases of Ordovician sedimentation were (1) a prolonged period of stable carbonate-platform deposition encompassing the first half of Ordovician time; (2) a progressive submergence of the platform, accompanied by marine limestone and initial siliciclastic sedimentation; and (3) filling of the resulting basin with marine and continental siliciclastic sediments. Each phase generated a different lithologic-sedimentologic association: the dolomite-

limestone, limestone, and siliciclastic associations, respectively.

DOLOMITE-LIMESTONE ASSOCIATION

Lithology

Rocks of the dolomite-limestone association are Early and early Middle Ordovician in age. They are dominated by thin- to thick-bedded dolomite and interbedded limestone. Dolomites are generally fine grained but include minor amounts of pelletal rocks (Figure 5–4). Much dolomite is secondary, replacing limestone. The dolomites contain numerous stromato-

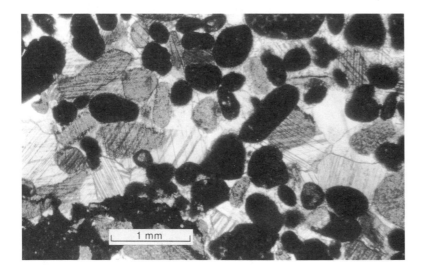

Figure 5–4. Photomicrograph of pelletal calcarenite of the dolomite-limestone association showing pellets, clastic calcite grains, and calcite cement. Plane-polarized light. The sample is from the Rockdale Run Formation, Pennsylvania Turnpike, Carlisle, Cumberland County.

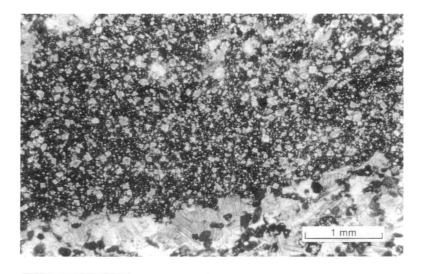

Figure 5–5. Photomicrograph of dolomitic intraclast (dark matrix) in recrystallized limestone. Plane-polarized light. The sample is from the Rockdale Run Formation, Pennsylvania Turnpike, Carlisle, Cumberland County.

lites and trace fossils, but few body fossils. The limestones are fine to coarse grained and include intraclast conglomerates (Figure 5–5), oolitic rocks, and crossbedded calcarenites. They contain more body fossils (notably trilobites and molluscs) than the dolomites. In many places, the limestones and dolomites are interbedded in shoaling-upward sequences.

Evaporites (mainly anhydrite) are rare but have been reported from the subsurface in western Penn-sylvania by Wagner (1966b). Terrigenous detritus is essentially absent; a few thin quartz sandstones occur in the upper parts of the section.

Stratigraphy and Paleoenvironments

Stratigraphic nomenclature applied to Ordovician rocks of the dolomite-limestone association is given in Figure 5–6. These rocks, everywhere assigned to the Beekmantown Group, reach 4,200 feet in thickness. Thickness trends are given in Figure 5–2. In general, the rocks are more dolomitic to the north and west. This association is rare in the Piedmont Lowland and is absent in the Hamburg klippe.

The dolomite-limestone association is, in many places, truncated above by a regional disconformity at the top of the Lower Ordovician. Karstic features were locally developed on this disconformity, which is the post-Knox unconformity or Sauk-Tippecanoe unconformity of Sloss (1963). It is commonly absent in eastern belts closer to the shelf edge, where deposition was more nearly continuous.

Rocks in the dolomite-limestone association were deposited in marine to marginal-marine environments. Facies belts extended northeast-southwest across the platform, generally parallel to the craton margin. The seas covering the platform shallowed progressively to the northwest, and environments of deposition became more intertidal and supratidal in that direction. The distribution of dolomite, while probably the result of diagenesis, was controlled by local hypersalinity, paleobathymetry, and tidal range.

LIMESTONE ASSOCIATION
Lithology

Rocks of the limestone association are Early, Middle, and Late Ordovician in age (Figure 5–6). They are dominated by fine-grained limestone and

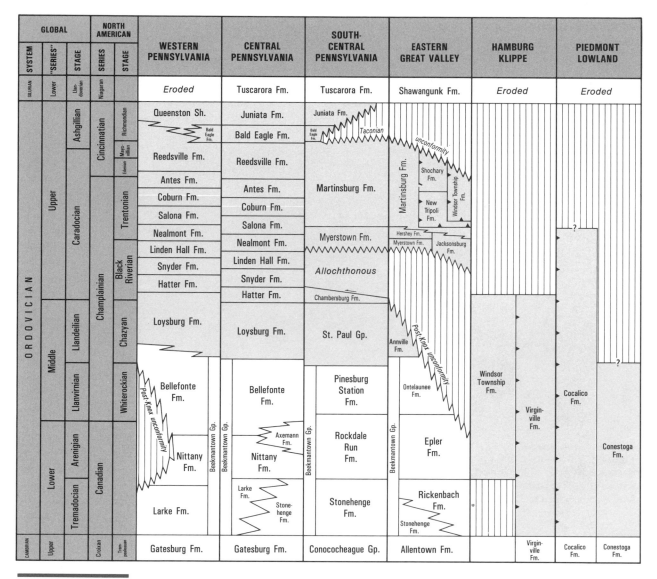

Figure 5–6. Generalized correlation chart of Ordovician strata in Pennsylvania showing lithologic-sedimentologic associations. Uncolored, dolomite-limestone association; gray tint, limestone association; colored tint, siliciclastic association. Data are from Wagner (1966b), Colton (1970), Gohn (1978), Lyttle and Drake (1979), Lash and others (1984), and Berg, McInerney, and others (1986).

include minor amounts of coarse-grained limestone and rare dolomite and terrigenous shale. These rocks are present over most of Pennsylvania and reach a thickness of 1,500 feet in central Pennsylvania.

Fine-grained limestones, the most abundant rocks, are laminated to thick bedded. These rocks are commonly dark gray to black, extensively bioturbated, and in some places fetid and carbonaceous; some are commercial-grade high-calcium limestones (see Chapter 41D). The coarser grained rocks include crossbedded pelletal and oolitic calcarenites and limestone-pebble conglomerates. Most rocks are abundantly fossiliferous (Figure 5–7).

Stratigraphy and Paleoenvironments

The stratigraphic nomenclature applied to rocks of the limestone association is given in Figure 5–6.

In the Piedmont Lowland, Lower and possibly Middle Ordovician fine-grained limestones of the Conestoga Formation truncate older rocks of the dolomite-limestone association. These limestones are facies of the platform edge and include both shallow- and deep-water types (Gohn, 1976).

In the eastern Great Valley, much of the section has been removed beneath an Upper Ordovician unconformity, the Taconian unconformity, which marks a hiatus that was of greater duration in the east (Figure 5–6). Upper Cambrian through Middle Ordovician limestones and terrigenous rocks of the Virginville Formation occur in the Hamburg klippe (Lash and Drake, 1984; Lash and others, 1984). These rocks include shales, deep-water limestones, and carbonate conglomerates (Figure 5–8) that occur as both coherent stratigraphic units and clasts in tectonic breccias. At least some rocks are Arenigian in age, based on conodonts (Repetski, 1984a, b).

The vertical sequence in the limestone association records a deepening basin floor and westward marine transgression. In central Pennsylvania, the lowest unit in this association, the Loysburg Formation, contains dolomite and stromatolites, suggesting tidal-zone deposition (Chafetz, 1969). Coarse-grained, fossiliferous limestones above the Loysburg suggest shallow-marine deposition above wave base (Rones, 1969). Fine-grained black limestones having graded bedding occur in the Salona and Coburn Formations at the top of the limestone association and suggest relatively anoxic, deep-water deposition below normal wave base (Newsom, 1983).

The basin floor subsided along a progressively deepening carbonate ramp (Read, 1980; Newsom, 1983). Facies belts trend generally northeast-southwest across the ramp, approximately parallel to the craton margin (Wagner, 1966b). These facies patterns record the downward flexing of the formerly stable carbonate platform along a basin hingeline that migrated west and northwest through Middle and Late Ordovician time.

Coincident with the subsidence was initiation of terrigenous clay deposition. Siliciclastic clay first appears as an impurity and as shale laminae in the Snyder and Linden Hall Formations (Figure 5–6) and indicates that detrital clay was now continually in the water mass. Graded limestone-shale bedding in the Salona and Coburn Formations (Figure 5–9) suggests lateral transport of shelf carbonate onto a clay-floored basin by turbidity currents.

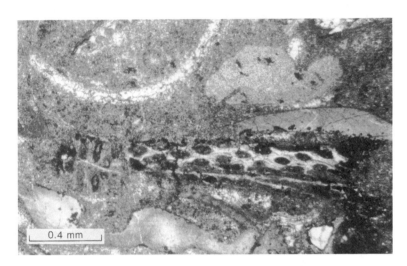

Figure 5–7. Negative print of acetate peel showing fine-grained, fossiliferous limestone of the limestone association. Brachiopod, mollusc, trilobite, and bryozoan debris are visible. The sample is from the Salona Formation, Pa. Route 453, Union Furnace, Huntingdon County.

Figure 5–8. Photomicrograph showing silty shale (dark) and laminae of fine-grained limestone from the Virginville Formation, Pa. Route 61, Mohrsville, Berks County. Strong slaty cleavage is nearly parallel to bedding. Plane-polarized light.

SILICICLASTIC ASSOCIATION

The siliciclastic association comprises up to 15,000 feet of shale, siltstone, sandstone, and conglomerate.

Figure 5–9. Interbedded fine-grained limestone (light beds) and terrigenous shale (dark beds) of the Coburn Formation along U.S. Route 322, Reedsville, Mifflin County. Limestones are parallel laminated and commonly have graded bedding (not visible in the photograph). The field notebook on the left provides scale.

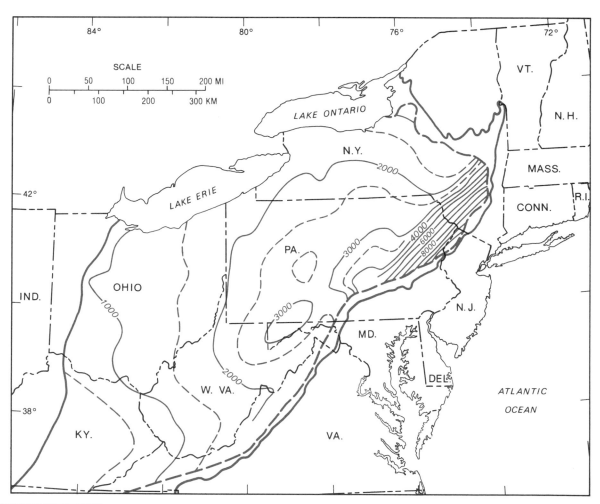

Figure 5–10. Isopach map showing thickness of Upper Ordovician rocks of the siliciclastic association (modified from Colton, G. W., *The Appalachian basin—its depositional sequences and their geologic relationships,* in Fisher, G. W., and others, eds., *Studies of Appalachian geology: central and southern,* Figure 16, p. 27, copyright © 1970 by Interscience Publishers, reprinted by permission of John Wiley & Sons, Inc.). Contour intervals are 500 feet (dashed colored lines) and 1,000 feet (solid colored lines). The heavy solid colored line represents the boundary of Colton's study area. The heavy dashed colored line represents the outer limit of outcrop of Upper Ordovician clastic rocks.

Siliciclastic-association rocks are of Late Ordovician age except in the Hamburg klippe and Piedmont Lowland, where they extend to Early Ordovician age (Figure 5–6). The maximum thickness of rocks in this association is developed in eastern and east-central Pennsylvania (Figure 5–10), and paleocurrents indicate westward and northwestward dispersal (Figure 5–11). Deposition was continuous west and northwest of Harrisburg and was terminated by Late Ordovician uplift and erosion that resulted in the Taconian unconformity in eastern and southeastern Pennsylvania (Figure 5–6).

The siliciclastic association contains two distinct groups of rocks: graywacke-shale flysch and sandstone-conglomerate molasse.

Graywacke-Shale

Pelagic shale and distal turbidites characterize the Martinsburg Formation, the lowest unit of the association. The graywacke sandstones exhibit graded bedding, load casts, and slump breccias. Larger scale features, such as channel fills and lag conglomerates, suggest channelized flow on submarine fans. Graptolites, trilobites, and trace fossils, in addition to the

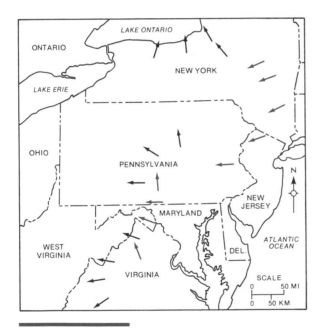

Figure 5–11. Generalized paleocurrent trends for rocks of the siliciclastic association in the central Appalachians. Black arrows, Juniata (Queenston in New York) and Bald Eagle (Oswego in New York) Formations; colored arrows, Martinsburg (Utica in New York) Formation. Data are from McBride (1962), Yeakel (1962), Zerrahn (1978), and Thompson (unpublished data).

sedimentologic features, point to deposition in deep water.

In the Great Valley west of Harrisburg, the Martinsburg shows vertical facies changes consistent with progressive basin filling. The lowest facies comprises 1,500 to 2,000 feet of graptolitic, calcareous pelagic shale with significant limestones but few sandstones. Above them lie fan/channel turbidites and flysch that become thicker, coarser grained, and nearer source upward. The highest facies contains massive, fine-grained, crossbedded, bioturbated sandstones containing wave-generated sedimentary structures and shallow-water faunas. These are interpreted to represent shallow-shelf deposition above wave base.

In the eastern Great Valley, the Martinsburg has been subdivided. Stose (1930) defined two members: a lower shale and an upper sandstone. This has been supported by Wright and Stephens (1978). Behre (1927) recognized three members: a lower shale (Bushkill Member), a middle sandstone (Ramseyburg Member), and an upper shale (Pen Argyl Member). More recent detailed mapping in the area (for example, that of Lyttle and others, 1986) supports the three-member interpretation.

In Lehigh and Berks Counties, Middle Ordovician rocks (the New Tripoli and Shochary Formations), which are thrust on the Martinsburg, comprise 10,000 feet of shale and calcareous turbidites (Lash and others, 1984). These rocks and their sedimentary characteristics are similar to those of the Reedsville Formation in central Pennsylvania (Lyttle and Drake, 1979).

Allochthonous siliciclastic rocks within the Hamburg klippe include pelagic red shale-chert sequences, graywacke-shale turbidites, and conglomerates of the Windsor Township Formation. In Lebanon County, the Windsor Township contains basaltic and andesitic igneous rocks, the Jonestown volcanics. The Windsor Township is thrust over the Shochary, New Tripoli, and Martinsburg Formations.

In the Piedmont Lowland in northern Lancaster County, Lower and Middle Ordovician shale of the Cocalico Formation is thrust over rocks of the limestone association.

In central Pennsylvania, rocks overlying the limestone association include gray calcareous shales of the Coburn Formation, graptolitic black shales of the Antes Formation, and interbedded shale, sandstone, and minor limestone of the Reedsville Formation (facies A in Figure 5–12). These sandstones are crossbedded and fossiliferous (Figure 5–13) and were probably deposited in shallow water above wave base (Conrad,

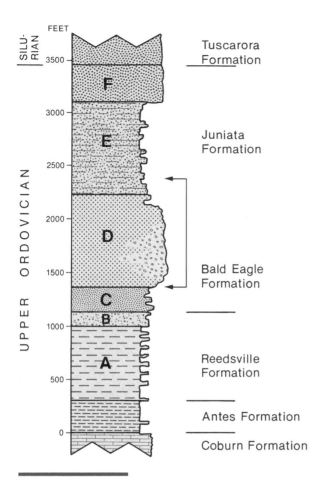

Figure 5–12. Schematic columnar section showing the stratigraphic nomenclature and the mappable lithofacies of the siliciclastic association in central Pennsylvania. The bracket indicates the stratigraphic range over which the color boundary between the gray Bald Eagle Formation and the red Juniata Formation fluctuates.

1985). The sandstones become thicker, burrowed, and more abundant upward (facies B in Figure 5–12).

Sandstone-Conglomerate

Strata overlying the Reedsville comprise nonfossiliferous sandstones, conglomerates, and mudstones of the Bald Eagle and Juniata Formations (Figure 5–6). Directly above the Reedsville lie marginal-marine, nonfossiliferous gray sandstones and minor shale (facies C in Figure 5–12; Horowitz, 1966; Thompson, 1970b). These are overlain by up to 1,200 feet of nonmarine, gray and red, crossbedded sandstone and conglomerate (Figure 5–14; facies D in Figure 5–12), the Lost Run conglomerate of Swartz (1955). These rocks are interpreted to be deposits of west-flowing, low-sinuosity streams on distal alluvial fans (Figures 5–15 and 5–16; Thompson, 1970b) and are the classical evidence for the Taconian orogeny in the central Appalachians.

The rocks of facies D are overlain by up to 1,000 feet of crossbedded red sandstone and burrowed, mud-cracked, red and gray mudstone (facies E in Figure 5–12) on which a paleosol developed (Feakes and Retallack, 1988). These rocks occur as fining-upward sequences (Figure 5–17) and were deposited in high-sinuosity meandering streams. They are locally overlain by red to gray sandstone and minor shale (facies F in Figure 5–12), which are transitional into overlying Silurian rocks (Thompson, 1970b).

The Bald Eagle-Juniata formation boundary is normally placed at the upward color change from

Figure 5–13. Interbedded sandstone, shale, and limestone of the Reedsville Formation (facies A) along Interstate Route 80, Milesburg Gap, Centre County. Sandstones (both light and dark) are lenticular, crossbedded, and hummocky bedded, have erosional upper surfaces, and in some places are size graded. The thick, light-colored bed at the left is fossiliferous limestone. Tops face left; the width of the outcrop is about 20 feet.

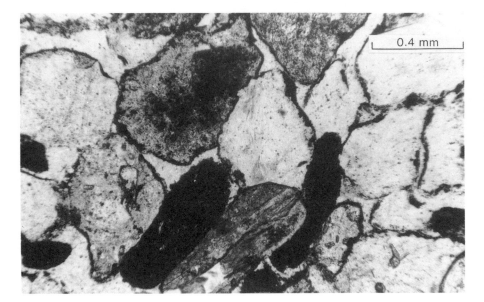

Figure 5–14. Photomicrograph of coarse-grained subgraywacke sandstone of the Juniata Formation (facies D) from an outcrop in East Waterford Gap, Juniata County. Note lithic-fragment grains, deformed and hematitized shale-clast grains, iron oxide grain coatings, and silica cement. Plane-polarized light.

Figure 5–15. Coarse-grained sandstone of the Juniata Formation (facies D) along Interstate Route 80, Loganton, Clinton County. Note the lack of interbedded shale and the prevalence of shallow-channel bedforms. The width of the outcrop is about 75 feet.

gray to red. That position varies locally by as much as 1,100 feet (Figure 5–12) and is probably of diagenetic rather than solely depositional origin (Thompson, 1970a). The Ordovician-Silurian boundary in central and western Pennsylvania is placed at the color change from red to white at the top of the Juniata. It, too, could be diagenetically controlled and may not have time (or age) significance.

Figure 5–18 shows a schematic restored cross section through the Taconian clastic wedge. The coarse clastic rocks (facies D) are confined to central Pennsylvania; they thin to both the northwest and the southeast. These rocks become coarser grained to the

southeast and pinch out above an unconformity atop the Martinsburg Formation. The pinching out marks the hingeline of the foreland basin.

STRATIGRAPHIC AND TECTONIC EVOLUTION

The principal components in the Ordovician evolution of eastern North America are illustrated in Figure 5–19. The carbonate platform of the Appalachian basin probably lay on the western margin of a small ocean basin, the eastern margin of which probably bordered a microcontinent. Subduction was initiated

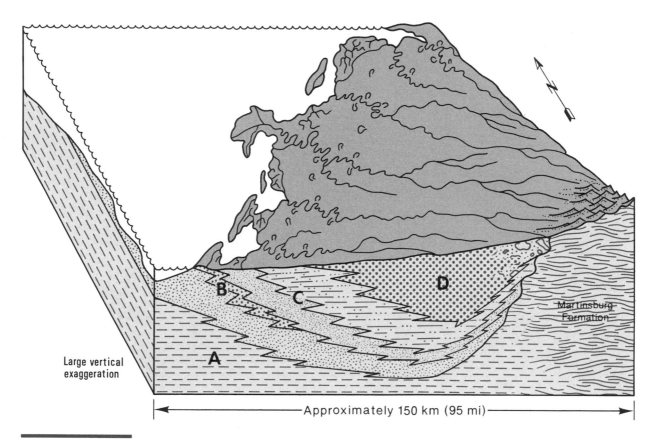

Figure 5–16. Inferred distribution of nearshore-marine and continental paleoenvironments during the marine regression associated with the early phases of deposition of the Taconian clastic wedge in central and eastern Pennsylvania (modified from Thompson, 1970b). Letters A through D refer to lithofacies defined in Figure 5–12.

Figure 5–17. Inter-bedded sandstone and shale of the Juniata Formation (facies E) along the Pennsylvania Turn-pike, Tussey Moun-tain, Bedford, Bed-ford County, show-ing two complete fining-upward sequences and the base of a third. These rocks in south-central Pennsylvania contain higher shale-to-sandstone ratios than equivalent rocks in central Pennsylvania. Tops face left.

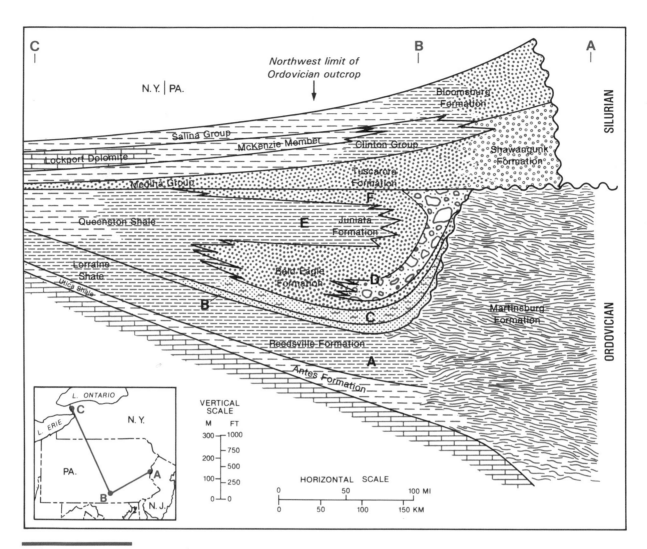

Figure 5–18. Schematic stratigraphic cross section through the Taconian clastic wedge, showing northwestward thinning of all units and southeastward coarsening and pinching out of the Bald Eagle and Juniata Formations (from Thompson and Sevon, 1982). Letters refer to lithofacies defined in Figure 5–12. Compare with Figure 5–3. Arrow marks the position of the Allegheny Front. Not palinspastic.

along this eastern margin during Middle Ordovician time, bringing about the eventual closing of the basin. The closing brought the carbonate platform partially beneath an east-dipping subduction complex along the eastern margin, giving rise to the Taconian orogeny.

The post-Knox unconformity records a widespread emergence of the eastern Laurentian craton in early Middle Ordovician time. It may represent erosion atop the peripheral bulge of flexed lithosphere that rose in response to coeval thrust loading of the craton margin to the east (Lash and Drake, 1984; Quinlan and Beaumont, 1984; Stanley and Ratcliffe, 1985).

The unconformity is probably slightly older in eastern Pennsylvania than it is in central Pennsylvania.

The distribution of facies shown in Figure 5–6 reflects the general westward migration of limestone- and siliciclastic-association deposition throughout Ordovician time, as the Appalachian basin evolved from passive margin to foreland basin in response to Taconian orogenic uplift. Creation of an accretionary prism began in easternmost Pennsylvania in Late Cambrian to Middle Ordovician time (Lash and Drake, 1984, Figure 34) as subduction was initiated. The sialic material above the subduction zone probably constituted a microcontinent of rifted North American crust.

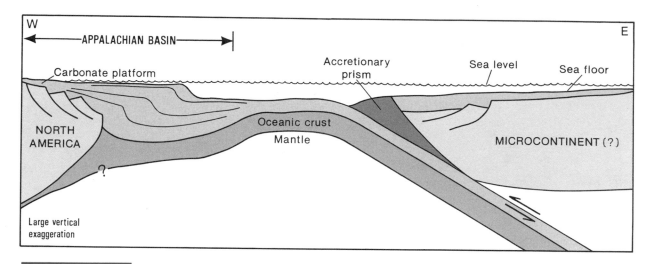

Figure 5-19. Schematic illustration of the major components of early Taconian orogenesis in the central Appalachians.

During closure of the oceanic basin in early Late Ordovician time, accretionary-prism slices (the Hamburg klippe) were emplaced atop the carbonate-platform sequence.

The thrusting created a tectonic highland (the Taconian mountains?) above the thrusts and led to the development of a foreland basin on the site of the former carbonate platform. Sediment for the Martinsburg, Bald Eagle, and Juniata Formations was derived primarily from this tectonic highland (Figure 5-16) and, later, from cannibalized sediment from the new eastern margin of the basin (Figures 5-18 and 5-20). The intensity of deformation decreased westward, and relations became conformable in central Pennsylvania.

Figure 5-20 shows, schematically, three stages in the evolution of the foreland basin. Early deposition in this basin included pelagic clay and distal turbidites of the Martinsburg Formation (Figure 5-20A).

Thickness and paleocurrent data (Figures 5-3 and 5-11) indicate a major post-Martinsburg depocenter in east-central Pennsylvania, in which terrigenous sediment was transported generally northwest in marginal-marine and fluvial depositional regimes during a regional marine regression (Figures 5-20B and 5-16). The conglomerates (facies D, Figure 5-12) reflect maximum regional stream gradients, which, in turn, reflect maximum uplift (Figure 5-16). The low-grade metamorphic, metavolcanic, and sedimentary-rock pebbles in the conglomerate suggest derivation from structurally high parts of the orogen (Leon, 1985).

Following maximum uplift, in late Late Ordovician time, regional paleoslope decreased, and low-gradient, floodplain-dominated fluvial facies of the middle Juniata Formation (facies E in Figure 5-12) became widespread in western Pennsylvania (Figure 5-20C). These more distal facies transgressed eastward into central Pennsylvania (Figure 5-18), where they passed upstream into more proximal, braided-stream sandstones of latest Ordovician and Silurian age.

In central Pennsylvania, the transition to Silurian deposition is continuous and records the encroachment of marine environments eastward across the Juniata land surface (Cotter, 1983a). In eastern Pennsylvania, Silurian continental rocks lie unconformably atop the eroded Martinsburg and Hamburg klippe sequences (Figures 5-6 and 5-18).

PROBLEMS AND FUTURE RESEARCH

The following topics, among many others, deserve further investigation:

1. Stratigraphic relations between the Antes-Reedsville sequence in central Pennsylvania and the New Tripoli-Shochary sequence in eastern Pennsylvania.
2. Stratigraphic relations between the Antes-Reedsville sequence and the Martinsburg Formation. This will involve an evaluation of the structural significance of Blue Moun-

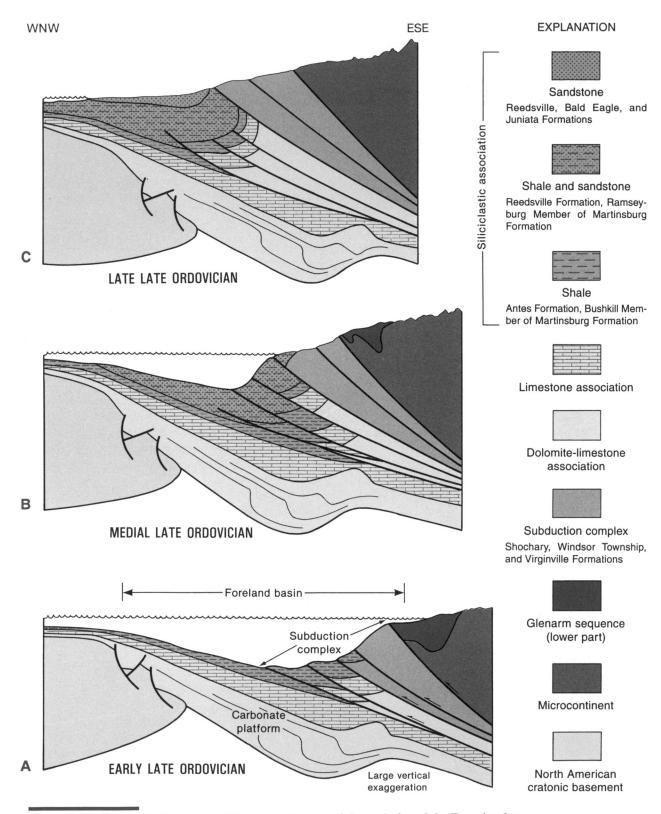

WNW   ESE   EXPLANATION

Sandstone
Reedsville, Bald Eagle, and
Juniata Formations

Shale and sandstone
Reedsville Formation, Ramsey-
burg Member of Martinsburg
Formation

Shale
Antes Formation, Bushkill Member of Martinsburg Formation

Limestone association

Dolomite-limestone
association

Subduction complex
Shochary, Windsor Township,
and Virginville Formations

Glenarm sequence
(lower part)

Microcontinent

North American
cratonic basement

C   LATE LATE ORDOVICIAN

B   MEDIAL LATE ORDOVICIAN

Foreland basin

Subduction complex

Carbonate platform

A   EARLY LATE ORDOVICIAN

Large vertical exaggeration

Figure 5–20. Schematic illustration of the inferred stages of the evolution of the Taconian fore-land basin and clastic wedge from deep-water marine clay deposition (A), represented by the Antes and Martinsburg Formations, to the continental sand and gravel deposition of the Bald Eagle and Juniata Formations (C). For earlier stages, see Lash and Drake (1984, Figure 34).

tain and the possibility of a major décollement there.

3. The origin of the color boundaries of the Juniata Formation, and the time-stratigraphic significance of the Ordovician-Silurian boundary in central Pennsylvania.

4. The sedimentologic and/or stratigraphic expression of the Late Ordovician glacioeustatic lowering of sea level documented elsewhere in the world.

5. Evaluation of synchrony of tectonism on either side of the Martic Line.

RECOMMENDED FOR FURTHER READING

Colton, G. W. (1970), *The Appalachian basin—its depositional sequences and their geologic relationships,* in Fisher, G. W., and others, eds., *Studies of Appalachian geology: central and southern,* New York, Interscience Publishers, p. 5–47.

Lash, G. G., and Drake, A. A., Jr. (1984), *The Richmond and Greenwich slices of the Hamburg klippe in eastern Pennsylvania—Stratigraphy, sedimentology, structure, and plate tectonic implications,* U.S. Geological Survey Professional Paper 1312, 40 p.

Read, J. F. (1980), *Carbonate ramp-to-basin transitions and foreland basin evolution, Middle Ordovician, Virginia Appalachians,* AAPG Bulletin, v. 64, p. 1575–1612.

Stanley, R. S., and Ratcliffe, N. M. (1985), *Tectonic synthesis of the Taconian orogeny in western New England,* Geological Society of America Bulletin, v. 96, p. 1227–1250.

Thompson, A. M. (1970), *Sedimentology and origin of Upper Ordovician clastic rocks, central Pennsylvania,* Society of Economic Paleontologists and Mineralogists, Eastern Section, Guidebook, 88 p.

_____ (1975), *Clastic coastal environments in Ordovician molasse, central Appalachians,* in Ginsburg, R. N., ed., *Tidal deposits—A casebook of recent examples and fossil counterparts,* New York, Springer Verlag, p. 135–143.

Wagner, W. R. (1966), *Stratigraphy of the Cambrian to Middle Ordovician rocks of central and western Pennsylvania,* Pennsylvania Geological Survey, 4th ser., General Geology Report 49, 156 p.

A

B

Figure 6–1. The physiography of the Appalachian Mountain section of the Ridge and Valley province is dominated by eroded folds with ridges that are underlain in part by sandstones of the Tuscarora Formation. A. View down the northwest flank of Stone Mountain in Huntingdon County. B. Talus slope of sandstone blocks derived from the Tuscarora, which caps the mountaintop 700 feet above the valley floor.

CHAPTER 6   SILURIAN AND TRANSITION TO DEVONIAN

CHRISTOPHER D. LAUGHREY
Bureau of Topographic and Geologic Survey
Department of Conservation and Natural
   Resources
400 Waterfront Drive
Pittsburgh, PA 15222

INTRODUCTION

Strata of Silurian age (405–430 Ma) constitute only about 10 percent of the relative volume of Paleozoic sedimentary rocks in the central Appalachian basin (Colton, 1970), but they impart a dominant and characteristic physiographic form to the Appalachian Mountain section of the Ridge and Valley province of central Pennsylvania (Figure 6–1). Good exposures of Silurian rocks occur in the eastern part of the state and in the Appalachian Mountain section (Figure 6–2). Silurian rocks in the subsurface are very important petroleum reservoirs in the western part of the state (see Chapter 38B). Knowledge of Silurian lithologies in the subsurface of western Pennsylvania is based on oil- and gas-well cores, drill-cutting samples, and geophysical data.

The demonstrable thickness of Silurian rocks in the state ranges from about 1,200 feet in northwestern Pennsylvania to almost 4,000 feet in eastern Pennsylvania (Figure 6–3). The Silurian System consists of two distinct depositional sequences: (1) a mainly Lower Silurian clastic sequence that extends throughout much of the state as a thin succession of sandstones, conglomerates, and subordinate mudrocks and carbonates; and (2) the Upper Silurian portion of a Silurian-Devonian carbonate sequence that consists of a moderately thick succession of limestones and dolomites and other minor, but significant, lithologies (Colton, 1970).

LOWER LLANDOVERIAN

In Early Silurian time, large volumes of clastic sediment were transported westward into central and northwestern Pennsylvania from eastern highlands raised during the Late Ordovician to Early Silurian Taconic orogeny. Three lithostratigraphic units in three geographic regions are recognized. These are the Shawangunk Formation in eastern Pennsylvania; the Tuscarora Formation in central Pennsylvania; and the Medina Group in northwestern Pennsylvania. The

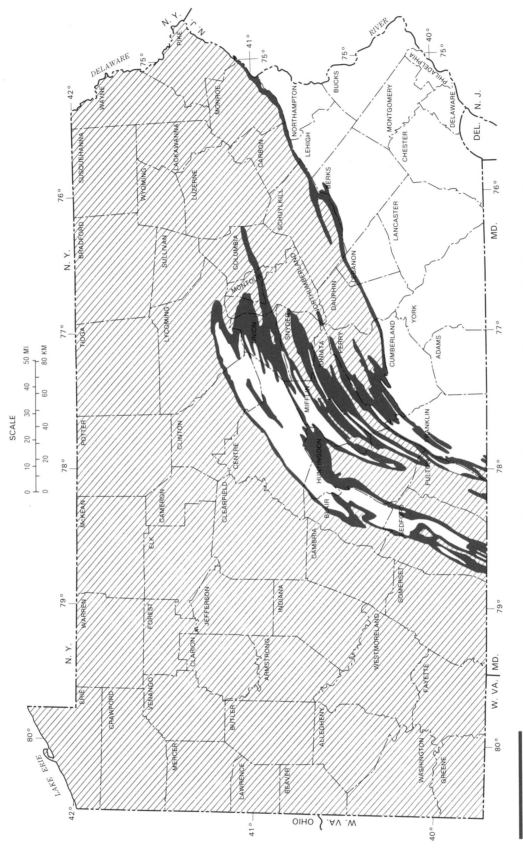

Figure 6–2. Distribution of Silurian rocks at the surface (solid color) and in the subsurface (line pattern) in Pennsylvania (from Pennsylvania Geological Survey, 1990).

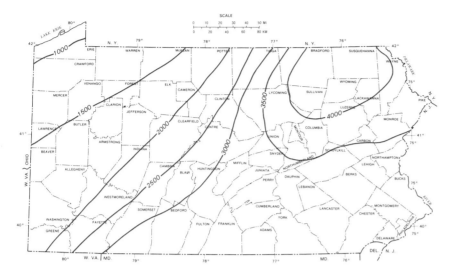

Figure 6–3. Isopach map showing the thickness of Silurian strata across Pennsylvania. Contour interval is 500 feet.

Shawangunk Formation is divided into members and facies (Epstein and Epstein, 1972), the Tuscarora Formation into facies (Cotter, 1982, 1983a), and the Medina Group into formations and informal facies (Piotrowski, 1981; Pees, 1983a; Laughrey, 1984).

Eastern Pennsylvania— Shawangunk Formation

In eastern Pennsylvania, the Shawangunk Formation comprises all of the Llandoverian and much of the Wenlockian Series (Berg, McInerney, and others, 1986). The maximum thickness of the Shawangunk occurs at the Delaware Water Gap, where the formation is 2,100 feet thick. The upper contact with the Bloomsburg Formation is irregular and transitional, whereas the contact with the underlying Martinsburg Formation is an angular unconformity (Epstein and Epstein, 1972). Lithologies in the Shawangunk include coarse conglomerate, quartzose sandstone, and shale. The Shawangunk is sparsely fossiliferous. Fragments of lingulid brachiopods, eurypterid remains, and rare Dipleurozoa (a class of jellyfishlike fossils in the phylum Cnidaria) occur in the Lizard Creek Member. Trace fossils reported from the Shawangunk include the feeding burrow *Arthrophycus alleghaniense* and the vertical burrow *Skolithos*. Epstein and Epstein (1972) interpreted the sedimentary characteristics of the Shawangunk as indicative of deposition in fluvial and paralic environments (Figure 6–4).

Central Pennsylvania— Tuscarora Formation

The Tuscarora Formation is distributed over a large area of central Pennsylvania. Through most of

this area, the thickness of the Tuscarora ranges between 492 and 656 feet. It thins to the northwest to a minimum thickness of about 200 feet. The Tuscarora Formation lies conformably on the Upper Ordovician (Ashgillian) Juniata Formation. Conformably above it is the Rose Hill Shale, which is appointed a late Llandoverian age. The Early Silurian age assignment for the Tuscarora is based on the ages of the juxtaposed formations because there are no datable fossils in the Tuscarora (Berry and Boucot, 1970). Rocks of the Tuscarora Formation consist of quartzose, sublithic, and argillaceous sandstones and shales (Folk, 1960; Cotter, 1982, 1983a; Wescott, 1982). Body fossils are conspicuously absent from the Tuscarora Formation, but a small number of trace fossils, including *Arthrophycus*, *Skolithos*, and *Monocraterion*, occur in varying abundance among different lithofacies (Cotter, 1982, 1983a). Cotter (1982, 1983a) interpreted the eastern part of the Tuscarora Formation as mostly fluvial in origin and the western part as mostly marine (Figure 6–5).

Western Pennsylvania—Medina Group

The Medina Group, which has no outcrops in Pennsylvania, is a sequence of quartzose, sublithic, and subarkosic sandstones, shales, and minor carbonates. It ranges in thickness from 200 feet to less than 140 feet. Workers in northwestern Pennsylvania generally report the Medina as disconformably overlying the red shales of the Ordovician Queenston Formation and conformably underlying the carbonates and shales of the Clinton Group. Body fossils are relatively common in the upper and middle parts of the Medina Group but are notably absent in the lowermost Whirlpool Sandstone (Fisher, 1954). Trace

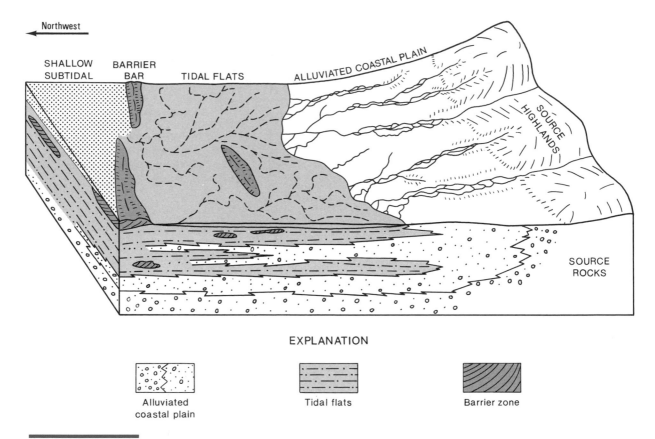

Figure 6–4. Block diagram showing sedimentary environments and major lithofacies in the Shawangunk Formation (from Epstein and Epstein, 1972, Figure 22).

fossils are abundant in the Medina Group and have proved quite useful for interpreting the origin of the rocks (Laughrey, 1984; Pemberton and Frey, 1984; Pemberton, 1987). Numerous workers have attributed the origin of the Medina Group to deposition in a variety of fluvial, deltaic, paralic, and marine sedimentary environments (Figure 6–6) (Kelley, 1966; Kelley and McGlade, 1969; Martini, 1971; Piotrowski, 1981; Laughrey, 1984; Duke and Fawcett, 1987).

Stratigraphic Correlations and Cyclicity

The correlation of lower Llandoverian lithostratigraphic units across western Pennsylvania is shown in Figure 6–7. A consensus developed among earlier workers that the extensive and unbroken continuity of Shawangunk, Tuscarora, and Medina lithologies across Pennsylvania and adjacent states represented a large, but simple, onshore-offshore complex from east to west (Yeakel, 1962; Knight, 1969; Martini, 1971; Smosna and Patchen, 1978; Piotrowski, 1981). This interpretation, most concisely presented by Yeakel (1962) and Smosna and Patchen (1978), implies that the Shawangunk and Tuscarora rocks are alluvial clastics deposited on a coastal plain, and the Medina rocks of western Pennsylvania are deltaic with offshore facies represented farther to the west (Figure 6–8). According to Smosna and Patchen (1978, p. 2,310), however, "Superimposed on this east-west gradation... is a dual origin recognized for the Tuscarora...." This twofold origin is apparent in all of the depositional schematics presented in Figures 6–4, 6–5, and 6–6. Facies analyses of the Shawangunk Formation, Tuscarora Formation, and Medina Group all reveal the imprint of fluvial or paralic and marine environments, although fluvial and transitional facies dominate the Shawangunk rocks of eastern Pennsylvania, and marine facies dominate the Tuscarora and Medina rocks of central and western Pennsylvania.

Cotter's (1983a) investigation of the Tuscarora Formation and work by Duke (1987b) employed contemporary techniques of "sequence stratigraphy," that is, "the attempt to analyze stratigraphic successions in terms of genetically related packages of strata" (Nummedal, 1987, p. iii). This approach promises to provide a dynamic and realistic understanding of Lower Silurian stratigraphy in Pennsylvania. Duke (1987b) has suggested subdivisions of the Medina Group based

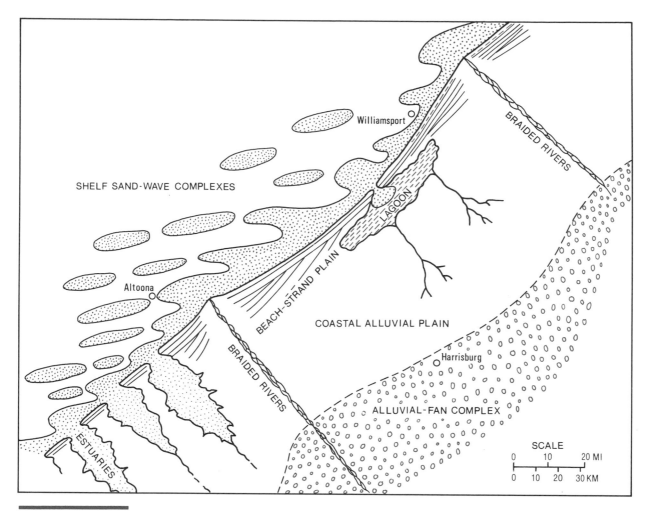

Figure 6–5. Cotter's interpretation of depositional environments in which the Tuscarora Formation originated during sea-level rise in earliest Llandoverian time (slightly modified from Cotter, 1983a, Figure 13, p. 42). Shoreline and shelf facies migrated southeastward over the coastal alluvial-plain sediments with rising sea level. Reprinted by permission of SEPM (Society for Sedimentary Geology).

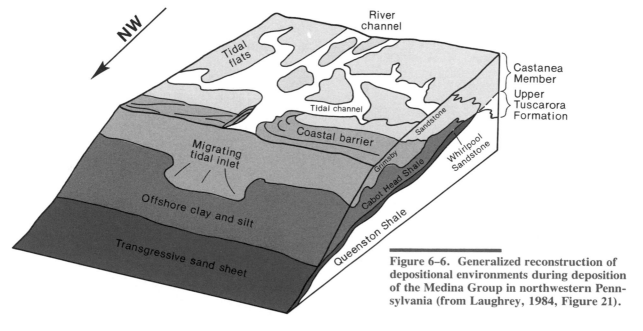

Figure 6–6. Generalized reconstruction of depositional environments during deposition of the Medina Group in northwestern Pennsylvania (from Laughrey, 1984, Figure 21).

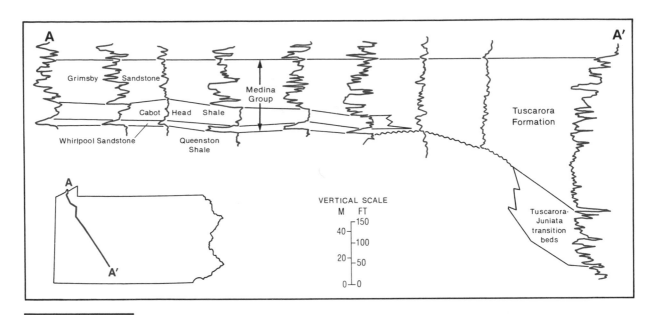

Figure 6–7. Correlation of lower Llandoverian lithostratigraphic units across western Pennsylvania (modified from Heyman, 1977, and Piotrowski, 1981). Correlations are based on subsurface geophysical (gamma-ray) logs.

upon the correlation of erosional unconformities bounding lithologically heterogeneous depositional cycles. The author has attempted to recognize these cycles in whole-diameter cores of the Medina Group from northwestern Pennsylvania and tentatively correlate them with those suggested by Duke (1987a) (Figure 6–9). Duke (1987a, p. 18) proposed that "The unconformity-bounded cyclic depositional sequences recognized in the Medina are essentially identical to depositional cycles recognized...by Cotter (1983a) in the time-equivalent Tuscarora Formation...." Cotter (1983a) ascribed the origin of depositional cycles in the Tuscarora Formation to the interplay of eustatic sea-level fluctuations with tectonic and depositional events. Duke and Fawcett (1987) stated that

depositional cycles in the Medina could be attributed to a number of possible causes, including tectonic processes, regional and/or global climatic variations, global sea-level fluctuations, or oscillatory process-response systems.

UPPER LLANDOVERIAN— LOWER WENLOCKIAN

The lithostratigraphic architecture of the Lower Silurian clastic sequence reveals a relatively uniform record of sedimentation across Pennsylvania and adjacent parts of the central Appalachian basin. A significantly different sedimentary pattern emerged during Middle Silurian time, however. This new pattern, defined by an elongate basin oriented northeast-southwest (Figure 6–10), prevailed into the Devonian Period (Dennison and Head, 1975). The central, or axial, part of the basin remained deeper than the margins through differential subsidence and limited sediment influx (Smosna and Patchen, 1978). Low-energy mud facies were deposited along the basin axis, whereas the southeast and northwest basin margins were regions of higher energy deposition.

Eastern Pennsylvania— Shawangunk Formation

In eastern Pennsylvania, the Middle Silurian is represented by the upper part of the Shawangunk Formation. Coarse-grained fluvial sands continued

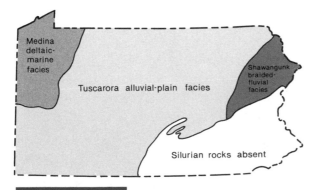

Figure 6–8. Interpretation of the Shawangunk, Tuscarora, and Medina lithologies across Pennsylvania as a simple onshore-offshore complex (modified from Piotrowski, 1981, Figure 3).

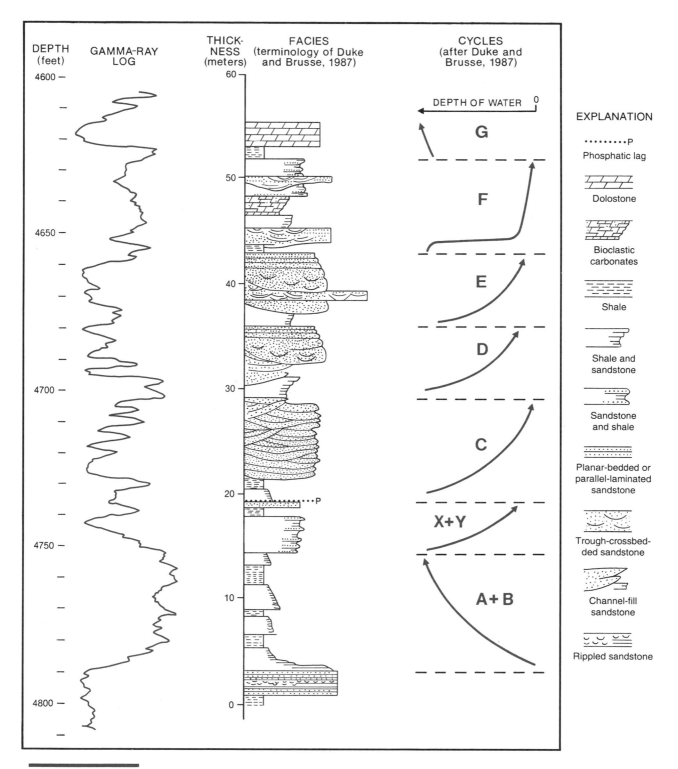

Figure 6–9. Allostratigraphic cycles in the Medina Group recognized in the Creacraft No. 1 well core from Crawford County. The gamma-ray log of the entire cored interval is shown on the left. The facies symbols used in the graphic core description are those of Duke and Brusse (1987). Letters and arrows on the right represent unconformity-bounded cyclic depositional sequences and relative sea-level changes proposed by Duke and Brusse (1987). The recognition of Duke and Brusse's cycles in the core supports their idea of cyclicity in these rocks and suggests that correlation of these Medina cycles with those recognized by Cotter (1983a) in the Tuscarora may be possible.

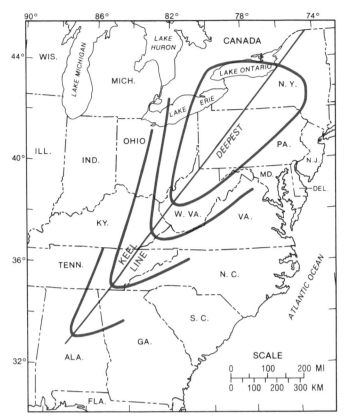

Figure 6–10. Map showing axis of elongate basin and "form lines" that indicate subsidence and sedimentary accumulation patterns during times of low detrital input during the middle and late Paleozoic (from Dennison, 1982, Figure 3). This basin architecture first appeared during Middle Silurian time.

The Keefer Formation conformably overlies the Rose Hill Formation (Figure 6–11). The Keefer contains quartz-cemented fossiliferous quartzose sandstone, hematitic oolitic sandstone, and minor mudrock. Sandstones of the Keefer Formation are very fine to coarse grained, silty, locally conglomeratic, crossbedded, and ripple bedded. Fossils include crinoid stems, brachiopods, and mollusc shells. The trace fossil *Skolithos* is locally abundant.

The Mifflintown Formation is composed of interbedded shallow marine mudrocks and limestones. It conformably overlies the Keefer Formation and underlies the Bloomsburg Formation (Faill and Wells, 1974).

Cotter and Inners (1986) suggested that the Rose Hill, Keefer, and Mifflintown Formations of central Pennsylvania accumulated on a submarine ramp that deepened from the proximal basin margin on the southeast to the basin axis at the approximate position of the modern Allegheny Front (Figure 6–12).

Cotter (1988, p. 242) recognized two "hierarchically superimposed cycles of sea-level fluctuations" in the medial Silurian succession of central Pennsylvania. His lithostratigraphic interpretations (Figures 6–11 and 6–12) suggest that five large-scale cycles of transgression and regression, with a mean recurrence interval of about 2.5 million years, occurred during Middle Silurian time, and that these cycles governed the development of the observed lithostratigraphic framework at the level of formations and members (Cotter, 1988, p. 242–245). Smaller scale cycles (3.3 to 9.8 feet in thickness) of sea-level fluctuations, possibly related to Milankovitch climate cycles, are superimposed on the larger scale transgressive-regressive cycles and are correlative between different contemporaneous facies (Cotter, 1988, p. 244–245).

to be deposited by streams bordering the southeastern margin of the newly developed basin (Smosna and Patchen, 1978). These deposits are identified as the Tammany Member, which is the uppermost member of the Shawangunk Formation (Lash and others, 1984). The underlying Lizard Creek Member of the Shawangunk, however, has much in common with basin-margin facies developed to the west (see comments by Lash and others, 1984, p. 83).

Central Pennsylvania—Rose Hill, Keefer, and Mifflintown Formations

The Middle Silurian succession in central Pennsylvania is represented by the Rose Hill, Keefer, and Mifflintown Formations (Figure 6–11). The Rose Hill Formation consists mostly of olive shale and also contains minor purplish shale and thin beds of hematitic sandstone (Cabin Hill and Center Members). The terms "lower shaly member," "middle shaly member," and "upper shaly member" are used informally to designate the intervals of Rose Hill mudrocks below, between, and above the hematitic sandstones. Thin beds of fossiliferous limestone also occur within the Rose Hill near the top of the upper shaly member.

Western Pennsylvania—Clinton Group

The Clinton Group constitutes Middle Silurian strata in western Pennsylvania. The dominant unit in these strata is the Rochester Shale (Figure 6–11), which consists of a variably fossiliferous, gray mud-

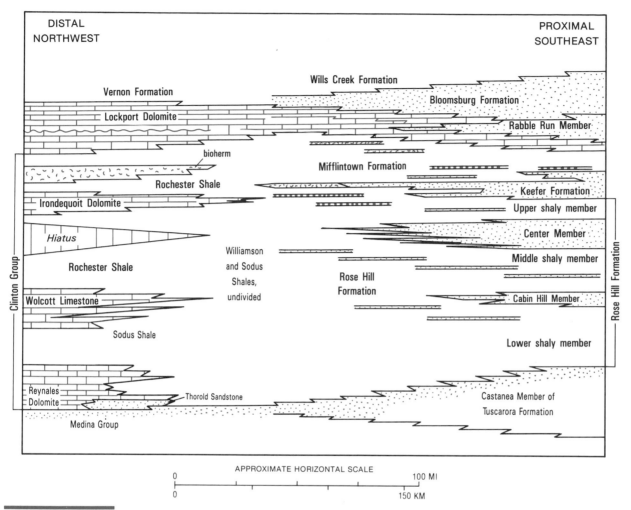

Figure 6-11. Cross section showing Middle Silurian stratigraphic units and lithofacies in central and western Pennsylvania. The cross section is oriented normal to the Appalachian basin axis in central and western Pennsylvania (from unpublished illustration by Edward Cotter, Bucknell University).

stone and numerous interbedded carbonates (Brett, 1983). The carbonate interbeds are interpreted as evidence for episodic, storm-dominated sedimentation on a gentle southeast-sloping ramp (Brett, 1983). Bioherms occur near the top of the Rochester interval toward the basin axis (Cuffey and others, 1985; Figure 6-13). The Rochester is recognized as a member of the Mifflintown Formation in central Pennsylvania (Berg, McInerney, and others, 1986).

The lower part of the Clinton Group consists of interbedded carbonate rocks (Irondequoit, Wolcott, and Reynales Dolomites, Figure 6-11), mudrocks (Williamson, Sodus, and Rochester Shales), and minor sandstone (Thorold Sandstone). These lithologies are equivalent to the Brassfield Limestone, which crops out in southern Ohio. The Brassfield splits westward in the subsurface into several carbonate rock units,

which are interbedded with the Rochester Shale (Nelson and Coogan, 1984). The lower units of the Clinton Group lose their identity to the southeast and merge into the distinctive Rose Hill-Keefer sequence (Heyman, 1977; Figure 6-11).

UPPER WENLOCKIAN—LOWER LUDLOVIAN

Eastern Pennsylvania— Bloomsburg Formation

The Bloomsburg Formation of Pennsylvania is composed of grayish-red claystone, siltstone, and clayey, very fine grained to coarse-grained sandstone with small amounts of conglomerate (Hoskins, 1961).

Figure 6–12. Interpretive model of Middle Silurian paleoenvironments in central Pennsylvania on the southeastern side of the Appalachian basin (from Cotter and Inners, 1986, Figure 14).

Foraminifera, bryozoans, brachiopods, molluscs, ostracodes, crinoids, and fish scales have been described from the Bloomsburg Formation, but most are rare except for brachiopods and ostracodes.

A generalized stratigraphic section of the Bloomsburg Formation and its correlative units is shown in Figure 6–14. The upper and lower contacts of the Bloomsburg are conformable. The entire Bloomsburg Formation represents a time-transgressive unit. Deposition of the Bloomsburg sediments began in late Wenlockian time and continued well into Ludlovian time. The top of the Bloomsburg Formation is increasingly young toward the east (Hoskins, 1961; Berry and Boucot, 1970).

Traced to the west and southwest from the type area in central Pennsylvania, the red beds of the Bloomsburg Formation thin and are separated into two red-bed units by the marine limestones and shales of the upper member of the Mifflintown Formation (Figure 6–14). The upper red unit continues to carry the name "Bloomsburg" in the west; the lower red unit is included in the Mifflintown Formation and is called the Rabble Run Member. The upper portion of the Bloomsburg Formation contains a persistent sandy unit named the Moyer Ridge Member that is traceable over much of central Pennsylvania.

The Bloomsburg Formation probably represents part of a large volume of deltaic sediments that were deposited over an area from Virginia into New York and possibly into northern Michigan (Hoskins, 1961; Smosna and Patchen, 1978). The sediments are thought to have been deposited in waters sufficiently saline to allow a brackish-water fauna to exist. A few local deposits of nonred quartzose sandstone are interpreted as bar or beach deposits that were reworked sufficiently to remove the clay and coloring matter.

Central Pennsylvania— McKenzie Formation

The McKenzie Formation of central Pennsylvania underlies and laterally interfingers with the

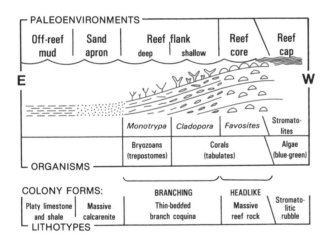

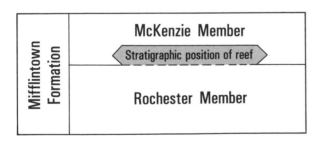

Figure 6–13. Paleoecological interpretation (top) and stratigraphic position (bottom) of a Middle Silurian reef near Lock Haven, Clinton County. Patch reefs such as this one developed on muddy Appalachian sea bottoms (from Cuffey and others, 1985, Figures 2 and 3).

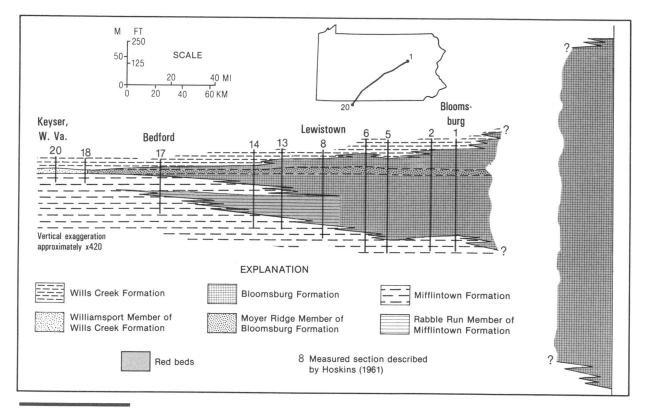

Figure 6–14. Generalized northeast-southwest stratigraphic section of the Bloomsburg Formation and its correlative units, approximately parallel to the Appalachian fold belt (modified from Hoskins, 1961, Figure 6).

Bloomsburg Formation. In much of central Pennsylvania, the McKenzie is designated as the upper member of the Mifflintown Formation; the McKenzie is given formational status in areas where other units of the Mifflintown Formation cannot be distinguished (see Berg, McInerney, and others, 1986).

The McKenzie Formation is composed of dark-olive to gray marine shales containing thin interbedded marine limestone and minor siltstone (Patchen and Smosna, 1975). It ranges in thickness from approximately 200 to 300 feet. The upper and lower boundaries are conformable. Fossils are sparse and include brachiopods, ostracodes, gastropods, and favositid corals (Cotter, 1983b). Coral/stromatoporoid bioherms in the McKenzie have been described by Patchen and Smosna (1975) and Inners (1984). Ripple marks, megaripple bedding, and trace fossils are common (Figure 6–15). The overall depositional envi-

Figure 6–15. Outcrop of limestone of the McKenzie Member of the Mifflintown Formation at Castanea, Clinton County (from Nickelsen and Cotter, 1983, Figure VIII–2A, p. 189). Note the megaripples and ripples on the surface of the limestone and the interbedded shale. The latter is the dominant lithology. Photograph by R. Sacks.

ronment was open marine to intertidal. These environments fluctuated with sea level during late Wenlockian time.

Western Pennsylvania—Lockport Dolomite

The McKenzie Formation grades laterally into the Lockport Dolomite in northwestern Pennsylvania. Although it consists predominantly of dolomite, the Lockport contains some limestone (Rhinehart, 1979; Laughrey, 1987). It has an average thickness of 200 feet in the subsurface of northwestern Pennsylvania. The Lockport is divided into five members at its outcrop in western New York (Zenger, 1965; Crowley, 1973). Such formational subdivisions cannot be resolved by the parastratigraphic format utilized to recognize operational units in the subsurface of northwestern Pennsylvania (Forgotson, 1957; Heyman, 1977). Only the basal DeCew Member can be recognized using the gamma-ray format (Figure 6–16).

Cores and well cuttings of the Lockport Dolomite appear brownish gray and buff to dark gray. The carbonate rocks are finely to moderately crystalline and contain intraclasts, ooids, peloids, and numerous fossils, including stromatoporoids, corals, echinoderms, bryozoans, molluscs, and brachiopods (Figure 6–17). The Lockport Dolomite is a shallowing-upward sequence (sensu James, 1979). Microfacies analysis (Wilson, 1975) suggests that most of the Lockport was deposited subtidally in reef and interreef environments (Zenger, 1965; Crowley, 1973; Rhinehart, 1979; Shukla and Friedman, 1983; Laughrey, 1987). In the upper part of the Lockport, however, some evidence exists for intertidal and supratidal deposition. This includes associations of ooids, stromatolites, and rip-up clasts, evaporite minerals, and sabkha-type dolomite (Shukla and Friedman, 1983; Laughrey, 1987).

UPPER LUDLOVIAN—LOWER PRIDOLIAN

Northeastern Pennsylvania—Poxono Island Formation and Bossardville Limestone

The Poxono Island Formation and Bossardville Limestone lack fossils that can be used for age assignment but are considered Pridolian in age on the basis of stratigraphic position (Berry and Boucot, 1970).

The Poxono Island Formation consists of laminated to finely bedded, mud-cracked, lenticular dolomite, limestone, and calcareous shale. Fossils include brachiopod fragments and ostracodes. The Poxono Island is approximately 140 to 200 feet thick and

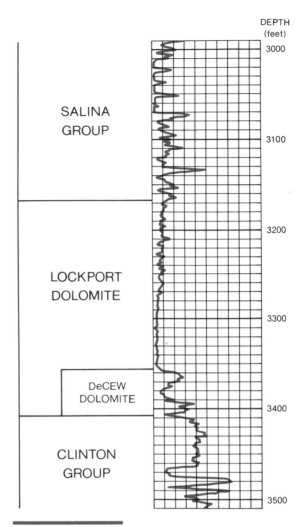

Figure 6–16. Gamma-ray geophysical log showing the stratigraphic position and geophysical character of the Lockport Dolomite and the DeCew Member in the subsurface of northwestern Pennsylvania. The log is from the Mary Mills No. 1 well, Erie County.

conformably overlies the Bloomsburg Formation. The Bossardville Limestone consists of very thin bedded to laminated, argillaceous limestones and lesser amounts of calcareous shale. Ostracodes are the dominant fossils. The Bossardville averages 100 feet in thickness. It and the subjacent Poxono Island Formation were deposited in supratidal, intertidal, and subtidal marine environments (Epstein and others, 1974). Epstein and Epstein (1967) stated that there was a deepening of the basin with time, causing a shift from supratidal deposition to subtidal deposition in a restricted lagoon.

Central Pennsylvania—Wills Creek and Tonoloway Formations

The Wills Creek and Tonoloway Formations represent the upper Ludlovian and lower Pridolian global

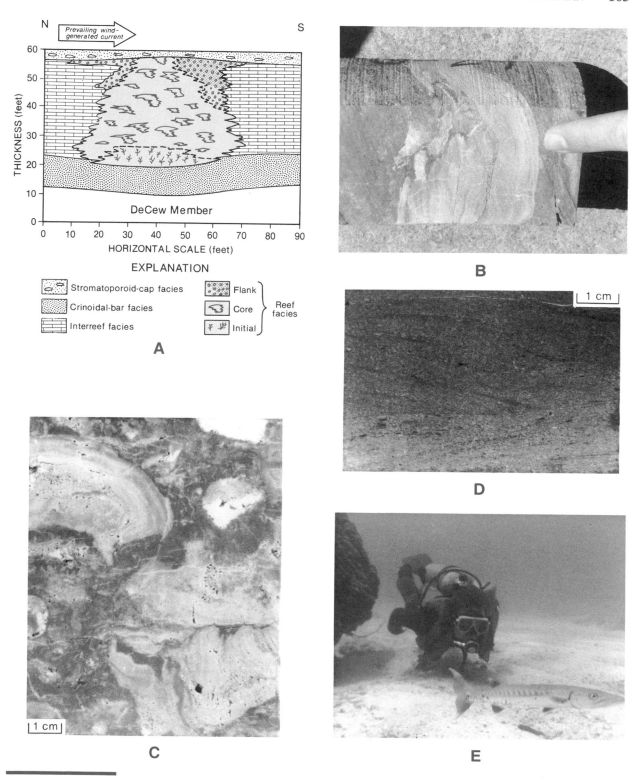

Figure 6–17. Composition and interpretation of reef and interreef lithofacies in the Lockport Dolomite of northwestern Pennsylvania. A. Schematic diagram showing the relative position of a reef-core, reef-flank, and interreef facies in the lower Lockport Dolomite (from Crowley, ©1973, Figure 12, p. 291, reprinted by permission of the American Association of Petroleum Geologists). B. Stromatoporoid in the reef-core facies of the Lockport Dolomite, G. W. Snyder well core, Mercer County. C. Stromatoporoid and coral rubble in a dolomite matrix from the reef-flank facies of the Lockport Dolomite, G. W. Snyder well core, Mercer County. D. Rippled oolitic dolomite in the interreef facies of the Lockport Dolomite, G. W. Snyder well core, Mercer County. E. Modern analog in the Florida Keys for the Lockport biostromal and biohermal lithofacies. The patch reef is just to the left of the diver. The diver and the barracuda hover over reef rubble and carbonate sand.

stages in central Pennsylvania. The Wills Creek Formation consists of variegated claystone, silty claystone, and argillaceous limestone. The thickness of the Wills Creek ranges from 250 to 500 feet. The upper and lower contacts are gradational and conformable.

The Tonoloway Formation conformably overlies the Wills Creek Formation. It consists mainly of laminated to thin-bedded limestone and a few thin beds of calcareous shale. Some thin to medium beds of dense microcrystalline limestone also occur. Faill and Wells (1974) reported the occurrence of pellet textures, ostracode shells, lenses of crystalline calcite, and sedimentary boudinage structures in the Tonoloway.

Both the Wills Creek and Tonoloway Formations consist of numerous shallowing-upward cycles that Lacey (1960), Tourek (1971), and Cotter and Inners (1986) have interpreted as repeated progradational events on very large tidal-sabkha flats (Figures 6–18 and 6–19).

Cyclicity in the Wills Creek-Tonoloway has been ascribed to both autogenic and allogenic mechanisms by different workers. Tourek (1971) proposed that localized basinal control on sedimentation is the principal mechanism governing the cyclicity observed in the sediments, whereas Anderson and Goodwin (1980) suggested eustatic control for the depositional events.

Western Pennsylvania— Salina Group

The Salina Group in northwestern Pennsylvania consists of interbedded carbonate and evaporite rocks. It ranges in thickness from over 2,000 feet in the southeastern part of the Appalachian Plateaus area to less than 400 feet at Lake Erie. Correlation of the Salina Group intervals with outcrop equivalents in central Pennsylvania is shown in Figure 6–20. Salt beds of Unit B in Figure 6–20 appear to be continuous from the Michigan basin into the Appalachian basin (Rickard, 1969). This unit contains the first known salt beds of the Salina deposited in Pennsylvania. Rickard (1969, p. 8) stated that the influx of terrigenous sediments of the Bloomsburg delta inhibited the deposition of evaporites in the Unit A rocks (Figure 6–20) of the central Appalachians. The

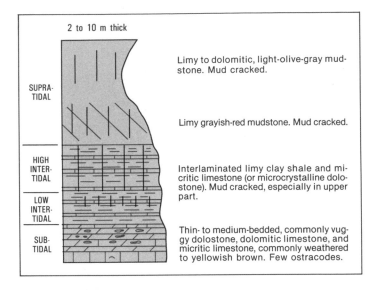

Figure 6–18. Sedimentary cycle in the Wills Creek Formation (from Cotter and Inners, 1986, Figure 16).

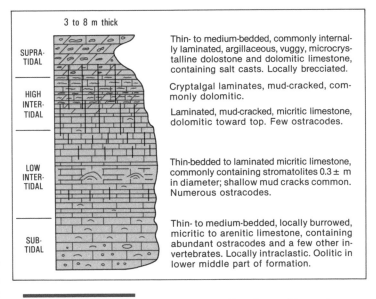

Figure 6–19. Sedimentary cycle in the Tonoloway Formation (from Cotter and Inners, 1986, Figure 16).

distribution of Unit B indicates that the development of a subbasin in north-central Pennsylvania was controlled by the location of Niagaran reefs, the eastward restriction of the Bloomsburg delta, and a higher platform area in southwestern Pennsylvania (Fergusson and Prather, 1968). The probable paleogeography of the Salina salt basin during mid-Cayugan time is illustrated in Figure 6–21.

SERIES		CENTRAL AND WESTERN NEW YORK (outcrop and subsurface) AND NORTH-CENTRAL PENNSYLVANIA (subsurface) (Rickard, 1969)		CENTRAL PENNSYLVANIA (outcrop)
UPPER SILURIAN (part)	Cayugan	Cobleskill-Akron Formation		Keyser Formation
		Salina Group	Bertie Formation	Unit H	
					?
			Camillus Formation	Unit G	
			Syracuse Formation	Unit F*	Tonoloway Formation
				Unit E*	
				Unit D*	
			Vernon Formation	Unit C	Wills Creek Formation
				Unit B*	
				Unit A	Bloomsburg Formation (part)

*Salt beds in Pennsylvania

Figure 6–20. Correlation of evaporite-bearing intervals in the Salina Group with outcrop equivalents in central Pennsylvania (from Cotter and Inners, 1986, Figure 18).

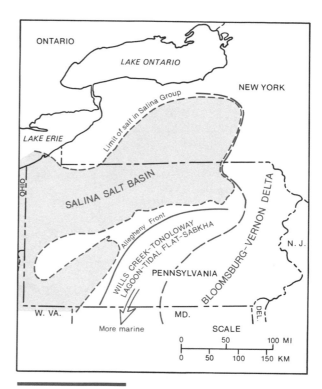

Figure 6–21. General paleogeography of the central Appalachian region in mid-Cayugan time (from Cotter and Inners, 1986, Figure 17).

UPPER PRIDOLIAN—LOWEST DEVONIAN

Eastern Pennsylvania—Keyser and Decker Formations

The Decker Formation is the youngest undisputed Silurian unit in northeastern Pennsylvania (Epstein and others, 1974). Conodonts collected by Denkler (1984) confirm the Pridolian (youngest Silurian) age of the Decker Formation. The interval is 80 to 90 feet thick in northeastern Pennsylvania and consists of arenaceous limestone and some argillaceous siltstone and sandstone. Fossils include ostracodes, brachiopods, bryozoans, stromatolites, and conodonts. The Decker formed as barrier beach and/or biostromal banks (Epstein and others, 1967) and thins to the southwest. The upper and lower contacts are conformable. In some parts of northeastern Pennsylvania, the Decker is overlain by the Andreas Red Beds. The age

of the Andreas is uncertain; it may be correlative with the upper part of the Decker Formation or the lowermost Devonian Rondout Formation (Lash and others, 1984; Berg, McInerney, and others, 1986).

The Keyser Formation in eastern Pennsylvania is made up of approximately 125 feet of gray, argillaceous, fossiliferous, nodular limestone and some interbedded calcareous shale (Inners, 1981). Basal and upper contacts are conformable. Inners (1981) interpreted the lower two thirds of the Keyser in eastern Pennsylvania as having formed in a shallow-marine, subtidal shelf environment. Deposition of the upper third of the formation was in shallow lagoons and on intertidal mudflats, similar to that of the subjacent Tonoloway Formation (Inners, 1981). Silurian fossils occur in the lower part of the Keyser, whereas Devonian fossils occur in the upper part, demonstrating that the systemic boundary lies within this formation (Berdan, 1964; Bowen, 1967).

Central Pennsylvania—Keyser Formation

The Keyser Formation of central Pennsylvania represents continuous carbonate sedimentation from Late Silurian into Early Devonian time. Both Silurian and Devonian fossils occur in the Keyser (Bowen,

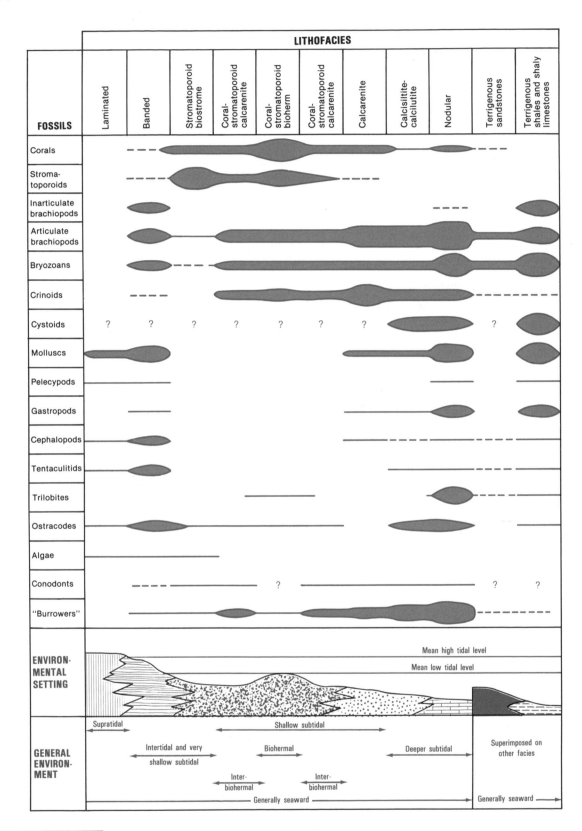

Figure 6–22. Head's (1969, Figure 33) interpretation of environmental relationships between lithofacies, fossils, and the sedimentary depositional setting of the Keyser Formation.

1967). The formation is recognized throughout the central Appalachian basin. The Keyser is a mainly gray, fossiliferous limestone. The upper part of the formation consists of laminated to thin-bedded limestone and dark-gray chert nodules. The rest of the formation is thin to very thick bedded. Stylolites commonly parallel the bedding. Fossils are typically, but not always, disarticulated. Fragments of brachiopods, crinoids, bryozoans, molluscs, and ostracodes are common, but unbroken specimens occur (Hoskins and others, 1983). The reported thickness of the Keyser ranges from 75 to 202 feet. The lower contact of the Keyser with the Tonoloway is sharp and conformable. The upper contacts with Lower Devonian lithologies are less distinctive. In east-central Pennsylvania, the upper Keyser limestones grade upward into cherty limestone and shale, which in turn grade upward into the Devonian Old Port Formation. To the west, the top of the Keyser Formation is marked by a distinct chert bed (Conlin and Hoskins, 1962). Head (1969) described the variations in marine sedimentary environments that existed in the central Appalachians during deposition of the Keyser Formation (Figure 6–22).

Western Pennsylvania—Keyser Formation and Equivalents

In west-central Pennsylvania, the Keyser Formation is recognized in the subsurface of the Appalachian Plateaus province (Heyman, 1977). Farther west and northwest, the lower part of the Keyser is equivalent to the Silurian Bertie Dolomite, Akron and Cobleskill Dolomites, and Bass Islands Dolomite. The uppermost part of the Keyser is equivalent to the Lower Devonian Manlius Formation. In extreme northwestern Pennsylvania, the basal lithologies of the Devonian Onondaga and Oriskany Formations lie directly on the Silurian rocks. This interval, from the base of the Devonian Onondaga Group to the top of the Salina Group, is one of very abrupt lithic changes (Heyman, 1977).

PROBLEMS AND FUTURE RESEARCH

A number of challenging problems and topics for further study await the geologist interested in Silurian sedimentation and stratigraphy in Pennsylvania. A review of these topics is beyond the scope of this article, and those who are curious should read publications listed in "Recommended For Further Read-

ing." A few of the unresolved subjects, however, warrant special mention. The provenance of the framework constituents in the sandstones and conglomerates of the Shawangunk Formation is enigmatic (Epstein and Epstein, 1972). Considerable work is still needed with regard to cyclicity and correlation in the Medina and Tuscarora intervals. The origin of channel deposits in the Grimsby Sandstone and the possible fluvial nature of the lower part of the Whirlpool Sandstone deserve careful attention (Duke and Brusse, 1987; Middleton and others, 1987). Silurian carbonates are mostly dolomitized in the subsurface of western Pennsylvania, whereas mostly limestones occur in the outcrop belt of central Pennsylvania. The differences in the diagenetic history of these rocks would make an excellent research project. Further resolution of the mechanisms controlling cyclicity in the Wills Creek-Tonoloway interval is needed. Finally, detailed correlation and stratigraphy of the interval between the top of the Salina Group and the base of the Onondaga Group would improve our understanding of the subsurface Upper Silurian and Lower Devonian rocks in western Pennsylvania.

RECOMMENDED FOR FURTHER READING

Berdan, J. M. (1964), *The Helderberg Group and the position of the Silurian-Devonian boundary in North America,* U.S. Geological Survey Bulletin 1180-B, 19 p.

Cotter, Edward (1982), *Tuscarora Formation of Pennsylvania,* Society of Economic Paleontologists and Mineralogists, Eastern Section, 1982, Guidebook, 105 p.

_____ (1983), *Shelf, paralic, and fluvial environments and eustatic sea-level fluctuations in the origin of the Tuscarora Formation (Lower Silurian) of central Pennsylvania,* Journal of Sedimentary Petrology, v. 53, p. 25–49.

Epstein, J. B., and Epstein, A. G. (1972), *The Shawangunk Formation (Upper Ordovician(?) to Middle Silurian) in eastern Pennsylvania,* U.S. Geological Survey Professional Paper 744, 45 p.

Fergusson, W. B., and Prather, B. A. (1968), *Salt deposits in the Salina Group in Pennsylvania,* Pennsylvania Geological Survey, 4th ser., Mineral Resource Report 58, 41 p.

Hoskins, D. M. (1961), *Stratigraphy and paleontology of the Bloomsburg Formation of Pennsylvania and adjacent states,* Pennsylvania Geological Survey, 4th ser., General Geology Report 36, 125 p.

Laughrey, C. D. (1984), *Petrology and reservoir characteristics of the Lower Silurian Medina Group sandstones, Athens and Geneva fields, Crawford County, Pennsylvania,* Pennsylvania Geological Survey, 4th ser., Mineral Resource Report 85, 126 p.

Smosna, Richard, and Patchen, Douglas (1978), *Silurian evolution of central Appalachian basin,* AAPG Bulletin, v. 62, p. 2308–2328.

Yeakel, L. S., Jr. (1962), *Tuscarora, Juniata, and Bald Eagle paleocurrents and paleogeography in the central Appalachians,* Geological Society of America Bulletin, v. 73, p. 1515–1540.

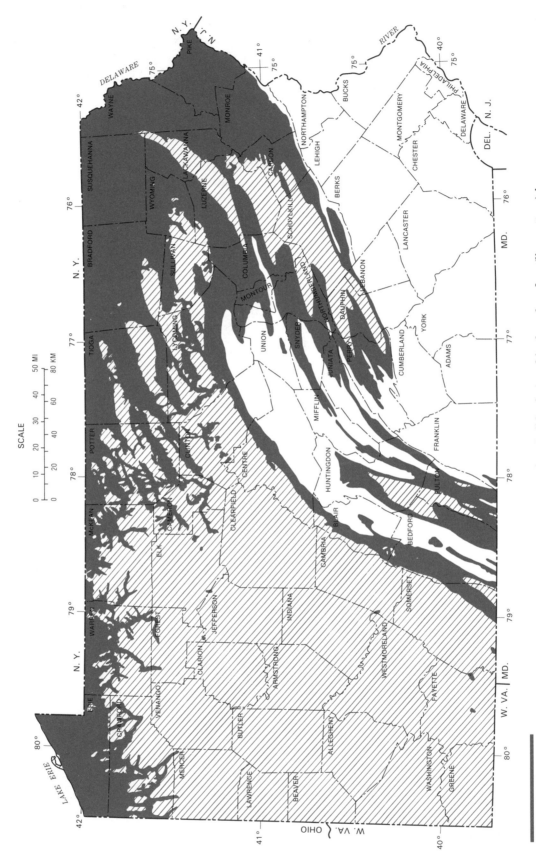

Figure 7-1. Generalized geographic extent of Devonian rocks at the surface (solid color) and in the subsurface (line pattern) in Pennsylvania (from Pennsylvania Geological Survey, 1990).

108

CHAPTER 7   DEVONIAN

JOHN A. HARPER
  Bureau of Topographic and Geologic Survey
  Department of Conservation and Natural
    Resources
  400 Waterfront Drive
  Pittsburgh, PA 15222

INTRODUCTION

Sedgwick and Murchison (1839) named the Devonian System on the basis of marine rocks exposed in Devonshire, England. At about the same time, the New York Geological Survey demonstrated that the Devonian section in New York was structurally less complex and stratigraphically more complete than the British section. The New York outcrop belt, recognized as the standard Devonian section in North America, would have been a much better systemic type section than the British section.

The Devonian System in Pennsylvania is thicker and more extensive than even the New York section, but much of it lies in the subsurface in western Pennsylvania (Figure 7–1). It is a westward-thinning wedge of sediments. Its thickness has been measured or estimated at 2,400 feet in Erie County and over 12,000 feet in eastern Pennsylvania (Figure 7–2). Mudrocks are dominant in the Devonian section; however, small amounts of chert and limestone are important constituents in the lower half, and larger quantities of siltstones, sandstones, and conglomerates dominate parts of the upper half. The upper and lower boundaries of the system are mostly conformable, but there are notable exceptions. In northwestern Pennsylvania, near the craton margin, the lower boundary is disconformable, whereas in eastern Pennsylvania, near the major sediment source areas, the upper boundary is disconformable.

The Devonian Period was a time of abundant life and significant changes or developments in biotic history. These include the Early Devonian development of widespread biohermal deposits ("reefs") dominated by stromatoporoids and corals, the rapid adaptive radiation of fishes, the appearance in the Late Devonian of the first land vertebrates, the rise of land plants and the development of primitive forests, and an important mass extinction event within the Upper Devonian (Senecan-Chautauquan boundary). Lower and Middle Devonian rocks in Pennsylvania have the best record of body fossils within the system, but the abundance and diversity of trace fossils in the

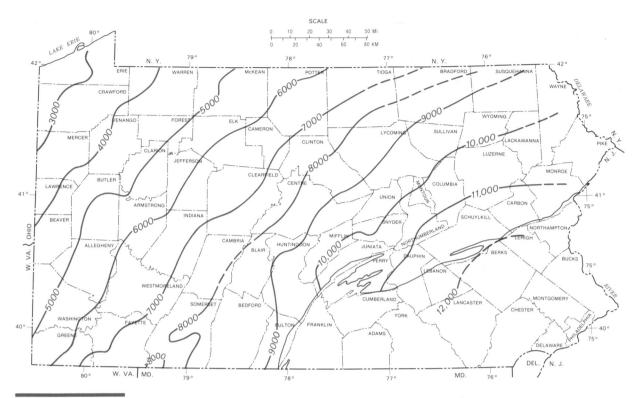

Figure 7–2. Isopach map showing the total thickness of the Devonian section in Pennsylvania, in feet (modified from Oliver and others, 1971, Sheet 7). Contour interval is 1,000 feet. The thin colored line represents the eastern limit of Devonian outcrop.

Upper Devonian indicate that large numbers of marine, freshwater, and terrestrial animals existed at the time of deposition (Hoskins and others, 1983). Land plants thrived in the deltaic plains and eventually formed localized thin layers of coal.

STRATIGRAPHY

Rocks of the Devonian System in Pennsylvania consist primarily of Lower Devonian marine carbonates, cherts, and shales, and Upper Devonian marine to nonmarine, coarse- to fine-grained terrigenous rocks deposited in the prograding Catskill deltaic system. The characteristic rocks of these two divisions interfinger in the Middle Devonian. The descriptions of formations that follow apply primarily to units exposed in central Pennsylvania. For equivalent formations and areas where various formation names are applicable, see Figures 7–3 and 7–4.

Lower Devonian

Rocks of the Lower Devonian consist of strata ranging from bioclastic shelf carbonates to very coarse grained detrital sandstones. Rocks of the Helderbergian Stage are typically limestones and include minor amounts of shale, chert, and detrital quartz (Figure 7–5). Quartz sandstones, siltstones, and shales make up the greatest part of Deerparkian Stage rocks, but limestones and cherts are important constituents, especially in central and eastern Pennsylvania (Figure 7–6). Coarse to fine detrital sediments characterize strata of the lower Onesquethawan Stage.

The basal Devonian unit in Pennsylvania, the Keyser Formation, is discussed in the preceding chapter. The non-Keyser portion of the Helderbergian Stage consists of the New Creek and Corriganville Limestones and the Mandata Shale (Figure 7–3). The limestones are distinguished from the underlying Keyser by their lighter color, lower chert content, and thicker, more massive bedding. Willard and others (1939) felt that the Keyser-New Creek boundary is disconformable throughout central Pennsylvania, but this was not substantiated by later investigations (e.g., de Witt and Colton, 1964; Faill and Wells, 1974). The New Creek Limestone is typically a coarse-grained, massive- to thick-bedded, fragmental biosparite ranging from 3 to 10 feet thick. It

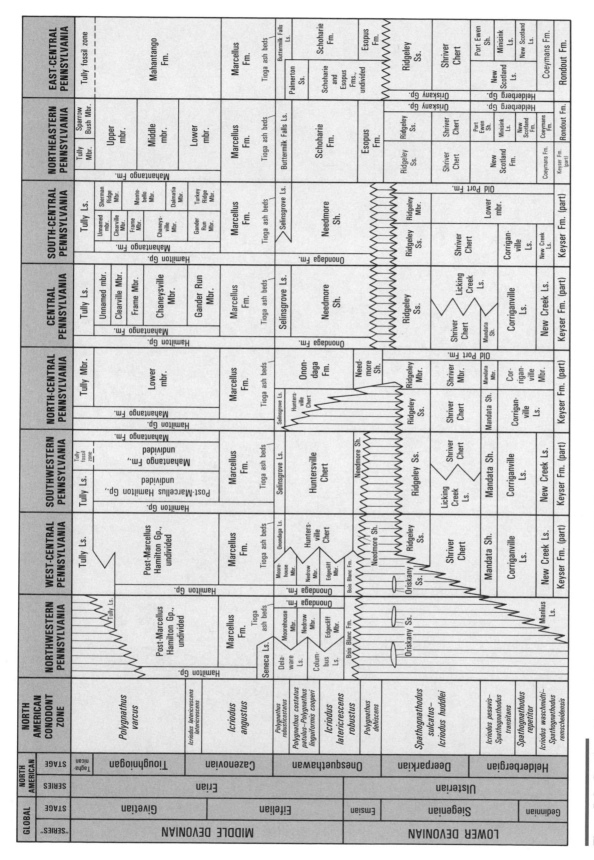

Figure 7-3. Stratigraphic correlation chart of Lower and Middle Devonian rocks in Pennsylvania (modified from Berg, McInerney, and others, 1986, and Rickard, 1975).

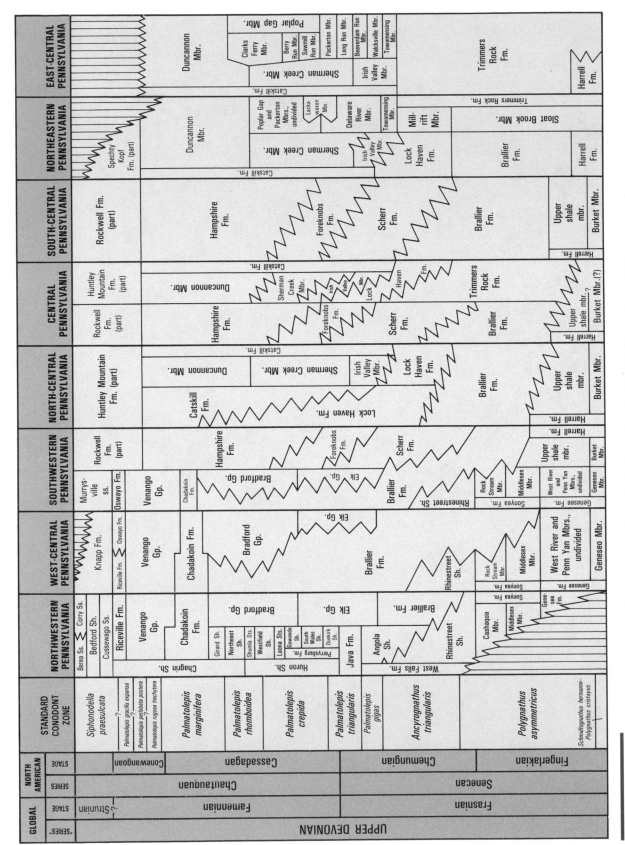

Figure 7–4. Stratigraphic correlation chart of Upper Devonian rocks in Pennsylvania (modified from Berg, McInerney, and others, 1986, and Rickard, 1975).

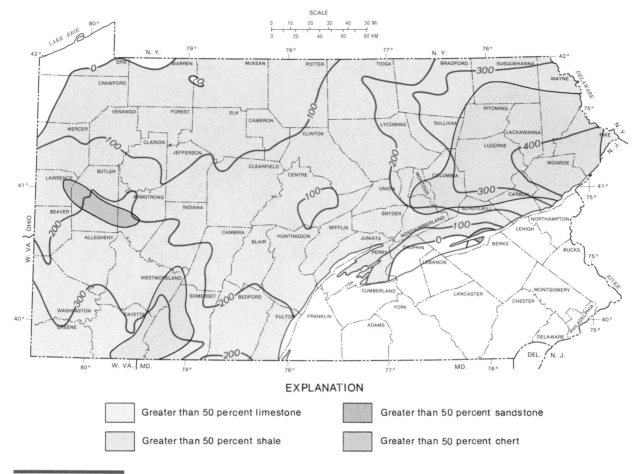

Figure 7–5. Generalized isopach and lithofacies map of the Helderbergian Stage in Pennsylvania (modified from Oliver and others, 1971, Sheet 2). Contour interval is 100 feet. The thin colored line represents the eastern limit of Devonian outcrop.

grades into the Corriganville Limestone, which consists of finely crystalline, thick- to thin-bedded limestones 10 to 30 feet thick. The New Creek is typically the more fossiliferous of the two. These limestone units are difficult to separate, especially in the subsurface (Heyman, 1977) (Figure 7–7). The Mandata Shale is dark gray to black, splintery, thin bedded, fissile to blocky, and siliceous. It contains interbedded chert and limestone layers and small nodules of phosphate. It grades into the Corriganville Limestone and ranges from 20 to 100 feet thick in central Pennsylvania. In northwestern Pennsylvania, the entire sequence of Helderbergian strata consists of carbonates that are referred to by the New York name, Manlius Limestone (Berg, McInerney, and others, 1986). The Manlius, including the Keyser portion, is commonly labeled "Helderberg" by drillers in the area.

The Shriver Chert, Licking Creek Limestone, and Ridgeley Sandstone constitute the strata of the Deerparkian Stage in central Pennsylvania. Light-colored, thin-bedded, cherty and silty mudstones and calcareous and siliceous siltstones characterize the Shriver throughout its outcrop, where it ranges from 80 to 170 feet thick. It grades laterally into the Licking Creek Limestone. The Licking Creek is about 90 feet thick at its type locality in Franklin County, south-central Pennsylvania. Both the Shriver and Licking Creek grade vertically into the Ridgeley Sandstone in an interval of cherty, calcareous siltstone and medium-grained calcareous sandstone or arenaceous limestone. The Ridgeley and its northwestern Pennsylvania equivalent, the Oriskany Sandstone, consist of lithologies ranging from calcareous, fine-grained sandstone to noncalcareous conglomerate, but the dominant lithology is generally white to light-gray, medium-grained, silica-cemented, quartzose sandstone (Figure 7–8).

The Ridgeley ranges in thickness from 8 to 150 feet in outcrop, and in the subsurface decreases from

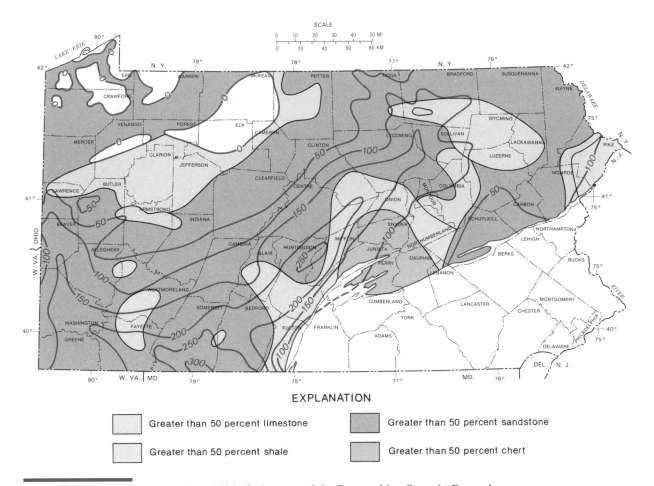

SCALE

EXPLANATION

| | Greater than 50 percent limestone | | Greater than 50 percent sandstone |
| | Greater than 50 percent shale | | Greater than 50 percent chert |

Figure 7–6. Generalized isopach and lithofacies map of the Deerparkian Stage in Pennsylvania (modified from Oliver and others, 1971, Sheet 3). Contour interval is 50 feet. The thin colored line represents the eastern limit of Devonian outcrop.

over 250 feet in Clearfield County to 0 feet along a pinch-out in northwestern Pennsylvania (Abel and Heyman, 1981). The Oriskany occurs as almost pure quartzose sandstone in patches less than 30 feet thick that generally follow the trends of salt-solution cavities in the Upper Silurian Salina Formation (Kelley and McGlade, 1969).

The Lower Devonian portion of the Onesquethawan Stage (Figures 7–3 and 7–9) is represented by the lower part of the Needmore Shale in central Pennsylvania (discussed under "Middle Devonian" below), the Bois Blanc Formation in the northwest, the lower part of the Schoharie Formation, and the Esopus Formation in the northeast. The Bois Blanc consists of less than 100 feet of sandstone grading upward to silty, shaly, and cherty limestones. It is tran-

Figure 7–7. Folded and tilted Keyser and Corriganville-New Creek limestones exposed in Everett, Bedford County, are typical of Helderbergian Stage limestones.

Figure 7–8. Mined outcrop of
the Deerparkian Ridgeley
Sandstone at a glass-sand
plant near Mount Union,
Huntingdon County.

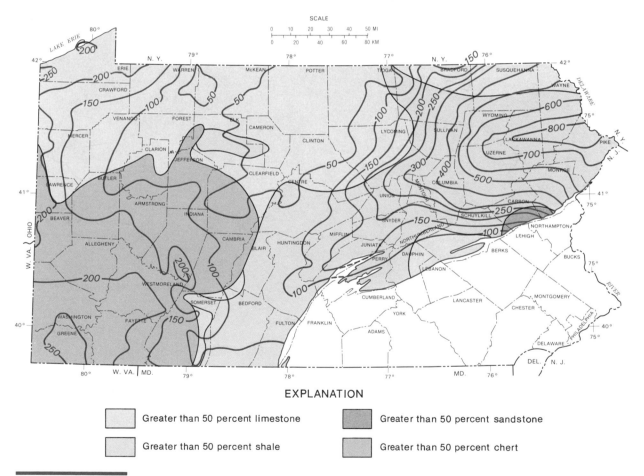

EXPLANATION

Greater than 50 percent limestone

Greater than 50 percent sandstone

Greater than 50 percent shale

Greater than 50 percent chert

Figure 7–9. Generalized isopach and lithofacies map of the Onesquethawan Stage in Pennsylvania (modified from Oliver and others, 1971, Sheet 4). Contour interval is 100 feet in northeastern Pennsylvania and 50 feet elsewhere. The thin colored line represents the eastern limit
of Devonian outcrop.

sitional with the overlying Onondaga Formation, but the basal contact is disconformable (Heyman, 1977). Drillers typically call the Bois Blanc "Oriskany" because of its sandy and silty nature (Harper, 1982). The correlative Esopus Formation consists of dark, light-gray, or brown shales, medium- to dark-gray silty shales, and argillaceous to finely arenaceous siltstones up to 300 feet thick (Epstein and others, 1967). It grades upward into the Schoharie Formation, and the two formations are essentially undifferentiable in the eastern counties.

Middle Devonian

Middle Devonian rocks range from basinal marine shales to nonmarine sandstones. Rocks of the upper Onesquethawan Stage (Figure 7–9) consist of marine cherts, shales, and limestone. The Cazeno-

vian and Tioughniogan Stage rocks (Figure 7–10) are dominated by marine-shelf shales and limestones at the northern and western basin margins, and by coarser nearshore and deltaic detrital rocks in the basin proper. The marine Tully Limestone and its detrital equivalents, where present, make up the rocks of the Taghanican Stage in the uppermost Middle Devonian.

In central Pennsylvania, the formations representing the Onesquethawan Stage are the Needmore Shale and the overlying Selinsgrove Limestone (Inners, 1979). The Needmore, a medium-gray to black, calcareous, commonly fossiliferous shale between 100 and 150 feet thick, grades into the Selinsgrove but lies disconformably on the Ridgeley Sandstone. In west-central Pennsylvania, the upper two thirds of the Needmore grades laterally into the dark-gray, slightly calcareous, locally glauconitic Huntersville Chert. The

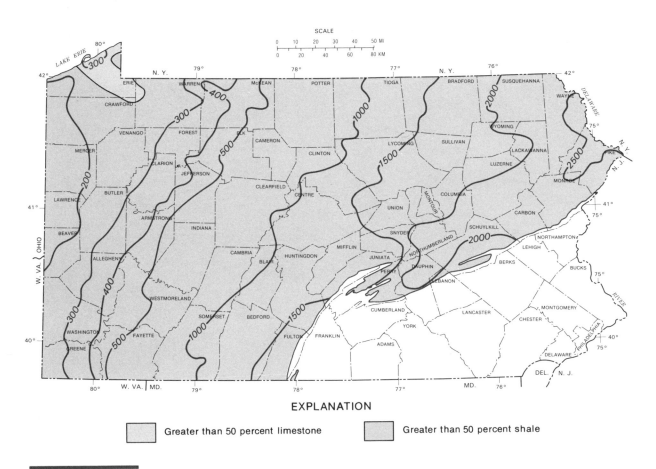

EXPLANATION

▢ Greater than 50 percent limestone   ▢ Greater than 50 percent shale

Figure 7–10. Generalized isopach and lithofacies map of the combined Cazenovian, Tioughniogan, and Taghanican Stages (Erian Series) in Pennsylvania (modified from Oliver and others, 1971, Sheet 5). Contour interval is 100 feet in western Pennsylvania and 500 feet elsewhere. The thin colored line represents the eastern limit of Devonian outcrop.

Huntersville is as thick as 250 feet in Fayette and Westmoreland Counties (Jones and Cate, 1957). It grades laterally into the very fine grained to crystalline, light- to dark-brownish-gray, somewhat argillaceous and cherty limestones of the Onondaga Formation in the subsurface of northwestern Pennsylvania (Fettke, 1961). The lower member of the Onondaga Formation, the Edgecliff, may contain a pinnacle-reef facies both in outcrop and in the subsurface (Piotrowski, 1976). To the east, the Onesquethawan section is dominated by argillaceous and calcareous siltstones and white, coarse- to fine-grained sandstones of the Schoharie and Palmerton Formations. The Buttermilk Falls Limestone, a thick (up to 200 feet in Monroe County), argillaceous, and silty formation, occupies the position of the Selinsgrove Limestone in this area (Epstein and others, 1967).

The Tioga ash zone, a series of at least six layers of brown, yellowish-brown, or brownish-gray micaceous shales of volcanic origin (Way and Smith, 1985), marks the approximate boundary between the Onesquethawan and Cazenovian Stages of the Middle Devonian (Figure 7–3). The Tioga, which occurs interbedded with Onesquethawan limestones and limy mudrocks and Cazenovian shales, contains up to 45 percent biotite, but the altered-clay fraction of the shale changes, depending on the surrounding formations (Roen and Hosterman, 1982). Way and Smith (1985) suggested that the Tioga resulted from three separate volcanic events.

A series of four formations, consisting mostly of shales with interbedded or intertonguing limestones, siltstones, and sandstones, constitutes the Hamilton Group (Cazenovian and Tioughniogan Stages) in New York (Rickard, 1975). In the subsurface of western Pennsylvania, these formations are increasingly coarse grained and indivisible to the south and east. In central and eastern Pennsylvania, the Hamilton Group is replaced by the Marcellus and Mahantango Formations (Figure 7–3). The Marcellus consists of 75 to 800 feet of dark-gray to black, highly fissile, homogeneous, carbonaceous shales containing locally abundant pyrite and few fossils. The Mahantango Formation is a complex series of interbedded shales, siltstones, and sandstones ranging from 1,200 to 2,200 feet thick in central and eastern Pennsylvania. The thickest coarse clastic sequences, particularly the Montebello Sandstone Member, occur near Harrisburg, and the average grain size decreases eastward, northward, and westward. Faill and others (1978) described the coarser elements of the Mahantango as a series of 6- to 250-foot-thick, asymmetrical, coarsening-upward

sequences that consist of olive-gray silty claystones at the bottom and light-olive-gray siliceous sandstones, conglomeratic sandstones, or conglomerates at the top (Figure 7–11). In western Pennsylvania, the Mahantango Formation grades laterally into the finer grained, undifferentiated upper Hamilton Group just west of the Allegheny Front (Harper and Piotrowski, 1979).

The Tully Limestone, or an equivalent shale or siltstone member of the Mahantango Formation, occupies the top of the Middle Devonian (Figure 7–12). Berg, McInerney, and others (1986) considered the Tully a member of the Mahantango Formation throughout most of its outcrop in the state. The Tully tends to be an olive- to medium-gray, fossiliferous shaly limestone or calcareous shale that may be thicker than 200 feet at some outcrops (Faill and Wells, 1974). In the subsurface, it comprises finely crystalline, brownish-gray, argillaceous limestone with interbedded dark-gray calcareous shales (Fettke, 1961) that are up to 150 feet thick in some areas (Piotrowski and Harper, 1979).

Upper Devonian

The marine and nonmarine rocks of the Upper Devonian (Figures 7–4 and 7–13) were formed from

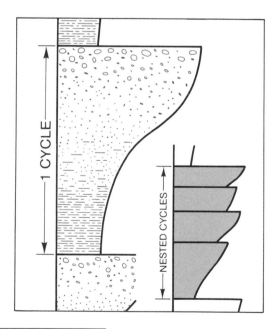

Figure 7–11. An idealized coarsening-upward cycle characteristic of the coarser elements of the Mahantango Formation (from Faill and others, 1978, Figure 1). Nested cycles consist of two or more cycles that have no sand-sized fraction.

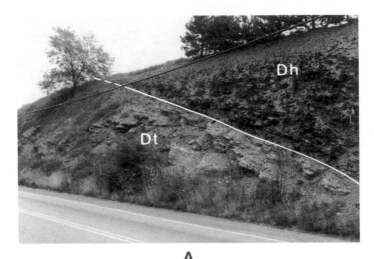

A

B

Figure 7–12. Tully Limestone exposures. A. In a roadcut near Newry, Blair County, the Middle-Upper Devonian boundary is prominent where the dark-colored Burket Member of the Harrell Formation (Dh) lies on the light-colored Tully Limestone (Dt). B. Southeast of the Laurel Hill anticline in western Pennsylvania, the Tully Limestone is thin, argillaceous to silty, and commonly nodular.

sediments deposited from east to west across the Appalachian basin (Figure 7–14) during progradation of the Catskill deltaic system. Sevon and Woodrow (1981, p. 11) called this system a series of "multiple contiguous deltas operating in the same sedimentary basin at approximately the same time." The Catskill deltaic system is the type example of a tectonic delta complex, a delta system dominated by orogenic sediments derived from the erosion of an active tectonic complex into a contiguous marine basin (Friedman

and Johnson, 1966). This system is the thickest integrated wedge of sediment in the basin and constitutes one of the most complex sequences of rock in North America. The interfingering and coarsening-upward rocks include typical flysch and molasse sequences, providing a classic example of the facies concept that is repeatedly cited in the literature (e.g., Caster, 1934). Because of this complexity, the rocks are categorized here in terms of facies rather than formations.

The rocks of the Upper Devonian can be incorporated into five broadly defined depositional and lithologic facies that form an overall progradational/regressive sequence in the Appalachian basin. They remain relatively consistent throughout the section despite differences in specific provenance, transport systems, and depositional settings (Figure 7–15). The depositional facies intercalate from offshore to onshore (generally speaking, from west to east and from bottom to top). For almost any given time interval in the Late Devonian of Pennsylvania, all five facies can be traced as lateral equivalents. Differences in lithology and depositional setting for these five facies are summarized in Table 7–1.

The dark-colored, organic-rich, basinal shales of Facies I, which are rarely fossiliferous except for styliolinids, lingulid brachiopods, and conodonts, dominate the lower third to half of the Harrell, Genesee, Sonyea, and West Falls Formations and the Huron Shale (Figures 7–4 and 7–16). These rocks are commonly interbedded with the lighter colored, less organic-rich shales and siltstones of Facies II and do not exceed 250 feet in thickness in any one formation (Piotrowski and Harper, 1979). Upper and lower contacts are normally sharply conformable or gradational through a short distance; in northwestern Pennsylvania, however, a major disconformity separates the black shales of the Middle and Upper Devonian (Figures 7–3 and 7–4).

Facies II consists of interbedded subfissile shales, fine- to coarse-grained, very thinly bedded siltstones, and rare thin-bedded, fine-grained sandstones deposited primarily on basin slopes (clinoform of Woodrow and Isley, 1983). Lundegard and others (1980) described the typical formation of Facies II, the Brallier Formation, as a series of turbidites having sharp planar bases and undulatory upper contacts (Figure 7–17).

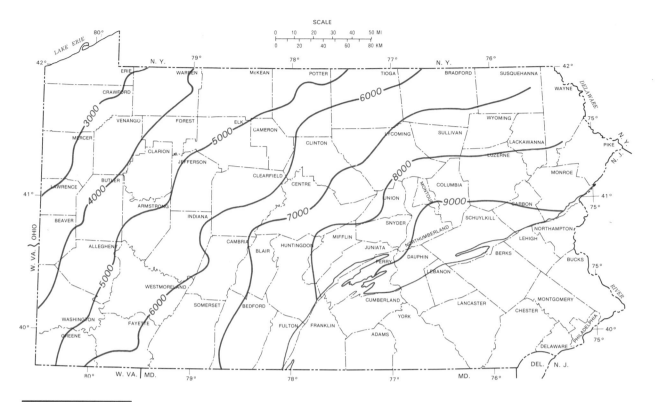

Figure 7–13. Generalized isopach map of the Upper Devonian in Pennsylvania (modified from Oliver and others, 1971, Sheet 6). Contour interval is 1,000 feet. The thin colored line represents the eastern limit of Devonian outcrop.

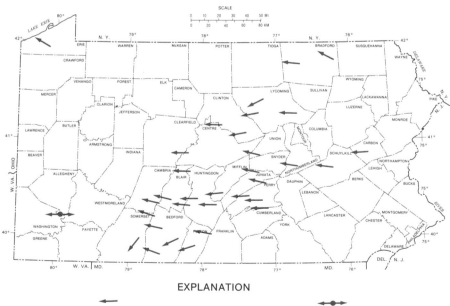

EXPLANATION

⟵ Average paleocurrent orientation

◆—●—◆ Oriented core and average paleo-current orientation

Figure 7–14. Average paleocurrent orientations in Upper Devonian rocks of Pennsylvania (data from Potter and others, 1981, and Lundegard and others, 1980). Paleocurrent orientations indicate that the direction of sediment transport was generally from east and southeast to west and northwest.

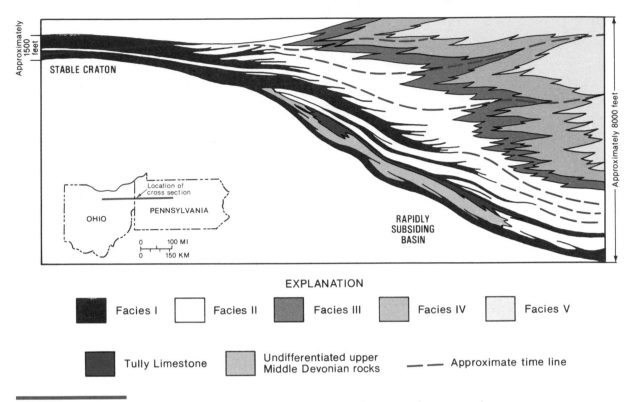

EXPLANATION

■ Facies I □ Facies II ▨ Facies III ▨ Facies IV ▨ Facies V

■ Tully Limestone ▨ Undifferentiated upper Middle Devonian rocks — — Approximate time line

Figure 7–15. Schematic representation of the Upper Devonian facies across the western Appalachian basin (see Table 7–1; slightly modified from Harper and Laughrey, 1987, Figure 10). The relationship of these facies and the formations of the upper Middle Devonian is shown.

They interpreted these sequences as submarine fan deposits, but the rock sequences are better explained as submarine ramp turbidites (*sensu* Heller and Dickinson, 1985). Thicknesses of Facies II rocks range from about 2,500 feet in the Brallier Formation of western and central Pennsylvania to a few tens or hundreds of feet in the Trimmers Rock and other formations (Frakes, 1967).

Facies III rocks are dominant in the Chadakoin, Riceville, and Oswayo Formations and are minor components of many other Upper Devonian formations. Facies III rocks are typically marine clastic rocks that vary extensively in color and texture (Table 7–1) but that are characteristically thin bedded and very fossiliferous. Their thickest occurrence is in the Chadakoin Formation, which exceeds 400 feet in western Pennsylvania.

Facies IV rocks are dominant in the Lock Haven, Scherr, and Foreknobs Formations in central and northeastern Pennsylvania and the Venango, Bradford, and Elk Groups of western Pennsylvania. They are also major components of the Trimmers Rock Formation in eastern Pennsylvania and minor components of the Catskill and Hampshire Forma-

tions. These rocks comprise varying amounts of interbedded multicolored mudrocks, shales, and thin- to thick-bedded siltstones, sandstones, and conglomerates (Figures 7–18 and 7–19). Although fossiliferous marine limestones are minor constituents of this facies, they are very important as stratigraphic markers, particularly in the subsurface. Specific lithologic differences between equivalent formations in Facies IV include little more than textural and color variations. For example, the Foreknobs and Scherr Formations contain rocks that are, overall, coarser grained and darker colored than rocks in the equivalent Lock Haven Formation. Thicknesses of the formations made up mostly of this facies range up to several thousand feet.

The complex multiple lithologies of the Catskill and Hampshire Formations (Figure 7–4) mostly belong to Facies V, which typically consists of red, green, or gray, nonmarine detrital rocks. These rocks are commonly interbedded with rocks of Facies IV in the lower portion of the formation. Individual members of the Catskill Formation range from 150 to 3,700 feet thick (the equivalent Hampshire Formation has not been subdivided), and the entire Catskill

Table 7–1. *Typical Lithologies and Depositional Environments of Upper Devonian Facies in Pennsylvania*

Facies	Lithology	Depositional environment
I	Dark-gray to black, somewhat calcareous, pyritic, sparsely fossiliferous shales.	Anoxic bottom muds of the basin proper (shallow or deep water).
II	Interbedded dark-gray shales and thin-bedded, light- to medium-gray siltstones; sparsely fossiliferous.	Turbidites of the delta-fed submarine ramp (slope).
III	Light- to dark-colored greenish, brownish, purplish, or reddish, highly fossiliferous shales, siltstones, and fine-grained sandstones.	Detrital sediments of the shallow-marine open shelf.
IV	Interbedded silty, micaceous mudrocks and fine- to coarse-grained, thin- to thick-bedded siltstones, sandstones, and conglomerates; moderately to highly fossiliferous. Occasional beds of sparsely to highly fossiliferous limestone.	Delta-derived detrital sediments of mixed fluvial-deltaic and linear-clastic shorelines; interspersed open-marine carbonates deposited during eustatic sea-level rises.
V	Gray to red, thin- to thick-bedded mudstones, claystones, siltstones, sandstones, and conglomerates; sparsely to moderately fossiliferous.	Mixed continental, fluvial-deltaic, and marginal-marine environments.

and Hampshire Formations range from 1,900 to 8,600 feet thick in central and eastern Pennsylvania. The upper and lower contacts of both formations are gradational, based essentially on percentages of red and gray rocks.

The uppermost Devonian rocks in central and eastern Pennsylvania consist of a series of mostly non-red, nonmarine sandstones and mudrocks spanning the Devonian-Mississippian systemic boundary. These rocks make up the Huntley Mountain and Spechty Kopf Formations in the northern counties and the Rockwell Formation in the southern counties. The stratigraphy of these transitional rocks is covered in the next chapter.

DEPOSITIONAL BASIN AND PROVENANCE

The Appalachian basin during the Devonian was part of an extensive inland sea receiving intermittent in-

Figure 7–16. Dark-colored, organic-rich shales of Facies I constitute the Burket Member of the Harrell Formation, exposed in a roadcut south of Newry, Blair County. The chippy weathering pattern of the shales is typical of this facies.

flux of terrigenous sediments from the eastern source area, Appalachia. Appalachia consisted originally of Precambrian(?) through Early Ordovician sedimentary, volcanic, and intrusive rocks that were uplifted and metamorphosed during the Taconian orogeny (see Chapter 33). Later tectonic activity during the Acadian orogeny added Middle Ordovician through Early Devonian sedimentary rocks to the eroding uplands. Additional terrigenous material has been reported from northern sources, such as the Canadian Shield and the Adirondacks (e.g., Stow, 1938), but these were probably only of minor influence. Continued sediment influx into the basin during periods of relative tectonic quiescence created an asymmetrical, wedge-shaped deposit due to differences in the subsidence and sedimentation rates at the opposite sides of the basin (Figures 7–2 and 7–15). Large volumes of coarse-grained sediment poured into the eastern trough area, whereas in the west, adjacent to the stable craton, the Devonian sediments were mostly fine-grained particles falling out of suspension.

Available data indicate that during the Devonian, the Appalachian basin lay in the southern hemisphere near the equator, as shown in Figure 7–20.

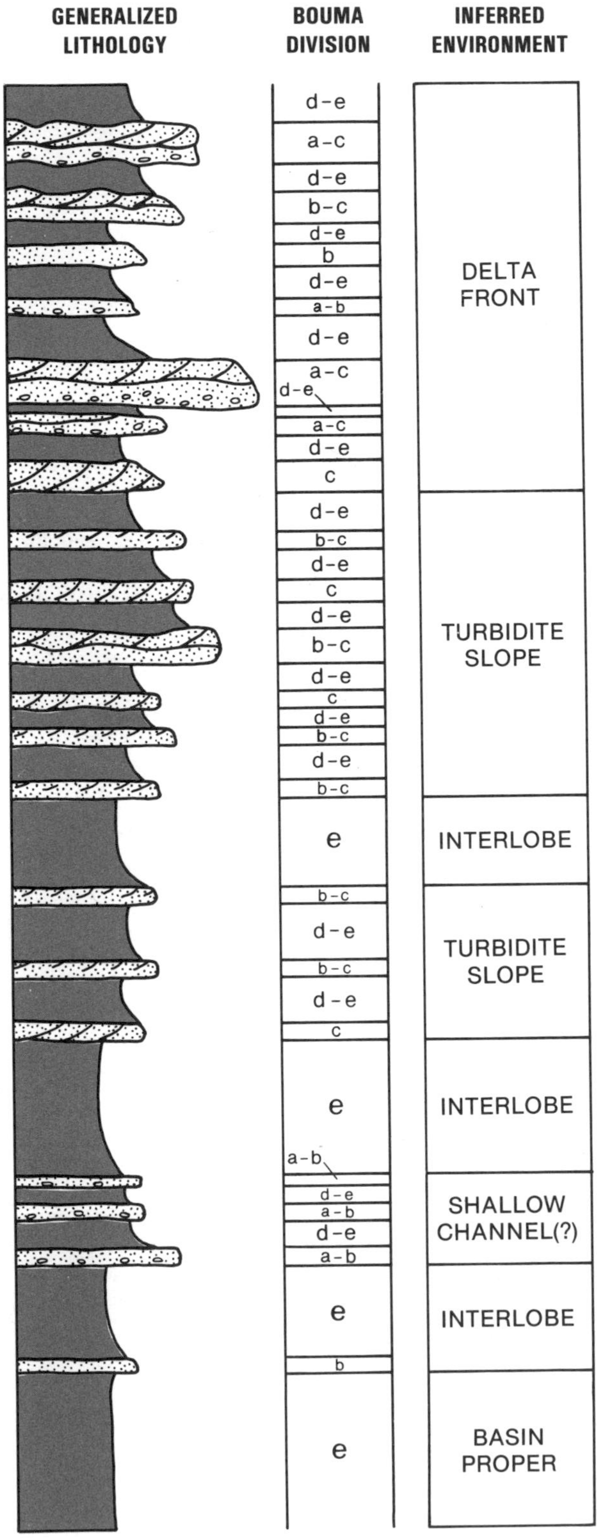

Figure 7–17. Generalized representation of Facies II turbidite sequences of the Brallier Formation in the central Appalachian basin (modified from Lundegard and others, 1980). The total thickness is approximately 1,000 feet. The inset, which has no scale, shows an idealized turbidite sequence and the Bouma divisions used to describe the diagnostic units. Not all divisions are present in all turbidite sequences. For example, Brallier turbidite sequences are rarely complete, consisting mostly of "acde" and "ade" Bouma divisions and subsidiary sequences such as "bcde." See Bouma (1962) for a discussion of turbidite sequences and their interpretation.

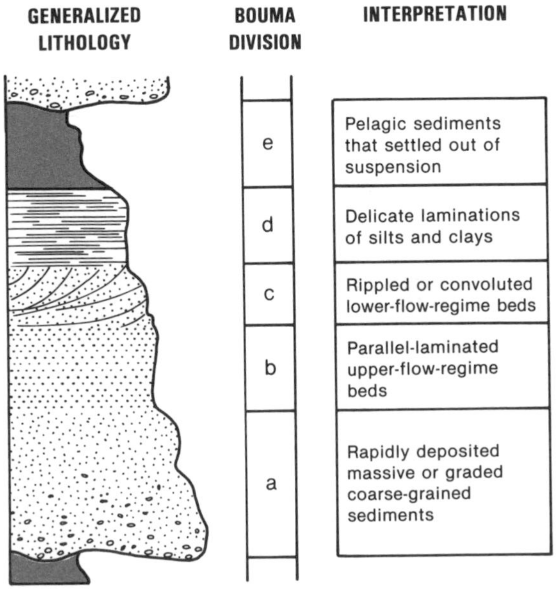

GENERALIZED LITHOLOGY	BOUMA DIVISION	INFERRED ENVIRONMENT
	d–e	
	a–c	
	d–e	
	b–c	
	d–e	
	b	
	d–e	DELTA FRONT
	a–b	
	d–e	
	a–c	
	d–e	
	a–c	
	d–e	
	c	
	d–e	
	b–c	
	d–e	
	c	
	d–e	
	b–c	TURBIDITE SLOPE
	d–e	
	c	
	d–e	
	b–c	
	d–e	
	b–c	
	e	INTERLOBE
	b–c	
	d–e	TURBIDITE SLOPE
	b–c	
	d–e	
	c	
	e	INTERLOBE
	a–b	
	d–e	
	a–b	SHALLOW CHANNEL(?)
	d–e	
	a–b	
	e	INTERLOBE
	b	
	e	BASIN PROPER

GENERALIZED LITHOLOGY	BOUMA DIVISION	INTERPRETATION
	e	Pelagic sediments that settled out of suspension
	d	Delicate laminations of silts and clays
	c	Rippled or convoluted lower-flow-regime beds
	b	Parallel-laminated upper-flow-regime beds
	a	Rapidly deposited massive or graded coarse-grained sediments

Woodrow and others (1973) determined that such a configuration would result in a hot climate with seasonally restricted rainfall. For example, the Late Devonian stratigraphic record, which contains as much as 80 percent of the total thickness of Devonian sediments, may be the result of long-term cyclic storm patterns affecting deposition on Catskill coastal plains and continental shelves.

The position of Appalachia with respect to the central basin is uncertain. Sevon and Woodrow (1981) suggested, however, that a distance of between 30 and 65 miles east of the present eastern outcrop limit is a reasonable estimate.

DEPOSITIONAL ENVIRONMENTS

During the Early Devonian, the Appalachian basin gradually deepened from supratidal mud flats of the Keyser to the stable, shallow-shelf, basin-axis facies of the New Creek and Corriganville Limestones (Head, 1972; Figure 7–3). The New Creek and Corriganville grade laterally into the more nearshore, clastic-rich limestones of the Coeymans and New Scotland Formations to the east (Epstein and

Figure 7–18. Sandstone and siltstone beds of variable thickness, color, and texture, separated by thicker layers of shale characterize Facies IV. Photograph of the Foreknobs Formation exposed near Entriken, Huntingdon County.

Figure 7–19. Portions of a depositional sequence of Facies IV from southwestern Pennsylvania. Fluvial-deltaic sandstones in the basal Venango Group exposed in a railroad cut in the Youghiogheny River gorge through Laurel Hill near Ohiopyle, Fayette County. From bottom to top, the sandstones exhibit plane beds (PB) of the channel floor, trough crossbeds (TC) and plane beds (PB) of a point-bar sequence, and (at the top left of the photograph) climbing ripple cross-laminations (CR) of the point-bar top.

others, 1967). The Mandata Shale, which overlies the Corriganville, represents the more anoxic bottom muds of the basin floor.

Later in the Early Devonian, the basin became shallower. The Shriver Chert was deposited below wave base as a combination of carbonate muds and shelf-derived silts in the central basin, whereas the Licking Creek Limestone represents deposition on the gently sloping carbonate shelf along the basin margins (Head, 1974). The Ridgeley and Oriskany Sandstones originated in shallow-water environments, such as shelf-bar complexes, beaches, and shorefaces.

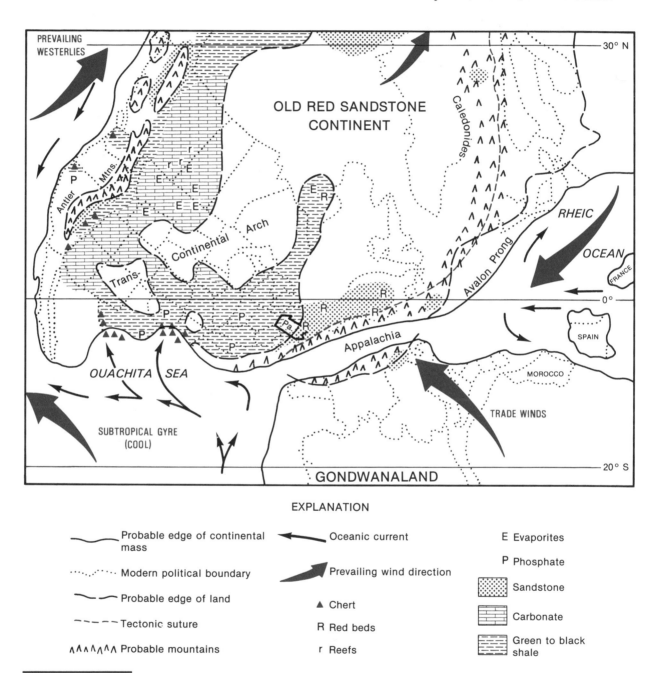

Figure 7–20. **Late Devonian paleogeography and lithofacies of North America. Diagram simplified and modified from Ettensohn and Barron (1981, p. 18) by Sevon and Woodrow (1981, Figure 3). This configuration probably also is approximately representative of the Early and Middle Devonian.**

Onesquethawan Stage rocks were deposited when the basin was once again deepening. The Bois Blanc Formation grades upward from reworked older formations to stable-shelf limestones and dolomites. The Needmore Shale was deposited along the axis of the basin as mud in stagnant, anoxic water, and the Huntersville Chert accumulated as radiolarian tests and sponge spicules, in part, in the shallower, more aerobic waters on the cratonic side of the basin (Inners, 1979). The Onondaga Formation represents shelf-margin limestones which became argillaceous (Selinsgrove Limestone) and silty (Buttermilk Falls Limestone) farther east. During a short period of volcanism at the end of the Onesquethawan Stage, volcanic ash blanketed the basin, forming the six ash beds of the Tioga ash zone (Way and Smith, 1985).

The Middle Devonian Marcellus Formation is commonly considered to have been deposited in deep anoxic waters (e.g., Potter and others, 1981). It should be emphasized, however, that the Devonian Appalachian sea was probably shallower than 300 feet, so it is unlikely that the shales can be considered "deep" in the same sense that the Atlantic Ocean is deep. It is more likely that the Marcellus Formation, and the Late Devonian black shales, were deposited in a variety of shallow-water anoxic environments, possibly at depths of less than 150 feet. The Mahantango Formation formed as a prograding marine shoreline during early Catskill delta building. The basin returned to more normal marine conditions, but with some terrigenous input, in the Taghanican Stage when the Tully Limestone was deposited. Heckel (1973) suggested a northern source for the carbonate muds and a southeastern source for the terrigenous muds of the Tully and its equivalents.

As the Catskill deltaic system prograded westward across the basin in the Late Devonian, the shape of the shoreline must have been very irregular due to variable rates of sediment supply, positions of different sediment-input systems, tectonic perturbations, and oceanic processes. Willard (1934) was the first to attempt the delineation of Late Devonian shorelines based on the outcrop of the "early Chemung" (the Scherr and lower Lock Haven Formations) in central and northeastern Pennsylvania. His three-lobed delta system was inaccurate, however, and it is unfortunate that this model has been perpetuated in the literature as being typical of the entire Upper Devonian depositional system. More recently, Sevon and Woodrow (1981) showed that sediment dispersal

occurred as a result of numerous systems, and Boswell (1988) illustrated the distinct changes in Devonian shoreline configurations through time (Figure 7-21).

The gradual increase in distance from source area to shoreline during progradation was accompanied by a decrease in transport gradient, creating a decrease in grain size and a concomitant increase in depositional complexity across the basin. Sediments ranged from muds, sands, and gravels of Facies V, which were deposited in alluvial fans, braided rivers, and other typical continental environments, to clays and muds of Facies I, which settled out of suspension onto the anoxic basin floor.

SEA-LEVEL VARIATIONS AND TECTONICS

Devonian sea-level variations were due to global eustatic sea-level changes and tectonic pulses. Global and Appalachian basin sea-level variations were correlated by Dennison and Head (1975), Johnson and others (1985), and Boswell (1988). Superimposed on these sea-level variations were tectonic effects of varying magnitudes. The Acadian orogeny was the most important tectonic event of the Devonian. Based on the volume of preserved rocks, the uplifted Acadian highlands poured more than 69,000 cubic miles of sediment into the Catskill deltaic system (Dott and Batten, 1976). Local tectonic pulses affected deposition around the basin, but because of subsequent distortion in the central and eastern areas, this activity is identifiable primarily in the northern and western Appalachian Plateau.

PROBLEMS AND FUTURE RESEARCH

Despite being one of the most studied systems of rocks in Pennsylvania, the Devonian still presents many problems that need to be resolved. Most of these problems are stratigraphic in nature, and many relate to the complex Upper Devonian Series. Some of the more important general problems are listed below.

1. Resolution of the Ridgeley-Oriskany relationship. Many workers feel that the Ridgeley and Oriskany Sandstones are a single unit and have identical source and depositional

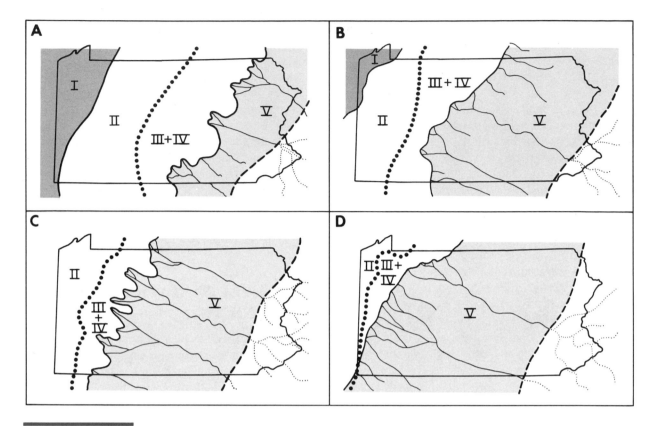

Figure 7–21. Changes in Late Devonian shoreline positions in Pennsylvania (modified from Boswell, 1988). Each diagram represents the hypothetical configuration of the Catskill depositional system during a particular instant of time within a stage: A, Middle Senecan; B, Early Chautauquan; C, Middle Chautauquan; and D, Late Chautauquan. Roman numerals refer to the facies of Figure 7–15. The heavy dotted line represents the shelf edge, and the dashed line represents the edge of the coastal plain.

regimes. Others believe that they are separate formations and that the Oriskany is only partially equivalent to the Ridgeley.

2. Determination of water depth in the Appalachian basin. Black shales (Facies I) have been considered by most authors to be representative of deep-basin deposition. There are, however, numerous indications that these shales were deposited in relatively shallow, stratified water.

3. Lithostratigraphic subdivision of the Catskill and Hampshire Formations. Most of the subdivision of the Catskill is based on the section occurring in northeastern Pennsylvania. The Hampshire Formation has not been subdivided at all.

4. Lithostratigraphic subdivision of the Venango, Bradford, and Elk Groups and the Lock

Haven, Foreknobs, and Scherr Formations. At the time of this writing, work was just beginning on the outcrop of the Foreknobs and Scherr. There are limestone marker beds within most of these formations that could be used for ultimate correlation.

5. Biostratigraphic zonation of the Upper Devonian, particularly of the Catskill nonmarine units. Palynology may be best suited for this monumental task.

6. Chronostratigraphic resolution of the Upper Devonian, particularly of the Catskill Formation, based on marine and nonmarine biozones.

7. Redefinition of the distributary systems of the Catskill deltaic complex. Much more needs to be done beyond the work of Sevon and Woodrow (1981) and Boswell (1988).

RECOMMENDED FOR FURTHER READING

Caster, K. E. (1934), *The stratigraphy and paleontology of northwestern Pennsylvania—Part I, Stratigraphy,* Bulletins of American Paleontology, v. 21, no. 71, 185 p.

Diecchio, R. J. (1985), *Regional controls of gas accumulation in Oriskany Sandstone, central Appalachian basin,* AAPG Bulletin, v. 69, p. 722–732.

Ellison, R. L. (1965), *Stratigraphy and paleontology of the Mahantango Formation in south-central Pennsylvania,* Pennsylvania Geological Survey, 4th ser., General Geology Report 48, 298 p.

Glaeser, J. D. (1974), *Upper Devonian stratigraphy and sedimentary environments in northeastern Pennsylvania,* Pennsylvania Geological Survey, 4th ser., General Geology Report 63, 89 p.

Gordon, E. A., and Bridge, J. S. (1987), *Evolution of Catskill (Upper Devonian) river systems: intra- and extrabasinal controls,* Journal of Sedimentary Petrology, v. 57, p. 234–249.

Johnson, J. G., Klapper, Gilbert, and Sandberg, C. A. (1985), *Devonian eustatic fluctuations in Euramerica,* Geological Society of America Bulletin, v. 96, p. 567–587.

McGhee, G. R., Jr., and Dennison, J. M. (1980), *Late Devonian chronostratigraphic correlations between the central Appalachian Allegheny Front and central and western New York,* Southeastern Geology, v. 21, p. 279–286.

Oliver, W. A., Jr., de Witt, Wallace, Jr., Dennison, J. M., and others (1967), *Devonian of the Appalachian basin, United States,* in *International Symposium on the Devonian System,* v. 1, Calgary, Alberta Society of Petroleum Geologists, p. 1001–1040.

Shepps, V. C., ed. (1963), *Symposium on Middle and Upper Devonian stratigraphy of Pennsylvania and adjacent states,* Pennsylvania Geological Survey, 4th ser., General Geology Report 39, 301 p.

Willard, Bradford, Swartz, F. M., and Cleaves, A. B. (1939), *The Devonian of Pennsylvania,* Pennsylvania Geological Survey, 4th ser., General Geology Report 19, 481 p.

Woodrow, D. L., and Sevon, W. D., eds. (1985), *The Catskill delta,* Geological Society of America Special Paper 201, 246 p.

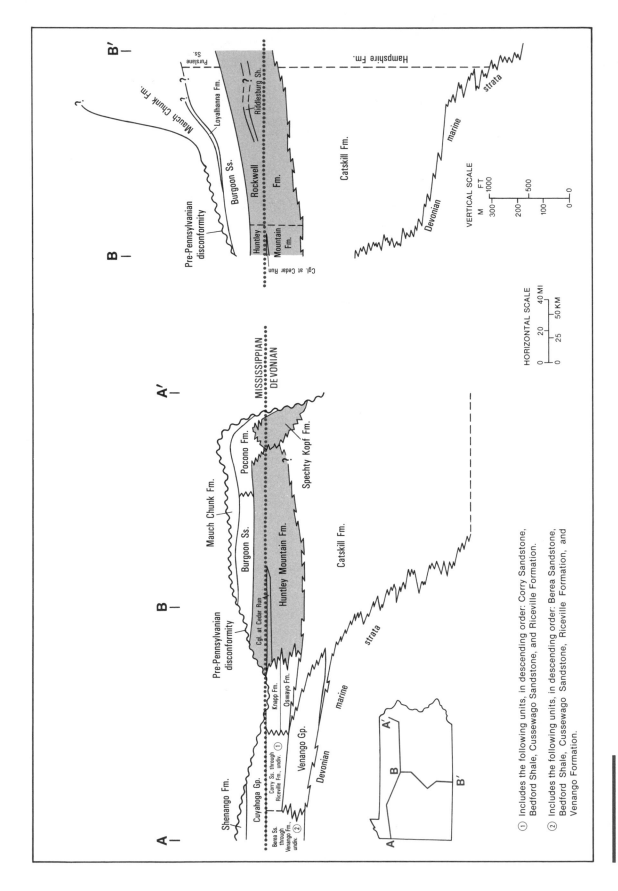

Figure 8–1. Lithostratigraphic cross sections showing the relationships among the Devonian-Mississippian transition formations (colored), overlying and underlying formations, and Mississippian and Upper Devonian marine units of northwestern Pennsylvania.

① Includes the following units, in descending order: Corry Sandstone, Bedford Shale, Cussewago Sandstone, and Riceville Formation.

② Includes the following units, in descending order: Berea Sandstone, Bedford Shale, Cussewago Sandstone, Riceville Formation, and Venango Formation.

128

CHAPTER 8   DEVONIAN-MISSISSIPPIAN TRANSITION

THOMAS M. BERG
Ohio Department of Natural Resources
Division of Geological Survey
4383 Fountain Square Drive
Columbus, OH 43224

INTRODUCTION

In central and eastern Pennsylvania, a variable and little-understood stratigraphic succession exists as a transition between underlying strata clearly defined as the Catskill Formation and the overlying Pocono Formation or Burgoon Sandstone (Figure 8–1). At different localities, this transition comprises the Spechty Kopf, Huntley Mountain, and Rockwell Formations (Figure 8–2). The boundary between the Devonian and Mississippian Systems occurs within these transitional formations, but its exact position is as yet undefined.

The development of a biostratigraphic framework that clearly defines the Devonian-Mississippian systemic boundary has been slow because geologic mapping and stratigraphic correlation in the Upper Devonian and Lower Mississippian have proceeded mostly within a lithostratigraphic framework, the interpretation of which has been evolving. The development of stratigraphic nomenclature in this succession has followed a course of mixed lithostratigraphic, chronostratigraphic, and biostratigraphic thinking. Gutschick and Moreman (1967) summarized paleontologic research on the Devonian-Mississippian boundary of the United States. Edmunds and others (1979) presented a brief overview of Mississippian biostratigraphy in Pennsylvania.

The marine stratigraphic succession embracing the systemic boundary in the northwestern part of the state (Figure 8–1) is fairly well known and has been examined by a number of workers during the twentieth century (Caster, 1934; Holland, 1958; Sass, 1960; de Witt, 1970; Dodge, 1992; Harper, 1993). The systemic boundary is now placed at the base of the Cuyahoga Group in western Pennsylvania. Laird (1941) examined the systemic boundary in the southwestern Pennsylvania inliers, and Reger (1927) and Girty (1928) reported on Carboniferous marine fossils in the "Pocono" Formation of the Broad Top area. Although Read and Mamay (1964) provided a framework for upper Paleozoic floral assemblages in the United States, there is presently no agreement

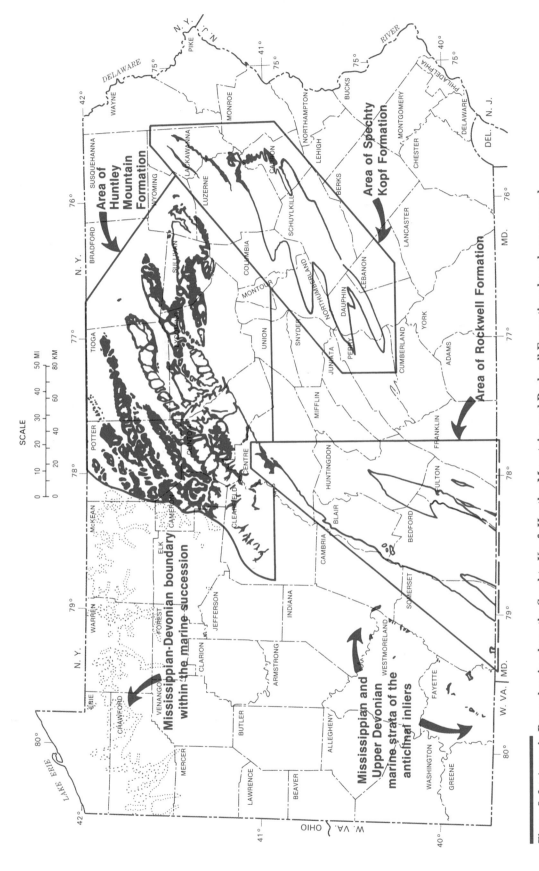

Figure 8-2. Areas in Pennsylvania where the Spechty Kopf, Huntley Mountain, and Rockwell Formations have been mapped (modified from Berg and others, 1980). The position of the boundary between Mississippian and Devonian strata of northwestern Pennsylvania is shown by the dotted line.

as to the exact position of the systemic boundary in the nonmarine, post-Catskill succession of north-central and eastern Pennsylvania.

Berg and Edmunds (1979) reviewed past usage of the name "Pocono," explaining that it was applied in a chronostratigraphic sense well beyond the borders of Pennsylvania. The "Catskill-Pocono" boundary became almost synonymous with "Devonian-Mississippian," and the name "Pocono" was geographically extended to rock sequences having no similarity whatsoever to the fluvial sandstones and conglomerates that fringe the anthracite fields and make up the Pocono Formation. As the mapping of Pennsylvania progressed, the name "Pocono" was applied to all the rocks between the red Catskill and Mauch Chunk Formations. The name was also extended to the western part of the state, even into areas where the bounding red-bed formations are not seen. Thus, the name was applied to the entire marine succession between the basal Pennsylvanian disconformity and the presumed Devonian-Mississippian boundary.

Where the red Catskill Formation grades westward to the marine Venango Group, a succession of marine siliciclastic rocks intervenes between the top of the Venango and what was considered to be the Devonian-Mississippian boundary by earlier workers who placed that systemic boundary at the base of the Cussewago Sandstone or Knapp Formation. This marine succession is called the Riceville Formation (sub-Cussewago) or Oswayo Formation (sub-Knapp). The "Oswayo," a New York stratigraphic term, was projected far eastward (Gray and others, 1960), mostly on the basis of interval, into north-central and central Pennsylvania and applied to nonmarine strata between a presumed Devonian-Mississippian boundary and Catskill red beds.

The 1980 state geologic map (Berg and others, 1980) shows three separate, distinct, and dominantly nonmarine formations that embrace the Devonian-Mississippian systemic boundary: the Spechty Kopf, Huntley Mountain, and Rockwell (Figures 8–1 and 8–2). The general paleogeographic setting at the time of deposition of these three formations is shown in Figure 8–3.

SPECHTY KOPF FORMATION

Trexler and others (1962) designated the dominantly gray and olive-gray beds below the Pocono Formation in the western part of the Southern Anthracite field the Spechty Kopf Member of the Catskill Formation. Sevon (1969b) included equivalent

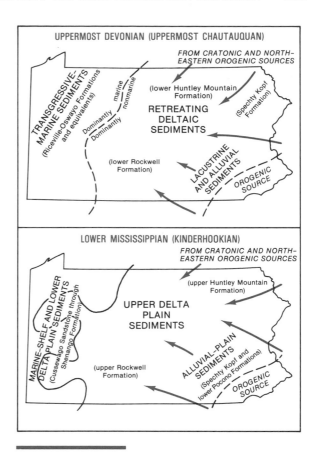

Figure 8–3. Paleogeographic maps showing generalized sedimentary environments during deposition of Devonian-Mississippian transition formations.

rocks in northeastern Pennsylvania as components of the Pocono Formation. The Spechty Kopf was raised to formation rank by Epstein and others (1974) and includes both of the aforementioned groups of rocks.

Over most of its outcrop belt in Pennsylvania, the Spechty Kopf Formation is dominantly sandstone (Figure 8–4). Other components include siltstone, shale, conglomerate, polymictic diamictite, pebbly mudstone, laminite, and coal. The sandstone, siltstone, and shale are mostly medium gray to olive gray, but yellowish-gray, brownish-gray, and some grayish-red colors occur. Most of the sandstones are trough crossbedded, but some planar bedding is present. An interesting, but genetically enigmatic, aspect of part of the Spechty Kopf is the widespread occurrence of an ordered vertical sequence (elements A, B, C, and D of Figure 8–4) in the lower and middle parts of the formation. Polymictic diamictite, pebbly mudstone, laminite, and planar-bedded sandstone occur as a laterally restricted, but recurring, stratigraphic succession (Sevon and Berg, 1986). These

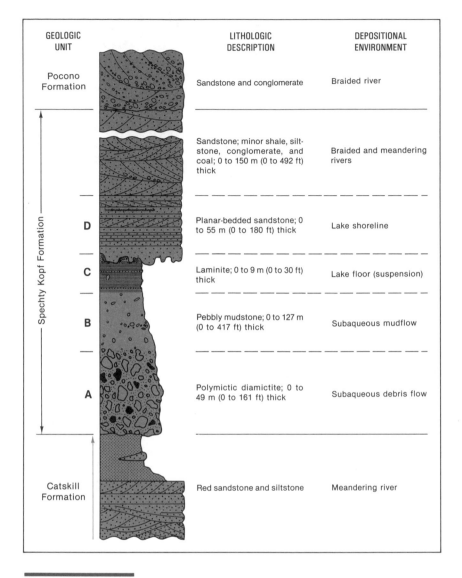

GEOLOGIC UNIT		LITHOLOGIC DESCRIPTION	DEPOSITIONAL ENVIRONMENT
Pocono Formation		Sandstone and conglomerate	Braided river
Spechty Kopf Formation		Sandstone; minor shale, silt-stone, conglomerate, and coal; 0 to 150 m (0 to 492 ft) thick	Braided and meandering rivers
	D	Planar-bedded sandstone; 0 to 55 m (0 to 180 ft) thick	Lake shoreline
	C	Laminite; 0 to 9 m (0 to 30 ft) thick	Lake floor (suspension)
	B	Pebbly mudstone; 0 to 127 m (0 to 417 ft) thick	Subaqueous mudflow
	A	Polymictic diamictite; 0 to 49 m (0 to 161 ft) thick	Subaqueous debris flow
Catskill Formation		Red sandstone and siltstone	Meandering river

Figure 8–4. Generalized stratigraphic column showing the character of the Spechty Kopf Formation and inferred depositional environments. The colored arrow marks a fining-upward cycle in the Catskill Formation.

may be separated from the overlying Pocono Formation by a disconformity (Wood and others, 1969; Epstein and others, 1974; Edmunds and others, 1979). The formation commonly ranges up to 390 m (1,280 ft) in thickness, but it is locally absent. Thickness ranges of individual components within the Spechty Kopf are given in Figure 8–4. Wood and others (1969) reported a maximum thickness of about 730 m (2,400 ft) near the type area in northern Dauphin County. Variations in overall thickness are probably due in part to the locations of multiple sediment-input systems (Sevon, 1985a). Variations in thickness of polymictic diamictite, pebbly mudstone, laminite, and planar-bedded sandstone are due to the configuration of the eroded upper surface of the Catskill alluvial plain, which subsided to form localized lake basins (Sevon and Berg, 1986).

Marine fossils have not been found in the Spechty Kopf Formation, even though many primary sedimentary structures, such as symmetric ripples, flutes, and tool marks, in the laminites and planar-bedded sandstones are identical to structures found in offshore marine deposits or tidal flats. Some burrows have been observed (Sevon, 1969b) but are not known to be marine. The primary structures are considered to be the result of deposition in ephemeral lakes. No nonmarine invertebrate fossils have been recorded. Plant fossils have been found, and thin coal beds have been observed. Wood and others (1969) reported *Adiantites* from the Spechty Kopf, supporting an Early Mississippian age for part of the formation. For the most part, Spechty Kopf sandstones, siltstones, conglomerates, and shales were deposited in fluvial systems, either braided or meandering. The unusual succession at the base of the formation has been interpreted by Sevon and Berg (1986) to be the result of deposition in

four elements are not present in every exposed section, but the vertical order appears to persist. The mostly nonsorted polymictic diamictites contain igneous, meta-igneous, and metasedimentary clasts, which suggests the sudden exposure of a widely polygenetic source area that was swiftly eroded. The derived sediments were rapidly transported to localized but isochronic nonmarine basins and probably represent a major event of considerable importance near the end of the Devonian. Whether that event was tectonic, climatic, or extraterrestrial is as yet undetermined.

The Spechty Kopf is separated from the underlying Catskill Formation by a disconformity, and it ephemeral lakes formed on the surface of the defunct Catskill alluvial plain. The polymictic diamictite and pebbly mudstone are unique in the upper Paleozoic of Pennsylvania and, as previously mentioned, probably represent a major event near the end of the Devonian. In context with the overlying laminites and planar-bedded sandstones, subaqueous debris flows and/or mudflows are likely agents of deposition (Figure 8–4). The laminite is interpreted as an offshore lacustrine facies where fine mud was deposited from suspension. Occasional "dropped in" pebbles, granules, and sand grains hint at debris-laden floating ice, but the equatorial climate of the Late Devonian (Ettensohn, 1985) casts considerable doubt on the possibility of ice floating on the ephemeral lakes. The origin of the dropped-in clasts in the laminites remains a mystery. The clean, planar-bedded sandstones most likely resulted from deposition on lake beaches or offshore lacustrine bars. The red siltstones and shales and the thin coals interbedded in the overlying Spechty Kopf fluvial sequence are interpreted as interfluve overbank and swamp deposits.

HUNTLEY MOUNTAIN FORMATION

The succession comprising the transition in north-central Pennsylvania (Figures 8–1 and 8–2) was named the Huntley Mountain Formation by Berg and Edmunds (1979). It is transitional from the Catskill Formation to the Burgoon Sandstone and was formerly mapped as a "lower part" of the Pocono Formation, plus the underlying Oswayo Formation. The Burgoon Sandstone is the homotaxial equivalent of the Pocono Formation of northeastern Pennsylvania.

The major rock type (Figure 8–5) of the Huntley Mountain Formation is greenish-gray to olive-gray, fine-grained, slab-

by to flaggy sandstone (Berg and Edmunds, 1979). Clearly a transition, sandstones in the lower half of the Huntley Mountain bear a close similarity to those of the underlying Catskill Formation, whereas sandstones in the upper half of the formation are similar in some respects to the overlying Burgoon sandstones. Minor lithologic components include red, gray, and olive siltstone and shale, intraformational and extraformational conglomerate, and pisolith beds. Sandstones display gentle trough crossbedding (Figure 8–6) and planar bedding. Siltstone and shale units are par-

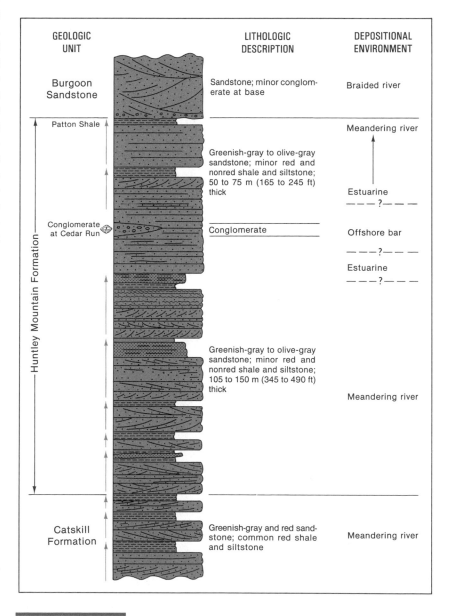

Figure 8–5. Generalized stratigraphic column showing the character of the Huntley Mountain Formation and inferred depositional environments. The colored arrows mark fining-upward cycles.

Figure 8–6. Outcrop of crossbedded sandstone in the lower part of the Huntley Mountain Formation at the type section in Lycoming County, near Waterville. The scale is marked in feet.

allel bedded and ripple bedded. The intraformational conglomerates are composed mainly of reworked lithic clasts, concentrated at the base of fining-upward cycles. One extensive, but thin, extraformational conglomerate within the upper half of the Huntley Mountain Formation, called the "conglomerate at Cedar Run" by Colton (1963), occurs over much of the western extent of the formation.

Like the underlying Catskill Formation, the Huntley Mountain Formation is characterized by fining-upward fluvial cycles (Figure 8–7). The cycles average about 17.5 m (57 ft) in thickness, but some exceed 30 m (100 ft). In general, the coarser grained lower members of the Huntley Mountain cycles are thicker than those of the Catskill, and the finer grained upper members are thinner than the equivalent members of the Catskill cycles (Berg and Edmunds, 1979). The overlying Burgoon Sandstone lacks fining-upward cycles.

The Huntley Mountain Formation ranges from 150 to 215 m (490 to 705 ft) in thickness. No systematic analysis of regional thickness changes has been made. In the northernmost part of the outcrop area, the Huntley Mountain appears to thicken to about 300 m (985 ft), possibly at the expense of the overlying Burgoon Sandstone (Edmunds and others, 1979), but such a relationship is speculative. In contrast to the Spechty Kopf-Catskill boundary, no disconformity exists at the base of the Huntley Mountain Formation. Criteria for separating the formation from the underlying "main body" of Catskill red beds

were given by Berg and Edmunds (1979). The upper contact with the Burgoon is conformable and relatively clear, because the medium-grained, buff sandstones of the Burgoon contrast well with the fine-grained, greenish-gray sandstones of the Huntley Mountain.

Figure 8–7. Fining-upward cycles in a flagstone quarry in the Huntley Mountain Formation in the Slate Run area, western Lycoming County. Planar-bedded sandstone is overlain by red siltstone that grades upward into olive-colored claystone just below the basal sandstone of the succeeding cycle (near the upper third of the highwall). The scale is 5 feet in length.

Fossil plants and some nonmarine invertebrates occur in the Huntley Mountain Formation (Berg and Edmunds, 1979). Marine invertebrates in the conglomerate at Cedar Run testify to a rapid marine transgression punctuating a large part of the area of this dominantly fluvial formation. Fossil brachiopods in this conglomerate appear to be Early Mississippian (Berg and Edmunds, 1979).

Fining-upward cycles, trough crossbedding, fossil plants, and sparse fossil freshwater invertebrates all indicate a fluvial environment of deposition for most of the Huntley Mountain Formation. The conglomerate at Cedar Run marks a very rapid transgression across the fluvial plain; beds just above and below this conglomerate may be estuarine or tidal-flat deposits. More lower-delta-plain and marginal-marine deposits may be expected in the region where the Huntley Mountain Formation grades westward into the Shenango-through-Oswayo succession (Figure 8-1). The Catskill Formation cycles in north-central Pennsylvania are inferred to be meandering-river deposits, whereas the Burgoon Sandstone is interpreted to be a braided-river deposit. The Huntley Mountain cycles are interpreted to be meandering-river deposits, but they were deposited by rivers that apparently carried a greater sand load than the Catskill rivers (Berg and Edmunds, 1979). Overbank deposits apparently had less time to stabilize, and channel stability was lower. A braided-river depositional system was probably approached late in Huntley Mountain time, just prior to deposition of the Burgoon Sandstone.

ROCKWELL FORMATION

The Rockwell Formation was named by Stose and Swartz (1912), who considered it to be the lower part of the "Pocono group." They named the rocks above the Rockwell the Purslane Sandstone. De Witt (1969) and Berg and Edmunds (1979) correlated the Purslane with the Burgoon Sandstone. The term "Rockwell" was first used on the 1980 state geologic map (Berg and others, 1980) to include the sequence between the Catskill red beds and the Burgoon Sandstone (Figures 8-1 and 8-2). The best exposure of the Rockwell Formation is at a very large roadcut in Maryland, close to the Pennsylvania border, where U.S. Route 40 passes through Sideling Hill. This exposure has been described and interpreted by Bjerstedt (1986) and should be considered the prime reference section.

As currently mapped, the Rockwell Formation is fairly heterolithic (Figure 8-8). Berg, Dodge, and

Lentz (1986) suggested that a large part of what has been mapped as Rockwell may be more closely allied to the more marine Mississippian strata below the Burgoon as exposed to the west at Conemaugh Gorge (Fettke and Bayles, 1945; Kaktins, Uldis, 1986) than to the Rockwell at Sideling Hill in Maryland.

The following generalizations can be made about the Rockwell in Pennsylvania. The lower quarter of the formation is predominantly sandstone. Reger (1927) called this interval "Berea," an overextension of an Ohio name. The middle of the Rockwell is a mixture of interbedded sandstone, siltstone, and shale, which is mostly olive gray or greenish gray, but some red beds are present. There are also brownish-gray to grayish-black shale intervals in the middle of the formation, including the marine, fossiliferous Riddlesburg Shale of Reger (1927). Other thin marine zones occur within the middle of the Rockwell. The upper quarter of the formation is sandy and shaly and contains the "Patton" red shale. There are fining-upward cycles in the Rockwell (Dodge and Berg, 1986), but the extent of that sedimentary pattern in the formation is not fully established. A number of relatively thin coals occur in the Rockwell in southern Bedford County, Fulton County, and in Maryland and West Virginia (Bjerstedt, 1986). In Fulton County, eastern Bedford County, and along Sideling Hill in Maryland, a polymictic diamictite (Figure 8-9) occurs at the base of the Rockwell (Sevon, 1979a, b; Bjerstedt, 1986). Relatively thin, calcareous, intraformational conglomerates containing nodules and pisoliths occur within the formation where fining-upward cycles are demonstrable.

The contact between the Catskill and the Rockwell is sharp and conformable. A minor disconformity may be interpreted where the diamictite occurs at the base of the Rockwell. The contact between the Rockwell and the overlying Burgoon Sandstone is also sharp and conformable, although the textural contrast between the two formations has led some workers to speculate that a minor disconformity may be present.

The Rockwell Formation is up to 315 m (1,035 ft) thick in the Broad Top region (Butts, 1945). At Horseshoe Curve, it is 180 m (590 ft) thick. Bjerstedt (1986) measured 191 m (627 ft) of Rockwell at Sideling Hill in Maryland. Terriere (1951) reported approximately 125 m (410 ft) at the Allegheny Front in Bedford County.

Multiple, contrasting depositional environments are represented by the Rockwell Formation (Figure 8-8). The predominant type of deposition appears to have been in fluvial systems, primarily high-sinuosity meandering rivers. However, deposition in marginal-

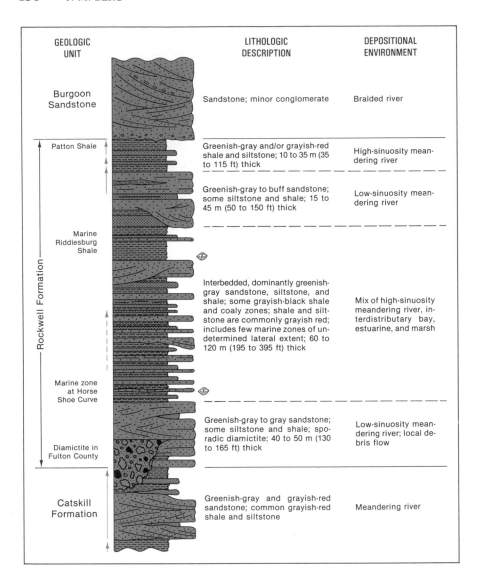

GEOLOGIC UNIT	LITHOLOGIC DESCRIPTION	DEPOSITIONAL ENVIRONMENT
Burgoon Sandstone	Sandstone; minor conglomerate	Braided river
Patton Shale	Greenish-gray and/or grayish-red shale and siltstone; 10 to 35 m (35 to 115 ft) thick	High-sinuosity meandering river
	Greenish-gray to buff sandstone; some siltstone and shale; 15 to 45 m (50 to 150 ft) thick	Low-sinuosity meandering river
Marine Riddlesburg Shale	Interbedded, dominantly greenish-gray sandstone, siltstone, and shale; some grayish-black shale and coaly zones; shale and siltstone are commonly grayish red; includes few marine zones of undetermined lateral extent; 60 to 120 m (195 to 395 ft) thick	Mix of high-sinuosity meandering river, interdistributary bay, estuarine, and marsh
Marine zone at Horse Shoe Curve		
Diamictite in Fulton County	Greenish-gray to gray sandstone; some siltstone and shale; sporadic diamictite; 40 to 50 m (130 to 165 ft) thick	Low-sinuosity meandering river; local debris flow
Catskill Formation	Greenish-gray and grayish-red sandstone; common grayish-red shale and siltstone	Meandering river

(Left margin bracket: Rockwell Formation)

Figure 8–8. Generalized stratigraphic column showing the character of the Rockwell Formation and inferred depositional environments. The colored arrows mark fining-upward cycles; the dashed arrow indicates that the interval contains some fining-upward cycles.

marine environments, including estuaries and interdistributary bays, also occurred. The coarser, sandier portions of the Rockwell, particularly the lower and upper quarters, represent deposition in low-sinuosity meandering rivers. The thin coals resulted from the development of sporadic marshes during Rockwell time. The diamictites near the base of the Rockwell resulted from deposition by debris flows in a standing body of water, either marginal-marine or lacustrine.

PROBLEMS AND FUTURE RESEARCH

Although there are some obvious similarities among the Spechty Kopf, Huntley Mountain, and Rockwell Formations, contrasts exist that give rise to questions that can only be answered by further research and analysis. For example, the Huntley Mountain and Spechty Kopf occur in close temporal and geographic proximity to each other. Why are there no diamictites or apparent lacustrine deposits in the Huntley Mountain? The Rockwell Formation has diamictites in south-central Pennsylvania and adjacent Maryland. Are they related genetically to the diamictites of the Spechty Kopf? Were there extensive lacustrine environments during Spechty Kopf deposition? Why is clear evidence of marine deposition lacking in the Spechty Kopf? Additional work will be required to relate the geologic events that gave rise to all aspects of the three formations that comprise the Devonian-Mississippian transition in Pennsylvania.

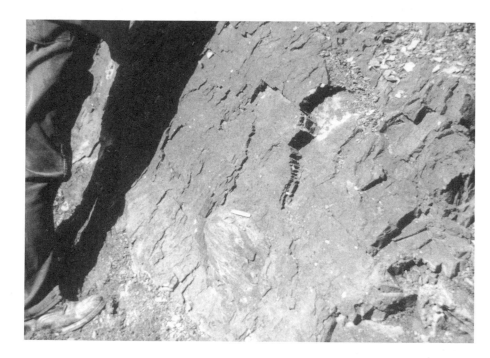

Figure 8–9. Polymictic diamictite in the lower part of the Rockwell Formation, exposed along the westbound lane of Interstate Route 70 in Bedford County, just west of the Bedford-Fulton County line. Note the abundant small pebbles in the mudstone matrix and the large clast (27 by 12 cm [11 by 5 in.]) just below the penknife. Photograph by J. A. Harper.

The western limits of the Rockwell and Huntley Mountain Formations are poorly understood, and considerable stratigraphic analysis will be necessary to relate these two formations to the well-established Devonian-Mississippian succession of western and northwestern Pennsylvania. New stratigraphic units will probably have to be established. The stratigraphic framework used by Schiner and Kimmel (1972) in northwestern Pennsylvania includes, in descending order, the Shenango Formation, the Cuyahoga Group, the Berea and Corry Sandstones, the Bedford Shale, the Cussewago Sandstone, and the Riceville Formation (Figure 8–1). Except for the Bedford Shale and the Cussewago Sandstone, Schiner and Kimmel's framework was extended into Warren County during reconnaissance mapping by the author during 1987 and 1988. The interval of mixed marine siliciclastic rocks between the Corry Sandstone and the Riceville Formation remains unnamed (Dodge, 1992). In eastern Warren County, the succession includes the Oswayo Formation and the overlying Knapp Formation, but that framework has not been extended eastward into McKean County. More detailed work needs to be done, including core drilling through the entire Mississippian and into the Venango or Catskill Formation. The relationships among the Rockwell Formation, the Lower Mississippian rocks exposed in Conemaugh Gorge, and the subsurface "Murrysville sand" of southwestern Pennsylvania need to be worked out in detail.

RECOMMENDED FOR FURTHER READING

Berg, T. M., and Edmunds, W. E. (1979), *The Huntley Mountain Formation: Catskill-to-Burgoon transition in north-central Pennsylvania,* Pennsylvania Geological Survey, 4th ser., Information Circular 83, 80 p.

Bjerstedt, T. W. (1986), *Regional stratigraphy and sedimentology of the Lower Mississippian Rockwell Formation and Purslane Sandstone based on the new Sideling Hill road cut, Maryland,* Southeastern Geology, v. 27, p. 69–94.

Caster, K. E. (1934), *The stratigraphy and paleontology of northwestern Pennsylvania—Part 1, Stratigraphy,* Bulletins of American Paleontology, v. 21, no. 71, 185 p.

Colton, G. W. (1963), *Devonian and Mississippian correlations in part of north-central Pennsylvania—a report of progress,* in Shepps, V. C., ed., *Symposium on Middle and Upper Devonian stratigraphy of Pennsylvania and adjacent states,* Pennsylvania Geological Survey, 4th ser., General Geology Report 39, p. 115–125.

Edmunds, W. E., Berg, T. M., Sevon, W. D., and others (1979), *The Mississippian and Pennsylvanian (Carboniferous) Systems in the United States—Pennsylvania and New York,* U.S. Geological Survey Professional Paper 1110-B, p. B1–B33.

Schiner, G. R., and Kimmel, G. E. (1972), *Mississippian stratigraphy of northwestern Pennsylvania,* U.S. Geological Survey Bulletin 1331–A, 27 p.

Sevon, W. D. (1969), *The Pocono Formation in northeastern Pennsylvania,* Annual Field Conference of Pennsylvania Geologists, 34th, Hazleton, Pa., Guidebook, 129 p.

Wood, G. H., Jr., Trexler, J. P., and Kehn, T. M. (1969), *Geology of the west-central part of the Southern Anthracite field and adjoining areas, Pennsylvania,* U.S. Geological Survey Professional Paper 602, 150 p.

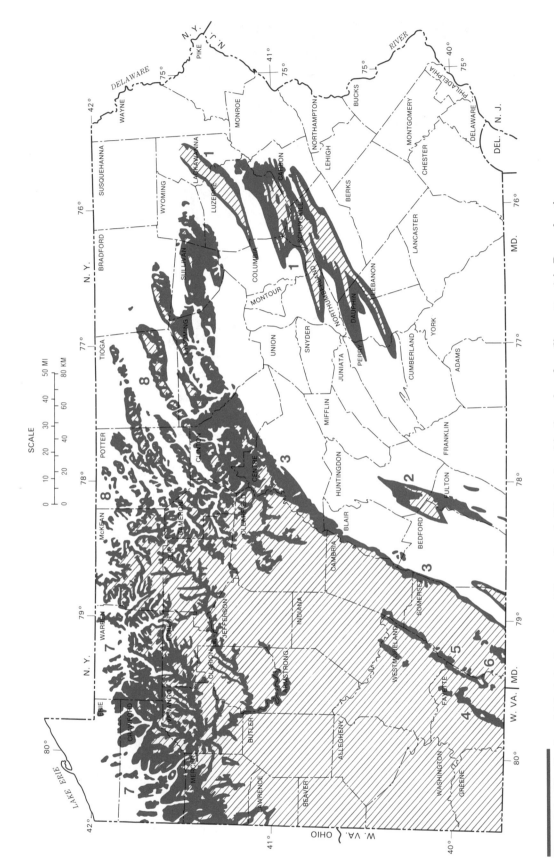

Figure 9–1. Distribution of Mississippian strata at the surface (solid color) and in the subsurface (line pattern) in Pennsylvania (from Pennsylvania Geological Survey, 1990). 1, Anthracite region; 2, Broad Top coal basin; 3, Allegheny Front; 4, Chestnut Ridge; 5, Laurel Hill; 6, Negro Mountain; 7, northwestern Pennsylvania; 8, north-central Pennsylvania.

138

CHAPTER 9   MISSISSIPPIAN

DAVID K. BREZINSKI
Maryland Geological Survey
2300 St. Paul Street
Baltimore, MD 21218

INTRODUCTION

Mississippian rocks are distributed at the surface in Pennsylvania in the Anthracite region, the Broad Top coal basin, along the Allegheny Front, along the axes of the Chestnut Ridge, Laurel Hill, and Negro Mountain anticlines, and in the northwestern and north-central parts of the state (Figure 9–1). Generally, Mississippian rocks are thickest in the Middle and Southern Anthracite fields and thin to the west and north (Figure 9–2).

The Mississippian Period of Pennsylvania represents a transition from the prograding deltas of the Middle and Late Devonian Period to the cyclic alluvial and paludal environments of the Pennsylvanian Period. The initial episode of sedimentation occurred as a continuation from the Late Devonian (Oswayo) transgression, which persisted through the Early Mississippian (Kinderhookian and Osagean Stages). This episode is responsible for the deposition of the Devonian-Mississippian marine sequence of northwestern Pennsylvania (Bedford, Berea, and Knapp Formations, and the Cuyahoga Group and Shenango Formation), as well as the Rockwell, Huntley Mountain, and Burgoon Formations of central Pennsylvania, and the Spechty Kopf through Pocono Formations of northeastern Pennsylvania (Figure 9–3). Late Mississippian deposition (Meramecian and Chesterian Stages) is represented by the Loyalhanna Limestone and Mauch Chunk Formation, including the coeval Greenbrier Limestone of the southwestern part of the state (Figure 9–3). These two depositional episodes are separated in the western half of the state by a period of widespread nondeposition and/or erosion that may span most of the Meramecian Stage. This unconformity becomes less distinct in central Pennsylvania and is not present in the eastern part of the state.

STRATIGRAPHY

Pocono Formation

The Pocono Formation has traditionally been considered the nonred, coarse-grained detrital strata

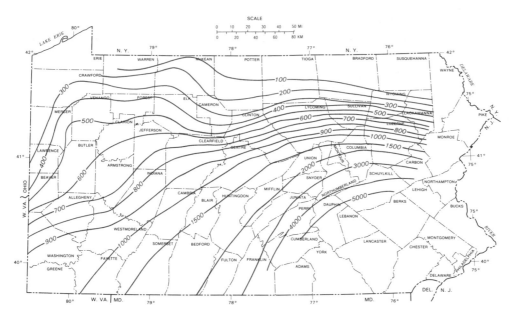

Figure 9–2. Generalized isopach map for Mississippian strata of Pennsylvania (modified from Colton, G. W., *The Appalachian basin—its depositional sequences and their geologic relationships,* in Fisher, G. W., and others, eds., *Studies of Appalachian geology: central and southern,* Figure 24, p. 38, copyright © 1970 by Interscience Publishers, reprinted by permission of John Wiley & Sons, Inc.). Contour intervals are 100, 500, and 1,000 feet.

occupying the interval between the Catskill red beds and the Mauch Chunk red beds, or the Loyalhanna Limestone where it is present (Swartz, 1965). In central and western Pennsylvania, marked differences in the lithologic character of the Pocono strata have led workers (Berg and Edmunds, 1979; Edmunds and others, 1979; Berg and others, 1986) to reassign this interval to the Rockwell, Huntley Mountain, and Burgoon Formations. Consequently, the term Pocono Formation is used only in the Anthracite region of northeastern Pennsylvania.

In the Northern Anthracite field, thinning and facies changes preclude subdivision of the Pocono into members (Sevon, 1969b). In the Middle and Southern Anthracite fields, it is subdivided into two members (Trexler and others, 1962). The lower member, the Beckville, consists of interbedded medium- to coarse-grained sandstone, siltstone, and conglomerate that lie unconformably upon diamictites and shaly strata of the Spechty Kopf Formation (see Chapter 8).

The upper member of the Pocono is known as the Mount Carbon Member. This member is characterized by crossbedded to massive, coarse-grained sandstone and conglomerate, and very minor silty intervals. Conglomeratic units commonly include large, rounded, white quartz pebbles and cobbles up to 3 inches in diameter (Figure 9–4). Generally, the Mount Carbon Member is much coarser than the underlying Beckville Member.

Pelletier (1958) proposed that the Pocono Formation of eastern Pennsylvania was deposited by high-gradient streams capable of carrying the coarse sand, pebbles, and cobbles present within this unit. These large clast sizes indicate that the Anthracite region was close to the source area (Pelletier, 1958) (Figure 9–5). Consequently, the Pocono, and especially the Mount Carbon Member, appears to have been deposited on a high-gradient alluvial plain or an alluvial fan.

Huntley Mountain and Rockwell Formations

In central Pennsylvania, two formations are recognized in the stratigraphic interval that has traditionally been termed the lower Pocono. The two formations, the Rockwell Formation in south-central Pennsylvania and the Huntley Mountain Formation in the north-central part of the state, straddle the Devonian-Mississippian boundary (see Chapter 8). The Huntley Mountain Formation consists of interbedded greenish-gray to tan, flaggy sandstone, sandy siltstone, and reddish-brown silty shale. The Rockwell consists of intertonguing marine (Riddlesburg Shale Member) and nonmarine strata in the lower part and interbedded lenticular sandstone and reddish-brown siltstone and mudstone in the upper part. The upper parts of both formations are equivalent to the Beckville Member of the Pocono Formation.

Berg and Edmunds (1979) postulated that the flaggy sandstones of the Huntley Mountain represent channel-phase sands, and the reddish-brown shales represent overbank flood deposits of alluvial-plain origin. This interpretation is similar to that proposed for the upper Rockwell by Bjerstedt and Kammer (1988).

Burgoon Sandstone

Overlying the Rockwell and Huntley Mountain Formations in central Pennsylvania is an interval

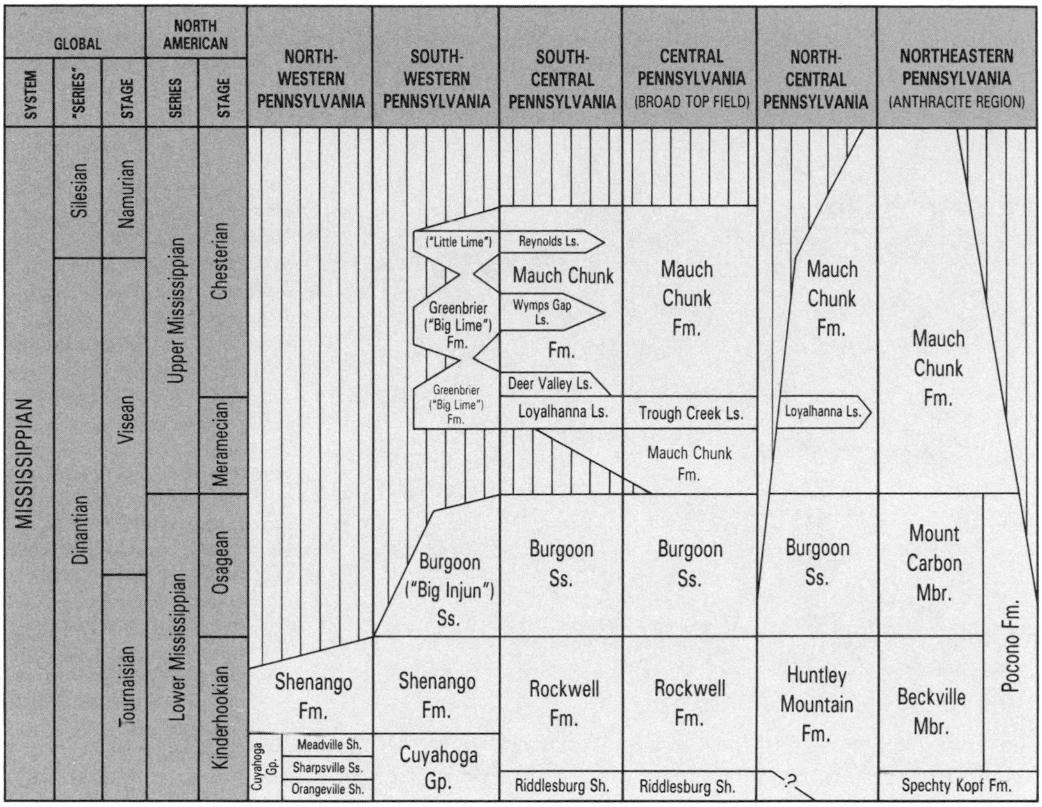

GLOBAL			NORTH AMERICAN		NORTH-WESTERN PENNSYLVANIA	SOUTH-WESTERN PENNSYLVANIA	SOUTH-CENTRAL PENNSYLVANIA	CENTRAL PENNSYLVANIA (BROAD TOP FIELD)	NORTH-CENTRAL PENNSYLVANIA	NORTHEASTERN PENNSYLVANIA (ANTHRACITE REGION)
SYSTEM	"SERIES"	STAGE	SERIES	STAGE						
MISSISSIPPIAN	Silesian	Namurian	Upper Mississippian	Chesterian		("Little Lime") / Greenbrier ("Big Lime") Fm.	Reynolds Ls. / Mauch Chunk / Wymps Gap Ls.	Mauch Chunk Fm.	Mauch Chunk Fm.	Mauch Chunk Fm.
	Dinantian	Visean		Meramecian		Greenbrier ("Big Lime") Fm.	Fm. / Deer Valley Ls. / Loyalhanna Ls.	Trough Creek Ls. / Mauch Chunk Fm.	Loyalhanna Ls.	
				Osagean		Burgoon ("Big Injun") Ss.	Burgoon Ss.	Burgoon Ss.	Burgoon Ss.	Mount Carbon Mbr.
		Tournaisian	Lower Mississippian	Kinderhookian	Shenango Fm. / Cuyahoga Gp. (Meadville Sh. / Sharpsville Ss. / Orangeville Sh.)	Shenango Fm. / Cuyahoga Gp.	Rockwell Fm. / Riddlesburg Sh.	Rockwell Fm. / Riddlesburg Sh.	Huntley Mountain Fm. / ?	Beckville Mbr. / Spechty Kopf Fm. (Pocono Fm.)

Figure 9–3. Correlation chart for Mississippian units in Pennsylvania (modified from Berg, McInerney, and others, 1986).

comprised predominantly of crossbedded, medium- to coarse-grained sandstone, which Butts (1904) termed the Burgoon Sandstone (Figure 9–6). Although the Burgoon is composed largely of crossbedded sandstone, thin, laterally discontinuous coal beds occur locally (Brezinski and Kertis, 1987).

The Burgoon Sandstone is equivalent to the Mount Carbon Member of the Pocono Formation but differs from the latter by an overall finer grain size and a lack of thick quartz-pebble conglomerates. Edmunds and others (1979) equated the Burgoon of Pennsylvania with the Logan Sandstone of Ohio and the "Big Injun" sandstone of drillers' terminology.

The only fossils known from the Burgoon Sandstone are plant fragments, which Read (1955) and Scheckler (1986) assigned to the *Triphyllopteris* zone. This zone characterizes the Lower Mississippian (mainly Osagean) of the Appalachian basin.

Cotter (1978) believed that the preponderance of crossbedding, lack of recognizable overbank deposits, and coarse grain size suggested that the Burgoon Sandstone of central Pennsylvania was deposited by high-gradient, braided streams.

Cuyahoga Group and Shenango Formation

In northwestern Pennsylvania, equivalents to the Rockwell and Huntley Mountain Formations of central Pennsylvania, and the Beckville Member of the Pocono Formation of the Anthracite region, consist of intertonguing sandstone, siltstone,

Figure 9–4. Quartz-pebble conglomerate within the Mount Carbon Member of the Pocono Formation at Jim Thorpe, Carbon County.

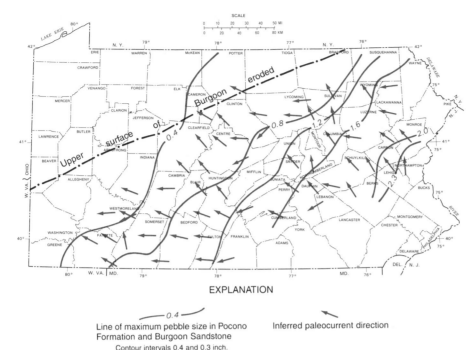

Figure 9–5. Inferred paleo-current directions and maximum pebble size for the Pocono Formation and Burgoon Sandstone (modified from Pelletier, B. R., 1958, *Pocono paleocurrents in Pennsylvania and Maryland,* Geological Society of America Bulletin, v. 69, Figure 16, p. 1055). Modified with permission of the publisher, the Geological Society of America, Boulder, Colorado USA. Copyright © 1958 Geological Society of America. Limit of erosion based on Pelletier (1958, Figure 3, p. 1038) and Edmunds and others (1979).

EXPLANATION

—0.4— Line of maximum pebble size in Pocono Formation and Burgoon Sandstone Contour intervals 0.4 and 0.3 inch.

↖ Inferred paleocurrent direction

and shale. This sequence is composed of the Cuyahoga Group and the Shenango Formation (Schiner and Kimmel, 1972; Edmunds and others, 1979). The Cuyahoga Group ranges in thickness from 200 to 240 feet, and is composed, in ascending order, of the Orangeville Shale, the Sharpsville Sandstone, and the Meadville Shale (Schiner and Kimmel, 1972). The Shenango Formation consists of thinly interbedded sandstone, siltstone, and shale and ranges in thickness from 150 to 180 feet; however, its upper limits have been removed by erosion.

The Cuyahoga Group and the Shenango Formation represent intricately interrelated facies created by the interplay of deltaic progradation and marine transgression.

Sub-Greenbrier Unconformity

During the Meramecian, much of western Pennsylvania appears to have experienced a period of either nondeposition or erosion prior to the deposition of the overlying Upper Mississippian strata (Adams, 1970). This presumed unconformity exhibits little erosional relief to support its existence. However, the sharp contact between the Burgoon and the Loyalhanna, the pervasive presence of a pitted zone in the upper Burgoon where it is overlain by the Loyalhanna, and the remnants of limestone beds not totally removed before Loyalhanna sedimentation began support the existence of an unconformity. Within the Broad Top coal field and to the east in the Anthracite region, the intertonguing relationship between the Burgoon and Pocono and the overlying Mauch Chunk Formation may indicate that the magnitude of the hiatus diminishes progressively eastward so that no significant break in sedimentation occurred in these areas.

Loyalhanna Limestone

Throughout most of southwestern Pennsylvania, the basal Upper Mississippian unit is the Loyalhanna

Figure 9–6. Crossbedded braided-stream deposits of the Burgoon Sandstone along U.S. Route 322 west of Port Matilda, Centre County.

Limestone. The Loyalhanna, named for exposures along Loyalhanna Creek in Westmoreland County (Butts, 1904), reaches a thickness of about 85 feet in southwestern Westmoreland and Fayette Counties (Adams, 1970). The Loyalhanna thins and interfingers to the east with clastics of the Mauch Chunk Formation (Brezinski, 1989b). The Loyalhanna is the most areally widespread of the Upper Mississippian marine units, extending from the southwestern corner of the state into Sullivan County (Wells, 1974). As of this writing, no macrofossils have been reported from the Loyalhanna of Pennsylvania, but brachiopods are known from the basal Loyalhanna in Maryland (Brezinski, 1989c). In thin section, fossil fragments, including bryozoans, brachiopods, echinoderms, and forams, are present.

Throughout the Allegheny Mountain section of the Appalachian Plateaus province of southwestern Pennsylvania, the Loyalhanna is present as a light-gray to grayish-green sandy limestone to calcareous sandstone containing large- to medium-scale crossbeds. It contains, on the average, 50 percent detrital quartz, but can contain from 11 to 82 percent detrital quartz. Carbonate sands are predominantly coated carbonate grains, but rounded endothyrid foraminifera and echinoderm fragments are also present. Adams (1970) has shown that the terrigenous component of the Loyalhanna generally increases to the north, indicating a northern (presumably eroded Burgoon) source area (Edmunds and others, 1979). A second, more subdued, source is suggested by the local presence of red clays and metamorphic rock fragments in the east. In these areas, the Loyalhanna takes on a reddish tint. The most diagnostic feature of the Loyalhanna in the Allegheny Mountain section is the pervasive, large-scale (up to 10 feet) crossbedding in which quartz-rich layers weather out in relief (Figure 9–7). Paleocurrent studies have shown that the major transport direction was from the southwest to the northeast (Adams, 1970; Hoque, 1975) (Figure 9–8).

In the Broad Top basin and in north-central Pennsylvania, the Loyalhanna is represented by interbedded crossbedded sandy limestone and red, mud-cracked, calcareous siltstone and mudstone (Gallagher and Parks, 1983; Brezinski, 1984, 1989b).

Mauch Chunk Formation

The most pervasive, and possibly most easily recognized, Mississippian formation in Pennsylvania is the Mauch Chunk Formation. Throughout most of its extent in the state, the

Mauch Chunk consists of red to reddish-brown mudstone and siltstone, and chocolate-brown, reddish-brown, and greenish-gray sandstone and conglomerate. The Mauch Chunk was named by Lesley (1876b) for exposures in the vicinity of the city formerly named Mauch Chunk, now called Jim Thorpe, in Carbon County. In the Southern Anthracite field, the Mauch Chunk has been estimated to be 3,000 to 4,000 feet thick, but it may reach a thickness of 6,000 to 7,000 feet. It can be subdivided into three informal members (Wood and others, 1969). The lower member displays an intertonguing of red siltstone and sandstone, typical of the Mauch Chunk, and tan to brown sandstone and conglomerate, similar to the Pocono. Reddish-brown to olive-gray lenticular sandstone and reddish-brown siltstone and mudstone characterize the middle member. The upper member consists of interbedded red sandstone and mudstone, and gray conglomerate more characteristic of the overlying Pennsylvanian Pottsville Formation (Figure 9–9).

The Mauch Chunk thins to the north and west from the Southern Anthracite field. To the north, the thinning appears to reflect not only a thinner original accumulation but also Late Mississippian erosion. The thinning of the Mauch Chunk into southwestern Pennsylvania is reflective of the more distal nature of these areas from the detrital source as well as a slower subsidence rate in the western part of the state. At maximum lateral extent, the Mauch Chunk extends to the southwestern corner of the state (Figure 9–10).

In southwestern Pennsylvania, the lower part of the Mauch Chunk exhibits numerous interbedded

Figure 9–7. Joint face exhibiting typical weathering character of the Loyalhanna Limestone in a quarry near Mount Davis, Somerset County. The Deer Valley Limestone (white unit at the top of the photograph) is approximately 10 feet thick.

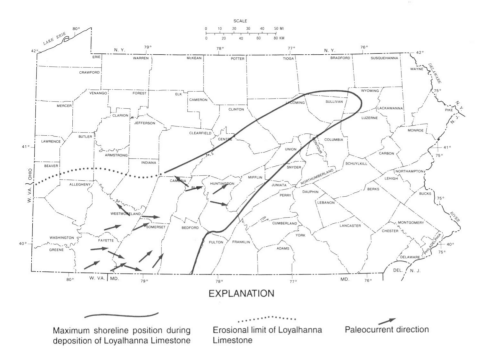

SCALE

EXPLANATION

Maximum shoreline position during
deposition of Loyalhanna Limestone

Erosional limit of Loyalhanna
Limestone

Paleocurrent direction

Figure 9–8. Maximum shoreline position and paleocurrents of the Loyalhanna Limestone. Shoreline position is from Edmunds and others (1979). Paleocurrent data are partly from Adams, R. W., *Loyalhanna Limestone—cross-bedding and provenance,* in Fisher, G. W., and others, eds., *Studies of Appalachian geology: central and southern,* Figure 14, p. 96, copyright © 1970 by Interscience Publishers, reprinted by permission of John Wiley & Sons, Inc.; and partly reprinted from Palaeogeography, Palaeoclimatology, Palaeoecology, v. 17, Hoque, M. U., *Paleocurrent and paleoslope—a case study,* Figure 4, p. 82, © 1975, with permission from Elsevier Science.

marine sandstones, shales, and limestones. In this area, the predominantly red coloration of the sediments is the only feature that allows this interval to be considered Mauch Chunk. Indeed, this part of the Mauch Chunk bears a greater resemblance to the Greenbrier Formation of Maryland and West Virginia than it does to the Mauch Chunk of the type area (Brezinski, 1989c). Several of the more significant limestone tongues include the Deer Valley and Wymps Gap (formerly the "Greenbrier of Pennsylvania") Limestones of Flint (1965), and the Reynolds Limestone ("Little Lime" of drillers' terminology of West Virginia) (Figure 9–11) (Brezinski, 1984; 1989a, b).

Greenbrier Formation

In Washington and Greene Counties in extreme southwestern Pennsylvania, the Loyalhanna and Wymps Gap Limestones, and perhaps the Reynolds, form a continuous sequence of carbonate that is not interstratified with Mauch Chunk clastics. This interval of limestone, known only from the subsurface, is named the Greenbrier Formation inasmuch as it is equivalent, at least in part, to the Greenbrier Group of West Virginia. Drillers refer to this unit in the subsurface as the "Big Lime." It can

also be correlated with the Maxville Group of Ohio. The limestone units in the Greenbrier are presumably separated from one another by unconformities, as is believed to be true for the limestones that make up the Maxville Group in Ohio (Collins, 1979). Therefore, from southwestern to northeastern Pennsylvania, the Upper Mississippian section changes from an unconformity-bound sequence of marine carbonates to a relatively complete nonmarine terrigenous interval.

Figure 9–9. Channel-phase lenticular sandstone, outlined in white, and adjacent fine-grained overbank deposits in the upper Mauch Chunk Formation near Hazleton, Luzerne County.

Basal Pennsylvanian Unconformity

Within the Northern Anthracite field, the Mauch Chunk and Pocono Formations thin to the north so that the overlying Pennsylvanian Pottsville strata lie disconformably upon progressively older strata. In northeastern Lackawanna, and in Susquehanna and Wayne Counties, Pottsville strata unconformably overlie Devonian strata of the Catskill Formation, and no Mississippian rocks are present. The magnitude of the hiatus diminishes to the south so that, within the Middle and Southern Anthracite fields, an intertonguing conformable relationship exists between the Mauch Chunk and Pottsville Formations. A regional discordance is present in northern Clearfield, Clinton, Lycoming, Tioga, and Bradford Counties, where Pottsville strata overlie sandstone of the Burgoon Formation. In much of northwestern and north-central

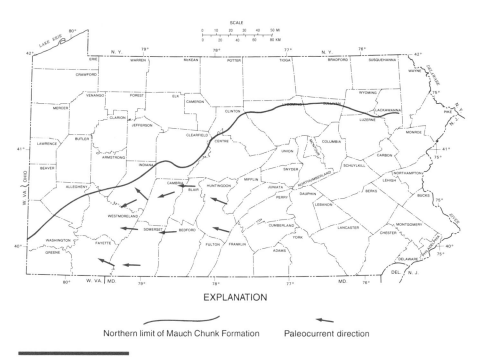

EXPLANATION

Northern limit of Mauch Chunk Formation   Paleocurrent direction

Figure 9–10. Areal extent of the Mauch Chunk Formation in Pennsylvania (from Berg and Edmunds, 1979, p. 45). Paleocurrent data are modified from Hoque (© 1968, Figure 1, p. 247, reprinted by permission of the American Association of Petroleum Geologists).

Pennsylvania, Pottsville strata overlie Lower Mississippian units of the Shenango or Huntley Mountain Formations. In southwestern and south-central Pennsylvania, evidence for a pre-Pennsylvanian unconformity is less distinct. Meckel (1970) postulated that

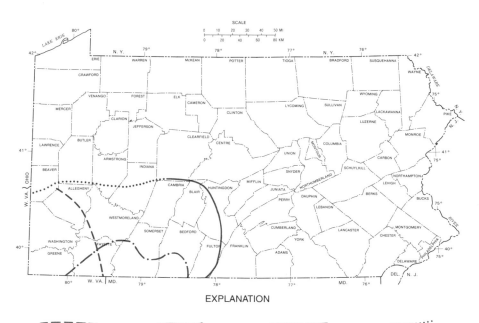

EXPLANATION

Maximum shoreline position during deposition of Reynolds Limestone

Maximum shoreline position during deposition of Wymps Gap Limestone

Maximum shoreline position during deposition of Deer Valley Limestone

Erosional limit of Wymps Gap and Reynolds Limestones

Figure 9–11. Relative maximum shoreline positions of the limestone members of the Mauch Chunk Formation in southwestern Pennsylvania (from Brezinski, 1984).

the pre-Pottsville surface was unconformable in most of Pennsylvania, with the exception of the Middle and Southern Anthracite fields. The dramatic lithologic change from the predominantly red, fine-grained deposits of the Mauch Chunk to the coarse-grained conglomerate of the Pottsville indicates that a major change in depositional environment occurred during this time interval.

PALEOGEOGRAPHY AND DEPOSITIONAL HISTORY

During the earliest Mississippian (Kinderhookian), marine waters extended into Pennsylvania from an extensive inland sea that covered much of the midcontinent. The marine embayment submerged most of eastern Ohio and inundated much of western Penn-

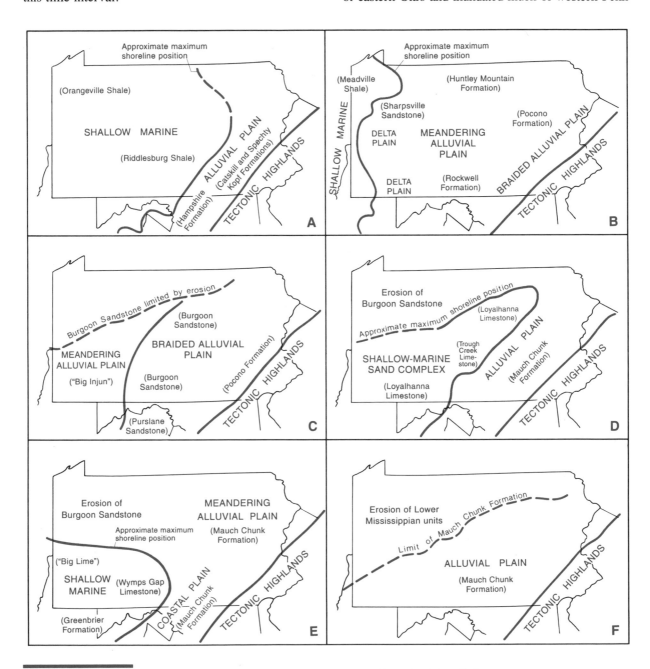

Figure 9–12. Generalized Mississippian paleogeography. A, Early Kinderhookian; B, Late Kinderhookian; C, Osagean; D, Late Meramecian; E, Early Chesterian; and F, Late Chesterian. See text for discussion.

sylvania as well. While this submergence resulted in the deposition of the Riddlesburg Member of the Rockwell Formation (Figure 9–12A) (Bjerstedt and Kammer, 1988), eroding tectonic highlands in eastern Pennsylvania continuously supplied clastic sediments. As marine regression occurred, deltas prograded westward into the marine embayment, and meandering streams deposited sediments to form what are now the upper Rockwell and Huntley Mountain Formations (Figure 9–12B). Pebbles and cobbles supplied from the tectonic highlands were transported westward by high-gradient, braided streams (Pocono Formation). As the gradients of the westward-flowing streams decreased, so did stream competency, and increasingly finer materials were deposited on an aggrading alluvial plain (Burgoon Sandstone) (Figure 9–12C). Alluvial-plain aggradation and progradation continued through much of the Early Mississippian, and by the Meramecian, a broad, low-lying alluvial plain lay across most of Pennsylvania (Berg and Edmunds, 1979).

During latest Meramecian, Pennsylvania once again marked the northern edge of a marine seaway that was oriented northeast-southwest and opened into the midcontinent in eastern Kentucky (Figure 9–12D). This seaway covered areas in West Virginia (producing the Greenbrier Formation) but only intermittently inundated the northern part of the depositional basin in Pennsylvania. Along its eastern extent, the sea was bordered by a broad alluvial plain on which red clastics (Mauch Chunk Formation) were deposited. Sediments were contributed to the northern end of the marine embayment from two sources. Large amounts of red clastics and metamorphic rock fragments were derived from an eastern source, presumably the tectonic highlands (Hoque, 1968; Adams, 1970). A more subdued source to the north contributed recycled quartz sand from the eroding Burgoon (Edmunds and others, 1979).

At the northern end of the marine embayment, in Pennsylvania, shallow estuarine conditions initially existed. This estuary was the site of a mixed transgressive carbonate and quartz sand-wave complex (Loyalhanna Limestone) that extended well into the north-central part of the state (Figure 9–12D). Although deepening of the marine waters continued into the Chesterian (Wymps Gap Limestone), the shoreline actually prograded westward as red Mauch Chunk sediments overwhelmed the marine conditions (Brezinski, 1989b) (Figure 9–12E). By latest Mississippian, red sediments of the Mauch Chunk had extended

into the southwestern corner of the state, and all but the most rapidly subsiding areas were undergoing erosion (Figure 9–12F).

PROBLEMS AND FUTURE RESEARCH

One of the most neglected Mississippian intervals is the one containing the Cuyahoga through Shenango marine units distributed throughout northwestern and north-central Pennsylvania. Future lithostratigraphic, as well as biostratigraphic, study of these units is needed. For the Upper Mississippian sequence, the most pressing need is for biostratigraphic study. Forams, which are common in many of the marine units, may prove useful in helping to unravel stratigraphic problems in this part of the Mississippian section.

RECOMMENDED FOR FURTHER READING

Adams, R. W. (1970), *Loyalhanna Limestone—cross-bedding and provenance,* in Fisher, G. W., and others, eds., *Studies of Appalachian geology: central and southern,* New York, Interscience Publishers, p. 83–100.

Bjerstedt, T. W., and Kammer, T. W. (1988), *Genetic stratigraphy and depositional systems of the Upper Devonian-Lower Mississippian Price-Rockwell deltaic complex in the central Appalachians, U.S.A.,* Sedimentary Geology, v. 54, p. 265–301.

Brezinski, D. K. (1989), *Late Mississippian depositional patterns in the north-central Appalachian basin, and their implications to Chesterian hierarchal stratigraphy,* Southeastern Geology, v. 30, p. 1–23.

Colton, G. W. (1970), *The Appalachian basin—its depositional sequences and their geologic relationships,* in Fisher, G. W., and others, eds., *Studies of Appalachian geology: central and southern,* New York, Interscience Publishers, p. 5–47.

Edmunds, W. E., Berg, T. M., Sevon, W. D., and others (1979), *The Mississippian and Pennsylvanian (Carboniferous) Systems in the United States—Pennsylvania and New York,* U.S. Geological Survey Professional Paper 1110-B, p. B1–B33.

Hoque, M. (1968), *Sedimentologic and paleocurrent study of Mauch Chunk sandstones (Mississippian), south-central and western Pennsylvania,* AAPG Bulletin, v. 52, p. 246–263.

Pelletier, B. R. (1958), *Pocono paleocurrents in Pennsylvania and Maryland,* Geological Society of America Bulletin, v. 69, p. 1033–1064.

Pepper, J. F., de Witt, Wallace, Jr., and Demarest, D. F. (1954), *Geology of the Bedford Shale and Berea Sandstone in the Appalachian basin,* U.S. Geological Survey Professional Paper 259, 111 p.

Swartz, F. M. (1965), *Guide to the Horse Shoe Curve section between Altoona and Gallitzin, central Pennsylvania,* Pennsylvania Geological Survey, 4th ser., General Geology Report 50, 58 p.

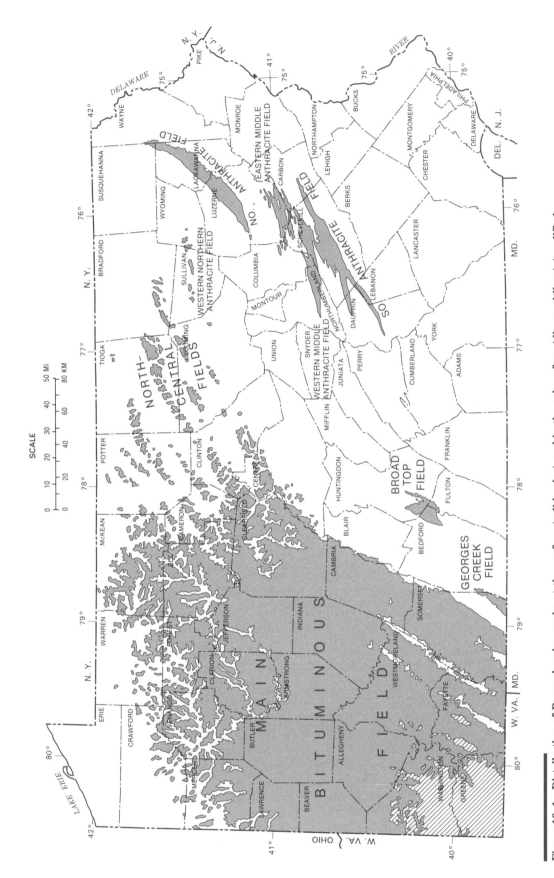

Figure 10–1. Distribution of Pennsylvanian rocks at the surface (solid color) and in the subsurface (diagonal lines) (modified from Berg and others, 1980), and the location of coal fields in Pennsylvania (from Pennsylvania Geological Survey, 1992).

148

CHAPTER 10   PENNSYLVANIAN

WILLIAM E. EDMUNDS
  Consulting Geologist
  263 Sassafras Street
  Harrisburg, PA 17102

VIKTORAS W. SKEMA
  Bureau of Topographic and Geologic Survey
  Department of Conservation and Natural
    Resources
  P. O. Box 8453
  Harrisburg, PA 17105

NORMAN K. FLINT*
  University of Pittsburgh
  Department of Geology and Planetary Science
  Pittsburgh, PA 15260

INTRODUCTION

The Pennsylvanian was originally named as a series within the Carboniferous System by H. S. Williams (1891) for exposures in Pennsylvania and was later raised to a system by Chamberlin and Salisbury (1905). It underlies about 35 percent of Pennsylvania, mostly in the Appalachian Plateaus physiographic province, but including important outliers elsewhere (Figure 10–1). It is probable that Pennsylvanian rocks originally covered the entire state, except in the southeastern source area. Pennsylvanian sediments were derived, principally, from southeastern orogenic highlands along the present margin of the North American plate. An important secondary source was the cratonic area to the north. Other possible sources were the Adirondack and Taconic highlands to the northeast. Pennsylvanian sedimentation took place in an elongate basin, aligned northeast to southwest, receiving sediments from all directions except the west and southwest. A rapidly subsiding geosynclinal trough to the southeast graded into an epicontinental shelf to the northwest (Figure 10–2).

Paleomagnetic studies show that Pennsylvania lay 5 to 10 degrees south of the equator during Pennsylvanian time (Scotese and others, 1979; Ross and Ross, 1985). Examination of Pennsylvanian flora by White (1913), Köppen and Wegener (1925), and Camp (1956) indicated a tropical to subtropical setting having abundant rainfall in the Early and Middle Pennsylvanian. Cecil and others (1985) have concluded that the Late Pennsylvanian was substantially more arid.

LITHOSTRATIGRAPHY

General

The rocks of the Pennsylvanian System in Pennsylvania are predominantly clastic and contain subordinate amounts of coal and limestone. The Pennsylvanian reaches a maximum theoretical composite thickness of about 4,800 feet and a maximum known thickness of about 4,400 feet near Llewellyn in Schuylkill County in the Southern Anthracite field, assuming that the top of this section is not Permian.

*Deceased.

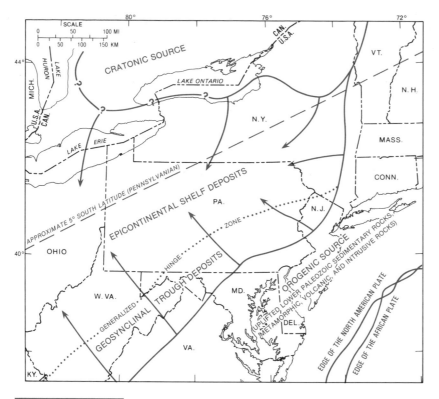

Figure 10–2. Generalized paleogeography of the Pennsylvanian depositional basin and source areas (after Edmunds and others, 1979).

In southwestern Pennsylvania, where the lower part of the system is absent, Pennsylvanian rocks are between 1,300 and 1,500 feet thick.

The bituminous coal fields of western Pennsylvania and the anthracite fields of eastern Pennsylvania each have their own stratigraphic nomenclature (Figure 10–3). The name "Pottsville" is employed in both areas, but with a different definition of the upper boundary. Nomenclature of the Broad Top and north-central areas of Pennsylvania is loosely tied to that of the western part of the state, but correlations are unclear, and each area has its own coal bed nomenclature.

The Mississippian-Pennsylvanian boundary in the Anthracite region is placed at the top of the highest red bed separating the Mauch Chunk and Pottsville Formations in the conformable and gradational sequence exposed near Pottsville, Schuylkill County (White, 1900). Rocks containing the systemic boundary are conformable throughout the Southern, Western Middle, and Eastern Middle Anthracite fields. Elsewhere in the state, the systemic boundary is disconformable, as some part of the earliest Pennsylvanian is absent (Figure 10–3).

The exact placement of the Pennsylvanian-Permian boundary is a complex and controversial problem that is discussed in Chapter 11. Conventionally, it is placed at the bottom of the Waynesburg coal bed.

Other than the base of the system, all principal stratigraphic subdivisions are defined using key-bed boundaries, mostly coals or their underclays. Many of these key beds lack continuity or lithologic distinctiveness. Therefore, interval and sequence are important factors in keeping track of various unit boundaries.

Except for the dominant sandstone and conglomerate composition of the Pottsville and Llewellyn Formations, there is no preponderant lithologic distinctiveness in any of the other major Pennsylvanian stratigraphic units. All are a more-or-less heterogeneous mixture of interbedded sandstones, siltstones, shales, claystones, limestones, and coals. Differences that do exist among the various parts of the section reflect the presence, absence, or variation in proportion of some lithologies or secondary characteristics (Figure 10–4).

The areal extent of individual lithosomes varies enormously, and none is known to be completely persistent. Individual lithosomes rarely exceed several tens of feet in thickness, although what are believed to be stacked sandstones may exceed a few hundred feet. Vertical and lateral gradation and interfingering among lithologies are very common. In western Pennsylvania alone, more than 100 individual lithosomes have been named, and many others are unnamed. In a general way, the various lithologies tend to be arranged in cycles that represent fluctuations between low-energy deposition (e.g., coals and limestones) and high-energy deposition (e.g., sandstones and conglomerates). Because the composition and order of lithologic sequences reflect such a wide variety of depositional settings, however, it is impossible to denote lithologic cycles or cyclothems in any concise, meaningful way.

Pottsville Formation of Western Pennsylvania

The Pottsville Formation in western Pennsylvania ranges from 20 to at least 250 feet in thickness. Its basal contact is apparently everywhere disconformable and from south to north overlies increas-

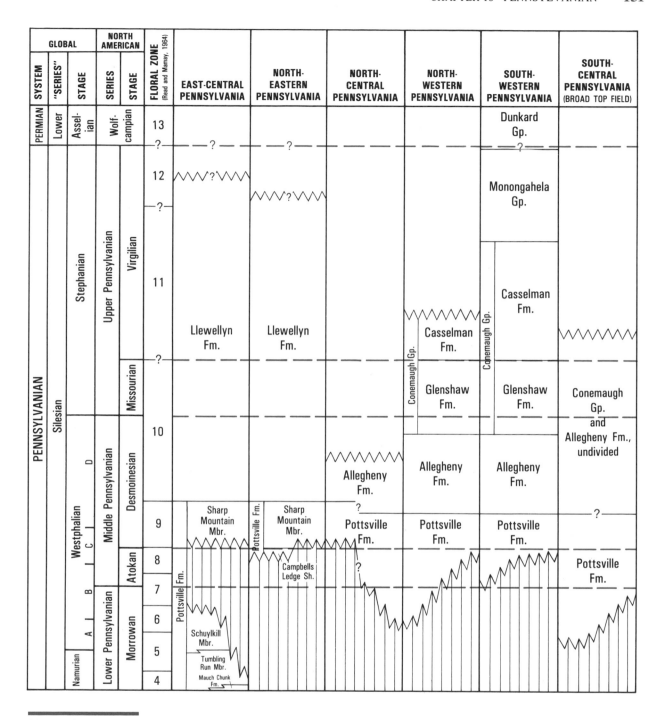

Figure 10–3. Correlation chart of Pennsylvanian stratigraphic units and floral zones (modified from Edmunds, 1993, Figure 4, p. 16, and Read and Mamay, 1964).

ingly older Mississippian and possibly uppermost Devonian rocks (Figure 10–5).

The base of the Brookville coal marks the upper boundary of the Pottsville Formation. The Pottsville (formerly a group) was divided into the Sharon, Connoquenessing, Mercer, and Homewood Formations,

in ascending order (Carswell and Bennett, 1963; Poth, 1963). It has proven to be very difficult to consistently apply this breakdown of the Pottsville beyond the area where it was originally established (Mercer County and parts of adjacent counties). In practice, the western Pottsville is usually divided into an upper

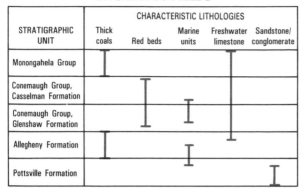

BITUMINOUS FIELDS

STRATIGRAPHIC UNIT	CHARACTERISTIC LITHOLOGIES				
	Thick coals	Red beds	Marine units	Freshwater limestone	Sandstone/ conglomerate
Monongahela Group					
Conemaugh Group, Casselman Formation					
Conemaugh Group, Glenshaw Formation					
Allegheny Formation					
Pottsville Formation					

ANTHRACITE FIELDS

STRATIGRAPHIC UNIT	CHARACTERISTIC LITHOLOGIES				
	Thick coals	Red beds	Marine units	Freshwater limestone	Sandstone/ conglomerate
Llewellyn Formation					
Pottsville Formation					

Figure 10–4. Stratigraphic distribution of definitive lithologic characteristics of the Pennsylvanian units in Pennsylvania.

sequence consisting of the Mercer coals and associated and overlying rocks, and a lower sequence dominated by sandstones (Figure 10–6).

In some places, the Pottsville is particularly thin, mainly because of depositional overlap with sequential loss of the basal elements of the group but partly because of the thinning or absence of internal units. Both cases are believed to reflect trends in the topographic relief of the pre-Pottsville erosion surface. A particularly important topographic feature of this erosion surface is the long, cuestalike ridge (or ridges) corresponding to the outcrop of the Mississippian Burgoon Sandstone and similar prominent sandstones near the base of the overlying Mauch Chunk Formation (Edmunds and Berg, 1971). This erosional high extends from at least as far east as

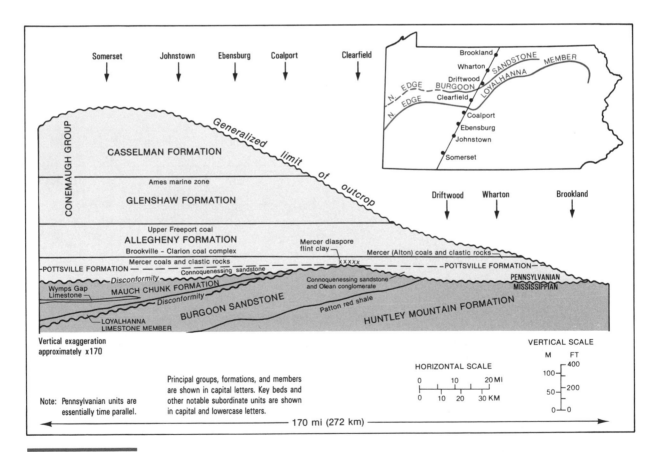

Figure 10–5. Generalized stratigraphic cross section of Pennsylvanian rocks from Somerset County to Potter County (modified from Edmunds and others, 1979).

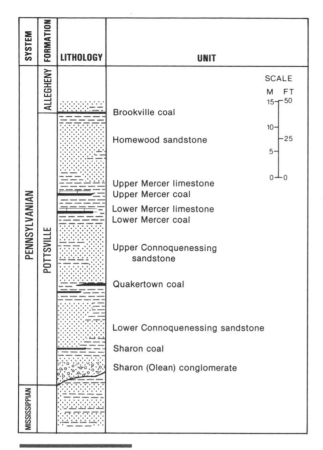

Figure 10–6. Generalized stratigraphic section of the Pottsville Formation of western Pennsylvania.

Clinton County across Centre and Clearfield Counties, and possibly west from there in the subsurface to connect with the "cuesta of Mississippian limestones" described by Wanless (1975) in eastern Ohio. The pre-Mercer Pottsville is missing along the ridge crests because of nondeposition. Thus, the pre-Mercer Pottsville is effectively separated into a northern sequence with a northern source and a southern sequence with a southeastern source, each largely isolated from and independent of the other (Figures 10–5 and 10–18C). It is along topographic highs that the unusual Mercer high-alumina hard clay formed as an apparent residual weathering product (Edmunds and Berg, 1971).

The pre-Mercer Pottsville, in both its northern and southern areas of occurrence, is dominantly sandstone and conglomeratic sandstone. Intervals of siltstone, shale, and thin coal are not uncommon and, in places, considerable parts of the section grade laterally into finer clastics. The pre-Mercer Pottsville is commonly divided into the upper and lower Connoquenessing sandstones, which are separated by a

shaly interval that includes the Quakertown coal (Figure 10–6). In northwestern Pennsylvania, the Connoquenessing sandstones are underlain by the Sharon coal and shale and the basal Sharon conglomerate, which are mostly confined to drainage channels cut into the pre-Pennsylvanian erosion surface. Farther east, the Olean conglomerate occurs at the same level. Meckel (1964, 1967) considered the Sharon and Olean to be separate, but contemporaneous, sediment lobes that were built from a northern source. There do not appear to be any clear equivalents to the Sharon and Olean in southwestern Pennsylvania.

In Pennsylvania, the pre-Mercer Pottsville is entirely nonmarine. Its thickness varies from 0 to as much as 175 feet. Recognition of the unconformable base of the Pottsville is often a problem, even in good exposures, because of the difficulty in separating Pottsville sandstones from those of the underlying Mauch Chunk, Burgoon, Shenango, and other formations.

The upper part of the Pottsville Formation, commencing with the lowest Mercer coal or its underclay, is a very complex, highly variable sequence between 20 and approximately 80 feet thick. It can contain several coals with intervening shales, underclays, and other clastics, and in Mercer and adjacent counties, it contains two marine limestones. Shales containing marine or brackish-water fauna occur widely, if irregularly, throughout western Pennsylvania. The upper part of the interval commonly contains one or more well-developed sandstones, which can displace many or all of the lower units.

Allegheny Formation

The Allegheny Formation includes those rocks from the base of the Brookville coal to the top of the Upper Freeport coal (Figure 10–7). It was specifically defined to include all of the economically significant coals present in that part of the Pennsylvanian sequence. The thickness of the formation is between 270 and 330 feet in Pennsylvania, and there is no obvious regional trend. The Allegheny Formation is a complex, repeating succession of coal, limestone, and clastics, ranging from claystone or underclay to coarse sandstone. A typical depositional cycle includes, in ascending order, coal, shale (marine or nonmarine), sandstone, and underclay (some with associated nonmarine limestone), but many variations occur. Interfingering and lateral gradation among the various lithologies are very common. No individual bed or lithosome is universally persistent, but some coals, marine shales, and limestones seem to be fairly continuous over thousands of square miles. The group

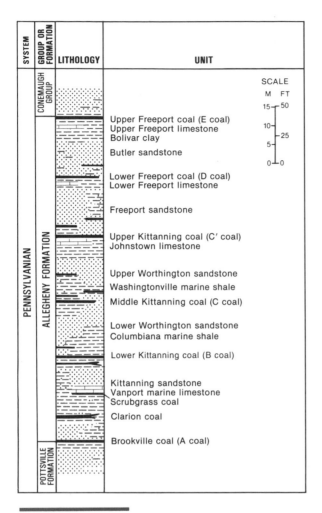

Figure 10–7. Generalized stratigraphic section of the Allegheny Formation of western Pennsylvania.

is fairly uniform in its lithologic diversity, except that marine units occur only below the Upper Kittanning underclay and, with minor exceptions, nonmarine limestones occur only at or above that unit (Figure 10–4). The Allegheny Formation contains six major coal zones. The coal in each zone may exist as a single, more-or-less continuous sheet, as a group of closely related individual lenses, or as a multiple-bed complex in which the various beds can be separated by tens of feet or merge into a single thick coal (see Chapter 37 for a discussion of individual coals).

Conemaugh Group

General

The Conemaugh Group is present at the surface throughout much of southwestern Pennsylvania. A few small, isolated outliers extend as far north as Elk County. The middle part of the Llewellyn

Formation of the Anthracite region of eastern Pennsylvania is stratigraphically equivalent to the Conemaugh. This group is stratigraphically defined as the rocks lying between the Upper Freeport coal horizon and the Pittsburgh coal (Figure 10–8). The thickness of this interval ranges from 520 feet in western Washington County to 890 feet in southern Somerset County. A gradual eastward thickening of the Conemaugh is apparent.

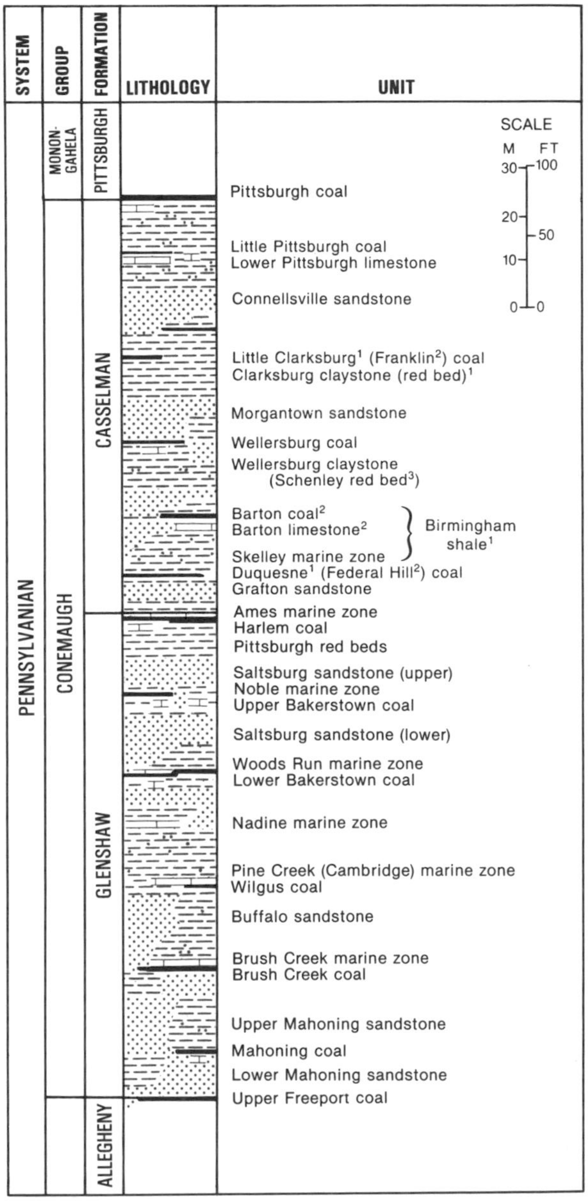

[1] Name used in Pittsburgh area and southwestern Pennsylvania excluding Somerset County.
[2] Name used exclusively in Somerset County.
[3] Name used exclusively in Pittsburgh area.

Figure 10–8. Generalized stratigraphic section of the Conemaugh Group of western Pennsylvania.

Flint (1965) subdivided the Conemaugh Group into a lower formation, the Glenshaw, containing several widespread marine units, and an upper formation, the Casselman, devoid of marine units except for the Skelley, which is of limited extent. The top of the marine Ames limestone was established as the boundary between the two formations. The Ames limestone is commonly present within a persistent marine zone that is traceable over much of the Appalachian Plateaus province.

In gross lithologic aspect, the Conemaugh is a clastic sequence dominated by siltstone, claystone, shale, and sandstone. In much of the section, primary bedding and other sedimentary structures have been destroyed by rootworking, bioturbation, and desiccation.

Calcareous and sideritic mineralization, in the form of nodules and fracture fillings, is commonly present. Iron-oxide-rich red beds and red and green mottled beds occur throughout the Conemaugh section. Most of these are caliche paleosols formed in an alternating wet-dry semiarid climate. Characteristic features include lack of bedding, hackly fracture, calcareous cutans, and small calcareous nodules. A few red beds situated in marine zones have undisturbed bedding and contain marine fossils. The red coloration in these beds is not a product of in-place soil formation but resulted from deposition of originally red detritus. Even though these beds are variable in thickness and laterally nonpersistent, some of them, especially those in the Glenshaw, roughly maintain their stratigraphic position. Coals in the Conemaugh, with local exceptions, are generally sparse, thin, and economically unimportant. Conemaugh underclays are generally impure, silty to sandy clay zones containing nodular freshwater limestone. Bedded limestones occur in some underclay zones and increase in abundance and thickness upward. The best development of the limestones is near the top of the group.

Glenshaw Formation

The thickness of the Glenshaw Formation ranges from a minimum of 280 feet in extreme western Pennsylvania to a maximum of 400 to 420 feet in Somerset County and southern Cambria County. The distinguishing feature of the Glenshaw Formation is the presence of several widespread marine units. The best developed of these, in upward succession, are the Brush Creek, Pine Creek, Woods Run, and Ames. These marine zones have both a limestone and a shale facies. The Brush Creek and Woods Run are always associated with a dark shale. The Pine Creek and Ames marine zones have a variety of lithofacies (Figure 10–9), including dark shales containing plant debris, gray-green crinoidal limestone, and red shales containing abundant and diverse marine fauna. A less prominent unit present in the Glenshaw is the Noble marine zone. This is a restricted marine to brackish shale overlying the Upper Bakerstown coal. Two other obscure Glenshaw marine zones, the Carnahan Run and the Nadine, have been reported in Pennsylvania. The Carnahan Run lies a few feet above the Woods Run limestone and appears to be of very local extent. It is separated from the Woods Run by dark fissile shale and is most likely a part of the Woods Run marine zone. The Nadine has a spotty occurrence over a much larger area, encompassing several counties. It lies a short distance below the Woods Run and is separated from it by the Lower Bakerstown coal. It is approximately 30 feet above the Pine Creek marine zone. The Nadine may be a poorly recognized, but discrete, marine zone. A zone of brackish-water fossils was found above the Mahoning coal in core from a hole drilled in 1981 by the Pennsylvania Geological Survey near Bakersville, Somerset County, and in another privately drilled hole near Blairsville, Indiana County, examined by Survey geologists in 1990. More work is needed to determine the nature and extent of this zone regionally; however, its presence suggests that there may be a

Figure 10–9. Ames limestone and associated strata of the Conemaugh Group along Pa. Route 28 near Creighton, Allegheny County. The Ames is about 3 feet thick here.

total of seven separate marine zones in the Glenshaw Formation.

Casselman Formation

The thickness of the Casselman Formation ranges from 230 feet in the extreme western part of the Appalachian Plateaus province to 485 feet in southern Somerset County. The lower part of the formation maintains the marine character of the underlying Glenshaw Formation. Marine fossils have been found in a shale overlying a thin coal 30 to 60 feet above the Ames marine zone. This marine zone covers an area from Somerset County, where it is present as a shale overlying the Federal Hill coal and containing a restricted marine to brackish fauna, to Pittsburgh, where it is represented by the distinctly marine Birmingham shale, which overlies the Duquesne coal (Raymond, 1911), to the Ohio border, where it is correlative with the Skelley Limestone of Ohio. This zone represents the last marine pulse of the Paleozoic in Pennsylvania.

The Casselman rocks above the Skelley marine zone are exclusively freshwater deposits, consisting of claystone, limestone, sandstone, shale, and coal. Much of this section is occupied by massive, impure, silty to sandy, commonly calcareous claystone of various colors, ranging from gray to dull red and pale green. Regionally, the red beds are discontinuous. Red beds are scattered throughout the formation along the western state border and make up a large percentage of the section. Eastward, they become thinner and fewer in number. This trend continues into eastern Somerset and Cambria Counties, where large areas of the Casselman Formation are completely devoid of red beds. Conversely, coals are nearly absent or very thin in the west but increase in quantity eastward. In Somerset County, a few coals are thick enough to mine. Sandy shales and sandstones are also more abundant eastward. The large lateral change in the overall thickness of the Casselman Formation and in its lithologic character makes correlation of individual units within it very difficult. The Casselman is also one of the least studied formations of the Pennsylvanian because of its lack of economically important rocks and paleontologically significant fossil zones. As a result, the stratigraphic nomenclature used in the literature is very confusing regionally and is only reliable locally.

Monongahela Group

The Monongahela Group extends from the base of the Pittsburgh coal to the base of the Waynesburg coal (Figure 10–10). It is divided into the Pittsburgh and Uniontown Formations at the base of the Uniontown coal. The group is about 270 to 400 feet thick in Pennsylvania, increasing in thickness irregularly from the western edge of the state to western Fayette County. It reportedly thins somewhat from there eastward to the Uniontown area in central Fayette County (Hickok and Moyer, 1940, p. 100). It is entirely nonmarine.

The Monongahela Group is a sedimentary sequence dominated by limestones and dolomitic limestones, calcareous mudstones, shales, and thin-bedded siltstones and laminites, all of which were deposited in a relatively low energy environment. Several coal beds are present.

The upper one half to two thirds of the Pittsburgh Formation consists principally of flat-lying, inter-

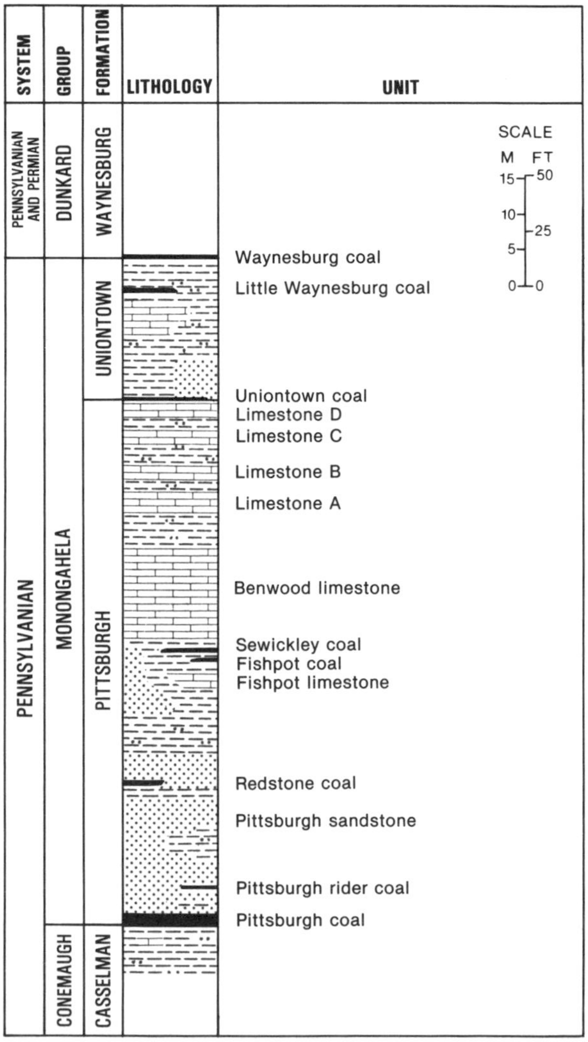

Figure 10–10. Generalized stratigraphic section of the Monongahela Group of western Pennsylvania.

layered limestones and calcareous mudstones, and relatively little coarse clastic rock (Figure 10–11). The only sandstone of significant thickness within the formation lies directly above the Pittsburgh coal complex. A major fluvial channel system, flowing north to northwest through what is now Greene and Washington Counties, deposited an elongate sandstone body up to 80 feet thick and several miles wide (Figure 10–12). To the west of this sandstone, the entire section is composed mostly of limestone and calcareous claystone. Eastward over a large area, the sandstone grades into a shale containing some thin, discontinuous sandstone bodies.

The Uniontown Formation consists mostly of thin-bedded sandstones and some channel-fill sandstones. It also contains siltstones and shales that may grade laterally into bedded limestones or cherty limestone.

Coals make up only a small part of the total Monongahela Group, but include, at the base, the Pittsburgh coal, which is generally 4 to 10 feet thick and unique in its areal continuity. Other coals can be locally thick, but lack lateral persistence (see Chapter 37 for a discussion of individual coals).

Pottsville Formation of the Anthracite Area

The Pottsville Formation of the anthracite fields of northeastern and east-central Pennsylvania (Figure 10–13) extends from the top of the highest red bed of the Mauch Chunk Formation, where the contact is conformable in the Southern and Middle Anthracite fields, to the base of the Buck Mountain (Red Ash) coal or its underlying shale (White, 1900; Wood and others, 1956). The top of the Pottsville Formation in eastern Pennsylvania and the top of the Pottsville in western Pennsylvania are not equivalent in that the Buck Mountain coal is generally correlated with the Lower Kittanning coal rather than the Brookville coal, which is the upper boundary in

the west (see Figure 10–7). The Pottsville is divided, in ascending order, into the Tumbling Run, Schuylkill, and Sharp Mountain Members (Wood and others, 1956).

The thickness of the Pottsville Formation ranges from a maximum of about 1,600 feet in the Southern Anthracite field to less than 100 feet in the Northern Anthracite field (Meckel, 1964; Wood and others, 1969). This northeastward thinning reflects the loss of the Tumbling Run and Schuylkill Members, which reach a maximum thickness of 600 and 700 feet, respectively, in the Southern field, but are absent in the Northern field, where the Sharp Mountain Member rests disconformably on Mississippian through Upper Devonian rocks (Figures 10–14 and 10–15). C. B. Read (Moore and others, 1944) concluded that there is a major disconformity between the Sharp Mountain Member and all underlying rocks, including the Schuylkill and Tumbling Run Members, throughout the entire Anthracite region (see also Edmunds, 1988; Inners, 1988). Wood and others (1969) and Meckel (1964) rejected the presence of this disconformity between the Sharp Mountain and Schuylkill Members in the Southern and Middle fields; they considered the loss of the Schuylkill and Tumbling Run Members to be a matter of depositional thinning and facies loss of the lower part of the Tumbling Run to the Mauch Chunk Formation.

The Pottsville Formation is approximately 50 to 60 percent cobble and pebble conglomerate and conglomeratic sandstone, 25 to 40 percent sandstone, and 10 to 20 percent finer clastics and coal. Most of the formation consists of fining-upward alluvial cycles. Pottsville rocks are mostly light gray to black, except the lower two thirds of the Tumbling Run,

Figure 10–11. Benwood and Fishpot limestones of the Pittsburgh Formation along Interstate Route 79 near Heidelberg, Allegheny County. The roadcut is approximately 100 feet high. See also Figure 12 in the color section.

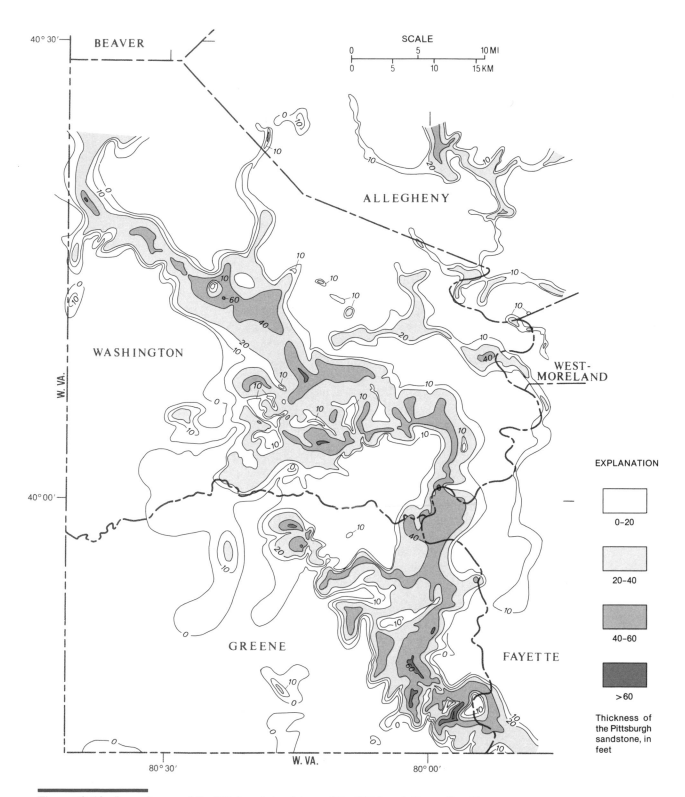

Figure 10–12. Isopach map of the Pittsburgh sandstone of the Pittsburgh Formation (from Roen and Kreimeyer, 1973). This channel deposit is from a major river that flowed generally northwest.

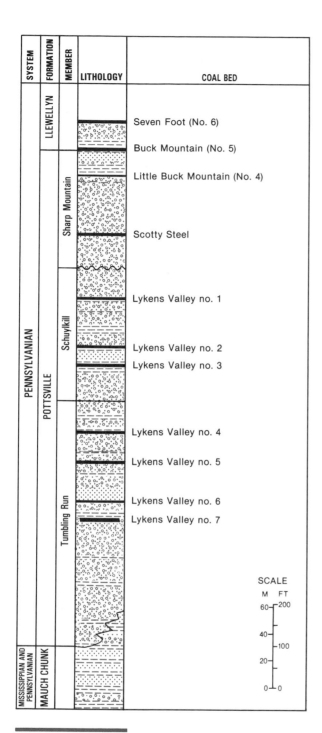

Figure 10–13. Generalized stratigraphic section of the Pottsville Formation in the Anthracite region of Pennsylvania.

which is olive to greenish gray. Fourteen coal beds have been named, but most are relatively discontinuous, and only a few persist outside the Southern field. The Pottsville is entirely nonmarine.

Llewellyn Formation

The Llewellyn Formation includes all remaining rocks in the Anthracite region above the base of the Buck Mountain (Red Ash) coal or the underlying shale (Figures 10–16 and 10–17). The greatest thickness of preserved section is about 3,500 feet. Lithologically, the Llewellyn is a complex, heterogeneous sequence of subgraywacke clastics, ranging from conglomerates to clay shale and containing numerous coal beds. Conglomerates and sandstones dominate. There are also a few thin, nonmarine limestones and, in the Northern Anthracite field, the marine Mill Creek limestone bed. Rapid lateral and vertical lithologic variability is characteristic throughout the Llewellyn.

The Llewellyn contains 40 coal beds that have sufficient persistence or minability to be named, plus numerous unnamed local coals and splits. The thickest and most persistent coals are confined to the lower 1,500 feet, and most of them occur in the lower 650 feet of the formation (see also Chapter 36). The maximum natural thickness of the coal beds generally does not exceed 50 to 60 feet, although in complex structural situations, where beds are folded back upon themselves or mass flow has occurred, thicknesses of 100 feet or more may occur.

PALEONTOLOGY AND BIOSTRATIGRAPHY

Because plants are the only fossil forms present in reasonable abundance throughout the stratigraphic and geographic extent of the Pennsylvanian System within Pennsylvania, paleobotany is the method used for general correlations. Early work produced large amounts of taxonomic data (Lesquereux, 1879, 1880, 1884) and limited correlation of certain beds and intervals (White, 1900, 1904), but it was not until the work of Darrah (1937, 1969) on the post-Pottsville and Read (Moore and others, 1944; Read and Mamay, 1964) on the entire Pennsylvanian that all-inclusive paleobotanical zonation was established (Figure 10–3). Gillespie and Pfefferkorn (1979) further refined the paleobotanical zonation of the Pennsylvanian standard section in West Virginia, work that should be applicable to the section in Pennsylvania as well.

The absence of Lower Pennsylvanian floral zones (zones 4, 5, and, in many places, 6), coupled with the loss of Mississippian floral zones, led White (1904) to recognize the widespread disconformity at the base of the Pennsylvanian throughout Pennsylvania, except in the Southern and Middle Anthracite fields (Figure 10–3). The apparent absence of Atokan-age flo-

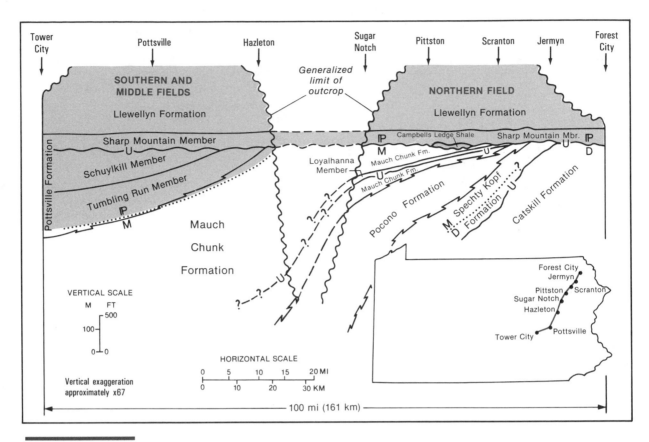

Figure 10–14. Generalized stratigraphic cross section of Pennsylvanian rocks from Tower City, Schuylkill County, to Forest City, Susquehanna County (from Edmunds, 1988).

ral zones (zones 7 and 8) in the Southern and Middle Anthracite fields indicated to Read (Moore and others, 1944) a major disconformity between the Sharp Mountain and the underlying Schuylkill and Tumbling Run Members of the Pottsville Formation.

Palynological studies have been conducted on a number of specific Pennsylvanian beds, mostly in limit-

ed areas, but have not been integrated into a biostratigraphic system (Cross and Schemel, 1952; Clendening and Gillespie, 1964; Gray, 1965a, b; Habib, 1965, 1966; Groth, 1966). Paleobotanical and palynological problems associated with the placement of the Pennsylvanian-Permian boundary are discussed in Chapter 11.

The distribution of fossil faunal assemblages within the Pennsylvanian System in Pennsylvania is strongly influenced by variations in depositional environments. Marine and marginal-marine forms are limited to two intervals in western and north-central Pennsylvania. The lower marine sequence extends from the Mercer shales and limestones of the Pottsville Formation to the Washingtonville shale of the Allegheny Formation (Figures 10–6

Figure 10–15. Basal conglomerate of the Sharp Mountain Member, disconformably overlying Mississippian strata along Interstate Route 84–380, 0.5 mile east of the Dunmore exit, Lackawanna County. The height of the roadcut is approximately 25 feet.

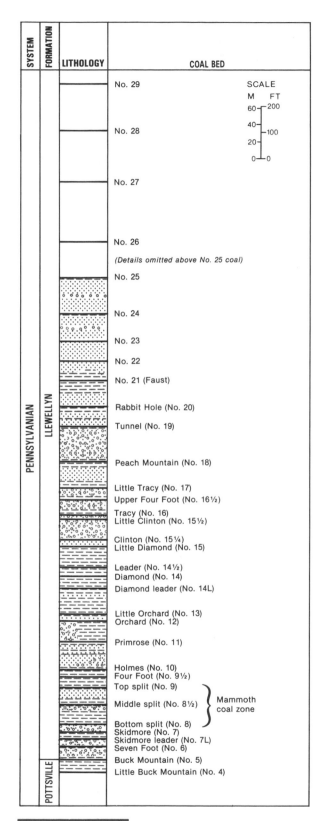

SYSTEM	FORMATION	LITHOLOGY	COAL BED
PENNSYLVANIAN	LLEWELLYN		No. 29
			No. 28
			No. 27
			No. 26
			(Details omitted above No. 25 coal)
			No. 25
			No. 24
			No. 23
			No. 22
			No. 21 (Faust)
			Rabbit Hole (No. 20)
			Tunnel (No. 19)
			Peach Mountain (No. 18)
			Little Tracy (No. 17)
			Upper Four Foot (No. 16½)
			Tracy (No. 16)
			Little Clinton (No. 15½)
			Clinton (No. 15¼)
			Little Diamond (No. 15)
			Leader (No. 14½)
			Diamond (No. 14)
			Diamond leader (No. 14L)
			Little Orchard (No. 13)
			Orchard (No. 12)
			Primrose (No. 11)
			Holmes (No. 10)
			Four Foot (No. 9½)
			Top split (No. 9)
			Middle split (No. 8½) } Mammoth coal zone
			Bottom split (No. 8) }
			Skidmore (No. 7)
			Skidmore leader (No. 7L)
			Seven Foot (No. 6)
	POTTSVILLE		Buck Mountain (No. 5)
			Little Buck Mountain (No. 4)

SCALE
M   FT
60 — 200
40 —
20 — 100
0 — 0

Figure 10–16. Generalized stratigraphic section of the Llewellyn Formation of the Southern and Middle Anthracite fields (adapted from Arndt, 1963, Figure 3).

SYSTEM	FORMATION	LITHOLOGY	UNIT
PENNSYLVANIAN	LLEWELLYN		No. 7 coal
			No. 6 coal
			No. 5 coal
			No. 4 coal
			(Details above No. 3 coal not available)
			No. 3 coal
			No. 2 coal
			No. 1 coal
			Mill Creek limestone (marine)
			Canal limestone
			Coal
			Upper Snake Island coal
			Lower Snake Island coal (George)
			Limestone
			Abbott coal (J, Hutchinson, Seven Foot, Eight Foot)
			Kidney coal (I, Mills, Five Foot)
			Hillman limestone
			Hillman coal (H, Four Foot)
			Upper Stanton coal
			Lower Stanton coal (G, Orchard, Diamond)
			Upper Lance coal
			Lower Lance coal (F, Five Foot, Forge, Rock)
			Upper Pittston coal (Baltimore, Cooper)
			Lower Pittston coal (E, Baltimore, Bennett, Big, Grassy)
			Skidmore coal (Marcy, New County)
			Upper Ross coal (D, Clark)
			Lower Ross coal (C, Clark)
			Upper Red Ash coal (B, Dunmore)
	POTTSVILLE		Lower Red Ash coal (B, Dunmore)

SCALE
M   FT
60 — 200
40 —
       100
20 —
0 — 0

Figure 10–17. Generalized stratigraphic section of the Llewellyn Formation of the Northern Anthracite field.

and 10–7). The upper marine interval extends from the Brush Creek marine zone (or possibly a Mahoning marine zone) in the lower Glenshaw Formation to the Skelley marine zone (Birmingham shale) in the lower Casselman Formation (Figure 10–8). Elements of this upper marine sequence occur in the Broad Top field (Edmunds and Glover, 1986), and one marine tongue reaches the Northern Anthracite field as the Mill Creek limestone in the Llewellyn Formation (Chow, 1951; Figure 10–17). Edmunds (1992) has demonstrated the presence of a marine fauna at the base of the Pottsville Formation in the southern Broad Top area. Potentially, nonmarine fauna should occur, at least intermittently, throughout the entire Pennsylvanian. Except for the comprehensive work of Williams (1960) on the macrofauna of the Allegheny Formation and the upper Pottsville Formation, most paleozoological studies have been narrowly limited with respect to stratigraphic interval, areal distribution, and faunal subject (Table 10–1).

Investigations by Shaak (1972), Donahue and Rollins (1974), Norton (1975), Rollins and Donahue (1975), Rollins and others (1979), Al-Qayim (1983), and Saltsman (1986) dealt with the relationships between marine ecosystems and their associated depositional environments for the various marine zones of the Glenshaw Formation. Studies have also been made of the relationship between the depositional setting of the Lower Kittanning coal (Allegheny Formation) and its petrography (Ting, 1967), its palynology (Habib, 1965, 1966), and the palynology of its overlying sediments (Groth, 1966).

CHRONOSTRATIGRAPHY

The rock sequence spanning the Mississippian-Pennsylvanian time boundary is conformable only in the Southern and Middle Anthracite fields. At the type section of the Pottsville Formation (an exposure through Sharp Mountain a few miles south of Pottsville in the Southern Anthracite field), the systemic time boundary falls, by definition, at the same stratigraphic position as the base of the Pottsville (Figure 10–3). Because the Pottsville-Mauch Chunk contact is defined as the top of the highest red bed and the stratigraphic position of the highest red bed rises somewhat to the north, the systemic boundary passes into the upper Mauch Chunk Formation (Wood and others, 1969; Berg and others, 1986). Elsewhere in Pennsylvania, the systemic boundary occurs within a regional disconformity below the Pottsville.

Where marine beds are present, the upper Pottsville Formation, the Allegheny Formation, and the

Table 10–1. *Summary of Paleozoological Studies of Pennsylvanian Rocks in Pennsylvania*

Northeastern Pennsylvania (Anthracite Area)
  Pottsville and Llewellyn Formations
    Insects: Carpenter (1960, 1967)
  Llewellyn Formation
    Mill Creek marine macrofauna: Chow (1951);
      Ashburner (1886)
Western Pennsylvania (Bituminous Area)
  Sub-Mercer Pottsville Formation: Edmunds (1992)
  Pottsville (upper part) and Allegheny Formations
    All macrofauna: Williams (1960)
    Fusulinids: Smyth (1974)
    Conodonts: Merrill (1970–71)
  Allegheny Formation
    Vanport Limestone cephalopods: Sturgeon (1964);
      Murphy (1966)
    Darlington (Lower Kittanning?) shale and Upper
      Freeport limestone vertebrates: Lund (1975)
    Columbiana shale macrofauna: Smith (1968)
  Glenshaw Formation
    Fusulinids: Smyth (1974)
    Conodonts: Merrill (1970–71)
    Brush Creek macrofauna: Seaman (1942); Donahue
      and others (1972); Shaak (1972); Brant (1971); see
      also Chow (1951)
    Brush Creek cephalopods: Murphy (1970)
    Brush Creek crinoids: Burke (1967, 1968)
    Brush Creek foraminifers: Norton (1975)
    Brush Creek gastropods: Knight (1941)
    Pine Creek (Cambridge) macrofauna: Seaman (1941);
      see also Chow (1951)
    Pine Creek (Cambridge) crinoids: Burke (1968)
    Ames macrofauna: Seaman (1940); see also Chow
      (1951)
    Ames crinoids: Burke (1968, 1970)
  Casselman Formation
    Skelley (Birmingham shale) macrofauna: Raymond
      (1911)
    Nonmarine bivalves: Eagar (1975)
    Vertebrates: Lund (1975)
  Monongahela Group
    Nonmarine bivalves: Eagar (1975)
    Vertebrates: Lund (1975)

Glenshaw Formation of western Pennsylvania and adjacent Ohio are correlated with a good degree of accuracy to the marine beds present in the type areas of the late Atokan, Desmoinesian, and Missourian Stages of the mid-continent (Sturgeon and Hoare, 1968). The ages of the lower part of the Pottsville Formation, the Casselman Formation, the Monongahela Group, and the controversial Pennsylvanian-Permian boundary in western Pennsylvania (see Chapter 11 and Barlow and Burkhammer, 1975) are based mainly upon paleobotanical, including palynological, correlations that are less clear.

Except for the Missourian Mill Creek marine zone in the Northern Anthracite field, all time equivalences in the Anthracite region are derived from paleobotanical correlations. The Pottsville Formation of the Southern and Middle Anthracite fields spans Morrowan through early Desmoinesian Stages but internally seems to be missing the Atokan equivalents (see Read in Moore and others, 1944; Edmunds, 1988). In the Northern field, the Pottsville, including the Campbells Ledge shale, is latest Atokan through early Desmoinesian (White, 1900; Read in Moore and others, 1944; Edmunds, 1988).

Age correlation of the Llewellyn Formation is more controversial. All agree that the lower part of the formation is middle and late Desmoinesian, but Read (Read and Mamay, 1964; Wood and others, 1969, Table 1) extended the Missourian equivalent above the middle of the formation (to the Faust coal), whereas Darrah (1969), using European time terminology, appears to have placed the Missourian-Virgilian boundary about 600 feet lower (approximately at the Diamond coal) and considered the upper two thirds of the Llewellyn to be Virgilian, if not partly Permian. Eggleston and others (1988) concluded that the flora of the No. 25 coal, 500 feet above the Faust coal and several hundred feet below the top of the formation, was probably equivalent to part of the Monongahela Group and, therefore, Virgilian in age.

The Pennsylvanian sequence of the Broad Top field in south-central Pennsylvania contains two or three marine zones that are believed to be equivalent to some of the Glenshaw marine zones of western Pennsylvania (Edmunds and Glover, 1986) and, therefore, are Missourian in age. The highest marine zone is at least 250 feet below the top of the section, presumably leaving room for some equivalent of the Virgilian Casselman Formation. Fossil lists (Gardner, 1913) suggest that most or all Desmoinesian-equivalent strata are present, but the maximum age beyond that is unclear. The use of marine invertebrates, macroflora, and microflora has permitted dating of the base of the Pottsville Formation in the southern Broad Top area as middle Morrowan (Edmunds, 1992).

Very little work has been done on the biostratigraphy of the 300-foot Pennsylvanian section of the North-Central fields. The presence of marginal-marine faunal zones suggests equivalency to some part of the upper Pottsville Formation to lower Allegheny Formation of western Pennsylvania and, therefore, a late Atokan to early Desmoinesian age. White (1904), Read (1946), and Pfefferkorn (personal communication, 1977) indicated that the fossil flora at

and near the Bloss (B) coal near the middle of the sequence is also equivalent to the upper Pottsville Formation to lower Allegheny Formation.

DEPOSITIONAL HISTORY

The Mississippian-Pennsylvanian contact is conformable only in the area of the Southern and Middle Anthracite fields in east-central Pennsylvania. Elsewhere in the state, the earliest Pennsylvanian rocks, as well as some or all of the Late Mississippian sequence, are unconformably missing. Englund (1979) has dated the onset of erosion associated with the unconformity in the central Appalachians as early Morrowan. This erosion followed deposition of earliest Morrowan sediments approximately equivalent to the lower two thirds of the Tumbling Run Member of the Pottsville Formation (Figure 10–18A).

The original extent of Late Mississippian (Chesterian) and very earliest Pennsylvanian rocks prior to the onset of erosion cannot be demonstrated directly within Pennsylvania. Since, however, it can be shown that the immediately preceding late Meramecian age Loyalhanna Member of the Mauch Chunk Formation extends across most of the state and that deposition of the Chesterian-earliest Morrowan sequence is continuous in east-central Pennsylvania and also in western Virginia and southern West Virginia, it is most likely that continuous Chesterian and earliest Morrowan rocks originally extended across all of Pennsylvania (except the source area in the southeast), and also westward into Ohio and northward into New York.

The early Morrowan erosion surface encompassed all of western and central Pennsylvania, but it did not extend into the east-central part of the state, where deposition was continuous (Figure 10–3). Whether or not the erosion surface extended into northeastern Pennsylvania in the area of the Northern Anthracite field cannot be determined, as that part of the section has been removed by a still later erosion surface.

The development of the early Morrowan erosion surface has been explained as the product of either structural arching of the area or eustatic sea-level decline. White (1904) proposed widespread epeirogenic uplift. Eustatic drop in sea level at the time of the Mississippian-Pennsylvanian boundary was considered to be a potential cause by Swann (1964) and Saunders and Ramsbottom (1986). Ettensohn and Chesnut (1989) observed that the onset of erosion in the central Appalachians occurred later than the Mississippian-Pennsylvanian boundary sea-level fall and concluded that the erosion surface was primarily the result of the rise of a peripheral tectonic bulge with, possibly, some subordinate influence from sea-level change.

In east-central and, possibly, northeastern Pennsylvania, where sedimentation was continuous, very coarse alluvial clastics built out from the southeastern orogenic highlands across the upper surface of the alluvial red beds of the Mauch Chunk Formation (Figure 10–18A) (Meckel, 1964, 1967; Wood and others, 1969). During middle and late Morrowan, interfluvial peat swamps developed in the more southerly part of the alluvial plain. Wet tropical conditions had clearly replaced the semiarid, seasonal wet-dry climate of Late Mississippian time.

Marine conditions briefly encroached across the erosion surface in south-central Pennsylvania in middle Morrowan time, followed by prograding alluvial coarse clastics (Edmunds, 1992).

A high-energy fluvial system, originating in New York, flowed southwestward across the northwest corner of the state, carrying the coarse clastics of the Sharon (Olean) conglomerates and sandstones into eastern Ohio and beyond (Figure 10–18B) (Fuller, 1955; Meckel, 1964; Rice and Schwietering, 1988). The Sharon fluvial system is at least as old as late Morrowan, based upon the flora of the overlying Sharon coal bed and shales, but was probably present as early as middle Morrowan.

The erosion surface in the rest of western Pennsylvania consisted of northern and southern positive areas separated by a higher west-east cuesta corresponding to the outcrop of the resistant Lower Mississippian Burgoon Sandstone.

In early and middle Atokan, coarse clastics of the Connoquenessing sandstones and finer grained equivalents buried the erosion surface in western and central Pennsylvania except for a narrow remnant of the Burgoon cuesta (Figure 10–18C).

At some time during the Atokan, the area of the Northern Anthracite field was uplifted and eroded down to Mississippian and uppermost Devonian rocks (Figure 10–18C). Read (Moore and others, 1944) and Edmunds (1988) concluded that this disconformity extends throughout the other anthracite fields, where it separates the Sharp Mountain Member from the lower members of the Pottsville Formation. Inners (1988) similarly concluded that this disconformity is present in the other anthracite fields, but below the Schuylkill Member. Meckel (1964) and Wood

and others (1969) rejected the presence of this disconformity outside the Northern Anthracite field.

Commencing in latest Atokan and continuing through the first half of Desmoinesian time, a general eastward shift of marine conditions introduced a series of shallow-marine transgressions into western Pennsylvania, resulting in deposition of the Mercer shales and limestones of the upper Pottsville Formation upward through the Washingtonville shale of the middle Allegheny Formation (Figure 10–18D through 10–18F). Depositional environments included a shallow-marine shelf, marine carbonate banks, coastal marshes and swamps, lagoons, and distributary deltas, which grade into alluvial-plain fluvial distributaries and interdistributary flood basins (Ferm, 1962, 1970, 1974, 1975; Williams and Ferm, 1964; Ferm and Williams, 1965; Weber and others, 1965; Ferm and Cavaroc, 1969; Williams and Bragonier, 1974; Cavaroc and Saxena, 1979).

Beginning at the same time as, or shortly after, deposition of the Mercer units in the west, a major incursion of very coarse alluvial clastics spread across northeastern Pennsylvania, which formed the conglomerates and sandstones of the Sharp Mountain Member of the Pottsville Formation. Beginning with the Llewellyn Formation in middle Desmoinesian time, the alluvial sediments of northeastern Pennsylvania became distinctly less coarse and included many widespread peat swamps (Wood and others, 1969). With one notable exception, a marine transgression discussed below, the depositional environment in the northeast remained basically unchanged throughout the remainder of the Pennsylvanian Period (Figure 10–18F through 10–18J).

During late Desmoinesian time, marine conditions withdrew westward into Ohio. The depositional environment in western Pennsylvania (Figure 10–18G) became entirely that of an alluvial plain with complex fluvial channels, large, isolated coal swamps, and freshwater lakes (Pedlow, 1977; Sholes and others, 1979; Skema and others, 1982). Rocks within the stratigraphic interval from the Johnstown limestone of the Allegheny Formation up through the Brush Creek coal of the Glenshaw Formation were the product of this deposition. Except for the discovery of a few brackish-water fossils above the Mahoning coal in two cored holes drilled in Somerset County in 1981 and Westmoreland County in 1990, there are no known marine units in this interval in Pennsylvania.

The Missourian and possibly very earliest Virgilian rocks from the Brush Creek marine zone of

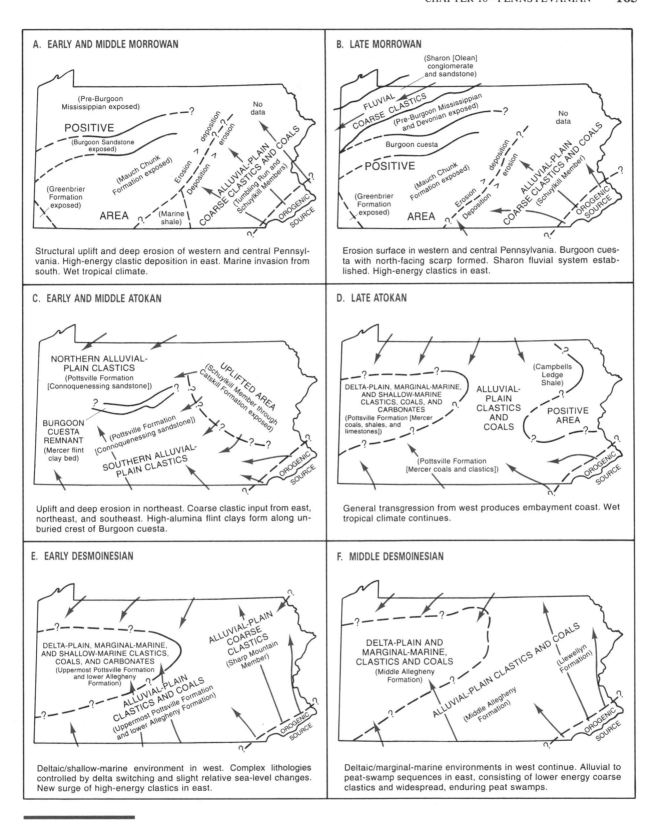

A. EARLY AND MIDDLE MORROWAN

(Pre-Burgoon Mississippian exposed)

POSITIVE

(Burgoon Sandstone exposed)

(Greenbrier Formation exposed)

(Mauch Chunk Formation exposed)

AREA

(Marine shale)

Erosion > Deposition > deposition > erosion

No data

ALLUVIAL-PLAIN COARSE CLASTICS AND COALS (Tumbling Run and Schuylkill Members)

OROGENIC SOURCE

Structural uplift and deep erosion of western and central Pennsylvania. High-energy clastic deposition in east. Marine invasion from south. Wet tropical climate.

B. LATE MORROWAN

(Sharon [Olean] conglomerate and sandstone)

FLUVIAL COARSE CLASTICS

(Pre-Burgoon Mississippian and Devonian exposed)

No data

Burgoon cuesta

POSITIVE

(Greenbrier Formation exposed)

(Mauch Chunk Formation exposed)

AREA

Erosion > deposition > erosion Deposition

ALLUVIAL-PLAIN COARSE CLASTICS AND COALS (Schuylkill Member)

OROGENIC SOURCE

Erosion surface in western and central Pennsylvania. Burgoon cuesta with north-facing scarp formed. Sharon fluvial system established. High-energy clastics in east.

C. EARLY AND MIDDLE ATOKAN

NORTHERN ALLUVIAL-PLAIN CLASTICS
(Pottsville Formation [Connoquenessing sandstone])

BURGOON CUESTA REMNANT
(Mercer flint clay bed)

(Pottsville Formation [Connoquenessing sandstone])

UPLIFTED AREA
(Schuylkill Member Catskill Formation through exposed)

SOUTHERN ALLUVIAL-PLAIN CLASTICS

OROGENIC SOURCE

Uplift and deep erosion in northeast. Coarse clastic input from east, northeast, and southeast. High-alumina flint clays form along unburied crest of Burgoon cuesta.

D. LATE ATOKAN

DELTA-PLAIN, MARGINAL-MARINE, AND SHALLOW-MARINE CLASTICS, COALS, AND CARBONATES
(Pottsville Formation [Mercer coals, shales, and limestones])

ALLUVIAL-PLAIN CLASTICS AND COALS

(Campbells Ledge Shale)

POSITIVE AREA

(Pottsville Formation [Mercer coals and clastics])

OROGENIC SOURCE

General transgression from west produces embayment coast. Wet tropical climate continues.

E. EARLY DESMOINESIAN

DELTA-PLAIN, MARGINAL-MARINE, AND SHALLOW-MARINE CLASTICS, COALS, AND CARBONATES
(Uppermost Pottsville Formation and lower Allegheny Formation)

ALLUVIAL-PLAIN COARSE CLASTICS
(Sharp Mountain Member)

ALLUVIAL-PLAIN CLASTICS AND COALS
(Uppermost Pottsville Formation and lower Allegheny Formation)

OROGENIC SOURCE

Deltaic/shallow-marine environment in west. Complex lithologies controlled by delta switching and slight relative sea-level changes. New surge of high-energy clastics in east.

F. MIDDLE DESMOINESIAN

DELTA-PLAIN AND MARGINAL-MARINE, CLASTICS AND COALS
(Middle Allegheny Formation)

ALLUVIAL-PLAIN CLASTICS AND COALS

(Llewellyn Formation)

(Middle Allegheny Formation)

OROGENIC SOURCE

Deltaic/marginal-marine environments in west continue. Alluvial to peat-swamp sequences in east, consisting of lower energy coarse clastics and widespread, enduring peat swamps.

Figure 10–18. Pennsylvanian paleogeography and depositional environments (modified from Edmunds and others, 1979).

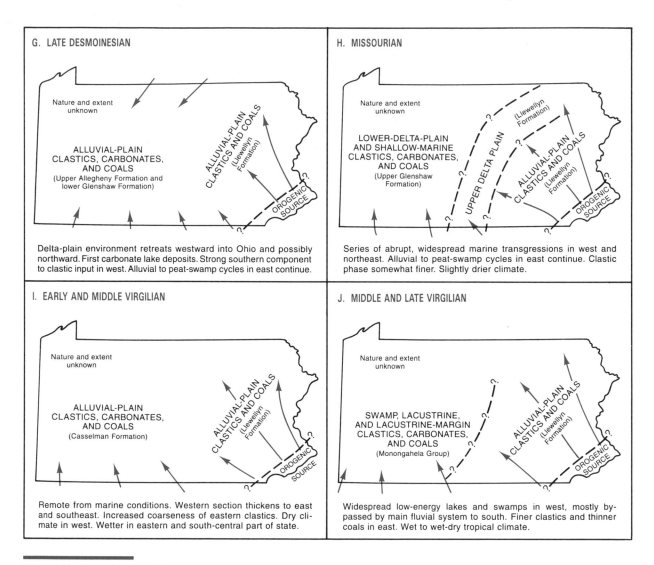

Figure 10–18. *(Continued).*

the Glenshaw Formation to the Skelley marine zone of the Casselman Formation are characterized by a series of sharp eastward marine transgressions (Figure 10–18H), which resulted in the establishment of shallow-marine, coastal-plain, and lower-delta-plain conditions across all of western Pennsylvania (Morris, 1967; Donahue and Rollins, 1974; Al-Qayim, 1983; Saltsman, 1986). Busch and Rollins (1984) described seven distinct marine transgressions (including the Mahoning event) in the Glenshaw Formation, which they ascribed to eustatic sea-level changes. There is, in addition, the eighth, and last, Skelley marine transgression in the lowest part of the Casselman Formation. Interspersed between the shallow-marine limestones and black shales are low-

energy, delta-plain distributary sediments, coastal-plain coals, freshwater limestones, and caliche-bearing red-bed paleosols. One marine transgression (commonly assumed to be Ames equivalent) reached as far east as the Northern Anthracite field, where the Mill Creek sideritic limestone is clearly a shallow-marine deposit and other beds for at least several tens of feet above and below the Mill Creek have sedimentary characteristics distinctly unlike the usual alluvial features of the Llewellyn Formation. In addition, the presence of nonmarine limestones in the 330-foot interval below the Mill Creek suggests a possible distal-alluvial-plain environment.

Near the beginning of the Virgilian Stage, marine conditions withdrew permanently from Pennsylvania (Figure 10–18I). Although there have been no systematic studies of the depositional setting of the early Virgilian Casselman Formation, the presence of freshwater limestones, discontinuous coals, and red beds suggests a relatively drier alluvial-plain setting. Any marine connection is very remote.

By the last half of Virgilian time, represented by the Monongahela Group, the northeastern end of the Appalachian basin was almost completely severed from any marine connection (Figure 10–18J). The main sediment input at this time was farther south across West Virginia, and there were only intermittent diversions northward into Pennsylvania. Sediment was also received from secondary sources to the north. The general environment appears to have been that of an isolated, relatively low-energy alluvial plain containing widespread coal swamps and freshwater lakes (Donaldson, 1969, 1974, 1979; Berryhill and others, 1971; Marrs, 1981). The Pittsburgh coal swamp apparently extended across all of southwestern Pennsylvania, but other coal swamps were more limited. Most of the late Virgilian sequence consists of thick deposits of interbedded limestone and calcareous claystone that were laid down in freshwater lakes. The sequence was terminated by a renewed influx of clastics.

DEPOSITIONAL CONTROLS

Geologists have long speculated upon the nature of the depositional environments and the factors operating thereon that have produced the complex Pennsylvanian sequence with its multiplicity of thin, interbedded lithologies. From the beginning, it was recognized that, in a general way, the rocks represented some sort of subtropical coastal lowland setting in which alluvial elements that emanated from the east interfaced with marine or lacustrine conditions to the west. Determining the degree of continuity of individual lithosomes has always been a particularly difficult problem. This question of lithologic persistence is important, not only from the abstract sedimentological standpoint, but also in matters of stratigraphic subdivision or correlation and the economic geology of the coal beds. For whatever reason, the concept that individual units have great lateral persistence steadily gained acceptance. By the time of the Second Pennsylvania Geological Survey (Lesley, 1879), certain sandstones and most coal beds were treated as widespread sheets and were made the official boundaries of all major stratigraphic subdivisions.

The cyclothem concept (i.e., the idea that thin, repetitive, laterally persistent lithologies reflect the effects of external (allocyclic) processes operating basin-wide) promised to provide the theoretical underpinning for the notion of widespread lithosome continuity. Decades were spent trying to fashion a representative Appalachian cyclothem or cyclothems (Reger, 1931; Stout, 1931; Cross and Arkle, 1952; Sturgeon, 1958; Beerbower, 1961; Branson, 1962). Eventually, it became apparent that no reasonable number of representative cyclothems could be devised that would hold up for any distance, laterally or vertically. Although it is usually not difficult to recognize cyclic alternations between low-energy sediments (such as peat) at one extreme and high-energy sediments (such as fluvial sandstone or conglomerate) at the other, the character, order, and extent of individual lithosomes are too variable to reduce to any simple order regulated by allocyclic controls alone.

Comparison of modern sedimentary systems and the internal (autocyclic) processes that control the nature and distribution of individual modern lithosomes with their ancient analogues has permitted interpretation of much of the complex lithologic variation encountered in the Pennsylvanian sequence (Donaldson, 1969, 1974, 1979; Ferm and Cavaroc, 1969; Ferm, 1970, 1979a, 1979b).

In spite of the success achieved in applying autocyclic depositional concepts, many of the broader aspects of the Pennsylvanian rocks have such general and wide-ranging influence that allocyclic factors must be at work as well. Without referring to specific lithologies, Busch and Rollins (1984) and Heckel (1986) reiterated the point that it is possible to recognize the effects of widespread transgressive-regressive couplets, at least in those parts of the section that include marine units. During the Pennsylvanian, the tropical climate of Pennsylvania ranged between persistently wet and semiarid seasonal wet-dry conditions. The pronounced depositional effects of these variations have been emphasized by Phillips and Peppers (1984), Cecil and others (1985), Donaldson and others (1985), Cecil (1990), and Winston (1990).

Williams and Holbrook (1985), remarking on the apparent very large discrepancy between the estimated 20,000 to 40,000 years needed to produce the rock sequence from one prominent coal zone to the next, and the average of 400,000 years this same interval would represent if all such intervals are distributed throughout the total time available, concluded that most of the missing time is incorporated in widespread erosional-surface paraconformities (see also Williams and others, 1965).

It appears, in fact, that both allocyclic and autocyclic controls were operating to a significant degree. These can be summarized as follows:

Allocyclic Controls

Geographic configuration of the basin
Tectonic or epeirogenic activity in the source area
Climatic changes
Eustatic sea-level changes
Differential subsidence and tectonic or epeirogenic activity within the basin

Autocyclic Controls

Sedimentary prograding
Delta and distributary switching
Alluvial-channel relocation
Channel, levee, and flood-basin (constructive) fluvial processes
Longshore coastal processes
Physical and chemical impact of large-scale plant development
Differential compaction

At any time and place, all of the above influences could have operated to some degree. When dealing with any particular aspect of the rocks in any selected interval and area, one must consider the *relative* influence of each of these controls.

PROBLEMS AND FUTURE RESEARCH

Research in the following areas is needed in order to gain a better understanding of the geology of the Pennsylvanian in the Commonwealth and to develop a more applicable model of Pennsylvanian stratigraphy.

Regional stratigraphic framework—Much of the stratigraphy currently in use was established at a time when some sandstones and most coals were erroneously considered to have great lateral persistence. It is now known that the areal extent of these beds varies enormously and that many are not nearly as widespread as first thought. The identification of the regionally persistent lithosomes and an accurate assessment of their distribution are needed in order to correct the stratigraphic errors present in the literature. This is especially true in the parts of the Pennsylvanian that lack economically important units and

consequently have been mostly ignored, such as the Casselman Formation.

Regional biostratigraphy—Many of the paleontological studies of the Pennsylvanian have been narrowly limited in scope. Much of the past work has concentrated on the fauna of the open-marine beds of the Glenshaw Formation and the Vanport Limestone of the Allegheny Formation. Studies of the more restricted marine and brackish beds present throughout the upper Pottsville Formation, the lower Allegheny Formation, and the Glenshaw Formation, and an attempt to link these to their better-known marine equivalents in Ohio, would greatly improve our understanding of biostratigraphy in the Pennsylvanian. This is especially true in the much-neglected North-Central fields. Paleobotanical correlations, although extensive, are still relatively vague in relation to the present understanding of lithostratigraphy. Floral zonation is almost the sole source of correlation between the anthracite fields and western Pennsylvania and needs further clarification and refinement. Palynological zonation of the Pottsville Formation of western Pennsylvania should help to resolve age, correlation, and depositional-history problems associated with this relatively thin, but apparently long-enduring, high-energy clastic unit.

Basal Pennsylvanian unconformity—More work is needed regarding the cause of the unconformity below the Pennsylvanian sequence in western Pennsylvania, in particular, whether it represents the development of a tectonic arch (peripheral bulge), the effects of eustatic sea-level decline, or some combination thereof. The question also remains as to why the overlying Pottsville Formation of this area is only a few hundred feet thick while more than 2,000 feet of presumably laterally equivalent rocks were deposited above the same unconformity farther south in the central Appalachians.

Paleoenvironmental reconstruction—Further research is necessary on the paleoenvironments present at the time of Pennsylvanian deposition, including the nature and relative impact of the various controlling allocyclic and autocyclic processes. Accurate paleoenvironmental models would provide a more rational basis for developing a workable new stratigraphic framework. This is especially needed in the anthracite fields. A more thorough understanding of the depositional environment and climate in this region will aid in correlating these coals and their associated rocks, which have undergone extensive structural deformation. The areas of the Casselman and Pottsville

Formations of the bituminous fields are also in need of this type of approach.

Existence, scale, and effects of intermittent widespread disconformities—It has been claimed, with considerable theoretical justification, that the amount of real time represented by the present Pennsylvanian stratigraphic sequence falls far short of the actual amount of time spanned by the Pennsylvanian Period, and that most of Pennsylvanian time may be tied up in frequent, widespread intervals of nondeposition and/or erosion. The existence, areal extent, temporal duration, erosional results, and soil development of such disconformities should be investigated further because, if present, their effect upon stratigraphic and depositional concepts could be profound.

RECOMMENDED FOR FURTHER READING

Berryhill, H. L., Jr., Schweinfurth, S. P., and Kent, B. H. (1971), *Coal-bearing Upper Pennsylvanian and Lower Permian rocks, Washington area, Pennsylvania,* U.S. Geological Survey Professional Paper 621, 47 p.

Busch, R. M., Wells, K. E., and Rollins, H. B. (1984), *Correlation of Carboniferous strata using a hierarchy of transgressive-regressive units,* Appalachian Basin Industrial Associates, v. 6, p. 4–44.

Donaldson, A. C. (1974), *Pennsylvanian sedimentation of central Appalachians,* in Briggs, Garrett, ed., *Carboniferous of the southeastern United States,* Geological Society of America Special Paper 148, p. 47–78.

Ferm, J. C., Horne, J. C., Weisenfluh, G. A., and Staub, J. R., eds. (1979), *Carboniferous depositional environments in the Appalachian region,* Columbia, S. C., Carolina Coal Group, University of South Carolina Department of Geology, p. 10–619.

Meckel, L. W., Jr. (1967), *Origin of Pottsville conglomerates (Pennsylvanian) in the central Appalachians,* Geological Society of America Bulletin, v. 78, p. 223–258.

Read, C. B., and Mamay, S. H. (1964), *Upper Paleozoic floral zones and floral provinces of the United States,* U.S. Geological Survey Professional Paper 454–K, 35 p.

Ross, C. A., and Ross, J. R. P. (1985), *Carboniferous and Early Permian biogeography,* Geology, v. 13, p. 27–30.

Wood, G. H., Jr., Kehn, T. M., and Eggleston, J. R. (1986), *Depositional and structural history of the Pennsylvanian Anthracite region,* in Lyons, P. C., and Rice, C. L., eds., *Paleoenvironmental and tectonic controls in the coal-forming basins of the United States,* Geological Society of America Special Paper 210, p. 31–47.

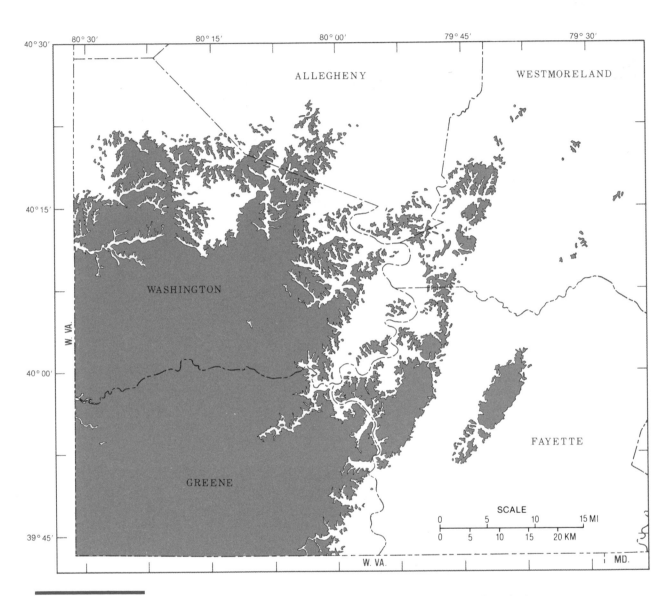

Figure 11–1. Areal distribution of the Dunkard Group (Permian and Pennsylvanian-Permian) in the southwestern corner of Pennsylvania (slightly modified from Berg and others, 1980).

170

CHAPTER 11   PENNSYLVANIAN-PERMIAN TRANSITION AND PERMIAN

WILLIAM E. EDMUNDS
Consulting Geologist
263 Sassafras Street
Harrisburg, PA 17102

INTRODUCTION

The strata conventionally considered Pennsylvanian-Permian and Permian in age comprise an 1,100-foot, dominantly clastic sequence forming the top of the stratigraphic section in southwestern Pennsylvania (Figure 11–1). These rocks are cradled in the center of the elongate Dunkard basin, where most dips are less than 100 feet per mile. The topographic expression of the Pennsylvanian-Permian and Permian sequence is that of a maturely dissected plateau having rounded uplands and steep valley slopes. Stream patterns are distinctively dendritic.

LITHOSTRATIGRAPHY

General

The portion of the stratigraphic sequence regarded as Pennsylvanian-Permian transition and Permian is identical with the Dunkard Group (Figure 11–2). By the current definition, the Dunkard Group extends from the base of the Waynesburg coal bed to the present topographic surface (Berryhill and Swanson, 1962; Berg, McInerney, and others, 1986). The Dunkard is divided into the Waynesburg, Washington, and Greene Formations, in ascending order. The boundary between the Waynesburg and Washington Formations is at the base of the Washington coal bed, and the boundary between the Washington and Greene Formations is at the top of the Upper Washington limestone bed. Prior to the revision by Berryhill and Swanson (1962), the Waynesburg coal was the uppermost unit of the subjacent Monongahela Group, and the other rock units in the Waynesburg Formation were considered part of the Washington Formation. The older definitions are still used in many recent publications.

To be effective, key-bed stratigraphy requires that the key beds be both distinctive and widely continuous. Within Pennsylvania, both the Waynesburg coal and the Upper Washington limestone are fairly persistent, although both deteriorate to the southwest in West Virginia and Ohio. The Washington coal is more

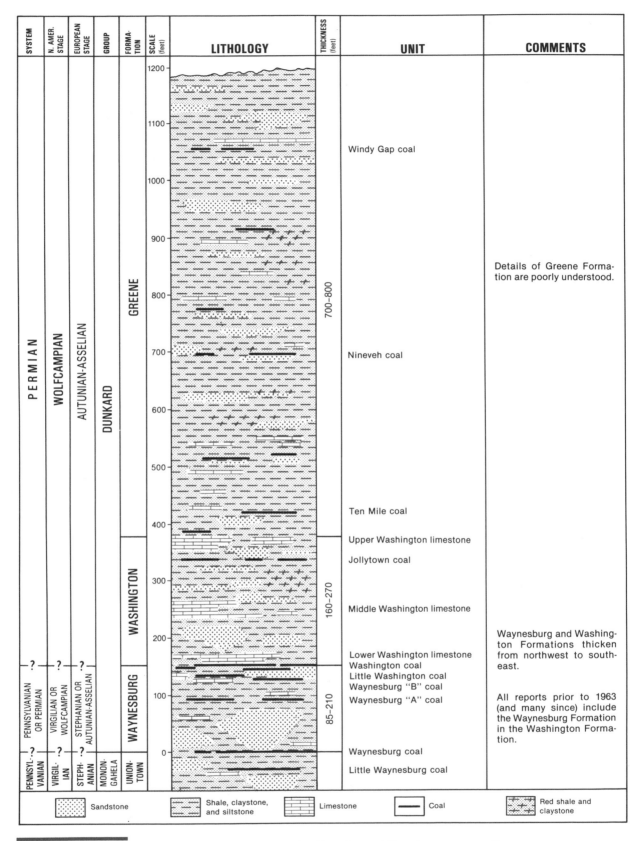

Figure 11–2. Stratigraphic column of the Pennsylvanian-Permian and Permian sequence of southwestern Pennsylvania.

commonly absent and can be confused with the Little Washington and Waynesburg "B" coals in some areas.

The Dunkard Group and its formational subdivisions are fundamentally lithostratigraphic units and have no inherent biostratigraphic or chronostratigraphic connotation. As it happens, however, these units and their key-bed boundaries are almost certainly time-parallel. Hence, biostratigraphic zones should closely parallel the formations. There are no known major disconformities or depositional hiatuses within the Dunkard, or between it and the underlying Monongahela Group.

The Dunkard Group is composed of varying proportions of interbedded sandstone, siltstone, claystone, shale, limestone, and coal (Figure 11–2). Such differences as do exist between the formations are mainly modest variations in the proportions of the constituent lithologies. Individual lithologic units vary in thickness from a mere trace to several tens of feet locally. No individual lithologic unit is persistent throughout the entire areal extent of the Dunkard Group in Pennsylvania, although a few, such as the Waynesburg coal and the Upper Washington limestone, are very widespread. Most lithologic units display more rapid lateral variations so that the detail of the overall sequence varies considerably from place to place. The Dunkard is entirely nonmarine, so far as is known.

In a very general way, the rocks of the Waynesburg and Washington Formations represent the high-energy to low-energy depositional alterations that, in a multitude of variations, are typical of the Pennsylvanian-Permian sequence of the Appalachian area. Beginning, arbitrarily, with a coal bed (minimum-energy setting), the depositional order tends to progress through silt shale and siltstone, sandstone (maximum-energy setting), silt shale and clay shale, limestone, claystone (underclay), and back to coal. Complete occurrences of this simple sequence are not common. The thicknesses of these cyclic intervals vary considerably, but most are in the 20- to 60-foot range. The pattern suggests an initial, high-energy infilling of a large, shallow peat swamp by coarser fluvial clastics, tailing off into low-energy, lacustrine, carbonate mud flats, and ultimately the reestablishment of a new peat swamp. The Greene Formation may exhibit a similar cyclicity; its lithologic character is not too different from the lower part of the Dunkard, although it seems to be dominated more by clastics and has fewer and more poorly developed coals and limestones.

A detailed description of the various lithologies of the Waynesburg and Washington Formations in the vicinity of Washington, Pa., was given by Berryhill and others (1971, p. 5–7 and Tables 1 and 2). Strictly speaking, their discussion is limited to that vicinity and includes the underlying Monongahela Group without distinction, but it is, nevertheless, probably applicable to the Dunkard Group throughout most of its extent in Pennsylvania. Figure 11–3 and the following discussion are mostly a summary of their observations.

Sandstones of the Dunkard Group range up to several tens of feet thick and are sheetlike, elongate (shoestring), or, less commonly, lobate in plan view (Figures 11–4 and 11–5). Most are fine- to very fine grained, feldspathic sandstones and are classified as subarkoses.

Siltstone, shaly siltstone, mudstone, and claystone occur as widespread lateral and vertical facies of the sandstones (Figures 11–6 and 11–7). Similarly, calcareous claystones and clay shales are interbedded with, or grade laterally into, limestones. Thin but widespread layers of claystone (underclay) occur below most coal beds. Illite is by far the most abundant clay mineral. Red beds (mostly red clay shale or claystone) are more common toward the southern border of the state, especially in the Washington and Greene Formations.

Limestones occur as sheetlike bodies up to 40 feet thick that grade laterally into other lithologies. Limestone units are generally made up of a series of individual limestone beds up to 3 feet thick separated by thin, commonly calcareous claystones (Figure 11–5). Using Pettijohn's (1957) classification of limestones and dolomites, about 70 percent of the samples studied by Berryhill and others (1971) were limestones or magnesium limestones. The rest were dolomitic limestones plus a few percent calcitic dolomites. Most are limestone breccias composed of reworked limestone fragments set in a microcrystalline matrix. Desiccation cracks are very common.

The Waynesburg coal and, to a lesser degree, the Waynesburg "A" and Washington coals are fairly persistent throughout much of the area. All other coal beds have much more limited areal continuity, and many grade laterally into carbonaceous shales.

Waynesburg Formation

The Waynesburg Formation, which extends from the base of the Waynesburg coal to the base of the Washington coal (Figure 11–2), is between 85 and 210 feet thick. The thickness increases generally from northwestern Washington County southward to south-central Greene County. Although the Waynesburg Formation is lithologically similar to the rest of the Dunkard Group, it tends to be somewhat sandier, its coal beds are thicker and more persistent, and it has few, if any, red beds.

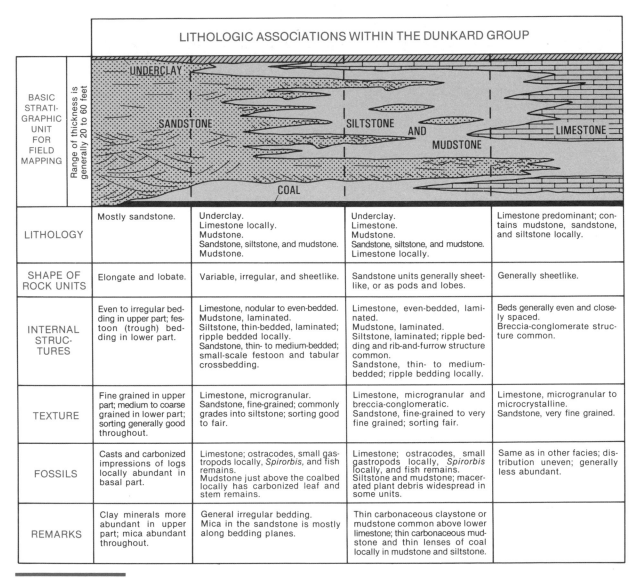

Figure 11–3. Lithofacies relations and summary of lithologic characteristics of the Dunkard Group of southwestern Pennsylvania (slightly modified from Berryhill and others, 1971, Figure 15).

Washington Formation

The Washington Formation is defined as the interval from the base of the Washington coal to the top of the Upper Washington limestone (Figure 11–2). It is 160 to 270 feet thick. The thickness increases generally, but irregularly, from northwestern and north-central Washington County to southeastern Greene County. It is distinguished by three widespread limestone units that occur at the top, at the middle, and near the base of the formation.

Greene Formation

The Greene Formation extends from the top of the Upper Washington limestone to the present erosion surface (Figure 11–2). The maximum thickness

of the Greene Formation is approximately 750 feet in southwestern Greene County (Stone, 1932b). The general character of the Greene Formation seems to be similar to the lower part of the Dunkard Group, although coals and limestones are more poorly developed. The stratigraphic details and continuity of individual beds are not well understood. A general section of the lower 500 feet of the Greene Formation was described by Kent (1972).

BIOSTRATIGRAPHY

The Dunkard Group is entirely nonmarine, and significant fossil suites are limited to plants and their spores, nonmarine aquatic invertebrates and vertebrates, terrestrial vertebrates, and insects.

Figure 11-4. Sandstone in the lower part of the Waynesburg Formation having festoon crossbedding, 5 miles east of the Washington area, Washington County (from Berryhill and others, 1971, Figure 4F).

Figure 11-5. Single, thick sheet of sandstone in the lower part of the Greene Formation (upper part of photograph) and closely spaced limestone beds of the Upper Washington limestone, Washington Formation (lower part of photograph), near the village of Vance, Washington County (from Berryhill and others, 1971, Figure 4D).

Figure 11-6. Shaly to thin-bedded siltstone and thin to thick, irregular sandstone beds in the middle part of the Washington Formation, near the village of Conger, Washington County (from Berryhill and others, 1971, Figure 4A).

The fossil flora includes forms that are transitional between the Upper Pennsylvanian and Lower Permian. Equivalency between the Dunkard paleobotanical suite and that of the standard Lower Permian stages of central Europe (Autunian Stage), Russia (Asselian Stage), and the rest of North America (Wolfcampian Stage) is unclear. Especially unclear is the significance of the Permian guide fossil *Callipteris conferta*. The problems are discussed at length in Barlow and Burkhammer (1975). Darrah (1969) placed the boundary between his Stephanian floral zone and, by exclusion, the Autunian-Asselian within the Waynesburg Formation-Washington Formation interval. Read and Mamay (1964) placed the division between their Pennsylvanian zone of *Danaeites* (zone 12) and their Permian zone of *Callipteris* (zone 13) somewhere within the Dunkard Group generally. Gillespie (Clendening and Gillespie, 1972; Gillespie and others, 1975) concluded that the floral forms of the Dunkard Group are entirely Pennsylvanian in age. Studies of Dunkard palynology by Clendening (1975) have led to the conclusion that the palynomorph suite is entirely of Pennsylvanian age.

Studying the nonmarine bivalves (mainly *Anthraconaia* spp.), Eagar (1975) concluded, tentatively, that the forms encountered in the Dunkard are dominantly Permian. He specified that the transition from Pennsylvanian to Perm-

Figure 11–7. Thin-bedded, laminated sandstone with an uneven basal contact overlying shaly mudstone, from the upper part of the Waynesburg Formation, 3 miles east of the Washington area, Washington County (from Berryhill and others, 1971, Figure 4C).

ian occurs "...somewhere within or not far outside the lower or upper boundaries of the Monongahela Group" (Eagar, 1975, p. 59). The distribution of conchostracan (estheriid) genera led Tasch (1975) to place the transition from Pennsylvanian to Permian suites at or below the Washington coal bed. The biostratigraphy of fossil vertebrates, both fish and tetrapods, has led Lund (1975) to place the boundary between Pennsylvanian and Permian suites at the base of the Benwood limestone of the Monongahela Group, making the Dunkard vertebrates Wolfcampian and probably also Leonardian in age. Olson (1975), also considering the vertebrate occurrences, did not find the data conclusive, but felt that the Dunkard forms were probably Permian. Based on examination of fossil insects, Durden (1975) concluded that those in the lower part of the Dunkard were Wolfcampian forms and those in the upper part were early Leonardian.

CHRONOSTRATIGRAPHY

Although, in a strict sense, biostratigraphic zonations and true age are separate entities, any date assigned to the Dunkard Group is totally dependent upon reference to its fossil suites. As the sequence is completely nonmarine, age determinations must rely solely on nonmarine fossils.

Based upon paleobotanical studies, the Dunkard was originally declared to be of Permian age by Fontaine and White (1880), setting off a century-long controversy that continues unabated. The range of opin-

ions place the Pennsylvanian-Permian boundary anywhere from as low as the Ames limestone of the Conemaugh Group, several hundred feet below the base of the Dunkard, to above the Dunkard's uppermost beds. The difficulty in resolving the boundary position involves not only the biostratigraphy of the Dunkard, but also questions of taxonomy, differences in time definition between individual paleontological subspecialties, problems in the North American and European standard sections, and the question of how accurately the paleontological forms available can be used to estimate true time. Readers requiring an extensive examination of the age problem are referred to Barlow and Burkhammer (1975).

It cannot be expected that the age problem will be settled soon, and because of the inertia of custom, the Dunkard Group will probably continue to be referred to the Permian Period. It does seem fairly clear, however, that the designation of the Waynesburg Formation alone as "Pennsylvanian-Permian transition" is a meaningless gesture, suggesting a nonexistent degree of certainty in the placement of the boundary.

Although not clearly demonstrated, it has been suggested that some of the higher beds of the Llewellyn Formation in the Southern Anthracite field in eastern Pennsylvania may be time equivalent to part of the Dunkard Group (Darrah, 1969, 1975).

DEPOSITIONAL HISTORY

The Dunkard Group is the uppermost remnant of the long Paleozoic sequence deposited in, and flanking, the Appalachian geosyncline along the eastern edge of the North American plate. It is likely that Dunkard-age sediments originally covered much of Pennsylvania and, as extrapolated from coal rank, were at least several thousand feet thicker than the remaining 1,100 feet (Hower and Davis, 1981). The principal sediment source lay to the southeast and south, and there was a secondary source to the north (Figure 11–8). Pennsylvania was located within a few degrees of the equator (Scotese and others, 1979; Ross and Ross, 1985) and received at least moderate rainfall.

The rocks of the Dunkard Group are entirely nonmarine, although marine equivalents presumably were deposited some undetermined distance to the west. The only remaining clue to the proximity of marine equivalents is the occurrence near the west-

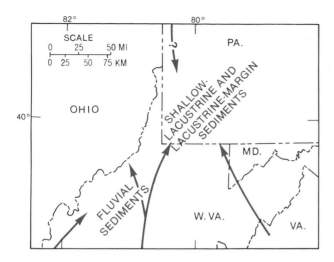

Figure 11–8. Regional paleogeography and depositional environments of the Dunkard Group. Arrows indicate sediment input trends (adapted from Berryhill, 1967, and Berryhill and others, 1971).

PROBLEMS AND FUTURE RESEARCH

Detailed stratigraphic correlations and studies of depositional environments of the Dunkard Group in Pennsylvania, especially above the Waynesburg Formation, are the most pressing needs. A large number of coal-company drill holes through the Dunkard exist and, if made available, would probably be the best source of data. Unquestionably, it would also be desirable to further clarify the biostratigraphy and resolve the position of the Pennsylvanian-Permian time boundary, but the problems are extremely complex and esoteric and, in many respects, reach far beyond the Dunkard itself.

RECOMMENDED FOR FURTHER READING

Arkle, Thomas, Jr., Lotz, C. W., Jr., Barlow, J. A., and others (1972), *I. C. White Memorial Symposium field trip*, West Virginia Geological and Economic Survey, 61 p.

Barlow, J. A., and Burkhammer, Susan, eds. (1975), *Proceedings of the First I. C. White Memorial Symposium [Morgantown, W. Va., 1972]—"The age of the Dunkard,"* West Virginia Geological and Economic Survey, 352 p.

Beerbower, J. R. (1961), *Origin of cyclothems of the Dunkard Group (Upper Pennsylvanian-Lower Permian) in Pennsylvania, West Virginia, and Ohio*, Geological Society of America Bulletin, v. 72, p. 1029–1050.

Berryhill, H. L., Jr. (1967), *Chapter A, Allegheny region*, in McKee, E. D., and others, *Paleotectonic investigations of the Permian System in the United States*, U.S. Geological Survey Professional Paper 515, p. 1–7.

Berryhill, H. L., Jr., Schweinfurth, S. P., and Kent, B. H. (1971), *Coal-bearing Upper Pennsylvanian and Lower Permian rocks, Washington area, Pennsylvania*, U.S. Geological Survey Professional Paper 621, 47 p.

Donaldson, A. C. (1974), *Pennsylvanian sedimentation of central Appalachians*, in Briggs, Garrett, ed., *Carboniferous of the southeastern United States*, Geological Society of America Special Paper 148, p. 47–78.

Fontaine, W. M., and White, I. C. (1880), *The Permian or Upper Carboniferous flora of West Virginia and S. W. Pennsylvania*, Pennsylvania Geological Survey, 2nd ser., Report PP, 143 p.

Martin, W. D., and Lorenz, D. M. (1972), *Lithofacies, paleocurrents, and environments of deposition of the Dunkard Group in Ohio, Pennsylvania, and West Virginia*, in *Pennsylvanian deltas in Ohio and northern West Virginia*, Appalachian Geological Society, p. 1–39.

ern outcrop limit in West Virginia and Ohio of the brackish-water brachiopod *Lingula* and orbiculoid brachiopods and gastropods. These fossils have been found in a thick parting in the Washington coal (Stauffer and Schroyer, 1920) and in the Elm Grove limestone a few feet above the Waynesburg coal (mentioned without citation in Cross, 1975).

The existing Dunkard Group appears to be an upper-delta-plain deposit. The portion in Pennsylvania was deposited in a relatively low energy lacustrine flood basin flanking the main fluvial input area to the south across central West Virginia (Berryhill, 1967; Berryhill and others, 1971; Donaldson, 1974). Depending upon the amount and size of clastic material diverted into the area, Dunkard depositional environments in southwestern Pennsylvania varied from lake deltas (complete with distributary sandstones and finer delta-margin clastics) to carbonate banks and peat swamps (Figure 11–8). Whether these periodic clastic diversions were purely autocyclic or had an ultimate allocyclic origin, such as climate change (Beerbower, 1961), is not clear.

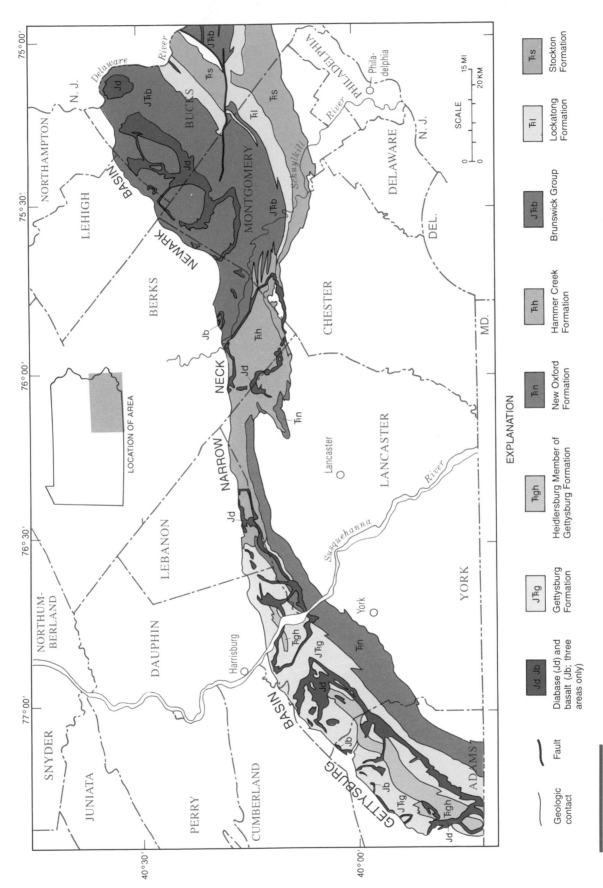

Distribution of Triassic and Jurassic rocks of the Newark and Gettysburg basins in Pennsylvania (modified from Berg and others, 1980). The major lithostratigraphic units are indicated.

EXPLANATION

Fault	Ẕs — Stockton Formation
Geologic contact	Ẕl — Lockatong Formation
	JẔb — Brunswick Group
	Ẕh — Hammer Creek Formation
	Ẕn — New Oxford Formation
Jd Jb — Diabase (Jd) and basalt (Jb; three areas only)	Ẕgh — Heidlersburg Member of Gettysburg Formation
	JẔg — Gettysburg Formation

SCALE

0   15 MI
0   20 KM

LOCATION OF AREA

CHAPTER 12   EARLY MESOZOIC

Lower Mesozoic sedimentary rocks occur within two half-graben basins that form a sinuous belt across southeastern Pennsylvania (see figure on facing page): the Newark basin, which extends eastward into New Jersey, and the Gettysburg basin, which extends southward into Maryland. The basins are part of a series of structural troughs in eastern North America (see Chapter 21) that formed during the continental rifting event that began during the Triassic Period and led to the opening of the Atlantic Ocean. The trend of the basins is subparallel to the dominant structural grain of the Appalachian orogen. The broad parts of the Newark and Gettysburg basins are joined by a constricted medial basin called the Narrow Neck (see figure on facing page). The strata in these basins are collectively referred to as the Newark Supergroup (Froelich and Olsen, 1985), which is composed of several thousand meters of nonmarine sedimentary rocks and basalt flows. A basal unconformity forms the southeastern edge of both basins, and strata generally dip toward the northwest margin, which is marked by normal faults (see Chapter 21). Although most of the sedimentary rocks are Upper Triassic, three small remnants of Lower Jurassic sedimentary rocks and basalt flows ("Jb" in figure on facing page) are preserved along the border faults of both basins in Pennsylvania. Lower Jurassic diabase sheets and dikes intrude the sedimentary rocks, which are thermally metamorphosed in aureoles of various widths.

—Joseph P. Smoot
A. J. Froelich
David Gottfried

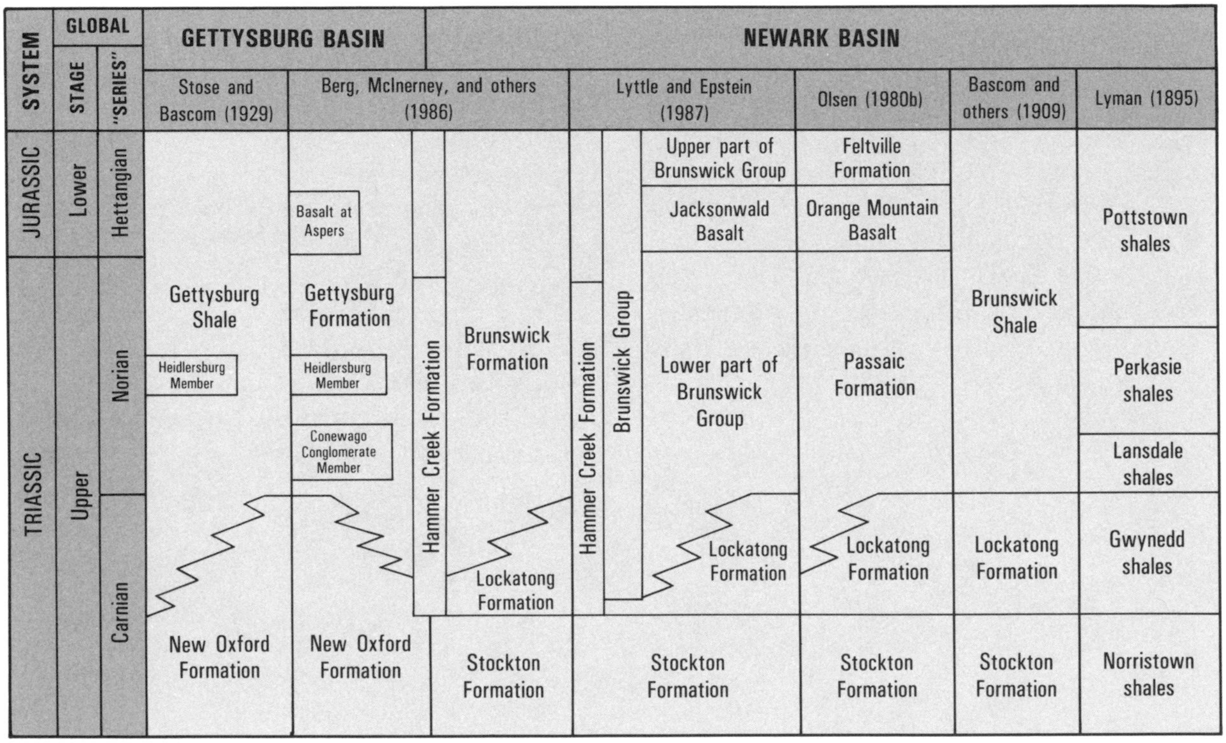

SYSTEM	GLOBAL STAGE	GLOBAL "SERIES"	GETTYSBURG BASIN – Stose and Bascom (1929)	GETTYSBURG BASIN – Berg, McInerney, and others (1986)	NEWARK BASIN – Lyttle and Epstein (1987)	NEWARK BASIN – Olsen (1980b)	NEWARK BASIN – Bascom and others (1909)	NEWARK BASIN – Lyman (1895)
JURASSIC	Lower	Hettangian		Basalt at Aspers	Upper part of Brunswick Group	Feltville Formation		Pottstown shales
					Jacksonwald Basalt	Orange Mountain Basalt		
TRIASSIC	Upper	Norian	Gettysburg Shale (Heidlersburg Member)	Gettysburg Formation (Heidlersburg Member) (Conewago Conglomerate Member)	Hammer Creek Formation / Brunswick Formation / Brunswick Group — Lower part of Brunswick Group	Passaic Formation	Brunswick Shale	Perkasie shales / Lansdale shales
		Carnian	New Oxford Formation	New Oxford Formation	Hammer Creek Formation / Lockatong Formation / Stockton Formation	Lockatong Formation / Stockton Formation	Lockatong Formation / Stockton Formation	Gwynedd shales / Norristown shales

Figure 12A–1. Correlation chart comparing nomenclature for stratigraphic units in the Newark and Gettysburg basins in Pennsylvania. The terminology used in this chapter is that of Lyttle and Epstein (1987) for the Newark basin and Berg, McInerney, and others (1986) for the Gettysburg basin. Historical relationships are from Luttrell (1989).

CHAPTER 12A   EARLY MESOZOIC— SEDIMENTARY ROCKS

JOSEPH P. SMOOT
U.S. Geological Survey
National Center, MS 926
Reston, VA 20192

INTRODUCTION

The sedimentary rocks of the Newark and Gettysburg basins consist of fluvial and lacustrine deposits exceeding 20,000 feet in thickness. The stratigraphic sequences in each basin are similar, but they are separated by distinctive coarse fluvial deposits in the narrow neck between the basins. The nomenclature for the Newark basin has changed several times, and the names used in Pennsylvania as of this writing differ from those used in New Jersey (Figure 12A-1). The stratigraphic names for the Gettysburg basin are nearly the same as those initially proposed by Stose and Bascom (1929). Glaeser (1963) introduced the Hammer Creek Formation for the rocks that lie in the narrow neck between the basins. Rocks in the Newark basin are generally better exposed than those of the Gettysburg basin and, consequently, are more completely described and better understood. The sedimentary rocks in both basins generally dip toward the border faults, except where they are deformed by intrusive diabase sheets and dikes or cut by faults (Figure 12A-2A, 2B). The lower part of the stratigraphic section in the Newark basin is partially repeated in three large fault blocks (Figure 12A-2A).

The sedimentary rocks, particularly black shales and gray siltstones, in both basins contain a rich assemblage of nonmarine fossils (Figure 12A-3), including plant remains, ostracodes, conchostracans, pelecypods, fish, aquatic reptiles, and tracks and trails of reptiles (Olsen, 1988). Root casts and burrows are locally abundant, and scattered remains of terrestrial reptiles have been reported. The rocks have been assigned a Late Triassic age, based largely on the macrofossil assemblage, but spores and pollen indicate an Early Jurassic age for sedimentary rocks immediately beneath and above the basalt flows (Cornet and Olsen, 1985).

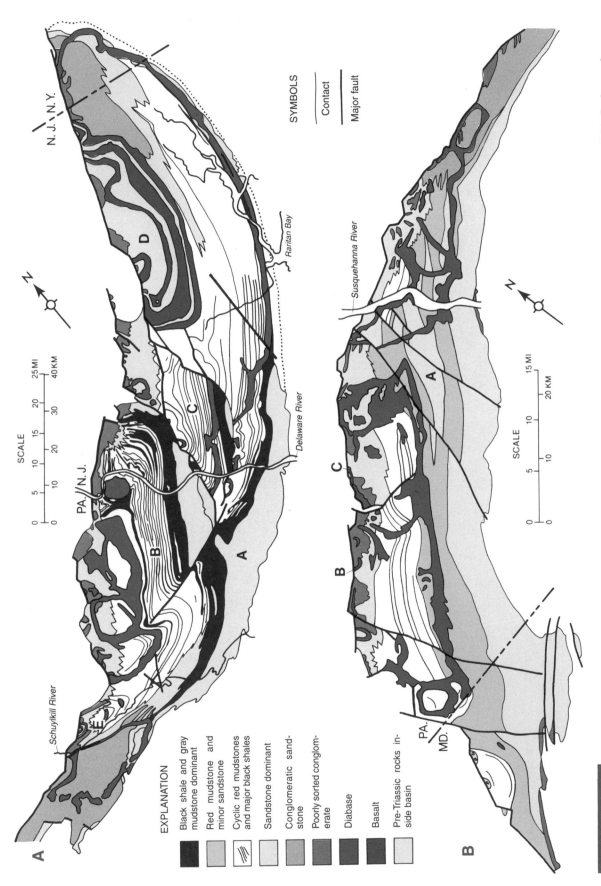

Figure 12A–2. A. Major lithologic units of the Newark basin in Pennsylvania and New Jersey (modified from Berg and others, 1980; Olsen, 1984; Parker and others, 1988; Ratcliffe, 1988; Olsen, P. E., and others, 1996, *High-resolution stratigraphy of the Newark rift basin (early Mesozoic, eastern North America)*, Geological Society of America Bulletin, v. 108, Figure 2, p. 42 [modified with permission of the publisher, the Geological Society of America, Boulder, Colorado USA; copyright © 1996 Geological Society of America]; and Smoot and others, in review). Structural provinces include the Montgomery-Chester fault block (A), Bucks-Hunterdon fault block (B), Sourland Mountain fault block (C), Watchung syncline (D), and Jacksonwald syncline, which includes the Jacksonwald Basalt near the border fault (E). Dotted lines along the southeastern margin denote the portion buried under coastal-plain deposits. B. Major lithologic units of the Gettysburg basin and preliminary distribution of black shale units (modified from Berg and others, 1980; reprinted with modifications from Root, S. I., *Structure and hydrocarbon potential of the Gettysburg basin, Pennsylvania and Maryland*, in Manspeizer, W., ed., *Triassic-Jurassic rifting—Continental breakup and the origin of the Atlantic Ocean and passive margins*, © 1988, Figure 14–1, p. 354, with permission of Elsevier Science; and modified from Smoot and Froelich, in review). Labeled units are the Conewago Conglomerate Member of the Gettysburg Formation (A), basalt at Aspers (B), and basalt east of Latimore (C).

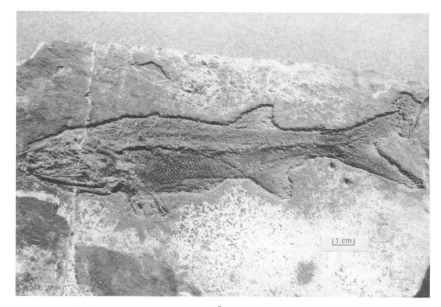

A

Figure 12A-3. A. *Turseodus* **sp. from the Lockatong Formation near Chalfont, Bucks County. B. Reptile footprint (*Rhynchosaurides hyperbates*) from the Lockatong Formation near Arcola, Montgomery County. Photographs courtesy of P. E. Olsen.**

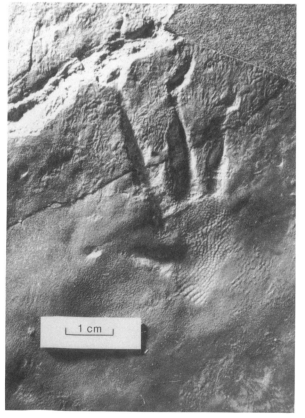

B

SEDIMENTOLOGY AND STRATIGRAPHY

The general lithologic characteristics and thicknesses of the major stratigraphic units in the Newark and Gettysburg basins are shown in Table 12A-1.

Although not strictly coeval, lithologic, stratigraphic, and sedimentological characteristics of the Stockton and New Oxford Formations are similar, so these two units will be discussed together. Relations are similar between the Brunswick Group and Gettysburg Formation, and they will also be considered together. Glaeser (1963) suggested that the Lockatong Formation and Heidlersburg Member are similar, but the Heidlersburg more closely resembles the portion of the Brunswick Group that includes the Graters and Perkasie Members. Therefore, the Lockatong Formation will be discussed separately, as will the Hammer Creek Formation.

Stockton and New Oxford Formations

The Stockton and New Oxford Formations, both mainly arkosic sandstone and siltstone (Table 12A-1), nearly merge across the Narrow Neck (see figure on p. 178). The provenance and crossbedding of both formations indicate northwesterly paleodrainages from Piedmont rocks to the southeast (Glaeser, 1966). Both formations thicken away from the Narrow Neck, and their overall grain size decreases up section. The Stockton is thicker and generally finer grained in the Bucks-Hunterdon fault block than in the Montgomery-Chester fault block.

Three major varieties of fluvial sandstone are present in the Stockton and New Oxford Formations: (1) Broad, thin sheets of pebbly sandstone containing trough and tabular foresets form irregularly spaced, fining-upward sequences 7 to 13 feet thick that alter-

Table 12A–1. *General Lithologic Descriptions of Newark Supergroup Stratigraphic Units in Pennsylvania*

NEWARK BASIN	NARROW NECK	GETTYSBURG BASIN
BRUNSWICK GROUP—Reddish-brown shale, silty mudstone, siltstone, and sandstone, commonly cyclic. Less abundant, cyclic, gray or black shale and red to gray siltstone and silty mudstone. Perkasie and Graters Members are each about 100 feet thick, and each contains several closely spaced, distinctive black shales. Lobate bodies of boulder-cobble conglomerate dominated by clasts of limestone, quartzite, shale, or metamorphic rocks occur adjacent to the border faults. Jacksonwald Basalt is about 500 feet thick, overlain by about 650 feet of sedimentary rock. Maximum thickness is estimated as 21,000 feet in the Jacksonwald syncline.	HAMMER CREEK FORMATION—Reddish-brown to buff, crossbedded sandstone, pebbly sandstone, and cobble conglomerate, and reddish-brown bioturbated siltstone. Pebbles are predominantly quartzite with some limestone clasts. Lenses of boulder to cobble conglomerate dominated by limestone clasts occur near the border fault. Maximum thickness is 9,100 feet.	GETTYSBURG FORMATION—Reddish-brown silty mudstone, siltstone, and sandstone, and less abundant, cyclic red, gray, or black shale and red to gray siltstone and silty mudstone, primarily in the Heidlersburg Member, which is about 4,700 feet thick. Lobate bodies of boulder-cobble conglomerate, dominated by clasts of limestone, quartzite, shale, and metamorphic rocks, occur adjacent to the border fault. About 200 feet of basalts at Aspers and east of Latimore are overlain by as much as 750 feet of sedimentary rocks. Crossbedded pebbly sandstone and conglomerate (including the 7,100-foot-thick Conewago Conglomerate Member) dominated by quartzite and, less commonly, limestone clasts, intertongue with sandstone and siltstone in the eastern part of the basin. Maximum thickness near Gettysburg is estimated to be 15,500 feet (Stose and Bascom, 1929) or 18,000 feet (Cornet, 1977).
LOCKATONG FORMATION—Cyclic gray siltstone, silty mudstone, and black shale interbedded with less abundant, cyclic red siltstone and silty mudstone and reddish-brown to buff sandstone. Very thin, fossiliferous laminated limestone and calcareous shale beds are common in the lower part. Maximum thickness is 3,800 feet along the Delaware River.		NEW OXFORD FORMATION—Gray to buff, crossbedded arkosic sandstone and pebbly sandstone, and reddish-brown arkosic sandstone, siltstone, and silty mudstone. Quartz-pebble conglomerate is common near the base, and thin beds of gray shale and limestone occur near the top. Unconformably beneath the quartz-pebble conglomerate, lenses as much as 800 feet thick consist of boulder-cobble conglomerate dominated by limestone clasts and interbeds of silty mudstone, gray shale, and limestone. Maximum thickness is about 6,800 feet near Gettysburg.
STOCKTON FORMATION—Gray to buff, crossbedded arkosic sandstone and pebbly sandstone, and reddish-brown arkosic sandstone, siltstone, and silty mudstone. Less abundant cobble conglomerate and gray siltstone. Maximum thickness is 6,000 feet.		

nate with similar thicknesses of bioturbated mudstone and siltstone (Figure 12A–4). These sequences are interpreted as braided-river deposits. (2) Regularly spaced lenses of coarse- to fine-grained, arkosic sandstone form fining-upward sequences 13 to 23 feet thick that grade into reddish-brown, bioturbated siltstone (Figure 12A–5). These sequences are interpreted as deposits of meandering or anastomosing streams. (3) Thin, inclined lenses of arkosic sandstone, commonly with carbonate-granule intraclasts, are interbedded with mudstone, forming uniformly spaced, fining-upward sequences 4 to 7 feet thick (Figure 12A–6). These sequences are interpreted as deposits of highly sinuous, muddy meandering streams. The first two varieties of fluvial sandstone form continuous ridges (McLaughlin, 1945), whereas the third

variety is commonly interbedded with thick sequences of bioturbated mudstone. Braided-river sandstones are most abundant near the base of the formations, and the others are more abundant up section. In the Newark basin, the braided-river pebbly sandstones are more abundant near the southeastern unconformable margin, apparently laterally equivalent to the lower ridge-forming meandering-river sandstones in the central part of the basin.

Poorly sorted, matrix-supported limestone conglomerates occur discontinuously at the base of the New Oxford Formation (see figure on p. 178, Figure 12A–2B, and Figure 16 in the color section). These deposits, the thicknesses of which vary considerably, occur where the basin overlies Paleozoic limestones (McLaughlin, 1960; Cloos and Pettijohn, 1973). The

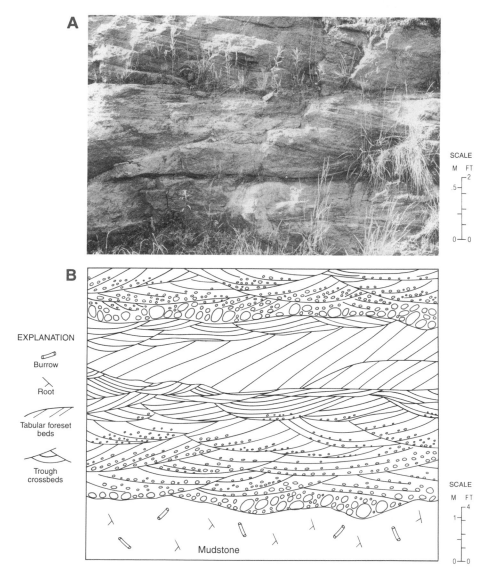

Figure 12A–4. A. Trough-crossbedded pebbly sandstone overlain by tabular foresets in the Stockton Formation exposed along the Pennsylvania Turnpike near Ambler, Montgomery County. The cut is perpendicular to the paleocurrent direction defined by the trough crossbeds. The lens cap is about 5 cm (2 in.) in diameter. **B.** Generalized sketch of typical fining-upward sequences in pebbly sandstones of the Stockton and New Oxford Formations. The base of the sequence consists of poorly sorted, grain-supported cobble conglomerate overlying an erosional surface. Trough crossbedding decreases in size upward and is interbedded with tabular foresets that may dip opposite to the trough crossbeds.

conglomerates have been interpreted as alluvial-fan deposits, and their irregular thicknesses have been attributed to deposition in local, fault-controlled subbasins (Manspeizer, 1981). Another interpretation (Smoot, 1991) is that they are local colluvial deposits, residuum, or karst breccias developed on the underlying Paleozoic limestones.

A few thin, black to gray siltstones containing ostracodes and conchostracans occur near the top of the Stockton Formation (Turner-Peterson, 1980), and fossiliferous black shales have been reported from near the base and near the top of the New Oxford Formation (Stose and Jonas, 1939; Cloos and Pettijohn, 1973). Not enough is known about the continuity and sedimentary characteristics of the shales to determine whether they were deposited in large lakes or in local ponds. Deltaic deposits have also been re-ported near the tops of both formations (Cornet, 1977; Turner-Peterson and Smoot, 1985).

Lockatong Formation

The Lockatong Formation differs from the Brunswick Group and Gettysburg Formation by the abundance of thick, finely laminated, fossiliferous black shales, particularly in the lower part. The Lockatong grades laterally into red beds of the Brunswick Group to the southwest, and thins markedly to the northeast in New Jersey and New York, where it intertongues with Stockton lithologies (Parker and others, 1988) (see figure on p. 178 and Figure 12A–2A). Where the Lockatong is adjacent to the border fault, the siltstone and shale grade into sandstone and conglomerate that are assigned to the Brunswick Group.

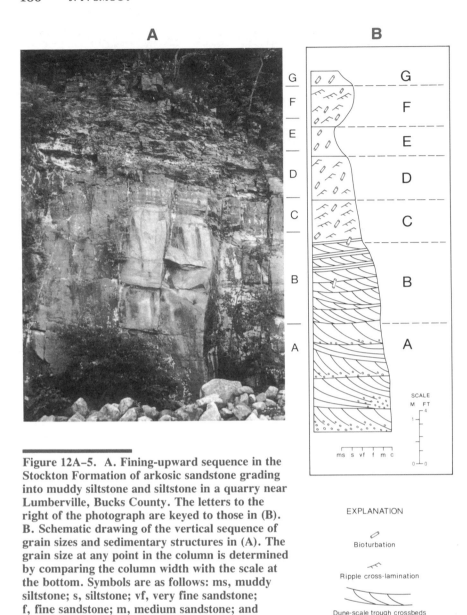

Figure 12A–5. A. Fining-upward sequence in the Stockton Formation of arkosic sandstone grading into muddy siltstone and siltstone in a quarry near Lumberville, Bucks County. The letters to the right of the photograph are keyed to those in (B). **B.** Schematic drawing of the vertical sequence of grain sizes and sedimentary structures in (A). The grain size at any point in the column is determined by comparing the column width with the scale at the bottom. Symbols are as follows: ms, muddy siltstone; s, siltstone; vf, very fine sandstone; f, fine sandstone; m, medium sandstone; and c, coarse sandstone.

EXPLANATION

Bioturbation

Ripple cross-lamination

Dune-scale trough crossbeds

The Lockatong typically consists of 7- to 23-foot-thick cyclic repetitions of black to gray shale grading up into massive gray silty mudstone (Figure 12A–7), called Van Houten cycles (Olsen, 1985a). Van Houten (1964) first recognized the cyclic nature of these deposits, which he divided into chemical and detrital cycles. These cycles are distinguished by their thickness, the amount of sandy material, and the presence of dolomite and analcime. Laminated black shales (Figure 12A–8A), commonly calcareous and often traceable for many miles, are interpreted as the deposits of deep lakes that covered most of the basin floor (Olsen, 1980a). Massive silty mudstones at the tops of cycles (Figure 12A–8B) indicate deposition under conditions ranging from shallow lakes to playa mud-flats (Smoot and Olsen, 1988; Smoot, 1991). Analcime, dolomite, and pseudomorphs after evaporite minerals occur within the Lockatong Van Houten cycles, particularly in the upper part, and have been used as evidence of arid alkaline lake conditions (Van Houten, 1965b). The predominance of thick, fossiliferous, black shales in the lower part of the cycles suggests an earlier, less arid climate, but also reflects an initially narrow half-graben basin (Schlische and Olsen, 1990). Van Houten cycles are believed to indicate the repeated rise and fall of lake level in closed-basin conditions (Smoot, 1985) in response to climatic change (Olsen, 1986). Sandstones within the Lockatong are mostly wave-formed and deltaic shoreline deposits near the tops of Van Houten cycles where they are near the border fault, or where the Lockatong grades into the Brunswick Group in the southwestern part of the basin.

Brunswick Group and Gettysburg Formation

Despite their lithologic heterogeneity (Table 12A–1), the Brunswick Group and the upper half of the Gettysburg Formation are notably similar. Both formations intertongue with the Hammer Creek Formation in the narrow neck between the basins, and both have Jurassic basalt flows near their tops (see figure on p. 178 and Figure 12A–2). The Brunswick Group gradationally overlies the Lockatong Formation, the contact having been arbitrarily placed where

A

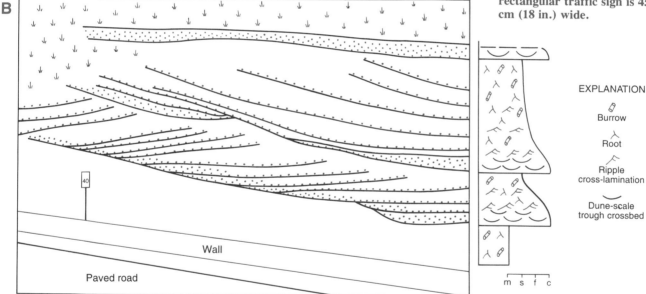

B

EXPLANATION

⬚ Burrow

⅄ Root

ⵉ Ripple cross-lamination

⌣ Dune-scale trough crossbed

m s f c

Figure 12A–6. A. Inclined beds of sandstone alternating with silty mudstone forming fining-upward sequences in the lower part of the Gettysburg Formation in a roadcut near Conewago Heights, York County. Similar fluvial deposits occur within the New Oxford and Stockton Formations. B. Sketch of (A) showing the distribution of sandstone (stippled) and silty mudstone (white) layers. The column to the right of the drawing shows the vertical distribution of grain size and sedimentary structures. Symbols are as follows: m, mudstone; s, siltstone; f, fine sandstone; and c, coarse sandstone. The rectangular traffic sign is 45 cm (18 in.) wide.

red mudstones predominate over gray. The Brunswick Group is also, in part, laterally equivalent to the Lockatong. The Gettysburg Formation gradationally overlies the New Oxford Formation.

The Brunswick Group is mostly composed of red and gray silty mudstones and shales forming Van Houten cycles (Figure 12A–7) similar to those of the Lockatong Formation, but with black shales thinner and less common. Cycles in the lowermost part of the Brunswick Group, including the Graters and Perkasie Members, contain thick black shales that are distinc-

tive and traceable across the length of the Newark basin (Olsen, 1985a). These laminated black shales are characteristically pyritic, lack lacustrine fossils, and contain evaporite pseudomorphs in their upper parts, reflecting elevated salinities (Smoot and Olsen, 1994). The Heidlersburg Member of the Gettysburg Formation also contains traceable black shales in Van Houten cycles similar to those in the lowermost part of the Brunswick Group. The black shales are thinner and less abundant upward in the Brunswick Group and Gettysburg Formation up to the basalts. Massive

A

SCALE

M   FT

8 — 30

— 20

4 — 10

0 — 0

Figure 12A–7. A. Cyclic black shales and gray massive mudstones in the Lockatong Formation in a quarry near Tradesville, Montgomery County. B. Two partial Van Houten cycles in the Perkasie Member of the Brunswick Group in a quarry at Ottsville, Bucks County. C. Sketch showing the sequence of sedimentary structures and the Van Houten cycle divisions (as defined by Olsen, 1985a) in (B). Symbols are as follows: l, laminated; t, thin bedded; and m, massive.

B

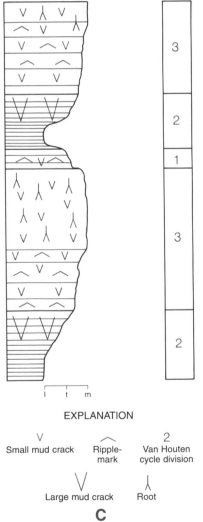

l   t   m

EXPLANATION

∨   ⌒   2
Small mud crack   Ripple-mark   Van Houten cycle division

∨   ⋏
Large mud crack   Root

C

Figure 12A–8. A. Laminated, calcareous black shale, rich in organic matter. The sample is
from the Lockatong Formation near Tradesville, Montgomery County. This was probably
deposited in a deep, stratified lake. Soft-sediment deformation of laminae at the base of the
sample is possibly due to earthquake-induced liquefaction (P. E. Olsen, oral communication).
B. Plan view of two rock surfaces representing the contact between thin-bedded mudstone,
brecciated by numerous mud cracks (light-colored area in lower right corner), overlain by
intensely mud-cracked massive mudstone (crumb fabric). White dots are cement-filled vugs
interpreted as vesicles. This rock type is interpreted as having formed on a playa mudflat. The
sample is from the Lockatong Formation along Pa. Route 32 north of Point Pleasant, Bucks
County. The coin is 1.8 cm (0.7 in.) in diameter. **C.** Plan view of massive mudstone with abundant cement-filled root structures (white). Dark spots are cavities formed by weathering of
carbonate cements and nodules. The sample is from the lower part of the Brunswick Group in
Bucks County.

silty mudstones at the top of Van Houten cycles in the lowermost part of the Brunswick Group are dominated by playa fabrics similar to those in the uppermost part of the Lockatong Formation (Figure 12A–8B). Root structures (Figure 12A–8C) become more important upward within the Brunswick Group, and playa fabrics are absent in the uppermost part. Playa fabrics and root structures are present in the lower part of the Heidlersburg Member, and, as in the Brunswick, root structures dominate in the upper part of the Gettysburg Formation. Pseudomorphs after evaporite minerals (Figure 12A–9) include distributions indicative of saline lakes, saline mudflats, and saline soils (Smoot, 1991; Smoot and Olsen, 1994).

From about 50 m (164 ft) below the Heidlersburg Member, the Gettysburg Formation consists mostly of red silty mudstone, siltstone, and sandstone, forming fluvial, fining-upward sequences similar to the finest grained variety of the New Oxford and Stockton Formations (Figure 12A–6), but with much more silty mudstone that is disrupted by root structures and polygonal, slickensided soil features. The fluvial beds intertongue with sandstone and conglomerate of the Conewago Conglomerate Member and with the Hammer Creek Formation. Similar fluvial deposits also intertongue with the cyclic lacustrine deposits of the Lockatong Formation, Brunswick Group, and Gettysburg Formation. Deltaic sandstone deposits (Figure 12A–10) are common where the fluvial and lacustrine deposits intertongue. Near the border faults of the Newark and Gettysburg basins, Van Houten cycles intertongue with sheetlike, thin-bedded sandstones that have ripple cross-lamination (Figure 12A–11), or that are poorly sorted and overlie irregular scour bases. These sandstones are interpreted as deltaic sheets and sheetflood deposits, respectively. Adjacent to the border fault, these sandstones intertongue with poorly sorted, commonly lobate conglomerate units containing clasts composed of Paleozoic limestone, quartzite, and shale, reflecting a local, northern provenance. Sedimentary features in the border conglomerates suggest deposition by debris flows (Figure 12A–12) and by shallow, flash-flooding streams. These features, and their restriction to the basin margin, indicate deposition as alluvial fans (Arguden and Rodolfo, 1986). Their lobate shape probably reflects later folding (Ratcliffe and others, 1986) rather than their depositional geometry. The sedimentary features of these conglomerates and their intercalation with lacustrine deposits near the border fault indicate that they were deposited as broad fans with low slopes, suggesting that fan apices were outside the present basin (Smoot, 1991).

Jurassic strata of the Brunswick Group overlying the Jacksonwald Basalt and of the Gettysburg Formation overlying the basalts at Aspers and east of Latimore include well-sorted, cross-stratified arkosic sandstone; fossiliferous, laminated, gray to black shale and limestone; ripple-cross-laminated siltstone; and poorly sorted boulder conglomerates. These strata are similar to the Feltville Formation of Olsen (1980b) in New Jersey, but different from the lower part of the Brunswick Group. Some sandstones above the basalts have sedimentary structures indicative of deposition

Figure 12A–9. Muddy siltstone containing abundant elongate crystal molds (black) partially filled with calcite cement (white) from the lower part of the Brunswick Group near Uhlerstown, Bucks County. Crystal molds are interpreted as former evaporites, possibly glauberite or gypsum. The mottled texture of the sediment is due to abundant root structures.

A

B

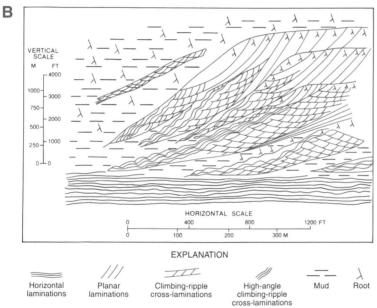

Figure 12A–10. A. Stacked large-scale planar foresets (oriented perpendicular to flow) in sandstone at the top of a coarsening-upward sequence in the lower part of the Brunswick Group in a quarry north of Norristown, Montgomery County. Each foreset bed contains planar lamination that grades downdip to ripple cross-lamination with shale partings. The locality is on strike with the Lockatong Formation. The man seated in front of the outcrop in the center of the photograph gives scale. B. Reconstruction of stacked delta foresets forming large-scale coarsening-upward sequences, based on observations of deltas in modern closed-basin lakes. The base of the sequence is a laminated to thin-bedded lacustrine silt; sand foresets contain planar lamination in the proximal portions and climbing ripple cross-lamination in the distal parts. The delta is encased in root-disrupted mud from shallow-lake and fluvial conditions.

by large rivers, whereas others have structures indicative of deltaic deposition.

Hammer Creek Formation

Thick tongues of quartzose, pebbly sandstone of the Hammer Creek Formation extend eastward, in the Newark basin, into the lowermost part of the Brunswick Group, including that equivalent to the Lockatong Formation, and extend westward into the Gettysburg Formation in the Gettysburg basin (see figure on p. 178 and Figure 12A–2). The Conewago Conglomerate Member is a tongue of the Hammer Creek Formation that is equivalent to the lower fluvial portion of the Gettysburg Formation. Hammer Creek clasts are predominantly Paleozoic quartzites and limestones, indicating a northern source (McLaughlin and Gerhard, 1953; Glaeser, 1966). Scattered paleocurrent data from crossbedding indicate an east-southeast flow for the Hammer Creek in the eastern part of the Narrow Neck and in the Newark basin, and a west-southwest flow for the Hammer Creek in the western part of the Narrow Neck and in the Gettysburg basin.

The Hammer Creek typically consists of poorly defined fining-upward sequences of crossbedded cobble to pebble conglomerate and coarse sandstone (Figure 12A–13), 7 to 30 feet thick, separated by locally thick sequences of reddish-brown, bioturbated silt-

VERTICAL SCALE
M   FT
3 —┬ 10
2 —┤
1 —┤— 5
0 —┴ 0

A

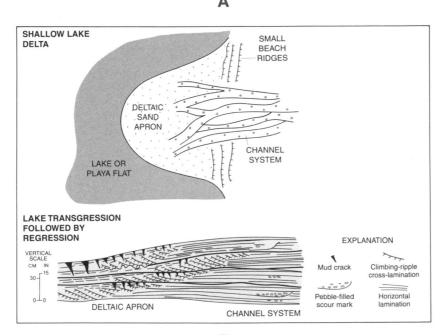

SHALLOW LAKE DELTA

SMALL BEACH RIDGES

DELTAIC SAND APRON

LAKE OR PLAYA FLAT

CHANNEL SYSTEM

LAKE TRANSGRESSION FOLLOWED BY REGRESSION

VERTICAL SCALE
CM   IN
30 —┬ 15
0 —┴ 0

EXPLANATION

Mud crack   Climbing-ripple cross-lamination

Pebble-filled scour mark   Horizontal lamination

DELTAIC APRON   CHANNEL SYSTEM

B

Figure 12A–11. A. Sheet sandstones (tabular bedding below the grassy slope) interbedded with massive silty mudstone in the lower part of the Brunswick Group in a quarry north of Kintnersville, Bucks County. Sandstone beds are 1 to 15 cm (0.2 to 6 in.) thick and contain climbing-ripple cross-lamination and mudstone partings disrupted by mud cracks. B. Schematic plan view and cross section of deltaic sheet sands in modern playa flats. A sheet of climbing-ripple cross-laminated sand (deltaic apron) with a mud drape is formed as a shallow lake transgresses over shallow braided streams during flooding. Following each flood, the lake recedes due to evaporation and seepage, and desiccation cracks develop. Deltaic aprons extend from a few tens of meters to a kilometer (0.6 mi) or more into the basin, and overlapping sheets may extend tens of kilometers parallel to the playa margin.

stone and fine-grained sandstone. McLaughlin (1957) interpreted the Hammer Creek conglomerates as the deposits of large alluvial fans. The thickness of fining-upward sequences and the presence of trough cross-beds up to 2 feet thick indicate deposition by braided rivers that could have been as much as 30 feet deep. The conglomerates and coarse sandstones deposited by these rivers are laterally equivalent to and intertongue with deltaic sandstones in the lowermost part

of the Brunswick Group and in the upper part of the Gettysburg Formation.

DIAGENESIS

The mineralogies and textures of sedimentary rocks in the Newark and Gettysburg basins suggest complicated diagenetic histories. Preliminary studies of diagenesis in the Newark Supergroup indicate

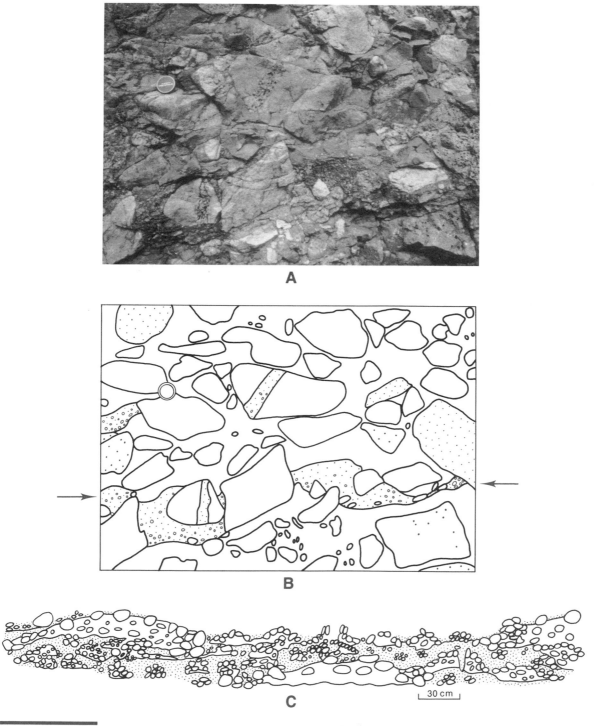

Figure 12A–12. A. Poorly sorted, matrix-supported boulder conglomerate, lower part of the Brunswick Group exposed in a railroad cut south of Reading, Berks County. Clasts are limestone and dolomite in a red, muddy matrix. An irregular layer of pebbly granule sandstone separates two debris-flow deposits. The lens cap is about 5 cm (2 in.) in diameter. B. Sketch of (A) with arrows marking the sandstone layer separating the debris flows. C. Schematic drawing of debris-flow and stream deposits from modern alluvial fans, similar to those in the Brunswick Group and Gettysburg Formation. Muddy matrix is white, and pebbly sands are stippled. Note the concentration of large clasts on the outer margins of debris flows and the isolated pods of boulders created by erosion of the muddy matrix.

Figure 12A–13. Trough crossbedded, coarse, pebbly sandstone near the base of a fining-upward sequence, Hammer Creek Formation along Wyomissing Creek south of Mohnton, Berks County. Foresets are about 40 cm (16 in.) thick and have a flow direction to the right and out of the picture. Cobbles and pebbles are mostly moderately rounded quartzite. The lens cap is about 5 cm (2 in.) in diameter.

very similar parageneses for mineralization in the Newark, Gettysburg, and Culpeper basins, particularly in the time-equivalent lacustrine intervals. The rocks have also been affected by intrusion of diabase (see Chapter 12B). No systematic studies of diagenesis in the Newark Supergroup of Pennsylvania have been made, so the timing and nature of mineral emplacement are poorly understood.

The most striking diagenetic feature of the early Mesozoic rocks is their nearly ubiquitous red color. The hematite that produces the red color is thought to reflect oxidizing conditions in the depositional environment or in the environment that existed shortly after deposition (see Hubert and others, 1978). Black and gray shaly mudstones contain organic matter, suggesting mostly reducing conditions. Mudstones beneath black shales are gray but contain desiccation features, root structures, and tracks, similar to the red strata, that indicate subaerial conditions. The sediments were apparently inundated with reducing fluids from the overlying lake that either prevented their oxidation or reduced limonitic oxides that later would have been converted to hematite.

Albite, quartz, and minor potassium feldspar occur as cements in sandstones and conglomerates of the Stockton and Hammer Creek Formations and Brunswick Group, primarily as syntaxial overgrowths (Oshchudlak and Hubert, 1988). Ferroan dolomite etched grains and replaced them in these coarse-grained deposits, and many dolomite layers within the mudstones of the Lockatong Formation and Brunswick Group are actually replaced silty beds (Figure 12A–14). Calcite and quartz cements are common in the border conglomerates of the Brunswick Group, Lockatong Formation, and Gettysburg Formation. Within the mudstones of the Lockatong Formation and the lower part of the Brunswick Group, there is a zonation of authigenic minerals that fill primary porosity (Smoot and Simonson, 1994). The Lockatong and the lowermost part of the Brunswick (up to unit D of McLaughlin, 1945) have analcime (Figure 12A–15) that is commonly overlain by, and partially replaced by, potassium feldspar. Both of these minerals are partially replaced by ferroan and nonferroan dolomite and calcite, which also fills the remaining pore space. The Brunswick Group overlying unit D to about one half the thickness below the Jacksonwald Basalt (to unit CC of Olsen and others, 1996) has a similar authigenic mineral assemblage, but there is no analcime and the earliest mineral is albite. The remainder of the Brunswick Group mudstones below the Jacksonwald Basalt has abundant calcite, nonferroan dolomite, and gypsum (or anhydrite) cements, which are partially replaced by albite and only minor potassium feldspar. The Brunswick Group mudstones and sandstones overlying the Jacksonwald Basalt have calcite as the primary authigenic mineral. In metamorphic aureoles near diabase intrusives, albite replaces grains and cements in sandstones and mudstones of the Stockton and Lockatong Formations and Brunswick Group (Van Houten, 1965a, 1971; Ratcliffe and Burton, 1988). The authigenic mineral assemblages of the Gettysburg

A

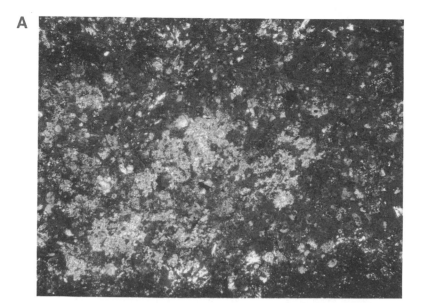

B

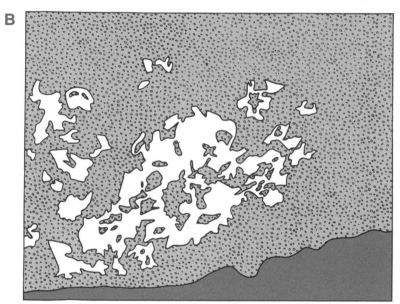

**Figure 12A–14. A. Photomicro-
graph of a single, large dolomite
crystal poikilitically encasing and
replacing a siliciclastic silt layer in a
mudstone. The sample is from an
outcrop of the Lockatong Formation along the Delaware River north
of Lumberville, Bucks County. The
siltstone layer resembles a dolomite
bed in outcrop. The field of view is
3 mm wide; partially crossed
nicols. B. Sketch of (A) showing
mudstone (color), siltstone (coarse
stipple on colored background), and
dolomite crystal (white).**

basin mirror those of the Newark basin, except that
there are no analcime-rich mudstones. In both basins,
the authigenic minerals are independent of depositional environments and have no geographic variability.
Furthermore, the potassium feldspar in the mudstones
of both basins provide similar ages of about 196 Ma,
independent of stratigraphic position (Kunk and others,
1995). This age is equivalent to that of the diabase intrusives. These observations suggest that the authigenic
minerals were not synsedimentary precipitates (Smoot
and Horowitz, 1988; Smoot and Simonson, 1994),
as had been generally assumed (Van Houten, 1964,
1965a).

DEPOSITIONAL ENVIRONMENTS

Most recent interpretations of depositional environments of the Newark and Gettysburg basins are
based on models after modern arid rift-valley basins
(for instance, Turner-Peterson, 1980), where the present border fault was the active fault margin of the basin and the present unconformable margin was the
other side. The Newark basin has received more attention in this respect than the Gettysburg basin, largely
due to its more complete sections and better exposure.
The depositional environments of the Newark basin
have been reconstructed showing formations as time-

Figure 12A–15. A. Photomicrograph of cement-filled vugs in massive mudstone with playa fabric. The sample is from an outcrop of the Lockatong Formation along the Delaware River north of Lumberville, Bucks County. The field of view is 3 mm wide; partially crossed nicols. B. Sketch of (A) showing mudstone (color), analcime cement (gray) filling vugs, and ferroan dolomite crystals (white) replacing the analcime along the vug margins.

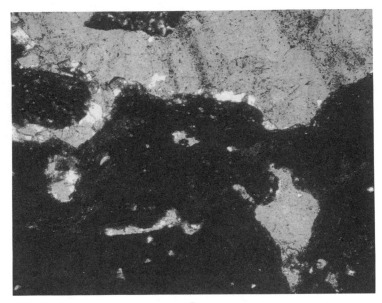

A

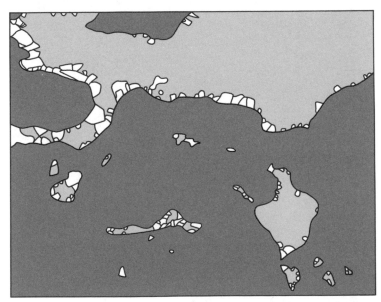

B

equivalent units (Figure 12A–16). The continuity of distinctive black shales of the Lockatong Formation and Brunswick Group in different fault blocks (see figure on p. 178 and Figure 12A–2A), and the consistent age differences indicated by spores and pollen (Cornet, 1977), however, dictate that intertonguing of stratigraphic units is limited. Furthermore, although long-term stability of depositional facies is implied by this interpretation, and although approximately 26,000 feet of sediment accumulated over a period of about 25 million years, radical changes in depositional facies occur vertically on the scale of several feet. The tectonic setting, paleolatitude, and variable facies assemblages indicate a depositional environment prone to changes.

A generally arid climate during deposition in the basins has been proposed, based upon the presence of red beds, evaporite pseudomorphs, alkaline minerals, and caliche, but some of these features may be diagenetic. Smoot and Olsen (1988) noted that depositional indicators of aridity appear to be stratigraphically restricted. Rock types indicative of arid conditions appear to be correlative between basins, which suggests long-term variations in early Mesozoic paleoclimate. These changes coincide with climatic changes postulated on variations in the palynoflora (Cornet, 1977) and are consistent with the early Mesozoic paleolatitude of the basins being near the border between subtropical and arid climate belts (Robinson, 1973). Each Van Houten cycle is interpreted to have resulted from climatic fluctuation in response to rhythmic astronomical influences (Olsen, 1986), such as

Milankovitch cycles. Lacustrine shales at the base of a cycle indicate higher inflow into the basins, and silty mudstones at the top of the cycles reflect drier conditions and lower inflow rates. Thus, paleoclimate was probably highly variable during deposition in the basins and should be considered an important control in deposition of the various facies. Some large-scale variations in fabrics, attributed to climatic fluctuations by Smoot and Olsen (1988), could have resulted from progressive broadening of the basin flood due to sediment infilling, from geographic variability

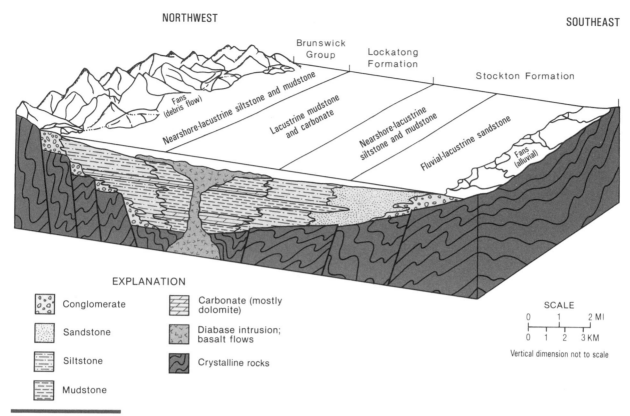

NORTHWEST

SOUTHEAST

Brunswick
Group

Lockatong
Formation

Stockton Formation

Fans
(debris flow)

Nearshore-lacustrine siltstone and mudstone

Lacustrine mudstone
and carbonate

Nearshore-lacustrine
siltstone and mudstone

Fluvial-lacustrine sandstone

Fans
(alluvial)

EXPLANATION

Conglomerate

Sandstone

Siltstone

Mudstone

Carbonate (mostly
dolomite)

Diabase intrusion;
basalt flows

Crystalline rocks

SCALE

0   1   2 MI

0   1   2   3 KM

Vertical dimension not to scale

Figure 12A–16. Generalized sketch of the distribution of sedimentary units in the Newark basin during deposition, assuming that formations are laterally equivalent facies (modified from Turner-Peterson, 1980). This model, based on observations within the Bucks-Hunterdon fault block (Figure 12A–2A), does not adequately explain the distribution of the Stockton Formation or the thin informal members of the Lockatong Formation and the lower part of the Brunswick Group in other fault blocks.

of the facies, and from changes in the subsidence rate (Olsen and Schlische, 1988).

A model for sequential change in depositional conditions of the Newark and Gettysburg basins is presented in Figure 12A–17. This model reflects the interplay of climatic and tectonic influences on sedimentation through various periods of the development of the basins. Other equally plausible interpretations are possible, based on the existing data.

During deposition of the Stockton Formation (Figure 12A–17A), rivers were probably through-flowing, as suggested by the hydrologic constraints of Smoot (1985) and the sparse paleocurrent data. Stockton sandstones and siltstones grade into border conglomerates, but these appear to be restricted to strata that intertongue with the Lockatong Formation (see figure on p. 178 and Figure 12A–2A). This interpretation for the New Oxford is more speculative because outcrop is restricted to the southeastern margin of the basin. The great thickness of the Stockton and New Oxford

Formations indicates basin subsidence during deposition. The evident basinward decrease of stream gradient in the Stockton and possible intermittent lacustrine conditions in the Stockton and New Oxford suggest restricted drainages, perhaps reflecting uplift along the northeast border fault. Black shales at the top of the New Oxford Formation could be time equivalent to the Lockatong (Cornet, 1977), as fluvio-deltaic equivalents of Lockatong-like deposits buried downdip, suggesting closed-basin conditions, or as lacustrine deposits on the New Oxford fluvial floodplain.

During deposition of the Lockatong Formation (Figure 12A–17B), the Newark basin was closed, as indicated by the cyclic lacustrine deposits and the intertonguing of strata equivalent to the Lockatong with alluvial-fan conglomerates derived from the northwest. Therefore, the abrupt transition from Stockton to Lockatong facies is better explained by tectonic rather than climatic changes. The basin closure at the initiation of Lockatong deposition could have been

A

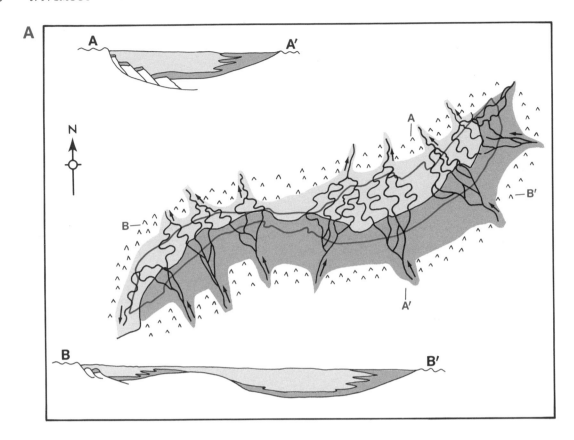

B

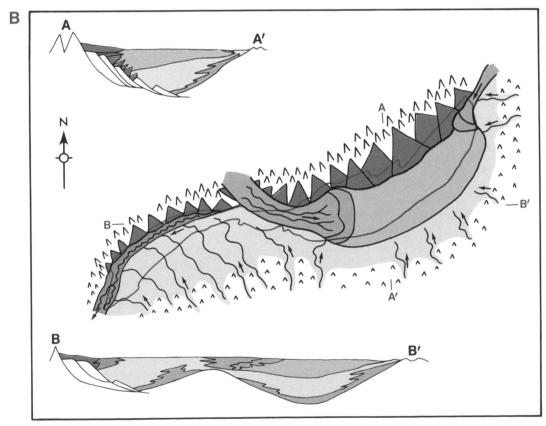

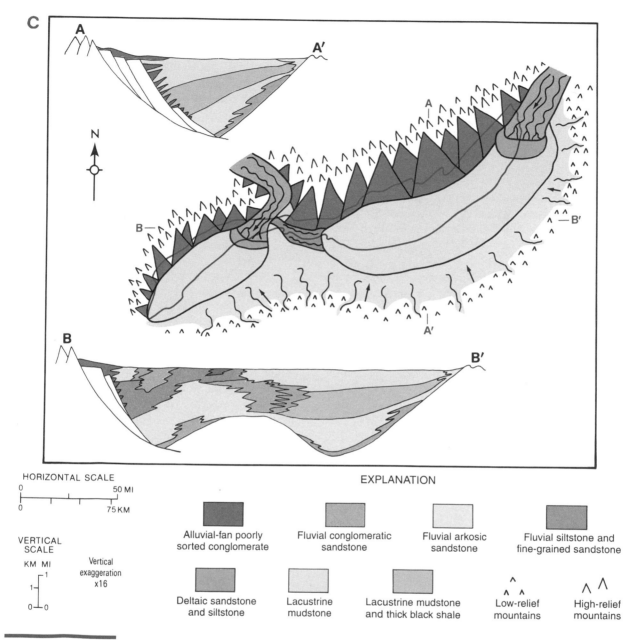

HORIZONTAL SCALE

0 ————————— 50 MI

0 ————————— 75 KM

VERTICAL
SCALE

KM MI

Vertical
exaggeration
x16

1 — 1

0 — 0

EXPLANATION

Alluvial-fan poorly
sorted conglomerate

Fluvial conglomeratic
sandstone

Fluvial arkosic
sandstone

Fluvial siltstone and
fine-grained sandstone

Deltaic sandstone
and siltstone

Lacustrine
mudstone

Lacustrine mudstone
and thick black shale

Low-relief
mountains

High-relief
mountains

Figure 12A–17. Reconstruction of the distribution of depositional facies during different periods of sedimentation in the Newark and Gettysburg basins. The present outlines of the basins are shown in color. Cross sections A–A´ and B–B´ illustrate three-dimensional facies relationships but do not model structural features within the basins. A. Stockton-lower New Oxford time: Fluvial systems from the southeast drain through the basins to the northwest. B. Lockatong-upper New Oxford time: Lacustrine mudstones in the Newark basin are cyclic, indicating a rise and fall of lake levels in a closed drainage system in which lakes are fed by axial river systems. All deposits thicken dramatically toward the faulted margin due to synsedimentary subsidence. Broad, low-angle alluvial fans with pedimentlike apices develop on faulted and uplifted terrain northwest of the basins. The Gettysburg basin still has open drainage, but it now has an axial component. C. Lower Brunswick-Heidlersburg time: The western axial river system switches from the Newark basin to the Gettysburg basin, and an eastern axial river builds out into the Newark basin. Lacustrine mudstones in the Gettysburg basin are cyclic, indicating the development of a closed drainage system.

caused by increased uplift along faults bordering the basin or by gradual broadening of the basin floor so that sediment infilling no longer kept up with subsidence (Olsen and Schlische, 1988). There is no evidence of large rivers extending across the basin during the many Lockatong subaerial episodes. This suggests that river inflow from the south ceased during Lockatong time, or that channel systems were drowned by expanding Lockatong lakes during floods, restricting fluvial deposits to an area south of the present basin margin (see Smoot, 1985). An arid climate during upper Lockatong deposition (Smoot and Olsen, 1988) could have caused the southern rivers to dry up while intermittent floods from the northern highlands allowed lakes to form between periods of playa conditions.

The Hammer Creek Formation and similar pebbly sandstones in the Gettysburg Formation represent major axial river systems that entered the basins near the Narrow Neck. The rivers initiated from the north and postdate the southern fluvial systems of the Stockton and New Oxford Formations. Tongues of Hammer Creek pebbly sandstone in the Newark basin grade into finer grained fluvial and deltaic deposits of the lower part of the Brunswick Group that intertongue with Lockatong lacustrine deposits (see figure on p. 178 and Figure 12A-2A). This suggests that drainages having a northern provenance became important when conditions changed from predominantly fluvial to lacustrine in the basin center (Figure 12A-17B). In the Gettysburg basin, however, black shales near the top of the New Oxford Formation, which are presumably equivalent to the Lockatong, are associated with sandstones having a southern provenance. This suggests that the shift in drainage patterns from a predominantly southern to a northern provenance occurred later in the Gettysburg basin than in the Newark basin.

During deposition of the lower part of the Brunswick Group and the Gettysburg Formation (Figure 12A-17C), arid conditions prevailed, although periods of wetter conditions increased in frequency toward the end of the Norian Age (Smoot and Olsen, 1988). Thick tongues of Hammer Creek pebbly sandstone are absent from the upper half of the lower part of the Brunswick Group, suggesting that the northwestern river system no longer entered the Newark basin. Pebbly sandstones restricted to the Narrow Neck (Figure 12A-2A) appear to be structurally uplifted and could be equivalents to Hammer Creek tongues near the base of the Brunswick Group. Hammer Creek pebbly sandstones in the Narrow Neck are also equivalent to the Gettysburg Formation. Pebbly sandstones

having provenance and sedimentary structures similar to those of the Hammer Creek occur in the Gettysburg Formation from near its base upward to levels equivalent to the Heidlersburg Member and higher (Figure 12A-2B). These relationships could reflect the shift from major river inflow into the Newark basin to inflow into the Gettysburg basin (Figure 12A-17C), perhaps by stream capture resulting from fault activity in the highlands. The Gettysburg basin may have been an open axial drainage system during deposition of the lower part of the Gettysburg Formation, as coarse fluvial deposits apparently grade westward into fine-grained fluvial deposits across the length of the basin. During Heidlersburg deposition, however, the basin was probably closed, as indicated by its cyclic lacustrine deposits.

The basalt flows in the Gettysburg and Newark basins are probably synchronous and equivalent to the Orange Mountain Basalt in New Jersey (Cornet, 1977; Olsen, 1980b). During deposition of the deposits overlying the basalt, deep, organic-rich lakes and large deltaic complexes were common, and playa conditions were absent. This suggests a climatic change to wetter conditions (Smoot and Olsen, 1988; Smoot, 1991). The return to deeper lakes may also be due to a narrowing and deepening of the basin resulting from an increase in tectonic activity (Schlische and Olsen, 1990). Deltaic deposits may also have extended further onto the basin floor during lowstands due to higher river discharge into a smaller basin.

PROBLEMS AND FUTURE RESEARCH

Most unresolved problems in the Triassic and Jurassic sedimentary rocks of Pennsylvania result from the paucity of outcrop and the lack of three-dimensional control due to homoclinal dip toward the border faults. The lateral and downdip relationships of depositional facies must be determined before questions concerning tectonic or climatic controls can be resolved. Some of these problems can be solved by careful mapping, but most need additional subsurface information from drilling or seismic-reflection data. Several of the major unresolved problems are presented below:

1. Paleocurrent data are scattered and poorly constrained for all stratigraphic units. Detailed measurements of different paleocurrent indicators, with particular attention to stratigraphic level and geographic position,

should help resolve questions such as the following: What was the effect of the border faults on Stockton and New Oxford paleo-drainages? Are the New Oxford and Stockton a continuous depositional unit or two similar units deposited in separate basins? Was the Hammer Creek deposited by two separate drainage systems during different time periods? Was the Narrow Neck a topographic high separating the Newark and Gettysburg basins during deposition?

2. Lateral facies changes can be examined along strike using lacustrine marker beds. Detailed studies of this nature will determine the effects of facies changes in the lacustrine beds relative to coeval fluvial and deltaic deposits. They may also establish the continuity of the different parts of Van Houten cycles. Paleomagnetic analysis of the Newark basin indicates a coherent pattern of reversals (Witte and others, 1991; Olsen and others, 1996) that may allow direct correlation to other early Mesozoic deposits. Such studies will help unravel the relative effects of climate and tectonics on sedimentation and address problems such as the following: Why are there no Lockatong-age Van Houten cycles in the Gettysburg basin? Is it possible to correlate individual lake cycles of the Brunswick Group and Gettysburg Formation between the two basins, particularly by use of magnetostratigraphy? Can the proposed climatic changes be recognized across facies boundaries?

3. Preliminary study of the diagenesis of the formations within the basins indicates similar histories despite different depositional successions. There is still a need for more systematic analysis of the diagenetic mineral parageneses in sandstones that intertongue with the mudstones and in deposits adjacent to diabase intrusives. The source of sodium for the authigenic minerals is still in doubt. Could a major portion of it have been derived from evaporite minerals? Could clay minerals have produced the sodium? How important were the intrusives to producing the authigenic mineral distributions and/or chemistries?

4. How do structural development, sedimentation, climatic changes, and igneous events in the Pennsylvania basins relate to those in other early Mesozoic rift basins in North America, Europe, and Africa?

RECOMMENDED FOR FURTHER READING

Froelich, A. J., and Robinson, G. R., Jr., eds. (1988), *Studies of the early Mesozoic basins of the eastern United States*, U.S. Geological Survey Bulletin 1776, 423 p.

Lorenz, J. C. (1988), *Triassic-Jurassic rift-basin sedimentology—history and methods*, New York, Van Nostrand Reinhold Company, 315 p.

Manspeizer, Warren, ed. (1988), *Triassic-Jurassic rifting—Continental breakup and the origin of the Atlantic Ocean and passive margins*, Amsterdam, Elsevier, Developments in Geotectonics, v. 22, 998 p.

Olsen, P. E. (1986), *A 40-million-year lake record of early Mesozoic orbital climatic forcing*, Science, v. 234, p. 842–848.

Robinson, G. R., Jr., and Froelich, A. J., eds. (1985), *Proceedings of the Second U.S. Geological Survey Workshop on the Early Mesozoic Basins of the Eastern United States*, U.S. Geological Survey Circular 946, 147 p.

Schlische, R. W. (1993), *Anatomy and evolution of the Triassic-Jurassic continental rift system, eastern North America*, Tectonics, v. 12, p. 1026–1042.

Smoot, J. P. (1991), *Sedimentary facies and depositional environments of early Mesozoic Newark Supergroup basins, eastern North America*, Palaeogeography, Palaeoclimatology, Palaeoecology, v. 84, p. 369–423.

Van Houten, F. B. (1964), *Cyclic lacustrine sedimentation, Upper Triassic Lockatong Formation, central New Jersey and adjacent Pennsylvania*, in Merriam, D. F., ed., *Symposium on cyclic sedimentation*, Kansas Geological Survey Bulletin 169, v. 2, p. 497–531.

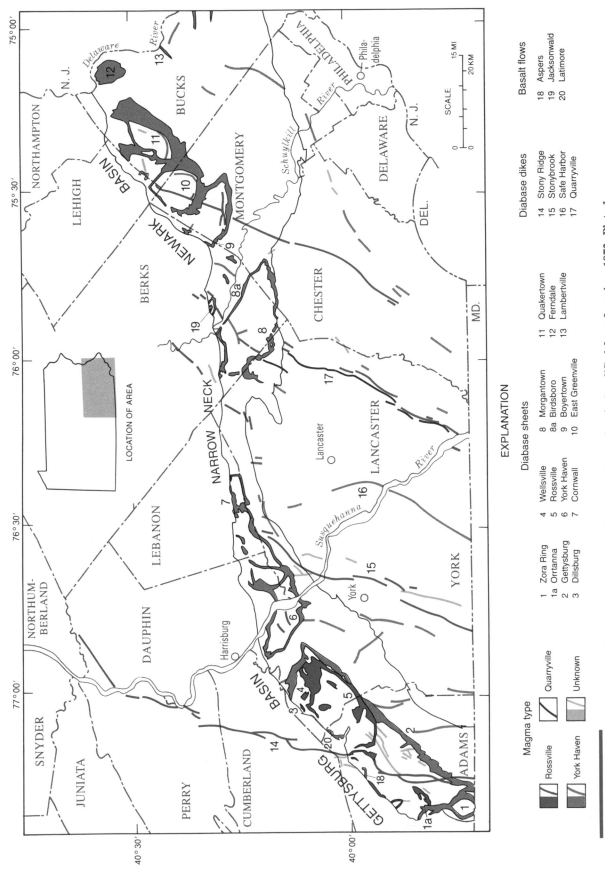

EXPLANATION

Magma type

Rossville

Quarryville

York Haven

Unknown

Diabase sheets

1	Zora Ring	8	Morgantown
1a	Orrtanna	8a	Birdsboro
2	Gettysburg	9	Boyertown
3	Dillsburg	10	East Greenville
4	Wellsville	11	Quakertown
5	Rossville	12	Ferndale
6	York Haven	13	Lambertville
7	Cornwall		

Diabase dikes

14 Stony Ridge
15 Stonybrook
16 Safe Harbor
17 Quarryville

Basalt flows

18 Aspers
19 Jacksonwald
20 Latimore

Figure 12B–1. Distribution of early Mesozoic igneous rocks in eastern Pennsylvania (modified from Lanning, 1972, Plate 1; Smith, R. C., II, and others, 1975, *Geology and geochemistry of Triassic diabase in Pennsylvania*, Geological Society of America Bulletin, v. 86, Figure 1, p. 944 [modified with permission of the publisher, the Geological Society of America, Boulder, Colorado USA; copyright © 1975 Geological Society of America]; Berg and others, 1980; and R. C. Smith, II, personal communication, 1996). Principal named diabase sheets, diabase dikes, and basalt flows are indicated by numbers.

CHAPTER 12B EARLY MESOZOIC—IGNEOUS AND CONTACT METAMORPHIC ROCKS

A. J. FROELICH*
U.S. Geological Survey
National Center, MS 926
Reston, VA 20192

DAVID GOTTFRIED
U.S. Geological Survey
National Center, MS 926
Reston, VA 20192

INTRODUCTION

Diabase sheets and dikes that form a complex igneous network have extensively intruded Triassic sedimentary rocks and comprise about one fifth of the basin fill of the Gettysburg and Newark rift basins (Figure 12B–1). Remnants of basalt flows intercalated with Lower Jurassic strata are preserved along the northwestern border fault (18, 19, and 20 on Figure 12B–1). Several swarms of through-going north- and northeast-trending diabase dikes extend from the Piedmont crystalline terrain on the southeast across the basins and into the folded and faulted Paleozoic sedimentary rocks to the north and west.

All diabase sheets, basalt flows, and most diabase dikes are quartz-normative continental tholeiites, but the Quarryville dike system (Figure 12B–1) is olivine-normative. The best estimate of the age of both intrusive and extrusive igneous rocks is Early Jurassic, or about 201 Ma. The quartz-normative diabase is subdivided into two principal magma types, York Haven and Rossville. Although Rossville-type sheets show little evidence of differentiation, the principal York Haven sheets, more than 2,000 feet thick, have well-developed cumulate zones and late-stage segregations of granophyre and ferrogabbro. The intrusive rocks in the basins are enclosed by thermal aureoles of contact metamorphosed Triassic sedimentary rocks of variable width and composition.

AGE OF IGNEOUS ROCKS

Prior to 1973, both intrusive and extrusive igneous rocks in the Gettysburg and Newark basins had been considered to be Late Triassic (King, 1971; Lapham and Root, 1971; Faill, 1973b). Abundant paleomagnetic data (M. E. Beck, 1965; De Boer, 1968) support the concept that basalt flows and diabase sheets and dikes in the eastern United States are all parts of the same general system, with paleopole positions reflecting about the same early Mesozoic age. Sutter and Smith (1979), using $^{40}Ar/^{39}Ar$ age spectrum techniques on diabase dikes and sheets in the southern part of the Gettysburg basin, determined that an Early Jurassic age (175 to 200 Ma) was likely. Later work on whole-rock and hornblende samples of diabases from the nearby Culpeper basin of Virginia and from the Newark basin in New Jersey indicated a mean age of 201 ± 1.3 Ma (2 sigma), which is Early Jurassic. This is interpreted as the best estimate of the age of intrusion and crystallization of diabase sheets and dikes (Sutter, 1985, 1988).

CHEMISTRY AND MINERALOGY OF IGNEOUS ROCKS

Before 1970, lower Mesozoic mafic igneous rocks of the eastern United States were considered essentially uniform in chemical and mineralogical character (Dana, 1873; De Boer, 1967). Later studies of the chemistry and petrology of Mesozoic diabase dikes in eastern North America (Weigand and Ragland, 1970) and of diabase sheets and dikes in eastern Pennsylvania (Smith and others, 1975) showed conclusively that the diabase consists of three distinct petrologic magma types, each homogeneous within itself. Samples from chilled margins show no overlap of titania (TiO_2) content between the three magmatic suites (Figure 12B–2). The two principal magma types that form both sheets and dikes in eastern Pennsylvania are quartz-normative. They are the low-TiO_2 Rossville type and the high-TiO_2 York Haven type. The chilled margins of the Rossville Diabase contain sparse, centimeter-sized calcic plagioclase phenocrysts (Figure 12B–3A), readily distinguishing it from the chilled margins of the York Haven Diabase (Figure 12B–3B), which are generally aphanitic and have microphenocrysts of clinopyroxene and plagioclase. Forming a single dike swarm, the Quarryville magma type is an olivine-normative tholeiite that contains abundant fresh olivine microphenocrysts in chilled zones (Figure 12B–3C).

The median major and minor oxide composition of the three types of diabase in eastern Pennsylvania are summarized in Table 12B–1. The basalt flows at Jacksonwald and Aspers (18 and 19 on Figure 12B–1) are of the York Haven type. Within each magma type, compositions are highly uniform, and many elements show no overlap of compositional range among diabase types. The chemical types, estimated thicknesses, volumes, and general characteristics of the principal diabase sheets are summarized in Table 12B–2.

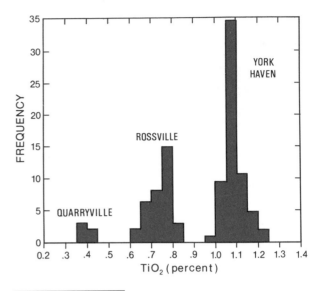

Figure 12B–2. Frequency distribution of TiO_2 in chilled margins of the three tholeiitic magma types in eastern Pennsylvania (modified from Smith, R. C., II, and others, 1975, *Geology and geochemistry of Triassic diabase in Pennsylvania*, Geological Society of America Bulletin, v. 86, Figure 3, p. 945). Modified with permission of the publisher, the Geological Society of America, Boulder, Colorado USA. Copyright © 1975 Geological Society of America.

The thickest and most extensive sheets are of the York Haven type, some of which are characterized by thick lower zones containing cumulus orthopyroxene (York Haven, Gettysburg, Boyertown, Morgantown, Ferndale, Quakertown, Lambertville) (Figure 12B–4). These orthopyroxene-rich lower zones typically occur in the southeastern parts of sheets. Lower contacts are approximately conformable to the bedding of the enclosing, gently northwest-dipping Triassic sedimentary rocks, but the other three margins commonly are crosscutting (Smith and others, 1975). The outcrop patterns produced by the variety of forms of diabase sheets have been analyzed and discussed by Hotz (1952). The northwestern margins of most sheets are generally characterized by abundant late-stage differentiates—syenitic granophyre, ferrogabbro (Figure 12B–5), diorite, pegmatite, and aplite (Zora Ring, Wellsville, Dillsburg, York Haven, Birdsboro). Some of these represent complementary fractions to the aforementioned cumulate-bearing sheets.

Variations in magnesia (MgO) and TiO_2 within the York Haven sheet are shown in Figure 12B–6. This pattern of enrichment and depletion of two oxides relative to chilled-margin contacts is typical of the geochemical variation of major elements, as well as trace elements and rare-earth elements, across most York Haven-type sheets (Smith, 1973; Husch, 1988).

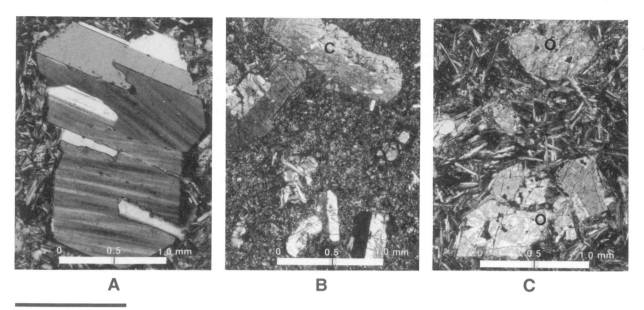

A   **B**   **C**

Figure 12B–3. Photomicrographs of chilled diabase margins formed from the three magma types. Crossed nicols. A. Rossville Diabase showing characteristic large calcic plagioclase phenocrysts (with rim overgrowths and oriented inclusions) enclosed in an aphanitic groundmass (sample D–7, courtesy of R. C. Smith, II, and A. W. Rose). B. York Haven Diabase with microphenocrysts of twinned clinopyroxene (C) and minor plagioclase and olivine in groundmass (sample D–107, courtesy of R. C. Smith, II, and A. W. Rose). C. Quarryville Diabase containing olivine microphenocrysts (O) that have chromium-aluminum spinel inclusions. The groundmass is plagioclase and clinopyroxene (sample Quarry–QT, courtesy of R. C. Smith, II, and A. W. Rose).

Table 12B–1. *Major and Minor Oxide Composition of Rossville, York Haven, and Quarryville Types of Diabase, Basalt at Aspers, and Jacksonwald Basalt*

(Oxide values reported in percent)

Oxide	Rossville Diabase median[1]	York Haven Diabase median[1]	Basalt at Aspers[2]	Jacksonwald Basalt[3]	Quarryville Diabase median[1]
SiO_2	50.56	51.84	51.10	51.7	46.60
Al_2O_3	16.56	14.34	[4]15.65	14.0	15.45
Fe_2O_3	1.07	1.18	2.30	3.8	1.66
FeO	9.02	8.75	7.74	7.2	8.42
MgO	6.79	7.72	7.15	7.47	13.10
CaO	10.81	10.73	10.95	11.4	10.55
Na_2O	1.95	1.96	1.91	1.85	1.57
K_2O	.39	.60	.38	.20	.35
H_2O^+	.46	.23	1.19	1.1	1.15
TiO_2	.74	1.09	1.19	1.17	.43
P_2O_5	.09	.12	.115	.14	.07
MnO	.18	.20	.17	.19	.17
CO_2	.12	.08	NA[5]	.03	.00
Total	98.74	98.84	99.85	100.25	99.52
Number of samples	20	30	1	1	15

[1]From Smith and others (1975).
[2]From Smith (1973).
[3]Unpublished data from U.S. Geological Survey, 1988.
[4]Possibly contaminated.
[5]NA, not analyzed.

Table 12B–2. *Estimated Thickness and Preserved Volume of Diabase in the Principal Sheets, Gettysburg and Newark Basins, Pennsylvania*

Map no.[1]	Name	Chemical type[2]	Area (square miles)	Thickness (feet)	Volume (cubic miles)	Remarks[3]
1	Zora Ring	YH	16	1,600	4.8	D (C, Db)
1a	Orrtanna	YH	5	1,250	1.2	D
2	Gettysburg	YH	36	1,800	12.3	C, Db
3	Dillsburg	R	10	350	.7	Db
		YH	10	1,000	2.0	D (Db)
4	Wellsville	R–YH	24	1,500	6.8	D, Db
5	Rossville	R	15	800	2.3	Db
6	York Haven	YH	64	2,000	24.3	C, D (Db)
7	Cornwall	YH	64	1,225	14.8	Db (C, D)
8	Morgantown	YH	150	780	22.5	Db (C)
8a	Birdsboro	YH	30	780	4.5	D
9	Boyertown	YH	15	1,200	3.5	Db, C, D
10	East Greenville	YH	25	1,500	7.1	Db, C, D
11	Quakertown	YH	84	1,800	28.6	Db, C (D)
12	Ferndale	YH	18	750	2.6	C
13	Lambertville	YH	2	1,000	.5	C (D, Db)

[1]See Figure 12B–1.
[2]R, Rossville type; YH, York Haven type.
[3]D, differentiates (granophyre, diorite, ferrogabbro, and so forth); C, cumulus orthopyroxenite; Db, "typical" diabase, or unknown volume of D and/or C; ( ), minor.

SUMMARY

York Haven-type (YH) sheets— 128.7 mi^3
Rossville-type (R) sheets— 3 mi^3
Mixed (R–YH) sheet— 6.8 mi^3
Minimum total diabase in
    principal sheets— 138.5 mi^3
*Minimum total diabase, sheets
    and dikes— 150.0 mi^3

*Explanation: The minimum total volume for diabase sheets and dikes was estimated by adding 5 mi^3 for dikes and 5 mi^3 for small diabase sheets, and by assuming that all sheets, except Zora Ring, York Haven, Cornwall, Morgantown, Quakertown, East Greenville, Boyertown, and Ferndale, extend to a depth of 0.6 mile.

Figure 12B–4. Photomicrograph of orthopyroxene-bearing cumulus zone in York Haven Diabase at York Haven, York County, showing a large bronzite phenocryst in a medium-crystalline matrix of mainly fresh plagioclase and slightly altered clinopyroxene (sample PYH–84–4, U.S. Geological Survey). Crossed nicols.

Figure 12B–5. Photomicrograph of late-stage, quartzose ferrogabbro differentiate of York Haven Diabase at Reesers Summit, York County (northern part of the York Haven sheet), showing fresh plagioclase phenocrysts, altered clinopyroxene, ilmeno-magnetite crystals (black), minor quartz (white), and secondary amphibole (sample PYRS 84–9, U.S. Geological Survey). Crossed nicols.

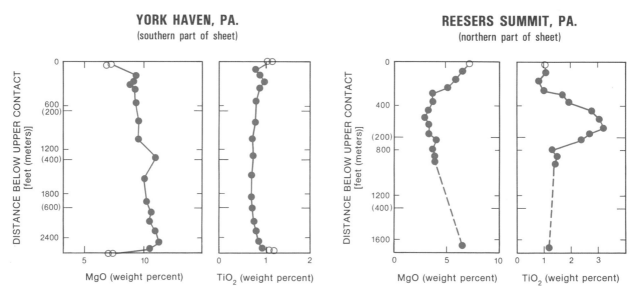

Figure 12B–6. Plot of the distance below the upper contact against weight percent MgO and TiO$_2$ for the southern part of the York Haven sheet, which is characterized by cumulus orthopyroxene, and for the northern part, which is dominated by a late-stage quartzose ferrogabbro. Open circles indicate data from the chilled margin. Data on the York Haven section are from Smith (1973).

None of the sheets of York Haven Diabase exhibit chemical mass balance in any given section across exposed tilted sequences. These geochemical and petrologic variations within the thick, widely distributed York Haven sheets are best explained by a process of wholesale lateral-flow differentiation, modified locally by gravitational settling (Smith, 1973) and by late-stage filter pressing of granophyric differentiates (Froelich and Gottfried, 1985).

The central part of the Gettysburg basin is characterized by Rossville sheets and dikes that extensively intrude the York Haven sheets as well as Triassic strata (Figures 12B–1 and 12B–7). The Rossville sheets are generally thinner than the York Haven

Figure 12B–7. Dike of Rossville Diabase, about 8 inches thick, cutting a sheet of York Haven Diabase in the footwall of the Cornwall open pit, Lebanon County. Carlyle Gray, Director of the Pennsylvania Geological Survey from 1953 to 1961, is at the right of the dike. Photograph courtesy of Donald Hoff, State Museum of Pennsylvania.

areas in the mantle or by complex melting processes. The Quarryville olivine tholeiite, however, could be parental to both or either of the quartz-normative tholeiites by crystallization of 30 to 45 percent of the Quarryville magma as olivine, minor clinopyroxene, plagioclase, or spinel, accompanied by assimilation of orthopyroxene (Smith and others, 1975).

CONTACT METAMORPHIC ROCKS

Thermally metamorphosed sedimentary rocks that enclose intrusive diabase bodies include the entire range of Triassic lithologies; for example, shale and siltstone are represented by hornfels, sandstone by quartzite, and limestone conglomerate by marble. The thickness of the thermal aureole is highly variable, ranging from 10 to 30 percent of the thickness of the intrusive sheet or dike. Aureoles are commonly zoned. Inner and outer zones are of variable mineral composition, depending upon the grade and the original host-rock lithology.

Hornfels, a brittle, gray to black, commonly spotted, massive rock with original bedding preserved but with subconchoidal fracture, is the most common contact metamorphic rock. Van Houten (1971) observed that high-grade calc-silicate hornfels, developed from Lockatong mudstone and argillite, commonly contains datolite, scapolite, fluorite, and tourmaline, suggesting volatile addition from the diabase; however, some of those minerals may have developed from residual brines. Lockatong feldspathic argillite is altered to hornfels that contains sanidine, anorthoclase, aegirine, riebeckite, and scapolite, whereas analcime-dolomite argillite is altered to hornfels containing cancrinite, natrolite-thomsonite, and, rarely, sodalite and nepheline (Van Houten, 1971). Where originally red siltstone and mudstone are adjacent to diabase intrusions, the hornfels consists of an inner black to dark-gray zone spotted with magnetite, biotite, and cordierite, and an outer purplish-gray zone containing specularite, chlorite, and epidote. Pseudomorphs and cavities after evaporite minerals, such as glauberite(?), have been attributed to thermal reactions with saline interstitial fluids (Wherry, 1916; Stose, 1919).

sheets, show little geochemical evidence of differentiation, and display neither well-developed cumulate zones nor abundant late-stage differentiates, although pods and dikes of pegmatoid and granophyre are locally present. Rossville sheets and dikes show less enrichment in light rare-earth elements, and lower incompatible trace-element abundances than are found in any of the York Haven sheets or dikes (Smith and others, 1975). Only a few Rossville dikes and one Quarryville dike are known in the Newark basin, but all three magma types are represented in the through-going dike systems outside both basins (Figure 12B–1).

The geochemical data for the quartz-normative tholeiites of the Gettysburg and Newark basins indicate that the York Haven and Rossville magmas are not related by any simple crystallization-differentiation process. They are either derived from separate source

Arkosic sandstone is commonly metamorphosed to quartzo-feldspathic granofels containing diopside, sphene, hornblende, myrmekitic quartz and feldspar, albite, muscovite, and tourmaline; quartzose sandstone is metamorphosed to quartzite containing andalusite, tourmaline, and muscovite; and limestone conglomerate is thermally recrystallized to calcite marble, commonly containing andradite, grossular, diopside, serpentine, epidote, tremolite, or actinolite (Stose and Glass, 1938).

GEOPHYSICS

Regional geophysical data, primarily aeromagnetic (Bromery and Griscom, 1967; Socolow, 1974; Phillips, 1985) and gravimetric (Hersey, 1944; Sumner, 1977; Daniels, 1985) surveys, have been used to delineate the diabase sheets and dikes and as a basis for preparing three-dimensional models of the diabase and the enclosing thermally metamorphosed rocks (see Chapters 23 and 24). The contrast in density and in magnetic susceptibility between the diabase and the Triassic sedimentary rocks makes the diabase uniquely suitable for subsurface definition and modeling (Daniels, 1985).

MINERAL DEPOSITS

Magnetite skarn deposits are spatially associated with large diabase sheets in contact with Paleozoic or Triassic carbonate units, typically along the margins of the Gettysburg and Newark basins (Lapham and Gray, 1973; Robinson, 1988; see Chapter 40B). In addition to the extensive iron oxide ore deposits at Cornwall and Morgantown, copper and iron sulfides enriched in cobalt, gold, and silver were produced as by-products (Smith, Berkheiser, and Hoff, 1988). Studies of the York Haven Diabase at Reesers Summit showed an order-of-magnitude enrichment of palladium in a late-stage ferrogabbro differentiate (Gottfried and Froelich, 1988; Gottfried and others, 1990). Although the iron ore deposits are not presently considered economic, the association of elements of strategic importance with the skarns and associated ferrogabbroic diabase may warrant their assessment as future low-grade sources of these elements (Robinson, 1985, 1988).

PROBLEMS AND FUTURE RESEARCH

Many questions on the geodynamic controls of magmatism during the early Mesozoic remain. How are the three Early Jurassic magma types in the Newark and Gettysburg basins related? Is the mantle laterally and vertically heterogeneous? How important a factor was crustal contamination? Additional work, including study of neodymium, rubidium, strontium, and lead isotopes and selected incompatible trace-element ratios, is needed before the interrelationships between magma types in Pennsylvania are firmly established.

What were the precise mechanism and role of physical and chemical differentiation during intrusion of the thick York Haven-type sheets? What were the intrusive mechanisms in relation to faulting, tilting, and other deformation? Accurate delineation of the orthopyroxene cumulate zones and the late-stage differentiates in each large sheet are needed to define the petrologic variations in the sheets, for better understanding of flow differentiation.

What are the specific chemical exchange reactions between diabase and host rocks? How important was metasomatism during contact metamorphism, especially in relation to potential hydrothermal ore deposits? What were the depth and temperature relationships during thermal metamorphism? Detailed geochemical studies of diabase and aureole rocks and minerals suited to geobarometry and geothermometry, as well as studies of fluid inclusions, are needed to address these problems.

RECOMMENDED FOR FURTHER READING

Bromery, R. W., and Griscom, Andrew (1967), *Aeromagnetic and generalized geologic map of southeastern Pennsylvania*, U.S. Geological Survey Geophysical Investigations Map GP-577, scale 1:125,000, 2 sheets.

Smith, R. C., II (1973), *Geochemistry of Triassic diabase from southeastern Pennsylvania*, University Park, Pennsylvania State University, Ph.D. thesis, 262 p.

Smith, R. C., II, Rose, A. W., and Lanning, R. M. (1975), *Geology and geochemistry of Triassic diabase in Pennsylvania*, Geological Society of America Bulletin, v. 86, p. 943–955.

Sumner, J. R. (1977), *Geophysical investigation of the structural framework of the Newark-Gettysburg Triassic basin, Pennsylvania*, Geological Society of America Bulletin, v. 88, p. 935–942.

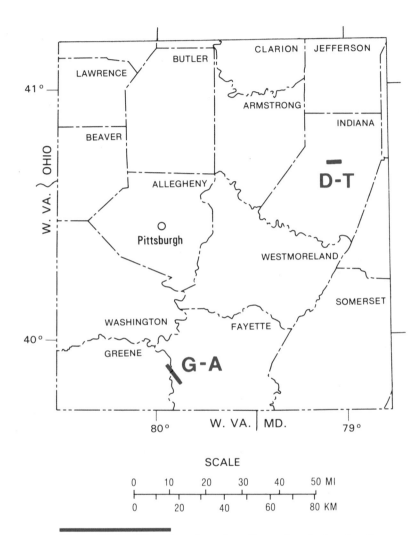

Figure 13–1. Map of southwestern Pennsylvania showing the locations of kimberlite dikes. D–T, Dixonville-Tanoma dikes; G–A, Gates-Adah dikes.

CHAPTER 13   JURASSIC KIMBERLITE DIKES

CHARLES H. SHULTZ
Department of Geology
Slippery Rock University
Slippery Rock, PA 16057

INTRODUCTION

Kimberlite dikes are known near Dixonville, Indiana County (Dixonville-Tanoma dikes), and near Masontown in Fayette and Greene Counties (Gates-Adah dikes) (Figure 13–1) in the Pittsburgh Low Plateau section of the Appalachian Plateaus physiographic province. Interest in kimberlites is economic, because they are an important source of diamonds, and scientific, because they contain suites of high-pressure–high-temperature minerals and xenoliths (foreign rock fragments) that provide insight into the nature of the upper mantle and lower crust.

The term "kimberlite" was originally coined by Lewis in 1887 for the diamond-bearing mica peridotite of the Kimberley pipe (diatreme) in South Africa. Kimberlite is a diverse and very complex class of rocks. Diamonds are no longer considered to be essential for the rock class, and no diamonds have been reported from Pennsylvania kimberlites. The Dixonville-Tanoma and Gates-Adah dikes are classed as massive carbonatitic phlogopite kimberlite belonging to the hypabyssal facies (Dawson, 1980).

Kemp and Ross (1907) were the first to publish a detailed description of the Gates-Adah dikes, and Honess and Graeber (1924) were the first to describe the Dixonville-Tanoma dikes. Subsequently, many investigations have been carried out, applying increasingly sophisticated techniques, including the carbon-isotope studies of Deines (1968) and the microprobe investigations of Hunter and Taylor (1984) and Hunter and others (1984). The Gates-Adah dikes have been the most intensively studied because of their accessibility. These dikes are part of a group of similar intrusions extending from eastern Tennessee and eastern Kentucky to the Finger Lakes region of New York (Zartman and others, 1967; Meyer, 1976). Using K-Ar techniques on phlogopite, Pimentel and others (1975) determined the age of the Gates-Adah dikes to be 185 ± 10 Ma, or lower Middle Jurassic. Other dikes in the group are reported to range in age from Mississippian in Tennessee to Early Cretaceous in New York.

DIXONVILLE-TANOMA DIKES

The Dixonville-Tanoma dikes are not exposed at the surface but were encountered underground in the Barr Slope coal mine and the Tanoma coal mine within a mile or two west-southwest of Dixonville in north-central Indiana County. Honess and Graeber (1926) reported the main dike to be 100 feet long and up to 45 feet thick. A second, much thinner dike parallels the main one. Honess and Graeber indicated a strike of N80°E but gave no dip (probably nearly vertical). The dikes intrude the Lower Freeport coal bed in the upper part of the Pennsylvanian Allegheny Formation in the Barr Slope mine. In the Tanoma mine, where the dikes strike N87°W and have a vertical dip (Robert C. Smith, II, personal communication, 1987), they intrude the Lower Kittanning coal bed in the lower third of the Allegheny Formation.

The dike in the Barr Slope mine is a strongly inequigranular rock with prominent megacrysts and sedimentary xenoliths embedded in a porous, mottled, yellowish-gray, fine-grained to aphanitic groundmass. The term "megacryst" is used herein for any mineral grain that is significantly larger than the surrounding groundmass, in order to avoid the genetic connotation of phenocryst or xenocryst (foreign crystal). A weak flow structure, shown by roughly parallel, shaly xenoliths and books of mica, is sporadically present. The rock has a strongly altered appearance and a rough, hackly fracture. Vuggy and netlike calcite veins cut megacrysts and matrix alike. Yellowish-orange serpentinized olivine, up to 0.75 inch long, and brownish-black phlogopitic mica dominate the megacryst suite (Table 13–1). Other megacrysts, in order of decreasing abundance, are purplish-red garnet (pyrope?), brilliant metallic magnesian ilmenite, and enstatitic orthopyroxene. Pyrrhotite is apparently abundant in the dike encountered in the Tanoma mine (Robert C. Smith, II, personal communication, 1987). Shale and coked coal are common xenoliths. These inclusions are strongly embayed by kimberlitic matrix and have vesicular margins that are now filled with calcite (amygdaloidal). Petrographic details of texture, mineralogy, and alteration are shown in Figures 13–2, 13–3, and 13–4.

GATES-ADAH DIKES

The Gates-Adah dikes are poorly exposed over a distance of 2.7 miles in eastern Greene County and western Fayette County. The best exposure is on the west side of a small, south-flowing tributary to Middle Run, 0.3 mile north of Gates near the Mononga-

Table 13–1. *Modes Observed in the Dixonville-Tanoma and Gates-Adah Dikes[1]*

(Quantities are in volume percent summed to 100 percent in each category)

Textural components	Dixonville-Tanoma	Gates-Adah (Nemacolin)	Gates-Adah (Middle Run)
Megacrysts (see below)	26.1	17.4	11.4
Xenoliths (foreign rock clasts)	.6	.3	.8
Carbonate veins	8.6	0	Tr[2]
Groundmass (see constituents below)	64.7	82.3	87.8
Megacrysts			
Olivine[3]	52.4	92.5	95.6
Garnet[4]	11.7	Tr	2.2
Magnesian ilmenite	2.1	Tr	2.2
Phlogopite[5]	33.3	Tr	Tr
Orthopyroxene	.4	7.5	0
Groundmass			
Olivine microphenocrysts[3]	24.8	26.9	33.4
Phlogopite (microphenocrysts and microlites)[5]	0	12.3	18.2
Opaques (magnetite and perovskite)[6]	13.3	8.7	9.3
Matrix	[7]61.9	[8]52.1	[9]39.1

[1]The dikes are highly variable and heterogeneous, but the data presented are representative.
[2]Tr, trace.
[3]Altered to serpentine and opaques, or replaced by carbonate or microcrystalline quartz. Relict olivine is 0 to 3.9 percent of volume.
[4]Includes alteration rims.
[5]Includes replacement carbonate.
[6]Mostly magnetite for Dixonville-Tanoma dikes. Coequal for Gates-Adah dikes. Perovskite is largely altered to leucoxene.
[7]Pseudomorphous bodies of calcite, rare dolomite rhombs, sparse apatite prisms, and minor serpentine embedded in micritic carbonate.
[8]Extremely minute, needlelike prisms of apatite; platelike prisms of melilite(?); some micritic carbonate; and minor serpentine within very irregular weblike patches of calcite that show unit extinction.
[9]Microgranular calcite, turbid micritic carbonate, and sparse pools of quartz.

hela River in western Fayette County (Figure 13–5). The main dike here is about 3 feet thick, but two parallel dikes, several inches thick, were reported about 100 feet to the northeast (Hickok and Moyer, 1940). Several hundred feet underground, in mines extracting the Pittsburgh coal, multiple dikes were also reported, and the main dike ranged up to 20 feet thick (Smith, 1912).

The Gates-Adah dikes were intruded into a zone of closely spaced fractures in an area up to 500 feet wide (Roen, 1968). Based on horizontal slickensides, Roen proposed that the fractures are part of a left-lateral strike-slip fault zone striking N51°W and having an essentially vertical dip. He speculated that displacement was a few tens of feet before intrusion. The fault is 4.4 miles long (Kent, 1969). A sandstone horst, uplifted 4.5 feet, presumably by forceful injection, occurs at the upper terminus of the dikes (Smith, 1912). Intruded strata in valley bottoms belong to the Uniontown Formation of the Upper Penn-

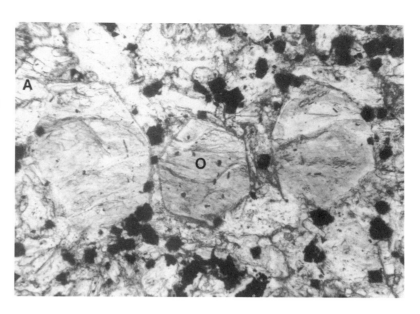

Figure 13–2. Photomicrograph of the Dixonville-Tanoma dike from the Barr Slope coal mine, Indiana County. Euhedral olivine microphenocrysts (O), entirely altered to serpentine, are embedded in a groundmass dominated by irregular patches of calcite that produce an almost mosaic texture. Other constituents include magnetite euhedra (uncommonly with perovskite rims) and prismatic apatite (A) partly replaced by carbonate. Width of photomicrograph is 0.73 mm. Plane-polarized light. Specimen contributed by James G. Tilton, Equitable Gas Company.

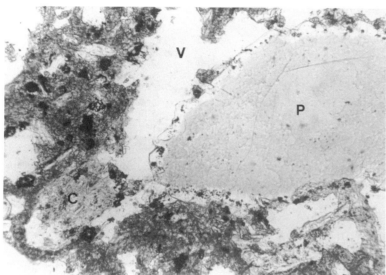

Figure 13–3. Photomicrograph of the Dixonville-Tanoma dike from the Barr Slope coal mine, Indiana County. Microphenocryst of phlogopite (P) is viewed normal to cleavage and is nearly surrounded by irregular microvesicles (V). Groundmass consists of clouded calcite crystals (pseudomorphs?) (C) with micritic rims and needlelike inclusions of apatite, phlogopite microlites, perovskite (nearly opaque), and dark, turbid micritic calcite. "Bleached" euhedral overgrowth of phlogopite on the microphenocryst developed mainly in contact with vesicles. Width of photomicrograph is 0.73 mm. Plane-polarized light. Specimen contributed by James G. Tilton, Equitable Gas Company.

Figure 13–4. Photomicrograph of the Dixonville-Tanoma dike from the Barr Slope coal mine, Indiana County. Phlogopite megacryst (P) was shredded by differential movement along a shear plane that is now healed by a vein of polygonal calcite (C). In order of decreasing abundance, the groundmass consists of irregular micropatches of calcite showing unit extinction and micritic margins; euhedral pseudomorphs of serpentine after olivine; opaques (equally abundant altered perovskite and magnetite with perovskite rims); prismatic apatite; and minor interstitial serpentine. Width of photomicrograph is 2.96 mm. Plane-polarized light. Specimen contributed by James G. Tilton, Equitable Gas Company.

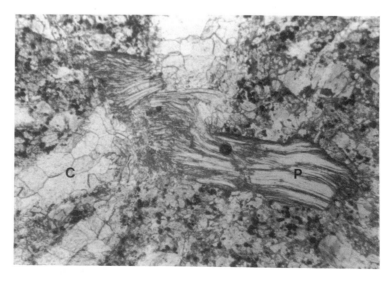

Figure 13–5. Close-up view of the Gates-Adah dike exposed near Middle Run, Fayette County. This is the center part of the dike, which is about 3 feet wide. The shape of the blocks is controlled by horizontal and vertical joint sets. Note the dark, egg-shaped olivine megacryst above the hammer point.

sylvanian Monongahela Group. Upper valley slopes are underlain by the Waynesburg Formation of the Pennsylvanian-Permian Dunkard Group. The dikes cut the Waynesburg coal bed at the base of the formation but do not appear to completely penetrate the sandstones lying just above the coal (Smith, 1912).

The main dike exposed near Middle Run, and shown in Figure 13–5, is a dark-gray to greenish-black, prominently inequigranular rock containing rounded, egg-shaped megacrysts in a sparkling micaceous, fine-grained to aphanitic matrix. It is remarkably free of xenoliths, although Hickok and Moyer (1940) reported abundant shale, limestone, and coal inclusions in places. Megacrysts, which show a vague clustering, are mostly olivine (entirely altered). Less common are magnesian ilmenite, garnets of two different colors, and traces of dark-colored phlogopitic mica (Table 13–1). Olivine grains are generally 0.2 to 0.4 inch in diameter (1.5 inches maximum), black (resembling coal at first glance), and waxy to very lustrous, having a phyllite-like surficial sheen. Magnesian ilmenite shows a brilliant metallic luster, excellent conchoidal fracture, and a microgranular perovskite rim. Garnets with alteration rims (kelyphitic) are either an intense purplish red or, more rarely, a lighter brownish red. Internal partings within the groundmass show a phyllite-like sheen caused by closely packed, parallel phlogopite microphenocrysts. The dike is cut by two kinds of veins, both of which

are parallel to the country-rock contact. More common are silky fibrolitic calcite veins, 0.1 to 0.2 inch wide, that bifurcate or occur in en echelon groups. The other veins are vuggy joint fillings dominated by granular to prismatic calcite and also containing sparse, doubly terminated quartz crystals. In some cases, the vuggy veins are slickensided, indicating movement in the fault zone after the dike was emplaced and solidified, and even after formation of the vein filling within the dike. A crude, spheroidal weathering has developed, and fresh internal spheroids are sharply bounded by a light-brown to greenish-gray weathered rind up to 0.6 inch thick. A photomicrograph of the Middle Run dike rock is shown in Figure 13–6. The mode is presented in Table 13–1.

Figure 13–7 shows a sample of a Gates-Adah dike from underground in the Nemacolin mine near the terminus of the dikes in Greene County, northwest of the Middle Run exposure. The mode is presented in Table 13–1. The margin of the dike, which is about 5 inches wide, is transected by closely spaced horizontal joints. Aphanitic chill zones are medium gray and in knife-sharp contact with intruded strata. The central part of the dike is medium brownish gray and is cluttered with nonuniformly distributed megacrysts up to 1.25 inches in length. A few rare xenoliths of limestone, sandstone, and peridotite are present. Photomicrographs of this section of the dike are shown in Figures 13–8 and 13–9.

Figure 13–6. Photomicrograph of the Gates-Adah dike from an exposure near Middle Run, Fayette County. Microphenocrysts of altered euhedral olivine (O) have magnetite-rich cores and serpentine rims (very light gray). Fresh euhedral phlogopite (P) has magnetite and perovskite euhedra embedded in the rim. The groundmass is nearly opaque perovskite (Pe) that is partly altered to leucoxene, magnetite (opaque, euhedral), apatite needles and prisms, melilite(?) plates (M), serpentine (S), and calcite (C). The letter C is on inclusion-free calcite that is part of a large, irregular, weblike plate showing unit extinction and covering almost the entire field of view. Width of photomicrograph is 0.73 mm. Plane-polarized light.

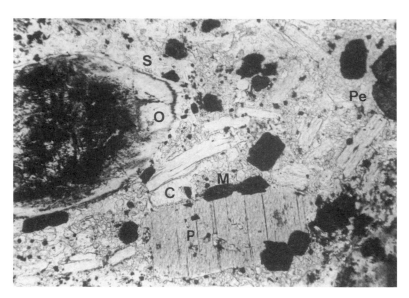

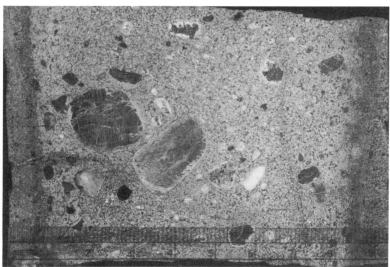

Figure 13–7. Cut-and-polished cross section of the Gates-Adah dike from its northwestern extension in the underground Nemacolin coal mine in Greene County. Note the strongly inequigranular texture, chilled composite contact margins, and uneven distribution of rounded megacrysts, which are mostly silicified olivine with calcite-impregnated rims. A vague internal contact, suggesting multiple injection, rises nearly vertically from between 7 and 8 on the scale (numbered divisions, cm; small divisions, mm). Specimen contributed by James G. Tilton, Equitable Gas Company.

Figure 13–8. Photomicrograph of the Gates-Adah dike shown in Figure 13–7. A rounded and embayed olivine megacryst is almost entirely replaced by chalcedonic quartz (white) and micritic carbonate (turbid). A few relicts (R) of olivine remain. These are surrounded by chalcedony, but a thin selvage of carbonate separates the two phases. An irregular rim of phlogopite, embedded in carbonate, also surrounds the relicts. An incomplete accretionary mantle composed of small phlogopite laths (autolithic) is to the right of the megacryst in the center of the photomicrograph. The general groundmass consists of phlogopite and olivine (entirely replaced by calcite) microphenocrysts, euhedral opaques, phlogopite laths, and patchy to micritic carbonate. Width of photomicrograph is 2.96 mm. Plane-polarized light.

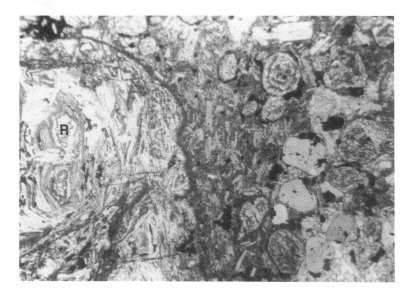

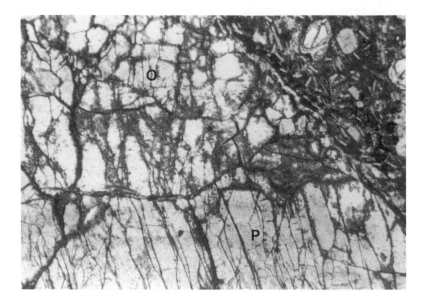

Figure 13–9. Photomicrograph of the Nemacolin segment of the Gates-Adah dikes in Greene County showing part of a peridotite nodule (mantle xeno-lith). Olivine (O) and pyroxene (P) have been entirely replaced by micro-granular quartz (chert), which in turn has been partly replaced by micritic carbonate (dark, turbid) along cracks. A thin, poorly developed, accretionary mantle of roughly parallel phlogopite laths in a micritic carbonate matrix appears in the upper right corner of the photomicrograph. Composite crystals (white) in the groundmass are pseudomorphs of calcite after olivine. Width of photomicrograph is 2.96 mm. Plane-polarized light. Specimen contributed by James G. Tilton, Equitable Gas Company.

DISCUSSION

Consideration of the chemistry, isotopic composition, and origin of the magma that produced the kimberlite dikes in Pennsylvania is beyond the scope of this paper. For detailed discussions, the interested reader is referred to the works of Deines (1968), Hunter and others (1984), Hunter and Taylor (1984), and Shervais and others (1987). Briefly, the kimberlite magmas probably originated near the base of the asthenosphere, or just below, and they were hybrid in character because of the mixing of separate magma batches.

The kimberlite magmas moved upward into the upper crust through zones of structural weakness. The Gates-Adah dikes occur in the strike-slip fault zone described by Roen (1968), and the Dixonville-Tanoma dikes occur within the Home-Gallitzin cross-structural lineament, which might represent a fracture zone (Parrish and Lavin, 1982; see Chapter 22). Both sets of dikes occur in the northeast-striking Greene-Potter fault zone, which is believed to be an extension of the Rome trough of West Virginia and Kentucky. The zone is thought to consist of a series of basement faults that were active during Cambrian and Ordovician time. Reactivation of these faults under tensional stresses associated with the opening of the Atlantic Ocean during the Mesozoic could have provided conduits for the ascent of the kimberlitic magmas.

The magma was probably very mobile and possibly fluidized by carbon dioxide gas and steam (wa-ter vapor). It was emplaced rapidly, possibly as a series of surges in close succession. The intrusion was probably emplaced near the surface, judging by the known thicknesses of Upper Pennsylvanian and Lower Permian strata. Microvesiculation and incipient fragmentation of the dike rock at the Dixonville-Tanoma dike in the Barr Slope coal mine can also be interpreted to indicate shallow depth. The magma was relatively cool and solidified rapidly because of its low volume, thin, sheetlike form, and emplacement at shallow depth where country-rock temperatures would have been relatively low. Sosman (1938) postulated an upper temperature limit of $520 \pm 30°C$ for the Gates-Adah dikes, based on analysis of coal inclusions. Relatively low temperatures are also supported by modest contact-metamorphic effects. Hickok and Moyer (1940) reported that shales are slightly baked or reddened and coal is dulled next to the Gates-Adah dikes. Honess and Graeber (1926) stated that within 8 inches of the contact, coal is coked adjacent to the thickest part (45 feet) of the Dixonville-Tanoma dike in the Barr Slope mine. In contrast, in the Tanoma coal mine, Robert C. Smith, II (personal communication, 1987), reported 2.8 inches of coke adjacent to a dike only 8 inches thick. Fluids of unknown origin caused extensive alteration of the original kimberlite minerals during or after solidification. They also deposited calcite, dolomite, and quartz within the kimberlite groundmass, in the adjacent country rock, and as thin veins.

PROBLEMS AND FUTURE RESEARCH

1. The Gates-Adah and Dixonville-Tanoma dikes should be assayed for diamonds.
2. The carbon-isotope composition of carbonate minerals (pseudomorphous after olivine, in the groundmass, and in veins) in the Gates-Adah dikes should be analyzed to determine if the carbon is derived from the mantle.
3. Isotopic K-Ar dating on both phlogopite megacrysts and microphenocrysts should be done for the Dixonville-Tanoma dikes.
4. Microprobe evaluations of megacrysts, similar to that done by Hunter and Taylor (1984) on the Gates-Adah dikes, should be done on the Dixonville-Tanoma dikes to determine if magma mixing occurred there as well.
5. A search for other kimberlite intrusions buried in the subsurface should be conducted. Peculiar seismic anomalies, recognized in the search for petroleum prospects in western Pennsylvania and eastern Ohio, have been interpreted as possible kimberlites (Richard W. Beardsley, personal communication, 1984). Howell and Vozoff (1953) suggested that a circular gravity and magnetic high in northeastern Tioga County (north-central Pennsylvania) on the New York border at the intersection of the Greene-Potter fault zone and the Attica-Easton lineament could be a buried kimberlite intrusion (see Chapter 23).

RECOMMENDED FOR FURTHER READING

Dawson, J. B. (1980), *Kimberlites and their xenoliths,* New York, Springer-Verlag, 252 p.

Deines, P. (1968), *The carbon and oxygen isotopic composition of carbonates from a mica peridotite dike near Dixonville, Pennsylvania,* Geochimica et Cosmochimica Acta, v. 32, p. 613–625.

Hickok, W. O., IV, and Moyer, F. T. (1940), *Geology and mineral resources of Fayette County, Pennsylvania,* Pennsylvania Geological Survey, 4th ser., County Report 26, 530 p.

Hunter, R. H., Kissling, R. D., and Taylor, L. A. (1984), *Mid- to late-stage kimberlitic melt evolution: phlogopites and oxides from the Fayette County kimberlite, Pennsylvania,* American Mineralogist, v. 69, p. 30–40.

Hunter, R. H., and Taylor, L. A. (1984), *Magma-mixing in the low velocity zone: kimberlitic megacrysts from Fayette County, Pennsylvania,* American Mineralogist, v. 69, p. 16–29.

Meyer, H. O. A. (1976), *Kimberlites of the continental United States: a review,* Journal of Geology, v. 84, p. 377–403.

Shervais, J. W., Taylor, L. A., and Laul, J. C. (1987), *Magma mixing and kimberlite genesis; mineralogic, petrologic, and trace element evidence from eastern U.S.A. kimberlites,* in Morris, E. M., and Pasteris, J. D., eds., *Mantle metasomatism and alkaline magmatism,* Geological Society of America Special Paper 215, p. 101–114.

Watson, K. D. (1967), *Kimberlites of eastern North America,* in Wyllie, P. J., ed., *Ultramafic and related rocks,* New York, John Wiley and Sons, p. 312–323.

Zartman, R. E., Brock, M. R., Heyl, A. V., and Thomas, H. H. (1967), *K-Ar and Rb-Sr ages of some alkalic intrusive rocks from central and eastern United States,* American Journal of Science, v. 265, p. 848–870.

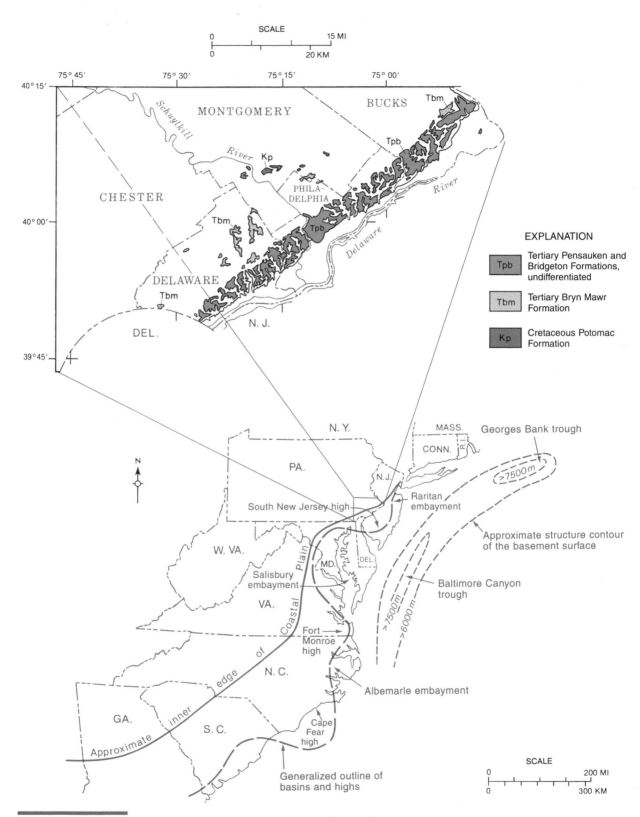

SCALE
0   15 MI
0   20 KM

EXPLANATION

Tpb	Tertiary Pensauken and Bridgeton Formations, undifferentiated
Tbm	Tertiary Bryn Mawr Formation
Kp	Cretaceous Potomac Formation

Approximate structure contour of the basement surface

Georges Bank trough

Raritan embayment

Baltimore Canyon trough

South New Jersey high

Salisbury embayment

Fort Monroe high

Albemarle embayment

Cape Fear high

Generalized outline of basins and highs

Approximate inner edge of Coastal Plain

SCALE
0   200 MI
0   300 KM

Figure 14–1. Map showing the pre-Cretaceous structural highs and lows of the Coastal Plain from Massachusetts to Georgia. Most of southeastern Pennsylvania was influenced by the South New Jersey high. Contours are in meters below sea level. The inset map shows the surface exposures of Cretaceous and Tertiary sediments in Pennsylvania (from Berg and others, 1980).

218

CHAPTER 14   CRETACEOUS AND TERTIARY

JAMES P. OWENS*
  U.S. Geological Survey
  National Center, MS 926A
  Reston, VA 20192

INTRODUCTION

Cretaceous and Tertiary sediments in Pennsylvania crop out in a narrow zone along the Delaware River in the southeasternmost part of the state and on a few upland surfaces west of this zone (Figure 14–1). The main area is part of the Atlantic Coastal Plain, and the upland areas are in the Piedmont province. The two provinces are separated by the Fall Line. A lack of datable material has made age dating of these deposits difficult, especially in the topographically higher and more isolated deposits. This has led to much speculation about their age. Deriving largely from the pioneering mapping of R. D. Salisbury and others (1891–1923) in New Jersey, and Salisbury's concept of four glacial-outwash sequences for the valley deposits, all of the post-Cretaceous deposits in the area were considered Pleistocene in age. This concept had great durability and is still considered correct by some (Jordan and Smith, 1983).

Owens and Minard (1975, 1979) and Owens and Denny (1979) proposed that parts of the valley fill are pre-Pleistocene and quantified the ages of the younger Pleistocene sands and gravels that are deposited in channels cut into Tertiary units.

DEPOSITIONAL SETTING

The Cretaceous and Tertiary deposits of southeasternmost Pennsylvania lie at the edge of the Coastal Plain, which comprises fill along the northwestern margin of the Atlantic Ocean. Once thought to be a simple oceanward thickening wedge of sediments, the Coastal Plain is now known to be a series of basins and arches (Figure 14–1). Tectonic activity associated with the Salisbury embayment, the South New Jersey high, and the Raritan embayment controlled deposition in southeastern Pennsylvania. The sources of sediment deposited on the Coastal Plain were diverse and related directly to the fluvial systems entering the coastal area. For southeastern Pennsylvania, these streams were the ancestral Schuylkill, Delaware, and Hudson Rivers, as well as smaller streams draining local areas. The sediment brought to the Coastal

*Deceased.

Plain varied from that which was highly feldspathic and rich in metamorphic minerals to that which was nonfeldspathic and impoverished in heavy minerals.

STRATIGRAPHY

The Cretaceous and Tertiary Coastal Plain sediments in southeastern Pennsylvania are subdivided into four units: Potomac Formation (oldest), Bryn Mawr Formation, Bridgeton Formation, and Pensauken Formation (youngest).

The names Patapsco Formation and Raritan Formation are used on the *Stratigraphic Correlation Chart of Pennsylvania* (Berg, McInerney, and others, 1986), and the name Patapsco(?) Formation is used on the *Geologic Map of Pennsylvania* (Berg and others, 1980), rather than the name Potomac Formation. However, for the purposes of mapping, most modern workers include all of the subdivisions of the Potomac Group, the Patuxent, Arundel, Patapsco, and Raritan Formations, in a single unit, the Potomac Formation. Because the name Potomac is used in adjacent states and will probably be used by the Pennsylvania Geological Survey in future revisions of the correlation chart and geologic map (W. D. Sevon, personal communication, 1989), the name Potomac Formation is used here.

Potomac Formation

The Potomac Formation occurs along the Delaware River between Delaware and Trenton, N. J., and is shown on some published maps (Owens and Minard, 1964; U.S. Geological Survey, 1967). However, the unit is almost totally covered by the Delaware River and by younger deposits, and the only mapped surface exposures in the area are near Camden and Trenton, N. J., and north of Conshohocken, Montgomery County, Pa. (Figure 14-1). Based on pollen analysis, the portion of the Potomac Formation in Pennsylvania is Late Cretaceous (early Cenomanian).

The Potomac is extremely variable, both vertically and horizontally, and consists of thick beds of pale-gray or grayish-orange sand interbedded with thin to thick beds of mottled pale-red or pale-gray, unctuous clay. Gravel beds are interstratified locally with the sands, especially near the base of the unit. The sandy beds comprise mainly quartz but contain some feldspar, and are mostly crossbedded and, less commonly, horizontally stratified (Figure 14-2). The finer sands typically contain significant concentrations of mica (mostly muscovite). The gravel consists almost totally of quartz and quartzite. Heavy minerals are sparse, but consist of zircon, rutile, tourmaline, and, locally, staurolite. Ilmenite and its weathering products are also present. The clay beds occur in thin to thick lenses (Greenman and others, 1961). The dominant clay mineral is kaolinite. There are localized high concentrations of illite. Only small amounts of mixed-layer illite/smectite occur. Small, reddish-brown to pale-gray pellets of siderite are locally abundant in the white or pale-gray clay beds.

The Potomac Formation has a very low, generally southeast dip and, in Pennsylvania, ranges from 0 to 150 feet thick. There is considerable variation in thickness because much of the formation occurs in a series of deep channels (Figure 14-3).

Figure 14-2. Crossbedded sandy beds of the Potomac Formation (Elk Neck beds equivalent) across the Delaware River from Philadelphia. The extensive large-scale planar crossbeds are common in the sandy facies of this unit. The shovel in the right center of the photograph provides scale.

The Potomac sediments accumulated in the nonmarine upper delta plain, part of a very large delta centered somewhere in central New Jersey. Sands accumulated in channels, and the clays were deposited as overbank or natural levee deposits.

Bryn Mawr Formation

The Bryn Mawr Formation, frequently called Bryn Mawr gravel, occurs as isolated sand and gravel deposits lying on uplands higher than 180 feet above sea level. Most of the deposits are in Delaware County, west of the Schuylkill River, and all known occurrences are shown on the *Geologic Map of Pennsylvania* (Berg and others, 1980) (Figure 14–1). Detailed mapping of some of the unit was presented by Bascom and others (1909) and Owens and Minard (1975). The history of nomenclature for the Bryn Mawr was well reviewed by Bascom (1925).

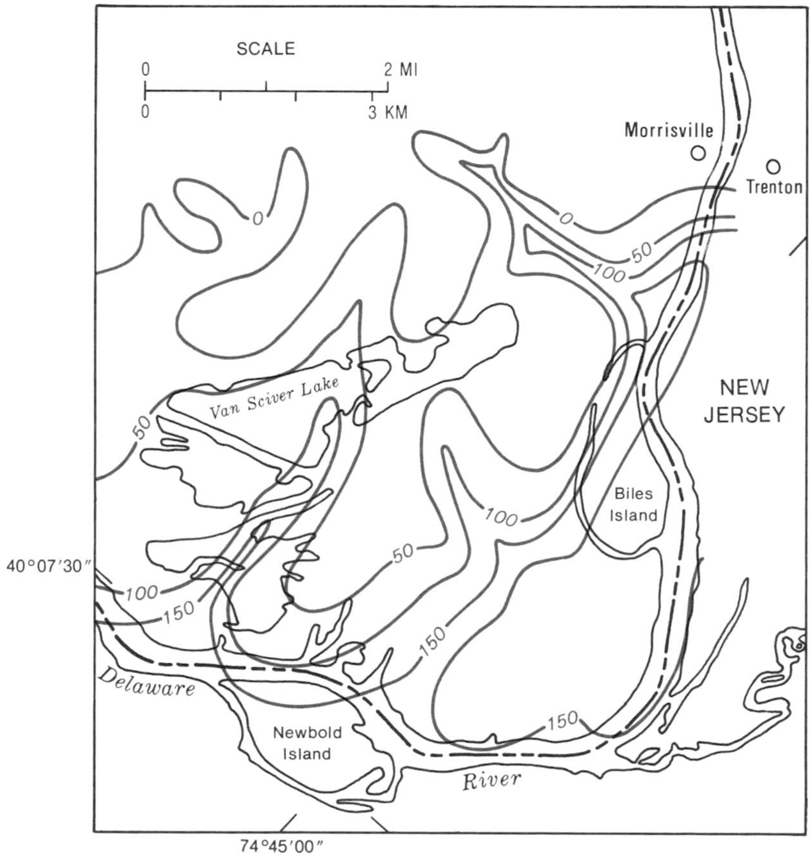

The Bryn Mawr comprises yellow gravel with some sand and a little clay. Clasts, some as large as 5 inches in diameter, are all quartz or quartzite, and the sand is all quartz. The gravel is commonly cemented by iron oxide into a hard rock. The thickness of the Bryn Mawr is generally unknown but is probably much less than 20 feet in most places.

The Bryn Mawr is a fluvial deposit that presumably represents the start of a period of erosion and deposition that has continued to the present. Not enough is known about the Bryn Mawr to speculate about the nature of the river, or rivers, that deposited the gravels, but it seems clear from the mature nature of the sediments that the source area was deeply weathered and that for materials of sand size or larger, only the most resistant material, quartz, was available for erosion.

The age of the Bryn Mawr Formation has been speculative because of the lack of datable materials and is usually thought to be early Quaternary or Pliocene. However, the upland position higher than the Bridgeton Formation indicates an older age, and Owens and Minard (1975) suggested a correlation with the Beacon Hill Formation of eastern New Jersey (Owens and Minard, 1979, p. D6–D8), which is assigned a Miocene age.

The Bryn Mawr (or upland gravels) was recently examined primarily in Maryland by Owens and Glaser (1989) and much more extensively by Pazzaglia (1993). The authors of both reports stressed the petrologic character of these deposits, noting the very mature nature (highly quartzose) of the sediments. The authors also discussed the difficulty of dating these unfossiliferous deposits. Based on a variety of criteria, Pazzaglia (1993) concluded that the Bryn Mawr was most likely late Miocene. Owens and Glaser (1989), on the other hand, concluded that the gravels were pre-middle Miocene and more likely late Oligocene in age. The latter age is the one accepted for the gravels in Pennsylvania in this report.

Figure 14–3. Map of the configuration of the base of the Potomac Formation in part of Bucks County, southeastern Pennsylvania. Structure contours are in feet below sea level; contour interval is 50 feet.

Bridgeton Formation

The Bridgeton Formation is part of the very large sequence of gravelly sands that covers much of the northern Atlantic Coastal Plain. Bridgeton deposits in Pennsylvania, shown on the *Geologic Map of Pennsylvania* (Berg and others, 1980) as part of the Pensauken-Bridgeton Formations, undifferentiated, occur in a discontinuous band paralleling the Delaware River between Delaware and Trenton, N. J. (Figure 14–1). The deposits occur on hilltops, generally at elevations between 100 and 140 feet. The area underlain by the Bridgeton is heavily urbanized, and exposures are few. These deposits constitute the highest level of gravelly sands within the Amboy-Salem trench, a former depositional lowland that parallels the Fall Line from Amboy to Salem, N. J.

The age of the Bridgeton Formation is now considered to be at least late Miocene on the basis of the stratigraphic relationship with the Pensauken Formation, which cuts the Bridgeton (Owens and Minard, 1979).

The Bridgeton is mainly a sand interspersed with gravelly beds (Figure 14–4). Boulders are a common constituent. The sand is typically pale orange to white, locally stained reddish brown by iron oxide. Small masses of black manganese oxide are common in the more weathered parts of the sand. A thin to thick bed of dark-maroon, very clayey sand is present at the top of most outcrops of the formation. This clay contains abundant vermiculite, kaolinite, and gibbsite, and has been interpreted to be the result of deep weathering. The Bridgeton has a high feldspar content in contrast to the older Potomac and Bryn Mawr Formations. Most of the feldspar is potassium feldspar, but, locally, plagioclase feldspar occurs in significant concentrations. Hornblende, epidote, tremolite, and actinolite are common heavy minerals in most of the Bridgeton sands. Ilmenite and its weathering products are the major opaque minerals, although magnetite is locally very abundant. High concentrations of halloysite and endellite in the clay-silt fraction of the sands below the upper clayey zone indicate that the formation is weathered to great depth. Illite is present but tends to decrease upward in most profiles.

The Bridgeton sands were deposited in a series of laterally migrating and upward-building channels, presumably in a braided-stream complex. Some of the channels within the trench were as much as 60 feet deep. There is little change in sand grain size in the Bridgeton throughout its outcrop in the Amboy-Salem trench. The sands are much less mature than those of the Bryn Mawr Formation and presumably

Figure 14–4. Sand facies of the Bridgeton Formation in the lower part of the Amboy-Salem trench near Woodstown, N. J. Large-scale crossbeds are typical of most of the Bridgeton throughout its outcrop in the trench and well into southern New Jersey. The shovel in the center of the photograph provides scale.

represent material eroded from less deeply weathered rock.

Pensauken Formation

The Bridgeton Formation in the central and southwestern end of the Amboy-Salem trench has been eroded, and a younger but similar-appearing gravel, the Pensauken Formation, has been deposited on the erosional surface. The type locality of the Pensauken is near Palmyra, N. J., just east of Philadelphia. The configuration of the Pensauken in the Middle Atlantic States is basically the same as that of the Bridgeton, except that the Pensauken lies at lower elevations and has been emplaced to the southwest of the main body of the Bridgeton (Owens and Minard, 1979). The only occurrence of Pensauken in Pennsylvania is at Turkey Hill, near Morrisville in Bucks County (Figure 14–5). Once one of the best exposures of the Pensauken (Salisbury and Knapp, 1917; Lockwood and Meisler, 1960; Owens and Minard, 1975, 1979), Turkey Hill has been almost totally removed by systematic mining. The Pensauken Formation has been established as upper middle to late Miocene on the basis of biostratigraphic evidence to the south in Delaware (Owens and Denny, 1979).

The Pensauken is mainly a sand, but it is also very gravelly in Pennsylvania. Quartzite boulders up to 5 feet in diameter were common at the Turkey Hill locality. The sands typically are medium to very coarse grained, poorly sorted, and commonly cemented by iron oxides, and have large-scale crossbedding averaging 3 feet or more in thickness. The gravel beds range from a few inches to a few feet thick and are horizontally bedded. Feldspar comprises 50 percent of the sand fraction and consists of both plagioclase and potassium feldspar, the latter being dominant. Most of the feldspar is altered by extensive weathering. The heavy minerals are similar to those in the Bridgeton. The Pensauken beds typically have more glauconite sand reworked from the Coastal Plain formations of New Jersey than does the Bridgeton Formation. The Pensauken sediments in eastern Pennsylvania are patchy in distribution because of extensive erosion. The maximum thickness in this area is about 40 feet.

The Pensauken Formation was deposited in a deltaic complex that, on its distal end in Delaware and Maryland, was flanked by a variety of shelf deposits. Such a sedimentary association is typical in most of the coastal formations in the Atlantic Coastal Plain (Owens and Sohl, 1969; Owens and Gohn, 1985).

PROBLEMS AND FUTURE RESEARCH

Except for the limited investigations by Owens and Minard (1964, 1975, 1979), there has been almost no research on the Cretaceous and Tertiary sediments in Pennsylvania in well over 50 years. Despite the intense urbanization of the area, limited outcrop accessibility and available subsurface information could be utilized to better define the areal distribution of the sediments. The Bryn Mawr Formation is known to occur at several different elevations, and it is possible that the deposits represent more than one depositional event. More detailed mapping is necessary.

Figure 14–5. The Pensauken Formation at Turkey Hill, near Morrisville in Bucks County. The Pensauken, like the Bridgeton, is primarily a sandy unit throughout its outcrop in the Amboy-Salem trench. Beds of gravel typically are interbedded with the sands in this area. This outcrop has been removed by surface mining.

RECOMMENDED FOR FURTHER READING

Doyle, J. A. (1977), *Spores and pollen: the Potomac Group (Cretaceous) angiosperm sequence*, in Kauffman, E. G., and Hazel, J. E., eds., *Concepts and methods of biostratigraphy*, Stroudsburg, Pa., Dowden, Hutchinson, and Ross, p. 339–363.

Doyle, J. A., and Robbins, E. I. (1977), *Angiosperm pollen zonations of the continental Cretaceous of the Atlantic Coastal Plain and its application to deep wells in the Salisbury embayment*, in Pierce, R. L., ed., *Proceedings of the Eighth Annual Meeting of the American Association of Stratigraphic Palynologists*, Palynology, v. 1, p. 43–78.

Glaser, J. D. (1969), *Petrology and origin of Potomac and Magothy (Cretaceous) sediments, middle Atlantic Coastal Plain*, Maryland Geological Survey Report of Investigations 11, 101 p.

Owens, J. P., and Glaser, J. D. (1989), *Cretaceous and Tertiary stratigraphy of the Elk Neck area, northeastern Maryland*, International Geological Congress, 28th, Guidebook, Field Trip T211, American Geophysical Union, Washington, D. C., 26 p.

Owens, J. P., Hess, M. M., Denny, C. S., and Dwornik, E. J. (1983), *Postdepositional alteration of surface and near-surface minerals in selected Coastal Plain formations of the Middle Atlantic States*, U.S. Geological Survey Professional Paper 1067-F, 45 p.

Pazzaglia, F. J. (1993), *Stratigraphy, petrography, and correlation of late Cenozoic middle Atlantic Coastal Plain deposits: implications for late-stage passive-margin geologic evolution*, Geological Society of America Bulletin, v. 105, p. 1617–1634.

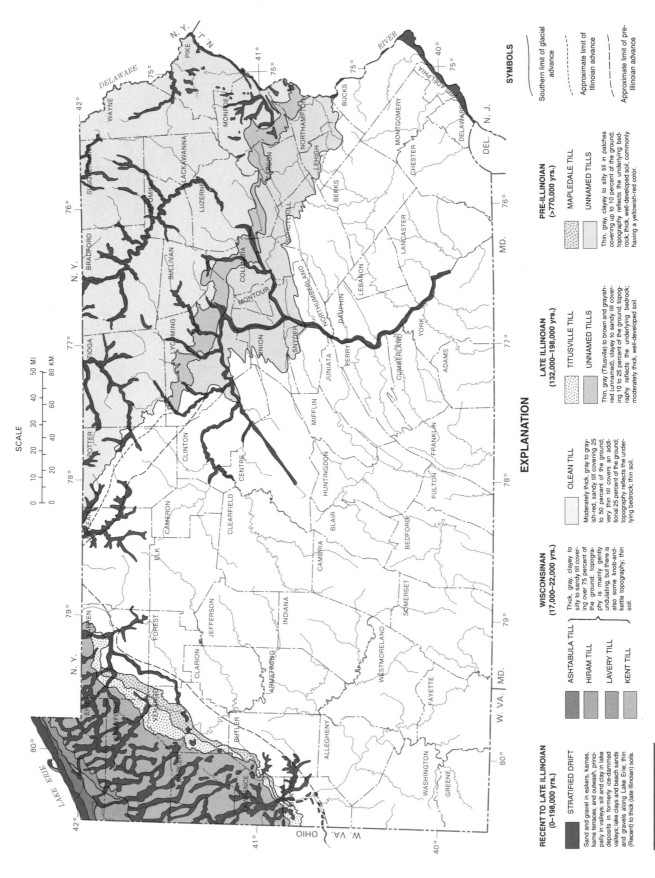

SCALE

0	10	20	30	40	50 MI		
0	20	40	60	80 KM			

EXPLANATION

RECENT TO LATE ILLINOIAN
(0–198,000 yrs.)

STRATIFIED DRIFT

Sand and gravel in eskers, kames, kame terraces, and outwash, principally in valleys; silt and clay in lake deposits in formerly ice-dammed valleys; lake clays and beach sands and gravels along Lake Erie; thin (Recent) to thick (late Illinoian) soils.

WISCONSINAN
(17,000–22,000 yrs.)

ASHTABULA TILL
HIRAM TILL
LAVERY TILL
KENT TILL

Thick, gray, clayey to silty to sandy till covering over 75 percent of the ground; topography is mainly gently undulating, but there is also some knob-and-kettle topography; thin soil.

OLEAN TILL

Moderately thick, gray to grayish-red, sandy till covering 25 to 50 percent of the ground; very thin till covers an additional 25 percent of the ground; topography reflects the underlying bedrock; thin soil.

LATE ILLINOIAN
(132,000–198,000 yrs.)

TITUSVILLE TILL
UNNAMED TILLS

Thin, gray (Titusville) to brown and grayish-red (unnamed), clayey to sandy till covering 10 to 25 percent of the ground; topography reflects the underlying bedrock; moderately thick, well-developed soil.

PRE-ILLINOIAN
(>770,000 yrs.)

MAPLEDALE TILL
UNNAMED TILLS

Thin, gray, clayey to silty till in patches covering up to 10 percent of the ground; topography reflects the underlying bedrock; thick, well-developed soil, commonly having a yellowish-red color.

SYMBOLS

Southern limit of glacial advance

Approximate limit of Illinoian advance

Approximate limit of pre-Illinoian advance

Figure 15–1. Glacial deposits of Pennsylvania (from Pennsylvania Geological Survey, 1981, and Sevon and Braun, 1997).

CHAPTER 15   QUATERNARY

GEORGE H. CROWL*
Department of Geography and Geology
Ohio Wesleyan University
Delaware, OH 43015

W. D. SEVON
Bureau of Topographic and Geologic Survey
Department of Conservation and Natural
   Resources
P. O. Box 8453
Harrisburg, PA 17105

INTRODUCTION

The Quaternary Period includes the last approximately 2.8 million years of geologic time (Beard and others, 1982). It is divided into the Pleistocene Epoch, which was marked by several northern- and southern-hemisphere continental glaciations, and the Holocene Epoch, which is the current interglacial period of time that started about 10,000 years ago. Most of the deposits associated with this interval in Pennsylvania are related directly or indirectly to glaciation. For purposes of discussion, the state is subdivided into two areas: (1) the glaciated parts of northwestern and northeastern Pennsylvania, and (2) the nonglaciated remainder of the state (Figure 15–1).

GLACIATED AREA

Four major periods of glaciation are identified in northwestern Pennsylvania (Shepps and others, 1959; White and others, 1969), and it is assumed that the same glaciations occurred in northeastern Pennsylvania, although evidence for the oldest glaciation is lacking. From oldest to youngest, these glaciations are pre-Illinoian (two), Illinoian, and late Wisconsinan (Woodfordian). Available data indicate that the younger pre-Illinoian glaciation was the most extensive, and that all of the glaciations followed similar patterns of advance and deglaciation (Braun, 1988). Most generalizations about glaciation in Pennsylvania are based on data obtained from deposits and erosional features of the last glaciation, the Woodfordian.

Continental glaciation in Pennsylvania derived from the Laurentide ice sheet, which spread south from its center over Hudson Bay in Canada. The ice sheet separated into lobes near its southern margin (Mickelson and others, 1983), and ice flow into Pennsylvania was via the Erie lobe in the northwest and the Lake Champlain-Hudson River lobe in the northeast (Figure 15–2). These lobes did not meet in Pennsylvania, and the unglaciated triangular part of Pennsylvania and New York between the two lobes is called the Salamanca Re-entrant. The maximum thickness of the ice is not known, but it certainly exceeded 1,000

*Deceased.

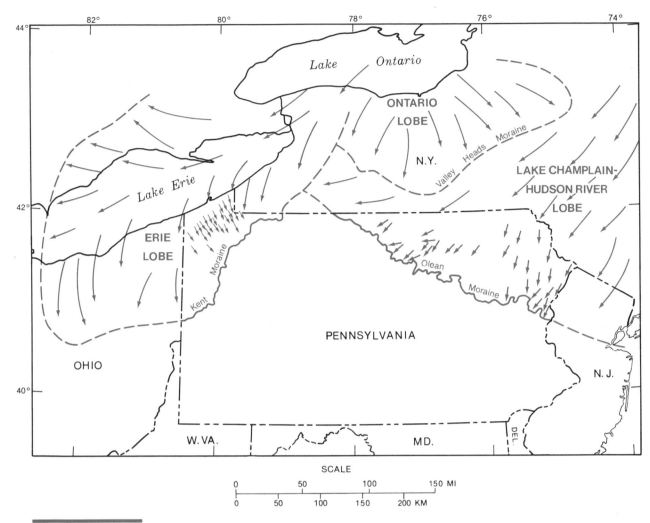

Figure 15–2. Directions of Laurentide ice flow into Pennsylvania during the late Wisconsinan. Ice-flow directions in northeastern Pennsylvania are derived from the orientation of glacial striae, and in northwestern Pennsylvania from linear landforms. Flow directions outside Pennsylvania are from Mickelson, D. M., and others, *The late Wisconsin glacial record of the Laurentide ice sheet in the United States,* in Porter, S. C., ed., *The late Pleistocene,* Volume 1 of Wright, H. E., Jr., ed., *Late-Quaternary environments of the United States,* Minneapolis, University of Minnesota Press, Figure 1–3, p. 5, copyright © 1983 by the University of Minnesota.

feet within a few miles of the southern margin (Sevon and others, 1975). Numerous vertical sequences in the northwest contain repetitions of a till with an intact soil zone at the top overlain by a younger till. These sequences indicate little erosion by ice during repeated advances. This lack of erosion was probably due to the relatively flat, frozen, and texturally homogeneous surface over which successive glaciations traversed. The preservation of multiple till sequences has allowed the development of a good glacial stratigraphy in the northwest (White and others, 1969).

In northeastern Pennsylvania, where topography is very irregular and surface materials heterogeneous, each glaciation eroded most, or all, of any older gla-

cial deposits, as well as some rock. Thus, vertical sequences of deposits of multiple glaciations are rare in the northeast, and knowledge of older glaciations is gained mainly where the deposits have not been overridden by a younger glaciation.

Till is the primary deposit directly associated with glaciation in Pennsylvania. The composition and texture of Woodfordian tills in the northeast very strongly reflect the character of the underlying bedrock (Epstein, 1969; Sevon and others, 1989). Local bedrock influence is considerably less in the northwest (White and others, 1969), presumably because of the lack of local erosion by successive ice advances. Woodfordian tills in the northwest are subdivided on the basis of texture, stratigraphic position, and areal separation by end moraines. Most Pennsylvania tills have a matrix dominated by silt, are stony, and are variable in surface morphology. Woodfordian till is widespread in the northwest and underlies relatively flat to undulating surfaces, whereas till in the northeast occurs primarily along the lower slopes of larger valleys or as fill in small valleys. The thickness of Woodfordian-age tills is variable. Total drift thickness in the northwest is commonly 50 feet or more, whereas the thickness is generally less than 20 feet in the northeast. Till greater than 3 feet thick covers 75 to 100 percent of the surface in the northwest but only 25 to 50 percent of the surface in the northeast.

Limited data on pre-Woodfordian tills suggest textural and compositional patterns similar to Woodfordian tills (White and others, 1969; Marchand, 1978; Wells and Bucek, 1980; Inners, 1981). Pre-Woodfordian tills, where not overridden and eroded by more recent glaciation, have been eroded sufficiently to now cover only a small percentage of the surface: 10 to 25 percent for Illinoian tills and less than 10 percent for pre-Illinoian tills. These deposits are rarely more than 10 feet thick.

Table 15–1 shows the stratigraphic terminology used by the Pennsylvania Geological Survey for glacial drift in Pennsylvania prior to 1989. The age assignments for the tills in northeastern and north-central Pennsylvania are based on comparative degrees of soil development (Sevon, 1974; Sevon and others, 1975), the amount of erosion of a specific till, and some radiocarbon dating (Crowl and Sevon, 1980; Cotter, 1983, 1985). Age assignments in the northwest are based primarily on stratigraphic position and mid-continent correlation (White and others, 1969). Marchand (1978) suggested additional terminology (Penny Hill, Laurelton, and White Deer) for some pre-Wisconsinan drift in north-central Pennsylvania, but the terminology has received limited use. The determination that there was no early Wisconsinan glaciation in Pennsylvania (Braun, 1988; Eyles and Westgate, 1987) required that age assignments shown in Table 15–1 be reevaluated. That reevaluation indicated that materials assigned an early Wisconsinan age are really Illinoian in age and all older materials are pre-Illinoian in age. Identification of lake clays having reversed polarity overlying till in north-central Pennsylvania allowed revision of age assignments in that area and indicated that pre-Illinoian-age materials are greater than 770,000 years old (Gardner and others, 1994).

Wisconsinan ice-contact sand and gravel deposits are common along valley sides in both glaciated parts of Pennsylvania. These deposits are characterized by extreme variability in bedding attitude and texture (Figure 15–3). The surface morphology of these de-

Table 15–1. *Stratigraphic Terminology Applied to Glacial Deposits in Pennsylvania by the Pennsylvania Geological Survey Prior to 1989*

		NORTHWESTERN White and others (1969)	NORTH-CENTRAL Wells and Bucek (1980)	Inners (1981)	NORTHEASTERN Berg and others (1977)
STAGE	SUBSTAGE	UNIT[1]			
Wisconsinan	Late (Woodfordian)	Ashtabula Till Hiram Till Lavery Till Kent Till	Olean drift	Nescopeck Loess Olean drift	Woodfordian drift
	Farmdalian	Paleosol	Paleosol	Paleosol	Paleosol
	Early (Altonian)	Titusville Till	Warrensville drift	Glen Brook Till	Altonian till
Sangamonian		Thick paleosol	Thick paleosol	Thick paleosol; pre-Nescopeck loess	Thick paleosol
Illinoian		Mapledale Till	Muncy drift	Muncy Till	Illinoian till
Pre-Illinoian		Slippery Rock Till			

[1] The term drift is used here where the name is applied to several different types of deposit (e.g., till, ice-contact sand and gravel, outwash, and so forth).

posits is variable, depending on whether the deposit is an esker, kame, kame terrace, delta, or some other type. Comparable pre-Illinoian deposits are rare but do occur locally (Inners, 1981).

Woodfordian outwash sand and gravel deposits occur within the glaciated parts of the state and along some river valleys outside the glaciated area (Figure 15–1). These deposits are flat surfaced, possess less textural variability than ice-contact deposits, and are locally many tens of feet thick. Outwash deposits of pre-Woodfordian glaciations occur mainly as isolated terrace deposits along major rivers.

Woodfordian ice-contact clay deposits occur locally in north-draining valleys that were dammed by ice during deglaciation. Extensive deposits of this type occur in the Cowanesque River valley in north-central Pennsylvania. These deposits are unstable and very susceptible to landslide. Preston (1977) described deposits of similar origin in western Pennsylvania. Older deposits of presumed similar origin are represented by the terrace materials of the Carmichaels Formation in southwestern Pennsylvania (Leverett, 1934; Jacobson and others, 1988).

Following Woodfordian deglaciation, many surface depressions in glaciated parts of the state became the sites of peat bogs. Northeastern Pennsylvania, particularly Pike and Monroe Counties, has the greatest concentration of peat (Cameron, 1970; Edgerton, 1969).

Figure 15–3. Woodfordian ice-contact sand and gravel near Blooming Grove, Pike County.

NONGLACIATED AREAS

During the Quaternary stages of glaciation, the nonglaciated part of Pennsylvania was the site of extensive periglacial activity, variable amounts of erosion, and limited fluvial deposition. Watts (1979) and Whitehead (1973) demonstrated the existence of a tundra environment, probably with continuous to discontinuous permafrost, in even the lower elevations of the state during the Woodfordian. Similar environmental conditions prevailed during each preceding glaciation. Tundra climate and permafrost are optimal conditions for periglacial activity.

The periglacial environment associated with the several glaciations caused extensive mass wasting throughout the nonglaciated part of Pennsylvania through extensive rock breakup and downslope movement of broken material. The hard sandstones that form the crests of linear ridges in the Appalachian Mountain section have numerous planes of bedding and fracture and thus are very susceptible to breakup by freeze-thaw cycles. Pleistocene periglacial activity probably lowered these crests several tens of feet (Cooper, 1944). The broken rock accumulated as talus (Figure 15–4) or became mixed with previously weathered, finer grained material to form stony colluvium. A complex interaction between available clast size, steepness of slope, and severity of periglacial activity produced the many variations of colluvial deposits. Some of these colluvial deposits have complex vertical stratigraphy and demonstrable age multiplicity (Hoover, 1983). Of some interest and economic importance are the numerous shale-chip-rubble deposits (*grèzes litées*) (Figure 15–5) associated with fine-grained rocks such as the Devonian Mahantango, Ordovician Martinsburg, and Ordovician Reedsville shales (Sevon and Berg, 1979).

Strikingly scenic deposits of periglacial origin occur on low slopes as boulder fields. Hickory Run in Carbon County (Figure 15–6) (Sevon, 1969a, 1987a), Blue Rocks in Berks County (Potter and Moss, 1968), Ringing Rocks in Bucks County, and Devils Racecourse in Dauphin County (Martin, 1971) are well-known examples (see Geyer and Bolles, 1979, for details of access).

Eolian deposits in the form of loess are widespread within Pennsylvania (Ciolkosz, Cronce, and Sevon, 1986) but have received little attention except in soils mapping. These surface deposits are in most places less than 5 feet thick and difficult to recognize

Figure 15–4. Talus composed of blocks of Silurian Tuscarora quartzite on the west slope of Brush Mountain near Altoona, Blair County.

Figure 15–5. Involutions of periglacial origin formed in shale-chip rubble developed from Ordovician Martinsburg shale near Jacksonville, Lehigh County.

except in subsurface vertical exposures. Loess has been mapped and named (Nescopeck Loess and pre-Nescopeck Loess) in Columbia County (Inners, 1981). A small area of dune sand occurs on the east side of the Susquehanna River in Northumberland County (Chase, 1977), and other areas may exist within the state. Both the loess and dune sand formed during the windy and cold periods associated with tundra climate.

A variety of small periglacial features occurs within the state, but these features are generally dif-

ficult to detect because they have subtle surface expression or can only be seen in subsurface vertical exposures. These features include ice-wedge casts (Figure 15–7), polygonal patterned ground, involutions (Figure 15–5), pingo scars, and solifluction lobes (Ciolkosz, Cronce, and Sevon, 1986).

Woodfordian outwash sand and gravel deposits occur along the valley bottoms of some of the major rivers in Pennsylvania outside the glaciated area (Figure 15–1) and are locally several tens of feet thick. The deposits are flat surfaced and possess less textural variability than ice-contact deposits. Similar deposits occur along some smaller streams, such as Loyalsock Creek and Lycoming Creek in Lycoming County. Older outwash occurs as isolated terrace deposits along the larger rivers, such as the Susquehanna (Peltier, 1949; Pazzaglia and Gardner, 1993). These various deposits are sometimes given a general age identification, but they have no formal name. Named deposits in southeastern Pennsylvania along the Delaware River include terrace deposits of the Van Sciver Lake beds and the Spring Lake beds, both part of the Trenton Gravel (Owens and Minard, 1979). These beds are texturally variable and have a pronounced down-gradient decrease in grain size. The deposits formed during different pre-Woodfordian periods of glacial to interglacial transition.

Fluvial deposits in the valley bottoms and on terraces of streams not heading in glaciated areas have received little attention in Pennsylvania, except for the work of T. L. Kaktins (1986) on the Juniata River. Deposits are present along most of these streams, and their history is complex.

A significant body of sand occurs in Lake Erie in the form of Presque Isle, a migrating, compound, recurved spit (Thomas and others, 1987) that is land tied at Erie. Other sand and gravel deposits in Erie County comprise onshore lake-parallel, glaciofluvial, glaciodeltaic, and glaciolacustrine sediments formed during former, higher glacial lake levels (Thomas and others, 1987), and offshore deposits associated with a cross-lake glacial moraine (Berkheiser, 1987).

Figure 15–6. Hickory Run Boulder Field, Hickory Run State Park, Carbon County. The smaller rounded boulders in the foreground are about 1 foot in diameter. The distance from the foreground to the treeline is about 1,000 feet.

Figure 15–7. Ice-wedge cast in Ordovician Reedsville Shale near Tusseyville, Centre County. Soil material fills the cast to a depth of 64 inches. The cast is 32 inches wide at the top. Sketch made from a photograph taken by Richard Cronce.

The geological observer should be aware that the several Quaternary glaciations were separated by interglacial periods, during which the climate was warmer than, or comparable to, the present climate, which is presumed to be that of another interglacial period. It is difficult to evaluate erosion and sedimentation events during the past interglacials because of the lack of datable materials. Processes occurring at present are probably not a good indicator because of the influence of man on erosion. However, descriptions of the precolonial landscape and streams in eastern North America (Trimble, 1974) suggest that, without the influence of man, physical erosion and sedimentation would be minimal under the present climate.

PROBLEMS AND FUTURE RESEARCH

The following aspects of Quaternary geology in Pennsylvania require research:

1. Determination of the ages of pre-Illinoian drift.
2. Delineation of Illinoian and pre-Illinoian drift boundaries.
3. Development of a colluvium stratigraphy.
4. Determination of the ages of various fluvial terraces in both glaciated and nonglaciated areas.
5. Continued detailed (1:24,000-scale) mapping of surficial materials.

RECOMMENDED FOR FURTHER READING

Flint, R. F. (1971), *Glacial and Quaternary geology*, New York, John Wiley and Sons, 892 p.

Goldthwait, R. P., ed. (1971), *Till—a symposium*, Columbus, Ohio State University Press, 402 p.

Mahaney, W. C., ed. (1976), *Quaternary stratigraphy of North America*, Stroudsburg, Pa., Dowden, Hutchinson, and Ross, 512 p.

Porter, S. C., ed. (1983), *The late Pleistocene*, in Wright, H. E., Jr., ed., *Late-Quaternary environments of the United States*, v. 1, Minneapolis, University of Minnesota Press, 407 p.

Wright, H. E., Jr., and Frey, D. G., eds. (1965), *The Quaternary of the United States*, Princeton, N. J., Princeton University Press, 922 p.

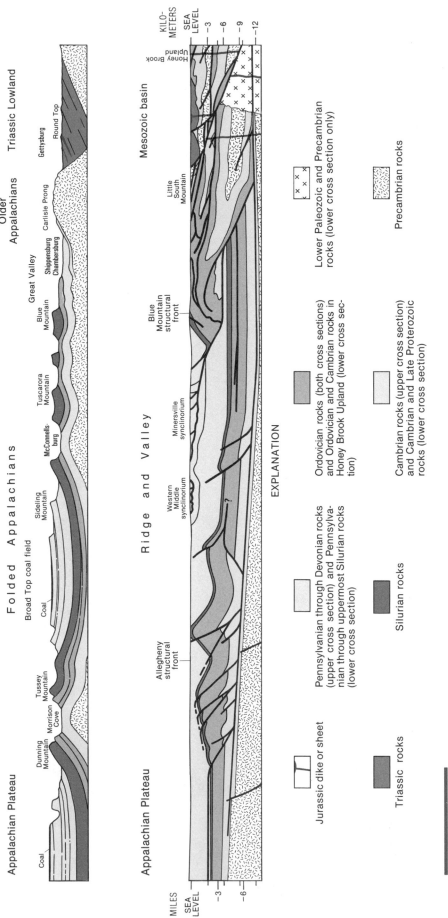

Changing interpretations of structural geology. The upper section represents concepts of deep structure from the Allegheny Front eastward to York County that were prevalent in the first half of the twentieth century (modified slightly from Lobeck, 1951). In this interpretation, Precambrian basement is involved in the folding that is expressed at the surface. The lower section represents a late-twentieth-century interpretation of the structural geology along the same general line of section (simplified from Faill, in preparation). In this example, relatively undisturbed deep Cambrian strata and Precambrian rocks are overridden by a thick allochthon made up of intricately faulted and folded Precambrian and Paleozoic rocks.

Part III

STRUCTURAL GEOLOGY AND TECTONICS

Most structures in the rocks of Pennsylvania can be genetically related to plate-tectonic activity. Convergence created three main orogenic episodes that caused structural deformation. These are the Grenville orogeny (circa 1,000 Ma), the Late Ordovician Taconic orogeny (circa 470 to 440 Ma), and the culminating Alleghanian orogeny (circa 300 to 245 Ma) at the end of the Paleozoic Era. Rifting, brought about by divergence, occurred in the late Precambrian (circa 700 Ma) and again in the Late Triassic to Early Jurassic (circa 230 to 190 Ma).

Even a casual glance at the geologic map of Pennsylvania shows that the structural grain of the state consists of a great curving arc that is convex toward the northwest. In a general way, the structural complexity decreases from southeast to northwest. For instance, structures in the rocks of the eastern Piedmont near Philadelphia were affected by all three orogenies and consist of imbricate thrust-bounded slabs and nappes, cored with Grenville gneisses, that have been subsequently displaced vertically along steep faults, causing arching or refolding. Conversely, in the western part of the state, surface strata are largely flat lying, disturbed only by indistinct folds of low structural relief.

Chapter divisions are based on physiographic provinces or sections, because each is characterized by a distinctive structural style or intensity, although there are important exceptions. For example, the structural styles of South Mountain and the western part of the Great Valley are identical, and the Reading Prong and the eastern part of the Great Valley belong to the same megastructural system. Common themes throughout Part III include thin-skinned tectonics (rootless structures floored by nonemergent décollements), multiple deformation, and the inheritance or reactivation of preexisting planes of weakness under different stress regimes.

—Charles H. Shultz

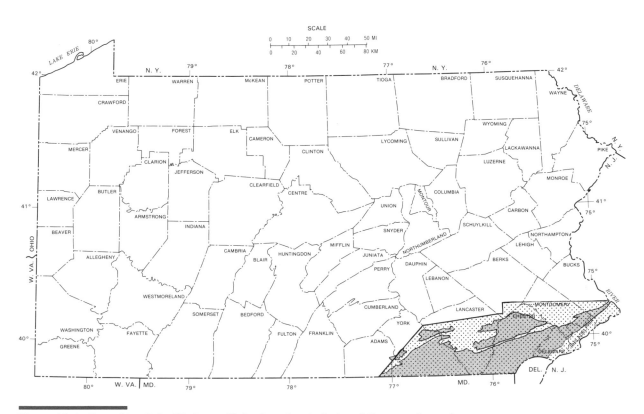

Figure 16–1. Location of the Piedmont Upland section (color) and the area shown in Figure 16–2 (stippled).

234

CHAPTER 16 PIEDMONT UPLAND

MARIA LUISA CRAWFORD
Department of Geology
Bryn Mawr College
Bryn Mawr, PA 19010

WILLIAM A. CRAWFORD
Department of Geology
Bryn Mawr College
Bryn Mawr, PA 19010

ALICE L. HOERSCH
Department of Geology and Physics
LaSalle University
Philadelphia, PA 19141

MARY EMMA WAGNER
Department of Geology
University of Pennsylvania
Philadelphia, PA 19104

INTRODUCTION

The Piedmont Upland section of the Piedmont physiographic province (Figure 16-1) is underlain by a group of metamorphosed and complexly deformed sedimentary, volcanic, and plutonic rocks and associated unmetamorphosed intrusive igneous bodies. As described in Chapter 3A, the metamorphosed units range in age from late Precambrian through early Paleozoic. The youngest intrusive rocks are Jurassic. For easy reference, the Piedmont Upland is subdivided into the Northern and Southern Uplands, which are separated by the Piedmont Lowland. Figures 16-2 and 16-3 show that the western part of the Piedmont Upland is overlain by Cambrian and Ordovician metacarbonate rocks, the eastern part is overlapped by Mesozoic clastic sedimentary strata on the north, and the southeastern part is overlapped by Cretaceous, Tertiary, and Quaternary sands and gravels of the Coastal Plain.

In the Piedmont Upland, the dominant structural grain trends northeast to east-northeast. The region consists of a series of thrust-bounded nappes and slabs that juxtapose rocks of various ages and degrees of metamorphism. These are described in more detail below. Superimposed on these thrust slabs, broad arches generate linear outcrop belts of Precambrian gneisses (metamorphosed during the Grenville orogeny, about 1,000 Ma) in the Honey Brook-Mine Ridge anticlinorium in the Northern Upland and the Buck Ridge-West Chester-Avondale anticlinorium in the Southern Upland (Figures 16-2 and 16-3). Between these structures lies a synclinorium consisting of the Whitemarsh syncline and, along strike to the southwest, the Peach Bottom synform. The Chester Valley, south of the Honey Brook Upland, is underlain by the northern limb of this fold. Major subvertical northeast-striking faults, including the Brandywine Manor fault, the Cream Valley fault, the Huntington Valley fault, and the Rosemont fault (Figure 16-2), cut through the blocks containing Grenville-age gneisses and juxtaposed them against younger rocks. Smaller scale structures, including minor folds, foliations, and lineations in the metamorphic rocks, generally parallel the regional structural trend.

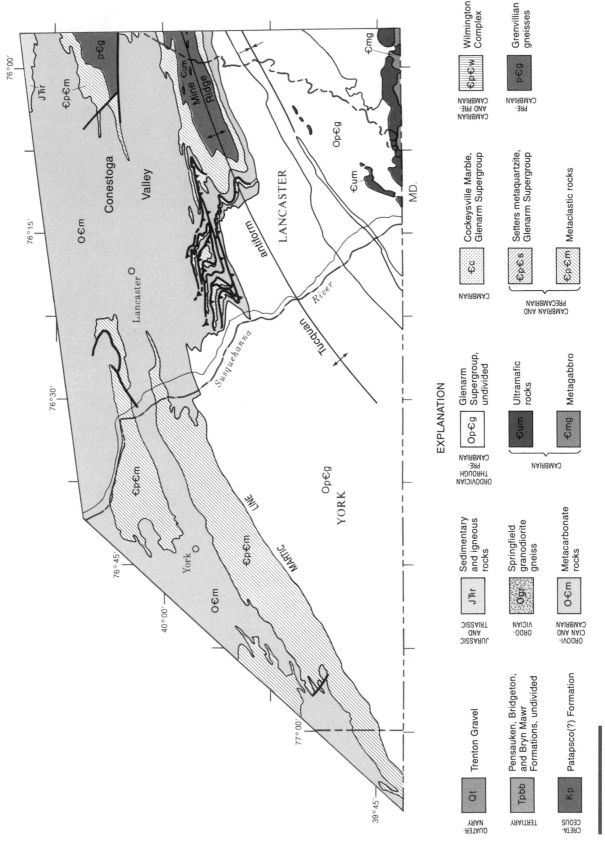

Figure 16–2. Geological features of the Piedmont Upland. Contacts and faults are modified from Berg and others (1980). Features identified by number are (1) Honey Brook anorthosite and (2) Arden pluton. Cross sections are shown in Figure 16–3.

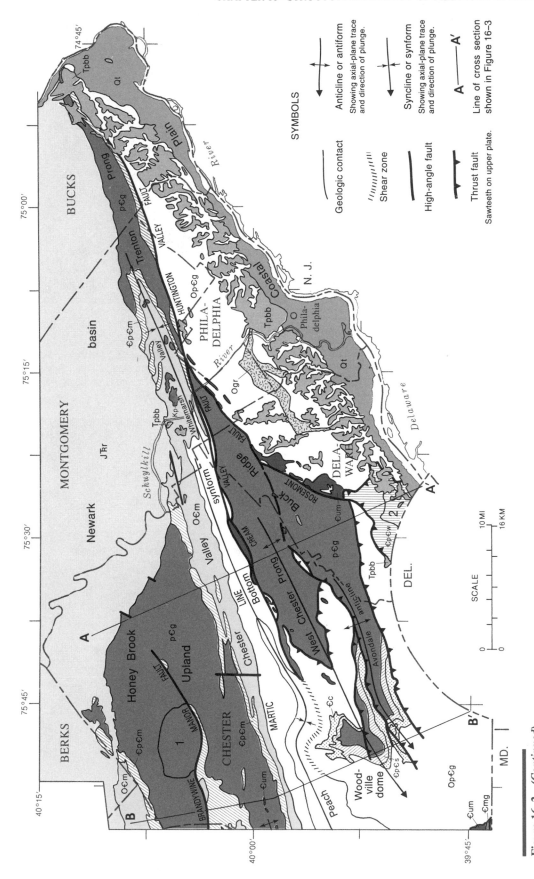

Figure 16-2. *(Continued).*

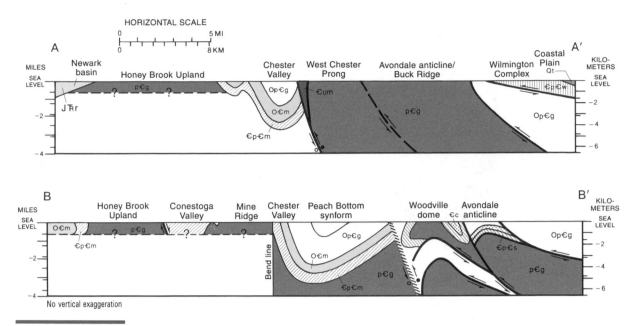

Figure 16–3. Generalized geologic cross sections through the Piedmont Upland. The lines of section are marked and patterns for lithologic units are explained on Figure 16–2. Thrust motion is indicated by arrows. Transcurrent motion is indicated by dots and circles: dot, motion toward viewer; circle, motion away from viewer. Units shown on Figure 16–2 that are of very limited extent or thickness are not shown in the cross sections.

NORTHERN UPLAND

In Mine Ridge and in the part of the Honey Brook Upland north of the Brandywine Manor fault, little is known of the structure because of very limited exposures. The region of the Honey Brook Upland south of the Brandywine Manor fault has more exposure, but detailed structural information is lacking. The principal structural elements of the crystalline rocks are a pervasive foliation (Figure 16–4) and compositional banding (Figure 16–5), which strike N75°E and dip steeply to the south. In some outcrops, the banding is isoclinally folded (Figure 16–6). The same trend characterizes the axial-plane orientation of isoclinal folds in the overlying late Precambrian through lower Paleozoic metasediments (Figure 16–2), and hence these folds developed during the Taconic orogeny in the Late Ordovician, or later. Aeromagnetic data (Crawford and Hoersch, 1984) suggest that the anorthosite massif in the northern part of the Honey Brook Upland (Figure 16–2) has steep contacts with the country rocks and that, from its eastern contact, the anorthosite extends a couple of miles under a thin cover of charnockite.

The following information suggests that the Honey Brook Upland and Mine Ridge are not rooted and are, perhaps, less than 1 km (0.6 mi) thick (Figure 16–3): (1) Only shallow rock units (less than 600 m [2,000 ft] deep) of appropriate susceptibility contrast were needed for computer modeling of aeromagnetic data for the

Figure 16–4. Foliated gneiss characteristic of Mine Ridge, along U.S. Route 30E bypass, west of Coatesville, Chester County.

anorthosite massif in the northern part of the Honey Brook Upland (Crawford and Hoersch, 1984); (2) the general pattern of magnetic anomalies in the Honey Brook Upland is similar to that of Mine Ridge and quite distinct from those of the Chester Valley and the Southern Upland, except possibly in the area of the West Chester Prong and the Avondale anticline (see Chapter 3A and Figure 16–2) (U.S. Geological Survey, 1978; Hoersch and Crawford, 1988); (3) a preliminary gravity profile across the Honey Brook Upland (Hoersch and Crawford, 1988) shows only the prevailing regional trend; and (4) a preliminary Bouguer anomaly map of Mine Ridge has no anomaly patterns that can be associated with the surficial geology and also shows only the prevailing regional trend (Hoersch and Crawford, 1988).

SOUTHERN UPLAND

The Grenville-age (1,000 Ma) gneisses south of the Chester and Whitemarsh Valleys occur in the Buck Ridge-West Chester-Avondale anticlinorium and reappear to the southwest in Maryland in the Baltimore-Washington anticlinorium. The gneisses of the Avondale anticline, the Woodville dome, and the Wilmington Complex, the rocks of the State Line ultramafic complex, and the metasedimentary rocks that surround them were tectonically emplaced as a series of ductile nappes and thrust slabs transported toward the North American continent before or during the Late Ordovician Taconic orogeny (about 440 Ma) (Wagner and Srogi, 1987; Figure 16–3). The stacked pile of thrust slabs and nappes was subsequently deformed by the uplift of the underlying basement, now exposed in the uparched and upfaulted blocks of the West Chester Prong and the eastern end of Buck Ridge. The age of this uplift is not known but is younger than the thrusting.

The uppermost thrust slab crops out in the southeasternmost exposed portion of the Piedmont. It contains the Wilmington Complex, which overlies the Wissahickon Formation (part of the Glenarm Supergroup) and has a nearly planar subhorizontal contact (Srogi, 1982). Crawford and Mark (1982) and Wagner and Srogi (1987) suggested that this contact is a major thrust fault (cross section A–A´ in Figure 16–3). North and west of the Wilmington Complex, the gneisses of the Woodville dome and the western end of the Avondale anticline, which are mantled by the Glenarm Supergroup, are in the cores of northwestward-directed recumbent nappes with sheared-off lower limbs (Mackin, 1962; cross section B–B´ in Figure 16–3). The Wissahickon schists that lie between the Wilmington Complex and the Woodville dome and Avondale anticline appear to lie in a separate thrust sheet (Alcock, 1994). The State Line ultramafic complex that lies along the Pennsylvania-Maryland border east of the Susquehanna River (Figure 16–2) is the northern edge of a similar group of thrust sheets and nappes mapped in the Maryland Piedmont (Fisher and others, 1979). The timing of the thrusting is not clear. The Wilmington Complex appears to have been emplaced no later than the Late Ordovician Taconic metamorphism (Crawford and Mark, 1982; Wagner and

Figure 16–5. Banded and foliated amphibolite-facies gneiss of the Honey Brook Upland, Little Conestoga Road, west of Marsh Creek Lake, Chester County.

Figure 16–6. Isoclinal folds in gneiss in the Honey Brook Upland, at the spillway on Marsh Creek Lake, Chester County.

Srogi, 1987). As noted in the previous section, the emplacement of the Mine Ridge-Honey Brook Upland slab may have occurred during the same time interval.

The rocks of Grenville age (1,000 Ma) in the core of the Buck Ridge-West Chester-Avondale anticlinorium are bounded by three steeply dipping faults: Cream Valley, Huntington Valley, and Rosemont (Figure 16–2). These three faults are interpreted to be related to vertical uplift of blocks of basement gneiss subsequent to nappe emplacement. The West Chester Prong is an upright anticline having a steeply overturned northern limb cut by the Cream Valley fault (see cross section A–A´ in Figure 16–3). The fault separates Grenville-age granulite- and amphibolite-facies rocks on the south from greenschist-facies rocks of the Glenarm Supergroup on the north. Slivers of amphibolite-facies Wissahickon Formation schists are caught up in the fault zone. Wagner and Srogi (1987) suggested that the West Chester Prong is autochthonous or parautochthonous; Elliott and others (1982) and Fisher (personal communication, 1982) suggested that this block forms a hanging-wall anticline. The West Chester Prong anticline also folds the overlying Woodville and Avondale nappes of Grenville-age basement and metasediments of the Glenarm Supergroup as shown by the hook pattern of the Woodville dome (Figure 16–2; cross section B–B´ in Figure 16–3). The Huntington Valley fault appears to be the eastward continuation of the Cream Valley fault (Bascom and others, 1909; Armstrong, 1941). It separates Baltimore Gneiss overlain by the Chickies and Ledger Formations on the north from Wissahickon Formation schist on the south. The Buck Ridge block is bounded on the southeast by the steeply dipping to vertical Rosemont fault. Textures in the metamorphic rocks along the faults suggest that faulting occurred after the peak of metamorphic activity and, therefore, was post-Ordovician.

The Wissahickon Formation has been complexly deformed. Along Wissahickon Creek, east of the Schuylkill River in northwestern Philadelphia, Amenta (1974) recognized three major episodes of deformation that coincided with the metamorphism of the schist. Weiss (1949), Amenta (1974), and Tearpock and Bischke (1980) noted that the structures dip to the northwest throughout much of the eastern part of the Wissahickon Formation schist belt (southeast of Buck Ridge and east of the Wilmington Complex) and steepen to vertical adjacent to the Rosemont and Huntington Valley faults. Foliations in the schists adjacent to and west of the Wilmington Complex also dip to the northwest, but near the Avondale anticline to the north, they dip southeast.

The greenschist-facies phyllite of the Octoraro Formation that lies between the Buck Ridge-West Chester-Avondale anticlinorium and the Chester and Whitemarsh Valleys is interpreted as representing a low-grade metamorphic equivalent of the Wissahickon Formation. The late Precambrian through Ordovician metaclastic and metacarbonate rocks of the Chester and Whitemarsh Valleys and the Octoraro phyllite lie in a syncline bounded by the Precambrian blocks of the Honey Brook Upland and Mine Ridge on the north, the West Chester Prong on the south, and the Trenton Prong to the east (Figures 16–2 and 16–3). The south limb of the syncline is cut off by the Cream Valley fault west of the Schuylkill River.

The nature of the contact between the Octoraro phyllite and the Cambrian and Ordovician metacarbonate rocks of the Chester and Whitemarsh Valleys has been the subject of considerable debate and contro-

versy. This contact is part of the Martic Line (Figure 16–2) and was interpreted as an overthrust by Knopf and Jonas (1929). The controversy arises in part because the age of the Glenarm Supergroup is unknown for certain and in part because the contact is poorly exposed. Detailed mapping by Cloos and Hietanen (1941) in the area between the end of Mine Ridge and the Susquehanna River, where Knopf and Jonas (1929) defined the Martic thrust, led them to conclude that the Martic Line is not a thrust fault but is simply the contact between the lower Paleozoic carbonate formations and the overlying phyllite. There is no evidence of any major stratigraphic offset at this contact either in the footwall or in the hanging wall. Cloos and Hietanen (1941) did, however, identify a series of north or northeasterly directed thrusts west of the end of Mine Ridge and south of Lancaster (Figure 16–2) that repeat the lower Paleozoic section north of the Martic Line. On the other hand, recent work (Lyttle, 1982; Duffy and Myer, 1984) supports the hypothesis advanced by Knopf (1931) that the phyllites, at least in part, have been tectonically deformed and recrystallized. Along the Susquehanna River, Freedman and others (1964) presented evidence that the phyllite-carbonate contact, whatever its nature, predates the deformation that has affected all units. Hill (1989) agreed with this interpretation and suggested that the deformation and low-grade metamorphism in a zone 1 to 3 km (0.5 to 2 mi) wide in the vicinity of the Martic Line is a feature associated with dextral-transcurrent movement along a ductile shear zone (cross section B–B´ in Figure 16–3). Because the deformation and metamorphism occurred later than the metamorphic and structural features associated with the Taconic orogeny, this shearing is post-Taconic in age.

Freedman and others (1964) pointed out that, in the Northern Upland, the uplift of Mine Ridge arched upward the formerly south-dipping foliations of the overlying late Precambrian through Ordovician clastic and carbonate metasediments (Tucquan antiform; see Figure 16–2). Therefore, in this area also, uplift of the basement-cored blocks is a relatively late event.

The Peach Bottom fold, cored by the Peters Creek Formation, the Cardiff Conglomerate, and the Peach Bottom Slate (all of the Glenarm Supergroup), is another controversial feature. Poor exposure has frustrated regional mapping in the southwestern Piedmont on either side of the Susquehanna River. Some workers (Knopf and Jonas, 1929; Agron, 1950; Southwick, 1969) classified the fold as a syncline based on their interpretation of stratigraphic relations. Higgins (1972), however, argued that sedimentary structures demonstrate that the fold is anticlinal. An analysis of the aeromagnetic map of the area (Fisher and others,

1979) suggests that units of the Wissahickon Formation in this region can be distinguished based on their magnetic signatures. Using this as a guide, Fisher and others (1979) concurred with the analyses of Freedman and others (1964) and Wise (1970), which suggest that much of the Piedmont south and west of the end of Mine Ridge is characterized by refolded folds; the Peach Bottom fold is one of these (see cross section B–B´ in Figure 16–3). Fisher and others (1979) included the Peters Creek Formation with the youngest subdivision of the Wissahickon and hence retained the interpretation that the Peach Bottom fold is synclinal. According to their interpretation, the metavolcanic units (part of the Wissahickon Formation) that crop out in the western Piedmont, in York County, also lie in the core of a synclinal structure.

TECTONIC INTERPRETATIONS

From the structural data, the authors interpret the tectonic evolution of the Piedmont Upland to reflect sedimentation along a late Precambrian-early Paleozoic stable continental margin, followed by tectonic transport of the offshore and continental-margin sedimentary units and of the crystalline rocks of the continental-margin basement toward the continent in thrust slabs and nappes. This tectonic telescoping was initiated by the emplacement of the Wilmington Complex, the base of a hot slab of metamorphic and igneous rocks, possibly the root of a volcanic arc. The Wilmington Complex thrust slab is analogous to the thrust slice containing the James Run volcanic rocks in the Maryland Piedmont, which were emplaced in a similar stratigraphic position (Crowley, 1976). The formation of large-scale recumbent nappes and thrust slices affected the entire lower Paleozoic section as far north as the northern boundary of the Great Valley (Chapters 4 and 18). The time of emplacement of the Avondale and Woodville nappes and of the Mine Ridge-Honey Brook Upland slab has not been established but must be 440 Ma (Taconic orogeny) or older. Metamorphism accompanied and outlasted the thickening of the crust by thrusting and nappe emplacement. Subsequently, the Piedmont units were uparched and upfaulted to produce the major upright anticlinoria and synclinoria. The timing of this is uncertain, but it was a postmetamorphic process. Potassium-argon dates (Lapham and Root, 1971) demonstrate that the metamorphic rocks had cooled significantly by Mississippian time. These data and the large volume of clastic material in the Silurian through Pennsylvanian units in the Appalachian Mountain section of the Ridge and Valley province suggest that uplift of the Piedmont occurred throughout the middle Paleozoic.

PROBLEMS AND FUTURE RESEARCH

A thorough study of structures in the Northern Upland and structures in the Southern Upland of Bucks, Lancaster, and York Counties is long overdue. Past and present work focuses primarily on the central part of the region.

As indicated in Chapter 3A, more detailed studies of the metamorphic histories of the rocks in the Piedmont Upland will help to decipher the history of burial and subsequent uplift during the Grenville and Taconic orogenies. The ages of deformational events are virtually unknown. A careful geochronological study is needed to determine the timing of faulting and other deformation. The age of the Glenarm Supergroup in Pennsylvania also remains unknown. This problem must be solved before the controversy concerning the nature of the contact between the Octoraro phyllite and the Cambrian and Ordovician metasediments that lie north of that phyllite (the Martic Line) can be resolved.

A series of ground magnetometer traverses across the ultramafic bodies should provide information concerning their shape and orientation in three dimensions. In Mine Ridge, as well as in the Southern Upland, this, in turn, might allow one to deduce the relationship between these bodies and shallow thrust faults.

RECOMMENDED FOR FURTHER READING

Amenta, R. V. (1974), *Multiple deformation and metamorphism from structural analysis in the eastern Pennsylvania Piedmont,* Geological Society of America Bulletin, v. 85, p. 1647–1660.

Cloos, Ernst, and Hietanen, A. M. (1941), *Geology of the "Martic overthrust" and the Glenarm Series in Pennsylvania and Maryland,* Geological Society of America Special Paper 35, 207 p.

Crawford, M. L., and Mark, L. E. (1982), *Evidence from metamorphic rocks for overthrusting, Pennsylvania Piedmont, U.S.A.,* Canadian Mineralogist, v. 20, p. 333–347.

Freedman, J., Wise, D. U., and Bentley, R. D. (1964), *Pattern of folded folds in the Appalachian Piedmont along Susquehanna River,* Geological Society of America Bulletin, v. 75, p. 621–638.

Mackin, J. H. (1962), *Structure of the Glenarm Series in Chester County, Pennsylvania,* Geological Society of America Bulletin, v. 73, p. 403–410.

Wagner, M. E., and Srogi, LeeAnn (1987), *Early Paleozoic metamorphism at two crustal levels and a tectonic model for the Pennsylvania-Delaware Piedmont,* Geological Society of America Bulletin, v. 99, p. 113–126.

Wise, D. U. (1970), *Multiple deformation, geosynclinal transitions and the Martic problem in Pennsylvania,* in Fisher, G. W., and others, eds., *Studies of Appalachian geology: central and southern,* New York, Interscience Publishers, p. 317–333.

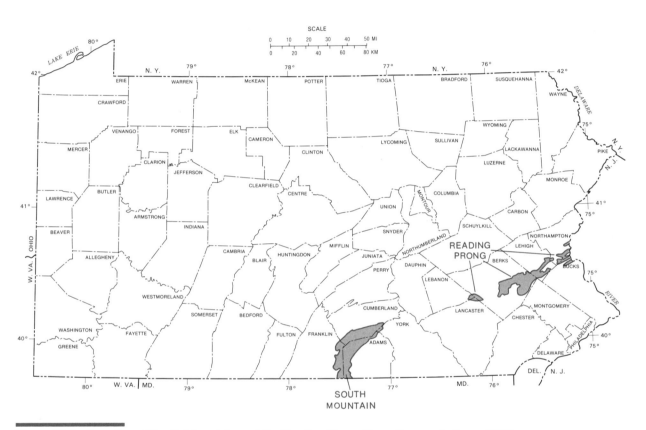

Figure 17–1. Location of South Mountain and the Reading Prong (from Berg and others, 1989).

CHAPTER 17   SOUTH MOUNTAIN AND READING PRONG

AVERY ALA DRAKE, JR.
U.S. Geological Survey
928 National Center
Reston, VA 20192

INTRODUCTION

South Mountain, which is the northern extremity of the Blue Ridge-South Mountain anticlinorium, and the Reading Prong are the largest external basement massifs in the central Appalachians (Drake and others, 1988) (Figure 17–1). Basement rocks, however, do not crop out in the Pennsylvania segment of South Mountain (Chapter 3B). These massifs differ both structurally and in their tectonic histories. The Reading Prong constitutes a complex nappe megasystem in which crystalline basement rocks and their sedimentary cover are involved in large, thrust-faulted, recumbent folds formed during the Taconic orogeny (Chapter 18). The nappe megasystem was later deformed by thrust faulting and attendant folding during the Alleghanian orogeny (Drake, 1978, 1980), leading to extremely complicated geologic relations.

South Mountain, on the other hand, has long been considered to be an extremely large, basement-cored anticlinorium formed by passive slip along cleavage (Cloos, 1971). With the advent of modern seismic-reflection techniques, however, it became apparent that, although it is an anticlinorium, South Mountain is a hanging-wall anticlinorium above a ramp in a deep thrust fault (Harris and others, 1982) (so-called "Eastern Overthrust Belt"). Deformation features in the igneous and metamorphic rocks of the anticlinorium can be related to features in even the youngest cover rocks (Chapter 18), and thereby would appear to be of Alleghanian age. To date, no pre-Alleghanian structural feature has been recognized within the rocks of South Mountain. The Reading Prong and South Mountain massifs, then, differ both in style and timing of deformation.

READING PRONG

The Middle Proterozoic rocks of the Reading Prong have had a long and complicated tectonic history. They were presumably first deformed during the Grenville orogeny at about 1 Ga. Subsequently, they experienced the entire Appalachian orogenic cycle from the Late Proterozoic through the Pennsylvanian-Permian. Finally, they were deformed during the extensional event related to the opening of the Atlantic Ocean during the Mesozoic. Their structure and current position are, therefore, the cumulative result of this long and complicated tectonic history.

Structures of Proterozoic Age

The structures formed during the Grenvillian orogenic event are not well understood. The metamorphosed sedimentary and volcanic-volcaniclastic rocks are both compositionally layered and foliated (Figures 3B–8 and 17–2). Most geologists think that the compositional layering is relict bedding, although some probably results from metamorphic differentiation. Many also think that the foliation in the rocks is mimetic after bedding because layering and foliation are roughly parallel in most exposures. Even if the layering is relict bedding, it may have little stratigraphic meaning, because units map out as lenses (Drake, 1967; Drake and others, 1967), suggesting regional transposition. Foliation, however, is not mi-

Figure 17–2. Light- and dark-layered biotite-quartz-feldspar gneiss on Chestnut Hill, Easton 7.5-minute quadrangle, Northampton County. The long dimensions of the biotite and feldspar crystals define a foliation. The coin at the base of the rock is 0.75 inch in diameter.

metic after bedding; observation of small, early, first-phase folds clearly shows that the foliation, which roughly parallels the layering on limbs, passes through the hinges rather than going around them.

Lineation is well to poorly developed in the Middle Proterozoic rocks and is mostly expressed by aligned minerals or streaks of minerals and, less commonly, by crenulations, rods, or fluted surfaces. The lineation everywhere appears to parallel second-phase fold axes.

Folds are common throughout the Middle Proterozoic terrane, although they are difficult to map because of poor exposure. The folds range from upright and open (Figure 17–3) to isoclinal overturned or isoclinal recumbent (Figures 3B–7, 3B–9, and 17–4). They range from a few inches in wavelength and magnitude to as much as 7 miles long parallel to the axis and 1 mile in width. All mapped folds are of foliation as well as layering (Figures 3B–7, 3B–9, 17–3, and 17–4), so none are first folds. Few geologists have mapped more than one fold phase. Two (possibly three) fold phases were mapped on South Mountain (of the Reading Prong) in Lehigh County (Figure 17–5). It is uncertain whether the east-north-east-trending folds in the western part of the map are a different phase than the north-northeast-trending folds in the eastern part of the area, because there is no overprinting relationship. It would appear, then, that the Middle Proterozoic rocks of the Reading Prong have experienced at least three (possibly four) phases of folding, the earliest of which produced the regional foliation. The concordant sheets of intrusive rocks appear to have been emplaced synkinematically during this fold phase, as their foliation and lineation parallel that in the layered rocks. The entire terrane then experienced the later deformations. Mineral lineation apparently formed during the first phase of folding and was transposed, so that it is now roughly parallel to the axes of second-phase folds and is refolded by the later phases.

Structures of Paleozoic Age

Early workers in eastern Pennsylvania recognized the complexity of the structural geology of the area, and Lesley and others (1883) likened it to that of the Alps. Nevertheless, most geologists considered the Reading Prong to be a large anticlinorium. Stose and Jonas (1935), however, proposed that the Middle Proterozoic crystalline rocks and Cambrian Hardyston Formation of the Reading Prong were part of a large thrust sheet lying upon the carbonate rocks of the Great Valley and that the carbonate-floored valleys within the crystalline terrane were tectonic windows.

Figure 17–3. Upright antiform-synform pair in biotite-quartz-feldspar gneiss on Chestnut Hill, Easton 7.5-minute quadrangle, Northampton County. The coin at the top of the antiform is 0.75 inch in diameter.

Figure 17–4. Isoclinal recumbent folds in potassic feldspar gneiss on Chestnut Hill, Easton 7.5-minute quadrangle, Northampton County. The field of view is about 4 feet by 2.5 feet.

Work since World War II led to the recognition of large recumbent nappes in the Great Valley (Chapter 18) and that thrust faults and overturned folds were a major factor in the distribution of the Middle Proterozoic crystalline rocks. A collation of these data with those gained from aeromagnetic surveying led to the interpretation that the Middle Proterozoic crystalline rocks were involved in the same Alpine structures as the rocks in the Great Valley and led Drake (1969, 1970) to make the rather naive suggestion that the Reading Prong constituted one gigantic nappe.

More recent geologic and geophysical work allows for a more sophisticated interpretation of Reading Prong geology. The Middle Proterozoic rocks are transported, as is clearly shown by the fairly abundant proprietary seismic-reflection profiles that suggest that basement is at a depth of about 15,000 feet in easternmost Pennsylvania and is perhaps as deep as 45,000 feet in the Reading area. Detailed map-

ping shows that the Pennsylvania segment of the Reading Prong consists of at least four nappes or, more properly, nappe systems that are defined largely by their cover sequences (Chapter 18) and that constitute the Reading Prong nappe megasystem (Drake, 1978). From west to east, these are the Lebanon Valley, Irish Mountain, Lyon Station-Paulins Kill, and Musconetcong nappe systems (Figure 17–6).

It must be pointed out that the Middle Proterozoic crystalline rocks were not folded as such with their lower Paleozoic cover, but were thrust into it. The crystalline rocks accommodated themselves to the nappe-form surfaces by movement on zones of ductile and brittle deformation (Drake, 1969, 1970).

Lebanon Valley Nappe System

The Lebanon Valley nappe system (Gray, 1959) was the first recognized element of the megasystem. Its crystalline core underlies Little South Mountain

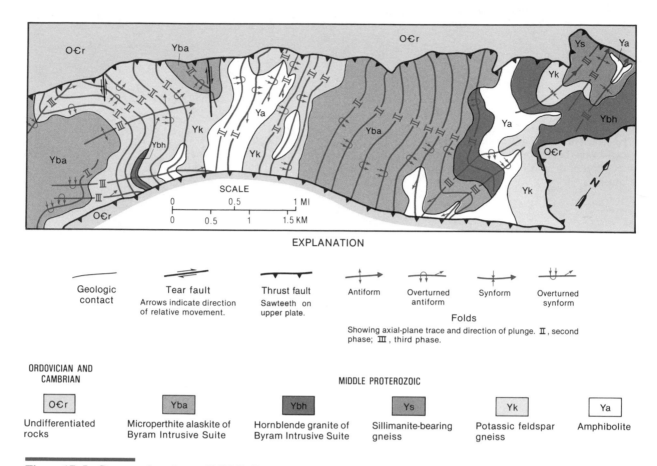

EXPLANATION

Geologic contact	Tear fault	Thrust fault	Antiform	Overturned antiform	Synform	Overturned synform
	Arrows indicate direction of relative movement.	Sawteeth on upper plate.				

Folds

Showing axial-plane trace and direction of plunge. II, second phase; III, third phase.

ORDOVICIAN AND CAMBRIAN

MIDDLE PROTEROZOIC

O∈r	Yba	Ybh	Ys	Yk	Ya
Undifferentiated rocks	Microperthite alaskite of Byram Intrusive Suite	Hornblende granite of Byram Intrusive Suite	Sillimanite-bearing gneiss	Potassic feldspar gneiss	Amphibolite

Figure 17–5. Structural geology of Middle Proterozoic rocks in part of South Mountain (Reading Prong) in the Allentown East 7.5-minute quadrangle, Lehigh County.

(Figure 17–6). These rocks resemble those of the Honey Brook Upland to the south (see Chapter 3A) more than the rocks of the Reading Prong nappes, which is in keeping with their cover of Lebanon Valley sequence rocks that have Piedmont affinities (MacLachlan, 1979). The crystalline rocks have been thrust over regionally inverted rocks of the Lebanon Valley sequence (Figure 17–7). East of Little South Mountain, the Lebanon Valley nappe system tectonically overlies the Irish Mountain nappe system on the Sinking Spring thrust fault (Figure 17–6).

Irish Mountain Nappe System

The Irish Mountain nappe system embraces all of the crystalline rocks, and their cover of Schuylkill sequence rocks (MacLachlan, 1983), from the Reading area in Berks County to the gap in outcropping basement rocks south of Hellertown (just southeast of Bethlehem in Northampton County) (Figure 17–6). A visualization of the Irish Mountain nappe system in the Reading area is given in Figure 17–8,

and in the Allentown area in Figure 17–9. The presence of carbonate rocks beneath outcropping crystalline rocks and Hardyston Formation is confirmed by water wells all along the Irish Mountain nappe trace (Wood and others, 1972). The crystalline rocks of the southern part of the Irish Mountain nappe system, as used herein, have a much higher content of radioactive minerals than the other crystalline rocks of the megasystem and may constitute another nappe (R. C. Smith, II, written communication, 1988). These rocks constitute the Applebutter thrust sheet of Drake (U.S. Geological Survey, 1973).

Lyon Station–Paulins Kill Nappe System

The Lyon Station–Paulins Kill nappe system occurs largely in the subsurface and was defined by Drake (1978) on the basis of aeromagnetic data and the mapping of cover rocks in windows. It lies beneath both the Irish Mountain and Musconetcong nappe systems (Figure 17–9). Its core, as shown by a magnetic anomaly, passes beneath the outcropping Middle Pro-

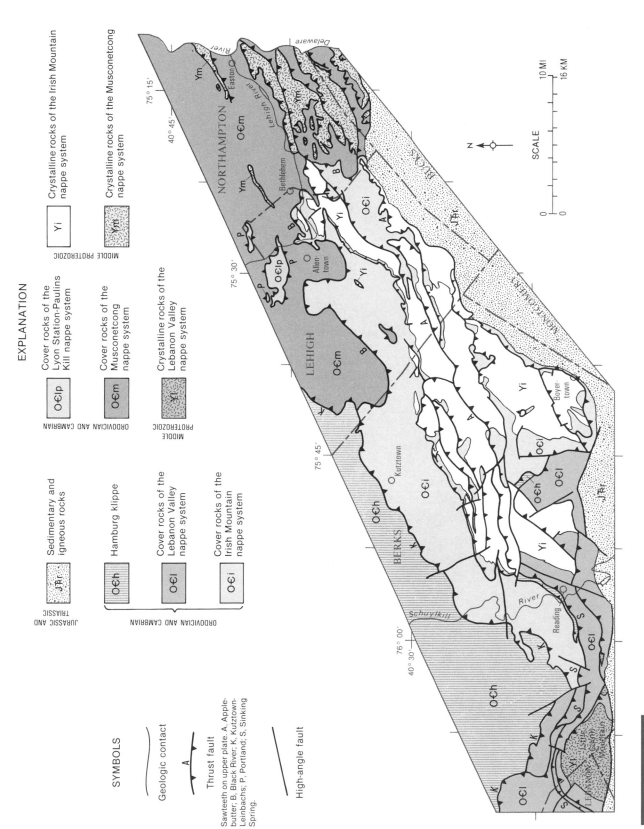

Figure 17-6. Tectonic sketch map of east-central Pennsylvania showing the distribution of nappe systems in the Reading Prong nappe megasystem (modified from Lyttle and Epstein, 1987, and Faill, in preparation).

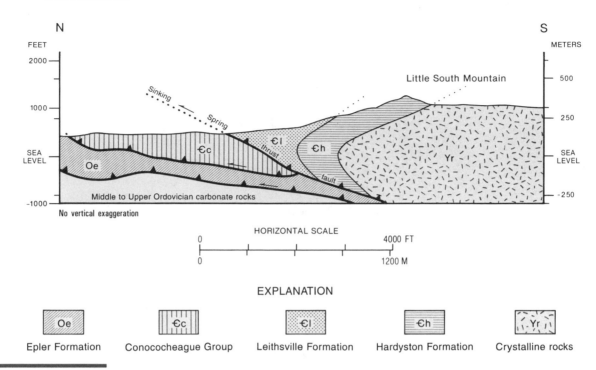

Figure 17–7. Geologic cross section through the brow and part of the lower limb of the Lebanon Valley nappe system in Little South Mountain (modified from Geyer and others, 1963, Plate 1, cross section C–C´).

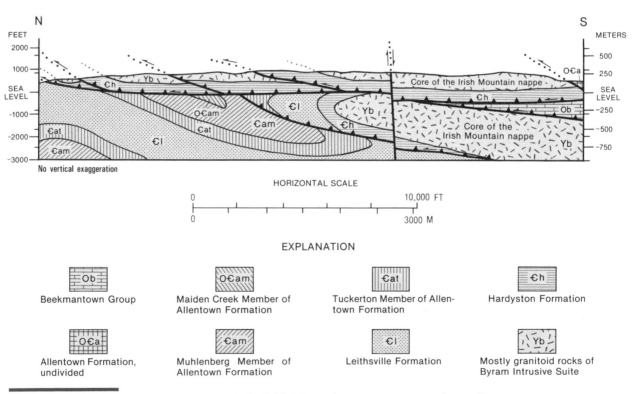

Figure 17–8. Geologic cross section through the Irish Mountain nappe system northeast of Reading (modified from MacLachlan, 1979). The high-angle normal fault is Mesozoic.

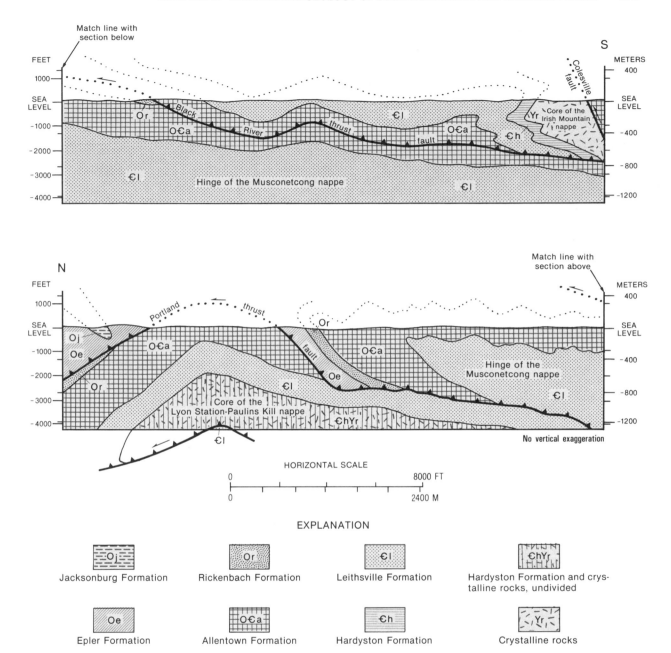

Figure 17–9. Geologic cross section showing the relationship of the Irish Mountain, Musconetcong, and Lyon Station-Paulins Kill nappe systems in the Allentown area (modified from Drake, 1978, Plate 3, Section B).

terozoic rocks of the Irish Mountain nappe system (Bromery and Griscom, 1967) and can be traced to the Delaware River but not into New Jersey.

Musconetcong Nappe System

The Musconetcong nappe system is made up of the basement massifs in eastern Pennsylvania that lie beneath the Black River thrust fault (Figure 17–6) and continue on into New Jersey. This nappe system was first interpreted by Drake (1969) to be one gigantic basement-cored structure produced by both folding and thrusting. The distribution of the crystalline rocks and their cover, as well as many recumbent folds and a regionally inverted sequence in eastern Pennsylvania (Figures 17–10 and 17–11), were thought to have resulted from the refolding of the nappe.

Abundant geologic mapping in eastern Pennsylvania and New Jersey since 1970 necessitates a new

interpretation of the structural geology. This interpretation of the Musconetcong nappe system along the Delaware River is shown in Figure 17-12. The interpretation relies greatly on thrust tectonics. Most of the faults that are shown have been known for many years. Those on the north margins of outcropping bodies of crystalline rock were incorrectly interpreted to be the Musconetcong thrust fault repeated by folding, whereas faults on the south margins were interpreted to be later thrust faults. The faults are now interpreted to constitute a thrust system. The basement

rocks shown in Figure 17-12 coalesce to the west and form a large, but faulted, massif, basement being brought onto basement. This massif was calculated to have a thickness of about 4,000 feet on the basis of aeromagnetic data (Bromery, 1960). This is taken to be the depth to the basal thrust fault of the Musconetcong nappe system in Pennsylvania. No geology is depicted beneath the basal thrust because seismic data are not available for this area.

The array of thrust faults shown in Figure 17-12 has the geometry of an imbricate-fan suite between a basal floor thrust and an eroded roof thrust, constituting a duplex or schuppen structure. Modern work has shown that basement rocks in both the external massifs and Pennine nappes in the Alps, the basement wedges of Cadisch (1946) and Umbgrove (1950), are giant crystalline duplexes (Boyer and Elliott, 1982). To date, three small duplexes or schuppen zones have been recognized in the Musconetcong nappe system. The roundhouse schuppen zone of Drake (unpublished data) contains five repetitions of crystalline rock and Leithsville Formation at the westernmost extremity of the Musconetcong system. Two other such zones have been mapped in New Jersey (Drake and others, 1993, 1994).

Time of Deformation

The time of deformation producing the Reading Prong nappe megasystem is uncertain, but it probably began during the Ordovician Taconic orogeny.

Tectonics

Lash and Drake (1984) presented a tectonic model for this part of the central Appalachians in which a relatively small ocean basin was opened between the Laurentian craton and a microcontinent (Baltimore terrane?) during the Late Proterozoic or earliest Cambrian (Figure 17-13A). Extension during this opening formed a number of listric normal faults on the Laurentian margin. If one does not accept the model of Lash and Drake (1984), one can consider the listric extensional faults to have formed on the Laurentian

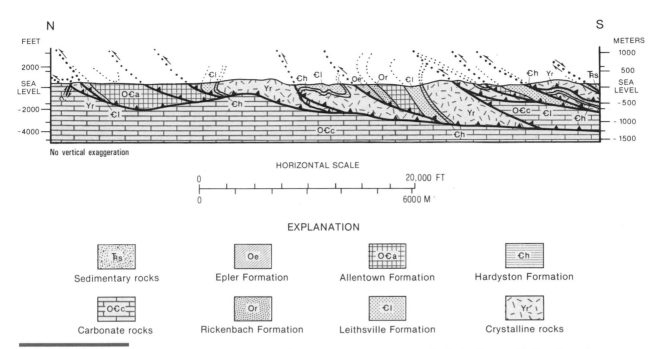

Figure 17-12. Geologic cross section through the Musconetcong nappe system in the Delaware Valley (based on and generalized from Drake, 1967, cross section D–D´, and Drake and others, 1967, Plate 3, cross section B–B´).

margin during the opening of the large Iapetus Ocean. In any case, the carbonate shelf on the cratonic margin collapsed during the attempted subduction of Laurentia beneath the microcontinent at the beginning of the Taconic orogeny, and the Martinsburg foreland basin was developed (Figure 17-13B). Subsequently, the basin closed and the listric extensional faults were reactivated as thrust faults along which wedges of basement rocks were driven into the carbonate and Martinsburg cover rocks, and the Reading Prong nappe megasystem was formed (Figure 17-13C).

SOUTH MOUNTAIN

In Pennsylvania and adjacent Maryland, the Blue Ridge-South Mountain anticlinorium is essentially a very large asymmetrical overturned fold that has a southeast-dipping axial surface. In Pennsylvania, particularly where it plunges out, the west limb of the fold is only slightly overturned.

Structural Geology

Smaller folds are developed within the anticlinorium and have the same style as folds in the Ridge and Valley province (Figure 17-14). They are characterized by straight, doubly plunging axes that can be traced for more than 25 miles. The rocks are well cleaved (Figures 17-15 and 17-16); the cleav-

age fans the folds (Figure 17-14). The cleavage surfaces are commonly marked with a downdip elongation lineation. The cleavage and downdip lineation are taken to define the South Mountain deformation plan of Cloos (1947), which has a very uniform relation over a wide area. Cloos interpreted the anticlinorium to have originated by laminar flow along the cleavage, which allowed great shortening without faulting, making it a large "shear fold." There are, however, several faults within the anticlinorium (Figure 17-17). The Carbaugh-Marsh Creek fault (Root, 1970), the most important of these faults, starts within the core of the anticlinorium as a right-slip fault. It passes westward into the carbonate rocks of the Cumberland Valley, where it turns to the southwest and becomes a steep thrust fault that can be traced at least as far south as the Potomac River (Root, 1970). The fault has an apparent lateral separation of 2.5 miles within the anticlinorium and a stratigraphic separation of about 4,700 feet at the Pennsylvania-Maryland border, bringing Lower Ordovician limestone onto Middle Ordovician shale. The array of thrust faults in the hanging wall (Figure 17-17) suggests that it might be the floor thrust of a sizable duplex. This type of fault, which begins as a strike-slip fault within the anticlinorium core and turns into a thrust fault within the carbonate valley, may be an important feature all along the length of the Blue Ridge-South Mountain structure, as at least two other

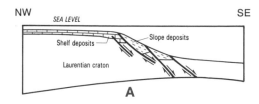

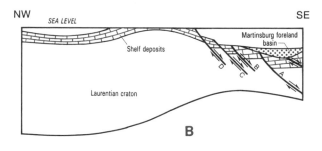

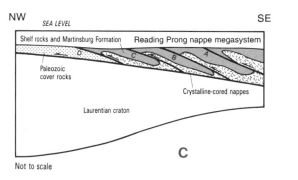

Not to scale

Figure 17–13. Schematic representation of the development of the Reading Prong nappe megasystem. A. Extensional faults related to the opening of a small ocean basin or the Iapetus Ocean formed on the margin of the Laurentian craton during the Late Proterozoic or earliest Cambrian. B. Shelf collapse related to the attempted subduction of Laurentia beneath the microcontinent at the beginning of the Taconic orogeny allowed the formation of the Martinsburg foreland basin during the Middle Ordovician. C. Closing of the small ocean basin or the Iapetus Ocean during the early Late Ordovician Taconic orogeny reactivated the extensional faults as thrust faults, forming the nappe megasystem. Thrust faulting during the Alleghanian orogeny greatly complicated the nappe megasystem. Rifting related to the opening of the Atlantic Ocean during the Late Triassic reactivated the thrust faults on the southeast as listric extensional faults. The amount, if any, of extensional movement of the other thrust faults is currently not known. The model presented here, therefore, suggests three periods of movement on the same faults: extensional, contractional, and extensional.

examples are known in Virginia. These faults may have been mechanisms to accommodate some of the regional shortening within the anticlinorium core.

The other faults shown in Figure 17–17 would appear to have less regional importance. The Antietam Cove fault was interpreted by Root (1971) to be a left-slip fault, that is, a second-order wrench fault, related to the Carbaugh-Marsh Creek fault. The Cold Springs, Reading Banks, and Piney Mountain faults are interpreted to be steep thrust faults, whereas the Laurel Forge and Clay Pit faults are thought to be high-angle normal faults (Root, 1970).

The above structural picture is a conservative reading of the field geology. More recently, however, geophysics and a better understanding of the mechanics of structural geology have allowed a much different solution. Geophysical data, particularly seismic reflection, summarized by Gwinn (1970) show that gently southeast-dipping basement rocks occur at a depth of greater than 25,000 feet beneath the Cumberland Valley. This, combined with the fact that the core rocks of the Blue Ridge-South Mountain anticlinorium had to be shortened as much as the rocks in the Great Valley and Appalachian Mountain sections of the Ridge and Valley province, led him to suggest that the anticlinorium was allochthonous above a deep thrust fault. Root (1970), also using geophysical data, came to the same conclusion, and the interpretative sections drawn by both geologists are essentially identical. David Elliott (personal communication, 1972) reported that the anticlinorium had to be allochthonous on the basis of data gained from unfolding the digitations on its west limb. Harris (1979) called attention to the geometry of the Blue Ridge-South Mountain anticlinorium and its similarity to that of the

Figure 17–14. Open concentric fold in the Cambrian Antietam Formation in Franklin County. The cleavage occurs in a fan. Photograph by J. M. Fauth.

Figure 17–15. Bedding and cleavage in the Cambrian Conococheague Group northeast of Scotland in the Caledonia Park 7.5-minute quadrangle. Bedding dips steeply left, and cleavage dips gently right. The hammer is 16.75 inches long. Photograph by J. M. Fauth.

Figure 17–16. Layering and cleavage in the Late Proterozoic Catoctin Formation, Iron Springs 7.5-minute quadrangle. Layering dips steeply right, and cleavage dips gently left. The arrow is about 18 inches long. Photograph by J. M. Fauth.

zone. Many thrust faults splay from this surface, forming an imbricate fan. The concept of duplex structure immediately comes to mind. A recent analysis of Ridge and Valley geology in central Pennsylvania (Chapter 19), however, suggests that the thrust system there lacks a roof thrust and thereby constitutes a "passive-roof duplex." The applicability of this solution to the imbricate fan associated with the Blue Ridge-South Mountain anticlinorium is beyond the scope of this paper.

In summary, the Blue Ridge-South Mountain anticlinorium is an allochthonous hanging-wall anticline above a major non-emergent thrust fault. The importance of such faults (Drake, 1978; Boyer and Elliott, 1982) cannot be overemphasized and should be considered in the analysis of any antiformal structure in a tectonic realm. The early proponents of an allochthonous Blue Ridge-South Mountain anticlinorium, George and Anna Jonas Stose, have been proved correct; the "Blue Ridge thrust" does not crop out at the base of the anticlinorium and does not emerge at the surface.

Powell Valley anticline in Virginia, the type hanging-wall anticline of the Appalachian orogen. He concluded that the anticlinorium was allochthonous and drew an interpretative section not far different from those of Gwinn (1970) and Root (1970). Harris and others (1982) reported on a seismic-reflection survey from the Ridge and Valley to the Atlantic Coastal Plain in central Virginia that showed the basal reflector passing beneath the anticlinorium, as well as the Piedmont, thereby proving that the anticlinorium is allochthonous. The depth to the basal reflector, the presumed sole thrust, is between 26,000 and 28,000 feet, depending on a choice of travel time. This is essentially the same depth that was proposed by Gwinn (1970) and Root (1970) and that is shown on the interpretative section (Figure 17–18) presented herein. The seismic section shown in Harris and others (1982) is the only published seismic section across the anticlinorium, but all of the available data suggest that the central Virginia survey is directly applicable to Pennsylvania.

The interpretation presented in Figure 17–18 suggests that the anticlinorium proper moved on a thrust within the Martinsburg Formation and that there are two major thrust faults beneath this slip

Time of Deformation

No structural feature has been observed within the pre-Silurian rocks of the anticlinorium that cannot be found in younger rocks to the west, a point first put forth by MacLachlan and Root (1966). Additional data were summarized by Drake (1980). South Mountain is overridden on the northeast by the polydeformed rocks of the Lebanon Valley nappe system on the Yellow Breeches thrust fault (Figure 17–17; Chapter 18). This terrane boundary is important (Drake, 1980), but it cannot be satisfactorily explained at this time. Mesozoic deformation must have been active along the east limb of the anticlinorium, which adjoins the Gettysburg basin. Presumably, the steep normal faults shown on Figure 17–18 are of Mesozoic age and may be reactivated Paleozoic faults like those in the Reading Prong.

Figure 17–17. Tectonic sketch map of the Blue Ridge-South Mountain anticlinorium in Pennsylvania (modified from Root, 1971, Figures 29 and 30).

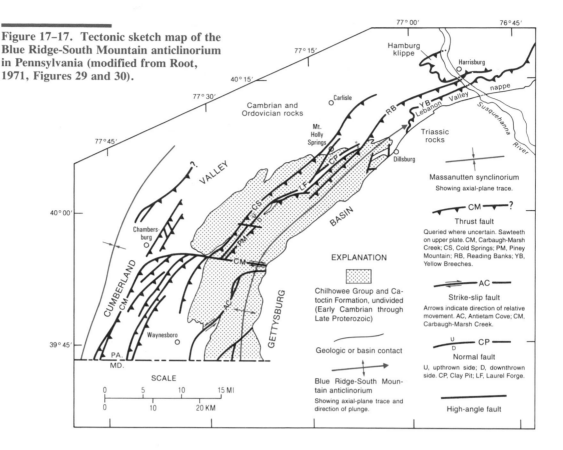

Tectonics

Many geologists have taken the Blue Ridge-South Mountain anticlinorium to lie along the transition of miogeoclinal rocks on the west to eugeoclinal rocks to the east. It has been suggested (Wehr and Glover, 1985) that the anticlinorium lies along the hinge zone related to the opening of the Iapetus Ocean. Certainly the immense quantities of volcanic rock and rift-facies rocks in the lower part of the Chilhowee Group (Chapter 3B) show that the Pennsylvania part of the anticlinorium contains rift-related rocks. Basement rocks exposed to the south contain vast quantities of Catoctin feeder dikes that in places constitute at least 50 percent of the rock volume. This mixture of rift-related igneous rocks and Laurentian granitoid rocks would appear to constitute the elusive "transitional crust" known only heretofore as the "stuff that makes squiggly lines" on reflection profiles. These relationships suggest that the hinge line of Wehr and Glover (1985) in Virginia can be transported to Pennsylvania with some validity. It is likely that the collision of Gondwana and Laurentia that caused the Alleghanian orogeny reactivated the extensional faults along the hinge zone as thrust faults of the Blue Ridge-South Mountain thrust system. This reactivation model differs little in concept from that put forth above for the Reading Prong, but differs greatly in timing and tectono-environment setting. The lack of volcanic rocks and feeder dikes in the Reading Prong basement supports the model of Lash and Drake (1984) of a small ocean that never progressed past the intracontinental phase. Therefore, although a fault-reactivation model is proposed for both the Reading Prong and the Blue Ridge-South Mountain anticlinorium, they formed at different places and at different times. The boundary between these two external basement massifs remains obscure. The Yellow Breeches thrust fault (Figure 17–17) is locally important, but it is doubtful that it is the prime contact.

PROBLEMS AND FUTURE RESEARCH

South Mountain and the Reading Prong have been almost completely mapped at the scale of 1:24,000 and constitute two ideal field laboratories for further research. The Middle Proterozoic deformational framework in the Reading Prong is not well understood. This would make an excellent topical study. Although the area is poorly exposed, there are many excellent outcrops that could be studied in detail by a researcher not hindered by the necessity of covering the ground.

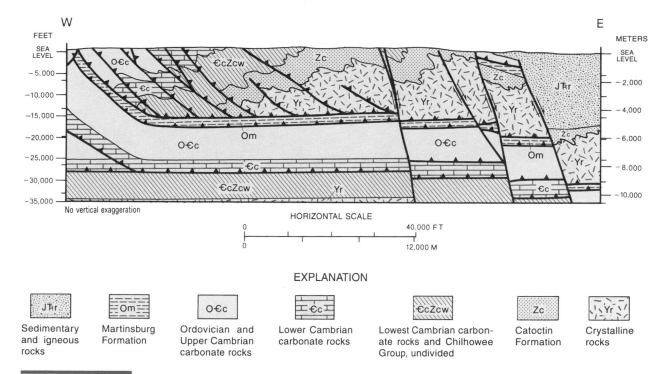

Figure 17-18. Geologic cross section through the Blue Ridge-South Mountain anticlinorium near the Maryland state line (modified from Berg and others, 1980, cross section D-D´).

Results from this work combined with those suggested in Chapter 3B would be of major importance in understanding the Grenvillian history of the Appalachians.

The effects of the Taconic and Alleghanian orogenies are difficult to separate in the Reading Prong. A concentrated effort to study the many faults in detail, as well as the relation of the basement to the cover rocks, should be undertaken. New laser techniques may be useful in dating different fabrics and, thereby, in separating the results of different orogenic periods.

Detailed topical structural studies should also be made in South Mountain to determine if evidence for pre-Alleghanian deformation might exist. The northern Blue Ridge is an anomaly in Appalachian external massifs because of its lack of Taconian deformation. Perhaps it is separated from the Reading Prong by a major strike-slip fault. A study of this possibility should be made.

RECOMMENDED FOR FURTHER READING

Cloos, Ernst (1965), *Appalachenprofil 1964*, Geologic Rundschau, v. 54, p. 812–834.

Fauth, J. L. (1968), *Geology of the Caledonia Park quadrangle area, South Mountain, Pennsylvania*, Pennsylvania Geological Survey, 4th ser., Atlas 129a, 133 p.

_____ (1978), *Geology and mineral resources of the Iron Springs area, Adams and Franklin Counties, Pennsylvania*, Pennsylvania Geological Survey, 4th ser., Atlas 129c, 72 p.

Freedman, Jacob (1967), *Geology of a portion of the Mount Holly Springs quadrangle, Adams and Cumberland Counties, Pennsylvania*, Pennsylvania Geological Survey, 4th ser., Progress Report 169, 66 p.

MacLachlan, D. B. (1983), *Geology and mineral resources of the Reading and Birdsboro quadrangles, Berks County, Pennsylvania*, Pennsylvania Geological Survey, 4th ser., Atlas 187cd, scale 1:24,000.

MacLachlan, D. B., Buckwalter, T. V., and McLaughlin, D. B. (1975), *Geology and mineral resources of the Sinking Spring quadrangle, Berks and Lancaster Counties, Pennsylvania*, Pennsylvania Geological Survey, 4th ser., Atlas 177d, 228 p.

MacLachlan, D. B., and Root, S. I. (1966), *Comparative tectonics and stratigraphy of the Cumberland and Lebanon Valleys*, Annual Field Conference of Pennsylvania Geologists, 31st, Harrisburg, Pa., Guidebook, 90 p.

Miller, B. L. (1944), *Specific data on the so-called "Reading Overthrust,"* Geological Society of America Bulletin, v. 55, p. 211–254.

Miller, B. L., and Fraser, D. M. (1935), *Comment on highlands near Reading, Pennsylvania; an erosion remnant of a great overthrust sheet—By George W. Stose and Anna I. Jonas (pages 757–780)*, Geological Society of America Bulletin, v. 46, pt. 2, p. 2031–2038.

Miller, B. L., Fraser, D. M., and Miller, R. L. (1939), *Northampton County, Pennsylvania*, Pennsylvania Geological Survey, 4th ser., County Report 48, 496 p.

Root, S. I. (1968), *Geology and mineral resources of southeastern Franklin County, Pennsylvania*, Pennsylvania Geological Survey, 4th ser., Atlas 119cd, 118 p.

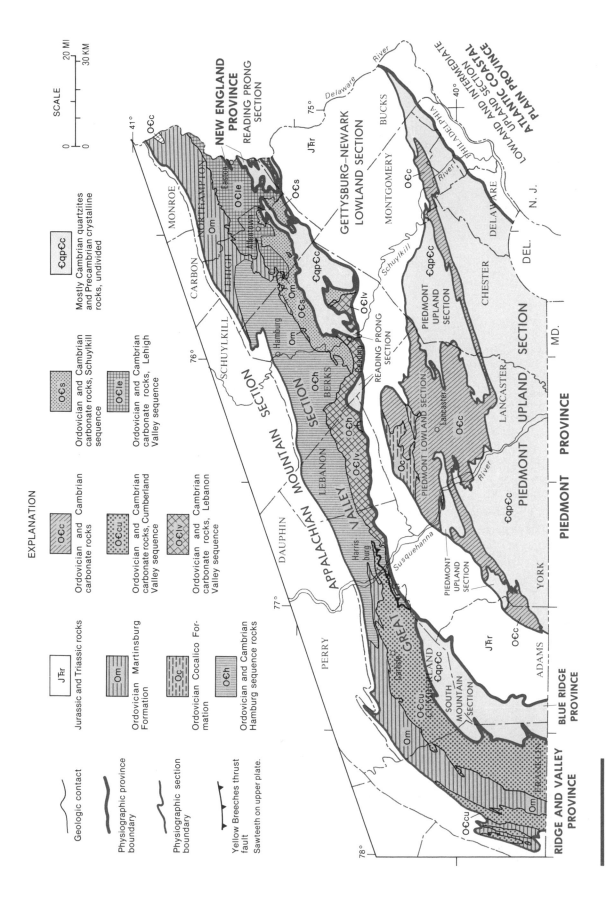

EXPLANATION

Geologic contact

Physiographic province boundary

Physiographic section boundary

Yellow Breeches thrust fault
Sawteeth on upper plate.

| JꞦr | Jurassic and Triassic rocks |

| Om | Ordovician Martinsburg Formation |

| Oc | Ordovician Cocalico Formation |

| OϵϨh | Ordovician and Cambrian Hamburg sequence rocks |

| OϵϨc | Ordovician and Cambrian carbonate rocks |

| OϵϨcu | Ordovician and Cambrian carbonate rocks, Cumberland Valley sequence |

| OϵϨlv | Ordovician and Cambrian carbonate rocks, Lebanon Valley sequence |

| OϵϨs | Ordovician and Cambrian carbonate rocks, Schuylkill sequence |

| OϵϨle | Ordovician and Cambrian carbonate rocks, Lehigh Valley sequence |

| ϵqpϵϨc | Mostly Cambrian quartzites and Precambrian crystalline rocks, undivided |

SCALE

0   20 MI
0   30 KM

Figure 18–1. Simplified geologic map of the Great Valley section of the Ridge and Valley province and the Piedmont Lowland section of the Piedmont province (modified from Berg and others, 1980, 1989; and Lyttle and Epstein, 1987).

CHAPTER 18   GREAT VALLEY AND PIEDMONT LOWLAND

CARLYLE GRAY
Carlyle Gray and Associates, Inc.
P. O. Box 66
Yorkville, CA 95494

SAMUEL I. ROOT
Department of Geology
The College of Wooster
Wooster, OH 44691

INTRODUCTION

The Great Valley section of the Ridge and Valley physiographic province comprises the area lying between the South Mountain-Reading Prong uplands and Blue Mountain, which is the first ridge of the Appalachian Mountain section of the province (Figure 18-1). The Great Valley is unified by a stratigraphic sequence consisting of a thick Cambrian and Ordovician carbonate sequence overlain by a thick Ordovician clastic sequence. In places, the clastic sequence contains allochthonous beds that are part of the Taconic Hamburg klippe. Two subprovinces are recognized: the Cumberland Valley subprovince, a fold terrane deformed during the Alleghanian (Permian) orogeny, and the Lebanon-Lehigh Valley subprovince, having large-scale thrust and fold nappes, formed during at least two periods of deformation, the Taconic (Late Ordovician) and Alleghanian (Permian) orogenies.

The Piedmont Lowland section, which is part of the Piedmont physiographic province, is structurally and stratigraphically linked to the Great Valley but is separated from it by the Mesozoic Gettysburg-Newark Lowland and parts of the Piedmont Upland.

LEBANON-LEHIGH VALLEY SUBPROVINCE

The tectonic style of the Lebanon-Lehigh Valley subprovince consists of refolded recumbent folds and thrust sheets, the Reading Prong nappe megasystem of Drake (1978), which includes at least four nappe systems. The rocks of the Lebanon-Lehigh Valley form the sedimentary cover of these crystalline-cored, tectonically superimposed nappes. From east to west, the nappes include the Musconetcong (New Jersey and easternmost Pennsylvania), Lyon Station-Paulins Kill (eastern Pennsylvania), Irish Mountain (Allentown to Reading), and Lebanon Valley (Reading to west of the Susquehanna). The Lyon Station-Paulins Kill nappe is the lowest of the four, lying beneath both the Musconetcong and Irish Mountain nappe systems and occurring largely in the subsurface. The other three nappes overlap from east to west, the easternmost Musconetcong nappe partially underlying the Irish Mountain nappe, which in turn partially underlies the Lebanon Valley nappe. The Hamburg klippe was thrust onto the Reading Prong nappe megasystem during the Taconic orogeny and in turn was overridden by late Taconic and Alleghanian thrust sheets (Lyttle and Epstein, 1987).

There are four orders of folds in the carbonate rocks: (1) the Reading Prong nappe megasystem, which has now been mapped from Musconetcong Mountain in New Jersey to the Susquehanna River in central Pennsylvania, a distance of more than 100 miles; the width of the nappes may be as much as 20 to 30 miles, much greater than the width of the Great Valley; (2) large digitations having amplitudes on the order of 1 mile, which can be mapped by tracing lithologies in exposures and float; (3) folds seen in single exposures that have amplitudes of a few feet to a few tens of feet; and (4) hand-specimen-sized folds visible in almost every exposure. Most of the third- and fourth-order folds are overturned and recumbent and have a flow cleavage that parallels the axial surfaces. A sense of movement is shown that is consistent with flowage out of the center of a large recumbent fold, overturned to the north.

There has been so much shortening that there are definite, though subtle, differences in the stratigraphic units in the different nappes of the megasystem. These have been named the Lehigh Valley sequence in the Musconetcong nappe (and in windows of the Lyon Station-Paulins Kill nappe [MacLachlan, personal communication, 1997]), the Schuylkill sequence in the Irish Mountain nappe, and the Lebanon Valley sequence in the Lebanon Valley nappe (MacLachlan, 1967, 1983).

In the Lehigh Valley, west of the Delaware River, Drake (1969, 1970) and his co-workers have shown that the carbonates and the Martinsburg Formation of the Lehigh Valley sequence wrap around the nose of the Musconetcong nappe and are thrust onto the Hamburg klippe on the Kutztown thrust (Figure 18–2). West of the Easton-Allentown area, the exposed parts of the individual nappes of the nappe megasystem are separated by major thrust faults. Lying above the Musconetcong nappe, and separated from it by the Black River thrust (Drake, 1987), is the gneiss-cored Irish Mountain nappe, which was first described by MacLachlan (MacLachlan and others, 1975; MacLachlan, 1979, 1983). MacLachlan recognized as many as four tectonic levels brought about by the superposition of nappes during two separate episodes of deformation.

In the Great Valley north of Reading, the Evansville thrust (which may be an extension of the Kutztown thrust) carries part of the Irish Mountain nappe onto the autochthonous Jacksonburg-Martinsburg sequence (Figures 18–2 and 18–3). In the Reading area, the Sinking Spring thrust brings the overturned lower limb of the Lebanon Valley nappe onto the Schuylkill sequence of the upper, right-side-up limb of the Irish Mountain nappe. MacLachlan (1979) considered this thrust and the Grings Hill thrust (see below) to be Alleghanian in age.

The carbonates of the Lebanon Valley sequence are overridden by the Grings Hill thrust (Figure 18–2), which brings Cambrian Hardyston quartzite and Precambrian gneiss in contact with carbonate rocks possibly as young as the Lower Ordovician Epler Formation. Drake (Chapter 17) states that this gneiss is from the core of the Lebanon Valley nappe. To the west, in Lebanon County, Cambrian and Lower Ordovician carbonates emerge as the Lebanon Valley sequence in the inverted limb of the Lebanon Valley nappe. The south side of the Lebanon Valley is bordered by the Mesozoic basin (Gray and others, 1958; Geyer and others, 1958).

As is typical of the Great Valley, exposures in the Lebanon Valley consist mostly of small outcrops of carbonate rock in farm fields; a few more extensive exposures occur in small quarries (Figure 18–4) and roadcuts. In most exposures, the beds are overturned and dip gently to the south. Even in the limited areas where the dip is to the north, primary structures show the beds to be overturned. Figure 18–5 is a map and cross section of a second-order fold, gently refolded, in which all exposures are inverted.

The lower limb of the Lebanon Valley nappe is continuously exposed westward (Geyer, 1970; MacLachlan, 1967) to 10 miles beyond the Susquehanna River, where it disappears beneath Triassic strata (Root and MacLachlan, 1978). The stratigraphic character and structural style of deformation are unchanged throughout this belt.

The Yellow Breeches thrust is an Alleghanian structure that brings rocks of the Hamburg sequence and the Lebanon Valley sequence to lie on rocks of the Cumberland Valley sequence in the area south and southwest of Harrisburg (Root and MacLachlan, 1978; Figure 18–1).

PIEDMONT LOWLAND SECTION

South of the Mesozoic basin, in the Piedmont Lowland, the Lebanon Valley sequence of carbonate rocks reappears (lumped with other Cambrian and

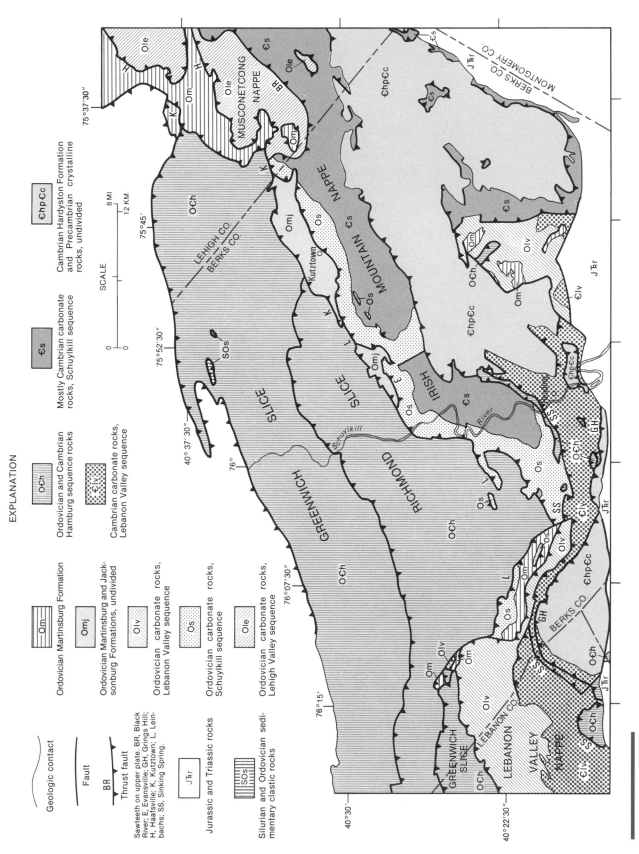

Figure 18-2. Geologic map of part of the Lehigh-Lebanon Valley subprovince of the Great Valley (modified from Berg and others, 1980; Lyttle and Epstein, 1987; and Faill, in preparation).

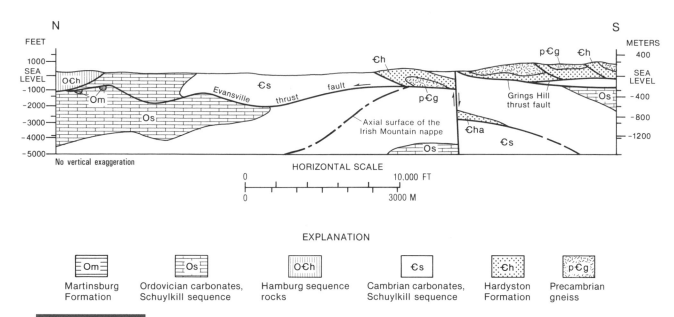

Figure 18–3. Cross section of the Great Valley north of Reading, Berks County (modified from MacLachlan, 1979, Plate 1, cross section B–B´).

Ordovician carbonate rocks labeled O€c in Figure 18-1). Mapping is not complete, but it appears that north of Lancaster, the rocks are again exposed in the inverted limb of a nappe (Meisler and Becher, 1971). Because of the lithologic similarity to the Lebanon Valley rocks, it is likely that this is part of the Lebanon Valley nappe. The Cocalico Formation (labeled

Oc in Figure 18-1) may be a correlative of the Martinsburg Formation, but it also has similarities to the rocks of the Hamburg klippe. West of Lancaster in the Piedmont Upland section, Chestnut Ridge and Chickies Rock, and their extension across the Susquehanna River (Hellam Hills), appear to be the core of a nappe. Further detailed mapping is required to establish whether this is the core of the Lebanon Valley nappe or another structure altogether.

HAMBURG KLIPPE

Stose (1946) proposed the presence of a klippe, analogous to the Taconic klippe in New England, in an area previously mapped as Martinsburg Formation. The klippe stretches from the west shore of the Susquehanna at Harrisburg to just east of Hamburg in Berks County (Figure 18-1). Stose observed the presence of red shales, limestones, graywackes, and other lithologies not found in the Mar-

Figure 18–4. Isoclinal folding in an abandoned quarry southeast of Annville, Lebanon County. The beds are part of the Ordovician Epler Formation.

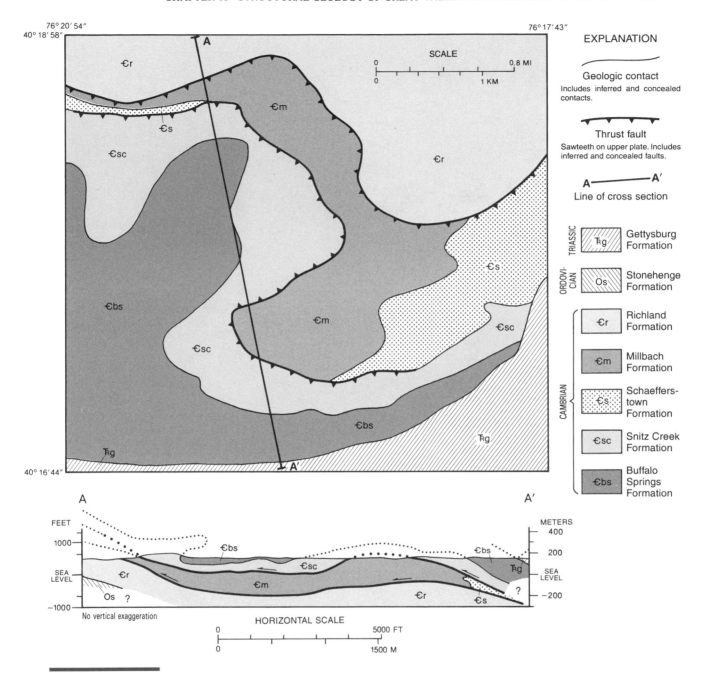

Figure 18–5. Map and cross section of a second-order fold, part of the Lebanon Valley nappe in southeastern Lebanon County, illustrating the map pattern brought about by the refolding of an inverted sequence (from Gray and others, 1958).

tinsburg Formation to the southwest and northeast. He presented evidence, based on a few scattered graptolite localities, that the rocks were older than typical Martinsburg. More recent work, beginning in the 1960's and still continuing, has confirmed and expanded on the concept.

Many new graptolite localities have been found, and their zonation has been established (Stephens and others, 1982). The Martinsburg to the east and west of the klippe contains graptolite faunas of *Diplograptus multidens* zone (zone 2) and three younger zones (Figure 18–6). Fossils of the older *Nemagraptus gracilis* zone (zone 1) have been found in all lithologies designated as anomalous by Stose (1946) except limestone and clean sandstone. Zone 1 fossils have been found in some dark shales of the klippe. Conodonts

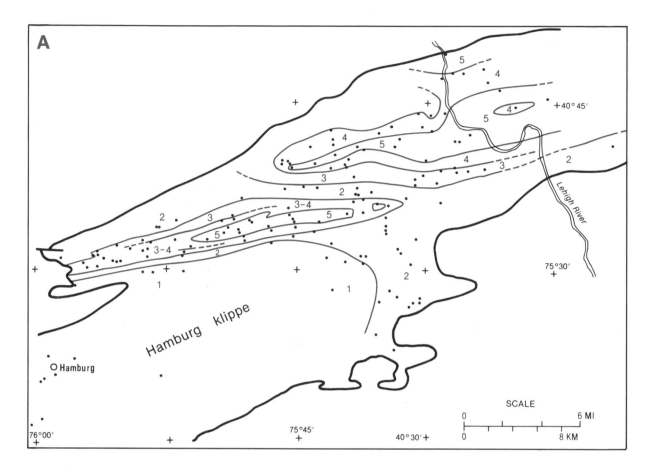

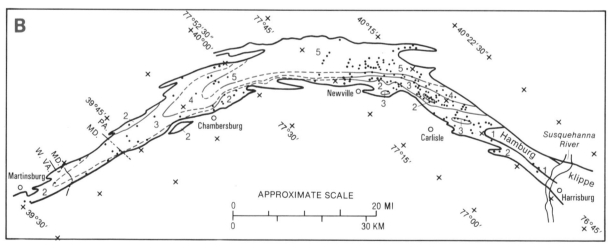

Figure 18–6. Fossiliferous-locality maps of graptolite faunas (slightly modified from Stephens and others, 1982, Figures 3 and 4). A, Martinsburg east of the Hamburg klippe; B, Martinsburg west of the Hamburg klippe. 1, *Nemagraptus gracilis*; 2, *Diplograptus multidens*; 3, *Corynoides americanus*; 4, *Orthograptus ruedemanni*; 5, *Climacograptus spiniferus*.

correlated with graptolites of the *Nemagraptus gracilis* zone have been found in some of the limestones. Conodonts that "suggest a Late Cambrian to Early Ordovician age" were reported in the klippe by Lash (1985). No graptolites of any of the younger zones have been found in the klippe area.

Work summarized by Lash and Drake (1984) shows that in its eastern end, the klippe consists of two tectonic slices (Figure 18–2), the Greenwich slice and the tectonically superimposed Richmond slice. The rocks of the Richmond slice constitute the Virginville Formation, and those of the Greenwich slice the Windsor Township Formation. The Windsor Township Formation has been recognized throughout the entire length of the klippe (Figure 18–1).

Several methods of emplacement have been suggested. Platt and others (1972) proposed that the klippe consisted of a number of separate gravity blocks that buried themselves in the Martinsburg muds. Fossil evidence now seems to rule this out. Wright and Stephens (1978) suggested that the klippe was a single sheet that slid by gravity into the Martinsburg basin in early Martinsburg time. More recently, Lash and others (1984) and Lash and Drake (1984) described the stratigraphy, sedimentology, and structure of the Richmond and Greenwich slices in the framework of plate tectonics. In their scenario, the older rocks of the Richmond slice were deposited on the northwest-facing slope of an offshore (southwesterly) microplate in Late Cambrian to Early Ordovician time. The Windsor Township Formation of the Greenwich slice was deposited as a fan in the trench separating the microplate from the North American continent. As the plate and continent converged, the Richmond slice was thrust onto the Greenwich slice, and both were thrust over the crystalline-cored nappes that were forming simultaneously at the continental margin. The entire picture is further complicated by later thrusts that brought Cambrian and Ordovician carbonate sequences of the Great Valley into contact with the klippe rocks.

CUMBERLAND VALLEY SUBPROVINCE

The Cumberland Valley stratigraphic sequence emerges from beneath the Yellow Breeches thrust in the area south and west of Harrisburg (Figure 18–1) and extends southwestward to Virginia with only minor facies changes. The major difference between the Cumberland Valley subprovince and the Lebanon-Lehigh Valley subprovince and Piedmont Lowland is their structural histories. In contrast to the complex tectonic history of rocks of the Lebanon-Lehigh Valley sequence described above, strata of the Cumberland Valley sequence were deformed only once during the terminal Paleozoic orogeny (Alleghanian). The result is a dominantly folded terrane above non-outcropping, low-angle detachment thrusts (Gwinn, 1964; Root, 1973b; Kulander and Dean, 1986). Near

Harrisburg, the deformed rocks of the Cumberland Valley sequence were overridden on a flat thrust by the Yellow Breeches thrust sheet. This thrusting represents a late Alleghanian deformation event. Later (Jurassic) normal faulting affected the Cumberland Valley sequence and Blue Ridge (Figures 18–7 and 18–8) near the border of the Mesozoic Gettysburg basin (Root, 1989).

The area of the present Susquehanna River is the western limit of the Reading Prong nappe megasystem, which is preserved on the late Alleghanian-age Yellow Breeches thrust sheet, and is also the western edge of the Hamburg klippe. During Taconic time, the area east of the river may have been structurally low, creating a site for the emplacement of the nappes and the klippe. A comparable setting may account for the later emplacement of the Yellow Breeches thrust sheet.

The structural style of Alleghanian deformation is the same across the Blue Ridge physiographic province and Great Valley and Appalachian Mountain sections of the Ridge and Valley physiographic province (Root, 1973b), so that treatment of any area as a distinct structural entity is arbitrary. Cambrian quartzites and Precambrian volcanics of South Mountain and younger quartzitic sandstones of the Ridge and Valley form the resistant mountain ridges bounding the Cumberland Valley. Fundamentally, the sedimentary strata in these three regions constitute a conformable lithologic sequence that has been folded and shortened and is geometrically and kinematically congruent. Structural contrasts are principally those of scale and result from lithologic differences and differences in the thickness of the overlying cover. The Paleozoic rocks are divisible into major lithotectonic units based on relative competency, bedding thickness, and heterogeneity (Root, 1973a). Folds of small wavelength and pervasive cleavage are developed in incompetent units (Lower and Middle Cambrian argillaceous limestones and the Ordovician Martinsburg shale), as shown in Figure 18–9. Folds having longer wavelengths and poor cleavage development occur in competent Upper Cambrian and Lower Ordovician massive carbonate rocks. Figure 18–10 shows an outcrop of the Ordovician St. Paul Group, a commonly massive limestone having a tectonite fabric imposed by the nearby Yellow Breeches thrust. All ridge-forming siliciclastics are ultracompetent. Thus, the scale of folds, development of cleavage, and propagation of thrust faults are all related to mechanical characteristics of lithotectonic units.

Three regional structural elements extend into the Cumberland Valley from the south. On the east

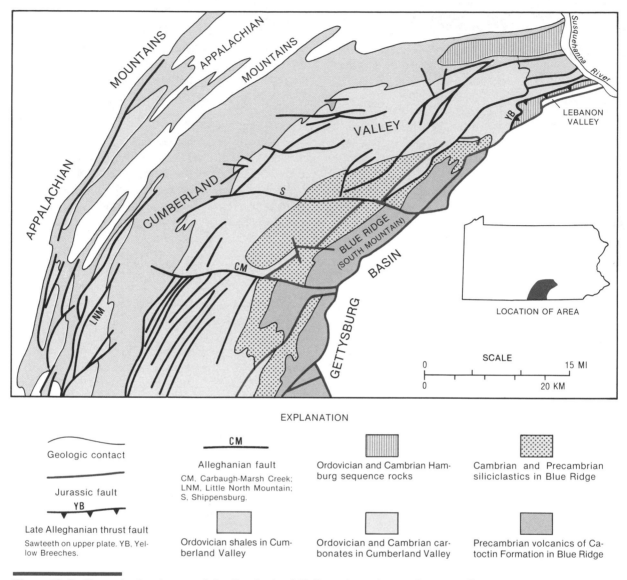

EXPLANATION

Geologic contact

Jurassic fault

YB
Late Alleghanian thrust fault
Sawteeth on upper plate. YB, Yellow Breeches.

CM
Alleghanian fault
CM, Carbaugh-Marsh Creek;
LNM, Little North Mountain;
S, Shippensburg.

Ordovician shales in Cumberland Valley

Ordovician and Cambrian Hamburg sequence rocks

Ordovician and Cambrian carbonates in Cumberland Valley

Cambrian and Precambrian siliciclastics in Blue Ridge

Precambrian volcanics of Catoctin Formation in Blue Ridge

Figure 18–7. Tectonic sketch map of the Cumberland Valley subprovince and surrounding areas (modified from Berg and others, 1980).

side is the South Mountain anticlinorium cored by Precambrian Catoctin metavolcanics (Figure 18–7). Passing through the center of the valley is the complementary Massanutten synclinorium, preserving Ordovician Martinsburg shales (Figure 18–1). The western limit is the Little North Mountain fault system (Kulander and Dean, 1988) that breaks into splays in Pennsylvania (Clark, 1970) and separates the Cumberland Valley from the Appalachian Mountain section of the Ridge and Valley province.

The South Mountain fold culminates along the Shippensburg fault (Figure 18–7). South of the fault, most folds plunge southwest, and north of the fault,

most folds plunge northeast. The associated Carbaugh-Marsh Creek fault, another major cross structure, is also significant because the strike of major structures changes dramatically across it (Root, 1970).

All folds adhere to the classic South Mountain deformation plan established by Cloos (1947), in which axial planes and fanning cleavage dip southeast, and lineation and extended oolites are in the cleavage plane normal to the fold axis (*ac* plane). Folds in the carbonates are cylindrical, flexural-slip type, plunging 15 to 20 degrees. Individual folds are as much as 25 miles long, but generally are less, and fold wavelengths average 1 to 2 miles. West-facing

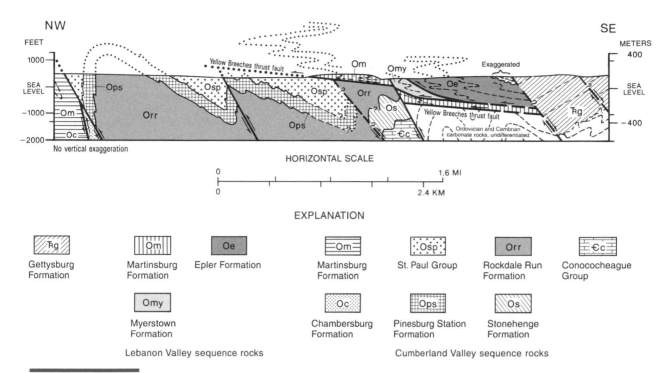

Figure 18–8. **Cross section near the west side of the Susquehanna River showing late Alleghanian out-of-sequence thrusting of the Lebanon Valley sequence over the Cumberland Valley sequence, which was deformed in the early Alleghanian (modified from Root, 1977, Plate 1). Note the Jurassic normal faulting truncating the Paleozoic strata on the southeast.**

Figure 18–9. **Small-scale folds in shale of the Ordovician Martinsburg Formation cut by nearly vertical, pervasive Alleghanian-age cleavage, in a roadcut along the Conodoguinet Creek west of Plainfield, Cumberland County. The coin in the synclinal hinge gives the scale.**

Figure 18–10. Finely banded limestone of the Ordovician St. Paul Group, dipping 25°SE, at the entrance to the village of Allendale, Camp Hill, Cumberland County. These beds occur close to the overlying Yellow Breeches thrust sheet and carry a tectonite fabric imposed by this later thrusting; each bedding surface is a movement surface bearing transport lineations.

limbs are subvertical to overturned, and east-facing limbs are upright, dipping less than 50 degrees. Folds in the structurally incompetent Martinsburg shales are geometrically identical to the folds in the carbonates, but an order of magnitude smaller, and are cleavage dominated.

Low-angle detachment thrusts within bedding are inferred to exist at great depths (>20,000 feet) ("Eastern Overthrust Belt"). Two types of steep thrusts are exposed: major ramp faults that dip 50° to 60°SE, such as the outcropping splays of the Little North Mountain detachment fault (Figure 18–7), and less extensive, east- and west-dipping faults developed across bedding planes during flexural-slip folding and directed toward the fold crest (Root, 1973a). All thrust traces are subparallel to the regional fold axes.

The subvertical, east-west-trending Shippensburg and Carbaugh-Marsh Creek faults occur at large angles to regional structural grain (Figure 18–7). Semi-independent shortening occurred across the faults during the Alleghanian deformation. It is suggested that these are reactivated segments of the Transylvania fault, an east-west fracture zone of probable Precambrian age embedded in the continental plate (Root and Hoskins, 1977).

PROBLEMS AND FUTURE RESEARCH

In spite of the recent publication of many excellent detailed geologic quadrangle maps, more mapping is needed to resolve some basic discrepancies between different workers and to revise some earlier work that was completed before present concepts had fully evolved. In particular, the Piedmont Lowland in Lancaster and York Counties lacks integration with the mapped nappes in the Great Valley.

To resolve major outstanding problems, future research in the Cumberland Valley should be directed to the following:

1. The amount of shortening of the rocks by transport on detachment horizons as well as by tectonic-directed solution or flow of material.
2. The depth and eastward extent of the detachment horizons. What oil and gas potential may occur beneath the detachment?
3. The age of the main phase of Alleghanian deformation and the age of the later emplacement of the Yellow Breeches thrust sheet. What was the westward extent of the Yellow Breeches thrust sheet; did it extend over the anthracite basins to the north?

RECOMMENDED FOR FURTHER READING

Davis, R. E., Drake, A. A., Jr., and Epstein, J. B. (1967), *Geologic map of the Bangor quadrangle, Pennsylvania-New Jersey*, U.S. Geological Survey Geologic Quadrangle Map GQ–665, scale 1:24,000.

Drake, A. A., Jr. (1967), *Geologic map of the Easton quadrangle, New Jersey-Pennsylvania*, U.S. Geological Survey Geologic Quadrangle Map GQ–594, scale 1:24,000.

Drake, A. A., Jr., McLaughlin, D. B., and Davis, R. E. (1967), *Geologic map of the Riegelsville quadrangle, Pennsylvania-New Jersey*, U.S. Geological Survey Geologic Quadrangle Map GQ-593, scale 1:24,000.

Geyer, A. R., Gray, Carlyle, McLaughlin, D. B., and Moseley, J. R. (1958), *Geology of the Lebanon quadrangle*, Pennsylvania Geological Survey, 4th ser., Atlas 167c, scale 1:24,000.

Gray, Carlyle (1954), *Recumbent folding in the Great Valley*, Pennsylvania Academy of Science Proceedings, v. 28, p. 96-101.

Lash, G. G., Lyttle, P. T., and Epstein, J. B., eds. (1984), *Geology of an accreted terrane: the eastern Hamburg klippe and surrounding rocks, eastern Pennsylvania*, Annual Field Conference of Pennsylvania Geologists, 49th, Reading, Pa., Guidebook, 151 p.

Root, S. I., and MacLachlan, D. B. (1978), *Western limit of the Taconic allochthons in Pennsylvania*, Geological Society of America Bulletin, v. 89, p. 1515-1528.

Stephens, G. C., Wright, T. O., and Platt, L. B. (1982), *Geology of the Middle Ordovician Martinsburg Formation and related rocks in Pennsylvania*, Annual Field Conference of Pennsylvania Geologists, 47th, New Cumberland, Pa., Guidebook, 87 p.

Stose, G. W., and Jonas, A. I. (1935), *Highlands near Reading, Pennsylvania; an erosional remnant of a great overthrust sheet*, Geological Society of America Bulletin, v. 46, p. 757-779.

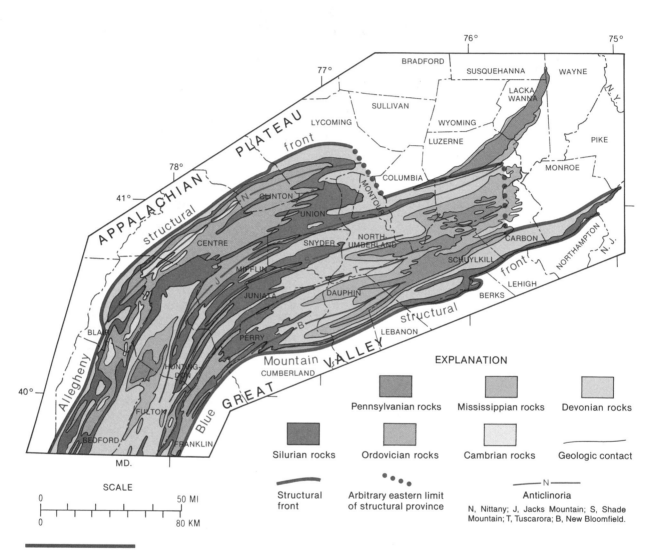

Figure 19–1. Generalized geologic map of the Valley and Ridge structural province in Pennsylvania. This province is bounded by a structural front on both the northwest and southeast sides; the northeast boundary is shown by arbitrary lines. The major anticlinoria are indicated. The outcrop patterns of the systemic units are also portrayed.

CHAPTER 19   APPALACHIAN MOUNTAIN SECTION OF THE RIDGE AND VALLEY PROVINCE

RODGER T. FAILL
  Bureau of Topographic and Geologic Survey
  Department of Conservation and Natural
    Resources
  P. O. Box 8453
  Harrisburg, PA 17105

RICHARD P. NICKELSEN
  Department of Geology
  Bucknell University
  Lewisburg, PA 17837

INTRODUCTION

The Valley and Ridge structural province has long been considered the classic example of a folded and faulted foreland mountain system.[1] The structures in this province were developed in one mountain-building episode, the Alleghany orogeny. This province is part of the Appalachian foreland, the slightly metamorphosed, deformed terrane of Cambrian to Pennsylvanian rocks between the craton and the main orogenic crystalline terranes to the southeast. The Valley and Ridge structural province crosses central Pennsylvania in a broad, arcuate (northwestwardly convex) belt, bounded on the northwest by the Allegheny structural front and the Appalachian Plateau and on the southeast by the Blue Mountain structural front and the metamorphic rocks of the hinterland (Figure 19-1). The province extends for 700 miles southwest to Alabama, but in eastern Pennsylvania, much of it terminates at the east end of the anthracite basins; a narrow (10-mile-wide) band continues to the northeast through New Jersey and New York into the Hudson and St. Lawrence Valleys (Rodgers, 1970).

Folds are the most obvious structures in the Valley and Ridge structural province (Figure 19-2), but the most fundamental tectonic element is the system of southeast-dipping thrust faults that rise through the stratigraphic column. These faults, both paralleling the bedding of certain ductile stratigraphic units as "flats" and "ramping" up to the northwest through more brittle rocks, are commonly "blind," not intersecting the surface of the earth.

All the Paleozoic rocks in the province have been transported to the northwest along a basal, flat floor thrust (décollement) in Cambrian strata. Imbricate thrusts ramping up through the 2-mile-thick Cambrian and Ordovician carbonate section from the dé-

---

[1] The Valley and Ridge structural province roughly corresponds to the Appalachian Mountain section of the Ridge and Valley physiographic province.

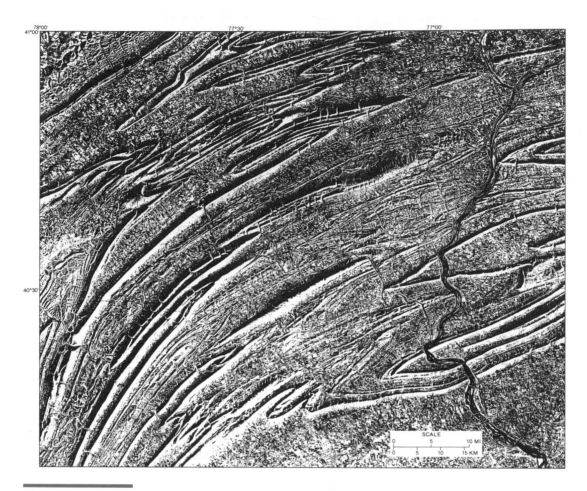

Figure 19–2. Synthetic-aperture radar image mosaic of part of the Harrisburg 1- by 2-degree quadrangle, illustrating the linear ridges and valleys characteristic of the Valley and Ridge structural province (from U.S. Geological Survey 1982 experimental edition, scale 1:250,000). This topography reflects both the subhorizontal to gently plunging folds and the contrasting lithologies throughout the Paleozoic section.

collement created a train of large, kink-shaped, fault-bend anticlines. The overlying Upper Ordovician to Pennsylvanian strata conform to the fold structures in the underlying duplex but contain other thrust faults and smaller folds. The large discontinuity in shortening between the carbonates and overlying rocks has not generally been recognized as a regional detachment in Pennsylvania, although intense deformation has locally been observed at the Upper Ordovician contact between the carbonates and the overlying predominantly clastic section. Distortion by extension jointing, dissolution, crenulation, and flow to form spaced or slaty cleavage, and by contractional or extensional faulting also contributed to the bulk strain of these rocks.

The Alleghanian foreland deformation in the Valley and Ridge structural province was initially thought to consist of large and very long folds along

with various subordinate structures, all of which were the result of buckling and flexural-slip folding of horizontal strata responding to a unidirectional horizontal compression. It is now recognized that the folds are but one of a number of stages of a deformation that extended over a period of time, during which the principal stress directions changed orientation. The deformation stages included pretectonic hydraulic jointing followed by tectonic cross-fold extension jointing and layer-parallel shortening, which is expressed as both rock cleavage and conjugate wedge and wrench faulting. Major flexural-slip folding overprinted all previous structures and led to layer-parallel extension on the steep limbs of folds. The last structures of the Alleghany orogeny were late strike-slip faults, which are sometimes associated with major transverse lineaments, and out-of-sequence high-angle reverse faults. It appears that the orientation of principal stresses changed during the sequence of stages, rotating clockwise in north-central and northeastern Pennsylvania and counterclockwise in the south-central part of the state (Geiser and Engelder, 1983; Nickelsen, 1988; Nickelsen and Engelder, 1989; Gray and Mitra, 1993).

FOLDS

The northwestward convex arc of geologic contacts and topography, the Pennsylvania salient of Nickelsen (1963) and Rodgers (1970, p. 4), and also named the Pennsylvania reentrant by Thomas (1977), reflects the progressive change in fold trend from 030° (azimuth) in south-central Pennsylvania to 080° in the east-central part of the state (Figure 19-1). Folds of all sizes, from first order (wavelength > 10 miles) to fifth order (hand-specimen size) (Nickelsen, 1963), pervade the province. The first-order anticlinoria extend for the most part around the salient from the

Breezewood transverse fault zone to the eastern limits of the province (Figure 19-3). In contrast, the smaller, second-order folds that are part of the anticlinoria are not as long—few have lengths greater than 60 miles.

In profile, the folds have planar limbs and hinges that are narrow with respect to the fold wavelengths (Figure 19-4). Bed thickness is constant throughout the limbs and hinges (except where thickened by faulting), which attests to the relative lack of ductile deformation within beds. Slickensides on bedding surfaces are perpendicular to the fold axes, indicating that slip between adjacent beds was the dominant fold mechanism. This fold geometry and kinematics is characteristic of kink folds (Figure 19-5) (Faill, 1969, 1973a). The folds are generally upright, though most verge to the northwest. The beds in the northwest limbs of some of the largest anticlines are vertical to overturned along the three (Allegheny, Jacks Mountain [Faill, in preparation], and

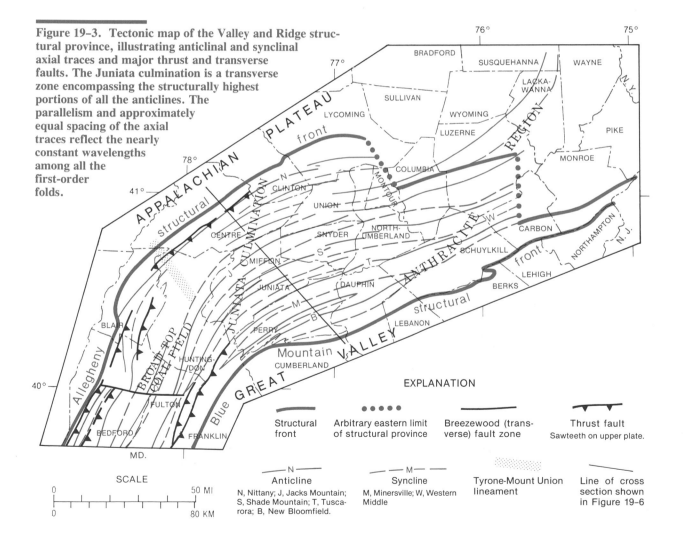

Figure 19–3. Tectonic map of the Valley and Ridge structural province, illustrating anticlinal and synclinal axial traces and major thrust and transverse faults. The Juniata culmination is a transverse zone encompassing the structurally highest portions of all the anticlines. The parallelism and approximately equal spacing of the axial traces reflect the nearly constant wavelengths among all the first-order folds.

EXPLANATION

Structural front

Arbitrary eastern limit of structural province

Breezewood (transverse) fault zone

Thrust fault
Sawteeth on upper plate.

SCALE

0   50 MI

0   80 KM

—N—
Anticline
N, Nittany; J, Jacks Mountain; S, Shade Mountain; T, Tuscarora; B, New Bloomfield.

— —M— —
Syncline
M, Minersville; W, Western Middle

Tyrone-Mount Union lineament

Line of cross section shown in Figure 19-6

Figure 19–4. An anticline and syncline in the Silurian Wills Creek Formation, along U.S. Route 22 at Charlie Hill, 6 miles northwest of Huntingdon, Huntingdon County. This fold pair exhibits the planar-limb and narrow-hinge geometry that is characteristic of folds of all sizes in the Valley and Ridge structural province. Note the person inside the outline of the fold limb in the lower right for scale.

Figure 19–5. Interbedded quartzites and argillaceous sandstones and siltstones of the Silurian Tuscarora Formation at the Laurel Creek Reservoir of the Lewistown Water Supply System, adjacent to U.S. Route 322, 12 miles north of Lewistown, Mifflin County. A 15-foot-wide kink band (its boundaries highlighted by the colored lines) dips moderately to the south (right) within the vertical, north-facing beds, which form part of the northwest limb of an anticline. The beds and kink band are offset by a few subhorizontal faults that have displaced the hanging walls to the north (left) by approximately 3 feet each.

Blue Mountain) structural fronts (Figure 19–1). Some of the folds in eastern Pennsylvania are recumbent (Epstein and others, 1974).

Wedge faults with slickenlines normal to the local fold axis are important ancillary structures; they occur in both the fold limbs and the hinges. Some of the wedges are contraction faults that preceded the folding during an early phase of layer-parallel shortening. Other wedges developed during the folding by simple shear on fold limbs and by filling the voids in the fold hinges.

In plan, Valley and Ridge kink folds are commonly many times longer than wide, an aspect that has impressed Appalachian geologists since folds were first studied in the province (e.g., Rogers, 1858a). The axial traces of the folds do not curve smoothly along their length, but consist of linear segments that change trend by as little as a few degrees or by as much as 20 degrees. Not all of the folds are simple. The hinges of the first-order anticlinoria often contain a number of second- or third-order en echelon folds. These smaller folds may lie over local thrusts that occur at different positions or in different stratigraphic levels along the length of the anticlinoria. Their trends are usually at a small angle (less than 15 degrees) to the overall trend of the anticlinorium. In central Pennsylvania, the trends of the individual folds are consistently more easterly. Some of the second-order folds are almost domal, having lengths only two or three times their widths (e.g., the east ends of the Nittany and Shade Mountain anticlinoria). Others are tens of miles long and are the hinges of the first-order anticlinoria before being replaced, en echelon, by other second-order folds (see, for example, the central part of the Shade Mountain anticlinorium, Figure 19–3).

The Valley and Ridge structural province (except that east of the anthracite basins) is underlain by a décollement flat in the Lower Cambrian Waynesboro shale, which ranges from 4 to 7 miles beneath the surface depending on location. Each first-order anticline developed over an imbricate thrust ramping up from this décollement (Figure 19–6). The synclines are passive structures, mere consequences of the growth of the adjacent anticlines. Anticlines grew during conversion of northwestward movement of the Paleozoic cover above the décollement into deformation of this cover. As the growing anticlines absorbed the décollement movement, the amount of horizontal tectonic transport at the northwest side of the province (the Allegheny structural front) was reduced to a small fraction of what it was at the southeast margin (the Blue Mountain structural front).

Each of the anticlines has Cambrian and Ordovician carbonates occupying its core, and each first-order anticline has roughly the same amplitude, despite the fact that on any traverse southeastward across the province, progressively younger rocks are exposed in the hinges of the anticlinoria. This trend does not reflect a diminishing amplitude of the anticlines; it is solely a consequence of the deepening of basement to the southeast (Figure 19–6).

The same cannot be said along trend. The structurally highest parts of many of the anticlinoria and synclinoria occur in the Juniata culmination (Gwinn, 1970). This culmination is a 20- to 25-mile-wide (broadening to 60 miles in the Nittany anticline) transverse belt that runs approximately north-south, oblique to the structural grain of the province (Figure 19–3). The folds east of the culmination plunge to the east, and those to the southwest plunge to the southwest, both away from the culmination. This structural high is not a basement feature, but instead reflects the additional amount of anticlinal relief that resulted from greater horizontal shortening here than to the east or southwest. The southwestward decrease of amplitude of the anticlines to the southwest of the culmination indicates that the folds were not absorbing the décollement movement. Rather, much of that movement appears in the thrust faults east and west of the Broad Top basin (Figure 19–3).

FAULTS

Faults are present at the surface in the Pennsylvania Valley and Ridge, but they are abundant only in the Anthracite region. Most of these faults are thrust faults, but strike-slip or wrench faults do occur individually or along major zones transverse to strike. Detachment faults are common at certain stratigraphic horizons. Extension faults (Faill, 1978) are rare and generally of small displacement.

The décollement in the Waynesboro shale probably extends southeastward under the Great Valley, Blue Ridge, Reading Prong, Mesozoic basins, and perhaps much of the Piedmont (Faill and MacLachlan, 1989; Faill, in preparation). On the northwest side, at the Allegheny structural front, it ramps upward from the Cambrian strata to the Silurian Salina Group (Figure 19–7), where it forms the principal basal detachment horizon under the Appalachian Plateau of northern and western Pennsylvania and New York State (Gwinn, 1964; Prucha, 1968; Frey, 1973). To the south in Maryland, Virginia, and West Virginia, two major detachment horizons have been delineated within the Valley and Ridge by Perry (1978), one in

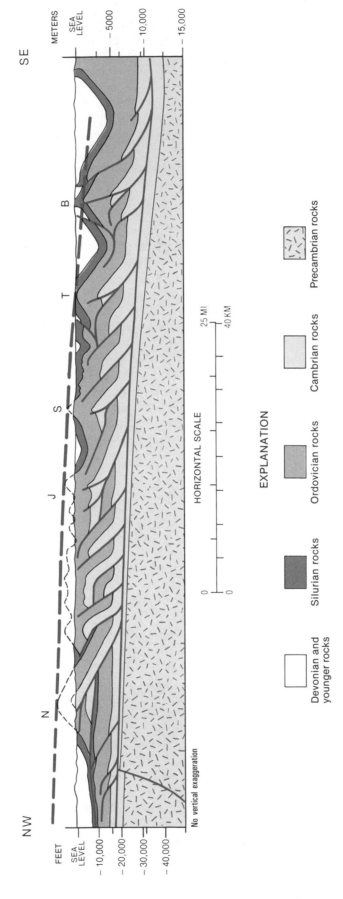

Figure 19–6. Cross section of the Valley and Ridge structural province portraying the major folds and their relation to the basal Waynesboro décollement and imbricates or ramps therefrom. The heavy dashed line connecting the crests of the top of Ordovician rocks in each anticline parallels the basal décollement, indicating that the fold structural relief across the province is constant. The location of the cross section and anticline names corresponding to the letters above the section are shown in Figure 19–3.

EXPLANATION

Devonian and younger rocks

Silurian rocks

Ordovician rocks

Cambrian rocks

Precambrian rocks

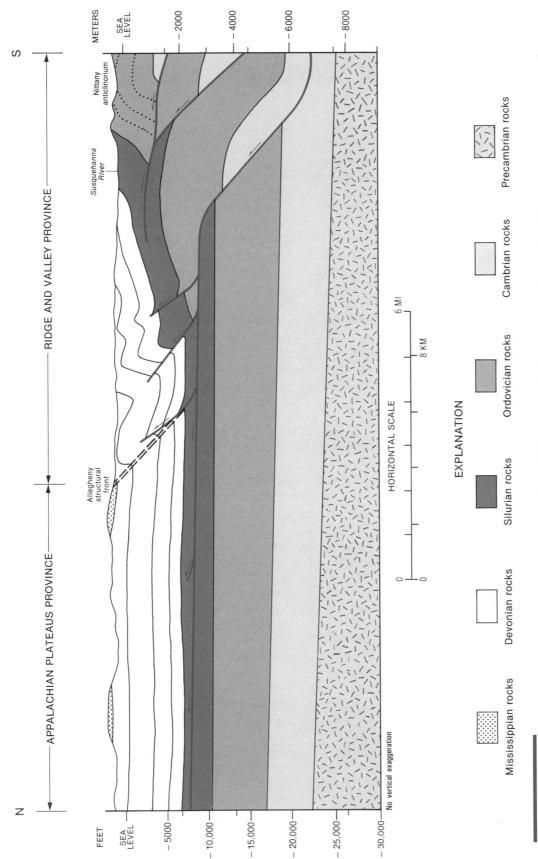

Figure 19–7. Cross section through the Allegheny structural front in the Williamsport vicinity, Lycoming County (modified from Faill and others, 1977b). Along much of the northwest margin of the Valley and Ridge structural province, the Allegheny structural front (indicated by the double dashed line) lies above or near a major ramp that extends from the basal décollement in the Cambrian Waynesboro Formation into the Silurian Salina Group or its equivalent. The front separates the moderate to tight folds of the Valley and Ridge structural province from the very open folds of the Allegheny Plateau.

the Cambrian Waynesboro (as in Pennsylvania) and the other at the base of the Upper Ordovician Martinsburg (Reedsville) Formation.

Within the Valley and Ridge structural province of Pennsylvania, detachment has been recognized at least locally at the following horizons: (1) the Upper Ordovician Antes shale and Salona or Coburn limestone (Pierce, 1966; Moebs and Hoy, 1959; Nickelsen, 1988), which is here named the Antes-Coburn detachment and is an equivalent of Pierce's (1966) Tuscarora fault and Perry's Martinsburg (Reedsville) detachment; (2) the Upper Ordovician Martinsburg Formation-Lower Silurian Shawangunk Formation contact (Epstein and others, 1974); (3) the Silurian Wills Creek and Poxono Island Formations (Epstein and others, 1974; Nickelsen, 1983b; J. Farley, personal communication, 1978), which are equivalent to the Salina Group; (4) the Middle Devonian Marcellus shale (Miller, 1961; Wood and Bergin, 1970; Epstein and others, 1974; Nickelsen, 1986); (5) the Devonian Tully Limestone-Burket shale contact (D. M. Hoskins and J. H. Way, personal communication, 1978); and (6) possibly near the bottom and the top of the Mississippian Mauch Chunk Formation of the Anthracite region (Wood and others, 1969). Although mesoscopic faults, rock cleavage, and disharmonic folds indicative of higher strain seem to occur more commonly at these horizons, many outcrops of the same intervals show no strain disharmony with strata above and below. Hence, movements on these horizons may be of only local extent.

Perhaps the most important of the detachment horizons is the Antes-Coburn, a basin-wide boundary separating two mechanically dissimilar lithic sequences, the underlying 2-mile-thick carbonate sequence and the overlying 5-mile-thick sequence of shales, siltstones, and sandstones. Some exposures of the Antes and the underlying Coburn show well-developed cleavage, fourth-order disharmonic folds, and/or small fault or cleavage duplexes, which suggests that the Antes-Coburn detachment is a boundary zone (Currie and others, 1962) between mechanically different sequences that have experienced different strains. Gwinn (1970, Figure 3) recognized that the underlying carbonate sequence had been shortened twice as much as the overlying rocks and that the Antes-Coburn (Gwinn's Reedsville) detachment extends under the whole synclinal Broad Top region. Mitra and Namson (1989, Figure 8) reinterpreted Gwinn's section, making it conform better to his concept of no differential shortening in the Cambrian and Ordovician section below the Reedsville detachment. Similarly, Perry (1978, Figures 2 and 8)

portrayed a Cambrian and Ordovician carbonate duplex (also shown by Boyer and Elliott, 1982, Figure 26) to the south in Maryland and Virginia with a floor thrust in the Waynesboro Formation and a roof thrust at the Reedsville (or Antes-Coburn) horizon. Herman and Geiser (1985) showed the necessity of this Upper Ordovician detachment horizon to explain section-balancing discrepancies.

The middle and upper Paleozoic rocks in eastern Pennsylvania display various deformational styles and have been divided into four lithotectonic units based upon contrasting fold geometries and amount of strain (Epstein and others, 1974). The four units (Martinsburg, Shawangunk and Bloomsburg, Poxono Island to Marcellus, and post-Marcellus) are separated by the Blue Mountain, Stone Ridge-Godfrey Ridge, and Weir Mountain décollements. Few folds cross these bounding detachment faults, and shortening is greater in the Martinsburg and Marcellus units.

The thrust faults that rise off the basal décollement and lie in the cores of the anticlines are probably synthetic, having movement in the same sense and direction as on the décollement. The thrusts tend to be moderately steep and parallel to the overlying bedding in the southeast limbs of the anticlines, whereas in the hinges and northwest limbs, they possess a low dip and cut across bedding (Figures 19-7 and 19-5; see also discussions of the Nittany anticline in Gwinn, 1970; Faill and others, 1977a; Faill, 1986b; and Faill and others, 1989). In contrast, thrust faults on the northwestern limb of the Jacks Mountain anticline cut up section from the Antes-Coburn detachment into Silurian rocks, and because of subsequent limb rotation, they now dip northwest (Nickelsen, 1988).

The Anthracite region, located on the diminishing, east-plunging, first-order folds in eastern Pennsylvania, is one of the most extensively faulted areas of the entire Appalachian orogen. The overwhelming majority of the faults are thrust faults originating as imbricates from the rising hypothetical Pottchunk décollement in the underlying Mauch Chunk Formation (Figure 19-8) (Wood and others, 1969). The Pottchunk may have been an early décollement with northward movement that was later folded (Wood and Bergin, 1970), or it may have simply been a detachment zone from which imbricate thrusts rose in response to crowding between the growing anticlines. Other interpretations of Anthracite region upper imbricate thrust fault relations to deep-seated décollements include those of (1) Berg and others (1980), who placed the décollement in the Silurian; (2) Lyttle and Epstein (1987), who placed the floor décollement for the imbricate thrusts in the Devonian Marcellus

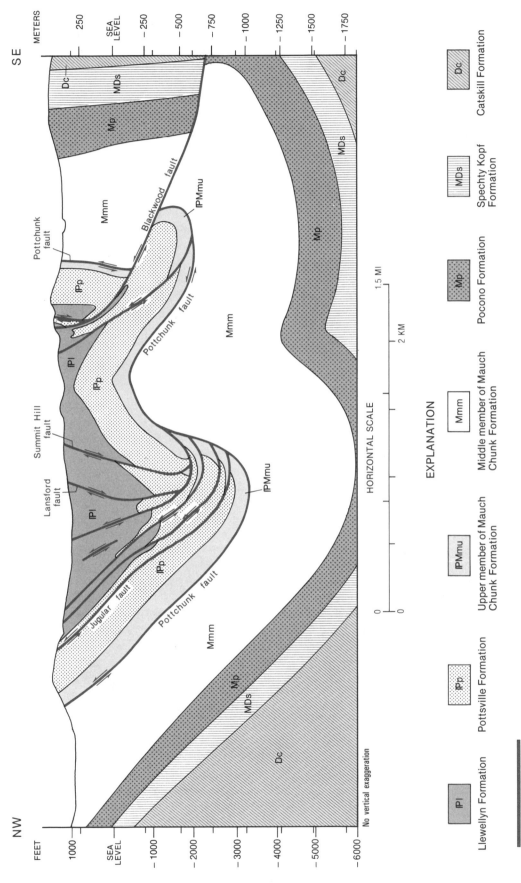

Figure 19-8. Cross section of the Minersville synclinorium (see Figure 19–3) in the southern Anthracite field near Tamaqua (modified from Wood, 1974b, cross section B–B'). Each surface fault is interpreted as a ramp from the décollement, which is the Pottchunk fault at the top of the middle member of the Mauch Chunk Formation. Offsets on faults (e.g., the Jugular) in the northwest limbs of the synclines are consistent with an early Alleghanian, prefolding northwestward movement on the Pottchunk décollement. The offsets are also consistent with out-of-the-syncline movements, which generally occur late in the folding. The Lansford and Summit Hill faults in the southeast limb exhibit reversal of early ramp offsets by the late out-of-the-syncline movements. The Blackwood fault is a late Alleghanian fault offsetting all other structures.

Formation above a basal Cambrian décollement; and (3) Gray (1991), who drew balanced cross sections of part of the southern Anthracite region that showed imbricate thrusts in the upper Paleozoic section rising off both the Pottchunk fault in a crowded Minersville syncline and from a deeper, probably Cambrian, major décollement.

Paleoisotherms established by conodont color alteration indexes, coal-rank differences, fluid inclusions, and mineral equilibria indicate that during the Alleghany orogeny of the Valley and Ridge structural province, there was a gradient of increasing temperature extending from central to northeastern Pennsylvania (Hosterman and others, 1970; Epstein and others, 1977; Nickelsen, 1983a; Levine, 1986). The presence of lower greenschist metamorphism ($300\pm50°C$) in the youngest beds of the Anthracite basins suggests either transport of hot fluids into this part of the foreland from the Piedmont or other deep-seated sedimentary section (Hearn and others, 1987), or the presence of an overlying thermal blanket which has since been eroded. Such a blanket could have been an unusually thick post-Llewellyn sedimentary cover, a 7-km- (4.3-mi-) thick autochthonous overburden created by folding and faulting within the Anthracite region as depicted in a balanced cross section by Gray (1991), or an Alleghanian overthrust of Reading Prong allochthonous rock onto the Anthracite region (Levine, 1986; MacLachlan, 1985). However, Levine has demonstrated that in the late Carboniferous time available for deposition, it is highly unlikely that sufficient sediment could have been accumulated to achieve the temperatures that have been measured. The apparent inversion of the temperature gradient suggests that the source of heat was from above the presently preserved rocks.

A number of large, subvertical, transverse, strike-slip faults have been mapped in localities such as the Nittany anticlinorium near Tyrone, Blair County, or along the southern edge of the Anthracite region. The longest zone of transverse faulting is the Transylvania fault zone of Root and Hoskins (1977) (part of which [Breezewood] is shown in Figure 19–3). A triangular area of transverse faults is present within and just outside the Valley and Ridge structural province between Altoona, Milesburg, and Clearfield (Figure 19–9) (Glass, 1971; Glass and others, 1977; Faill, 1981). Slickenlines on some transverse faults are parallel to bedding, indicating a strike-slip movement prior to folding (Figure 19–10). Overprinting by other slickenlines at various angles to bedding points to continued movement on the transverse faults as folding progressed. Such slickenlines are particu-

larly well displayed in the Anthracite region (Nickelsen, 1979), at Pine Creek north of Jersey Shore, and in the gaps along the Nittany anticline (Canich and Gold, 1985).

Many of the linear Tuscarora quartzite ridges throughout the province possess smooth crests of uniform elevation, but on the northwest limbs of some of the larger anticlines, these ridges exhibit an uneven, knobby form (Figure 19–11). Each knob consists of a coherent block of quartzite that has been rotated so that its bedding strikes north of the ridge trend at a small to moderate angle (e.g., Pierce, 1966; Nickelsen, 1988). The blocks are in a zone that is bounded on both sides of the ridge by major thrusts or steep reverse faults, but within the zone two kinds of faults can be found. Imbricate faults that strike parallel to the bedding in the quartzite blocks cause multiple duplications of the red Juniata-Tuscarora section, whereas transverse west-striking faults with right-lateral separation pass through the swales separating the knobs. Interpretations differ on how this structure evolved (Main, 1978; Nickelsen, 1988).

The last faults developed during the Alleghanian orogeny were the low-angle extensional faults that are restricted to vertical and overturned beds in the northwest limbs of the anticlines. These faults commonly occur as mutually offsetting conjugate pairs dipping southeast and northwest, and bound extensional wedges related to layer-parallel extension (Figures 19–12 and 19–5). They were formed when the bedding was perpendicular to the horizontal maximum principal stress and extension was vertical.

Long lineaments transverse to the folds have been delineated in Pennsylvania (Chapter 22; Kowalik and Gold, 1976), the most prominent being the one between Tyrone and Mount Union (Figure 19–3). It stands out because the valleys of the Little Juniata and Juniata Rivers are parallel. Evidence cited for it includes slickensided transverse faults, mesoscopic disharmonic folds, high fracture density, and terminations of third- and second-order folds. It may be a deep-seated crustal zone, perhaps formed during the Precambrian, that has since been intermittently active (Canich and Gold, 1985).

PENETRATIVE DEFORMATION

Attention has previously focused on the folds and faults that shape the major structures and topography, but more recently, geologists became aware that flow and dissolution were also significant deformational processes. Evidence of these processes appears in several forms: (1) distorted mud-crack

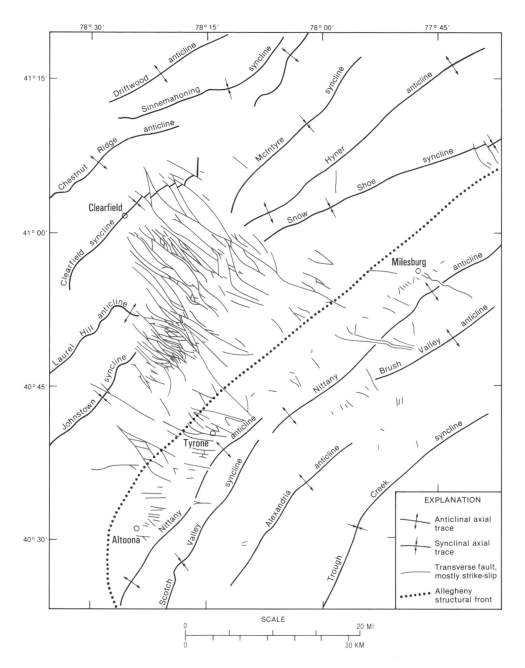

Figure 19-9. Strike-slip, transverse faults in the Altoona-Milesburg-Clearfield triangle straddling and northwest of the Allegheny structural front. This conjugate array of faults is developed in an area of northeastward extension formed at the juncture between northeast-trending folds to the northeast and more northerly trending folds to the southwest.

polygons, reduction spots, and fossils; (2) clay-carbon partings; (3) stylolites; and (4) spaced to slaty cleavage (Nickelsen, 1972; Faill and Nickelsen, 1973; Epstein, 1974; Nickelsen, 1986).

The penetrative deformation occurred in two phases. The first was a pre-Alleghanian compaction perpendicular to bedding, indicated by distorted fossils and reduction spots, and bed-parallel stylolites. In argillaceous rocks, the compaction was primarily by a mechanical rotation of phyllosilicate grains during expulsion of water. Dissolution removed carbonate material along bed-parallel stylolites in the limestones.

Reduction spots were compacted 20 to 30 percent into oblate ellipsoids (pancake-shaped, parallel to bedding).

Layer-parallel shortening constituted the second phase at the initiation of Alleghanian folding. This shortening, perpendicular to the axial planes of the folds, is revealed by mud-crack polygons on bedding planes that are longer parallel to cleavage traces and fold axes (Figure 19-13). Initially spherical reduction spots were first compacted and then flattened to oblate ellipsoids lying parallel to cleavage (Figure 19-14). Along the strain path between oblate ellipsoidal shapes, first parallel to bedding and then parallel to cleavage,

Figure 19–10. Slickenlines on a small transverse fault in the Devonian Lock Haven Formation 1.2 miles west of Altoona, Blair County. Bedding dips moderately to the west (left); the transverse fault is subvertical, trending down the bedding dip. The parallelism of the slickenlines to the bedding-fault intersection suggests that the movement on the fault either preceded folding or occurred very early in the folding.

Figure 19–11. Knobby topographic expression of Little Scrub Ridge as seen looking south from U.S. Route 522 at its intersection with Pa. Route 475, 7 miles north of McConnellsburg, Fulton County. This ridge occurs on the northwest limb of the McConnellsburg anticline and is similar to Tuscarora ridges on the northwest limbs of other first-order anticlines in the province. Each sag contains a transverse fault separating the intact beds of the adjacent knobs. Development of these faults resulted in an extension strain parallel to the ridge (and fold axis).

the reduction spots passed through a period of elongation parallel to cleavage-bedding intersections and fold axes (Graham, 1978). In areas of high strain along the West Branch Susquehanna River between Milton and Watsontown, Northumberland County, they ended as triaxial ellipsoids with X:Y:Z axial ratios of 1.3:1:0.5, where X is down the dip of cleavage, Y is parallel to the strike of cleavage and fold axes, and Z is perpendicular to the cleavage, a nearly 50 percent flattening perpendicular to cleavage (Nickelsen, 1983b).

Distortion of fossils is another indication of early layer-parallel shortening (Figure 19–15). Measurements on crinoid columnals in the bedding surface

indicate 5- to 15-percent layer-parallel shortening perpendicular to the fold axes throughout the Valley and Ridge structural province, although locally somewhat higher values were obtained in strongly cleaved rocks (Faill, 1977; Faill and others, 1977a). The same amount of strain is found in the Appalachian Plateau of Pennsylvania and in New York beyond the northern edge of the Alleghanian folds (Nickelsen, 1966; Engelder and Engelder, 1977). Layer-parallel-shortening strain is approximately the same across the Valley and Ridge and Appalachian Plateau.

Cleavage is probably the most variable of the penetrative structures, both geographically and strati-

Figure 19-12. Vertical quartzite and argillaceous siltstone beds in the Montebello Member of the Devonian Mahantango Formation along U.S. Route 22–322 on the east side of the Susquehanna River water gap north of Harrisburg, just north of Blue Mountain (north is to the left). These beds are transected by mutually offsetting extensional faults that formed late in the folding, after the bedding had reached its present orientation. Responding to the horizontally directed, maximum deforming stress, the fault system allowed the rocks to be extended vertically, parallel to bedding. The outcrop is 40 feet wide at the base.

Figure 19-13. Extremely deformed mud polygons in the Silurian Wills Creek Formation in southernmost Huntingdon County, 1.2 miles northeast of Burnt Cabins. These mud polygons were originally equidimensional but were shortened perpendicular to the fold axial plane (long axes are parallel to the fold axis) by flow and dissolution during the layer-parallel shortening of the Alleghanian deformation. The view is looking down on the bedding surface. Polygons are about 1 by 4 inches in size.

Figure 19-14. Bits of organic material entrained in red siltstone beds of the Silurian Bloomsburg Formation produced local environments which reduced the ferric ions, resulting in small volumes of green spots. Where the original material was equidimensional, the resulting green spots were probably spherical; thus, the distorted spots are good strain indicators for the period of the Alleghanian penetrative deformation. This example is from the quarry at the Watsontown Brick and Crystal Fabricator near Watsontown, Northumberland County, 15 miles north of Sunbury. The view is 8 inches wide.

graphically. It is best developed in the Bloomsburg mudstones, but it is also common in the Reedsville, Mifflintown, Keyser, Mahantango, and Catskill Formations. Cleavage is also best developed in the steeply dipping to overturned beds of the anticlinal northwest limbs, especially adjacent to the structural fronts. It is particularly strong north of Blue Mountain in eastern Pennsylvania, and along the west and north branches of the Susquehanna River. It occurs both as a continuous cleavage (where grain rotation dominated) and as a spaced cleavage (where dissolution was the predominant mechanism) (Figure 19-16). Some of the cleavage is perpendicular to bedding regardless of the dip of the bedding, which indicates that it developed prior to folding during layer-parallel shortening. In numerous other localities, the cleavage is axial planar, indicating that its original attitude has been modified during folding. Where distinct differences in lithology occur, cleavage has also been rotated (or "refracted") by shear movements between beds during the folding (Figure 19-17).

Figure 19–15. Distorted fossils are common throughout the Valley and Ridge structural province and are evidence of a widespread flow early in the folding. On this bedding surface from the Upper Devonian Trimmers Rock Formation along Pa. Route 54, 2.5 miles north of Danville, Montour County, the originally circular crinoid columnals are now elliptical in shape, having the long axes parallel to the bedding strike and the fold axis.

The two categories of penetrative-deformation mechanisms that produced the distortion and cleavage in the Valley and Ridge structural province are (1) volume loss by dissolution of quartz and calcite with residual accumulation of phyllosilicates and carbon (Nickelsen, 1972, 1974); and (2) volume-constant flow. The latter includes intragranular twin and translation gliding, and intergranular cataclastic flow, grain-boundary sliding, or crenulation (grain rotation). The dominant mechanism that was utilized was a function of rock type, lithologic association, and structural position. But in most situations, the distortion and cleavage developed by a combination of two or more mechanisms.

Figure 19–17. Rotated cleavage and early calcite vein in the Silurian Mifflintown Formation along U.S. Route 11, 3 miles west of Danville, Montour County, and 11 miles east-northeast of Sunbury, Northumberland County, on the north branch of the Susquehanna River. The cleavage in the argillaceous beds, which was probably initially perpendicular to bedding, has been rotated clockwise by the simple shear between the overlying and underlying limestone beds, so that cleavage now dips only 20 degrees more steeply to the southeast than the bedding. The shape of the white calcite vein is strongly influenced by cleavage and ductility contrasts among the various beds. It was an early vein, emplaced before folding and offset by clockwise flexural slip as the beds were folded.

Figure 19–16. Cleavage in shales of the Silurian Rose Hill Formation in the hinge of the Hartleton syncline at the Laurel Creek Reservoir of the Lewistown Water Supply, adjacent to U.S. Route 322, 12 miles north of Lewistown, Mifflin County. The dark, folded and faulted band is a very thin siltstone bed in which cleavage did not develop. This siltstone bed gives a measure of shortening achieved by the cleavage development.

SEQUENCE OF EVENTS

The Alleghanian deformation in the Valley and Ridge structural province can be divided into a number of stages in which one or another process was predominant. An exceptional exposure of folds and associated structures at Bear Valley in the Western

Middle Anthracite basin (Figure 19–18) provides evidence for seven stages of structural development in this area and, by analogy, throughout the entire Valley and Ridge (Nickelsen, 1979, 1983b).

Pre-Alleghanian deformation left a record of regional, extensional (Stage I) joint sets in coals of the Appalachian Plateau (Nickelsen and Hough, 1967) and Anthracite region (Nickelsen, 1979). Evidence of Alleghanian deformation is preserved in overprinted episodes of layer-parallel shortening, which produced extension joints in shales and sandstones, spaced cleavage, small-scale folding, and conjugate wrench faulting and thrusting (Stages II–IV). The major folding constitutes Stage V. In late stages of folding, layer-parallel extension in the outer arc of folds and on the steep (>45-degree dip) limbs produced joints and both strike and transverse extensional wedges (Stage VI) (Figure 19–19). Stage VII strike-slip faults cut all previous structures and appear to be restricted to major gaps located on lineaments (Nickelsen, 1983b).

Once the sequence of stages of Alleghany deformation had been established, it was realized that the principal stresses changed orientations throughout the structural history of the Valley and Ridge. On the Appalachian Plateau and extending into the Valley and Ridge, the presence of several overprinted, pre-Alleghanian, extensional joint sets imply different stress orientations that resulted from epeirogenic movements and/or early Alleghanian layer-parallel shortening (Nickelsen and Hough, 1967). Then, during the following Alleghanian layer-parallel shortening, there was a progressive change in the orientation of Alleghanian structures as documented by overprinted structures at Bear Valley (Nickelsen, 1979, 1980; Faill,

Figure 19–18. The "whaleback" anticline in the Pennsylvanian Llewellyn Formation, in the Bear Valley strip mine, 2.5 miles west of Shamokin, Northumberland County, in the Western Middle field (Minersville synclinorium, Figure 19–3) of the Anthracite region. The primary surface exposed on the anticline is a sandstone, which formerly was beneath a coal bed. Structures in this sandstone include transverse faults, multiple slickenlines, extensional wedges, thrust faults, and strike-slip faults. The view is to the east. The steeply north-dipping sandstone bed in the upper right is the same bed as that exposed on the anticline. A syncline lies between the two exposures. The same syncline is exposed in younger beds in the highwall at the east end. Slip along the intervening coal and shale resulted in this disharmonic relation of a synclinal hinge over an anticlinal hinge. The absence of a kink geometry in these folds is a consequence of the very large ductility contrast between the coal and sandstone. Note the person at the plane table in the lower right for scale.

Figure 19–19. View of the north limb of the "whaleback" anticline shown in Figure 19–18, looking down on the steeply north-dipping to vertical sandstone bed. Numerous transverse faults that formed late during the folding cross the bedding at a large angle. Subhorizontal conjugate fault pairs produced grabens parallel to the bedding strike and the fold axis; subvertical conjugate fault pairs produced grabens downdip of bedding. The field of view is approximately 80 feet at the base of the outcrop. Circular depressions in the sandstone bedding surface are molds of ironstone concretions.

1979, 1986a). The overprinting of early Lackawanna phase structures by Main phase structures (correlated with Nickelsen's Stages V and VI) in northeastern Pennsylvania and adjacent New York documents a progressive clockwise rotation of stress axes throughout the Alleghanian orogeny (Engelder and Geiser, 1980; Geiser and Engelder, 1983). In contrast, along the southern plungeout of the Jacks Mountain anticline in south-central Pennsylvania, the Stage IV Stone Mountain duplex was overprinted by Stage V folding and a later out-of-sequence steep reverse fault, both of which demonstrate a counterclockwise rotation of stress axes. Further evidence of counterclockwise overprinting of later stages of the Alleghany orogeny is provided by the angular relation between a Stage IV slip line in the Birmingham window that was overprinted by a Stage V fold trend (Nickelsen and Engelder, 1989).

PROBLEMS AND FUTURE RESEARCH

At first glance, the Valley and Ridge structural province appears to be structurally simple and well understood, but each new investigation challenges old ideas and points to new opportunities for reinterpretation. The fact that the total strain is partitioned among extension fractures, faults, folds, flow, and dissolution indicates that the structure is anything but simple.

Problems for future research in the Pennsylvania Valley and Ridge structural province include the following:

1. Deep drilling, seismic data, and projections of surface data have defined the depth to basement and the top of the Paleozoic carbonates throughout most of the province; however, cross sections cannot be balanced because the amount of shortening occurring in the Cambrian and Ordovician carbonates exceeds that in overlying clastic rocks. An explanation may exist in (a) reinterpretation of the roof thrust at the top of the carbonates; (b) analysis of back thrusting, flow, and dissolution that would recognize more layer-parallel shortening in rocks above the roof thrust within the Valley and Ridge; or (c) absorption of the shortening above the roof thrust by layer-parallel shortening of the clastic rocks of the Appalachian Plateau, west of the Valley and Ridge (Geiser, 1988).

2. Crinoid columnals and brachiopod shells of post-Ordovician strata above roof thrusts usually exhibit 5- to 15-percent layer-parallel shortening, whereas mud-crack polygons, reduction spots, and pedogenic slickensides (Gray and Nickelsen, 1989) (all large, lithologically homogeneous strain markers) record layer-parallel-shortening strain of 25 to 50 percent. Twinning of calcite crystals com-

monly records less than 5 percent layer-parallel-shortening strain. Clearly, not all strain indicators are equally representative of the total strain in the rocks, and this must be considered during the area balancing of sections.

3. The high thermal maturity of the rocks in the northeastern part of the province indicates excess heating in the youngest, Pennsylvanian Llewellyn strata that cannot be correlated with any known igneous heat source. An explanation for this temperature anomaly, in which paleoisotherms are oriented perpendicular to strike, and temperature increases toward the northeast along strike, must be sought in either migration of hot fluids from a deep basin in an adjacent province or imposition of a sedimentary or tectonically emplaced thermal blanket that has since been eroded.

4. Recent data on both the northeast and southwest parts of the Pennsylvania salient suggest that the sequential deformation of the Alleghany orogeny has operated in a rotating stress field. In the northeast, earlier Lackawanna trends striking 050° to 065° are overprinted by Main trends striking 085°, a clockwise sequential rotation. In the southwest part of the Pennsylvania salient, Lackawanna trends of 050° are overprinted by trends of 022° to 033° in a counterclockwise sequential rotation. Are these data valid, or are they an artifact of the observed strike differences between first-order and second- or third-order folds at many places in the province? If valid, how do these sequentially overprinted, different transport directions relate to the plate collision that produced the Alleghany orogeny?

5. First-order anticlines all have roughly the same amplitude and wavelength. What controls their development? Thickness of the Paleozoic sheet above the décollement? Horse spacing in the Cambrian and Ordovician carbonate duplex?

6. First-order folds probably formed in succession, either from southeast to northwest, or from northwest to southeast. By what criteria can the proper in-sequence succession be determined?

7. Out-of-sequence, steep reverse faults overprint all previous structures on the northwest limbs of two first-order anticlines of the province—Jacks Mountain and McConnellsburg Cove. What are the different environmental parameters controlling the different fault fabrics of these and other yet-to-be-found, out-of-sequence structures?

8. The Broad Top basin is a relatively undeformed island within the province. Very little structure exists beneath it (Jacobeen and Kanes, 1975), but extensively thrust-faulted anticlines lie immediately to the west and east of it, and the Juniata culmination rises to the northeast. Why were the Broad Top rocks not similarly deformed?

9. All the first-order anticlinoria in central Pennsylvania diminish in size eastward by plunging out and are absent in eastern Pennsylvania, leaving only a narrow belt of Valley and Ridge structures adjacent to the Blue Mountain structural front. In addition, the rocks in the east possess a more pervasive cleavage and contain more extensive brittle structures, such as wedges. What is the cause of this substantial change in the Valley and Ridge structural province?

RECOMMENDED FOR FURTHER READING

Boyer, S. E., and Elliott, David (1982), *Thrust systems*, AAPG Bulletin, v. 66, p. 1196–1230.

Nickelsen, R. P. (1983), *Aspects of Alleghanian deformation*, in Nickelsen, R. P., and Cotter, Edward, eds., *Silurian depositional history and Alleghanian deformation in the Pennsylvania Valley and Ridge*, Annual Field Conference of Pennsylvania Geologists, 48th, Danville, Pa., Guidebook, p. 29–39.

———— (1987), *Sequence of structural stages of the Alleghany orogeny at the Bear Valley strip mine, Shamokin, Pennsylvania*, in Roy, D. C., ed., *Northeastern Section of the Geological Society of America*, Geological Society of America Centennial Field Guide, v. 5, p. 55–58.

Rodgers, John (1970), *Central Pennsylvania sector*, in *The Valley and Ridge province—central Pennsylvania to central Alabama*, Chapter 3 in *The tectonics of the Appalachians*, New York, Wiley-Interscience, p. 31–36.

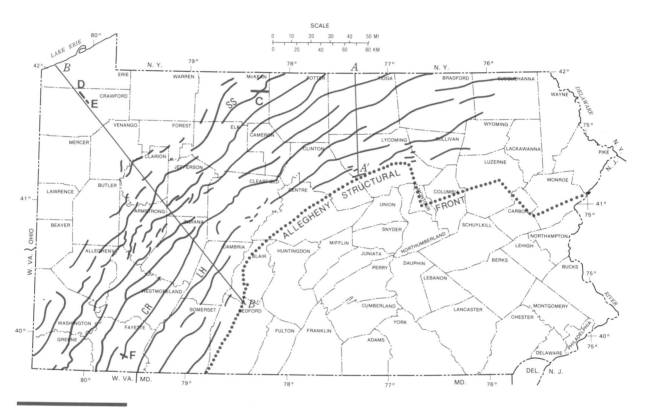

Figure 20–1. Generalized location of surface anticlines in the Appalachian Plateaus province of Pennsylvania (from Berg and others, 1980). Cross sections shown in Figures 20–3 and 20–4 are located along A–A′ and B–B′, respectively. Seismic sections shown in Figures 20–2, 20–6, 20–11, and 20–12 are located at C, D, E, and F, respectively. The Chestnut Ridge, Laurel Hill, and Smethport-Sharon anticlines are labeled CR, LH, and SS, respectively. The location of the Allegheny structural front is from Faill (in preparation).

286

CHAPTER 20   APPALACHIAN PLATEAUS

RICHARD W. BEARDSLEY
   Columbia Natural Resources
   900 Pennsylvania Avenue
   Charleston, WV 25302

RICHARD C. CAMPBELL
   Columbia Natural Resources
   900 Pennsylvania Avenue
   Charleston, WV 25302

MAURICE A. SHAW
   The Mitre Corporation
   Attn: HSD/YAQ
   Building 624W
   Brooks AFB, TX 78235

INTRODUCTION

The study of Appalachian Plateau structures and tectonism in Pennsylvania began in 1835 with the work of H. D. Rogers. Rogers and his contemporaries (see reviews by Sherrill, 1934, and Rodgers, 1949) recognized and described such features as the general northwestward decrease in the intensity of deformation, the occurrence of asymmetrical folds, and the great length and striking parallelism of fold axes in the Appalachian Plateaus province. Most of their theories concerning the events that formed the Appalachian Plateau structures have since been superseded.

The depth of deformation in the Plateau region has been a controversial subject for many years. Until the late 1950's, most geologists believed in basement involvement in Appalachian folding (Gwinn, 1964). However, studies by Woodward (1959), Rodgers (1963, 1970), Gwinn (1964, 1970), Prucha (1968), Harris (1970), Frey (1973), and Wiltschko and Chapple (1977) have demonstrated the "thin-skinned" nature of deformation in the Appalachian Plateau. These studies have shown that the incompetent rocks of the Silurian Salina Group (and, in some places, sections of the Silurian Tonoloway Formation and Ordovician Reedsville Shale) have been deformed, creating the Plateau structures. Anticlines and synclines extend downward only to a décollement surface near the base of the Salina Group.

The question of whether the strata above the décollement surface slid southeastward on Salina salt or were thrusted northwestward as an extension of the Ridge and Valley Alleghanian system has been another point of discussion. Most early geologists concluded that relative tectonic transport had occurred from southeast to northwest because of the character of the Ridge and Valley folds and the general northwestward decrease in the amplitude of Plateau folds. Other workers noted the oversteepened nature of the southeast limb of most of the Plateau anticlines, which suggested movement from the northwest. Gwinn (1964) referred to the work of Rubey and Hubbert (1959), who pointed out the near impossibility of thrusting a large slice of incompetent rocks northwestward. Frey

(1973) stated that the downdip southeasterly sliding of the post-Salina section is a possibility in the Plateau region of Pennsylvania. Wiltschko and Chapple (1977) suggested that flowage of salt-bearing rock from synclines to anticlines formed most of the structures. Others have postulated that salt solution and removal initiated the formation of the Plateau structures.

GENERAL FEATURES OF PLATEAU STRUCTURES
Surface Features

The folds of the Plateau region of Pennsylvania are arcuate and parallel to the Ridge and Valley system (Figure 20–1; see Fettke, 1954, for details of the features described below). These folds are broad, gentle features having wavelengths that range between 5 and 20 miles and structural relief from a few hundred to greater than 2,500 feet (Wiltschko and Chapple, 1977). Generally, the amplitudes of the folds decrease to the northwest. Most of the folds are asymmetric with the steep flank facing southeast. Surface dips of the folds are generally low. Most anticlines commonly have dips ranging from 3 to 5 degrees on their northwestern flanks and from 4 to 6 degrees on their southeastern flanks. Dips between 10 and 60 degrees have been measured at scattered localities (Cathcart, 1934; Hickok and Moyer, 1940; Ebright and others, 1949; Woodrow, 1968).

The Plateau structures die out in northeastern Pennsylvania. Frey (1973) concluded that the areal extent of the folds was related to the Salina salt pinch-out in this area. Seismic surveys support his conclusion. In areas where Salina salt is present, seismic data display salt-induced folding.

Few faults have been recognized at the surface in the Plateau region of Pennsylvania. Fettke (1954) and Glover (1970) recognized and described high-angle faults oriented perpendicular to fold axes in Clearfield County. Other faults were described by Cathcart (1934), Hickok and Moyer (1940), Finn (1949), Shaffner (1958), Berg and Glover (1976), and Pohn and Purdy (1982).

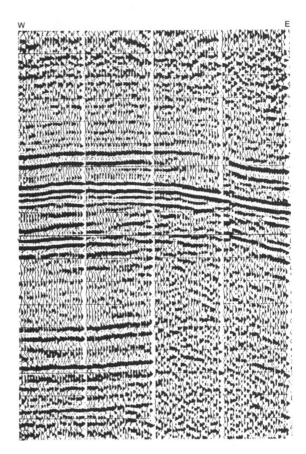

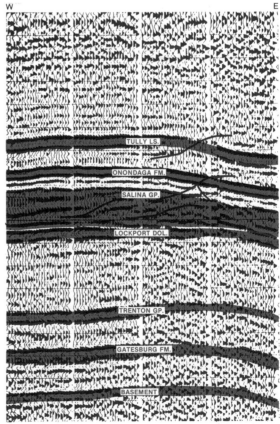

Figure 20–2. Seismic section across the Smethport-Sharon anticline in McKean County (see Figure 20–1 for location). The seismic section on the bottom is an interpreted version of the section on the top. Note the monoclinal flexures at the Lockport and Trenton horizons. The length of the seismic line is 6 miles.

Subsurface Features

The subsurface of the Plateau region of Pennsylvania varies in its structural complexity, which is in contrast to the surface structural pattern (Cate, 1962). In the area of surface anticlines, the Onondaga-Salina interval is faulted extensively. The Onondaga-Ridgeley zone is characterized by high-angle reverse faults (see Fettke, 1954, and Gwinn, 1964, for case studies of the structure at this level). Most of the anticlines at this level have steep southeast limbs with associated northwest-dipping reverse faults. These faults die out in the overlying Devonian shales. Beneath the Onondaga-Ridgeley units, the fault planes flatten and pass into a décollement surface in the Salina Group.

Beneath the Salina Group, the structure is less complex. Monoclinal flexures are the major features in the Middle Silurian to Upper Ordovician interval in most of the Plateau region (see Figures 20–2, 20–3,

and 20–4). Seismic data suggest that faulting does occur in this interval, especially near the Ridge and Valley province, where a series of low-angle thrust faults are present in the Upper Ordovician shales. The Middle Ordovician and Cambrian section contains growth faults, which appear to be related to reactivated normal faults in Grenvillian basement rocks (Root, 1978).

DEVELOPMENT OF PLATEAU STRUCTURES

Cambrian Extension

Surface and subsurface structures and tectonism in the Pennsylvania Plateau region are influenced by features in the Precambrian Grenville terrane beneath the Paleozoic strata. At the beginning of Cambrian deposition in the Plateau region of Pennsylvania, three

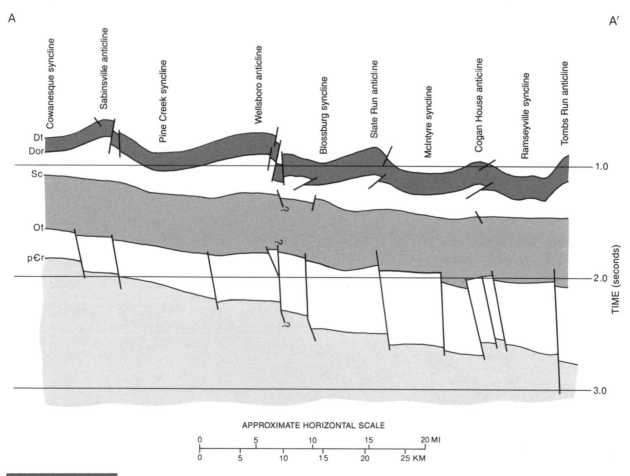

Figure 20–3. Regional cross section based on seismic data in Tioga and Lycoming Counties (see Figure 20–1 for location). Note the uniform seismic time interval between the Clinton (Sc) and Trenton (Ot) horizons and reverse "keystone" grabens at the Tully (Dt) and Ridgeley (Dor) horizons at the Sabinsville and Wellsboro anticlines. The top of crystalline basement is assumed to be the top of the Precambrian (pЄr).

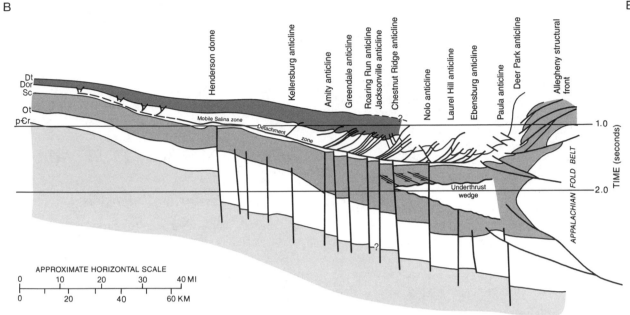

Figure 20–4. Regional cross section based on seismic data from Erie County to Blair County (see Figure 20–1 for location). Note the change in structural style from northwest of the Chestnut Ridge anticline to southeast of the anticline. The Tully (Dt) to Ridgeley (Dor) interval is not illustrated southeast of the Chestnut Ridge anticline due to the structural complexity within this zone. Other horizons shown are Clinton (Sc), Trenton (Ot), and the top of the Precambrian (p€r). The Henderson dome structure, in northwestern Pennsylvania, was first identified in Mercer County and has been traced into Venango County, where it is intersected by cross section B–B´.

major structural grains were inherent from the Grenville event (about 1 Ga) (Figure 20–5). Incipient zones of failure were the décollement ramps (Figure 20–6), tear faults, and transform faults generated by the Grenville event. Rifting due to extension in Cambrian time rejuvenated some of these older fault zones (Figure 20–7), creating the northwest boundary of the Rome trough system (Wagner, 1976; Root, 1978; see Figure 20–8). The development of this structure initiated much of the subsequent growth faulting in the Cambrian section in the Plateau region. Reversal of movement along the Grenvillian ramps produced

Figure 20–5. Major Grenvillian structural grains in the Plateau region at the beginning of Cambrian deposition. These grains represent the orientations of the majority of the Grenvillian structural features (faults, folds) in each area. The location of the Allegheny structural front is from Faill (in preparation).

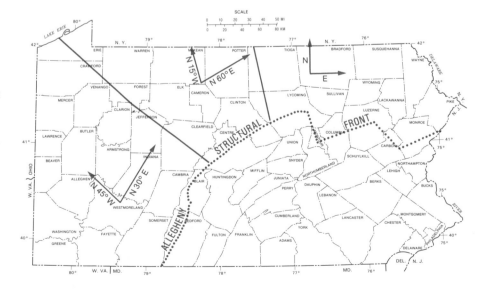

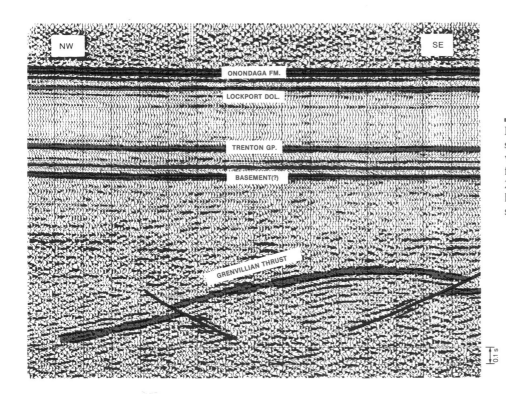

Figure 20–6. Seismic section across a Grenvillian thrust in Crawford County (see Figure 20–1 for location). The length of the seismic section is 3.3 miles.

Figure 20–7. Sequence of events leading to the rejuvenation of Grenvillian thrust faults. A. Thrusting of Grenvillian basement rocks. B. Deposition of Eocambrian sediments and subsequent erosion and faulting due to extension. C. Deposition of Cambrian and Ordovician sediments. Eocambrian sediments are metamorphosed. Some fracturing in Grenvillian rocks caused by basin fill. D. The Grenvillian thrust is rejuvenated by loading, which causes further deformation of the Grenvillian rocks and growth faulting in the Cambrian and Ordovician section. Each section is approximately 6 miles across. No vertical scale. Horizons: Ot, Trenton; Obr, Black River; €g, Gatesburg; and €p, Potsdam.

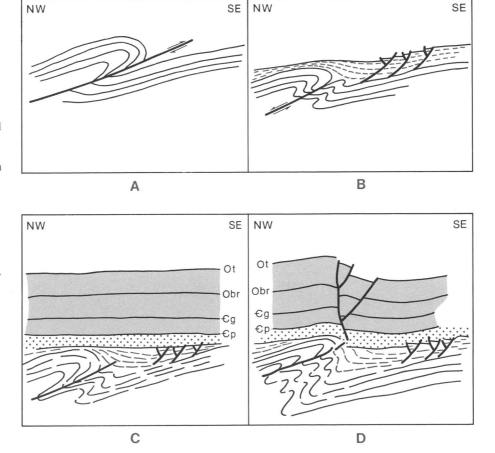

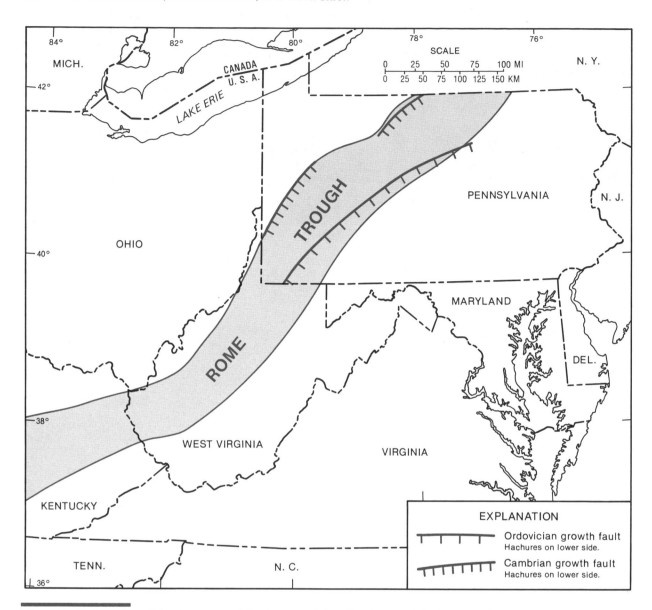

Figure 20–8. Location of the Rome trough in the central Appalachians and the location of Cambrian and Ordovician growth faults in Pennsylvania (faults from Wagner, © 1976, Figures 7 and 10, p. 422 and 425, reprinted by permission of the American Association of Petroleum Geologists).

normal displacement on the faults penetrating the Cambrian section (Figure 20–7), allowing the deposition of as much as 5,000 feet of additional section below the Ordovician Trenton section.

Taconic Compression

Growth faulting terminated near the end of Ordovician Black River deposition as the eastern margin of the present Appalachian basin again was subjected to compressive forces (Colton, 1970). Differential compaction and sedimentation formed a series of monoclinal flexures across the old growth-faulted terrane.

These flexures acted as both barriers to and sources for clastic deposits across the Plateau. Compaction features dominate the Plateau structure from the Ordovician Trenton through the Silurian Clinton sections, as shown in Figure 20–3 by the uniform seismic time intervals between the Clinton and Trenton Groups.

Acadian/Caledonian Extension

At the approximate time of the Lower Devonian regressive event, major downwarping developed along the monoclinal flexures associated with Cambrian growth faults, resulting in increased basin slope to the

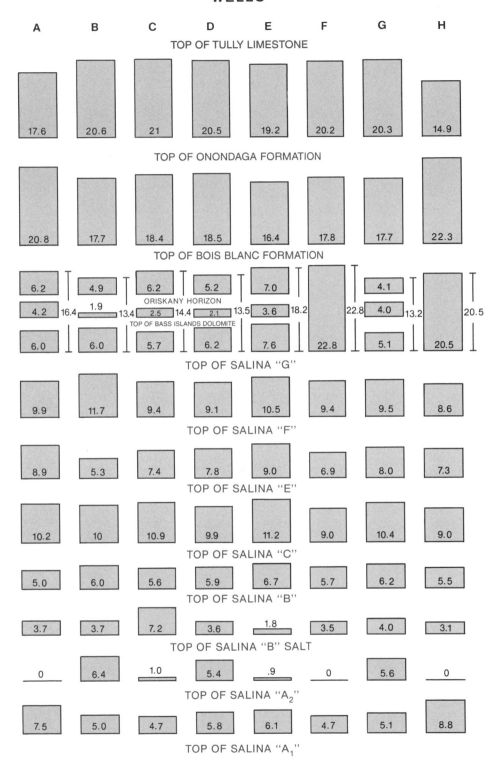

Figure 20–9. A histogram comparison of the percent of total depositional thickness of units between the top of the Salina "A_1" and the top of the Tully Limestone. This comparison provides a means for determining the time of salt migration by demonstrating the subsequent formation thickness adjustment in the overburden. Each vertical column represents a well, and numbers are percent of total interval for each stratigraphic unit.

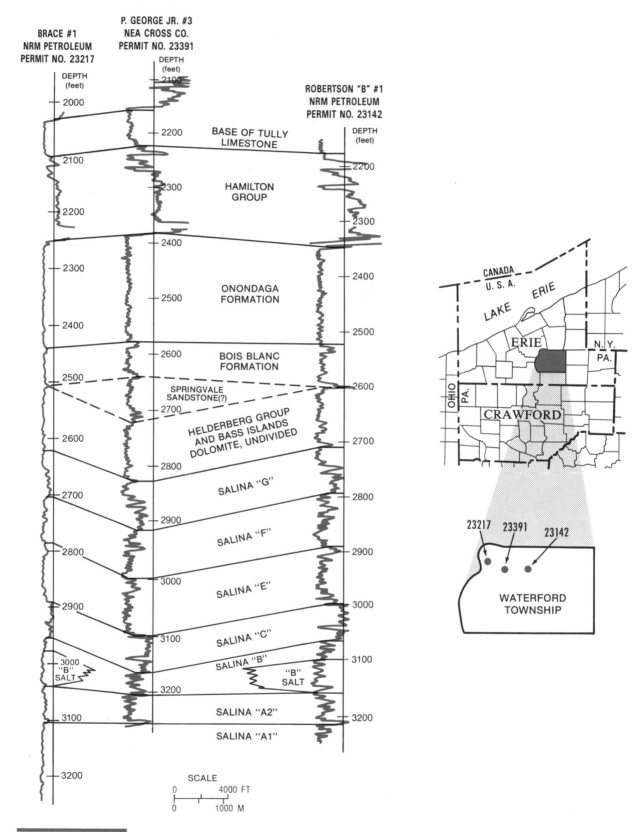

Figure 20–10. Three gamma-ray signatures for wells in Waterford Township, Erie County. The signatures demonstrate, in cross section, formation adjustment during Helderberg-Bois Blanc time due to Salina "B" salt migration.

southeast. This event occurred about 390 Ma (Trainer, 1932). The basin extension and rotation, coupled with the mobility of the Salina "B," "C," "D," "E," and "F" units, formed many structural features that are unique to the Appalachian Plateau region. These features are related to, but not rooted in, the configuration of the pre-Paleozoic Grenville province. Movement from northwest to southeast in the northwest Plateau region occurred only in Lower Devonian rocks. This movement can be detected as early as the Early Devonian. To the southeast, movement continued through the Middle Devonian, involving both Lower and Middle Devonian rocks. The faults associated with this movement were high-angle normal to high-angle reverse in the northwest and lower angle reverse toward the southeast. Present shallow structures coincide with the reset tectonic limits of the "B," "D," "E," "F_1," "F_2," "F_3," and "F_4" salts of the Salina Group. Devonian structures are characterized by steep-faulted southeast limbs, indicating movement from northwest to southeast.

Migration of the Salina "B" salt and the subsequent structural adjustment has been studied in Waterford Township, Erie County. Random wells were chosen beyond the Salina "D" salt pinchout but within the extent of the "B" salt. This constraint allowed study of subsequent deposition as it related to the migration of salt through time without the complication of monitoring more than one salt unit.

When tectonic and overburden stresses are placed upon a salt-bearing formation, the salt may either act as a glide surface for the overburden or migrate away from the stressing force. The subsequent depressions developed on the surface will cause beds deposited after the stress adjustment to be anomalously thick. The stratigraphic location of these anomalies pinpoints the onset of salt migration and, therefore, the time when significant stress first affected the area in question.

The necessity of choosing wells between the salt pinchouts placed them in an area near the edge of the basin. The basin-edge effect was filtered out by evaluating the percent of total depositional thickness (%t) of the various definable formations (base of the Tully to top of the Salina "A_2").

Eight wells were evaluated, and histograms were constructed of the %t of the formations (Figure 20-9). Three separate cases of salt migration and depositional adjustment can be observed. Well C has minimal (1%t) salt deposition. This disparity from the calculated norm of 5.7%t for Salina "B" salt is compensated for by the total (dolomite and anhydrite) Salina "B" %t and is, therefore, a result of a stratigraphic facies change and not migration of the salt.

Wells B, D, and G can be considered average for the interval, as the %t of individual formations are all close to calculated averages. Strata in these wells either experienced no stress and no salt "reaction" or an equal amount of salt migrated from each well. The former explanation is the simplest.

Wells A, E, F, and H show little or no residual "B" salt. Evaluation of the %t of the overlying formations in wells A and E reveals that no single interval compensates for the loss of the salt. Rather, the individual histograms for the Salina "G" through Bois Blanc interval show higher than average %t, suggesting gradual or perhaps spasmodic adjustment. The presence of several unconformities in this Silurian-Devonian interval supports this hypothesis.

Wells F and H also show compensation in the Salina "G" through Bois Blanc interval. Formation

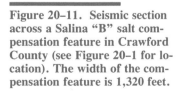

Figure 20-11. Seismic section across a Salina "B" salt compensation feature in Crawford County (see Figure 20-1 for location). The width of the compensation feature is 1,320 feet.

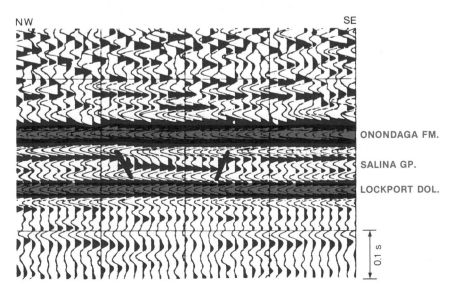

NW

SE

ONONDAGA FM.

SALINA GP.

LOCKPORT DOL.

0.1 s

WNW   ESE

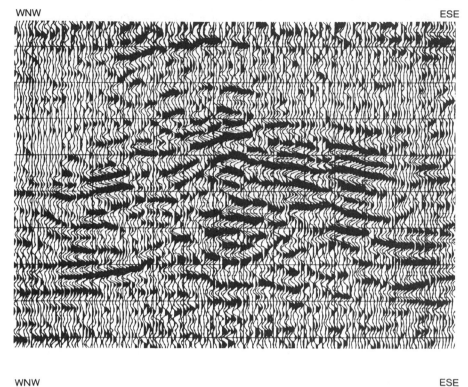

WNW   ESE

PIEDMONT COAL CO. #2
Dor: − 4664 feet
                                              HEYN #1
                                              Dor: − 4466 feet
PIEDMONT COAL CO. #1   THOMPSON #1
Dor: − 4857 feet   Dor: − 5322 feet

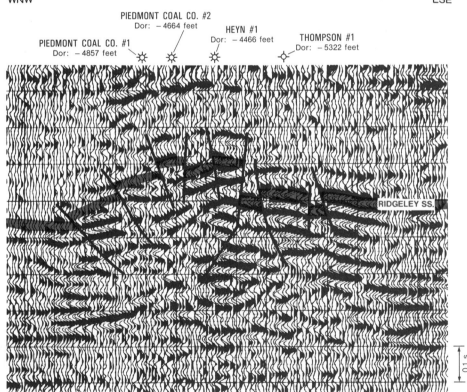

RIDGELEY SS.

0.1 s

Figure 20–12. Seismic section across the Chestnut Ridge anticline in Fayette County (see Figure 20–1 for location). The bottom seismic section is an interpreted version of the top section. The wells shown at the top of the seismic section are in the Summit field. The altitude of the subsea top of the Ridgeley Sandstone is given below each well name. The length of the seismic section is 3 miles.

tops were not recognizable from the logs. Well cuttings retained from this interval in adjacent productive wells showed that the predicted Bass Islands limestones and dolomites were replaced by well-sorted, winnowed, subspherical, slightly calcitic, unconsolidated quartz sandstone. This interval has produced gas (10 to 25 million cubic feet per day) or water in at least five wells. The gamma-ray logs from three wells in Erie County are shown in Figure 20-10. The P. George Jr. #3 well is well F in Figure 20-9. Clearly, the Salina "B" salt is absent in this well, and formation adjustment occurs after Salina "G" deposition. The Brace #1 and Robertson "B" #1 wells (Figure 20-10) are 4 miles apart.

Figure 20-11 is a seismic section showing the character of a salt-adjustment structure. Opposing associated faults are marked. The Brace and Robertson wells (see Figure 20-10) would fall outside these faults. The George well (see Figure 20-10) lies within the structure between the faults. Close examination of the seismic signature reveals relaxation of the overlying reflector.

Acadian Compression

In Middle Devonian time, the Plateau region was affected by compression that stabilized gravity tectonism in the Plateau and subsequently overprinted low-angle, northwest-dipping gravity faults with southeast-dipping Appalachian components in the Allegheny Mountain section of the Plateau. This combination of events is responsible for the great contrast in structural style and relief between the Allegheny Mountain section and the other Plateau sections (see Figure 20-4). Generally, these overprinted structures are limited to a narrow band proximal to the fold belt in the Nittany anticlinorium east of the Allegheny Front. Figure 20-12 represents an area on the Chestnut Ridge anticline in Fayette County where both Acadian

and Alleghanian orogenic events have contributed to the present structure.

PROBLEMS AND FUTURE RESEARCH

Many aspects of Appalachian Plateau structure and tectonics remain to be explained adequately. Even with the extensive research on salt tectonics, the initiation, mechanism(s), and direction of movement of the Salina salt in the Plateau region are not clearly understood.

Recent seismic data are only beginning to shed light on the configuration of the Grenville terrane. Although this terrane appears to have ultimately affected most Paleozoic structures and sedimentation patterns, it is far from being adequately understood.

RECOMMENDED FOR FURTHER READING

Colton, G. W. (1970), *The Appalachian basin—Its depositional sequences and their geologic relationships*, in Fisher, G. W., and others, eds., *Studies of Appalachian geology: central and southern*, New York, Interscience Publishers, p. 5-47.

Frey, M. G. (1973), *Influence of Salina salt on structure in New York-Pennsylvania part of Appalachian Plateau*, AAPG Bulletin, v. 57, p. 1027-1037.

Gwinn, V. E. (1964), *Thin-skinned tectonics in the Plateau and northwestern Valley and Ridge provinces of the central Appalachians*, Geological Society of America Bulletin, v. 75, p. 863-900.

Rodgers, John (1949), *Evolution of thought on structure of middle and southern Appalachians*, AAPG Bulletin, v. 33, p. 1643-1654.

———— (1970), *The tectonics of the Appalachians*, New York, Wiley-Interscience, 271 p.

Wagner, W. R. (1976), *Growth faults in Cambrian and Lower Ordovician rocks of western Pennsylvania*, AAPG Bulletin, v. 60, p. 414-427.

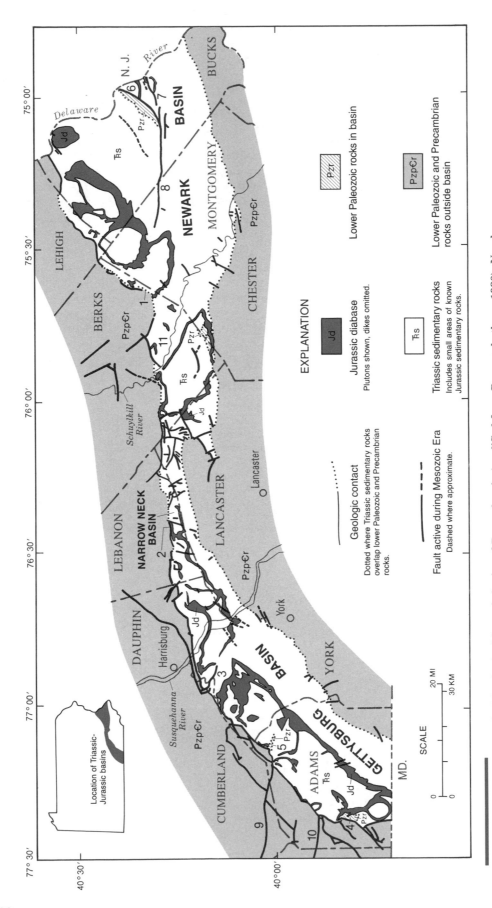

Figure 21-1. Map showing faulting in the Mesozoic basins of Pennsylvania (modified from Berg and others, 1980). Numbers refer to localities and structures cited in the text: 1, Boyertown; 2, Cornwall; 3, Lisburn fault; 4, Paleozoics at Fairfield; 5, Paleozoics at York Springs; 6, Furlong-Flemington fault; 7, Hopewell fault; 8, Chalfont fault; 9, Shippensburg fault; 10, Carbaugh-Marsh Creek fault; and 11, Jacksonwald syncline. Numbered faults are wrench faults; the others are normal faults, down-dropped on the southeast. Overlying Quaternary, Tertiary, and Cretaceous sediments in the area are not shown.

298

CHAPTER 21   GETTYSBURG-NEWARK LOWLAND

SAMUEL I. ROOT
  Department of Geology
  The College of Wooster
  Wooster, OH 44691

DAVID B. MacLACHLAN*
  Bureau of Topographic and Geologic Survey
  Department of Conservation and Natural
    Resources
  P. O. Box 8453
  Harrisburg, PA 17105

REGIONAL SETTING

The linked Newark-Narrow Neck-Gettysburg basin complex (Figure 21–1) is the largest of a series of exposed rift basins of Late Triassic to Early Jurassic age, extending intermittently from Nova Scotia to North Carolina. It is filled with fluvial and lacustrine clastic deposits. The characteristic structural form of these basins is a tilted fault block or half graben, with strata commonly dipping into major normal faults that bound the basins on the northwestern side.

CONFIGURATION OF THE BASINS

The basins form a 140-mile arc across Pennsylvania, closely following the Appalachian structural grain. They extend into New Jersey on the northeast and into Maryland on the south. The maximum width of the Gettysburg basin is 18 miles, and strata dip dominantly northwesterly at 25 to 30 degrees (Figure 21–2). It is joined on the northeast to the Newark basin by the Narrow Neck basin, which diminishes in width to 4 miles and has variable northerly stratal dips, mostly in the range of 20 to 40 degrees. The Newark basin widens to 30 miles. Strata generally dip 5° to 15°N, except where folded near the north margin (Faill, 1973b; MacLachlan, 1983).

The basins are bordered on the northwest by one or more major normal faults. Locally, but especially at the Susquehanna River, a narrow, thin belt of overlapping basal Triassic strata, having a subhorizontal to slight southeast dip, is preserved north of the border fault (Faill, 1973b; Root, 1977) on the passive north shoulder of the rift basin. Probably most overlap conditions at the north margin represent this type of relation. Despite ideas to the contrary (Faill, 1973b), the authors consider the basins to be bordered by a continuous, complex system of normal faults.

*Retired.

299

Figure 21-2. Triassic red beds of the Gettysburg basin dipping 35°NW in roadcuts just south of exit 16, Interstate Route 83, near Lewisberry, York County.

NATURE OF THE BORDER FAULT

Low-angle extensional faulting at the northwest border of the Newark basin, demonstrating normal-fault reactivation of prior Alleghanian thrusts, was established by Ratcliffe and others (1986). They showed that the border fault just south of the Delaware River dips 25° to 30°SE (Figure 21-3). Proprietary seismic data near the Delaware River reportedly show a reflector surface, interpreted as the border fault of the Newark basin, that dips southeast at about 25 degrees. About 5 miles southeast of the border fault, in the Riegelsville 7.5-minute quadrangle, the Cabot-KBI #1 well bottomed in beds of the Triassic Stockton Formation at 10,500 feet. Proprietary seismic data suggest that basement in this area may be at a depth of 18,000 feet. At Boyertown (Figure 21-1), the border fault dips 35° to 45°SE (Hawkes and others, 1953), and at Cornwall, the border fault dips 25°SE (Lapham and Gray, 1973). At the Susquehanna River, the Paleozoic-Triassic contact dips 45°SE, and the Triassic beds dip at 20 degrees into the contact (Wherry, 1913). Low-angle normal faulting may persist westward to the Lisburn fault (Figure 21-1).

In a structural sense, the Gettysburg basin begins at the Lisburn fault. It differs from the Narrow Neck and Newark basins to the east because it lacks the im-

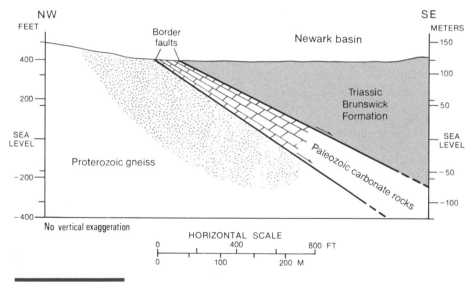

Figure 21-3. Geologic cross section across the northwest border of the Newark basin, near the Delaware River. The Mesozoic border fault here dips 25° to 30°SE and is interpreted as a normal-fault reactivation of an earlier Alleghanian thrust fault. Modified from Ratcliffe, N. M., and others (1986), *Low-angle extensional faulting, reactivated mylonites, and seismic reflection geometry of the Newark basin margin in eastern Pennsylvania,* **Geology, v. 14, Figure 3, p. 767. Modified with permission of the publisher, the Geological Society of America, Boulder, Colorado USA. Copyright © 1986 Geological Society of America.**

press of pervasive wrench tectonics apparent as en echelon folds adjacent to the border fault. The straight trace of the normal fault across high-relief terrain (Figure 21–4) and the 60° to 70°SE dips of minor normal faults in the basin suggest steep normal faulting at the surface (Root, 1988, 1989). However, gravity data show the deepest part of the basin toward the present basin center (Sumner, 1977; Root, 1977, Figure 24), not adjacent to the border fault. Consideration of these structural elements led Root (1988, 1989) to model the border fault as a listric normal fault; it is steep at the surface and flattens out at depth (Figure 21–5).

NORMAL FAULTING WITHIN THE BASIN

At or near the major border faults are a series of lesser faults that formed either contemporaneous with or slightly later than the border faults. The Lisburn fault (Figure 21–1), which offsets the border fault, appears to be a later stage fault. It is presumed to be steep because associated normal faults dip 60°SE. East of the Lisburn fault and extending to Cornwall (Figure 21–1), small, probably steep, faults offset the border fault.

Normal faults associated with basin development occur both transverse and parallel to the structural grain within and beyond the basin (Figure 21–1). Transverse faults are best known in the Narrow Neck basin, where there are abundant conglomerate reference beds. Faults parallel to the grain are difficult to recognize, but are at least locally abundant where exposure is superior (e.g., Watson, 1958). Relatively few faults parallel to the grain have been mapped in

the basin, but several are mapped at the south, overlap margin of the Gettysburg basin (Figure 21–1). In Maryland, several more such faults are mapped at the south margin (Root, 1988), some attaining vertical displacements of 2,800 feet. These faults form minor half grabens on the major Gettysburg half-graben structure (location map, Figure 21–5). Faults that were formed after diabase intrusion are present and appear to be part of the latest (post-folding) development of the basin.

Some faults were apparently active early in the development of the basin and affected distribution of coarse fluviatile sediments (MacLachlan, 1983). The Lisburn fault is apparently such a fault; early activity produced a thick clastic wedge south of the fault, and later activity offset the border fault. Few such faults have been identified to date, indicating little syndepositional faulting within the present limits of the basin.

Normal faults, related to Mesozoic rifting, are now recognized west of the Gettysburg basin in the Precambrian and Paleozoic basement (Root, 1988) and in basement rocks north of the Jacksonwald syncline (Figure 21–1). Additional faults of this type are present to the east of the basin in the Piedmont, but complex structure and stratigraphy obscure their recognition (Root, 1988, 1989).

WRENCH FAULTING

Manspeizer (1981) interpreted the Furlong-Flemington and Hopewell faults of the Newark basin as right-lateral antithetic faults and the Chalfont fault as a left-lateral synthetic fault generated by major left-lateral wrenching of the basin (Figure 21–1). Ratcliffe

Figure 21–4. View across plains developed on northwest-dipping Triassic red beds. South Mountain, in the background, is an extension of the Blue Ridge Mountains and is formed by resistant Precambrian metavolcanics and quartzites. The Mesozoic border fault, located at the foot of the mountain, forms a straight trace. The view is to the northwest from near Dillsburg, in northern York County.

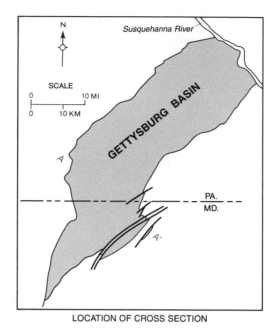

LOCATION OF CROSS SECTION

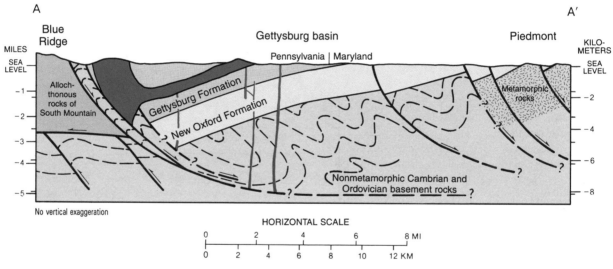

Figure 21–5. Geologic cross section through the Gettysburg basin showing the half-graben structure of the basin, uniform dip across the basin of the Mesozoic New Oxford and Gettysburg Formations, and listric normal faults at the border (reprinted with modifications from *Tectonophysics*, v. 166, Root, S. I., *Basement control of structure in the Gettysburg rift basin, Pennsylvania and Maryland*, p. 286, © 1989, with permission from Elsevier Science). Diabase sheets and dikes are shown in the darkest brown. Note the sliver of Paleozoic limestone caught up in the border faults adjacent to the Blue Ridge (South Mountain) and the minor listric faults toward the south end of the basin that form a series of smaller half grabens.

and Burton (1985) considered the former to be right-normal oblique faults. The amount of displacement on these faults is considerable; for example, the apparent vertical displacement required to uplift the Paleozoic basement block on the Furlong-Flemington fault is on the order of 20,000 feet.

The east-west-trending Shippensburg and Carbaugh-Marsh Creek faults (Figure 21–1) are major pre-Mesozoic faults (Root and Hoskins, 1977) that were reactivated during structural development of the Gettysburg basin; they have wrench-fault attributes. Right-lateral offset of the border fault and deflection of Triassic strata indicate 2 miles of offset on the Shippensburg fault. Paleozoic basement rocks are caught as a sliver along this fault within the basin at York Springs, Adams County (Figure 21-1). On the Carbaugh-Marsh Creek fault, wrenching offset of the border fault is much less. However, considerable wrench-fault displacement was transferred by folding of the Triassic strata and the development of two northwest-striking, left-lateral antithetic faults. One of these forms the border fault from Fairfield (Figure 21-1) into Maryland. Between the two faults, a block of Paleozoic basement is upfaulted in the basin at Fairfield.

FOLDING

Considerable folding occurs through the Narrow Neck and into the western Newark basin. Folds are best developed at the north margin of the basin and are truncated by the border fault (Figure 21-6). The most prominent fold is the Jacksonwald syncline (Figures 21-1 and 21-6), which extends southeasterly for at least 10 miles and has limb dips up to 55 degrees. A stereonet plot of poles to bedding from MacLachlan (1983) defines a syncline plunging 309°/016° (Figure 21-6). Other folds examined in the Newark basin by Lucas and others (1988) show comparable fold

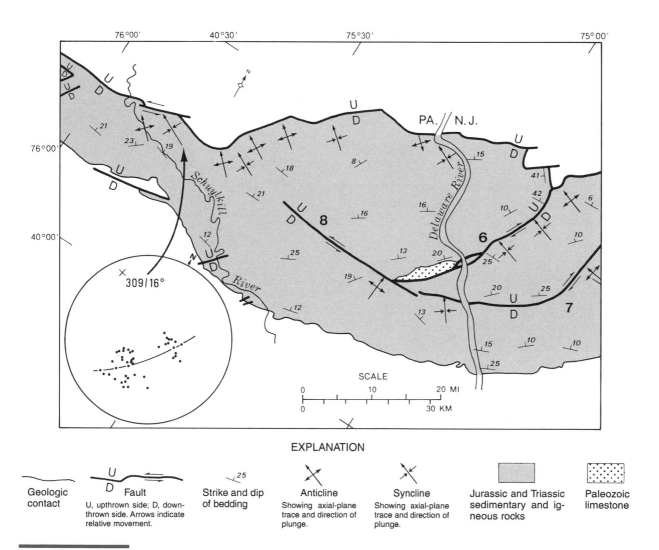

EXPLANATION

Geologic contact	U D Fault	↙25 Strike and dip	Anticline	Syncline	Jurassic and Triassic	Paleozoic

Geologic contact

Fault
U, upthrown side; D, downthrown side. Arrows indicate relative movement.

Strike and dip of bedding

Anticline
Showing axial-plane trace and direction of plunge.

Syncline
Showing axial-plane trace and direction of plunge.

Jurassic and Triassic sedimentary and igneous rocks

Paleozoic limestone

Figure 21-6. Structure map of the Newark basin showing major Mesozoic faults and the large number of associated folds (from Olsen, 1980b). Refer to Figure 21-1 for the names of the numbered faults. The inset stereonet plot shows poles to bedding in the Jacksonwald syncline (from MacLachlan, 1983). The poles define a chevron fold plunging 309°/016°.

orientations and are characterized as upright folds having subangular hinges and straight planar limbs, typical of chevron folds. The fold trend in the Newark basin is oblique to the basin margin and all older structures but is consistent with the left-lateral motion proposed by Manspeizer (1981).

The few folds mapped in the Gettysburg basin are related to the Mesozoic reactivations of the older, east-west-trending Carbaugh-Marsh Creek and Shippensburg faults (Root, 1988, 1989). At the southern end of the basin, principally in Maryland, are several northerly trending, en echelon folds related to the development of the antithetic northwest-trending border fault at Fairfield (Figure 21–1). The largest fold extends for 8 miles through Maryland and just into Pennsylvania, southeast of Fairfield. The other folds are less than 2 miles in axial length (Root, 1988).

Wrenching along the eastward extension of the Shippensburg fault within the Gettysburg basin and south of the fault block of Paleozoic basement at York Springs (Figure 21–1) formed a fold pair. For a distance of 7 miles in an east-west zone, folding occurs as a regional deflection of the northeast-striking Triassic beds into nearly east-west-striking beds (Root, 1989). A stereonet plot of bedding attitudes here defines a fold plunging 335°/032°.

IGNEOUS STRUCTURE

Numerous vertical diabase dikes, not shown on Figure 21–1, trend north to northwesterly across the basin. The dikes, which are up to tens of miles long, have been considered the result of regional extensional reactivation of an inherited basement weakness (Smith and others, 1975). A less likely explanation is that they are products of regional left-lateral wrenching (Swanson, 1982).

Extensive diabase sheets occur, generally in an elliptical pattern elongated along strike (Hotz, 1952). The sheets are folded concordantly with enclosing strata on their up-dip margins in the central parts of the basins, but they generally show discordant relations toward the north margin.

The diabase sheets and associated Lower Jurassic basalt flows (Cornet, 1977) are truncated by the border fault, demonstrating that emplacement clearly preceded faulting and most likely preceded folding as well. Paleomagnetic studies of the diabase sheets by Volk (1977) suggested that most of the emplacement occurred when the enclosing strata were still horizontal or only rotated less than 10 degrees.

INTERPRETATION AND DISCUSSION

The following structural inferences are derived principally from surface data:

1. During deposition of the Mesozoic strata, the Narrow Neck basin may have structurally separated the Gettysburg basin from the Newark basin by a slight amount.

2. Within each basin, syndepositional faulting was negligible. This derives from the lateral persistence of thin lacustrine units (Olsen, 1985b) and the lack of significant unconformities in each basin as shown by the general concordance of bedding attitudes.

3. The generally uniform northwest dip of strata across the basin militates against progressive downfaulting and significant rotation of the basin concurrent with deposition. However, if only minor rotation (less than 5 degrees) occurred, then syndepositional faulting at the northwest margin could have been active at times and not be apparent in the present dips (Root, 1988).

4. Major basin rotation and development of the border faults are related to regional, post-Early Jurassic (probably Toarcian) rifting. This was slightly preceded by folding and igneous activity.

5. Overall deformation in the Gettysburg basin is of an extensional character. Vertical Mesozoic diabase dikes in the basin are thought to indicate the principal plane of stress, which represents principal extension oriented at about 105°/285°. This simple model seems to fit in the Maryland portion of the basin, at least, where this direction is normal to the trend of the border faults (Root, 1988).

6. The Newark and Narrow Neck basins are structurally more complex than the Gettysburg basin, and their calculated stress fields are more speculative. Ratcliffe and Burton (1985) proposed that simple extensional reactivation of a complex system of curvilinear thrust-ramp structures can explain the deformational structures and fault geometry of these basins. Their figures indicate a principal extension oriented at about 160°/340°. Lucas and others (1988) recognized one model that involves normal rifting in the northeast-trending Mesozoic rift basins and produces left-

lateral transtension in the easterly trending Narrow Neck and Newark basins as a consequence of their orientation relative to the stress field. This particular model is appealing because it has the principal extension oriented at about 110°/290°, similar to that suggested for the Gettysburg basin.

7. The striking congruence of the configuration of the Mesozoic basins and arcuation of the older Appalachians suggests a genetic relation between the two (see discussion by Swanson, 1986). Based on a study of the relation of cleavage in basement rocks to the Mesozoic border faults in the Gettysburg basin, Root (1989) concluded that the Mesozoic rifting was developed along the late Precambrian rift zone that formed the original margin of the Appalachians.

PROBLEMS AND FUTURE RESEARCH

Lack of subsurface data from deep oil- and gas-well drilling and detailed seismic work impedes substantive elucidation of the structural evolution and origin of these basins, particularly regarding the nature and distribution of local orogenic clastic wedges, extent and sequence of syndepositional faulting within the basin, and nature and variation of the regional stress field. These problems form the provenance of future studies.

RECOMMENDED FOR FURTHER READING

Faill, R. T. (1973), *Tectonic development of the Triassic Newark-Gettysburg basin in Pennsylvania*, Geological Society of America Bulletin, v. 84, p. 725–740.

Hotz, P. E. (1952), *Form of diabase sheets in southeastern Pennsylvania*, American Journal of Science, v. 250, p. 375–388.

Ratcliffe, N. M., Burton, W. C., D'Angelo, R. M., and Costain, J. K. (1986), *Low-angle extensional faulting, reactivated mylonites, and seismic reflection geometry of the Newark basin margin in eastern Pennsylvania*, Geology, v. 14, p. 766–770.

Root, S. I. (1989), *Basement control of structure in the Gettysburg rift basin, Pennsylvania and Maryland*, Tectonophysics, v. 166, p. 281–292.

Root, S. I., and Hoskins, D. M. (1977), *Lat 40°N fault zone, Pennsylvania: a new interpretation*, Geology, v. 5, p. 719–723.

Sumner, J. R. (1977), *Geophysical investigation of the structural framework of the Newark-Gettysburg Triassic basin, Pennsylvania*, Geological Society of America Bulletin, v. 88, p. 935–942.

Swanson, M. T. (1982), *Preliminary model for an early transform history in central Atlantic rifting*, Geology, v. 10, p. 317–320.

———— (1986), *Preexisting fault control for Mesozoic basin formation in eastern North America*, Geology, v. 14, p. 419–422.

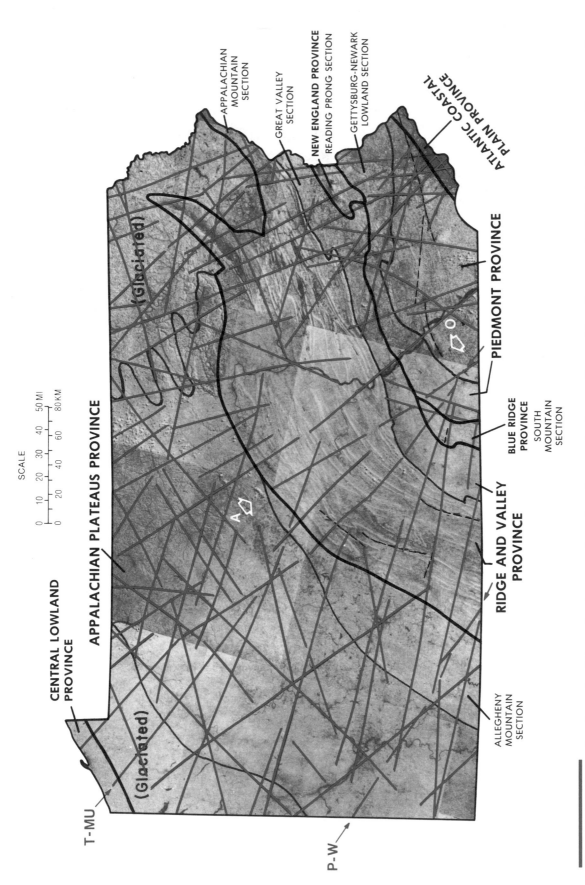

Figure 22–1. This Landsat–1 mosaic of Pennsylvania was used as a base for mapping intermediate and long lineaments (solid lines) and also provides a synoptic view of the major physiographic provinces (modified from Gold and others, 1974, Figure 1, p. 47). One notable physiographic feature is the crescent-shaped area (dark tone) of the Wyoming Valley "anthracite basin" of northeastern Pennsylvania. The Pennsylvania orocline (axis indicated by the arrows A and O) is apparent from the curvature of the Appalachian Mountain section of the Ridge and Valley province (curvilinear tonal pattern). Note the discordant attitude of many lineaments to the regional structural grain and their independence of the major physiographic and tectonic boundaries (e.g., Tyrone-Mount Union lineament [T–MU] and Pittsburgh-Washington lineament [P–W]). The variable ages (Precambrian to Mesozoic) of ore deposits along some lineaments suggest that they are long-lived, periodically rejuvenated features. Some of the lineaments are discernible in Tertiary coastal-plain sediments, and others are evident in Pleistocene glacial deposits. The dashed lines represent the traces of selected, conventionally mapped faults.

CHAPTER 22   LINEAMENTS AND THEIR INTERREGIONAL RELATIONSHIPS

DAVID P. GOLD
Department of Geosciences
The Pennsylvania State University
University Park, PA 16802

INTRODUCTION

In no other states are physiographic provinces and the curved nature of the Appalachian fold belt better displayed than in Pennsylvania (Figure 22–1). These coincide with different tectonic regimes and also reflect the dominant northeast-trending structural grain of the basement rocks (see Chapters 3, 23, and 24). The axis of the bend in the fold belt, which is so apparent on Figure 22–1, coincides with the axis of a broad culmination (the Juniata culmination) that extends across the Ridge and Valley fold belt from Centre County southeastward through Cumberland and York Counties. Along this culmination, south-southwest-plunging folds to the south are separated from northeast-plunging folds to the northeast.

Other transverse linear morphological features are revealed on topographic or drainage maps of both regional (megascopic) and local (macroscopic) scales. The study of these remarkably linear features, termed "lineaments" by Hobbs (1904), has gained impetus with the development of space-age remote-sensing systems and the production of ortho-images in the visible, infrared, and microwave bands. Until about 15 years ago (Gold, 1980), little attempt was made to separate lineaments parallel to the regional structure (strike parallel) from those exhibiting transverse (cross-strike) orientations. This paper will focus on the cross-strike lineaments because they are difficult to reconcile with conventional structures, such as faults and dikes.

NATURE OF LINEAMENTS

That lineaments represent more than two-dimensional geomorphic alignments is demonstrated in their expression on derived maps such as gravity- and magnetic-anomaly (Lavin and others, 1982), lithofacies (Gwinn, 1964), or fracture-density (Sites, 1978) maps. Offsets in gravity and magnetic anomalies along some lineaments (Chapters 23 and 24) and their coincidence with earthquake epicenters indicate a deep-seated root. The coincidence of some lineaments with zones of anomalously high gas leakage (Rodgers and Anderson, 1984) or groundwater well yields (Parizek, 1975) suggests a subsurface fracture zone.

Most of the regional-scale lineaments mapped in Pennsylvania (Figure 22–1) are essentially two-dimensional linear and curvilinear alignments of stream and valley segments plus wind and water gaps. Short lineaments and fracture traces (Lattman, 1958) are expressed on aerial photographs by the alignment of stream segments, swales, gullies, and changes in the vegetation and soils. These latter phenomena generally are manifest as tonal changes on aerial photographs. The terminology and typical sizes of linear features are listed in Table 22–1. The distribution, orientations, and lengths of the lineaments shown in Figure 22–1 are depicted in a rose diagram and histogram in Figure 22–2.

Most strike-parallel lineaments are defined by dipping strata, which form cuesta scarps or hogbacks. In contrast, cross-strike lineaments are inferred to represent zones of high fracture density in bedrock. These zones are more susceptible to weathering and erosion than the surrounding rocks. Great care must be taken in lineament mapping to filter out cultural features such as fences, roads, pipelines, power lines, and animal trails from the perceived natural vegetational and morphological alignments. If a lineament is shown by subsequent mapping to be a shear zone,

fault, or dike, or a physiographic feature, such as a cuesta scarp or hogback, the formal structural or geomorphic term would supercede photogeologic designation. Most Pennsylvania lineaments are zones of fracture concentration with little or no cumulative displacement across them. They are nearly vertical zones of increased porosity and permeability that should be considered in engineering projects, groundwater exploitation, and oil and gas exploration.

CONCEPTUAL MODEL

The conceptual model of a lineament is a zone of strained rocks, bounded by semirigid crustal domains (blocks). The zone might be long-lived but not necessarily continuously active. Lineaments might be likened to "megajoints" that separate crustal blocks, which are "jostled" daily by earth tides. Two sets of intersecting lineaments (Figure 22–1), those oriented north-northwest with a 30- to 40-mile spacing, and the longer west-northwest set with a 25- to 30-mile spacing, are inferred to define crustal blocks that are independent of the Appalachian orogen. The shorter set of lineaments that fan with the Appalachian orocline apparently are related to Appalachian deformations.

A model of some Pennsylvania lineaments is depicted in Figure 22–3, which shows a lateral ramp and strain boundary emanating from a basement fault. Nearer the surface, this strain boundary is marked by the termination of small folds (see Chapter 19). Two of the longest lineaments that traverse Pennsyl-

Table 22–1. *Scale of Some Linear Traces That Have No Obvious Displacements*

Surface feature	Size	Mapping base	Possible structure
Joint traces	Inches to tens of yards	Outcrop maps; large-scale aerial photographs	Joints; bed forms
Fracture traces	Approximately 100 yards to 1 mile	Aerial photographs; large-scale topographic maps	Narrow, steeply dipping zones of joint concentrations up to 100 feet wide
Lineaments	Short: 1 to 6 miles	Topographic maps; small-scale aerial photographs	Broad zones up to a few miles wide of disrupted rocks, including concentrations of narrow fracture zones
	Intermediate: 6 to 60 miles	Topographic maps; relief models at approximately 1:250,000 scale; high-altitude imagery	Petrographic provinces and aligned volcanic centers, rift valleys, aulacogens, and continental sutures as much as 60 miles wide
	Long: 60 to 300 miles	Satellite imagery; small-scale relief models	
	Megalineaments	Satellite imagery; mosaics	

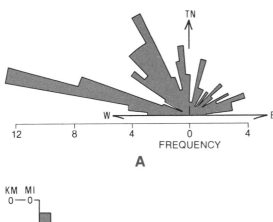

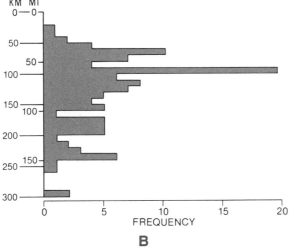

Figure 22–2. A. Rose diagram showing the strike frequency of the intermediate and long lineaments mapped on the Landsat mosaic of Pennsylvania (Figure 22–1) and adjacent areas. The longer cross-strike lineaments account for the dominant west-northwest and north-northwest trends; some of these cut across tectonic provinces and are even discernible in Pleistocene glacial till and Tertiary coastal-plain sediments. The shorter lineaments tend to fan with the bend in the Appalachian fold belt. B. Histogram of the lengths of the intermediate and long lineaments mapped on the Landsat mosaic of Pennsylvania (Figure 22–1). The uneven frequency distribution probably is due to the small population (n=115). Figure 22–2 is from Gold, D. P., *Structural geology*, in Siegal, B. S., and Gillespie, A. R., eds., *Remote sensing in geology*, Figure 14–17b and 14–17c, p. 443, copyright © 1980 by John Wiley & Sons, Inc. Reprinted by permission of John Wiley & Sons, Inc.

vania (Tyrone-Mount Union and Pittsburgh-Washington) coincide with the landward projections of transform faults associated with the mid-Atlantic ridge system (Lavin and others, 1982). They may represent zones of weakness over extensions of the fossil transform faults (pre-Iapetus) that may be re-

activated under favorably oriented stress conditions. The northwest-trending lineaments are probably inactive now; essentially they are locked by the contemporary northeast-southwest-trending maximum horizontal stress regime (Zoback and Zoback, 1980). The north-south-striking lineament near Lancaster appears to be seismically active today (Sbar and Sykes, 1973; Stockar, 1986) (see Chapter 53).

Base-metal deposits of different ages are exposed along some lineaments, such as Perkiomen Creek (Figure 22–4), and between Tyrone and Mount Union (Rose, 1970). Such distinct alignments suggest episodic infiltration of ore fluids into fractures that comprise the lineaments. The location of kimberlite dikes in some lineaments in Fayette, Greene, and Indiana Counties (Chapters 13 and 23) suggests fracture control to great depth.

The Tyrone-Mount Union lineament probably has been studied in more detail than any other large cross-strike lineament in Pennsylvania. It is characterized by an alignment of discontinuities and, in places, en echelon valley segments for some 250 miles through central Pennsylvania. It is expressed best in the Ridge and Valley province by transverse valley segments of the Juniata and Little Juniata Rivers, especially where they cross the folds of the Nittany anticlinorium. Although its morphologic expression northwestward into the Appalachian Plateaus province is more subtle, it is nevertheless recognized for some 150 miles as (a) valley and stream alignments on Landsat images, (b) terminations of fold axes, (c) linear topographic depressions, (d) a zone of anomalous hydrocarbon leakage (Rodgers and Anderson, 1984), and (e) terminations and displacements in gravity and magnetic anomalies (Parrish and Lavin, 1982). Local tear faults in the Great Valley section of the Ridge and Valley province, a fracture zone in the South Mountain section of the Blue Ridge province, and displaced gravity and magnetic anomaly patterns suggest an extension of some 100 miles to the southeast (Canich and Gold, 1985). Between Tyrone and Mount Union, fractures observed at three scales bear a hierarchical geometric relationship (Figure 22–5), predicted in the second-order shear model of McKinstry (1953). Displacements on the dominantly strike-slip mesoscopic-scale faults compensate in sense to produce no displacement across the lineament. Superimposed slickenlines on these fault planes are interpreted to indicate rotation coincident with Alleghanian folding (Canich and Gold, 1985).

The Port Matilda-McAlevys Fort lineament in central Pennsylvania near State College was shown

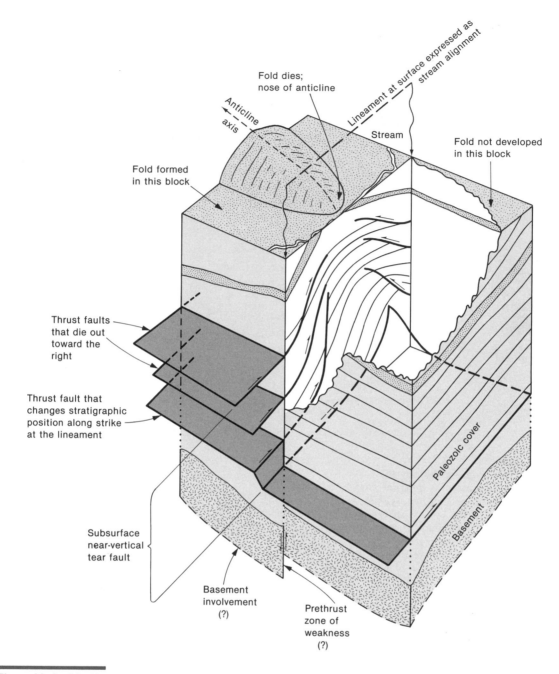

Figure 22–3. Idealized block diagram showing the postulated three-dimensional structure of a "Gwinn-type" lineament (slightly modified from Kowalik and Gold, 1976, Figure 7, p. 244). The lineament is the topographic expression, commonly a linear valley segment, of a strain discontinuity between two semi-independent thrust blocks, which may be linked by a stepped tear fault. The effect is to create a discontinuity that is not necessarily a fault everywhere along the plane. This enables the strain in adjacent blocks to be manifest in different ways, for example, blocks having folds of different forms and noncoincidence of fold axes between blocks. The strain boundary is envisaged as an essentially vertical zone, as much as 1.5 miles wide, of anomalously high fracture density (joints and minor faults). Decoupling of regional stress across this fracture zone may be a "thin-skinned" manifestation above a décollement, or it may be caused by rejuvenation of a deep-seated fault.

by Hunter (1977) to coincide with a structurally disturbed zone dominated by tear faults. Other lineaments such as French Creek, Transylvania, Home-

Gallitzin, Mason-Dixon, and Blairsville-Broadtop (Parrish and Lavin, 1982) deserve closer scrutiny. A major strike-parallel lineament, which defines the

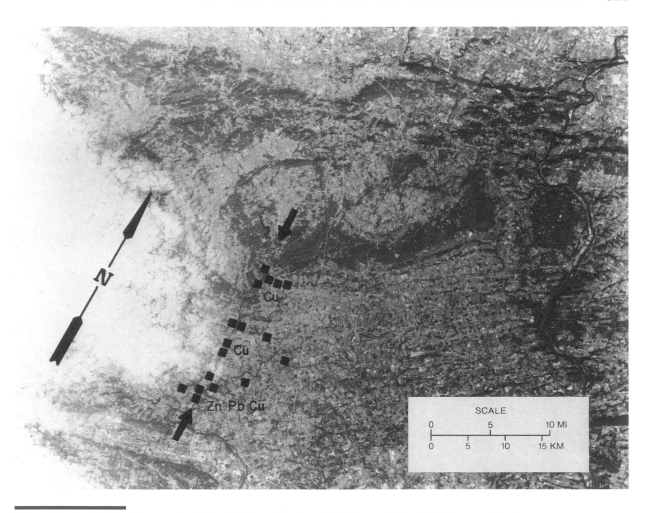

Figure 22–4. Skylab photograph (SL3, S190B, orbit 44, roll 87, frame 296) of Perkiomen Creek lineament and known mineral deposits along its length (from Gold and Kowalik, 1976, Figure 4–23, p. 4–57 and 4–58). The lineament, as shown here, extends from east of Phoenixville (Chester County) northward to Perkiomenville (Montgomery County). The dark circle at the north end of the lineament is tree-covered Jurassic diabase of the East Greenville pluton (sheet). Allentown (Lehigh County) is located at the right-angle bend in the Lehigh River to the north. Clouds (white) are visible on the left, and the meandering Delaware River is visible on the right edge of the photograph.

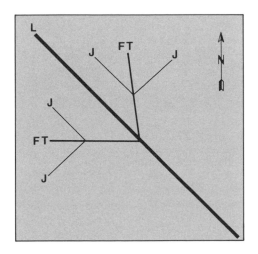

boundary between the Appalachian Plateaus and the Ridge and Valley provinces, was traced by its aeromagnetic signature (King and Zietz, 1978) from Alabama to New York (Chapter 24).

APPLICATIONS

The subsurface nature of lineaments probably was not appreciated by early railroad and highway engineers who sited their access routes along them, but dam builders learned early

Figure 22–5. Geometric relationship of "fractures" of different scales in the vicinity of the Tyrone-Mount Union lineament. The strike-parallel lineaments and fold axes trend northeast and have been omitted from this scaled, second-order shear model (from Canich, 1976, Figure 19, p. 50).

of the permeable conditions of many valley bottoms. On a more limited scale, the short lineaments and fracture traces are likely to be narrow, fractured zones of high porosity and permeability, suitable for both the storage or movement of groundwater and other fluids. The enhanced yields of water wells located on fracture traces and short lineaments, particularly on the intersections of such features, has been demonstrated by Parizek (1975). The nature of these subsurface fractured and/or weathered zones should be accommodated in the design of highways (landslide hazard), and tunnels or underground mine openings (Blackmer, 1987), where unstable roof conditions might be hazardous.

PROBLEMS AND FUTURE RESEARCH

Mapping lineaments is a simple task, usually performed in the office on an appropriate satellite image or aerial photograph. Lineaments are difficult to characterize physically because of their large size,

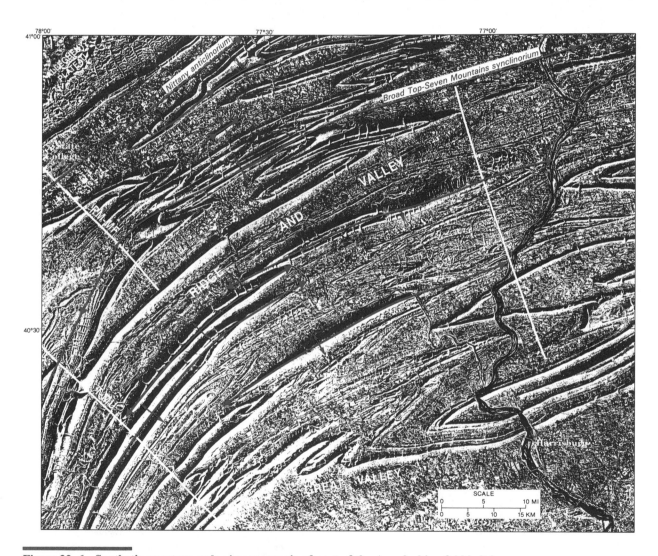

Figure 22–6. Synthetic-aperture radar image mosaic of part of the Appalachian fold belt between State College and Harrisburg (image from U.S. Geological Survey 1982 experimental edition, scale 1:250,000). The northwest look ensures maximum reflection (illumination) on the southeast slopes and portrays well the fold form defined by the positive relief of the Silurian Tuscarora and Ordovician Bald Eagle Formations. The traces of the Tyrone-Mount Union (T–MU) lineament, the Port Matilda-McAlevys Fort (PM–MF) lineament, and an unnamed lineament north of Harrisburg are shown in white. The doubly plunging folds, common in this part of the Appalachian oroclinal axis, are shown in color, along with the axes of a major anticlinorium and a major synclinorium.

the paucity of subsurface data, and their composite nature. More detailed ground-based studies are needed.

A more satisfactory base for mapping short and intermediate-length lineaments in hilly terrain has become available in the form of maps produced from side-looking radar systems (SAR and SLAR images). In the Harrisburg 1- by 2-degree quadrangle (Figure 22–6), the folds and strike-parallel lineaments are well portrayed because of enhanced reflections from slopes nearly at right angles to the sensoring beam. Even though the flight line (northeast) is in the least optimum direction for imaging northwest-trending features, the cross-strike lineaments are apparent and in greater detail than on other satellite (Landsat and SPOT) images of comparable scale. The virtue of this microwave system is its ability to penetrate a leaf canopy and to record local vertical features. The 1:250,000-scale SLAR series (U.S. Geological Survey, available from EROS Data Center) shows details of stream networks and surface roughness with greater clarity than the 1:50,000-scale topographic quadrangle maps.

The future trend is to characterize the size, orientation, and density of fractures by their fractal dimensions. Not only can bulk permeability and porosity be deduced from the fractal parameters, but this analysis also facilitates the comparison of fractures on many scales and from region to region (Barton and others, 1985).

RECOMMENDED FOR FURTHER READING

Blanchet, P. H. (1957), *Development of fracture analysis as exploration method*, AAPG Bulletin, v. 41, p. 1748–1759.

Gold, D. P. (1983), *Application of remote sensing to structural geology and tectonics*, in Colwell, R. N., and others, eds., *Manual of remote sensing*, 2nd ed., Falls Church, Va., American Society of Photogrammetry, v. 2, p. 1777–1782.

Gold, D. P., and Pohn, H. A. (1985), *The nature of cross-strike and strike-parallel structures in central Pennsylvania*, in Gold, D. P., and others, *Central Pennsylvania geology revisited*, Annual Field Conference of Pennsylvania Geologists, 50th, State College, Pa., p. 138–143.

Lattman, L. H., and Nickelsen, R. P. (1958), *Photogeologic fracture-trace mapping in Appalachian Plateau*, AAPG Bulletin, v. 42, p. 2238–2245.

Lattman, L. H., and Parizek, R. R. (1964), *Relationship between fracture traces and the occurrence of ground water in carbonate rocks*, Journal of Hydrology, v. 2, p. 73–91.

Nur, Amos (1981), *The tensile origin of fracture-controlled lineaments*, in O'Leary, D. W., and Earle, J. L., eds., *Proceedings of the Third International Conference on Basement Tectonics [Durango, Colo., 1978]*, Denver, Basement Tectonic Committee, Publication 3, p. 155–167.

Pohn, H. A. (1983), *The relationship of joint and stream drainage in flat-lying rocks of south-central New York and northern Pennsylvania*, Zeitschrift für Geomorphologie, v. 27, p. 375–384.

Saunders, D. F., and Hicks, D. E. (1979), *Regional geomorphic lineaments on satellite imagery—their origin and applications*, in Podwysocki, M. H., and Earle, J. L., eds., *Proceedings of the Second International Conference on Basement Tectonics [Newark, Del., 1976]*, Denver, Basement Tectonics Committee, Publication 2, p. 326–352.

Segall, Paul, and Pollard, D. D. (1983), *From joints and faults to photo-lineaments*, in Gabrielsen, R. H., and others, eds., *Proceedings of the Fourth International Conference on Basement Tectonics [Oslo, Norway, 1981]*, Salt Lake City, International Basement Tectonics Association, Publication 4, p. 11–20.

Southworth, C. S. (1986), *Side-looking airborne radar image map showing cross-strike structural discontinuities and lineaments of the central Appalachians*, U.S. Geological Survey Miscellaneous Field Studies Map MF–1891, scale 1:500,000, 14 p. text.

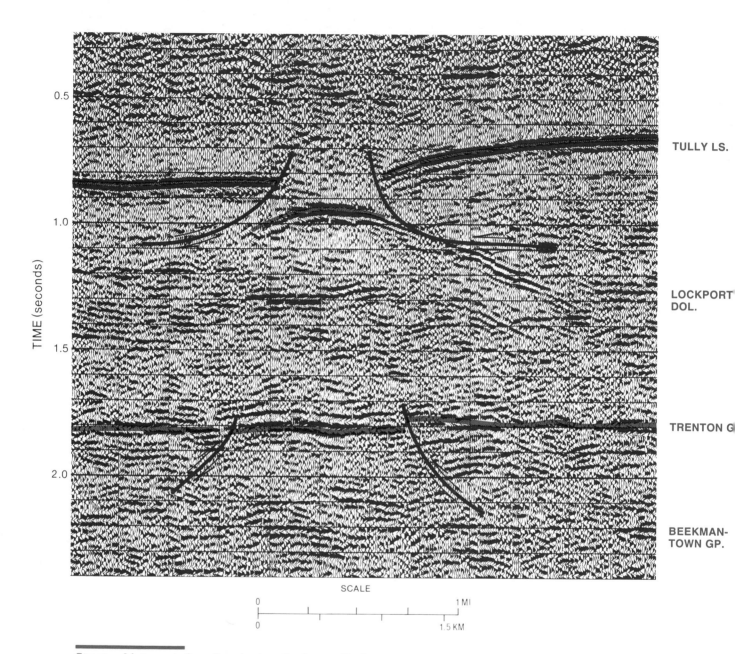

TULLY LS.

LOCKPORT DOL.

TRENTON G

BEEKMAN-
TOWN GP.

TIME (seconds)

0.5

1.0

1.5

2.0

SCALE

0   1 MI

0   1.5 KM

Structural interpretation of a seismic-reflection profile from north-central Pennsylvania. Notice that a block including the Middle Devonian Tully Limestone has been displaced about 1,000 feet along high-angle reverse faults. Other prominent recognizable reflectors are the Silurian Lockport Dolomite, Upper Ordovician Trenton Group, and Lower to Middle Ordovician Beekmantown Group. Sections such as this are generated with artificially induced seismic waves in the exploration for possible petroleum traps.

314

Part IV

REGIONAL GEOPHYSICS

Until the beginning of this century, knowledge of the earth was gained almost entirely from observations and measurements made at its surface and at relatively shallow depths in caves, drill holes, mines, and other excavations. Most observations were constrained by physiographic obstacles and the earth's curvature, and little was known of the earth beneath the sea.

From about 1900, though, the development of instrumentation technologies accelerated phenomenally, enabling detailed study of the earth by a broad spectrum of quantitative physical methods. In due course, applications of physics to geology were made at sea as well as on land. Geophysical techniques later were adapted to aircraft, and now they are well established in space. The profound revolution in geological thought of the late twentieth century was based almost entirely on geophysical investigations, which resulted in broad acceptance of the theory of plate tectonics.

The geophysical framework of Pennsylvania is explored in Part IV. An area that lacks geophysical anomalies contains little to be discussed. Pennsylvania's geophysical framework is as varied as its geology. Some of the anomalies in the state have been interpreted to the satisfaction of many. Others may be subjects for puzzled speculation far into the future.

—*Reginald P. Briggs*

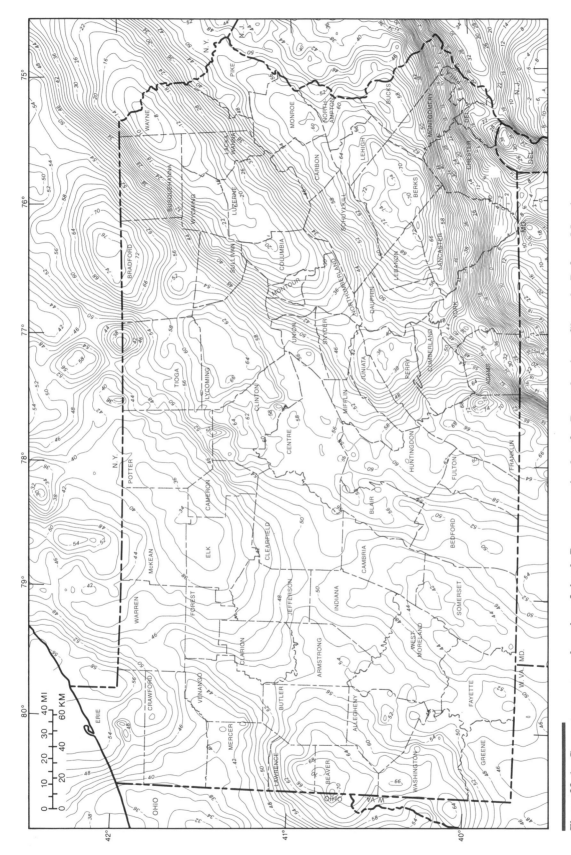

Figure 23–1. Computer-contoured version of simple Bouguer gravity data for Pennsylvania on file at the Defense Mapping Agency as of 1980 (contour interval is 2 mGal). All data have been adjusted to the International Gravity Standardization Net 1971 and have been corrected using the 1967 Geodetic Reference System formula (Woollard, 1979). Free-air and Bouguer corrections (Dobrin, 1976) were applied using a sea-level datum and a crustal density of 2.67 g/cm³. Lack of smoothness of the contours and some of the shortest wavelength features may be artifacts of the computer processing and/or transcription errors resulting from entering the data into the computer; however, these perturbations are not significant for regional-scale analysis.

CHAPTER 23   GRAVITY

PETER M. LAVIN*
443 Deike Building
Department of Geosciences
The Pennsylvania State University
University Park, PA 16802

INTRODUCTION

This discussion is based on the simple (no terrain corrections) Bouguer gravity anomaly map of Pennsylvania (Figure 23-1) prepared for this article, and the review and integration of the work of many other investigators. Major emphasis is placed on the interpretation of regional gravity anomalies as an aid to determining the framework for regional and local geologic studies.

Gravity stations are irregularly distributed across the state at an average station spacing of about 5 km (3 mi). Closer spacing of 1 km (0.6 mi) is common in parts of southeastern Pennsylvania; wider spacing on the order of 8 km (5 mi) is common in some areas of high relief. The simple Bouguer anomaly values are accurate to within 1 mGal (1 mGal$=0.001$ cm/s^2) or better. Terrain corrections are not included here because their typical magnitude (0.3 to 3 mGals) will not significantly alter the interpretation of the regional anomalies.

Variations in the simple Bouguer anomaly values result from any condition giving rise to a lateral change in density (plus topographic effects not accounted for in the map). Relative gravity "highs" (or positive anomalies above background) are due to mass excesses; gravity "lows" result from mass deficiencies. Likely sources for lateral density variations include folded and faulted beds, sedimentary basins, igneous intrusions, lithologic variations, basement uplifts, and variations in crustal structure and/or thickness.

The relative magnitude and shape of a gravity anomaly depend on the magnitude of the density contrast between the anomalous mass and the surrounding material and the depth, shape, and size of the mass anomaly. Unfortunately, there is no unique solution for a given gravity anomaly. Broad (long-wavelength) anomalies may be due to broad, shallow structures or to more concentrated, deeper structures. Sharper (shorter wavelength) features of any significant amplitude are due to shallower sources.

*Retired.

REGIONAL FEATURES ON THE BOUGUER ANOMALY MAP OF PENNSYLVANIA

The major gravity gradient that extends from Canada to Alabama, paralleling the structure of the Appalachians, is visible just inside the southeastern corner of Pennsylvania (Lancaster marks the approximate midpoint of the gradient in Figure 23–2). It is thought to mark the edge of the late Precambrian-early Paleozoic North American craton (Ando and others, 1983) and thus could represent a suture zone between colliding continental plates in later Paleozoic time (Kane, 1983). A thinner crust and/or a major increase in density southeast of the zone can account for the gradient. The Mesozoic basins of Pennsylvania lie just to the northwest of the gradient and are seen in the detailed gravity data of Sumner (1977). Gravity lows over the basins show that the major offsets along faults occur southeast of the inferred position of the northeast-trending border faults (Shaub, 1975). Relative gravity highs, represented in the detailed data, outline some of the diabase sheets in the area.

The Pennsylvania gravity map is characterized by a number of northeast-trending, long-wavelength gravity highs and lows (Figure 23–2). They appear to reflect changes of thickness of the sedimentary rocks (depth to basement) and crustal structure rather than changes in lithology within the sedimentary or shallow-basement sections (see Chapter 24 for the magnetic map, which primarily reflects lithologic changes in the basement complex). However, recent detailed high-quality data obtained in western Pennsylvania show a significant correlation between local short-wavelength gravity anomalies and sedimentary structures (Muller and others, 1979).

The Beaver Falls gravity low (BFGL) dominates the western part of Pennsylvania and eastern Ohio. Geologic, gravity, and magnetic data suggest the presence of a deep (greater than 8 km [5 mi]) sedimentary basin, which is distinct from the basin to the east (Woollard, 1943; Rodgers, 1963; Wagner, 1976; Chaffin, 1981).

The Somerset gravity high (SOGH) coincides with a regional basement high that is about 6 km (3.5 to 4 mi) below the surface. Although several lower Paleozoic depositional axes are present, the thick sequences of carbonates do not appear to be dense enough to produce the observed anomaly. Net-

tleton (1941) suggested deeper sources for this anomaly. A slight thinning of the crust (0.6 km [0.4 mi]) was used by Chaffin (1981) to improve the fit to the gravity anomaly.

The Chambersburg gravity low (CGL) is part of a broad, northeast-trending gravity low (Lyons and O'Hara, 1982) that extends the length of the Appalachian Mountain system. Its expression to the northeast is masked, in part, by the Scranton gravity high (SGH) but can be seen in the flanking Williamsport and Reading lows (WGL and RGL). Woollard (1943) suggested a deep Paleozoic sedimentary basin and/or increased crustal thickness as the source of the anomaly. Gravity modeling by Chaffin (1981) showed the anomaly to be consistent with a basement low approximately 8.5 km (5.3 mi) below the surface and perhaps a slight increase (less than 1 km [0.6 mi]) in the crustal thickness.

Diment and others (1972) reported on their detailed gravity survey in the region of the SGH, suggesting the emplacement of mafic material during late Precambrian rifting as the likely cause. Revetta (1970) presented several possible alternative models, including a thick (3.5 km [2 mi]) sequence of mafic volcanics in a rift, emplacement of dense mantle material into the crust, and upwarping of the mantle resulting in a thinning of the crust.

Hawman (1980) reinterpreted the data of Diment and others (1972) in terms of elastic bending of the lithosphere in order to account for the flanking WGL and RGL. His final model shows an asymmetrical sedimentary basin extending over the region marked by the SGH and the flanking gravity lows, reaching a maximum depth of about 10 km (6 mi) near the axis of the SGH. A mafic block intruded through the entire crustal section would account for the SGH. Up to 3 km (2 mi) of the almost 8 km (5 mi) downwarp of the Moho under the axis of the anomaly (to a depth of approximately 40 km [25 mi]) can be explained by isostatic adjustment subsequent to the emplacement of the intrusion. Lack of a significant magnetic anomaly precludes the existence of extensive basaltic volcanism, which would be expected in a mature rift system. Creation of the rift structure likely exerted an important control on the early sedimentary history of the Appalachian basin. The Scranton anomaly is coincident with the thick clastic rocks of Devonian age (Colton, 1970). The Newport gravity high (NGH), because of its associated magnetic high (see Chapter 24), is believed by Fleming and Sumner (1975) to be a sep-

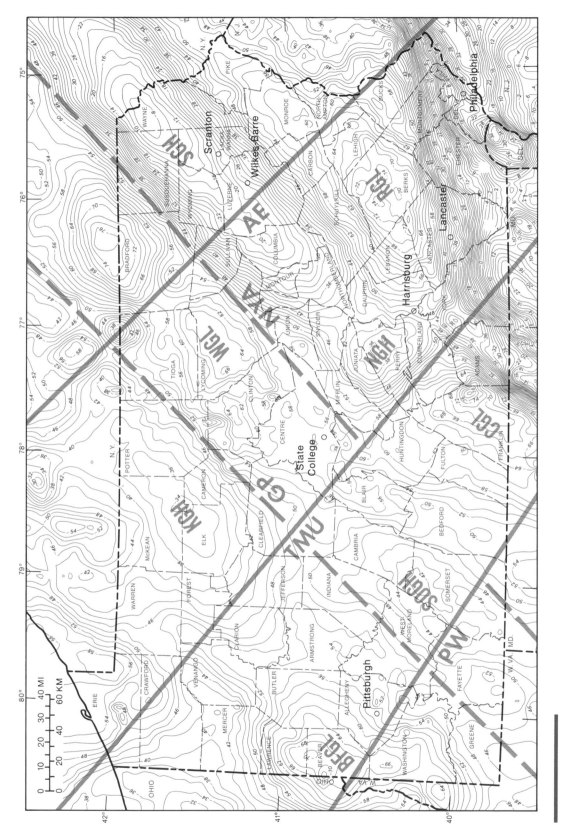

Figure 23–2. Simple Bouguer gravity anomaly map of Figure 23–1 with selected geophysical features marked. Dashed lines are structure-parallel features: GP, Greene-Potter fault zone; NYA, New York-Alabama lineament. Solid lines mark major cross-structural lineaments: AE, Attica-Easton lineament; TMU, Tyrone-Mt. Union lineament; and PW, Pittsburgh-Washington lineament. Gravity lows (GL) and highs (GH) are identified by place names: BF, Beaver Falls; K, Kane; SO, Somerset; W, Williamsport; C, Chambersburg; N, Newport; S, Scranton; and R, Reading.

arate (although related) feature and might represent the site of a triple junction (Rankin, 1976).

The Kane gravity high (KGH) marks the area of a paleotopographic high that controlled the sedimentation patterns and composition in the Pennsylvanian (Williams and Bragonier, 1974; Chapter 10 in this volume). Stratigraphic evidence along the extension of the Tyrone-Mt. Union fracture zone (TMU) at the southern boundary of the gravity high indicates uplift from Early Devonian through Early Pennsylvanian time (Rodgers and Anderson, 1984). The gravity data along the southeastern edge of the block can be explained by a 1.5-km (1-mi) down-to-the-east normal basement fault (Parrish, 1978) on strike with the Greene-Potter (GP) fault zone of structure-parallel basement faults that have been reactivated from Cambrian through post-Triassic time (Root, 1978). The axis of this northeast-trending zone can be clearly seen in the gravity data and extends from central New York through West Virginia. It lies west of the New York-Alabama lineament (NYA) and is the locus of kimberlite intrusions (Parrish and Lavin, 1982; Chapter 13).

At least three major cross-structural lineaments marking crustal fracture systems are seen in the gravity data (see Chapter 22; Figure 23-2). The Tyrone-Mt. Union lineament connects the features described by Gold and Parizek (1976) and Rodgers and Anderson (1984). The Pittsburgh-Washington (PW) lineament is marked by a major magnetic gradient as well as the minor changes in gravity patterns (Lavin and others, 1982). These two lineaments are believed to bound a major crustal block (Lake Erie-Maryland block) that underwent 60 to 100 km (37 to 62 mi) of relative northwestward movement from late Precambrian to Early Ordovician time. Gravity and magnetic expression of the New York-Alabama (NYA) lineament within this block is weak. Subsequent uplift of the region of the Kane gravity high (KGH) may have started as early as Late Ordovician time. The Attica-Easton (AE) lineament (line X of Diment and others, 1980) intersects the northeast-trending fault that bounds the KGH in the vicinity of a circular gravity and magnetic high that might be due to a buried kimberlite intrusion (Howell and Vozoff, 1953). Other cross-structural lineaments having less pronounced correlation with gravity and magnetic data (Parrish and Lavin, 1982) are probably confined to the sedimentary sequence or shallow basement.

PROBLEMS AND FUTURE RESEARCH

Changes in gravity (and magnetic) trends and patterns can provide important information on the regional geologic framework, as well as more detailed information for local geologic studies. The intersection of structure-parallel and cross-cutting crustal lineaments that likely have been reactivated many times during the geologic past has led to the concept of the blocklike structure of the crust. It is believed that block structures, as inferred for Pennsylvania, are prevalent in the eastern United States (Matthews, 1982; Kane, 1983; Rice, 1983) and are significant in terms of their control on subsequent sedimentation patterns, intrusion history, and regional seismicity (Alexander and Lavin, 1983).

Distinguishing long-wavelength anomalies caused by crustal variations from those resulting from broad, near-surface sedimentary basins has always been a problem. Isostatic gravity data on a 4-km (2.5-mi) grid (Jachens and others, 1985) should aid in such studies. Reexamination of many of the regional anomalies is in order, using filtering and other data-enhancement techniques (Ruder and Alexander, 1986). The correlation of short-wavelength anomalies with structure in the sedimentary section, particularly in western Pennsylvania, calls for more detailed surveys in areas of interest.

RECOMMENDED FOR FURTHER READING

Ackermann, H. D., and Howell, B. F., Jr. (1962), *Gravity investigations in northeastern and central Pennsylvania,* Pennsylvania Academy of Science Proceedings, v. 36, p. 218–224.

Bacon, L. O. (1954), *Gravity surveys of central Pennsylvania,* American Geophysical Union Transactions, v. 35, p. 495–502.

Dennison, J. M. (1983), *Comment, in Comment and reply on 'Tectonic model for kimberlite emplacement in the Appalachian Plateau of Pennsylvania,'* Geology, v. 11, p. 252–253.

Hersey, J. B. (1944), *Gravity investigation of central-eastern Pennsylvania,* Geological Society of America Bulletin, v. 55, p. 417–444.

Hutchinson, D. R., Grow, J. A., and Klitgord, K. D. (1983), *Crustal structure beneath the southern Appalachians: nonuniqueness of gravity modeling,* Geology, v. 11, p. 611–615.

Nettleton, L. L. (1976), *Gravity and magnetics in oil prospecting,* in the collection *McGraw-Hill international series in the earth and planetary sciences,* New York, McGraw-Hill, 464 p.

Simpson, R. W., Jachens, R. C., Blakely, R. J., and Saltus, R. W. (1986), *A new isostatic residual gravity map of the conterminous United States with a discussion on the significance of isostatic residual anomalies,* Journal of Geophysical Research, v. 91, p. 8348–8372.

Thomas, M. D. (1983), *Tectonic significance of paired gravity anomalies in the southern and central Appalachians,* in Hatcher, R. D., Jr., and others, eds., *Contributions to the tectonics and geophysics of mountain chains,* Geological Society of America Memoir 158, p. 113–124.

Woollard, G. P. (1968), *The interrelationship of the crust, the upper mantle, and isostatic gravity anomalies in the United States,* in Knopoff, Leon, and others, eds., *The crust and upper mantle of the Pacific area—International Upper Mantle Project, Science Report 15,* American Geophysical Union Geophysical Monograph 12, p. 312–341.

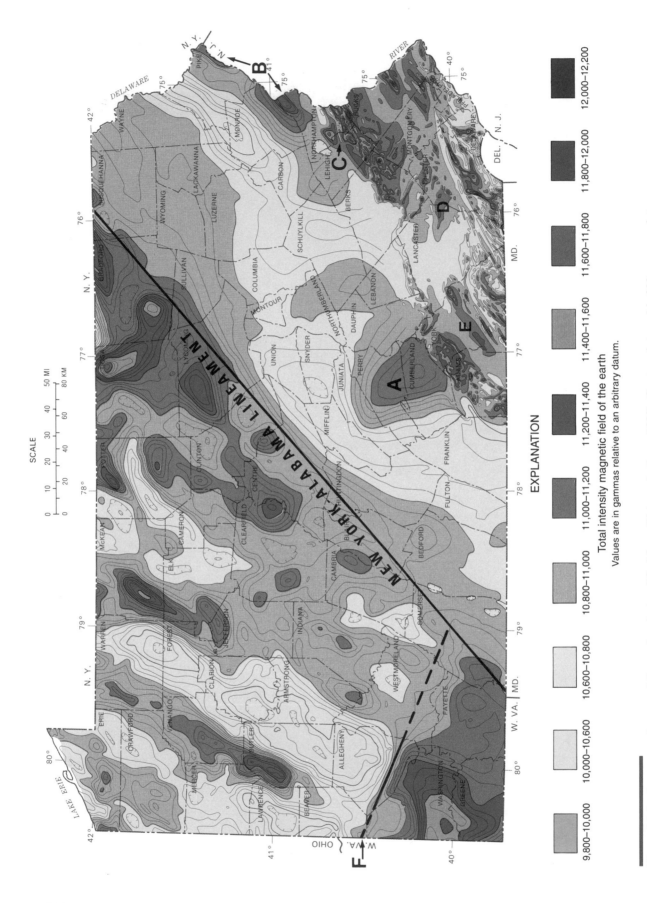

Figure 24-1. Aeromagnetic map of Pennsylvania (modified from Zietz and others, 1980). Contour interval is 200 gammas; intermediate 50-gamma contours are omitted in the southeast. A, New Bloomfield high; B and C, subsurface nappes; D and E, anomalies over largely subsurface Proterozoic rocks; F, inferred basement fault.

EXPLANATION

9,800–10,000   10,000–10,600   10,600–10,800   10,800–11,000   11,000–11,200   11,200–11,400   11,400–11,600   11,600–11,800   11,800–12,000   12,000–12,200

Total intensity magnetic field of the earth
Values are in gammas relative to an arbitrary datum.

SCALE

0   10   20   30   40   50 MI
0   20   40   60   80 KM

CHAPTER 24   AEROMAGNETICS

ELIZABETH R. KING
U.S. Geological Survey
National Center, MS 927
Reston, VA 20192

INTRODUCTION

Aeromagnetic mapping began in Pennsylvania in 1944 with a survey over Boyertown using a flux-gate magnetometer. This was the first test of this method in the western hemisphere (Hawkes and others, 1953). The area was selected because of the effectiveness of ground magnetic investigations of Cornwall-type magnetite deposits by the U.S. Geological Survey and the U.S. Bureau of Mines in the early to mid-1940's. In 1948, a major new "blind" iron orebody was located at Morgantown by a private company using similar equipment (Jensen, 1951). That orebody was subsequently developed as the Grace mine by the Bethlehem Mines Corporation. In the following years, Pennsylvania was completely covered by surveys by or under the auspices of the U.S. Geological Survey, most of which were in cooperation with the Pennsylvania Geological Survey (Joesting and others, 1949; Henderson and others, 1963; Popenoe and others, 1964; Bromery and Griscom, 1967; U.S. Geological Survey, 1969, 1974a–g). A more recent survey covering the whole state at a flight-line spacing of 3 to 6 miles was made by the U.S. Department of Energy under the National Uranium Resource Evaluation (NURE) Program (see Chapter 25).

A composite magnetic map based on these surveys (Figure 24–1) shows a profound contrast between southeastern Pennsylvania, where the exposed rocks have highly complex magnetic anomaly patterns, and the Appalachian basin, where broad, smooth magnetic anomalies reflect the deeply buried rocks of the crystalline basement. Nearly all the component surveys were flown north-south, but flight-line spacing varied widely, from 0.25 mile to as much as 6 miles in one area. Flight altitudes also varied, from 500 feet aboveground to a barometric altitude of 3,000 feet above sea level (Figure 24–2; Table 24–1). For areas where the distance from the sources of the anomalies is great, as it is in most of the state, these differences in flight level are tolerable.

SOUTHEASTERN PENNSYLVANIA

Most of southeastern Pennsylvania is covered by a survey made by the U.S. Geological Survey in

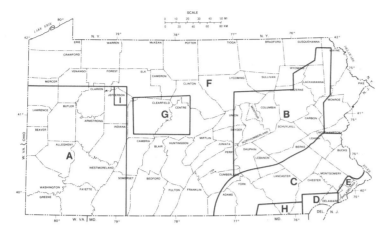

Figure 24–2. Index map of aeromagnetic surveys used to produce the aeromagnetic map of Pennsylvania shown in Figure 24–1. Parameters of each survey are given in Table 24–1.

Table 24–1. *Flight-Line Direction, Altitude, Spacing, and Source of Data for the Aeromagnetic Map of Pennsylvania*

Area[2]	Flight-line direction	Altitude[1] (feet)	Spacing (miles)	Source of data
A	N-S	500	1	Popenoe and others (1964)
B	N-S	[3]3,000	2	U.S. Geological Survey (1969)
C	N-S	500	¼	Bromery and Griscom (1967)
D	N-S	1,000	½	Henderson and others (1963)
E	N-S	[3]1,000	1	U.S. Geological Survey (1974g)
F	N-S	1,000	4	U.S. Geological Survey (1974a–f)
G	N-S	1,000	½	Joesting and others (1949)
H	E-W	500	½	U.S. Geological Survey, unpublished data
I	E-W	500	6	High Life Helicopters and QEB (1982)

[1]Aboveground unless indicated otherwise.
[2]Shown on index map in Figure 24–2.
[3]Barometric altitude.

1956 and 1957 with the primary goal of locating Cornwall-type iron ore deposits. The resulting series of 77 maps at 1:24,000 scale was used to locate numerous concentrations of iron ore, which were drilled by private industry. Socolow (1974) made brief interpretations of each map, describing correlations and noncorrelations of the magnetic anomalies with surface geology, and Bromery and Griscom (1967) prepared a composite magnetic map of the entire area on a geologic base with a detailed interpretation of the magnetic patterns on the map.

The predominantly clastic rocks of the Newark and Gettysburg basins (Figure 24–3) do not have a significant magnetic susceptibility. They have been intruded by a number of highly magnetic saucer-shaped bodies of diabase that are delineated by magnetic anomalies with oval or looplike map patterns.

The diabase anomalies terminate abruptly along the northern edge of the basins, where the Mesozoic rocks have been downfaulted against Proterozoic and Paleozoic rocks. Near the southern margin of the Newark basin, the clastic rocks thin, and the underlying basement rocks give rise to a couple of broad northeast-trending highs (Socolow, 1974, p. 55–57, 69). A prominent magnetic anomaly over Buckingham Mountain (see Figure 24–3) is produced by a fault-bound sliver of Proterozoic and Paleozoic rock that forms a northeast-trending ridge, dividing the Newark basin into two parts. The faults (the Furlong and others; see Chapter 21) cut the Mesozoic rocks and bound small diabase sheets on the north just as the larger sheets are bounded along the northern boundary fault. The Buckingham magnetic high indicates a large subsurface ridge of magnetic Proterozoic rocks extending 15 miles southwest from the state line. Models calculated from the magnetic data (Zietz and Gray, 1960) indicate a Proterozoic basement sloping to the south that is 7,000 feet deep 3 miles south of the exposed Proterozoic rocks.

Magnetic rocks occur just north of the Mesozoic basins in the Reading Prong and Blue Ridge (Figure 24–3). The intricate, closely spaced pattern of magnetic anomalies over the Reading Prong is produced by a complex of magnetite-rich, gneissic Proterozoic rocks at the surface (Bromery and Griscom, 1967). Work by Drake (1970) indicates that these rocks are allochthonous and form the core of a huge nappe system overthrust from the southeast. North of the exposed Proterozoic rocks of the Reading Prong, there is a northeast-trending magnetic high (C in Figure 24–3) with a dip or saddle near Allentown. Bromery and Griscom (1967) concluded that it was caused by similar Proterozoic rocks at depth beneath the Paleozoic sedimentary rocks of the Great Valley. Drake (1978) calculated from the magnetic data that these Proterozoic rocks form the core of the Lyons Station-Paulins Kill nappe at a depth of 1.6 km (l mi). A broader magnetic high to the northeast (B in Figure 24–3) may indicate an even deeper nappe or thrust sheet. Recent drilling and a Vibroseis profile near the Pennsylvania-New Jersey border (Ratcliffe and others, 1986) show that the fault boundary between the Newark basin and the Proterozoic rocks dips gently southward. These data also indicate that there is a series of imbricate thrust slices in the Proterozoic rocks of the footwall block (Ratcliffe and

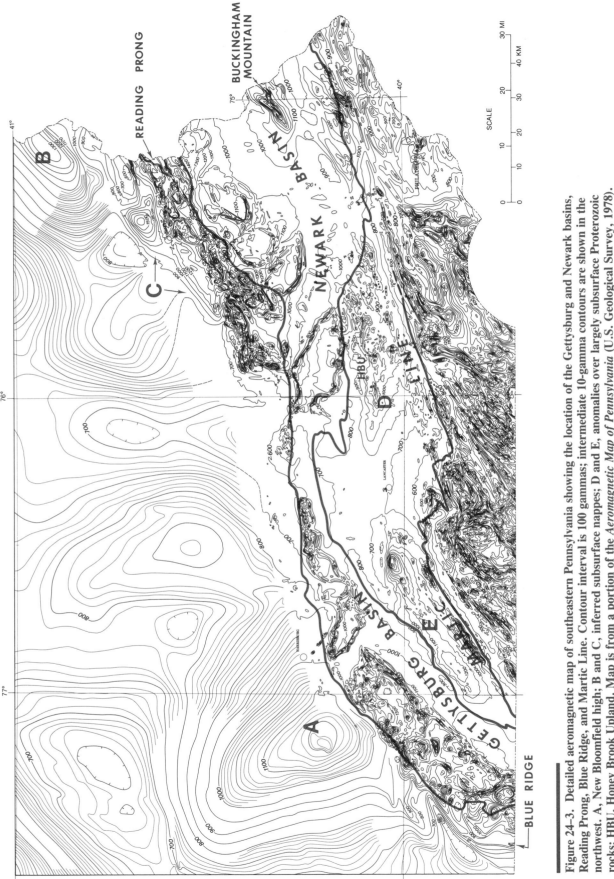

Figure 24-3. Detailed aeromagnetic map of southeastern Pennsylvania showing the location of the Gettysburg and Newark basins, Reading Prong, Blue Ridge, and Martic Line. Contour interval is 100 gammas; intermediate 10-gamma contours are shown in the northwest. A, New Bloomfield high; B and C, inferred subsurface nappes; D and E, anomalies over largely subsurface Proterozoic rocks. Map is from a portion of the *Aeromagnetic Map of Pennsylvania* (U.S. Geological Survey, 1978).

others, 1986), which is compatible with the magnetic data.

The smoother pattern over the Catoctin metavolcanic rocks of the Blue Ridge anticlinorium (Figure 24-3) indicates that these rocks are only moderately magnetic. The Blue Ridge anticlinorium south of Pennsylvania is typically marked by a pair of large, linear magnetic highs. The Catoctin is mostly metabasalt to the south, but in Pennsylvania, less magnetic metarhyolite predominates (Espenshade, 1970).

The region south of the Mesozoic basins is divided by a pronounced northeast-trending magnetic lineament (Martic Line in Figure 24-3) into an intensely magnetic southern province and a less magnetic, more heterogeneous region to the north. The eastern part of this lineament coincides with the Martic Line (Stose and Jonas, 1935), but the western part is slightly south of the traditional Martic Line, which Wise (1970) distinguished from the "magnetic Martic Line." South of this lineament, the rocks consist of a thrust stack of highly magnetic "eugeosynclinal" rocks, including ophiolitic fragments. To the north, much less magnetic carbonate and clastic rocks predominate. Socolow (1974, p. 73–75) suggested that the magnetic line may be a function of magnetic susceptibility controlled by the preexisting mineralogy (mineralization?) of the metasediments rather than structure.

North of the Martic Line, most of the magnetic anomalies are related to Proterozoic basement rocks. An area of numerous small anomalies east of Lancaster (D in Figure 24-3) coincides with a domal area of Middle Proterozoic gneisses exposed in the Mine Ridge anticline and related structures. The magnetic data indicate similar rocks at shallow depths both to the west toward Lancaster and to the east of the Honey Brook Upland (HBU in Figure 24-3) under the Triassic basin. A southwest-trending magnetic high west of Lancaster (E in Figure 24-3), having peaks at either end over exposed mafic Proterozoic rocks, indicates a shallow basement ridge or thrust sheet.

South of the Martic Line, Middle Proterozoic basement gneisses are exposed in several domelike structures that are marked by characteristic magnetic lows. These lows have an open pattern that is in sharp contrast to the pattern of the surrounding highly magnetic units of the overlying Glenarm Supergroup. These so-called domes include the Woodville, Avondale, and West Chester, and the smaller Mill Creek dome east of Philadelphia, which was first identified from magnetic data (Higgins and others, 1973). McKinstry (1961) concluded that these were domal uplifts, but Bailey and Mackin (1937), Mackin (1962), and later Fisher and others (1979) concluded that

these were refolded nappes. Bromery (1968), in a study of similar domes north of Baltimore, was able to trace the magnetic expression of the surrounding rocks under the gneisses. More recent geological and gravity studies by Muller and Chapin (1984) have shown that these structures are part of a refolded nappe system.

THE APPALACHIAN BASIN

The broad, low-gradient magnetic anomalies typical of the Appalachian basin are produced by magnetic rock units in the Precambrian crystalline basement underlying the thick sedimentary sequence, which is essentially nonmagnetic. Only a few drill holes have penetrated basement, all in the western part of the basin (Saylor, 1968). Vacquier and others (1951) developed and tested mathematical techniques for determining the depth and shape of a magnetic body using several of the early surveys made by the U.S. Geological Survey, including a survey in an area northwest of State College in central Pennsylvania (area G in Figure 24-2). Depth calculations indicated that the basement surface is 19,000 to 22,000 feet below the surface in the western part of this area and slopes to much greater depths to the southeast (Joesting and others, 1949). Prior to the availability of aeromagnetic data, there was much uncertainty about the degree of basement involvement in the Appalachian deformation. In the controversy between advocates of so-called thick-skinned deformation versus those favoring thin-skinned tectonics (Rodgers, 1949), magnetic mapping provided independent evidence that the crystalline basement was not involved in the folds mapped at the surface. The major basement trends determined from the magnetic surveys are independent of the surface trends of the mapped Appalachian folds in Pennsylvania.

Other aeromagnetic surveys have added information on the basement. Analysis of an aeromagnetic survey of a large area in western Pennsylvania (area A in Figure 24-2) showed that the basement slopes from about 8,000 feet below sea level at the northwest corner of the area to over 20,000 feet below sea level in the southeast, near 79° west longitude (Beck and Mattick, 1964). In 1974, a drill hole (#1 Leonard Svetz) penetrated the Upper Cambrian at 18,980 feet below sea level in Somerset County, close to the location of the magnetic calculation. Data from a regional survey across southwestern Pennsylvania (Zietz and others, 1966), which indicated a profound deepening of the basement to the east toward the Blue Ridge where exposed Proterozoic rocks have been overthrust toward the basin, were used by Gwinn

(1970) to back up his arguments for thin-skinned deformation in the central Appalachian fold belt. The same survey also revealed the presence of a large wedge-shaped block of strongly magnetic rocks in southwest Pennsylvania and adjacent West Virginia. On the northeast, the block has a sharp, linear boundary (F in Figure 24–1) that is 100 miles long and appears to be fault controlled. Lavin and others (1982) have proposed that this magnetic boundary, along with other geophysical and geologic data, delineates a much longer feature, the Pittsburgh-Washington lineament, that is one of several cross-structural lineaments involving basement rocks in the northeastern United States (Parrish and Lavin, 1982; Rodgers and Anderson, 1984; also see Chapter 22).

As soon as magnetic coverage became available for the entire Appalachian basin (King and Zietz, 1978), a major magnetic lineament was apparent along its entire length. The New York-Alabama lineament divides the basement into two magnetically distinct areas (Figure 24–1). To the southeast, the few anomalies present are very broad and have gentle gradients consistent with the profound basement depths of the region adjacent to the Blue Ridge. To the northwest, numerous anomalies indicate a basement composed of large units of rocks with strongly contrasting magnetic properties. Several anomalies have well-defined northeast trends that are discordant with the more easterly trends of the fold axes at the surface, and other anomalies trend north or northwest.

The New York-Alabama lineament may mark the edge of a stable craton of older Precambrian rocks that limited the strong Appalachian deformation on the east, as arcuate salients of the fold belt in both Tennessee and Pennsylvania are tangential to it. The linearity of this feature suggests that it may be a strike-slip fault analogous to the strike-slip faults of the Tibetian Plateau that are associated with the collision of India with the Asian continent (King and Zietz, 1978).

Southeast of the New York-Alabama lineament and west of Harrisburg, there is a large triangular anomaly (A in Figure 24–1) that has an associated positive gravity anomaly. Fleming (1975) modeled both magnetic and gravity data for this feature, which he called the New Bloomfield high. He concluded that it is caused by a large block of basaltic material in the Proterozoic basement, possibly related to Catoctin metabasalts at the surface and emplaced in late Precambrian time during continental rifting and the opening of the proto-Atlantic ocean.

PROBLEMS AND FUTURE RESEARCH

Although Pennsylvania has been in the forefront in the development and application of aeromagnetic techniques, the available data are uneven in quality. The older surveys, such as the one for southeastern Pennsylvania, were recorded in analogue form with a fluxgate magnetometer. Much of the Appalachian basin is covered by data spaced 3 or 4 miles apart. Simultaneous acquisition of aeromagnetic data by modern proton magnetometers and gamma-ray data where gamma-ray coverage is currently inadequate (see Chapter 25) would be very worthwhile.

An updated database would aid in resolving many of the questions about the Precambrian basement. Perhaps the most important problem concerns the degree of participation of the basement in the deformation of the overlying sedimentary rocks in the plateau area, where basement control of some of the surface lineaments and small kimberlite intrusions has been postulated by Parrish and Lavin (1982) (see Chapters 13 and 20). The location and configuration of the Rome trough in western Pennsylvania is poorly known and might be delineated by high-precision aeromagnetic data.

RECOMMENDED FOR FURTHER READING

Bromery, R. W., and others (1959–61), *Aeromagnetic maps of southeastern Pennsylvania*, U.S. Geological Survey Geophysical Investigations Maps GP–200–210, 213–245, and 254–287, scale 1:24,000.

Fisher, G. W., Higgins, M. W., and Zietz, Isidore (1979), *Geological interpretations of aeromagnetic maps of the crystalline rocks in the Appalachians, northern Virginia to New Jersey*, Maryland Geological Survey Report of Investigations 32, 43 p.

Fisher, G. W., Pettijohn, F. J., Reed, J. C., Jr., and Weaver, K. N., eds. (1970), *Studies of Appalachian geology: central and southern*, New York, Interscience Publishers, 460 p.

Nettleton, L. L. (1971), *Elementary gravity and magnetics for geologists and seismologists*, Society of Exploration Geophysicists Monograph Series 1, p. 73–121.

Socolow, A. A. (1974), *Geologic interpretation of aeromagnetic maps of southeastern Pennsylvania*, Pennsylvania Geological Survey, 4th ser., Information Circular 77, 85 p.

Telford, W. M., Geldart, L. P., Sheriff, R. E., and Keys, D. A. (1976), *Applied geophysics*, Cambridge, England, Cambridge University Press, p. 105–217.

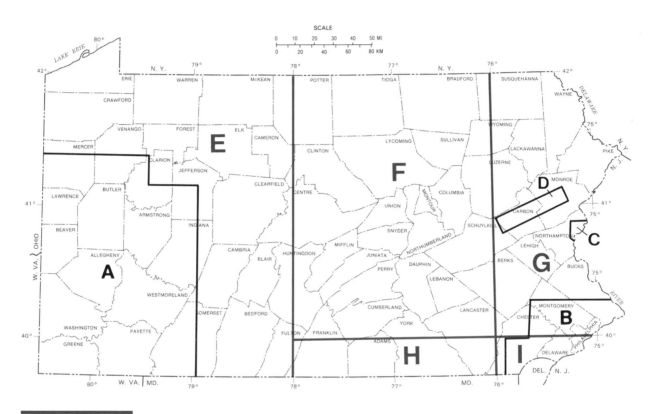

Figure 25–1. Aeroradioactivity surveys in Pennsylvania. The colored lines separate NURE
surveys of different flight-line directions and spacings. The NURE surveys (E, F, G, H, and I)
cover the entire state, and the other surveys (A, B, C, and D) are total-count surveys that
cover parts of the state. The total-count surveys were flown at 500 feet above the ground, and
the NURE surveys were flown at 400 feet. Flight-line spacings of the surveys were as follows:
A and B, N–S 1 mile; C, N–S 0.5 mile; D, NE–SW 0.25 mile; E, E–W 6 miles, N–S 18 miles;
F, N–S 3 miles, E–W 12 miles; G, E–W 3 miles, N–S 18 miles; H, E–W 3 miles, N–S 18 miles;
and I, E–W 6 miles, N–S 18 miles.

328

CHAPTER 25   AERORADIOACTIVITY

ELIZABETH R. KING
U.S. Geological Survey
National Center, MS 927
Reston, VA 20192

JOSEPH S. DUVAL
U.S. Geological Survey
National Center, MS 927
Reston, VA 20192

INTRODUCTION

Aeroradioactivity surveying began after World War II when sensitive scintillometers that could be mounted in aircraft were developed to explore for uranium. Scintillometers measure gamma radiation produced by certain radioactive elements in the ground, primarily potassium and members of the uranium and thorium decay series. The early equipment measured only the combined signal (total counts per second) produced by all gamma-emitting elements, but the more recently developed spectral radiometry measures the signals of the different elements separately (Bristow, 1979; Grasty, 1979; Killeen, 1979).

Although radiometric surveys are often made concurrently with magnetic surveys, the radiometric survey parameters are much more restrictive (Pitkin and Duval, 1980). Gamma radiation is rapidly attenuated by the atmosphere, so that the maximum useful flight elevation is about 600 feet above the ground, and most surveys are flown with a nominal ground clearance of 400 feet. At 400 feet, the surface area contributing to the measurement is limited to a width of about 0.25 mile. Because spacings greater than 0.25 mile between the flight lines are often used, surveys miss anomalous sources of radioactivity between the lines.

Most of the gamma radiation comes from the top 18 inches of soil and is very sensitive to the presence of water. If, however, the surface materials are representative of deeper material, the data provide a relative indication of the radioactivity of the underlying rocks. Heavily fertilized farmland sometimes produces anomalously high signals because of radium in phosphate fertilizers. In spite of their limitations, aeroradioactivity surveys provide much valuable geologic information.

AVAILABLE DATA

Most of the aeroradioactivity data for Pennsylvania were collected under two national programs. The Aerial Radiological Measuring Surveys (ARMS)

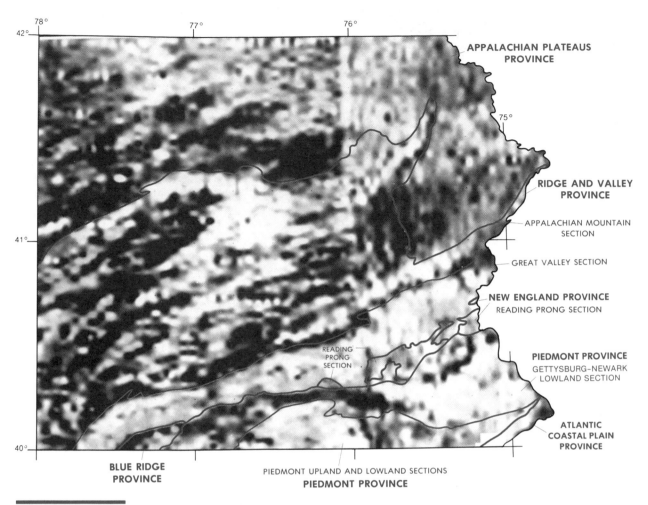

Figure 25–2. Composite aeroradioactivity image of eastern Pennsylvania north of the 40° parallel showing physiographic provinces and sections. Light areas indicate higher radioactivity. Generalized geologic units of the same area are shown on the facing page. Image compiled from NURE data; geologic units modified from Pennsylvania Geological Survey (1982); physiographic areas slightly modified from Berg and others (1989).

were made for the U.S. Atomic Energy Commission to determine the background gamma radiation of rectangular areas, averaging 100 miles on a side, that surround major nuclear installations in the United States (Guillou, 1964). Two areas in Pennsylvania were flown: the Pittsburgh area, about two thirds of which is in Pennsylvania (Bates, 1964, 1966) (Figure 25–1, area A); and the Camden-Delaware Valley area, a small part of which is in southeastern Pennsylvania (Guillou, 1961) (Figure 25–1, area B). Both of these surveys measured total counts per second.

The entire state of Pennsylvania was surveyed by regional radiometric surveys conducted by the U.S. Department of Energy from 1976 to 1981 to systematically assess the occurrence of uranium in

the United States. In this program, the National Uranium Resource Evaluation (NURE) Program, total-count plus uranium, thorium, and potassium channels, and aeromagnetic data were recorded in digital form for each 1- by 2-degree quadrangle. The data for the state of Pennsylvania are reported in LKB Resources (1977, 1978a–c), Texas Instruments (1978), Carson Helicopters and Texas Instruments (1980), Geodata International (1980), and High Life Helicopters and QEB (1982). Line spacing and direction vary from quadrangle to quadrangle and are listed in the caption of Figure 25–1.

Total-count gamma-ray surveys of two small areas (areas C and D in Figure 25–1) in eastern Pennsylvania were made by the U.S. Geological Survey.

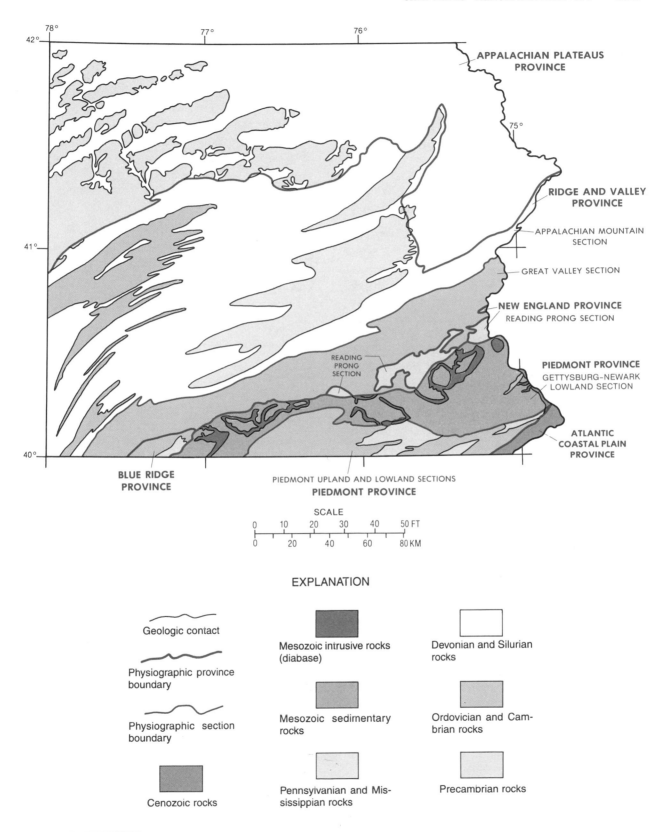

Figure 25–2. *(Continued).*

Area C is part of a survey of the Reading Prong, in which the radioactivity survey was an adjunct to an aeromagnetic survey (Boynton and others, 1966a, b). Area D is a strip 25 miles long that was surveyed in 1954 to investigate occurrences of uranium in eastern Pennsylvania.

MAPS OF RADIOMETRIC DATA

The older radiometric surveys were recorded in analogue form and compiled as sets of profiles or as maps of levels or ranges of counts per second (cps). These levels, which could be identified on a number of adjacent profiles, were used to divide the maps into zones that could be correlated with the geology of the area (Guillou, 1964; Pitkin and others, 1964). The data for areas A, B, and D on Figure 25-1 were compiled into maps of radioactivity levels. Eventually, such maps were replaced by contour maps, which are able to provide much greater detail. The contour maps of area C (Figure 25-1) and the other maps of this survey in adjacent New Jersey show coherent patterns that can be related to the mapped geology.

Both the older maps of radioactivity levels and the newer contour maps show a strong correlation of radiometric data with geologic units. For example, in area A, the Mississippian carbonate rocks on the flanks and crests of anticlines in the southeast corner of the mapped area have an excellent correlation with elongate areas of lower radioactivity (Bates, 1966).

Figure 25-2 (p. 330) shows a black-and-white version of a color composite of the three channels (uranium, thorium, and potassium) in which the three sets of data, each assigned a different color, are superimposed to give a single image (Duval, 1983). The data are from the NURE surveys for the Williamsport, Harrisburg, Scranton, and Newark 1- by 2-degree quadrangles (Figure 25-1, areas F and G), where the flight-line spacing was 3 miles. In Figure 25-2, the light areas indicate where all three components are present in higher amounts, and the dark areas indicate where they are lower.

Geologic units are shown on the second map in Figure 25-2 (p. 331) to illustrate the correlation of lithologies with the radiometric patterns. The shaly rocks of the Great Valley stand out as a broad belt having higher radioactivity than the adjacent lithologies. A similar light pattern coincides with the clastic rocks of the Newark basin and with the metamorphic terrane farther south, which includes abundant phyllite. Separating these two light areas is a narrow, dark belt of lower radioactivity over parts of diabase intrusions and coarser Mesozoic clastic rocks of the Gettysburg basin and over some units in the Blue Ridge province. The Appalachian fold belt is characterized by northeast-trending areas of alternating higher and lower radioactivity, and the plunging folds coincide with interfingering light and dark areas. Because these data are regional and measure less than 10 percent of the surface area (Pitkin and Duval, 1980), they do not provide precise correlations with the geologic units, but more closely spaced data would provide better correlations with the geology.

RELATIONSHIP OF DATA TO URANIUM DEPOSITS

Exploration for uranium deposits has provided the main impetus for aeroradioactivity surveys. There are known deposits (Klemic, 1962; Rose, 1970) in the eastern part of the state in Upper Devonian to Mississippian and Upper Triassic clastic rocks and in some of the gneisses and skarns of the Reading Prong (see Chapter 39). A small strip, area D on Figure 25-1, was flown over a cluster of occurrences in Carbon County, but only one has an associated radiation anomaly, and no other promising anomalies were detected in spite of the 0.25-mile flight-line spacing. The NURE data, which were collected for the entire state at intervals of 3 to 6 miles, delineate the Reading Prong and indicate several anomalous locations in eastern Pennsylvania in areas underlain by clastic rocks, especially those of continental origin. However, known uranium deposits in three areas in the Williamsport 1- by 2-degree quadrangle (Figure 25-1, north half of area F) did not have associated aeroradioactivity anomalies in the survey data (Smith and Hoff, 1984; LKB Resources, 1978c), and others could have been missed because of the wide flight-line spacing.

PROBLEMS AND FUTURE RESEARCH

Many areas of research could benefit from more closely spaced aeroradiometric data. Detailed contour maps, gray-scale images, and composite-color maps of such data can provide information on faults, facies changes, and other lithologic features in sedimentary rocks and assist in unravelling the complex structures of the igneous-metamorphic terrane of southeastern Pennsylvania, particularly gneisses and mafic intrusions. Radon-pollution studies have recently generated great interest (see Chapter 55B) and would benefit from detailed aeroradioactivity data. Another very interesting area of research is in petroleum exploration (Saunders and others, 1987), as some investigators see a correlation of radioactivity with oil fields. Such studies might have applications in western Pennsylvania.

RECOMMENDED FOR FURTHER READING

Adams, J. A. S., and Gasparini, Paolo (1970), *Gamma-ray spectrometry of rocks*, Amsterdam, Elsevier, 295 p.

Adams, J. A. S., and Lowder, W. M., eds. (1964), *The natural radiation environment*, University of Chicago Press, 1,069 p.

Dobrin, M. B. (1960), *Introduction to geophysical prospecting,* 2nd ed., New York, McGraw-Hill, p. 374–397.

Hood, P. J., ed. (1979), *Geophysics and geochemistry in the search for metallic ores*, Geological Survey of Canada Economic Geology Report 31, 811 p.

Telford, W. M., Geldart, L. P., Sheriff, R. E., and Keys, D. A. (1976), *Applied geophysics*, Cambridge, England, Cambridge University Press, p. 736–770.

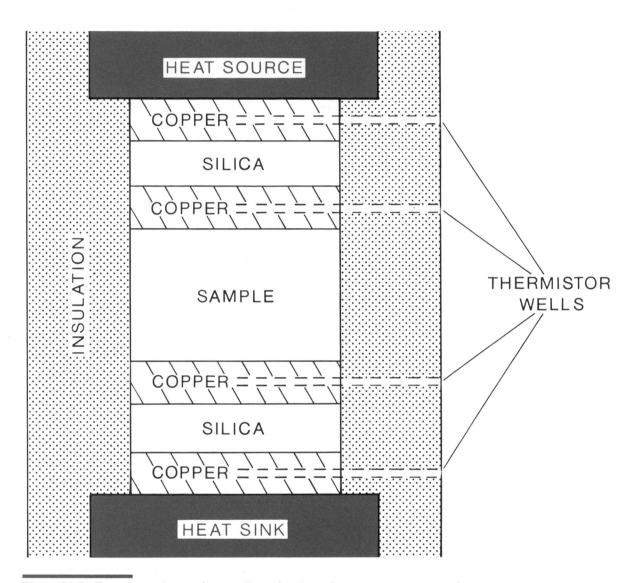

Figure 26–1. Experimental setup for one-dimensional steady-state measurements of thermal conductivity in rock samples (modified from Birch, Francis, 1950, *Flow of heat in the Front Range, Colorado,* Geological Society of America Bulletin, v. 61, Figure 14, p. 601). Modified with permission of the publisher, the Geological Society of America, Boulder, Colorado USA. Copyright © 1950 Geological Society of America.

CHAPTER 26   TERRESTRIAL HEAT-FLOW DENSITY

YORAM ECKSTEIN
  221 McGilvrey Hall
  Department of Geology
  Kent State University
  Kent, OH 44242

GARRY MAURATH
  221 McGilvrey Hall
  Department of Geology
  Kent State University
  Kent, OH 44242

INTRODUCTION

Terrestrial heat flow is the quantity of heat transferred from a variety of heat sources in the interior of the earth to the earth's surface. This heat is predominantly radiogenic in nature. Within the crust, heat is transferred largely by crystalline-lattice conduction, although considerable convective heat transfer may occur where local geological conditions involve substantial movement of fluids. Heat transfer by radiation, at temperatures prevalent within the upper crust, is negligible.

In a geologic context, terrestrial heat-flow density (q_z) is expressed as the vertical component of heat conducted through the drillable portion of the outer crust:

$$q_z = k_z(\partial T/\partial z) \qquad (1)$$

where $\partial T/\partial z$ is the rate of increase of temperature (T) with depth (z) within a rock formation of thermal conductivity k_z, measured in the vertical (z) direction. This is a simplification based on the assumption that heat is transferred through the crust solely by conduction, along a path normal to the surface of the earth. Therefore, anomalies in measured heat-flow density may be attributed either to anomalous thermal properties of the rock formation, an anomalous heat source, and/or convective heat transfer. Measurements of heat-flow density are generally reported in SI units as mW/m^2 (milliwatts per square meter; 1 mW = 0.000239 calorie per second).

THERMAL CONDUCTIVITY OF ROCK FORMATIONS

Thermal conductivity of a rock formation is usually estimated on the basis of laboratory measurements conducted on selected rock samples. Various transient methods of in situ measurements have been developed (Beck, 1957), but their applicability is commonly limited to fine-grained unconsolidated sediments, particularly in marine or lacustrine heat-flow surveys. Conductivity measurement techniques may be divided into two broad categories: (a) one-dimensional steady state, and (b) two-dimensional transient or steady state.

In the most commonly used one-dimensional steady-state technique, a disc machined out of the rock sample is sandwiched between two reference discs of known conductivity. This entire "sandwich" is placed between a heat source and a heat sink (Figure 26–1). Temperature gradients measured across the two reference discs are used to determine the quantity of heat flowing per unit time across a unit area down the stack. This quantity is used in conjunction with the temperature gradient measured across the central disc to determine the thermal conductivity of the sample. A detailed description of the technique and a review of the inherent experimental errors are given by Beck (1965). Descriptions of alternative steady-state techniques are presented by Benfield (1939), Schroder (1963), and Creutzburg (1964).

Two-dimensional thermal conductivity measurements employ a long, cylindrical heat source inserted into the investigated medium (usually unconsolidated sediment), which is heated at a carefully controlled rate per unit length. The resulting rise of temperature at a given radial distance from the linear heat source is a function of the thermal conductivity of the surrounding material. The theoretical background for this methodology is described in Carslaw and Jaeger (1959).

Thermal conductivity of rock materials is dependent on both temperature and pressure. Conductivity is directly proportional to pressure (Hurtig and Brugger, 1970) and, in general, is inversely proportional to temperature, within the range of crustal temperatures (Kappelmeyer and Haenel, 1974).

Thermal conductivity is commonly expressed in either of the two following units:

$$1 \text{ Watt m}^{-1}\text{K}^{-1} = 2.391 \text{ mcal cm}^{-1}\text{s}^{-1}\,^{\circ}\text{C}^{-1}$$

Typical values of most common rocks, at 25°C and 1 atmosphere, range from an average of 0.35 W/m^{-1}K^{-1} for obsidian to about 6.71 W/m^{-1}K^{-1} for quartzite (Kappelmeyer and Haenel, 1974).

A detailed treatment of the methodology for measurements of thermal conductivity in sediments and rock formations can be found in Beck (1988) or Jessop (1990).

GEOTHERMAL GRADIENT

The geothermal gradient is commonly defined as the rate of increase of temperature (T) with depth (z) within a rock formation ($\partial T/\partial z$ in equation 1). The gradient is usually measured in boreholes at discrete intervals, utilizing thermistors, or as a continuous temperature log.

The effects of numerous cyclic and noncyclic environmental temperature perturbations are superimposed upon the geothermal gradient. Short-term cyclic effects, such as those associated with the diurnal or annual oscillations of surface temperature, are generally attenuated within 20 to 50 m (66 to 164 ft) of the surface. The effects of long-term cyclic effects, such as Pleistocene glaciation, may be observed to depths of hundreds of meters, and the raw data must be corrected (Birch, 1948; Cermak, 1976). One of the noncyclic temperature perturbations most commonly observed is caused by variations in topography and may be corrected in a manner similar to that used in gravity surveys. An excellent summary of the various methods used to correct for topographic effects is given by Blackwell and others (1980). Other perturbations resulting from uplift, erosion, subsidence, sedimentation, surface drainage, and groundwater movement may require individual corrections (Kappelmeyer and Haenel, 1974).

An extensive description of the techniques of measuring the geothermal gradient and the associated problems can be found in Beck and Balling (1988).

TERRESTRIAL HEAT-FLOW DENSITY IN PENNSYLVANIA

Nine measurements of heat-flow density have been made in Pennsylvania (Figure 26–2). The initial measurement, 54 mW/m^2, was taken in the north-central part of Pennsylvania by Joyner (1960). Six additional measurements have been made by Urban (1971). The two most recent measurements were made by the authors in 1979 (Maurath, 1980). Measurements range from a low of 38 mW/m^2 in the southeastern part of the state to a high of 84 mW/m^2 in Venango County. The mean heat-flow-density value is 57 mW/m^2, which closely approximates the global mean heat flow of 59 mW/m^2 (Chapman and Pollack, 1975).

A generalized picture of the regional thermal regime in Pennsylvania may be derived from the map of the geothermal gradient approximated from the groundwater temperatures at about 30-m (100-ft) depth and the bottom-hole temperatures for 439 oil and gas wells in Pennsylvania and adjacent states (Figure 26–2). Whenever possible, temperatures were obtained from continuous-temperature logs of deep wells. Where these logs were not available, recorded bottom-hole temperatures or maximum recorded temperatures from various other geophysical logs were used.

DISCUSSION

Because only nine measurements of heat-flow density have been made within Pennsylvania, a detailed analysis of regional heat flow is not possible. The mean observed heat-flow density of the six measurements in the Appalachian Plateaus province prob-

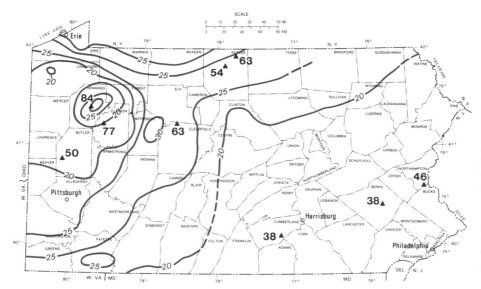

Figure 26–2. Map of Pennsylvania showing (1) location of terrestrial heat-flow sites (triangles) with values in mW/m^2, and (2) contours representing the generalized temperature gradient derived from bottom-hole temperature measurements in 439 selected oil and gas wells (modified from Maurath, 1980). Since such wells are generally absent from the southeastern third of the state, there are no contours. Contour interval is 5°C/km (0.2743°F/100 ft).

ably represents the regional conductive heat flow. The two measurements of heat-flow density made by the authors (84 and 77 mW/m^2) are anomalously high as a result of local geologic conditions. Thickening of highly radiogenic Pennsylvanian and Mississippian shales could result in local increases in the concentration of heat-producing elements within the upper crust. The three low values observed in eastern Pennsylvania are part of a southwest-northeast-trending regional heat-flow low associated with the folded Appalachians (Urban, 1971) and are not associated with the adjacent Reading Prong. Assuming an upper mantle heat-flow density of 16.7 mW/m^2 (Roy and others, 1968) and a two-layer crustal model, the observed heat flow in the Appalachian Plateaus province of Pennsylvania indicates an average crustal thickness of 45 km (28 mi). Although this estimate is based upon many simplifying assumptions, it is in general agreement with a crustal thickness of 36 to 45 km (22 to 28 mi) determined by other geophysical methods (Pakiser and Steinhart, 1964).

PROBLEMS AND FUTURE RESEARCH

There is an extensive gap in heat-flow-density data for central Pennsylvania. Considerable work needs to be done within the eastern part of the Appalachian Plateaus province and the Ridge and Valley province that could possibly provide information useful in constraining models of the Appalachian orogeny, crustal thickness, and maturation and distribution of the Appalachian hydrocarbons. Unresolved problems include an unexplained temperature-gradient high in the Pittsburgh area, which may be an artifact of thermal convection in Paleozoic aquifers in the area. In addition,

the subnormal heat flow observed in eastern Pennsylvania needs to be examined in much greater detail. High heat-flow-density values should be expected in the region of the Reading Prong, where Eckstein and others (1982) reported high radiogenic heat production.

RECOMMENDED FOR FURTHER READING

Beck, A. E. (1965), *Techniques of measuring heat flow on land,* in Lee, E. H. K., ed., *Terrestrial heat flow,* American Geophysical Union Monograph 8, p. 24–50.

Beck, A. E., Garven, Grant, and Stegena, Lajos, eds. (1987), *Hydrogeological regimes and their subsurface thermal effects,* American Geophysical Union Geophysical Monograph 47, 158 p.

Blackwell, D. D., Steele, J. L., and Brott, C. A. (1980), *The terrain effect on terrestrial heat flow,* Journal of Geophysical Research, v. 85B, p. 4757–4772.

Chapman, D. S., and Pollack, H. N. (1975), *Global heat flow—a new look,* Earth and Planetary Science Letters, v. 28, p. 23–32.

Diment, W. H., Urban, T. C., and Revetta, F. A. (1972), *Some geophysical anomalies in the eastern United States,* in Robertson, E. C., ed., *The nature of the solid earth,* New York, McGraw-Hill, p. 544–572.

Haenel, R., Rybach, L., and Stegena, L., eds. (1988), *Handbook of terrestrial heat-flow density determination—with guidelines and recommendations of the International Heat Flow Commission,* Dordrecht, Netherlands, Kluwer Academic Publishers, 486 p.

Jessop, A. M. (1990), *Thermal geophysics,* Amsterdam, Elsevier, 306 p.

Kappelmeyer, O., and Haenel, R. (1974), *Geothermics—with a special reference to application,* Geoexploration Monograph Series 1, no. 4, 238 p.

Roy, R. F., Blackwell, D. D., and Decker, E. R. (1972), *Continental heat flow,* in Robertson, E. C., ed., *The nature of the solid earth,* New York, McGraw-Hill, p. 506–543.

Sass, J. H., Blackwell, D. D., Chapman, D. S., and others (1981), *Heat flow from the crust of the United States,* in Touloukian, Y. S., and others, eds., *Physical properties of rocks and minerals,* New York, McGraw-Hill, p. 503–548.

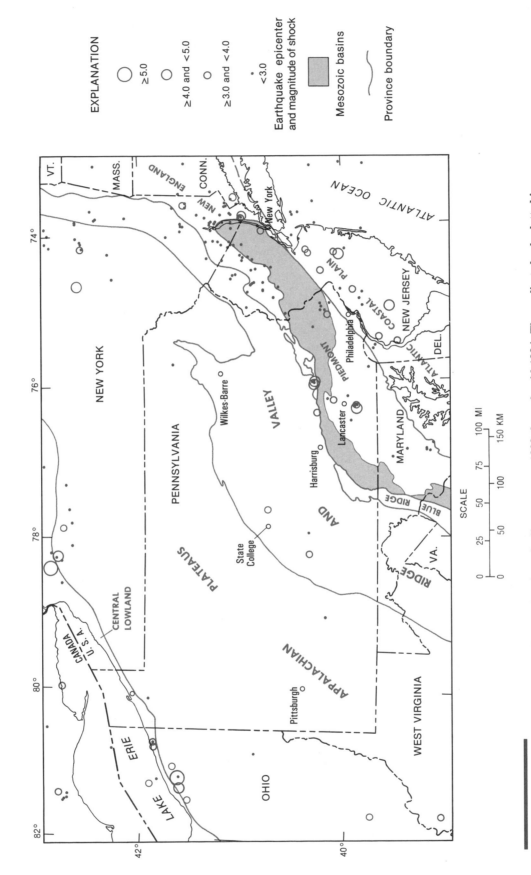

Figure 27-1. Instrumental seismicity of Pennsylvania and adjacent states, 1929 through mid-1994. The earliest shock plotted is the magnitude 5.2 New York State shock of August 12, 1929 (42.9°N/78.4°W). Probably all shocks of magnitude 4.0 or greater that have occurred since the late 1930's are plotted.

338

CHAPTER 27   SEISMOTECTONIC FRAMEWORK

JAMES W. DEWEY
    U.S. Geological Survey
    National Earthquake Information Center
    Denver Federal Center
    Box 25046, MS 966
    Denver, CO 80225

DAVID W. GORDON*
    U.S. Geological Survey
    National Earthquake Information Center
    Denver Federal Center
    Box 25046, MS 966
    Denver, CO 80225

Note: On September 25, 1998, a magnitude 5.2 earthquake occurred in northwestern Pennsylvania near the Ohio border (epicenter at 41.4°N latitude and 80.4°E longitude). This was the largest earthquake yet recorded that was centered in the state. Early damage reports suggested a maximum intensity of VI. The earthquake occurred after this book went to press and is not included in the text discussion.

*Retired.

INTRODUCTION

Twice per decade, on average, an earthquake occurs within Pennsylvania that is large enough (magnitude 3 or greater) to be felt in an area of several hundred square kilometers (about a hundred square miles) or more. The largest shocks in the historical era have had magnitudes of 4 to 4.6. These shocks were felt in areas exceeding several tens of thousands of square kilometers (about ten thousand square miles), and they produced effects such as cracked masonry and objects shaken from shelves. Pennsylvania also is shaken occasionally by earthquakes that originate outside the borders of the state. A number of small shocks occur each year within the borders of the state that are too small to be felt but that can be detected by seismographs in the region. This chapter focuses on the relationship of seismicity to geologic structure; the seismic hazard posed by Pennsylvania earthquakes is considered in Chapter 53.

THE INSTRUMENTAL RECORD OF PENNSYLVANIA SEISMICITY

Figure 27–1 shows epicenters of earthquakes that have been located using the arrival times of elastic waves recorded on seismographs. These epicenters should be the most reliable in the overall catalog of Pennsylvania earthquakes and therefore the most suitable for evaluating the relationship of earthquakes to geologic structure. Events that are known or strongly suspected of being explosions or mine cave-ins and whose effects are therefore not primarily to the release of tectonic strain energy have not been plotted. Also omitted from Figure 27–1 are earthquakes that occurred before the installation of adequate seismographs and whose epicenters must therefore be estimated from the distribution of shaking intensity as reflected in minor damage and human perceptions. Epicenters of felt, but instrumentally unrecorded, earthquakes are plotted in Figure 53–1 of Chapter 53.

The distribution of operating seismographs in and around Pennsylvania is shown in Figure 27–2.

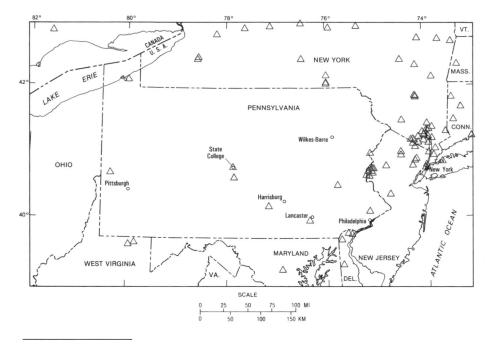

Figure 27-2. Locations of seismographs (triangles) in Pennsylvania and adjacent states in the mid-1990's.

These instruments should enable the estimation of epicenters of earthquakes occurring anywhere in Pennsylvania that have magnitudes of about 3 or more. Shocks of magnitude less than 3 are locatable where seismograph distribution is dense, but not throughout the state. The relative scarcity of earthquakes having magnitudes less than 3 in Pennsylvania compared with New Jersey (Figure 27-1) is in part a consequence of the lower density of seismographs in Pennsylvania. Figure 27-3 is an example of the seismograms that are analyzed to determine the location and time of a shock in the region.

ASSOCIATION OF PENNSYLVANIA EARTHQUAKES WITH TECTONIC PROCESSES AND GEOLOGIC STRUCTURE

The tectonic stresses that produce earthquakes in most source regions of Pennsylvania probably result principally from the forces that move or impede the North American plate. The orientation of the axis of maximum compressive stress is quite uniform over the interior of the North American plate and is approximately parallel to predicted plate-moving or plate-resisting stresses (Zoback and Zoback, 1981). Most Pennsylvania earthquakes probably represent slip along preexisting faults or zones of weakness that are so

oriented that tectonic shear stress is high across their planes. As in many other midplate regions, however, there is not a consensus on the geologic characteristics of these faults or on the conditions that have predisposed them to be seismogenic while other preexisting faults have not been seismogenic. Spatial variations in the elasticity of the crustal rock or in the ductility of the lower crust may perturb the overall midplate stress field so that some sites are more highly stressed than others. Variations in crustal pore-fluid pressure may cause some faults to be weaker than others.

Southeastern Pennsylvania has historically been the most seismically active part of the state. Earthquakes in this region occur principally on the margins of the Mesozoic Newark basin, in a zone of diffuse activity that extends into Delaware, New Jersey, and southern New York (Figure 27-1). Within the southeastern Pennsylvania part of this zone, smaller regions of persistent activity have been identified near Lancaster (Scharnberger and Howell, 1985; Armbruster and Seeber, 1987) and Philadelphia (Bischke, 1982).

In contrast to the situation in many plate-boundary regions, the earthquakes of southeastern Pennsylvania and vicinity apparently occur on faults that strike at a large angle to the first-order structural grain of the region. Seismographic data imply that the largest of these shocks in recent decades have involved slip on north-northeast- to northwest-striking planes in regions where the border faults of the Newark basin locally trend, respectively, east-west and northeast (Alexander and Stockar, 1984; Armbruster and Seeber, 1987). It is commonly thought that slip occurs preferentially on north-northeast- to northwest-trending faults because midplate shear stress is higher across faults of these orientations than across faults trending east-west and northeast. The individual seismogenic faults of southeastern Pennsylvania, however, have not been reliably identified. Faults suggested by seismographic data are not mapped at the ground sur-

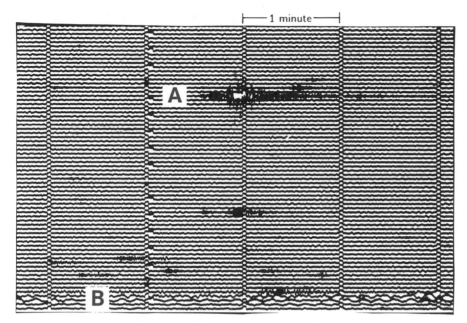

|—— 1 minute ——|

Figure 27-3. Section of a seismogram recorded at State College, Pa., on May 12, 1964. Each wiggly horizontal line represents the motion of the ground as a function of time. Displacements on the seismogram are approximately 100,000 times larger than the corresponding displacements of the ground itself. Time increases from left to right on each line, and the temporal order of the lines is from top to bottom. The large-amplitude wiggles following (to the right of) "A" represent the motion of the ground from a magnitude 3.2 earthquake that occurred north of Lancaster on May 12, 1964, at a distance of 135 km (84 mi) from the seismograph. "B" identifies several lines that record ground motions from a magnitude 5.3 earthquake in Alaska, 5,500 km (3,400 mi) from the seismograph.

face (Armbruster and Seeber, 1987), and there has never been an observation of tectonic fault rupture at the ground surface accompanying a Pennsylvania earthquake.

The Appalachian Plateaus and the Ridge and Valley provinces of Pennsylvania have had very low rates of earthquake activity in historic times. Earthquakes widely felt in northern and western Pennsylvania were centered in other states or Canada. Some of the events that have been cataloged as earthquakes in the Ridge and Valley or Appalachian Plateaus provinces were not tectonic earthquakes but mine explosions or ground settling caused by collapse of subsurface mines. For example, two episodes of mine subsidence caused appreciable damage in a neighborhood of Wilkes-Barre in February 1954 (Coffman and von Hake, 1973). Although such events are frequently included in earthquake catalogs, they are not indicative of current tectonism. The Clover Creek earthquake of July 15, 1938 (40.4°N/78.2°W), is an example of

a small, apparently tectonic, earthquake occurring in the Ridge and Valley province (Landsberg, 1938).

PROBLEMS AND FUTURE RESEARCH

In order to recognize potentially seismogenic faults that have not historically produced earthquakes, earth scientists must better characterize the faults that have produced earthquakes. The seismologist's contribution to the eventual solution of this problem will consist of accurate locations of earthquake epicenters and focal depths, which are necessary to determine the geographic locations of seismogenic structures, and well-constrained earthquake focal mechanisms, which are necessary to determine the strike, dip, and rake of seismogenic shear failure. Acquisition of these earthquake parameters will, in turn, require maintenance and, preferably, augmentation of the seismograph network in Pennsylvania and adjacent states.

RECOMMENDED FOR FURTHER READING

Beavers, J. E., ed. (1981), *Earthquakes and earthquake engineering: the eastern United States*, Ann Arbor, Mich., Ann Arbor Science Publishers, 2 v., 1,189 p.

Bolt, B. A. (1988), *Earthquakes,* San Francisco, W. H. Freeman and Company, 282 p.

Dewey, J. W., Hill, D. P., Ellsworth, W. L., and Engdahl, E. R. (1989), *Earthquakes, faults, and the seismotectonic framework of the contiguous United States,* in Pakiser, L. C., and Mooney, W. D., eds., *Geophysical framework of the continental United States,* Geological Society of America Memoir 172, p. 541–575.

Richter, C. F. (1958), *Elementary seismology*, San Francisco, W. H. Freeman and Company, 768 p.

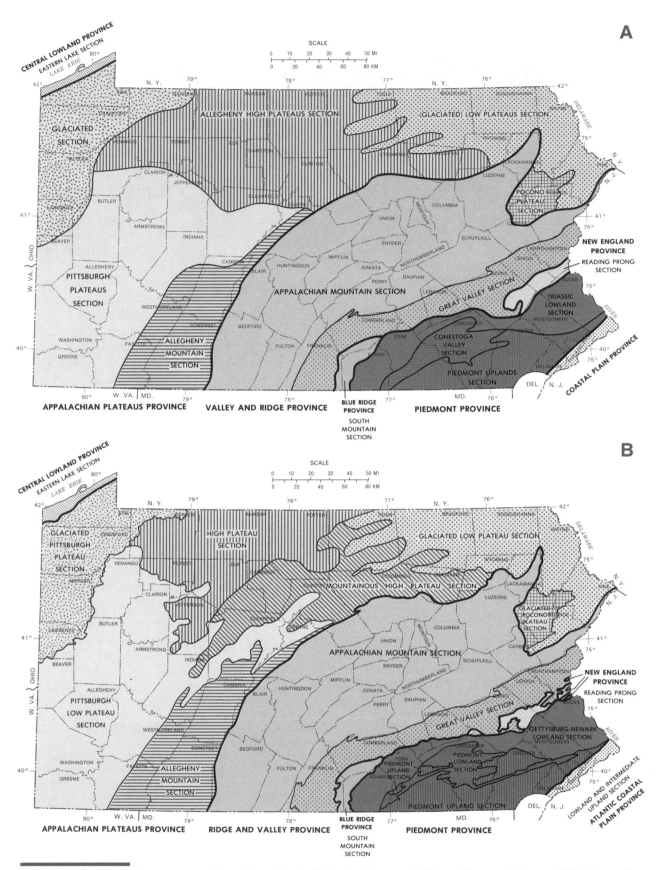

Physiographic maps of Pennsylvania (from Pennsylvania Geological Survey, 1962; and Berg and others, 1989). Two editions of Map 13 were published by the Pennsylvania Geological Survey at the time of this writing. The first edition (A), published in 1962, was superseded by the second edition (B) in 1989. The new version shows considerably greater detail, especially in the Appalachian Plateaus province, the Piedmont province, and the Reading Prong section. Another notable change is that the Triassic Lowland section was renamed the Gettysburg-Newark Lowland section.

Part V

PHYSIOGRAPHY

Pennsylvania's landscape is characterized by a clear and spectacular relationship between bedrock type and topography. This relationship was beautifully illustrated by Rogers (1858b, p. 919–927). In general, well-indurated sandstones and quartzites form the highest elevations, and carbonates almost universally underlie the lowest areas. Differential rates of weathering and erosion of the various rocks have produced the landscape of today, but the broad scope of landscape evolution in Pennsylvania has long been controversial.

Davis' (1889) classic paper "The Rivers and Valleys of Pennsylvania" was the first substantial discussion of Pennsylvania's landscape. His arguments for geographic cycles and peneplains generated decades of peneplain research (Sevon and others, 1983). Davis' proposed major peneplain remnants were (1) the Fall Zone (highest), (2) the Schooley, (3) the Harrisburg (or Chambersburg), and (4) the Somerville (lowest).

Theory required that these surfaces be (1) eroded to plains that had elevations near sea level, (2) uplifted, and (3) planated to lower elevation. Accordant summits at various elevations were inferred to be the remnants of former peneplains.

The concept of peneplanation fell into disrepute in the 1940's. Mathews (1975) concluded from the volume of offshore sediments that an average thickness of 2 km (1.2 mi) of rock had been removed from the Appalachians during the Cenozoic, thus discounting the survival of any peneplain. The principle of dynamic equilibrium (Hack, 1960, 1965), in which all elements of the landscape are adjusted to one another so that downwasting proceeds at the same rate on ridges, slopes, and lowland areas, has been the serious challenge to the peneplain concept.

Sevon (1985c, 1989c) presented an excellent review of the development of Pennsylvania's landscape. He argued that the current Appalachian landscape is polygenetic, with climate and isostatic rebound being the dominant controls of landscape evolution in Pennsylvania. The collection of papers in Gardner and Sevon (1989) is, as of this writing, the best available summary of geomorphic information for the Appalachians as a whole.

The chapters that follow contain discussions of the relationship between bedrock and topography in the various regions of Pennsylvania, and the problems specific to those regions.

—Noel Potter, Jr.

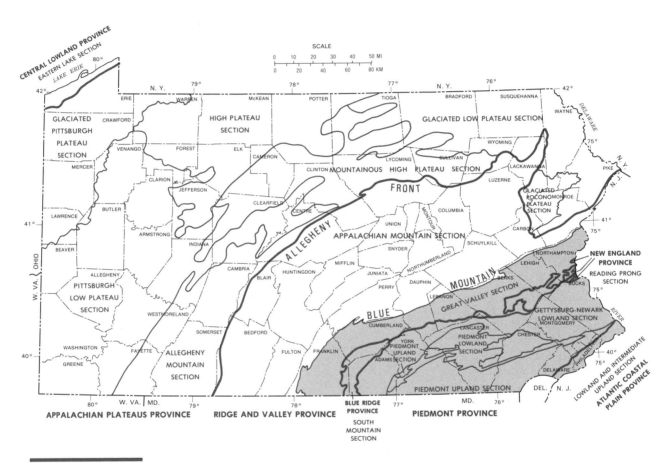

Figure 28–1. Map showing the physiographic provinces of Pennsylvania and the area covered by this chapter.

344

CHAPTER 28   SOUTHEAST OF BLUE MOUNTAIN

NOEL POTTER, JR.
Department of Geology
Dickinson College
Carlisle, PA 17013

INTRODUCTION

The major physiographic provinces in Pennsylvania southeast of Blue Mountain are shown in Figure 28–1. These provinces were defined by Fenneman (1938) and have been used by most workers since with only minor modification.

Since the late Mesozoic, differential erosion has produced a distinctive topography in each section, and sharp boundaries can be drawn between sections, or subprovinces, in most places. The relationships between lithology and topography are illustrated (a) in the *Atlas of Preliminary Geologic Quadrangle Maps of Pennsylvania* (Berg and Dodge, 1981), which shows geologic contacts superimposed on 7.5-minute topographic quadrangles for much of the state; or (b) by comparison of the 1:500,000-scale map *Rock Types of Pennsylvania* (Berg and others, 1984) with topographic maps of the same scale.

GREAT VALLEY SECTION

The Great Valley section of the Ridge and Valley province (see Figure 8 in the color section) is bounded on the west and north by Blue Mountain from the Maryland line to the Delaware Water Gap in Monroe County. On the east and south, the Valley is bounded, successively from Maryland to New Jersey, by South Mountain, the Gettysburg-Newark Lowland, and the Reading Prong, most of which stand in relief above the Valley.

The Ordovician Martinsburg Formation along the northern part of the Great Valley lies 700 to 1,500 feet lower than the more resistant sandstones of the Silurian Tuscarora Formation that underlies Blue Mountain. The northern third to two thirds of the valley is underlain by shale. These shale uplands are commonly 400 to 700 feet in elevation, and stream valleys cut 100 to 150 feet below that surface. In the eastern part of the valley, north of Allentown in Lehigh County, where there is slate rather than shale, the elevations and relief are 100 to 200 feet greater. These shale uplands commonly stand as much as 100 feet above the carbonate terrain to the south.

The southern part of the Great Valley is underlain by a thick sequence of Cambrian and Ordovician carbonates. There, the relief is somewhat less than on the shale, on the order of 50 to 100 feet, and elevations are commonly 400 to 500 feet. Higher elevations occur at drainage divides farthest from the major southeast-flowing rivers. Subdued karst topography is common on the carbonates, as discussed in Chapter 49A.

Minor variations in lithology, within both the shale and the carbonates, produce linear ridges. Sandy units within the shale stand out, and cherty and silicified units in the carbonates stand above the adjacent, more soluble, units. Drainage density is low on the carbonates but relatively high on the shales, because precipitation seeps below the surface of the carbon-

ates into solution passages and moves considerable distances underground to reemerge in springs. In contrast, on the relatively impermeable shales, a higher percentage of precipitation runs off directly on the surface.

SOUTH MOUNTAIN AND THE READING PRONG

South Mountain and the Reading Prong are similar in topography, and both are bounded by the Great Valley on the north. The South Mountain section, the northern extension of the Blue Ridge province into Pennsylvania, extends northward from the Maryland line to near Dillsburg, west of the Susquehanna River in western York County. Here, this complex anticlinorium plunges beneath younger Cambrian and Ordovician carbonates and Mesozoic rocks.

South Mountain is underlain by resistant quartzites of the Precambrian-Lower Cambrian Chilhowee Group and somewhat less resistant Precambrian metavolcanics (see Chapter 3B). The elevation of the crest is 1,800 to 2,000 feet. Locally, relief is as high as 800 to 1,400 feet within the South Mountain section.

The part of the Reading Prong section of the New England province that is in Pennsylvania (Figure 28–2) extends from Reading in eastern Berks County to the New Jersey line. It lies between the Great Valley and Gettysburg-Newark Low-

Figure 28–2. Reading Prong, Lehigh County. The forested ridge, looking west, is underlain by granitic gneiss. Saucon Valley, on the left, is underlain by Cambrian and Ordovician carbonates. The Great Valley, at the upper right, is also underlain by Cambrian and Ordovician carbonates. The flat-topped feature in the left center is the tailings area for the New Jersey Zinc Company's Friedensville mine (now closed), and the quarry in the lower left is part of the Ueberroth zinc mine (see Chapter 40D). Photograph courtesy of the Pennsylvania Department of Transportation.

land in a setting similar to that of South Mountain. A smaller outlier ("Little South Mountain") of the Reading Prong occurs at the junction of Lebanon, Lancaster, and Berks Counties. Both the Reading Prong and the outlier are cored by Precambrian granitic gneiss and Cambrian Hardyston quartzite (see Chapter 3B). Elevations in the Reading Prong are as great as 1,000 to 1,300 feet.

GETTYSBURG-NEWARK LOWLAND

The Gettysburg-Newark Lowland section of the Piedmont province extends from the Maryland line south of Gettysburg in Adams County eastward to Bucks County on the New Jersey line, and varies in width from 4 to 30 miles. The red sedimentary rocks of the Mesozoic basins include sandstones, siltstones, shales, and, locally, conglomerates (see Chapter 12A). Average elevations of these rocks are 450 to 550 feet, and relief is typically 100 to 150 feet. However, some of the more resistant units of hard shale and conglomerates rise to 800 to 1,200 feet. The resistant Hammer Creek Formation reaches elevations of 1,200 feet in northwestern Lancaster County and southeastern Lebanon County. Belts of contrasting lithologies, where tilted, commonly produce distinct parallel ridges.

The Mesozoic rocks are intruded by numerous thick sills and thin dikes of diabase (see Chapter 12B) that almost invariably stand out in relief above the adjacent sedimentary rocks. On larger intrusives, such as the Gettysburg pluton in Adams County, the Dillsburg pluton in northern York County, and the Quakertown pluton in Montgomery and Berks Counties, elevations can reach 1,000 to 1,300 feet and commonly are at least 900 feet. Some of the diabase dikes extend well outside the belt of Mesozoic strata, both to the north and, especially, to the south. The dikes commonly produce low ridges that stand a few tens of feet above adjacent rocks. Soils on the diabase are almost always stony, so that they are forested and easily recognizable on aerial photographs and satellite images.

PIEDMONT LOWLAND

The Piedmont Lowland section extends through northern Lancaster County and central York County, bounded on the north by the Gettysburg-Newark Lowland section and on the south by the Piedmont Upland section. It is underlain dominantly by Cambrian and Ordovician carbonates, but Precambrian-Lower Cambrian quartzites (Figure 28–3) and Ordovician shale are also present. The carbonates underlie lowland areas, typically at elevations of 300 to 400 feet, but

Figure 28–3. The Piedmont Lowland section along the Susquehanna River, looking south from near York Haven. The Hellam Hills on the right, in York County, are underlain by Precambrian-Lower Cambrian quartzites. The lowland on the left, in Lancaster County, is underlain by Cambrian carbonates. In the upper left corner, beyond the town of Marietta at the sharp bend in the river, is the famous Chickies Rock anticline (see Figures 4–7 and 4–8). Photograph courtesy of the Pennsylvania Department of Transportation.

are lower or higher depending on their distance from the Susquehanna River. As in the Great Valley, the shale terrain stands about 50 to 100 feet above the carbonates, and the Cambrian sandstones produce ridges as much as 400 to 500 feet above the adjacent carbonates. Subdued karst topography is common on the carbonates.

PIEDMONT UPLAND

The Piedmont Upland section extends from southern York County across the southeastern part of the state to southern Bucks County north of Philadelphia, and is bounded on the north by the Piedmont Lowland and Gettysburg-Newark Lowland sections and on the southeast by the Atlantic Coastal Plain province. The underlying complex of metamorphic rocks is dominated by schists and gneisses to the south and felsic igneous and metamorphic rocks in northern Chester County and near West Chester (see Chapter 3A). Upland elevations on the schists are typically 400 to 500 feet, but elevations in southern York County are as high as 1,000 feet. Locally, there is as much as 100 to 200 feet of relief between the schists and adjacent rock types. Relief on the schists in southern York and Lancaster Counties is as great as 300 to 450 feet (Figure 28-4).

East of Lancaster, Mine Ridge of the Piedmont Upland section rises 300 feet above the carbonate rocks of the Conestoga Valley of the Piedmont Lowland section to the north and west. South of Mine Ridge is Chester Valley of the Piedmont Lowland section (Figure 28-5), a prominent linear feature (see Chapter 16) that is 1 to 3 miles wide and extends from south-central Lancaster County 55 miles to southern Montgomery County north of Philadelphia. It is underlain by carbonates and is several hundred feet lower than the adjacent uplands. North of the Chester Valley, in northern Chester County, is the Honey Brook Upland of the Piedmont Upland section, which is underlain by Precambrian metamorphic and igneous rocks. Elevations in the Honey Brook Upland range from 550 to 900 feet.

ATLANTIC COASTAL PLAIN

A narrow belt of the Atlantic Coastal Plain province extends along the west side of the Delaware River through Philadelphia and southeastern Bucks and Delaware Counties (Figure 28-6). It is separated from the Piedmont Upland section by a jagged boundary. Coastal Plain sediments lap onto the Piedmont crystalline rocks and have been partly removed by fluvial erosion, resulting in an irregular border between sediments on ridges and crystalline rocks in valleys. Relief on the Coastal Plain is low. Tertiary and Quaternary gravels and sands occur at elevations up to 180 feet (Owens and Minard, 1975).

Figure 28-4. The Piedmont Upland section underlain by schist along the Susquehanna River south of Holtwood Dam, looking south. The Norman Wood Bridge carries Pa. Route 372 between York County, on the right, and Lancaster County. Photograph courtesy of the Pennsylvania Department of Transportation.

Figure 28–5. Chester Valley on the left, within the Piedmont Lowland section, is underlain by Cambrian-Ordovician Conestoga limestone at Parkesburg, Chester County, looking west. The ridge on the right is underlain by Precambrian-Lower Cambrian clastics in the foreground and Precambrian gneiss of the Mine Ridge anticline in the upper right. Photograph courtesy of the Pennsylvania Department of Transportation.

Figure 28–6. The Atlantic Coastal Plain, looking northwest toward Levittown, southeastern Bucks County. The foreground is underlain by Quaternary gravel, and the urban area is underlain by Tertiary sediments and islands of Wissahickon schist of the Piedmont Upland section. Photograph courtesy of the Pennsylvania Department of Transportation.

GEOMORPHOLOGY

It is ironic that more is known about the Paleozoic history than the late Mesozoic and Cenozoic history of the Appalachians. Reconstruction of the amount of rock removed from southeastern Pennsylvania is more difficult than for the Appalachian Mountain section to the north because of the uncertainties of thickness of the former Paleozoic cover where erosion has removed all but the Precambrian and earliest Paleozoic rocks. However, Poag and Sevon (1989) used the sedimentary deposits from the Atlantic continental margin to infer an erosional history for the central Appalachians. Braun (1989) used their data to calculate that more than 0.6 mile has been eroded from the Appalachians since the middle Miocene, and that an average of 390 to 490 feet has been removed during the Quaternary.

Some of the erosional history of southeastern Pennsylvania has recently been inferred from the following: (1) fluvial terrace deposits along the lower Susquehanna River, (2) carbonate residuum and overlying quartzitic gravel fans in the Great Valley, and (3) saprolite in the Piedmont.

Pazzaglia (1993) and Pazzaglia and Gardner (1993) mapped fluvial terraces along the lower Susquehanna River and correlated the terraces to dated Coastal Plain deposits. They distinguished upland terraces of middle to late Miocene age 260 to 460 feet above the present river channel and lower terraces of Pliocene to Pleistocene age up to 150 feet above the present channel. They used the warped terraces to infer flexural isostatic upwarping of the continental margin as the area beneath the Coastal Plain sank.

The process of downwasting of the carbonates in southeastern Pennsylvania is particularly complex. In the Great Valley, for example, low-pH rainwater runs off the siliceous quartzites of South Mountain with little chemical reaction, and when it reaches the carbonates at the base of the mountain runs deep underground to dissolve them. Classic karst topography and depths to bedrock of 100 to as much as 450 feet attest to the prolonged solution that has occurred there. Solution of the carbonates lowers the landscape and provides a trap for coarse alluvium washed from the quartzitic mountains. The coarse debris protects the fine-grained residuum of insolubles from subaerial removal and has preserved a thickness of well over 100 feet of these residual silts and clays in places. Sevon and others (1991) and Sevon (1994) illustrated the complexity of the downwasting processes at the Mainsville quarry south of Shippensburg, where clay residuum has been injected upward into the overlying gravels. Pierce (1965) described a site at the northwestern base of South Mountain at Pond Bank, Franklin County, where he inferred that a Late Cretaceous (Tschudy, 1965) lignite deposit rests on more than 170 feet of residuum. He used the insoluble residue content of the underlying rocks (about 10 percent) to infer that, in the process of accumulation, the residuum has been lowered more than 1,400 feet. This is considerably greater than the present height of South Mountain above the present floor of the Great Valley.

Alluvial gravels are common at the base of quartzitic ridges, particularly where they are trapped on weathering carbonates, such as at the base of South Mountain in the Great Valley. Some of these gravels may be as old as Late Cretaceous, for they overlie the Pond Bank lignite (Pierce, 1965) and clearly predate late Pleistocene or older sinkholes formed on their surfaces (Potter, 1985). Alluvial terrace gravels, often preserved only as a thin veneer of quartzite cobbles, occur up to 150 feet above many Great Valley streams that originate on quartzite ridges. The only recent study of these gravels is by Pierce (1966) in Franklin County. The gravels probably preserve a long record of stream incision, but the problem will be in dating the gravels.

Saprolites, from which soluble constituents have been removed, but in which insoluble constituents are still preserved, are common on uplands in the Piedmont. There are differences of opinion regarding the age of these saprolites. Cleaves and Costa (1979) inferred that some of the saprolites are relict from a past climate, whereas Pavich (1986) believed that saprolite development and removal are in dynamic equilibrium and are relatively young materials. The controversy was reviewed by Sevon (1988).

PROBLEMS AND FUTURE RESEARCH

Little is known of the detailed processes of weathering and erosion that have produced the topography of southeastern Pennsylvania. Some problems and questions that deserve more attention are as follows:

1. For each common rock type, what is the relative importance of removal and downwasting by solution compared to removal as particulate matter? Few studies of the detailed mechanisms of weathering and removal are available from Pennsylvania, and these pro-

cesses deserve careful description and quantification. The work of Bricker and others (1968) and Cleaves and others (1970) on weathering of the Wissahickon schist in the Piedmont province in Maryland suggests that chemical weathering there is considerably more important today than is mechanical weathering. The problem of measurement of modern denudation rates in the face of human activity, which overinflates inferred past denudation rates, is addressed by Sevon in Chapter 35. The controversy over the age of Piedmont saprolites should be resolved, for very different interpretations of Appalachian denudational history follow from the views of those on each side of the issue.

2. How long has it taken to produce the topography we now see? Has the topography been nearly as it is now since the late Mesozoic or early Cenozoic, or has it changed significantly through time? Is much of the topography we now observe relict from an earlier time (see Sevon, Chapter 35), or has it uniformly downwasted, as Hack (1960) suggested?

3. What has been the role of changing climate in producing the present landscape? Periglacial features such as block streams, sorted patterned ground, and tors have been identified on South Mountain (Clark, 1991). We know that, at least for the Quaternary, the climate changed during glaciation to the north, and there were probably climatic changes in the Mesozoic and earlier Cenozoic, too. Changing climate surely changed weathering and erosion rates, but it is difficult to distinguish climatic versus tectonic effects on erosion.

4. What is the relation between sediments preserved beneath the Atlantic Coastal Plain province and continental shelf and the inferred erosional history we have for the Appalachians? Too little attention has been paid to the connections between the two,

for most workers tend to devote their work to only one or the other. The studies of Pazzaglia (1993) and Pazzaglia and Gardner (1993) are a model for future work.

5. What has been the Cenozoic tectonic history of southeastern Pennsylvania? Little is known about Cenozoic rates and amounts of tectonic uplift in southeastern Pennsylvania, but Hack (1980, 1982) reviewed the evidence for differential uplift in the Piedmont and Blue Ridge and concluded that uplift occurred in the Piedmont in the Cenozoic. His evidence includes higher relief in some parts of the Piedmont than elsewhere, particularly in southern York County and adjacent areas in Maryland, the steep gradient beneath the Coastal Plain in that area, and major river profiles that steepen as they approach the Coastal Plain. His inferences are generally supported by Pazzaglia (1993) and Pazzaglia and Gardner (1993) along the lower Susquehanna, but what of elsewhere in southeastern Pennsylvania?

RECOMMENDED FOR FURTHER READING

Berg, T. M., and Dodge, C. M., compliers and eds. (1981), *Atlas of preliminary geologic quadrangle maps of Pennsylvania*, Pennsylvania Geological Survey, 4th ser., Map 61, 636 p.

Davis, W. M. (1889), *The rivers and valleys of Pennsylvania*, National Geographic Magazine, v. 1, no. 3, p. 183–253.

Gardner, T. W., and Sevon, W. D., eds. (1989), *Appalachian geomorphology,* Amsterdam, Elsevier, 318 p. [reprinted from Geomorphology, v. 2, no. 1–3].

Hack, J. T. (1965), *Geomorphology of the Shenandoah Valley, Virginia and West Virginia, and origin of the residual ore deposits*, U.S. Geological Survey Professional Paper 484, 84 p.

_____ (1980), *Rock control and tectonism—their importance in shaping the Appalachian highlands*, in *Shorter contributions to stratigraphy and structural geology, 1979*, U.S. Geological Survey Professional Paper 1126–B, p. B1–B17.

Sevon, W. D. (1989), *The rivers and valleys of Pennsylvania— Then and now*, Annual Geomorphology Symposium, 20th, Carlisle, Pa., 1989, Guidebook, Harrisburg Area Geological Society, 59 p.

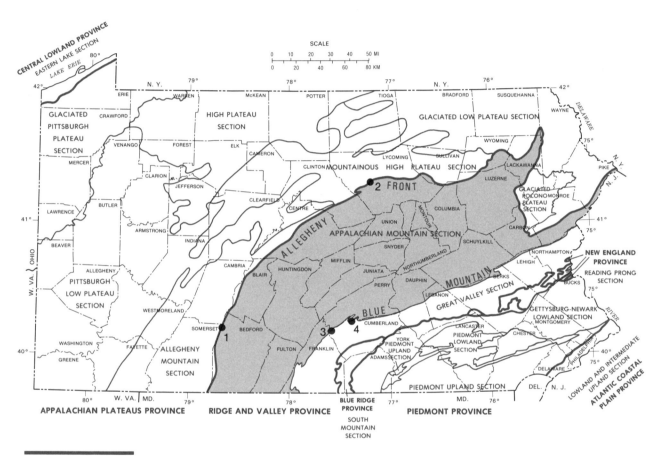

Figure 29–1. Map of Pennsylvania showing the location of the Appalachian Mountain section of the Ridge and Valley physiographic province (from Berg and others, 1989). Approximate locations are shown for the maps and cross sections in Figures 29–2 and 29–3 as follows: 1, Figure 29–2A; 2, Figure 29–2B; 3, Figure 29–3A; and 4, Figure 29–3B.

CHAPTER 29 APPALACHIAN MOUNTAIN SECTION OF THE RIDGE AND VALLEY PROVINCE

JOHN H. WAY
Department of Geology and Physics
Lock Haven University
Lock Haven, PA 17745

INTRODUCTION

The Endless mountains, so called from a translation of the Indian name bearing that signification...are not confusedly scattered and in lofty peaks overtopping one another, but stretch in long uniform ridges scarce half a mile perpendicular in any place above the intermediate vallies. Their name is expressive of their extent.... The mountains are almost all so many ridges with even tops and nearly of a height. To look from these hills into the lower lands is but, as it were, into an ocean of woods swelled and deprest here and there by little inequalities, not to be distinguished one part from another any more than the waves of a real ocean (Evans, 1755, p. 7–9).

This early description of the Appalachian Mountain section in Pennsylvania gives some indication of the aesthetic appeal that has drawn explorers, travelers, journalists, and scientists to these mountains. The Appalachian Highlands of eastern North America (Fenneman, 1938) has been one of the most intensely studied mountain belts in the world, and its Appalachian Mountain section stands as *the* model for orogenically deformed sedimentary rock sequences. Thornbury (1965) pointed to the marked parallelism of the ridges and valleys, streams running transverse to regional structure, striking trellis drainage patterns, accordant summit levels, and numerous wind and water gaps cutting resistant rock ridges as outstanding features characterizing the province (Figure 35–2). The Appalachian Mountain section occupies a truly unique position as a "source place and proving ground for concepts" that were first applied here and later adopted throughout the world (Mackin, 1938). It remains a classic area for geologic studies today.

EXTENT OF THE APPALACHIAN MOUNTAIN SECTION

The Ridge and Valley physiographic province (Figure 29–1), synonymous with the more general terms "folded Appalachians" or "folded belt," is subdivided into two sections, the Appalachian Mountain

A

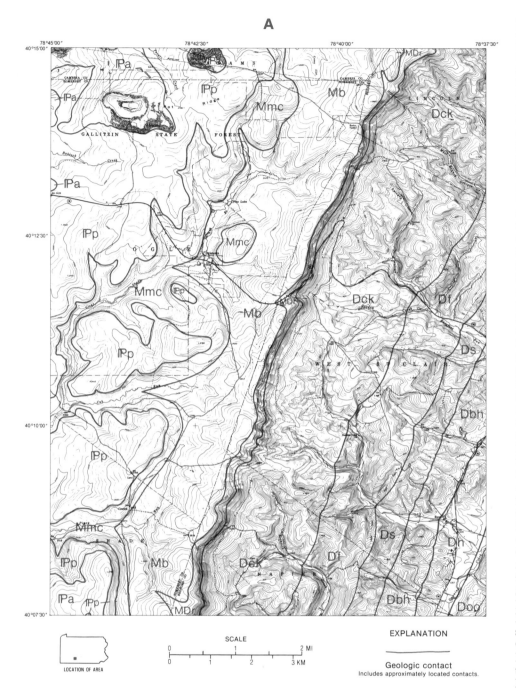

SCALE

LOCATION OF AREA

EXPLANATION

Geologic contact
Includes approximately located contacts.

Figure 29–2. The Allegheny Front, a major topographic escarpment, marks the northern and western boundary of the Appalachian Mountain section of the Ridge and Valley province in Pennsylvania. A. The geologic map of the Ogletown 7.5-minute quadrangle, Bedford, Cambria, and Somerset Counties, illustrates the topographic character of the Allegheny Front (see Figure 29–1) (slightly modified from Berg and Dodge, 1981, p. 435). In this region, the Front has developed on the Catskill Formation (Dck). Caprock sandstones of the Rockwell Formation (MDr) separate the gently dipping Mississippian and Pennsylvanian strata on the Plateau from the moderately to steeply dipping Devonian units of the Appalachian Mountain section. Doo, Onondaga and Old Port Formations, undivided; Dh, Hamilton Group; Dbh, Brallier and Harrell Formations, undivided; Ds, Scherr Formation; Df, Foreknobs Formation; Mb, Burgoon Sandstone; Mmc, Mauch Chunk Formation; IPp, Pottsville Formation; IPa, Allegheny Formation.

section, discussed here, and the Great Valley section, discussed in Chapter 28. The alternating ridges and valleys that make up the Appalachian Mountain section have developed on folded and faulted, unmetamorphosed rocks that extend 1,200 miles from New York to Alabama. A Paleozoic sedimentary sequence that reaches an estimated thickness of 40,000 feet underlies this region in east-central Pennsylvania (Colton, 1970, p. 13).

The topographic grain of the Appalachian Mountain section (Figure 35–2) reflects the trends of subparallel, plunging folds. In Pennsylvania, the trend of this fold belt changes from west-southwest (approximately 250 degrees) between New Jersey and the Susquehanna River to south-southwest (approximately 200 degrees) from the Susquehanna River to Maryland. Extending from the vicinity of New York City to southern Virginia, this pronounced curvature,

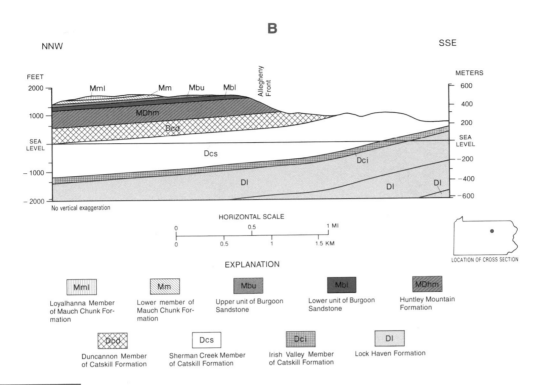

Figure 29-2. (Continued). B. A cross section drawn through the Allegheny Front in north-central Pennsylvania (modified from Faill and others, 1977b, Plate 1), approximately 10 miles northwest of Williamsport, Lycoming County (see Figure 29–1). The Front here is underlain by rocks of the Huntley Mountain Formation. The top of the lower cliff-forming unit of the Burgoon Sandstone marks the top of this escarpment.

called the Pennsylvania salient, is one of a series of arcs that are convex to the northwest along the length of the Appalachian chain.

The Appalachian Mountain section in Pennsylvania is about 230 miles long. About 45 miles wide near the Maryland border, it increases to a maximum width of almost 70 miles through central Pennsylvania and narrows to less than 2.5 miles in width for the Pennsylvania portion parallel to the Delaware River at the New Jersey border. The Allegheny Front, an east-southeast-facing topographic escarpment at the eastern edge of the Appalachian Plateaus province, bounds the section on the northwest (Figure 29–2). Blue Mountain, the first major ridge north and west of the Great Valley, forms much of the southern and eastern boundary of the section (Figure 29–3).

GENERAL CHARACTER OF THE SECTION

Henry Darwin Rogers, in his 1858 report as the first state geologist (Rogers, 1858b), devoted nearly half his introductory chapter to a description of the Appalachian Mountain chain. Beyond appreciating the

"extraordinary length, slenderness, evenness of summit and parallelism of [the] multitudinous crests or ridges" of this, his Second District, Rogers wove structural concepts into his geomorphic portraits: anticlinal waves of strata, synclinal coves, and large monoclinal ridges.

Rogers' picturesque descriptions characterize the Appalachian Mountain section as well as any worker since. In general, mountains are long, narrow, and even-crested. Intervening valleys are highly variable in width and elevation, and a trellis drainage pattern is well developed throughout the section. As folds plunge beneath the surface, resistant units converge upon themselves, resulting in fishtail, canoe-shaped, and zigzag topographic configurations (Figure 29–4).

The development of this landscape occurred primarily as a result of the evolution of the drainage systems. Multiple Pleistocene glacial advances subsequently modified a large part of the landscape in northeastern Pennsylvania. Since the retreat of the last ice sheet, the landscape appears to have undergone little change (Sevon, 1985c).

Both the composition and structure of the rock units played a major role in the shaping of the land-

A

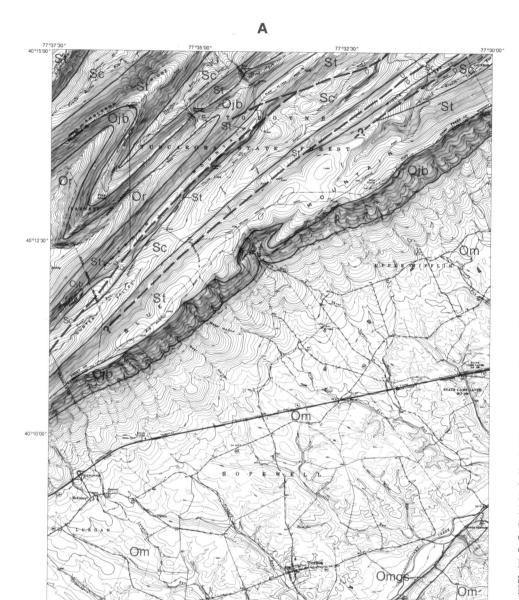

Figure 29-3. The southern boundary of the Appalachian Mountain section is marked by Blue Mountain, which separates it from the Great Valley section (discussed in Chapter 28) to the south and east. A. The geologic map of the Newburg 7.5-minute quadrangle, Perry, Cumberland, and Franklin Counties, illustrates the topographic character of Blue Mountain in the area just north of Shippensburg (see Figure 29-1) (from Berg and Dodge, 1981, p. 415). Here, the Ordovician Juniata and Bald Eagle Formations (Ojb) form a prominent southeast-facing escarpment, and the Silurian Tuscarora Formation (St) underlies the broad crest of the ridge. Omgs, Martinsburg Formation, shale and graywacke; Om, Martinsburg Formation; Or, Reedsville Formation; Sc, Clinton Group.

EXPLANATION

SCALE

LOCATION OF AREA

0   1   2 MI
0   1   2   3 KM

Geologic contact
Includes approximately
located contacts.

U
— — — — — — — ?
D
Fault
Location inferred; queried where uncertain.
U, upthrown side; D, downthrown side.

forms. Marked differences in resistance to weathering and erosion of the various lithologies account for differences in topographic relief. For example, coarse-grained, quartz-rich rocks form most of the prominent ridges of the section (Figure 29-5). From the Susquehanna River westward, the Silurian Tuscarora Formation (see introduction to Part X, p. 802) and underlying sandstones of the Ordovician Juniata and Bald Eagle Formations form the major ridges. The less resistant Cambrian and Ordovician carbonates, Silurian mudstones and limestones, and Devonian marine mudstones floor most valleys. Moderately resistant strata, including interbedded sandstone, siltstone, and mudstone sequences, and cherty and silicified units within the carbonates, underlie the minor ridges, foothills, and slopes. To the east, in the Anthracite region, the Mississippian Pocono and Pennsylvanian Pottsville sandstones and conglomerates are the ridge makers, and the siltstones and mudstones of the Mississippian Mauch Chunk Formation underlie the valleys.

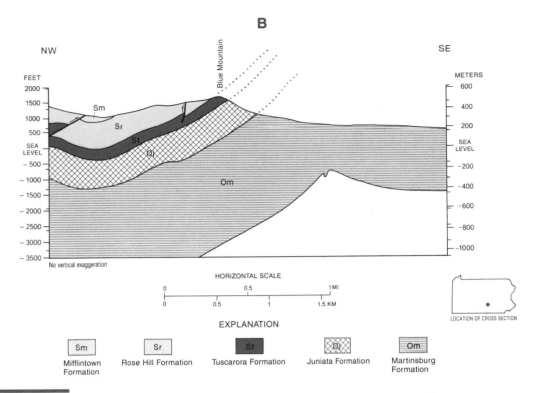

Figure 29–3. *(Continued).* **B. The structural relations of the stratigraphic units discussed in Figure 29–3A are shown in this geologic cross section drawn through Blue Mountain at the eastern margin of the Andersonburg 7.5-minute quadrangle, about 10 miles to the northeast of the Newburg area (see Figure 29–1) (from Miller, 1961, Plate 2).**

With the exception of the major trunk-stream valleys, the regional drainage pattern can be characterized as comprising long, straight stretches parallel to the structures and short stretches at right angles to them. This trellis pattern shows conspicuously, even in the road network, and occurs as a result of the alternating resistant and nonresistant folded strata within the section.

Ridge elevations generally decrease from the southwest (2,400 to 2,700 feet) to the northeast (1,600 to 1,900 feet), and from the Allegheny Front (2,000 to 2,700 feet) to Blue Mountain (1,600 to 2,400 feet). Valley elevations follow similar trends (740 to 420 feet in the southwest; 480 to 300 feet in the northeast). The lowest elevations in the section are at the Susquehanna River water gap through Blue Mountain north of Harrisburg, Dauphin County, and at the Delaware Water Gap through Kittatinny Mountain near Stroudsburg, Monroe County.

NOTEWORTHY ELEMENTS WITHIN THE SECTION

Two of the most prominent regions of the Appalachian Mountain section, the Nittany Valley and the Broad Top synclinorium, lie west of the main branch of the Susquehanna River. A third feature, the Anthracite region, lies between the Susquehanna and Lehigh Rivers and appears as a topographic contrast to the rest of the section.

Nittany Valley

The first fold southeast of the Allegheny Front, and the largest valley in the section in Pennsylvania, is the Nittany Valley (Figure 29–5). This 10-mile-wide valley extends along the western edge of the section for nearly 60 miles, from the vicinity of Altoona, Blair County, northeastward to near Lock Haven, Clinton County. The Nittany Valley, ranging in elevation from 800 to 1,500 feet, is underlain by complexly folded and faulted Cambrian and Ordovician carbonate rocks. Variably thick residual soils blanket much of the valley, and thicknesses of weathered mantle exceeding 365 feet have been documented (Parizek and White, 1985). Dolomitic rocks, some rich in chert and clastic quartz, underlie the broad, gently sloping valley uplands. These low-relief, strike-parallel hills range in elevation from 1,200 to 1,500 feet. The remaining parts of the valley parallel the surrounding ridge flanks as bands at elevations between 800 and 1,200 feet and

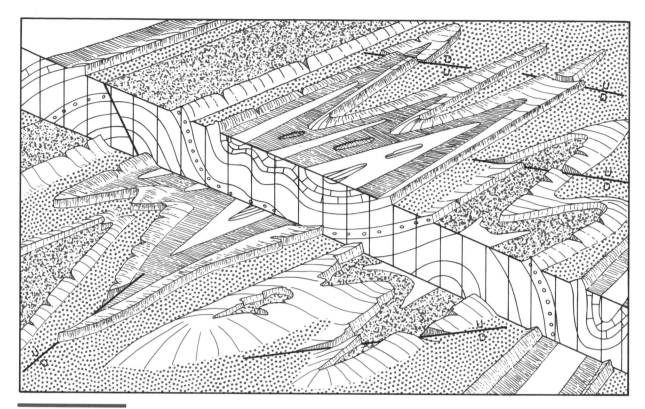

Figure 29–4. Block diagram showing the outcrop patterns that occur when plunging anticlines and synclines are eroded (modified from Lobeck, 1939, p. 598).

display greater evidence of karst topography. Pinnacles, surface sags and closed depressions, and sparse surface drainage characterize the cavernous limestones at the valley margins.

Most of the anticlinal valleys that dominate the region west of the Susquehanna River are geomorphologically similar to the Nittany Valley. With the exception of the westernmost valleys, where Cambrian and Ordovician carbonates are present, most of the valley lowlands are underlain by a thick succession of Middle Silurian through lower Middle Devonian rocks dominated by carbonates. These carbonates typically display a subdued karst topography, characterized by sinkholes and pinnacle weathering, but are much less well developed compared to the solution features formed in the valleys containing Cambrian and Ordovician carbonates. Some stratigraphic units—for example, the Silurian-Devonian Keyser Formation—are considerably more susceptible to solution weathering than others. Prominent, double-crested, quartz-rich sandstone ridges ranging from 2,000 to 2,400 feet in height surround the canoe-shaped lowlands.

Broad Top Synclinorium

South of the Nittany Valley and some 25 miles east of the Allegheny Front, in Bedford, Fulton, and

Huntingdon Counties, is the Broad Top synclinorium (Figure 29–5). It extends from Pennsylvania southward 250 miles into southern Virginia. This 10- to 20-mile-wide synclinal complex comprises gently folded Mississippian and Pennsylvanian strata dipping toward the center of the basin, surrounded by steeply dipping Devonian and older rocks.

The Broad Top is a high, dissected tableland of low relief. Its shape has been compared to that of the mesas of the southwestern United States (Gardner, 1913). However, unlike those mesas, it is not flat on top; elevations across the Broad Top range between 900 and 2,400 feet. Folding and subsequent erosion of the strata have left some of the more resistant Pennsylvanian-age sandstones standing as higher knobs and ridges surrounded by a dendritic stream network. An escarpment, developed in the softer strata of the Mauch Chunk Formation, accentuates the mesalike profile. Overall, the landscape, the coal-bearing strata, and the geologic structure give the Broad Top the appearance of a displaced portion of the Appalachian Plateaus province within the Appalachian Mountain section.

Anthracite Region

The Anthracite region occupies much of the Appalachian Mountain section east of the Susquehanna

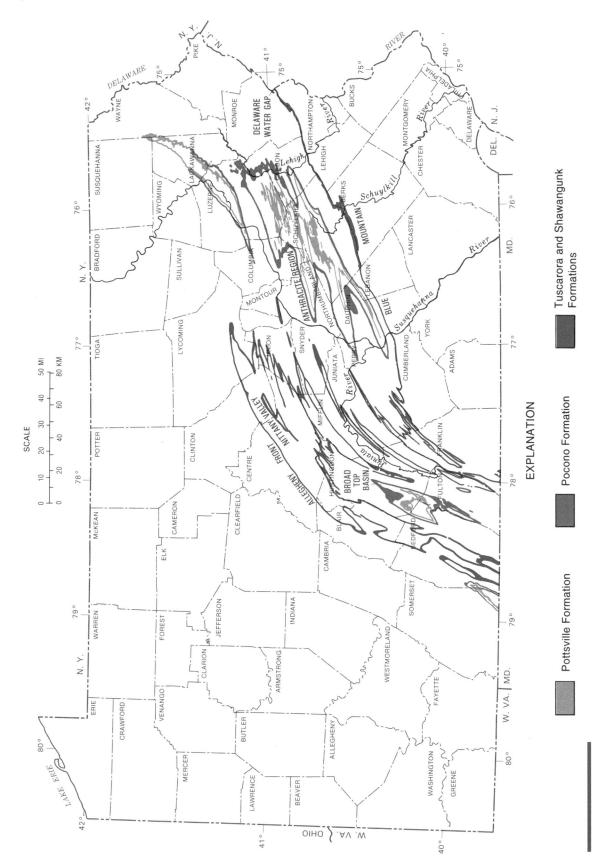

EXPLANATION

Pottsville Formation

Pocono Formation

Tuscarora and Shawangunk
Formations

Figure 29-5. Throughout the section, quartz-rich stratigraphic units underlie the major ridges (geologic units from Berg and others, 1980). West of the Susquehanna River, the Silurian Tuscarora Formation is the most extensive ridge former (the eastern limit of the Tuscarora is in Lebanon County; the stratigraphically equivalent Shawangunk Formation is mapped from Lebanon County to the Delaware River). East of the Susquehanna, the Mississippian Pocono Formation and the Pennsylvanian Pottsville Formation underlie the ridges and form a zigzag outcrop pattern around the anthracite basins.

River (Figure 29–5) and is characterized by a series of complexly deformed anticlinoria and synclinoria (Wood and Bergin, 1970). Set in a structural depression between the Juniata culmination to the west (Gwinn, 1970) and the gently deformed rocks of the Pocono Plateau to the east, the region is dominated by clastic Devonian- through Pennsylvanian-age rocks at the surface. The apparent anomalous preservation of the younger Pennsylvanian rocks in this part of the folded belt reflects the decreasing plunge of the folds to the northeast and the southwestward-plunging basement (Faill, 1985b).

Topography in this part of the section, especially in Schuylkill County and southern Luzerne County, is unusual compared to the rest of the folded belt. The major ridge tops are extremely broad, have low relief, and take on a plateaulike appearance. Intensely faulted rocks of the Pocono and Pottsville Formations form these broad, anticlinal ridges (Figure 29–5), which have elevations ranging from 1,500 to 1,700 feet. Intervening valleys display parallel, riblike configurations of resistant rock units but lack the continuous, elongated nature so characteristic of the valleys to the southwest. Underlain by the less resistant rocks of the Mauch Chunk Formation, these valleys vary in elevation from 500 to 900 feet. When viewed from the air, the topography of this region appears blurred in contrast to the sharp ridge crests and parallel valleys and ridges that characterize the rest of the section. Variations in lithology, structure, degree of glacial imprint, and response to weathering between the regions may account for this apparent dissimilarity. Another factor, the large amounts of high-quality anthracite occurring throughout this region, may indirectly contribute to this contrast. As a result of more than 150 years of mining activities, culm banks (waste), deeply scarred terrain, and hundreds of small lakes have been created and remain as significant modifications to this landscape.

WATER AND WIND GAPS

Sporadic breaks in ridges, water gaps and wind gaps, are historically notable and inherently interesting features occurring throughout this section. The Delaware Water Gap, cut by the Delaware River through Kittatinny Mountain along the eastern margin of Pennsylvania (see Chapter 57 and Figure 31 in the color section), has received much attention and is considered one of the most attractive because of the sinuous course the river has taken through the folds and the rocky, steep-walled gap it has carved. Other large, yet less spectacular, water gaps occur where the Lehigh, Schuylkill, and Susquehanna Rivers have cut through Blue Mountain at nearly right angles.

Marking the positions of abandoned stream courses, wind gaps occur at various elevations and have an irregular distribution. The one named "Wind Gap" has been referred to as the "finest example of a wind gap in the Northern Appalachians" (Ver Steeg, 1930). It breaches Blue Mountain a few miles southwest of the Delaware Water Gap.

Ideas related to gap formation are integral parts of theories explaining Appalachian landform evolution. Chance location, superposition from earlier drainages (Johnson, 1931), position control by structure and topography inherited from Permian-initiated drainage (Myerhoff and Olmsted, 1936), and headward piracy accompanying northwestward-moving drainage divides (Thompson, 1949) are among the explanations proposed for the gaps. Most recently, a detailed study by Epstein (1966) of six gaps in the Stroudsburg area of Monroe County, including both the Delaware Water Gap and Wind Gap, suggested that structure was the effective control in determining the location of the gaps.

THEORIES OF APPALACHIAN GEOMORPHOLOGY

The fascination with Appalachian Mountain geomorphology over the years has resulted in the creation of numerous models by geologists attempting to explain the development of the landscape. Well-known geologists, including Davis, Johnson, Meyerhoff, Thompson, and Hack, have contributed theories and generated vigorous debate. The main concepts of these models are summarized by Potter at the beginning of Part V.

Most analyses of Appalachian landform evolution in the 1970's and 1980's stressed the importance of tectonism and climate. These aspects were either ignored or assumed to be inconsequential by earlier workers. Both seismic activity and vertical crustal movements, although modest in comparison to active plate boundaries, have been documented throughout the Appalachian fold belt (Brown and Oliver, 1976). These data challenge the assumptions of earlier workers that extensive erosion surfaces resulted from prolonged periods of tectonic quiescence. Furthermore, repeated changes in climate, often to extremes, have been shown to produce significant modifications to the landscape (Budel, 1982). Late Cretaceous kaolinite, bauxite, iron ore deposits, and thick saprolites of the Nittany Valley (Parizek and White, 1985) contrast with Pleistocene glacial and periglacial features less than 47 miles to the northeast, attesting to such paleoclimatic extremes.

When viewed in its totality, the present Appalachian landscape comprises landforms and deposits that do not appear to be attributable to any one evolutionary scheme, no matter how complex or integrated that synthesis may be. Sevon (1985b, c) characterized the geomorphology of this region as polygenetic, that is, having been produced by many geologic processes and environments, each operating within a framework of varying diastrophic activity and more than one climatic condition for an unknown period of time. It is likely, then, that future research dealing with the geomorphology of this classic region will include such considerations.

PROBLEMS AND FUTURE RESEARCH

With the recognition that tectonics and climate play a significant role in geomorphic interpretations, qualitative studies focusing upon these subjects may prove fruitful in future investigations. Recently, workers have given greater attention to the varied surficial deposits throughout the section. What climatological information can these deposits provide about the processes and rates of the physical and chemical breakdown of rocks? Do local concentrations of clays, iron- and aluminum-rich sediment, residual soils and their insoluble residues, or thick saprolites have information to offer? Can multiple soil horizons and organic accumulations within residual soils be correlated from region to region, and what can serve as keys to this correlation? Are these keys present in datable deep-sea marine sediments or ice cores? Does the Mesozoic-Cenozoic post-rifting clastic wedge, the Atlantic Coastal Plain, contain clues that could be used in reconstructing the tectonic and weathering history of the region?

RECOMMENDED FOR FURTHER READING

Davis, W. M. (1909), *Geographical essays*, Boston, Ginn and Co., 777 p.

Fenneman, N. M. (1938), *Physiography of eastern United States*, New York, McGraw-Hill, 714 p.

Flemal, R. C. (1971), *The attack on the Davisian system of geomorphology, a synopsis*, Journal of Geological Education, v. 19, p. 3–13.

Melhorn, W. N., and Flemal, R. C., eds. (1975), *Theories of landform development*, Binghamton, N. Y., State University of New York, Annual Geomorphology Symposia Series, 6th, Proceedings, p. 1–68, 129–143.

Oberlander, Theodore (1965), *The Zagros streams: a new interpretation of transverse drainage in an orogenic zone*, Syracuse University, Department of Geology, Syracuse Geographical Series 1, 168 p.

Sevon, W. D., Potter, Noel, Jr., and Crowl, G. H. (1983), *Appalachian peneplains: an historical review*, in Jordan, W. M., ed., *History of geology and geological concepts in the northeastern United States*, Earth Sciences History, v. 2, p. 156–164.

Twidale, C. R. (1976), *Analysis of landforms*, Sydney, John Wiley and Sons Australasia Pty., Ltd., 572 p.

Wood, G. H., Jr., Trexler, J. P., and Kehn, T. M. (1969), *Geology of the west-central part of the Southern Anthracite field and adjoining areas, Pennsylvania*, U.S. Geological Survey Professional Paper 602, 150 p.

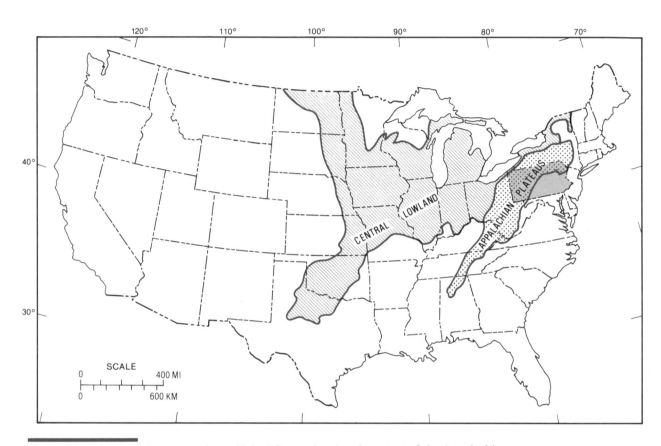

Figure 30–1. Map of the conterminous United States showing the extent of the Appalachian Plateaus province and the Central Lowland province relative to Pennsylvania (modified from Lewis, 1977, p. 906). Adapted with permission from "United States of America" in *Encyclopædia Britannica,* 15th edition, © 1978 by Encyclopædia Britannica, Inc.

362

CHAPTER 30

APPALACHIAN PLATEAUS PROVINCE AND THE EASTERN LAKE SECTION OF THE CENTRAL LOWLAND PROVINCE

REGINALD P. BRIGGS
Geomega, Inc.
101 Algonquin Road
Pittsburgh, PA 15241

APPALACHIAN PLATEAUS PROVINCE

The Appalachian Plateaus province extends northeastward from Alabama into New York (Figure 30–1). In Pennsylvania, this province occupies more than 26,000 square miles, almost 60 percent of the area of the state, including all or parts of 41 of its 67 counties (Figure 30–2). The northwestern boundary of the province in Pennsylvania is the prominent scarp in Erie County that drops 300 to 600 feet to the Eastern Lake section of the Central Lowland province. The impressive Allegheny Front is the southeastern boundary across most of Pennsylvania, from the Maryland border to the termination of the Front in northern Luzerne County. Macfarlane (1873, p. 102–104) provided an early description of the Front and its hinterland that, even today, cannot be much improved upon. With his focus on coal, he wrote the following:

> The most important feature of the North-American Continent in connection with our subject is the Alleghany Mountain...which contains, or rather is the eastern boundary of, the largest...of the coal-regions. The whole length of this mountain is about 1,300 miles...the most remarkable peculiarity about this mountain is the great regularity of outline of the east or southeast summit of the ridges. It is not of an unusual height...being usually about 1,000 feet above the adjoining valley...but it pursues a remarkably straight course, sometimes hardly diverging from a straight line for a distance of 50 or 60 miles. Throughout its entire length it pursues a uniformly northeast course, and from the North Branch of the Susquehanna in Pennsylvania to the line between Tennessee and Alabama...it is one continuous, unbroken range of high table-land...and throughout this whole length there is no clean cut through the range.... [It is] parallel with the Appalachian Mountain-chains east of it, many of whose ridges rise within its borders and insulate valleys of the coal-bearing strata.

From the Allegheny Front for a short distance through northeastern Luzerne County, the provincial boundary is obscure. Thereafter, it follows a

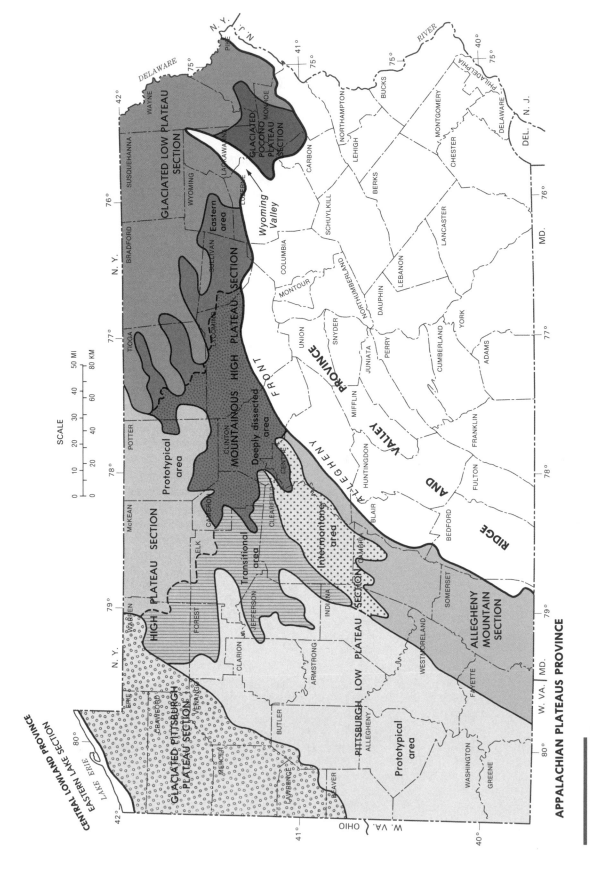

Figure 30–2. Map of Pennsylvania showing the locations and names of sections and areas of the Appalachian Plateaus province, and the Eastern Lake section of the Central Lowland province.

generally well-defined but erratic course along escarpments that enclose the Wyoming Valley prong of the Ridge and Valley province, circle the southern part of the Glaciated Pocono Plateau, and ultimately resume a northeasterly trend through Pike County and into New York (Figure 30–2). The Appalachian Plateaus province in Pennsylvania currently is divided into seven sections, as shown in map B (Berg and others, 1989) in the introduction to Part V (p. 342). Comparing map B with Figure 30–2, the reader will note some differences in delineation of sections of this province. These chiefly arise from the methods used in defining sections. Boundaries of sections shown in Figure 30–2 were mostly based on topographic comparisons illustrated in Figures 30–3, 30–4, and 30–5. The reader will further note that the similarities between section boundaries of map B and Figure 30–2 are greater than the differences, particularly when the gradational nature of boundaries between sections and provinces is taken into account. In addition, for the purpose of this chapter, three of the sections are subdivided, each into two parts, making a total of 10 descriptive units (Figure 30–2). The upland Plateau surfaces of these sections everywhere are more than 1,200 feet above sea level, except in the extreme northwest part of the state adjacent to the Eastern Lake section. They range upward in regionally gentle and locally abrupt increments to extensive areas of high plateaus and mountain ridges well in excess of 2,000 feet (Figure 30–3). Within individual sections, high and low upland surface elevations generally differ by 400 feet or less; the maximum range is about 700 feet in the Allegheny Mountain section (Figure 30–4). Absolute maximum elevations in the sections are obscured in Figure 30–3 by generalization. They range from about 1,800 feet in the Prototypical area of the Pittsburgh Low Plateau section to 3,213 feet in the Allegheny Mountain section (Table 30–1).

All sections of the province have undergone uplift and dissection, but only in the Mountainous High Plateau section does depth of dissection greater than 800 feet generally prevail. Sizable areas having less than 400 feet of local relief are present in all sections except the Prototypical area of the High Plateau section and the Mountainous High Plateau section (Figure 30–5). In most sections, local relief generally varies by 400 feet or less (Figure 30–4). Gross relief of most sections ranges from 1,100 to 1,800 feet but is about 2,300 feet in both the Allegheny Mountain and Glaciated Low Plateau sections. Total relief in the province in Pennsylvania is about 2,780 feet, from Mount Davis to the Delaware River (Table 30–1).

The predominant bedrock stratigraphy in the province ranges from Upper Devonian in the Glaciated Po-cono Plateau and Glaciated Low Plateau sections to Pennsylvanian and Permian in the Prototypical area of the Pittsburgh Low Plateau section (Table 30–2). Relatively high resistance to erosion characterizes units from the Mississippian-Devonian Huntley Mountain and Rockwell Formations upward to the Pennsylvanian Pottsville Formation. Areas in which these rocks are exposed generally are higher than areas in which younger Pennsylvanian and Permian strata predominate in outcrop, though the change in elevation is gradational. In contrast, the contact between the Huntley Mountain Formation and the more readily eroded Upper Devonian Catskill Formation is on escarpment faces.

Geologic structure is an important factor in defining most sections, particularly in the high and strongly folded Allegheny Mountain section. Lesser degrees of folding are significant in differentiating other sections. Where folds are of very low amplitudes and strata are close to horizontal, upland surfaces are nearly horizontal true plateaus, as in the Prototypical area of the Pittsburgh Low Plateau section (Figures 30–6 and 30–7) and the Glaciated Pittsburgh Plateau section. Some faults also occur in the province, but these largely are not well expressed topographically and are unimportant to general physiographic description (Table 30–2). Joints, however, seem well expressed in some areas by linear segments of rivers and streams, though Ferguson (1967) has cast doubt on whether this really is control by jointing in the conventional sense. Many apparently joint-controlled stream segments are parallel or normal to fold axes, as is expectable, but others have divergent orientations. Examples of the former are many short reaches and the general northwesterly trace of the Kiskiminetas and Conemaugh Rivers through the Prototypical area of the Pittsburgh Low Plateau section. The latter are illustrated by the alternating, generally north-south and east-west segments of the Allegheny River northeast of Pittsburgh (Figure 30–6).

The Appalachian Plateaus province in Pennsylvania chiefly is drained by four master streams to widely divergent waters of the Atlantic Ocean (Figure 30–8). In order of approximate basin area in the plateaus in Pennsylvania, they are the Ohio River via the Mississippi River to the Gulf of Mexico (15,600 square miles); the Susquehanna River to Chesapeake Bay (8,000 square miles); the Delaware River to Delaware Bay (2,000 square miles); and Lake Erie and the Genesee River via Lake Ontario to the St. Lawrence River and the Gulf of St. Lawrence (400 square miles).

Sections of the province are presented in Figures 30–2 and 30–4 and in Tables 30–1 and 30–2 and are discussed below in order from the east westward to the High Plateau section. The remaining order is chiefly based on comparability.

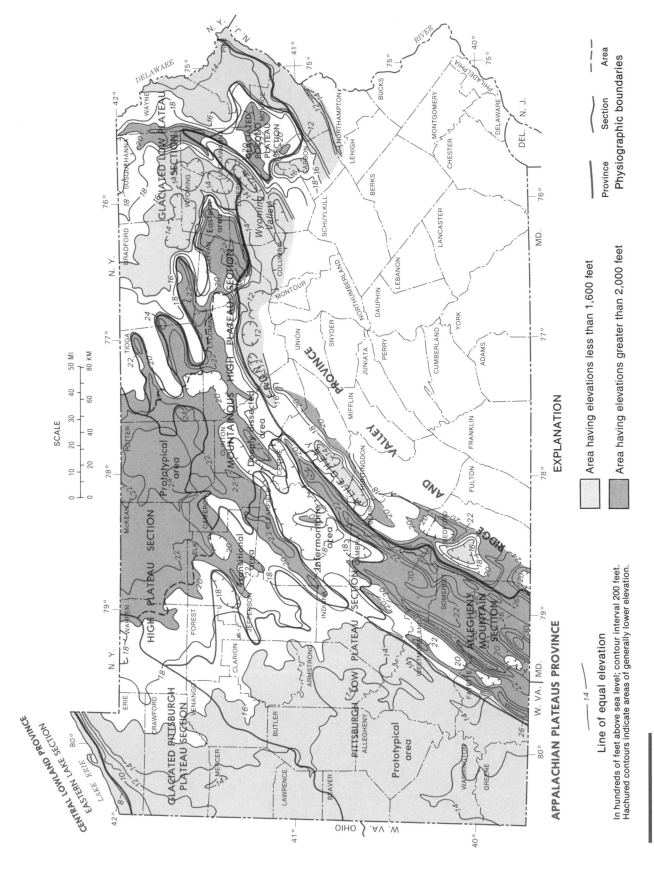

Figure 30–3. Map of Pennsylvania showing generalized topography of the upland surface in the Appalachian Plateaus province, Eastern Lake section of the Central Lowland province, and adjacent parts of the Ridge and Valley province. This map was first prepared at scale 1:500,000 by joining equal contours of areas 5 miles or less apart, a level of generalization that suppressed most river and stream valleys while retaining most of the important features of the upland surface.

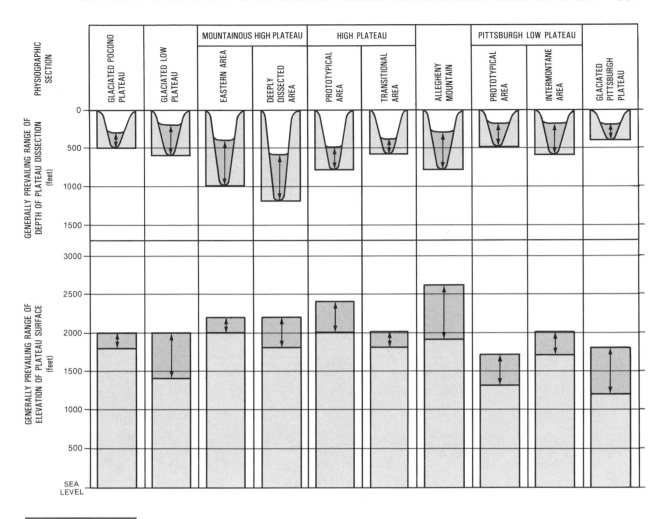

Figure 30–4. Graphs showing generally prevailing ranges of elevation and depths of dissection (i.e., local relief) of the Appalachian Plateaus province in Pennsylvania. Arrows indicate ranges.

Glaciated Pocono Plateau Section

The Glaciated Pocono Plateau section is the smallest and most homogeneous of the sections, is bounded on almost all sides by escarpments, and is essentially defined by the 1,800-foot contour on Figure 30–3. The large-scale pattern of drainage is rectangular. The headwaters of the Lehigh River are parallel to the northeast-trending, synclinal Wyoming Valley (Figure 30–8), and some tributaries are normal to the syncline. Overprinted on this is a loose dendritic pattern with a general north-south emphasis that is a result of glacial action. The Wisconsinan Woodfordian terminal moraine occupies the south edge of the section. With generalized relief mostly around 400 feet, the overall aspect of the section is a monotonous rolling upland characterized by sparse outcrops, numerous boulders, sandy soil, and small ponds and swamps.

Glaciated Low Plateau Section

Trending north from the northern end of the Wyoming Valley to the New York State line is a relatively small (about 200 square miles) part of the Glaciated Low Plateau section that has affinities to the Glaciated Pocono Plateau in both upland elevation and relief (Figures 30–3 and 30–5). It contains Elk Hill, Mount Ararat (Table 30–1), and other monadnocks. This zone divides the 4,100-square-mile Glaciated Low Plateau section into an eastern part, in which the generalized upland surface falls away almost imperceptibly to the Delaware River, and a large western part, chiefly draining similarly to the "North Branch" Susquehanna River. Glacial action has resulted in a modified rectangular to dendritic pattern of drainage elongated generally north-south. Streams flowing north or south are offset laterally toward the

Table 30-1. *Approximate Areas, Maximum and Minimum Elevations, and Gross Relief in the Sections of the Appalachian Plateaus Province in Pennsylvania*

Glaciated Pocono Plateau section—800 square miles
    Highest point—Big Pine Hill in western Lackawanna County .... 2,291 feet
    Lowest point—indefinite, in the headwaters of the Lehigh River in Luzerne County........................ ~1,200 feet
    Gross relief .... ~1,100 feet

Glaciated Low Plateau section—4,100 square miles
    Highest point—Elk Hill in southeastern Susquehanna County, the highest point in eastern Pennsylvania   2,698 feet
    Second highest point—Mount Ararat in northwestern Wayne County.. 2,669 feet
    Lowest point—Delaware River near Matamoras, Pike County .... ~430 feet
    Gross relief .... ~2,270 feet

Mountainous High Plateau section—Eastern area—900 square miles
    Highest point—North Mountain at west end of Huckleberry Mountain ridge, southern Sullivan County   2,593 feet
    Northern high point—Armenia Mountain in easternmost Tioga County .... 2,458 feet
    Lowest point—indefinite, on a number of streams draining the section .... ~1,000 feet
    Gross relief .... ~1,600 feet

Mountainous High Plateau section—Deeply Dissected area—2,100 square miles
    Highest point—slopes of Cedar Mountain, southwestern Tioga County .... ~2,400 feet
    Lowest point—West Branch Susquehanna River, near Lock Haven, Clinton County .... ~570 feet
    Gross relief .... ~1,800 feet

High Plateau section—Prototypical area—2,100 square miles
    Highest point—Cobb Hill, at the common junction of the Allegheny, Genesee, and Susquehanna River
      basins in Potter County .... 2,608 feet
    Lowest point—indefinite, near Kinzua Dam on the Allegheny River in Warren County and other valleys . ~1,300 feet
    Gross relief .... ~1,300 feet

High Plateau section—Transitional area—2,300 square miles
    Highest point—at lookout tower near Brockway Reservoir, southernmost Elk County .... 2,372 feet
    Lowest point—Allegheny River near Tidioute, Warren County.. ~1,100 feet
    Gross relief .... ~1,300 feet

Allegheny Mountain section—2,800 square miles
    Highest point—Mount Davis, in southern Somerset County, the highest point in Pennsylvania .... 3,213 feet
    Second highest point—Blue Knob, an anomalous feature on the curvilinear Allegheny Front, northwest-
      ern Bedford County .... 3,136 feet
    Lowest point—Youghiogheny River near South Connellsville, Fayette County .... ~910 feet
    Gross relief .... ~2,300 feet

Pittsburgh Low Plateau section—Prototypical area—6,500 square miles
    Highest point—indefinite, on slopes leading to adjacent higher sections .... ~1,800 feet
    Lowest point—Ohio River at the junction of Pennsylvania, Ohio, and West Virginia, Beaver County... ~665 feet
    Gross relief .... ~1,150 feet

Pittsburgh Low Plateau section—Intermontane area—1,100 square miles
    Highest point—indefinite, on slopes leading to adjacent higher sections .... ~2,000 feet
    Lowest point—West Branch Susquehanna River east of Clearfield, Clearfield County .... ~900 feet
    Gross relief .... ~1,100 feet

Glaciated Pittsburgh Plateau section—3,600 square miles
    Highest point—west of Youngsville, northwestern Warren County.. 1,994 feet
    Lowest point—Beaver River near Koppel, Beaver County .... ~730 feet
    Gross relief .... ~1,250 feet

Appalachian Plateaus province—26,300 square miles
    Highest point—Mount Davis, Somerset County.. 3,213 feet
    Lowest point—Delaware River near Matamoras, Pike County .... ~430 feet
    Gross relief .... ~2,780 feet

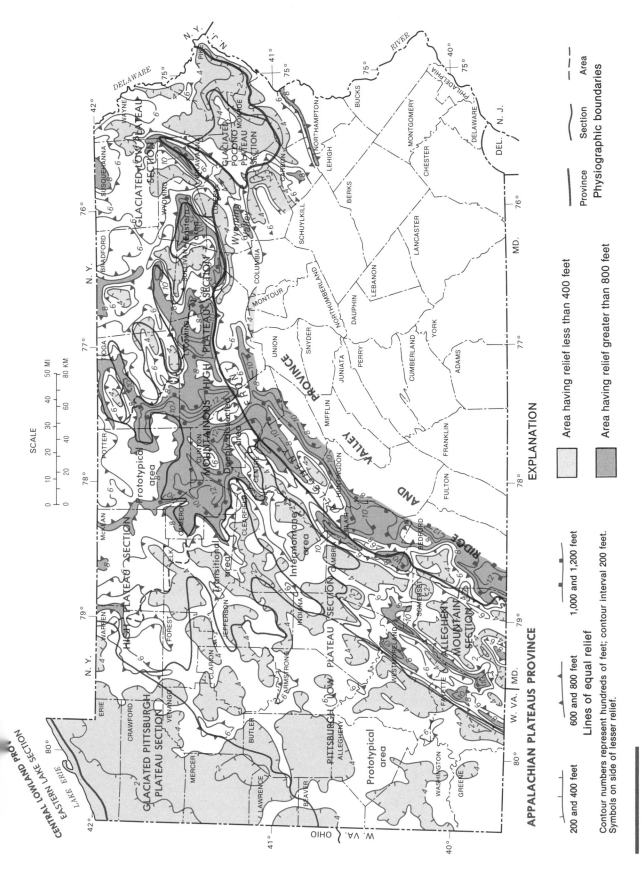

Figure 30-5. Map of Pennsylvania showing generalized local relief, or depth of dissection of the upland surface, in the Appalachian Plateaus province, Eastern Lake section of the Central Lowland province, and adjacent parts of the Ridge and Valley province. This map was first prepared at scale 1:500,000 by comparing the original map of Figure 30-3 with a map in which equal contours were joined where they crossed perennial streams 5 miles or less apart. Differences in elevation between the generalized base level of the latter and the generalized upland surface of the former were contoured to yield generalized local relief.

Table 30–2. *Bedrock Stratigraphy, Structure, and Geomorphic Factors in Development of the Sections of the Appalachian Plateaus Province in Pennsylvania*

Section	Predominant bedrock stratigraphy[1]	Geologic structure at the surface[1]	Predominant geomorphic factors
Glaciated Pocono Plateau	Upper Devonian Catskill Fm.	Gentle east-northeast-trending folds that decrease in amplitude toward the east.	Isolated high plain on the divide between the Susquehanna and Delaware Rivers, mostly bordered by cliff-forming units; glacial scour and deposition.
Glaciated Low Plateau	Upper Devonian Catskill and Lock Haven Fms.	East-northeast-trending folds in the western part, curving to the north parallel to, and becoming gentler away from, the Wyoming Valley prong of the Ridge and Valley province.	Preglacial major drainage patterns(?); glacial scour and deposition; postglacial erosion.
Mountainous High Plateau—Eastern area	Pennsylvanian Pottsville Fm. Mississippian Mauch Chunk, Burgoon, and Pocono Fms. Mississippian-Devonian Huntley Mountain Fm. Upper Devonian Catskill Fm.	Relatively broad, east-northeast-trending folds that decrease in amplitude northward.	Synclinal highlands, mostly surrounded by escarpments of cliff-forming units, probably largely isolated by preglacial erosion; glacial scour and deposition; postglacial erosion.
Mountainous High Plateau—Deeply Dissected area	Pennsylvanian Allegheny and Pottsville Fms. Mississippian Burgoon Fm. Mississippian-Devonian Huntley Mountain Fm. Upper Devonian Catskill Fm.	Relatively broad, northeast- to east-northeast-trending folds that decrease in amplitude northwestward. A few faults, normal to folds.	Fold-mountain ridges, chiefly anticlinal, more synclinal toward the east-northeast because of variations in erodibility of exposed rocks; deep dissection by the West Branch Susquehanna River and tributaries before, during, and after glaciation; strong structural control both parallel and normal to fold trends.
High Plateau—Prototypical area	Pennsylvanian Pottsville Fm. Mississippian Burgoon Fm. Mississippian-Devonian Huntley Mountain Fm.	Relatively broad, northeast-trending folds that decrease in amplitude northward.	Chiefly anticlinal fold-mountain ridges; uplift; moderate dissection.
High Plateau—Transitional area	Pennsylvanian Pottsville Fm. Mississippian Shenango and Burgoon Fms. Mississippian-Devonian Huntley Mountain Fm. Upper Devonian Venango Gp. and Catskill Fm.	Gentle southwest dip overprinted by relatively broad, northeast-trending folds that decrease in amplitude northwestward and southwestward.	Essentially the now-modified erosional slope between the High Plateau prior to significant dissection and the base level of the Pittsburgh Low Plateau; some valleys significantly modified by glacial outwash and valley-fill deposits.
Allegheny Mountain	Pennsylvanian Conemaugh Gp. and Allegheny and Pottsville Fms. Mississippian Mauch Chunk and Burgoon Fms. Mississippian-Devonian Rockwell Fm.	Relatively tight, narrow, north-northeast-trending anticlines and broad, intervening synclines. West-dipping homocline on the Allegheny Front is locally cut by significant cross-strike faults.	Strongly folded anticlinal mountain ridges; variations in erodibility of exposed rocks; northwestern and northeastern borders with less-folded terrain probably relate to deep-seated tectonic activity; uplift; erosion.
Pittsburgh Low Plateau—Prototypical area	Permian-Pennsylvanian Dunkard Gp. Pennsylvanian Monongahela and Conemaugh Gps., and Allegheny and Pottsville Fms.	Very gentle southwest dip overprinted by gentle, northeast-trending folds that decrease in amplitude northwestward.	Base leveling; subsequent uplift and dissection; concurrent(?) subdued folding; extensive river terraces related to glacial outwash.
Pittsburgh Low Plateau—Intermontane area	Pennsylvanian Conemaugh Gp. and Allegheny and Pottsville Fms. Mississippian Burgoon Fm.	Relatively broad, north-northeast- to northeast-trending folds having sinuous traces. Swarm of northwest-striking faults in southeastern Clearfield County and vicinity.	Anticlinal ridges chiefly surrounded by higher areas; headward erosion from the northeast by the West Branch Susquehanna River and tributaries.
Glaciated Pittsburgh Plateau	Pennsylvanian Allegheny and Pottsville Fms. Mississippian Shenango Fm. and subjacent rocks Upper Devonian Riceville Fm. and Venango Gp.	Very gentle south dip with minor irregularities.	Like the Prototypical area of the Pittsburgh Low Plateau, but much modified by glacial scour and deposition of till; deep valley-fill deposits.

[1]Bedrock stratigraphy and structure chiefly based on Berg and others (1980). Lists of stratigraphic units are not intended to be all-inclusive. Other units of similar ages are also present.

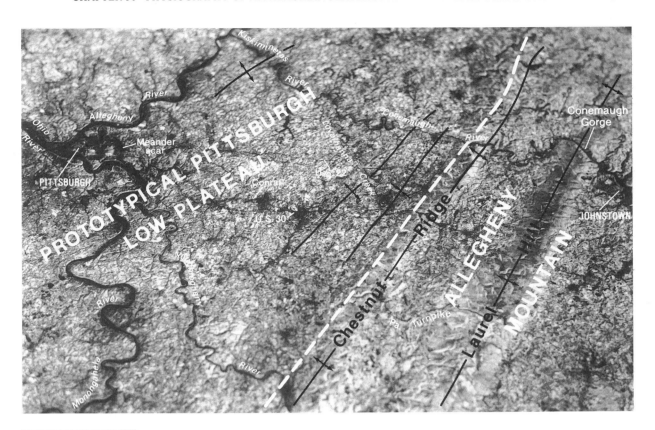

Figure 30–6. High-angle oblique photograph of a Landsat Thematic Mapper image of parts of the Proto-typical area of the Pittsburgh Low Plateau section and Allegheny Mountain section, looking just west of due north from an imaginary position over southeastern Fayette County. The dashed line is the approximate section boundary. Chestnut Ridge and Laurel Hill are prominent anticlines. Parallel linear features in the Prototypical area of the Pittsburgh Low Plateau section, three of which are delineated as examples, are topographic reflections of much more subdued folds. The airline distance from Pittsburgh, in Allegheny County, to Johnstown, in Cambria County, is about 55 miles. The relatively straight east-west features through the center of the scene are highway and railway rights-of-way. The Pennsylvania Turnpike from Laurel Hill to Chestnut Ridge also is clearly defined.

rivers by fairly straight segments that may be controlled by jointing, such as occur on Tunkhannock Creek and the Lackawaxen River (Figure 30–8). Local relief is somewhat greater in the western part of the Glaciated Low Plateau than in the eastern part (Figure 30–5). The general aspect of the section is one of relatively straight, but not closely oriented, valleys with irregular, somewhat knobby intervening ridges, generally moderate but varying relief, and many small bodies of water.

Mountainous High Plateau Section— Eastern Area

The Eastern area of the Mountainous High Plateau section includes disconnected parts that are spatulate eastward and rise abruptly above the Glaciated Low Plateau. Upland surfaces are synclinal and mostly shaped like elongated bowls. The streams run approximately along the synclinal axes, and high points are

along the rims of the plateaus. In all but the north-westernmost part, streams flow in a rectangular pattern that locally has trellis characteristics; then, with steepened gradients, they drop off the plateau to tributaries of the "North Branch" or West Branch Susquehanna River (Figure 30–8). Numerous small ponds, lakes, and swamps testify to glacial action. The north-westernmost segment of this area, in contrast, has been transected by antecedent streams. Rather than a single, massive topographic unit, this segment is a linear series of steep-sided, almost mesa-like, hills.

Mountainous High Plateau Section— Deeply Dissected Area

In the Deeply Dissected area of the Mountainous High Plateau section, headward erosion by the West Branch Susquehanna River has created an awesome landscape of high ridges and deep valleys. The area has a strong, large-scale trellis drainage pattern. Straight

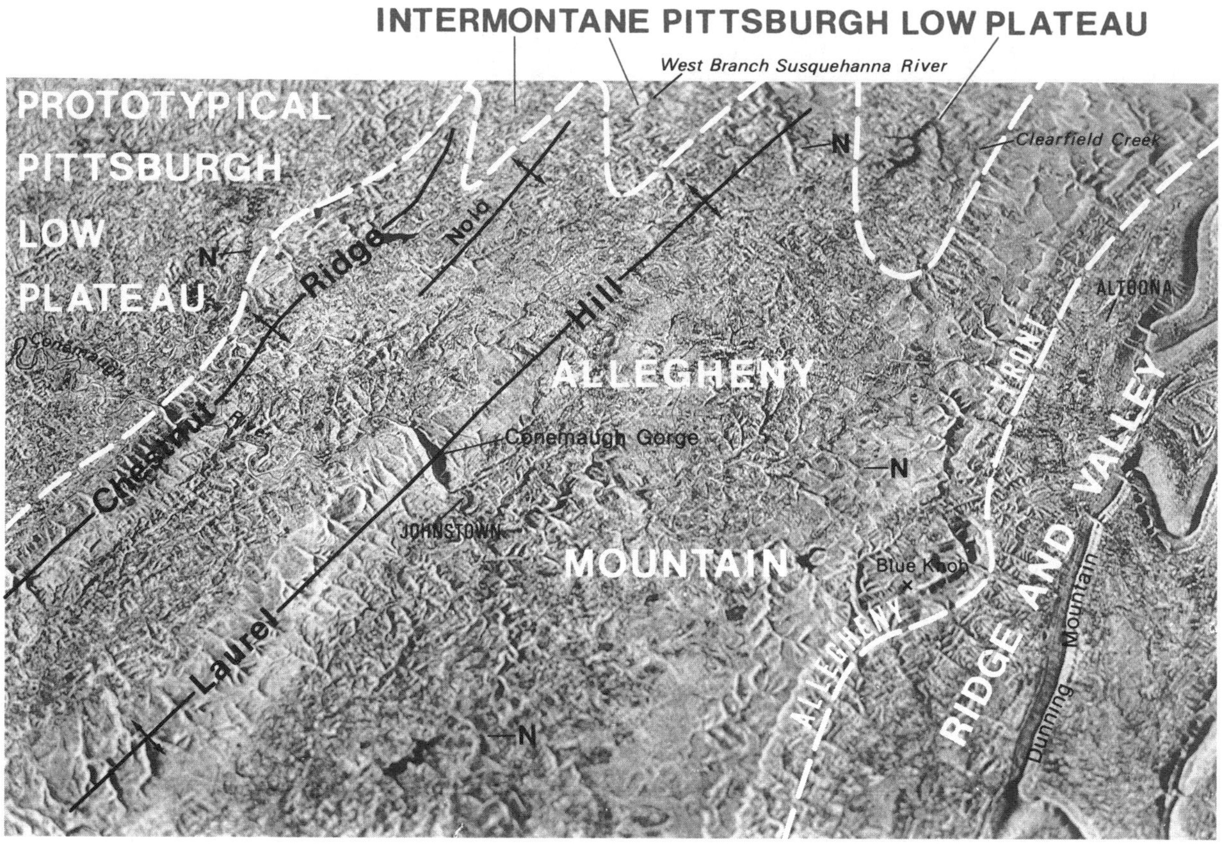

Figure 30–7. High-angle oblique photograph of part of the Pittsburgh 1- by 2-degree synthetic aperture radar map showing parts of the Prototypical and Intermontane areas of the Pittsburgh Low Plateau section and Allegheny Mountain section of the Appalachian Plateaus province, and part of the Appalachian Mountain section of the Ridge and Valley province, looking north from an imaginary position over southwestern Bedford County. The dashed lines are approximate physiographic boundaries. Note the anomalous pattern in the vicinity of Blue Knob on the Allegheny Front. Some puzzling, north-trending features are indicated by "N." The airline distance from Johnstown, in Cambria County, to Altoona, in Blair County, is about 32 miles. The radar image was acquired by the U.S. Geological Survey in 1982.

to wandering, subsequent stream segments are parallel to folding, and cross-structure reaches are mostly normal to folds (Figure 30–9). Though some of this pattern passes into adjacent sections, it is a commanding characteristic of this area only. In this, it bears a greater similarity to the Appalachian Mountain section of the Ridge and Valley province than it does to other plateau sections. Nevertheless, the Deeply Dissected area of the Mountainous High Plateau section is properly part of the Appalachian Plateaus province chiefly because the relatively broad ridge tops are at elevations similar to those of adjacent plateau areas (Figure 30–4). Moreover, a greater percentage of the Deeply Dissected area of the Mountainous High Plateau section is covered by ridges than by valleys, whereas the Appalachian Mountain section has more area covered by valleys than by ridges.

In the eastern part of the Deeply Dissected area is one of the scenic wonders of Pennsylvania, Pine Creek Gorge, also called "The Grand Canyon of Pennsylvania," which extends along the valley for about 55 miles through western Tioga and Lycoming Counties (Figures 30–8 and 30–9). Near its north end, the gorge is more than 800 feet deep and is about 4,000 feet across from rim to rim. It reaches its maximum depth of 1,450 feet near its south end. Equally great valley depths occur elsewhere in the Deeply Dissected area (Geyer and Bolles, 1979, p. 89–90, 105, 110–114).

High Plateau Section—Prototypical Area

The Prototypical area of the High Plateau section is moderately to deeply dissected. Local relief is generally 500 to 800 feet (Figure 30–4). Compared

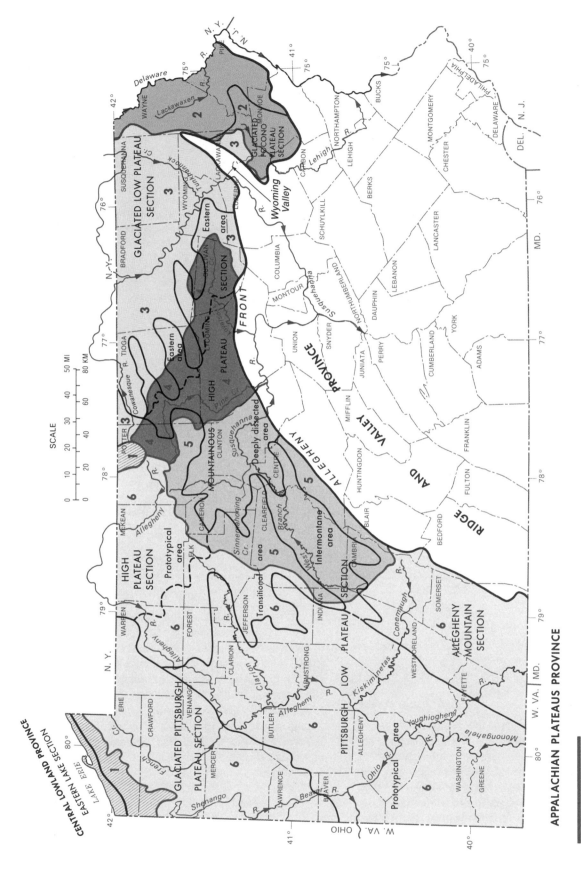

Figure 30-8. Map of Pennsylvania showing the relation of physiographic sections and areas (outlined in black) of the Appalachian Plateaus province and the Eastern Lake section of the Central Lowland province to major drainage basins and subbasins (outlined in color). Drainage is as follows: 1, to the St. Lawrence River; 2, to the Delaware River; 3, to the Susquehanna River except the West Branch; 4, chiefly to Pine and Loyalsock Creeks, then to the West Branch Susquehanna River outside the province; 5, to the West Branch Susquehanna River within the province; and 6, to the Ohio River. Relatively minor parts of stream basins in the Allegheny Mountain section that drain to the Potomac and Susquehanna Rivers are not delineated.

Figure 30–9. Topographic map of parts of Clinton, Potter, Tioga, and Lycoming Counties and adjacent areas showing a striking, large-scale trellis drainage pattern chiefly in DDMHP, the Deeply Dissected area of the Mountainous High Plateau section. Selected anticlinal traces demonstrate structural control. Pine Creek Gorge is shown by the colored dots. PHP, Prototypical area of the High Plateau section; GLP, Glaciated Low Plateau section; EMHP, Eastern area of the Mountainous High Plateau section; THP, Transitional area of the High Plateau section; IPLP, Intermontane area of the Pittsburgh Low Plateau section; AM, Allegheny Mountain section; RV, Ridge and Valley province.

to the Mountainous High Plateau section, however, this area is not truly rugged. Upland surfaces have a more rolling aspect, valley walls have moderate slopes, and valleys are broader relative to depth. Drainage patterns are generally dendritic, though rectangular elements are important in the southern part of the area. The general aspect is more spacious, less confining than in adjacent areas to the southeast and east (for example, see Geyer and Bolles, 1979, p. 103–104).

High Plateau Section—Transitional Area

As the name indicates, the Transitional area of the High Plateau section is one of changing character. To the northeast, it abuts the Prototypical area of the High Plateau section and there has a character similar to, but generally lower than, that area. The structural control in the eastern part of the Transitional area resembles that in the Mountainous High Plateau section. From these zones, the Transitional area declines gently in elevation southwesterly, assuming gradually the character of the Prototypical area of the Pitts-

burgh Low Plateau section. Patterns of drainage in the Transitional area have a general dendritic aspect. However, some large streams have preferred west-southwesterly sets (Figure 30–8), and straight reaches at various orientations suggest some structural control. Some valleys were widened by glacial outwash and have broad, flat bottoms floored by valley fill, notably in Warren County.

Allegheny Mountain Section

Though the Allegheny Mountain section is part of the Appalachian Plateaus province, "plateau" is a misnomer here. The long and orderly, high anticlinal ridges and the broad synclinal valleys have a greater affinity to the Appalachian Mountain section of the Ridge and Valley province, as was recognized by Macfarlane (1873). Even though the area of generalized upland surface higher than 2,400 feet is not much larger in area in the Allegheny Mountain section than that in the Prototypical area of the High Plateau section, variations in upland surface elevation and relief are substantially greater (Figures 30–3, 30–4, and 30–5). The highest discrete peaks in Pennsylvania are in the Allegheny Mountain section. They are more than 400 feet higher than the highest points in any other section (Table 30–1). As is true regarding the Deeply Dissected area of the Mountainous High

Plateau section, but for different reasons, an argument could be put forward that the Allegheny Mountain section perhaps should be an adjunct to the Ridge and Valley province rather than the Appalachian Plateaus province. However, general elevation and position at the top of the Allegheny Front, among other similarities to the plateaus, are more persuasive in keeping the section within the Appalachian Plateaus province.

The eastern and western boundaries of the Allegheny Mountain section are sharply defined by the Allegheny Front and the west slope of Chestnut Ridge, respectively. Steepest dips of strata on flanks of the longest anticlinal ridges, Chestnut Ridge and Laurel Hill, commonly are 20 degrees or more in the southern part of the section, appreciably greater than those that generally prevail in any other section of the province. The folds decrease in amplitude north-northeastward, and the ridges lose height and definition across the gradational boundary with the Intermontane area of the Pittsburgh Low Plateau section (Figure 30–7). The crest of the Allegheny Front, however, retains its considerable elevation appreciably farther northeastward (Figures 30–3 and 30–9). On the Allegheny Front, at the boundary between Bedford and Blair Counties, is a structural anomaly centering on Blue Knob, the origin of which is not well understood (Figure 30–7). A similar feature occurs in northern Blair County. The Conemaugh and Youghiogheny Rivers and other streams cut northwestward, creating water gaps through the ridges. These water gaps provide impressive exposures of strata within the anticlines. The most notable is Conemaugh Gorge, the walls of which are more than 1,300 feet high (Figures 30–6 and 30–7; Geyer and Bolles, 1979, p. 141-143). Some streams flowing in the north-northeast-trending synclinal valleys meet the crosscutting rivers and streams at close to right angles, but others are oriented more northerly (Figure 30–7), and still other streams are dendritic. The pattern of drainage, thus, is a much modified trellis.

Pittsburgh Low Plateau Section— Prototypical Area

Occupying about 6,500 square miles, the Prototypical area of the Pittsburgh Low Plateau section forms the largest unit of the Appalachian Plateaus province in Pennsylvania (Table 30–1). Customary usage is to combine the 1,100 square miles of the Intermontane area of the Pittsburgh Low Plateau section with the Prototypical area, but here the two are separated, for the purpose of discussion, chiefly on the basis of differences in generally prevailing elevation and somewhat greater depth of dissection and structural

involvement in the Intermontane area of the Pittsburgh Low Plateau section (Figure 30–4 and Table 30–2).

In comparison to its gradational boundary on the northeast, the Prototypical area of the Pittsburgh Low Plateau section is sharply defined along the west flank of Chestnut Ridge (Figures 30–6 and 30–7) and along the boundary with the Glaciated Pittsburgh Plateau section (Figure 30–2). As is clear from Figure 30–3, the upland surface of the Prototypical area forms a true plateau. Base level is developed in the mostly homogeneous bedrock, shale and chiefly subordinate, but locally dominant, sandstone, siltstone, and limestone. Most strata are gently folded, with amplitudes decreasing northwestward; dips greater than 5 degrees are rare. Subdued anticlines and synclines commonly are reflected by equally subdued linear topographic highs and lows (Figure 30–6). Jointing apparently is an important factor, for incised stream valleys display many straight segments (Figure 30–6). In contrast, there also are a number of incised meanders. A dendritic pattern is generally expressed in headwater streams on upland surfaces. Locally, near the current mainstem river valleys, abandoned meander scars are moderately incised in the uplands. A complex scar at Pittsburgh (Heyman, 1970) is shown by an irregular, concave-upward, dark area in Figure 30–6. Glacial outwash terraces and benches are common along the sides of deeper valleys.

The overall aspect of the Prototypical area of the Pittsburgh Low Plateau section is one of broad, rolling interfluves separated by relatively narrow, steep-walled, moderately incised valleys. The crests of most neighboring interfluves are at essentially equal elevations, so only relatively rarely can one see a distant horizon.

Pittsburgh Low Plateau Section— Intermontane Area

With upland surface elevations that are almost entirely less than 2,000 feet, the Intermontane area of the Pittsburgh Low Plateau section is bounded on almost all sides by higher ground. Only to the west-southwest is it bounded by lower ground, that of the Prototypical area of the Pittsburgh Low Plateau section, which is lower by about 400 feet in average upland-surface elevation (Figures 30–3 and 30–4). Broad, relatively flat anticlinal ridges characterize the Intermontane area, but structural control of topography is subdued compared to higher areas to the northeast and southwest. An anomalous high ridge in Clearfield County and a number of linear reaches of the West Branch Susquehanna River and its tributaries trend northerly, oblique to the generally northeasterly structural grain (Figures 30–3 and 30–7). The drainage pattern is generally rectangular, but patterns of shorter streams are modified dendritic. Small-scale incised meanders characterize the bottoms of many valley reaches that themselves in large scale are essentially straight.

Glaciated Pittsburgh Plateau Section

In earlier physiography, the Glaciated Pittsburgh Plateau section was simply labeled "Glaciated section" (see map A in the introduction to Part V, p. 342). This was misleading, for the name carried the false implication that no other sections in the province had been glaciated. The name was changed on the basis that absent glaciation, this section largely would not have been distinguishable from the Prototypical area of the Pittsburgh Low Plateau section. The areal extent of the Glaciated Pittsburgh Plateau is defined by the limits of glacial deposits as mapped by Shepps and others (1959) and by the escarpment facing the Eastern Lake section of the Central Lowland province in Erie County. The glacial deposits typically range from 50 to 150 feet in thickness and locally exceed 300 feet in thickness in buried stream valleys. Outcrops of bedrock are sparse and relief is low (Figures 30–4 and 30–5), except where rivers and their tributaries have incised the upland surface, such as in northwestern Warren County. Geologic structure has had minimal effect on the topographic expression of the section.

Prior to Pleistocene time, drainage across the section was north-northwesterly toward the ancestral Lake Erie basin. Incursion by the glaciers blocked this route and diverted Allegheny River and Monongahela River flow to the ancestral Ohio River. Upon slow retreat of the ice, streams in the section developed a generally southerly flow, and now almost all of the section drains to the Ohio River (Figure 30–8; Heyman, 1970). The Glaciated Pittsburgh Plateau clearly owes its morphology almost exclusively to glaciation, unlike the other glaciated sections of the province in Pennsylvania, where other factors also played significant roles in creating the landscape.

The general aspect of the section is one of rolling, subparallel ridges oriented generally south-southeasterly, deranged wandering streams, and large and small marshes and other bodies of water. Pymatuning Reservoir, a naturally occurring wetland now dammed and somewhat enlarged, covers about 25 square miles on and adjacent to the state boundary in Crawford County. Other glacial features include kames and kame complexes, ground and terminal moraines, drumlins, and eskers (Geyer and Bolles, 1979, p. 17–22, 24–25, 36–38).

CENTRAL LOWLAND PROVINCE, EASTERN LAKE SECTION

The Eastern Lake section in Pennsylvania is limited to a band 2 to 5 miles wide extending about 40 miles along the Lake Erie shore in Erie County (Figure 30–2). It includes about 150 square miles, less than 0.4 percent of the state. It is the only section of the very large Central Lowland province represented in Pennsylvania (Figure 30–1).

The Eastern Lake section rises from the approximate mean water level in Lake Erie of 571 feet to an elevation of about 800 feet at the bottom of the escarpment that rises to the Glaciated Pittsburgh Plateau section of the Appalachian Plateaus province (Figure 30–3). Nearly horizontal Devonian shale bedrock is concealed by glacial and beach deposits everywhere except low in shoreline cliffs on Lake Erie and in the lower reaches of some streams draining to the lake. The thickness of till resting on bedrock probably is in the general range of 40 to 80 feet at most places in the section. The beach deposits that rest on the till are reworked glacial materials. Some of the shoreline cliffs and walls of incised valleys exceed 100 feet in height. Otherwise, the surface is as described by Tomikel and Shepps (1967, p. 7):

> The surface of the lake plain is extremely flat except for abrupt rises up onto former beaches created by higher levels of the lake.... Behind the rises, to the south, a higher, flat level continues.... In southern areas of the lake plain, the surface becomes hummocky and irregular because... glacial deposits...there [were] never overrun by lake waters and consequently...never smoothed.

Centrally located on the Pennsylvania portion of the Lake Erie shore, Presque Isle is a complex arcuate sand spit about 6 miles long. It has been modified extensively by wind, wave, and current action since Europeans first saw it, and it remains mobile, to the discomfiture of many (see Chapter 55A).

PROBLEMS AND FUTURE RESEARCH

From Chapters 34 and 35, the origin of the landscape in the Appalachian Plateaus province briefly is as follows. The late Paleozoic Alleghanian orogeny created a very high mountain chain well to the southeast of the current plateaus, from which rivers carried sediment generally northwesterly to northerly across Pennsylvania, ultimately to the vicinity of Hudson Bay. During the Triassic and Jurassic Periods, the Atlantic basin opened as a result of seafloor spreading. Owing to new and steep stream gradients eastward, the remnants of the highlands in eastern Pennsylvania were eroded away, and the divide between Atlantic and

Hudson Bay drainage migrated northwestward. At about the end of the Mesozoic Era, its position approximated the current line of the Allegheny Front. Erosion rates probably were great during the latest Paleozoic and much of Mesozoic time, but erosion rates during the Cenozoic are postulated to have been much slower. Thus, the plateaus had taken on their general shape and size by about 70 million years ago. Pleistocene glaciation completed matters, with considerable modifications to plateau drainage.

This general history seems well grounded, but many problems on regional and local scales remain. The youthful aspect of the ridges of the Allegheny Mountain section is the most striking paradox. In the adjacent Intermontane area of the Pittsburgh Low Plateau section, most rivers and streams drain northeasterly in the West Branch Susquehanna River basin. These streams have generally moderate gradients; the fall on the West Branch from its source in northern Cambria County to southern Clinton County is about 1,200 feet in about 120 miles, or 10 feet per mile. Drainage in the Allegheny Mountain section is northwesterly. From its source, also in Cambria County, to the Allegheny River, the Kiskiminetas-Conemaugh River drops about 1,200 feet in 80 miles, or about 15 feet per mile. Therefore, it is a reasonable supposition that streams in the Allegheny Mountain section are cutting headward more rapidly than those in the Intermontane area of the Pittsburgh Low Plateau section. If so, it also becomes a reasonable speculation that the West Branch may once have drained the Allegheny Mountain section northeastward, and that these segments have been captured by northwest-flowing streams. If one accepts this, then a number of questions arise. How did the streams cut headward through Chestnut Ridge and Laurel Hill? Did the water gaps through these ridges exist previously? Or did the ridges form during or after the emplacement of the water courses, with incision of the streams keeping pace with folding? In the Prototypical area of the Pittsburgh Low Plateau section, streams cut through much gentler ridges precisely centered over anticlines, subtler but perhaps more persuasive of late folding, here after base leveling of a lithologically homogeneous terrain.

In short, did the Alleghanian orogeny persist long after the Paleozoic, perhaps with essentially aseismic movement on fault splays in Silurian salt? Investigation could include theoretical modeling of rock character and denudation rates and exceedingly precise mapping of terraces and determination of the depths of alluvium along transverse streams, perhaps best along the Conemaugh-Kiskiminetas continuum. Or, if one is really thinking "recent," one could obtain, as precisely as possible, early levels of the Pennsyl-vania Canal and the railroad for comparison to current first-order lines of levels.

The Eastern Lake section is relatively well known, so no suggestions for future research in the section are offered. Other topics concerning the Appalachian Plateaus province that are deserved objects of rewarding research are as follows:

1. Investigations by Ferguson (1967) place in question the common assumption that joints are responsible for the many straight valley reaches in the plateaus. What is the true nature of the apparently real structural control of these features?

2. When and how did the invasion of the plateaus by the West Branch Susquehanna River happen, and why did it occur where it did?

3. What are the origins of the antecedent streams that cut through the northern part of the Eastern area of the Mountainous High Plateau section?

4. Why do the Glaciated Pocono Plateau section and a smaller, similar plateau in the Glaciated Low Plateau section north of the Wyoming Valley persist on the divide between the upper Delaware River and "North Branch" Susquehanna River?

5. Not on the plateaus, but significant to them, is the strikingly underfit Raystown Branch of the Juniata River that flows east from the Allegheny Front in Bedford County. What is the history of this stream? Where were its headwaters?

RECOMMENDED FOR FURTHER READING

Campbell, M. R. (1903), *Brownsville-Connellsville folio, Pennsylvania*, U.S. Geological Survey Geologic Atlas of the United States, Folio 94, 19 p.

Davies, W. E. (1968), *Physiography*, in U.S. Geological Survey and U.S. Bureau of Mines, *Mineral resources of the Appalachian region*, U.S. Geological Survey Professional Paper 580, p. 37–48.

Davis, W. M. (1909), *Geographical essays,* New York, Dover Publications (unabridged reprint of 1909 edition), 777 p.

Geyer, A. R., and Bolles, W. H. (1979), *Outstanding scenic geological features of Pennsylvania*, Pennsylvania Geological Survey, 4th ser., Environmental Geology Report 7, pt. 1, 508 p.

Leverett, Frank (1904), *Glacial gravels*, in Butts, C. R., *Kittanning folio, Pennsylvania*, U.S. Geological Survey Geologic Atlas of the United States, Folio 115, p. 9–10.

Thornbury, W. D. (1965), *Regional geomorphology of the United States*, New York, John Wiley and Sons, 609 p.

Wagner, W. R., Heyman, Louis, Gray, R. E., and others (1970), *Geology of the Pittsburgh area*, Pennsylvania Geological Survey, 4th ser., General Geology Report 59, 145 p.

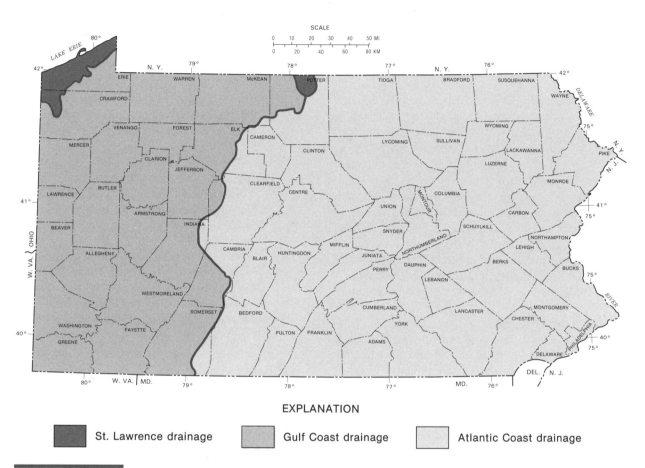

SCALE

| 0 | 10 | 20 | 30 | 40 | 50 MI |
| 0 | 20 | 40 | 60 | 80 KM |

EXPLANATION

St. Lawrence drainage   Gulf Coast drainage   Atlantic Coast drainage

Figure 31–1. Regional drainage divides in Pennsylvania (modified from Click, this volume, Figure 45–1).

378

CHAPTER 31   DRAINAGE BASINS

ULDIS KAKTINS
  Department of Geology and Planetary Science
  University of Pittsburgh at Johnstown
  Johnstown, PA 15904

HELEN L. DELANO
  Bureau of Topographic and Geologic Survey
  Department of Conservation and Natural
    Resources
  P. O. Box 8453
  Harrisburg, PA 17105

INTRODUCTION

Drainage patterns are perhaps the most conspicuous geomorphic characteristics of a region and have long been used as indicators of the effects of other geologic factors on landscape. Ongoing adjustments of drainage systems can indicate recent or continuing tectonic activity or climatic changes. The drainage systems of Pennsylvania (Figure 31–1) range from very old (the Atlantic drainage having been established by some time in the Mesozoic Era) to quite young (the entire Lake Erie and Genesee basins were covered by Wisconsinan ice). All of the drainages have undergone adjustment in response to geologic events since their establishment.

Sixty-four percent of Pennsylvania is drained by streams and rivers flowing to the Atlantic Coast via the Chesapeake and Delaware Bays (Figure 31–1). The bulk of this drainage is provided by the Susquehanna River, while the Delaware River basin occupies the easternmost part of the state and the Potomac River drains a relatively small part of south-central Pennsylvania (Figure 31–2). The Susquehanna drains about 46 percent of the land area of the state (Table 31–1). Its total drainage area, including portions in New York and Maryland, is about 27,500 square miles and is the largest of any drainage basin on the east coast.

Drainage from the western part of Pennsylvania (Figure 31–2) flows away from the Atlantic Coast of the United States to either the Gulf of Mexico or to the Great Lakes and St. Lawrence River. About 15,000 square miles, or 34 percent of the area of the state (Table 31–1) is drained by the Ohio River, which is tributary to the Mississippi River. The Allegheny River, which rises in Potter County, flows into New York before turning south and returning to Pennsylvania. At Pittsburgh, it joins the Monongahela, which flows north from West Virginia, to form the Ohio (Figures 31–3 and 31–4). The two remaining areas of the state, which drain to the north, are the 508-square-mile Pennsylvania portion of the Lake Erie basin, in Erie and Crawford Counties, and the very small (less than 100 square miles) Pennsylvania portion of the Genesee River basin. The Genesee be-

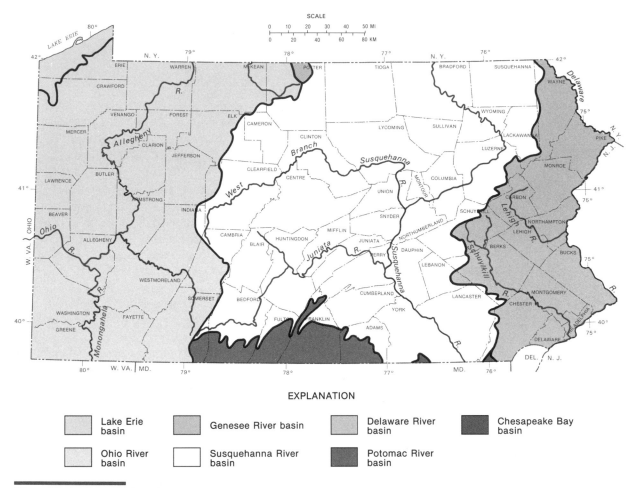

EXPLANATION

▢	Lake Erie basin	▢ Genesee River basin	▢ Delaware River basin	▢ Chesapeake Bay basin
▢	Ohio River basin	▢ Susquehanna River basin	▢ Potomac River basin	

Figure 31–2. Boundaries of major drainage basins (from Click, this volume, Figure 45–1) and major drainage courses in Pennsylvania.

gins near the triple junction of the Allegheny, West Branch Susquehanna, and Genesee basins in Potter County (Figure 31–3) and flows north across New York to Lake Ontario.

ATLANTIC COAST DRAINAGE

The Susquehanna rises in two branches, the "North Branch" and the West Branch (Figure 31–3). The West Branch heads in Cambria County on the dissected Appalachian Plateau and remains entirely in Pennsylvania. The "North Branch" originates at Otsego Lake on the glaciated plateau of upstate New York. The Delaware River also begins in New York, arising along the western slopes of the Catskill Mountains and on the plateau to the north. The course of the "North Branch" and lower Susquehanna shows a remarkable subparallelism to the Delaware as these two rivers flow through the physiographic provinces of eastern Pennsylvania. The lower Schuylkill River is

Table 31–1. *Drainage Basin Areas in Pennsylvania*[1]

Basin	Area (square miles)	Percentage of drainage area in Pennsylvania
Gulf Coast	[2]15,611	34.5
Ohio	[3]15,181	33.6
Major subbasins		
Allegheny	9,765	21.6
Monongahela	2,654	5.9
Atlantic Coast	[4]29,615	65.5
Susquehanna	20,888	46.2
Major subbasins		
West Branch	6,955	15.4
North Branch	5,047	11.2
Juniata	3,404	7.5
Delaware	6,468	14.3
Major subbasins		
Lehigh	1,361	3.0
Schuylkill	1,912	4.2
Potomac	1,582	3.5
St. Lawrence	602	1.3
Lake Erie	508	1.1
Genesee	94	.2

[1]Data from Shaw and Busch (1970) and Click (this volume, Figure 45–1).
[2]Includes 430 square miles that are drained by tributaries of the Ohio River that head in Pennsylvania but join the Ohio downstream in other states.
[3]The area drained by the Ohio River and tributaries that join it within Pennsylvania.
[4]Includes 75 square miles that are drained by small streams that flow directly into the Chesapeake Bay.

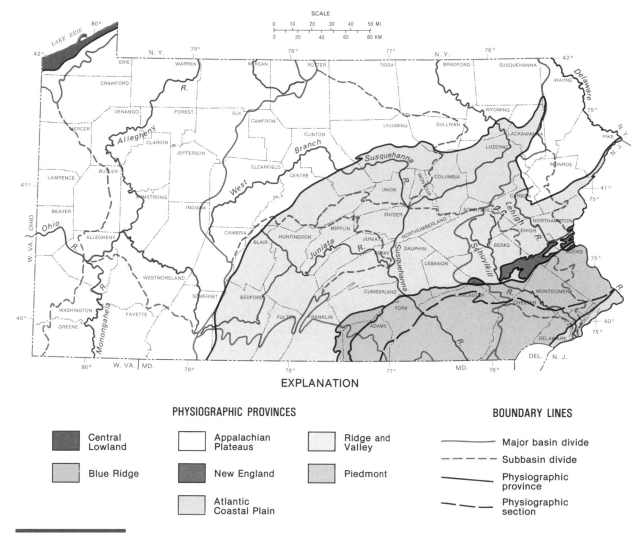

EXPLANATION

PHYSIOGRAPHIC PROVINCES

▮ Central Lowland

▮ Blue Ridge

☐ Appalachian Plateaus

▮ New England

☐ Atlantic Coastal Plain

▮ Ridge and Valley

▮ Piedmont

BOUNDARY LINES

———————— Major basin divide

– – – – – Subbasin divide

———— Physiographic province

– – – – Physiographic section

Figure 31–3. Major drainage courses, subbasin boundaries, and physiographic provinces in Pennsylvania. The dashed physiographic section boundary is the southeast border of the Gettysburg-Newark Lowland section. See Figure 31–2 for names of major drainage basins. Physiographic boundaries are from Berg and others (1989); boundaries of major basins are from Click (this volume, Figure 45–1).

also subparallel to the Susquehanna and the Delaware as these rivers flow across the Gettysburg-Newark Lowland and the Piedmont. The Lehigh River, on the other hand, is deflected northeastward by the Reading Prong to join the Delaware at Easton (Figure 31–3). The main western tributaries of the Susquehanna (West Branch Susquehanna and Juniata Rivers) flow in a general eastward direction and exhibit a somewhat less well developed subparallelism of their own.

The Ridge and Valley province of Pennsylvania provides excellent examples of the relationship between structure, physiography, and drainage. Whereas major stream segments are often transverse to structure, most tributaries are subsequent and exhibit a pronounced trellis drainage pattern. Perhaps the best ex-

amples of this type of drainage occur in the Juniata basin, the West Branch Susquehanna basin within the Appalachian Mountain section, and the Potomac basin. Numerous water and wind gaps, formed by drainage transverse to the linear ridges, further characterize the folded Appalachians of Pennsylvania.

Speculation about the origin of transverse drainage, wind and water gaps, and the subparallelism of major stream segments has spurred investigation and discussion for over 100 years. The controversy was initially kindled by the strongly transverse nature of many stream segments. Because such stream behavior was thought to be anomalous, numerous hypotheses were advanced purporting to solve the dilemma. Although it is now apparent that the development of

Figure 31–4. Photograph of the confluence of the Allegheny River (upper left) and Monongahela River (center right) at Pittsburgh, forming the Ohio River (lower left). Point State Park is the triangular tract between the Allegheny and Monongahela Rivers.

drainage transverse to structure is rather common in fold belts (Oberlander, 1985), some questions remain. Still unresolved is the question concerning the timing and nature of a regional drainage reversal. Sedimentological evidence clearly indicates that, from the Ordovician to the end of the Pennsylvanian, the regional drainage pattern was one of streams draining highland areas to the east and flowing in a northwesterly direction into the Appalachian basin. The sequence of events that resulted in the subsequent reversal of the drainage direction and the development of the present regional drainage divide (Figure 31–1) is complex.

Hypotheses addressing this problem can be divided into two general categories: those that maintain that the present, southeasterly drainage evolved without any structural or lithologic control, and those that envision such control as either a primary or secondary factor. Advocates of the former position hypothesize regional drainage superposition from consequent streams that developed on a Cretaceous marine sediment cover that had been deposited on a previously peneplaned surface of the folded Appalachians. Because Cretaceous marine deposits do not occur within the Appalachian fold belt, a subsequent episode of peneplanation was also required. The present position of through-flowing streams would, therefore, have little, if any, correlation with structure or lithology. This proposal is seriously impaired by its reliance on both the questionable concept of peneplanation and the purely hypothetical Cretaceous marine cover. Rather than a marine transgression covering the folded Appalachians, there is evidence that this region was a highland during the Cretaceous (Groot, 1955; Pierce, 1965). Regional superposition is further invalidated by the fact that Appalachian drainage is by no means completely independent of structural or lithologic control.

The remaining early hypotheses all included some degree of structural control. A number of investigators believed that the drainage was subsequent in origin and that its position was controlled by transverse faults. However, the inability to correlate most water and wind gaps with transverse faults seemed to leave the field to the proponents of regional superposition. It should be stressed that the question of "structural control" that has generated so much controversy cannot be interpreted simply in terms of transverse faults but involves much more varied and, in some cases, subtle controls. As Epstein (1966) and Hoskins (1987b) have demonstrated, a number of lithologic and structural factors can influence gap development. Furthermore, transverse faulting is not the only type of faulting that can localize gaps. For example, Theisen (1983) has described a prefolding wrench fault associated with the Susquehanna River water gap north of Harrisburg. Nor can large-scale structural features be ignored in any discussion of regional drainage. Meyerhoff (1972), Liebling and Scherp (1984), and Oberlander (1985) have pointed out that the course of the middle Susquehanna is between the transverse axes of the major anticlinorium and synclinorium of the fold belt. Also, it has been known since the work of Hobbs (1904) that parts of the Susquehanna, Delaware, and Potomac Rivers correspond to the traces of major lineaments, a fact that is probably related to the subparallelism of the major stream courses. For yet another approach to drainage evolution, see Chapter 34.

Another concern involves the formation and subsequent migration, if any, of the divide between the Atlantic and Gulf Coast drainages. Meyerhoff (1972) adopted the position that drainage reversal had already occurred by the Permian Period. Therefore, the existing regional drainage would represent Permian streams that developed in response to an inferred regional postorogenic slope. The original divide would, therefore, have been close to the Allegheny Front, and the major drainage courses would have undergone only minor modification since the Permian. In contrast, Davis (1889) proposed that parts of major transverse streams, such as the Susquehanna, Schuylkill, and Lehigh, represent westward-draining Permian stream valleys, the drainage of which was reversed in the Triassic Period by downfaulting along the Newark basin. Thompson (1949) placed the original divide along the Blue Ridge-Reading Prong axis, but differed from Davis in advocating reversal by headward piracy by steep-gradient streams draining to the southeast. This imbalance in stream gradients was attributed to foundering of the Atlantic coastal margin during the Jurassic Period.

Indeed, the evolution of the Atlantic drainage can be, perhaps, best understood by looking at the tectonic history of the Atlantic continental margin. Steckler and others (1988) believed that rift-flank uplifts along the Atlantic border would have been in excess of 3,000 feet. The resulting uplifted area would have served as the regional divide between the Gulf drainage and that of the proto-Atlantic. Any hypothesis requiring antecedent drainage across the rift valleys at this time is also negated by the nature and distribution of fluvial deposits in the Newark basin (McLaughlin, 1932; Carlston, 1946; Van Houten, 1969). Manspeizer and Cousminer (1988) noted that the perennial fluvial systems during that time would have flowed along the basinal axis, draining the flexured margins, while small ephemeral streams deposited coarse clastics along the rifted margins. In any case, the development of modern drainage across this part of the rift valley had to postdate the Newark deposits that extend into the Early Jurassic (Cornet and others, 1973).

On a regional scale, Judson (1975) placed the beginning of the drainage reversal to coincide with foundering of the continental margin sometime in the Jurassic. Such subsidence is supported by the presence of interbedded Jurassic shallow-marine and nonmarine sediments along the continental margin. Whether any of these coastal sediments represent southeasterly drainage that is ancestral to the present drainage network is conjectural.

More apparent is the relationship between existing drainage and the Salisbury embayment, a major structural embayment along the coast in the area of the Chesapeake Bay (see Chapter 14). The embayment represents a downdropped crustal block and, according to Mixon and Newell (1977), movement associated with this block may have been initiated as early as the Cretaceous. Therefore, the final tectonic adjustments responsible for the present coastal drainage configuration seem to have begun in the Cretaceous.

Throughout the Cenozoic, base-level fluctuations caused by a combination of tectonic and eustatic factors affected the downstream segments of major transverse streams such as the Susquehanna, Potomac, and Delaware. The mid-Tertiary was a time of rejuvenation brought on by intermittent tectonism in the Chesapeake Bay area (Mixon and Newell, 1977) and a eustatic drop in sea level during the Miocene (Keller and Barron, 1983). It is also at this time that the earliest evidence of the ancestral Susquehanna channel formed on the erosional surface of Miocene coastal sediments (Shideler and others, 1984). Dissection of the coastal margin seems to have continued into the Pliocene Epoch and, at least initially, was accomplished by southeast-flowing drainage.

However, the present courses of the upper estuaries of the Potomac, Susquehanna, and Delaware Rivers make a sharp turn to the southwest at the Fall Zone and show a remarkable southwest-northeast alignment. Hack (1982) proposed that the Potomac estuary, just below Washington, D. C., was diverted from its original southeast course to the southwest in late Tertiary time by southwest tilting of a downdropped crustal block. Because the estuaries of the Delaware and Susquehanna also show a southwest jog, they were probably similarly affected. Furthermore, a drowned Susquehanna channel that can be traced to the mouth of the Chesapeake Bay (Harrison and others, 1965) implies that the Pliocene Susquehanna might have gathered drainage from the Potomac, Rappahannock, York, and James Rivers.

As pointed out by Hack (1982), both the Susquehanna and the Potomac Rivers exhibit nonequilibrium conditions in their downstream reaches. The nonequilibrium (convex upward) Susquehanna profile contrasts strongly with profiles of the West Branch Susquehanna, Juniata, Delaware, Schuylkill, and Lehigh Rivers (see Figure 31–5A to F). The nonequilibrium condition of the Susquehanna can be traced upstream slightly past Harrisburg. That the effects of rejuvenation have not migrated much past the mouth of the Juniata River can be inferred from the lack of a pronounced convexity in the downstream profile of the Juniata (Figure 31–5C). If this nonequilibrium condition does date to base-level changes initiated in the

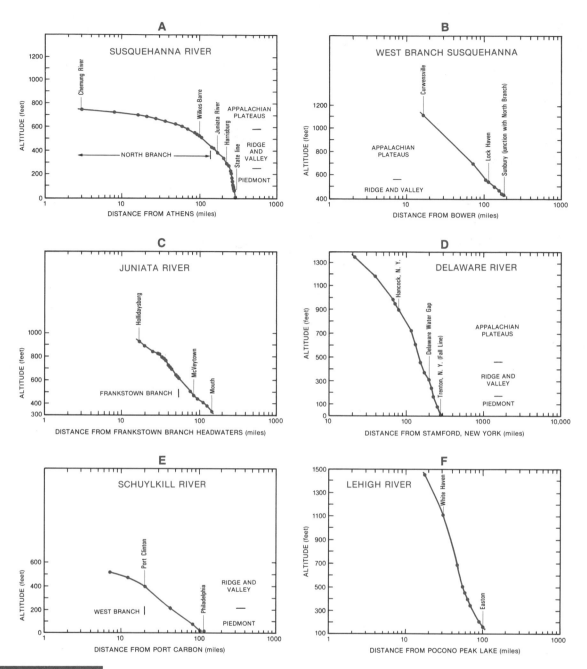

Figure 31–5. The longitudinal profiles of major rivers in central and eastern Pennsylvania, plotted on semilogarithmic graphs to compare the channel slopes of rivers of varying lengths and the slopes of upstream versus downstream sections of each river. Because the relationship between slope and discharge is logarithmic, the normal concave-up longitudinal profile that would be shown on an arithmetic graph approximates a straight line on a semilog graph. Departures from a straight line indicate deviations from the normal discharge-slope relationship. A convex-upward curve on the semilogarithmic profile does not necessarily indicate that the true profile of the stream is convex upward, but rather that the upward concavity is less than that of a normal stream. This approach to longitudinal profiles has been described by Hack (1973). Refer to Figure 31–2 for geographic locations. Profiles are as follows: A, Susquehanna River from Athens (just downstream from the New York state line) to the mouth (data adapted from Hoyt and Anderson, 1905); B, West Branch of the Susquehanna River from Bower (upstream of Curwensville) to Sunbury (data adapted from Hoyt and Anderson, 1905); C, Juniata River from the Frankstown Branch headwaters near Hollidaysburg to the mouth (data adapted from Hoyt and Anderson, 1905); D, Delaware River from Stamford, N. Y., to Trenton, N. J. (data adapted from Gannett, 1901, and New York State Department of Health, Water Pollution Control Board, 1960); E, Schuylkill River from Port Carbon to the mouth at Philadelphia (data adapted from Gannett, 1901); and F, Lehigh River from Pocono Peak Lake (30 miles upstream from White Haven) to the mouth at Easton (data adapted from Gannett, 1901, and Miller and others, 1941).

late Tertiary, then the Susquehanna has adjusted its gradient at least 80 miles upstream from its mouth in the last 6 to 10 million years. Although sea-level changes associated with Pleistocene glaciation are no doubt superimposed on the tectonic effects, they are not sufficient by themselves to account for a gradient change so far upstream. Hack (1982) suggested that tectonic movement in this area has continued into the Quaternary. Evidence of relatively recent tectonic readjustments is provided by the gradient reversal of the drowned Pleistocene-age Susquehanna channel in Chesapeake Bay (Harrison and others, 1965).

Thus, the system of drainage to the Atlantic, although its origins seem to go back to the late Mesozoic, is still undergoing some adjustment. There is scant evidence that the system has experienced prolonged periods of standstill; rather, the available evidence points to tectonism as the major and continuing driving force behind the evolution of the system.

GULF COAST AND ST. LAWRENCE DRAINAGES

Western Pennsylvania drainages have inspired less controversy than the eastern drainages. Some major points in the evolution of drainage patterns in western Pennsylvania were described over a century ago, but there is disagreement on the details, and there is little or no evidence of the drainage patterns that existed during the Mesozoic and most of the Cenozoic.

Carll (1880) noted that oil-well-drilling records revealed the existence of buried valleys under glacial deposits in northwestern Pennsylvania that are up to 500 feet thick. He considered these and the northward slope of the general upland surface as evidence that the pre-Pleistocene drainage of all of western Pennsylvania had been to the northwest, into the area now covered by Lake Erie. Leverett (1902, 1934) and Leggette (1936) supported this basic premise, but differed in detail with Carll and each other. The diversion of the present upper Ohio drainage to the Gulf of Mexico was considered to be effected by Pleistocene glaciation. There is no evidence for the timing of the establishment of the northwestward drainage, other than that it must have occurred after the end of the Permian, when the youngest sediments of the Appalachian basin were deposited, and long enough before the Pleistocene reversal for the development of the fairly wide and deep bedrock channels that are now filled with glacial deposits in the northwest. Before the Pleistocene, the Monongahela drainage was similar to that of the present, but about 200 feet higher.

The Allegheny River below the mouth of the Clarion was also essentially established in its present course. The rest of the drainage, however, was significantly different, as shown in Figure 31-6. The locations of the outlets into the Lake Erie area are known from locations of buried bedrock valleys. Most of this early northward drainage was diverted to the southwest by the breaching of one major divide and the reversal of flow direction of several channel sections.

There was general agreement that major drainage changes occurred at the time of the earliest Pleistocene glaciation of the area. This had been presumed to be Illinoian, in accordance with the traditional interpretation of the age of the earliest tills in Pennsylvania. The ice of the Erie lobe came into the area from the northwest, damming the north-flowing streams. In the "Upper Allegheny" and "Middle Allegheny" drainages, as the individual streams were blocked, water backed up until it flowed over the lowest ice-free divides. Because the direction of ice advance was so nearly opposite the drainage direction, the low points were near the ice front, and the present course of the Allegheny River above Franklin closely parallels the position of maximum ice advance.

Farther west, the "Lower Allegheny-Monongahela" and "Ancestral Ohio" system was also dammed. Lessig (1963) described deposits of the Calcutta Silt near East Liverpool, Ohio (Figure 31-6). He indicated that this is a remnant of the deposits from the earliest ponding when the ice blocked the ancestral Ohio drainage. This fine-grained, water-laid sediment was deposited on bedrock benches at elevations from 1,080 to 1,180 feet near East Liverpool in Columbiana County, Ohio. This supports I. C. White's (1896) description of "glacial Lake Monongahela," which submerged the Ohio-Monongahela-Allegheny area below about 1,100 feet. White attributed the extensive deposits of fine-grained sediment along the high terraces of the Monongahela and its tributaries to this proglacial lake. Other workers, such as Leverett (1934), believed that the maximum elevation of the lake was sustained for only a short time, and that the extensive deposits have a later origin. In any case, the drainage backed up until it found an outlet over a divide near New Martinsville, West Virginia, and established the present course of the Ohio River. More recently, new data and correlations by Jacobson and others (1988) have shown that the earliest terrace deposits (upper portion of the Carmichaels Formation) in the Monongahela drainage include sediments having reversed magnetic polarity that were deposited in the early Pleistocene, prior to 772,000 years ago. These are correlated with the Calcutta Silt and with the similar

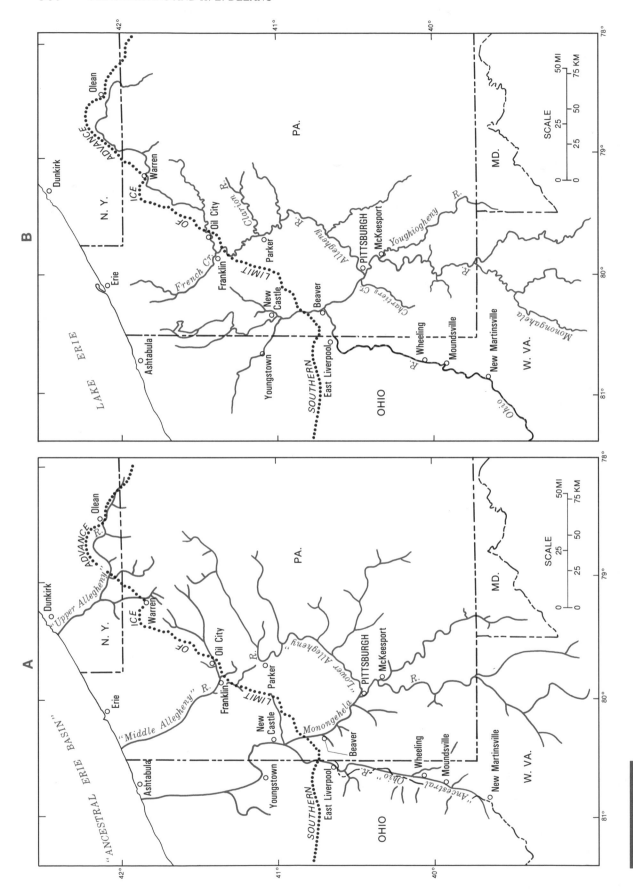

Figure 31-6. Comparison of the preglacial (A) and present (B) drainage systems of western Pennsylvania (maps adapted from Wagner and others, 1970).

Minford Silt of the Teays drainage in southern Ohio and West Virginia. Lower slackwater deposits, having normal magnetic polarities, are younger than 772,000 years B.P. and probably represent damming by Illinoian and Wisconsinan outwash sediments. Alluvial terraces below the level of the Calcutta Silt along the Ohio River between New Martinsville, W. Va., and Beaver, Pa., indicate northward drainage after the earliest ponding. Lower terraces correlated with the presumed Illinoian-age lower Carmichaels Formation and covered with Illinoian gravel indicate southward flow through the same section. These data constrain the age of the Ohio River reversal to sometime between the magnetic reversal at 772,000 years B.P. and the Illinoian (302,000 to 132,000 years B.P.).

The pre- or early Pleistocene drainage is preserved in the modern Allegheny and Monongahela basins in a series of abandoned stream channels and cutoff meander bends. The elevations of the rock floors of these channels range from about 200 to 300 feet above present river levels. This series of wide, flat valleys is known as the Parker Strath, named for the very well developed meander cutoff across the Allegheny from Parker in Armstrong County. Other good examples occur at locations near Pittsburgh (Figure 31–7) and south along the Monongahela and Youghiogheny Rivers.

Valleys and terraces at the Parker Strath level along the Allegheny and Ohio Rivers and tributaries are floored with pre-Wisconsinan outwash. The Monongahela drainage lacked the glacial-sediment supply but was ponded by the extensive sediment deposits in its lower reaches to the north (Leverett, 1934). The streams responded by building up their valley floors with alluvial deposits of silt, sand, and some gravel derived from the local bedrock. These deposits, known as the Carmichaels Formation, are discussed by Campbell (1902, 1903a), Richardson (1904), and White (1896).

After deposition of the Carmichaels Formation and equivalent pre-Wisconsinan outwash in the streams draining the glaciated areas, there was extensive channel erosion. The Parker Strath surface was incised by the Allegheny River to about 50 feet below the present channel bed. This "deep stage" erosion event was presumably related to the new base level for the re-

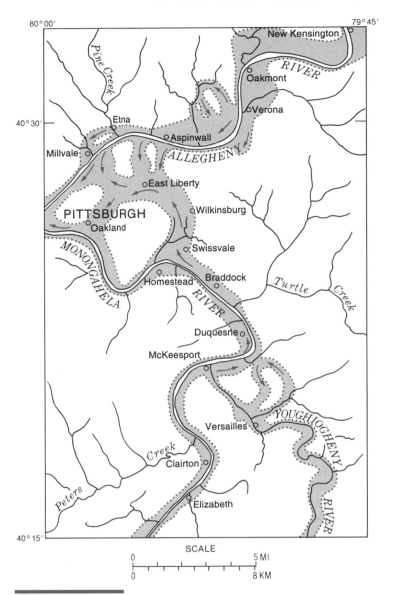

Figure 31–7. Map of old channels near Pittsburgh (from Wagner and others, 1970, p. 89, adapted from Leverett, 1934). The shaded area indicates channels and terraces approximately 200 feet above the present drainage. The reconstruction of flow directions is based on the distribution of deposits of pre-Wisconsinan glacial outwash brought down the Allegheny River, and of the fine-grained, locally derived sediments, known as the Carmichaels Formation, in the unglaciated areas drained by the Monongahela River. The unusual anastomosing pattern between the Allegheny and Monongahela may be related to high discharge and heavy sediment loads during deglaciation.

versed Ohio drainage and the increase in drainage area for the Allegheny and Ohio basins after the drainage reversal. The pre-Wisconsinan bedrock channel profile for the upper Ohio River and the present channel profile are shown in Figure 31–8.

Although the Wisconsinan glaciers covered parts of the newly established drainage network and sup-

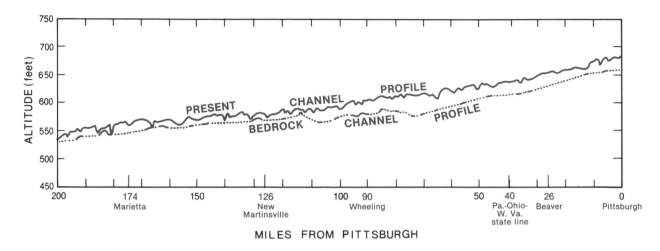

Figure 31–8. Longitudinal profile of the pre-Wisconsinan (bedrock) and present channels of the upper Ohio River from Pittsburgh to below Marietta, Ohio (modified from Carlston, 1962). The solid-line segments of the bedrock channel profile were positioned based on detailed test-boring data. Note the bedrock high point at mile 114, north of New Martinsville.

plied meltwater and outwash sand and gravel to the northern part of the upper Ohio drainage basin, the basic drainage pattern remained unaltered. Wisconsinan outwash deposits fill the valleys of the Allegheny, Beaver, and Ohio Rivers and form terraces 10 to 30 feet above the present rivers. Wisconsinan terraces at similar elevations along the Monongahela drainages are composed of fine-grained sediments, reflecting the local, rather than glacially transported, origin of the material.

Preston (1977) and Watson (1989) offered different interpretations of the Pleistocene drainage history of parts of Butler and Lawrence Counties. Philbrick (1976) outlined the drainage changes in the upper Allegheny near the site of Kinzua Dam in Warren County.

The Ohio drainage system could still be adapting to the change in drainage direction. Fridley and Eddy (1964) cited differences in gradient and channel form between streams draining to the Ohio and the Monongahela as evidence that the Ohio system is not in equilibrium. They described Ohio River tributaries as downcutting, while across the divide to the east, Monongahela River tributaries are aggrading.

Genesee Basin

The Genesee River is the only tributary of Lake Ontario that extends south of the Valley Heads moraine in New York. Muller and Prest (1985) described the complex late Pleistocene drainage history of the lower parts of this river, which drained at various times to the Allegheny River, Susquehanna River, Lake Erie basin, Mohawk River, and finally Lake Ontario. There is no evidence for changes in the Pennsylvania portion of the Genesee basin since the late Wisconsinan deglaciation.

Lake Erie Basin

As discussed previously, the preglacial drainage of the Lake Erie basin was to the northwest, into the present lake area. An old bedrock channel ("Middle Allegheny" River of Figure 31–6A), now filled with Pleistocene sediments, entered the lake near modern Crooked Creek (Figure 31–9). Other large buried valleys occur in Ohio and New York. Pleistocene glaciation had a profound effect on the Great Lakes area, but erosion and sediment deposition have obscured most details of the early history. As ice retreated from the area, a series of proglacial lakes occupied the basins. Calkin and Feenstra (1985) described the changes in the Erie basin from 14,500 B.P. until establishment of the present system. Early lakes in the Erie basin drained to the west through at least five different outlets, all higher than the present outlet through the Niagara River to the northeast. Beach and delta deposits from these very early lake levels occur in western Erie County, as well as in Ohio, Michigan, and Ontario.

The first easterly drainage of the Lake Erie basin during the Wisconsinan was during an interstade at about 13,300 B.P., when an outlet was open near Buffalo, N. Y. (Calkin and Feenstra, 1985). This drainage eroded channels in till and earlier lake deposits to levels more than 100 feet below the present lake level. Returning ice blocked the northeast outlet, establishing another series of high lakes that once again drained to the west. Strandlines related to two of

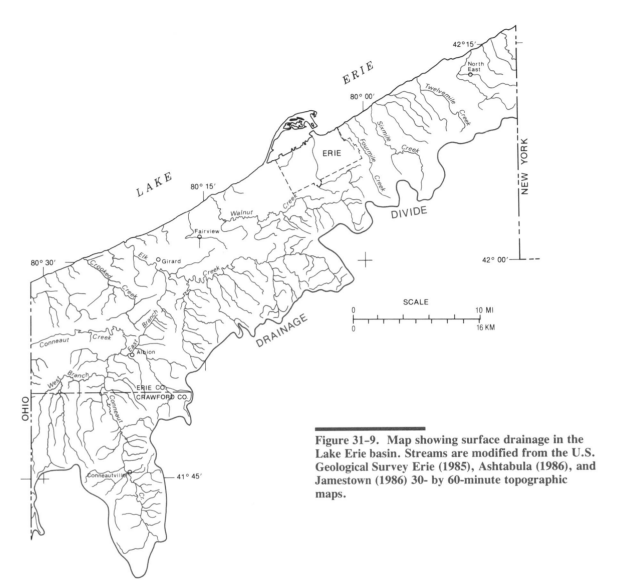

Figure 31–9. Map showing surface drainage in the Lake Erie basin. Streams are modified from the U.S. Geological Survey Erie (1985), Ashtabula (1986), and Jamestown (1986) 30- by 60-minute topographic maps.

these, Lake Whittlesey and Lake Warren, have been mapped in Pennsylvania (Schooler, 1974). These cliffs, terraces, and sand and gravel deposits were later tilted by the postglacial isostatic uplift of the Niagara area. After ice retreat allowed the lake level to fall to the Niagara River level for the last time, direct glacial influence in the basin stopped, and a much lower Lake Erie was established by about 12,500 B.P.

The level of early Lake Erie was controlled by the elevation of the outlet across the Niagara Peninsula and by the greatly varying inflow of water at the western end. Coakley and Lewis (1985) offered one detailed interpretation of postglacial lake-level history, which includes a possible temporary highstand as much as 16 feet above the present level.

The modern streams draining the lake plain have cut deeply into the glacial and lacustrine sediments. Many flow on bedrock floors, and most of the small

streams take a straight northwesterly course down the slope of the land surface. Most of the major streams, such as Conneaut, Elk, and Walnut Creeks, are diverted to the west by moraines into old glacial-meltwater drainageways before turning back toward the lake (Figure 31–9). The Lake Erie basin drainage is the youngest in Pennsylvania and is in the process of adjusting to ongoing changes in base level due to lake fluctuations and bluff recession (see Chapter 55A).

PROBLEMS AND FUTURE RESEARCH

Only a few of the questions concerning drainage in the folded Appalachians are mentioned here. Both Judson (1975) and Hack (1980) have pointed out that, although the divide between Gulf and Atlantic drainage coincides with the negative gravity anomaly in the southern and central Appalachians, in Pennsylvania and New York the divide has, at least in part, migrated past the western edge of the anomaly onto the Appalachian Plateau. Future study may explain the circumstances that enabled this part of the divide to achieve its present position. Another interesting relationship between gravity anomalies and drainage can be seen in the course of the Susquehanna. Both the "North Branch" and the main trunk of the Susquehanna are generally flanked by areas of gravity lows. The Delaware shows a similar, though less well defined, relationship. These relationships should be examined more closely to see whether or not they hold up to more detailed analysis. If cause and effect can be demonstrated, it would certainly help to explain some of the real drainage trends.

There are also questions remaining in the western drainages. The timing of many of the details of the evolution of the Ohio River system is poorly known. The pre-Pleistocene drainage of western Pennsylvania was moderately entrenched. Is there a tectonic explanation for this apparent evidence of uplift? The dates and manner of deposition of the high-level terrace deposits along the major rivers is of interest, both for applications in engineering geology, such as the siting of dams and industrial facilities, and in the increasingly active area of archeological geology. The causes of Holocene trends in the level of Lake Erie and other lakes are not entirely understood and may be

a worthy target for future research. In 1986, the level of Lake Erie reached a historic record high, causing flooding and erosion of shoreline property (see Chapter 55A). The question of future trends of lake level is not just of academic interest.

RECOMMENDED FOR FURTHER READING

Calkin, P. E., and Feenstra, B. H. (1985), *Evolution of the Erie-basin Great Lakes*, in Karrow, P. F., and Calkin, P. E., eds., *Quaternary evolution of the Great Lakes*, Geological Association of Canada Special Paper 30, p. 149–170.

Judson, Sheldon (1975), *Evolution of Appalachian topography*, in Melhorn, W. N., and Flemel, R. C., eds., *Theories of landform development*, Binghamton, N.Y., State University of New York, Annual Geomorphology Symposia Series, 6th, Proceedings, p. 29–44.

Leverett, Frank (1934), *Glacial deposits outside the Wisconsin terminal moraine in Pennsylvania*, Pennsylvania Geological Survey, 4th ser., General Geology Report 7, 123 p.

Mills, H. H., Brakenridge, G. R., Jacobson, R. B., and others (1987), *Appalachian mountains and plateaus*, in Graf, W. L., ed., *Geomorphic systems of North America*, Geological Society of America Centennial Special Volume 2, p. 5–50.

Muller, E. H. (1965), *Quaternary geology of New York*, in Wright, H. E., Jr., and Frey, D. G., eds., *The Quaternary of the United States*, Princeton, N. J., Princeton University Press, p. 99–112.

Oberlander, T. M. (1985), *Origin of drainage transverse to structures in orogens*, in Morisawa, M., and Hack, J. T., eds., *Tectonic geomorphology*, Boston, Allen and Unwin, p. 155–182.

Philbrick, S. S. (1976), *Kinzua Dam and the glacial foreland*, in Coates, D. R., ed., *Geomorphology and engineering*, Stroudsburg, Pa., Dowden, Hutchinson and Ross, p. 175–197.

COLOR SECTION

FIGURE 1. False-color thematic-mapper (TM) imagery of southeastern Pennsylvania. The area covered includes the eastern parts of the Ridge and Valley province and the South Mountain section of the Blue Ridge province, plus the Reading Prong section of the New England province and the Piedmont province. Data and imagery contributed by NOAA/EROS Data Center, November 1982 (TM 190, 40109–15134, FCC).

FIGURE 2. Generalized geologic map of Pennsylvania (reproduced from Pennsylvania Geological Survey, 1990).

FIGURE 3. Map of surficial materials of Pennsylvania (reproduced from Sevon, 1989b).

FIGURE 4. Color infrared image of the Appalachian Mountain section of the Ridge and Valley province, central Huntingdon County and southwestern Mifflin County (from U.S. Geological Survey National High Altitude Photograph 333–94, May 11, 1983). The northern end of the Broad Top synclinorium and its northeast extension, the Trough Creek syncline, trend north-northeastward across the western half of the area. The rim of the synclinorium is clearly outlined by a ridge underlain by the Devonian-Mississippian Rockwell Formation. The asymmetrical, faulted Jacks Mountain anticline trends subparallel to the synclinorium across the eastern half of the area. Dips on the steeper west flank range up to 75°W. The gentler east limb is marked by the highly resistant sandstone of the Silurian Tuscarora Formation, which forms the crest of Jacks Mountain. Ordovician carbonates are exposed in the breached core of the anticline. West of the Broad Top synclinorium, the partially dammed Raystown Branch meanders to the Juniata River. The open black arrow in the center indicates the U.S. Silica Company plant 1 mile north of Mapleton, Huntingdon County. The dashed white brackets show the location of the 6-mile-long quarries of U.S. Silica in the Ridgeley Member of the Lower Devonian Old Port Formation. The dashed white box in the southeast outlines quarries in the Tuscarora Formation, stockpiles, and plant of the former Harbison-Walker Refractories at Mount Union, Huntingdon County.

FIGURE 5. Color infrared photograph of a deeply dissected part of the Mountainous High Plateau section of the Appalachian Plateaus province, western Lycoming County and northeastern Clinton County (from U.S. Geological Survey National High Altitude Photograph 319–618, May 6, 1983). The walls of Pine Creek Gorge, "The Grand Canyon of Pennsylvania," expose gently folded strata of the Devonian Catskill Formation and the overlying resistant Devonian-Mississippian Huntley Mountain Formation and Mississippian Burgoon Sandstone. The plateau surface is capped by the Burgoon Sandstone and the overlying Mississippian Mauch Chunk Formation. The Pennsylvanian Pottsville Formation is preserved at the top of a few hills. The dashed white box outlines quarries in the Pottsville. Relief from the valley bottom at Jersey Mills (open black arrow) to the plateau is greater than 1,300 feet.

FIGURE 6. Map showing the distribution of Pennsylvania coals (reproduced from Pennsylvania Geological Survey, 1992).

FIGURE 7. Map showing the oil and gas fields of Pennsylvania (reproduced from Pennsylvania Geological Survey, 1993).

FIGURE 8. Enhanced Landsat imagery of south-central Pennsylvania (taken on September 19, 1984; contributed by Earth Satellite Corporation and David P. Gold). The western portion shows part of the Allegheny Plateaus province and its characteristic dendritic drainage pattern. The central and northeast portion shows the hogback ridges of the Appalachian Mountain section of the Ridge and Valley province. The boundary between these two provinces is the Allegheny Front. The Blue Mountain Front separates the Appalachian Mountain section and the Great Valley section to the southeast. The South Mountain section of the Blue Ridge province and the Gettysburg-Newark Lowland section of the Piedmont province appear in the southeast corner.

FIGURE 9. First geologic map of Pennsylvania. Published in 1824 in the *Geographical, Historical and Statistical Repository,* v. 1, no. 2, by William Darby, it is the earliest known map that presents the geology of a single state. The map is based on Maclure's 1817 geologic map of the United States. Darby improved on Maclure's depiction of Pennsylvania by delineating what is now the contact between shales and carbonates in the Great Valley section of the Ridge and Valley province.

FIGURE 10. Cutface exposure of the transition zone between the marine Lock Haven Formation and the overlying nonmarine Catskill Formation, along the south side of the connecting channel between the Tioga and Hammond Reservoirs, at Tioga, Tioga County. The white sandstone may be a beach facies. Photograph by W. D. Sevon, July 1981.

FIGURE 11. Outcrop of planar-bedded quartzitic sandstone of the Spechty Kopf Formation, on the east rim of the Lehigh River gorge, about 1 mile north of Jim Thorpe, Carbon County. Photograph by W. D. Sevon, 1967.

FIGURE 12. Exposure of the Pittsburgh Formation of the Upper Pennsylvanian Monongahela Group, just south of the Carnegie interchange on Interstate Route 79, Allegheny County. The top of the Redstone Member is exposed at the base of the cut. The Redstone is overlain by the Fishpot Member (chiefly dark mudstone and siltstone), the Sewickley Member (chiefly light-colored limestone), and the upper member (alternating dark shale and light limestone). Photograph by Reginald P. Briggs, 1982.

FIGURE 13. Alternating red and green mudrocks and sandstones of the Upper Devonian Catskill Formation, Raystown Lake, Huntingdon County. Photograph by John A. Harper, September 1986.

FIGURE 14. Duncannon Member of the Upper Devonian Catskill Formation, showing fining-upward alluvial cycles having erosional bases, along U.S. Route 322 (northbound) in the Juniata River valley, 3 miles south of Millerstown, Perry County. Photograph by Charles H. Shultz, December 1988.

FIGURE 15. Planar crossbedding etched by differential solution in alternating calcareous sandstone and arenaceous limestone of the Upper Mississippian Loyalhanna Formation, exposed in the Keystone Limestone Company quarry on the east flank of Negro Mountain anticline, 1.5 miles south of Savage, Somerset County. The bedding was formed by large-scale subtidal sand waves on a shallow marine shelf. Photograph by Paul W. Garrett, Jr., May 1989.

FIGURE 16. Limestone conglomerate of the Conoy Creek fanglomerate, which occurs at the base of the Upper Triassic New Oxford Formation, 3 miles southwest of Elizabethtown, Lancaster County. Vertical grooves are drill holes. Photograph by Charles H. Shultz, September 1967.

FIGURE 17. Outcrop of megaripples on a bedding surface of quartzite of the Lower Cambrian Antietam Formation exposed in the quarry of Mount Cydonia Sand Company near Fayetteville, Franklin County. Megaripples were probably generated by waves during shallowing of water at the time of deposition. Photograph by W. D. Sevon, July 1980.

FIGURE 18. Current-ripple marks in fine-grained sandstone overlain by shale in the Upper Ordovician Juniata Formation along U.S. Route 322 in the Mann Narrows gap of Kishicoquillas Creek through Jacks Mountain, about 2 miles northwest of Burnham, Mifflin County. Photograph by Charles H. Shultz, September 1967.

FIGURE 19. Pinnacle weathering in limestone of the Ordovician Rockdale Run Formation, southwest of Carlisle, Cumberland County, at the Plainfield exit of Interstate Route 81. The area was stripped for fill during construction of the highway and is now buried. Photograph by Noel Potter, Jr., June 1971.

FIGURE 20. "Ribbon" limestone of the Lower Ordovician lithotectonic unit 2 of the Hamburg sequence in a small quarry on the west side of Pa. Route 61, Mohrville, Berks County. Gray bands of relatively pure limestone alternate with black silty shale. Note the disruption of limestone layers and other evidence of soft-sediment deformation. Photograph by Charles H. Shultz, October 1982.

FIGURE 21. Isoclinal fold in Precambrian amphibolite-grade gneiss of the Honey Brook Upland on the west side of the Marsh Creek dam spillway, Chester County. Photograph by William A. Crawford, 1981.

FIGURE 22. Thrust fault dipping steeply to the right (south) in the center of a small syncline in the dark-colored Mississippian Mauch Chunk Formation, northbound lane of Interstate Route 81, south of Hazleton, Luzerne County. The light-colored upper portion of the cut is the lower part of the Pennsylvanian Pottsville Formation. Photograph by W. D. Sevon, 1978.

FIGURE 23. Complex recumbent fold in limestone and dolostone beds of the Lower Ordovician Epler Formation. The outcrop (now removed) was located on the southeast side of Annville, Lebanon County. Photograph by Donald Hoff, November 1974.

FIGURE 24. Complex similar folds interrupted by irregular masses of milky quartz in the Cambrian-Ordovician Conestoga Formation on the east side of U.S. Route 222, 2 miles south of Lancaster, Lancaster County. Relatively pure limestone (gray) alternates with silty argillaceous limestone; low-grade metamorphism has converted the rock to a fine-grained marble. Photograph by Charles H. Shultz, September 1986.

FIGURE 25. Kink folds in the shaly phase of the Lower Silurian Tuscarora Formation in a quarry adjacent to the Laurel Creek dam, 2.5 miles northwest of Milroy, Mifflin County. Pink sandstone is interbedded with dark-colored shale. Near-vertical fold limbs are steeply overturned to the northwest. A gently dipping thrust fault cuts the lower part of the outcrop. Photograph by Donald W. Watson, April 1975.

FIGURE 26. Close-up view of kink folds and thrust faults visible in the lower center part of Figure 25. Photograph by Eberhard Werner, July 1976.

FIGURE 27. Tightly folded, 100-foot-high anticline known as the "whaleback," a third-order disharmonic fold, plunging discordantly beneath an overlying synclinal trough in the Bear Valley mine, approximately 3 miles southwest of Shamokin, Northumberland County. Anthracite of the Pennsylvanian Llewellyn Formation was stripped to expose the core of the anticline. Photograph by Richard Nickelsen, 1971.

FIGURE 28. Two wind gaps on the southeast side of Tuscarora Mountain in the Appalachian Mountain section of the Ridge and Valley province. The view is to the northwest from Pa. Route 17 just east of Ickesburg, Perry County. The gap on the left is traversed by Pa. Route 74. The ridge is supported by quartzites of the Lower Silurian Tuscarora Formation, and the valley in the foreground is underlain by mudrocks of the Upper Silurian Bloomsburg and Wills Creek Formations. Photograph by Charles H. Shultz, December 1988.

FIGURE 29. Lower part of a giant pothole, about 24 feet long and 10 feet in diameter at the base, cut in schist of the lower Paleozoic(?) Wissahickon Formation on Peavine Island in the Holtwood gorge of the Susquehanna River, about 0.5 mile downstream from the Norman Wood Bridge on Pa. Route 372, York County. Photograph by Charles H. Shultz, May 1988.

FIGURE 30. Another view of the giant pothole shown in Figure 29, showing its full 24-foot length (depth). Photograph by Charles H. Shultz, May 1988.

FIGURE 31. Delaware Water Gap, cut through a hogback composed of sandstones and conglomerates of the Lower Silurian Shawangunk Formation. Interstate Route 80 in New Jersey is in the center; Monroe County, Pa., is on the right. Photograph by Charles H. Shultz, March 1989.

FIGURE 32. Part of the Holtwood gorge of the Susquehanna River, looking south, about 0.5 mile down-

stream from the Norman Wood Bridge on Pa. Route 372, York County. Peavine Island is on the right. This is a subsidiary rock channel cut into schist of the lower Paleozoic(?) Wissahickon Formation. Photograph by Charles H. Shultz, May 1988.

FIGURE 33. Aerial photograph of elongate entrenched meanders of Conodoguinet Creek west of Camp Hill, Cumberland County. The view is to the north across the Great Valley, toward Blue Mountain. Photograph by Noel Potter, Jr., February 1970.

FIGURE 34. The Susquehanna River water gap between Cove Mountain (Perry County) on the left and Second Mountain (Dauphin County) on the right. The view is in an upstream direction from the Rockville Bridge, just north of Harrisburg. Photograph by Donald Hoff, July 1973.

FIGURE 35. Oblique aerial photograph (looking northeast) of the Susquehanna River water gap at West Pittston (bottom center), Luzerne County. The hogback is the northwest flank of the Lackawanna syncline, supported by the Mississippian Pocono Formation and the Pennsylvanian Pottsville Formation. Photograph by Charles H. Shultz, winter 1963.

FIGURE 36. Anthracite strip mine at the Greenwood operation of Bethlehem Mines. The view is eastward from the rim of the mine near Tamaqua, Schuylkill County. This is a multiseam, two-level pit in which several beds of the lower part of the Pennsylvanian Llewellyn Formation are being extracted. Photograph by Jane R. Eggleston, summer 1979.

FIGURE 37. Bituminous strip mine of Adobe Mining Company, Marion Township, northern Butler County. The view is to the west, toward the 115-foot highwall. The dragline is excavating overburden to expose Clarion and Brookville coal beds at the base of the Pennsylvanian Allegheny Formation. Photograph by Charles H. Shultz, April 1988.

FIGURE 38. Marion 8700 dragline with 300-foot boom and 85-cubic-yard bucket excavating the overburden to expose the Mammoth coal bed (anthracite) of the Pennsylvanian Llewellyn Formation in the Ebervale mine of the Jeddo-Highland Coal Company, Big Black Creek basin, Luzerne County. The station wagon near the bottom of the photograph indicates scale. Photograph by Charles H. Shultz, October 1988.

FIGURE 39. Photograph showing a shuttle car being loaded in an underground mine developed in the Pittsburgh coal bed, Greene County, 1987.

FIGURE 40. Stripping in a typical bituminous coal mine, Armstrong County. A 3-foot-thick layer of Upper Freeport coal at the top of the Pennsylvanian Allegheny Formation is exposed behind the shovel. The overburden is shale and siltstone. The shovel is on the underclay at the base of the coal. Photograph taken in July 1988.

FIGURE 41. Miner checking for loose rock in the roof of an underground mine developed in the Pittsburgh coal bed, Greene County, 1987.

FIGURE 42. View of part of the Pennreco refinery in Karns City, Butler County. Products produced include kerosene, petrolatum, and white oil. Most of the crude oil is from local wells, but some is shipped in from Louisiana and Texas. The original plant was built in 1878 by the Pennsylvania Refining Company. Photograph by G. Jeffrey Hoch, September 1989.

FIGURE 43. Replica of the second derrick and engine house built at the Drake well, near Titusville, Crawford County. The original structure burned two months after production began in 1859. The present building, its appearance based on old photographs of the original building, was constructed in 1946 on the grounds of the Drake Well Museum. Photograph by G. Jeffrey Hoch, May 1989.

FIGURE 44. Replica of the Densmore Car, the first successful railroad tank car for oil, at the Drake Well Museum, near Titusville, Crawford County. This type of car, which was designed by Amos Densmore in the summer of 1865, remained in service until 1869. Each tank held 42 to 45 barrels of oil. Photograph by G. Jeffrey Hoch, May 1989.

FIGURE 45. Electrically operated pumping jack, typical of many used throughout western Pennsylvania. This one, located in Warren County, is removing oil from the Upper Devonian Bradford Group. Photograph taken in February 1987.

FIGURE 46. Modern shallow-well drilling rig and logging truck at the site of a 3,800-foot-deep gas well in Indiana County. Electric logging techniques were being used to determine the thickness of sands of the Upper Devonian Bradford Group. Pipes visible on the racks were used to case the hole. The well was treated with sand and water to increase the flow rate of the gas. Photograph taken in July 1988.

FIGURE 47. "Pennsylvania" standard metal rig at the Drake Well Museum near Titusville, Crawford County, consisting of a tall derrick and walking beam, powered by a steam engine, which is just out of the view to the left. Rigs of this size were capable of drill-ing in excess of 5,000 feet using cable tools. Photograph by G. Jeffrey Hoch, May 1989.

FIGURE 48. Surface facility of Bethlehem Steel's Grace mine, Morgantown, Berks County. The pelletizing plant is in the foreground, and in the left background is a structure (headframe of the A-shaft) used to lift ore to the surface. The mine is now flooded, and the two shafts are sealed. Most of the surface structures have been removed, including the pelletizing plant and the exhaust stack. Photograph by Donald Hoff, October 1973.

FIGURE 49. Old West, Dickinson College, Carlisle, Cumberland County, built in 1804. The building was designed by Benjamin Latrobe and is an example of the use of natural stone in classic Georgian architecture. The walls are Cambrian-Ordovician limestone, and the trim is red Triassic sandstone. Photograph by Noel Potter, Jr., January 1988.

FIGURE 50. Stoddard slate quarry (abandoned) in the Lehigh-Northampton district near Pen Argyl, Northampton County. Steeply dipping bedding is cut by horizontal axial-plane cleavage, a condition conducive to deep rectangular quarry development. Each bench, marked by horizontal traces on the quarry walls, is about 12 feet high. The bottom of a waste pile is visible across the road in the upper right corner, and the contiguous Doney No. 2 quarry can be seen on the right. Photograph by S. W. Berkheiser, Jr., 1984.

FIGURE 51. Limestone quarry of the Thomasville Stone and Lime Company, Thomasville, York County. The quarry face is Cambrian Kinzers Formation. The operation produces a high-calcium limestone. Photograph by W. D. Sevon, April 1982.

FIGURE 52. Doney No. 1 slate quarry, Pen Argyl, Northampton County. This is a typical operation, with steeply dipping bedding and horizontal benches parallel to cleavage. The benches are 45 to 65 feet long, 14 feet wide, and 12 feet high. A core-drilling machine is visible in the lower left corner, and a bin of white abrasive sand is visible in the lower center of the photograph. A large slab of slate is being hoisted to the right of the shed. Photograph by S. W. Berkheiser, Jr., 1984.

FIGURE 53. Rheems quarry in the Lower Ordovician Epler Formation (Beekmantown Group), 2 miles southeast of Elizabethtown, Lancaster County. Alternating layers of limestone and dolostone have been deformed into a recumbent fold that has younger rocks in the core. Dolostone beds show boudinage (upper center) and carbonate-filled gash fractures (white). Photograph by Charles H. Shultz, June 1967.

Captions continued on page 411

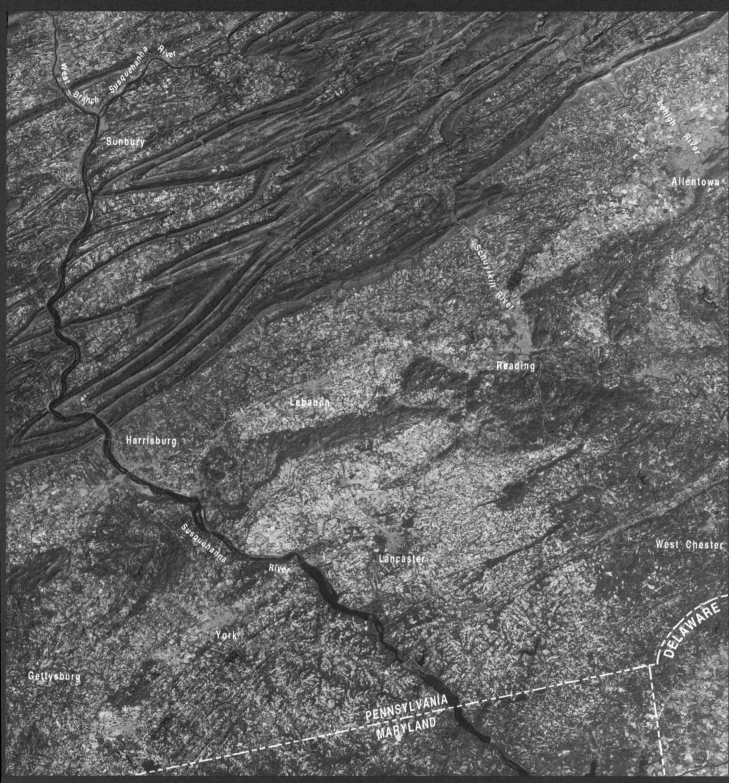

FIGURE 1

395

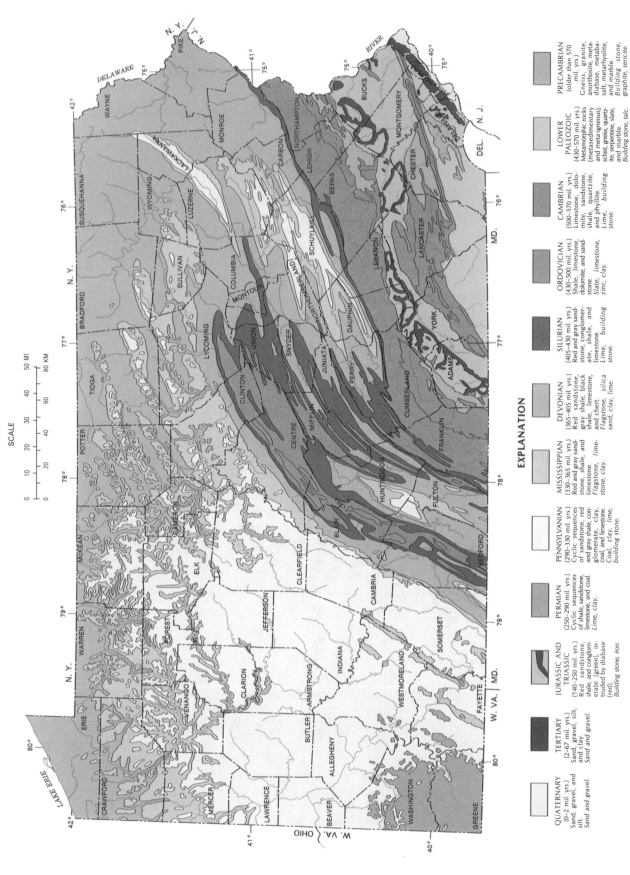

SCALE

```
0        10   20   30   40   50 MI
0   20      40      60      80 KM
```

EXPLANATION

QUATERNARY
(0–2 mil. yrs.)
Sand, gravel, and
silt.
Sand and gravel.

TERTIARY
(2–67 mil. yrs.)
Sand, gravel, silt,
and clay.
Sand and gravel.

**JURASSIC AND
TRIASSIC**
(140–250 mil. yrs.)
Red sandstone,
shale, and conglom-
erate (green), in-
truded by diabase
(red).
Building stone, iron.

PERMIAN
(250–290 mil. yrs.)
Cyclic sequences
of shale, sandstone,
limestone, and coal.
Lime, clay.

PENNSYLVANIAN
(290–330 mil. yrs.)
Cyclic sequences
of sandstone, red
and gray shale, con-
glomerate, clay,
coal, and limestone.
*Coal, clay, lime,
building stone.*

MISSISSIPPIAN
(330–365 mil. yrs.)
Red and gray sand-
stone, shale, and
limestone.
*Flagstone, lime-
stone, clay.*

DEVONIAN
(365–405 mil. yrs.)
Red sandstone,
gray shale, black
shale, limestone,
and chert.
*Flagstone, silica
sand, clay, lime.*

SILURIAN
(405–430 mil. yrs.)
Red and gray sand-
stone, conglomer-
ate, shale, and
limestone.
*Lime, building
stone.*

ORDOVICIAN
(430–500 mil. yrs.)
Shale, limestone,
dolomite, and sand-
stone.
*Slate, limestone,
zinc, clay.*

CAMBRIAN
(500–570 mil. yrs.)
Limestone, dolo-
mite, sandstone,
shale, quartzite,
and phyllite.
*Lime, building
stone.*

**LOWER
PALEOZOIC**
(430–570 mil. yrs.)
Metamorphic rocks
(metasedimentary
and meta-igneous);
schist, gneiss, quartz-
ite, serpentine, slate,
and marble.
Building stone, talc.

PRECAMBRIAN
(older than 570
mil. yrs.)
Gneiss, granite,
anorthosite, meta-
diabase, metaba-
salt, metarhyolite,
and marble.
*Building stone,
graphite, sericite.*

FIGURE 2

396

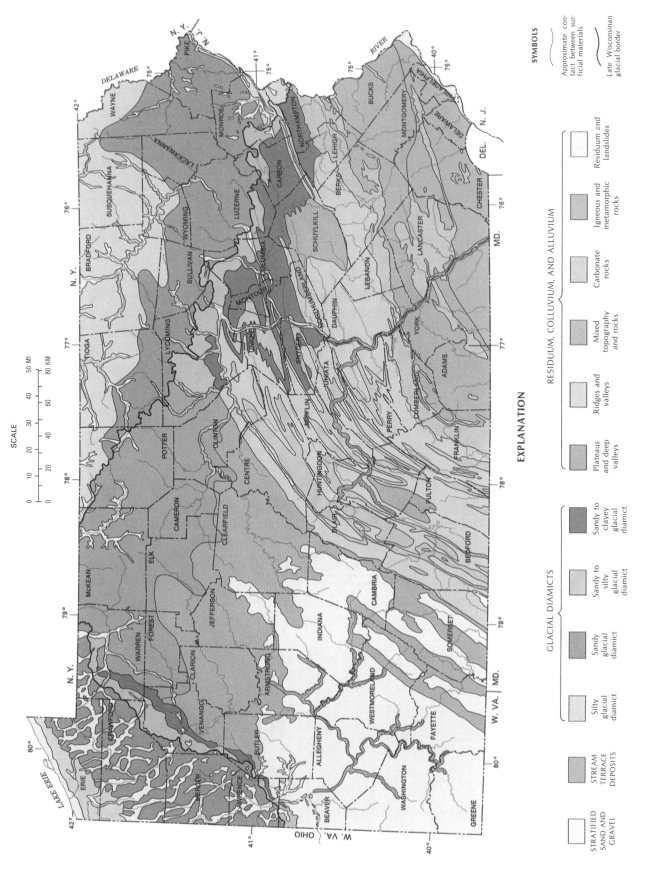

SCALE

| 0 | 10 | 20 | 30 | 40 | 50 MI |
| 0 | 20 | 40 | 60 | 80 KM |

EXPLANATION

GLACIAL DIAMICTS

Silty glacial diamict

Sandy glacial diamict

Sandy to silty glacial diamict

Sandy to clayey glacial diamict

STREAM TERRACE DEPOSITS

STRATIFIED SAND AND GRAVEL

RESIDUUM, COLLUVIUM, AND ALLUVIUM

Plateaus and deep valleys

Ridges and valleys

Mixed topography and rocks

Carbonate rocks

Igneous and metamorphic rocks

Residuum and landslides

SYMBOLS

Approximate contact between surficial materials

Late Wisconsinan glacial border

FIGURE 3

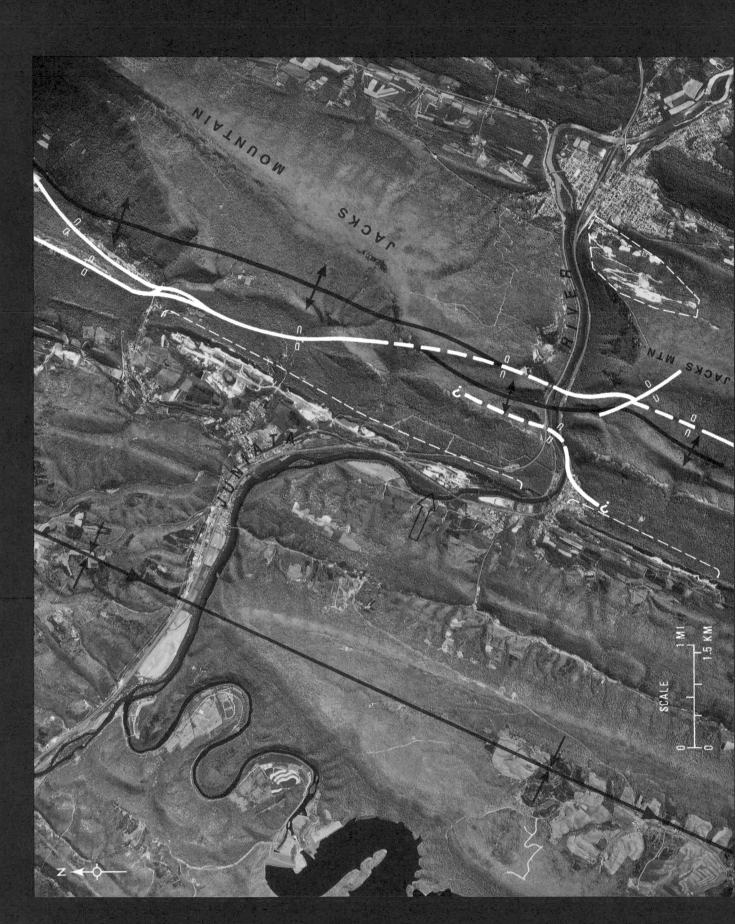

MOUNTAIN

JACKS

JUNIATA

RIVER

JACKS MTN

SCALE

1 MI

1.5 KM

0

0

N

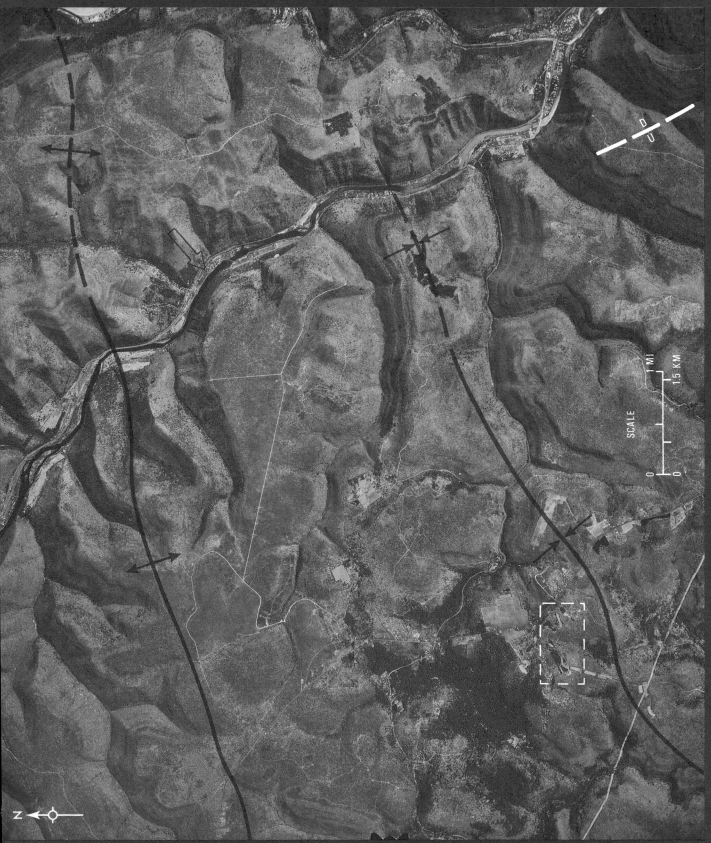

SCALE

1 MI

1.5 KM

N

FIGURE 5

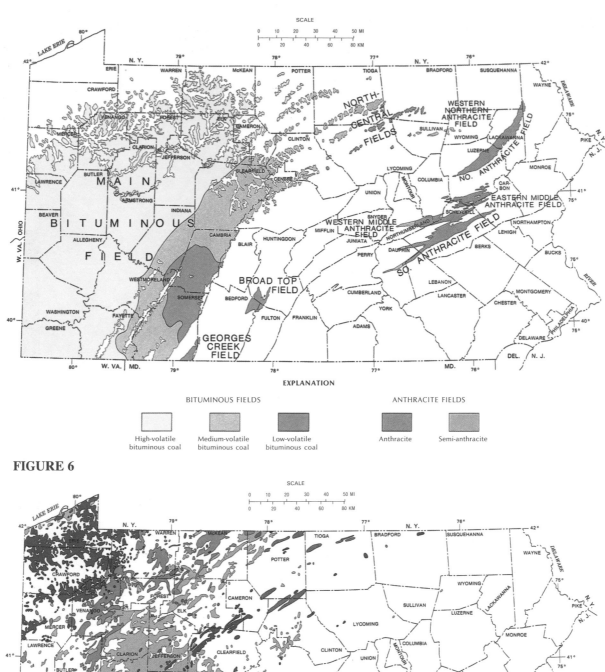

EXPLANATION

BITUMINOUS FIELDS

High-volatile bituminous coal   Medium-volatile bituminous coal   Low-volatile bituminous coal

ANTHRACITE FIELDS

Anthracite   Semi-anthracite

FIGURE 6

SCALE
0   10   20   30   40   50 MI
0   20   40   60   80 KM

EXPLANATION

Shallow oil field   Shallow gas field   Deep gas field   Gas storage area

FIGURE 7

400

FIGURE 8

FIGURE 9

FIGURE 10

FIGURE 11

FIGURE 12

FIGURE 13

FIGURE 14

FIGURE 15

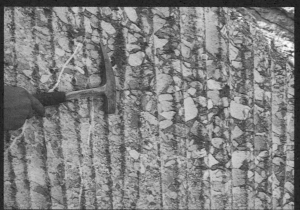

FIGURE 16

FIGURE 17

FIGURE 18

FIGURE 19

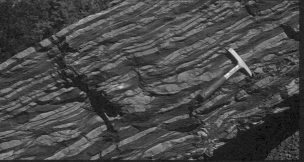

FIGURE 20

403

FIGURE 21

FIGURE 22

FIGURE 23

FIGURE 24

FIGURE 25

FIGURE 26

FIGURE 27

FIGURE 28

FIGURE 29

FIGURE 30

FIGURE 31

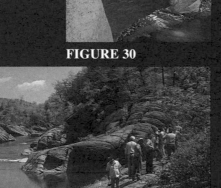

FIGURE 32

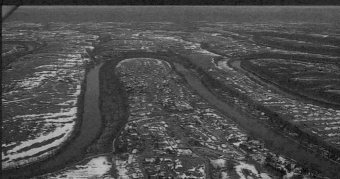

FIGURE 33

FIGURE 34

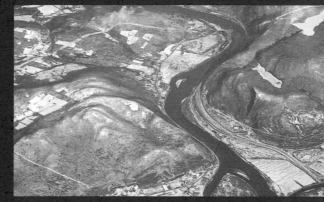

FIGURE 35

FIGURE 37

FIGURE 36

FIGURE 38

FIGURE 39

FIGURE 40

FIGURE 41

FIGURE 42

FIGURE 43

FIGURE 44

FIGURE 45

FIGURE 46

FIGURE 47

FIGURE 48

FIGURE 49

FIGURE 50

FIGURE 51

FIGURE 52

FIGURE 53

FIGURE 54

FIGURE 56

FIGURE 57

FIGURE 55

FIGURE 58

FIGURE 59

FIGURE 60

FIGURE 61

FIGURE 62

FIGURE 63

FIGURE 64

FIGURE 65

FIGURE 66

FIGURE 54. House destroyed by a landslide (slump) triggered by fill placement over colluvium, in Brentwood Borough, Allegheny County. Photograph by James V. Hamel, May 1984.

FIGURE 55. Sinkholes that caused collapse of Bullfrog Valley Road west of Hershey, Dauphin County. The site is underlain by limestone of the Ordovician Epler Formation. The town of Hershey is visible in the background. Photograph by Noel Potter, Jr., April 1979.

FIGURE 56. Aerial view of flooding of the Carlisle water-treatment plant along Conodoguinet Creek, Longs Gap Road, north of Carlisle, Cumberland County, as a result of tropical storm Agnes in 1972. Photograph by Noel Potter, Jr., June 1972.

FIGURE 57. Alluvial deposits and damage to buildings on the west side of Pa. Route 8, at the south edge of Franklin, Venango County, caused by a small-stream flash flood resulting from 4.5 inches of rain dumped by a very large thunderstorm on June 9, 1981 (see Appendix 52B). Photograph by Charles H. Shultz, June 1981.

FIGURE 58. Alluvium stained by iron oxides ("yellow boy") produced by acidic mine drainage contaminating Rolling Stone Run at its junction with the West Branch of the Susquehanna River near Karthaus, Clearfield County. The pH of the water was 2.5 on the day the photograph was taken. Photograph by Bob Helm, June 1979.

FIGURE 59. Boulder field at Big Boulder Ski Resort, Big Boulder Lake, Carbon County. The surface is the top of a periglacial accumulation of rocks derived from nearby outcrops of the Devonian Catskill Formation. Boulders were rounded during periglacial transport. Photograph by W. D. Sevon, October 1971.

FIGURE 60. An outcrop of Devonian Oriskany Sandstone known as Pulpit Rock, Warrior Ridge, Huntingdon County. This exposure was identified and described by geologists of the First Pennsylvania Geological Survey in 1836. The costumed figure (W. D. Sevon) is helping to recall this event. Photograph taken by Steve Hanes during the 50th Field Conference of Pennsylvania Geologists, October 1986.

FIGURE 61. Cucumber Falls, formed where Cucumber Run drops 25 feet from an overhanging sandstone ledge near the base of the Pennsylvanian Clarion Formation. The falls are just above the confluence of Cucumber Run and the Youghiogheny River in Ohiopyle State Park, Fayette County. Photograph by Helen L. Delano, April 1983.

FIGURE 62. Ohiopyle Falls on the Youghiogheny River in Ohiopyle State Park, Fayette County, underlain by resistant sandstones of the Pennsylvanian Pottsville Formation. Photograph by Glenn H. Thompson, about 1968.

FIGURE 63. Lititz Spring, a large spring emanating from solution openings in the Lower Ordovician Stonehenge Formation (Beekmantown Group) in Lititz Springs Park, Lititz, Lancaster County. Its median discharge is 1,200 gallons per minute. Photograph by Charles H. Shultz, November 1988.

FIGURE 64. View of the Gettysburg plain looking west from the Union Army position on Cemetery Ridge at Little Round Top in Gettysburg National Military Park, Adams County. The ridge on the horizon is South Mountain. Diabase blocks in the foreground were derived from the Lower Jurassic Gettysburg pluton. The rock pile across the road, visible in the center of the photograph, is called Devils Den. Photograph by Charles H. Shultz, May 1978.

FIGURE 65. Devils Den, 3.5 miles south of Gettysburg, Adams County, in Gettysburg National Military Park, was occupied by Confederate sharpshooters during the Battle of Gettysburg on July 2, 1863. The "boulders" result from spheroidal weathering of Lower Jurassic diabase of the Gettysburg pluton. Photograph by Charles H. Shultz, May 1978.

FIGURE 66. A dripstone column, approximately 3 feet in height, developed in nearly horizontal layers of limestone of the Middle Cambrian Elbrook Formation in Carnegie Cave, Shippensburg, Cumberland County. Part of the cave is under Interstate Route 81. Photograph by Charles E. Miller, Jr., August 1974.

Diorama depicting a Pennsylvanian coal swamp. The large amphibian is *Eryops*. The treelike plants in the upper center are *Calamites*, and the large trunk on the right is *Sigillaria*. The display is housed in the Benedum Hall of Geology, Carnegie Museum, Pittsburgh. Photograph courtesy of the Carnegie Museum.

Part VI

GEOLOGIC HISTORY

The decipherable geologic history of Pennsylvania began with the formation of the Precambrian basement complex, which was metamorphosed, intruded, and severely deformed during the Grenville orogeny (circa 1,000 Ma). The age of formation and nature of the parent rocks of Grenville gneisses are unknown and perhaps unknowable, but events creating the diverse and complex geology of Pennsylvania certainly began well in excess of 1 billion years ago.

This historical narrative is organized by era. The boundary between Precambrian and Paleozoic is marked by the onset of significant fossil deposition, but there is no evidence of changes in climate or gross physical process. During the transitions from the Paleozoic to Mesozoic and Mesozoic to Cenozoic Eras, no rocks were formed in Pennsylvania. The nearly continuous deposition with concomitant subsidence that characterized the Paleozoic of most of Pennsylvania, culminating in the Alleghanian orogeny during the suturing of Pangea, was replaced by a regime of uplift and erosion that continues episodically to the present. Post-Paleozoic deposits ranging from Late Triassic to Holocene are restricted to certain parts of Pennsylvania.

The reader will find considerable overlap from chapter to chapter. This not only emphasizes continuance of process, but the principle of inheritance as well, namely that early events and their effects set the stage for later ones in a kind of domino effect. Among the many processes involved are mountain building and deformation, volcanism, igneous intrusion, long periods of erosion and landscape evolution, transgression and regression of oceans and shallow seas, glaciation, epeirogenic uplift and downwarping, crustal subsidence, rifting, mineralization, and deposition of thousands of feet of sediment.

Readers will discover here an outstanding synthesis of a vast store of geologic fact and thought, punctuated with inventive new insights and creative original ideas.

—Charles H. Shultz

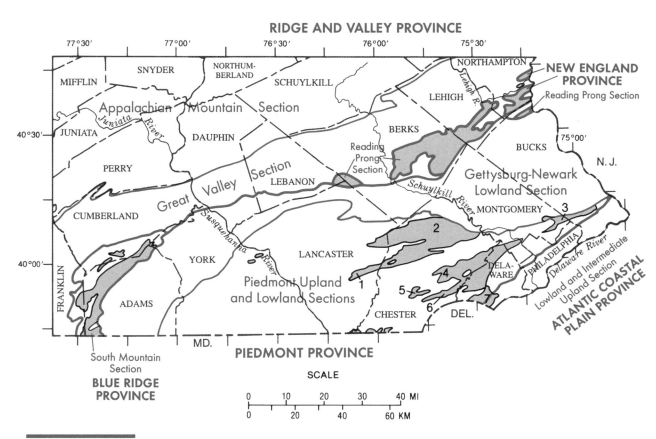

Figure 32–1. Map of southeastern Pennsylvania showing regions where Precambrian rocks are exposed (light brown). Geologic and cultural boundaries are modified from Berg and others (1980) and Pennsylvania Geological Survey (1990). Physiographic boundaries are from Berg and others (1989). 1, Mine Ridge; 2, Honey Brook Upland; 3, Trenton Prong; 4, West Chester Prong; 5, Woodville dome; 6, Avondale anticline; 7, Wilmington Complex.

414

CHAPTER 32   PRECAMBRIAN

MARIA LUISA CRAWFORD
Department of Geology
Bryn Mawr College
Bryn Mawr, PA 19010

WILLIAM A. CRAWFORD
Department of Geology
Bryn Mawr College
Bryn Mawr, PA 19010

ALICE L. HOERSCH
Department of Geology and Physics
LaSalle University
Philadelphia, PA 19141

MARY EMMA WAGNER
Department of Geology
University of Pennsylvania
Philadelphia, PA 19104

The Precambrian rocks in Pennsylvania (Figure 32-1) can be divided into two groups. The older ones, exposed in the Reading Prong and Piedmont Upland, are crystalline gneisses metamorphosed during the Grenville orogeny and yielding radioisotope ages of approximately 1,000 Ma. Unconformably overlying these gneisses in South Mountain and, locally, in the Reading Prong are a group of uppermost Precambrian (<750 Ma; Rankin and others, 1969) to Cambrian metavolcanic and metasedimentary units. The tectonic history outlined below is based on the igneous, metamorphic, and structural events described in Chapters 3A, 3B, and 16. Additional details are provided in reports by Wagner and Crawford (1975), Crawford and Crawford (1980), Crawford and Hoersch (1984), Drake (1984), Wagner and Srogi (1987), and Hoersch and Crawford (1988).

The oldest rocks record several periods of igneous and sedimentary activity and at least two major metamorphic events: the Grenville orogeny ($\sim 1,000$ Ma) and the Late Ordovician Taconic orogeny (~ 440 Ma). The nature of the Grenville orogeny has been the subject of much debate; many, following the analysis of Dewey and Burke (1973), suggest it was the result of plate collision. More recent interpretations of structural data in the Grenville rocks exposed in the Adirondacks (McLelland and Isachsen, 1980) suggest that continental collision and underthrusting is a reasonable tectonic model for that part of the Grenville orogenic belt. On the other hand, Baer (1981) proposed a mechanism of intraplate and intracontinental deformation by plate "jostling" that differs from the plate-edge types of deformation characteristic of the Phanerozoic. Geological relations in the Grenville rocks of eastern Canada and adjacent New York (Rivers and others, 1989) support the former interpretation.

The Grenville rocks exposed in Pennsylvania vary considerably in lithology and metamorphic grade. Many of these metamorphic rocks have a whole-rock chemistry that resembles the chemistry of igneous rocks, but metasedimentary units also occur. The latter can be recognized by their quartzitic, calcareous, or aluminous compositions. The high grade of metamorphism that has thoroughly recrystallized the rocks, the complex deformation that they have undergone, and limited exposure preclude correlation between exposed areas of Pennsylvania's Grenville-age rocks and restrict interpretation of their geologic history. During the Grenville orogeny, the rocks were deeply buried and heated sufficiently to generate metamorphic assemblages belonging to the granulite and amphibolite facies (see Table 3A–1). The highest metamorphic grade is preserved in the granulite gneisses of the West Chester Prong in the Piedmont Upland (Figure 32–1), but granulite-facies rocks also are common in the Honey Brook Upland (Figure 32–1), the Reading Prong, and in the subsurface in northwestern Pennsylvania.

In the Honey Brook Upland, the oldest crustal rocks, the charnockites (hypersthene-bearing granitic gneisses), were intruded by an anorthosite massif (see Figure 3A–2). This association also characterizes Grenville terranes in New York and Quebec. Overlying the charnockites are a group of volcanic rocks of the basalt-andesite-dacite-rhyolite series and associated volcaniclastic sediments (see Crawford and Hoersch, 1984, for a discussion of the geologic history of the Honey Brook Upland). During the Grenville event, the charnockite and intrusive anorthosite reached granulite-facies metamorphic conditions while the covering volcanic pile reached upper-amphibolite-facies conditions.

The lack of age determinations on rocks of Mine Ridge (Figure 32–1) makes it difficult to correlate the events there with those of the Honey Brook Upland. The mineral assemblages in Mine Ridge crystalline rocks indicate that they were metamorphosed under lower-amphibolite-facies conditions, whereas the mantling lower Paleozoic metasediments reached upper greenschist facies. Both have retrograded to lower greenschist facies (Hoersch and Crawford, 1988). It is not clear whether the lower-amphibolite-facies metamorphism of the crystalline core is the same age as the upper-greenschist-facies assemblages in the metasediments or if it is, perhaps, of Grenville age.

In the West Chester Prong, the granulite-grade metamorphism has so thoroughly recrystallized the rocks that there is little hope of deciphering their pre-Grenville history, or even whether they had igneous or sedimentary protoliths (parent rocks). Diabase dikes intruded the West Chester Prong granulite gneisses and those of the Honey Brook Upland and Mine Ridge after the Grenville orogeny but before the Paleozoic, as they do not cut the Cambrian

clastic rocks. The dikes have chilled borders, and most are undeformed and display relict ophitic texture, even though they were metamorphosed together with their host rocks during the Taconic orogeny. They can be clearly distinguished from later Mesozoic diabase dikes on the basis of this metamorphism. It is possible that the dikes are the same age as the late Precambrian Catoctin metavolcanic units in South Mountain.

During the Taconic metamorphism, some of the Grenville-age gneisses of the West Chester Prong were partially recrystallized at high pressure (9 to 10 kb) in a static metamorphism of dry rocks. Elsewhere, where water had access and the rocks were deformed, the Precambrian rocks were recrystallized to amphibolite-facies assemblages that tend to obliterate evidence of the Precambrian metamorphic event.

In the Reading Prong, the oldest rocks appear to be an oceanic suite overlain by a thick pile of metavolcanic rocks called the Losee Metamorphic Suite (see Chapter 3B). This is overlain, in turn, by calcareous and quartzo-feldspathic metasediments. All of these units are metamorphosed to uppermost amphibolite and granulite facies and, locally, have undergone partial anatexis, generating the granitic rocks of the Byram Intrusive Suite that occurs throughout the Reading Prong. These Grenville-age rocks show little or no evidence of Late Ordovician (Taconic) metamorphism.

Uppermost Precambrian units unconformably overlie the Grenville sequence in South Mountain (the Catoctin Formation and the Chilhowee Group) and in the Reading Prong (the Chestnut Hill Formation; see Chapter 3B). Rankin (1976) proposed that the peralkaline rhyolite and basalt of the Catoctin volcanic suite are diagnostic of a continental-rift environment. The overlying Chilhowee clastic sequence, which may represent rift-related sedimentation, grades upward into the lower Paleozoic miogeoclinal sequence.

In the Southern Upland of the Piedmont, the Glenarm Supergroup (of unknown age) lies unconformably above rocks of Grenville age (see Figure 16–2). Some have correlated the lowermost Glenarm units with the lithologically similar Cambrian-Ordovician miogeoclinal sequence that mantles Mine Ridge, the Honey Brook Upland, and the northern side of the Trenton Prong. However, some parts of the Wissahickon Formation could be late Precambrian in age, and Higgins (1972) pointed out that much of the Wissahickon is considered correlative with much of the Chilhowee Group. The Wissahickon Formation probably represents turbidites and basalt flows deposited in a marginal basin, in part on oceanic crust and in part on downwarped continental crust. The nature of the contact between the Wissahickon Formation schists and the Ordovician formations in the Chester-Whitemarsh and Conestoga Valleys (the Martic Line) is discussed in Chapter 16.

During the Taconic orogeny, or perhaps earlier, a thick plate of hot, uppermost Precambrian(?) Wilmington Complex gneisses (Figure 32–1) was thrust onto the North American continent (Crawford and Mark, 1982; Wagner and Srogi, 1987). The only evidence for the age of the complex is the 502 Ma date obtained from the Arden pluton that intrudes the Wilmington Complex (Foland and Muessig, 1978). The heat of the Wilmington Complex plate was responsible, in part, for the high-grade Taconic metamorphism of the underlying Wissahickon Formation. Wagner and Srogi (1987) considered the Taconic metamorphism in the West Chester Prong to be due to heating during deep burial of this part of the North American continent under the combined thicknesses of the advancing Wilmington Complex plate, of basement-involved nappes (Avondale anticline and Woodville dome), and of deformed marginal-basin sediments (Wissahickon Formation). The Taconic deformation also transported the gneisses of the Reading Prong north over the lower Paleozoic units of the Great Valley.

Following these events, probably in the middle to late Paleozoic, folding and faulting raised blocks of Precambrian gneiss to their present position, deforming the overlying cover rocks and leading to the present outcrop pattern of the Precambrian units (Figure 32–1).

PROBLEMS AND FUTURE RESEARCH

Radiometric ages for many of the Precambrian units are needed. In most of the Piedmont Upland, the original ages of the rocks that were metamorphosed during the Grenville orogeny are not known. In addition, the ages of the Glenarm Supergroup and the Wilmington Complex remain unknown. The age of the successive metamorphic recrystallization events that affected the Precambrian rocks is also uncertain, especially in Mine Ridge and the Avondale anticline.

Based on whole-rock chemical analyses, the parent rocks of the Grenville-age rocks in the Reading Prong, Honey Brook Upland, Mine Ridge, and West Chester Prong are not similar. Geophysical evidence suggests that the Reading Prong, Honey Brook Upland, and Mine Ridge are not rooted; rather, they are allochthonous. Are the Grenville-age rocks all part of the same original terrane, or have they separate origins? When were the Precambrian blocks transported to their present positions? How can the histories of these Precambrian blocks be correlated with those in similar geological settings in Maryland, to the south, and New York, to the north?

RECOMMENDED FOR FURTHER READING

Crawford, M. L., and Crawford, W. A. (1980), *Metamorphic and tectonic history of the Pennsylvania Piedmont,* Journal of the Geological Society of London, v. 137, p. 311–320.

Crawford, M. L., and Mark, L. E. (1982), *Evidence from metamorphic rocks for overthrusting, Pennsylvania Piedmont, U. S. A.,* Canadian Mineralogist, v. 20, p. 333–347.

Crawford, W. A., and Hoersch, A. L. (1984), *The geology of the Honey Brook Upland, southeastern Pennsylvania,* in Bartholomew, M. J., ed., *The Grenville event in the Appalachians and related topics,* Geological Society of America Special Paper 194, p. 111–125.

Drake, A. A., Jr. (1984), *The Reading Prong of New Jersey and eastern Pennsylvania—an appraisal of rock relations and chemistry of a major Proterozoic terrane in the Appalachians,* in Bartholomew, M. J., ed., *The Grenville event in the Appalachians and related topics,* Geological Society of America Special Paper 194, p. 75–109.

Hoersch, A. L., and Crawford, W. A. (1988), *The Mine Ridge of the SE Pennsylvania Piedmont,* Northeastern Geology, v. 10, p. 181–194.

Wagner, M. E., and Crawford, M. L. (1975), *Polymetamorphism of the Precambrian Baltimore Gneiss in southeastern Pennsylvania,* American Journal of Science, v. 275, p. 653–682.

Wagner, M. E., and Srogi, LeeAnn (1987), *Early Paleozoic metamorphism at two crustal levels and a tectonic model for the Pennsylvania-Delaware Piedmont,* Geological Society of America Bulletin, v. 99, p. 113–126.

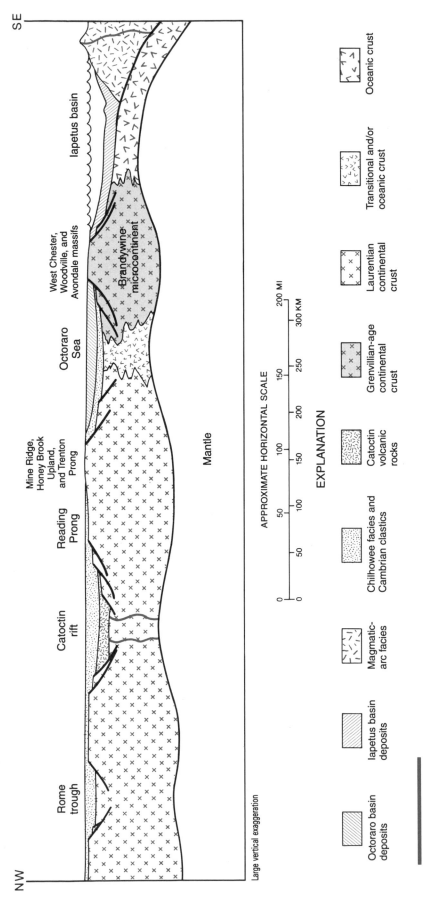

Figure 33–1. Schematic cross section through the eastern margin of Laurentia, showing the relative positions of the four rifts. Heavy colored lines represent volcanic vents.

SE

Iapetus basin

West Chester,
Woodville, and
Avondale massifs

Brandywine
microcontinent

Octoraro
Sea

Mine Ridge,
Honey Brook
Upland,
and Trenton
Prong

Reading
Prong

Catoctin
rift

Rome
trough

Mantle

NW

Large vertical exaggeration

APPROXIMATE HORIZONTAL SCALE

200 MI

300 KM

EXPLANATION

Octoraro basin
deposits

Iapetus basin
deposits

Chilhowee facies and
Cambrian clastics

Catoctin volcanic
rocks

Magmatic-
arc facies

Grenvillian-age
continental
crust

Laurentian
continental
crust

Transitional and/or
oceanic crust

Oceanic crust

418

CHAPTER 33   PALEOZOIC

RODGER T. FAILL
Bureau of Topographic and Geologic Survey
Department of Conservation and Natural
  Resources
P. O. Box 8453
Harrisburg, PA 17105

INTRODUCTION

It began with rifting. Three orogenies later, the Appalachian orogen stood as a high mountain system. In the early part of the formation of this orogen, marginal oceanic basins and microcontinents were thrust onto the carbonate shelf above the eastern Laurentian continental margin; subsequently, the continental Appalachian basin formed, filled, and was deformed—only to undergo rifting, again. So passed the Paleozoic Era in Pennsylvania.

The Taconic, Acadian, and Alleghany were the three principal orogenies. The Taconic telescoped and metamorphosed Cambrian and Ordovician shelf rocks and various microcontinental and marginal oceanic terranes into an assemblage of thrust sheets that defines much of the present-day distribution of terranes in southeastern Pennsylvania. The Middle Devonian Acadian deformed (to some minor extent) and uplifted this Taconic assemblage, but its greater influence was in generating the tremendous volume of sediment that was deposited in the Appalachian basin. The Permian Alleghany further telescoped southeastern Pennsylvania into its present configuration. Through décollement tectonics, the Alleghany also created the Blue Ridge province, may have overthrust the Anthracite region, and generated in the Appalachian basin the foreland folds and faults for which the Appalachians are so famous.

THE INITIAL CONFIGURATION

Crustal extension late in the Neoproterozoic separated the ancient North American continent, Laurentia, from Baltica and Gondwana. The separation fragmented the eastern margin of the Laurentian craton into a number of rifts and microcontinents. To the east, a magmatic arc formed in the Iapetus, the Late Proterozoic-early Paleozoic proto-Atlantic ocean. Four rifts were developed: the Rome trough, the Catoctin rift, the Octoraro Sea, and the Iapetus basin (Figures 33–1 and 33–2).

The Rome trough, in the west, was the youngest and least developed of the rifts. Lying unconformably on presumably Laurentian rocks, the age of the oldest rift deposits is probably Late Cambrian. The very limited deep drilling in Pennsylvania suggests the deposits are mainly carbonates and sandstones (Wagner, 1966b).

The Catoctin rift, some 250 km (155 mi) to the southeast (Figure 33–2), is also floored with presumably Laurentian crustal rocks (Clarke, 1984). In contrast to the Rome trough, a thick sequence of volcanic rocks, the Catoctin volcanics, represents the earliest deposits. These are overlain by quartzites, slates, and phyllites of the Chilhowee Series.

Another segment of the Laurentian continent rose east of the Catoctin rift. From this horst would come the various Taconic nappes that make up the Musconetcong nappe megasystem (Drake, 1984). The eastern edge of this horst was to become a fundamen-

tal boundary during the early Paleozoic—the southeast edge of the carbonate shelf on the craton margin. Southeast of this horst stretched the Octoraro Sea, in which were deposited the shales, graywackes, sandstones, and a few volcanic rocks that compose a large fraction of the siliciclastic Piedmont terrane in York and central Lancaster Counties.

Southeast of the Octoraro Sea were perhaps two microcontinents, both Grenville-age fragments of uncertain provenance: the Baltimore, from which the Baltimore gneiss-domes were derived (the Towson block of Muller and Chapin, 1984); and the Brandywine, which would form the West Chester, Woodville, and Avondale nappe massifs with their Glenarm Supergroup cover (Faill and MacLachlan, 1989). The marginal oceanic basin of a magmatic arc lay farther southeast. Within it developed the felsic to mafic

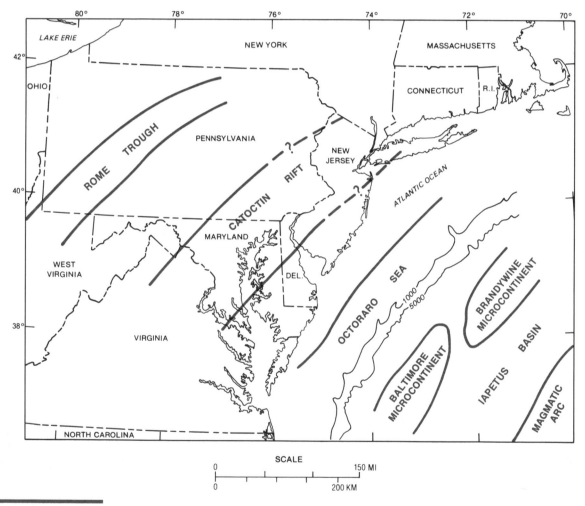

Figure 33–2. Paleogeographic map of the mid-Atlantic area on the eastern margin of Laurentia at the end of the Neoproterozoic. Both the Rome trough and Catoctin rift were well established, the Baltimore and Brandywine microcontinents had probably separated from Laurentia, and the Iapetus basin was growing. Contours show the depth of the present-day ocean over the continental shelf, in feet.

and the ultramafic rocks from which the Wilmington Complex and the James Run Formation in Maryland would be derived. Farther to the east, a portion of the Iapetus would form the siliciclastic sequence (Wissahickon Formation) that now underlies much of Philadelphia.

THE CONTINENTAL MARGIN

The oldest deposits of the newly formed Laurentian continental margin, found in the Catoctin rift, are the Precambrian (latest Neoproterozoic) Catoctin sequence of volcanic rocks. Uplift in the craton to the west probably began during the Neoproterozoic and earliest Paleozoic, initiating an eastward transport of sand and mud that accumulated in the rift as the oldest Chilhowee sediments, overlying the waning emissions from the earlier rift volcanism (Figure 33–3). By the close of the Proterozoic, this clastic material had largely filled both the Catoctin rift and the Rome trough, and began to cover the continental margin to the southeast as well. To the northeast, only the youngest beds of the Chilhowee Series (the Hardyston Formation) were deposited.

The deepening and filling of the Catoctin rift was ending by the start of the Cambrian, and this eastern part of the Laurentian craton became a passive continental margin. Gradual subsidence resulted in the westward transgression of a basal quartzitic sandy beach (represented by the Hardyston, Antietam, and Potsdam Formations of the Chilhowee Group) across this submerging shelf, reaching western Pennsylvania

by the late Middle Cambrian. Seaward (eastward) of this beach edge, carbonate deposition occurred in shallow water. In the absence of any prominent source areas on or near the shelf, this carbonate deposition spread from the shelf edge progressively westward, following the westward march of the leading beach deposits.

A pattern developed on this carbonate shelf that persisted into the Middle Ordovician (Figure 33–4). Dolomites formed in the shallower (supratidal to occasionally subtidal) western waters, and limy beds formed in the deeper (peritidal and subtidal) waters farther east toward the shelf edge (see Chapters 4 and 5). Occasional impulses of well-sorted sand from the west (e.g., in the Cambrian Waynesboro and Gatesburg Formations) added quartzose intervals to the carbonate sections. Subsidence was faster in the east, resulting in greater accumulations there. Either an uplift of the craton during the Early Ordovician suspended deposition across the western shelf, or early Middle Ordovician uplift caused extensive erosion of Lower Ordovician units. However, this hiatus, called the Knox unconformity, did not affect the eastern shelf.

Seven distinct carbonate sequences (see Figure 33–4) developed across the broad lower Paleozoic carbonate bank, their differences depending on such factors as proximity to carbonate bank sources, depth of water, and currents. These separate environments were rather stationary through much of the carbonate-shelf history, but, late in the Middle Ordovician, a northwestward progression of environments began in response to the growing Taconic orogeny to the southeast.

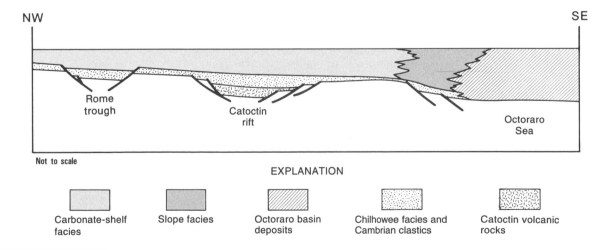

Figure 33–3. Schematic cross section of the eastern North American continental margin (in the mid-Atlantic region) in the early Late Ordovician. The thick sequences of the carbonate shelf grade southeastwardly through the slope facies into the basin deposits of the Octoraro Sea. These overlie the siliciclastic rocks of the Chilhowee Series and their lateral equivalents, which, in turn, largely covered the late Neoproterozoic and Cambrian rift structures.

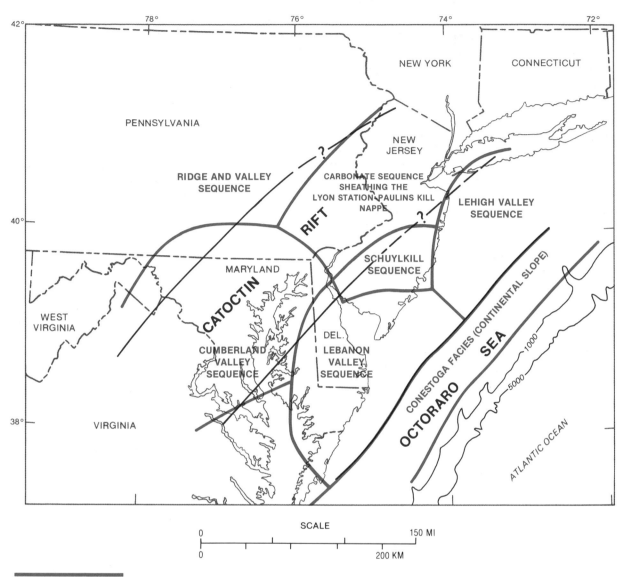

Figure 33–4. Paleogeographic map of the Cambrian-Ordovician carbonate shelf, showing the relative positions of the various carbonate sequences. The sequences probably graded laterally into one another. Contours show the depth of the present-day ocean over the continental shelf, in feet.

THE CONTINENTAL SLOPE AND BASINS TO THE SOUTHEAST

Meanwhile, another story was unfolding to the southeast on the continental slope and in the Octoraro Sea and Iapetus basin. This fundamental contrast in sedimentation was initiated during the latest Proterozoic and persisted for the next 150 million years.

The shallow water at the carbonate bank edge (the southeast boundary of the carbonate shelf) passed southeastwardly into deeper water. Carbonate detrital material from the bank edge and fine-grained siliciclastic material from the adjoining Octoraro Sea mixed

to produce an intertonguing limestone and argillaceous limestone sequence, the Cambrian-Ordovician Conestoga Formation, on the continental slope. This "hybrid" unit graded laterally into the shelf carbonates to the northwest, and into the basin pelites to the southeast (Figure 33–3).

The Octoraro Sea and Iapetus basin lay southeast of the continental slope and surrounded the microcontinents. At what stage they had originally formed during the Neoproterozoic (relative to the Catoctin rift) is not known, but the sedimentation was initially quite different (see Chapter 3A). No quartzose-carbonate succession overlay the oceanic to transitional crust—

the initial sediments were pelagic and did not become hemipelagic and turbiditic until the Middle Ordovician (Lash and Drake, 1984). The shales and siltstones in the basins northwest of the microcontinents (from which the Hamburg klippe hailed) were derived from both the continent and the microcontinents. The pelites farther to the southeast were extensively interbedded with volcanic flows and intrusions (Baltimore Complex) that were largely derived from the mature magmatic arcs (James Run Formation and Wilmington Complex) that lay either within the Iapetus basin, or on its eastern margin (Muller and Chapin, 1984). Volcanism did not reach the western parts of the Octoraro Sea until the Middle Ordovician (e.g., Sams Creek Formation of Maryland and in York County).

On the Baltimore and Brandywine microcontinents, a lithic sequence developed that is grossly similar to the lower part of the shelf sequences. A quartzose unit, the Setters Formation, was deposited on Grenville gneisses over much of the Baltimore microcontinent and over part of the Brandywine block of Grenville gneisses; above this, a fairly impure to pure carbonate, the Cockeysville Marble, was laid down. Although no real correlation exists between these rocks and the shelf rocks, this succession of quartzites and carbonates unconformably overlying the Grenville rocks of the Baltimore block and the southwestern part of the Brandywine block could indicate that these two microcontinental fragments did not separate from Laurentia until the beginning of the Cambrian. On the other hand, the fragmentation of the Laurentian margin could have been much earlier, in which case the similarities of the postunconformity lithic sequences merely reflect similar depositional environments. In either case, continued and more rapid subsidence of the microcontinental region resulted in pelagic and hemipelagic sediments spreading over the carbonates and some of the formerly emergent gneisses.

THE TACONIC OROGENY: ASSEMBLAGE

Reversal of plate motion stopped the spreading of Iapetus; the convergence that followed generated the Taconic orogeny. The initial aspect of the orogeny was a southeastward subduction of the Iapetus oceanic crust under the magmatic arc farther east (Rankin, 1975; Muller and Chapin, 1984). The resulting mafic to ultramafic igneous suite of rocks became interbedded with the pelagic sediments in, and adjacent to, the trench. When the Brandywine and Baltimore microcontinents reached the trench (probably in the Middle

Ordovician), their buoyancy prevented further subduction. But the convergence continued.

The crushing of the magmatic arc against the microcontinents changed the character of the carbonate shelf. The collision zone gradually rose, and the subsidence of the adjacent carbonate shelf to the northwest accelerated slightly, causing a regional northwestward shift in the depositional environments. Water depths increased throughout the Black Riverian and Trentonian Ages (Late Ordovician), changing the former dolomitic tidal deposition to a largely subtidal limestone environment. Also during the Trentonian, volcanic activity (presumably in the vicinity of the magmatic arc) dispersed numerous ash falls across the carbonate shelf. Continued elevation of the collision zone to the southeast generated increasing volumes of siliciclastic detritus that began to encroach upon the shelf. The westward spread of this terrigenous material first covered southeastern Pennsylvania in the latter part of the Trentonian, resulting in deposition of the Martinsburg Formation, and extended across the rest of the state throughout the Edenian and Maysvillian Ages as the Reedsville Shale. Concomitantly, the dolomite and limestone associations migrated farther northwest onto the craton. The Taconic clastic wedge had begun to form (see Chapter 5).

Coeval with these shifts in depositional environments, Taconic structures began to appear near the collision zone and on the shelf to the west. One of the earliest events was the pushing of large slabs of Cambrian to Middle Ordovician terrigenous sediments from the Octoraro Sea up onto the shelf. The one slab that arrived in Pennsylvania, the Hamburg klippe, developed in front of the Lebanon Valley nappe. As the Octoraro Sea rose, the klippe, a group of perhaps as many as eight or more blocks and slices of various lithologic sequences, slid into the Martinsburg pelites that were accumulating above the drowned carbonate shelf (MacLachlan and others, 1975). Smaller pieces spalled off the edges of the klippe to form a wildflysch imbedded within shales of the surrounding Martinsburg sediments.

The creation of the Hamburg klippe was merely the icing, so to speak. The main action lay farther to the southeast. During the continuing convergence at the collision zone, several large nappes containing masses of Precambrian Grenville gneiss and overlying cover rocks were "flaked" off the Laurentian crust and driven northwestward on low-angle thrusts into the Martinsburg shales and siltstones being deposited toward the craton on the continental shelf (Figure 33–5) (see Chapter 17). Most of the nappes contained a crystalline core of Grenville rocks overlain by, or even wrapped in (as in a recumbent fold), a mostly carbonate cover. Converging from different parts of the continental shelf, they were tectonically superimposed. However, they were not stacked one upon the other but, rather, partially overlapped along the Appalachian trend (Figure 33–6). These nappes are the Lebanon Valley (perhaps the only one without a Grenville core), the Irish Mountain (the core of which is the northern part of the Reading Prong), the Applebutter (forming the southern part of the Reading Prong and Buckingham Mountain), the Musconetcong (forming the northeasternmost part of the Reading Prong in Pennsylvania and into New Jersey), and the Lyon Station-Paulins Kill (forming the Reading Prong in New Jersey and descending into the subsurface in Pennsylvania). Together, these nappes compose the Musconetcong nappe megasystem (Drake, 1978).

The piling up of these nappes on the eastern part of the shelf produced a growing highland that shed increasing amounts of detritus westward into what was then becoming the Appalachian basin. The elevation of this Taconic mountain system permanently changed the carbonate shelf on a passive continental margin into a continental basin adjacent to a very active continental margin. Previously open to the ocean, this western Appalachian basin region would from now to the end of the Paleozoic be separated from eastern

seas by the Taconic mountains and two succeeding mountain systems.

The westward migration of shale deposition across the shelf from the Trentonian to the Maysvillian Age was the beginning of the Taconic clastic wedge. With continued rising of the highlands to the east, the sediments increased in volume and in coarseness. By the end of the Late Ordovician, the Appalachian basin was covered by a sequence of sandstones, mudstones, and conglomerates. In contrast, the Martinsburg underlying the eastern part of the basin was truncated by an unconformity.

And still the convergence continued. Now additional slabs were flaked off the Brandywine microcontinent and carried northwestward onto the shelf, along with their overlying beds and parts of the basin deposits containing fragments of oceanic crust. To the southwest, the Baltimore nappe was thrust over the Liberty Complex and Westminster terranes of Maryland and York County, which had been derived from the Octoraro Sea at the foot of the Laurentian continental slope. Farther to the northeast, the Brandywine nappe(s), comprising the West Chester, Avondale, and Woodville massifs, along with associated surrounding Glenarm rocks, were pushed up and onto the Octoraro Sea deposits and the Reading nappes already emplaced on the shelf. From behind, the graywacke,

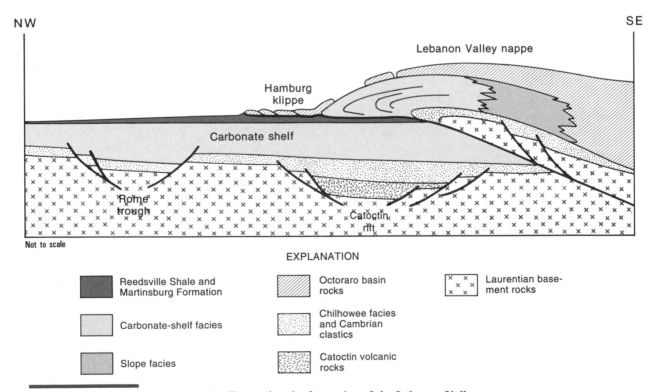

Figure 33–5. Schematic cross section illustrating the formation of the Lebanon Valley nappe during the Taconic orogeny.

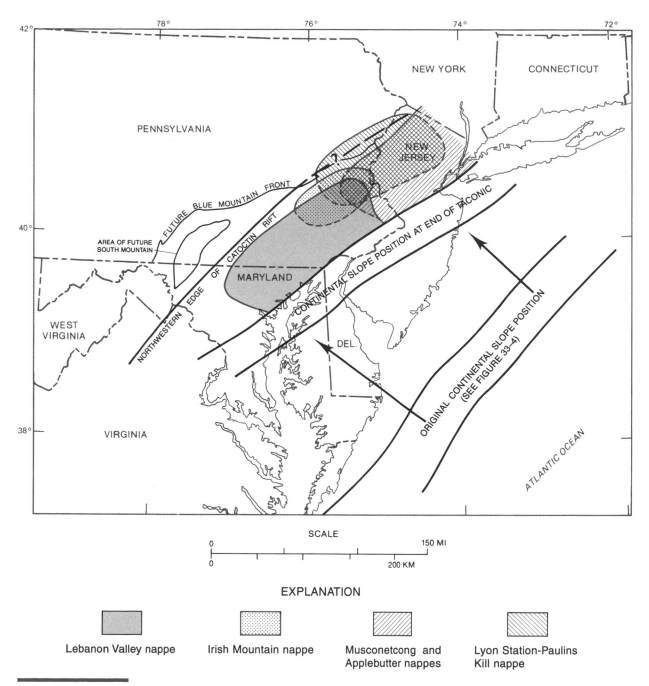

Figure 33–6. Paleogeographic map showing the overlapping of the various nappes (cores and overlying carbonate sequences) at the end of the Taconic orogeny at the close of the Ordovician. From highest structural level to lowest structural level, the order of nappes is as follows: Lebanon Valley, Irish Mountain, Musconetcong and Applebutter, and Lyon Station-Paulins Kill. Contours show the depth of the present-day ocean over the continental shelf, in feet.

mafic, and ultramafic rocks of the Iapetan basin, along with the James Run and Wilmington Complex magmatic arcs and the Wissahickon (Philadelphia terrane) east of the Rosemont fault, were thrust against and over the microcontinental Baltimore and Brandywine nappes (Figure 33–7).

A widespread, low- to high-grade metamorphism affected the Piedmont from the Taconic to the Acadian (Crawford and Crawford, 1980). The degree to which the lower grade metamorphism in the west was simply a burial metamorphism is moot—the coincidence of upper-greenschist facies with the hinge of

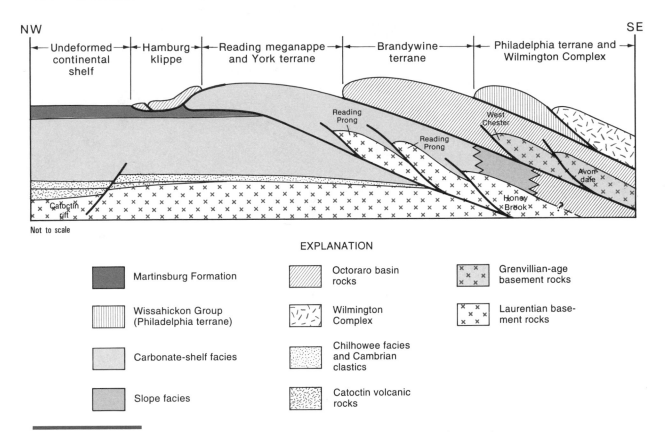

Figure 33–7. Schematic cross section illustrating the telescoping and stacking of the various Taconic nappes.

the Tucquan antiform (Faill and Valentino, 1989) suggests simple uplift of regional, bed-parallel gradations in the degree of metamorphism (see Figure 16–2 for the location of the Tucquan antiform). In the eastern Piedmont, the telescoping and overriding of the various nappes produced considerable heat in the rocks, probably in excess of 600°C in the deeper parts, causing a widespread Barrovian regional metamorphism. A center of low-pressure granulite-grade metamorphism developed around the Wilmington Complex (Crawford and Mark, 1982), probably related to its emplacement over the Brandywine nappes (Wagner and Srogi, 1987). Heating persisted in these rocks for more than 50 million years, until uplifts, possibly produced by the Acadian orogeny, occurred. A retrograde greenschist metamorphism that is widespread throughout the Piedmont may have coincided with Alleghany transpressional tectonics.

THE APPALACHIAN BASIN: FROM FLYSCH TO PARALIC SEA

So, the Taconic orogeny transformed most of the carbonate shelf into the Appalachian basin. Uplift and erosion of the Taconic highlands along the south-eastern part of the basin provided the detritus that flowed northwestward and filled the basin. The Taconic began a lithologic sequence that would continue to accumulate over the next 180 million years. This accumulation would record the tectonic events taking place in the active Appalachian orogen to the southeast in the suture between the jostling, colliding cratons.

By the end of the Carboniferous, the Appalachian basin was very deep, having accepted up to 8,000 m (26,000 ft) of sediment. The basin was also widespread, extending at its maximum from Canada southwestward to Alabama along the western side of the Appalachian Mountains. It was also asymmetric, rapidly thinning to the east to what had been an ever-shifting strandline. To the west, the basin tapered gradually, merging imperceptibly into the cratonal mid-continental deposits.

But back to the beginning. The initial Late Ordovician Martinsburg/Reedsville flysch deposits were conformably succeeded by Richmondian Age molassic siltstones, sandstones, and conglomerates of the Bald Eagle and Juniata Formations (lower part of the Taconic molasse in Figure 33–8). These beds thin and pinch out southeastwardly. Whether they were deposited and subsequently eroded, or were never deposited at

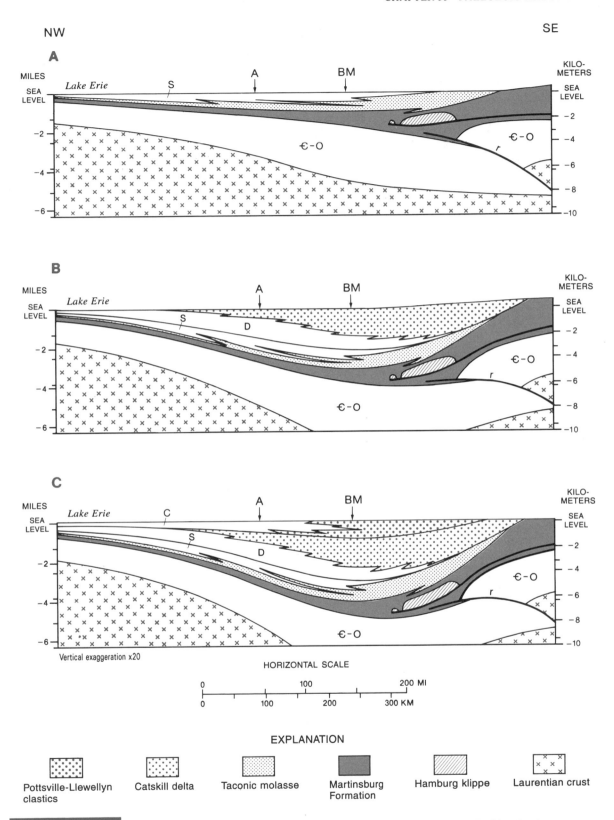

Figure 33–8. Schematic cross sections illustrating the Paleozoic development of the Appalachian basin in Pennsylvania: A, at the end of the Silurian; B, at the end of the Devonian; and C, at the end of the Carboniferous. Symbols in the sections are as follows: A, position of the Alleghany structural front; BM, position of the Blue Mountain Front; r, Reading nappe thrust; C, Carboniferous rocks; D, Devonian rocks; S, Silurian rocks; and €-O, Cambrian and Ordovician rocks of the carbonate shelf.

all, is not known. The beveling of Taconic structures indicates that erosion did occur in eastern Pennsylvania along Blue Mountain. In northwestern Pennsylvania, erosion or nondeposition also marks the Richmondian.

The Taconic orogeny had probably ended by the beginning of the Silurian Period, but the detritus eroded from its mountains would continue to affect the Appalachian basin through the Niagaran Epoch and into the Cayugan Epoch. These sediments form the upper part of the Taconic clastic wedge, which was most extensive at the beginning of the Silurian, but gradually shrank in size with time. The fluvial quartz arenites of the Shawangunk Formation dominated eastern Pennsylvania and graded westwardly into the more marine Tuscarora and Medina Formations (see Chapter 6). As the detrital input decreased in the latter part of the Niagaran, the sandy facies retreated eastward and were succeeded in the western part of the state by the finer grained, detrital Clinton beds. Limestone and, farther west, dolomite deposits also crept eastward on the heels of the Clinton. East-west shifting of these deposits was in response to sporadic increases of sediments from the eastern highlands (e.g., the Bloomsburg delta).

Slow subsidence and sparse sediment input then prevailed for the remainder of the Silurian, enabling carbonate deposition to dominate much of the Appalachian basin. The environments suitable for carbonate deposition passed into more evaporitic environments to the west and north. In these areas, anhydrite and salt, which would play a significant tectonic role some 130 million years later, were precipitated.

More-normal shallow-marine conditions became established near the end of the Late Silurian Cayugan Epoch. The overlying heterogeneous mixture of Lower Devonian Helderbergian and Deerparkian Age limestones, cherts, and shales, capped by the Ridgeley (Oriskany) Sandstone (see Chapter 7), suggests more-restricted (areally) and variable environments. The widespread late Deerparkian erosion (which began in the Cayugan in northwestern Pennsylvania) was particularly severe on the Auburn Promontory northeast of Harrisburg, where rocks of the Onondaga Formation lie on rocks as old as the Bloomsburg Formation. In contrast, sedimentation was apparently continuous in eastern Pennsylvania.

The period of Deerparkian erosion, however, was short-lived. Early Onesquethawan Age muds were overlain by Onondaga limestone. Paralic stability, it seems, had returned to the Appalachian basin.

But then it ended, abruptly.

ACADIAN STIRRINGS, THE CATSKILL DELTA, ET CETERA

One could say the Acadian orogeny in Pennsylvania started with a bang—certainly the Tioga ash fall at the top of the Onondaga Formation represents a volcanicity that the central Appalachians had not experienced since the early part of the Late Ordovician, some 70 million years before. The Tioga was widespread, it was distinctive, and it marked the beginning of a terrigenous sedimentation that was to proceed for the next 110 million years, up to and through the late Carboniferous Alleghany orogeny.

Nothing is really known of Early to Middle Devonian Acadian activity in the Appalachian orogen east of Pennsylvania. Aside from the evidence in New England and the southern Appalachians, the principal evidence for an Acadian orogeny is recorded in the rocks of the Appalachian basin and in the probable Acadian structures in the Piedmont in southeastern Pennsylvania. First, the Piedmont.

After Taconic tectonism ended, the elevated temperatures in the orogen persisted for a long time. The rise of the Taconic highlands at the end of the Ordovician did not allow the rocks to cool enough to interrupt the process of metamorphism, and tectonic inactivity during the Silurian kept these rocks nicely buried and hot. The Acadian spoiled it, even though its extent was limited—the farthest northwest that Acadian tectonism reached in Pennsylvania was the Piedmont. The subhorizontal Taconic cleavage and isoclinal folding were transected by subvertical slip surfaces and folded into open, upright, regional folds (Freedman and others, 1964). The Tucquan antiform, cored by upper-greenschist-grade rocks, and Mine Ridge are the primary examples of this folding. Uplift of the Piedmont at this time is corroborated by the fact that the earliest metamorphic clasts from the Piedmont are found in the uppermost Upper Devonian rocks in the Appalachian basin, those in the lower part of the Spechty Kopf Formation. Presumably, only the cover rocks over the Piedmont were exposed to erosion before then. In addition, most of the radiometric ages in the Piedmont, which are cooling dates, cluster in the 360 to 320 Ma age span (largely early Carboniferous).

The absence of Acadian deformational structures northwest of the Piedmont (see Faill, 1985a) means that the only evidence of the Acadian orogeny in the Appalachian basin is the record of sedimentologic changes (see Chapter 7). The Tioga ash fall was immediately followed by a rapid subsidence within the basin in which the black shales of the Marcellus Formation accumulated. The rising terranes to the southeast created subaqueous deltas composed of upward-coarsening cycles that graded laterally northward, northwestward, and westward into the siltstones, shales, and limestones that filled the more distal parts of the basin. A decrease in sediment input brought the Middle Devonian to a close with the spread of the argillaceous Tully Limestone across much of the basin.

The depositional patterns that followed during the Late Devonian in response to the presumably continued Acadian tectonism and uplift to the east and southeast were quite different. The central Appalachian basin (i.e., in Pennsylvania) encompasses a wide variety of lithologies that are complexly related (see Chapter 7). Basically, the basin was still an elongate trough paralleling the Appalachian orogen, bounded by open-marine conditions on the craton to the west and a large source of terrigenous material to the east. These two influences interacted in the Appalachian basin, which was rapidly and asymmetrically deepening, the greatest deepening occurring in the east.

Rapid subsidence at the beginning of the Upper Devonian terminated the rather shallow-water Middle Devonian deltas and must have shifted the strandline markedly to the east, as evidenced by the spread of black shale (Harrell Formation) deposition across the entire basin. Throughout most of the Fingerlakian Age, the deltas that probably existed east of Pennsylvania generated enough turbiditic flysch sedimentation to push the black shale deposits into western Pennsylvania. The thicker, coarser grained beds of the proximal Trimmers Rock Formation in the eastern part of the basin passed westward into thinner, less coarse, distal siltstones of the Brallier Formation, which graded into the Genesee and Sonyea shales in the western part of the state.

The rising of the highlands to the east must have persisted, because the Catskill delta, which had been forming in southern New York as early as the Middle Devonian, expanded into eastern Pennsylvania during the early Chemungian Age of the Upper Devonian. By the end of the Chemungian, the delta strandline had established itself in central Pennsylvania.

The Catskill delta continued to prograde westward across the basin throughout the remainder of the Late Devonian, pushing the marine environments ahead of it. Bursts of coarse detritus passed through the strandline to form the shallow-marine sandstones of the Elk and Bradford Groups, but in westernmost Pennsylvania, black shales remained dominant. On the Catskill delta to the east, the red siltstones and mudstones of the lower- and upper-delta-plain environments also crept westward behind the shoreline. The thickest and coarsest grained sequences of braided-river deposits accumulated in the area of the Lehigh River, indicating that a large input center was located there. Throughout the Middle and Late Devonian, input centers such as this shifted from one location to another (Sevon, 1985a).

The Acadian orogeny in the northern Appalachians had largely ended by the close of the Late Devonian, but in Pennsylvania, important changes were occurring in the Appalachian basin. Near the end of the Late Devonian, the upward-fining cyclicity of the Catskill Formation (Duncannon Member) gave way conformably (except in eastern Pennsylvania) to sandier intervals that passed upward into the quartzitic beds of the Mississippian Pocono Formation. Throughout the Lower Mississippian, the fluvial quartzitic sandstones, siltstones, and conglomerates of the Spechty Kopf and Pocono Formations spread westward across the former Catskill delta plain and graded laterally into the quartzitic sandstones of the Huntley Mountain and Burgoon Formations in western and southwestern Pennsylvania. Marine sandstones and shales continued to dominate the northwestern part of the state. However, in the eastern part of the state, a brief, but significant, disconformity developed at the top of the Catskill. On this disconformity, coarse-grained polymictic diamictites were deposited in localized lake basins, forming the base of the Spechty Kopf Formation. The presence of low-grade metamorphic rock fragments among the clasts in the Spechty Kopf indicates that the metamorphic core of the Piedmont had finally been exposed by the end of the Devonian. Their absence in every younger stratigraphic unit in the basin suggests that the source of the metamorphic clasts was soon blocked (Sevon, 1985a). In short, the gradual increase in sediment volume and coarseness, the termination of red-bed sedimentation, and the Spechty Kopf disconformity and diamictites reflected some tectonic activity that increased highland elevations to the southeast. Yet, the lack of renewed heating in the Piedmont and the absence of deformation in the basin (Faill, 1985a) indicate that no major orogenic collision was occurring.

The reduction of sediment input from the now lowering eastern highland during the Meramecian Age, along with continued subsidence, enabled a marine incursion to transgress the Burgoon delta, bringing in the distinctively crossbedded calcareous sandstones of the Loyalhanna Formation. In contrast to underlying units, the detrital source of the Loyalhanna was mostly from the north, principally from the Burgoon sandstones that were being eroded as a consequence of possible uplift of the Canadian Shield that began in the Early Mississippian. At the same time, fluvial-deltaic red beds began to accumulate in the southeast on the Mauch Chunk alluvial-deltaic plain.

Gradually increasing deposition on this alluvial-deltaic plain forced an early Chesterian westward regression of the sea, during which the Mauch Chunk red beds reached as far as southwestern Pennsylvania, where they repeatedly intertongued with marine limestones and shales. The delta may have extended across northern Pennsylvania as well, although lateral facies changes in the upper Mauch Chunk in the Lackawanna syncline suggest that the strandline was nearby. In either case, continued uplift to the north subsequently caused extensive erosion across north-central Pennsylvania, which, by the end of the Mississippian, had beveled formations as old as the uppermost Catskill.

Once again, at the beginning of the Pennsylvanian, the Appalachian basin underwent an important change (see Chapter 10). Accelerated uplift to the southeast gradually increased sediment volume and coarseness so that the Mauch Chunk delta became transformed into a Pottsville alluvial plain; far to the southwest, it merged into a coastal marine/nonmarine environment. Across northern Pennsylvania, the Pottsville, Sharon, and Olean sandstones and conglomerates had a northern cratonal source. The absence of red beds in the Pottsville indicates that the climate probably had changed to more steadily humid conditions. Although the renewal of coarse-detrital input to the basin from the southeast points to a resumption of tectonic activity in that direction, this activity was not the major collision between Africa and Laurentia that produced the Alleghany orogeny, because more than 25 million years of coal, sandstone, and limestone deposition lay ahead, a sequence that shows little evidence of syndepositional folding.

Two major sequences of cyclic coal deposition, interspersed with marine and freshwater limestones, followed the Pottsville. The lower one, the Allegheny Formation, accumulated on a lower delta plain during the Desmoinesian Age. The subsequent, relatively "barren" interval containing red beds, the Conemaugh Group of western Pennsylvania, reflects a westward progradation of the delta plain in the Missourian. A series of marine beds (the Glenshaw Formation) transgressed eastward during the late Missourian Age. The presence of the Mill Creek limestone (part of the Llewellyn Formation) in the Northern Anthracite field indicates that major Alleghany folding had not yet commenced. By the middle of the Virgilian Age, the delta plain had reestablished itself across Pennsylvania, and the second sequence of coal measures, the Monongahela Group, was forming in the western half of the state. In the Anthracite region, equivalent Virgilian coals comprise the middle part of the Llewellyn Formation.

The similarity of the Permian rocks of southwestern Pennsylvania to the underlying Pennsylvanian sequences indicates that the Carboniferous alluvial and delta plains persisted well into the Wolfcampian Age (see Chapter 11). The presence of some red beds, the paucity of coals, and the absence of marine zones point to a moderately arid, temperate climate, for the most part at a substantial distance above the strandline. How much additional sediment was deposited upon these youngest preserved beds before, during, or even after the Alleghany orogeny is not known. Some studies (e.g., Friedman, 1987) suggest thicknesses in excess of several kilometers.

And so closed the Paleozoic Appalachian basin in Pennsylvania. Slightly younger Permian beds of the Dunkard Group are present to the southwest in West Virginia, but there the sedimentary record stops. The next youngest preserved deposits in Pennsylvania are of Late Triassic age, but by then, the Appalachian orogen had changed tremendously. The Alleghany orogeny had done its work.

CLIMAX! THE ALLEGHANY OROGENY

The Alleghany was the final blow. Throughout the Paleozoic, Baltica, which probably consisted of several microcontinents, and who knows what else, had piled against this eastern margin of Laurentia, each collision leaving its tectonic imprint on the Appalachian orogen. Now it was Africa's turn.

Whatever was left of the proto-Atlantic ocean, Iapetus, was consumed in this last convergence, which was between Africa and that part of the eastern Laurentian margin that was to become the central and southern Appalachians. The tectonic uplifts throughout the Carboniferous, and perhaps even in the Late Devonian, could have been indirectly related to the consumption of this ocean basin. Even though Carboniferous convergence may have created the uplifts that continued to fill the Appalachian basin, it was not until the cratons met that the continent-to-continent collision, and the consequent Alleghany orogeny, began in earnest.

The date the orogeny commenced is not precisely known and could have varied along the orogen. The Dunkard basin lies at the outermost fringe of the Alleghany folds, and the depositional environment does not seem to have been much disturbed by any growing folds to the southeast. From this, one could argue that the foreland folding did not begin until after the Early Permian or, considering the several kilometers of sediment that have probably been eroded, perhaps even later. Despite paleomagnetic data that suggest a late Carboniferous age for the Alleghany folding (Van der Voo, 1979), significant foreland folding could not have started before deposition of the late Carboniferous (Missourian) Mill Creek limestone, or else this limestone would never have extended as far eastward as the Anthracite region. But then, foreland folding did not really mark the beginning of the Alleghany. In fact, Alleghany tectonism was expressed in three phases: an early, layer-parallel shortening; the main folding of the foreland; and a late, low-angle thrusting (Figure 33–9).

The Alleghany orogeny commenced with horizontal telescoping of the Laurentian crust in response to the African impingement. (This is not to imply that Africa escaped unscathed. Its western edge also underwent an orogenic deformation.) The telescoping took the form of southeast-dipping, low-angle thrust faults through the Grenville and older crustal rocks, perhaps utilizing, in part, earlier Taconic fault surfaces. Rising to the west, one or more of these thrusts broke through the upper surface of Precambrian Grenville into the Cambrian-Ordovician rocks of the early Paleozoic shelf, over which the Taconic assemblage of crustal "flakes" and shelf-edge, slope, and basin deposits had been thrust. That is to say, the faults "surfaced" from basement into the Paleozoic rocks somewhere beneath, or southeast of, the present Piedmont terrane.

Upon entering the well-bedded Paleozoics, the faults became concentrated in the shaly layers between the basal siliciclastics and the overlying carbonates, and followed this slippery zone northwestward. Having now merged and become a décollement, the faults carried the entire crystalline terrane westward in the hanging wall. As these rocks advanced, they pushed on the layered Paleozoic rocks of the foreland, generating a horizontally directed stress. The foreland rocks responded with a layer-parallel shortening that included fracturing, dissolution, flow, and twinning. The structures that resulted from this early phase of deformation are joints, bedding-plane wedges, distorted fossils and mud cracks, and cleavage (see Chapter 19).

Continuing collision engendered additional movement up the thrusts and along the décollement. Within the crystalline rocks, splays branched upward from the main thrusts across the Taconic and Acadian structures. In the layered Paleozoic rocks of the foreland, a different process developed. Splays from the basal décollement in the Cambrian rocks cut up through the overlying beds, but because of the mechanical anisotropy inherent in the bedded Paleozoic sequence, kink folding accompanied the faulting. As a consequence, long, first-order anticlines grew above each splay, each containing second- and higher order kink folds and lesser faults. It is not known definitively whether the first fold developed in the northwest with subsequent ones appearing progressively to the southeast, or if the first fold was in the southeast, and additional folds were generated in front as the folded mass moved northwestward. As of this writing, opinions heavily favor the latter, the "bulldozer" scenario (see Butler, 1987), but some evidence supports the former view (Faill, 1991).

The foreland basin contains two important boundaries. The northwesternmost is the Allegheny structural front, the boundary between the Valley and Ridge and the Appalachian Plateaus structural provinces. At the surface, the subvertical beds of the Nittany anticline (and its equivalents) pass directly into the gently dipping beds of the Plateau folds. At depth, the front consists of a major ramp of the décollement from the Cambrian strata to the salt layers in the Upper Silurian (Figure 33–9). Subordinate décollement horizons are present in the Cambrian shales and the Upper Ordovician Reedsville Shale near the front, but most of the Plateau folds terminate downward at the Salina interval (see Chapter 20).

The other boundary, the Blue Mountain structural front, separates the Appalachian Mountain section of the Ridge and Valley province from the Great Valley section. Two cleavages exist along the Great Valley from the Delaware River to approximately Carlisle, Cumberland County. The earlier, Taconic, slaty cleavage is more systematic, dipping gently to moderately to the southeast. The later, Alleghany, cleavage is generally more steeply dipping, but it is a fracture cleavage that has a more variable dip.

Of the various crustal thrusts that were active during the Alleghany, all but one emerged from the

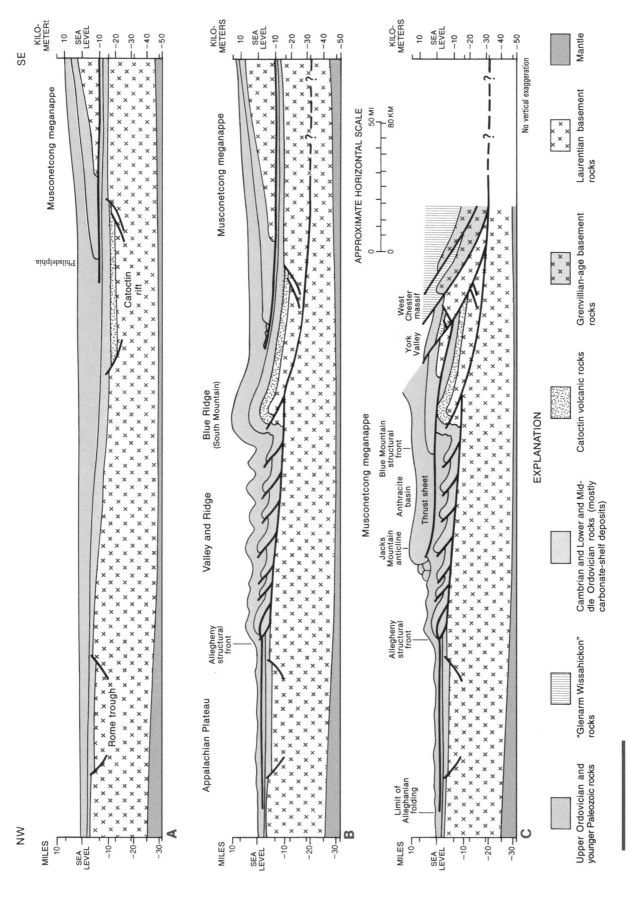

Figure 33-9. Composite schematic cross sections illustrating Alleghany tectonism in Pennsylvania. Each section is a hypothetical composite showing elements from different parts of the orogen: A, at the end of the late Carboniferous, just before the Alleghany commenced; B, at the end of the main folding phase; and C, after late thrusting.

Proterozoic rocks east of the Catoctin rift. In contrast, the westernmost thrust intercepted the trough, bringing up in its hanging wall much of the Late Proterozoic volcanic and transitional rocks that had been deposited there. These rocks rode up a splay on the southeast side of the Great Valley, forming the South Mountain anticlinorium.

And the collision between Laurentia and Africa continued. Late in the Alleghany, a complex of low-angle thrusts (including the Yellow Breeches, Grings Hill, and Oregon thrusts, among others) advanced the Piedmont and Reading Prong crystalline terranes to the north-northwest, overriding the largely overturned beds of the Taconic nappes (Figure 33–9C). These thrusts (or higher thrusts that have since been eroded) carried a regional nappe (now eroded) over the Blue Mountain front and onto the Anthracite region beyond. The presence of this Alleghany nappe and the heat generated by its movement may have elevated the temperatures in the anthracite beds to 300°C, imparting to them a lower-greenschist-facies metamorphism.

Alleghany thrusts were also active within the Piedmont. The most prominent ones, the Oregon and Chickies thrusts, carried the eastern continuation of the Blue Ridge up and over the Taconic nappe rocks of northern Lancaster County and Chester County. In York Valley, the proximity of limestones exhibiting only Alleghany-style folding to the Taconic metamorphosed pelites suggests that the intervening Stoner thrust had Alleghany movement. Other, as yet unrecognized, thrusts may lay farther to the southeast in the crystalline rocks.

This late thrusting seems to have been the last event of the Alleghany orogeny, which left behind an Appalachian highland consisting of long, parallel mountains in the foreland and a more irregular topography to the southeast on the stacked and overthrust nappes. Apparently, the Appalachian basin continued to accumulate sediments west of the newly folded foreland. But any direct record of this phase of the orogeny and its highlands is now gone, recycled into other, younger deposits.

EPILOGUE: AGAIN THE RIFTING

So passed the Paleozoic in Pennsylvania. It was a busy schedule covering a span of 300 million years. The three orogenies, accompanied by first shelf and then basin deposition, have provided a rich and varied geology within the Appalachian orogen. Follow-

ing the climax of the Alleghany orogeny, the preserved record becomes vacant (there may have once been a full record) and remains so until the beginning of the Late Triassic. By then, the Appalachian world was quite different, and a tectonism of an entirely different kind was beginning. Yes, it was rifting, again! But that story is for the next chapter.

PROBLEMS AND FUTURE RESEARCH

The most pressing problem, in terms of the Paleozoic history in Pennsylvania, is the delineation of tectonic boundaries in the southeastern part of the state. In order to trace these boundaries, the included areas need lithic, metamorphic, and structural descriptions by which they may be distinguished. Without these, restoration of the pre-Taconic paleogeography by unscrambling the Taconic assemblage and subsequent Alleghany thrusting is impossible. In the absence of restoration, any study of more than local extent might unsuspectingly compare rocks of entirely different provenances and histories.

The remainder of the Paleozoic rocks in Pennsylvania are much better understood. A stratigraphy exists that has generally withstood the test of time; décollement tectonics explains much of the structure, and the newest kid on the block, layer-parallel shortening, is providing insights into the early stages of Alleghany deformation. This is not to say that additional work is not needed. Each good project reveals insights and expands our understanding, as numerous studies have shown.

RECOMMENDED FOR FURTHER READING

Crawford, M. L., and Mark, L. E. (1982), *Evidence from metamorphic rocks for overthrusting, Pennsylvania Piedmont, U.S.A.*, Canadian Mineralogist, v. 20, p. 333–347.

Drake, A. A., Jr. (1980), *The Taconides, Acadides, and Alleghenides in the central Appalachians,* in Wones, D. R., ed., *Proceedings of "The Caledonides in the USA,"* Blacksburg, Virginia Polytechnic Institute, Department of Geological Sciences, Memoir 2, p. 179–187.

Root, S. I. (1973), *Structure, basin development, and tectogenesis in the Pennsylvania portion of the folded Appalachians*, in De Jong, K. A., and Scholten, Robert, eds., *Gravity and tectonics*, New York, John Wiley and Sons, p. 343–360.

Wagner, M. E., and Srogi, LeeAnn (1987), *Early Paleozoic metamorphism at two crustal levels and a tectonic model for the Pennsylvania-Delaware Piedmont*, Geological Society of America Bulletin, v. 99, p. 113–126.

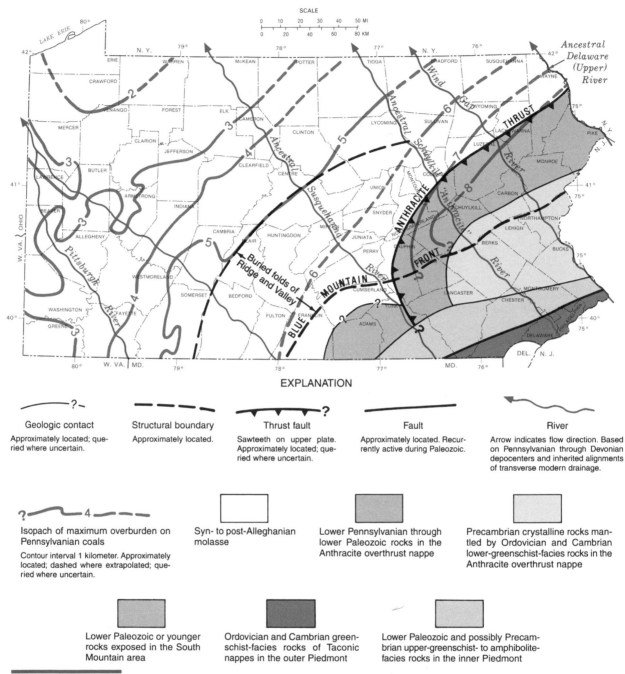

SCALE

0 10 20 30 40 50 MI

0 20 40 60 80 KM

EXPLANATION

?—	——	⏄ ?	——	⬳
Geologic contact	Structural boundary	Thrust fault	Fault	River
Approximately located; queried where uncertain.	Approximately located.	Sawteeth on upper plate. Approximately located; queried where uncertain.	Approximately located. Recurrently active during Paleozoic.	Arrow indicates flow direction. Based on Pennsylvanian through Devonian depocenters and inherited alignments of transverse modern drainage.

?—⌇—4—	▢	▨	▨
Isopach of maximum overburden on Pennsylvanian coals	Syn- to post-Alleghanian molasse	Lower Pennsylvanian through lower Paleozoic rocks in the Anthracite overthrust nappe	Precambrian crystalline rocks mantled by Ordovician and Cambrian lower-greenschist-facies rocks in the Anthracite overthrust nappe
Contour interval 1 kilometer. Approximately located; dashed where extrapolated; queried where uncertain.			

▨	▨	▨
Lower Paleozoic or younger rocks exposed in the South Mountain area	Ordovician and Cambrian greenschist-facies rocks of Taconic nappes in the outer Piedmont	Lower Paleozoic and possibly Precambrian upper-greenschist- to amphibolite-facies rocks in the inner Piedmont

Figure 34–1. Post-Alleghanian paleogeology in Pennsylvania. Isopachs of overburden material in the coal regions represent the approximate amount of material eroded since the Alleghany orogeny. Most of the area southeast of the molasse was subject to erosion during the deposition of the molasse, and most of the erosion in the extreme southeastern part of the state took place during this time.

CHAPTER 34   MESOZOIC

DAVID B. MacLACHLAN*
Bureau of Topographic and Geologic Survey
Department of Conservation and Natural
  Resources
P. O. Box 8453
Harrisburg, PA 17105

INTRODUCTION

According to the geologic time scale accepted for The Decade of North American Geology (DNAG) Project (Palmer, 1983) and used herein, the age of the beginning of the Mesozoic Era is 245 Ma. The climax of the Alleghany orogeny in terms of foreland folding and thrusting was about 25 million years before this and marks the dividing point between processes that are essentially Paleozoic and those that are essentially Mesozoic in character. The thermal development of coals in Pennsylvania indicates a thick sedimentary cover, which is proposed to be a post-Alleghanian molasse; however, there is no distinct record of this interval or of the earliest Mesozoic in eastern North America. This fact is simply a reflection of the dominant theme of Pennsylvania's Mesozoic history: massive erosion, somewhat episodic and provincially variable with respect to timing, but generally decreasing in intensity with time.

The most spectacular events, those that were precursors to and associated with continental rupture near Paleozoic sutures in the Late Triassic and Early Jurassic, giving rise to the Atlantic Ocean, are interesting in their own right, but they are literally and figuratively only peripheral events in the Mesozoic evolution of Pennsylvania. The Late Triassic to Early Jurassic faulted basins, intrusions, and other related phenomena of the oceanic rifting are conspicuous by their preservation, but they are relatively small elements in the total Mesozoic history. They are, in part or entirely, the subject of several chapters of this volume (Chapters 12, 13, 21, and 40B), and they will be mentioned here only to document their position in the historical record.

The time from the Alleghany orogeny to the end of the Mesozoic Era was approximately 200 million years. During this time, with the exception of a possible brief Early Cretaceous marginal marine incursion in the extreme southeastern part of the state, Pennsylvania was entirely continental. Local Mesozoic terrestrial deposits that survive in southeastern Pennsylvania represent a total of probably less than 10 million years, though additional deposits that were

*Retired.

not strictly ephemeral can be deduced. Most of the state, however, was subject to subaerial erosion for all of the Mesozoic, and all of the state was subject to it for a major fraction of the time. The principal story is one of denudation. Some consideration has been given to the contributions of classical geomorphology, but emphasis is placed on datable events suitable for reconstructing removal in space and time.

The accepted age of the Cretaceous-Tertiary boundary is about 67 Ma. By this time, only the Appalachian Plateau appears to have still required significant modification to achieve its present form. The Ridge and Valley province was rising, and it may have risen 1,000 feet or more during the Cenozoic Era. Commensurate erosion is indicated, but the topographic aspect was probably little changed. Whereas some Cretaceous cover has been removed from the southeastern part of the Piedmont, the impression is that the total Cenozoic erosion was less in the Piedmont than in the Ridge and Valley. It appears that less than 10 percent of the material eroded since the Alleghany orogeny was removed during the Cenozoic.

IN THE BEGINNING

Slingerland and Furlong (1989) inferred that the mountain system that existed at the close of the Alleghany orogeny had an average relief of 11,500 to 15,000 feet and was developed on a 155- to 185-mile-wide accretionary wedge superposed on essentially Laurentian crust. The toe of this wedge was near the Allegheny Front, and the proximal end lay in the upper Chesapeake Bay region. This is in excellent agreement with a number of models of Paleozoic evolution of the continental margin that place the suture between Laurentian and Avalonian or African crust in this area. The data of the Slingerland and Furlong model are independent of this fact, and the coincidence adds confidence that their critical wedge is a sufficient explanation of the gross geometry of the Alleghanian Mountains in Pennsylvania. Slingerland and Furlong do not attempt to explain the location of the subsequent Atlantic rupture. When under extension, continental crust has been shown to be weakest where it is thickest (Vink and others, 1984), and the true axis of the Alleghanian disturbed zone was probably about at the present continental-shelf margin. The full width of the zone, including its eastern flank, which is represented by the Mauritanides of Africa, was not less than two and one-half times the width of the western wedge deduced by Slingerland and Furlong, and the maximum relief with re-

spect to the axial zone was commensurately somewhat higher.

The post-Alleghanian paleogeologic map shown in Figure 34–1 is based in part on Paleozoic sedimentation and provenance but is primarily based on various data derived from thermal metamorphism and radiometric and structural ages. The least known feature of this map is the Anthracite overthrust (Levine, 1983, 1985; MacLachlan, 1985), which was deduced to explain the very thick overburden required for anthracite metamorphism. Reflectance anisotropy of anthracite in Pennsylvania indicates that the thermal maximum was attained during deformation (Levine, 1983). Silurian and Lower Devonian conodonts in the anticline separating the Middle and Northern Anthracite fields (Harris and others, 1978) have a lower alteration temperature than the Pennsylvanian coals about 10,000 feet higher in the section. This relationship denies the possibility of a crustal heat anomaly, which has occasionally been proposed to explain supposedly anomalous anthracite metamorphism, and demonstrates an inverted geothermal gradient of a type known to be associated only with major overthrusts. The conodont alteration isotherms are, nevertheless, deflected in this area, and this pattern has been used to help define the probable configuration and limits of the thrust sheet. MacLachlan (1985) proposed that the thrust cut the upturned Paleozoic section above Blue Mountain and came to the present erosion surface in the low-angle Alleghanian thrusts associated with the Reading Prong. Although demonstrable post-Carboniferous cover reached a maximum thickness in the Southern Anthracite field, total post-Alleghanian erosion is a few miles less in that field than it is through much of the Ridge and Valley province. This is an anomalous feature in the general pattern of Appalachian denudation. The explanation of this anomaly may be that the Anthracite overthrust emplaced well-lithified Paleozoic and possibly Precambrian rocks over the Southern Anthracite field at a level elsewhere occupied only by poorly lithified Alleghanian molasse. The consequent reduction in erosion rate would be sufficient to explain the observed difference. The erosional anomaly thus tends to confirm the Anthracite overthrust by criteria independent of those from which it was deduced.

In the area west and north of Blue Mountain, the paleogeologic map (Figure 34–1) shows isopachs of overburden on Pennsylvanian coals deduced from coalification, clay diagenesis, and degree of metamorphism using the median figures of Levine (1983), Paxton (1983), and Paxton and Williams (1985). These figures are sensitive to the assumed paleogeothermal gradient, but the maximum probable uncertainty is ±20 percent. (If data such as paleoelevations and burial and erosion estimates were reported in metric units in the original sources, the metric units have been retained herein.) Beyond the limits of the Anthracite thrust, this cover must have been composed of a wedge of Alleghanian molasse, which was deposited after the deformation (Levine, 1983) and completely buried the underlying folds. The subsequent removal of this thick wedge increases the amount of post-Paleozoic erosion that must have occurred beyond that accounted in most classic geomorphic reconstructions. Given that Pennsylvania was in the tropical rain belt at this time (see Figure 34–3 for paleolatitudes), we may be assured that this wedge was traversed by major northwestward- to northward-flowing streams, the headwaters of which were near or beyond the present coastline. Modern investigators argue that major drainageways are rarely displaced by uplift (Oberlander, 1965). We may, then, reasonably suppose that the post-Alleghanian streams are survivors of those that supplied the delta plains of the Late Devonian and Carboniferous. Based on the location of middle to late Paleozoic depocenters, it seems probable that these streams approximated the alignment of many modern drainage segments. Though the pattern of through drainage has been significantly modified by tributary captures and fracture-zone alignments (especially in the strongly folded beds of differing erosional resistance in the Ridge and Valley province), there is a strong basis for believing that major modern drainage elements are inherited from the Late Devonian drainage. The direction of flow in the eastern two thirds of the state was, of course, reversed during the evolution of the Atlantic margin.

Southeast of Blue Mountain, the paleogeology of the earliest Mesozoic surface is more speculative. In the extreme southeast, the Paleozoic thermal maximum occurred in the Early Ordovician, when the maximum tectonic overburden was at least 35 km (20 mi) above the West Chester Prong (Wagner and Srogi, 1987). Uplift and erosion that started in the Late Ordovician are clearly established by the Taconic clastic wedge and radiometric cooling ages. Allowing for shortening of the supradécollement Paleozoic rocks during the Alleghany orogeny, depositional facies of Paleozoic sediments to the northwest clearly indicate that the Philadelphia area had been eroded to the level of the sillimanite isograd in the amphibolite facies by the time of deposition of the uppermost Devonian-lowermost Mississippian Spechty Kopf Formation. This represents not less

than 5 to 6 miles of erosion in southeasternmost Pennsylvania during this 80-million-year interval. Subsequent Paleozoic deposits document the continuation of substantial erosion to the southeast. The 110-million-year period from the time of Spechty Kopf deposition to the Alleghany orogeny surely permits comparable erosion, perhaps approximately 12 miles during the interval from the Taconic to the Alleghany orogeny. This leaves approximately 9 miles as the maximum thickness eroded from the time of the Alleghany orogeny to the present. A major part of this erosion must have been the reduction of the initial Alleghanian relief, which Slingerland and Furlong (1989) judged was accomplished in 30 million years and is reflected in the Alleghanian molasse; this was the only plausible load to provide the observed coal ranks across the Appalachian Plateau. The plateau region of the state was, in any case, reduced to near its present level by the Early Cretaceous and was topographically lower than the central part of the state by no later than the early Late Jurassic.

The thermal maximum of metavolcanics in South Mountain was attained about 360 Ma (Early Mississippian) (Rankin and others, 1969; Lapham and Root, 1971), shortly after the end of Catskill deposition. In the subaerial environment of the Catskill Formation, erosion probably started immediately after the maximum sediment loading; potassium-argon cooling ages indicate that erosion was initiated at least by 330 Ma (the start of the Pennsylvanian) and continued through the late Paleozoic. The rate of uplift implied by the radiometric cooling ages and the warm, humid climate of the Pennsylvanian suggest that erosion possibly extended down into the Ordovician rocks on the crest of South Mountain by the climax of the Alleghany orogeny.

Potassium-argon dates of about 320 to 330 Ma are also widespread through the Piedmont, and a general pattern of uplift and erosion in the late Paleozoic is implied. This is apparently reflected by greenschist-grade metamorphic-rock fragments in the exposed proximal beds of the Pottsville and Llewellyn Formations of the Anthracite region, which suggests significant exposure of lower Paleozoic and upper Precambrian(?) metamorphic rocks in the Piedmont before the Alleghany orogeny.

The Reading Prong represents a special case, as these Precambrian rocks were never sufficiently buried during the Paleozoic to generally reset the potassium-argon system in the manner of South Mountain. These rocks were apparently mantled by lower Paleozoic rocks similar in type and thickness to those now found in the Great Valley and northern Lancaster County, but they must have been located well southeast of the locus of maximum thickness of middle and upper Paleozoic deposits before Alleghanian thrusting. Slate chips in Pennsylvanian conglomerates are probably of this provenance, and much of the lower Paleozoic section was probably still present over these rocks at the climax of the Alleghany orogeny.

Such are the elements from which our present geography evolved, a process largely accomplished during the Mesozoic Era except on the Appalachian Plateau, where Cenozoic erosion played a proportionately greater part. The northwestward slope clearly implied by the isopachs of coal overburden (Figure 34–1) suggests drainage toward Hudson Bay. Figure 34–2 shows the regional constraints controlling this drainage, which evidently persisted until the drainage of western Pennsylvania was captured by the Mississippi River system at some time in the Cretaceous. Headward erosion of the Mississippi system toward Pennsylvania probably proceeded along the weak shales presently occupied by Lake Erie and the Maumee-Wabash drainage of Ohio and Indiana. Prior to capture, the ultimate northern outlet was the Sverdrup basin, a major depocenter in the Mesozoic.

ALLEGHANY OROGENY TO MIDDLE TRIASSIC

Although Slingerland and Furlong (1989) would allow the first half of the 60-million-year interval from the Alleghany orogeny to the Middle Triassic for primary reduction of the Alleghanian relief and, by extrapolation, deposition of the aggradational prism required to produce observed coalification, definite preserved deposits of Pennsylvania provenance from this interval are unknown. The molasse probably represents only a fraction of the ephemeral deposits that came from the reduction of the primitive Appalachians and episodic rejuvenations thereof. These deposits were transported northwest and entirely removed from Pennsylvania during the Mesozoic. Paleoclimatic models (see Barron, 1989) tend to emphasize increasing aridity, not only because of latitudinal drift, but also because of the extreme interior position of the Appalachians after the Pangean assembly. The factor that seems insufficiently accommodated in these models, as pertains to Appalachian denudation, is elevation. The area of Pennsylvania was drifting from 5 degrees south latitude to less than 20 degrees north latitude during this time (Figure 34–3A, 3B) and lay squarely in the tropical rain belt during the earlier half of the interval. The distance from the crest of the modern, tropical Andes to

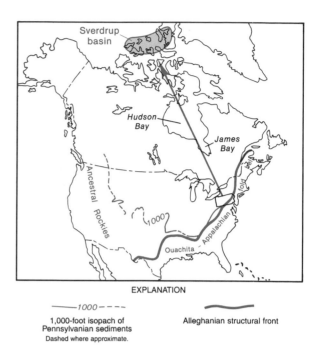

EXPLANATION

——1000 – – – –
1,000-foot isopach of
Pennsylvanian sediments
Dashed where approximate.

Alleghanian structural front

Figure 34–2. Regional controls on post-Alleghanian drainage. Northwest drainage (arrow) was constrained by late Paleozoic uplift to the southeast and thick Pennsylvanian clastic wedges to the south and west. The isopach for Pennsylvanian sediments (not shown in south-central United States) roughly delimits presumed uplands. Modern shorelines are shown for geographic orientation. Isopach and structural front are simplified from Cook and Bally (1975, p. 106); copyright © 1975 by Shell Oil Company; reproduced by permission of Shell Oil Company.

the mouth of the Amazon River is barely less than the distance was from the crest of the Late Permian Appalachians to the Tethys Ocean, and the former is entirely an area of excess precipitation. Differences in the global geography of continents may indeed attenuate this effect, but the volume of flow implied by the transport of a few miles of sediments across nearly the full width of the state, and considerably greater amounts for somewhat lesser distances, on the possibly rain-shadowed side of the Appalachians is much greater than what would be expected in Barron's "tropical desert." Indeed, even though the flow could have been evaporatively reduced crossing the horse latitudes, the volume of water required to move the sediments was likely sufficient to support through drainage to tidewater, which was probably somewhere in the northern Hudson Bay area. Based on simple isostatic considerations, the present elevation of the Allegheny Front and the 3 to 4 miles of total erosion deduced there are consistent with an

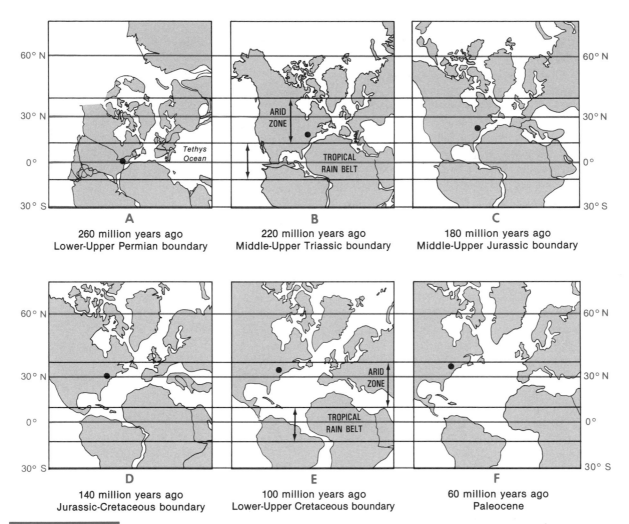

Figure 34–3. Continental positions 260 to 60 million years ago. A is modified from Scotese, C. R., and others, *Paleozoic base maps*, Journal of Geology, v. 87, Figure 43, p. 277 (published by University of Chicago; © 1979 by the University of Chicago Press), B is modified from Keppie (1977, Figure 7, p. 43), which is modified from Smith and others (1973, Figure 9, Map 4), and the remaining maps are modified from Barron and others (1981, Plates 1, 3, 5, and 7; reproduced by permission of Birkhäuser Verlag AG). The nominal ages approximately coincide with series boundaries except in F, which represents a time about 7 million years after the end of the Cretaceous. The general positions of the tropical rain belt and the arid zone of the subtropical convergence of global circulation are indicated, although distributions of land and water masses and orography will produce substantial variations. The Tethys Ocean is labeled in A, and the position of Pennsylvania is indicated by a black bullet on each map.

elevation of a few miles in that area for the top of the Alleghanian molasse in the Middle Triassic. A modern analog with many elements of geomorphologic similarity is "mile-high" Denver, which is about 1,700 river miles to tide. Given the longer run to probable tide, there is a close consistency between the isostatically implied elevation and that which can be deduced from the hydraulic gradient. This residual elevation, after reduction of local Alleghanian relief, presumably increased somewhat toward the Appalachian core, and it had a nontrivial impact on the local climate that endured at least into the Early Jurassic (Cornet and Olsen, 1989).

The latter half of the interval from the Alleghany orogeny to the Middle Triassic was a time when Pennsylvania was drifting into the subtropical convergence, and some measure of aridity is certain. Judging from the deposits and biota of the Upper Triassic, which are even more firmly set in arid latitudes, the precipitation deficit was less than that of the present Great Basin of the intermontane west. Much of the latter is too biologically productive to constitute true desert, and the Triassic deposits verge on subhumid, at least during the more pluvial phases of well-documented cyclic oscillations of climate. The increasing aridity may have been instrumental in preserving the molasse across the Appalachian Plateau from erosion until a much later date. East of the Allegheny Front, however, substantial erosion must have persisted. In fact, significant uplift of the Ridge and Valley province relative to the Plateau is implied at this time. It is not clear whether this uplift was purely isostatic, but it could have been, as the geometry of the Alleghanian wedge clearly implies a basement flexure near the Allegheny Front that is not apparent in modern seismic sections. The possible elimination of this flexure without apparent fault discontinuity clearly favors isostatic rebound flexure in this area during post-Paleozoic time.

The best measure of this erosion comes from the central Ridge and Valley province, where Roden and Miller (1989) determined apatite fission-track annealing ages for the Tioga metabentonite. They suggested an 85°C temperature for the lower limit of the annealing, though as little as 70°C has also been suggested (M. J. Johnson, 1984). These temperatures imply an overburden of less than 3.5 km (11,400 ft) and possibly as little as 2 km (6,600 ft) at the annealing times, which approximately coincide with the onset of deposition in the Gettysburg-Newark basin. These lower Middle Devonian metabentonites are about 2 miles below the coals, which had a cover of 3 to 4 miles of molasse in the Early Permian. Thus, it appears that two thirds to three quarters of all post-Alleghanian erosion in the Ridge and Valley occurred before the Late Triassic. As the remaining cover on the Tioga extends to about the base of the Pottsville Formation, these figures suggest that the Ridge and Valley anticlines may have been breached to the level of the Pottsville Formation by this time. Furthermore, the general courses of the lower Susquehanna River and part of the West Branch Susquehanna River could already have been locked approximately into their modern positions.

On the southeastern crop of the Tioga metabentonite, annealing ages range well up into the Jurassic. This reflects both a greater initial overburden and the fact that the analyzed samples lay beneath the Anthracite overthrust, where much of the well-lithified upper plate was more resistant to erosion than was the upper Paleozoic molasse.

The Newark Supergroup is underlain by an unconformity that was tilted northwestward during the Newark deposition and that emerges on the southeast side of the early Mesozoic basins. The maximum pre-Newark erosion after the Taconic orogeny might have been as much as 7 miles where the Newark Supergroup rests on the Precambrian rocks of the Trenton Prong near the eastern side of the state. Major ero-

sion in this area probably started by at least the Carboniferous, contributing detritus to the Alleghanian clastic wedge. The total erosion is thus incommensurable with that in the Ridge and Valley province. Border conglomerates along the northwest margin of the Gettysburg-Newark basin suggest that, north of the basin, little Precambrian rock was unroofed by the very Late Triassic. If there was only lower Paleozoic cover on South Mountain and the Reading Prong at the beginning of this interval (Figure 34–1), the erosion there probably did not exceed 2.5 miles, and comparable erosion at the south margin of the basin is plausible. However, this is, perhaps, twice the amount of the cumulative erosion from the Jurassic to the Holocene, exclusive of eroded Mesozoic cover. The erosion surface beneath the Newark Supergroup has sinkholes where it was developed on carbonate rock (Figure 34–4), and it has generally low relief. The most conspicuous exception is the broad elevation that was precursor to the Honey Brook Upland area of Lancaster and Chester Counties, which is indicated by the thinning and onlap of the Stockton and New Oxford Formations.

LATE TRIASSIC TO EARLY JURASSIC

The onset of Late Triassic sedimentation about 230 Ma marks a profound change in the evolution of Pennsylvania. The event that triggered the sedimentation, of course, was crustal stretching prior to the opening of the Atlantic Ocean. The Newark-Gettysburg basin is the extreme northwestern margin of the extension zone that extended southeastward to the continental margin (Figure 34–5) and onward into Africa. No significant general crustal thinning is apparent within the state. Thinning increases offshore, and any surviving elevation of the Appalachian core was much reduced by loss of crustal support once any thermal anomaly associated with the stretching was dissipated. The basement profile shown in Figure 34–6 is extrapolated from other sections that generally show the major attenuation extending about 60 miles westward from the East Coast Magnetic Anomaly (ECMA).

Although the Stockton and New Oxford Formations, which make up the lower part of the Newark sediments, are of southeasterly provenance, a drainage reversal was effected, and the major portion of the Newark sediments was derived from the north and west. The first indication of this reversal is in the lowest conglomerates of the Hammer Creek Formation, which show mixed provenance and inter-

Figure 34–4. Upper Triassic paleokarst. Red sandstone of the Upper Triassic Stockton Formation infilling a sinkhole (paleokarst) in Cambrian dolomite near Norristown, Montgomery County.

finger with the upper parts of the Stockton and New Oxford Formations near Terre Hill, Lancaster County. These are the first deposits of the south-flowing ancestral Schuylkill River (Anthracite River of Davis, 1889). Deposits from the ancestral Susquehanna River appeared slightly later, the first being the Conewago Conglomerate of York County, but the total volume of coarse sediments in this area is much smaller. The implication is that the Susquehanna was a less substantial stream than the Schuylkill, and Davis (1889) was correct in stating that the upper Susquehanna was pirated from the headwaters of the ancestral Schuylkill at a later time. The lower Delaware River makes no apparent contribution to the Newark sedimentation where it presently meets the Newark basin, and this reach is probably the product of several piracies below Port Jervis, N. Y., which may even be entirely post-Mesozoic. If the upper reach is projected down the presumed paleoslope, it emerges near the mouth of the Hudson River, where it could have contributed to a sedimentary influx (comparable

to the Hammer Creek Formation) that was deposited predominantly(?) by the ancestral Hudson River at the northeast end of the Newark basin. The coarse fluvial facies of the southeast-flowing ancestral Schuylkill and Hudson Rivers represent the coarse fraction of a major part of the basin fill and should not be confused with the border fanglomerates.

Faults bounding the northwestern margin of the basin suggest that Newark sedimentation extended little north of the present exposure, though local overlaps with the faults are still discernible. In New Jersey, there is nearly a mile of sedimentary strata and basalt flows above the youngest Lower Jurassic rocks equivalent to those exposed in Pennsylvania, and there is no reason to doubt that such cover rocks were once present in Pennsylvania. The Jacksonwald Basalt and overlying beds in Berks County are certainly equivalent to the Orange Mountain Basalt and the Feltville Formation of New Jersey (Cornet, 1977). The basalt at Aspers, Adams County, in the Gettysburg basin, is of the same age and composition (York Haven type) as the Orange Mountain Basalt. It is uncertain if this is only a related flow or an actual erosional outlier of the Orange Mountain Basalt. These thick sediments extended well south of their present limits, as evidenced by the advanced coalification of logs in the Lockatong Formation (Hatcher and Romankiw, 1985). As much as 20,000 feet of overburden is implied if normal geothermal gradients prevailed, though a higher thermal gradient associated with the volcanism might significantly reduce this figure. The ultimate southeastern extent of the Newark sediments is indefinite but could have been south of Pennsylvania. The necessity of subsequently stripping such rock may largely account for the apparently small amount of post-Triassic erosion of crystalline rocks in southeastern Pennsylvania.

The youngest preserved rocks of the Newark basin are of earliest Jurassic age. Only rocks of the lower Hettangian Stage remain in Pennsylvania, whereas the sequence in New Jersey reaches into the lower Sinemurian (Olsen and others, 1982). Because carbonaceous material in the Towaco Formation, less than 3,300 feet below the top of the section exposed in New Jersey, is coalified consistent with 2.5 to 3 km (8,200 to 9,850 ft) maximum overburden (Hatcher and Romankiw, 1985), the additional thickness of implied sediment may extend original Newark sedimentation into the Pliensbachian Stage.

Klitgord and Hutchinson (1985) claimed that, offshore, the "breakup unconformity" characteristic of rifted continental margins truncates some Newark equivalents and underlies some Lower Jurassic(?)

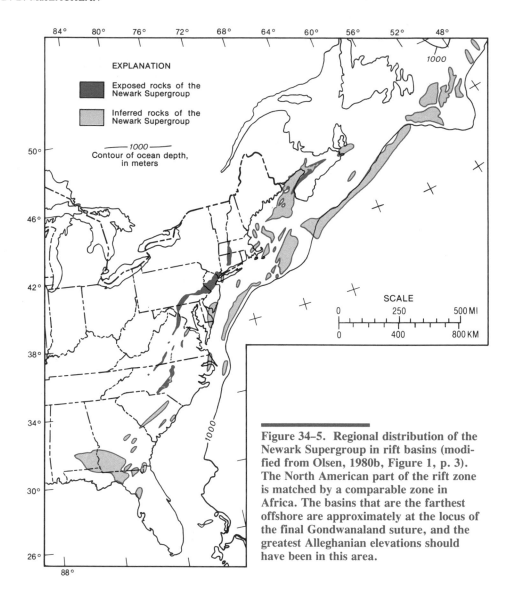

Figure 34–5. Regional distribution of the Newark Supergroup in rift basins (modified from Olsen, 1980b, Figure 1, p. 3). The North American part of the rift zone is matched by a comparable zone in Africa. The basins that are the farthest offshore are approximately at the locus of the final Gondwanaland suture, and the greatest Alleghanian elevations should have been in this area.

rocks that extend onto oceanic basement (Figure 34–6). Poag and Sevon (1989) provided a better description of these rocks than was available when Figure 34–6 was prepared, but their more detailed data largely support the generalizations made here from the figure. The breakup implies final reduction of Appalachian core relief and the initiation of a climatic regime characterized by an increase in available moisture. The west end of the section shown in Figure 34–6 is located about 44 miles north-northwest of Cape Charles, Va., on the west side of the Chesapeake Bay, where debris of Pennsylvania provenance are anticipated. Another section, through the COST B3 well off the coast of New Jersey, is dominated by Hudson River deposits (Libby-French, 1984), and there are significant differences in lithologies

and indicated rates of sedimentation between these two sections.

MIDDLE JURASSIC

Middle Jurassic deposits of the Baltimore Canyon trough pinch out against the steep basement slope offshore. The thin edge of the wedge is evidently terrestrial, but restricted-marine carbonates and evaporites are predominant (Schlee, 1981) in the lower part of unit MJ of Figure 34–6. This is the consequence of having highlands, a result of thermal uplift, immediately adjacent to the newly formed oceanic basement. A Holocene example is in the region of the Red Sea, where sabkhas develop in an analogous geographic and climatic situation. Streams

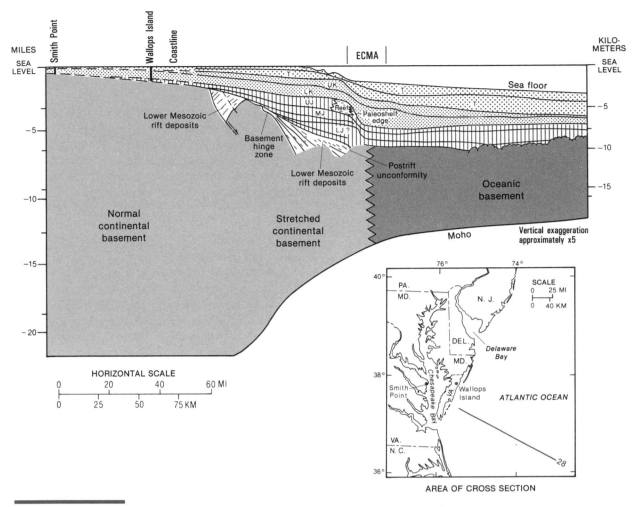

Figure 34–6. Cross section of the southern Baltimore Canyon trough along U.S. Geological Survey seismic line 28 and the area westward to Smith Point (adapted from Klitgord and Hutchinson, 1985). This section, which extends from the Atlantic Ocean through the Chesapeake Bay, receives most Pennsylvania drainage and shows the amount of sediment accumulation with time. Basement structure has been added by analogy with other sections for which complete geophysical analyses of the deep structure have been published.

from Pennsylvania had not yet reached the Atlantic at this time, but available moisture implies accelerating erosion. Apatite from the Tioga metabentonite on the southeast margin of the Ridge and Valley province became closed to fission-track annealing in this epoch, and erosion of the Anthracite thrust sole back to somewhere in the Great Valley is indicated. Erosional debris accumulated as ephemeral deposits to the southeast, presumably in the Coastal Plain area.

With the decay of the Middle Jurassic thermal uplift, the major southeast drainage reached the Atlantic basin. The Middle Jurassic unit of Figure 34–6 attained a thickness of about 6,500 feet in less than 20 million years. The major part of this great influx was probably derived from poorly consolidated lower Mesozoic rocks, including much of the Newark Supergroup. The lower reaches of trunk streams were fixed essentially in their modern positions as they were superposed on the Lower Jurassic diabase sheets.

LATE JURASSIC

The Atlantic Ocean was about 1,000 miles wide by the end of the Jurassic, and it is presumed that moisture availability had ceased to be a factor limiting erosion. The Atlantic deposits of the Late Jurassic lapped up on crystalline rocks of the outer Coastal Plain, but they accumulated more slowly than in the preceding epoch. The system was largely flushed of the lower Mesozoic debris, and the decline in sedimentation was apparently attributable entirely to the greater resistance of the older source rocks now being very actively reduced. The Late Jurassic strandline was not far seaward of the present coast, and predominantly sandy sediments extended nearly to a reef that was located on a well-defined escarpment a little beyond the present slope break (Schlee, 1981). The deep-water deposits were probably terrigenous shales.

The east-coast drainage was developing vigorously at this time and had probably fully claimed the fold belt. Capture of the upper Anthracite River by a Susquehanna tributary, as advocated by Davis (1889), could have occurred at this time. Pennsylvania was about at the present latitude of Florida, and rain was presumably abundant across the state. Erosion in the western part of the state, however, was inhibited by the long run to the Arctic. The principal trunk stream in western Pennsylvania (shown as the Pittsburgh River in Figure 34–1), inherited from Permian and possibly earlier drainage, probably consisted of the alignment of the Potomac, Monongahela, and Beaver Rivers. The northwestward-flowing part of this alignment in the Tertiary was called the Pittsburg [sic] River by Tight (1903), and it reached the Atlantic Ocean via the Laurentian River (proto-St. Lawrence and lower Great Lakes). The St. Lawrence intercept, however, was not established until the Late Cretaceous or the Tertiary (Ziegler and others, 1985). Although provenance in Pennsylvania cannot be proven, Late Jurassic and Early Cretaceous fluvial deposits in the Moose River basin (James Bay area) of Canada (Scott and Aiken, 1982) suggest the persistence of the drainage established in the Permian. Conditions, thus, were optimum for westward migration of the Atlantic divide.

EARLY CRETACEOUS

The Coastal Plain deposits are described by Owens (Chapter 14). It is sufficient to note that the Potomac Group, mostly Lower Cretaceous to lower Upper Cretaceous, forms a great seaward-thickening wedge (Figure 34–7) that extended inland at least to Norristown, northwest of Philadelphia. Remnants there, identified as Patapsco Formation by early workers (Bascom and others, 1909), were preserved in part because of Cenozoic solution of the underlying carbonate rock, and they lie topographically below relatively young saprolite (Pavich, 1989) developed on schist on adjacent hills. The particular significance of these exposures is that some lie less than a

mile south of pre-Carnian Stage Triassic karst at the present margin of the Newark basin. It follows that general reduction of southeasternmost Pennsylvania was within a thousand feet or so of completion before Patapsco deposition, and, other than the removal of some apparently rather thin Cretaceous sediments and the incision of Neogene streams, little was required to complete the modern configuration.

Offshore deposits of the Early Cretaceous have the greatest volume of any of the deposits in the Baltimore Canyon trough. They differ from the Late Jurassic deposits primarily because the reef on the outer shelf was submerged, but they had somewhat more than twice the time to accumulate the moderately greater thickness. Poag and Sevon (1989) concluded that the volume of siliciclastic detritus delivered offshore in any constant time interval is relatively insensitive to climatic variations, which are accorded great significance in most geomorphic models. Episodic uplift, largely isostatic or flexural response to offshore loads, seems to be the major controlling parameter.

Continued reduction of the Appalachian fold belt is indicated, but the task was perhaps 90 percent complete before the Late Cretaceous. The erosion in the Appalachian Plateau was relatively much less complete, and significant erosion may have been only beginning in parts of this area. As development of the Mississippi embayment implies a much shorter run to tide in the Early Cretaceous, it seems likely that the northern drainage route could have been abandoned before the mid-Tertiary(?) diversion to the Laurentian River. The development of the modern drainage of western Pennsylvania is no older than Late Pliocene, though it includes recombination and reversal of a number of older drainage elements, some of which (as suggested above) had considerable antiquity.

LATE CRETACEOUS

Apatite fission-track ages from the Allegheny Front to the west and north decrease from Early Cretaceous to Eocene, according to Roden and Miller (1989). Although the extended persistence of a few miles of the Alleghanian molasse into the Eocene in the Altoona area (44 Ma site of Roden and Miller) pushes the limit for a plausible, purely erosional interpretation of the Allegheny Plateau cooling ages, it is significantly upstream from the 141 Ma Tyrone locality, where the denudational origin should be sufficient. The original thickness of the molasse was

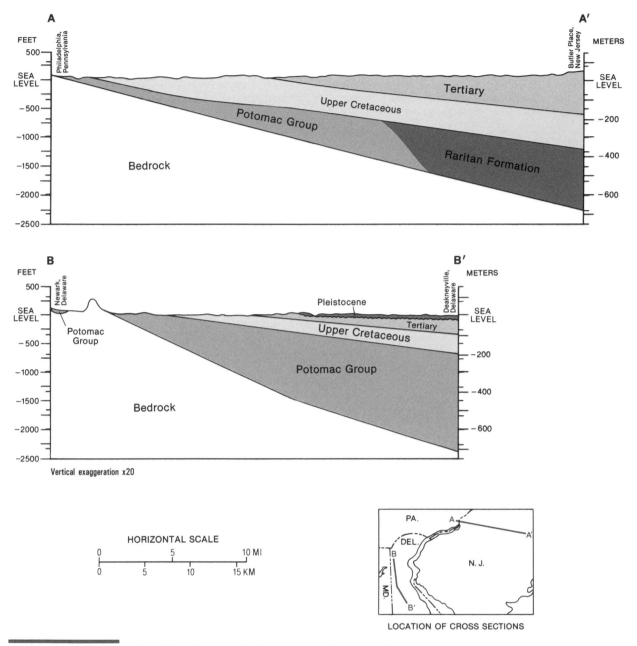

Figure 34-7. Cross sections of the inner half of the Atlantic Coastal Plain in New Jersey and Delaware (U.S. Geological Survey, 1967). Section A–A´, from Philadelphia to Butler Place, N. J., is about 45 miles north of section B–B´, from Newark, Del., to Deakneyville, Del. The major deposit is the Lower Cretaceous Potomac Group, forming a conspicuous wedge that thickens seaward and southward toward the Salisbury embayment. Upper Cretaceous deposits show southward thinning, but much less thinning than the Potomac Group in the landward direction. The implied northwestern limit of original deposition lies well within the Pennsylvania Piedmont.

at least 6,500 feet greater at Altoona than at Tyrone, and as the former is at the extreme headwaters of a more vigorous drainage that supplanted one that accomplished essentially no net erosion in over 100 million years, the purely erosional interpretation for

all the Plateau observations of Roden and Miller is within the pale. The substantial observation that induced them to deduce a reheating event is the shortening and broadening of the fission-track length distribution curve. This phenomenon could also result

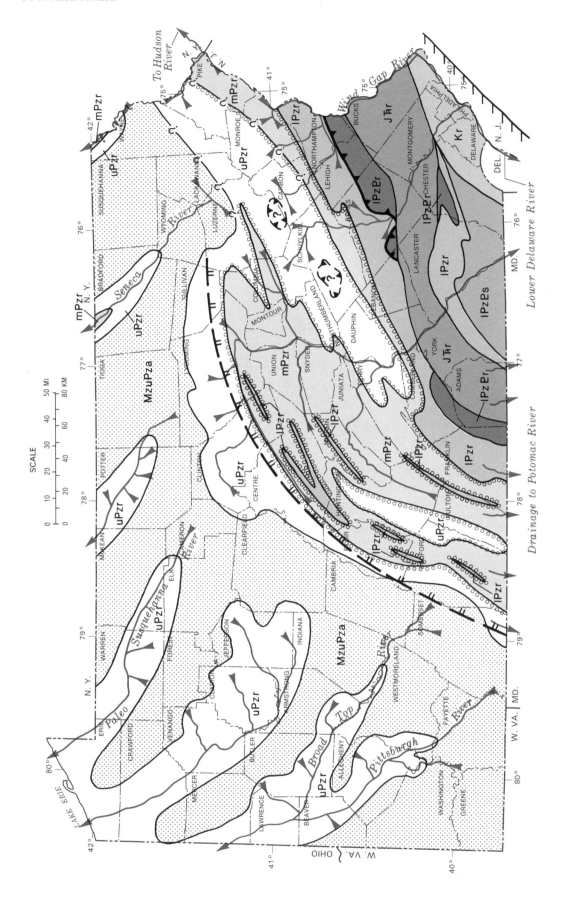

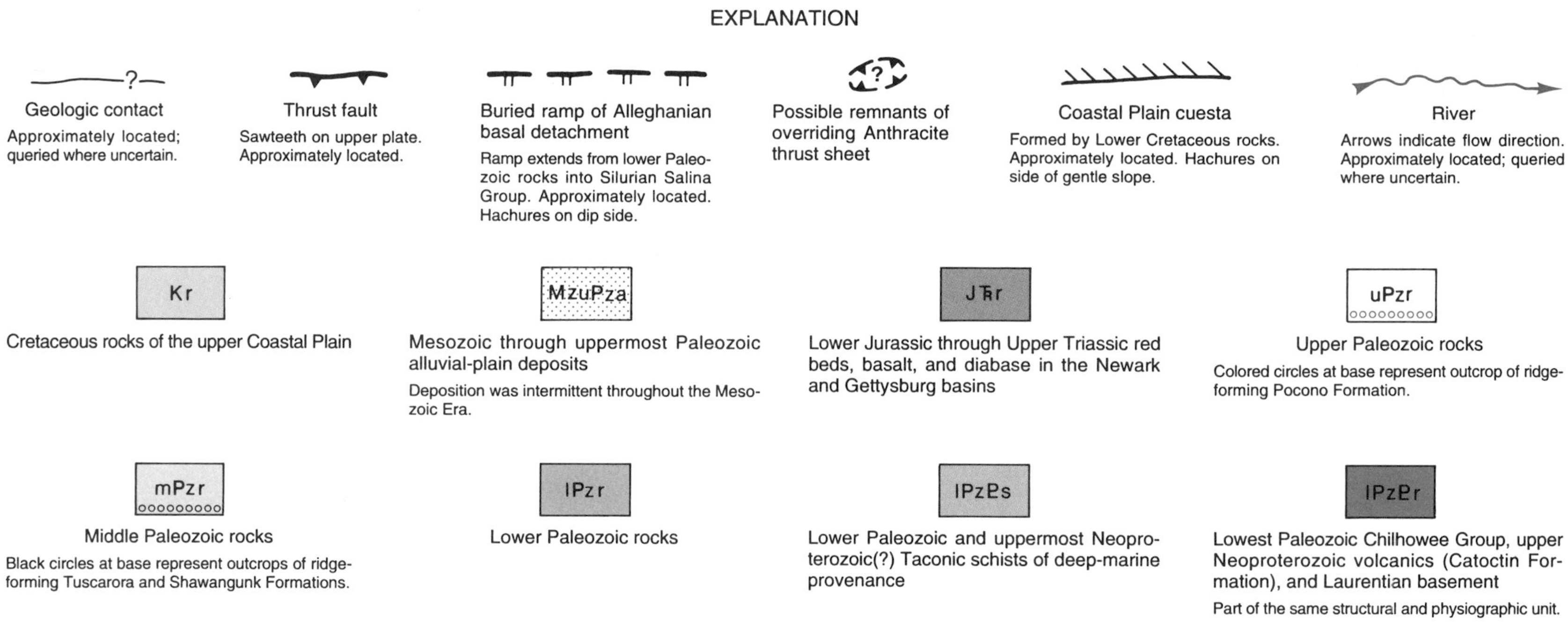

EXPLANATION

Geologic contact
Approximately located; queried where uncertain.

Thrust fault
Sawteeth on upper plate. Approximately located.

Buried ramp of Alleghanian basal detachment
Ramp extends from lower Paleozoic rocks into Silurian Salina Group. Approximately located. Hachures on dip side.

Possible remnants of overriding Anthracite thrust sheet

Coastal Plain cuesta
Formed by Lower Cretaceous rocks. Approximately located. Hachures on side of gentle slope.

River
Arrows indicate flow direction. Approximately located; queried where uncertain.

Kr
Cretaceous rocks of the upper Coastal Plain

MzuPza
Mesozoic through uppermost Paleozoic alluvial-plain deposits
Deposition was intermittent throughout the Mesozoic Era.

JRr
Lower Jurassic through Upper Triassic red beds, basalt, and diabase in the Newark and Gettysburg basins

uPzr
Upper Paleozoic rocks
Colored circles at base represent outcrop of ridge-forming Pocono Formation.

mPzr
Middle Paleozoic rocks
Black circles at base represent outcrops of ridge-forming Tuscarora and Shawangunk Formations.

lPzr
Lower Paleozoic rocks

lPzЄs
Lower Paleozoic and uppermost Neoproterozoic(?) Taconic schists of deep-marine provenance

lPzЄr
Lowest Paleozoic Chilhowee Group, upper Neoproterozoic volcanics (Catoctin Formation), and Laurentian basement
Part of the same structural and physiographic unit.

Figure 34–8. **Paleogeologic map of Pennsylvania at the end of the Cretaceous Period. The buried ramp of the Alleghanian basal detachment separates Plateau-style deformation from Ridge-and-Valley-style deformation and essentially coincides with the modern Allegheny Front. Drainage in the eastern half of the state was approaching its modern form; however, the age of significant stream piracies during the Mesozoic is uncertain. Drainage patterns in the western part of the state were radically modified in the late Cenozoic. Reconstructions of mid-Cenozoic drainage show many modern segments realigned, but with flow reversed in some cases. This older pattern is readily derived from the persistence of northwesterly flow associated with deposition of the Alleghanian molasse. At the end of the Cretaceous, these streams were still flowing well above the present upland surface of the Appalachian Plateaus, which does not appear to have been deeply incised until much later. The streams may have, thus, shifted and meandered some, but the present position of the surviving older reaches has been accepted as the best approximation of drainage alignments at the end of the Mesozoic.**

from extended initial residence near the critical 80°C level, which is consistent with the very low erosion rates noted above.

The Late Cretaceous was an epoch of maximum transgression associated with worldwide eustacy. It was a time of exceptional warmth, and temperate vegetation existed well into the Boreal zones. Marine-shelf deposits extended well onto the Coastal Plain, although Late Cretaceous sediments are shallow marine east of Trenton, N. J., and they may be fluvial within the area of their occurrence on Figure 34–8. There was considerably less material deposited both offshore and onshore than in preceding epochs, and the offshore material was rather calcareous. It is likely that major reduction of the Pennsylvania Appalachians was complete, and a somewhat subdued erosion surface, mimicking the present Ridge and Valley topography and more or less identifiable with the "Schooley peneplain," was developing. It is evident from Figure 34–7 that Late Cretaceous Coastal Plain deposits formerly extended over southeastern Pennsylvania. Figure 34–8 presents a conservative projection based on the sections shown in Figure 34–7.

It now seems to be generally accepted that Hack (1960) was correct in stating that erosionally resistant rocks subjected to humid, subaerial erosion will retain considerable relief with respect to less resistant rocks almost indefinitely. A classical peneplain in the folded Appalachians is, thus, an impossibility. During the Late Cretaceous, the trunk streams of the Ridge and Valley province were probably at easy grade to tide and were flowing at about 1,000-foot elevation in broad saddles in the resistant ridges that lay above the steep gorges of many of the Tertiary water gaps. The present elevation of the area probably represents over 500 feet of post-Mesozoic uplift. When the extreme climate saprolitized even the resistant sandstones, the ridges were somewhat reduced by mass wasting to the adjacent valleys, even though clastic debris was largely retained in the drainage basins by vegetative cover. Thus, the local relief would have been somewhat less than it is at present but would have had the same general form as is seen today.

The intervening valleys developed a deep weathering mantle that is preserved where lowered by solution of underlying limestone. Parizek and White (1985) discussed this process in the Nittany Valley, although their material is tentatively dated Eocene. Definite Late Cretaceous lignite occurs in the Cumberland Valley of Franklin County (Pierce, 1965; Tschudy, 1965). It is preserved in a karst situation

with colluvial cover, and the original extent is unknown. Its present position is consistent with the magnitude of Cenozoic lowering of the carbonate valleys previously suggested. The Late Cretaceous valley floor erosion surface is, thus, the true Schooley peneplain. The approximately accordant summit levels above this surface, which form the classical Schooley peneplain, are the natural consequence of equilibrium erosion.

AND THEN

The paleogeologic map for the end of the Cretaceous (Figure 34–8) is generalized and, necessarily, less certain in many details than the pre-Mesozoic map. Measurement of the timing of denudation is, inevitably, indirect and less precise than that of the datable effects of deposition and deformation. Figure 34–8 represents an effort to synthesize the effects of the Mesozoic evolution as deduced above from sources too numerous to fully document in a brief presentation. With at least 6 miles, and possibly 10 miles, of overburden eroded from parts of Pennsylvania since the Alleghany orogeny, of which less than 300 feet is attributed to Cenozoic erosion, it is presumed that substantial departure at the scale of this map from the Holocene distribution of exposed geologic units will be found only in areas of low dip in western Pennsylvania and in the Coastal Plain. The extent of subsequently eroded deposits portrayed here is intended to be conservative.

PROBLEMS AND FUTURE RESEARCH

The author presumes that problems associated with any part of the Mesozoic evolution that are concerned with data deemed sufficient to merit separate chapters in this volume have been addressed by the authors of these respective chapters. Of the more nebulous matters concerning missing rocks, paleotopographic surfaces that have largely evaporated into the sky, presumed uplifts that are not always adequately datable, and related phenomena that form a major part of this chapter, almost every assertion of this text is a legitimate target for further examination.

Among studies likely to be immediately productive, the radiometric and geochemical studies of datable isothermal or isobaric surfaces, including the contemporary regolith, can be both expanded geographically and extended to other materials. Extension of the analysis of offshore and Coastal Plain deposits to determine the total volume of deposits associated with each specific epoch could lead to a considerably more refined chronology of Atlantic-slope denudation. It appears that the paleoclimatologists need to refine their models to match the accessible fragments of ground truth, but the effort could well be worthwhile. Classical geomorphic studies, unaugmented by sophisticated measurement techniques, may have reached saturation in Pennsylvania, at least for studies having regional implications, but comparative studies of erosion in other folded mountain belts having a maximum variety of topographic and climatic conditions could yet reveal some insights on processes bearing on peneplains (if any) and related topics of the classic curriculum.

RECOMMENDED FOR FURTHER READING

For further information on the evolution of the lower Mesozoic rifts and more specific information on Mesozoic strata, consult Chapters 12, 13, 21, and 40B of this volume and the references recommended below.

The volume by Gardner and Sevon (1989) was published after this manuscript had passed through review, and its impact is only partly reflected by last-minute revisions. To a considerable degree, the authors of papers in that volume that are relevant to the nondepositional history of the Mesozoic support the conclusions independently derived by this author from the more obvious and accessible sources. They bring to bear, however, expertise from a variety of disciplines, many remote from classical geomorphology, and a breadth of knowledge that this author cannot hope to emulate. Several contributions are individually cited in this chapter, but the whole volume is highly recommended.

Gardner, T. W., and Sevon, W. D., eds. (1989), *Appalachian geomorphology,* Amsterdam, Elsevier, 318 p. [reprinted from Geomorphology, v. 2, no. 1–3].

Hack, J. T. (1960), *Interpretation of erosional topography in humid temperate regions,* American Journal of Science, v. 258–A, p. 80–97.

Sevon, W. D. (1985), *Pennsylvania's polygenetic landscape,* Harrisburg Area Geological Society Annual Field Trip, 4th, Guidebook, 55 p.

Sevon, W. D., Potter, Noel, Jr., and Crowl, G. H. (1983), *Appalachian peneplains: an historical review,* in Jordan, W. M., ed., *History of geology and geological concepts in the northeastern United States,* Earth Sciences History, v. 2, p. 156–164.

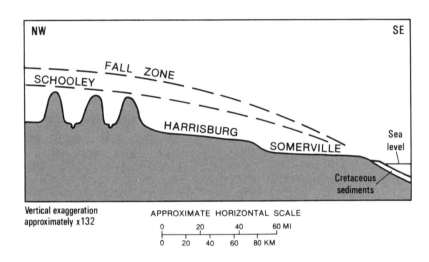

Figure 35–1. Schematic cross section showing relative positions of the four most widely identified peneplains in Pennsylvania. The Fall Zone is preserved only under Cretaceous sediments; the Schooley corresponds to the crests of the highest curvilinear ridges in the Ridge and Valley province; the Harrisburg corresponds to the higher uplands of the dissected terrain of the Martinsburg Formation and Hamburg sequence immediately south of Blue Mountain; and the Somerville corresponds to the low-relief carbonate terrain in areas such as Allentown in Lehigh County.

CHAPTER 35   CENOZOIC

W. D. SEVON
Bureau of Topographic and Geologic Survey
Department of Conservation and Natural
    Resources
P. O. Box 8453
Harrisburg, PA 17105

INTRODUCTION

There is little record of what happened in Pennsylvania during the last 66 million years except for the glacially related sediments of the Pleistocene Epoch (last 2.6 million years). This lack of preserved deposits has contributed significantly to the idea that erosion was the main geological activity in Pennsylvania during the Cenozoic Era.

During the first half of this century, identification of peneplains, the presumed end result of long-term erosion that reduces a landscape to base level (Davis, 1889), consumed the energies of many workers but contributed little to our understanding of Cenozoic history (Sevon and others, 1983). The various peneplains (Figure 35–1) were identified by correlation of presumed accordant surfaces, but there never was total agreement about the reality of peneplains, and there was considerable disagreement about the ages of the presumed peneplains. For example, ages assigned to the Schooley peneplain range from Jurassic to post-late Tertiary (Sevon and others, 1983). The only presumed peneplain to receive widespread recognition by many workers and to be identified by means other than accordant surfaces is the Harrisburg peneplain.

Campbell (1903b) defined the Harrisburg peneplain on the basis of presumed accordance of uplands developed on the Martinsburg Formation and Hamburg sequence in southeastern Pennsylvania. He extended the surface by topographic correlation throughout the state, and other workers correlated similar surfaces elsewhere in the Appalachians, principally in Maryland, Virginia, and Tennessee. Campbell suggested a mid-Tertiary age for the peneplain and calculated downcutting since the Miocene (1933, p. 572–573).

It has long been suggested that secondary, residual mineral deposits of bauxite, manganese, and iron found throughout the Appalachians were formed during the development of the Harrisburg peneplain (Bridge, 1950; Hewett, 1916; Parizek and White, 1985), because these deposits appear to be related to a topographic position on the presumed peneplain.

During the second half of this century, there has been general rejection of the reality of peneplains in the Appalachians and widespread acceptance of the dynamic-equilibrium concepts of Hack (1960, 1975). Hack argued that topographic irregularity results from erosion under disequilibrium conditions, such as tectonic uplift, and that once equilibrium conditions are established, the whole landscape is eroded at an equal rate, thus preserving the topographic irregularity and never achieving a peneplain. At the time of this writing, research attention is directed generally to understanding the processes that carve the landscape and the rates at which these processes work.

A basic problem related to interpreting the erosional history of Pennsylvania during the Cenozoic is that of initial conditions—the character of the landscape at the end of the Mesozoic. Assuming the model for Mesozoic history presented in Chapter 34 is correct, then the overall structural level of Pennsylvania was higher at the beginning of the Cenozoic than it is at present. The form of that landscape is unknown.

THE CENOZOIC: TIME OF CHANGE

During the first 50 million years of the Cenozoic, from the Paleocene through the early Miocene, temperature and rainfall increased in the Appalachians, and a megathermal rain-forest ecosystem evolved in the coastal region of eastern North America (Wolfe and Upchurch, 1987).The maximum temperature of this system was reached in the Eocene (Wolfe, 1978; Frederickson, 1984). Under such prolonged warm and humid conditions, chemical weathering proceeded to considerable depths beneath the land surface while vegetation inhibited physical erosion of the surface. Presumably, minimal change of the land surface occurred during this time interval. This scenario is supported by the middle Atlantic offshore sediment record, which shows the Paleocene-early Miocene period to have the lowest sediment-accumulation rate of any period since the Atlantic opened (Poag and Sevon, 1989).

The extensive chemical weathering produced thick saprolites both in Pennsylvania (Sevon, 1975, 1988, 1990) and elsewhere in the Appalachians (Costa and Cleaves, 1984). Most of the saprolite has been lost to erosion, and those saprolites still preserved represent only the basal remnants of what was once a very thick mass of weathered rock. The base of the original extensive saprolites was presumably irregular in profile, reflecting variations in rock type and structure (Sevon, 1990).

It is probable that the secondary residual mineral deposits mentioned above formed at this time also, not because of any relationship to a peneplain, but because of the weathering conditions.

Not all geologists accept the above scenario. Pavich (1989) believed that saprolite production and erosion is an ongoing process and that there are no old saprolites. Cleaves (1989) also questioned the age of the Piedmont saprolites. In addition, Hack (1965) argued that the secondary iron and manganese deposits are forming today and thus have no time or topographic significance.

The topographic surface of Pennsylvania produced by this extended period of chemically dominated weathering is problematic. Its surface was everywhere at a higher structural level than the surface of today. Streams were probably nowhere entrenched. The curvilinear ridges of the Ridge and Valley province probably had much less relief than they do today. The surface may have had relatively low relief everywhere and may have approximated a partial peneplain. However, the actual appearance of the surface is strictly conjecture.

Dramatic climatic changes occurred during the middle Miocene. A pronounced decrease in temperature (Savin, 1977; Pollack, 1982; Miller and others, 1987) was accompanied by changes in precipitation. A humid subtropical climate developed in the central Appalachians, and a period of intense physical erosion, which has continued to the present, was initiated (Poag and Sevon, 1989). It is this erosion that has produced the finely etched topography (Figure 35–2) we see today in that part of the state draining to the Atlantic Ocean.

The detailed topographic reflection of variations in rock hardness and structure evident in Figure 35–2 when viewed closely is the result of chemical weathering followed by physical erosion. Figure 35–3A suggests a hypothetical amount of erosion and change in topography for an area in Mifflin County.

Data from the offshore sediment record (Poag and Sevon, 1989) indicate that in excess of 3,000 feet of rock must have been removed from the eastward-draining land area in order to account for the volume of sediments accumulated since the middle Miocene (Braun, 1989). Because of the general lack of preserved saprolite in the more inland parts of the source area, in contrast to the more seaward parts, it is assumed that more erosion occurred inland than seaward. Regardless, all of the eastward-draining parts of Pennsylvania have been lowered several hundred feet during the last 16 million years. This removal

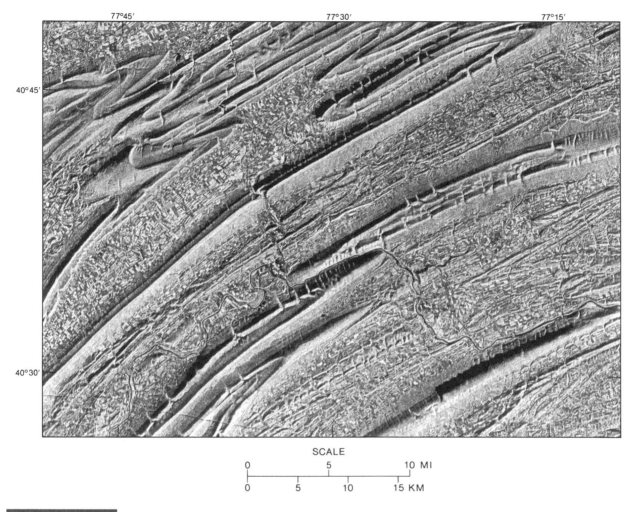

Figure 35–2. Part of the Harrisburg, Pa., synthetic-aperture radar imagery mosaic published by the U.S. Geological Survey in 1982 at 1:250,000 scale (near range, X-band, northwest look). When viewed closely, the finely etched topographic reflections of variations in rock and structure resulting from chemical weathering and ensuing physical erosion are evident. The prominent southwest-northeast-trending ridge just north of center is Jacks Mountain. The Juniata River is visible in the lower half of the view, and Lewistown is slightly southwest of center.

of material has presumably been balanced by isostatic uplift so that the surface elevation relative to sea level has probably changed little.

The highest upland terraces along the lower Susquehanna River have been correlated with the late Miocene Bryn Mawr Formation in Maryland (Pazzaglia and Gardner, 1993), and the lower terraces are Pliocene or younger in age. Pazzaglia and Gardner (1993) demonstrated that the terrace positions are controlled by isostatic adjustment on a passive margin in response to denudation and sediment loading. Terrace deposits occurring along the Juniata River (Figure 35–3B) (Kaktins, T. L., 1986) have not been dated but, like those along the lower Susquehanna

River, represent erosion and deposition subsequent to middle Miocene cutting.

Sand and gravel of the Bryn Mawr Formation (Chapter 14) in extreme southeastern Pennsylvania presumably represent late Miocene deposits of the Schuylkill River, but their correlation and age are speculative. The Bridgeton and Pensauken Formations of late Miocene to Pliocene age (Chapter 14) occur along the Delaware River, but Owens and Minard (1979) indicated a source outside the state for these sediments.

A number of diamicts of unknown age were deposited on undissected weathered surfaces in some areas of the state (Pierce, 1966; Sevon, 1981), and

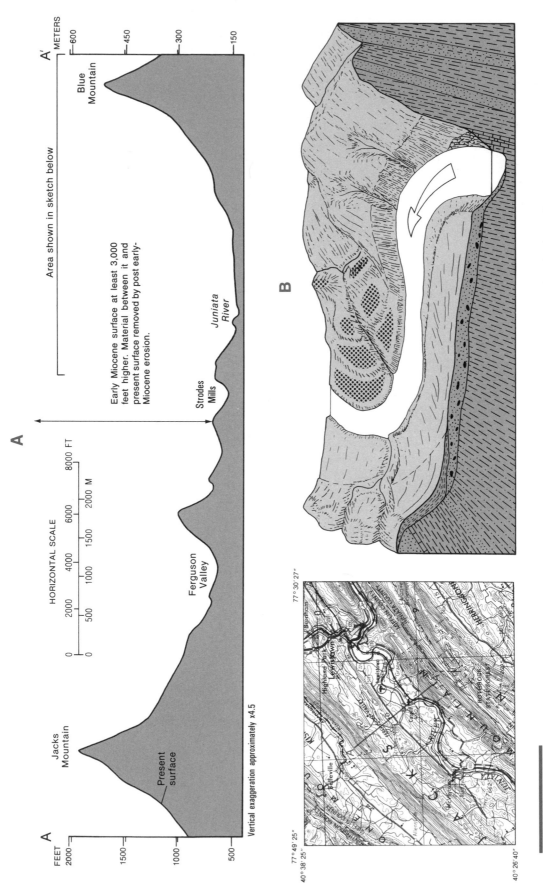

Figure 35–3. A. Cross section showing the present topographic surface of an area in Mifflin County. The surface in the early Miocene would have been at least 3,000 feet higher and would have had an unknown configuration. The location of the cross section is shown on the index map. B. Diagrammatic sketch of part of the Juniata River and adjacent terrace levels (from Kaktins, T. L., 1986, Figure 10). The line of cross section A–A´ is left-right through the center of the block. The coarse stippling shows areas of terrace gravels. The terrace levels were formed as the Juniata River cut downward and migrated laterally to the left (north). All the terrace gravels are Pleistocene in age, and the highest terrace gravel may be more than 780,000 years old.

remnants of these deposits still exist. The diamicts probably formed during a period of climatic change, possibly early Pleistocene, but the exact conditions and time of origin are unknown.

Little is known about the pre-Pleistocene Cenozoic in western Pennsylvania. Erosion must have occurred, but there is currently no measure of how much. The amount was probably considerably less than in the eastern part of the state.

The Pleistocene Epoch had a severe effect on Pennsylvania, producing both erosion and deposition, the effects of which are discussed in detail in Chapter 15. In addition, during the Pleistocene, there were considerable drainage modifications in western Pennsylvania. Former northwest-flowing drainage, including the Allegheny and Monongahela Rivers, was reversed and diverted to its present course through specific changes related to one or more ice advances (Wright, 1914; Leverett, 1934). Glaciation mainly enhanced drainage changes already in progress prior to the Pleistocene. Those changes were realignment of drainage from northwest flow to southwest flow through updip headward erosion (Sevon, 1992). Lake Erie, along with the other Great Lakes, was presumably excavated by ice during one or more advances of continental glaciers (Shepard, 1937). That a well-established preglacial drainage system tied the present lake basins together (Spencer, 1891) is speculative, but not improbable. It is assumed that during the whole Cenozoic, most or all streams draining to the Atlantic flowed in locations and directions comparable to those of today.

Continental ice of the Laurentide ice sheet advanced into Pennsylvania via the Erie lobe in the northwest and the Lake Champlain-Hudson River lobe in the northeast. Four major periods of glaciation are known: pre-Illinoian (two periods), Illinoian, and late Wisconsinan (Woodfordian). Each glaciation left behind numerous deposits, mainly till and ice-contact sand and gravel, north of its glacial border, as well as fluvial outwash sediments beyond the border. Many deposits of successive glaciations are well preserved in western Pennsylvania, but in eastern Pennsylvania, each successive ice sheet eroded earlier glacial deposits and, for the most part, older deposits occur only at sites south of subsequent glacial advances.

During glaciation, most of the nonglaciated part of the state was subjected to a rigorous cold climate with optimal conditions for periglacial activity. Freeze-thaw breakup of hard rock created abundant talus and probably lowered ridge crests many tens of feet in the Ridge and Valley province. Finer grained materials moved downward via solifluction and accumulated on lower parts of many slopes. Presumably, much of the removal of previously weathered material was accomplished during these intensive periods of erosion, but the actual amount is unknown.

The several interglacial intervals, including the current one, have imprinted weathering and soil development on the surficial deposits of each preceding glacial interval but have left no marked impression on the bedrock.

At present, a humid continental climate characterized by seasonal temperature extremes and moderate rainfall controls erosion in Pennsylvania. In an undisturbed landscape, these climatic conditions produce minimal physical and chemical weathering (Budel, 1982). However, the activities of man have accelerated physical erosion locally (Sevon, 1989a) and, in some areas of surface mining, have dramatically altered the form of the landscape.

PROBLEMS AND FUTURE RESEARCH

The following aspects of Cenozoic history in Pennsylvania require research:
1. Determination of the ages of various fluvial terraces in nonglaciated areas.
2. Determination of the age of remnant saprolites.
3. Determination of the mechanism and rate of fluvial erosion of resistant rocks such as the Tuscarora Formation.
4. Determination of the form of the pre-late Miocene landscape surface.
5. Comprehensive study of drainage changes in western Pennsylvania.

RECOMMENDED FOR FURTHER READING

Gardner, T. W., and Sevon, W. D., eds. (1989), *Appalachian geomorphology,* Amsterdam, Elsevier, 318 p. [reprinted from Geomorphology, v. 2, no. 1–3].

Pioneer Run on Oil Creek in 1865, during the first great oil rush, which was in Crawford and Venango Counties. Parts of 17 oil wells are visible in the scene, some with derricks overlapping. Hard lessons had yet to be learned about reservoir geology and geometry, and very close well spacing was the rule. The bare slope probably was stripped for lumber for construction. Environmental awareness was far in the future. Photograph by John A. Mather, from the Mather collection at the Drake Well Museum, Titusville.

456

Part VII

MINERAL RESOURCES

Before Europeans settled in Pennsylvania, Indians here mined the earth for flint, talc, tar, and perhaps other minerals. The European colonists, however, had a much more advanced mining tradition, which was put to good use from about 1700 onward.

Nonmetals, clay for brick and limestone for burnt lime, were the first minerals recorded as produced by the settlers, followed by glass sand. Iron was the first metal produced from Pennsylvania rocks, and until recently, iron as well as other metals was mined in the state. Metals were important contributors to the economy, but nonfuel mineral production now is entirely nonmetals, dominated by crushed stone and cement. Nonmetals were valued at $844 million in 1991.

Pennsylvania's coal was first utilized in about 1751, and coal mining grew into a huge industry during the great industrial expansion from 1830 to 1920. Production was well over 100 million tons annually for decades, though it has declined in the latter part of this century. Colonel Drake's oil well in Venango County in 1859 ushered in the petroleum industry. "Pennsylvania crude" still is produced, but natural gas now is more important; annual production in recent years has averaged about 160 billion standard cubic feet.

Pennsylvania for many years led the nation in production of a wide variety of mineral resources. In spite of this long history of mineral extraction, a significant part of the state's large though finite mineral heritage remains intact for the use of future generations.

—Reginald P. Briggs

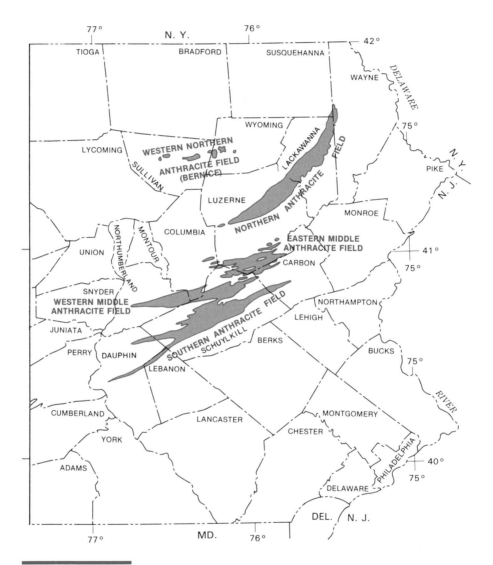

SCALE

| 0 | 10 | 20 | 30 | 40 | 50 MI |
| 0 | 20 | 40 | 60 | 80 KM |

Figure 36–1. Location map of the Anthracite region, eastern Pennsylvania (from Pennsylvania Geological Survey, 1992).

CHAPTER 36   ANTHRACITE

JANE R. EGGLESTON
U.S. Geological Survey
227 North Bronough Street
Suite 3015
Tallahassee, FL 32301

THOMAS M. KEHN*
U.S. Geological Survey
301 Thirteenth Street
St. Augustine, FL 32084

GORDON H. WOOD, JR.**
U.S. Geological Survey
National Center, MS 956
Reston, VA 20192

INTRODUCTION

The Anthracite region is largely in the Ridge and Valley physiographic province of northeastern Pennsylvania and is drained by the Schuylkill, Susquehanna, and Lehigh Rivers. It contains most of the nation's anthracite resources in four major coal fields covering parts of 10 counties (Figure 36–1). These northeast-trending fields range from about 24 to 70 miles in length and from 1 to 8 miles in width. They generally occupy valley floors that range in elevation from 500 to 1,700 feet; the elevations of surrounding ridge tops range from 1,200 to 2,200 feet. Approximately 5.5 billion tons of anthracite has been removed from these fields since 1820 (revised from Arndt and others, 1968). The Bernice basin, or Western Northern Anthracite field, approximately 35 miles west of the Northern Anthracite field, contains semianthracite, but this basin is traditionally included within the North-Central (bituminous) fields and is, therefore, described in the chapter of this book on bituminous coal (Chapter 37).

GEOLOGIC SETTING

Coal-bearing strata within the Anthracite region are Pennsylvanian in age. Areas between the coal fields are underlain, in general, by rocks of Devonian and Mississippian age (Figure 10–14). Resistant strata of the Pottsville Formation of Pennsylvanian age form high ridges around each field, and the overlying less resistant Pennsylvanian Llewellyn Formation floors the valleys within each field.

The Pottsville Formation (Lower and Middle Pennsylvanian) is about 80 percent conglomerate, conglomeratic sandstone, and sandstone; the remainder includes shale, siltstone, and several coal beds. It is more than 1,500 feet thick along the southern edge of the Southern Anthracite field and thins northward to less than 100 feet in the Northern field (see Chapter 10). The Pottsville Formation is divided into three members, each of which is a thick sequence that fines upward from massive conglomerates at the base through

*Retired.
**Deceased.

sandstone and siltstone to shale at the top. As many as 10 lenticular to persistent coal beds are recognized in the Pottsville Formation in the Southern Anthracite field; in contrast, few Pottsville coal beds are recognized in the Eastern and Western Middle fields and Northern field (Figure 36–2).

The Llewellyn Formation (Middle and Upper Pennsylvanian) includes all strata in this region that are above the Pottsville Formation. In most places, the lower contact is located at the base of the underclay or shale underlying the Buck Mountain coal, and the upper contact is the modern erosional surface. The known maximum thickness of the formation, approximately 3,500 feet, is preserved in the Southern field near Llewellyn. The formation is a predominantly nonmarine sequence of conglomerate, sandstone, siltstone, shale, and coal beds. A few thin beds of limestone have been identified in the upper part of the formation in the Northern field; only the thin, lenticular Mill Creek limestone of Ashburner (1886) is marine or marginal marine in origin (Chow, 1951). By generally adopting the system used by the coal industry and earlier geologists, Wood and Trexler (1968) and Wood and others (1968) identified 40 coal beds by name and/or number for usage by the U.S. Geological Survey in the Southern field, starting with No. 5 (Buck Mountain) at the base and moving upward to No. 29 at the top (Figure 36–2). Fewer coal beds have been identified in the fields to the north. Names and numbers for coal beds in the Northern field were similarly adopted for usage by the U.S. Geological Survey, but uncertainties in bed correlations precluded the use of names adopted in the other fields. Only one name is listed for many coal beds in Figure 36–2, although perhaps several different names might be used for each by mining companies. Correlations of the coal beds between fields are based on the relative stratigraphic position and interval. Many unnamed or unnumbered beds are known to exist, but they are usually thin and lenticular, and generally cannot be correlated.

The depositional history of the Anthracite region during Pennsylvanian time records the latest stages of development of the Appalachian geosyncline. A series of sedimentary pulses from the southeast, giving rise to coarse conglomerates, define each member of the Pottsville Formation. These are separated by the terrestrial-fluvial-swamp units consisting of interbedded sandstone, siltstone, shale, and coal. The swamps were generally short lived and laterally discontinuous, particularly toward the north. The end of Pottsville deposition was marked by the development of a widespread swamp in which the Buck Mountain coal bed formed. Sediments of the Llewellyn depositional basin accumulated on a broad, fairly flat, slowly subsiding floodplain as fluvial and swamp deposits. This basin was bounded on the west and northwest by a distant, fluctuating coastline. On the southeast, it was bounded by a nearby highland area, which was periodically uplifted and yielded fine to coarse detritus that washed onto the floodplain over the swamp. In the Northern field, the presence of the fossiliferous Mill Creek limestone indicates that marine brackish waters from the west extended into the northern part of the region during early Late Pennsylvanian time. The Llewellyn Formation represents a period of accumulation of fine to coarser sediments and thick, persistent coal beds. The Buck Mountain coal bed contains plant fossils of late Middle Pennsylvanian age (Wood and others, 1956, Table 2), but the rest of the Llewellyn is of Late Pennsylvanian age. Oleksyshyn (1982) used paleobotany to confirm that the shale just below the Buck Mountain is of late Middle Pennsylvanian age (Westphalian D), equivalent to the middle and upper parts of the Allegheny Formation in western Pennsylvania. Identifiable plant fossils have been found in the roof shale of the No. 25 coal bed (Eggleston and others, 1988), and these indicate that the upper part of the Llewellyn could be equivalent to the Monongahela Group.

The Anthracite region is in a northeast-trending structural depression within the Ridge and Valley province, bounded by the Pocono Plateau to the east, the Pennsylvanian culmination to the west, the Appalachian structural front to the north, and the Blue Mountain structural front to the south (Wood and Bergin, 1970). Each field is a complexly folded and faulted synclinorium having structural trends between N55°E and N85°E. Deformation is most complex to the southeast, where it is characterized by hundreds of thrust, reverse, tear, and bedding faults and tightly folded, commonly overturned folds (Figure 36–3). The four fields are underlain by a large décollement located at approximately the lower contact of the upper member of the Mauch Chunk Formation. High-angle reverse and thrust faults are more common in relatively competent rocks; in contrast, incompetent rocks are characteristically broken by low-angle thrust, décollement, and bedding faults.

COAL RESOURCES

Principal coal beds of the Anthracite region are illustrated in the columnar sections of Figure 36–2.

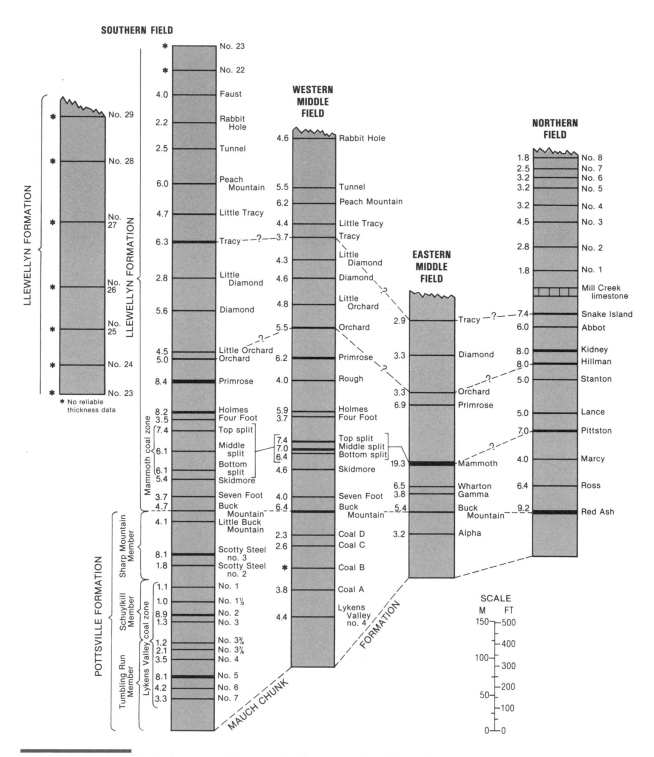

Figure 36–2. Generalized columnar sections showing the names of coal beds, the average thickness of each coal in feet, and the intervals between coal beds in the Pennsylvania anthracite fields (modified from Arndt and others, 1968, p. 130).

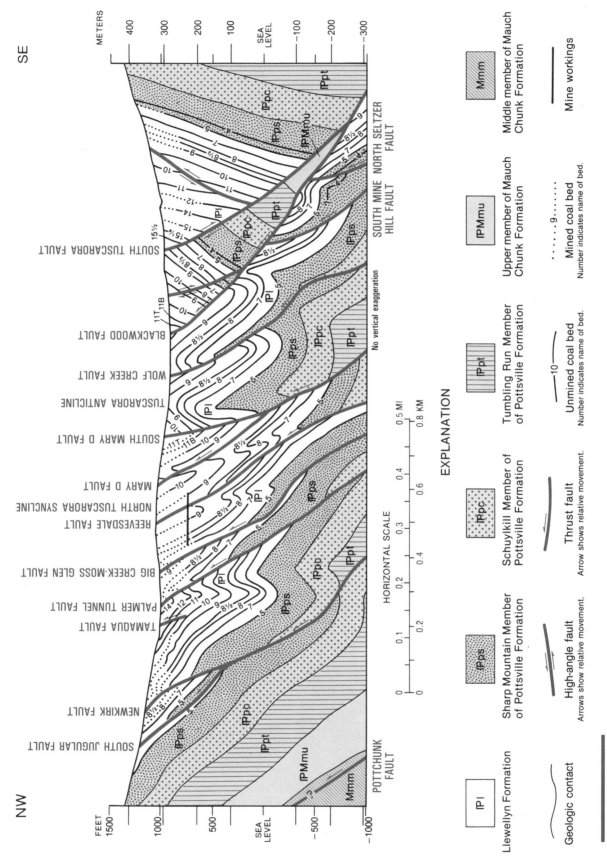

Figure 36–3. Geologic cross section across the east end of the Southern Anthracite field (from Wood, 1974a).

EXPLANATION

Mmm	Middle member of Mauch Chunk Formation
IPMmu	Upper member of Mauch Chunk Formation
IPpt	Tumbling Run Member of Pottsville Formation
IPpc	Schuylkill Member of Pottsville Formation
IPps	Sharp Mountain Member of Pottsville Formation
IPl	Llewellyn Formation

Mine workings

.......9....... Mined coal bed
Number indicates name of bed.

——10—— Unmined coal bed
Number indicates name of bed.

Thrust fault
Arrow shows relative movement.

High-angle fault
Arrows show relative movement.

Geologic contact

The coal bed names shown on the columnar sections are the most commonly used names; however, alternative names for these beds are presented in parentheses in the following paragraphs. Many of the upper beds are of local occurrence and limited economic value. About 90 percent of the mined coal came from beds in the lower part of the section, including the Lykens Valley coal beds, Buck Mountain (No. 5, Red Ash, Dunmore), Seven Foot (No. 6, Gamma, Clark, Ross), Skidmore (No. 7, Wharton, New County, Marcy, Twin, Church), Mammoth (No. 8, No. 8½, No. 9, Baltimore, Pittston, Big, Grassy), Holmes (No. 10, Rock, Lance, Checker, Five Foot), Primrose (No. 11, Diamond, Stanton, Orchard), and Orchard (No. 12, Hillman). The Diamond (No. 14, Kidney), Little Diamond (No. 15, Abbott), and Tracy (No. 16, Snake Island) are the more productive coal beds of the upper section.

The Pottsville Formation in the Southern field contains 10 coal beds of economic importance: Lykens Valley Nos. 7, 6, 5, and 4 in the Tumbling Run Member; Lykens Valley Nos. 3, 2, and 1 in the Schuylkill Member; and Scotty Steel no. 2 and no. 3 and Little Buck Mountain in the Sharp Mountain Member. In the Western Middle field, the Little Buck Mountain and a few of the Lykens Valley coal beds have been mined, whereas in the Eastern Middle and Northern fields, the only Pottsville coal beds are the Alpha and "A" coal beds, respectively.

The Buck Mountain (No. 5) coal bed, at the base of the Llewellyn Formation, averages 7 to 10 feet in thickness but in places is more than 20 feet thick. The Buck Mountain has been identified in the three southern fields and is correlated with the Red Ash (or Dunmore) in the Northern field. It is second only to the Mammoth beds in economic importance.

The Seven Foot (No. 6) coal bed, 30 to 100 feet above the Buck Mountain, averages 4 feet in thickness. It is not as economically important in the Southern field as in the other fields. In the Eastern Middle field, it is sometimes called the Gamma bed, and in the Northern field, it is tentatively correlated with the Ross (or Clark) bed.

The Skidmore (No. 7) coal bed, 50 to 150 feet above the Seven Foot, averages 4 to 6 feet in thickness. In the Eastern Middle field, it is often called the Wharton; in the Northern field, it is probably the Marcy (or New County, Twin, or Church).

The Mammoth coal zone lies about 200 to 300 feet above the Buck Mountain coal bed. In some places, it occurs in as many as three splits, Top (No. 9), Middle (No. 8½), and Bottom (No. 8), which

total as much as 65 feet of coal. Where it occurs as only one bed, it measures 50 feet in thickness in some places. Because of its persistence and unusual thickness, the Mammoth coal zone is easily recognized in drilling logs and is used as a marker bed for correlations. In the Northern field, it could be the Pittston (or Baltimore, Big, or Grassy) coal bed.

The Holmes (No. 10) coal bed lies 50 to 200 feet above the Mammoth and averages about 6 feet in thickness, except in the western part of the Southern field, where it is as much as 8 feet thick, including shale partings. In most places in the central and western parts of the Western Middle field, the Holmes is split, each split being about 4 feet thick. In the Northern field, the Holmes is tentatively correlated with the Lance (or Rock, Checker, or Five Foot) and averages about 9 feet in thickness.

The Primrose (No. 11) coal bed, 100 to 250 feet above the Holmes, is as much as 21 feet thick in the western part of the Southern field and averages about 10 feet in thickness in the rest of the field. The Primrose is also important in the Western Middle field, where it is in two splits that total about 14 feet in thickness, including partings. It is probably the Stanton (or Diamond or Orchard) coal bed in the Northern field, where it averages 8 feet in thickness.

The Orchard (No. 12) coal bed and the overlying Little Orchard bed (No. 13) are 30 to 180 feet above the Primrose. The Orchard averages 16 feet in thickness, but most of the bed consists of shale partings. The Little Orchard averages only 4 to 5 feet in thickness. In the Northern field, the Orchard is at the approximate position of the Hillman, which averages about 7 feet in thickness and is useful as a key bed for correlations. Generally, the Orchard is of minor economic importance.

Coal resources of the Anthracite region were originally estimated by Smith (1895) and Ashmead (1926) and were later revised by Ashley (1945) and Edmunds (1972), primarily on the basis of production figures. In a resource study funded by the U.S. Bureau of Mines (Resource Technologies Corporation, 1984), more recently published geologic maps and available mine maps were used to reevaluate resources and to estimate reserves for three mining methods: shallow surface mining (strip mining), deep surface mining (open-pit mining), and underground mining. These estimates indicate that, as of January 1981, a total of 19,582 million short tons of anthracite remained in the four fields (Table 36–1). The study showed about 1,505 million short tons as recoverable, 1,150 million short tons by conventional strip mining

Table 36–1. *Remaining Pennsylvania Anthracite Resources as of 1981[1]*
(Quantities are in short tons)

Field	Total remaining resources	Tonnage above 1,000 feet (demonstrated reserve base)	Recoverable tonnage by conventional strip mining, underground mining, and open-pit mining (reserves)
Northern	2,762,383,000	2,306,957,000	253,000,000
Western Middle	3,352,009,000	1,820,096,000	440,000,000
Southern	13,294,649,000	2,966,149,000	716,000,000
Eastern Middle	172,811,000	167,052,000	96,000,000
TOTALS	19,581,852,000	7,260,254,000	1,505,000,000

[1]From Resource Technologies Corporation (1984).

and underground mining and 355 million short tons by open-pit mining. Recoverable coal is defined as coal lying above the mine-water pool level, under undeveloped land-surface areas, and minable using current technology. Open-pit mining reserves are further defined as less than 1,000 feet deep, and were estimated only for the Western Middle and Southern fields, where sufficient contiguous unmined reserves are known to make open-pit mining economically viable. In addition to in-the-ground resources, 620 million cubic yards of coal refuse and silt (silt-sized coal and rock), which are scattered in banks throughout the four fields, were estimated to contain approximately 84 million short tons of anthracite. This material remained from past mining and processing. The silt collected in settling ponds after coal processing and is believed to contain an average of 40 percent coal, whereas other refuse from mechanical cleaning contains about 10 to 15 percent coal.

In general, the coal in the four fields has a high Btu value, ranging from 14,430 to 15,450 (moisture- and ash-free), and 13,000 to 14,000 on an as-received basis. Btu value and volatile-matter content of the coal generally show an increase regionally toward the west. The carbon content of anthracite averages 74 to 82 percent. Figures 37–5 and 37–6 in the following chapter show the distribution of carbon content and Btu values, respectively, in coals of the Anthracite region. Moisture content is low, particularly in coal from the western part of the region, and ranges from 0.5 to 14.6 percent. Sulfur content is generally low, ranging from 0.3 to 1.2 percent (as-received). Therefore, Pennsylvania anthracite represents a large resource of low-sulfur coal in the eastern United States. Ash content ranges from 7.0 to 24.0 percent (as-received) and averages about 12.2 percent. Hydrogen ranges from

2.5 to 3.1 percent (as-received), and nitrogen ranges from 0.7 to 1.1 percent (as-received); both tend to increase toward the west. Oxygen ranges from 3 to 7 percent.

Anthracite is the highest ranking coal, with 92 to 98 percent fixed carbon and 2 to 8 percent volatile matter (dry, ash-free basis). In the western parts of the Southern and Western Middle fields, the anthracite is of slightly lower rank, where it grades into semianthracite. According to Levine and Davis (1983), the west-to-east increase in rank across the region is attributed to increasing depth of burial. Levine (1986) believed that, in order to reach the coalification temperatures of 200° to 250°C required for anthracite, the coal beds must have been buried by 6 to 9 km of overburden during a 10- to 15-million-year interval. He proposed that a large downwarp occurring during the Alleghanian orogeny could account for this rapid accumulation of thick overburden.

PRODUCTION, MINING, AND USES OF ANTHRACITE

A chronological history of the anthracite mining industry is presented in Table 36–2. Anthracite mining in the United States began in the mid-1700's, but anthracite was known to exist in Pennsylvania as early as 1698. It was first used by blacksmiths in forging but soon became popular in home heating and various industrial markets. Coal production reached a peak of 100.4 million short tons in 1917 and has steadily declined since then. In 1995, anthracite production was 8.8 million short tons (Pennsylvania Department of Environmental Protection, 1995). Figure 36–4 shows a summary of production trends since 1890 for

Table 36–2. *History of the Anthracite Industry*[1]

Year	Event
1762	Parshall Terry and some Connecticut pioneers discovered coal at the mouth of Mill Creek, near Wilkes-Barre.
1769	Obadiah Gore, a blacksmith, used anthracite for fuel in his forge.
1775	First shipment of coal from Wilkes-Barre to Harrisburg down the Susquehanna River.
1788	Judge Jesse Fell of Wilkes-Barre made nails using anthracite as a heat source.
1791	Coal was discovered on Mauch Chunk Mountain by Philip Ginter.
1792	Lehigh Coal Mining Company, the first coal-mining company in America, was organized by Colonel Jacob Weiss.
1802	Oliver Evans burned anthracite in a grate in Philadelphia.
1807	First regular anthracite trade was begun by the Smith brothers, of Plymouth, Pa., who bought coal lands and began shipping coal by arks down the Susquehanna River.
1825	Schuylkill Navigation Company opened a canal from Mount Carbon to Philadelphia.
1826	Mauch Chunk Railroad, the first steam railroad in Pennsylvania, was completed.
1842	First train from Philadelphia to Pottsville (Philadelphia and Reading Railroad).
1844	First mechanical breaker was introduced.
1846	Canal system had expanded to 643 miles.
1867	Canals had lost most of their business to railroads.
1871	Philadelphia and Reading Coal and Iron Company was chartered.
1915	Large-scale surface-mining excavation equipment became available.
1917	Anthracite production peaked.
1925	Series of labor strikes began.
1961	Surface-mine production first exceeded deep-mine production.
1991	Bank recovery exceeded both surface and underground mining.

[1]Modified from Stoek (1902).

underground mining, surface mining, and bank recovery. Although underground mining was once the dominant method of production, it declined to a mere 5 percent of Pennsylvania's anthracite production in 1995. Surface mining dominated production from 1961 until 1991, and both surface and underground mining are now surpassed by bank recovery.

Surface mining is done by long-pit and block-pit mining, and production averages about 10 tons/man-day. Long-pit mining is a continuous operation in which miners advance along the outcrop of one or two closely spaced beds. In contrast, block-pit mining concentrates on a particular areal block of coal and overburden, and is especially useful in variable geologic conditions and discontinuous beds. The block pits average 150 to 200 feet in depth, but a few have been mined to depths of 600 feet, and there is growing interest in the mining of even deeper pits (Figure 36–5).

Underground mining is done by the breast-and-pillar method, and entry is by tunnel (adit), slope, or shaft. Initially, two horizontal headings are driven parallel to the strike of the coal bed from the entry.

The lower heading, or gangway, is used for haulage; the upper heading, or monkey, provides access for breast development up the dip of the coal bed through the full thickness of coal for distances of 200 to 300 feet (Figure 36–6). Coal is drilled and blasted and falls by gravity into a waiting coal car in the gangway. Because of the large amount of manual labor required, underground mine production averages only 4 tons/man-day.

Anthracite in refuse and silt, which remains from previous cleaning and preparation operations, is currently recovered by reprocessing the materials through preparation plants. Productivity is high, and anthracite recovery averages about 40 tons/man-day. The dredging of waterways for discarded or eroded coal reached a peak in 1941, when 1.5 million tons of coal was recovered, but this source has been depleted.

Most anthracite is cleaned and sized at a preparation plant (Figure 36–7). Ten specific sizes are produced for various markets (Table 36–3). Residential and commercial heating are the major markets for anthracite, but electric utilities, coke making, and cement plants are also markets. In past years, foreign con-

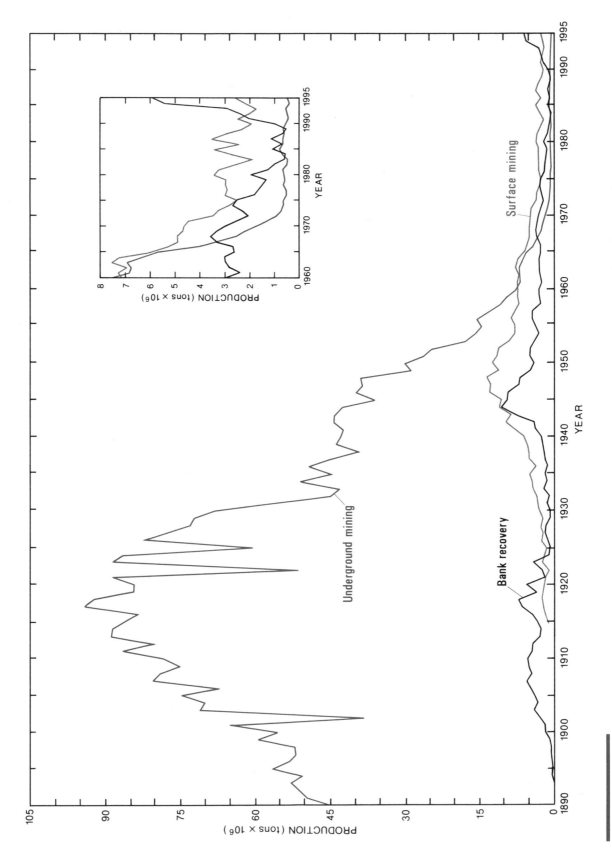

Figure 36–4. Pennsylvania anthracite production, 1890–1995 (based on data from Pennsylvania Department of Environmental Protection, 1995, p. 22–24). An enlargement of the part of the graph showing production trends from 1960 to 1995 is shown in the inset.

sumption was an expanding market, but demand has recently decreased. Currently, most anthracite is moved to preparation plants and to the marketplaces by truck, but railroad restoration is underway, and rail could again provide an alternative transportation system.

PROBLEMS AND FUTURE RESEARCH

The decline in anthracite production has been dramatic, particularly as the demand for bituminous coal and other fuels has generally been increasing. Some of the reasons for the decline include the availability of cheaper and cleaner fuels; labor disputes and the consequent unreliability of the anthracite supply; inconvenience in handling anthracite and ash in home heating; labor-intensive mining; difficulty in mechanization of mines because of such geologic conditions as hard rock and contorted, steeply

Figure 36–5. Deep block-pit mining operation of the Reading Anthracite Company at Wadesville, Schuylkill County, in the Anthracite field (note the drill, which is circled, for scale). The dashed line emphasizes structure.

dipping, highly faulted coal beds; depletion of the more easily accessible coal beds; and costly mandated responsibilities to rectify such problems as mine water,

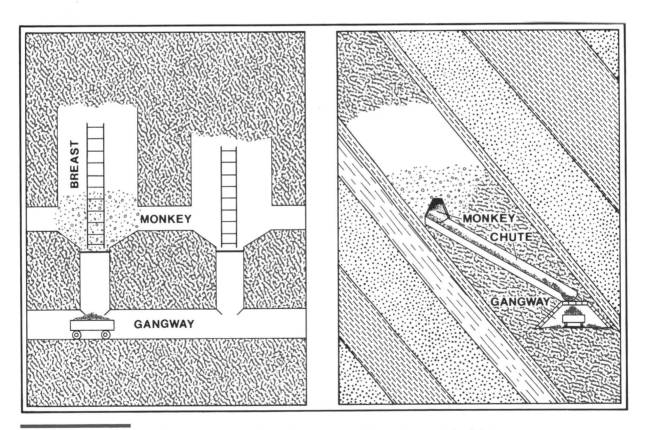

Figure 36–6. Two schematic cross-sectional views of breast-and-pillar underground mining.

Figure 36–7. Reading Anthracite Company's Saint Nicholas Breaker, Schuylkill County, with loaded coal cars in the foreground.

subsidence, mine fires, burning culm piles, and the so-called "lunar" landscapes (highwalls, gaping pits, and massive spoil piles) left by mining. Each anthracite field has a network of interconnected mine workings filled with acid mine water. These networks ex-

Table 36–3.	*Standard Sizes of Anthracite Coal for Sales*
Size	Round test mesh (inches)
Broken	Through 4-3/8 Over 3-1/4 to 3
Egg	Through 3-1/4 to 3 Over 2-7/16
Stove	Through 2-7/16 Over 1-5/8
Chestnut	Through 1-5/8 Over 13/16
Pea	Through 13/16 Over 9/16
Buckwheat No. 1	Through 9/16 Over 5/16
Buckwheat No. 2 (rice)	Through 5/16 Over 3/16
Buckwheat No. 3 (barley)	Through 3/16 Over 3/32
Buckwheat No. 4	Through 3/32 Over 3/64
Buckwheat No. 5	Through 3/64

tend for many miles and are fed by rivers, such as the Susquehanna, as well as by local streams and surface runoff. Water in the resultant mine pools gains access to surface streams through mine openings, strip-mine pits, air vents, and fractures. Although the anthracite resources available for future mining are enormous, companies that develop mines are responsible for treating the water to meet acceptable standards and are liable for any costs of pumping, neutralization, and purification; these are costly procedures that affect the economics of anthracite mining.

Subsidence is a long-term serious problem in the region, mostly because of the large number of consecutive beds that have been mined underground. Despite attempts to lessen subsidence in inhabited areas by backfilling abandoned deep mines, human lives and structures continue to be lost. Renewed mining would require dewatering of previously mined beds, which, in turn, would withdraw roof support and increase the danger of additional subsidence.

Mine fires and the spontaneous combustion of coal or adjacent carbonaceous shale in mined areas affect many square miles of the Anthracite region, posing a threat to populations, as at Centralia in southern Columbia County, and impeding future mining. Another reason that anthracite is in little demand is that its combustive nature differs from that of bituminous coal. Industrial plants must be designed for the particular characteristics of anthracite, such as high ignition and burning temperatures and greater grinding difficulty. Many companies are reluctant to build a plant specifically for anthracite burning when the anthracite market is so limited in comparison to that of bituminous coal.

Anthracite, on the other hand, has many advantages as a fuel. These advantages include (1) a relatively high Btu content, high fixed-carbon content, and low volatility, which, combined, produce long, slow combustion; (2) a low-sulfur content that is appealing because of tightening SO_2 emission standards; and (3) a source area that is close to northeastern markets and East Coast port facilities. Remaining coal resources in the region are vast and will be tapped if the cost of anthracite can become competitive with that of other fuels and the supply can be relied upon to meet long-term needs. Development of anthracite-specific technology, possibly moving toward larger open-pit operations and increasing state-of-the-art underground mechanization, could possibly help to reduce costs and turn the anthracite industry in a positive direction. In addition, the Anthracite region could be a future source of natural gas, and further research is needed to identify a means of tapping this resource.

There is still much to be learned about the geology of the region, particularly the Northern and Eastern Middle fields, where little mapping has been done. Correlation with the bituminous fields could be improved by additional paleobotanical and stratigraphic studies. Further research is also needed to improve our understanding of (1) the structural history of the region; (2) the depositional system that could create such thick coal beds; and (3) the cause of the elevation of the coal to the anthracite rank.

RECOMMENDED FOR FURTHER READING

Deasy, G. F., and Griess, P. R. (1963), *Atlas of Pennsylvania coal and coal mining, Part II, Anthracite*, Bulletin of the Mineral Industries Experiment Station, Pennsylvania State University, No. 80, 123 p.

Edmunds, W. E., and Eggleston, J. R. (1989), *Characteristics of the mid-Carboniferous boundary and associated coal-bearing rocks in the Northern Appalachian basin*, International Geological Congress, 28th, Field Trip Guidebook T352, Part 1, 37 p.

Levine, J. R. (1986), *Deep burial of coal-bearing strata, Anthracite region, Pennsylvania: sedimentation or tectonics?*, Geology, v. 14, p. 577–580.

Majumdar, S. K., and Miller, E. W. (1983), *Pennsylvania coal: resources, technology, and utilization*, The Pennsylvania Academy of Science, 594 p.

Oleksyshyn, John (1982), *Fossil plants from the anthracite coal fields of eastern Pennsylvania*, Pennsylvania Geological Survey, 4th ser., General Geology Report 72, 157 p.

Wood, G. H., Jr., Kehn, T. M., and Eggleston, J. R. (1986), *Depositional and structural history of the Pennsylvania Anthracite region*, in Lyons, P. C., and Rice, C. L., eds., *Paleoenvironmental and tectonic controls in coal-forming basins in the United States*, Geological Society of America Special Paper 210, p. 31–47.

Wood, G. H., Jr., Trexler, J. P., and Kehn, T. M. (1969), *Geology of the west-central part of the Southern Anthracite field and adjoining areas, Pennsylvania*, U.S. Geological Survey Professional Paper 602, 150 p.

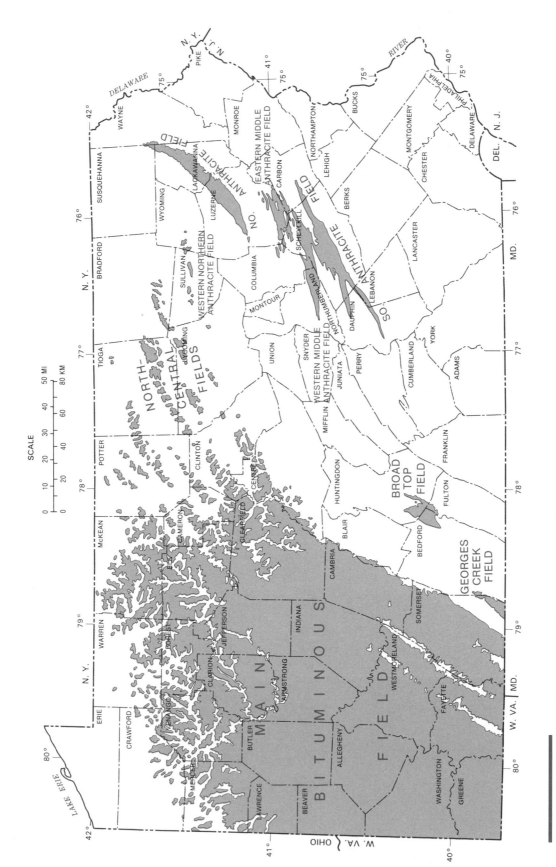

Figure 37-1. Coal fields of Pennsylvania (from Pennsylvania Geological Survey, 1992).

470

CHAPTER 37   BITUMINOUS COAL

WILLIAM E. EDMUNDS
Consulting Geologist
263 Sassafras Street
Harrisburg, PA 17102

BITUMINOUS COAL FIELDS

Pennsylvania is located at the northern end of the Appalachian coal basin. Coal beds underlie about 15,000 square miles of the state (Figure 37–1). Most bituminous coal occurs in the Main Bituminous field. Much smaller amounts exist in the Georges Creek and Broad Top fields and the several small coal areas known collectively as the North-Central fields. The coal in the Western Northern Anthracite field (Bernice field) is actually semianthracite, but has, in recent years, been associated more with the easternmost of the North-Central fields than with the anthracite fields, so is included in this chapter. The Georges Creek field is included with the Main Bituminous field for purposes of discussion.

All significant coal beds in Pennsylvania are Pennsylvanian or Permian. The stratigraphically lowest beds in the anthracite fields are the oldest, and the highest beds in the Main Bituminous field are the youngest. Coal bed names employed (Figures 37–2, 37–3, and 37–4) are well established in modern usage, although older reports may use somewhat different terminology. General stratigraphic correlations within each field are reasonably well established, but correlations between fields are so doubtful that separate bed names are used.

The system of coal bed names is, to a considerable degree, an oversimplification of stratigraphic reality. Coal beds carrying the same name in different areas do not necessarily represent a continuous lithosome or even exactly contemporary deposits. Individual coal lithosomes reflect their original depositional settings. Accordingly, real areal continuity of a bed can range from a few acres to thousands of square miles. A coal can occur as a widespread sheet having scattered holes or as a number of sizable, but isolated, bodies, or as both. Many named coal seams are actually multiple-bed complexes in which the best developed bed may change from place to place. In some areas, two or more beds of a complex may merge into a single coal. Even so, the sequence of bed nomenclature is sufficiently applica-

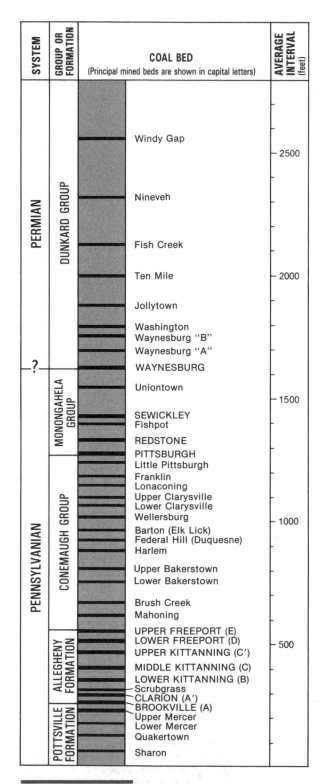

Figure 37–2. Coal beds of the Main Bituminous and Georges Creek coal fields (modified from Edmunds and others, 1979, Figure 16).

ble in practice that coals identified by the same name from place to place are in most cases not greatly different in stratigraphic position, age, and genetic affinity.

All of the principal economic coals of the Main field are confined to two intervals: the Allegheny Formation, and the Monongahela Group plus the Waynesburg coal at the base of the Dunkard Group (Figure 37–2). Although correlations are unclear, it

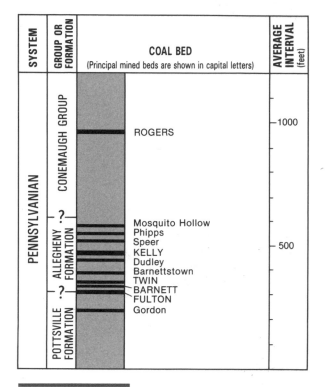

Figure 37–3. Coal beds of the Broad Top coal field (modified from Edmunds and others, 1979, Figure 16).

SYSTEM	FORMATION	COAL BED (Principal mined beds are shown in capital letters)	AVERAGE INTERVAL (feet)
PENNSYLVANIAN	POTTSVILLE AND ALLEGHENY	Rock SEYMOUR (CUSHING) MORGAN CANNEL One Foot BLOSS Bear Creek Kidney	300 200 100

Figure 37–4. Coal beds from the North-Central coal fields (modified from Edmunds and others, 1979, Figure 16).

is believed that most of the minable coals of the Broad Top and North-Central fields are equivalent to part of the Allegheny Formation (Figures 37–3 and 37–4). The Allegheny Formation is about 270 to 330 feet thick. The Monongahela Group is 275 to 375 feet thick, increasing in thickness from west to east. Both groups are heterogeneous sequences made up of relatively thin units of clastics (claystone to coarse sandstone), coal, and limestone.

DEPOSITIONAL ENVIRONMENTS

The depositional environments of coal beds and related rocks influence a number of economically important coal characteristics, such as physical dimensions, continuity, mineral-matter content, sulfur content, and some aspects of mining conditions (Horne and others, 1978).

Coals and associated strata of the lower Allegheny Formation (Brookville through Middle Kittanning coals) were deposited during a general eastward marine transgression. The setting was a shifting complex of marine to brackish embayments, lower-delta-plain distributaries, and interdistributary to coastal-margin swamps, grading inland to an upper-delta-plain fluvial and interfluvial swamp system (Williams, 1960; Williams and Ferm, 1964; Ferm and Williams, 1965; Ferm and Cavaroc, 1969; Ferm, 1970, 1974). The upper Allegheny Formation (Upper Kittanning through Upper Freeport coals) was deposited in a relatively high energy, upper-delta-plain fluvial and interfluvial lake and swamp environment during a period of general marine regression (Sholes and others, 1979; Skema and others, 1982). The Monongahela Group was developed in a relatively low energy, marginal upper delta plain having extensive lake and swamp development (Berryhill and others, 1971; Donaldson, 1974).

STRUCTURAL GEOLOGY

Various aspects of geologic structures have an important effect upon coal-mine design, operations, and safety. In the bituminous area, folds are very broad and shallow and have dips that rarely exceed 2 degrees, except in the Broad Top field, where dips can be up to 75 degrees. Widespread faulting with significant displacement occurs within a zone from Cambria County to Clinton County, where numerous high-angle tear faults are present. There are a few major thrust faults along some major anticlines.

Small faults with a few feet of displacement are common throughout the bituminous area.

Jointing generally occurs in paired, right-angle sets oriented with the sharp, planar-faced "systematic" joints normal to the folding trend and the more irregular and poorly developed "nonsystematic" joints parallel to the folds (Nickelsen and Hough, 1967). Jointing within coal, termed "cleat," is generally very distinct and closely spaced. Underground mining is commonly directed to take advantage of the tendency of coal to break out easily along the systematic joints ("face cleat"). Although jointing by itself is usually not a primary cause of roof falls, it provides ready detachment planes for collapse instigated by other factors. In mines that have serious roof problems, reorientation of the mining direction to an angle between joint directions may be helpful (Kent, 1974).

PHYSICAL AND CHEMICAL PROPERTIES

Coal displays a variety of physical and chemical properties that reflect variations in depositional environments and postdepositional diagenetic and metamorphic influences. Some properties have geographic or stratigraphic trends, whereas others are more local.

Specialized Terminology

Coal technology is laden with specialized terminology that is so pervasive it cannot be avoided, and coal cannot be discussed in other terms. The following are simplified definitions of some of the more common terms:

Proximate analysis. The nonelemental analysis procedure for coal in which percentages of four compounds or groups of compounds are determined. The four are as follows:

Moisture. Water, other than that which is chemically bound, adhering to the surface ("surficial" or "casual" moisture) or adsorbed in the coal ("inherent" or "bed" moisture).

Volatile matter. Coal compounds that volatilize by nonoxidizing, destructive distillation to 950°C. It consists mostly of compounds containing hydrogen, oxygen, carbon, and nitrogen.

Fixed carbon. The solid organic residue remaining after nonoxidizing, destructive distillation to 950°C. It is mostly carbon.

Ash. The inorganic residue left after all moisture has been evaporated and all other constituents have been oxidized or vaporized. It is different from "mineral matter," which includes partly combustible minerals (mostly pyrite) and water of hydration. Ash is mainly silicon, aluminum, and iron oxides.

As-received basis. Proximate-analysis results giving percentages of all four standard test items listed above.

Moisture-and-ash-free (MAF) basis. Proximate-analysis results that include only fixed-carbon and volatile-matter data, recalculated to 100 percent.

Moisture-and-mineral-matter-free (MMF) basis. Proximate-analysis results that include only fixed-carbon and volatile-matter data, recalculated to 100 percent and adjusted mathematically for the partial combustion and volatilization of certain mineral constituents.

Rank

Coal rank is the extent to which a coal has advanced along the continuous series from lignite to meta-anthracite under the influence of low-grade metamorphism. The parts of this metamorphic sequence relevant to Pennsylvania include the following (fixed-carbon percentages listed below are all MMF basis):

> High-volatile bituminous: less than 69 percent fixed carbon
>
> Medium-volatile bituminous: 69 to 78 percent fixed carbon
>
> Low-volatile bituminous: 78 to 86 percent fixed carbon
>
> Semi-anthracite: 86 to 92 percent fixed carbon
>
> Anthracite: 92 to 98 percent fixed carbon
>
> Meta-anthracite: 98 through 100 percent fixed carbon

Because of the small difference and simpler calculation, analyses of fixed carbon are done using MAF basis rather than MMF basis in actual practice.

Fixed-carbon content (MAF) increases from about 55 percent in the extreme western part of Pennsylvania to over 98 percent in the anthracite area of eastern Pennsylvania (Figure 37–5). Rank also tends to increase stratigraphically downward. In both cases, the increase is believed to have been caused by high-

er temperatures, reflecting greater maximum depths of burial.

Calorific Value

The calorific value of Pennsylvania bituminous coals (MAF basis) increases from about 14,700 Btu/lb (British thermal units per pound) near the west edge of the state to about 15,800 Btu/lb in Cambria and Somerset Counties and in the Broad Top field (Figure 37–6). The as-received calorific value of a particular coal depends upon its moisture and ash content as well, and will be proportionately lower.

Moisture Content

The total moisture content of Pennsylvania bituminous coal varies widely, depending upon exposure to extraneous surficial water. Inherent moisture content mainly ranges from 0.5 to 6 percent, and most coals have inherent moisture content from 2 to 4 percent. Inherent moisture decreases as rank increases. It averages about 4 percent in Lawrence County and adjacent counties and about 2 percent in the Broad Top field.

Ash and Mineral Content

The ash content of a typical coal is about 90 percent of the total mineral matter. The other 10 percent is weight that is lost in expelling water of hydration and in the conversion of iron sulfide to iron oxide. About 60 to 80 percent of the mineral content is illite, sericite, and kaolinite. Quartz, siderite, and pyrite are always present in moderate amounts, and many other minerals regularly occur in small quantities (Stach and others, 1982).

Mineral matter is introduced at various stages in the development of a coal. A small amount is inherent in the original plant material. Most minerals are syngenetic or very early diagenetic and include clastic sediments, such as clays, quartz grains, and accessory minerals, and authigenic chemical precipitates and alteration products, such as siderite, silica, and some pyrite. Later epigenetic minerals and alteration products, such as sulfates and additional pyrite, are minor constituents.

Peat beds form in low-energy environments, and low-ash coal generally reflects this remoteness from strong currents needed to carry in clastics. Maximum mineral-matter concentrations occur at the base and top of most coal beds and as internal clastic bands, termed "partings." Coal beds can also show an in-

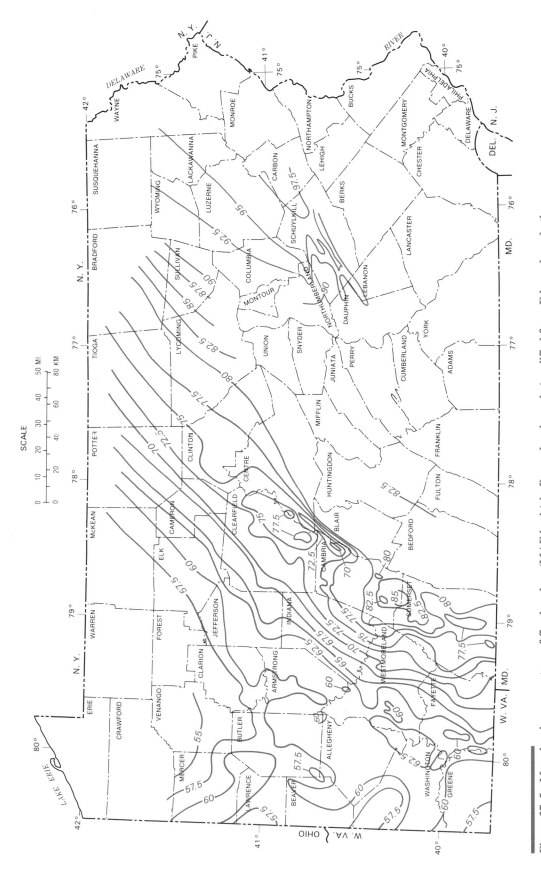

Figure 37-5. Map showing percentage of fixed carbon (MAF basis) in Pennsylvania coals (modified from Edmunds and others, 1979, Figure 15). Contour interval is 2.5 percent.

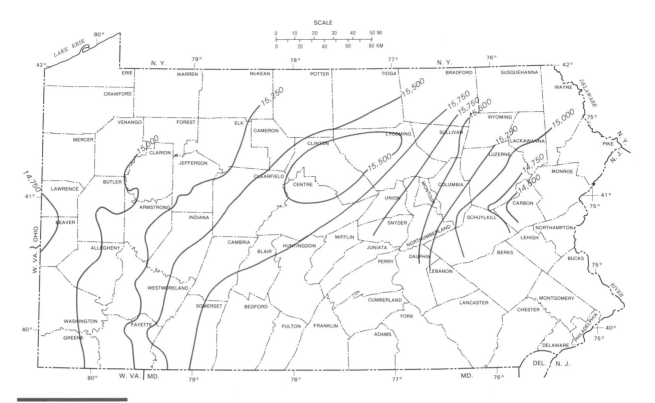

Figure 37-6. Map showing the average calorific value of Pennsylvania coals (MAF basis) (modified from Socolow and others, 1980, Figure 1). Contour interval is 250 Btu/lb.

crease in mineral matter near their geographic margins (i.e., the original swamp margins), reflecting their proximity to adjacent fluvial systems (Sholes and others, 1979). Although there is a tendency for ash content to increase as rank increases because of proportional loss of moisture and volatile matter, ash distribution is more directly related to local variations in the original depositional and postdepositional environments.

The fusion (melting) temperature of coal ash is an important factor in slag and ash buildup in combustion chambers. In general, a proportional increase in silicon, aluminum, and titanium produces higher fusion temperatures, and an increase in iron and alkali metals lowers fusion temperatures (Singer, 1981). Fusion temperatures of Pennsylvania bituminous coal range widely between 1900°F and 3100°F.

Sulfur Content

Sulfur occurs in coal as organic sulfur within the organic molecular structure, as iron sulfide (pyrite), and as calcium or iron sulfates. The amount of each has a major impact upon acid mine drainage, coking potential, and cleaning potential.

Organic sulfur is important because it cannot be removed by conventional cleaning operations. It is inherent in the original plant material and is also introduced chemically or biochemically in the early stages of coalification. Organic sulfur content is commonly between 0.35 and 1 percent and rarely exceeds 1.5 percent. Most of the remaining sulfur contained in Pennsylvania bituminous coal occurs as iron sulfide (pyrite) in the form of lenses, nodules, flakes, or fine particles. All but the last can be removed fairly readily by conventional cleaning processes. Sulfates are insignificant in most fresh coals and can be readily washed out.

Most of the variation in sulfur content is a variation in the amount of pyrite. Pyrite accumulates syngenetically and diagenetically throughout the coalification process and later as secondary mineralization. To a large extent, pyrite content varies locally, reflecting differences in depositional and diagenetic environments. Sulfur content is higher at the bottom and top of most coals; it was at these horizons that sulfate-bearing water mixed with that of the swamp or lagoon, causing the precipitation of iron sulfide that infiltrated the porous peat. Similarly, sulfur content is higher toward the lateral limits of many coal beds as a result of the influx of sulfate-bearing water from beyond the original swamp margin (Sholes and others, 1979; Skema and others, 1982). Coal directly underlying a sandstone commonly will show a higher level of sulfur, suggesting postdepositional infiltration of sulfate-bearing water from above.

Sulfur concentration also displays distinct regional and stratigraphic trends. Sulfur content is markedly higher in coals overlain by sediments deposited in brackish or marine conditions (Guber, 1972). This is illustrated by the lower-delta-plain Mercer through Middle Kittanning coals, which show a strong westward increase in sulfur (Williams and Keith, 1963).

Coking Properties

The processing of coal into coke, mainly for use in the steel industry, involves heating the coal in a reducing atmosphere to drive off the volatile fraction, thus producing a porous, high-carbon fuel that has a strong resistance to crushing and minimum amounts of sulfur, ash, and other impurities. Few coals have all the desired properties for coking, and almost all require cleaning to remove sulfur and ash. Pennsylvania medium-volatile bituminous coal is close to ideal for coking, but relatively little remains. Most coke produced today is a blend of different coals from different areas, usually 20 to 30 percent low-volatile bituminous coal for mechanical strength and 70 to 80 percent high-volatile bituminous for fluidity and porosity.

PRINCIPAL ECONOMIC COAL BEDS

Virtually all of the economically minable bituminous coal resources of Pennsylvania are confined to 10 important coal beds in the Allegheny Formation, and the Monongahela Group plus the Waynesburg coal at the base of the Dunkard Group, in the Main Bituminous field (Figure 37–2). The smaller fields and other coal beds in the Main field can be locally important but are only a small part of the total resources.

Brookville-Clarion Coal Complex

The Brookville and Clarion, along with one or two other minor coals, form an interrelated set of discontinuous beds. In at least one area, they merge into a single thick coal seam. They are strip mined in some areas and are mined underground in a few

areas. Coals of the Brookville-Clarion complex generally tend to be high in sulfur and ash and are difficult to clean.

Lower Kittanning Coal Complex

The Lower Kittanning coal complex consists of up to four or five closely related beds, one of which is distinctly thicker and more persistent than the rest. In most places, the most persistent bed is the one identified as "Lower Kittanning," but, in some places, one of the other members of the complex may be better developed and will assume the name. The Lower Kittanning is normally strip mined throughout its extensive outcrop area and is also mined underground in many places (Sholes and Skema, 1974; Socolow and others, 1980). The sulfur content increases from east to west, and in most places, the ash content is lower than that of most Pennsylvania bituminous coals. It is high-quality coking coal in parts of Cambria and Somerset Counties. The Lower Kittanning ranks third in terms of remaining resources.

Middle Kittanning Coal

The Middle Kittanning coal seems to be widely present but generally thin (Sholes and Skema, 1974). The degree of bed continuity is not well understood. Several rider coals occur locally in association with the Middle Kittanning coal. It is commonly strip mined but is not commonly mined underground. The few analyses available show a wide range in quality with little obvious regional trend.

Upper Kittanning Coal

The Upper Kittanning coal is irregularly present throughout the Main Bituminous field, but it is best developed in Cambria and Somerset Counties (Sholes and Skema, 1974), where it is extensively mined, both on the surface and underground, and displays good to excellent quality. It is also reported to be well developed in parts of Indiana and Armstrong Counties, where it has been widely miscorrelated as Lower Freeport (W. A. Bragonier, personal communication, 1987).

Lower Freeport Coal Complex

Although one or more coal beds are present at the stratigraphic position of the Lower Freeport coal in much of the Main field, they tend to be discontinuous, separated by areas of nondeposition or erosion. The Lower Freeport coal complex is best developed in the northeastern counties of the Main field, where the coals are of excellent quality and have been widely stripped and mined underground (Sholes and Skema, 1974). Elsewhere, the coals tend to be thinner, more discontinuous, and of poorer quality.

Upper Freeport Coal

The Upper Freeport coal is fairly persistent as a single bed of highly variable thickness across the northern and eastern parts of the Main Bituminous field. It may be absent in limited areas because of nondeposition or erosion. To the southwest, the Upper Freeport occurs more as extensive bodies of thick coal that are isolated from one another by wide areas of nondeposition. The thickness and quality vary widely and, in many places, abruptly. It is mined extensively, both on the surface and underground. Its general persistence, many areas of impressive thickness (Sholes and Skema, 1974; Socolow and others, 1980), and general good quality make the Upper Freeport the secondmost important bed in terms of mining and reserves.

Pittsburgh Coal

The Pittsburgh coal is the most important seam in Pennsylvania. In spite of extensive mining, it still represents one third of the recoverable reserves over 36 inches thick and almost all of the reserves over 60 inches thick. Most of the remaining Pittsburgh coal bed is in Washington and Greene Counties. It is a single, very persistent bed, generally between 4 and 10 feet thick, and is absent only in relatively limited areas (McCulloch and others, 1975; Socolow and others, 1980). It is of excellent quality overall and has been widely used for metallurgical coke. Except in northwestern Washington County and eastern Greene County, its sulfur content is less than 2 percent (Socolow and others, 1980). Almost all production of the Pittsburgh coal, past and present, is from underground mines.

Redstone Coal

Although irregularly present in the five southwestern counties (Allegheny, Fayette, Greene, Washington, and Westmoreland), the Redstone coal is rarely thick enough to mine underground and only intermittently suitable for strip mining (Sholes and Skema, 1974). Where mined, the sulfur content tends to be somewhat lower than that of most Pennsylvania bituminous coals, and the ash content tends to be somewhat higher.

Sewickley Coal

The Sewickley coal is well developed only in southern Greene and Fayette Counties, where it is up to 6 feet thick (Sholes and Skema, 1974). The sulfur and ash content are low in Greene County, but both increase eastward into Fayette County. There is a sizable reserve available for underground mining in southern Greene County.

Waynesburg Coal

The Waynesburg coal is largely confined to the five southwestern counties. It appears to be a single, fairly continuous bed, 2 to 4 feet thick, that contains from one to three thick claystone partings (Sholes and Skema, 1974). The ash content and, commonly, the sulfur content are high. The thick clastic partings make the Waynesburg difficult to mine underground, but it is commonly mined in surface operations, where the partings can be more readily separated.

UTILIZATION

Pennsylvania bituminous coal is mined for four markets: electric power generation, metallurgical coke, industrial use, and foreign export. The distribution varies, but in 1986, electric utilities consumed 72 percent, coke production 11 percent, industrial use 7 percent, and export 10 percent. The amount of coal used for electric power has increased steadily for many years, while the production for coke and export has declined.

MINING OPERATIONS

In 1993, output of bituminous coal fell to its lowest level in the twentieth century. Production from 1985 through 1993 was between 58 and 70 million tons annually. In 1993, 65 percent of the coal mined came from underground operations, and 35 percent came from surface mines (including stripping, augering, and refuse reprocessing). More than 98 percent of production from underground mines comes from two areas. One area is in Greene and Washington Counties, where most production is from the Pittsburgh coal. The other area extends across southern Armstrong, southern Indiana, Cambria, and Somerset Counties, where production is mainly from the Lower Kittanning, Upper Kittanning, Lower Freeport, and

Upper Freeport coals. Surface mining is scattered across the entire bituminous area.

The great majority of underground production is from large mines employing longwall panel systems, which may be augmented by continuous miners. Room-and-pillar mining systems are still used in most smaller deep mines and some older large mines. It is expected that most future large underground mines will be designed around high-capacity longwall systems. The rugged hilly topography of western Pennsylvania controls the type of surface mining, as well as the type and size of equipment. Most surface mines are hillside contour strippings in which mining follows the outcrop of coal beds as they wrap around the sides of hills and ridges (Figure 37–7). Additional coal is obtained from strip mines by augering, a procedure in which the bed is drilled and extracted horizontally by a large spiral auger. After mining, most coal is processed in complex cleaning facilities to reduce the amount of pyrite and mineral matter (Figure 37–8).

RESOURCES

Remaining recoverable resources from Pennsylvania bituminous coal beds over 28 inches and 36 inches thick as of January 1, 1984, are estimated to be 21 billion tons and 11 billion tons, respectively (Table 37–1). The total of all bituminous coal production in Pennsylvania through 1991 is estimated to have been approximately 11 billion tons, almost all from beds over 28 inches thick. From this, it follows that the total original recoverable resources over 28 inches was about 32 billion tons. Allowing for a factor of between one third and one half for coal lost in mining, original in-place resources were between 45 billion and 60 billion tons.

PROBLEMS AND FUTURE RESEARCH

The most valuable geologic contributions that could be made at this time are complete, integrated studies of the economic geology of specific coal lithosomes or complexes, as they actually exist (see Sholes and others, 1979, and Skema and others, 1982). Well over a century of invaluable, but disconnected, background work into all aspects of coal geology (i.e., stratigraphy and stratigraphic correlations, sedimentology, depositional environments and paleogeography, distribution and controls on physical and chemical properties, coal petrography, structural features, premining analysis of potential mining hazards, and so forth) has now made it possible to deal with coals as definable, physical entities, rather than to continue the antiquated and unrealistic practice of treating all coals as imaginary, single, continuous sheet deposits.

Figure 37–7. Kent No. 55 strip-mine operation of the Rochester and Pittsburgh Coal Company on the Upper Freeport coal, near Jacksonville, Indiana County.

Figure 37–8. **Keystone cleaning plant of the Rochester and Pittsburgh Coal Company, near Elderton, Armstrong County.**

Table 37–1. *Remaining Recoverable Identified Bituminous Coal Resources of Pennsylvania to January 1, 1984[1]* (Quantities are in millions of short tons)		
County	Total over 28 inches[2]	Total over 36 inches[2]	Strippable[3]
MAIN BITUMINOUS FIELD (INCLUDING GEORGES CREEK FIELD)[4]		
Allegheny	630	210	29
Armstrong	960	760	133
Beaver	350	200	62
Blair	8	3	NE
Butler	830	350	223
Cambria	900	300	46
Cameron	13	0	NE
Centre	65	3	NE
Clarion	390	46	115
Clearfield	600	45	127
Clinton	8	3	NE
Elk	100	42	NE
Fayette	2,100	1,100	75
Greene	3,900	2,600	44
Indiana	1,500	520	45
Jefferson	850	250	71
Lawrence	140	75	27
McKean	96	5	NE
Mercer	76	19	69
Somerset	1,600	610	84
Venango	70	5	NE
Washington	3,600	2,500	142
Westmoreland	1,900	1,200	26
Field total	21,000	11,000	1,300

Table 37–1. *(Continued)*		
County	Total over 28 inches[2]	Total over 36 inches[2]	Strippable[3]
BROAD TOP FIELD		
Bedford	64	56	NE
Fulton	7	4	NE
Huntingdon	16	5	NE
Field total	87	65	—
NORTH-CENTRAL FIELDS		
Bradford	3	1	NE
Lycoming	14	3	NE
Sullivan[5]	3	0	NE
Tioga	5	2	NE
Field total	25	6	—
PENNSYLVANIA TOTAL	21,000	11,000	—

[1]Figures rounded to first two digits (first digit if 9.5 million or less). Numbers may not total exactly because of independent rounding.
[2]Revised from Edmunds (1972).
[3]Adapted from U.S. Bureau of Mines (1971, Table A63). Based upon 120 feet maximum cover less 20 percent mining loss. NE, not estimated.
[4]Excludes small resources from Crawford, Forest, Potter, and Warren Counties.
[5]Semianthracite.

RECOMMENDED FOR FURTHER READING

Ashley, G. H. (1928), *Bituminous coal fields of Pennsylvania—General information on coal,* Pennsylvania Geological Survey, 4th ser., Mineral Resource Report 6, Pt. 1, 241 p.

Briggs, Garrett, ed. (1974), *Carboniferous of the southeastern United States,* Geological Society of America Special Paper 148, 361 p.

Cassidy, S. M., ed. (1973), *Elements of practical coal mining,* New York, Society of Mining Engineers, 614 p.

Dapples, E. C., and Hopkins, M. E., eds. (1969), *Environments of coal deposition,* Geological Society of America Special Paper 114, 204 p.

Edmunds, W. E., Berg, T. M., Sevon, W. D., and others (1979), *The Mississippian and Pennsylvanian (Carboniferous) Systems in the United States—Pennsylvania and New York,* U.S. Geological Survey Professional Paper 1110-B, p. B1–B33.

Ferm, J. C., Horne, J. C., Weisenfluh, G. A., and Staub, J. R., eds. (1979), *Carboniferous depositional environments in the Appalachian region,* Columbia, S. C., Carolina Coal Group, University of South Carolina, 760 p.

Majumdar, S. K., and Miller, E. W., eds. (1983), *Pennsylvania coal: resources, technology, and utilization,* Pennsylvania Academy of Science, 594 p.

Socolow, A. A., Berg, T. M., Glover, A. D., and others (1980), *Coal resources of Pennsylvania,* Pennsylvania Geological Survey, 4th ser., Information Circular 88, 49 p.

Stach, E., Mackowsky, M.-Th., Teichmüller, M., and others (1982), *Stach's textbook of coal petrography* [English translation], Berlin, Gebrüder Borntraeger, 535 p.

"Colonel" Edwin L. Drake (in top hat) and his close friend, Titusville pharmacist Peter Wilson, in front of the famous Drake well, 1861. The engine house and derrick were actually the second to be built for the well. The original building burned late in 1859, and no picture of it exists. Photograph courtesy of the Drake Well Museum, Titusville, Pa.

CHAPTER 38   PETROLEUM

The story of oil and natural gas in Pennsylvania is one of firsts, largests, and deepests. Many are aware that the world's first commercial oil well, drilled expressly for the purpose of finding oil, was operated by "Colonel" Edwin Drake at Titusville, Pa., in 1859. But how many are aware that waterflooding, one of the most commonly used methods of enhanced oil recovery, began as an accident in Pennsylvania's oil fields in the 1800's when rainwater flowing into abandoned wells increased production in nearby holes? John Carll, a geologist with the Second Geological Survey of Pennsylvania (1874–88), is considered by many to have founded the science of petroleum geology. And many of the early drillers who became famous for discovering the enormous oil fields of Texas and Oklahoma started their careers in Pennsylvania.

The natural gas industry also began in Pennsylvania when George Westinghouse, the inventor, realized that gas could make Pittsburgh the greatest manufacturing city in the world. Prior to Westinghouse's contribution, natural gas was tolerated by some in the oil industry and condemned by others who felt that it was a dangerous nuisance. Only a few forward-thinking individuals, companies, and municipalities saw the advantages of gas as a cheap, efficient fuel and source of light. Now it is considered to be the best source of readily available, clean energy in our environment-conscious world.

—John A. Harper

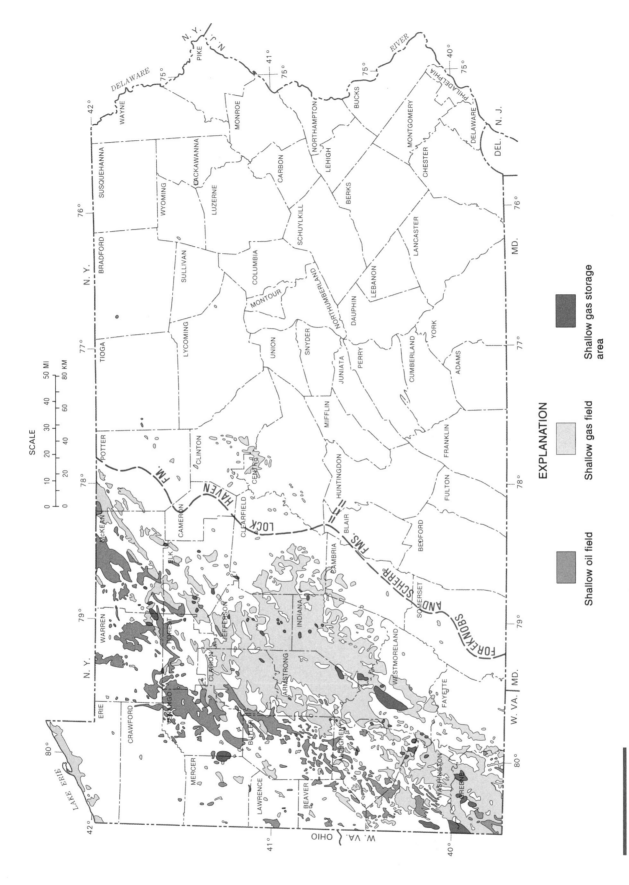

SCALE

0	10	20	30	40	50 MI		
0	20	40	60	80 KM			

EXPLANATION

Shallow oil field

Shallow gas field

Shallow gas storage area

Figure 38A–1. Distribution of shallow oil and gas fields in Pennsylvania (modified from Pennsylvania Geological Survey, 1993). The dashed line through central Pennsylvania marks the boundary between the discrete Upper Devonian reservoir formations in the west (the Venango, Bradford, and Elk Groups) and the undifferentiated formations to the east (the Lock Haven Formation in north-central Pennsylvania and the Foreknobs and Scherr Formations in south-central Pennsylvania). The boundary is from Piotrowski and Harper (1979).

484

CHAPTER 38A   PETROLEUM—SHALLOW OIL AND NATURAL GAS

JOHN A. HARPER
   Bureau of Topographic and Geologic Survey
   Department of Conservation and Natural
      Resources
   400 Waterfront Drive
   Pittsburgh, PA 15222

DEREK B. TATLOCK
   Tatlock Exploration, Inc.
   920 Woodland Road
   Pittsburgh, PA 15237

ROBERT T. WOLFE, JR.
   Consultant
   94 Fiske Avenue
   Bradford, PA 16701

INTRODUCTION

In Pennsylvania, a "shallow" well is one that does not penetrate the boundary between the Middle and Upper Devonian Series, that is, the Tully Limestone or its equivalent. Shallow wells normally range between 500 and 5,000 feet deep.

Shallow oil and gas have been produced historically from broad belts that cross the state from Greene County in the southwest corner to Potter County in north-central Pennsylvania (Figure 38A–1). A few seemingly anomalous shallow fields occur in northeastern Pennsylvania, but there is little available information concerning them.

Pennsylvania's oil and gas industry has its own terminology for many of the formations penetrated in the state. Key beds and producing sandstones were informally named for geographic areas (e.g., the Sheffield sand), farms (Gordon sand), physical characteristics of the rock (Thirty-Foot sand), and relative stratigraphic position (Bradford Third sand). The complexity of drillers' nomenclature in the Upper Devonian and its relationship to formal stratigraphy is shown in Figure 38A–2.

HISTORICAL SUMMARY

Oil and gas have been known in Pennsylvania for over 200 years. Owen (1975) referred to a 1748 citation on the occurrence of oil springs along Oil Creek in what is now Crawford and Venango Counties. Such springs were exploited by the American Indians and European settlers for medicinal purposes. Natural gas was recognized early in the 1800's for its value as boiler fuel and for its use in lighting.

Numerous occurrences of hydrocarbons associated with brine aquifers in salt-well operations established early on that oil and gas could be found in the subsurface by drilling to the reservoirs. The modern oil and gas industry began in Pennsylvania in 1859 with the successful drilling of the Drake well in Ve-

GROUP OR FORMATION	DRILLERS' SAND NAMES	
	NORTHWESTERN	SOUTHWESTERN
RICEVILLE FORMATION	Riceville, Oswayo, Drake	Oswayo
VENANGO GROUP	Venango First, Tuna, Panama Red Valley	Gantz Hundred-Foot Fifty-Foot
	Lytle, Rosenberry Venango Second, Salamanca	Thirty-Foot, Upper Nineveh Snee, Lower Nineveh
	Venango Third Stray, Gray, Knox Third, Shira Venango Third, Knox Fourth, Wolf Creek, Clarion	Gordon Stray, Boulder Gordon, Third
	Knox Fifth	Fourth, Washington
		Fifth, McDonald Fifth A
	McGee Hollow	Bayard Bayard Stray
CHADAKOIN FORMATION	Pink Rock	Elizabeth Elizabeth Stray
BRADFORD GROUP	Warren First	First Warren
	Warren Second	Second Warren
	Bradford First, Eighty-Foot, Queen Glade	Third Warren
	Clarendon Stray, Watsonville, Sugar Run Clarendon, Kinzua, Upper Balltown Dewdrop, Lower Balltown, Gartland	Upper Speechley Speechley Stray Speechley
	Speechley, Cherry Grove Tiona, Bradford Second	Tiona
	Cooper Stray, Sliverville Cooper	First Balltown
	Klondike, Harrisburg Run Deerlick	Second Balltown
	Bradford Third Lewis Run	Sheffield, Third Balltown
	Upper Kane Lower Kane	Bradford Kane
ELK GROUP	Sartwell	
	Haskill	Riley, Elk
	Humphrey	Benson Alexander

Figure 38A–2. Generalized stratigraphic correlation chart of Upper Devonian drillers' sand names most commonly used in Pennsylvania. Most of the names in the Bradford Group originated in northwestern Pennsylvania and were misapplied in the southwestern part of the state.

nango County using salt-well drilling techniques. Drake's well produced only about 2,000 bbl (barrels) of oil that first year, but it succeeded in stimulating the active search for hydrocarbons around the world. Drake's well was only 69.5 feet deep, a truly shallow well.

Early exploration for hydrocarbons in Pennsylvania focused on shallow oil (Figure 38A–3), and, for this reason, most of the geological and engineering information concerning subsurface reservoirs pertains to the oil fields. Natural gas was typically considered a nuisance, but a few enterprising people saw a lucrative market for the gas in larger manufacturing towns such as Pittsburgh. Natural gas eventually became important in the late 1800's when utility companies were formed and pipelines were laid from the fields to the cities and towns. As the shallowest and most easily produced fields became depleted, and as technology improved, drillers began probing to greater depths in search of additional production (Figure 38A–4).

Figure 38A–3. Well-head assembly and pump jack on a shallow combination oil and gas well in Westmoreland County. Equipment like this has been used on wells throughout Pennsylvania's oil fields for many years, often replacing the original cable-tool rig that was used to drill the well.

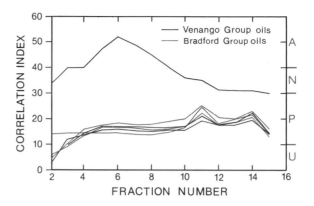

Figure 38A-5. Correlation index curves for Upper Devonian oils from northwestern Pennsylvania. Oils were distilled using the U.S. Bureau of Mines Hempel distillation method. Data are from Lane and Garton (1938) and Dickey and others (1943). See Smith (1940) for an explanation of the correlation index. Most Pennsylvania Grade crude oils are paraffinic throughout the range of distillation cuts, indicating their superior lubricating qualities. Some oils, however, such as those obtained from the Venango First sand in the Franklin-Oak Forest field, Venango County, are naphthenic to aromatic in the lower cuts (2 to 6) and provide high-octane gasoline. This discrepancy is apparently due to biodegradation (Hunt, 1979). A, aromatic; N, naphthenic; P, paraffinic; U, ultra-paraffinic.

Figure 38A-4. Typical modern rotary rig used for drilling most of the shallow oil and gas wells in Pennsylvania. Unlike cable-tool rigs, which use the weight of heavy, steel, chisellike bits to smash and chip the rock at the bottom of the hole, rotary rigs spin toothed bits to grind the rock. Rotary drilling is superior to cable-tool drilling in speed and depth of penetration.

CRUDE OIL AND NATURAL GAS

Pennsylvania Grade crude oil has a paraffin base and low sulfur content (Table 38A-1 and Figure 38A-5) and has long been noted for its excellent lubricating qualities. In contrast, Pennsylvania's natural gas is not chemically or physically unusual (Table 38A-2). Methane content is typically greater than 90 percent, and the heating value almost always exceeds 1,000 Btu (British thermal unit)/ft^3.

The main controlling factor for hydrocarbon production in Pennsylvania is price. A dramatic increase in drilling and production between 1975 and 1985, for example, was the direct result of the equally dramatic increase in oil and gas prices worldwide following the establishment of the Organization of Petroleum Exporting Countries (OPEC) in 1973 (Table 38A-3).

Pennsylvania produced more than half of the world's petroleum until the discovery of the giant oil fields in Texas in the early 1900's. At the time of this writing, Pennsylvania's annual production is less than 1 percent of the national total, but it is still significant because of the unique qualities of Pennsylvania Grade crude oil. The history of oil production in Pennsylvania through 1986 is illustrated in Figure 38A-6.

Figure 38A-7 illustrates the primary-production decline curves of three shallow oil wells in Pennsylvania. A well producing over 1,450 bbl during its first year is above average and should produce in excess of 4,500 bbl over a 12-year period. An average well will produce 3,000 bbl of oil over a period of 10 years, and a below-average well will have a production life of 8 years and produce only 1,500 bbl.

Natural gas production in Pennsylvania never achieved the notoriety accorded crude oil production in the late 1800's. Although most shallow gas wells drilled in Pennsylvania are considered "successful," some do not produce large amounts of gas or pay back the investment necessary to drill. A truly successful commercial well will return the initial in-

Table 38A-1. *General Characteristics of Some Representative Samples of Pennsylvania Grade Crude Oil From Upper Devonian Reservoirs in Pennsylvania[1]*

Group (reservoir)	County	API gravity (degrees)	Specific gravity	Sulfur (percent)	Color
Venango (Hundred-Foot)	Allegheny	45.4	0.800	0.10	Pale orange
Venango (Venango First)	Venango	32.3	.864	<.10	Green
Venango (Third)	Butler	46.5	.795	<.10	Light green
Venango (Gordon)	Washington	45.4	.800	.10	Dark green
Venango (Fifth)	do.	43.2	.810	.11	Green
Bradford (Glade)	Warren	45.2	.801	.15	Dark red
Bradford (Speechley)	Butler	45.6	.799	.12	Dark red
Bradford (Watsonville)	McKean	47.2	.792	.11	Light green
Bradford (Bradford Third)	do.	44.7	.808	<.10	Green
Bradford (Kane)	do.	45.6	.799	<.10	Light green

[1]Data from Lane and Garton (1938) and Dickey and others (1943).

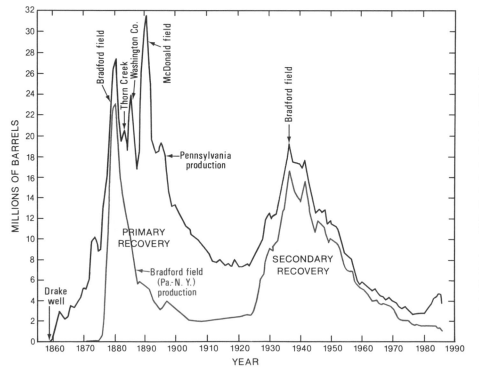

Figure 38A-6. Annual production of crude oil in Pennsylvania, 1859-1986 (from Harper, 1987, p. 4). Important discoveries and events that affected production are labeled. Production by natural means (pumping only) peaked in the late 1800's. The introduction of waterflooding in the Bradford field in 1920 began a new surge in production that peaked from 1935-45. Pennsylvania's crude oil production has generally declined ever since.

Table 38A–2. *Representative Gas Analyses From Selected Shallow Geologic Units in Pennsylvania*

Geologic unit (reservoir)	County	Field	Methane	Ethane	Propane	N-butane	Isobutane	N-pentane	Isopentane	Cyclo-pentane	Hexanes plus	Nitrogen	Oxygen	Argon	Helium	Hydrogen	Hydrogen sulfide	Carbon dioxide	Btu value
								Constituents (percent)											
Conemaugh Group (Little Dunkard sand)	Washington	Tenmile	77.2	5.1	5.1	3.3	2.2	1.3	0.9	0.3	1.5	2.6	0.0	Tr¹	0.0	0.0	0.5	Tr	1,373
Allegheny Formation (Gas sand)	Venango	Speechley	87.1	6.8	1.8	.8	.6	.6	.1	.1	1.0	.0	.0	0.0	.0	.0	.1	0.10	1,183
Pottsville Formation (Salt sand)	Greene	Waynesburg	85.9	11.3	.0	.0	.0	.0	.0	.0	.0	2.3	.3	.0	.0	.0	.2	.13	1,073
Mauch Chunk Formation (Maxton sand)	do.	Garrison	80.6	10.9	3.9	1.3	.4	.5	.2	.1	.5	1.3	.0	.0	.0	.0	.2	.09	1,230
Burgoon Sandstone (Big Injun sand)	Allegheny	Forward	92.7	4.7	.9	.2	.2	.1	.1	Tr	.1	.8	.0	Tr	.0	.0	.1	.10	1,074
Cussewago Sandstone (Murrysville sand)	Armstrong	Johnetta	95.3	2.4	.4	.0	.0	.0	.0	.0	.0	1.6	.0	Tr	.0	.0	.1	.15	1,019
Venango Group (Fifty-Foot sand)	Washington	Vanceville	91.5	4.3	1.3	.4	.2	.1	.2	.1	.4	1.3	.0	Tr	.0	.0	.1	.09	1,095
Venango Group (Venango Third sand)	Venango	Guitonville	76.2	9.8	6.3	2.7	1.5	.7	.8	.1	.6	1.1	Tr	Tr	.0	.0	.2	.09	1,351
Venango Group (Elizabeth sand)	Greene	Jefferson	90.2	5.2	1.5	.6	.4	.1	.2	Tr	.3	1.2	.0	Tr	.1	.0	.1	.10	1,108
Bradford Group (Speechley sand)	Westmoreland	Bagdad	92.3	4.9	1.2	.3	.1	.1	.1	Tr	.1	.8	.0	Tr	Tr	.0	.0	.11	1,081
Bradford Group (Balltown sand)	Indiana	Blairsville	92.5	4.1	1.2	.3	.5	.1	.1	Tr	.1	.7	.0	.0	.1	.1	.0	.10	1,083
Bradford Group (Third Bradford sand)	Westmoreland	Saltsburg	95.5	2.4	.2	.0	.0	.0	.0	.0	.0	1.5	.3	Tr	.0	.0	Tr	.09	1,016
Elk Group (Elk sand)	Elk	Boone Mountain	95.4	3.0	.5	.1	Tr	Tr	Tr	Tr	.1	.4	.0	Tr	.0	.0	.3	.09	1,042
Elk Group (Haskill sand)	Jefferson	Millstone	88.9	6.1	1.5	.5	.1	.1	.1	Tr	.1	2.3	.0	.0	.1	.0	.1	.10	1,083
Lock Haven Formation (Elk sand)	Centre	Council Run	95.1	2.5	.3	.1	Tr	.1	.0	.1	.2	1.2	.1	Tr	.1	.0	Tr	.15	1,038
Lock Haven Formation (not named)	Lackawanna	Ransom	67.6	.0	Tr	.0	.0	.0	.0	.0	.0	31.6	.1	.4	Tr	.0	Tr	.25	685

¹Tr, trace.

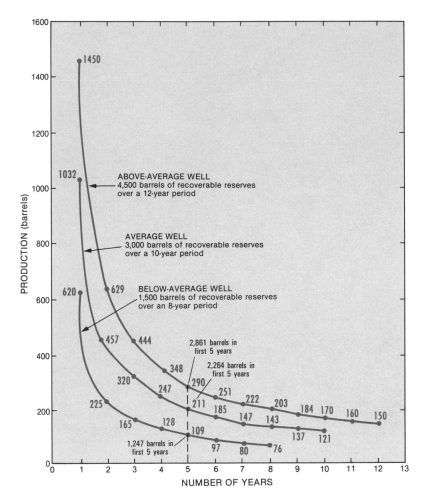

Figure 38A–7. Primary oil production decline curves for above-average, average, and below-average shallow oil wells producing from the Upper Devonian Bradford Group sandstones in northwestern Pennsylvania.

Figure 38A–8. Gas production decline curves for above-average, average, and below-average shallow gas wells producing from the Upper Devonian Bradford Group sandstones in southwestern Pennsylvania.

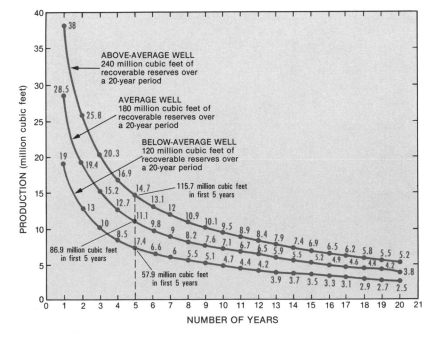

Table 38A–3. *Production, Unit Price, and Total Value of Oil and Gas Produced in Pennsylvania (1960–86)[1]*

	Crude oil			Natural gas			Total oil and gas value (dollars)
Year	Production[2] (bbl)	Average yearly price (dollars/bbl)	Total value (dollars)	Production[3] (Mcf)[5]	Average yearly price[4] (dollars/Mcf)[5]	Total value (dollars)	
1960	5,942,000	4.57	27,154,940	119,671,000	0.26	31,114,460	58,269,400
1961	5,580,000	4.76	26,560,800	98,318,000	.26	25,562,680	52,123,480
1962	5,238,000	4.63	24,251,940	87,308,000	.26	22,700,080	46,952,020
1963	5,014,000	4.63	23,214,820	92,340,000	.26	24,008,400	47,223,220
1964	5,113,000	4.48	22,906,240	85,322,000	.26	22,183,720	45,089,960
1965	4,859,000	4.20	20,407,800	82,668,000	.26	21,493,680	41,901,480
1966	4,349,000	4.33	18,831,170	91,365,000	.26	23,754,900	42,586,070
1967	4,409,000	4.35	19,179,150	89,966,000	.26	23,391,160	42,570,310
1968	4,160,000	4.35	18,096,000	87,987,000	.28	24,636,360	42,732,360
1969	4,448,000	4.29	19,081,920	79,134,000	.26	20,574,840	39,656,760
1970	4,015,000	4.27	17,144,050	77,535,000	.27	20,934,450	38,078,500
1971	3,798,000	4.47	16,977,060	76,451,000	.30	22,935,300	39,912,360
1972	3,441,000	4.60	15,828,600	73,958,000	.45	33,281,100	49,109,700
1973	3,282,000	5.73	18,805,860	78,514,000	.45	35,331,300	54,137,160
1974	3,399,000	8.43	28,653,570	82,735,000	.50	41,367,500	70,021,070
1975	3,199,000	9.26	29,622,740	84,772,000	.80	67,817,600	97,440,340
1976	2,950,000	11.51	33,954,500	89,974,000	.85	76,477,900	110,432,400
1977	2,659,000	14.22	37,810,980	92,293,000	1.00	92,293,000	130,103,980
1978	2,820,000	14.77	41,651,400	97,763,000	1.25	122,203,750	163,855,150
1979	2,817,000	23.67	66,678,390	96,313,000	1.40	134,838,200	201,516,590
1980	2,940,000	37.42	110,014,800	97,439,000	1.50	146,158,500	256,173,300
1981	3,729,000	36.33	135,474,570	122,454,000	2.00	244,908,000	380,382,570
1982	4,282,000	31.42	134,540,440	121,111,000	2.80	339,110,800	473,651,240
1983	4,491,000	28.18	126,556,380	118,372,000	3.00	355,116,000	481,672,380
1984	4,825,000	27.64	133,363,000	166,342,000	3.25	540,611,500	673,974,500
1985	4,851,000	25.12	121,857,120	150,541,000	3.15	474,204,150	596,061,270
1986	3,783,000	15.66	59,241,780	159,889,000	2.50	399,722,500	458,965,642

[1]Data from Harper (1987, Figure 23, p. 23).
[2]Oil production figure courtesy of the Penn Grade Crude Association.
[3]Gas production figure courtesy of the American Gas Association.
[4]Gas prices estimated only.
[5]Mcf, thousand cubic feet.

Figure 38A–9. "Flowing back" of a shallow gas well after hydraulic fracturing of the sandstone reservoir. Fracturing is accomplished by forcing a fluid, such as water, and a propping agent, such as sand, into the well under high pressure. The fluid fractures the rock, forcing the propping agent into the cracks. When the pressure is released, the fluid flows back out of the fractures but leaves the propping agent in place to provide artificial permeability.

vestment within four years. Assuming a gas price of $3.00/Mcf (thousand cubic feet), an average well, costing $160,000 to drill and having a net revenue interest of 87.5 percent, will return the initial investment within approximately 34 months. A below-average or

"marginal" well would not generate a return on the investment for almost six years.

Figure 38A–8 illustrates the production history of three shallow gas wells in western Pennsylvania. Without flow restrictions due to purchase curtailments, an

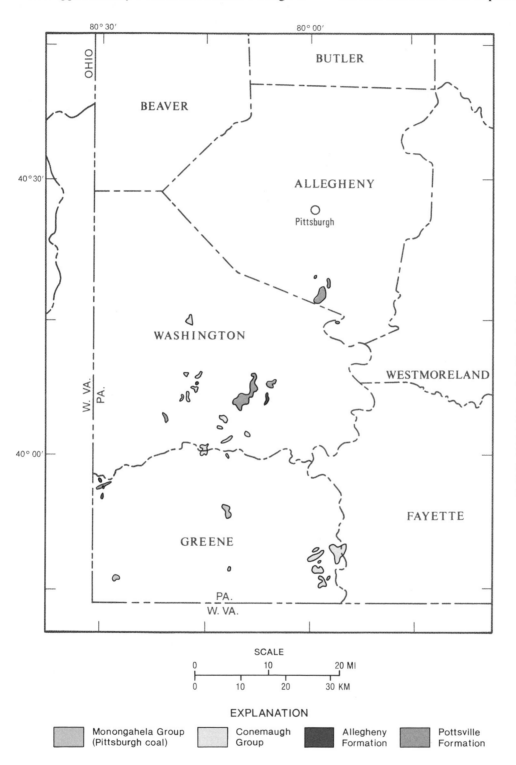

SCALE

0   10   20 MI

0   10   20   30 KM

EXPLANATION

Monongahela Group (Pittsburgh coal)   Conemaugh Group   Allegheny Formation   Pottsville Formation

Figure 38A–10. Distribution of fields and pools in southwestern Pennsylvania from which oil and gas have been produced from Pennsylvanian reservoirs (slightly modified from Harper and Laughrey, 1987, p. 9). Monongahela Group production is restricted to coalbed methane from the Pittsburgh coal.

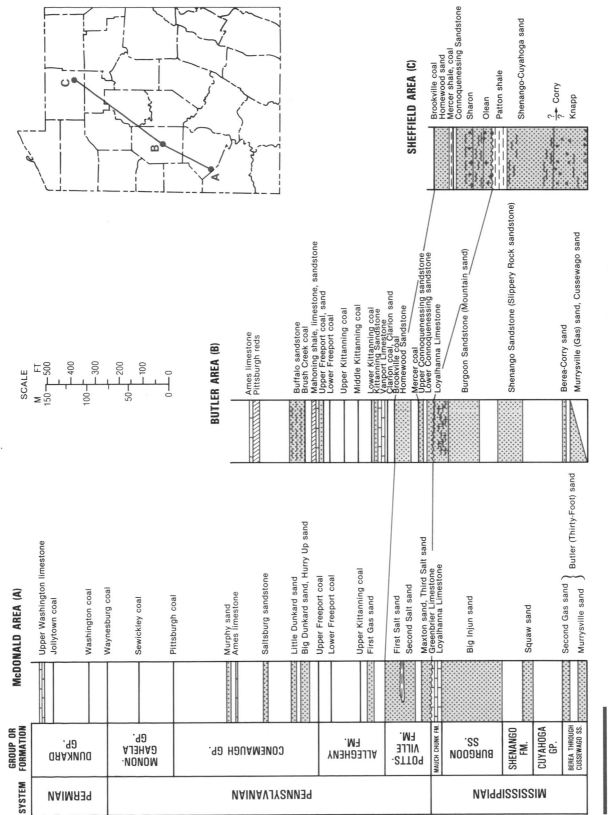

Figure 38A–11. Generalized stratigraphic column and correlation chart of Pennsylvanian and Mississippian groups and formations and drillers' nomenclature associated with them (modified from Edmunds and others, 1979, p. B30).

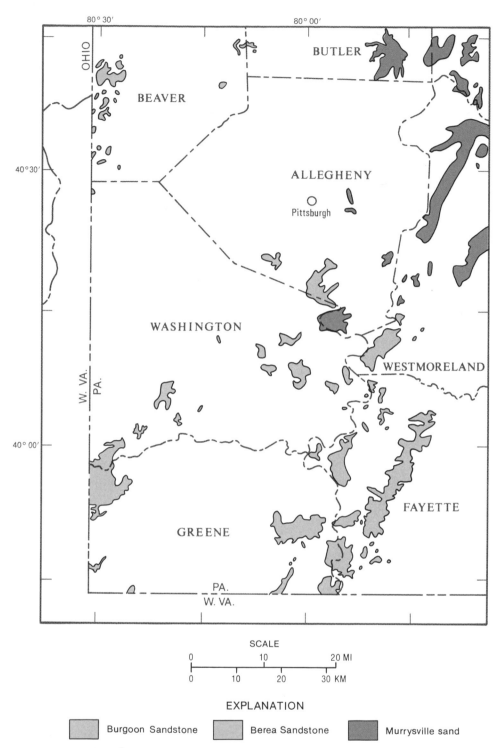

Figure 38A–12. Distribution of fields and pools in southwestern Pennsylvania from which oil and gas have been produced from Mississippian reservoirs (from Harper and Laughrey, 1987, p. 17).

SCALE

EXPLANATION

Burgoon Sandstone   Berea Sandstone   Murrysville sand

average Upper Devonian well will produce 180 MMcf (million cubic feet) over a period of 20 years. Half of this amount will be produced in the first five years. An above-average well could have reserves of 240 MMcf for the same period, whereas a below-average well could produce less than 120 MMcf.

Although shallow oil and gas fields occur throughout western and parts of north-central Pennsylvania, the oil fields in the northwestern counties and the gas fields in the central-western part of the state are currently the most active and the most productive. The reservoirs in many of these fields are low-porosity,

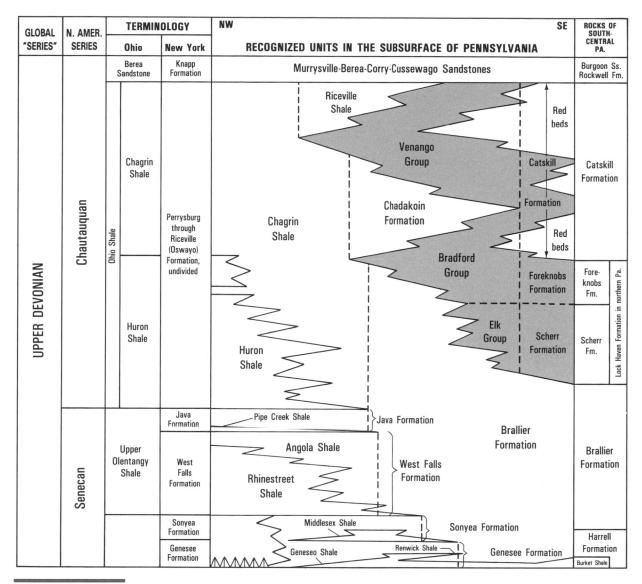

Figure 38A–13. Schematic diagram of Upper Devonian stratigraphic units in western and central Pennsylvania (slightly modified from Harper, 1987, p. 30). Primary reservoir rocks in Pennsylvania are colored.

low-permeability sandstones that have to be stimulated by hydraulic fracturing (Figure 38A–9) or by exploding a nitroglycerine torpedo in order to obtain and maintain a flow. Stimulation also allows greater recovery of reserves within a shorter period of time, thus enhancing the economics of the well. It is not uncommon for a stimulated well to have an after-treatment open flow 20 times its natural flow.

SHALLOW RESERVOIRS

Sandstones of Pennsylvanian, Mississippian, and Late Devonian age constitute the shallow reservoirs in Pennsylvania. The Late Devonian reservoirs are the most important in the state.

Pennsylvanian Reservoirs

Pennsylvanian reservoirs are sporadically located throughout the southwestern quarter of western Pennsylvania (Figure 38A–10). With few exceptions (e.g., several small pools in Greene County), these reservoirs produce natural gas. The primary Pennsylvanian reservoirs are sandstones of the Conemaugh Group and Allegheny and Pottsville Formations (Figure 38A–11). However, the thicker coal seams (the Pittsburgh,

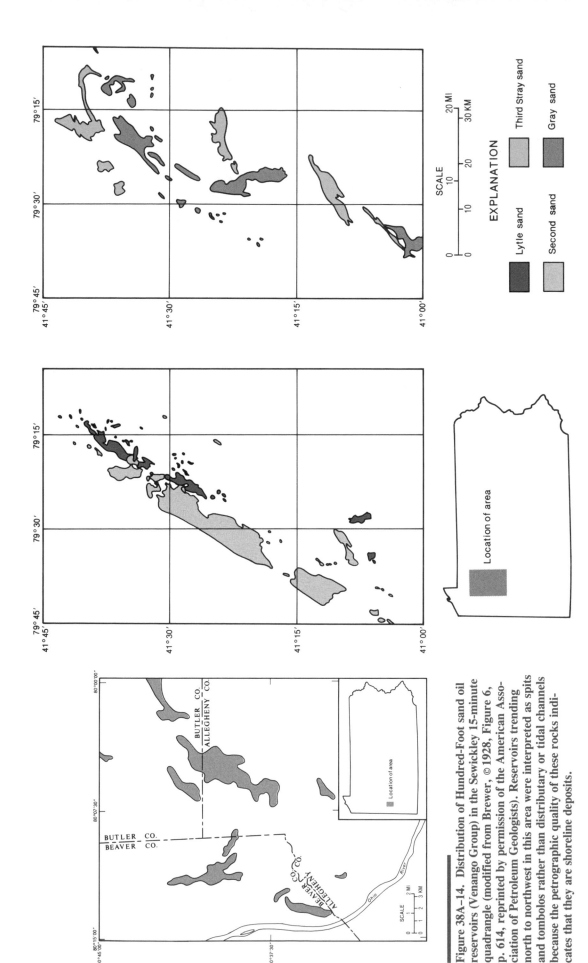

Figure 38A–14. Distribution of Hundred-Foot sand oil reservoirs (Venango Group) in the Sewickley 15-minute quadrangle (modified from Brewer, © 1928, Figure 6, p. 614, reprinted by permission of the American Association of Petroleum Geologists). Reservoirs trending north to northwest in this area were interpreted as spits and tombolos rather than distributary or tidal channels because the petrographic quality of these rocks indicates that they are shoreline deposits.

Figure 38A–15. Distribution of various Venango Group oil reservoirs in a portion of northwestern Pennsylvania (modified from Dickey and others, 1943, p. 24). These sandstones were interpreted as offshore bars. The Third Stray sand was deposited as a series of en echelon bars, some with recurved spits. The arcuate nature of the Gray sand reservoirs suggests that they could be reworked sands from an abandoned delta lobe.

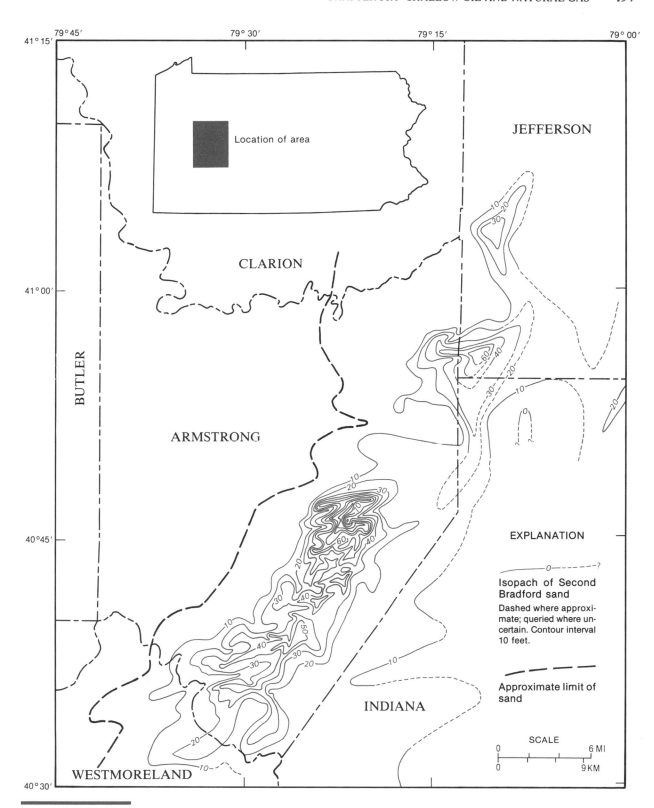

Figure 38A–16. Isopach map of the Second Bradford sand (Bradford Group) in Armstrong, Jefferson, Indiana, and Westmoreland Counties (from Wolfe, 1963, p. 257). This reservoir was interpreted as an offshore bar.

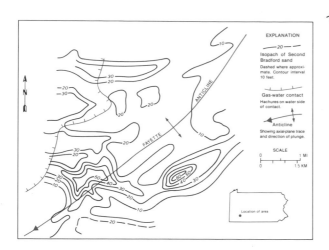

Figure 38A–17. Isopach map of the Second Bradford sand (Bradford Group) in the Latrobe field, central Westmoreland County. This map possibly illustrates the effects of syndepositional tectonics on reservoir geometry. It appears that sediment influx from the southeast was interrupted by the uplift of the Fayette anticline, resulting in a channel deposit paralleling the structure. Uneven development of the anticline, however, would have created low areas in the subsea topography, allowing sediment passage to the northwest.

Figure 38A–18. Isopach map of the Sliverville sand (Bradford Group) in the Music Mountain field, McKean County (modified from Fettke, © 1941, Figure 2, p. 498, reprinted by permission of the American Association of Petroleum Geologists). The "shoestring" geometry of this field suggests an offshore-bar configuration. The Sliverville sand is only locally developed and may represent an anomalous depositional condition.

EXPLANATION

- ● Flowing oil well
- ● Oil well
- ✳ Flowing oil well having upper gas pay
- ✳ Oil well having upper gas pay
- ✳ Gas well
- ✿ Show of gas
- ✦ Dry hole in Sliverville sand
- ⚓ Well drilled prior to August 24, 1937

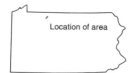
Location of area

SCALE
0 — 3000 FT
0 — 900 M

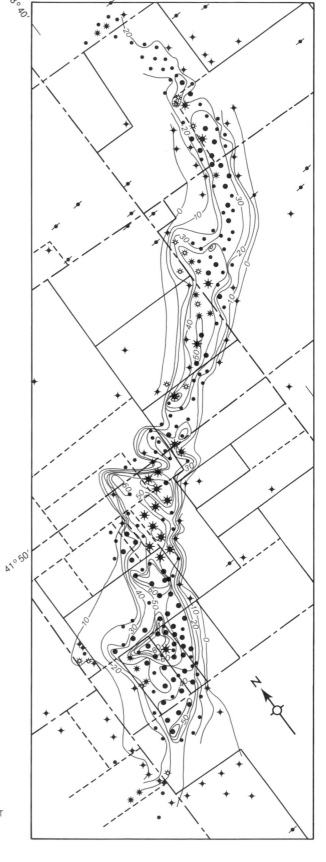

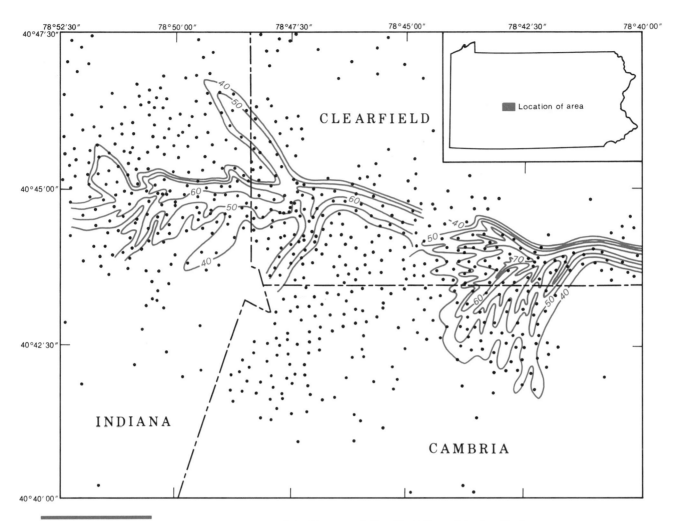

Figure 38A–19. Gross-interval isopach map of the Kane sand (Bradford Group) in the Cush Cushion and adjacent fields in Indiana, Clearfield, and Cambria Counties. The Kane sand in this area was interpreted as part of a small-scale submarine fan system with long axes trending west-northwest (S. S. Johnson, 1984). Solid dots represent well locations. Contour interval is 10 feet.

Upper Freeport, and Lower Kittanning) may eventually prove to be good sources of natural gas (see Chapter 38C).

Mississippian Reservoirs

Mississippian reservoirs consist of sandstones of varying compositions, textures, porosities, and permeabilities. Major reservoirs include the Burgoon, Berea, and Cussewago Sandstones (Figure 38A–11), whereas sandstones of the Mauch Chunk Formation, Shenango Formation, Cuyahoga Group, and Corry Sandstone represent minor or subsidiary reservoirs. Mississippian oil and gas reservoirs are scattered throughout western Pennsylvania and commonly are secondary targets in predominantly Upper Devonian fields (Figure 38A–

12). Fields and pools in which Mississippian reservoirs dominate do occur, but are limited primarily to the extreme southern and western edges of the state.

Upper Devonian Reservoirs

The primary reservoir rocks in Pennsylvania and adjacent states, and the targets of more than 80 percent of all drilling, are the Upper Devonian multi-tiered marine sandstones of the Venango, Bradford, and Elk Groups (Figure 38A–13). These groups consist of several thousand feet of interbedded sandstones, siltstones, and shales, in which the lenticular sandstones and some siltstones act as reservoirs. Traps are primarily stratigraphic and diagenetic, but structure, particularly fracturing, has had a bearing on many of the reservoirs.

Upper Devonian reservoirs consist of nearshore marine sequences (beach, bar, and subaqueous channel deposits) to slope turbidites (as interpreted by Bayles, 1949; Wolfe, 1963; Piotrowski and Harper, 1979; S. S. Johnson, 1984; Laughrey and Harper, 1986; and others). Figures 38A–14 through 38A–19 illustrate some representative Upper Devonian reservoir geometries in western Pennsylvania.

In general, compaction, cementation, and replacement processes destroyed the primary porosity in the sandstones and siltstones, and secondary porosity resulted when the cements, replacement minerals, and unstable grains were dissolved. There is also a scattered amount of fracture porosity present in these rocks (Laughrey and Harper, 1986).

Average porosities in the Upper Devonian rocks range from 14.3 percent in the oil district of northwestern Pennsylvania (Fettke, 1938; McGlade, 1964; Lytle, 1965; Dixon, 1974) to 8.5 percent in the gas-producing belt throughout the rest of western and north-central Pennsylvania (Kimmel and Fulton, 1983). Permeabilities in the oil district range from 0.1 md (millidarcy) to more than 33 md (some reservoir permeabilities are measured in whole darcies), and, in the gas belt, the average reported in-situ permeability of Bradford Group sandstones is 0.0031 md (Laughrey and Harper, 1986). Areas of significantly higher permeabilities do occur in these rocks (e.g., those identified by Laughrey, 1982), but they are relatively insignificant in terms of the volume of existing and potential reservoirs in the Upper Devonian of the Appalachian basin. Core evaluations of some representative Upper Devonian reservoir rocks are shown in Figures 38A–20 through 38A–22.

POTENTIAL FUTURE HYDROCARBON RESERVOIRS

In general, there are three stratigraphic sequences that show good potential for future recoverable hydrocarbon resources:

1. The Lock Haven Formation in north-central and northeastern Pennsylvania and the Foreknobs and Scherr Formations in south-central Pennsylvania (Figure 38A–1). Small quantities of natural gas were found in the Lock Haven sandstones in north-central Pennsylvania as early as 1864, and a small but economical amount of oil was first produced in 1898. Lock Haven sandstones are very simi-

lar to Bradford sandstones in most reservoir characteristics. They also are prolific producers of natural gas in several areas. By comparison, production from the equivalent Foreknobs and Scherr Formations in south-central Pennsylvania is minor at present. Only a few wells in Cambria County have recorded marginally economical production of gas (no oil) from these rocks. Standard geological and engineering studies, such as log interpretation (Figure 38A–23) and mapping, supplemented by seismic and geochemical work, should help determine which areas of these "fringe" formations have the best potential for future production.

2. Upper Devonian shales. Natural gas has been produced from Upper Devonian shales along the Lake Erie shoreline in Pennsylvania (Figure 38A–1), where extensive fracturing due to glacial rebound occurs at depths of less than 1,500 feet. Most of the shale wells in Pennsylvania were drilled for domestic purposes. The volumes of gas in these wells are typically small, but the wells have long lives, making them ideal for homes and small businesses that have limited heating needs. Briggs and Tatlock (1983) estimated potential resources of shale gas in Pennsylvania at 8,395 billion cubic feet (see Chapter 38C).

3. Pennsylvanian coal seams. Small quantities of coal-bed methane have been produced from the Pittsburgh seam in Greene and Washington Counties and from several seams in Westmoreland County (Figure 38A–24). It is only within the last decade that real attention has been focused on coal-bed methane as a resource, but production to date remains small. Natural gas ranges from 32 to 356 cf/t (cubic feet per ton) in bituminous coals (Iannacchione and Puglio, 1979). Where it exceeds 500 feet in depth, the Pittsburgh coal averages 150 cf/t (Byrer and others, 1984). Briggs and Tatlock (1983) estimated potential recoverable resources of natural gas from Pennsylvania's bituminous and anthracite coals at 2,645 billion cubic feet.

RECOMMENDED FOR FURTHER READING

Carll, J. F. (1880), *The geology of the oil regions of Warren, Venango, Clarion, and Butler Counties,* Pennsylvania Geological Survey, 2nd ser., Report III, 482 p.

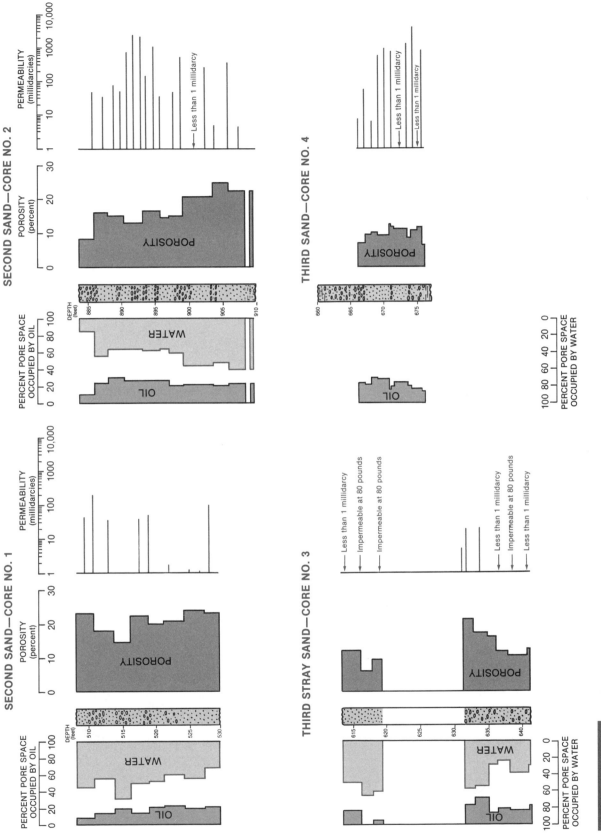

Figure 38A–20. Representative core-analysis profiles from the Venango Second, Venango Third Stray, and Venango Third sands in Venango County (from Sherrill and Matteson, 1941, p. 42).

Figure 38A–21. Representative core-analysis profile from the Glade sand (Bradford Group) in Warren County (slightly modified from Lytle, 1965, p. 36).

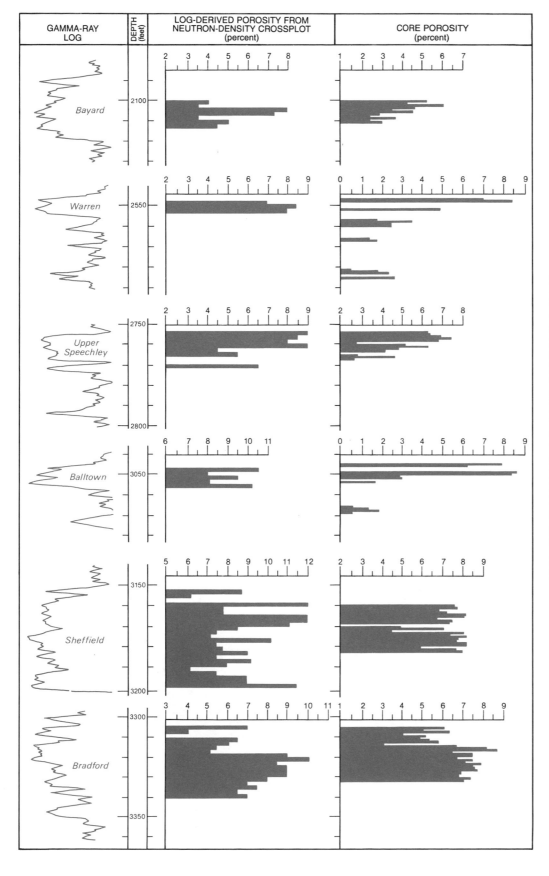

Figure 38A–22. Comparisons of core-derived and log-derived porosity values for six Upper Devonian reservoir sandstones in the Louden Properties #1 Good, Lahr, and Kaufman well, Indiana County (from Laughrey and Harper, © 1986, Figure 19, p. 36, reprinted by permission of the American Association of Petroleum Geologists).

Figure 38A–23. Geologist evaluating a set of geophysical logs (gamma ray, neutron, density, temperature, and resistivity). Geophysical-log analysis provides the geologist with an excellent tool for determining subsurface reservoir conditions, projecting production trends, and searching for new reservoirs.

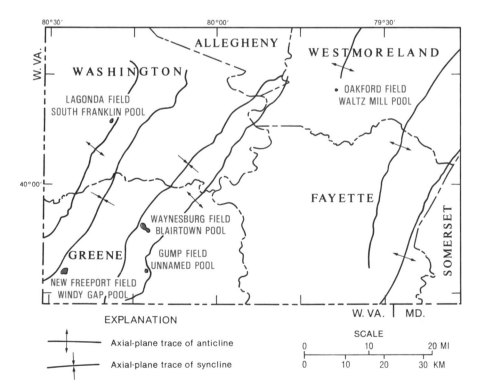

Figure 38A–24. Locations of established coal-bed methane production in southwestern Pennsylvania circa 1990. The pools in Greene and Washington Counties produce from the Pittsburgh coal (Monongahela Group), and the pool in Westmoreland County produces from various coals in the Allegheny Formation.

Grow, G. C., Jr. (1964), *Gas production near hard coal areas of Pennsylvania,* World Oil, v. 159, no. 4, p. 79–81.

Kelley, D. R. (1967), *Geology of the Red Valley sandstone in Forest and Venango Counties, Pennsylvania,* Pennsylvania Geological Survey, 4th ser., Mineral Resource Report 57, 49 p.

Lytle, W. S. (1950), *Crude oil reserves in Pennsylvania,* Pennsylvania Geological Survey, 4th ser., Mineral Resource Report 32, 256 p.

_____ (1963), *Underground gas storage in Pennsylvania,* Pennsylvania Geological Survey, 4th ser., Mineral Resource Report 46, 31 p.

Miller, E. C. (1974), *Pennsylvania's oil industry,* Pennsylvania Historical Association, Pennsylvania History Studies 4, 69 p.

Sisler, J. D., Ashley, G. H., Moyer, F. T., and Hickok, W. O., IV (1933), *Contributions to oil and gas geology of western Pennsylvania,* Pennsylvania Geological Survey, 4th ser., Mineral Resource Report 19, 94 p.

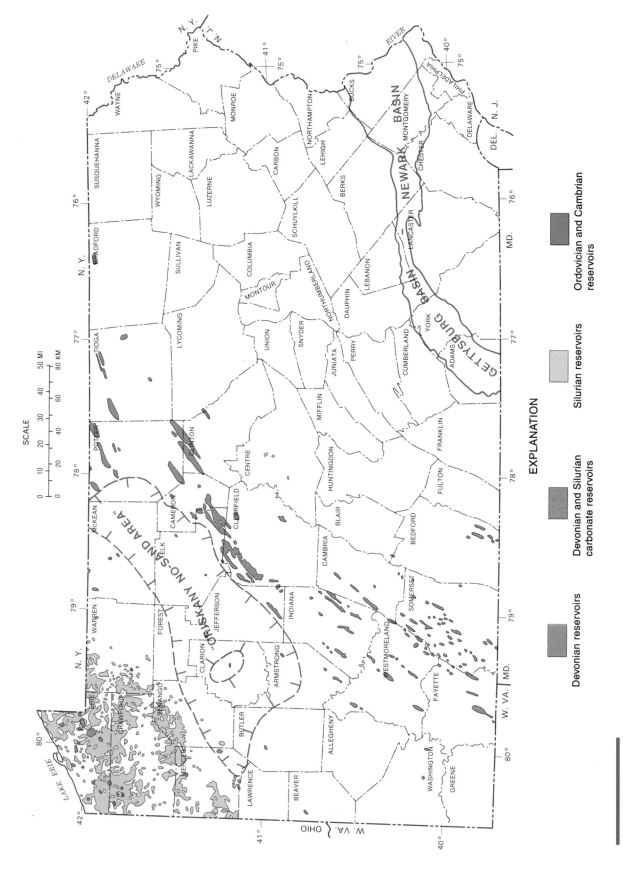

Figure 38B–1. Distribution of deep oil and gas fields (modified from Pennsylvania Geological Survey, 1993) and the locations of "Oriskany no-sand area" and the Gettysburg and Newark basins in Pennsylvania. The outline of the Gettysburg and Newark basins was taken from Berg and others (1989). Geologic units for each reservoir category are discussed in the text.

EXPLANATION

Devonian reservoirs

Devonian and Silurian carbonate reservoirs

Silurian reservoirs

Ordovician and Cambrian reservoirs

CHAPTER 38B   PETROLEUM—DEEP OIL AND NATURAL GAS

JOHN A. HARPER
   Bureau of Topographic and Geologic Survey
   Department of Conservation and Natural
      Resources
   400 Waterfront Drive
   Pittsburgh, PA 15222

DANA R. KELLEY*
   D. R. Kelley Consulting
   200 Hightower Boulevard
   Pittsburgh, PA 15205

EARL H. LINN
   Meridian Exploration Corporation
   3514 Fifth Avenue
   Pittsburgh, PA 15213

INTRODUCTION

A "deep" well, as defined in Pennsylvania, is one that penetrates the boundary between the Middle and Upper Devonian Series, that is, the top of the Tully Limestone or its equivalent. Because of the wedge-shaped nature of the Appalachian basin, the actual depth of this boundary varies from about 1,000 feet near Lake Erie to over 7,000 feet in south-central Pennsylvania. In most of central and eastern Pennsylvania, the deep horizons crop out. Figure 38B–1 shows the distribution of Pennsylvania's deep oil and gas fields. Table 38B–1 is a list of deep formations and the names applied to them by drillers.

The first deep well reported in Pennsylvania, Presque Isle Natural Gas Company's "Erie deep well" (circa 1889), penetrated to Middle Ordovician carbonates at 4,460 feet. The well had a show of gas in the Lower Silurian Medina Group, but was aban-

Table 38B–1.   *Selected Deep Geologic Units and Corresponding Drillers' Terminology*

Geologic unit	Drillers' name
Selinsgrove Limestone	Onondaga
Huntersville Chert	Chert
Ridgeley Sandstone	Oriskany
Licking Creek Limestone	Helderberg
Shriver Chert	do.
Mandata Shale	do.
Corriganville Limestone	do.
New Creek Limestone	do.
Salina Group	Salt
Lockport Dolomite	Newburg
Medina Group	Clinton
Bald Eagle Formation	Oswego
Gatesburg Formation	Rose Run

*Deceased.

doned without commercial production (Fettke, 1950). The first commercially successful deep well, the Peoples Natural Gas #1 Booth and Flinn well in McCance, Westmoreland County, produced gas from the Middle Devonian Huntersville Chert at 6,817 feet in 1920. Deep drilling was ignited by the discovery of gas in the Lower Devonian Ridgeley Sandstone in the Tioga field, Tioga County, in 1930. The Tioga field produced 37.2 Bcf (billion cubic feet) of gas before it was converted to a storage field in 1935 (Lytle and others, 1961).

Deep drilling in Pennsylvania has resulted in two Appalachian basin records. The Leidy Prospecting #2 Finnefrock well in the Leidy field, Clinton County, had a natural open flow from the Ridgeley Sandstone estimated at 145,000 Mcfgpd (thousand cubic feet of gas per day), the largest reported flow to date in the basin. The deepest well in the basin is the Amoco Production Company #1 Svetz well in Somerset County, a dry hole that reached total depth in the Middle Cambrian at 21,460 feet.

DEEP RESERVOIRS

In Pennsylvania, major production from deep reservoirs is limited to the Lower Devonian Ridgeley Sandstone and associated formations, and to the Lower Silurian Medina Group. Proven deep reservoirs, however, range from the Middle Devonian to the Upper Cambrian (Table 38B–2).

Devonian Reservoirs

Deep Devonian reservoirs include the Middle Devonian Onondaga Formation and Huntersville Chert

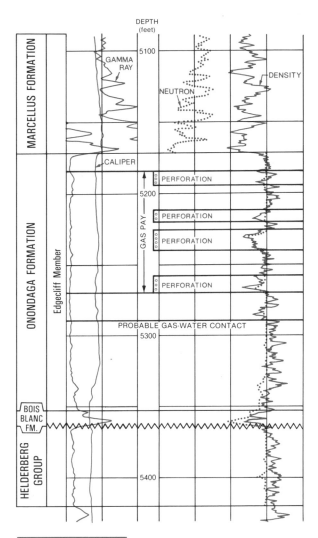

Figure 38B–2. Wire-line log section through the Onondaga reef (from the Amoco #1 Witco, discovery well of the Cyclone pool, Bradford field) in McKean County (slightly modified from Piotrowski, 1976, p. 31). The gamma-ray log signature indicates that the Edgecliff Member was developed as a pinnacle reef to the exclusion of the normally overlying Moorehouse and Nedrow Members. Pay zones, shown where the casing and formation were perforated, were recognized as porous intervals with high gas saturations on the neutron and density logs. Production from the well was 200 Mcfgpd natural and 3,000 Mcfgpd after treatment with acid.

Table 38B–2. *Cumulative Deep Gas Production in Pennsylvania by Producing Geologic Unit*

Producing geologic unit	Date of first production	Cumulative production at end of 1987 (Mcf)
Marcellus Formation	1979	75,930
Onondaga Formation	1974	1,883,619
Oriskany Sandstone	1946	5,953,706
Huntersville Chert and Ridgeley Sandstone	1922	1,267,662,353
Bois Blanc Formation through Salina Group	1984	787,948
Lockport Dolomite	1966	5,465,265
Medina Group	1947	148,842,015
Tuscarora Formation	1964	3,140,264
Bald Eagle Formation	1983	1,792,160
Gatesburg Formation and Little Falls Dolomite	1964	207,200

and the Lower Devonian Oriskany Sandstone and Ridgeley Sandstone. The Middle Devonian Marcellus Formation, which produces small amounts of gas from several wells in southwestern Pennsylvania, is more important as a hydrocarbon source than as a reservoir.

Onondaga Formation

Natural gas, gas condensates, and oil occur in Onondaga Formation reefs and other high-porosity reservoirs in southern New York and northwestern Pennsylvania. One reef has been found in Pennsylvania, in McKean County (Figures 38B–2 and 38B–3). Other Onondaga reservoirs exist because of subtle differences in lithology. Reef exploration can pro-

ceed by geophysical prospecting, but the discovery of subtle reservoirs requires intensive evaluation of standard geophysical logs.

Oriskany Sandstone

The Oriskany Sandstone has a patchy distribution throughout northwestern Pennsylvania (Kelley and McGlade, 1969). Traps occur where subdued structures coincide with development of the sandstone (Figures 38B–4 and 38B–5). Productive wells tend to have short lives because of the eventual invasion of water into the gas-producing zone. The Summit storage pool in Erie County (Figure 38B–6) is the largest Oriskany reservoir in the state. Before

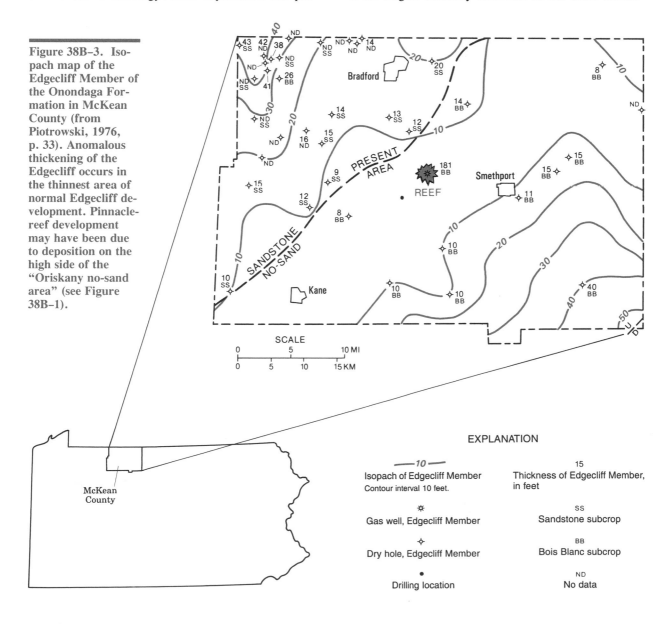

Figure 38B–3. Isopach map of the Edgecliff Member of the Onondaga Formation in McKean County (from Piotrowski, 1976, p. 33). Anomalous thickening of the Edgecliff occurs in the thinnest area of normal Edgecliff development. Pinnacle-reef development may have been due to deposition on the high side of the "Oriskany no-sand area" (see Figure 38B–1).

SCALE

0   5   10 MI
0   5   10   15 KM

McKean County

EXPLANATION

— 10 —
Isopach of Edgecliff Member
Contour interval 10 feet.

15
Thickness of Edgecliff Member, in feet

✳
Gas well, Edgecliff Member

SS
Sandstone subcrop

✦
Dry hole, Edgecliff Member

BB
Bois Blanc subcrop

•
Drilling location

ND
No data

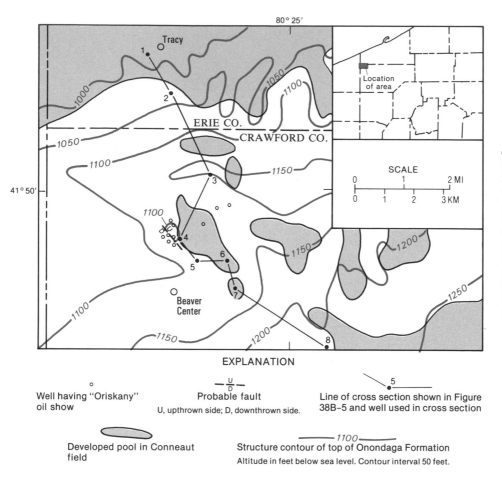

Figure 38B–4. Structure map of the top of the Onondaga Formation in a portion of Erie and Crawford Counties, showing the location of wells having oil shows from the Oriskany and of the cross section shown in Figure 38B–5 (from Harper, 1982, p. 4).

EXPLANATION

○ Well having "Oriskany" oil show

—U—D— Probable fault
U, upthrown side; D, downthrown side.

5 Line of cross section shown in Figure 38B–5 and well used in cross section

⬭ Developed pool in Conneaut field

——1100—— Structure contour of top of Onondaga Formation
Altitude in feet below sea level. Contour interval 50 feet.

conversion to a natural gas storage area, the pool had a cumulative production of 4.9 Bcf over 13 years.

Huntersville Chert and Ridgeley Sandstone

The most productive deep Devonian reservoirs are the combined Middle Devonian Huntersville Chert and Lower Devonian Ridgeley Sandstone. The Huntersville is not in direct contact with the Ridgeley, but because of interconnection by fractures, both formations may constitute a single reservoir.

Early exploration and development of Huntersville-Ridgeley reservoirs occurred on major surface anticlines of western and north-central Pennsylvania. More recent drilling established production low on the flanks of and even between the anticlines when it became evident that more than folding was responsible for the distribution of natural gas in the rocks. The Huntersville-Ridgeley interval is commonly faulted and fractured, and the locations of pools are governed by the distribution of fault blocks and associated connate water and rock pressures. Although attempts

have been made to map faults in this interval (Figures 38B–7 and 38B–8), the true complexity of faulting can only be appreciated by intensive, high-quality seismic surveying and processing (Figure 38B–9).

The entrapment of gas in Huntersville-Ridgeley reservoirs is primarily structural, but combined structural and stratigraphic traps occur along the southeastern edge of the "Oriskany no-sand area" (Figure 38B–1) where porosity decreases and the reservoir pinches out (e.g., the Elk Run pool, described by Heyman, 1969). In general, Huntersville-Ridgeley reservoirs occur on the overthrust flanks of complex, centrally depressed anticlines (Figures 38B–10 and 38B–11). Production is mainly from fractures. Except for a narrow zone close to the reservoir pinchout, where dissolution of both cements and feldspar grains has enhanced porosity (Figure 38B–12), neither the Huntersville nor the Ridgeley has notable intergranular porosity.

Small Huntersville-Ridgeley pools of 1 or 2 wells have reserves ranging from 0.5 to over 8 Bcf, whereas larger pools of 10 or 15 wells can have reserves rang-

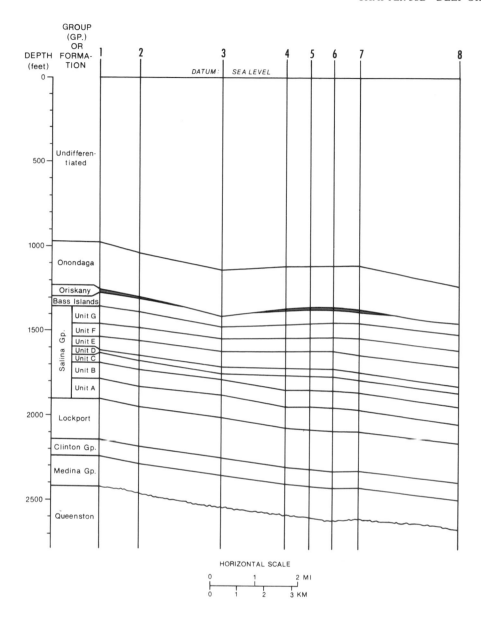

Figure 38B–5. Cross section of the area in western Erie and Crawford Counties shown in Figure 38B–4, highlighting the distribution of the Oriskany Sandstone in relation to structure (modified from Harper, 1982, p. 6). Paleostructure studies indicate that the Oriskany was deposited in swales formed by the dissolution of salt in the Salina Group (see Chapter 20). Subsequent regional deformation raised the swales and created anticlinal traps in the Oriskany.

ing from 15 to 20 Bcf. A single well having reserves of 1 Bcf may produce for 25 years (Figure 38B–13). The production from Huntersville-Ridgeley wells averages between 1.5 and 2 Bcf per well and is affected by drilling control and type of completion.

Devonian and Silurian Carbonate Reservoirs

Lower Devonian and Upper Silurian carbonate reservoirs are known to be subsidiary reservoirs in Oriskany and Ridgeley fields. Since 1880, the carbonate rocks of the Devonian Onondaga, Bois Blanc, and Manlius Formations and the Silurian Bass Islands Dolomite and Salina Group have produced large quanti-

ties of oil and natural gas in a faulted section of these rocks in western New York. The trend of the fault (Figure 38B–14) suggested that production could also be found in Pennsylvania, and in 1983, the Greenley pool in Erie County was found in the Pennsylvania portion of the trend (Harper, 1985). Gas production in this pool comes from the entire carbonate sequence (Figure 38B–15). Not enough is known about this reservoir at the time of this writing to adequately discuss its impact on future production in the state.

Silurian Reservoirs

Production from Silurian reservoirs is generally natural gas. In addition to natural gas production, the

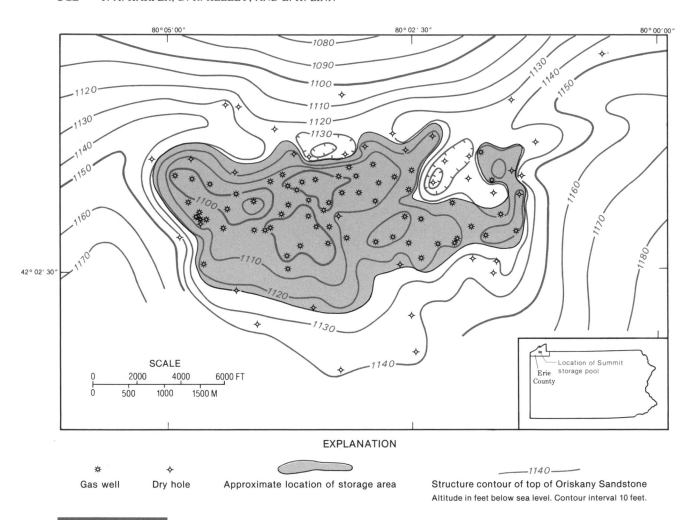

Figure 38B–6. Structure map of the top of the Oriskany Sandstone in the Summit storage pool, Erie County (from Lytle, 1963, p. 26). The undulatory nature of the Oriskany is the result of patchy deposition of sand combined with salt movement in the underlying Salina Group.

Lower Silurian Medina Group sandstones have produced small amounts of oil, and the Upper Silurian Lockport Dolomite has had significant shows of oil.

Lockport Dolomite

The Lockport Dolomite has produced natural gas in Pennsylvania since the discovery of the Kilgore pool in the Wolf Creek field, Mercer County, in 1966. Subsequent drilling has not greatly expanded the limits of production, but the cumulative production of gas from this small pool is very high (Table 38B–2). The Lockport produces from the "Newburg sand," a high-porosity zone of vuggy, reef-derived rubble in a grainstone matrix (Figure 38B–16). The Kilgore pool is situated on the southwest flank of the

anomalous Henderson dome, a large circular structure associated with basement faulting. The accumulation of natural gas in the Lockport is apparently due to a combination of porosity and structure.

Medina Group

Small amounts of natural gas were first obtained from the Medina Group near North East, Erie County, as early as 1914, but the first commercial production was from the Corry field in eastern Erie County in the late 1940's. Medina gas was subsequently found in western Crawford County in 1957; Medina oil was found less than 10 years later. Medina oil production commonly makes up more than two percent of the total state production (Table 38B–3). Drilling in-

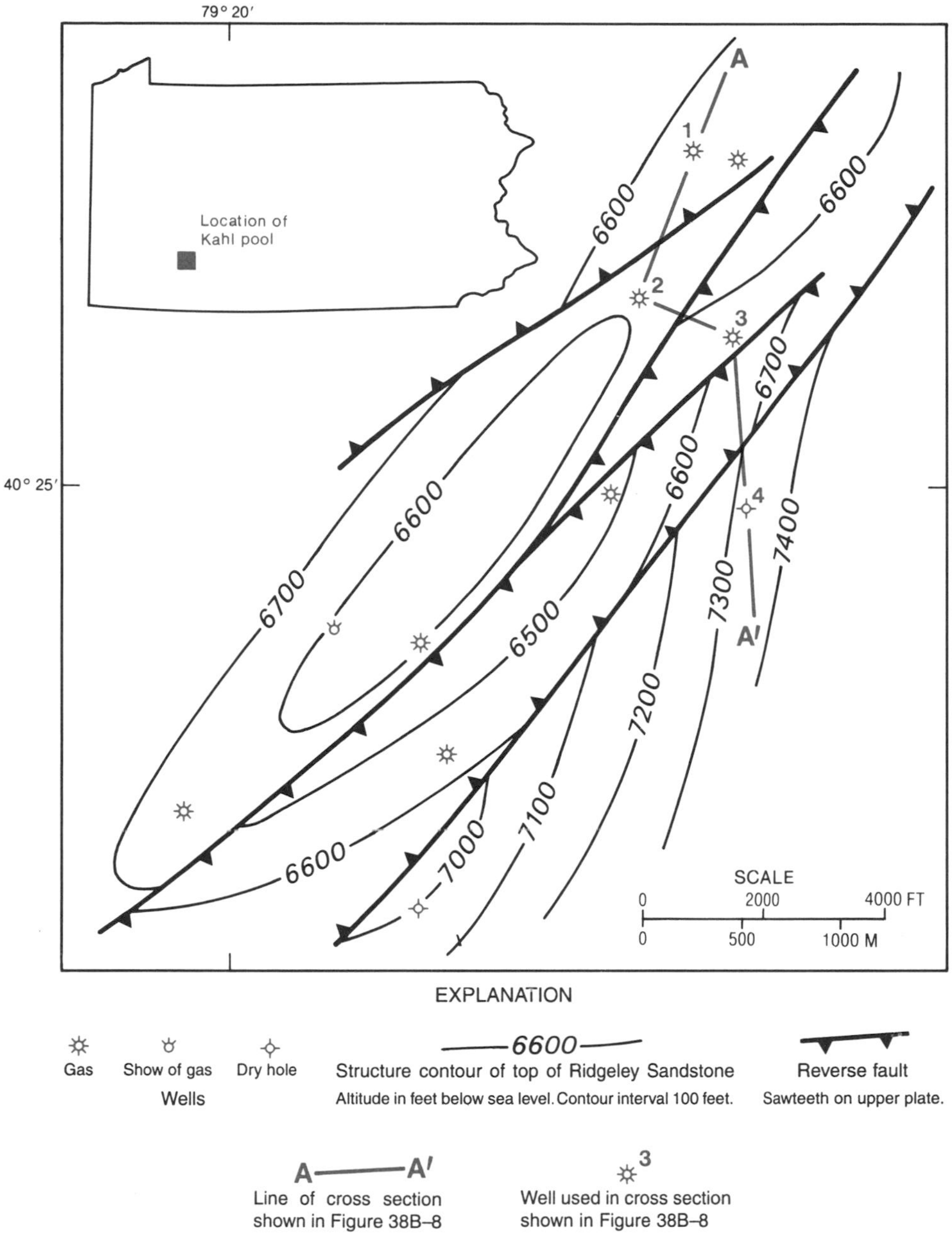
79° 20′
40° 25′
Location of Kahl pool
A
A′
1
2
3
4
6600
6700
6500
7000
7100
7200
7300
7400
SCALE
0 2000 4000 FT
0 500 1000 M
EXPLANATION
Gas
Show of gas
Dry hole
Wells
6600
Structure contour of top of Ridgeley Sandstone
Altitude in feet below sea level. Contour interval 100 feet.
Reverse fault
Sawteeth on upper plate.
A——A′
Line of cross section shown in Figure 38B–8
Well used in cross section shown in Figure 38B–8

Figure 38B–7. Structure map of the top of the Ridgeley Sandstone in the Kahl pool, Westmoreland County (modified from Lytle and others, 1964, p. 27). This map was constructed solely from drillers' records and logs, without benefit of seismic information. Cross section A–A′ is shown in Figure 38B–8.

creased dramatically in northwestern Pennsylvania after passage of the Natural Gas Policy Act in 1978. More than 1,500 wells were completed in a five-county area during the next seven years, resulting in the coalescence of many of the originally discrete fields and pools (Figure 38B–1).

Production from the Medina Group, a series of interbedded sandstones, siltstones, and shales exhibiting varied porosities and permeabilities (Figure 38B–17), is controlled by stratigraphic or combined stratigraphic and structural traps (Kelley and McGlade, 1969; Laughrey, 1984). Porosity in the sandstones is mainly secondary and is due to dissolution of feldspars, carbonate minerals, and lithic fragments. Fracture porosity is also present, especially in areas of plunging anticlinal structures and cross-strike structural discontinuities, which are common in northwestern Pennsylvania (Pees, 1983b). The best production comes from rock sequences that include numerous interbedded sublithic sandstones and shales; this is

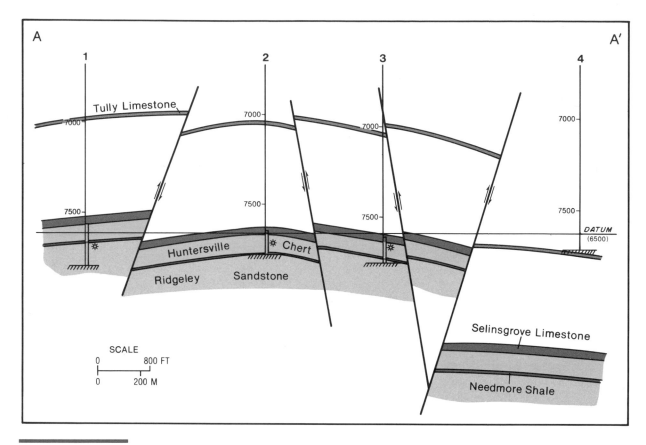

Figure 38B-8. Cross section through the Kahl pool, Westmoreland County, along the line shown in Figure 38B-7 (modified from Lytle and others, 1964, p. 28). The datum is given in feet below sea level. Measurements on vertical drill lines are depths below the surface in feet.

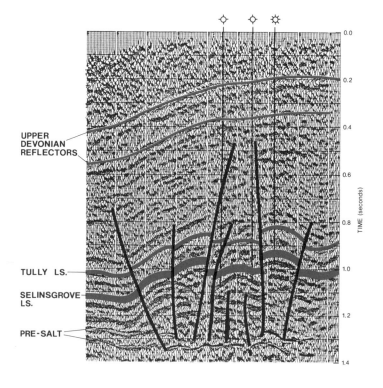

Figure 38B-9. Interpreted seismic cross section of a major anticline in western Pennsylvania. Compare this figure with Figure 38B-8.

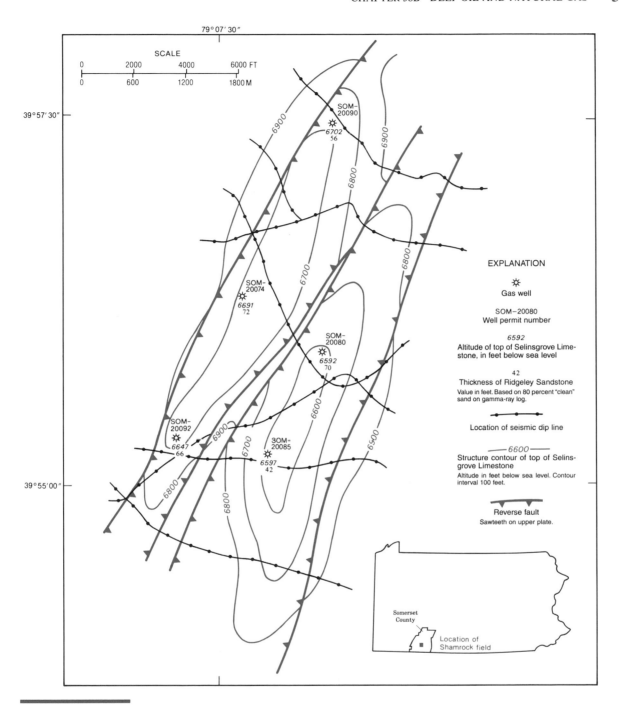

Figure 38B–10. Structure map of the top of the Selinsgrove Limestone (Onondaga) in the Shamrock field, Somerset County. Gas production from the Huntersville Chert and Ridgeley Sandstone occurs on upthrown blocks on the flanks of an anticline, whereas the crest of the anticline is downfaulted and does not contain producible hydrocarbons.

presumably because of high secondary porosity development in those sandstones containing more labile (unstable) material. Figures 38B–18 and 38B–19 illustrate the structural attitude and isolithic distribution of the Medina in a typical field.

Commercial production from the Medina Group generally occurs only after hydraulic fracturing of the reservoir rocks. Medina wells neither produce large volumes of gas nor have long lives; total reserves for wells on a 40- to 60-acre spacing typically

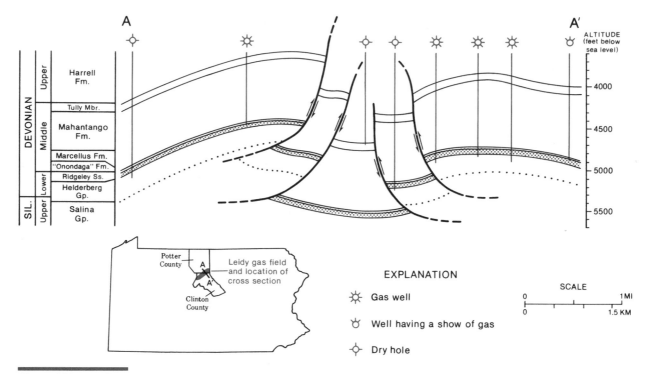

Figure 38B–11. Structural cross section of the Leidy field in Clinton County (from Harper, © 1990, Figure 6, p. 166, reprinted by permission of the American Association of Petroleum Geologists). The structural datum is sea level. Gas production from the Ridgeley Sandstone occurs only on overthrusted flanks.

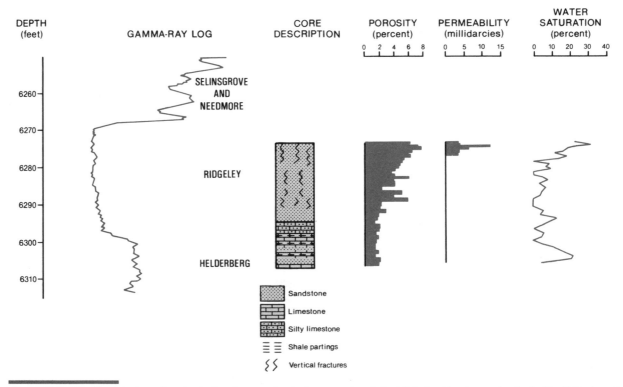

Figure 38B–12. Correlation of geological and petrophysical properties of the Ridgeley Sandstone in the Leidy field, based on core data (from Harper, © 1990, Figure 11, p. 172, reprinted by permission of the American Association of Petroleum Geologists, courtesy of Consolidated Gas Supply Corporation). Porosity and permeability are greatest in the upper 4 or 5 feet, but so is water saturation. Porosity and permeability have been enhanced by dissolution of calcite cement in this zone.

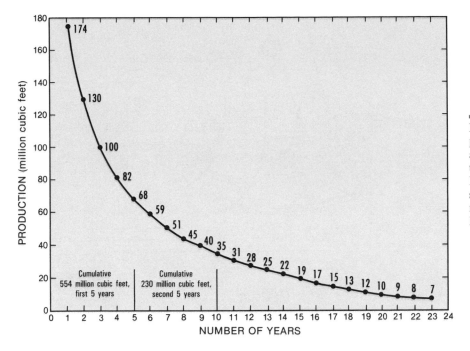

Figure 38B–13. Gas production-decline curve for a typical well producing from the Huntersville Chert and Ridgeley Sandstone in Somerset County. Such wells commonly have reserves of at least 1 Bcf.

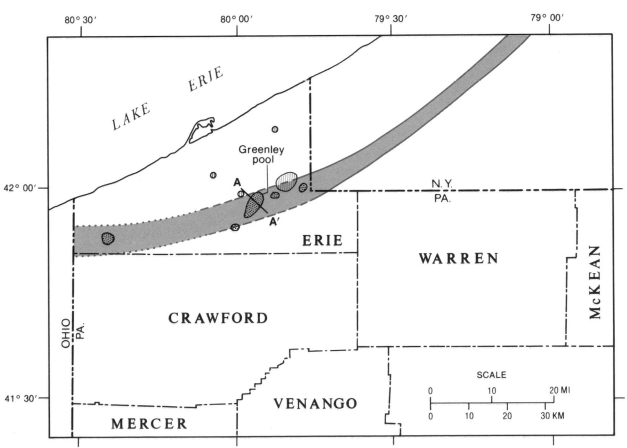

Figure 38B–14. Location of the "Bass Islands trend" of New York (colored area) and related production in Pennsylvania. Areas producing from the Onondaga Formation through Salina Group interval, dot pattern; areas producing from the Onondaga Formation, vertical-line pattern. Cross section A–A´ is shown in Figure 38B–15.

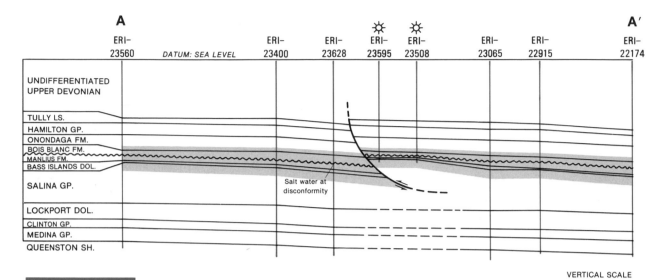

Figure 38B–15. Generalized cross section of the Greenley pool, Erie County, located in the Pennsylvania extension of the "Bass Islands trend" (from Harper, 1985, p. 11). The New York portion of the trend is more faulted than the Pennsylvania portion shown here. Variations in thickness across the fault zone indicate that faulting was probably penecontemporaneous with deposition. Gas production occurs from the lower part of the Middle Devonian down into the Upper Silurian carbonate section, from the Onondaga Formation to the carbonate rocks at the top of the Salina Group.

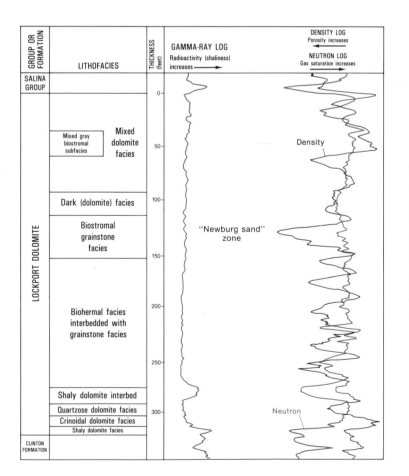

Figure 38B–16. Generalized lithofacies (based on Rhinehart, 1979) and geophysical log signatures in the Lockport Dolomite. The productive "Newburg sand" zone, part of the biostromal grainstone facies, is most recognizable by the combination of high porosity readings on the density log and high gas-saturation readings on the neutron log. Notice that there are other zones of potential gas production indicated by the neutron and density logs.

Table 38B-3. *Deep Oil Production From the Medina Group by Year*

Year	Amount (bbl)	Percent of state total
1965	4,422	0.1
1966	11,921	.3
1967	21,954	.5
1968	58,991	1.4
1969	45,000	1.0
1970	65,000	1.6
1971	65,000	1.7
1972	78,000	2.3
1973	76,000	2.3
1974	58,000	1.7
1975	67,000	2.1
1976	63,000	2.1
1977	37,405	1.4
1978	61,616	2.2
1979	70,440	2.5
1980	73,218	2.5
1981	64,327	1.7
1982	71,380	1.7
1983	88,718	2.0
1984	120,976	2.5
1985	163,118	3.4
1986	163,912	4.3
1987	134,580	4.1

fall between 150,000 and 250,000 Mcf per well, and well life varies from 7 to 30 years, the average being 15 years. Assuming a constant flow with no mechanical problems or purchaser restrictions, almost half of the total reserves to be produced by any given well will be produced in the first five years (Figure 38B-20).

Tuscarora Formation

Of 11 wells drilled into the Tuscarora Formation in Pennsylvania, only 5 were successful. The most productive Tuscarora well, the Amoco/UGI #1 Texasgulf well (CEN-20006), was the discovery well for the Devils Elbow field in Centre County (Figure 38B-21). Drilled into an overpressured reservoir (bottom hole pressure was 6,940 psi [pounds per square inch]), the well had a natural open flow estimated at over 30,000 Mcfgpd. Tuscarora gas typically has low heating values due to high nitrogen content (Table 38B-4); therefore, conversion of the gas to an acceptable heating value resulted in a net flow of about 7,000 Mcfgpd. In the first 512 days, the well produced 2.7 Bcf, but

water production increased from 1 to almost 20 bbl per 1,000 Mcf. Production in the Tuscarora Formation is controlled by fracture porosity and bedding-plane partings resulting from intense structural deformation associated with thrust-fault-bounded anticlines. Some of the fractures in the rock are visibly propped open by large quartz crystals (Nickelsen and Cotter, 1983), and it appears that these fractures constitute the most productive reservoir in the rock. Other than the Texasgulf discovery well, Tuscarora tests are difficult to assess because of sporadic or nonexistent production.

Ordovician and Cambrian Reservoirs

Ordovician and Cambrian production in Pennsylvania is uncommon. Natural gas from the Upper Ordovician Bald Eagle sandstones and gas and gas condensate from the Upper Cambrian Gatesburg and Little Falls carbonates have been produced in substantial quantities over short periods of time (Table 38B-2).

Bald Eagle Formation

Commercial production from the Bald Eagle Formation started in 1983 when the Texaco #1 Pennsylvania State Forest Tract 285 well (CLI-20276), the discovery well of the Grugan field, was completed in Clinton County (Figures 38B-1 and 38B-22). Originally drilled as a 19,365-foot Cambrian test, the well was plugged back and completed between 12,900 and 13,030 feet with an open flow of 3,847 Mcfgpd and a rock pressure of 9,220 psi. The multitiered Bald Eagle sandstones in this reservoir are fine to medium grained and tightly cemented (porosity is generally less than 2 percent). The rock is highly fractured (Harper and Laughrey, 1986), probably the result of deep-seated faulting (Henderson and Timm, 1985; Figure 38B-22). The well yielded over 300,000 Mcf in its first 4 months of production, and over 1 Bcf over the first 16 months. Other wells drilled to locate Bald Eagle gas reserves since the discovery of the Grugan field have been less successful. In early 1988, only two Bald Eagle wells were producing natural gas.

Gatesburg Formation and Little Falls Dolomite

Despite numerous shows of oil and gas in the lower Paleozoic carbonate rocks in western Pennsylvania, only a few one-well pools have had any production from these rocks. In western Crawford County, the "Upper Sandy member" of the Gatesburg Forma-

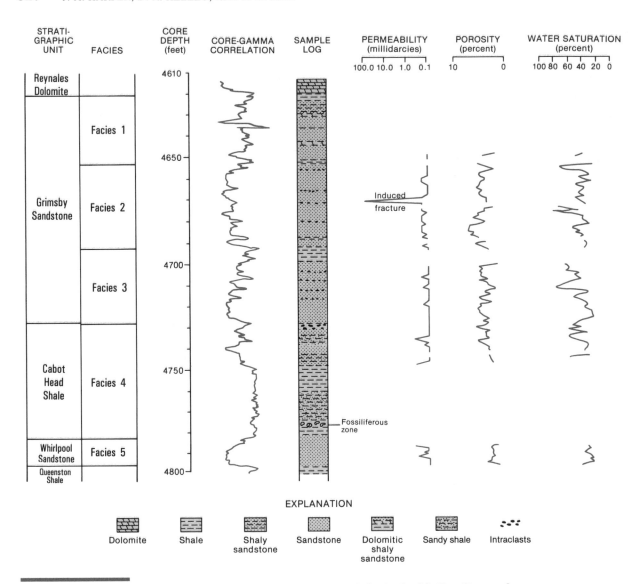

Figure 38B–17. Correlation of lithology and reservoir characteristics in the Medina Group of Crawford County (from Laughrey, 1984, p. 13). Porosity, permeability, and water saturation vary greatly over the interval of the core and from well to well. See Laughrey (1984) for an explanation of the significance of these variations.

tion produced gas for a short time in the Scull and Beaver Center pools in the Conneaut field (Figures 38B–23 and 38B–24). These pools produced for 18 months before being shut in and eventually abandoned due to excessive water in the formation. Total production during the 18 months was 190,000 Mcf and 1,100 bbl of condensate. The Minard Run pool in the Bradford field, McKean County (Figure 38B–23), which was discovered in 1974, produced 2.2 Bcf from the Little Falls Dolomite before being taken out of commercial use in 1988.

In the Gatesburg pools, the gas and condensate occur in reservoir rocks having combined structural and stratigraphic trapping mechanisms where the formation was truncated by a Late Cambrian-Early Ordovician unconformity on plunging anticlinal flexures (Figures 38B–25 and 38B–26). The Gatesburg pinches out updip at the unconformity, and it is difficult to project this pinch-out without close control. Wells must be located favorably using both structural controls and subcrop relationships. Seismic programs can locate the structures, but the proper reser-

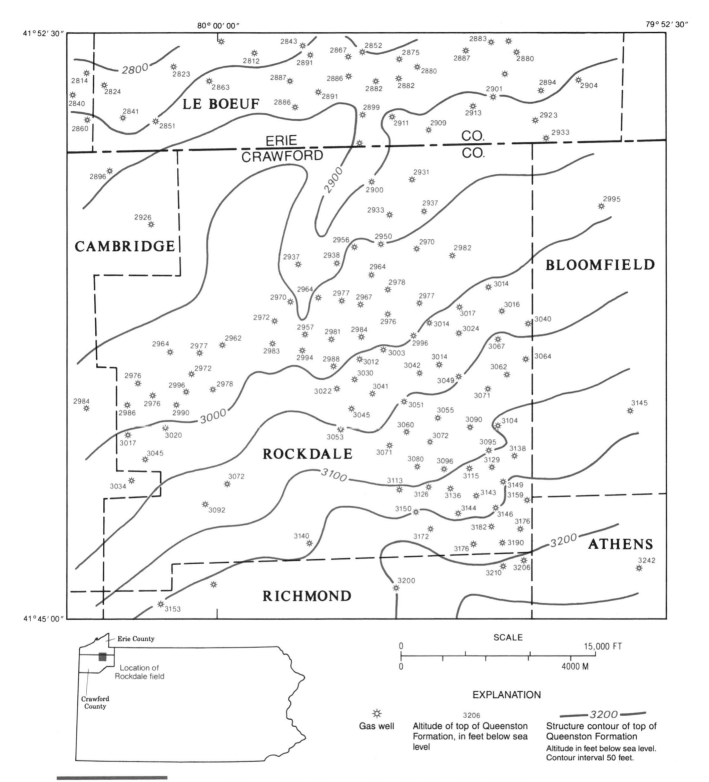

Figure 38B–18. Structure map of the top of the Queenston Formation (base of the Medina Group) in the Rockdale field, Crawford County. The structural attitude shows a gentle dip toward the basin axis to the southeast, but small discontinuities and structural nosings, such as in the northern part of the field, are common.

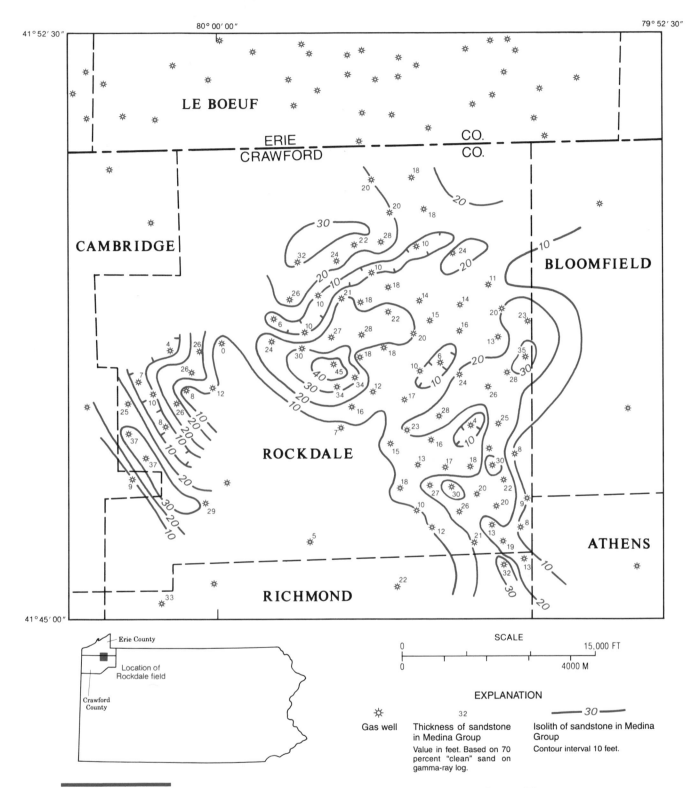

Figure 38B–19. Isolith map of the productive "clean" sandstones of the Medina Group. The contours are based on 70 percent sandstone or greater as picked on gamma-ray logs and 7 percent porosity or greater as picked on density logs. The most productive wells occur where the net thickness of "clean" sandstone is 10 feet or greater.

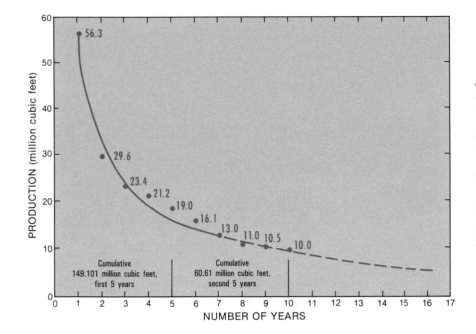

Figure 38B–20. Gas production-decline curve for a typical well producing from the Medina Group in north-western Pennsylvania. In general, a Medina well must have reserves between 150,000 and 200,000 Mcf of gas in order to be considered commercial. This particular well has estimated reserves of over 300,000 Mcf.

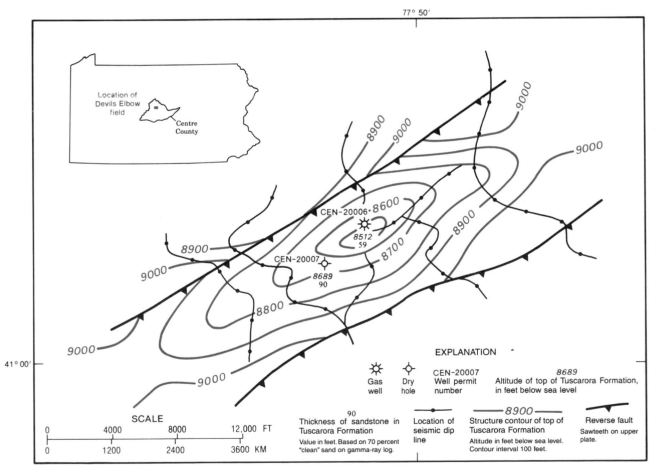

Figure 38B–21. Structure map of the top of the Tuscarora Formation in the Devils Elbow field, Centre County.

Table 38B–4. *Representative Gas Analyses From Selected Deep Geologic Units in Pennsylvania*

Geologic unit	County	Field	Methane	Ethane	Propane	N-butane	Isobutane	N-pentane	Isopentane	Cyclo-pentane	Hexanes plus	Nitrogen	Oxygen	Argon	Helium	Hydrogen	Hydrogen sulfide	Carbon dioxide	Btu[1] value
Oriskany Sandstone	Erie	Erie	77.8	11.4	3.9	1.0	0.0	0.0	0.2	0.0	0.0	5.1	0.3	0.0	—	0.2	0.0	0.0	1,133
do.	do.	North East	80.1	11.3	3.7	.8	.3	.1	.2	Tr[2]	.1	2.9	.0	Tr	0.2	.1	.0	.1	1,165
Huntersville Chert	Indiana	Cherry Hill	96.7	1.7	.1	.0	.0	.0	.0	.0	.0	1.1	.2	Tr	Tr	.0	.0	.2	1,013
do.	Somerset	Ohiopyle	96.5	1.5	.1	Tr	Tr	Tr	Tr	.0	.1	1.6	.0	Tr	Tr	.0	.0	.1	1,012
Huntersville Chert and Ridgeley Sandstone	Fayette	do.	97.5	1.7	.1	.0	.0	.0	.0	.0	.0	.6	.0	.0	Tr	.0	.0	.1	1,021
do.	Indiana	Jacksonville	97.2	2.0	.2	.0	.0	.0	.0	.0	.0	.4	.0	Tr	Tr	.0	.0	.2	1,026
do.	Westmoreland	Murrysville	96.6	2.5	.2	.0	.0	.0	.0	.0	.0	.6	.0	.0	Tr	.0	.0	.1	1,029
Ridgeley Sandstone	Armstrong	Roaring Run	96.2	3.0	.2	.0	.0	.0	.0	.0	.0	.4	.0	Tr	.0	.0	.0	.1	1,033
do.	Bedford	Artemas	98.4	.3	.0	.0	.0	.0	.0	.0	.0	1.2	.0	.0	.1	.0	.0	Tr	1,002
do.	Cambria	Rager Mountain	98.0	1.2	.0	.0	.0	.0	.0	.0	.0	.6	.0	.0	Tr	.0	.0	.2	1,014
do.	Clearfield	Penfield	96.0	1.9	.2	.0	.0	.0	.0	.0	.0	1.5	.0	Tr	Tr	.0	.0	.4	1,012
do.	Jefferson	Frostburg	97.1	2.1	.0	.0	.0	.0	.0	.0	.0	.6	.0	.0	Tr	.0	.0	.2	1,021
do.	Potter	East Fork-Wharton	95.5	2.9	.5	.1	Tr	.1	Tr	Tr	.1	.5	Tr	Tr	Tr	.0	.0	.2	1,045
do.	Somerset	Somerset West	98.0	1.1	.1	.0	.0	.0	.0	.0	.0	.6	.0	.0	.1	.0	.0	.2	1,015
do.	Tioga	Tioga	98.9	.0	.0	.0	.0	.0	.0	.0	.0	.6	.1	.0	.0	.0	.0	.4	1,259
do.	Westmoreland	Crabtree	96.6	1.9	.3	.0	.0	.0	.0	.0	.0	.5	Tr	.0	Tr	.0	.0	.7	1,020
Medina Group	Crawford	Athens	93.0	3.4	.5	.1	Tr	.1	Tr	Tr	.1	2.7	.0	.1	Tr	.0	.0	Tr	1,029
do.	do.	Conneaut	85.8	4.7	1.3	.5	.2	.1	.2	Tr	.1	6.5	.3	Tr	.2	Tr	.0	.1	1,029
do.	Erie	do.	90.7	3.8	.9	.3	.1	.1	.0	Tr	.1	3.9	.1	Tr	.2	.0	.0	.0	1,033
do.	do.	North East	80.1	11.3	3.7	.8	.3	.1	.2	Tr	.1	2.9	.0	Tr	.1	.0	.1	.2	1,165
do.	Venango	Wesley	95.2	2.2	.1	Tr	Tr	.0	.0	.0	.0	2.5	.0	.0	.0	.0	.0	.0	1,009
Tuscarora Formation	Centre	Devils Elbow	74.6	2.4	.1	.1	.0	.1	Tr	Tr	Tr	22.3	Tr	Tr	.2	Tr	.0	.1	809
do.	Fayette	Summit	83.6	1.7	.2	.0	.0	.0	.0	.0	.0	13.9	.0	.0	.2	Tr	.0	.4	883
Beekmantown Group	Bedford	—	60.1	.1	Tr	.0	.0	.0	.0	.0	.0	38.5	.2	.2	.3	.1	.0	.6	612
Gatesburg Formation	Erie	Conneaut	—	—	—	—	—	—	—	—	—	—	—	—	—	—	—	—	1,060

Constituents (percent)

[1] Btu, British thermal unit.
[2] Tr, trace.

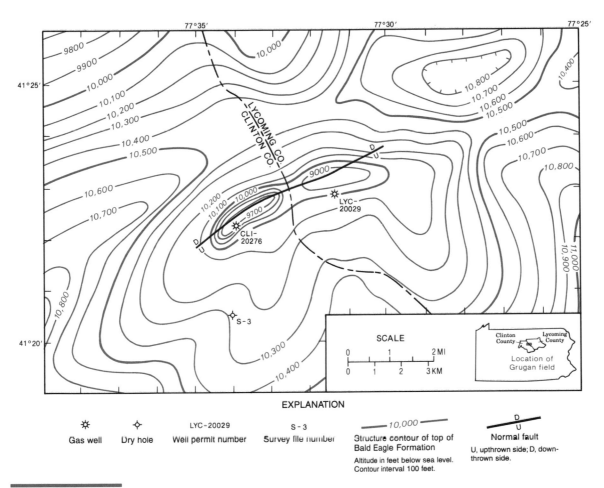

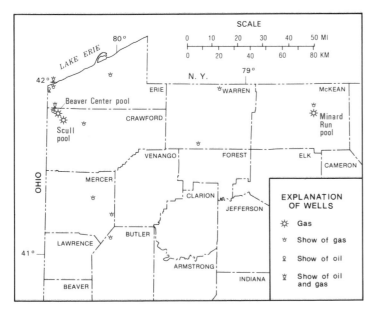

Figure 38B–22. Structure map of the top of the Bald Eagle Formation in the Grugan field, Clinton and Lycoming Counties. The fault on the northwest side of the field was interpreted from seismic data to have offset the Middle Ordovician carbonates (and possibly deeper). It could project into the Bald Eagle and be principally responsible for intense fracturing in the formation.

Figure 38B–23. Locations of wells known to have had shows or production of gas, oil, or condensate from the Ordovician and/or Cambrian carbonate section.

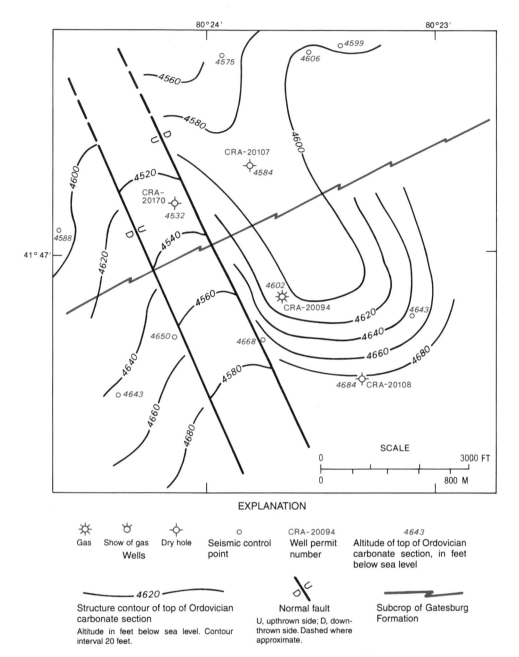

Figure 38B–24. Structure map of the top of the Ordovician carbonate section in the vicinity of the Scull pool, Crawford County. The Scull pool produced gas and condensate from the Gatesburg Formation. The top of the Ordovician carbonates (Trenton limestone of drillers) was used for structural control because it is easily recognized from drill cuttings and gamma-ray logs.

EXPLANATION

☼ Gas	♉ Show of gas	◇ Dry hole	○	CRA-20094	*4643*
	Wells		Seismic control point	Well permit number	Altitude of top of Ordovician carbonate section, in feet below sea level

——— *4620* ———
Structure contour of top of Ordovician carbonate section
Altitude in feet below sea level. Contour interval 20 feet.

Normal fault
U, upthrown side; D, downthrown side. Dashed where approximate.

Subcrop of Gatesburg Formation

---

voir conditions within the sandstone can only be delineated by drilling.

POTENTIAL FUTURE HYDROCARBON RESERVOIRS

Approximately 60 percent of 26,000 square miles of prospective area, or 17 percent of 90,000 cubic miles of prospective section volume, remain virtually unevaluated for economic hydrocarbon potential just in the Appalachian Plateaus province of Pennsylvania

(Kelley and others, 1970; Harper, 1981). Future consideration should be given to the following:

1. Deep drilling in the "Eastern Overthrust Belt" of the Ridge and Valley province (Figure 38B–27). Despite numerous tests, only three Ridgeley Sandstone fields have produced gas in this large structural province in Pennsylvania. At the time of this writing, however, a certain optimism about the area remains among the major companies. Source-rock studies indicate that certain strata are still actively generating hydrocarbons, and these

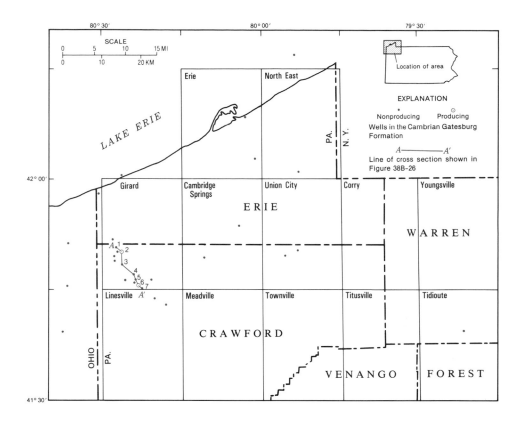

Figure 38B–25. Locations of wells that penetrated the Cambrian in northwestern Pennsylvania, including those used in constructing the cross section in Figure 38B–26 (modified from Wagner, 1966a, Figure 1, p. 152). Boundaries and names of U.S. Geological Survey 15-minute quadrangles are shown for reference.

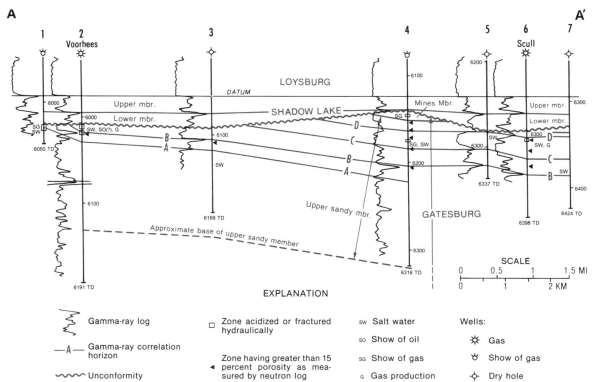

Figure 38B–26. Cross section of Lower Ordovician and Upper Cambrian formations in western Crawford County (modified from Wagner, Figure 3, 1966a, p. 153). Gas production in the Beaver Center (Voorhees well) and Scull pools was related to structure and the presence of an unconformity at the top of the Cambrian section. See Figure 38B–25 for the location of the cross section. Vertical measurements are depth in feet.

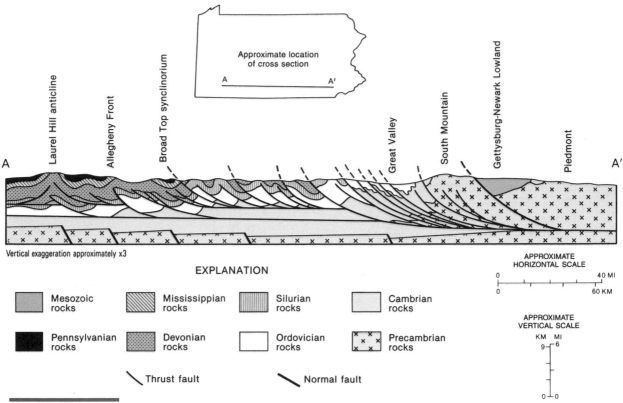

Figure 38B–27. Generalized cross section across the "Eastern Overthrust Belt" in southern Pennsylvania (modified from Harper and Laughrey, 1982, p. 5). Multiple repetitions of potential reservoir rocks occur in the highly distorted stratigraphic section. Essentially undisturbed sedimentary rocks may occur beneath the lowest décollement surface, and these rocks may have the greatest potential for undiscovered hydrocarbon resources in the belt.

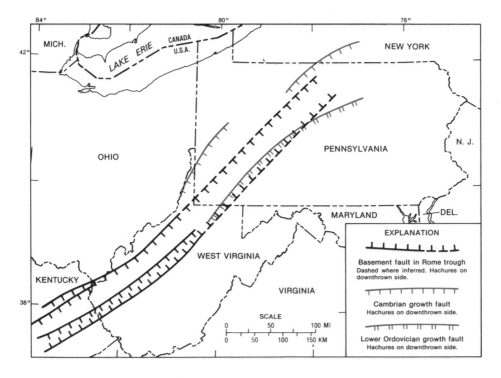

Figure 38B–28. The approximate location of the Rome trough in Pennsylvania. This series of down-to-the-east basement faults, the existence of which is known for certain only in Kentucky and West Virginia, can be inferred from growth faults in Cambrian and Ordovician rocks (position of growth faults from Wagner, © 1976, Figures 7 and 10, p. 422 and 425, reprinted by permission of the American Association of Petroleum Geologists). Cambrian and Ordovician rocks deposited in the Rome trough during fault movement may be hydrocarbon reservoirs, but this has yet to be confirmed.

rocks, as well as the relatively unaltered section beneath the severely deformed section, may hold the key to future production.

2. Deep drilling along the northern extension of the Rome trough (Figure 38B–28). Some of Pennsylvania's larger companies may be interested in attempting to locate potential traps in the Ordovician and Cambrian carbonate sections associated with deep-seated faulting (e.g., the Cambrian growth faults of Wagner, 1976). The Cambrian and Ordovician sections represent the greatest potential for significant new hydrocarbon resources in western Pennsylvania. Little serious attention has yet to be directed to these rocks.

3. Deep drilling in the Mesozoic rocks of the Gettysburg and Newark basins (Figure 38B–1) in southeastern Pennsylvania.[1] Some oil and gas have been found in the Mesozoic rift basins south of the Gettysburg and Newark basins, and correlative basins on the west coast of Africa have had commercial production for many years. Two wells drilled in the Newark basin in 1985 and 1987 were

[1]Although Mesozoic rocks are significantly younger than Middle Devonian, wells in these rocks are considered to be "deep" primarily because of their depths.

unproductive, but one had gas shows over a 3,000-foot interval in the Triassic Lockatong Formation. The proximity of the basins to the large gas markets along the eastern seaboard makes further exploration for commercial hydrocarbons from Triassic and Jurassic sediments highly attractive.

RECOMMENDED FOR FURTHER READING

Diecchio, R. J. (1985), *Regional controls of gas accumulation in Oriskany Sandstone, central Appalachian basin,* AAPG Bulletin, v. 69, p. 722–732.

Ebright, J. R., Fettke, C. R., and Ingham, A. I. (1949), *East Fork-Wharton gas field, Potter County, Pennsylvania,* Pennsylvania Geological Survey, 4th ser., Mineral Resource Report 30, 43 p.

Harper, J. A., Laughrey, C. D., and Lytle, W. S., compilers (1982), *Oil and gas fields of Pennsylvania,* Pennsylvania Geological Survey, 4th ser., Map 3, scale 1:250,000, 2 sheets.

Piotrowski, R. G. (1981), *Geology and natural gas production of the Lower Silurian Medina Group and equivalent rock units in Pennsylvania,* Pennsylvania Geological Survey, 4th ser., Mineral Resource Report 82, 21 p.

Wescott, W. A. (1982), *Nature of porosity in Tuscarora Sandstone (Lower Silurian) in the Appalachian basin,* Oil and Gas Journal, v. 80, no. 34, p. 159–173.

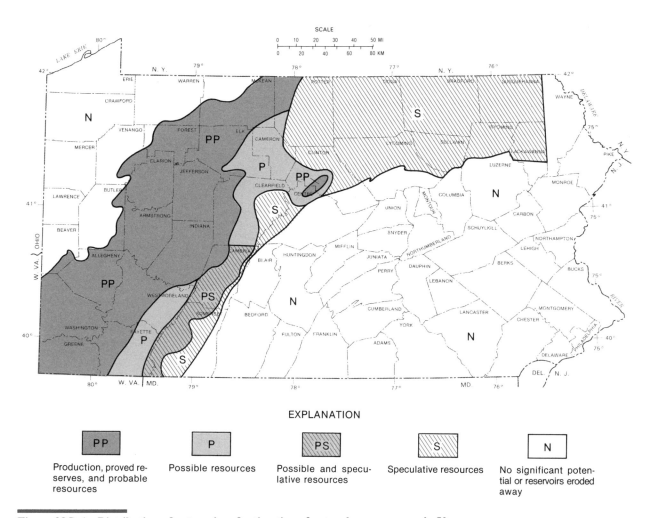

SCALE

| 0 | 10 | 20 | 30 | 40 | 50 MI |

| 0 | 20 | 40 | 60 | 80 KM |

EXPLANATION

PP — Production, proved reserves, and probable resources

P — Possible resources

PS — Possible and speculative resources

S — Speculative resources

N — No significant potential or reservoirs eroded away

Figure 38C–1. Distribution of categories of estimation of natural gas resources in Upper Devonian and Mississippian sandstones.

530

CHAPTER 38C   PETROLEUM—GUIDE TO UNDISCOVERED RECOVERABLE NATURAL GAS RESOURCES

REGINALD P. BRIGGS
Geomega, Inc.
101 Algonquin Road
Pittsburgh, PA 15241

DEREK B. TATLOCK
Tatlock Exploration, Inc.
920 Woodland Road
Pittsburgh, PA 15237

This chapter is an abbreviated and revised version of a report (Geomega, Inc., 1983) prepared by the authors for the Pennsylvania Oil and Gas Association (POGA) and the Pennsylvania Natural Gas Association, and it is with POGA's kind permission that the report is reviewed here. The 1983 report was based on data through 1982. This version was completed in early 1989 and includes adjustments of estimated resources to reflect post-1982 developments.

INTRODUCTION

The total quantity of natural gas in the rocks of Pennsylvania is vast. The purpose of this chapter is to provide estimates of how much of this gas ultimately will prove recoverable. When working within the huge framework of Pennsylvania's gas resources, it is necessary to be consciously conservative. In considering the estimates presented, readers must bear this conservative attitude in mind. The gas-resource categories used by the authors are consistent with the categories of nationwide resource estimates used by the Potential Gas Agency (1983). The categories of undiscovered recoverable resources are defined, generally, as follows:

Probable—Resources that are believed discoverable and recoverable without significant advances over discovery and/or recovery techniques employed at the time of this writing.

Possible—Resources having a lesser degree of assurance of discovery and recovery, chiefly because of sparse data and information.

Speculative—Resources estimated chiefly on the basis of the geological framework and having a still lower degree of assurance of discovery. It is generally implied that advances in technology would be required for discovery and/or recovery. Unlike the practice of the Potential Gas Agency, however, this category is not restricted, necessarily, to new formations or provinces.

To the authors' knowledge, there are no other publicly available estimates of undiscovered natural gas resources in Pennsylvania. The Potential Gas Agency annually makes estimates for groups of states, however, and Pennsylvania is one of 19 states in the agency's Reporting Area A. The U.S. Geological Survey (Dolton and others, 1981) also has provided estimates for regions of the country but used divisions based on geologic rather than state boundaries. It is the opinion of Gordon Dolton, lead author of the

U.S. Geological Survey report, that the portion of a regional resource estimate assignable to an individual state is probably about the same ratio as the annual gas production of the region to the annual gas production of the state (personal communication, 1983). Applying this rule of thumb to the U.S. Geological Survey regional estimates, one arrives at the following estimates of potential resources in Pennsylvania: 2,000 billion cubic feet at the 95-percent confidence level; 6,300 billion cubic feet at the 50-percent confidence level; and 14,300 billion cubic feet at the 5-percent confidence level. Application of the same general rule to the 1983 estimates by the Potential Gas Agency yields the following results: probable resources, 8,400 billion cubic feet; possible resources, 2,500 billion cubic feet; speculative resources, 10,300 billion cubic feet; and total potential resources in the state, 21,200 billion cubic feet. The U.S. Geological Survey's estimates do not include inferred resources, which, by the Survey's definition, are more or less comparable to probable resources as defined by the Potential Gas Agency. Accordingly, the Survey's estimates are more conservative than those of the Agency.

The above extrapolations of regional estimates from the U.S. Geological Survey and the Potential Gas Agency provide useful frames of reference for the state, from the top down as it were. Working rather from the bottom up, the authors of this chapter estimated resources in seven general geologic settings, grouped as one of two types, conventional or unconventional. The authors consider resources in conventional settings as those that could be recoverable with equipment and practices currently available to the petroleum industry. Those settings labeled unconventional have generally different conditions. The settings used are as follows:

Conventional

Upper Devonian and Mississippian sandstones
Lower and Middle Devonian Huntersville/ Ridgeley interval and related Upper Silurian to Lower Devonian reservoirs
Lower Silurian Medina Group and related Silurian stratigraphic-trap reservoirs
Lower Silurian Tuscarora Formation and deeper structural- and structural/stratigraphic-trap reservoirs
Cambrian and Ordovician strata beneath the décollement of the "Eastern Overthrust Belt"

Unconventional

Middle and Upper Devonian shales
Pennsylvanian and Permian coal beds

Another geologic setting that was considered conventional is the Mesozoic rocks of the Newark and Gettysburg basins. However, two test wells drilled into Mesozoic rocks in York County in 1962 yielded no natural gas, and two other wells, one each in Bucks and Montgomery Counties, drilled in 1985 and 1987, were also unfavorable for commercial production. In the 1987 test well, hydrocarbons were encountered in the Triassic Lockatong Formation, but they had undergone a heating event and, as a result, are overmature (John A. Harper, personal communication, 1989). Accordingly, speculation on Mesozoic natural gas resources appears unjustified at this time.

Although there is conventional production locally from Pennsylvanian and Permian coal beds and Devonian shales, they are labeled unconventional for the chief reason that widespread and large-scale recovery of natural gas from these settings is viewed as requiring significantly changed gas-supply, economic, technological, and/or legal conditions.

Methods used in the estimation of potential resources differed from setting to setting, chiefly owing to differences in available data and the geology. Factors used in each setting are given in Table 38C–1, and most are self-explanatory. Cultural constraints include urbanized areas. Institutional constraints are mainly state and federal forests and parks. The principal industrial constraints are gas-storage fields. The significance of factors to individual settings was largely a function of the availability and completeness of data. For example, there has been no production from strata under the "Eastern Overthrust Belt" décollement; therefore, production data were of no significance to the estimation. Significance in some cases, however, was a matter of judgment. Provided at the bottom of Table 38C–1 is the authors' confidence of the estimates for each setting. By rating two settings 9, the authors considered that other investigators of comparable experience, working independently and conservatively with the same data, would develop estimates of resources for these reservoirs not greatly different (neither larger by a third, nor smaller by a quarter) from those of the authors'. The rating of 2 for strata under the "Eastern Overthrust Belt" means that other investigators might well arrive at very different estimates.

NATURAL GAS IN UPPER DEVONIAN AND MISSISSIPPIAN SANDSTONES

Figure 38C–1 shows the distribution of resource categories in Upper Devonian and Mississippian sand-

Table 38C–1. *Relative Significance of Factors Used in Estimation of Potential Natural Gas Resources[1] and Confidence in Estimates*

Factor	Geologic setting						
	Upper Devonian and Mississippian sandstones	Huntersville-Ridgeley interval and related reservoirs	Medina Group and related reservoirs	Tuscarora Formation and deeper reservoirs	Cambrian and Ordovician strata beneath the "Eastern Overthrust Belt"	Middle and Upper Devonian shales	Pennsylvanian and Permian coal beds
Areal extent of units	S	S	S	S	S	S	S
Thickness, volume, and/or tonnage of units	S	U	S	M	S	S	S
Structural relations	U	S	M	S	S	S	M
Proximity to producing areas	S	U	S	U	M	U	M
Production histories and/or declines	S	S	S	U	M	U	U
Open-flow, emission, and/or pressure data	S	S	U	U	M	S	S
Success rates	S	S	S	S	M	M	M
Cultural, institutional, and/or industrial constraints	S	U	S	M	M	S	U
Terrain constraints	S	M	U	M	M	U	U
Extraregional and/or out-of-state information	M	M	U	M	S	S	M
Authors' confidence in estimates, from 10 (greatest) to 1 (least)	9	7	8	4	2	5	9

[1]S, significant; U, useful; M, marginal to insignificant.

stones. Based largely on published sources (Piotrowski and Harper, 1979; Berg and others, 1980; Harper and others, 1982), the "shallow-gas-producing belt" was identified and subsequently subdivided into areas of probable, possible, and speculative potential. The sandstones thin westward and northwestward. In those directions, they become oil-bearing in part and have questionable gas potential; therefore, estimates were not made for the northwestern counties. Reservoirs in this setting are almost entirely the sandstones themselves. Gas recovery is from zones of relatively high primary porosity, which, in recent decades, are commonly enhanced by stimulation. Relatively impermeable enveloping shales entrap the gas. Over 90 percent of the wells drilled in this setting were completed as producers. However, 10 percent of these completions were commercially marginal, so a conservative success factor of 80 percent was used. Estimates of recoverable resources for each county are presented in Figure 38C–2.

NATURAL GAS IN THE HUNTERSVILLE-RIDGELEY INTERVAL AND RELATED RESERVOIRS

Huntersville-Ridgeley production, traditionally "Onondaga-Oriskany" in industry practice, is mostly from structural traps, chiefly upthrown blocks parallel to the trend of the Appalachian Mountains. There has been relatively minor production from other units in generally similar structural settings, for example, the Upper Silurian to Lower Devonian Keyser Formation and Helderberg Group carbonate sequence. For the present purpose of resource estimation, such units are included with the Huntersville-Ridgeley interval. Traditional exploration targets have been the crests of surface anticlines, identified by geologic mapping, and these targets largely have been tested with significant success. Refinements in seismic exploration techniques

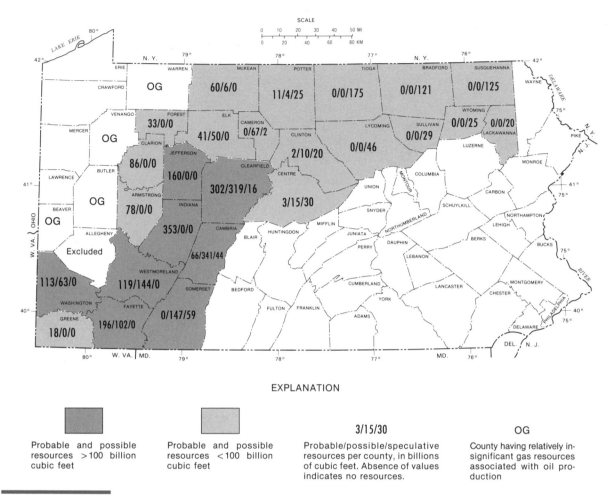

EXPLANATION

Probable and possible resources >100 billion cubic feet	Probable and possible resources <100 billion cubic feet	

3/15/30

Probable/possible/speculative resources per county, in billions of cubic feet. Absence of values indicates no resources.

OG

County having relatively insignificant gas resources associated with oil production

Figure 38C–2. Estimated undiscovered natural gas resources in Upper Devonian and Mississippian sandstones. No estimates were made for Allegheny County in the belief that the press of urbanization made significant additional natural gas activity unlikely.

now allow the identification of previously obscure targets not identifiable at the surface. In particular, the vicinity of western Somerset County has been thoroughly explored seismically and tested by drilling, with appreciable success. To acquire a grasp on what proportion of untested acreage elsewhere may contain similar traps, the Somerset area was used as a model. Drilling in the model area was chiefly in two discrete periods, 1957 through 1965 for targets found using traditional methods, and 1973 through 1981 for targets based on seismic evaluation. Data from these two periods were compared in detail, and a rationale was developed that allowed extrapolation of the structurally obscure target situation to other parts of the state. Figure 38C–3 shows the location of the model area and the distribution of areas of greater to lesser favorability that were developed. Within each of these areas, the authors projected different acreages and proportions of probable, possible, and speculative resources. Areas

of past and existing Huntersville-Ridgeley production and gas-storage fields were excluded from the calculations, as were areas of other deep-gas production. Figure 38C–4 shows estimates, by county, of undiscovered resources recoverable from this setting.

NATURAL GAS IN THE MEDINA GROUP AND TUSCARORA FORMATION AND RELATED RESERVOIRS

For the purpose of estimating potential gas resources, the stratigraphically equivalent basal Silurian Medina and Tuscarora strata were separated into two "packages." The Medina Group package includes other Silurian reservoirs, such as the Lockport Dolomite, that locally are productive within the area dominated by Medina production and potential. The Tus-

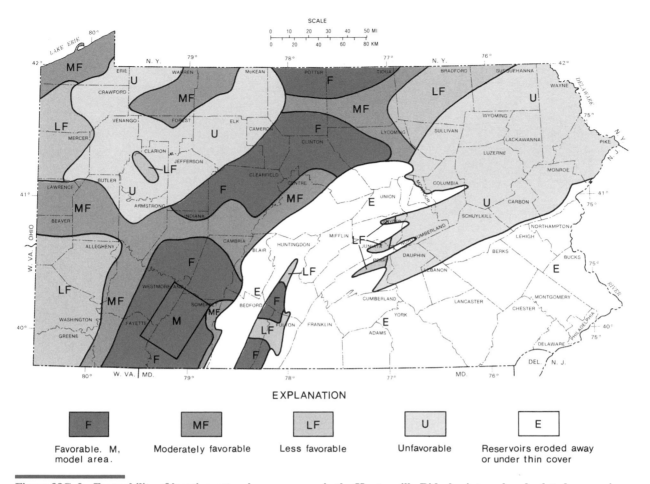

EXPLANATION

F	MF	LF	U	E
Favorable. M, model area.	Moderately favorable	Less favorable	Unfavorable	Reservoirs eroded away or under thin cover

Figure 38C–3. Favorability of locating natural gas resources in the Huntersville-Ridgeley interval and related reservoirs.

carora Formation package includes the Tuscarora plus the Ordovician Oswego and Bald Eagle Formations, Utica Shale, and Trenton-Black River carbonates, and the Cambrian and Ordovician clastics and carbonates. The rationale is that gas from the Medina package is mostly stratigraphically controlled, whereas gas from the Tuscarora package occurs mostly in structurally controlled fracture-porosity traps. An exception to the latter case occurs in northwestern Pennsylvania, where the potential for production from the Ordovician Beekmantown Group and Upper Cambrian carbonates or clastics is related to unconformity traps.

Lower Silurian Medina Group and Related Silurian Stratigraphic-Trap Reservoirs

The Medina Group and related reservoirs have resource potential in northwestern Pennsylvania (Figure 38C–5). The southeastern limit of this area coincides generally with the zone where the Cabot Head Shale thins and the Grimsby and Whirlpool Sand-

stones coalesce to form the Tuscarora Formation (Piotrowski, 1981; Harper and others, 1982).

Areas where the potential is considered probable are associated with existing fields and include developments within known fields and extensions approximately 2 miles beyond major fields or clusters of fields (Figure 38C–5). The remainder of the Medina area is considered to contain possible natural gas resources. Historically, 90 to 95 percent of wells completed in the Medina Group in Erie County, northern Crawford County, and western Warren County have been successful; hence, a 90-percent success factor was utilized in these areas. A slightly lower success rate, 84 percent, was used elsewhere.

Lower Silurian Tuscarora Formation and Deeper Structural-Trap and Structural/Stratigraphic-Trap Reservoirs

The Tuscarora and deeper formations are recognized as high-risk exploratory targets and have

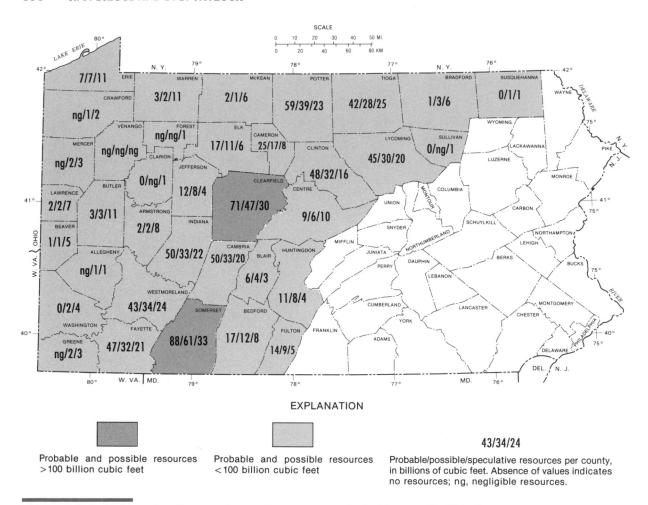

EXPLANATION

Probable and possible resources >100 billion cubic feet

Probable and possible resources <100 billion cubic feet

43/34/24

Probable/possible/speculative resources per county, in billions of cubic feet. Absence of values indicates no resources; ng, negligible resources.

Figure 38C–4. Estimated undiscovered natural gas resources in the Huntersville-Ridgeley interval and related reservoirs.

been placed in the speculative category, except for relatively small areas of possible potential that are on trend or adjacent to known fields. The reservoirs in the Tuscarora Formation package have little effective primary porosity. Locally, fractured reservoirs for gas accumulation are present owing to faulting, folding, or possible draping over relict structures. Fracturing also has facilitated dolomitization of carbonates, such as in the Trenton-Black River sequence, forming potential reservoirs.

Gas was discovered in only three of a total of 19 test wells drilled to the Tuscarora through 1985, a 16-percent success rate. During the period from 1963 through 1965, 14 test wells were drilled into Cambrian strata in Crawford County; two of these produced gas from the Gatesburg Formation. Two successful wells were drilled to Oswego (Bald Eagle) strata in Clinton and Lycoming Counties in the 1980's.

Because reservoir porosity is structurally controlled, an area of deformation most likely to have affected the Tuscarora and deeper rocks was identified. This area is essentially bordered on the east by the Allegheny Front and on the west and northwest by the Chestnut Ridge and Sabinsville anticlines (see Chapter 20). It is identified as the larger of the more favorable prospective areas (TS1) on Figure 38C–5. The less favorable TS2 area west of the large TS1 area has a lesser likelihood of widespread fracture porosity. An area in Bedford, Fulton, and Huntingdon Counties could have undergone deformation greater than that west of the Allegheny Front, but here the Tuscarora is at a relatively shallow depth and locally could be badly broken up. If that is the case, any gas that it contained would probably have been largely vented to the atmosphere. This area is labeled partly TS1 and partly TS2 on Figure 38C–5. The large TS2

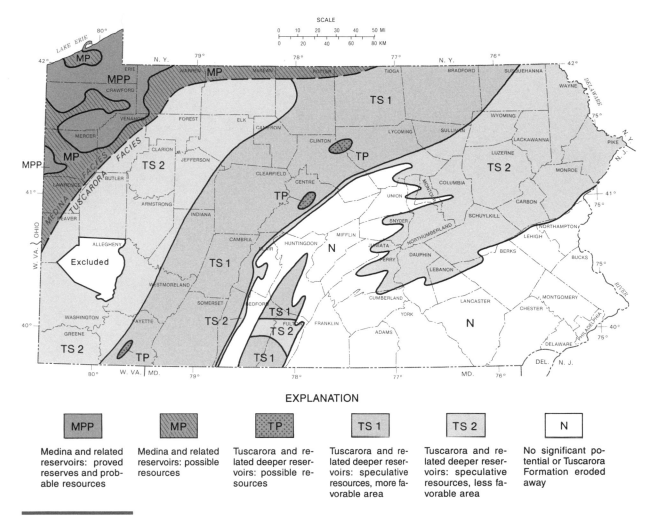

EXPLANATION

MPP	MP	TP	TS 1	TS 2	N
Medina and related reservoirs: proved reserves and probable resources	Medina and related reservoirs: possible resources	Tuscarora and related deeper reservoirs: possible resources	Tuscarora and related deeper reservoirs: speculative resources, more favorable area	Tuscarora and related deeper reservoirs: speculative resources, less favorable area	No significant potential or Tuscarora Formation eroded away

Figure 38C–5. Distribution of categories of estimation of natural gas resources in the Medina Group and Tuscarora Formation and related reservoirs. No estimates were made for Allegheny County in the belief that the press of urbanization made significant additional natural gas activity unlikely.

area in the eastern part of the state was assigned this status chiefly because of sparse data. It is a reasonable speculation that the Tuscarora package beneath the anthracite coal fields in this area (see Chapter 36) may have been subjected to excessive heat and, therefore, possibly contains no extractable hydrocarbons. Zones in this TS2 area where strata of the package are at a shallow depth may have some potential. The part of the area labeled N in Centre County and vicinity on Figure 38C–5 is underlain by potential reservoirs deeper than the Tuscarora but above the "Eastern Overthrust Belt" décollement, such as the Gatesburg Formation. Test wells have been drilled in this area without known success, so the authors hesitate to assign potential for gas production here. Figure 38C–6 shows estimates by county for the Medina, Tuscarora, and related reservoirs.

SPECULATIVE NATURAL GAS UNDER THE "EASTERN OVERTHRUST BELT"

The theory of the "Eastern Overthrust Belt" suggests that the highly faulted and folded metamorphic and igneous rocks of the eastern United States Piedmont, and the rocks of much of the folded and faulted Appalachians, are a detached allochthonous mass above a deep, nearly horizontal décollement that overlies relatively less disturbed, largely non-

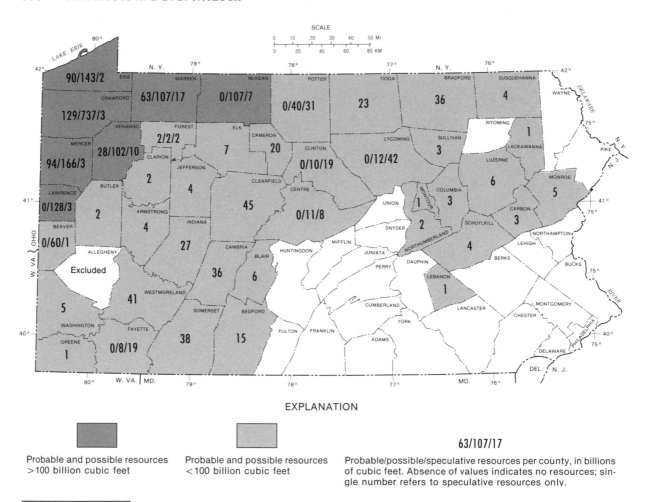

EXPLANATION

Probable and possible resources
>100 billion cubic feet

Probable and possible resources
<100 billion cubic feet

63/107/17

Probable/possible/speculative resources per county, in billions
of cubic feet. Absence of values indicates no resources; single number refers to speculative resources only.

Figure 38C–6. Estimated undiscovered natural gas resources in the Medina Group and Tuscarora Formation and related reservoirs. No estimates were made for Allegheny County in the
belief that the press of urbanization made significant additional natural gas activity unlikely.
Counties and parts of counties included in the large eastern TS2 area and the small south-
central TS1 and TS2 areas of Figure 38C–5 that contain no numbers are considered to have
negligible natural gas potential.

metamorphosed Cambrian and Ordovician strata. It
is widely understood that significant shows of natural gas have been encountered in rocks beneath the
décollement plane in the Carolinas, but no confirma-
tion of production has been reported. If gas is present under the décollement south of Pennsylvania, it
is possible that gas is also present under the décollement in Pennsylvania. Results of a 1983 test in a relatively shallow overthrust area northeast of Albany,
N. Y., were negative, however.

Publicly available data bearing on the overthrust
in Pennsylvania are sparse. Geologists of the Pennsylvania Geological Survey projected deep thrusting
in cross sections accompanying the *Geologic Map of
Pennsylvania* (Berg and others, 1980). A deep test

well in Somerset County in 1974 may have penetrated
the décollement. A 1982 test well in Mifflin County
was rumored to have been aimed at the décollement,
but faulting was encountered, and the well was completed as a dry hole at a depth appreciably less than
that suggested for the décollement. No shows of gas
were reported.

Figure 38C–7 shows subdivisions of Pennsylvania relevant to the "Eastern Overthrust Belt." The
line separating area S from area D is the northwest
limit of the overthrust for the present purpose. In
central Pennsylvania, it coincides with the Allegheny
Front. To the southwest, it is shown crossing west
of the Front on the basis of differences in structural
style at the surface and data from West Virginia. To

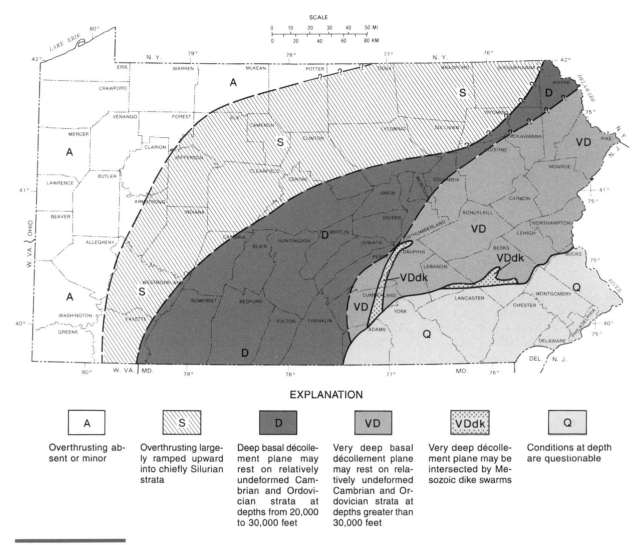

EXPLANATION

A	S	D	VD	VDdk	Q
Overthrusting absent or minor	Overthrusting largely ramped upward into chiefly Silurian strata	Deep basal décollement plane may rest on relatively undeformed Cambrian and Ordovician strata at depths from 20,000 to 30,000 feet	Very deep basal décollement plane may rest on relatively undeformed Cambrian and Ordovician strata at depths greater than 30,000 feet	Very deep décollement plane may be intersected by Mesozoic dike swarms	Conditions at depth are questionable

Figure 38C–7. Subdivisions relevant to the "Eastern Overthrust Belt."

the northeast, it is carried northwest of the arc of the Wilkes-Barre–Scranton (Wyoming Valley) synclinal basin. Potential resources in areas A and S exist in settings other than the "Eastern Overthrust Belt." Area Q includes all outcropping rocks from the northern and northwestern borders of the Mesozoic Newark and Gettysburg basins south and southeastward to the state line. No speculation on potential gas under the overthrust in area Q is justified, owing to the lack of even speculative consensus on the nature of the rocks at depth and to the likely presence of Mesozoic dike swarms. Because Mesozoic dikes also crop out in the areas labeled VDdk, these areas are also excluded from calculation.

In areas D and VD, the décollement plane possibly dips generally southeasterly from a depth of

about 20,000 feet to more than 30,000 feet. To find gas in Cambrian and Ordovician clastics and carbonates under the "Overthrust" in area D, one probably would have to drill deeper than 20,000 feet; in the areas labeled VD, deeper than 30,000 feet. To produce commercially from such depth, each well must be enormously productive. Accordingly, a yield of 10 million cubic feet of gas per acre was assumed for estimation. It was further assumed that just 1 percent of area D may produce and that 0.5 percent of area VD may produce. On this highly speculative basis, the total recoverable resource may be 850 billion cubic feet (Table 38C–2). There is no justification for "Overthrust" estimates by county.

It is emphasized that this speculative total does not duplicate estimates provided for other settings

Table 38C–2. *Speculative Recoverable Natural Gas Resources in Strata Beneath the "Eastern Overthrust Belt" in Pennsylvania*

	Area (square miles)	Speculative resources (billion cubic feet)[1]
Area D	10,100	650
Area VD	6,200	200
Total	16,300	850

[1]Standard cubic feet measured at 60°F and 1 atmosphere pressure.

that coincide areally with the "Overthrust." For example, estimates for the Tuscarora package in Somerset County (Figure 38C–6) are in addition to the "Overthrust" estimates; these reservoirs lie above the décollement.

NATURAL GAS IN DEVONIAN SHALES

Erie County accounts for almost all shale-gas production in Pennsylvania. Local shale-gas production, or potential for production, has been reported from sporadically located wells in eight other counties, and shows are reported from another 15 of the 32 counties considered in the Devonian shale estimates (Figure 38C–9).

It is well documented that all shale-gas production in Ohio and West Virginia has been from areas where black-shale sections are at least 100 feet thick (Tetra Tech, Inc., 1981b, d), and the same is believed to be true in Pennsylvania. No significant quantities of gas are known to have been produced from shales more than 5,000 feet below ground surface in Pennsylvania or in nearby parts of adjacent states.

Natural fracture permeability is the key to shale-gas production now and for at least the middle-term future. In the Erie County shale-gas fields, where most of the shales are less than 1,000 feet deep, the locally intense fracture systems that form reservoirs (Piotrowski, 1978) may be attributable to glacial isostasy. In the Middle Devonian shales near the Allegheny Front, significant fracturing also is likely, because the subjacent Huntersville-Ridgeley sequence is

highly faulted locally. The extent of natural fracturing in shales elsewhere in Pennsylvania is not known. However, a small-scale LANDSAT lineament map of Pennsylvania (Kowalik and Gold, 1976) shows extensive linear features that may be interpreted as deep fracture systems. An analysis of a more detailed West Virginia LANDSAT lineament map (Reynolds, 1979) shows that, in northern West Virginia, adjacent to Pennsylvania, 12 percent of the area is within 0.5 mile of zones where three or more lineaments intersect each other; another 15 percent is within 1 mile. On the basis of structure-to-stress ratios (Komar and Bolyard in Tetra Tech, Inc., 1981a, b, c, d), a similar distribution is predictable for Pennsylvania. Perhaps 12 percent of the ground is favorable for shale-gas drilling, 15 percent is moderately favorable, and the remainder is of lower or questionable favorability.

Figure 38C–8 shows the relative favorability for shale-gas exploration in various parts of the state based on black-shale thickness (100 feet or greater), depth to shale (less than 5,000 feet), proximity to known productive wells and shows of gas, and the projected density of intersecting fractures. No estimates of potential gas recovery were made for areas indicated as unfavorable on this basis. Gas estimates were calculated using a factor of 0.2 cubic feet of gas from each cubic foot of shale, based on estimated Erie County production and shale volumes. This ratio is consistent with laboratory determinations (Tetra Tech, Inc., 1981a, b, c, d).

Figure 38C–9 shows shale-gas estimates by county. "Probable" for shale-gas purposes suggests that, at some future time, this gas volume may well prove extractable, given appropriate economic conditions and/or modest technical advances. "Possible" suggests that advances would be required in both exploration methodology and stimulation techniques, and that more favorable economic conditions would have to prevail. "Speculative" mostly implies that startling breakthroughs in stimulation techniques would be required to allow production.

According to Tetra Tech, Inc. (1981c), "about 29 trillion cubic feet of gas are expected to be recoverable using presently available methods" from shales in the Appalachian, Illinois, and Michigan basins. Proportionally, it then appears that perhaps 7.5 trillion cubic feet could be recovered from shale in Pennsylvania using current practices. The phrase "presently available methods" suggests that this amount would be comparable to the estimate for the authors' "probable" category. If such is the case, then, in the authors'

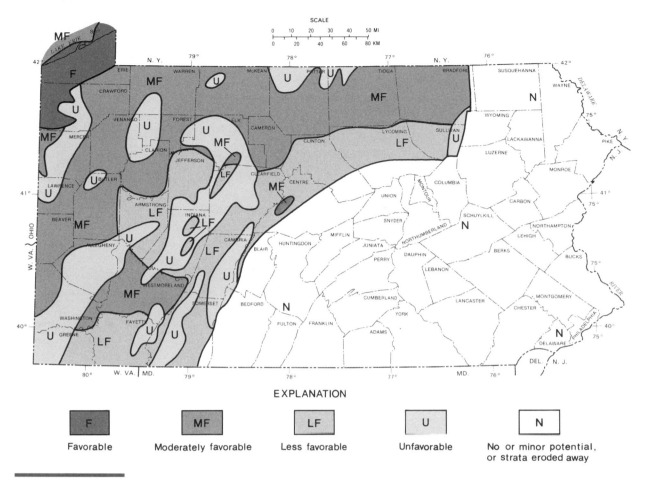

Figure 38C–8. Favorability of locating natural gas resources in Devonian shales.

view, the projection of 7.5 trillion cubic feet is most unlikely. The estimate of probable shale gas given herein is 768 billion cubic feet, an order of magnitude lower. The authors' total estimate, more than two-thirds (highly) speculative, is of the same order of magnitude as the "expected" 7.5 trillion cubic feet.

NATURAL GAS IN COAL BEDS

Natural gas in coal beds is called "methane" by the coal-mining industry, but the methane molecule, CH_4, is the dominant constituent of virtually all natural gas, so the usage by the coal industry is misleading. In actuality, coal-bed gas is indistinguishable from natural gas in some conventional reservoirs (Price and Headlee, 1937).

Natural gas is common in essentially all coal beds. For example, as a safety measure, about 8.8 billion cubic feet of gas was vented to the atmosphere from just four mines in Greene and Washington Counties during 1972 (McCulloch and others, 1975). Moreover, since the 1890's, natural gas has been produced conventionally from coal-bed reservoirs in a few localities. Production for consumption, though, has been minor compared to the quantities vented. Only since the 1970's has much attention been focused on the resource potential of natural gas in coal beds (Deul, 1975). Low reservoir pressure probably is the chief technical constraint to greater use of coal-bed gas as a fuel. The legal status of natural gas in coal in Pennsylvania, however, is a still greater constraint to significant development. Owners of natural gas rights claim that coal-bed gas is theirs to capture, whereas owners of coal in place claim they own the contained gas. A 1978 court ruling in Greene County was generally in favor of the owners of gas rights, but it was later nullified by a ruling of the Superior Court of

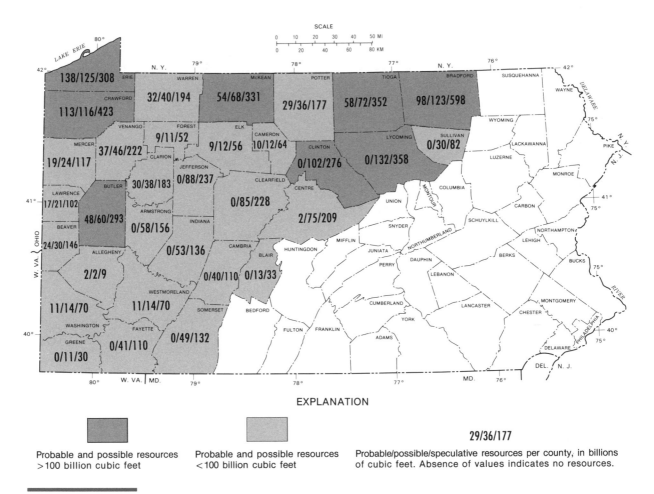

Figure 38C–9. Estimated undiscovered natural gas resources in Devonian shales.

Pennsylvania. Without this legal constraint, a significant part of the coal-bed gas characterized as "probable" could be counted as reserves.

Most data on coal-bed gas in Pennsylvania are from the blocky, high-volatile bituminous Pittsburgh coal bed of the Pennsylvanian Monongahela Group. Five hundred feet or more beneath ground surface, its gas content averages approximately 150 cubic feet per ton of coal. Adsorbed gas released by coal beds ranges from about 60 percent in blocky coal beds to as much as 96 percent in friable coal beds (McCulloch and others, 1975). To be conservative in the determination of estimated gas, values of gas content and recoverability from the blocky Pittsburgh coal bed were applied to all bituminous coal beds. Sixty percent of 150 cubic feet of gas per ton of coal means that 90 cubic feet per ton will be recoverable. At any given depth, anthracite coal adsorbs at least twice as much

gas as high-volatile bituminous coal (Kim, 1977), so anthracite estimates were based on the potential recovery of 180 cubic feet of gas per ton of coal.

The remainder of the method was essentially a specialized coal-reserve study culminating in the multiplication of the resulting coal tonnages by the above gas constants. In the bituminous fields, coal-bed areas within 2 miles of outcrops or mines were excluded. Estimates for gas in the Allegheny Formation and Monongahela Group were calculated separately. Coal beds in the Pottsville Formation and Conemaugh Group are of such sporadic occurrence in outcrop that projection to depth was not justifiable. No estimates were made for the Broad Top coal field, chiefly in Huntingdon County, or the "Bloss" coal beds, chiefly in Tioga County. In the anthracite fields, areas less than 1 mile from the outcrop of the Llewellyn Formation were excluded to reflect steeply dipping strata. Only

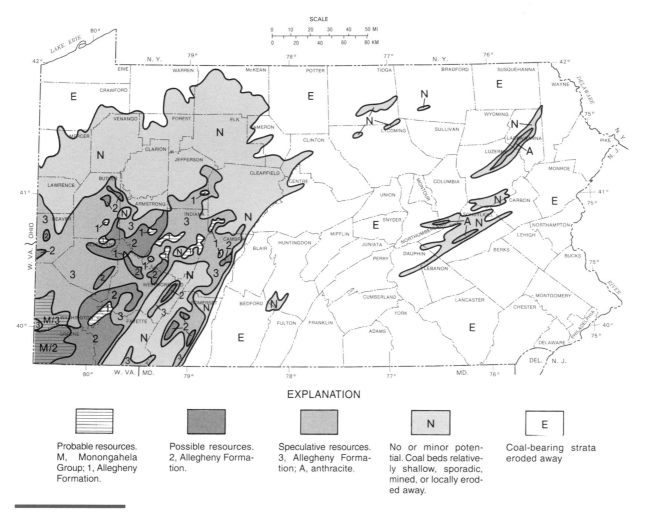

EXPLANATION

Probable resources. M, Monongahela Group; 1, Allegheny Formation.	Possible resources. 2, Allegheny Formation.	Speculative resources. 3, Allegheny Formation; A, anthracite.	N — No or minor potential. Coal beds relatively shallow, sporadic, mined, or locally eroded away.	E — Coal-bearing strata eroded away

Figure 38C–10. Distribution of categories of estimation of natural gas resources in Pennsylvanian and Permian coal beds (see footnote 1 in Table 38C–3).

coal beds more than 5 feet thick in the lower 500 feet of the Llewellyn were included in the calculation. Because there are several other relatively thick coal beds in the Llewellyn Formation and the subjacent Pottsville Formation, resulting estimates of anthracite coal-bed gas are believed to be conservative.

Figure 38C–10 shows the general distribution of the natural gas resource categories for coal beds. Figure 38C–11 shows estimates of undiscovered natural gas resources in coal beds by county. In Table 38C–3, estimates for bituminous and anthracite coal beds are presented.

Kim (1975) estimated that virgin Pittsburgh coal in Greene County contained 375 billion cubic feet of natural gas, and McCulloch and others (1975) reported that the same coal bed in Greene and Washington Counties combined contained over 500 billion

cubic feet of natural gas. Applying the factor of 60-percent recoverable gas, these become, respectively, 225 and 300 billion cubic feet. The authors' total estimates for natural gas in the Monongahela Group in Greene County and in Greene and Washington Counties combined are 260 and 344 billion cubic feet, respectively (Geomega, Inc., 1983). Because the thick Pittsburgh coal bed is the predominant coal bed in the Monongahela Group, this comparison is justification for a superior degree of confidence in the estimates of potentially recoverable coal-bed gas presented here (Table 38C–1).

The estimate for the anthracite region is wholly speculative. However, the large gas constant reported, 675 cubic feet per ton of coal (Kim, 1977), suggests that additional investigation for coal-bed gas in this region may be rewarded.

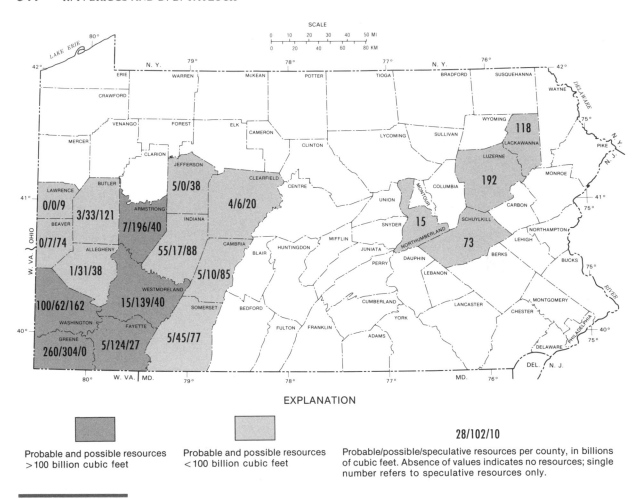

EXPLANATION

Probable and possible resources
> 100 billion cubic feet

Probable and possible resources
< 100 billion cubic feet

28/102/10

Probable/possible/speculative resources per county, in billions
of cubic feet. Absence of values indicates no resources; single
number refers to speculative resources only.

Figure 38C–11. Estimated undiscovered natural gas resources in coal beds.

Table 38C–3. *Estimates of Recoverable Natural Gas Resources in Coal Beds*

(Quantities are in billions of cubic feet)

	Probable	Possible	Speculative	Total
Bituminous coal beds				
Monongahela Group[1]	345	0	0	345
Allegheny Formation	120	973	820	1,913
Subtotal	465	973	820	2,258
Anthracite coal beds	0	0	397	397
Total	465	973	1,217	2,655

[1] Includes relatively minor amounts of coal-bed gas from the Pennsylvanian-Permian Dunkard Group.

SUMMARY OF ESTIMATES

The estimated total of probable, possible, and speculative undiscovered, recoverable natural gas in conventional settings in Pennsylvania is 8,560 billion cubic feet. The total volume of recoverable natural gas resources in unconventional settings may be 11,050 billion cubic feet, for a grand total of 19,610 billion cubic feet. These totals are broken down by individual geologic setting in Table 38C–4 and by counties in Table 38C–5. These estimates in total are not greatly different from and lie between the extrapolations made from the U.S. Geological Survey and Potential Gas Agency regional results, which are given in the introduction.

Figure 38C–12 shows the spatial distribution of estimated total recoverable natural gas resources. For large gas reserves in conventional settings, Figure 38C–12 and Table 38C–5 indicate that one might explore Crawford County, Clearfield County, or counties southwest of Clearfield County. The best gas prospects in unconventional settings are in Crawford and Erie Counties (shale gas), Greene County (mostly coal-bed gas), and Butler County (both shale gas and coal-bed gas). Of interest, too, is the very large, though mostly highly speculative, shale-gas potential in Brad-

Table 38C–4. *Estimates of Undiscovered Recoverable Natural Gas Resources in Pennsylvania by Category and Geologic Setting*

(Quantities are in billions of cubic feet)

	Probable	Possible	Speculative	Total
Conventional settings				
Upper Devonian and Mississippian sandstones	1,641	1,268	737	3,646
Huntersville-Ridgeley interval and related reservoirs	675	474	364	1,513
Medina Group and related reservoirs	406	1,448	0	1,854
Tuscarora Formation and deeper reservoirs	0	188	509	697
Cambrian and Ordovician strata beneath the "Eastern Overthrust Belt"	0	0	850	850
Subtotal	2,722	3,378	2,460	8,560
Unconventional settings				
Devonian shales	768	1,662	5,965	8,395
Pennsylvanian and Permian coal beds	465	973	1,217	2,655
Subtotal	1,233	2,635	7,182	11,050
Grand total	3,955	6,013	9,642	19,610

Possible and probable resources combined

Conventional settings	6,100
Unconventional settings	3,868
Total	9,968

ford County. The occurrence of natural gas under the "Eastern Overthrust" décollement also is highly speculative but remains an exciting challenge to the nerves and wallets of explorationists (Harper and Cozart, 1992, p. 53–54).

NATURAL GAS DEVELOPMENTS DURING THE 1980'S

As is stated in the note at the bottom of the title page of this chapter segment, rationale, methodology, and estimates based on data available for 1982 and earlier years were contained in a report published in 1983 (Geomega, Inc., 1983). The estimates contained in that report were adjusted for this chapter in 1989 to accomodate post-1982 developments. There were 13,667 new gas wells and old gas wells drilled deeper from 1980 through 1989 (Harper and Cozart, 1992, p. 39, Figure 35). Most of these wells produce gas from Upper Devonian sandstones in Indiana, Clearfield, Armstrong, Westmoreland, and Jefferson Counties or from the Medina Group reservoirs in Erie, Crawford, Mercer, Venango, and Warren Counties, and there were Upper Devonian gas discoveries in Clinton and Centre Counties as well (Harper and

Cozart, 1992, p. 42, 50). Despite these developments and activity into the 1990's, the authors believe that their estimates by and large remain valid within the degrees of confidence stated in Table 38C–1, an indication of the overall magnitude of the resource.

PROBLEMS AND FUTURE RESEARCH

National and regional estimates of gas resources are institutionalized in the annual reports of the Potential Gas Agency and in the sporadic estimates prepared by the U.S. Geological Survey. If these are justified, then perhaps it is also appropriate to consider, as an institutional necessity, complete reexamination of potential natural gas resources in Pennsylvania every decade or so.

RECOMMENDED FOR FURTHER READING

Dolton, G. L., Carlson, K. H., Charpentier, R. R., and others (1981), *Estimates of undiscovered recoverable conventional resources of oil and gas in the United States,* U.S. Geological Survey Circular 860, 87 p.

Table 38C–5. *Estimates of Undiscovered Recoverable Natural Gas Resources in Pennsylvania by Category and County*

(Quantities are in billions of cubic feet)

County	Probable[1] C[2]	Probable[1] U[2]	Possible[1] C[2]	Possible[1] U[2]	Speculative[1] C[2]	Speculative[1] U[2]	Total[1] C[2]	Total[1] U[2]
Allegheny	0	3	1	33	1	47	2	83
Armstrong	80	7	2	254	12	196	94	457
Beaver	1	24	62	37	6	220	69	281
Bedford	17	0	12	0	23	0	52	0
Blair	6	0	4	13	9	33	19	46
Bradford	1	98	3	123	164	598	168	819
Butler	3	51	3	93	13	414	19	558
Cambria	116	5	374	50	99	195	589	250
Cameron	25	10	84	12	30	64	139	86
Carbon	0	0	0	0	3	0	3	0
Centre	12	2	32	75	48	209	92	286
Clarion	86	30	0	38	2	183	88	251
Clearfield	373	4	366	91	91	248	830	343
Clinton	50	0	52	102	55	276	157	378
Columbia	0	0	0	0	3	0	3	0
Crawford	129	113	737	116	5	423	871	652
Elk	58	9	61	12	12	56	131	77
Erie[3]	97	138	152	125	13	308	262	571
Fayette	243	5	142	165	40	137	425	307
Forest	35	9	2	11	3	52	40	72
Fulton	14	0	9	0	5	0	28	0
Greene	18	260	2	304	4	0	24	564
Huntingdon	11	0	8	0	4	0	23	0
Indiana	403	55	33	70	48	224	484	349
Jefferson	172	5	8	88	8	275	188	368
Lackawanna	0	0	0	0	21	118	21	118
Lawrence	2	17	130	21	10	111	142	149
Lebanon	0	0	0	0	1	0	1	0
Luzerne	0	0	0	0	6	192	6	192
Lycoming	45	0	42	132	108	358	195	490
McKean	62	54	114	68	13	331	189	453
Mercer	94	19	168	24	6	117	268	160
Monroe	0	0	0	0	5	0	5	0
Montour	0	0	0	0	1	0	1	0
Northumberland	0	0	0	0	2	15	2	15
Perry	0	0	0	0	1	0	1	0
Potter	70	29	84	36	79	177	233	242
Schuylkill	0	0	0	0	4	73	4	73
Somerset	88	5	208	94	130	209	426	308
Sullivan	0	0	0	30	32	82	32	112
Susquehanna	0	0	1	0	130	0	131	0
Tioga	42	58	28	72	224	352	294	482
Venango	28	37	102	46	10	222	140	305
Warren	66	32	109	40	28	194	203	266
Washington	113	111	65	76	9	232	187	419
Westmoreland	162	43	178	174	65	211	405	428
Wyoming	0	0	0	0	25	0	25	0
Subtotal	2,722	1,233	3,378	2,635	1,610	7,182	7,710	11,050
Reservoirs beneath the "Eastern Overthrust Belt"	0	0	0	0	850	0	850	0
Grand total	2,722	1,233	3,378	2,635	2,460	7,182	8,560	11,050
Conventional and unconventional settings combined	3,955		6,013		9,642		19,610	

[1]County estimates for conventional settings do not include reservoirs beneath the "Eastern Overthrust Belt" (see discussion in text).
[2]C, conventional setting; U, unconventional setting.
[3]Includes the Pennsylvania segment of Lake Erie, all of which is in Erie County.

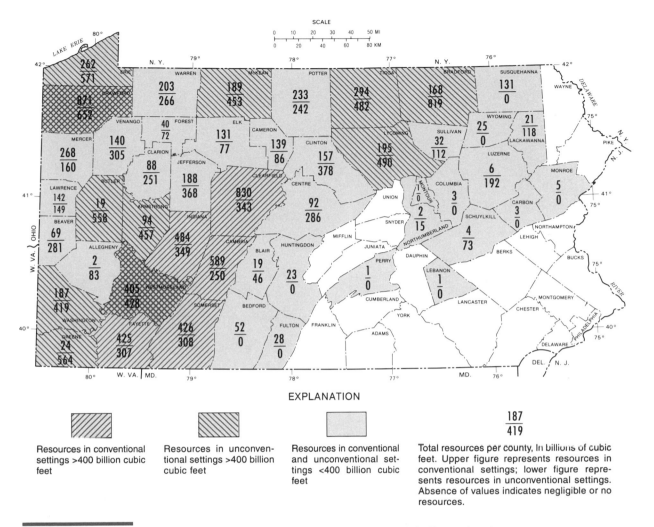

EXPLANATION

Resources in conventional settings >400 billion cubic feet	Resources in unconventional settings >400 billion cubic feet	Resources in conventional and unconventional settings <400 billion cubic feet	$\dfrac{187}{419}$ Total resources per county, in billions of cubic feet. Upper figure represents resources in conventional settings; lower figure represents resources in unconventional settings. Absence of values indicates negligible or no resources.

Figure 38C–12. Estimated undiscovered recoverable natural gas resources in Pennsylvania. Estimates for conventional settings do not include resources in strata below the "Eastern Overthrust Belt."

Geomega, Inc. [Briggs, R. P., and Tatlock, D. B.] (1983), *Estimates of undiscovered recoverable natural gas resources in Pennsylvania,* Bradford, Pa., Pennsylvania Oil and Gas Association, 33 p.

Harper, J. A., and Cozart, C. L. (1992), *Oil and gas developments in Pennsylvania in 1990 with ten-year review and forecast,* Pennsylvania Geological Survey, 4th ser., Progress Report 204, 85 p.

Harper, J. A., Laughrey, C. D., and Lytle, W. S., compilers (1982), *Oil and gas fields of Pennsylvania,* Pennsylvania Geological Survey, 4th ser., Map 3, scale 1:250,000, 2 sheets.

Kim, A. G. (1973), *The composition of coalbed gas,* U.S. Bureau of Mines Report of Investigations 7762, 9 p.

Pees, S. T., and Burgchardt, C. R. (1985), *What to expect from a typical Medina gas well,* World Oil, v. 200, no. 2, p. 37–40, 65.

Piotrowski, R. G. (1981), *Geology and natural gas production of the Lower Silurian Medina Group and equivalent rock units in Pennsylvania,* Pennsylvania Geological Survey, 4th ser., Mineral Resource Report 82, 21 p.

Tetra Tech, Inc. (1981), *Evaluation of Devonian shale potential in Pennsylvania,* U.S. Department of Energy, DOE/METC-119, 56 p.

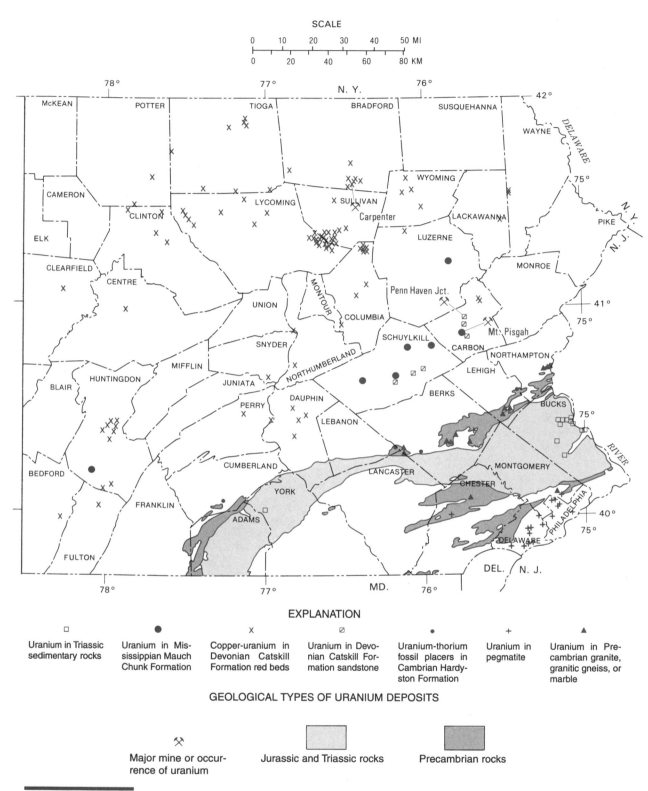

SCALE

0   10   20   30   40   50 MI

0   20   40   60   80 KM

EXPLANATION

□	●	X	◪	•	+	▲
Uranium in Triassic sedimentary rocks	Uranium in Mississippian Mauch Chunk Formation	Copper-uranium in Devonian Catskill Formation red beds	Uranium in Devonian Catskill Formation sandstone	Uranium-thorium fossil placers in Cambrian Hardyston Formation	Uranium in pegmatite	Uranium in Precambrian granite, granitic gneiss, or marble

GEOLOGICAL TYPES OF URANIUM DEPOSITS

⚒ Major mine or occurrence of uranium

☐ Jurassic and Triassic rocks

▨ Precambrian rocks

Figure 39–1. Map of eastern Pennsylvania showing the locations of uranium occurrences, divided according to geological types. Data are from Rose (1970), Ballieul and others (1980), Popper and Martin (1981), Popper (1982), Roe and Martin (1982), and Smith and Hoff (1984). Geologic contacts are from Pennsylvania Geological Survey (1990).

548

CHAPTER 39   URANIUM

ARTHUR W. ROSE
Department of Geosciences
The Pennsylvania State University
University Park, PA 16802

INTRODUCTION

The uranium minerals uraninite, autunite, and torbernite (Table 39–1) were reported by early mineral collectors in pegmatites near Philadelphia prior to 1874 (Genth, 1876). Additional, similar occurrences, as well as carnotite near Jim Thorpe, were discovered by 1922 (Gordon, 1922). During the uranium boom of the 1950's, numerous occurrences were discovered throughout the Paleozoic rocks of the folded Appalachians. About 300 tons of ore was mined from adits of the Mount Pisgah locality (Figure 39–1) near Jim Thorpe. During the renewed boom in the late 1970's, many additional occurrences were discovered (Ballieul and others, 1980; Popper and Martin, 1981; Popper, 1982; Roe and Martin, 1982; Smith and Hoff, 1984), though none appear economic. Thus, Pennsylvania has not yet produced significant uranium, but it ranks high among states of the eastern part of the country in potential for future discoveries.

The distribution of known localities of uranium minerals or distinctly anomalous radioactivity is summarized on Figure 39–1. Most of these are merely

Table 39–1. *Some Minerals Containing or Related to Uranium in Pennsylvania*

Uraninite	UO_{2+x}
Coffinite	$U(SiO_4)_{1-x}(OH)_{4x}$
Carnotite	$K_2(UO_2)_2(VO_4)_2 \cdot 3H_2O$
Tyuyamunite	$Ca(UO_2)_2(VO_4)_2 \cdot 5{-}8H_2O$
Autunite	$Ca(UO_2)_2(PO_4)_2 \cdot 10{-}12H_2O$
Meta-autunite	$Ca(UO_2)_2(PO_4)_2 \cdot 2{-}6H_2O$
Torbernite	$Cu(UO_2)_2(PO_4)_2 \cdot 8{-}12H_2O$
Metatorbernite	$Cu(UO_2)_2(PO_4)_2 \cdot 8H_2O$
Uranophane	$Ca(UO_2)_2Si_2O_7 \cdot 5H_2O$
Clausthalite	$PbSe$

mineral localities, and only one (Mount Pisgah) has definitely produced even a small amount of ore. As can be seen, the occurrences are scattered through the eastern two thirds of the state.

Types of deposits in Pennsylvania are classified geologically in Table 39–2, using analogies to types recognized elsewhere in several cases.

The occurrences in pegmatites and the fossil uranium-thorium placers are not discussed further, because they appear to be of mainly mineralogic interest (Gordon, 1922; Smith, 1978).

OCCURRENCES IN GRANITE, GNEISS, AND MARBLE

Most occurrences in this group are in the Reading Prong (see Chapter 3B) and are associated with Precambrian granite, granitic gneiss, and marble. Some occurrences are also in the vicinity of pegmatite. Thorium is associated with uranium in most of the occurrences. In airborne surveys, the Reading Prong furnishes many more radioactivity anomalies than adjacent regions and is apparently enriched in uranium and thorium (LKB Resources, 1977).

In detail, some uranium occurs in leucogranite, a very light colored variety of granite, and some in granodiorite that has traces of molybdenite (R. C. Smith, personal communication, 1986). Other occurrences are in gneissic granites. At one of these, near Oley in Berks County, the anomalous radioactivity can be traced along poorly exposed shear zones in an area about 0.6 mile long and 0.3 mile wide, in which the uranium content is 0.005 to 0.05 percent (Pennsylvania Geological Survey, 1978). A third group of occurrences is in a belt of Precambrian Franklin Marble near Easton, Northampton County, where the marble is highly altered to serpentine and a variety of other minerals in association with pegmatite. The best known locality is the Williams quarry (Montgomery, 1969), which contains uraninite as well as molybdenite and several secondary uranium minerals.

Some uranium occurrences in this group appear to result from metamorphism of rocks originally containing above-average amounts of uranium. They are also associated with the intrusion of granitic magmas and partial melting, followed by redistribution and concentration of uranium and molybdenum by high-temperature aqueous fluids. Grauch and Ludwig (1979) reported a $^{207}Pb/^{206}Pb$ age of 948 Ma for a uranium-rich sample from the Easton area.

Table 39–2. *Geological Types of Uranium Deposits and Occurrences in Pennsylvania*

Terrane	Class
I. Igneous and metamorphic	A. Pegmatite
	B. Occurrences in granite, gneiss, and marble
II. Sedimentary	A. Fossil uranium-thorium placers, mainly in the basal Cambrian Hardyston Formation
	B. Wyoming-type roll-front sandstone uranium occurrences in the Devonian Catskill Formation
	C. Red-bed copper-uranium occurrences in the Devonian Catskill Formation
	D. Colorado Plateau-type sandstone uranium occurrences in the Mississippian Mauch Chunk Formation
	E. Uranium in Triassic sedimentary rocks

Prospects of the same types were discovered in similar rocks in New Jersey (Ballieul and others, 1980; Popper and Martin, 1981), and R. C. Smith (personal communication, 1986) reported others in Chester County.

WYOMING-TYPE SANDSTONE URANIUM

The major occurrence of Wyoming-type sandstone-uranium deposits in Pennsylvania is in the Devonian Catskill Formation at Penn Haven Junction, on the west side of the Lehigh River about 4 miles north of Jim Thorpe in Carbon County (Figure 39–1). The uranium occurs in a zone several feet thick that curves across bedding in a "roll" (Figure 39–2), similar to those found in major deposits in the state of Wyoming (Klemic and others, 1963; Harshman, 1972). The uranium, at least partly in the form of uraninite, is localized just beneath a relatively coarse grained conglomeratic channel sandstone. Sandstone in the interior of the "roll" is hematite stained, similar to the oxidation observed in the Wyoming deposits, whereas rock composing the "roll" and outside the "roll" is relatively reduced (Schmiermund, 1977; Sevon and others, 1978). A larger, more complex "roll" is present on the east side of the Lehigh River, and other occurrences are sporadically exposed for about a mile downstream. A uranium content of about 0.1 percent appears typical for the zone. Clausthalite (Table 39–1), traces of pyrite, and elevated values of arsenic and vanadium accompany the uranium.

Four exposures on the Lehigh River, about 5 miles south of Penn Haven Junction and just south of Jim Thorpe at Packerton Junction, show similar mineralization in rocks of almost the same stratigraphic interval. Additional occurrences in a similar stratigraphic position occur near Hecla in Schuylkill County.

The uranium of these occurrences is believed to have been transported to the locality in oxidizing groundwater flowing through unconsolidated, permeable channel sandstones of Catskill age, and to have been precipitated by a change from oxidizing to reducing conditions. The sediments have since been consolidated by deep burial and have been folded. The consistent occurrence of uranium in all good exposures of this horizon suggests that more extensive deposits could be present in the vicinity.

RED-BED COPPER-URANIUM OCCURRENCES

A very large number of small copper-uranium occurrences are known in local reduced lenses within the dominantly red mudrock and sandstone of the Catskill Formation in central Pennsylvania (McCauley, 1961; Sevon and others, 1978; Smith and Hoff, 1984; Smith and Rose, 1985) (Figure 39–1). The uranium is in small lenses containing carbonaceous plant fragments. The lenses have typical lateral dimensions of 3 to 30 feet and thicknesses of 4 inches to 6 feet. The copper sulfides chalcocite and digenite are accompanied by small amounts of uranium (20 to 1,000 ppm), rarely as recognizable uraninite, along with enrichments in arsenic, lead, and vanadium. Oxidation has produced a variety of arsenates and other minerals. At two localities of this type, the Carpenter mine in Bradford County and the Avery Brothers mine near Beaver Lake in Lycoming County, small amounts of copper ore having associated uranium have been produced. However, neither these nor other known occurrences of this group are large enough to be economic, though several companies explored and drilled in the region in the 1970's.

These occurrences are thought to have originated by mobilization of copper and uranium from the oxidized host sediments into reducing environments during diagenesis (Smith and Hoff, 1984; Smith and Rose, 1985; Rose and others, 1986).

SANDSTONE-TYPE OCCURRENCES IN MISSISSIPPIAN ROCKS

The major occurrence of this type is the Mount Pisgah deposit in calcareous conglomerate and sandstone of the Mississippian Mauch Chunk Formation, exposed in roadcuts of U.S. Route 209 just north of Jim Thorpe (Figures 39–1 and 39–4). The uranium, in part as coffinite (Table 39–1), occurs as several lens-shaped bodies 3 to 20 feet thick and several tens of feet long in a zone about 2,000 feet long (Figure 39–3). Reserves of 2×10^6 pounds of U_3O_8 were estimated to be present by Rocky Mountain Energy Company, which drilled about 20 holes in the zone (C. Voss, oral presentation to 43rd Annual Field Conference of Pennsylvania Geologists, 1978). About 300 tons of ore is reported to have been mined from the short adits along the highway and sold to the former Atomic Energy Commission (McCauley, 1961). Grades are typically 0.05 to 0.2 percent U_3O_8, though one sample of 2.6 percent U_3O_8 and 1.3 percent V_2O_5 across 11 inches was recorded (D. T. Hoff and R. C. Smith, personal communication, 1984). Vanadium accompanies the uranium, generally at levels several times higher than uranium. Oxidation has produced tyuyamunite-carnotite, uranophane, and other minerals (Table 39–1). Carbonaceous matter in the conglomerate has apparently provided a reducing environment to localize the uranium. The high vanadium and the lack of an oxidation interface at the locality is analogous with deposits in the Salt Wash Member of the Morrison Formation in Colorado and Utah (Fischer, 1970) and, perhaps, with the Ambrosia Lake deposits in New Mexico (Rautman, 1980).

The Mount Pisgah deposit is believed to have formed from slightly oxidizing, uranium-bearing groundwaters that encountered a reducing zone shortly after deposition of the enclosing sediments. The sediments have since been highly indurated, strongly folded, and locally faulted and sheared.

URANIUM IN TRIASSIC SEDIMENTARY ROCKS

A number of uranium occurrences are recognized in Triassic arkose and argillite of the Stockton and Lockatong Formations in the Newark Supergroup of Bucks County, near the Delaware River (Figure 39–1). Anomalously high radioactivity extends along bedding in lenses approximately 3 feet thick and extending tens to hundreds of feet lateral-

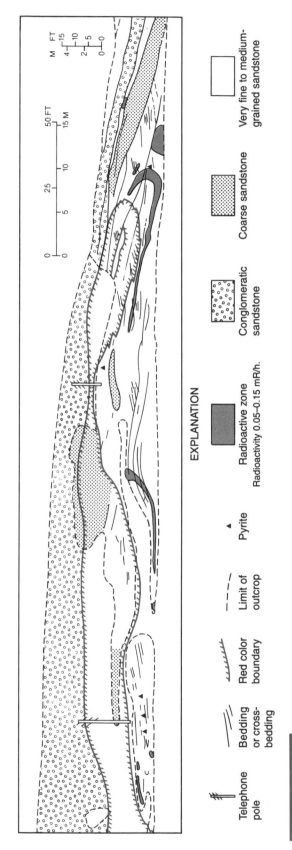

Figure 39–2. Sketch (near-vertical section) of railroad cut showing uranium-bearing beds of the Catskill Formation at Penn Haven Junction, Carbon County (modified from Sevon and others, 1978, Figure 15, which was modified from Schmiermund, 1977, Plate 3); mR/h, milliroentgens per hour.

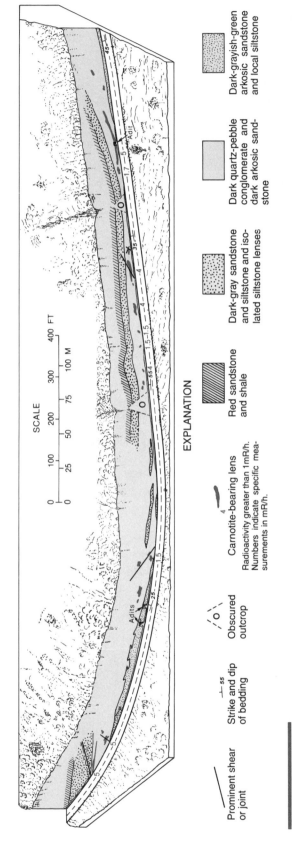

Figure 39–3. Sketch of roadcut showing uranium-bearing beds of the Mount Pisgah occurrence near Jim Thorpe, Carbon County (modified from McCauley, 1961, Figure 4).

Figure 39–4. View of the uranium-bearing sandstone and backfilled adit (behind marker) along U.S. Route 209 at the Mount Pisgah occurrence near Jim Thorpe, Carbon County. About 300 tons of ore was mined from this vicinity in the 1950's.

ly. Concentrations of uranium are typically 50 to 200 ppm.

The uranium appears to have been emplaced by oxidizing Triassic groundwaters that flowed downward along bedding in fluvial arkose until encountering reducing conditions in the lake sediments of the Lockatong or nearby sandstones (Turner-Peterson, 1977).

PROBLEMS AND FUTURE RESEARCH

The nature and number of uranium prospects and occurrences in Pennsylvania suggest a potential for economic deposits as good as any area in the east-ern United States. However, a truly economic discovery has yet to be made and would probably face severe challenge by environmentally conscious residents. If these conditions change, the development of geological concepts leading to an economic discovery is a significant challenge.

RECOMMENDED FOR FURTHER READING

McCauley, J. F. (1961), *Uranium in Pennsylvania*, Pennsylvania Geological Survey, 4th ser., Mineral Resource Report 43, 71 p.

Sevon, W. D., Rose, A. W., Smith, R. C., II, and Hoff, D. T. (1978), *Uranium in Carbon, Lycoming, Sullivan, and Columbia Counties, Pennsylvania*, Annual Field Conference of Pennsylvania Geologists, 43rd, Hazleton, Pa., Guidebook, 99 p.

Hopewell Furnace, showing the casting house, furnace stack, and, in the background, the connecting shed leading to the charcoal house. Hopewell Village is the only surviving example of the 16 blast-furnace plantations in Pennsylvania that were in operation during the Revolutionary War. It has been restored to the condition of its prosperous 1820–40 period and is now part of the Hopewell Furnace National Historic Site in Berks County.

CHAPTER 40   METALLIC MINERAL DEPOSITS

Although Pennsylvania has never produced metals in great quantities, metal mining has had considerable historic significance in this state. For instance, iron cannon and shot produced by Pennsylvania ironmasters from Cornwall-type magnetite deposits made a significant contribution to the Revolutionary War effort. Residual limonite deposits from southeastern Pennsylvania did likewise for the Civil War. In the nineteenth century, Pennsylvania was a world leader in the production of nickel and chromium from ore produced at the Gap nickel mine on Mine Ridge in Lancaster County and the numerous chromite mines in the serpentinite belt in southern Lancaster and Chester Counties.

Though there is no current metal production in Pennsylvania, two operations that closed for economic reasons in the 1970's and 1980's reportedly still have significant reserves. They are the Friedensville zinc mine in Lehigh County, shut down in 1983 and now flooded, and the Grace mine near Morgantown in Berks County, a Cornwall-type magnetite operation that closed in 1977. Other metals that have been produced in the state, typically as by-products of mining operations, include lead, copper, cobalt, gold, and silver. Cobalt is of particular interest. It was recovered from pyrite in magnetite ores mined at Cornwall mines in Lebanon County. These mines, which closed in 1973, were the only source of cobalt in the United States. Metallic resources within the state are not depleted, but their exploitation in the foreseeable future is unlikely because most known deposits are small and of low grade. Modern environmental regulations and urbanization in metalliferous terrane in southeastern Pennsylvania are likely to deter development.

—Charles H. Shultz

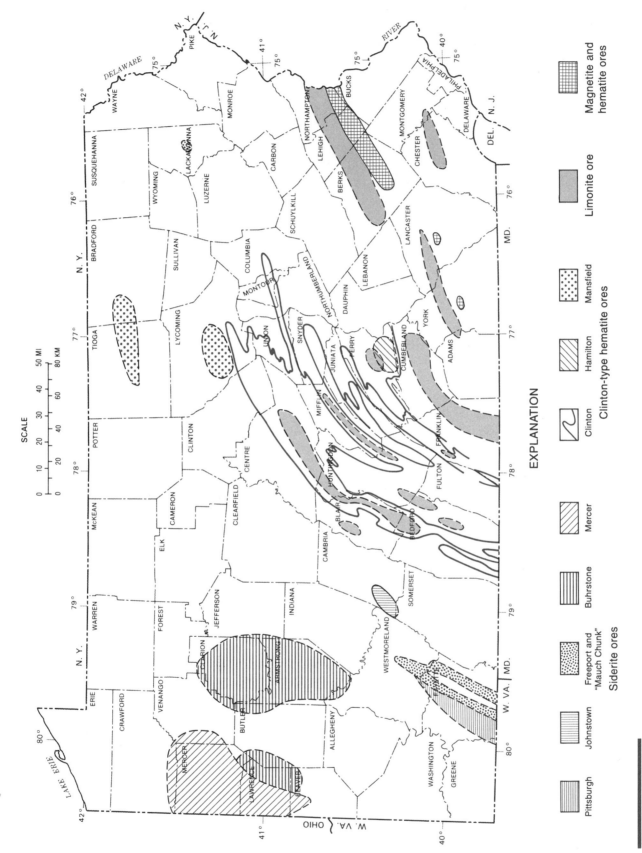

Figure 40A–1. General geographic distribution of mined sedimentary and metasedimentary iron ores. Boundaries are dashed where approximately located.

SCALE

EXPLANATION

Pittsburgh

Johnstown

Freeport and "Mauch Chunk"

Buhrstone

Siderite ores

Mercer

Hamilton

Clinton

Clinton-type hematite ores

Mansfield

Limonite ore

Magnetite and hematite ores

556

CHAPTER 40A   METALLIC MINERAL DEPOSITS— SEDIMENTARY AND METASEDIMENTARY IRON DEPOSITS

JON D. INNERS
Bureau of Topographic and Geologic Survey
Department of Conservation and Natural
   Resources
P. O. Box 8453
Harrisburg, PA 17105

Iron deposits discussed in this chapter can be grouped into the following four classes: (1) magnetite and hematite ores in Precambrian, Eocambrian, Cambrian, and Ordovician(?) rocks; (2) goethite-limonite ores in Precambrian, Cambrian and Ordovician, Silurian, Devonian, Mississippian, and Cretaceous(?) rocks (residual brown ores) and Quaternary surficial deposits (bog ores); (3) Clinton-type hematite-chamosite ores in Silurian and Devonian rocks; and (4) siderite-limonite ores in Mississippian and Pennsylvanian rocks. The general geographical distribution of these deposits is shown in Figure 40A–1. Iron deposits that are excluded here are the important Cornwall-type deposits, which are described in Chapter 40B.

CRYSTALLINE ORES: MAGNETITE AND HEMATITE

Precambrian Magnetite and Hematite in the Reading Prong

Magnetite and hematite deposits occur in Precambrian gneisses at numerous places in Bucks, Lehigh, Berks, and Northampton Counties (Figure 40A–1). Orebodies are gneissoid, pod-shaped lenses up to 15 feet thick and 3,000 feet long parallel to strike that conform to general gneissic foliation and mineral lineation (Bayley, 1910, 1941).

Magnetite was the most important ore mineral mined, but hematite-rich ore was obtained on Mine Hill at Durham. The ores averaged 45 percent iron (Miller and others, 1941). Silica was the most objectionable impurity.

The origin of these iron deposits apparently varies from strictly igneous and hydrothermal (Rittenhouse Gap, Vera Cruz, and Rattlesnake Hill at Durham) to metasedimentary (Seizholtzville and Mine Hill at Durham). All formed during a period of tectonism and migmatization in the Late Proterozoic (840 million years ago) (Drake, 1970).

Mining of the Precambrian iron deposits began as early as 1698 at Durham and prior to 1785 at Rittenhouse Gap. The most active exploitation took place between 1870 and 1895 at locations that include Seizholtzville, Vera Cruz, Durham, and Rittenhouse Gap. Both underground and open-cut methods were used to mine the Reading Prong ores.

The total production of magnetite ore from the Precambrian gneisses probably exceeded 1 million long tons.

Martic Ores of York and Lancaster Counties

Exploitation of at least two deposits of metasedimentary iron ore took place in the Martic Line area of the Piedmont Upland of southeastern Pennsylvania, mainly during the last half of the nineteenth century.

A deposit of specular hematite, the "Codorus ore," in the Eocambrian Harpers Phyllite was once mined near Strickhousers, southwest of York. Three stratabound ore zones, each up to 80 feet thick and 3,000 feet long, make up the ore zone. The ore itself is a heavy, medium-gray phyllitic schist that contains up to 50 percent specular hematite and about 10 percent euhedral magnetite. Between 1854 and the late 1870's, open cuts and drift mines of the York Iron Company yielded over 100,000 tons of this ore, averaging 36 percent iron (Frazer, 1876; Gray and Socolow, 1961).

Magnetite disseminated through schists of the Antietam Formation about 1.25 miles southeast of Conestoga, Lancaster County, yielded a small amount of low-grade iron ore at various times between 1881 and 1903 (Price, 1953). Although the ore ran only 15 to 30 percent magnetite, it was upgraded to about 70 percent using magnetic concentrators before being placed in the furnaces.

LIMONITE ORES

Limonite iron deposits of Pennsylvania consist of residual limonites and bog ore. Both types originate from weathering processes. The residual ores were the most important source of iron in the state prior to the mid-1880's, probably reaching peak production between 1865 and 1875 (Pennsylvania Department of Internal Affairs, 1944a).

Residual Limonite

Residual limonite, often called brown iron ore, occurs in a great variety of geologic settings throughout Pennsylvania (Table 40A–1). Of greatest importance to the historic economy of the state were the "mountain," "valley," and "Barrens" ores developed in the Cambrian and Ordovician carbonates and immediately subjacent clastics of southeastern and central Pennsylvania (Figure 40A–2).

Typical residual iron deposits are nodular, botryoidal, cellular, and stalactitic masses of limonite and goethite in variegated, kaolinitic clay (Foose, 1945a). Larger masses, classified as "lump" ore, could be shipped without beneficiation, but smaller fragments, called "wash ore," had to be washed free of clay matrix before shipment. The mined ores generally ranged from 35 to 50 percent iron, and deleterious phosphorus commonly exceeded 0.18 (the Bessemer limit). Manganese, zinc, and silica were other undesirable constituents that were locally abundant.

Most of the mined residual limonite ores were supergene enrichment deposits apparently related to the development of thick saprolitic residuum on the Harrisburg erosion surface (Foose, 1945a). The iron was ultimately derived from the weathering of pyrite, iron silicates, and iron carbonates in the parent rocks of the enclosing saprolitic clays. Several recent studies suggest that the Harrisburg surface and its associated secondary mineral deposits (iron, manganese, kaolinitic clay, and bauxite) formed during a period of intense chemical weathering in the Late Cretaceous to early Tertiary (approximately 70 to 40 million years ago) (Parizek and White, 1985; Sevon, 1985; Chapter 35).

Residual limonite deposits were worked in countless open pits, called "banks," throughout central and southeastern Pennsylvania (Figure 40A–3). For example, 261 old limonite mines are known from Lehigh County alone (Miller and others, 1941). Other counties that boasted more than 100 such mines include York, Lancaster, Cumberland, Berks, Huntingdon, Centre, and Mifflin. Most banks were relatively small, but a few exceeded 1,000 feet in length. The total thickness of the iron-ore-bearing clays in the mined areas varied from less than 50 to more than 300 feet.

Brown ore apparently "worked" well in both the old charcoal (Figure 40A–4) and newer anthracite (Figure 40A–5) furnaces, and in many cases produced an excellent foundry iron and gun metal (Lesley, 1892). The annual production of limonite probably exceeded 1 million tons during peak years between 1865 and 1880. The last significant production of limonite in Pennsylvania took place between 1910 and 1915.

Bog Iron Ore

Bog iron ore is a soft, spongy deposit of impure hydrous iron oxide (limonite) that forms in bogs, marshes, and shallow lakes as a precipitate from acidic, iron-bearing water. It is typically "iron red" in color and is found in tubular, pisolithic, nodular,

Table 40A-1. *Distribution and Host Rock of Residual Limonite Ores in Pennsylvania*

Type	Distribution Physiographic area	County	Host rock Age	Geologic unit	Rock type	References
"Gneiss" ore	Piedmont (Honey Brook Upland)	Chester	Precambrian	Pickering Gneiss	Graphitic gneiss	Rogers (1858b); Lesley (1883)
"Piedmont" ores	Piedmont (especially Conestoga Valley area)	York, Lancaster, Chester, Montgomery	Mostly Cambrian; some Ordovician	Antietam-Vintage Fms. (also Chickies, Ledger, and Conestoga Fms.)	Dolomite, limestone, quartzite	Frazer (1876, 1880); Lesley (1883)
"Mountain" ores	Reading Prong (South Mountain)	Lehigh, Berks, Northampton	Cambrian	Hardyston Fm. (some Leithsville Fm.)	Quartzite, limestone	Rogers (1858b); d'Invilliers (1883); Miller and others (1939, 1941)
do.	South Mountain	Cumberland, Franklin, York	do.	Antietam-Tomstown Fms.	Quartzite, dolomite, phyllite	d'Invilliers (1887); Lesley (1892); Foose (1945a, b)
"Valley" ores	Lehigh Valley (including Saucon and Oley Valleys)	Lehigh, Berks, Northampton	Mainly Ordovician	Beekmantown Group, Allentown Fm.[1]	Limestone, dolomite	d'Invilliers (1883); Miller and others (1939, 1941)
do.	Cumberland Valley	Cumberland, Franklin	do.	Beekmantown Group[1]	do.	d'Invilliers (1887)
"Barrens" ores	Nittany Valley-Morrisons Cove area	Centre, Bedford, Blair, Huntingdon	Cambrian and Ordovician	Chiefly Gatesburg Fm.; also Beekmantown Group[1]	Dolomite, limestone	Rogers (1858b); Platt (1881); Lesley (1892)
Helderberg ore	Juniata Valley	Mifflin, Bedford, Blair	Silurian and Devonian	Tonoloway-Keyser-Old Port Fms.	Limestone, limy shale, chert	Platt (1881); d'Invilliers (1891)
"Oriskany" and "Marcellus" ores	do.	Perry, Mifflin, Huntingdon	Devonian	Mainly Onondaga Fm.; also Old Port and Marcellus Fms.	Limestone, limy shale, chert	Dewees (1878); Claypole (1885); d'Invilliers (1891)
Mauch Chunk ore	Broad Top area	Bedford, Huntingdon	Mississippian	Mauch Chunk Fm.	Red shale and sandstone	Lesley (1859)
Patapsco(?) ore	Piedmont	Montgomery	Cretaceous (also Tertiary?)	Patapsco Fm. (also Bridgeton and Pensauken Fms.)	Clay and sand	Lewis (1881); Hopkins (1899)

[1]Many other limestone units contain small pods of residual limonite.

laminated, or irregular aggregates, many of which are impregnated with plant debris and mineral material (Corbin, 1922). Bog ore deposits are particularly common in northwestern and northeastern Pennsylvania, but they occur in other areas as well. These ores formed primarily in Quaternary time under presently existing or colder climatic conditions.

Accumulations of bog ore are invariably small, but in Franklin County, bog ore developed from the leaching of pyrite in Ordovician Martinsburg shale was used at Richmond Furnace east of Mercersburg

(d'Invilliers, 1887). The old Erie Furnace at Erie was supplied with bog ore from the head of Presque Isle Bay (Sharp and Thomas, 1966).

CLINTON-TYPE HEMATITE ORES

Grayish-red, oolitic, calcareous, and often chamositic hematite ores of the "Clinton type" occur in central and north-central Pennsylvania in the Lower Silurian Clinton Group, the Middle Devonian Mahantango Formation (Hamilton Group), and the Upper De-

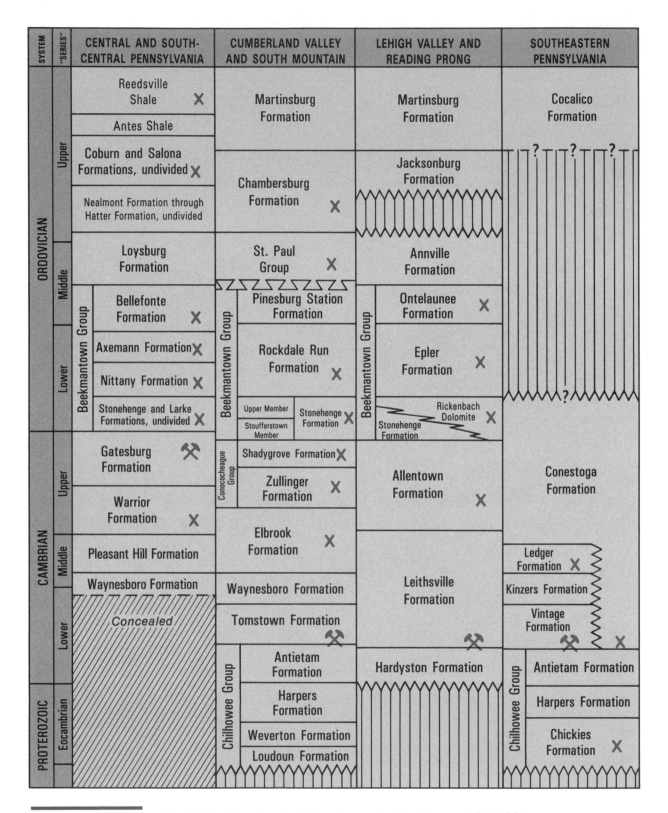

Figure 40A–2. Stratigraphic distribution of residual limonite ores in Cambrian and Ordovician rocks (mainly carbonates). Quarry symbol indicates regionally important ore; x indicates locally important ore. Correlation of stratigraphic units is based on Berg, McInerney, and others (1986).

Figure 40A–3. **Moselem mine, reportedly the largest open-pit residual limonite mine in Berks County, located 1.3 miles northwest of Moselem Springs, Richmond Township. Cherty, limonite-bearing residual clays filled a 2,000-foot-long pocket in Middle Ordovician Onte-launee dolomite (MacLachlan, 1979).**

vonian Lock Haven Formation. These deposits are typically thin, lenticular, and stratabound. They are of primary sedimentary origin, having formed in near-shore, shallow-marine depositional environments.

Clinton Ores

The Clinton hematite ores *sensu stricto* are widely distributed throughout the Lower Silurian outcrop belt in the Appalachian Mountain section of central Pennsylvania (Figure 40A–1), occurring mainly in the Rose Hill and Keefer Formations (Figure 40A–6). The two chief varieties of Clinton ore beds are the "fossil ores" and the "block ores." The "fossil ores" are typically hematitic, bioclastic calcarenites and calcirudites composed of crinoid ossicles and frag-

ments of bryozoans, brachiopods, and trilobites. The "block ores" are siliceous, oolitic ores associated with low-grade hematitic sandstones.

Hematite in the Clinton ores occurs as both primary, somewhat earthy, grayish-red oolitic coatings on shell fragments and quartz grains and as secondary, shiny black and metallic, acicular clusters of specularite that transect primary features (Cotter, 1983). Typical chemical analyses range from 20 to 50 percent metallic iron. Phosphorus content is relatively high (0.2 to 0.8 percent), and the ores are nearly all of high-phosphorus, non-Bessemer grade.

Clinton iron ores were mined by both open-cut and underground methods (Dewees, 1878). Surface mining was especially effective in areas of shallow dip on the noses of anticlinal folds. Underground mine

Figure 40A–4. **Carlisle (Boiling Springs) Furnace stack, on the north bank of Yellow Breeches Creek at Boiling Springs, South Middleton Township, Cumberland County. Built in 1815, the furnace used a mixture of residual "mountain" ore from banks on the north flank of South Mountain and Cornwall-type magnetite ore from near Dillsburg, south of the mountain (Lesley, 1859). The piping indicates conversion of the furnace to hot-blast in its later history.**

Figure 40A–5. Shawnee Furnaces of the Chestnut Hill Iron Ore Company at Columbia, Lancaster County. This large complex consisted of three anthracite-fired steam furnaces that were erected between 1842 and 1868. Most of the ore used here came from the Chestnut Hill limonite banks in nearby West Hempfield Township. The last of the Shawnee Furnaces ceased operation in 1894. Photograph courtesy of the Lancaster County Historical Society.

openings consisted of drifts, slopes, tunnels, or shafts, depending on local topography, structure of the ore beds, and drainage conditions (Figure 40A–7).

Major developments of Clinton ores were undertaken between 1840 and 1875. Because more than 1.3 million tons of hematite (mainly Clinton) was mined in the waning years of the industry after 1880 (Pennsylvania Department of Internal Affairs, 1944a), the total production of Clinton hematite ore could have exceeded 5 million tons.

Hamilton Oolitic Ores

Hamilton oolitic hematite deposits occur at the top of thick, coarsening-upward sedimentary cycles in the middle and upper parts of the Middle Devonian Mahantango Formation (upper part of the Hamilton Group) in Perry, Juniata, and Dauphin Counties (Kaiser, 1972; Sarwar, 1984). The ores were mined only in Perry County, however (Figure 40A–1).

The ore beds, typically 1 to 3 feet thick where mined (Claypole, 1885), consist of bioturbated sandy silt shales that contain a profusion of black "chamosite" oolites 0.2 to 2 mm in diameter. Analyzed samples of oolitic ore reportedly varied from 25 to 35

percent iron. The total tonnage mined from shallow drifts and tunnels between 1830 and 1875 may have amounted to several hundred thousand tons.

Mansfield Ores

The Mansfield ores are erratically distributed through parts of Tioga, Bradford, and Lycoming Counties (Figure 40A–1). Typical ore is grayish-red, calcareous, oolitic, fossiliferous and very hematitic sandstone that occurs in lenticular beds at different levels in the upper part of the Upper Devonian Lock Haven Formation (Luce, 1981; Figure 40A–8). Most analyses of Mansfield ores ran 30 to 40 percent iron and more than 0.35 percent phosphorus (Sherwood, 1878). These ores were extensively mined during the middle 50 years of the nineteenth century.

SIDERITE ORES

Sideritic iron deposits are present at many stratigraphic horizons in rocks of Pennsylvanian age (Figure 40A–9). Most deposits that at one time had economic significance occur in the western part of the state (Figure 40A–1), but a limited amount of mining was also carried on in the Anthracite region in eastern

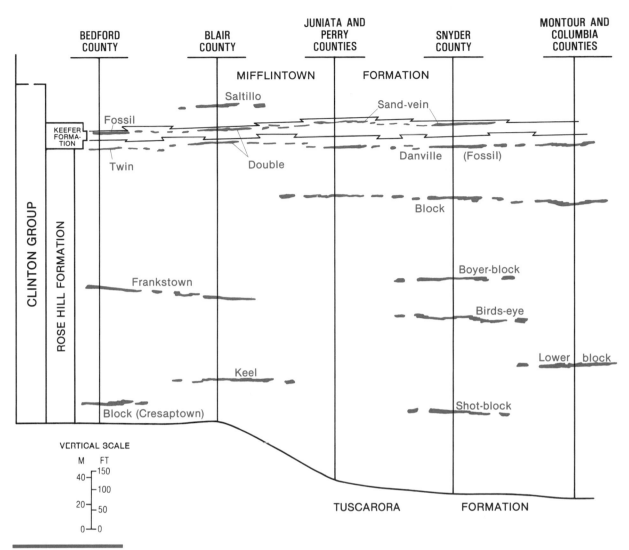

Figure 40A–6. Correlation diagram of Clinton hematite-ore beds in central and south-central Pennsylvania. Names are those used by local miners and adopted by the Second Pennsylvania Geological Survey.

Pennsylvania. Nearly all of the ores are nodular and concretionary, with the notable exception of the bedded Buhrstone ore.

The Buhrstone ore occurs at the top of the Vanport Limestone in the lower part of the Allegheny Formation. It is named for the light-bluish-gray chert, or "buhrstone," that commonly occurs between the ore bed and the main body of the limestone (Rogers, 1858b). Unweathered buhrstone is typically medium-gray, sparsely fossiliferous calcitic siderite that turns brick red and hematitic on slight oxidation. The ore bed in the old mines was generally between 6 and 12 inches thick (Chance, 1880). Locally, weathering of the ore bed and associated siderite nodules formed thick pockets of secondary limonite.

Siderite, or clay-ironstone, nodules at the other ore horizons (Figure 40A–9) are typically bluish gray where unweathered and are finely crystalline. They break with a sharp conchoidal fracture and generally occur in dark shale. Enriched, secondary limonite deposits commonly developed from weathering of the carbonate nodules.

Mined buhrstone and nodular siderite ores generally ranged from 30 to 40 percent iron, whereas the enriched limonitic derivatives averaged about 50 percent (White, 1877; Chance, 1880). The ore was typically siliceous and moderately high in phosphorus (greater than 0.15 percent). In the early charcoal-iron days, the lower grade, unaltered siderite ores were mixed with supergene limonite ores from the same mine to act as both flux and auxiliary iron source.

Mining of siderite ores was done by a variety of surface and underground methods. Some of the more advanced mines were those of the Cambria Iron Com-

Figure 40A-7. Reopened portal of a Clinton ore tunnel on the east side of Tussey Mountain at Tatesville, near Everett, Bedford County. Glamorgen Iron Company, of Lewistown, mined the "Sand-vein" ore from this 200-foot-long crosscut. The borough of Everett currently uses the tunnel, as well as a longer one nearby, for water supply.

Figure 40A-8. Mansfield-type ore bed (hammer) in a shallow underground mine, 0.35 mile south of Austinville, Bradford County. The ore occurs about 50 feet below the basal red shale unit of the overlying Catskill Formation.

pany at Johnstown, where a longwall system was used to mine the "Johnstown" ore (Platt and Platt, 1877).

The great era of carbonate-charcoal iron production in western Pennsylvania lasted from 1825 to 1855. During this period, more than 50 furnaces were erected in the wilds of Clarion and Venango Counties alone (Sharp and Thomas, 1966). The last extensive mining of carbonate ore took place in the Connellsville Coke District of Fayette and Westmoreland Counties prior to 1900.

PROBLEMS AND FUTURE RESEARCH

Prospects for renewed mining of any of these sedimentary and metasedimentary ores in the near future are extremely remote. Not only are all of the deposits of limited size, but they are also invariably of low grade.

Despite this bleak potential, interest in these ores has revived periodically. During World War II, local exploration activity in old Clinton hematite and residual-limonite districts proved disappointing (Miller, 1942; Foose, 1945a). About 15 years later, investigators at the Pennsylvania State University studied the potential tonnages and beneficiation possibilities of the Centre iron sandstone in Perry County. Although they concluded that approximately 100 million short tons of low-grade (10 to 20 percent iron) ore existed in the area studied (Swartz and Hambleton, 1958), beneficiation of this siliceous, hematitic

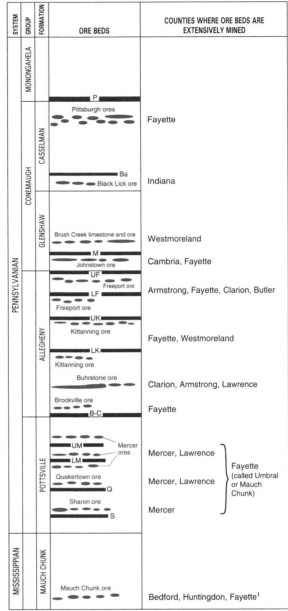

SYSTEM	GROUP	FORMATION	ORE BEDS	COUNTIES WHERE ORE BEDS ARE EXTENSIVELY MINED

Footnote: ¹Also Lackawanna County in northeastern Pennsylvania.

Figure 40A–9. Main siderite iron-ore horizons in Pennsylvanian rocks of western Pennsylvania.
Coal beds are as follows: P, Pittsburgh; Ba, Barton; M, Mahoning; UF, Upper Freeport; LF, Lower Freeport; UK, Upper Kittanning; LK, Lower Kittanning; B-C, Brookville-Clarion; UM, Upper Mercer; LM, Lower Mercer; Q, Quakertown; and S, Sharon.

sandstone appeared to be noneconomic (Lovell and Leonard, 1958).

Much geologic work remains to be done, however, on the genesis of many of the sedimentary and

metasedimentary ores, particularly the crystalline magnetite and hematite deposits and the residual limonite deposits. For example, Sevon (1985c), Parizek and White (1985), and Ciolkosz and others (1980) have shown that a better understanding of the geomorphic history of the region is necessary to decipher the origin of the residual limonite ores.

Many of the abandoned mines also pose local environmental challenges. Instances of damaging subsidence, collapsed water wells, groundwater contamination, dewatered aquifers, and highway construction delays are well documented in central Pennsylvania (Inners and Williams, 1983; Inners and others, 1984). An increased knowledge of the extent and configuration of the old workings would greatly facilitate dealing with such problems.

RECOMMENDED FOR FURTHER READING

Bartholomew, C. L., and Metz, L. E. (1988), *The anthracite iron industry of the Lehigh Valley,* Easton, Pa., Center for Canal History and Technology, 222 p.

Bining, A. C. (1979), *Pennsylvania iron manufacture in the eighteenth century,* 2nd ed., Harrisburg, Pennsylvania Historical and Museum Commission, 215 p.

Hunter, R. E. (1970), *Facies of iron sedimentation in the Clinton Group,* in Fisher, G. W., and others, eds., *Studies of Appalachian geology, central and southern,* New York, Interscience Publishers, p. 101–121.

Inners, J. D., and Williams, J. H. (1983), *Clinton iron-ore mines of the Danville-Bloomsburg area, Pennsylvania: their geology, history, and present-day environmental effects,* in Nickelsen, R. P., and Cotter, E., eds., *Silurian depositional history and Alleghanian deformation in the Pennsylvania Valley and Ridge,* Annual Field Conference of Pennsylvania Geologists, 48th, Danville, Pa., Guidebook, p. 53–63.

Lesley, J. P. (1859), *The iron manufacturer's guide,* New York, John Wiley, 772 p.

Loose, J. W. W. (1982), *Anthracite iron blast furnaces in Lancaster County, 1840–1900,* Journal of the Lancaster County Historical Society, v. 86, p. 78–117.

Miller, B. L., Fraser, D. M., Miller, R. L., and others (1941), *Lehigh County, Pennsylvania,* Pennsylvania Geological Survey, 4th ser., County Report 39, 492 p.

Perry, D. K. (1994), *"A fine substantial piece of masonry"—Scranton's historic iron furnaces,* Pennsylvania Historical and Museum Commission and Anthracite Heritage Museum and Iron Furnaces Associates, 47 p.

Sharp, M. B., and Thomas, W. H. (1966), *A guide to the old stone blast furnaces in western Pennsylvania,* Pittsburgh, Historical Society of Western Pennsylvania, 90 p.

Sternagle, A. M. (1986), *Iron furnaces of Blair and Huntingdon Counties,* in Sevon, W. D., ed., *Selected geology of Bedford and Huntingdon Counties,* Annual Field Conference of Pennsylvania Geologists, 51st, Huntingdon, Pa., Guidebook, p. 41–50.

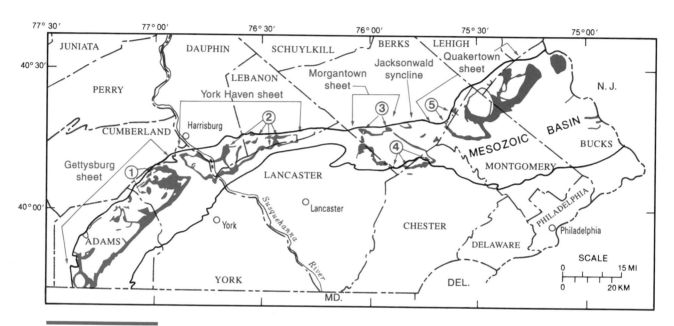

Figure 40B–1. Map showing the location of the larger Cornwall-type magnetite deposits and the diabase sheets in southeastern Pennsylvania (after Lapham and Gray, 1973, p. 285; and Berg and others, 1980). 1, Dillsburg deposits; 2, Cornwall deposits; 3, Wheatfield and Fritz Island deposits; 4, Morgantown-French Creek group; 5, Boyertown deposits.

566

CHAPTER 40B METALLIC MINERAL DEPOSITS—CORNWALL-TYPE IRON DEPOSITS

CARLYLE GRAY
Carlyle Gray and Associates, Inc.
P. O. Box 66
Yorkville, CA 95494

INTRODUCTION

Spencer (1908) first recognized that the replacement iron deposits at Cornwall, Lebanon County, represent a type of deposit found in many places in Pennsylvania (Figure 40B–1). All of the deposits occur at the contact of Jurassic (Berg, McInerney, and others, 1986) diabase intrusives with carbonate rock. Magnetite is the principal ore mineral, and chalcopyrite and cobaltian pyrite are common accessories.

Historically, the deposits have been important sources of iron ore, but at the time of this writing, none are being mined. Smith and others (1988) estimated the total ore production at Cornwall to have been 106 million tons, and at the Grace mine in Berks County to have been 45 million tons. Other occurrences that had a production of over 1 million tons in the nineteenth and early twentieth centuries are the Boyertown, French Creek, and Dillsburg deposits (Rose, 1970).

CORNWALL DEPOSITS

The deposits at Cornwall, located about 5 miles south of Lebanon, in Lebanon County, consist of two major replacement orebodies (Figure 40B–2) and several smaller ones. The deposits, with one exception, occur at the upper contact of a diabase sheet with carbonate rocks of Cambrian age, probably the Buffalo Springs Formation. The diabase sheet, of the York Haven type, is 1,000 to 1,200 feet thick and dips to the south at 10 to 45 degrees (Figure 40B–3).

Lapham and Gray (1973) reported that the western orebody had an outcrop length of 4,400 feet and a maximum dip length of 1,000 feet. The maximum thickness of the ore was 150 feet. The eastern orebody did not crop out; the highest point was 150 feet below land surface. It was discovered by a dip-needle survey in 1919. The orebody had the general shape of a lima bean and had a dip length of more than 1,000 feet and a maximum strike length of 2,500 feet. Its maximum thickness was 200 feet.

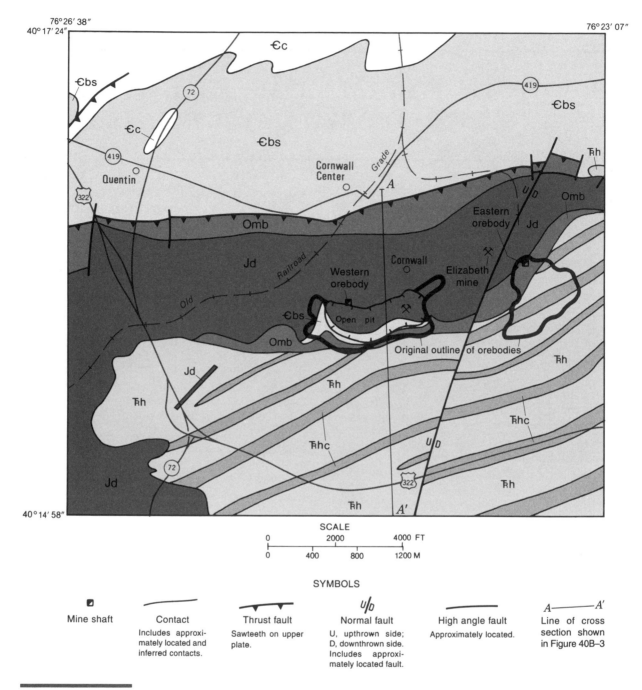

76°26′38″
40°17′24″

76°23′07″

€c

€bs

€c

72

€bs

419

€bs

Ŧh

419

€c

Cornwall
Center

Grade

A

Omb

322

Quentin

U D

Omb

Eastern
orebody

Jd

Omb

Jd

Railroad

Cornwall

Western
orebody

Elizabeth
mine

Old

€bs

Open pit

Original outline of orebodies

Ŧh

Omb

Jd

Ŧh

Ŧh

Ŧhc

72

U D

Ŧhc

Jd

322

Ŧh

Ŧh

A′

40°14′58″

SCALE

0   2000   4000 FT

0   400   800   1200 M

SYMBOLS

■
Mine shaft

Contact
Includes approxi-
mately located and
inferred contacts.

Thrust fault
Sawteeth on upper
plate.

U/D
Normal fault
U, upthrown side;
D, downthrown side.
Includes approxi-
mately located fault.

High angle fault
Approximately located.

A———A′
Line of cross
section shown
in Figure 40B–3

Figure 40B–2. Map showing the location of orebodies at Cornwall in southern Lebanon County (after Gray and Lapham, 1961, p. 2; and Lapham and Gray, 1973, Plate 21). Jd, Jurassic diabase; Ŧh, Hammer Creek Formation; Ŧhc, Hammer Creek conglomerate; Omb, "Mill Hill slate" and "Blue conglomerate," undivided; €bs, Buffalo Springs Formation; €c, Cambrian carbonate units, undivided.

The Buffalo Springs Formation in the hanging wall of the western orebody is a crystalline limestone, commonly having thin shaly laminae, alternating with dense dolomite and magnesian limestone. The con-

tact between the ore and the limestone is quite sharp, but irregular tongues of ore extend out along favored beds (Figure 40B–4). Two local units, a hornfels called the "Mill Hill slate" and a metamorphosed breccia

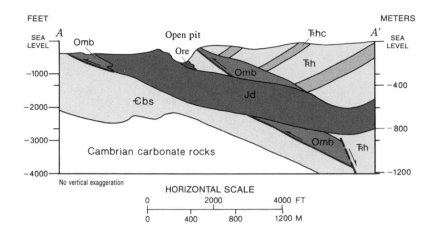

Figure 40B–3. Cross section of the western orebody at Cornwall, Lebanon County (from Lapham and Gray, 1973, Plate 21). See Figure 40B–2 for explanation.

called the "Blue conglomerate," constitute the hanging wall of the eastern orebody. These units are contact metamorphosed shale and wildflysh of the Cambrian and Ordovician Hamburg sequence (D. B. MacLachlan, personal communication, 1988) and are overlain by north-dipping Triassic sandstones and conglomerates.

The ore averaged about 40 percent iron, the principal ore mineral being magnetite. Chalcopyrite and pyrite also were recovered. The copper content of the ore was about 0.4 percent; gold and silver were recovered from copper refining. The pyrite concentrates averaged 1.1 percent cobalt (Smith and others, 1988). The principal gangue minerals are actinolite, diopside, chlorite, calcite, and dolomite.

Mining was begun in 1742 and continued without a break until 1973. The ore was almost exhausted at that time, but closing was hastened by flooding of the underground workings as a result of tropical storm Agnes in 1972.

MORGANTOWN-FRENCH CREEK GROUP

This group includes two important deposits, the Grace mine at Morgantown and the French Creek mine at St. Peters. It also includes the interesting Pine Swamp prospect and several minor deposits, including the Jones, Hopewell, and Warwick deposits. All are replacement orebodies and are located at the upper contact of the Morgantown sheet (numbers 3 and 4 in Figure 40B–1).

Grace Mine

The magnetite deposit at the Grace mine at Morgantown in Berks County was discovered by Bethlehem Steel Corporation through an airborne magnetometer survey in 1947 and confirmed by diamond drilling in 1948 (Sims, 1968). The highest point of the orebody was 600 feet below sea level.

Figure 40B–4. Western orebody open pit, spring of 1948. The diabase footwall is above the road at the right. The ore (medium-gray) forms the floor of the pit and fingers into the limestone hanging wall (white), which is overlain by the "Blue conglomerate" at the upper left. Photograph by G. David Graeff.

The orebody is a replacement of Cambrian carbonate of the Buffalo Springs Formation (formerly Elbrook Formation). The 1,000-foot-thick Morgantown sheet (York Haven Diabase; Smith and others, 1975) strikes about N60°W and dips 20 degrees to the northeast, cross-cutting both the Cambrian carbonates and the overlying Triassic sandstones and conglomerates (Figure 40B–5).

The orebody is approximately 3,500 feet long (on the 20°N80°E plunge) and 700 to 1,500 feet wide. The thickness varies from 50 feet to over 400 feet (Figure 40B–6).

The ore is fine to medium grained. The principal metallic mineral is magnetite, and the principal gangue minerals are serpentine (antigorite), talc, and chlorite. Accessory metallic minerals include cobaltian pyrite, chalcopyrite, and pyrrhotite, which is locally abundant.

The grade of the ore averaged 40.5 percent magnetic iron. Sulfide concentrates yielded iron, copper, cobalt, and gold (Sims, 1968). Ore production began in 1958, and by 1964, annual production was 2.8 million tons. The mine closed in 1977 after having produced about 45 million tons of ore (Smith and others, 1988).

French Creek Mine

The French Creek deposit is located just north of the village of St. Peters in Chester County, about 10 miles east of Morgantown. The carbonate host rock is a lens of marble in Precambrian gneiss (Smith, 1931).

The deposit, which was mined from the mid-nineteenth century until it was exhausted in 1928, consisted of two "shoots" of ore (Figure 40B–7). The principal orebody is in a lens of marble that is not everywhere in contact with the diabase. A barren lens of marble nearby is nowhere in contact with the diabase. It appears that some contact with diabase is essential for ore formation.

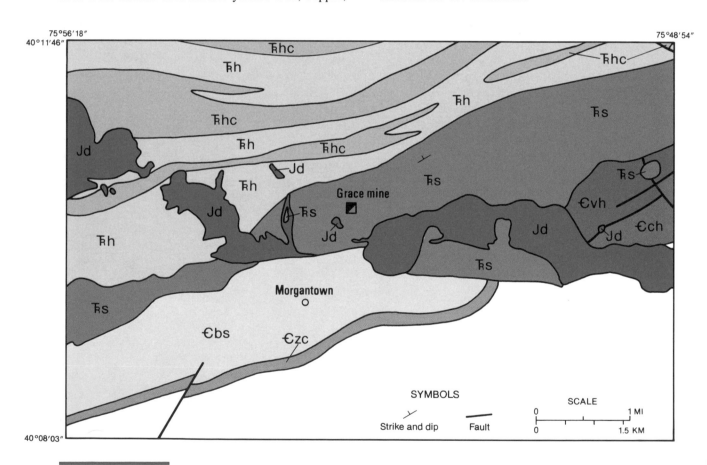

Figure 40B–5. Geologic map of the vicinity of Morgantown in southern Berks County (from Berg and Dodge, 1981, p. 195 and 393). Jd, Jurassic diabase; Ꞇh, Hammer Creek Formation; Ꞇhc, Hammer Creek conglomerate; Ꞇs, Stockton Formation; Ꞓbs, Buffalo Springs Formation; Ꞓzc, Zooks Corner Formation; Ꞓvh, Vintage, Antietam, and Harpers Formations, undivided; Ꞓch, Chickies Formation.

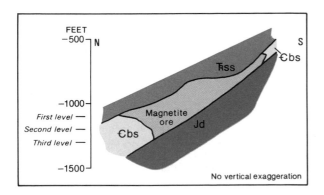

Figure 40B–6. Typical cross section of the orebody at the Grace mine in southern Berks County (from Tsusue, 1964, p. 3). Jd, Jurassic diabase; Ƒss, Triassic sandstone and shale; €bs, Buffalo Springs Formation.

In addition to the usual ore minerals, pyrrhotite and cobaltite were present (Smith, 1978). Gangue minerals included actinolite, serpentine, and garnet.

Other Deposits

The Pine Swamp prospect, 1.25 miles east of the French Creek mine, is a magnetic anomaly almost as large in area and amplitude as the Grace mine anom-aly (Socolow, 1959a). The anomaly was described by Gedde (1965).

Several minor deposits occur on the northern limb of the Morgantown sheet near Reading (number 3 in Figure 40B–1). All are small, and none have been worked since early in this century. The most important were the Wheatfield and the Fritz Island mines (Spencer, 1908).

BOYERTOWN DEPOSITS

The principal deposit of the Boyertown group lies directly under the borough of Boyertown in Berks County. Two minor deposits are nearby. The Boyertown deposit is a replacement orebody that occurs at the contact of Cambrian and Ordovician carbonates and York Haven Diabase of the Quakertown sheet (number 5 on Figure 40B–1). The ore is generally on top of the diabase (Figure 40B–8).

The mines closed in the 1890's. They were dewatered in the period 1916–17, but production was never resumed. The deposit was the first to be surveyed by airborne magnetometer (Hawkes and others, 1953). The survey indicated the existence of ore remaining in the ground, which was confirmed by drilling by the U.S. Bureau of Mines. The ore is not of commercial interest.

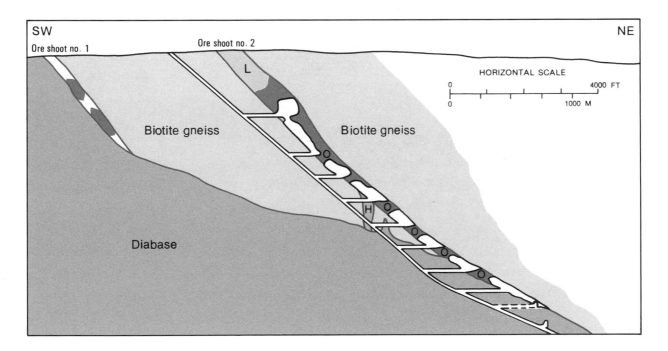

Figure 40B–7. Cross section of orebodies at the French Creek mine in northern Chester County (from Smith, 1931, p. 14). L, limestone; O, magnetite ore; H, hornblende syenite gneiss.

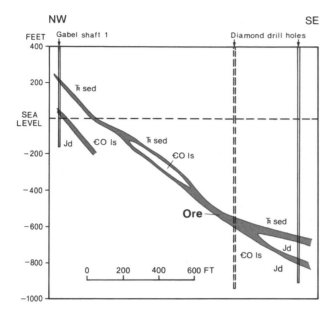

Figure 40B–8. Cross section of orebodies at Boyertown in eastern Berks County (from Hawkes and others, 1953, Plate 19). Jd, Jurassic diabase; Ŧsed, Triassic conglomerate, sandstone, shale, and their metamorphosed equivalents; ₵Ols, Cambrian and Ordovician limestone.

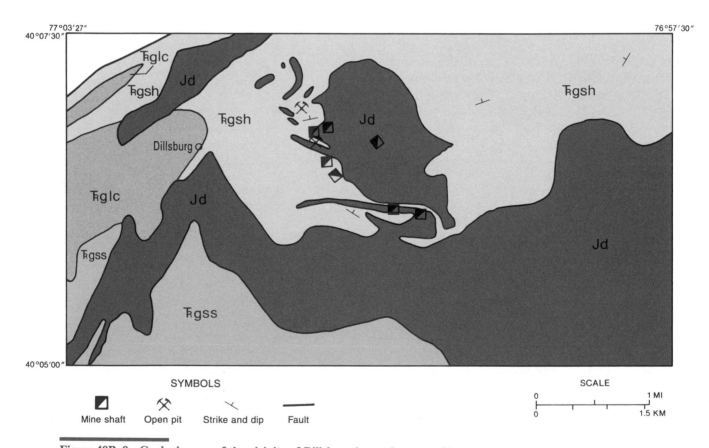

Figure 40B–9. Geologic map of the vicinity of Dillsburg in northwestern York County (modified from Hotz, 1950, Plate 3; and Wood, 1980, Plate 1). Jd, Jurassic diabase; Ŧgss, Gettysburg sandstone; Ŧglc, Gettysburg limestone conglomerate; Ŧgsh, Gettysburg shale.

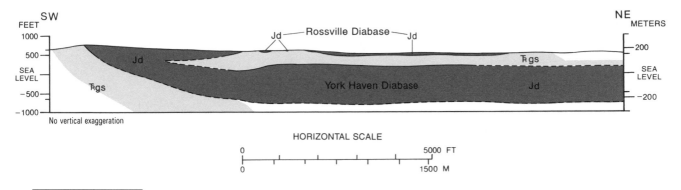

Figure 40B–10. Cross section through orebodies in the Dillsburg iron district, York County (after Hotz, 1950, Plate 4). Jd, Jurassic diabase; Ŧgs, Gettysburg sandstone and shale. Gray shading indicates metamorphosed zone.

DILLSBURG DEPOSITS

The Dillsburg deposits (number 1 in Figure 40B–1) are a group of small orebodies occurring as replacements of Triassic limestone conglomerate, located 0.5 mile east of Dillsburg in northern York County. Figure 40B–9 is a geologic map showing the location of the mines. The diabase at Dillsburg is part of the Gettysburg sheet and occurs as a compound, multiple-intrusive, horizontal sheet (Smith and others, 1975). Triassic sedimentary rocks are caught between an erosional remnant of Rossville Diabase and a thick, lower sheet of York Haven Diabase (Figure 40B–10). Because the ore formed as a replacement of carbonate lenses interbedded with ordinary Triassic detrital rocks, the orebodies are small and scattered.

The mines were opened in 1855 and were worked for 60 years. About 1.5 million tons of ore was recovered (Stose and Jonas, 1939). Later, diamond drilling by the U.S. Bureau of Mines failed to find any significant quantities of ore, but did provide valuable geologic information (Hotz, 1950).

ORIGIN OF THE ORES

A detailed summary of the origin of the ores was provided by Lapham and Gray (1973). Briefly, they believed that the intrusive contact of the diabase provided a channel for the ore-forming solutions. The ores formed following contact metamorphism associated with the diabase intrusion and resulted from a separate hydrothermal event. Diabase magma and the hydrothermal solutions had the same ultimate source.

The evidence at Cornwall is conclusive that the diabase sheets had solidified and cooled before the ore formed. Eugster and Chou (1979) presented a quantitative model for the deposition of the Cornwall-type magnetite deposits. Rose and others (1985) have shown, by studies of oxygen and sulfur isotopes, that the ore-forming fluids had an important component of connate and meteoric water. They recognized the magma as the source of the copper and cobalt, if not all of the iron.

PROBLEMS AND FUTURE RESEARCH

One remaining puzzle is the mechanism for separation of iron from titanium. All of the magnetite in the late differentiates of the diabase is intergrown with ilmenite. The Cornwall-type ores are all notably low in titanium.

RECOMMENDED FOR FURTHER READING

Hickok, W. O., IV (1933), *The iron ore deposits at Cornwall, Pennsylvania,* Economic Geology, v. 28, p. 193–255.

Lapham, D. M. (1968), *Triassic magnetite and diabase at Cornwall, Pennsylvania,* in Ridge, J. D., ed., *Ore deposits of the United States, 1933–1967,* New York, American Institute of Mining, Metallurgical, and Petroleum Engineers, p. 72–94.

Peets, R. B. (1957), *Mining history of Cornwall, Pennsylvania,* Mining Engineering, v. 9, p. 741–746.

Shale, S. J. (1953), *After two centuries of mining Cornwall keeps its methods up-to-date,* Mining Engineering, v. 5, p. 670–675.

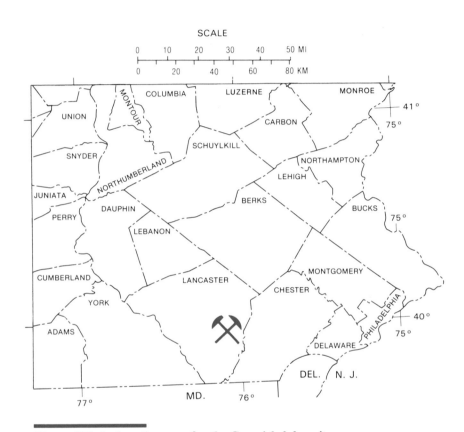

Figure 40C–1. Location map for the Gap nickel deposit.

CHAPTER 40C METALLIC MINERAL DEPOSITS—NICKEL-COPPER DEPOSIT (GAP MINE)

JAMES M. McNEAL
U.S. Geological Survey
910 National Center
Reston, VA 20192

INTRODUCTION

The Gap nickel deposit is the only known nickel-copper deposit in Pennsylvania (Rose, 1970) and was the sole North American producer of nickel for more than 25 years (1863–88) (Ashley, 1931a). The deposit was probably formed by magmatic segregation of sulfide minerals in intrusive rocks of probable Precambrian age that were initially gabbroic but were later largely altered to amphibolite. The nickel content of the Gap deposit was overlooked in favor of copper for about 140 years following its discovery in 1718. Four or five unsuccessful small-scale attempts to mine the deposit for copper were made before the 1840's (Frazer, 1880). The last two attempts were on a much larger scale than earlier efforts. In 1849, mining began for copper, but after nickel was discovered in the deposit in about 1853, the deposit was mined for nickel. After failing in 1860, the mine was bought in 1862, and the deposit was successfully mined for nickel from 1863 to 1893, largely because of a new refining process. Cobalt and copper were also recovered. The mine closed when it could no longer compete with nickel from Sudbury in Canada and from New Caledonia. The Gap Nickel Mining Company and the American Nickel Works (refinery at Camden, N. J.) were sold to the International Nickel Company (INCO) of Canada in 1902. Drilling by INCO in 1942 determined that the remaining resource of nickel and copper in the deposit was insufficient to resume mining.

The Gap nickel deposit is located in Lancaster County (Figure 40C–1) about 12 miles southeast of Lancaster and about 1.5 miles north of Bart. The mined location is in a wooded area in the Gap 7.5-minute quadrangle at 39°57'25"N/76°05'05"W, about 0.25 mile west of the road between Nickel Mines and Nickel Mines Mission. The smelter was located about 1 mile north of the deposit. The surface rights of the deposit are privately owned, and the mineral rights are owned by a subsidiary of INCO (Good, 1955).

GEOLOGY

The Gap nickel deposit occurs in the Piedmont province and is situated on the Mine Ridge anticline (Knopf and Jonas, 1929). According to Avery A. Drake (personal communication, 1986), the bulk of the anticline is most likely metasedimentary Pickering Gneiss, which is highly variable in composition and includes mica schist, as occurs at the Gap nickel deposit. The main metasedimentary sequence is quartzose and biotitic gneiss, with sequences of felsic to intermediate and mafic gneisses. Small bodies of serpentinite and metagabbro occur within the gneiss. Rocks from Mine Ridge have not been dated but are presumed to be of Grenville age (about 1,000 Ma) (see Chapter 3A).

The Gap nickel deposit occurs at the base of the largest known mafic intrusive body in Mine Ridge; it has been largely altered to amphibolite (Rose, 1970). Kemp (1895a) noted that the intrusion consists mainly of secondary green hornblende altered from ortho-rhombic pyroxene and olivine. Small pegmatite and quartz veins intrude both the country rock and the amphibolite body (Phemister, 1924; Moyd, 1942). The original composition of the intrusive is uncertain, but it is most likely to have been either a peridotite or a pyroxenite.

In plan view, the lenticular mafic body is about 2,000 feet long and up to 500 feet wide and is oriented with the long axis approximately east-west (Figures 40C–2 and 40C–3). Yates (1942) described the body as possibly the remnant of the bottom of a synclinal fold of a peridotite sill. Frazer (1880) presented a map (Figure 40C–3) of the deposit showing a probable eastward extension of the intrusion. The bulk of the ore came from the eastern end along both the southern and northern margins (Figure 40C–2) at the nearly vertical, sharp contact of the intrusion with mica-schist country rock. This ore zone ranged from 4 to 30 feet thick (Frazer, 1880) and averaged 20 feet thick (Phemister, 1924).

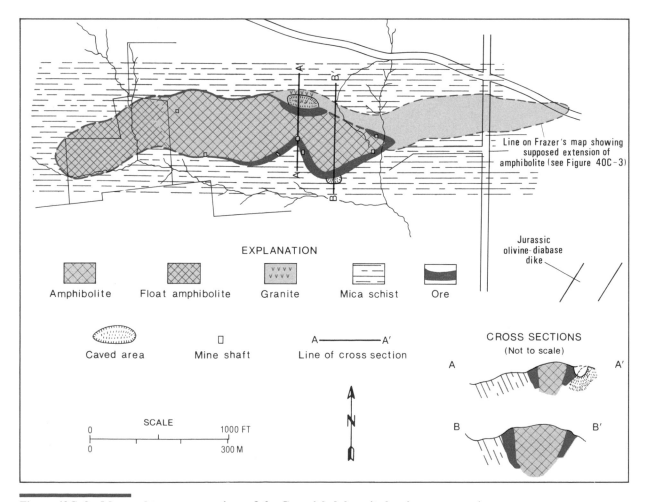

Figure 40C–2. Map and two cross sections of the Gap nickel deposit showing ore zones in relation to the amphibolite body (modified from Kemp, 1895b, p. 5).

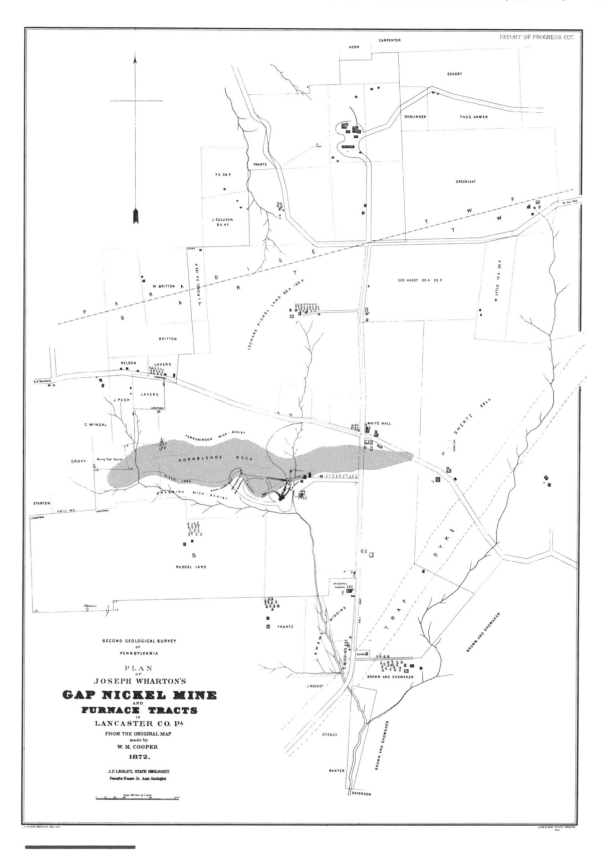

Figure 40C–3. Map of the Gap nickel deposit showing cultural features, property boundaries, and probable eastern extension of the ultramafic intrusive (from Frazer, 1880).

The origin of the ore deposit was the subject of some debate for nearly 50 years. Phemister (1924) proposed that the deposit was formed by hydrothermal solutions, but the early opinion of Kemp (1895a, b) and later of Moyd (1942) that the deposit was formed by magmatic segregation of sulfides is now commonly accepted (Yates, 1942; Rose, 1970).

The principal ore minerals are pyrrhotite containing exsolved pentlandite $(Fe,Ni)_9S_8$, millerite (NiS), and chalcopyrite (Figure 40C-4). The abundance of these minerals varies. Chalcopyrite increases toward the hanging wall, and pyrrhotite increases toward the footwall (Dickeson, 1860). Pyrrhotite with pentlandite lamellae had been discarded in early mining as "mundic" (an old Welsh term for pyrite) prior to the discovery of nickel. Millerite (Figure 40C-5) was the ore mineral produced from the Millerite shaft, which was the richest part of the deposit. The millerite and minor violarite $[Ni(Fe,Ni)_2S_4]$ were probably formed by supergene alteration of the primary nickel-bearing minerals.

Smith (1978) described the mineralogy, geology, and history of the deposit. The history of the deposit is also described in Henfry (1797) and Frazer (1880). Some old photographs of the mine and miners are shown in Figure 40C-6.

MINING PRODUCTION

Detailed information is not available on the production or grade of the deposit. Reports (Genth, 1875; Frazer, 1880; Day, 1885; and Ashley, 1931a) on the grade of the ore vary (Table 40C-1), but a reasonable grade estimate is 2 to 2.5 percent nickel, 0.1 percent cobalt, and 1 percent copper.

For the period 1863–93, the mine is estimated to have produced about 5.3 million pounds of nickel, 190,000 pounds of cobalt oxide, and about 3.9 million pounds of copper. During this time, the mine produced essentially all of the nickel and cobalt mined in the United States (Day, 1894). This amounted to about one third of the U.S. consumption of cobalt oxide and, until 1883, most of the U.S. consumption of nickel. An estimated 0.8 million pounds of nickel was produced from 1853 to 1862.

MINING METHODS

Shafts, drifts, and stopes were used in mining. The drifts were generally 60 feet apart, and the intervening ore was removed by stoping either upward or downward. Below 60 to 70 feet, the rock was sufficiently hard that the ore had to be blasted, and no timbers were necessary. Frazer (1880) described 10 or 11 vertical shafts ranging from 60 to 235 feet deep along both the northern and southern edges of the deposit. Yates (1942) published a map (Figure 40C-7) showing the locations of many of the shafts and other features of the mine.

The ore was brought to the surface in skips or buckets. Steam engines were used to power the hoists and pumps. About one third of the mined material was waste. The ore was crushed, then set on fire at

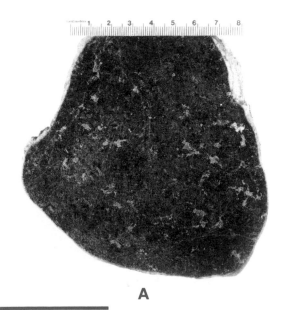

A   B

Figure 40C-4. Photographs of polished amphibolite samples from the Gap nickel deposit.
A. The medium-gray mineral is pyrrhotite. B. The minerals in the stringers are chalcopyrite (light gray) and pyrrhotite (medium gray).

A

Figure 40C–5. Photographs of millerite (NiS) by Breck P. Kent (Smithsonian sample NMNH 123056). A. Top view showing botryoidal form. The field of view is about 8 inches high. B. Side view showing fibrous radial or spherulitic structure. The field of view is about 3 inches wide.

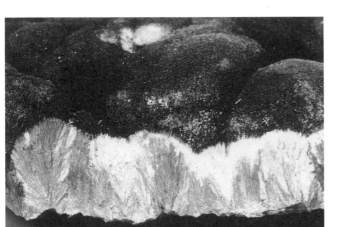

B

the deposit was discovered in 1718. Henfrey (1797) reported that a spring from the mine area containing "water of pale green color, of an acid, sweet, austere, inky, nauseous taste" flowed at the rate of "700 or 800 hogsheads in 24 hours" (about 2,000 gallons per hour). Where this water overflowed the fields, grass could not be grown for a number of years, and the fish were killed downstream. Benjamin Franklin was reported to have visited the area several times and experimented with the water by submerging his knife blade and observing the resulting copper coating (Henfrey, 1797). Several other interesting stories were recounted by Henfrey, some of which were reported by Smith (1978).

RECENT STUDIES

Good (1955) used biogeochemical and soil geochemical exploration procedures over the western portion of the deposit and concluded that nickel in soil was useful in locating potential mineralization to a depth of at least 200 feet. Stephens and Colman (1979), using geophysical and geochemical techniques over the eastern end of the deposit, concluded that (1) contacts between the amphibolite and country rock could easily be detected using ground magnetic geophysical techniques, and (2) additional mineralization at depth was indicated.

Two holes (numbers 1 and 3, about 180 and 390 feet deep, respectively) were drilled about 0.6 mile due north of the Gap deposit in the late 1960's by the Pennsylvania State University (Arthur W. Rose, personal communication, 1985), in the vicinity of an aeromagnetic high. Detailed ground geophysical surveys located ground magnetic and self-potential (s-p) anomalies about 1,000 feet apart. No gravity anomalies were found. Hole 1 in the s-p anomaly showed nothing of economic interest. The bulk of the rock was quartzose chlorite-muscovite schist containing local tourmaline but no sulfides.

the nearby smelter to remove sulfur. The fire, once set, would burn for four or five weeks without additional fuel. After smelting with quartz or limestone flux, the matte (melted mixed sulfides) was crushed and shipped to the refinery at Camden, N. J. The products included metallic nickel and copper, and cobalt oxide.

A drilling program of more than 35 holes was conducted by INCO in 1942. The reserves of the deposit (Yates, 1942) were estimated to be 750,000 tons of ore averaging 0.44 percent copper and 0.69 percent nickel. Yates (1942) reported a negligible precious-metal content.

ENVIRONMENTAL CONCERNS

The environmental impact of the Gap nickel mine and surrounding area is probably no greater today than that which was occurring naturally when

Table 40C–1. *Reported Ore Grade for the Gap Nickel Mine*
(All values are percentages)

	Nickel	Cobalt	Nickel and cobalt	Copper
Frazer (1880)	1.3	0.05–0.15	—	0.3–1.0
Genth (1875)	—	—	2.0–2.9	—
Day (1885)	2.0–2.5	0.1	—	—
Ashley (1931a)	—	—	1.5–4.23	1.10–2.26

Figure 40C–6. Old photographs of the Gap nickel mine (reproduced from Smith, 1978, Figure 134, p. 280–81). A. Workers at the mine, about 1880. B. General view of mine buildings, about 1880. C. Another general view of mine structures and excavations as viewed from the east in April 1894. D. Open cut on the south side of the deposit at the contact between mica schist (under blocks at right) and the amphibolite body (exposed on the left). The view is toward the east, and the photograph was taken in April 1894.

Hole 3 in the ground magnetic anomaly showed two zones containing minor sulfides, the lower zone containing about 20 feet of low concentrations of pyrrhotite, chalcopyrite, pyrite, and pentlandite(?) in an actinolite schist bearing talc and chlorite. This hole bottomed in gneiss. The pervasive hydrothermal alteration of the rocks in both holes, indicated by the presence of chlorite and tourmaline in hole 1, and chlorite, talc, and actinolite in hole 3, reflects the known alteration of the whole area.

Villaume (1969) mapped on the Mine Ridge anticline and located additional metagabbroic or altered ultramafic bodies that are not likely to contain economic amounts of nickel and copper (Villaume and others, 1969).

Recent geochemical evidence corroborates earlier interpretations that the Gap deposit was formed by magmatic segregation. Six samples containing sulfide minerals were analyzed by the author for trace-element and precious-metal content using semiquantitative procedures, and for their sulfur-isotope composition. For the one sample that had platinum values greater than the detection limit, the values of $Pt/(Pt+Pd)$ (0.6) and $Cu/(Cu+Ni)$ (0.62) were found to be reasonably similar to the accepted range for Sudbury, Canada (Naldrett, 1981). Similarly, the sulfur-isotope values, which range from 1.3 to 2.6 per mil (mean=2.04 per mil, n=7) (McNeal, 1985), are similar to values reported by Naldrett (1981) for Sudbury.

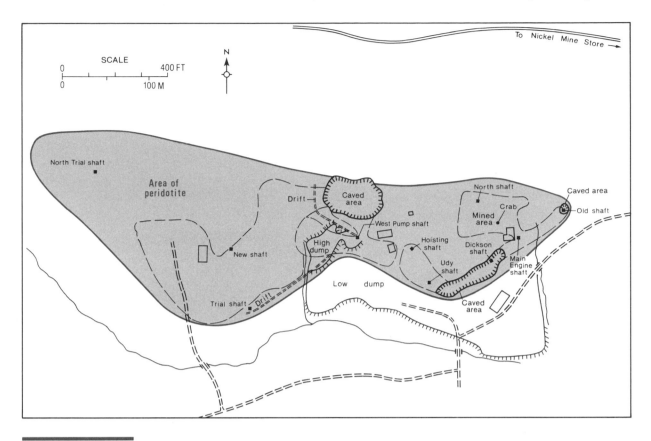

Figure 40C-7. Map of the Gap nickel deposit showing some shaft names and areas of workings (from Yates, 1942).

PROBLEMS AND FUTURE RESEARCH

Significant extensions of the Gap deposit are not likely to be found. Except for the possibility of blind metagabbroic bodies, it is unlikely that additional nickel-copper deposits of the Gap nickel type will be found on Mine Ridge.

RECOMMENDED FOR FURTHER READING

Dickeson, M. W. (1860), *Report of the geological survey and condition of the Gap Mining Company's property: Lancaster County,* Philadelphia, J. B. Chandler, 26 p.

Frazer, Persifor, Jr. (1880), *The geology of Lancaster County,* Pennsylvania Geological Survey, 2nd ser., Report of Progress CCC, p. 163–176.

Good, R. S. (1955), *A chromographic study of nickel in soils and plants at the Lancaster Gap mine, Pennsylvania,* University Park, Pennsylvania State University, M.S. thesis, 53 p.

Henfrey, Benjamin (1797), *A plan with proposals for forming a company to work mines in the United States; and to smelt and refine the ores, whether of copper, lead, tin, silver, or gold,* Philadelphia, Snowden and McCorkle, 34 p.

Kemp, J. F. (1895), *The nickel mine at Lancaster Gap, Pennsylvania, and the pyrrhotite deposits at Anthony's Nose, on the Hudson,* American Institute of Mining Engineers Transactions, v. 24, p. 620–633.

Moyd, Louis (1942), *Evidence of sulphide-silicate immiscibility at Gap nickel mine, Pennsylvania,* American Mineralogist, v. 27, p. 389–393.

Naldrett, A. J. (1981), *Nickel sulfide deposits: classification, composition, and genesis,* in Skinner, B. J., ed., *Seventy-fifth anniversary volume, 1905–1980,* Economic Geology, p. 628–685.

Phemister, T. C. (1924), *A note on the Lancaster Gap mine, Pennsylvania,* Journal of Geology, 5th ser., v. 32, p. 498–510.

Smith, R. C., II (1978), *The mineralogy of Pennsylvania, 1966–1975,* Friends of Mineralogy, Pennsylvania Chapter, Special Publication 1, 304 p.

Stephens, G. C., and Colman, C. S. (1979), *Geophysical and geochemical exploration of the Gap nickel mine, Lancaster County, Pennsylvania,* Pennsylvania Academy of Science Proceedings, v. 53, p. 209–211.

Villaume, J. F. (1969), *A reconnaissance study of the rocks of the Precambrian core of the Mine Ridge anticline, Gap, Pennsylvania, 7.5' quadrangle, Lancaster County, Pennsylvania,* Lancaster, Pa., Franklin and Marshall College, B.A. thesis, 33 p.

Villaume, J. F., Freedman, J., and Al-Mishwt, Ali (1969), *Geochemical and geophysical study of mafic and ultramafic rocks in Mine Ridge, southeastern Pennsylvania,* Pennsylvania Academy of Science Proceedings, v. 43, p. 169–171.

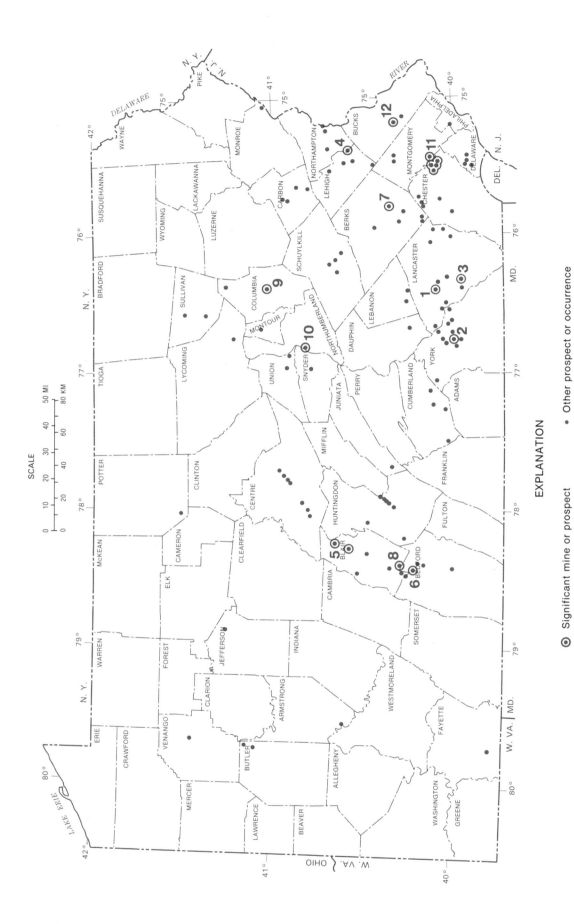

Figure 40D–1. Zinc and lead mines, prospects, and occurrences in Pennsylvania (based largely on Smith, 1977; and Smith, personal communication, 1984). Numbered mines and prospects are as follows: 1, Bamford mine; 2, York Stone quarry; 3, Pequea mine; 4, Friedensville mines; 5, Sinking Valley mines; 6, Woodbury prospect; 7, Oley Valley quarry; 8, Soister iron mine; 9, Almedia mine; 10, Doughty mine; 11, Phoenixville mines; and 12, New Galena mine.

CHAPTER 40D   METALLIC MINERAL DEPOSITS— ZINC-LEAD-SILVER

ARTHUR W. ROSE
Department of Geosciences
The Pennsylvania State University
University Park, PA 16802

The earliest recorded mining of lead and zinc in Pennsylvania was during the Revolutionary War, when small mines were operated in Sinking Valley, Blair County, to supply lead for Washington's army. Small-scale mining of lead began near Phoenixville, Chester County, in 1808, and near Bloomsburg, Columbia County, in 1816. Between 1850 and 1893 and between 1958 and 1983, the mines at Friedensville (Figure 40D-1) were among the largest zinc producers in the United States. They have now closed, though the ore is by no means exhausted. A number of other small mines were developed near Lancaster and Tyrone in the period 1850-95, and minor amounts of ore were produced. Numerous prospects and old mines suggest the possibility for discovery of concealed orebodies.

The important deposits, geologic host formations, and deposit types are summarized in Table 40D-1. Most of the important mines and prospects occur in Paleozoic dolomite and limestone. Other host rocks are Silurian quartzite, Precambrian gneiss, and Triassic sandstone and shale. Smith (1977), Miller (1924), and Rose (1970) described zinc and lead deposits in Pennsylvania and mentioned many occurrences in other rock types, but at present, none of these appear to be of significance. Geographically, the mines are concentrated in the Great Valley section of the Ridge and Valley province and in the Piedmont province in the southeastern quarter of Pennsylvania, in clusters near Bethlehem, Lancaster, and Phoenixville. A few mines and prospects are farther west in the Appalachian Mountain section of the Ridge and Valley province (Figure 40D-1).

No precise data are available on the total production or reserves of lead and zinc in Pennsylvania, but some approximate values are listed in Table 40D-1. For zinc, the bulk of the production has been from the Friedensville area in Lehigh County. Total production of zinc metal and zinc oxide between 1853 and 1924 is estimated to have been be-

Table 40D–1. *The More Important Zinc and Lead Mines and Prospects in Pennsylvania*[1]

Map no.[2]	Name	County	Host rock	Type[3]	Ore production[4]; metals
1	Bamford mine	Lancaster	Cambrian Ledger dolomite	A	67,000 tons of 12% Zn (Pb, Ag)[5]
2	York Stone quarry	York	do.	A	None; Zn
3	Pequea mine	Lancaster	Cambrian Vintage dolomite	A	2,000 tons of 0.5% Pb (Ag)
4	Friedensville mines	Lehigh	Ordovician Rickenbach dolomite	B	11,000,000 tons of 7% Zn
5	Sinking Valley mines	Blair	Ordovician Chazy limestone(?)	C	3,500 tons of 12% Zn + Pb
6	Woodbury prospect	Bedford	Ordovician Bellefonte dolomite and others	C	Small(?); Zn + Pb
7	Oley Valley quarry	Berks	Ordovician Ontelaunee dolomite	C	None; Zn
8	Soister iron mine	Blair	Ordovician Nittany dolomite	B	None; Fe (Zn)
9	Almedia mine	Columbia	Silurian Tonoloway limestone	D	2,000 tons of high Pb, Zn
10	Doughty mine	Northumberland	do.	D	100 tons of 20% Zn + Pb
11	Phoenixville mines	Chester, Montgomery	Precambrian gneiss; Triassic sandstone and shale	E	>55,000 tons of 5% Pb, 5% Zn, 1% Cu
12	New Galena mines	Bucks	Triassic shale	E	>200 tons of high Pb, Zn

[1]Data from Smith (1977) and Miller (1924).
[2]See Figure 40D–1.
[3]Types (modified after Smith, 1977): A, replacement zones, commonly parallel to bedding in Cambrian carbonate rocks; B, solution collapse breccia in dolomite of Ordovician Beekmantown Group; C, veins, commonly cross-cutting, in Ordovician carbonate rocks; D, veins cutting Silurian carbonate rocks of hypersaline origin; and E, veins, in part cutting Triassic sediments and possibly related to Jurassic diabase.
[4]Figures for production of ore are incomplete; based on data in Smith (1977) and Miller (1924).
[5]Parentheses indicate minor by-products.

tween 120,000 tons (Miller, 1924) and 240,000 tons (Smith, 1977, and personal communication, 1984). Figures quoted by Smith (1977) for the New Hartman mine at Friedensville for production for 1958 to 1975, plus extrapolated production through 1983, suggest an additional 700,000 tons of zinc, giving a total of at least 820,000 tons of zinc for the district. The New Hartman mine produced the largest tonnage of ore, amounting to about 11 million tons averaging about 6.5 percent zinc. The next largest zinc-producing mine, at Bamford in Lancaster County, produced ore containing about 8,000 tons of zinc, and other mines appear to have produced less than about 1,000 tons of zinc. For lead, the largest pro-

ducers appear to have been the Phoenixville and New Galena areas (Figure 40D–1), which produced ore containing perhaps 3,000 and 100 tons of lead, respectively.

FRIEDENSVILLE AREA

The Friedensville ores occur in a block of Cambrian and Ordovician carbonate rocks nearly surrounded by Precambrian rocks of the Reading Prong (Callahan, 1968). The ore is in the Ordovician Rickenbach Formation, a limy dolomite member of the Beekmantown Group, which contains very similar ores to those near Knoxville, Tennessee (Hoagland, 1971).

In the vicinity of the mines, the formation is folded into a sharp, asymmetrical anticline, the axis of which plunges about 20 degrees to the southwest. Beds on the north limb of the anticline dip nearly vertically and contain the large Ueberroth orebody (Figures 40D–2 and 40D–3). The south limb of the anticline dips 20 to 30 degrees and hosts the other mines. The ore mined in the Triangle, Correll, and New Hartman mines is part of a single ribbon-shaped ore zone approximately conformable to bedding and plunging about 20 degrees southwest, parallel to the anticlinal axis. The ore zone is up to 150 feet thick and 500 to 1,500 feet wide and extends down plunge for at least 6,000 feet, to a depth of more than 1,500 feet.

Sphalerite and pyrite in the major orebody fill the interstices of a breccia zone (Figure 40D–4). This breccia probably formed by collapse caused by dissolution of carbonate either by ancient meteoric

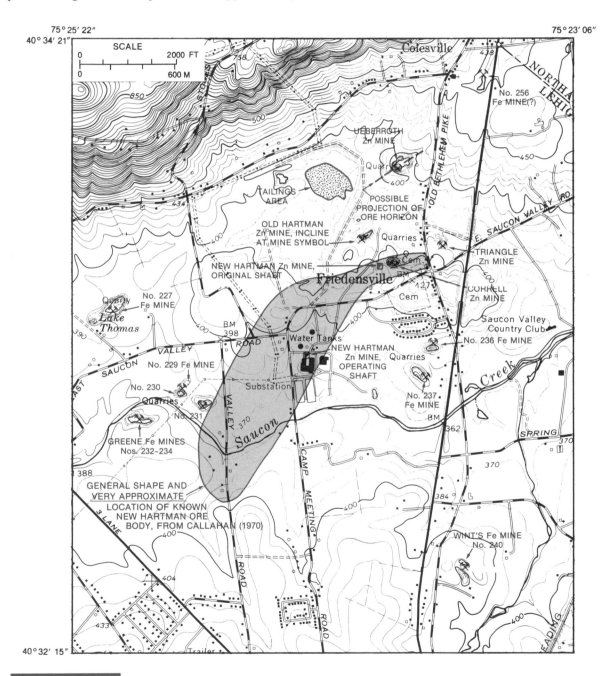

Figure 40D–2. Zinc and iron mines in the Friedensville area, Lehigh County (from Smith, 1977, p. 85).

Figure 40D-3. View of the northeast end of the Ueberroth open cut showing vertical bedding, underground drifts (white arrow) following selected beds or veins, and white secondary sulfate incrustations (black arrow) (from Smith, 1977, p. 148). See Figure 28-2 for an aerial view.

waters (karst processes) or by hydrothermal ore-forming fluids, as postulated for east Tennessee (Hoagland, 1971). Sphalerite, pyrite, dolomite, and quartz fill the matrix between breccia fragments of host-rock dolomite. The average grade of recently mined ore was 6 to 6.5 percent zinc, with minor cadmium, no lead, and only traces of copper. The footwall ore is relatively high grade and has a sharp basal boundary, whereas the hanging-wall ore is leaner and has a gradationally decreasing grade. Some veinlike bodies of oxidized ore were mined prior to 1890.

Much of the mining from 1853 to 1893 extracted high-grade oxidized zinc ore (>25 percent zinc) composed mainly of hemimorphite, possibly with some smithsonite and other oxidized zinc minerals. Much of this ore was mined from four large open pits that later were extended downward into a network of underground openings. Influx of water from the carbonate host rocks was a major problem, and one of the world's largest pumps was operated in the mines even during working of the shallower mines (to 250 feet) in the 1800's.

The now-flooded New Hartman mine of the New Jersey Zinc Company closed in 1983, apparently because of the high cost of pumping (Metsger, 1979) and the depressed condition of the zinc market, even though considerable additional ore of a grade similar to that mined is apparently still present.

PHOENIXVILLE AND NEW GALENA AREAS

The mines of these two areas exploited lead-copper-zinc veins cutting Precambrian and Triassic

Figure 40D-4. Sphalerite-bearing ore in rubble breccia, top of rib dividing Old Hartman open pit, Friedensville, Lehigh County (from Smith, 1977, p. 106).

Figure 40D–5. Looking northeast in the 80-foot stope of the Ecton mine, showing the former width of the vein (from Smith, 1977, p. 261). A thin veneer of rich ore remains on both walls in many places.

rocks. The veins were possibly related to Mesozoic diabase, which served as a heat source. They contain sphalerite, galena, and chalcopyrite in a gangue of quartz, ferroan dolomite, and barite. The veins are commonly 1 to 5 feet in width (Figure 40D–5) and were oxidized to pyromorphite, cerussite, anglesite, smithsonite, and other species to depths of several tens of feet. Small amounts of silver were reported in old assays.

PROBLEMS AND FUTURE RESEARCH

The future of lead and zinc mining in Pennsylvania is very problematical. Until there is a major change to a long-term shortage of these metals, and much higher prices, it seems unlikely that any mines will operate, even though "ore reserves" still exist at Friedensville. The environmental problems are an additional negative factor for metal mining in Pennsylvania.

Scientifically, the origin and age of the hydrothermal fluids forming the lead and zinc deposits remain a problem. For example, if the fluids forming the deposits at Friedensville were expelled from a sedimentary basin, as is postulated for similar deposits elsewhere, what basin supplied them, what was their flow path, and during what geologic period did this flow occur? What are the relative ages of mineralization and tectonic/sedimentologic events at Friedensville? Do more such deposits exist, and if so, where? Additional large, undiscovered deposits extending into the weathering zone seem unlikely, but major deposits at depth are quite possible.

RECOMMENDED FOR FURTHER READING

Howe, S. S. (1981), *Mineralogy, fluid inclusions and stable isotopes of lead-zinc occurrences in central Pennsylvania,* University Park, Pennsylvania State University, M.S. thesis, 155 p.

Metsger, R. W. (1979), *Mining problems in a karst valley—technical and social,* Bulletin of the Association of Engineering Geologists, v. 16, p. 427–447.

Miller, B. L. (1924), *Lead and zinc ores of Pennsylvania,* Pennsylvania Geological Survey, 4th ser., Mineral Resource Report 5, 91 p.

Smith, R. C., II (1977), *Zinc and lead occurrences in Pennsylvania,* Pennsylvania Geological Survey, 4th ser., Mineral Resource Report 72, 318 p.

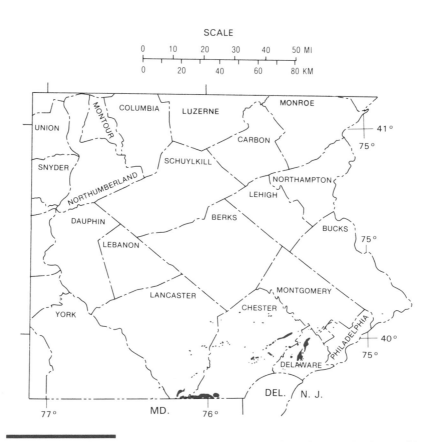

Figure 40E–1. Serpentinite bodies in Pennsylvania (from Berg and others, 1980).

588

CHAPTER 40E   METALLIC MINERAL DEPOSITS— CHROMITE

ANN G. WYLIE
Laboratory for Mineral Deposits Research
Department of Geology
University of Maryland
College Park, MD 20742

PHILIP A. CANDELA
Laboratory for Mineral Deposits Research
Department of Geology
University of Maryland
College Park, MD 20742

INTRODUCTION

Chromite, the only ore of chromium, was discovered in the United States in 1810 at Bare Hills, Md. Exploration for other deposits in southeastern Pennsylvania and northeastern Maryland soon followed. During the period between 1825 and 1865, mining activity was at its height, and the region led the world in the production of chromite. Over 40 mines and prospects are known, and total production reached almost 300,000 tons. This is about one quarter of all the chromite ever produced in the United States. The depletion of many of the mines and the discovery of chromite in Turkey and California contributed to the demise of the chromite mining industry in this region by 1882, although small-scale placer mining and reworking of some mine dumps continued intermittently until 1928. Nonetheless, today the region remains a center for the chemical and pigment manufacturing industries that were started in Baltimore, Md., because of the proximity of chromite ore.

ORIGIN AND GEOLOGY OF CHROMITE DEPOSITS

The chromite deposits occur in serpentinized ultramafic bodies that are an integral part of the Baltimore Mafic Complex, which forms part of the Piedmont of Maryland, Delaware, and Pennsylvania (Figures 40E-1 and 40E-2). The complex is composed primarily of variably metamorphosed gabbro and ultramafic rocks and lesser amounts of quartz diorite and albite granite. Most of the ultramafic rocks are variably altered to serpentine and talc. The complex extends 150 miles from Laurel, Md., at its most southerly limit, through Baltimore, Harford, and Cecil Counties in Maryland, and into York, Lancaster, Chester, and Delaware Counties in Pennsylvania. Smaller ultramafic bodies occur in many Maryland and Pennsylvania counties, but their relationship to

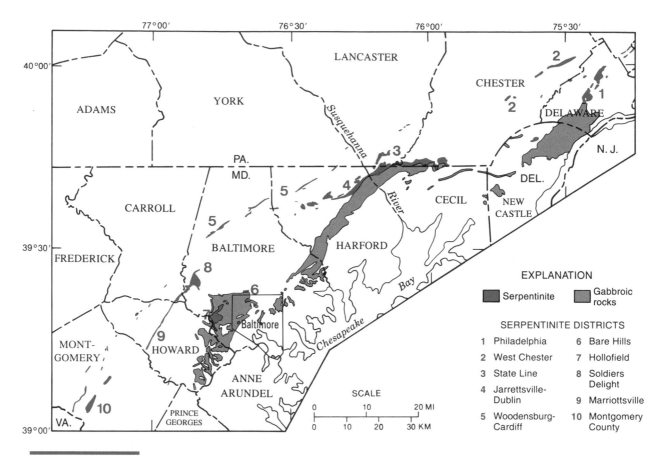

Figure 40E–2. The Baltimore Mafic Complex and other serpentinite bodies (from Spoljaric and Jordan, 1966, Cleaves and others, 1968, and Berg and others, 1980). The serpentinite districts (from Pearre and Heyl, 1960, Figure 65, and Larrabee, 1966) of the complex are indicated.

the Baltimore Mafic Complex is not clear. The two main mafic-ultramafic belts of the complex diverge near the Maryland-Pennsylvania state line, where the larger and more southerly belt crosses the regional strike (Lapham and McKague, 1964). A preliminary Nd-Sm isotope dating for the complex (Shaw and Wasserburg, 1984) yields an age of 490 ± 20 Ma, which places the crystallization of the igneous protolith at the earliest stages of the Taconic orogeny.

Hopson (1964) considered the Baltimore Mafic Complex to represent a huge folded and faulted sheet formed by magmatic intrusion into flat-lying strata, with deformation occurring during crystallization. Thayer (1967) concluded that it was instead an "alpine" body, crystallizing in the upper mantle-lower oceanic crust and later emplaced tectonically into its present position. This classification now carries with it a strong connotation of an ophiolitic association (Morgan, 1977); that is, it is a piece of oceanic lithosphere that formed at a mid-oceanic ridge. Thayer's

criteria for classifying the complex as alpine included the close association of gabbroic, ultramafic, and felsic rocks, the podiform shape of the chromite deposits, and the high ratio of magnesium olivine to pyroxene. However, the complex also possesses attributes that are distinctly uncharacteristic of alpine systems. The occurrence of hypersthene-bearing gabbros (norites) having high concentrations of iron and calcium plagioclase (Southwick, 1970) suggests that the complex assimilated aluminous country rock (Bowen, 1928) and is not a simple alpine (ophiolitic) system. Furthermore, Southwick (1970) showed that the rocks of the complex differentiated to produce iron-rich rocks more closely related to stratiform intrusions than to other alpine systems. An additional piece of evidence that further complicates the simple ophiolitic picture is the presence of numerous deposits of titanium-rich magnetite in the ultramafites of the complex (Pearre and Heyl, 1960), which are uncommon in ophiolitic serpentinites; abundant amounts of titanium point toward an affinity with stratiform ultramafic complexes. Furthermore, Shaw and Wasserburg (1984), in their Nd-Sm and Rb-Sr isotope study of the complex, showed that its isotopic composition was quite dissimilar from that of most ophiolite complexes and was consistent with mafic magma that had assimilated a rather large quantity of old crustal material. Hence, isotopic, petrologic, and mineralogic criteria suggest a continental or island-arc origin for the Baltimore Mafic Complex.

The simplest mechanism proposed for the precipitation of chromite in layered complexes is pressure variation during eruption (Cameron, 1980), which in the case of the Baltimore Mafic Complex may have been via island-arc volcanism. The podiform nature of chromite ore would then be a product of deformation following recrystallization.

CHROMITE MINES IN PENNSYLVANIA

Massive (lode), disseminated, and placer are the three types of chromite deposits that have been mined in Pennsylvania. Massive, or lode, ore is a dense aggregate of almost pure chromite. Serpentine-group minerals and pink or purple "kämmererite" (a chromian chlorite) are commonly associated with it, as are brucite, magnesite, "genthite," zaratite, and the low-temperature alteration product of serpentine termed "deweylite." Disseminated ore is referred to as birdseye ore because it is composed of discrete, rounded grains of chromite embedded in serpentinite (Figure 40E–3). Disseminated deposits mined in the past av-

eraged about 35 percent chromite. Massive and disseminated deposits were most common along the northern margins of the serpentinite bodies. They were highly irregular in shape. Some were pipelike or veinlike, whereas others were highly irregular, sackform masses. Still others were tabular. Small but widespread placer ores were found in stream valleys. Workable deposits ranged from a few inches to 4 or 5 feet in thickness.

Chromite, $Fe(Cr,Al,Fe^{3+})_2O_4$, is a member of the spinel group of minerals. Its composition is variable. Most of the chromite mined in the region had a fairly low aluminum content, which resulted in a melting temperature that was too low for it to be useful as a refractory material, a major use of much of the chromite mined today. However, the chromite ore was excellent for manufacturing chromium chemicals for use primarily as pigments and dyes. By 1845, a thriving chemical industry that used chromite from Pennsylvania and Maryland as its major raw material had developed in Baltimore. The chromite analyses given by Pearre and Heyl (1960) indicate that some of the deposits would be suitable as a source of metallurgical chromite, which normally requires a Cr_2O_3 (chromic oxide) content in excess of 48 weight percent and a chromium to iron ratio of 3:1 or more. In particular, chromite from the Line Pit and Red Pit mines (Figure 40E–4) in Pennsylvania conforms to these specifications. This chromite is also high in magnesium (McKague, 1964). In fact, some Pennsylvania chromite was used in the production of steel during World War I. Generally, the iron content of Pennsylvania chromite is reported to be higher in the placer

Figure 40E–3. Specimen of birdseye ore from a dump near the North Rock Springs mine in Lancaster County (see Figure 40E–4 for location). The black bands are chromite. The surrounding material is mostly serpentine and chlorite.

deposits than in the massive ores (Pearre and Heyl, 1960). This is probably due to the coating of magnetite that surrounds almost all disseminated chromite grains, the source of most placer chromite.

The major production of chromite came from lode deposits. Little beneficiation was necessary. Chromite was hand sorted and shipped as it came from the mine. Disseminated ore was ground, and the chromite was concentrated by gravity sorting. Placer "sand chromite" was sieved and washed in a concentrator known as a buddle. In some deposits, notably the placer ores of Delaware and Philadelphia Counties, garnet was abundant and could not be separated from the chromite by these techniques, thus rendering the deposits uneconomical.

The major chromite mines were located in the State Line serpentinite district, where 24 lode chromite mines are known to have been worked, including the very productive Wood and Red Pit mines (Figure 40E–4). The Jarrettsville-Dublin serpentinite district (Figure 40E–2), where the third largest mine of the area, the Reed mine, was located, was also important. Only a few small mines are known from the West Chester district, all having production of less than 250 long tons (Pearre and Heyl, 1960). The Soldiers Delight and Bare Hills serpentinite districts in Maryland also produced moderate to substantial amounts of chromite.

The principal chromite mines in Pennsylvania are listed in Table 40E–1 and are shown in Figure

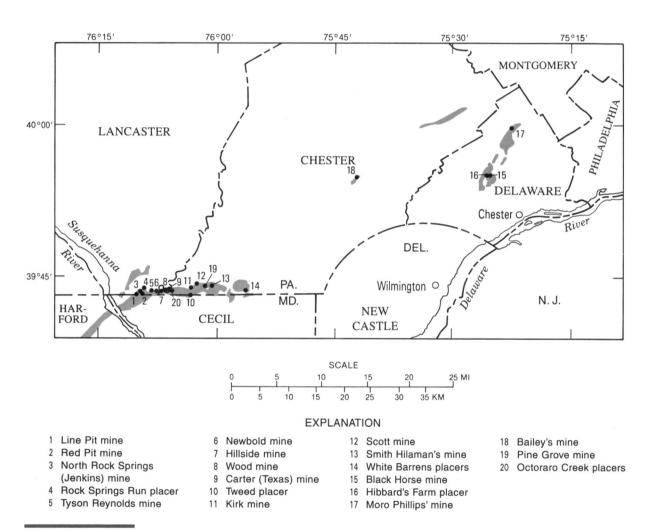

EXPLANATION

1 Line Pit mine	6 Newbold mine	12 Scott mine	18 Bailey's mine
2 Red Pit mine	7 Hillside mine	13 Smith Hilaman's mine	19 Pine Grove mine
3 North Rock Springs (Jenkins) mine	8 Wood mine	14 White Barrens placers	20 Octoraro Creek placers
4 Rock Springs Run placer	9 Carter (Texas) mine	15 Black Horse mine	
5 Tyson Reynolds mine	10 Tweed placer	16 Hibbard's Farm placer	
	11 Kirk mine	17 Moro Phillips' mine	

Figure 40E–4. The major chromite mines, quarries, and placers in Pennsylvania (slightly modified from Pearre and Heyl, 1960, Plates 41 and 42). Large serpentinite bodies (from Berg and others, 1980; and Cleaves and others, 1968) are shown in color.

Table 40E–1. *Chromium Mining Localities in Pennsylvania[1]*

Name of mining locality	Location	Minerals reported	Notes
STATE LINE DISTRICT, LANCASTER AND CHESTER COUNTIES, PA.			
Line Pit mine	¾ mile north of Rock Springs, Md., on the state line	Quartz, hematite, brucite, magnesite, hydromagnesite, clinochlore, "penninite," "kämmererite," antigorite, "williamsite," chrysotile, talc, "deweylite," sepiolite, chromite, maucherite, millerite, and serpentine	
Red Pit mine	0.3 mile northeast of Mason Dixon milepost 21	"Genthite," amphibole, asbestos, chromite, "williamsite," magnetite, and serpentine	Large producer; closed by explosion in 1868
North Rock Springs (Jenkins) mine	220 yards southwest of Rock Springs Church	Hydromagnesite, "williamsite," clinochlore, "genthite," zaratite, "kämmererite," chromite, and serpentine	
Tyson Reynolds mine	Approximately ¾ mile north of state line, 1 mile south of Wrightsdale		
Newbold mine	1 mile east of Geiger pits and ½ mile west of Hillside mine within a bend of Octoraro Creek	Tremolite, chromite, and serpentine	
Hillside mine	¼ mile west of Wood mine, on Octoraro Creek	Magnetite, "kämmererite," chromite, "williamsite," and serpentine	
Wood mine	3½ miles southeast of Lyles, Pa.	Hematite, "limonite," quartz, brucite, aragonite, magnesite, hydromagnesite, dolomite, zaratite, clinochlore, "penninite," "kämmererite," vermiculite, antigorite, "williamsite," chrysotile, "deweylite," chromite, maucherite, millerite, and serpentine	Largest of all the mines
Carter (Texas) mine	¼ mile northeast of Wood mine	Same as Wood mine; zaratite more plentiful	
Scott mine	½ mile southwest of Nottingham (Chester County)	"Kämmererite," magnesite, chromite, and serpentine	Produced about 3,000 tons
Kirk mine	1 mile southwest of Scott mine, 2½ miles east of Octoraro Creek	Chromite and serpentine	
Pine Grove mine	¾ mile south of Nottingham	Amphibole, asbestos, serpentine, and crystals of talc, zaratite, and chromite	Called Moro Phillips' mine (Chester County) by Pearre and Heyl (1960)
Smith Hilaman's mine	1 mile southeast of Nottingham	Chromite and serpentine	
Rock Springs Run placer	Approximately ½ mile north of the state line, near Rock Springs Church	Placer chromite and serpentine	One of several known as the Conowingo Creek placers, located between Lyles, Pa., and Oakwood, Md.
Octoraro Creek placers	Along the Octoraro Creek and its tributaries, West Nottingham Township	Placer chromite and serpentine	
Tweed placer	On the state line near Stone Run		
White Barrens (Little Elk Creek) placers	Between Hickory Hill and Chrome	Placer chromite and serpentine	
PHILADELPHIA DISTRICT			
Moro Phillips' mine	Southwest of Darby Creek, south corner of Radnor Township	Massive and disseminated chromite and serpentine	Early mine; there were two mines in Delaware County having this name
Black Horse mine	Schertz's farm, Mineral Hill, 2 miles west of Media	Massive and disseminated chromite and serpentine	
Hibbard's Farm placer	Middletown Township	Placer chromite and serpentine	
WEST CHESTER DISTRICT			
Bailey's mine	1½ miles northeast of Unionville	Chromite and serpentine	

[1] Modified from Hartford (1980).

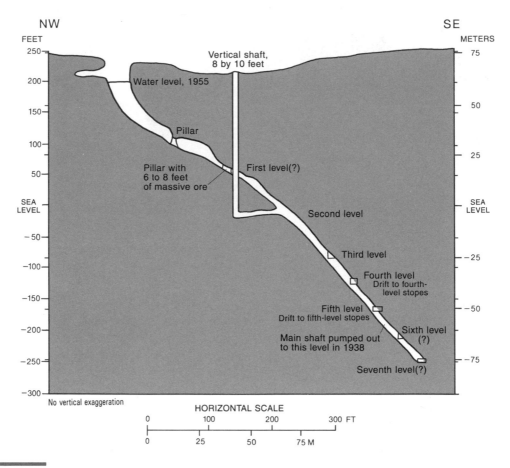

NW   SE

Figure 40E–5. Cross section of the Wood mine, Lancaster County (after Pearre and Heyl, 1960, Plate 47; see Figure 40E–4 for location).

40E–4. The largest and deepest chromite mine in the United States was the Wood mine (Figure 40E–5). It had a 720-foot-long inclined shaft that opened into stopes that followed an irregularly shaped, massive orebody of almost pure chromite. The most extensive openings covered a horizontal distance of 800 feet. At the surface, the orebody was 30 feet long and 6 feet wide, striking approximately east. At depth, the orebody had a northerly strike and increased in size to up to 70 feet by 300 feet. Ore shoots and branches of the main orebody, some veinlike with alteration zones in the serpentinites, extended for tens of feet into the wall rock. The ore ranged from 48 to 63 weight percent Cr_2O_3. The mine produced 400 to 500 tons per month from 1828 until the Civil War, after which it produced 500 to 600 tons per year, for a total production in excess of 96,000 tons (Pearre and Heyl, 1960).

The Red Pit mine, located just north of the Pennsylvania-Maryland state line, was reported to be almost as large as the Wood mine. Exact production figures are lacking, but estimates range as high as 150,000 tons of ore of greater than 50 weight percent Cr_2O_3 (Pearre and Heyl, 1960). It is thought to have been over 500 feet deep, but it was closed abruptly by an explosion of unknown origin in 1868, and no descriptions of the mine workings exist. The name of the mine came from a magnetite-bearing, red, siliceous gangue material.

The Line Pit mine, also known as Lowe's mine, was divided by the Mason-Dixon line. Although both shafts were in Lancaster County, Pa., most of the underground workings were in Maryland. The Line Pit orebody is an irregular, pipelike body of massive chromite that has short stringers extending into the surrounding rock. The orebody was worked to a depth of 241 feet, and at the bottom of the mine, it was 4 feet by 11 feet in plan. An unusual feature of the deposit is that it was encased by a 1-foot-thick zone of translucent, emerald-green "williamsite," a variety of antigorite that contains disseminated chromite and is highly prized as a semiprecious stone. Smith and Speer (1980) reported that the Line Pit orebody contains trace maucherite and millerite, also known in ore from the Wood mine.

Three mining localities were worked in the Philadelphia district, all in Delaware County. Less than 600 tons of chromite was produced, all prior to 1900.

Placer mining took place in most of the stream valleys that drain the chromiferous areas in all the serpentinite districts. Production was small and throughout the nineteenth century totaled only a little more than 20,000 tons of concentrate. Some of the deposits had concentrations as high as 40 percent chromic oxide, but most were much lower. The largest producing area in the State Line district was along Rock Springs Run in Lancaster County (number 4 in Figure 40E–4).

PROBLEMS AND FUTURE RESEARCH

Many reports indicate that the mines were not all worked out during the nineteenth century, and the potential for undiscovered orebodies is good. In 1937, the Wood mine was dewatered and partially explored, but no ore was discovered (Pearre and Heyl, 1960). Several other mines have also been studied, but no significant ore production resulted. Between 1932 and 1937, and again in 1941, the U.S. Bureau of Mines, in cooperation with private industry and the U.S. Geological Survey, made several attempts to locate new orebodies by gravimetric, magnetic, and resistivity surveys and drilling, but none of these efforts proved successful. Several mining companies have also made geophysical surveys and are reported to have drilled anomalous areas without finding ore. However, geophysical surveys usually are not effective in chromite exploration, and the negative results they have produced are not conclusive. In fact, even today, prospecting goes on, although the huge reserves in South Africa and Zimbabwe discourage all but the most determined. However, future success depends on the development of a model for the genesis of massive chromite deposits, which in turn depends on future research. Until such a model is developed, the likelihood of a rejuvenated chromite mining industry in Pennsylvania appears remote.

RECOMMENDED FOR FURTHER READING

Hartford, W. H. (1980), *Chromium deposits of Maryland and eastern Pennsylvania,* Rocks and Minerals, v. 55, no. 2, p. 52–59.

Lapham, D. M., and McKague, H. L. (1964), *Structural patterns associated with the serpentinites of southeastern Pennsylvania,* Geological Society of America Bulletin, v. 75, p. 639–660.

Pearre, N. C., and Heyl, A. V. (1959), *The history of chromite mining in Pennsylvania and Maryland,* Pennsylvania Geological Survey, 4th ser., Information Circular 14, 27 p.

Pearre, N. C., and Heyl, A. V., Jr. (1960), *Chromite and other mineral deposits in serpentine rocks of the Piedmont Upland, Maryland, Pennsylvania, and Delaware,* U.S. Geological Survey Bulletin 1082–K, p. 707–833.

Arthur A. Long hefts a "gute bushel" of burnt lime (1982) from his restored batch-kiln in Northumberland County, symbolizing both Pennsylvania's mineral heritage and the people who extracted these resources, making Pennsylvania a leading mineral-producing state. Superimposed is a graph of Pennsylvania's nonfuel-mineral value by year from 1910 to 1988. Data were compiled from U.S. Geological Survey (1911–27) and U.S. Bureau of Mines (1927–34, 1933–90).

CHAPTER 41   NONMETALS

Pennsylvania has a diversified economy, and mining continues to play a major role in that economy. For every citizen of the Commonwealth, 10 tons of nonfuel-mineral commodities was produced in 1987. That is 55 pounds per day for every man, woman, and child! The total value of this production in 1987 exceeded $1 billion for the first time in the state's history. Approximately 80 percent of this tonnage and 45 percent of the value came from crushed-stone production, which was the highest ever reported by a single state in one year.

This should come as no surprise, as the Keystone State has been blessed with a rich variety and abundance of mineral resources. Pennsylvania had led the nation, and sometimes the world, in the production of nonfuel commodities such as portland cement, lime, refractories, glass, bricks, sand and gravel, crushed stone, feldspar, slate, and mineral pigments.

Industrial minerals have played an increasingly significant role in the Commonwealth's economy. In 1911, approximately 5 percent of the value of all mineral production in Pennsylvania (including fuels) could be attributed to industrial minerals; by 1987, this figure had risen to about 37 percent. For Pennsylvania's mineral industry to continue to be a significant factor in supporting our society and the economy of the United States, the Commonwealth must continue to develop and nurture a competitive mining industry.

—*Samuel W. Berkheiser, Jr.*

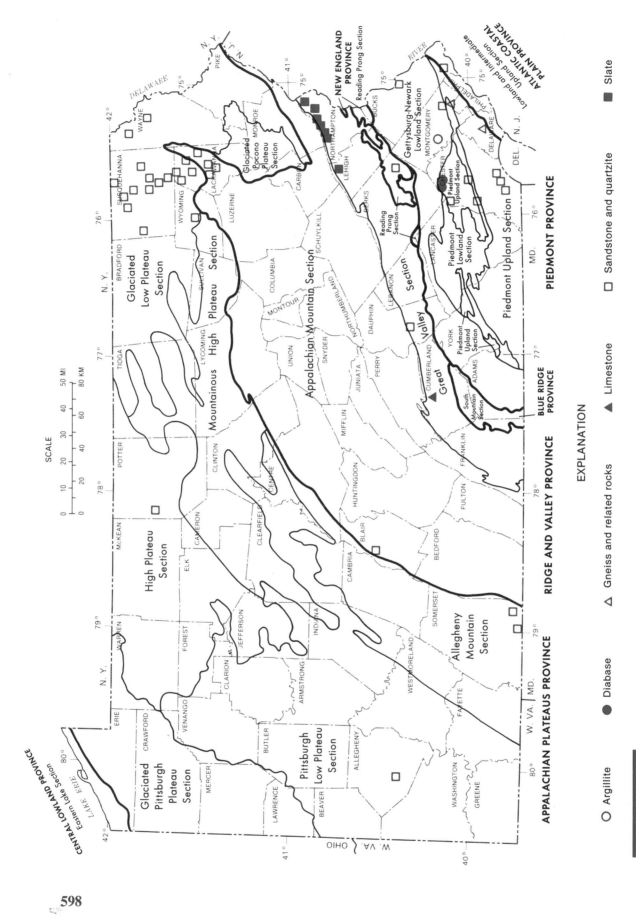

Figure 41A–1. Locations of dimension-stone operations (from Berkheiser and others, 1985) within the physiographic provinces of Pennsylvania (from Berg and others, 1989).

598

CHAPTER 41A NONMETALS—DIMENSION STONE

G. ROBERT GANIS
Tethys Consultants, Inc.
2001 North Front Street
Harrisburg, PA 17102

INTRODUCTION

Dimension stone is natural rock that is shaped or cut and sometimes polished. It is used for a variety of purposes, including the construction of buildings or structures, as well as curbing, monuments, veneers, roofing slate, flagging, laboratory furniture, industrial plates, and ornaments. In Pennsylvania, this industry produces approximately 0.5 million cubic feet of dimension-stone products annually, having an estimated value of about $8 million (Prosser and Smith, 1987b). Pennsylvania's most notable dimension-stone products are slate, flagstone ("bluestone"), and diabase ("black granite"). Dimension stone includes building stone, which is a term generally used for materials employed in masonry construction.

Dimension-stone operations vary widely in size, value-added dressing, and end-product usage. In every region of the state, local stone is used for foundations or structural walls and for a myriad of miscellaneous uses. Stone for these applications is obtained from the most convenient source available, which can include deposits of colluvium, alluvium, residual stone, and glacial material. In some places, exposed rock ledges have become small quarries to suit these purposes. The material chosen for these small-scale operations is whatever is at hand, which has resulted in the use of practically every kind of resistant rock throughout the state. The estimated production and value for this low-value "fieldstone" are not recorded.

At a significantly larger scale are regional commercial building-stone sources that produce rough stone on a regular basis for the construction industry. This category consists of commercial quarries that ship to a limited regional market. Stone from these sources is often sorted or sized as is, sometimes with little or no trimming, and is commonly referred to as "rubble" or rough stone. Many of Pennsylvania's construction-aggregate quarries contribute to this market on an "as-needed" basis, but there are also quarries that produce this material as their sole product. It is estimated that this segment represents about 32 percent of the market volume, and these building-stone products sell in the range of $3 per cubic foot (Prosser and Smith, 1987b).

Finally, there are commercial dimension-stone operations that supply rough and dressed stone materials that are distinctive in color, texture, structural properties, and/or physico-chemical composition. These are products such as roofing slates, structural and sanitary slabs, flooring slates, and monuments. The unique character and/or aesthetic appeal of these products allows their marketing to regional, national, and, in some cases, international markets. These higher-value products require strict attention to quality control and specification requirements. A good review of the specifications and rock properties that are required for dimension stone can be found in Power (1975). The dressed-stone or value-added segment of this industry represents about 92 percent of the total value and about 68 percent of the total volume (Prosser and Smith, 1987b).

The character of Pennsylvania's dimension-stone industry has gradually changed from many small operations serving limited markets to fewer and larger operations serving regional markets. In 1932, Pennsylvania had approximately 200 dimension-stone quarries operating in all but five counties (Stone, 1932a; Behre, 1933); however, recently there were 50 operations in 17 counties, and 90 percent of these operations were located in the eastern half of the state (Figure 41A–1). The evolution of modern transportation systems, improvements in mechanized equipment, development of man-made substitutes, and the extensive development of construction-aggregate operations supplying by-product building stone have led to this change.

This review of past and present aspects of Pennsylvania's dimension-stone industry is organized by physiographic province or section. Refer to Part V of this volume for general geomorphic characteristics and bedrock. To complete this summary, the writer drew heavily on the works of Stone (1932a), *Building Stones of Pennsylvania,* and Berkheiser and others (1985), *Directory of the Nonfuel-Mineral Producers in Pennsylvania.* Stone's work is exhaustive and comprehensive.

PIEDMONT PHYSIOGRAPHIC PROVINCE

The Piedmont physiographic province is divided into three sections (Figure 41A–1). In the Piedmont Upland section, there are two active building-stone operations in the lower Paleozoic Wissahickon Formation, one in Delaware County and one in Montgomery County (Berkheiser and others, 1985). Gneisses

and schists of the Wissahickon Formation have long provided materials for construction in the greater Philadelphia metropolitan area. The quartzites of the Cambrian Setters Formation and the Precambrian Chickies Formation are also notable current and past building-stone producers. White marble from the Cambrian Cockeysville Marble was formerly produced from quarries near Downingtown, Chester County (Stone, 1932a). Serpentinite dimension stone used for building facings was formerly produced from the West Chester district (Pearre and Heyl, 1960). A slate district was formerly operated at Peach Bottom in York County (Stose and Jonas, 1939).

In the Piedmont Upland section, mostly in central York and Lancaster Counties, the most notable dimension-stone unit utilized is the Precambrian Chickies quartzite. White limestone rubble from the Cambrian Kinzers Formation in the Piedmont Lowland section is supplied by construction-aggregate quarries in York.

In the Gettysburg-Newark Lowland section, the brownstone industry formerly boasted a number of large quarries. A notable center for production was near Hummelstown in Dauphin County. Although widely used, these brown or maroon sandstones are not overly durable and spall upon exposure to long periods of weathering. A better-quality red and gray quartzitic sandstone from the Triassic Stockton Formation has been quarried for dimension stone near Lumberville in Bucks County since the mid-eighteenth century (Stone, 1932a), and is still quarried. Argillite from the Triassic Lockatong Formation has been quarried for dimension stone in Montgomery County.

A very beautiful Triassic rock, sometimes called "Potomac Marble," is composed of well-cemented limestone-fanglomerate breccia. A small operation in West Donegal Township, Lancaster County, has produced an ornamental material called "Donegal Marble" for items such as tabletops (Thompson, 1983).

The Mesozoic basin of Pennsylvania contains extensive diabase intrusions (traprock). The area around St. Peters in Chester County has been a center for production of "black granite," as it is commercially called, since the mid-eighteenth century. Today, there are two active quarries in this area, the Fox Hill (Figure 41A–2) and Cherry Hill quarries, which produce rough blocks for monuments, industrial surface plates, and building facings (Roy Strickland, Pennsylvania Granite Corporation, personal communication, 1987). The rough blocks are shipped to Barre, Vt., Elberton, Ga., and Cold Spring, Minn., for fabrication and finishing. Formerly there were black granite operations near Gettysburg in Adams County and in Bucks County (Stone, 1932a).

Figure 41A–2. Fox Hill "black granite" quarry near St. Peters, Chester County. Rough blocks of diabase are removed by drilling closely spaced holes (at left) that are then filled with expansive cement, forcing the blocks loose. A subhorizontal set of fractures forms the floor of lifts (horizontal sheets bounded by joints).

NEW ENGLAND PROVINCE

Both the Precambrian crystalline rocks in the cores of nappes and the overlying Cambrian quartzites have been sources of dimension stone in this province. Quartzite of the Cambrian Hardyston Formation is currently being used for building stone from an operation in Berks County (Figure 41A–1). Historically, the Hardyston Formation has been widely used as a local source of building stone. Stone (1932a) described granite quarries at Seisholtzville, Berks County, that were once important sources of dimension stone for Bethlehem and Reading.

In Northampton County, serpentinite dimension stone was produced in the early twentieth century from quarries in Chestnut Ridge north of Easton, Northampton County (Stone, 1932a). These quarries, which are now closed, produced serpentinite from the Precambrian Franklin Limestone, which was serpentinized by igneous solutions (Miller and others, 1939).

BLUE RIDGE PROVINCE

In the Blue Ridge province of south-central Pennsylvania, Precambrian metavolcanic units are unconformably overlain by Lower Cambrian(?) to upper Precambrian clastics of the Chilhowee Group. Quartzite, greenstone, and vein quartz rubble were the principal building-stone materials used in the past. Many of the metarhyolite units are vividly colored in shades of purple, red, and green, in some places intermixed as breccia flows. The potential use of this stone for ornamental purposes in Adams County was described by Stose (1925); however, to date, significant exploitation has not occurred.

RIDGE AND VALLEY PROVINCE

The folded Paleozoic sedimentary rocks of this province account for about 30 percent of the dimension-stone producers and approximately 60 percent of the total value (Prosser and Smith, 1987b). In the eastern part of the Great Valley section are the famous Pennsylvania slate quarries of Northampton and Lehigh Counties (Figure 41A–1). Fine-grained homogeneous slate with pervasive axial-plane cleavage has yielded commercial slate deposits in the Pen Argyl Member of the Ordovician Martinsburg Formation (Behre, 1933; Drake and Epstein, 1967; Berkheiser, 1985b). The slate is marketed throughout the United States. The quarries are very picturesque (Figure 41A–3), and the manufacture of slate products is a master craftsman's enterprise (Figure 41A–4). The slate is used for traditional purposes, such as roofing and flooring tiles, as well as for more exotic purposes, such as billiard tables and electrical insulators (Berkheiser, 1985b).

In the Great Valley section of Cumberland County, Caretti, Inc., operates a limestone quarry in the Ordovician Chambersburg Formation solely for building stone (Pennsylvania Geological Survey, 1986). However, the many construction-aggregate quarries in carbonate units throughout the Ridge and Valley province also provide building stone as a by-product.

Quartzite, sandstone, and carbonate units have been widely used as building stone on a local basis in the Appalachian Mountain section.

APPALACHIAN PLATEAUS PROVINCE

This province contains almost 40 percent of the known active dimension-stone operations in Pennsylvania (Berkheiser and others, 1985). The majority of these produce the famous bluestone (flagstone) from

Figure 41A–3. Slate quarry in the Lehigh-Northampton district, Northampton County (from Berkheiser, 1985b, p. 31). The near-vertical bedding in the Pen Argyl Member of the Martinsburg Formation is cut horizontally by axial-plane cleavage, allowing deep, rectangular quarry development. Each bench is approximately 12 feet high.

Figure 41A–4. Roofing slates being split and trimmed at the Penn Big Bed mill, Lehigh County (from Berkheiser, 1985b, p. 29).

Devonian sandstones and graywackes of the High Plateau, Mountainous High Plateau, and Glaciated Low Plateau sections (Figure 41A–1). Near the margin of the Appalachian Mountain section of Lackawanna County, at the transition to the Appalachian Plateau, are building-stone and flagstone operations developed in both Devonian graywackes and conglomeratic Devonian-Mississippian transition rocks.

The flagstone district of northeastern Pennsylvania is also known as the Endless Mountains region (Figure 41A–5), and the geology is discussed in an informative pamphlet by Glaeser (1969). Krajewski and Williams (1971) studied this industry and concluded that rocks deposited in ancient beach settings will have the greatest volume of minable stone, whereas those deposited in fluvial or tidal channels will have the best overall durability. In addition to the active flagstone operations, the region contains numerous small, inactive pits (Figure 41–6).

In the various sections of the Appalachian Plateaus province in western Pennsylvania, massive Car-

boniferous sandstones have been extensively used for building stone. Active operations listed in Berkheiser and others (1985) include two Carboniferous sandstone sources producing flagstone and building stone in the Allegheny Mountain section and an operation in the Monongahela Group sandstones in the Pittsburgh Low Plateau section (Figure 41A–1).

The Mississippian Loyalhanna Formation, a siliceous limestone, was formerly a source of paving blocks for the Pittsburgh area. Today, the Loyalhanna is an important aggregate unit and still provides rubble blocks for construction.

PROBLEMS AND FUTURE RESEARCH

Pennsylvania contains some valuable dimension-stone resources. As with other open-pit mining, dimension-stone producers share in the conflicts resulting from environmental and land use concerns. Contrary to some misconceptions, dimension stone is not obsolete, although substitutes such as precast concrete have replaced a great part of the industry.

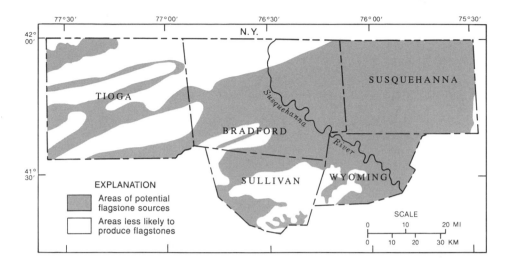

Figure 41A–5. Map of the Endless Mountains region showing potential sources of flagstone (slightly modified from Glaeser, 1969, p. 4).

Pennsylvania maintains a position of national importance in the production of slate, flagstone (bluestone), and diabase (black granite). It should be of prime importance to support these industries and ensure the availability of future reserves.

Pennsylvania also has some unrealized potential in dimension stone. Further exploration and possible development of the metarhyolites of the Blue Ridge province and the serpentinites of the Piedmont province are but two examples. The finishing and fabrication centers in the United States make development of new dimension-stone operations more feasible. Pennsylvania's architects should be kept informed of the various quality sources of native dimension stone.

General problems of the industry, which Pennsylvania's producers share, include competing with cheap imports, finding uses for waste rock, and protecting their market share from inexpensive resin-bonded composites (for example, "cultured marble").

Several factors have contributed to a renewed interest in natural stone for construction. Advances in the technology of hanging cut stone slabs as thin as 0.75 inch (compared to 3 inches in the past) are making stone construction much more competitive. Aesthetic interest in natural stone is again very popular.

There is a continuing incentive to develop faster and more economical ways

to extract stone. Improvements in this area should be expected.

RECOMMENDED FOR FURTHER READING

Berkheiser, S. W., Jr. (1985), *Pennsylvania's slate industry: alive and well,* in Glaser, J. D., and Edwards, J., eds., *Twentieth Forum on the Geology of Industrial Minerals [Baltimore, Md., 1984],* Maryland Geological Survey Special Publication 2, p. 23–33.

Geyer, A. R. (1977), *Building stones of Pennsylvania's capital area,* Pennsylvania Geological Survey, 4th ser., Environmental Geology Report 5, 47 p.

Glaeser, J. D. (1969), *Geology of flagstones in the Endless Mountains region, northern Pennsylvania,* Pennsylvania Geological Survey, 4th ser., Information Circular 66, 14 p.

Miller, B. L. (1934), *Limestones of Pennsylvania,* Pennsylvania Geological Survey, 4th ser., Mineral Resource Report 20, 729 p.

Stone, R. W. (1932), *Building stones of Pennsylvania,* Pennsylvania Geological Survey, 4th ser., Mineral Resource Report 15, 316 p.

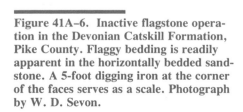

Figure 41A–6. Inactive flagstone operation in the Devonian Catskill Formation, Pike County. Flaggy bedding is readily apparent in the horizontally bedded sandstone. A 5-foot digging iron at the corner of the faces serves as a scale. Photograph by W. D. Sevon.

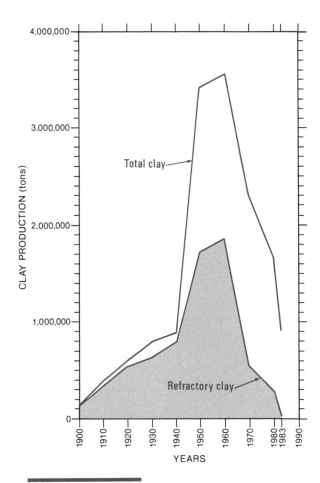

Figure 41B-1. Clay and shale production in Pennsylvania from 1900 to 1983. Data from 1900 to 1940 represent clay that was mined and sold as clay. They do not include clay that was burned into clay products by the producers. The total-clay curve includes kaolin, clay and shale for cement manufacture, pottery clay, and clay products such as tiles and bricks. Data compiled from Middleton (1901, 1911, 1923), Tyler and Linn (1943), Pennsylvania Department of Internal Affairs and others (1944a), Gunsallus and Ritenour (1953), Thomson and others (1961), Cooper (1972), Kebblish and Tuchman (1982), and Prosser and others (1984).

CHAPTER 41B   NONMETALS—CLAY AND SHALE

SAMUEL W. BERKHEISER, JR.
   Bureau of Topographic and Geologic Survey
   Department of Conservation and Natural
      Resources
   P. O. Box 8453
   Harrisburg, PA 17105

JOHN H. BARNES
   Bureau of Topographic and Geologic Survey
   Department of Conservation and Natural
      Resources
   P. O. Box 8453
   Harrisburg, PA 17105

INTRODUCTION

Clay working is undoubtedly one of the world's oldest mining activities. Clay was used by the Early Woodland Indians in Pennsylvania to make pottery in about 1000 B.C. (B. Kent, personal communication, 1985). According to Bishop (1861), William Penn gave instructions to Dutch agents in 1684 to build principally with brick. People must have taken Penn's advice; Hopkins (1900) reported that Philadelphia was the leading brick-producing city in America for more than two centuries. The Commonwealth was also an early producer of earthenware, stoneware, and whiteware pottery. Traditional industries of Pennsylvania, such as steel and glass, relied heavily on the state's refractory clays and shales.

Clays and shales that are produced for industrial applications in Pennsylvania fall into six general categories: alluvial deposits, glaciolacustrine deposits, marine shales, residual clays, soils, and underclays (Table 41B–1).

The production of clays in Pennsylvania reached a peak of 3.5 million tons in about 1960. Recent production of clay and shale has dropped to about 1 million tons annually, with face brick, firebrick, and portland cements consuming about 90 percent of this production, according to the U.S. Bureau of Mines (Kebblish, 1984b) (Figure 41B–1). The average price for all clay and shale mined in the state is about $6 per ton, whereas fireclay, or refractory clay, of which Pennsylvania has consistently been a major producer, averages about $19 per ton (Ampian, 1984).

CONSTRUCTION SOURCES AND USES

Borrow and General Fill

The largest tonnage of clay and shale can probably be attributed to this application. Most producers of borrow and fill are located in the Ridge and Valley province and the northeastern part of the Appalachian Plateaus province (Figure 41B–2). About 200 producers were noted by Berkheiser and others (1985). These resources, which include shale-chip rubble

Table 41B–1. *General Classification of Clays and Shales and Some of Their More Common Uses*

Material	Definition	Borrow and general fill	Impermeable barriers	Bricks, tiles, and pottery	Light-weight aggregate	Cement manufacture	Refractory clays	White clay
Alluvial (terrace), Pleistocene	Sediment deposited on a terrace above present stream level, such as the Carmichaels Formation	X	X	X				
Glaciolacustrine, Pleistocene	Sediment deposited by meltwater in lakes bordering glaciers	X	X	X				
Marine shales, Paleozoic–Mesozoic	Fine-grained sediment deposited in a normal, aqueous, saline environment	X		X	X	X		
Residual clays, Eocene–Holocene	Clay formed in place by alteration of minerals or removal of soluble minerals	X	X	X		X	X	X
Soils, Holocene	Material containing clays, other mineral matter, and organic constituents	X						
Underclays, Paleozoic	Fine-grained detritus below a coal; former soil in which coal-forming plants grew	X	X	X	X	X	X	

(Sevon and Berg, 1979), are popular because they are easily mined and loaded without regard to sizing.

Impermeable Barriers

Certain clay minerals are among the components used in the construction of impermeable barriers used in lagoons, landfills, and the cores of earth-fill dams. Ideally, these materials should be free of rock fragments, have a uniform density, and have a suitable cation exchange capacity. Much of Pennsylvania is underlain by materials that have the potential to be suitable for this purpose (Table 41B–1).

Bricks, Tiles, and Pottery

Early settlers found most of Philadelphia underlain by at least 3 feet of residual and alluvial clays, which became known as the Philadelphia Brick Clay. By 1880, there were 78 companies employing about 3,000 people and producing about $1,700,000 worth of handmade red bricks in Philadelphia (Hopkins, 1900).

Some residual clays overlying limestone in the Conshohocken area of Montgomery County were

used for manufacturing earthenware (unvitrified red flowerpots) and stoneware (glazed and partly vitrified) (Hopkins, 1900).

Commercial brick construction in Pittsburgh probably did not commence until around 1800 (Hice, 1911). The pottery industry in western Pennsylvania did not become established until the mid- to late 1800's. The New Brighton area in Beaver County was an early, major producing center of many kinds of pottery goods. Alluvial, or terrace, clays were mixed with underclays of the Pennsylvanian Lower Kittanning coal. Whiteware was manufactured with materials brought from across the state, such as kaolin, feldspar, and "flint" from pegmatites in southern Chester and Delaware Counties and vein quartz from Adams and York Counties (Hopkins, 1898, 1900).

Specialty bricks and tiles were manufactured around the turn of the century in Adams, Berks, Cumberland, Franklin, Lehigh, and Monroe Counties. White and colored vitrified bricks and tiles were manufactured using white, kaolinitic, and siliceous clays associated with the "valley" or "brown" iron ores (d'Invilliers, 1883; Hopkins, 1900; Hice, 1911;

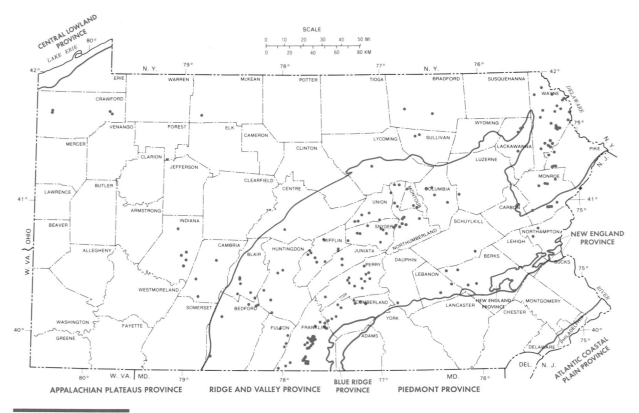

Figure 41B–2. Map showing borrow-and-fill producers (modified from Berkheiser and others, 1985) in relation to the major physiographic provinces of Pennsylvania (from Berg and others, 1989).

Peck, 1922b; Stose, 1932). White siliceous clays associated with the upper contact of the Hardyston Formation were mined near Longswamp in Berks County around the turn of the century for fillers and pigments in linoleum, and later as a filler in joint compounds and as an ingredient in chemical-resistant bricks, tiles, and coatings (A. A. Boova, Atlas Minerals and Chemicals, Inc., personal communication, 1983).

Many clays and shales can be used for the manufacture of construction brick (Figure 41B–3). Successful manufacturing depends upon proper blending of raw materials so that the "green" (unfired) mix exhibits plasticity for molding and can be economically burned to a pleasing color without undue shrinkage or cracking. Calcareous materials are undesirable because they act as a flux and reduce the temperature difference between incipient vitrification and melting (Leighton, 1941). An account of a modern brick manufacturing process in Northumberland County is given by Berkheiser and Inners (1984). Potential resources for brick manufacturing, as identified by O'Neill and others (1965), Hoover

and others (1971), and O'Neill and Barnes (1979, 1981) are incalculably large.

In Cumberland County, a black manganiferous residual clay from the old Reading Banks iron ore deposit is reportedly mined for use as a coloring ingredient in the production of stoneware. Tile and flue-liner producers generally mine underclays associated with the Pennsylvanian Lower Kittanning and Clarion coals in western Pennsylvania.

Lightweight Aggregate

Lightweight aggregate is used primarily for thermal and acoustical insulation, although other beneficial properties include weight reduction, fire resistance, and toughness (McCarl, 1983). Williams and others (1974, 1985) have identified Pennsylvanian marine shales with high illite:kaolinite ratios, especially within the basinal axes, as prime exploration targets. Sampling and testing by O'Neill and others (1965), Hoover and others (1971), and O'Neill and Barnes (1979, 1981) led to the identification of the

Pennsylvanian Pittsburgh coal underclay, and shales of the Cambrian Cocalico, Ordovician Martinsburg and Reedsville, Devonian Mahantango, Pennsylvanian Casselman and Glenshaw, and Triassic Lockatong Formations as having good expandable characteristics for the production of lightweight aggregate.

Cement Manufacture

Clays and shales provide alumina needed to manufacture portland cement. Overburden from limestone quarrying is a common source of this material. White cement manufacture, however, requires a light-colored, low-iron clay that can also be used as a whitening agent. Residual white, siliceous, kaolinitic clays, usually associated with the contact between a carbonate rock and a sandstone (quartzite), have been mined for this purpose in Monroe and Cumberland Counties (Epstein and Hosterman, 1969; Hosterman, 1969). An active white-clay mine near Narvon, Lancaster County, and a recently discovered deposit in Berks County (Berkheiser and Smith, 1984), could supply similar material.

REFRACTORY CLAY SOURCES

Refractory clays, or fireclays, are characterized by the ability to withstand temperatures greater than 1424°C (2595°F), because they have high fusion (melting) points, measured as pyrometric cone equivalents (PCE). Their most common use is for handling molten metals, particularly in blast furnaces. Only the highest classes of fireclay brick (high duty with a minimum PCE of 31½ and super duty with a minimum PCE of 33) still have a significant market (Figure 41B–1). High-alumina brick (made from imported bauxite) and basic refractories (dolomite and magnesite) are replacing fireclay in the more modern steel-making processes. Table 41B–2 lists fireclays that have a PCE of 31 or greater. Figure 41B–4 is a generalized location map of these fireclays and indicates the relative stratigraphic position of the Carboniferous underclays.

The basic types of commercial fireclays mined in Pennsylvania are underclays categorized as nodule, flint (hard with a conchoidal fracture), semi-flint, and plastic (becomes soft with the addition of water). In general, nodule clays, which are the most

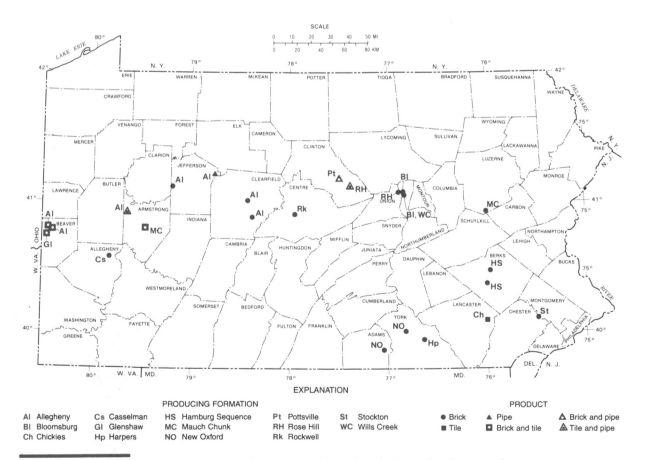

Figure 41B–3. Map showing the producing formation and location of clay and shale currently mined for the manufacture of bricks, tiles, and pipe (modified from Berkheiser and others, 1985).

Table 41B–2. *Refractory Clays Having PCE's of 31 or Greater*

Stratigraphic unit[1]	Thickness	PCE[2]	Reference
BERKS COUNTY			
Hardyston Formation	12 and 10 feet	31	Berkheiser and Smith (1984)
BLAIR COUNTY			
Gatesburg Formation	4 to 5 feet	31–32	O'Neill and others (1965)
CAMBRIA COUNTY			
Brookville (Cambria)	4 feet	32–34	Leighton (1941)
Mercer	2 to 6 feet	34	Leighton (1941)
CAMERON COUNTY			
Brookville (Clermont)	4.5 to 6 feet	31	Leighton (1941)
CENTRE COUNTY			
Brookville	3 to 5 feet	31	Leighton (1941)
Mercer	6 feet	32	Shaw (1928)
CLARION COUNTY			
Lower Kittanning	10 feet(?)	31–32	O'Neill and others (1965)
Mercer	2 to 8 feet	33–34	Leighton (1941)
CLEARFIELD COUNTY			
Allegheny Formation	?	32½	Shaw (1928)
Brookville or Mercer	6 to 7 feet	35	Shaw (1928)
Clarion (Bigler)	?	33+	Edmunds (1968)
Mercer	2 to 10 feet	31½–34	Shaw (1928), Leighton (1941), O'Neill and others (1965), Edmunds (1968)
Mercer or Clarion	4 to 8 feet(?)	31–33	Shaw (1928)
Pottsville Formation	?	32	Shaw (1928)
CLINTON COUNTY			
Brookville(?)	3 to 7 feet	33–34	Shaw (1928)
Upper Kittanning	4 feet	33½	Shaw (1928)
Mercer(?)	0.5 to 4 feet	31–33	Leighton (1941)
ELK COUNTY			
Lower Kittanning(?)	?	32	Leighton (1941)
FAYETTE COUNTY			
Upper Freeport	10 feet	32	Shaw (1928)
Lower Kittanning	3 to 4 feet	32–34	O'Neill and others (1965)
INDIANA COUNTY			
Upper Mercer	8 feet	32	Shaw (1928)
JEFFERSON COUNTY			
Lower Freeport(?)	4 feet	31	Leighton (1941)
Lower Kittanning	2 to 3½ feet	32	Leighton (1941)
Mercer	4 to 11 feet	32½–33	Leighton (1941)
LYCOMING COUNTY			
Brookville or Mercer	4 feet	31½–33	Leighton (1941)
SOMERSET COUNTY			
Clarion	8 feet	34	Shaw (1928), Flint (1965)
Upper Freeport	5 feet	32	Shaw (1928)
Lower Kittanning	4 to 14 feet	32–34	Shaw (1928), Leighton (1941)
Upper Kittanning	4 feet	31½–32	Shaw (1928)
Mercer	1 to 3 feet	34+	O'Neill and others (1965)
WESTMORELAND COUNTY			
Mercer	>5 feet	32	Shaffner (1958)
Pittsburgh	1 foot	32	Leighton (1932)

[1]Units refer to underclays unless otherwise indicated.
[2]PCE, pyrometric cone equivalent.

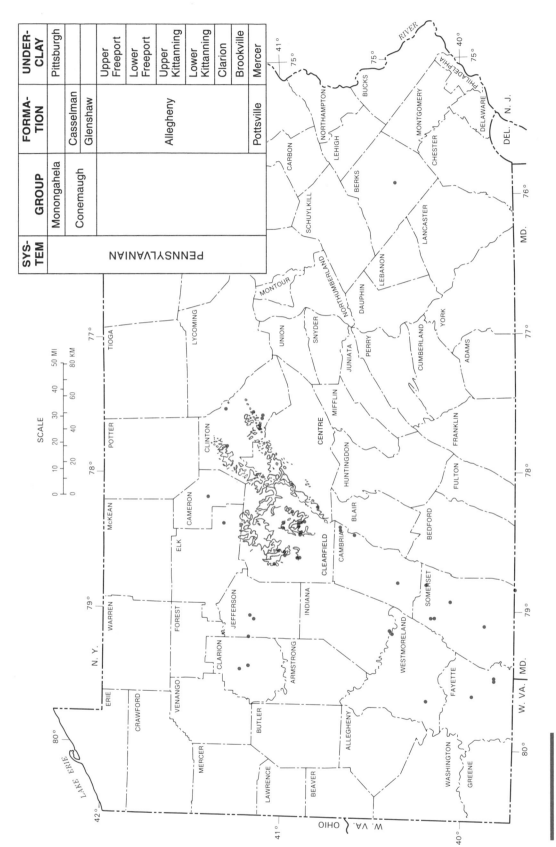

Figure 41B-4. Map showing the location of underclays having a PCE of 31 or greater. The stratigraphic column shows the relative position of some Pennsylvanian-age underclays. Generalized crop lines are shown for the Mercer clay horizon in Centre, Clearfield, and Clinton Counties (from Weitz and Bolger, 1964). See Table 41B-2 for general characteristics.

refractory, contain diaspore and boehmite; flint clays are essentially pure kaolinite; and plastic clays are a mixture of kaolinite, illite, and quartz (Grim, 1962; Williams and Bragonier, 1985). Usually, these different kinds of clays are mixed in various proportions, depending on the properties desired.

Most of the flint clays and nodule clays occur as lenses. Williams (1972), Bragonier (1970), and Williams and Bragonier (1985) suggested that the better refractory clays formed in freshwater, swampy areas, or close to the continental-marine transition zone, and were formed on paleostructural highs, now located on the margins of the bituminous coal basin. A higher kaolinite:mica ratio in the underclay of the Lower Kittanning coal in such depositional settings led Williams and Holbrook (1985) to interpret these underclays as paleosols, which are indicated by other criteria to have formed during hiatuses of up to 200,000 years. Intense chemical weathering (leaching) presumably increased the total amount of alumina.

The most exploited Pennsylvania fireclay is the Mercer underclay (Pennsylvanian Pottsville Formation), which has mineable thicknesses mainly in Clearfield, Centre, and Clinton Counties. The Lower Mercer flint clays are geographically sporadic in their occurrence. Williams (1960, 1972), Bragonier (1970), and Williams and Bragonier (1985) suggested prospecting in areas where the Upper Connoquenessing sandstone (laterally equivalent to the Mercer flint clays) is absent, and in areas of structural and topographic highs. Williams and Bragonier (1985) further hypothesized that these clays may have been derived from the underlying sandstones, based on physical and mineralogical associations.

During World War II, nodular (diaspore-bearing) portions of the Mercer flint clays were investigated as a potential source of aluminum metal. Foose (1944) reported that millions of tons of "ore," containing more than 35 percent Al_2O_3 and not suitable for refractory products because of high iron content, were identified in Clearfield County in the well-established Curwensville and Morgan Run districts. Foose's "burnt nodular" variety, characterized as having a rusty-brown, porous, cindery appearance, commonly has Al_2O_3 values in the 70 to 75 percent range.

The once-robust fireclay industry in Pennsylvania has dwindled to the mining of the Mercer underclay in Clearfield and Clinton Counties and the Clarion underclay in Somerset County, and minor production from the Lower and Middle Kittanning underclays in Clearfield and Lawrence Counties (Berkheiser and others, 1985).

The anthracite underclays (generally dark-colored argillites) contain some minor refractory minerals, such as kaolinite and pyrophyllite. However, Al_2O_3 rarely exceeds about 25 percent (O'Neill and others, 1965; Hosterman and others, 1970). Of the few samples tested, only one, from Schuylkill County, has marginal low-duty potential (O'Neill and others, 1965). The presence of carbonate minerals limits the refractory potential of most occurrences of these underclays.

WHITE CLAY SOURCES

Most significant kaolinitic and siliceous white clays have at least 20 percent alumina and are the apparent result of weathering and alteration along clastic-carbonate contacts or transition zones (Table 41B–3). This upland-valley and clastic-carbonate interface has generated many residual kaolinite-rich clay deposits in eastern Pennsylvania and is a prime exploration target for this material. The locations of these and of less significant deposits in central Pennsylvania are shown in Figure 41B–5. It is not uncommon for these deposits to be associated with limonite iron ore and cryptomelane-pyrolusite manganese mineralization. Most exploited occurrences of white clay were initially iron mines and pits, active around 1880. Similar clay from a hand-dug shaft near Reading was used to make horse liniment in the mid-twentieth century (G. Waldbiesser, Eastern Industies, Inc., personal communication, 1987).

The Narvon Mines near Narvon, Lancaster County, and the Lehigh Portland Cement operation near Kunkletown, Monroe County, are the only active pits producing products for the agricultural, filler, refractory, and cement industries. A washed clay product was produced prior to 1930 from many now-abandoned fine-grained, silica-rich deposits for fillers in paper, china, paint, rubber, tile, and linoleum. Approximately 1.4 million tons of kaolin was mined in Pennsylvania between 1900 and 1940 (Pennsylvania Department of Internal Affairs and others, 1944a).

PROBLEMS AND FUTURE RESEARCH

Many clay materials that have been produced in Pennsylvania in the past are no longer produced, or are produced in much smaller quantities, because of changes in manufacturing processes that have rendered past applications obsolete or because of the development of higher-quality sources in other states. The clay use that seems to hold potential for growth in Pennsylvania, and upon which additional research to locate better sources and methods of beneficiation is warranted, is that of impermeable liners for landfills. As outlined above, these materials should be free of rock fragments, have a uniform density, and have a suitable cation-exchange capacity. Much of Pennsylvania is underlain by either kaolinite-rich plastic clays, alluvial (terrace) clays, glaciolacustrine clays, underclays associated with bituminous coal, or other residual clays, such as those forming from limestone, all of which have the potential to be suitable for this purpose.

	Geologic unit(s) and thickness	Uses	References
		Table 41B–3. *White Clays in Pennsylvania*	
Location	Geologic unit(s) and thickness	Uses	References
KUNKLETOWN-SAYLORSBURG AREA			
Monroe County	Bossardville Limestone through Buttermilk Falls Limestone. Best ore near base of "Oriskany." Mostly 8 to 26 feet; locally more than 110 feet.	White cement manufacturing, paper, rubber, paints, refractory; early uses include soap and brick	Peck (1922a, b), Leighton (1934), Epstein and Hosterman (1969), and Hosterman (1984)
SOUTHEASTERN PENNSYLVANIA			
Berks County	Hardyston Formation, 20 to 60 feet	Bricks and tiles (including chemically resistant), fire brick, fillers, pigments, coatings, white china, porcelain, paper, paper hangings, and horse liniment	Genth (1875), d'Invilliers (1883), Brown and Ehrenfeld (1913), and Berkheiser and Smith (1984)
Lancaster County	Chickies Formation, 70 feet	Filler, insecticide carrier, ceramics, and water purification	Leighton (1934, 1941), and Hosterman (1984)
SOUTH MOUNTAIN AREA			
Cumberland County	Antietam and Tomstown Formations, 22 to more than 145 feet	White cement manufacturing, brick and tile, linoleum, matches, refractory cement, chinaware, paper, and paint	d'Invilliers (1887), Stose (1907b, 1932), Leighton (1934), Stose and Jonas (1939), Freedman (1967), and Hosterman (1969, 1984)
CENTRAL PENNSYLVANIA			
Bedford, Blair, Centre, and Huntingdon Counties	Gatesburg Formation, 5 to 75 feet	Refractory cement and lining, saggars, ladles, cupolas, and paper	Moore (1922), Leighton (1934), Hosterman (1972, 1984)
Blair, Huntingdon, and Mifflin Counties	"Oriskany" Sandstone and Shriver Chert, 6.5 to 30 feet	Refractories: furnace linings, fire brick, and cement	Peck (1922a), Leighton (1934), and Hosterman (1984)

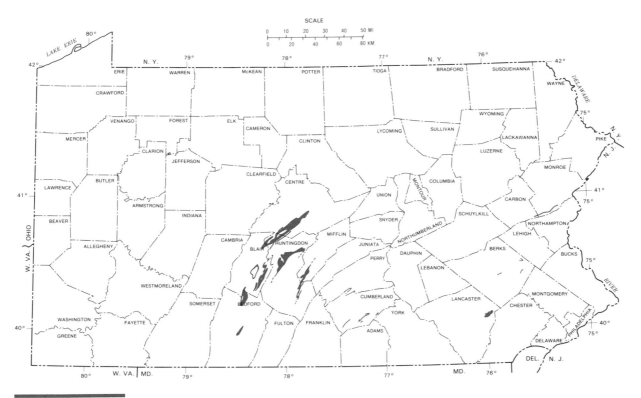

Figure 41B-5. Map showing the location of some known and potential residual white-clay sources in Pennsylvania. See Table 41B-3 for general characteristics and uses.

RECOMMENDED FOR FURTHER READING

Crookston, J. A., and Fitzpatrick, W. D. (1983), *Refractories,* in Lefond, S. J., and others, eds., *Industrial minerals and rocks,* 5th ed., New York, American Institute of Mining, Metallurgical, and Petroleum Engineers, v. 1, p. 373–386.

Gold, D. P., Canich, M. R., Cuffey, R. J., and others (1985), *Central Pennsylvania geology revisited,* Annual Field Conference of Pennsylvania Geologists, 50th, State College, Pa., Guidebook, 290 p.

Hosterman, J. W. (1984), *White clays of Pennsylvania,* U.S. Geological Survey Bulletin 1558-D, 38 p.

Leighton, Henry (1934), *The white clays of Pennsylvania,* Pennsylvania Geological Survey, 4th ser., Progress Report 112, 19 p.

———— (1941), *Clay and shale resources in Pennsylvania,* Pennsylvania Geological Survey, 4th ser., Mineral Resource Report 23, 245 p.

O'Neill, B. J., Jr., Lapham, D. M., Jaron, M. G., and others (1965), *Properties and uses of Pennsylvania shales and clays,* Pennsylvania Geological Survey, 4th ser., Mineral Resource Report 51, 448 p.

Patterson, S. H., and Murray, H. H. (1983), *Clays,* in Lefond, S. J., and others, eds., *Industrial minerals and rocks,* 5th ed., New York, American Institute of Mining, Metallurgical, and Petroleum Engineers, v. 1, p. 585–651.

Shaw, J. B. (1928), *Fire clays of Pennsylvania,* Pennsylvania Geological Survey, 4th ser., Mineral Resource Report 10, 69 p.

Williams, E. G. (1972), *Structural control of high-alumina refractory clays in western Pennsylvania,* Earth and Mineral Sciences, v. 41, no. 7, p. 53–54.

A

B   C

**Figure 41C1–1. Test for soundness of aggregates using sodium sulfate (Pennsylvania Test Method 510).
A. Sample preparation. The crushed gravel (bottom) passed through a sieve having 3/8-inch openings
(right) and was retained on a No. 4 sieve (four openings per inch; left). Sieves are 8 inches in diameter.
B. One of five soak-and-dry cycles. A saturated solution of sodium sulfate is poured onto the samples
after they have been dried in an oven and then cooled to room temperature. C. End of test. The final
separation is made on a sieve having slightly smaller openings than that used in the original separation
(No. 5 sieve, five openings per inch). In this example, the material, shown on the right, that broke down
enough to pass through the No. 5 sieve is only 3 percent of the original sample, shown on the left.**

614

CHAPTER 41C, PART 1   NONMETALS— CONSTRUCTION AGGREGATES: GEOTECHNICAL ASPECTS

RICHARD H. HOWE
2911 Chestnut Street
Camp Hill, PA 17011

INTRODUCTION

The search for suitable geologic materials for use by the construction-aggregate industry presents many challenges. The goal is to make a product that has engineering properties acceptable to the market from materials that have inherent, but often hidden, variations.

Construction aggregates are inert, granular materials, commonly composed of stone, gravel, sand, or slag. These materials are used either with a cementing medium to form mortars or concretes, or alone to form pavement base courses, railroad ballasts, and so forth (American Society for Testing and Materials, 1988a). In Pennsylvania in 1983, about 12 million tons of sand and gravel, 29 million tons of crushed stone, 3 million tons of iron slag, and 1 million tons of steel slag were processed for use in construction (Prosser and others, 1985b). Recent prices of aggregate in Pittsburgh and Philadelphia, F.O.B. plant, ranged from $6 to $11 per ton (Engineering News Record, 1989). Aggregates of lesser required quality, but suitable for use as backfill around foundation walls, subbases beneath pavements, or abrasives for icy roads, are not discussed here. These aggregates are frequently produced from the same sources as aggregates meeting the more stringent requirements for use in making concrete.

The intent here is to provide some guidance to geologists in evaluating existing or potential sources of construction aggregates in Pennsylvania. The space given to sampling, testing, and specifications indicates their relative importance in producing a marketable product. The emphasis is on the characteristics of coarse (gravel-sized) aggregates, which are produced from geologic materials and which are suitable for use in building roads and bridges. Fine (sand-sized) aggregates must meet similar requirements. Suitable lithologies are diverse (Table 41C1-1). Sources are mostly rock quarries and gravel pits but also in-

615

clude some mines and dredges (Berkheiser and others, 1985; Pennsylvania Department of Transportation, 1988).

SAND AND GRAVEL SOURCES

Most of the sands and crushed gravels suitable for use as construction aggregate are produced from unconsolidated materials of Illinoian, Wisconsinan, and Recent ages. The composition of the particles tends to reflect the composition of the bedrock that was traversed by glaciers and glacial meltwater. In western Pennsylvania, the result of this is an abundance of siltstone and sandstone particles. The siltstones are often laminated, and the sandstones are in some places poorly cemented. In some gravel deposits, several percent ferruginous (sideritic) concretions are present. When they are exposed to repeated freezing and thawing, the laminated particles become wafers, the poorly cemented ones become sand, and the ferruginous particles turn into small fragments and, in many cases, stain cement-concrete surfaces. Where they are close to the surface of cement concrete, the ferruginous concretions and laminated particles may expand enough to cause "popouts," which are small, saucer-shaped depressions. On pavements, the disintegrated particles are readily plucked from the surface by traffic, leaving pits and pockets.

In eastern Pennsylvania, the gravels contain better-indurated siltstones and sandstones, and freeze-thaw durability is less often a problem. Nevertheless, ferruginous concretions have been known to cause thousands of lenticular popouts in a few miles of cement-concrete pavement. Shale particles in the coarse-aggregate sizes have caused popouts and pitting. Because the shales of eastern Pennsylvania are older and better indurated, some of the more durable shale particles occur in gravels. Where these shales contain very finely disseminated iron sulfides, they may disintegrate, resulting in the formation of siderite and gypsum (Evenson and others, 1975). These minerals may have an adverse effect on portland-cement concrete in its plastic state, or even in its hardened state, depending on the size and abundance of the authigenic gypsum particles. It is from the bedrock, however, rather than from the gravels, that the greatest volume of construction aggregate is obtained.

CRUSHED-ROCK SOURCES

In southeastern Pennsylvania, there are important sources of aggregate in argillite, siltstone, hornfels, and diabase of Triassic age. Most of the sources are in the argillite of the Lockatong Formation.

In western Pennsylvania, the quarries that provide most of the construction aggregates are in the Vanport marine limestone of the Pennsylvanian Allegheny Formation and in the calcareous sandstone and sandy limestone of the Mississippian Loyalhanna Formation. Sandstone from other Mississippian units provides aggregate in both the east and west. Sandstone aggregate is also produced from the Pennsylvanian Llewellyn and Pottsville Formations in the east and from the Pennsylvanian Burgoon and Pocono Formations in the west.

From the Devonian Catskill and Trimmers Rock Formations, argillite, siltstone, and sandstone are produced in central and eastern Pennsylvania. About an equal number of sources provide marine limestone from the Silurian-Devonian Keyser Formation and Silurian Tonoloway Formation (or equivalent formations). Aggregate is also obtained from sandstone of the Devonian Palmerton Formation and calcareous sandstone of the Silurian Decker Formation.

There are more than 70 sources of con-

Table 41C1–1. *Distribution of Crushed-Stone Coarse-Aggregate Sources by Lithology and Geologic Age*[1]

	Triassic	Pennsylvanian	Mississippian	Devonian	Silurian	Ordovician	Cambrian	Uncertain
Argillite	16			3				
Hornfels	2							
Diabase	3							
Sandstone[2]		4	5	9		1	7	
Siltstone	1			4				
Calcareous sandstone			10		1			
Limestone		11			15	24	3	
Dolomite						6	8	
Limestone and dolomite					2	18	10	
Serpentinite								1
Gneiss								3

[1]Generalized from Berkheiser and others (1985) and Pennsylvania Department of Transportation (1986).
[2]Sandstone includes quartzite and quartz phyllite.

struction aggregate in Cambrian and Ordovician carbonate rocks of central and southeastern Pennsylvania. Several quartzites and a quartz-phyllite aggregate are produced from the Cambrian Antietam and Hardyston Formations and Precambrian Chickies Formation. Of less certain age are rocks in a quarry where serpentinite is produced and three quarries where gneisses are produced. A concise discussion of certain Cambrian-Ordovician and Silurian-Devonian carbonate stratigraphic units as sources of construction aggregate in Pennsylvania is provided by Ganis (1983).

SPECIFICATIONS AND TEST METHODS

For a material to be acceptable as a construction aggregate, it must meet the buyer's requirements. Commonly, these are based on standards published annually by the American Society for Testing and Materials (ASTM), and a part of these, with minor modifications, is published by the American Association of State Highway and Transportation Officials (AASHTO) (1986). The tests that provide information on the physical properties commonly specified include soundness, abrasion, particle shape, deleterious shale, and absorption tests. Users of large quantities of construction aggregates, such as the Pennsylvania Department of Transportation (PennDOT), issue their own standards, but the specification limits and test methods for the same uses are similar to those of ASTM (Pennsylvania Department of Transportation, 1986, 1987).

Soundness tests provide an estimate of freeze-thaw durability. Samples of aggregates are soaked in a saturated solution of sodium sulfate and then drained and dried in an oven; this procedure is repeated for a total of five cycles (Figure 41C1–1). The test may be considered an analog of cyclic freezing and thawing. Weakly cemented sandstones, weathered rock of several types, and shales tend to disintegrate during this test. The results of engineering tests such as this one, when carried out on samples of aggregate from the same source, in some cases differ by more than 15 percent of the average. In such cases, careful investigation typically shows that the samples or the test procedures, or both, were not identical.

The abrasion test distinguishes poorly indurated and brittle materials from those that are hard, dense, and tough. The test was developed to identify those aggregates that would not break down while being compacted by a heavy, steel-wheeled roller. The method is shown in Figure 41C1–2. Low abrasion loss is generally associated with low weight loss in the soundness test on crushed stone (Table 41C1–2). Diabases, argillites, and hornfelses are among those aggregates that have the lowest abrasion losses.

A test for particle shape is applied to crushed stone to determine the number of thin and elongated particles, those having a length greater than five times their thickness. These platy or pencil-shaped particles do not readily compact, allowing a high interparticle void content. Their high surface area to volume ratio causes an increase in the amount of fine aggregate and cement or asphalt required to fill the voids. In addition, these particles tend to have a preferred orientation, which provides a potential direction of weakness. A tendency to develop platy particles occurs in some argillites, siltstones, and argillaceous limestones, but in the selection and operation of the crushing equipment, this tendency can be minimized.

A test for particle angularity is applied to gravel. For most uses, the gravel must be crushed, and the required weight percent having one or more fractured faces is usually specified. Angularity is important for the interlocking of aggregate particles. Also, in seal-coat roadway surfacing ("oil and chips"), where a single-particle-thick layer of aggregate is broadcast over a sprayed-on film of asphalt, the importance of having angular particles is readily apparent. In some sources, the gravel is not coarse enough to provide economically the required number of fractured particles in the desired sizes. On the other hand, crushing of the gravel tends to beneficiate the coarser aggregate, because the less well indurated particles become sand.

The amount of shale permitted in coarse aggregate for use with cement and asphalt is very limited, because shale particles weaken the cemented mass of aggregate particles. Also, the particles tend to disintegrate when exposed to the weather. Contrary to popular opinion, asphalt does not effectively waterproof the aggregate particles in a bituminous mixture. Positive identification of shale, however, is often a problem in construction, because any platy fragment of very fine grained rock will be called "shale" by someone. PennDOT uses the following operational definition for shale: deleterious shale splits and cracks after four cycles of soaking in water and drying in an oven. Only 2 percent by weight of deleterious shale is permitted in coarse aggregate in asphalt and cement concrete by PennDOT specifications.

Acceptance tests for gravels include absorption. Gravels with high absorption tend to have high soundness losses (Table 41C1–2). The more water an aggregate absorbs, the more likely it is to disintegrate when frozen and the longer it will take to dry before being added to a hot asphalt mixture. Also, highly absorptive materials are quite porous and, therefore, of lower strength than those same materials when they have lower porosity.

The skid-resistance level (SRL) ratings are an additional requirement imposed on aggregates used

Figure 41C1–2. Test for resistance to degradation of small-sized coarse aggregate by abrasion and impact in the Los Angeles machine (Pennsylvania Test Method 662). A. The Los Angeles machine. The diameter of the drum is 28 inches. B. Inside the drum as the test begins. Part of the charge of crushed stone and steel balls is being raised by an internal shelf. The steel balls are 1-7/32 inches in diameter. C. Inside the steel drum at the end of the test. The charge of crushed stone and steel balls is shown after 500 revolutions.

deterioration of concrete in Pennsylvania; these aggregates were rarely tested for their reactivity. The potential for such problems, however, was recognized. Reviews of aggregate reactivity by Diamond (1978), Walker (1978), and Dolar-Mantuani (1983) contain many references to the extensive literature on the subject.

Some test results disclose unexpected variations in properties that have engineering significance. At one site, deeper dredging leads to a higher quality product, whereas at another site, it leads to a lower quality product. In limestones, a change from a 5 percent insoluble residue (quartz sand) to one of 20 percent may improve the skid-resistant properties, although a change from limestone to fine-grained dolomite may not. In a single stratum of alluvial sandstone, the massive parts may have good durability, but the crossbedded part may have poor durability. These variations commonly reveal details of the geologic history that are useful in planning future production.

Where ferruginous concretions caused a problem in one concrete pavement, the pattern of pop-outs indicated that most of the concretions had come from a narrow zone in the source gravel deposit. Later, detailed mapping of the pertinent quadrangle (Inners, 1978) revealed that the concretions, which may have formed originally in argillaceous rock and later weathered out, were deposited in older, topographically higher Pleistocene gravels. The concretions were eroded later from these older gravels and redeposited, forming thin, lenticular deposits in the upper part of a frontal kame. Once this interpretation had been made, suitable precautions could be taken and satisfactory concrete aggregate obtained with confidence.

SAMPLING

Sampling is as important as testing, and it is necessary to follow appropriate procedures if the evaluation is for commercial use (American Society for Testing and Materials, 1988b). Furthermore, it is generally not recognized that the excavation, crushing, and sizing will change the material. For example, if three lithologies in a quarry face are in equal proportions, those three lithologies will not be in equal proportions in the stockpiles of sized material (West and others, 1969). Lithologies less resistant to impact will tend to be more abundant in the smaller particle sizes. Consequently, glacial-gravel aggregate tends to have fewer limestone particles in the smaller sizes, because siltstone and sandstone particles are weaker and have broken down. In summary, tests on processed aggregate may give results that are somewhat different than tests on the exploratory samples.

on asphalt road surfaces in Pennsylvania. The average daily traffic volume (ADT) of each road determines the SRL rating that is required. This, in turn, determines which aggregates may be used in the surface of the road. To the extent possible, the SRL rating for each aggregate source is determined by measuring the skid resistance (friction coefficient) on several road surfaces containing that aggregate. When enough measurements are obtained to allow calculation of the least squares regression line for the rate of decreasing skid resistance with increasing traffic volume, the SRL for that aggregate source is determined. For rating a new aggregate source before it can be used in any pavements, both petrographic analyses and laboratory polishing tests are used to extrapolate from sources previously rated by road tests. The list of aggregate sources compiled by PennDOT shows the SRL rating for each source.

As of 1989, only a few cases were recognized where alkali-reactive aggregates have caused serious

Table 41C1–2. *Distribution of Crushed-Gravel Coarse-Aggregate Sources by Soundness and Absorption*[1]
(Test results for AASHTO Gradation #8; 3/8-inch nominal maximum size)

Absorption (percent weight gain)	Soundness (percent weight loss)								
	0 to 1	2 to 3	4 to 5	6 to 7	8 to 9	10 to 11	12 to 13	14 to 15	16 to 17
1.00 to 1.49	1	4	1	2					
1.50 to 1.99	2	2	4	1	2		1		1
2.00 to 2.49		3	2	2	4	3			
2.50 to 2.99				1		4	1	1	
3.00 to 3.49					1		1		
3.50 to 3.99				1					1

[1]Adapted from Pennsylvania Department of Transportation (1986) and unpublished data.

PROBLEMS AND FUTURE RESEARCH

Although this discussion of construction aggregates is primarily about natural materials, industrial by-products and waste materials have been, and will continue to be, used in significant amounts. Geologic materials must compete in the marketplace with iron and steel slags and increasingly with power-plant ashes, incinerated mine waste, and municipal incinerator residue. If the cost of producing construction aggregates from geologic materials increases, and if the cost of disposing of ashes and cinders also increases, then ashes and cinders tend to become attractive alternative materials when processed to conform to the same standards of acceptability.

Adequate quality control of aggregate production requires new, efficient test methods that will provide answers in a few hours, if not sooner. This may mean different tests for different lithologies. If tests for quality could be used reliably on shot-hole drill cuttings, development of new sources would be expedited.

The development of expert computer systems may expedite the training of petrographers in the evaluation of construction aggregates, especially for resistance to weathering, tire polishing, and reaction to sulfates and alkalies. Computer systems can also be of assistance to aggregate producers in obtaining maximum quality and uniformity of product. Expert systems can improve the analysis of production, transportation, and storage costs to determine when it is practicable to develop stockpiles of durable, polish-resistant aggregate in critical urban areas.

Because there is an increasing reliance on the service record of an aggregate for its approval for certain uses, the producer may find it necessary to keep better records that show what work incorporates his product.

This will also require better procedures to evaluate performance both quantitatively and objectively.

In the cost-effective evaluation and development of sources of construction aggregates, and in the efficient processing, marketing, and utilization of these aggregates, there are abundant challenges for effective combinations of geological science and materials engineering, only some of which have been mentioned here. But in all of this, now perhaps more than ever before, there is a never-ending need for attention to detail.

RECOMMENDED FOR FURTHER READING

American Society for Testing and Materials (1978), *Significance of tests and properties of concrete-making materials,* ASTM Special Technical Publication 169B, 872 p.

Berkheiser, S. W., Jr., Barnes, J. H., and Smith, R. C., II (1985), *Directory of the nonfuel-mineral producers in Pennsylvania,* 4th ed., Pennsylvania Geological Survey, 4th ser., Information Circular 54, 165 p.

Craft, J. L. (1979), *Quality of gravel resources in northwestern Pennsylvania,* Pennsylvania Geological Survey, 4th ser., Information Circular 86, 54 p.

Dolar-Mantuani, Ludmila (1983), *Handbook of concrete aggregates: a petrographic and technological evaluation,* Park Ridge, N. J., Noyes Publications, 345 p.

Gandhi, P. M., and Lytton, R. L. (1984), *Evaluation of aggregates for acceptance in asphalt paving mixtures,* American Asphalt Paving Technologists, Proceedings, v. 53, p. 525–558.

Henningsen, D. (1980), *Relationship between petrography and texture of rocks and their properties as road material,* International Association of Engineering Geology Bulletin 22, p. 191–193.

Hudec, P. P. (1983), *Aggregate tests—their relationship and significance,* Durability of Building Materials, v. 1, p. 275–300.

Primel, L., and Peter, M. A., eds. (1984), *International Symposium on Aggregates,* International Association of Engineering Geology Bulletin 29, 470 p.; Bulletin 30, 482 p.

O'Neill, B. J., Jr. (1974), *Greater Pittsburgh region construction aggregates,* Pennsylvania Geological Survey, 4th ser., Mineral Resource Report 67, 60 p.

Orchard, D. F. (1976), *The properties and testing of aggregates,* v. 3, in Orchard, D. F., *Concrete technology,* 3rd ed., New York, John Wiley and Sons, 282 p.

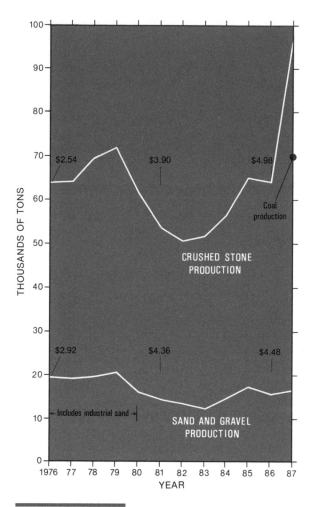

Figure 41C2–1. Crushed stone and sand and gravel production in Pennsylvania from 1976 to 1987 showing average sale prices in dollars per ton (F.O.B. plant) posted for 1976, 1981, and 1986 (data from Kebblish, 1979, 1981a, 1981b, 1984a; Kebblish and Tuchman, 1982, 1983; Prosser and others, 1985a; Prosser and others, 1986; Prosser and Smith, 1987a, 1989; and Prosser and Berkheiser, 1988). Production estimate for bituminous and anthracite coal is based on Pennsylvania Department of Environmental Resources (1987).

620

CHAPTER 41C, PART 2 NONMETALS— CONSTRUCTION AGGREGATES: ECONOMIC ASPECTS

SAMUEL W. BERKHEISER, JR.
  Bureau of Topographic and Geologic Survey
  Department of Conservation and Natural
    Resources
  P. O. Box 8453
  Harrisburg, PA 17105

INTRODUCTION

In 1987, more than 50 pounds per day of construction aggregate was produced for each citizen of the Commonwealth, with a daily per-person value of less than 13 cents. It would be difficult to find a more economical and yet useful commodity. Indeed, one of the major attributes of aggregate is low cost per volume (Figure 41C2-1). Toughness and durability are the other principal attributes.

Construction aggregates can be natural or manufactured materials, including crushed stone, sand, gravel, and slag. Their major function is to provide strength and bulk to concrete and bituminous mixes, mortars, and plasters, products that society depends upon every day. In terms of volume and value, they are the primary nonfuel mineral commodity of Pennsylvania, which in 1987 ranked first in the production of crushed stone and set a national record for production by an individual state. In that year, for the first time in the state's history, cumulative crushed-stone tonnage exceeded the production tonnage of coal (Prosser and Smith, 1989).

Two rules of thumb generally can be applied to the economics of construction aggregates: (1) the more effort it takes to produce a ton of material, the more it will cost the producer; and (2) the longer the distance it must be transported, the more it will cost the consumer. Hence, unconsolidated glacial materials having little overburden should be less expensive to produce than bedrock deposits, especially Carboniferous bedrock, from which up to 150 feet of overburden must be removed (Figure 41C2-2). Traditionally, most land-transported aggregates—excluding those used for railroad ballast—are consumed within a 30-mile radius of their source. At this limit, truck-haulage costs approximately double the value of the product. It is estimated that about 50 percent of the sand and gravel production in 1986 was dedicated to highway construction and maintenance (Figure 41C2-

A

B

Figure 41C2–2. Production faces of bedrock mining in the southwestern part of the Appalachian Plateaus province versus sand-and-gravel mining in the northeastern part of the Ridge and Valley province. A. In southern Somerset County, the approximately 50 foot thick, light-colored basal limestones (Mississippian Loyalhanna Formation and Deer Valley Limestone) are mined for construction aggregate, whereas the overlying darker claystones, siltstones, and sandstones (Mississippian Mauch Chunk Formation) constitute a bedrock overburden that must be removed. B. An approximately 150 foot thick, unconsolidated frontal kame fan of the late Wisconsinan glacial terminus is mined for sand and crushed gravel along the Susquehanna River in southwestern Luzerne County. Typically, less than 10 feet of unconsolidated overburden is removed.

3). Crushed-stone uses probably have parallel trends, although it is difficult to separate uses for general construction from uses for highway construction.

WHERE DOES IT COME FROM AND HOW IS IT MINED?

Sand and Gravel

Sand and gravel should be the most economical construction aggregate because of the ease with which it is mined (little overburden and no blasting) and the ease of preparation (crushing and sizing). However, other than some limited outwash valley trains, sand-and-gravel resources are mostly confined to areas of low population density that were covered by Pleis-

tocene glaciers (see Figure 3 in the color section, and Figure 41C2–4). Consequently, many of Pennsylvania's population centers are in regions that are deficient in sand and gravel, a situation that has helped contribute to some of the highest unit prices of aggregates in the United States. Furthermore, these limited resources are intimately linked to the local bedrock on which they occur and from which they derive part of their composition. This is an unfortunate circumstance, because a large part of the bedrock underlying the northwestern and northeastern parts of the glaciated areas of the Appalachian Plateaus province is composed of unsound laminated shales and siltstones. There are over 240 sources of sand and gravel in Pennsylvania, most of which are small open-pit operations, but less than 30 percent

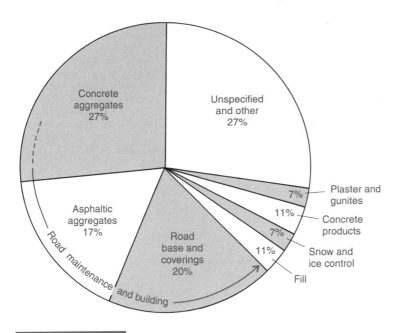

Figure 41C2–3. Major use categories of construction sand and gravel in Pennsylvania, based on 1986 U.S. Bureau of Mines data (modified from Prosser and Berkheiser, 1988).

are approved by the Pennsylvania Department of Transportation (PennDOT) for highway construction (Figure 41C2–5). Most of the PennDOT-approved sand-and-gravel aggregate is produced by a handful of dredging operations (Figure 41C2–6). It is ironic that one of the most potentially economical sources of high-friction aggregate in Pennsylvania is also one of the most expensive. Less than 20 percent of the construction-aggregate market has been captured by sand and gravel in Pennsylvania (Figure 41C2–5).

Crushed Stone

Carbonates are the second most common aggregate source mined after sand and gravel, and they have captured more than 60 percent of the construction-aggregate market (Figure 41C2–5). Almost 90 percent of the carbonate sources are approved by PennDOT and, unlike sand and gravel, are located within the densely populat-

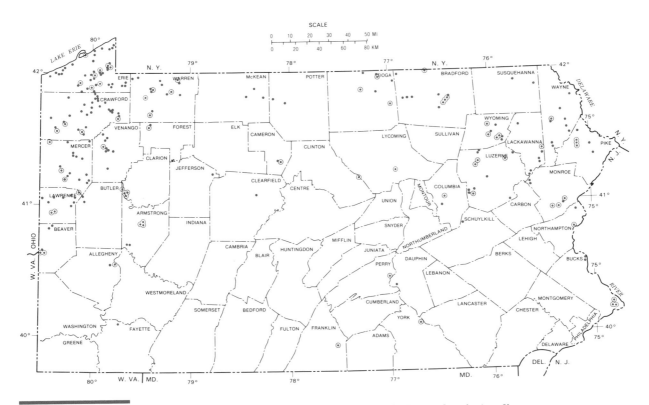

Figure 41C2–4. Sources of sand and gravel for construction aggregate in Pennsylvania (modified from Berkheiser and others, 1985). Circled sources are approved by the Pennsylvania Department of Transportation.

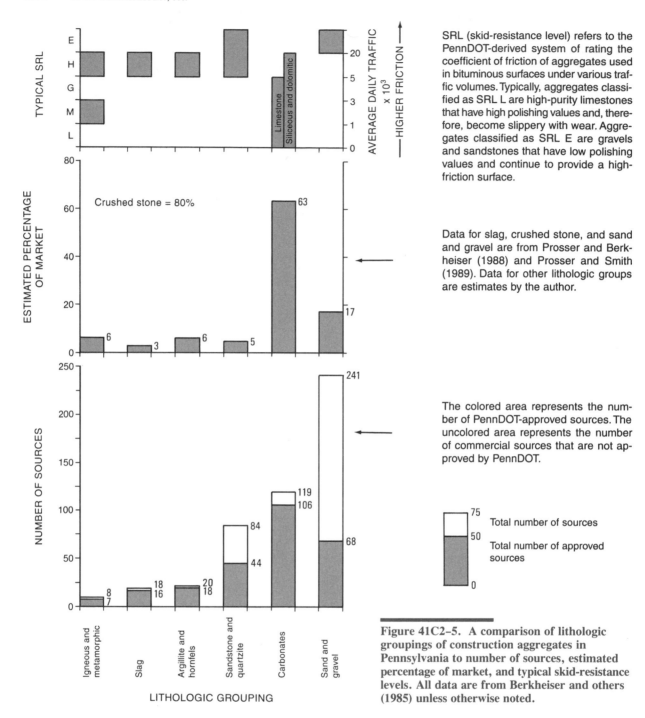

SRL (skid-resistance level) refers to the PennDOT-derived system of rating the coefficient of friction of aggregates used in bituminous surfaces under various traffic volumes. Typically, aggregates classified as SRL L are high-purity limestones that have high polishing values and, therefore, become slippery with wear. Aggregates classified as SRL E are gravels and sandstones that have low polishing values and continue to provide a high-friction surface.

Data for slag, crushed stone, and sand and gravel are from Prosser and Berkheiser (1988) and Prosser and Smith (1989). Data for other lithologic groups are estimates by the author.

The colored area represents the number of PennDOT-approved sources. The uncolored area represents the number of commercial sources that are not approved by PennDOT.

Figure 41C2–5. A comparison of lithologic groupings of construction aggregates in Pennsylvania to number of sources, estimated percentage of market, and typical skid-resistance levels. All data are from Berkheiser and others (1985) unless otherwise noted.

ed parts of the state (see Figures 41D–3 and 41C2–7). In fact, approximately 70 percent (68 million short tons) of crushed stone was produced by quarries in the southeastern part of the state in 1987 (Prosser and Smith, 1989). Generally, the economies of thin overburden, ease of crushing, product flexibility (see Chapter 41D), and local availability have made these Paleozoic-age carbonate rocks the primary aggregate source within the Piedmont and Ridge and Valley provinces.

The Appalachian Plateaus province is limited with respect to all types of construction aggregate. Minable carbonates are particularly sparse in the clastic-dominated Carboniferous portion of the Plateaus. Minable areas of the thin (generally less than 20 feet thick), but relatively pure, Pennsylvanian Vanport Limestone are limited to the west-central part of the state. The thicker and more siliceous Mississippian Loyalhanna Formation is only minable near

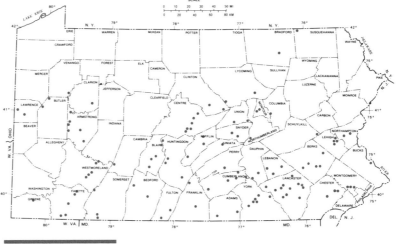

Figure 41C2–7. Carbonate sources mined for construction aggregate in Pennsylvania (modified from Berkheiser and others, 1985).

Figure 41C2–6. Clamshell-type dredge in western Pennsylvania, capable of producing 1 million tons of construction sand and gravel annually, working on the Allegheny River north of Kittanning, Armstrong County.

the crests of anticlines in the southwestern part of the state. Both of these sources are exploited by contour strip mining and room-and-pillar underground methods. With overburden stripping ratios of up to 9:1, product costs are generally higher than elsewhere in the state.

Sandstones and quartzites occupy a unique position within the state's construction-aggregate picture. Generally, they yield some of the best high-friction aggregates, similar to sand and gravel. But, also like sand and gravel, they have some of the worst performance records in terms of abrasion and soundness. Slightly more than half of the approximately 80 sources are PennDOT approved (Figure 41C2–5). Furthermore, the abrasive nature of these rocks causes excessive wear on production equipment. They are, however, the most widespread source of crushed stone and manufactured sand within the state, in part because they occur in almost every physiographic province (Figure 41C2–8).

Argillites and hornfelses are economical to crush but have limited geographic extent. They generally produce a high-friction aggregate and are quarried in the southeastern part of the Gettysburg-Newark Lowland section, a very densely populated part of the state (Figures 41C2–5 and 41C2–9). Perhaps the most valuable commodity that these quarries supply is large, dry holes in the ground, many of which could be modified for use as landfills (Figure 41C2–10). With average landfill tipping fees approaching $100 per ton

in this area, the space created by mining could be more valuable than the commodity originally mined!

Crystalline igneous and metamorphic rocks are quarried in the Piedmont and New England provinces, where the population density is high (Figures 41C2–5 and 41C2–9). Most of them qualify as high-friction aggregates. Because they are generally composed of interlocking, high-density, abrasive minerals, they, too, are more costly to produce than the more abundant carbonates. Most of these operations compete by producing large annual tonnages (greater than 1 million short tons) and marketing high-quality railroad ballast.

Annual production of railroad ballast is estimated to be approximately 4 million tons. Carbonates account for more than 50 percent of the sources, but igneous and metamorphic sources probably account for the greatest production (Figure 41C2–11). Traditionally, the Mississippian Loyalhanna Formation (quartz-sand-bearing limestone) of southwestern Pennsylvania provided significant amounts of ballast for use in western Pennsylvania and states to the west. The most common ballasts in the eastern part of the state are produced from diabase, serpentinite, and argillite.

Slag

Air-cooled slag from blast furnaces generally provides a tough, durable, approved aggregate. It is especially desirable in applications where lighter weight aggregates are beneficial, such as bridge decks and the construction of high-rise buildings. Slag is a welcome source in the aggregate-poor Appalachian Plateaus province. Its use is limited by its availability, which in turn is linked to the production of pig iron. Production in the 1980's showed a downward trend, as sources became depleted, to less than 3 million short tons annually.

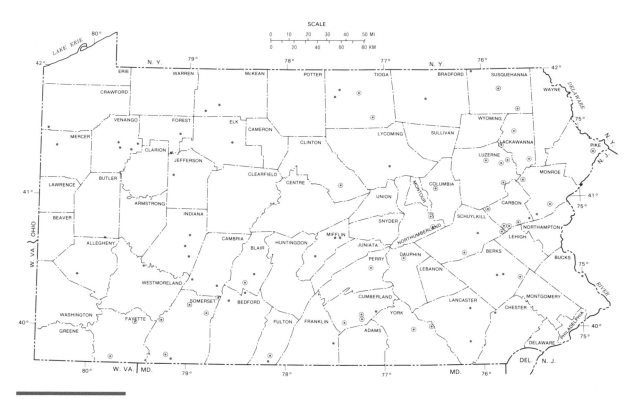

Figure 41C2–8. Sandstone sources mined for construction aggregate in Pennsylvania (modified from Berkheiser and others, 1985). Circled sources are approved by the Pennsylvania Department of Transportation.

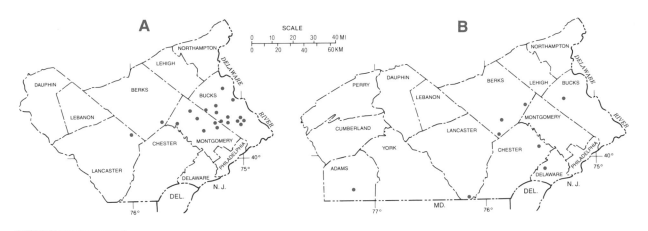

Figure 41C2–9. Igneous and metamorphic sources of construction aggregate in Pennsylvania (modified from Berkheiser and others, 1985). A. Location of argillite and hornfels sources in the southeastern part of the state. B. Location of igneous and metamorphic sources exclusive of argillites and hornfelses in the southeastern part of the state.

PROBLEMS AND FUTURE RESEARCH

In the late 1980's, Pennsylvania's construction-aggregate industry was reaping the benefits of an expanding economy and continued maintenance of an industrialized infrastructure in the heavily populated mid-Atlantic area. United States aggregate producers have been considered attractive acquisitions to foreign investors because of this perceived growth.

However, the following trends, which could affect the industry, should be considered: (1) few citizens want a quarry as a neighbor; (2) a majority of the population of Pennsylvania lives within a 50-mile radius of five international ports; and (3) abundant resources of sand and gravel exist on the continental shelf.

As the cost of aggregates rises in Pennsylvania due to environmental considerations, resource limitations, supply-and-demand economics, and more restrictive manufacturing specifications, different op-

Figure 41C2-10. Typical argillite quarry in the southwestern part of Mongomery County that is mined for construction aggregate and has potential as a future landfill site.

RECOMMENDED FOR FURTHER READING

Bates, R. L. (1987), *Stone, clay, glass—how building materials are found and used,* Hillside, N. J., Enslow Publishers, 64 p.

Bates, R. L., and Jackson, J. A. (1982), *Our modern stone age,* Los Altos, Calif., William Kaufmann, 136 p.

Berkheiser, S. W., Jr. (1987), *Erie Sand and Gravel Company—Suction hopper dredging on Lake Erie,* Pennsylvania Geology, v. 18, no. 3, p. 2-6.

Dunn, J. R. (1983), *Construction materials—Aggregates—sand and gravel,* in Lefond, S. J., and others, eds., *Industrial minerals and rocks,* 5th ed., New York, American Institute of Mining, Metallurgical, and Petroleum Engineers, v. 1, p. 96–110.

McCarl, H. N., Eggleston, H. K., and Barton, W. R. (1983), *Construction materials—Aggregates—slag,* in Lefond, S. J., and others, eds., *Industrial minerals and rocks,* 5th ed., New York, American Institute of Mining, Metallurgical, and Petroleum Engineers, v. 1, p. 111–131.

Pennsylvania Geological Survey (1984), *An outstanding mineral producer—Martin Stone Quarries, Inc.,* Pennsylvania Geology, v. 15, no. 5, p. 2-4.

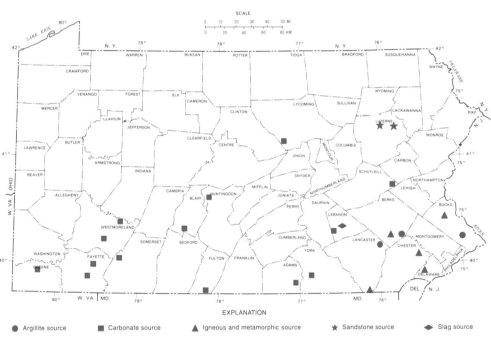

Figure 41C2-11. Lithologies and sources of aggregates mined for railroad ballast in Pennsylvania (modified from Berkheiser and others, 1985).

EXPLANATION

● Argillite source   ■ Carbonate source   ▲ Igneous and metamorphic source   ★ Sandstone source   ◆ Slag source

tions, such as imported aggregates, underground mining and processing, seabed mining of sand and gravel, alternate transportation modes, aggregate recycling, and physical and chemical upgrading of substandard sources, become more feasible. Individuals who have vision, creativity, and entrepreneurial spirit will research and commit themselves to these types of projects in the future. However, more immediate concerns within this industry revolve around being a good community neighbor, coping with government rules and regulations concerning asbestos and silica, and interpreting the state rules and regulations affecting noncoal mining operations.

_____ (1985), *Keystone Lime Company, Inc.—Making the most from what's available,* Pennsylvania Geology, v. 16, no. 5, p. 2-5.

_____ (1986), *Limestone production in Pennsylvania's Allegheny Plateau—Allegheny Mineral Corporation,* Pennsylvania Geology, v. 17, no. 2, p. 10-13.

Schenck, G. H. K., and Torries, T. F. (1983), *Construction materials—Aggregates—crushed stone,* in Lefond, S. J., and others, eds., *Industrial minerals and rocks,* 5th ed., New York, American Institute of Mining, Metallurgical, and Petroleum Engineers, v. 1, p. 60-80.

Smith, R. C., II, and Berkheiser, S. W., Jr. (1989), *An unusual aggregate source: getting the squeal out of the pig-iron,* Pennsylvania Geology, v. 20, no. 3, p. 2-5.

Figure 41D–1. Recently restored vertical batch-type lime kilns in Northumberland County. The charging level of these 1850-vintage, 450-bushel-capacity kilns contains ruins of smaller kilns, probably similar to those used by Pennsylvania's earliest settlers.

CHAPTER 41D NONMETALS—LIMESTONE-DOLOSTONE: SPECIALTY USES

SAMUEL W. BERKHEISER, JR.
Bureau of Topographic and Geologic Survey
Department of Conservation and Natural
   Resources
P. O. Box 8453
Harrisburg, PA 17105

INTRODUCTION

The carbonate rock of the Commonwealth played an important role in the agricultural and industrial development of Pennsylvania and was probably the first type of bedrock mined in significant quantities in the "New World" north of Mexico. Colonists were attracted to the carbonates because of their occurrence in valley settings beneath farmlands near early centers of population, their ease of mining and crushing, and their recognized value as a source of construction and agricultural material.

As early as the seventeenth century, settlers burned limestone (Figure 41D-1) for construction materials such as mortar and plaster. William Penn (1685) published a letter from Robert Turner of Philadelphia reporting that "Samuel Carpenter is our lime-burner on this wharf. Brave Lime Stone found here, as the workmen say being proved." Apparently, the benefits of adding lime to agricultural soils to neutralize acidity were also understood in the late 1600's. According to Bining (1979), the earliest Pennsylvania ironworks, which used limestone as a flux, were developed in the eastern part of the state in 1716. During the mid-1800's, the manufacture of natural cement thrived in Pennsylvania. The building of the canal system at this time stimulated the production of domestic hydraulic cement, because of its ability to harden or set underwater. David O. Saylor, of Lehigh County, founder of Coplay Cement Company, is credited with establishing the first commercial portland cement plant in the United States in the 1870's (Peck, 1908; Miller and others, 1941). The advent of a reliable gasoline engine spawned the increased demand for crushed roadstone, which is a major carbonate end use today.

Within the nation, Pennsylvania has traditionally ranked among the leading producers of carbonate products such as crushed stone, aggregate, flux, lime, portland cement, and masonry cement. Prior to 1900, the Commonwealth annually produced about half of the total mineral wealth of the United States (Pennsylvania Department of Internal Affairs and others, 1944b). On a tonnage basis, carbonate rock currently represents about 80 percent of all nonfuel rocks being mined in Pennsylvania.

Limestone (rich in calcium carbonate [$CaCO_3$]) and dolostone or dolomite (rich in magnesium carbonate [$MgCO_3$]) are among the most versatile of the rocks used by mankind. The potential resources of these carbonate rocks in Pennsylvania are enormous (Figure 41D-2). Some of the carbonate rock uses, other than aggregate and dimension stone, ranked by decreasing order of tonnage, include raw materials for portland cement and cement mortars; lime for the steel industry and for neutralizing acidity; fluxstone for the steel, chemical, and glass industries; pulverized limestone and dolostone for agriculture; refractories; and pulverized products, including fillers, extenders, abrasives, and whiting. The methods and sophistication of their preparation for market vary widely among these uses. This value-added processing can range from simple size classification to ultrafine wet and dry pulverizing, and can include pyroprocessing, as in the manufacture of cement, lime, and basic refractory products. In 1985, about 16 million tons of carbonate rocks was mined for these uses in Pennsylvania, with an as-mined value of about $91 million (Prosser and Smith, 1987a).

DISTRIBUTION AND MINING

Figure 41D-2 shows the distribution of carbonate rocks in the major physiographic provinces of Pennsylvania. Figure 41D-3 illustrates the general distribution of the more valuable, easily mined, high-purity carbonates. Limestones that have average analyses of at least 90 percent $CaCO_3$ are herein considered to be high purity. High-purity dolostones are those that have average analyses of at least 40 percent $MgCO_3$.

Appalachian Plateaus Province

The subhorizontal Devonian and Carboniferous rock sequences of the Appalachian Plateaus province typically contain a few thin (1- to 3-foot thick) marine limestones. More commercially significant, thicker limestone sequences exist and are noted in Table 41D-1.

Open-pit contour mining generally prevails throughout the Plateau. However, when the ratio of overburden to rock becomes excessive (e.g., greater than 2:1), underground room-and-pillar mines are commonly developed (Figure 41D-4).

Ridge and Valley and New England Provinces

The limestones and dolostones in the folded Ridge and Valley and New England provinces that are the most economically important are of Ordovician age (Table 41D-1). Significant Silurian and Devonian limestones also occur in this area. Carbonate sequences ranging from 100 feet to more than 1,000 feet in thickness are not uncommon.

Open-pit mining prevails. Some quarries produce from more than one formation in this folded terrain. Selective mining can produce stone for various end-use products from one quarry. Most high-calcium limestones also are, or have been, mined by underground methods (Figure 41D-5).

Piedmont Province

The Piedmont probably yields the greatest value of high-purity carbonates in the Commonwealth (Table 41D-1). Both open-pit and underground mining produce carbonate stone from this structurally and stratigraphically complex province. Metamorphism has changed some Paleozoic sedimentary carbonates to generally light-colored marbles, such as the Wakefield and Cockeysville Marbles and, locally, the Kinzers Formation (Figure 41D-6).

SOME SELECTED USES

In general, the chemical, lime, and glass industries require the highest $CaCO_3$ content, commonly 98 percent or more. Some of these uses are better met by raw carbonate rock, and some by lime (decarbonated). Low iron content is desirable for most uses and is critical for glass manufacture. The manufacture of pulverized limestone and dolostone for agricultural purposes generally requires a minimum of about 90 percent total carbonates. A common requirement for most end uses is a low silica content. High silica content, in the mineralogical form of quartz and its cryptocrystalline varieties, is a respirable health hazard and causes manufacturing equipment to wear excessively. A primary requirement for the portland cement industry is limestone having a low $MgCO_3$ content (about 6 percent or less). The basic refractories industry, conversely, prefers high-density, high-purity dolostone containing 1 percent or less silicon dioxide (SiO_2). A relatively new use of limestone and lime is in the removal of SO_2 emissions from stack gases. High-calcium (more than 95 percent $CaCO_3$) limestone appears to be most effective; magnesia content to 5 percent may be beneficial.

Basic Refractories

The only manufacturer in the United States of dolomite grain (granular sintered dolomite), used for the production of a refractory (heat-resistant) dolomite

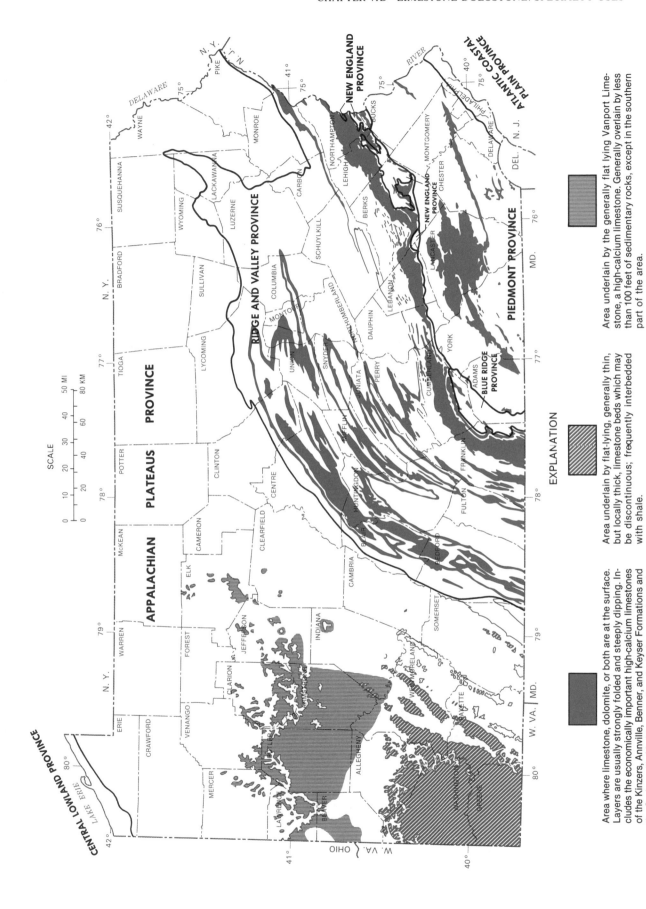

Figure 41D–2. **Distribution of carbonate rocks (from Pennsylvania Geological Survey, 1984) in the physiographic provinces of Pennsylvania (from Berg and others, 1989).**

EXPLANATION

Area where limestone, dolomite, or both are at the surface. Layers are usually strongly folded and steeply dipping. Includes the economically important high-calcium limestones of the Kinzers, Annville, Benner, and Keyser Formations and the Cockeysville Marble, as well as the high-magnesium dolomites of the Ledger Formation and the Cockeysville Marble.

Area underlain by flat-lying, generally thin, but locally thick, limestone beds which may be discontinuous; frequently interbedded with shale.

Area underlain by the generally flat lying Vanport Limestone, a high-calcium limestone. Generally overlain by less than 100 feet of sedimentary rocks, except in the southern part of the area.

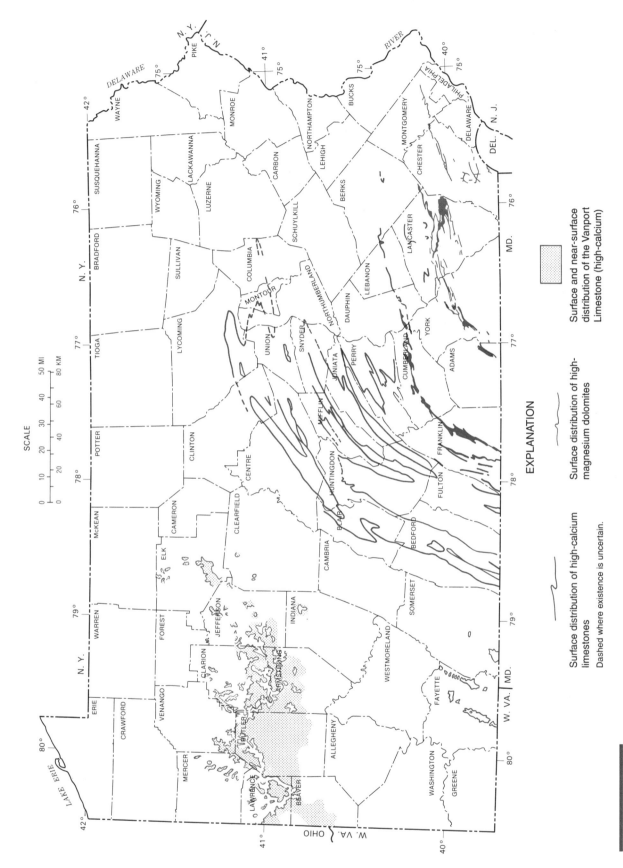

Figure 41D-3. Surface and near-surface distribution of high-purity carbonate rocks in Pennsylvania (modified from O'Neill, 1976, and Berg and others, 1980).

EXPLANATION

Surface distribution of high-calcium limestones

Dashed where existence is uncertain.

Surface distribution of high-magnesium dolomites

Surface and near-surface distribution of the Vanport Limestone (high-calcium)

Table 41D–1. *Quality, Distribution, and Specialty Uses of Pennsylvania's Carbonate Rocks by Physiographic Province*

Geologic age	Group or formation	General thickness and quality	Current uses
APPALACHIAN PLATEAUS PROVINCE			
Pennsylvanian	Allegheny Formation, Vanport Limestone	Greater than 20 feet thick in Lawrence, Butler, and Armstrong Counties. Best developed in northeastern Lawrence County and northwestern Butler County. Ninety (90) to 96 percent $CaCO_3$; $MgCO_3$ less than 2 percent (O'Neill, 1976).	Cement, coal-mine rock dust, limestone for agriculture, fluxstone, and lime manufacture. Early uses included both fluxstone and "buhrstone iron ore" (siderite) for the steel industry (Miller, 1934).
Mississippian	Mauch Chunk Formation; Deer Valley and Wymps Gap Limestones (equivalent to the Greenbrier Formation)	Massive, fossiliferous limestone beds, the purest generally about 10 feet thick in southern Fayette and Somerset Counties. No published analyses of greater than 90 percent $CaCO_3$ (Miller, 1934; Hickok and Moyer, 1940; Flint, 1965).	Pulverized limestone for agriculture (89 percent $CaCO_3$ equivalent).
RIDGE AND VALLEY PROVINCE			
Silurian and Devonian	Keyser Formation	"Calico rock" (basal dark limestone containing white calcite crystals) is best developed in Blair County (35 feet of 95 percent $CaCO_3$), Mifflin County (65 feet of 96 percent $CaCO_3$), Lycoming County (30 feet of 96 percent $CaCO_3$), and Union County (40 feet of 94 percent $CaCO_3$), according to Miller (1934) and Faill (1976). Thicker sequences of less pure limestone are available throughout the province (O'Neill, 1976).	Pulverized limestone for agriculture and fillers. Early uses included fluxstone and lime (Miller, 1934).
Ordovician	Jacksonburg Formation	Cement rock (argillaceous limestone), up to 800 feet thick, and cement limestone ($CaCO_3$ between 70 and 90 percent), up to about 400 feet thick in Berks, Lehigh, and Northampton Counties (Sherwood, 1964). Structural complexities and rapid lateral facies variations make measurements and distinctions difficult.	Cement. Some Jacksonburg containing 95 percent $CaCO_3$ was used earlier for lime manufacture (Miller, 1934).
Ordovician	Benner or Linden Hall Formation, Valentine Member	Purest and thickest development in the Bellefonte and Pleasant Gap areas, where it ranges from 60 to 90 feet thick and averages greater than 96 percent $CaCO_3$ (Miller, 1934; O'Neill, 1976; Berkheiser, 1985c). Other members of the Benner, Nealmont, and Snyder Formations average greater than 90 percent $CaCO_3$ in the province (O'Neill, 1976).	Limestone for agriculture, coal-mine rock dust, lime manufacture, fluxstone for metals and glass, and chemical limestone.
Ordovician	Annville Formation	Maximum thickness of about 250 feet attained near the Dauphin-Lebanon County line. Greater than 96 percent $CaCO_3$ is not uncommon (MacLachlan, 1967; O'Neill, 1976). Thins rapidly both east and west. Alpine-type nappe structure prevails.	Limestone for agriculture, fluxstone, lime manufacture, cement manufacture, acid neutralization, and filler.
Ordovician	St. Paul Group	The St. Paul Group may be up to 1,000 feet thick. Generally, in Cumberland and Franklin Counties, the upper 35 to 175 feet of this sequence ranges between 90 and 95 percent $CaCO_3$, and the lower 85 feet of the sequence ranges between 94 and 96 percent $CaCO_3$ (Root, 1968, 1971; O'Neill, 1976).	Potential is not developed due to complex geology and local presence of chert. Possible whiting potential in Cumberland County (Berkheiser, 1983).
PIEDMONT PROVINCE			
Ordovician	Annville Formation	Maximum thickness is in Lancaster County and generally does not exceed 90 feet; $CaCO_3$ content is 94 percent or more (O'Neill, 1975; Berkheiser, 1983).	Limestone for agriculture, fluxstone, filler, cement manufacture, and acid neutralization.
Cambrian	Cockeysville Marble	Maximum thickness is in Chester County and is thought to be less than 500 feet. Up to 40-foot-thick coarsely crystalline dolomite sequences, containing less than 1 percent impurities. Possible high-calcium marble also available (Bascom and Stose, 1932; Berkheiser, 1983).	Not currently being exploited. Some whiting, refractory, and pharmaceutical potential (Berkheiser, 1983). Early uses included lime and dimension stone.
Cambrian	Ledger Formation	A coarsely crystalline dolomite, generally thought to be about 1,000 feet thick in Adams, York, and Lancaster Counties. Commonly contains less than 1 percent impurities (Jonas and Stose, 1930; Stose and Jonas, 1939).	Dolomite for agriculture, coal-mine rock dust, fillers, fluxstone, refractory products, and lime manufacture.
Cambrian	Kinzers Formation	Locally contains a middle sequence of white high-calcium marble having a maximum thickness of about 600 feet in York County (Stose and Jonas, 1939; Cloos, 1968). $CaCO_3$ content of 95 percent or more is not uncommon (O'Neill, 1976; Berkheiser, 1983).	Limestone for agriculture; cement manufacture; fluxstone for metals and glass; fillers and extenders, including whiting; and lime manufacture.
Cambrian	Vintage Formation	Locally, in Lancaster County, contains a coarsely crystalline (less than 1 percent impurities) dolomite (Miller, 1934). Thickness ranges from about 200 feet to 1,400 feet in York and Lancaster Counties (Jonas and Stose, 1930; Stose and Jonas, 1939).	Dolomite for agriculture and fillers. May have other high-magnesium carbonate potential.

Figure 41D–4. Underground room-and-pillar mine developed in the Wymps Gap Limestone (Greenbrier equivalent) of the Mauch Chunk Formation in southern Somerset County. The Keystone Lime Company works this 8- to 10-foot-thick fossiliferous limestone during the winter months for agricultural limestone.

Figure 41D–5. Service shaft used to hoist high-calcium Valentine Limestone from the 960-foot level of Warner Company's Bell mine in Centre County (see Berkheiser, 1985c).

Figure 41D–6. Northwest-looking view of White Pigment's quarry in York County, developed in white mottled marble of the Kinzers Formation. A near-vertical 3-foot-wide Mesozoic diabase dike is visible in the north face, near the center of the quarry.

brick, is located in Pennsylvania, and that manufacturer also is a major producer of other basic refractory products. The Cambrian Ledger Formation in York County is the source of raw material for this use. Historically, "roasted" (sintered) dolostone has been produced in Pennsylvania since the early 1900's, mostly for patching and lining open-hearth furnaces in steel mills. Today, a dolomite or dolostone brick product is being used as a lining in AOD (argon oxygen decarburization) vessels and in ladles for the steel industry;

a refractory brick liner is being used for the burn and transition zones of rotary cement and lime kilns (Hopkins, 1985).

Cement

Following about 50 years (around 1830 to 1880) of production of natural hydraulic cement, the more durable portland cement was manufactured by finely grinding and blending limestones with secondary ingredients to an accurately controlled composition. Eastern Pennsylvania was fortuitously blessed with a combination of enterprising individuals and the Ordovician Jacksonburg Formation. The transition zone within the Jacksonburg between low-$MgCO_3$ fossiliferous limestone ("cement limestone") and low-$MgCO_3$ dark argillaceous limestone ("cement rock") happened to be of the correct chemical composition for portland cement manufacture. By 1880, commercial portland cement manufacture was established in the Lehigh district (Peck, 1908; Miller and others, 1941), which continues to be a leading producing region (Figure 41D–7). Ames and Cutcliffe (1983) discussed modern aspects of cement production and marketing, and showed locations of cement plants.

The high-calcium Annville Formation is used as a "sweetener" to increase the $CaCO_3$ content of cement mixes made from the cement rock facies of the $CaCO_3$-poor Jacksonburg Formation. In western Pennsylvania, the Vanport Limestone traditionally has been, and still is, a source of $CaCO_3$ for cement manufacture in Butler and Lawrence Counties. Here, other Pennsylvanian rocks provide shale for aluminum oxide (Al_2O_3), sandstone for SiO_2, and coal for kiln fuel. In Allegheny County, a cement plant uses limestone from the Greenbrier Limestone, mined underground about 9 miles south of Pennsylvania in West Virginia, and barged down the Monongahela River. White portland cement is manufactured in York County, where the middle part of the Kinzers Formation is used as a source of low-iron $CaCO_3$, and white kaolinitic clays from the Kunkletown area in Monroe County

are used as a source of Al_2O_3 and SiO_2. Most calcitic limestones that contain less than 6 percent $MgCO_3$ have the potential for being used as a source of $CaCO_3$ in the manufacture of portland cement.

Masonry cement, which has essentially replaced lime mortars, is generally made by intergrinding crushed limestone and portland cement clinker. This mixture is used because it improves workability and plasticity, although small additions of lime may also benefit the mortar.

Crushed Stone

Crushed and variously sized high-purity carbonate rocks are used as fluxstone in the metal and glass industries to lower melting temperatures and absorb impurities. Carbonate lime is also used. In addition to acting as a fluxing agent in the glass industry, carbonate or lime improves the chemical and physical properties of glass by making it less soluble and less brittle, and by improving luster (Boynton, 1980). For most applications in the metals industry, magnesian fluxes are less destructive to refractory materials.

Since the 1950's, significant quantities of limestone and dolostone have been used in agriculture for the neutralization of organic acids in soil (Figure 41D–8). Agricultural limestone (and dolostone) must have a minimum calcium carbonate equivalent of 89 percent calculated as percent $CaCO_3$ + (1.19 x percent $MgCO_3$). Minimum specifications for size gradation also exist, because a fine grind is required to attain the maximum available surface area, and, hence, the maximum acid neutralization.

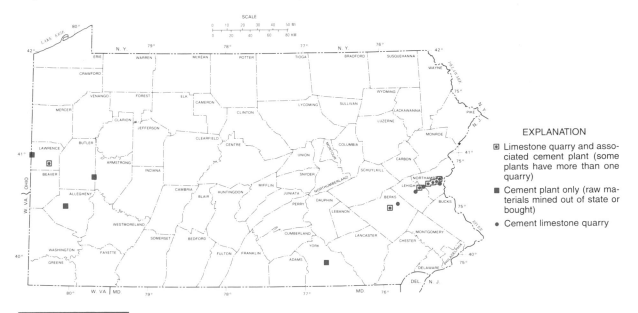

Figure 41D–7. Distribution of cement plants and limestone mined for cement manufacture in Pennsylvania (modified from Berkheiser and others, 1985).

Some lesser known uses of crushed or pulverized carbonates include sewage plant filter beds; fillers for "clay pigeons"; poultry grit; abrasives and scouring agents; mineral feeds for livestock; fillers in plastics, resins, and fertilizers; and the manufacture of mineral wool. Coal-mine rock dust is used to reduce the likelihood of coal dust explosions in underground mines; it should be light in color, finely ground, noncaking, and contain not more than 5 percent free and combined SiO_2.

Environmental Applications

Activities and processes related to increased population pressures generate wastes that require treatment. Mankind has become increasingly aware of this problem and is concerned with mitigating the damage. As a result, the use of ground carbonate products and limes for pollution abatement has become the most recent major new market. Carbonate products are in increased demand for water and sewage treatment, the neutralization of acid mine drainage and acid rain, and the desulfurization of flue gas, including applications in fluidized-bed boilers. Lime used for water treatment functions as a softening, purification, and coagulation agent (Boynton, 1980).

Lime

Early settlers in the eastern part of "Penn's Woods" probably first quarried carbonate rocks to make plaster, mortar, and whitewash from lime. Colonial buildings had interior lime-plaster walls made from a mixture of hair, hydrated or slaked lump lime, and sand. This early lime was prepared by removing the carbon dioxide (CO_2) from the carbonate in small, vertical batch-type kilns (Figure 41D–1). Berkheiser and Hoff (1983) described the early methods and hardships of mining and producing lime in this manner. The industry flourished in parts of Pennsylvania until about the mid-1930's. Many farmers worked their own kilns and quarries during the winter months. Numerous ruins of this type of kiln are found throughout the state, wherever carbonates crop

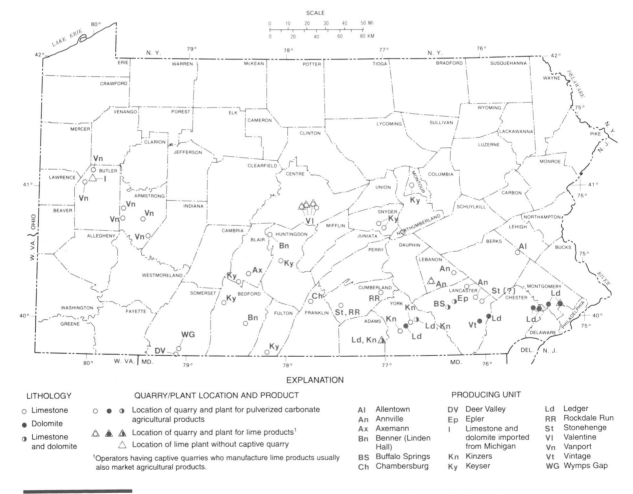

Figure 41D–8. Sources of carbonates for agricultural uses and lime manufacture in Pennsylvania (modified from Berkheiser and others, 1985).

out. Agriculture was a major end use of burned lime up to about 1950, after which time the more economical pulverized limestone and dolostone became popular.

The steel industry is the major consumer of both calcium and magnesium limes, calcined in modern rotary and vertical shaft kilns. These limes are used to purify molten steel by fluxing unwanted compounds into the slag. Steel companies have held many captive carbonate mines in the Commonwealth and are responsible for much of the nonaggregate use of carbonate today. Other important end uses of lime include applications in the refining of nonferrous metals, the treatment of liquid wastes, and the manufacture of chemicals, pulp and paper, and glass. The principal advantages of lime are speed of reaction, absence of CO_2, and smaller amounts of material needed compared to raw carbonates. Figure 41D-8 illustrates the locations of lime plants and associated quarries in Pennsylvania.

Whiting

High-purity, finely ground (97 percent, minus-325 mesh), white carbonate products are used by the plastics, paint, sealant, carpet, rubber, flooring, and paper industries as fillers and coatings. The total annual demand in the United States is relatively small (about 4 million tons per year) but is growing steadily as this product becomes more popular, especially in plastics and paper manufacturing. High brightness, whiteness, and chemical purity are desired. Limestone is preferred over dolostone. Pennsylvania's production of whiting is from the Cambrian Kinzers Formation in the York area. The lower Paleozoic Cockeysville Marble in Chester County and, locally, the Ordovician St. Paul Group in Cumberland County also have some whiting potential (Berkheiser, 1983). Whiting can be manufactured by pulverizing carbonate rocks or by chemical precipitation from lime. Chemical precipitates have the advantage of high whiteness and controlled particle size. They are more expensive to produce, but they also command a higher price.

PROBLEMS AND FUTURE RESEARCH

As the value-added price of these products increases, transportation costs become less significant, allowing international trade to develop. A favorable regulatory climate and a society that recognizes the benefits of maintaining domestic mineral production will be required to avoid import dependence.

Mineral beneficiation research will become increasingly important to specialty-use carbonate pro-

ducers as manufacturers set more restrictive physical and chemical specifications. Innovations in improving the chemistry, color, and size of the product will allow producers to meet these specifications, and will convert ordinary carbonate resources into additional value-added reserves.

Standardized tests of carbonate rock used for flue-gas desulfurization and acid mitigation must be established. This would allow direct comparison of the potential effectiveness of various carbonate intervals for this purpose.

More chemical and physical analyses of representative samples from Pennsylvania's carbonate rocks are needed. Grindability, chemical purity, and grain size should continue to be useful parameters by which to characterize these rocks for industrial use. These analyses are needed because Pennsylvania, with its abundant resources, transportation system, and proximity to major markets, continues to be a major producer of carbonate materials.

RECOMMENDED FOR FURTHER READING

Ames, J. A., and Cutcliffe, W. E. (1983), *Construction materials—Cement and cement raw materials,* in Lefond, S. J., and others, eds., *Industrial minerals and rocks,* 5th ed., New York, American Institute of Mining, Metallurgical, and Petroleum Engineers, v. 1, p. 133–159.

Boynton, R. S. (1980), *Chemistry and technology of lime and limestone,* 2nd ed., New York, Interscience Publishers, 563 p.

Boynton, R. S., and Gutschick, K. A. (1975), *Lime,* in Lefond, S. J., ed., *Industrial minerals and rocks,* 4th ed., New York, American Institute of Mining, Metallurgical, and Petroleum Engineers, p. 737–756.

Carr, D. D., and Rooney, L. F. (1983), *Limestone and dolomite,* in Lefond, S. J., and others, eds., *Industrial minerals and rocks,* 5th ed., New York, American Institute of Mining, Metallurgical, and Petroleum Engineers, v. 2, p. 833–868.

Eckel, C. E. (1928), *Cements, limes, and plasters; their materials, manufacture, and properties,* 3rd ed., New York, John Wiley and Sons, 699 p.

Lamar, J. E. (1961), *Uses of limestone and dolomite,* Illinois Geological Survey Circular 321, 41 p.

Miller, B. L. (1934), *Limestones of Pennsylvania,* Pennsylvania Geological Survey, 4th ser., Mineral Resource Report 20, 729 p.

O'Neill, B. J., Jr. (1964), *Atlas of Pennsylvania's mineral resources—Part 1, Limestones and dolomites of Pennsylvania,* Pennsylvania Geological Survey, 4th ser., Mineral Resource Report 50, pt. 1, 40 p.

_____ (1976), *Atlas of Pennsylvania's mineral resources—Part 4, The distribution of limestones containing at least 90 percent $CaCO_3$ in Pennsylvania,* Pennsylvania Geological Survey, 4th ser., Mineral Resource Report 50, pt. 4, 2 p.

Peck, F. B. (1908), *Geology of the cement belt, in Lehigh and Northampton Counties, Pa., with brief history of the origin and growth of the industry and a description of the methods of manufacture,* Economic Geology, v. 3, p. 37–76.

638

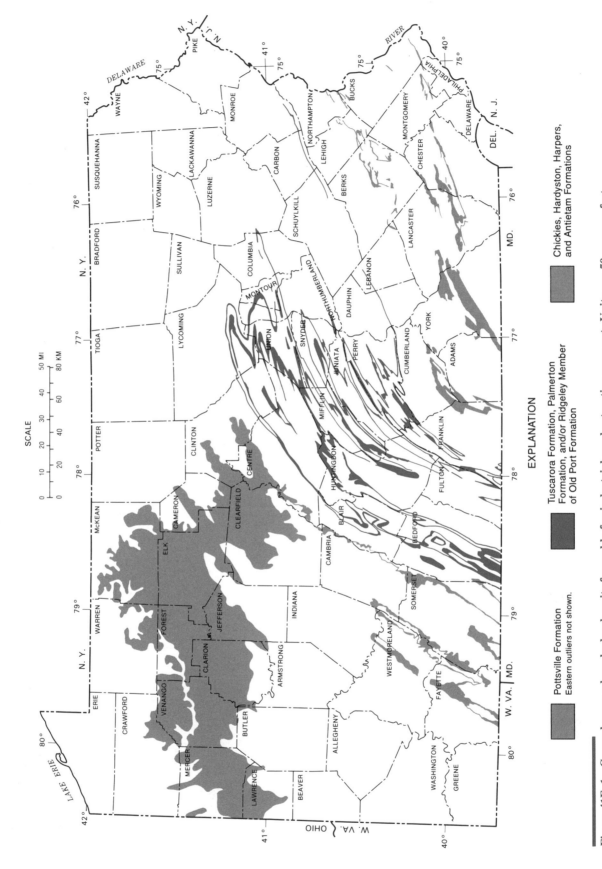

EXPLANATION

Pottsville Formation
Eastern outliers not shown.

Tuscarora Formation, Palmerton
Formation, and/or Ridgeley Member
of Old Port Formation

Chickies, Hardyston, Harpers,
and Antietam Formations

Figure 41E–1. General areas where bedrock units favorable for industrial-sand extraction crop out. Units are 50 or more feet thick in most of these areas (after Berg and others, 1980, and Berkheiser, 1985a).

CHAPTER 41E   NONMETALS—INDUSTRIAL SAND

REGINALD P. BRIGGS
  Geomega, Inc.
  101 Algonquin Road
  Pittsburgh, PA 15241

SUSAN M. CARULLI
  Consultant
  18 Long Street
  Burgettstown, PA 15021

UTILIZATION

Industrial sand as discussed in this chapter is quartz (silica) sand of varying degrees of purity used in many applications. Smooth and round "refractory pebble" and angular "refractory ganister" are mostly coarser than sand, but they are included in this broad category because they are chiefly quartz. Such "sands" are used in manufacturing refractory brick for lining furnaces and ovens. Sand that has been washed and screened to a specified size range is the simple end product for some applications, such as engine sand for traction on railroads, filter sand in waste-water treatment plants, fire sand on furnace floors, and sand for sandblasting and other coarse abrasive uses. Sized sand having a low iron oxide content is supplied for white golf-course traps. Tinted sand is used for architectural decoration. Molding sands for casting metals mostly are blended mixtures of sand and clay. Sand is ground for use as filler to toughen rubber and give body to asphalt, paint, plaster, and plastics. Important additional applications are sand for grinding and polishing, mineral wool for insulation, additives to cement, and glazes and other ceramic uses. The rigidly controlled manufacture of glass is the most complex processing of industrial sand.

Physical characteristics such as particle size and shape are critical to some industrial-sand applications. For example, angular particles contribute to the strength of refractory brick, whereas equant to spherical particles are desirable for filter sand. Specific minerals also can play a part. For example, zircon, even in minor quantities, is detrimental in the manufacture of plate glass (Samuel W. Berkheiser, Jr., written communication, 1987). Chemical content, too, can be critical, especially in glassmaking. The most common chemical impurities occurring in industrial sands are alumina and iron oxides (Table 41E–1). Relatively low alumina amounts increase optical fidelity and the hardness of glass. Relatively high alumina amounts enhance chemical durability and make glass less brittle. Excessive iron oxides cause tinting of glass and induce heat-transfer problems during manufacture. Glass sand is not the only raw ma-

Table 41E–1. *Typical Alumina and Iron Oxide Content of Raw Silica Used in the Manufacture of Some Products[1]*

Product	Al_2O_3 (ppm)[2]	Fe_2O_3 (ppm)[2]
Synthetic quartz crystals for electronic and optical uses (from lasca[3])	20–40	2–8
Colorless glass	≤800	≤250
Refractory brick (from refractory pebble[4])	≤1,400	≤600
Metallic silicon	<1,500	<1,000
Ferrosilicon	≤1,500	≤1,000
Yellow or amber glass	≤2,500	≤1,500
Refractory brick (from refractory ganister[5])	≤6,200	≤1,700

[1]After Berkheiser (1985a, Table 14).
[2]ppm, parts per million; 1,000 ppm=0.1 percent.
[3]High-purity natural crystalline quartz.
[4]Smooth, rounded quartzose granules and pebbles, 2 to 64 mm in diameter.
[5]Angular fragments of crushed quartzite.

terial for making glass. Plate glass and bottle glass also require calcium, magnesium, and sodium oxides, which commonly come from dolomitic limestone (see Chapter 41D) and soda ash. The silica content of these types of glass normally is about 70 percent, though specialty glasses range widely in silica content (Maloney, 1975).

DEMAND

The earliest documented industrial use of sand in Pennsylvania was in 1763, when Henry Stiegel, a German settler, made leaded crystal glass in Lancaster County (Polak, 1975). However, iron manufacture took place in the state more than 20 years earlier than glass manufacture (see Chapter 40B), so it is a reasonable speculation that molding sand rather than glass manufacture was the first industrial application. With the Industrial Revolution, demand for sand grew greatly. During the decade of the 1920's, for example, an average of 1,880,000 tons was produced each year from Pennsylvania sources, not including refractory "sand" (Pennsylvania Department of Internal Affairs, 1944a). However, by the 1970's, industrial sand production had declined to just over 1,000,000 tons per year, and through 1987 there was a further significant decline, with some recovery thereafter (Table 41E–2).

Factors bearing on the decline in demand for Pennsylvania sand are too many to detail here, but

important among them are technological advances in user industries and competition from plastics.

During the 1920's, grinding and polishing sand, chiefly used in the glass industry, and glass sand together made up more than 50 percent of all industrial sand, and the bulk of the remainder was molding and engine sand. Currently, about 40 percent of the industrial-sand market is related to the glass industry, with abrasives, paints, filters, insulation, ceramics, molds, and plastics collectively making up most of the remaining market (Samuel W. Berkheiser, Jr., oral communication, 1995).

RESOURCES

Prior to the Industrial Revolution, sand used in various applications probably was taken mostly from easily excavated surficial deposits. In this century, however, most industrial sand produced in Pennsylvania has been crushed and graded sandstone and quartzite. Principal bedrock units of past, current, and potential interest are the Eocambrian and Cambrian Chickies, Hardyston, Harpers, and Antietam

Table 41E–2. *Annual Production and Value of Industrial Sand in Pennsylvania, 1975–92[1]*

Year	Tons produced (thousands)	Average price (dollars per ton)	Value ($1,000)
1975	1,005	7.08	7,120
1976	1,063	7.30	7,757
1977	1,120	7.23	8,095
1978 est.[2]	1,160	8.93	10,400
1979	1,102	10.62	11,709
1980 est.	1,040	11.79	12,300
1981 est.	970	13.18	12,800
1982	969	14.02	13,589
1983 est.	820	14.32	11,700
1984 est.	790	14.30	11,300
1985	693	14.21	9,846
1986	688	14.67	10,091
1987 est.	670	14.50	9,700
1988 est.	860	14.50	12,500
1989 est.	900	14.50	13,100
1990 est.	930	14.50	13,500
1991 est.	1,080	14.50	15,600
1992 est.	900	14.50	13,000

[1]From U.S. Bureau of Mines Minerals Yearbooks for the indicated years.
[2]For years labeled "est.," the numbers shown are estimates believed accurate to within 10 percent. Estimates are provided because, in the Yearbooks, statistics for industrial-sand production and value were grouped with the statistics for other commodities rather than being cited separately.

Formations (see Chapters 3B and 4), the Silurian Tuscarora Formation (see Chapter 6), the Devonian Palmerton Formation and the Ridgeley Member of the Old Port Formation (see Chapter 7), and sandstone units in the Pennsylvanian Pottsville Formation (see Chapter 10). The Ridgeley Member is "Oriskany Sandstone" in industrial and earlier stratigraphic nomenclature. Figure 41E-1 shows general areas where quartzites or sandstones in these units mostly exceed 50 feet and locally are more than 500 feet thick, constituting an essentially limitless resource. Smaller potential resources include quartz veins in Adams County and adjacent areas and in Chester County. Ranges of chemical analyses of some of the bedrock units are provided in Table 41E-3. Berkheiser (1985a) has shown that beneficiation can reduce alumina in selected samples from these units by factors of approximately 5 to 30, and can reduce iron oxides by factors of 3 to 35.

The source of sand used in Stiegel's pioneering glass plant is uncertain; it may have been weathered Chickies Formation quartzite (Charles H. Shultz, written communication, 1987). In any case, it was soon recognized that Pennsylvania had plentiful resources for glassmaking, sand, limestone, and fuel, and the industry burgeoned. Glass sand is reported to have been produced in the past from the Tuscarora Formation in Schuylkill County; the Ridgeley Member of the Old Port Formation in Bedford, Blair, and Mifflin Counties; the Mississippian Burgoon Formation in Tioga County; and the Pottsville Formation in 10 other counties. Glass is also believed to have been produced from alluvial sand in Allegheny County. In 1992, the only glass sand produced in the state was from the Ridgeley Member at the very large Mapleton operation of the U.S. Silica Company in Huntingdon County (Figure 41E-2). Earlier in this century, the Pittsburgh Plate Glass Company (now PPG Industries, the largest glassmaker in the state) produced much of its sand from a quarry in the Pottsville in Venango County (Fettke, 1919), but in recent decades the company has relied on out-of-state glass-sand sources. During the mid-1980's, however, a part of its annual requirement of 400,000 tons for Pennsylvania operations came from Mapleton (Bill Schuler, oral communication, 1995).

U.S. Silica's Mapleton operation also was the most diversified producer in the state during the 1980's, producing sand for all applications described except refractory brick, mineral wool, cement additives, golf-course traps, and architectural decoration. The Tuscarora Formation has favorable crushing characteristics for "refractory ganister," and this was produced from the Tuscarora in Huntingdon County as well as in Blair County. The Palmerton Formation in Monroe and Schuylkill Counties provided "refractory pebble." The Refractory Sand Company in Schuylkill County also produced mineral wool, golf-trap sand,

Table 41E-3. *Ranges of Published Chemical Analyses of Several Stratigraphic Units[1]*

Stratigraphic units (number of samples)	SiO_2 (percent)	Al_2O_3 (ppm)[3]	Fe_2O_3 (ppm)[3]	Other[2] (ppm)[3]
Cambrian				
Hardyston Formation (3)	97.20-97.92	8,000-10,800	8,500-13,500	3,700-4,300
Chickies Formation (3)	97.10-97.80	9,200-13,900	8,600-12,500	2,600-4,200
Silurian				
Tuscarora Formation (13)	97.70-98.11	7,800-9,300	6,700-10,100	2,400-4,700
Devonian				
Ridgeley Member[4] of Old Port Formation ("Oriskany") (9)	98.75-99.89	200-5,200	100-5,000	Trace-4,900
Palmerton Formation (2)	98.64-98.75	1,200-2,300	7,300-7,900	3,400-4,000
Pennsylvanian				
Lower Pottsville Formation sandstones (4)	96.08-98.35	8,100-23,500	600-8,600	900-11,300

[1]From Berkheiser (1985a, Tables 1, 3, 4, 5, and 6).
[2]Chiefly CaO, TiO_2, and combined H_2O.
[3]ppm, parts per million.
[4]Some Ridgeley samples may have been beneficiated.

Figure 41E–2. U.S. Silica Company operation in the Juniata River valley at Mapleton, Huntingdon County, looking north from the top of the quarry in the Ridgeley Member. The plant is at the left; storage silos are in the left center, the water treatment plant is in the upper center, external sand storage is in front of the plant, and an unprocessed rock pile is in the lower center. The railroad siding with covered hopper cars leads to the Conrail main line, hidden by trees. The Ridgeley Member, here about 190 feet thick (Berkheiser, 1985a), has been quarried for about 6 miles along strike. Quarrying in 1988 took place about 3 miles to the right of the scene. The rock remnant at the right illustrates the typical attitude of the rock, here striking about N65°E and dipping 70°NW. Photograph by C. H. Shultz.

and sand for cement additives, and a quarry in Carbon County produced cement additives. The Mount Cydonia sand quarry in the Antietam Formation in Franklin County (see Figure 17 in the color section) was the only producer of colored sand. Industrial sand for unspecified uses also was reported to have been extracted during the 1980's from unspecified sources in Allegheny, Armstrong, Luzerne, and Venango Counties. Figure 41E–3 shows the 10 counties that produced industrial sand during the 1980's, and 20 other counties that are reported to have been sites of production of industrial sand in the past. Construction sand has been produced commercially in at least 22 of the 37 counties that have no pattern in Figure 41E–3, and some of this sand probably was used in unreported industrial applications from time to time and place to place.

PROBLEMS AND FUTURE RESEARCH

Additional research is needed on lithofacies in the Tuscarora, Ridgeley, and Palmerton Formations, and on the chemical migration of elements in groundwater, in order to predict and define zones of sandstones of greater purity large enough for economical selective mining. The same can be said generally for the Pottsville Formation sandstones, though they have somewhat lower promise because of relatively higher alumina and clay-mineral content. Detailed mapping of the Cambrian quartzitic formations is needed to better characterize their potential. Berkheiser (written communication, 1987) believes that the Antietam Formation, in particular, has superior potential as a diversified source of industrial sand.

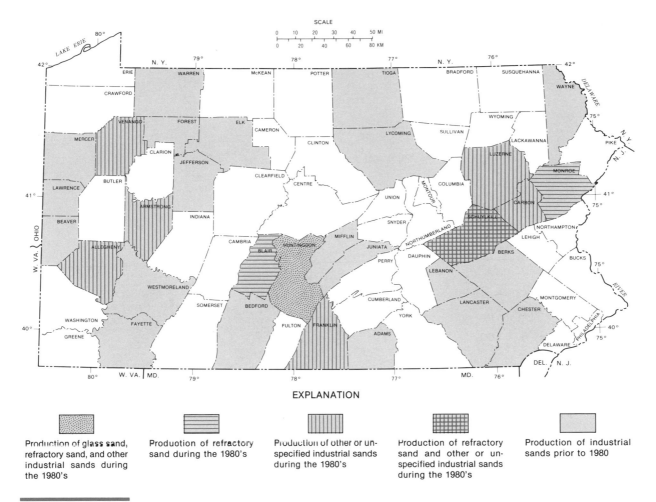

Figure 41E–3. Counties that had industrial-sand production during the 1980's, and counties that are reported to have had earlier production (from O'Neill, 1977; Prosser and others, 1984; Berkheiser, 1985a; Berkheiser and others, 1985; Prosser and Berkheiser, 1987; and historical sources).

Thick quartz veins in Adams County and vicinity are another possibility, but they, too, are not well mapped. Vein samples collected by Berkheiser (1985a) indicate superior in situ purity and response to beneficiation. His investigation was prompted by a relatively small but real demand for lasca, very pure quartz used as a nutrient in the growth of synthetic quartz crystals.

RECOMMENDED FOR FURTHER READING

Ashley, G. H. (1931), *A syllabus of Pennsylvania geology and mineral resources,* Pennsylvania Geological Survey, 4th ser., General Geology Report 1, 160 p.

Berkheiser, S. W., Jr. (1985), *High-purity silica occurrences in Pennsylvania,* Pennsylvania Geological Survey, 4th ser., Mineral Resource Report 88, 67 p.

Fettke, C. R. (1919), *Glass manufacture and the glass sand industry of Pennsylvania,* Pennsylvania Geological Survey, 3rd ser., Economic Report 12, 278 p.

Hoover, K. V., ed. (1970), *Proceedings—Fifth forum on geology of industrial minerals,* Pennsylvania Geological Survey, 4th ser., Mineral Resource Report 64, 278 p.

Moore, E. S., and Taylor, T. G. (1924), *The silica refractories of Pennsylvania,* Pennsylvania Geological Survey, 4th ser., Mineral Resource Report 3, 100 p.

Stone, R. W. (1928), *Molding sands of Pennsylvania,* Pennsylvania Geological Survey, 4th ser., Mineral Resource Report 11, 94 p.

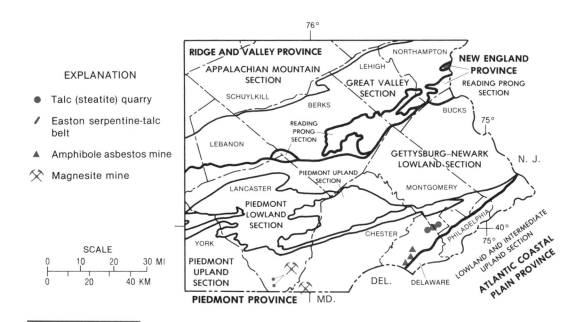

EXPLANATION

● Talc (steatite) quarry

/ Easton serpentine-talc belt

▲ Amphibole asbestos mine

⚒ Magnesite mine

SCALE

0   10   20   30 MI

0   20   40 KM

RIDGE AND VALLEY PROVINCE

APPALACHIAN MOUNTAIN SECTION

SCHUYLKILL

BERKS

LEBANON

READING PRONG SECTION

76°

NORTHAMPTON

LEHIGH

GREAT VALLEY SECTION

NEW ENGLAND PROVINCE

READING PRONG SECTION

BUCKS

75°

GETTYSBURG–NEWARK LOWLAND SECTION

N. J.

PIEDMONT UPLAND SECTION

LANCASTER

MONTGOMERY

PIEDMONT LOWLAND SECTION

YORK

CHESTER

PHILADELPHIA

40°

75°

LOWLAND AND INTERMEDIATE UPLAND SECTION

ATLANTIC COASTAL PLAIN PROVINCE

PIEDMONT UPLAND SECTION

DEL.

DELAWARE

PIEDMONT PROVINCE | MD.

Figure 42–1. Map of southeastern Pennsylvania showing talc, serpentine, asbestos, and magnesite extraction localities. At least six magnesite prospect pits occur near the eastern magnesite mine in Chester County. Data are from Peck (1911), Bayley (1941), and Pearre and Heyl (1960). Physiographic boundaries are from Berg and others (1989).

CHAPTER 42   MINOR RESOURCES

DONALD T. HOFF
5840 Chambers Hill Road
Swatara, PA 17111

INTRODUCTION

This chapter treats mineral deposits and occurrences having diverse geologic and economic characteristics. A few examples of characteristics that demote these resources to minor status include excessive overburden, small tonnages, low ore grade, foreign competition, expensive exploration and development costs, and saturated markets. Of all the mineral resources covered in this chapter, current production is limited to metabasalt for roofing granules.

TALC, SERPENTINE, ASBESTOS, AND MAGNESITE

Deposits of talc, serpentine, asbestos, and magnesite occur in Pennsylvania in the following geologic environments: altered ultramafic intrusions (serpentinites) of probable lower Paleozoic age in the Piedmont Upland section of the Piedmont province, and contact metamorphosed Precambrian Franklin Marble in the Reading Prong section of the New England province, which does not include magnesite (Figure 42–1). See Figure 40E–1 for a map of serpentinite bodies. Chromite remains as the most important economic mineral in the serpentinite belt.

Deposits in Serpentinites

The American Indians quarried talc, variety steatite, from several localities near Christiana, Lancaster County, to make "soapstone" bowls during the Transitional Period, 1800–800 B.C. (Pennsylvania Archaeological Site Survey file, State Museum of Pennsylvania, Harrisburg). More recently, steatite was quarried intermittently from before 1800 to 1911 at three Philadelphia-area localities (Figure 42–1) and used primarily for heat-resistant linings, for doorsills, and as a filler in paper and paint manufacture (Pearre and Heyl, 1960).

A talc occurrence near New Texas, Lancaster County, was investigated in the 1970's by a major talc mining company. However, the deposit was not deemed conclusively economic. The occurrence is

645

located in the footwall of a large serpentinite body approximately 100 feet from the contact with schist (Robert C. Smith, II, personal communication, 1986). Lapham and McKague (1964) reported considerable steatitization in the same general area.

Green serpentine cut by white carbonate vein-lets (i.e., verde antique) was quarried for decorative purposes at Cardiff, Md., near the Pennsylvania-Maryland line (Pearre and Heyl, 1960). Similar deposits could probably be found in Pennsylvania.

Amphibole asbestos was mined at three locali-ties in Delaware County (Figure 42–1), but produc-tion was small and probably ceased by about 1900. Gordon (1922) reported that talc occurred with the asbestos at two of the localities. In 1940, a small quantity of amphibole asbestos was mined in Chester County by the Foote Mineral Company (Pearre and Heyl, 1960).

Gordon (1922) reported a number of chrysotile asbestos occurrences in Chester, Delaware, and Lan-caster Counties. However, the chrysotile was proba-bly not exploited on a commercial basis.

Magnesite deposits located in southern Chester and Lancaster Counties (Figure 42–1) were the most important national source of magnesia for the synthe-sis of Epsom salt during the earlier part of the nine-teenth century. Production from mines east of Goat Hill, Chester County, amounted to more than 10,000 tons in 32 years, and then ceased in 1871 due to im-ports of German kieserite (Stone, 1922; Pearre and Heyl, 1960).

In 1921, development work in the old workings near Goat Hill yielded unsatisfactory results. Stone (1922) reported that white amorphous magnesite oc-curred as a network of veins in brecciated serpentine. Two veins, each approximately 1 foot thick, were ob-served, but most were less than 1 inch thick.

Frazer (1880) reported a magnesite mine on the Spence farm and a quarry where magnesite was abun-dant on the Gray farm, both in Fulton Township, Lan-caster County. A Baltimore-based company was re-ported to have produced 400 or 500 tons of magne-site by 1828, probably from the Boyce (Spence) farm (Pearre and Heyl, 1960).

Deposits in Franklin Marble

Serpentine-talc deposits occur north of Easton, Northampton County, in a several-mile-long zone of metamorphosed Franklin Marble (Figure 42–1). Mont-gomery (1955, 1957) reported that certain dolomitic and sometimes highly siliceous beds were partially converted to serpentine, talc, and other silicates such as tremolite (Figure 42–2) by late Precambrian ther-

Figure 42–2. Tremolite asbestos from the Verdolite quarry, Easton, Northampton County (State Museum of Pennsylvania specimen m1193).

mal and hydrothermal metamorphism related to gra-nitic pegmatite intrusions.

Peck (1911) described 13 quarries and open cuts developed in the Pennsylvania part of the serpentine-talc belt to provide decorative slabs and mineral pulp. Bayley (1941) reported the production of stucco, ter-razzo, and roofing granules from the Easton serpen-tines, in addition to decorative dimensional slabs. The mixed serpentine-talc-tremolite rock was favored for production of mineral pulp used as a pigment and for fillers in paper, rubber, and so forth.

FELDSPAR

The feldspar deposits of Pennsylvania are lo-cated in the Piedmont Upland section of the Pied-mont province (Figure 42–3), and consist of two types: granitic pegmatites intruded into Precambrian and probable lower Paleozoic crystalline rocks, and albitite dikes intruded into serpentinites of probable lower Paleozoic age.

Granitic pegmatites contain perthitic microcline as the most abundant feldspar of commercial inter-est (Stone and Hughes, 1931). The most productive quarries were located near Elam, Delaware County; from these, feldspar was obtained for 30 years, until 1917. Production occurred from a pegmatite reported as being approximately 70 feet thick with a low dip and a known length of about 0.9 mile. The Avondale-Chatham area in Chester County was also an impor-tant feldspar-producing district (Bascom and Stose, 1932).

Unusual sodic pegmatites (albitite dikes) were extensively worked in southwestern Chester County near Nottingham (Figure 42–4). Sodium-rich pla-gioclase (albite and subsidiary oligoclase) was the feldspar of commercial interest. The albitite dikes

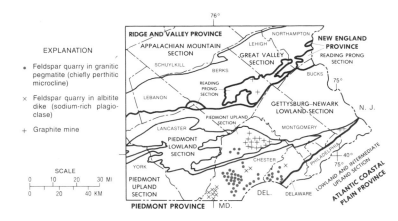

Figure 42–3. Map of southeastern Pennsylvania showing feldspar and graphite extraction localities. A few of the perthitic microcline quarries and the northeasternmost graphite mine may be prospects with no confirmed production. Data are from Miller (1912), Stone and Hughes (1931), Bascom and Stose (1932), and Pearre and Heyl (1960). Physiographic boundaries are from Berg and others (1989).

are usually highly deficient in quartz and mica, common constituents of most pegmatites, but they do contain hornblende and sparse biotite as accessory minerals (Gordon, 1921; Pearre and Heyl, 1960).

Pennsylvania produced about 265,000 short tons of all feldspars between 1900 and 1920, and ranked second among the states in 1907 as a producer of crude feldspar (Stone and Hughes, 1931). Feldspar production in Pennsylvania ceased in about 1928 (Stone, 1939).

GRAPHITE

Graphite was first mined in Pennsylvania in about 1750 near Trevose in Bucks County, according to Miller (1912a), who also reported that graphite deposits have been mined or prospected in Chester, Berks, Bucks, and Lehigh Counties in the southeast-

ern section of Pennsylvania (Figure 42–3). A total of 26 occurrences was discussed by Miller (1912a). The ores contained abundant flake graphite and also minor foliated graphite similar to Ceylon-type ore.

The most important graphite deposits are located in the Piedmont Upland section of the Piedmont province in northern Chester County, especially in an east-northeast-trending belt approximately 8 miles long and 0.5 mile wide in the valley of Pickering Creek (Figure 42–5). This area may contain more coarse flake graphite than any other known district in the United States (Cameron and Weis, 1960).

The extensive Chester County deposits occur in the Precambrian Pickering Gneiss, which typically consists of dominant quartz and lesser amounts of feldspar (orthoclase, microcline, and plagioclase), biotite, and hornblende. Zones containing abundant flake graphite are often associated with accessory pyrite and pyrrhotite. In worked deposits, the graphite-bearing zones were commonly calcareous and between 5 and 100 feet thick with or without sharp boundaries, and in some places contained lenses of graphitic marble. The ore zones were reported to contain 3 to 16 percent graphite with a probable average of less than 6 percent (Bascom and Stose, 1938).

In 1948, the U.S. Bureau of Mines evaluated the graphite deposits of the Benjamin Franklin and Just mines in the Pickering district (Sanford and Lamb, 1949). The tenor of the deposit was determined by drilling and trenching to be about 1.5 percent graphite. Cameron and Weis (1960) reported that the Benjamin Franklin and Just graphitic zone was traced along strike for about 3,200 feet. The zone has a proven width of at least 400 feet. The reported graphitic rocks are micaceous quartz schist, nearly pure metaquartzite, and feldspathic

Figure 42–4. Sparvetta feldspar quarry in 1975, located about 2.5 miles southwest of Nottingham, Chester County. Photograph courtesy of the Pennsylvania Geological Survey.

Figure 42–5. Open cut of Chester Graphite Company in 1986, located about 0.6 mile south-southeast of Chester Springs, Chester County. This open cut is about 300 feet long. The width of the cut varied considerably at the bottom, where there was a railroad track for mine cars.

quartz-muscovite gneiss. Pegmatites up to 5 feet thick were observed in the gneiss. A zone of nearly pure graphite up to 2 inches thick occurred along the foot-wall of a small pegmatite.

Sanford and Lamb (1949) reported that the Benjamin Franklin-Just property produced 178.8 tons of graphite from January 1947 to January 1948, when the operation was shut down. The greatest productive year for all of Pennsylvania may have been 1889, when 2,721 tons of graphite was produced. During the World War I era of 1916–18, Pennsylvania's graphite production was 1,458 tons.

CORUNDUM

Corundum deposits in Pennsylvania are located chiefly in the Piedmont Upland section of the Piedmont province, and also at two localities in the Reading Prong section of the New England province (Figure 42–6).

Corundum occurs in the Piedmont as granular masses and euhedral crystals irregularly distributed in the albite or oligoclase of sodic pegmatites (albitite dikes) located in Chester and Delaware Counties. The corundum-bearing pegmatites occur as intrusions in serpentinite bodies and in serpentinite-schist contact zones. Erratic records between 1839 and 1882 indicate production of 650 to 750 tons of high-grade corundum ore and concentrates from mines in Chester and Delaware Counties. However, the records do not include the very productive 1886–92 period at Corundum Hill, near Unionville, Chester County (Pearre, 1958).

The two Reading Prong corundum localities were reported by Hall (1883) as respectively situated 0.5 mile due north and approximately 0.45 mile north-northwest of the present four-cornered intersection in Shimerville, Lehigh County. Stone (1939) reported that the deposit due north of Shimerville was worked by trenches and a shaft during 1882 and 1883. Several tons of corundum crystals were separated from highly weathered gneiss and shipped. Miller and others (1941) reported that the corundum probably occurs in a pegmatite, which cuts Precambrian hornblende gneiss.

SHEET MICA

Geyer and others (1963) reported two abandoned sheet muscovite workings located in an outlier (Little South Mountain) of the Reading Prong, northern Lancaster County (Figure 42–6). The most recent activity occurred at the southwest opening (Walters mine) in 1951, and some small shipments of mica were reported. The Walters pegmatite dike is zoned and occurs in granitic gneiss. It has an outer zone of pink microcline, perthite, and sparse biotite, and has a quartz-muscovite core about 3 feet thick. The muscovite crystals were reported as being free from physical imperfections but as averaging only 2 to 3 inches in diameter.

SERICITIC PHYLLITE

Dennis J. Knox (personal communication, March 21, 1996) reported that phyllite was mined from two open pits near Mt. Hope, Adams County, from 1965 to 1992 (Figure 42–6). The pits are situated in a 200-

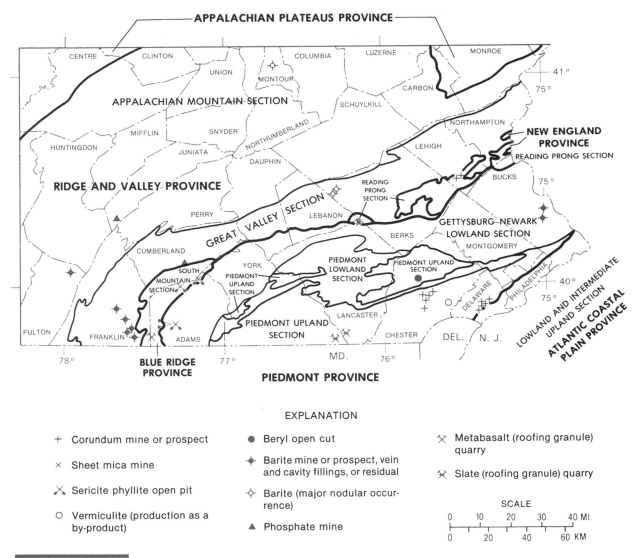

Figure 42-6. Map of central and eastern Pennsylvania showing corundum, mica, sericitic phyllite, vermiculite, beryl, barite, phosphate, and roofing granule extraction and prospect localities. Data are from Hall (1883), Stose (1909), Bascom and Stose (1932), Gault and others (1959), Socolow (1959b), Pearre and Heyl (1960), Geyer and others (1963), Carter (1969), Way and Smith (1983), Berkheiser (1984), and Pennsylvania Geological Survey (1985). Physiographic boundaries are from Berg and others (1989).

foot-wide zone of greenish-gray phyllite located between metarhyolite and metabasalt members of the Precambrian Catoctin Formation (Fauth, 1978).

The quarried phyllite was hauled 22 miles to a drying, grinding, and closed-air classification mill at Aspers, Adams County. The standard product was a finely ground mixture composed mainly of muscovite and quartz and traces of feldspar and chlorite. It was used for fillers in plastics, pipe enamel, rubber products, and so forth, as well as a carrier in insec-

ticides, fungicides, and phosphatic fire-extinguishing compounds (Pennsylvania Geological Survey, 1985).

Sericitic phyllite was also mined at an open pit near Gargol and from 1963 to 1965 at an open pit located approximately 2.4 miles northwest of Bendersville. Both sites are located in Adams County and are situated in the Precambrian Catoctin Formation. Pyrophyllite is also present in phyllite at the Gargol pit (Robert C. Smith, II, personal communication, April 22, 1986).

VERMICULITE

Vermiculite is commonly present in zones adjacent to the previously described albitite dikes in serpentinites, and it occurs at some localities as masses in the albitite. The vermiculite represents an altered biotite and could be produced as a by-product in mining sodium-rich plagioclase (Gordon, 1921; Pearre and Heyl, 1960).

Vermiculite was produced as a by-product during the former quarrying of serpentinite dimensional stone at Brinton's quarry, near West Chester, Chester County (Figure 42–6). The vermiculite variety jefferisite was calcined and used to make paint of a bright gold color (Bascom and Stose, 1932). Stone (1939) reported that a storage shed on the Brinton property held up to 250 cubic feet of vermiculite in reserve.

BERYL

Gordon (1922) reported more than 50 occurrences of beryl in Delaware, Chester, Montgomery and Philadelphia Counties, but the only known commercial production of beryl in Pennsylvania was from a complex granitic pegmatite located about 0.7 mile south of Wagontown, Chester County (Figure 42–6). The owner and producer was the late Frank Steidler. The Foote Mineral Company (personal communication, November 1, 1985) reported a June 1962 shipment of 10,138 pounds of Steidler's hand-cobbed beryl (Figure 42–7) containing 11.67 percent BeO (beryllium oxide).

The beryl occurs as crude yellowish-brown crystals up to about 20 inches in diameter. Ferrocolumbite as crystals up to 4.4 pounds is closely associated with the beryl. A chemical analysis of the ferrocolumbite yielded 62.4 percent N_2O_5 (niobium oxide) and 8 percent Ta_2O_5 (tantalum oxide) (Smith, 1978). Considerable beryl and ferrocolumbite may remain in place.

BARITE

Barite occurs in Pennsylvania as veins and cavity fillings, nodular deposits, and residual deposits. A significant occurrence of vein and cavity-filling barite is located near Ft. Littleton, Fulton County (Figure 42–6), where barite was mined for paint filler prior to 1882 (Stevenson, 1882). Socolow (1959b) reported that 1957-vintage development at this locality exposed a highly brecciated and mineralized fault zone,

up to 15 feet wide, in limestone of the Upper Silurian Tonoloway Formation. Major barite and minor pyrite and chalcopyrite were noted as cavity fillings between breccia fragments and in gash fractures, and also as replacements of wall rock and breccia. The fault can be traced for approximately 2,000 feet, but the lateral extent of mineralization is not known.

At least two fault-zone barite deposits are located in Bucks County (Figure 42–6). Near Buckmantown, a 150- by 450-foot area on the south side of Holiday Hill contains abandoned barite mines and prospect pits (Gault and others, 1959). The barite occurs as cavity fillings in brecciated red sandstone of the Upper Triassic Brunswick Formation and is thought to be genetically related to a nearby diabase intrusion (Tooker, 1949).

Vein and cavity-filling barite occurs as a gangue mineral in the Ordovician carbonate zinc-lead ores of Sinking Valley, Blair County; with sphalerite and galena in the tectonically brecciated Lower Silurian Tuscarora Formation at Milesburg Gap, Centre County; and in the lead-copper-zinc ores of Chester and Montgomery Counties (Smith, 1977).

Nodular barite deposits occur in Cambrian and Ordovician black shales of the allochthonous Hamburg sequence in western Berks County (Figure 42–6). Berkheiser (1984) reported 11 occurrences of crystalline, nodular barite (Figure 42–8) in a 6-square-mile area. The barite is relatively pure, dark colored, and

Figure 42–7. Frank Steidler and the large beryl crystals from his open cut near Wagontown, Chester County. Courtesy of the late Frank Steidler.

Figure 42–8. Fragment of a crystalline barite nodule collected about 0.9 mile northeast of Mount Aetna, Berks County (Berkheiser, 1984, Figure 11).

emits a fetid odor when scratched or fractured. It is probably of syngenetic origin.

Way and Smith (1983) reported nodular barite containing sphalerite and pyrite near Washingtonville, Montour County (Figure 42–6). The barite-bearing interval of interbedded, massive limestones and shale is probably equivalent to the Purcell limestone, an informal member of the Middle Devonian Marcellus Formation. John H. Way and Robert C. Smith, II (personal communication, 1985) reported numerous similar occurrences of nodular barite in the Ridge and Valley province near this same horizon.

Minor deposits of residual barite associated with Cambrian and Ordovician carbonates and sandstones occur near Waynesboro and Chambersburg, Franklin County (Figure 42–6). Stose (1909) noted five abandoned barite mines and prospects in this area. Stose (1904) reported that barite was typically discovered as masses, 6 to 8 inches in average diameter, in red-clay residuum, and that several tons had been shipped from the sites he visited.

PHOSPHATE

Phosphate deposits in Pennsylvania were mined and prospected at several Juniata County occurrences and also mined in Cumberland County (Figure 42–6).

Phosphate occurrences associated with the Devonian Old Port and Onondaga Formations in the Reeds Gap-East Waterford area of Juniata County were first reported by Ihlseng (1896). His chemical

analyses of selected float, such as white porous rock, red nodules, and blue limestone fragments, yielded a range of phosphoric acid values from greater than 12 percent to 30 percent.

Subsequent to Ihlseng's work, phosphate occurring as a secondary wavellite-crandallite enriched zone several feet thick at the top of the Old Port Formation (Figure 42–9) was mined between 1899 and 1904 on the Newman farm near East Waterford, Juniata County (Carter, 1969). The total phosphate production during the 5-year period was 4,000 long tons. This figure may include production at two similar localities in the general area (Hovey, 1904).

Stose (1907a) reported that clay prospecting along the western and northern flank of the Blue Ridge province ("Tomstown ore belt") led to the discovery of wavellite-bearing nodules in white clay near Moors (Moores) Mill, Cumberland County. An open-cut phosphate mine in the basal portion of the Lower Cambrian Tomstown Formation was then initiated in 1900. The sequence at this site, as revealed by a nearby shaft, was phosphate ore in white clay from a depth of 12 feet down to 52 feet that was followed

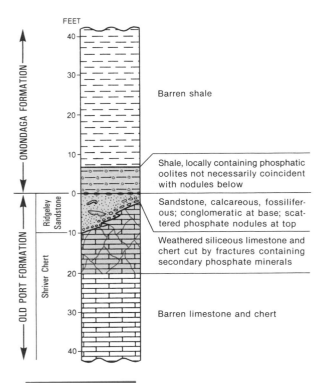

Figure 42–9. Stratigraphic column showing the distribution of phosphatic material in the Devonian Old Port and Onondaga Formations at the W. L. Newman farm, Juniata County (from Carter, 1969, Figure 3).

by 16 feet of manganese oxide ore. The greatest production probably occurred in 1905, when 400 tons of phosphate ore was reduced in furnaces for the manufacture of matches. Stone (1939) reported that mining ceased in about 1906.

ROCK SALT

Salt beds of possible economic importance make up part of the Upper Silurian Salina Group in northern and western Pennsylvania (Figure 42–10). Mining the salt beds would not be economic at present, as their depth of burial ranges from 2,200 feet in Erie County (northwestern Pennsylvania) to 8,200 feet in Fayette County (southwestern Pennsylvania) and 8,900 feet in Bradford County (northeastern Pennsylvania). However, solution mining techniques could prove technically successful in extracting the salt. The total thickness of salt ranges from 80 feet in Erie County to 542 feet in Fayette County and 776 feet in Bradford County (Fergusson and Prather, 1968).

METABASALT AND SLATE FOR ROOFING GRANULES

The GAF Corporation quarries metabasalt from the Precambrian Catoctin Formation in Adams and Franklin Counties (Figure 42–6) for the production of artificially colored, ceramic-coated roofing granules. Metabasalt is the preferred raw material because of these favorable characteristics: good heat and weathering resistance, toughness, low porosity, opacity to ultraviolet energy, yields equidimensional granules when crushed, and accepts coloring. The large GAF metabasalt quarry (Figure 42–11) and roofing-granule mill (Figure 42–12) are located near Gladhill (Greenstone PO), Adams County. Native copper (Figure 42–13) is locally considered a nuisance during crushing operations (Michael Shelbert, personal communication, 1986).

Stone (1923) reported roofing-granule operations near Delta, York County, and at Peach Bottom Station, Lancaster County (Figure 42–6). The granules were produced from the Peach Bottom Slate, of probable lower Paleozoic age. Michael Shelbert (personal communication, April 28, 1986) reported that the GAF Corporation's roofing-granule operation near Delta was closed down during November 1970.

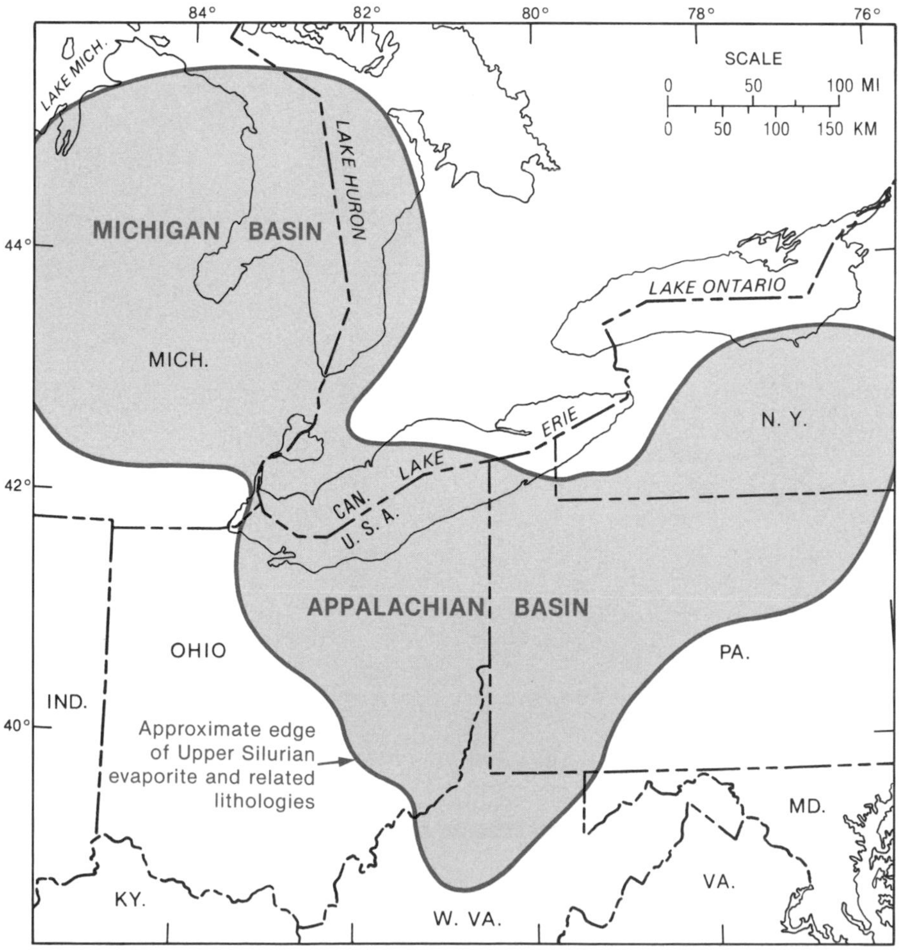

Figure 42–10. Distribution of Upper Silurian rock salt in Pennsylvania and other states. The rock salt occurs inside the colored line (from Alling and Briggs, © 1961, Figure 2, p. 517, reprinted by permission of the American Association of Petroleum Geologists).

GEMSTONES

The pegmatite-rich, metamorphic terrane of the Piedmont Upland section of the Piedmont province has yielded fine gemstones. The best localities are located within a 37-mile radius of central Philadelphia. Gordon (1922) reported a number of occurrences of beryl, colored quartz, garnet, and the feldspar group in this area. Unfortunately, the best localities are now inaccessible.

Sinkankas (1959) refined Gordon's (1922) list of occurrences for the best gem stock and excellent crystals. Only a few of the more notable localities are discussed here.

Beautiful aquamarine and golden beryl crystals were discovered in dimension-stone quarries near Swarthmore and Chester, Delaware County. Gem

stock was usually small, but an excellent golden beryl from Leiper's quarry near Swarthmore was cut into a 35.7 carat gem.

A locality near Kennett Square, Chester County, yielded brilliant oligoclase, variety sunstone, comparable to Norwegian material. Microcline, variety amazonite, and albite, variety moonstone, were found on Mineral Hill near Media, Delaware County. Gem-quality almandine possessing a deep blood-red color was recovered from gravels in Greens Creek, Aston Township, Delaware County. Exceptional colorless to pale-brown, transparent diaspore crystals, up to 2 inches in length, were found associated with corundum at Corundum Hill, near Unionville, Chester County.

Many beautiful specimens of colored and rutilated quartz were collected from localities in Dela-

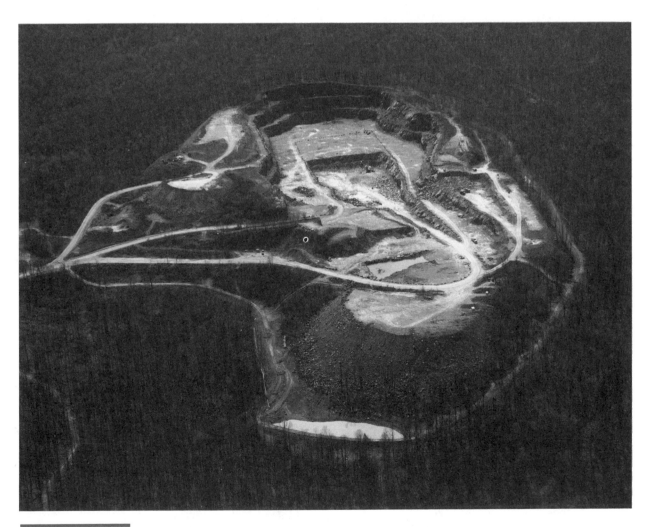

Figure 42–11. Aerial view looking south-southwest of GAF Corporation's West Ridge quarry (April 1983), located 0.6 mile northwest of Greenstone PO, Adams County. Photograph courtesy of GAF Corporation.

Figure 42–12. GAF Corporation's roofing-granule plant, located about 0.4 mile southwest of Greenstone PO, Adams County. The crushing facility is in the foreground, and the ceramic coating mill is in the background on the ridge.

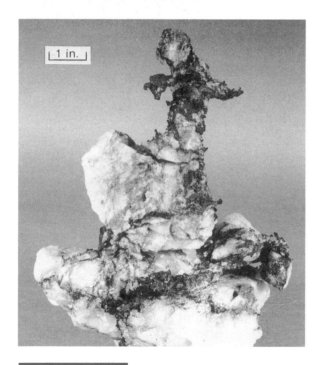

Figure 42–13. Late native copper in fractured quartz, and associated with secondary azurite and malachite, from GAF Corporation's West Ridge quarry, Adams County (State Museum of Pennsylvania specimen m17).

ware County. Notable are the fine groups of smoky-purplish crystals from Shaw and Esrey's quarry near Boothwyn; excellent deep-purple amethyst crystals from two localities near Media; and the fine rutilated quartz found near Boothwyn. Excellent smoky quartz crystals were collected from a sand pit in Lansdowne.

Presently (1996), several types of gem and ornamental stones are available if property owners permit access to localities. The most noteworthy are copper-bearing aporhyolite (Figure 42–14) from the Bigham copper prospect, 1 mile north of Gladhill (Greenstone PO), Adams County; moss agate and other varieties of agate (Figure 42–15), 0.25 to 1 mile west-southwest of Jenkins Corner, Fulton Township, Lancaster County (Sinkankas, 1959); and antigorite, variety williamsite, from southern Lancaster County localities such as the Cedar Hill quarry and Red Pit chromite mine in Fulton Township, and the Wood chromite mine in Little Britain Township (Gordon, 1922; Geyer and others, 1976).

PROBLEMS AND FUTURE RESEARCH

Most of the mineral resources discussed in this chapter will probably remain in a noncommercial, academic framework for the basic reasons given in the introduction.

Presently, a positive project commitment and improved beneficiation of Pennsylvania's graphite ores will probably not make them competitive with cheaply produced, high-grade foreign deposits. Zoning laws would probably present the greatest obstacle to production of the large graphite deposits in Chester County (Samuel W. Berkheiser, Jr., personal

Figure 42–14. Polished slab of aporhyolite containing amygdules of epidote, quartz, native copper, and cuprite. The pale-pink aporhyolite "groundmass" is irregularly pigmented by green epidote and orange cuprite. Bigham copper prospect, Adams County.

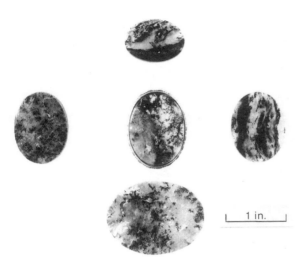

Figure 42–15. Moss agate from near Jenkins Corner, Lancaster County. Collected by, and cabochon cuts by, Dennis McGill.

communication, 1988). Zoning laws would also present great problems in Delaware County relative to feldspar production with a possible by-product of sheet mica or beryl.

The production of talc from the altered ultramafics (serpentinites) is presently precluded, in part because of associated tremolite and actinolite (Robert C. Smith, II, personal communication, 1988).

Exploration is needed to find deposits of relatively pure sericitic phyllite or muscovite schist for fillers. High whiteness and brightness of the finely ground standard product is required in joint com-

pounds and so forth. Mining and milling costs probably could be reduced in the production of roofing granules if advances in ceramic-coating technology would allow the use of rock other than metabasalt for the base rock (Samuel W. Berkheiser, Jr., personal communication, 1988).

Bedded barite deposits may be associated with the major nodular barite occurrences in Pennsylvania. The previously described barite-bearing interval of the Middle Devonian Marcellus Formation would serve as an interesting exploration target for an economic barite deposit (Robert C. Smith, II, personal communication, 1988).

RECOMMENDED FOR FURTHER READING

Berkheiser, S. W., Jr. (1984), *Fetid barite occurrences, western Berks County, Pennsylvania,* Pennsylvania Geological Survey, 4th ser., Mineral Resource Report 84, 43 p.

Fergusson, W. B., and Prather, B. A. (1968), *Salt deposits in the Salina Group in Pennsylvania,* Pennsylvania Geological Survey, 4th ser., Mineral Resource Report 58, 41 p.

Geyer, A. R., Smith, R. C., II, and Barnes, J. H. (1976), *Mineral collecting in Pennsylvania,* Pennsylvania Geological Survey, 4th ser., General Geology Report 33, 260 p.

Miller, B. L. (1912), *Graphite deposits of Pennsylvania,* Pennsylvania Geological Survey, 3rd ser., Report 6, 147 p.

Pearre, N. C., and Heyl, A. V., Jr. (1960), *Chromite and other mineral deposits in serpentine rocks of the Piedmont Upland, Maryland, Pennsylvania, and Delaware,* U.S. Geological Survey Bulletin 1082–K, p. 707–833.

Sanford, R. S., and Lamb, F. D. (1949), *Investigation of the Benjamin Franklin graphite mine (government owned) and the Just graphite mine, Chester County, Pennsylvania,* U.S. Bureau of Mines Report of Investigations 4530, 17 p.

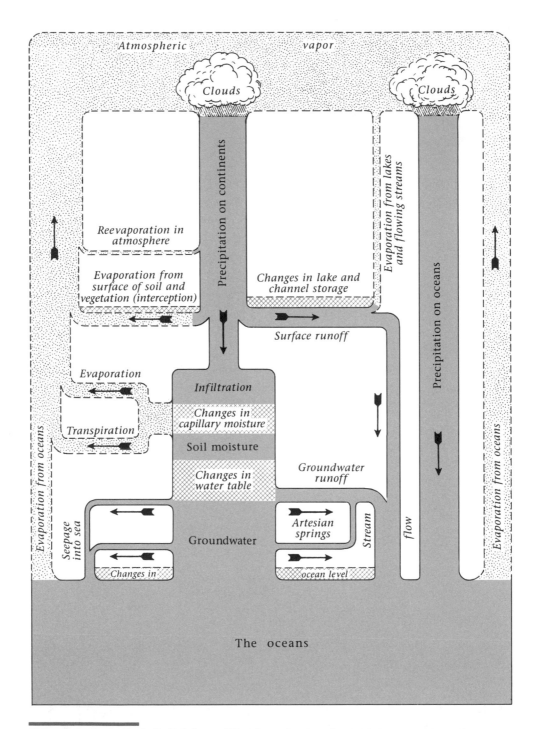

"The Hydrologic Cycle," slightly modified from the drawing by Adolph F. Meyer for the frontispiece of the classic volume *Hydrology*, edited by Oscar E. Meinzer (1942).

Part VIII

WATER RESOURCES

Though in the number of chapters it is one of the shortest parts of this volume, the brevity of Part VIII in no way reflects the importance of water to Pennsylvania. Water is our most vital resource. Annual precipitation across the state averages about 42 inches, and surface-water inflow from adjacent states provides the equivalent of an additional 6 inches, making the income part of Pennsylvania's average annual water budget about 48 inches. This is balanced by equal average outgo, or expense, of which about 28 inches is surface-water outflow and about 20 inches consists of evaporation and transpiration. In addition to this transient water, there is the equivalent of more than 60 inches of precipitation in long-term storage as groundwater in surficial deposits and bedrock.

Owing to practices of the past, the contamination of surface waters of the state was widespread. Much improvement has been made, but at the time of this writing, about a quarter of the state's major-stream miles still failed to meet water-quality standards. In contrast, the quality of groundwater in the state generally is good.

Clearly, Pennsylvania normally is well provided with water, for the average water budget equals almost 3,200,000 gallons for each resident per year. No year is perfectly average, and unusually low precipitation over significant periods can result in drought conditions, just as unusually high precipitation can cause flooding. It is the quality, and not the quantity, of the water supply that is the larger issue in Pennsylvania. Protection and improvement of the quality of the state's water supply is of vital concern for the health and safety of all its citizens.

—Reginald P. Briggs

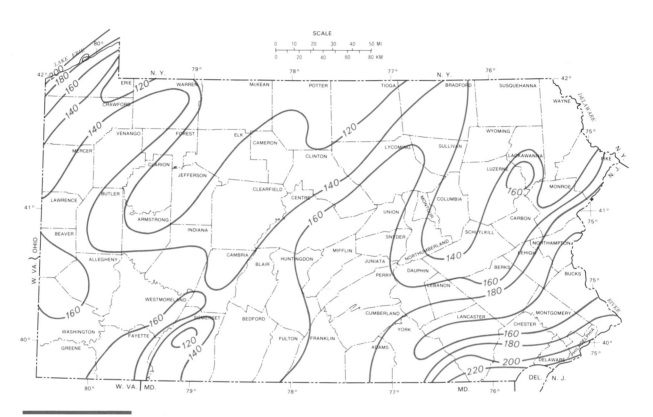

Figure 43–1. Mean freeze-free period per year, based on data for the period 1951–80 (U.S. National Oceanic and Atmospheric Administration, 1984a). Contour interval is 20 days.

658

CHAPTER 43   CLIMATE

THERESA ROSSI
  National Weather Service Forecast Office
  192 Shafer Road
  Coraopolis, PA 15108

INTRODUCTION

Pennsylvania is generally considered to have a humid continental type of climate, characterized by large annual ranges in temperature and an even distribution of precipitation. Its climate is not purely continental, however, due to the influences of the Great Lakes, the Atlantic Ocean, and the diversity of physiographic features within the state (U.S. National Oceanic and Atmospheric Administration, 1977a).

The Appalachian Mountains are a powerful influence on the climate of Pennsylvania. The relatively high elevations and general linearity of the mountains make them an effective obstacle to airflow. The mountains deflect the tracks of storm systems and may temporarily block the passage of air masses in lower levels of the atmosphere. If winds are strong enough to force air masses across the Appalachians, the forced ascent and descent profoundly alters the temperature and the distribution of precipitation. Ascending air currents cool, causing condensation and precipitation on the windward side of the mountains. Descending air currents on the lee side are stabilized, resulting in warmer and drier conditions.

The Great Lakes also influence the climate of Pennsylvania, acting as an important source of moisture. This is especially the case in times of northwesterly airflow. In addition, temperature variations between land, water, and air have stabilizing and destabilizing effects, which vary from season to season. Wind speed and direction are altered by these temperature variations as well as by frictional differences between land and water.

Most of the weather disturbances that affect Pennsylvania are carried from the interior of the continent by prevailing westerly winds. The Atlantic Ocean, therefore, has a limited influence on the climate of the western half of the state, but it is a major moisture source in the east. Storms are also fueled by moisture from the Gulf of Mexico; this moisture is pumped into the area by southerly winds.

TEMPERATURE

Temperatures across the state normally remain between 0°F and 100°F and average from 43°F in the north-central mountains to 55°F in the southeast. The highest temperature ever recorded was 111°F at Phoenixville in Chester County, just northwest of Philadelphia, on July 9 and 10, 1936. The lowest ever recorded was –42°F at Smethport in McKean County on January 5, 1904 (U.S. National Oceanic and Atmospheric Administration, 1977a).

High temperatures of 90°F or above occur about 10 days per year at any one location, but southeastern localities may experience more than twice this number. Ranges of daily temperature from maximum to minimum are commonly around 20°F during the summer and are a few degrees less during the winter. Freezing temperatures occur on an average of 100 or more days per year, and the greatest number of occurrences is in the Appalachian Plateaus province in north-central Pennsylvania. The southeast (near sea level) and northwest (adjacent to Lake Erie) sections of the state have the longest freeze-free period (Figure 43–1).

Figures 43–2 through 43–5 show mean maximum and mean minimum temperatures for the months of July and January. During July, the warmest month, high temperatures normally range from the upper 70's in northern areas of the state to the mid-80's in southern areas of the state. Minimum temperatures for this month range from the upper 60's in the southeast to the lower 50's in the north-central mountains.

During January, the coldest month, most of the state experiences low temperatures in the teens and high temperatures in the 30's. High temperatures usually remain near or below the freezing point during this month in northern sections of the state. In southern sections, high temperatures hover in the mid- to upper 30's.

PRECIPITATION

Precipitation is fairly evenly distributed; the maximum occurs during late spring or summer, primarily from thunderstorms. Annual amounts are normally between 34 and 51 inches (Figure 43–6). Precipitation tends to be greater in the eastern sections owing to coastal influences and the orographic effects of topography on easterly airflow from the Atlantic Ocean. Prevailing westerly winds cause a secondary precipitation maximum on the western slopes

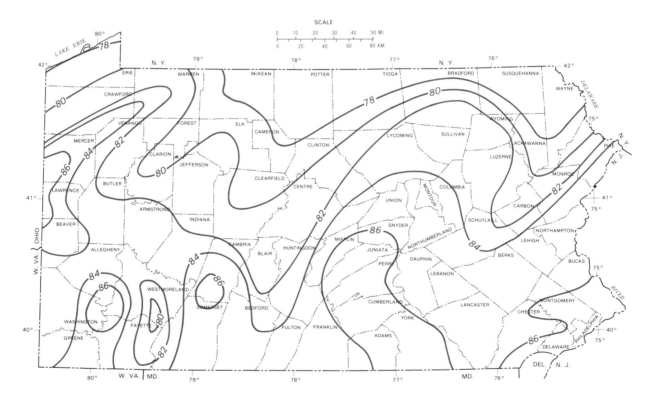

Figure 43–2. Mean maximum temperature in July, based on data for the period 1951–80 (U.S. National Oceanic and Atmospheric Administration, 1984a). Contour interval is 2°F.

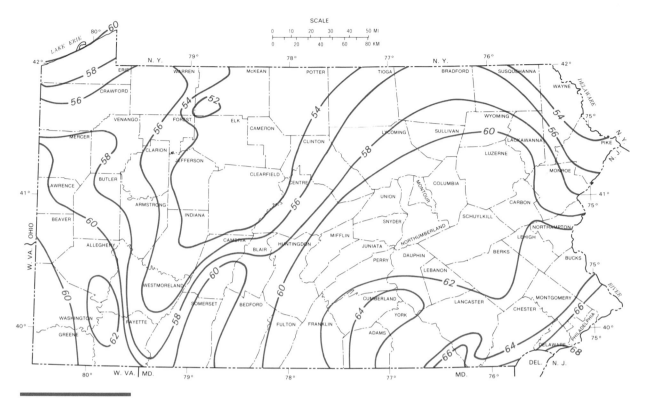

Figure 43–3. Mean minimum temperature in July, based on data for the period 1951–80 (U.S. National Oceanic and Atmospheric Administration, 1984a). Contour interval is 2°F.

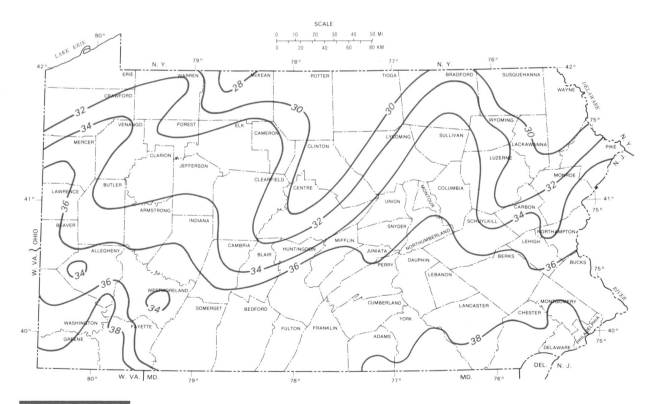

Figure 43–4. Mean maximum temperature in January, based on data for the period 1951–80 (U.S. National Oceanic and Atmospheric Administration, 1984a). Contour interval is 2°F.

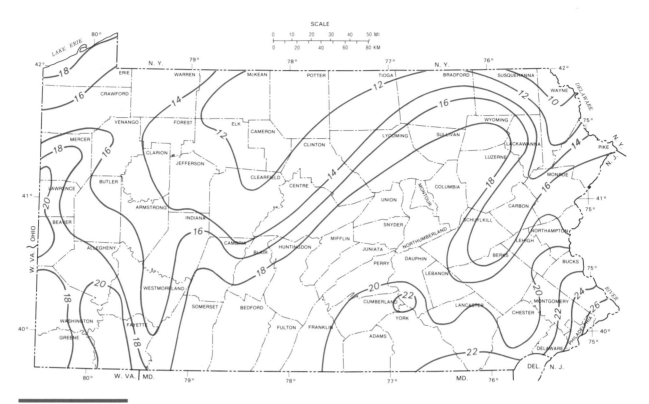

Figure 43–5. Mean minimum temperature in January, based on data for the period 1951–80 (U.S. National Oceanic and Atmospheric Administration, 1984a). Contour interval is 2°F.

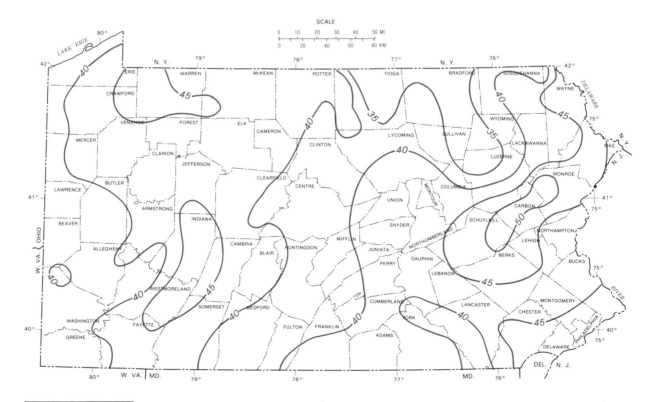

Figure 43–6. Mean annual precipitation, based on data for the period 1951–80 (U.S. National Oceanic and Atmospheric Administration, 1984a). Contour interval is 5 inches.

of the Allegheny Mountain section of the Appalachian Plateaus province in western Pennsylvania.

The average annual snowfall ranges from 23 inches in the southeast to over 80 inches in the northwest and northeast (Figure 43–7). Storms tracking up the east coast tap into Atlantic moisture, whereas the Great Lakes supply the moisture and instability for heavy snow squalls in the northwest. Orographic lift enhances snowfall over higher elevations (note particularly the higher snowfall in Somerset County in the Allegheny Mountain section). The snowfall season is November through April, and amounts are generally below 1 inch during October and May. The greatest monthly snowfalls occur in December and January, and maximum amounts for individual storms occur in March as the moisture supply begins to increase with rising temperatures (Daily, 1971).

Dry spells, during which monthly precipitation may total less than one-quarter inch, may occur and persist for several months. These periods rarely affect all sections of the state at once, nor are they confined to a particular season (U.S. National Oceanic and Atmospheric Administration, 1977a).

SEVERE WEATHER

Major flooding along principal rivers can occur during any month of the year in Pennsylvania (see Chapter 52). Flooding is most frequent and widespread during the spring thaw, when heavy rains combine with snowmelt. In addition, owing to steep slopes and narrow valleys, especially in the western part of the state, Pennsylvania is highly prone to flash flooding caused by heavy downpours during intense summer thunderstorms (see Chapter 55C). Serious local flooding can also result from ice jams, and sometimes storms of tropical origin cause flooding, especially in eastern sections of the state. Floods of notable severity and magnitude occur about once every 8 years. Major, widespread flooding occurs on an average of once in every 18- to 20-year period (Daily, 1971). Serious historical flood events in the state include tropical storm Agnes in June 1972 (see Chapter 52, Appendix A), during which 50 lives were claimed and property damage was in the billions of dollars (U.S. National Oceanic and Atmospheric Administration, 1972). After a very large thunderstorm stalled over the area, 10 feet of water was reported in the streets of Johnstown during the Johnstown flood of July 19, 1977, which claimed 74 lives and caused over $50 million in property damage (U.S. National Oceanic and Atmospheric Administration, 1977b).

Tornadoes and severe thunderstorms also occur in Pennsylvania. On an average, eight tornadoes are observed annually, with most occurring in June (U.S.

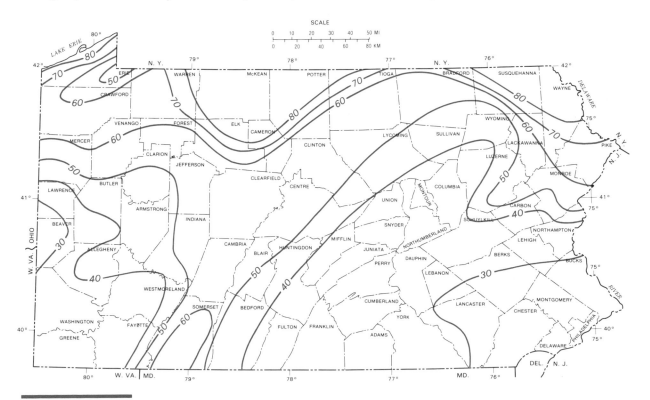

Figure 43–7. Average annual snowfall, based on data for the period 1951–80 (U.S. National Oceanic and Atmospheric Administration, 1984a). Contour interval is 10 inches.

National Oceanic and Atmospheric Administration, 1982b). Thunderstorms are normally observed between 30 and 40 days per year across the state, and there are about four lightning deaths annually (U.S. National Oceanic and Atmospheric Administration, 1984b). Seventeen tornadoes tracked across the state during a devastating tornado outbreak on May 31, 1985, resulting in the deaths of 65 persons (U.S. National Oceanic and Atmospheric Administration, 1985).

CLIMATIC ZONES

The various physiographic provinces of Pennsylvania (see map B, p. 342) exhibit distinctive climatic characteristics.

Atlantic Coastal Plain and Piedmont Provinces

The Appalachian Mountains to the west and the Atlantic Ocean to the east moderate the climate of the Atlantic Coastal Plain and Piedmont provinces. Warm summers and mild winters are characteristic of this climatic zone. Daily temperatures reach 90°F or above on an average of 24 days during the summer season, and the area occasionally experiences uncomfortable warm periods of light winds and high relative humidity (U.S. National Oceanic and Atmospheric Administration, 1984a).

During the winter months, there are normally about 116 days that have minimum temperatures at or below the freezing point. Minimum temperatures of 0°F or lower generally occur one or two times per year. The freeze-free season averages 170 to 200 days (U.S. National Oceanic and Atmospheric Administration, 1984a).

Precipitation is fairly evenly distributed throughout the year; maximum amounts occur during the late summer months. Annual precipitation averages 43 inches, and mean seasonal snowfall is 28 inches, the lowest for the state. Fields are normally snow covered about one third of the time during the winter season (Daily, 1971).

Ridge and Valley Province

The Ridge and Valley province has many of the characteristics of a mountain-type climate. Mountain and valley influences cause greater temperature extremes and an increase in daily ranges. The freeze-free season is generally between 140 and 180 days (U.S. National Oceanic and Atmospheric Administration, 1984a).

Maximum temperatures in most years are not excessively high; temperatures equal to or above 90°F occur on an average of only 18 days during the summer season. Temperatures above 100°F are seldom recorded. Minimum temperatures during January, February, and March are commonly below freezing, but are seldom below 0°F (U.S. National Oceanic and Atmospheric Administration, 1984a).

The average annual precipitation is 44 inches, similar to that of the Atlantic Coastal Plain and Piedmont provinces. A larger percentage of this precipitation falls in the form of snow, which averages 42 inches during the winter season (U.S. National Oceanic and Atmospheric Administration, 1984a).

Appalachian Plateaus Province

The Appalachian Plateaus province is fairly typical of a continental-type climate having changeable temperatures and more frequent precipitation than other parts of Pennsylvania. Latitude and elevation make the northern part of the province the coldest area of the state. Daily temperature ranges exceed those of other areas, averaging between 20°F and 30°F (U.S. National Oceanic and Atmospheric Administration, 1984a).

Because of the rugged topography, the freeze-free season is variable, ranging from 130 days in the north to 180 days in the south. Daily high temperatures reach 90°F or above on an average of 10 days during the summer season, but temperatures rarely exceed 100°F. During the winter months, there are normally about 145 days when temperatures dip to or below the freezing point. Low temperatures equal to or below 0°F generally occur 8 days per season. In northern sections, subzero temperatures occur twice as often (U.S. National Oceanic and Atmospheric Administration, 1984a).

Mean annual precipitation is 40 inches, and seasonal snowfall is normally about 50 inches. The greatest amounts occur in the northern regions, where some areas average more than 80 inches annually. Fields are usually snow covered three fourths of the time during the winter season (Daily, 1971).

Central Lowland Province

The influence of Lake Erie is profoundly evident in the climate of the Central Lowland province. The lake has a moderating effect on temperatures, and the freeze-free season is normally extended to about 200 days. Temperatures above 90°F or below 0°F are extremely rare. The lake also reduces daily temperature ranges to less than 20°F in most months (U.S. National Oceanic and Atmospheric Administration, 1984a).

Temperature differences between the air and water produce cloudiness and frequent snowfalls during the winter months. The lake also acts as an important moisture source for the region. At Erie, mean annual snowfall averages about 60 inches, and annual precipitation averages close to 40 inches. Just inland of the lake, snowfall averages about 80 inches per year due to the added effect of orographic influences (U.S. National Oceanic and Atmospheric Administration, 1984a).

PROBLEMS AND FUTURE RESEARCH

Technological advances continue to increase the number of high-quality observations available for climatological studies and the ability to process this vast amount of information. Automatic observing stations make it possible to reduce the scale of the observing network while subsequently increasing the library of normals, means, and extremes. High-powered computer processing systems compile and organize this information very efficiently into climatological summaries. Sophisticated communications systems increase the ability to maintain accurate statistics on significant weather events. As the quantity and quality of records increase, so will the ability to describe the climate of Pennsylvania.

The biggest concern for the future of the state is urbanization in flood-prone areas. Areas that were once covered with trees and grass are being replaced by pavement, shopping malls, and high-rise buildings. This urbanization increases the amount of run-off and the potential for flash flooding, which is the most serious weather-induced threat to the state.

RECOMMENDED FOR FURTHER READING

Anthes, R. A., Panofshy, H. A., and Cahir, J. J. (1975), *The atmosphere,* Columbus, Ohio, Charles E. Merrill, p. 55-93.

Berry, F. A., Jr., Bollang, E., and Beres, N. R. (1973), *Handbook of meteorology,* New York, McGraw-Hill, p. 927-996.

Trewartha, G. T. (1961), *The earth's problem climates,* Madison, Wis., University of Wisconsin Press, p. 251-306.

U.S. National Oceanic and Atmospheric Administration (1982), *Climate of Pennsylvania,* Environmental Data and Information Service, National Climatic Center, Ashville, N. C., p. 1-7.

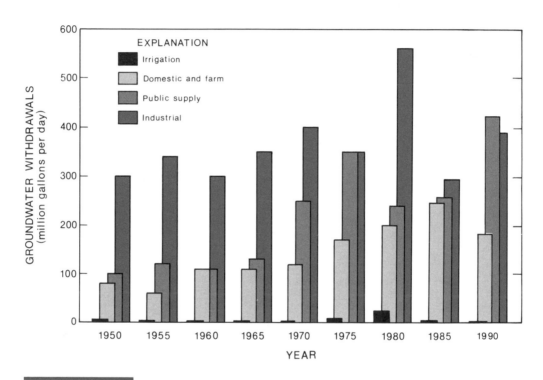

Figure 44–1. Trends in groundwater withdrawals in Pennsylvania, based on data from MacKichan (1951, 1957), MacKichan and Kammerer (1961), Murray (1968), Murray and Reeves (1972, 1977), and Solley and others (1983, 1988, 1993). Public systems supplying small- and moderate-sized communities are numerically the largest single user group.

666

CHAPTER 44   GROUNDWATER

ALBERT E. BECHER*
U.S. Geological Survey
Water Resources Division
840 Market Street
Lemoyne, PA 17043

INTRODUCTION

The groundwater hydrology of Pennsylvania is as complex, heterogeneous, and segmented as the geology. Most groundwater in the Piedmont physiographic province (see map B, p. 342) discharges within several miles of its entrance into the subsurface. Some subsurface systems drain areas of 100 square miles or more from valleys in the Appalachian Mountain section of the Ridge and Valley physiographic province. Deep, regional groundwater systems exist but transport little water except in aquifers of the Atlantic Coastal Plain province. Development of the groundwater resources has progressed with improvement in technology but even more with increased knowledge of local geology and groundwater-flow systems.

DEVELOPMENT AND USE OF GROUNDWATER

Early users of groundwater depended on the abundant springs and seeps in Pennsylvania. By the seventeenth century, wells were hand dug to supply water to places or in amounts not possible from springs. In the nineteenth century, the crude cable-tool drilling techniques, used to construct small-diameter boreholes for the removal of salt deposits, were adapted to water-well construction. Prospecting for water deep in bedrock then was possible almost anywhere. By the start of the twentieth century, the development of groundwater had progressed substantially.

Some information on groundwater use by communities appears in the early groundwater-resource reports published by the Pennsylvania Geological Survey (Lohman, 1941). Beginning in 1950, the U.S. Geological Survey has published estimates of statewide water use at 5-year intervals (MacKichan, 1951, 1957; MacKichan and Kammerer, 1961; Murray, 1968; Murray and Reeves, 1972, 1977; Solley and others, 1983, 1988, 1993). A summary of these estimates for fresh groundwater withdrawals in Pennsylvania

*Retired.

(Figure 44–1) shows the temporal trend in groundwater use.

The 1984 estimates of groundwater withdrawals for all uses, by county, are shown in Figure 44–2. About 30 percent of the population depended on groundwater for potable supply in 1984. Groundwater withdrawals in counties in the southeastern part of the state, where population, industry, and farming are concentrated and some of the highest yielding aquifers are located, accounted for 31 percent of the statewide total. The county having the largest withdrawal (average of 54 Mgal/d [million gallons per day]) of groundwater was Allegheny County; it was followed closely by Montgomery County, which had an average withdrawal of 53 Mgal/d. Withdrawals in Allegheny County were divided fairly evenly among public supply, industrial supply, and mineral-resource development; however, in Montgomery County, 75 percent of the withdrawals were for public supply.

OCCURRENCE OF GROUNDWATER

Most groundwater occupies heterogeneous planar openings, such as joints and bedding-plane separations, in bedrock. The remainder occupies the intergranular spaces in glaciofluvial deposits (see Figure 3 in the color section), colluvium on the flanks of ridges in the Ridge and Valley province, regolith throughout Pennsylvania where the water table is above bedrock, carbonate-cemented sandstone beds where the cement has been removed, and the wedge of unconsolidated sand and clay layers under the Atlantic Coastal Plain province.

Differences in the size and spacing of bedrock openings cause large variations in permeability both within and between rock units. Planar openings commonly are better developed along strike than across strike; as a result, responses to hydraulic stresses within the bedrock tend to be anisotropic. In general, per-

Figure 44–2. Withdrawal of groundwater by county in 1984, based on data from Loper and others (1989). Counties in southeastern Pennsylvania were the largest users, but many rural counties obtained more than 75 percent of all water used from groundwater sources.

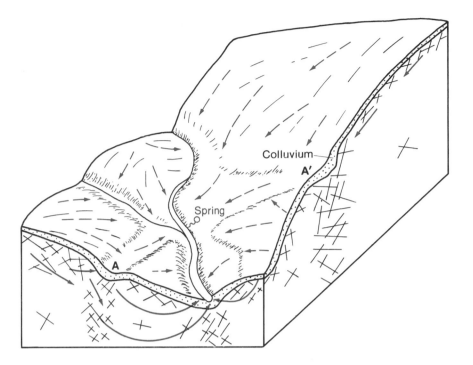

Figure 44–3. Generalized diagram of a local groundwater-flow system. Arrows show flow directions and are dashed where below the surface on which they appear. A–A´ is the linear surface expression of an underlying fracture zone.

meability decreases with increasing depth, as do the size and number of openings.

Most groundwater-flow systems discharge locally and drain areas that range from less than 1 square mile to several tens of square miles. Figure 44–3 shows a local groundwater-flow system typical of low-relief terrains throughout the state.

Many areas are underlain by more than one flow system, commonly as a result of irregularities in topography (Freeze and Cherry, 1979, p. 195). Flow beneath local groundwater systems bypasses local streams and discharges to distant streams at lower elevations. The flow systems shown in Figure 44–4 are typical of val-

leys underlain by folded carbonate rocks in the Ridge and Valley province. Multiple flow systems have been identified in the Appalachian Plateaus province (Figure 44–5). Wells that penetrate more than one flow system may provide a conduit between shallow and deeper systems. Under natural conditions, these systems are not well connected, and differences in head may be large.

AVAILABILITY OF GROUNDWATER

Ultimately, the availability of groundwater depends on lithology. Lithology controls the response of bedrock to the physical stresses and chemical pro-

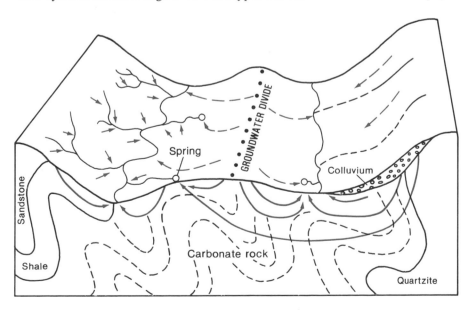

Figure 44–4. Generalized diagram showing multiple flow systems in a carbonate valley. Arrows show flow directions and are dashed where below the surface on which they appear. Large amounts of water move through conduits formed by the solution of carbonate rocks, under the local stream and groundwater divide, and discharge in the adjacent drainage basin. The diagram is analogous to conditions documented in Becher and Root (1981).

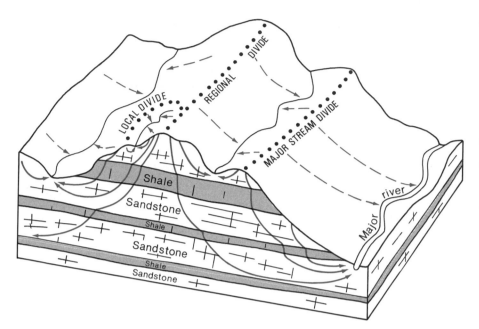

Figure 44–5. Generalized diagram of multiple flow systems in flat-lying rocks of the Pocono Plateau, reported by Carswell and Lloyd (1979). Arrows show flow directions and are dashed where below the surface on which they appear. The sparsity of fractures in shale beds between fractured sandstone beds restricts hydraulic, vertical connection.

cesses that produce fracture openings. Wells in rocks of similar lithology have similar yields. The lithologic variability within rock formations and diversity in structural and topographic settings cause differences in well yields.

Figure 44–6 shows the availability of groundwater based on yield data from more than 18,000 wells in the U.S. Geological Survey Ground Water Site Inventory (GWSI) database. Yields from bedrock wells were divided into four physiographic settings and grouped by major lithology. Unconsolidated sediments are shown separately, regardless of lithology or physiographic location.

In general, wells in sand and gravel and wells in carbonate rock formations have the largest yields. Maximum yields of 3,000 and 8,000 gal/min (gallons per minute), respectively, were obtained from wells in these units during test pumping. The relation of topography to well yield shows the same trends regardless of rock type or physiographic setting (Taylor and others, 1983; Meisler and Becher, 1971). In general, well yields are least from hilltop sites, are intermediate from hillside sites, and are greatest from valley sites.

MONTHLY, SEASONAL, AND LONG-TERM VARIABILITY IN WATER LEVELS

Groundwater levels generally rise in winter and spring and decline through summer and fall. Although precipitation is slightly greater in summer than in winter months, there is little recharge to groundwater systems during the warm part of the year, as most precipitation that reaches land and does not run off is lost to evapotranspiration. Figure 44–7 shows the seasonal trend in groundwater levels and their relation to precipitation typical of valley and hillside wells. Water levels in valley wells fluctuate less and commonly are shallower than in wells at higher topographic positions.

The quantiles of the monthly cumulative frequency distributions of daily low water levels in five observation wells are plotted for the period of record in Figure 44–8. Plots for three of the wells, those in Chester (B), Huntingdon (C), and Wayne (D) Counties, clearly show the same seasonal trend of water levels in the annual hydrograph. All three wells are shallow and yield abundantly from openings less than 90 feet below land surface. The remaining plots, for wells in Montgomery (A) and Indiana (E) Counties, have diffuse trends. Both of these wells are deep, have substantial yields from zones more than 140 feet below land surface, and have deep water levels. Therefore, seasonal cycles or multiyear periods of drought have a less pronounced effect on water levels in these wells compared to those in shallower wells.

WATER QUALITY

Temperature, specific conductance, hardness, and pH are useful indicators of general water quality. In Pennsylvania, groundwater temperature averages about 51°F, ranges from about 48°F to 54°F, and varies ac-

PIEDMONT PROVINCE

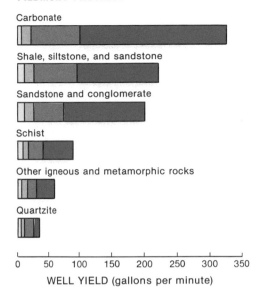

Carbonate

Shale, siltstone, and sandstone

Sandstone and conglomerate

Schist

Other igneous and metamorphic rocks

Quartzite

WELL YIELD (gallons per minute)

EXPLANATION

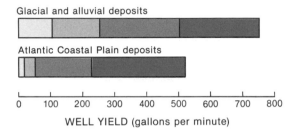

75 50 25 10

Percent > tip value

UNCONSOLIDATED SEDIMENTS

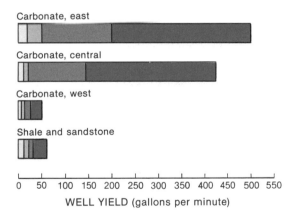

Glacial and alluvial deposits

Atlantic Coastal Plain deposits

WELL YIELD (gallons per minute)

GREAT VALLEY SECTION, RIDGE AND VALLEY PROVINCE

Carbonate, east

Carbonate, central

Carbonate, west

Shale and sandstone

WELL YIELD (gallons per minute)

APPALACHIAN MOUNTAIN SECTION, RIDGE AND VALLEY PROVINCE

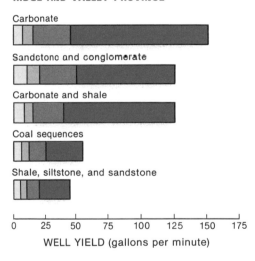

Carbonate

Sandstone and conglomerate

Carbonate and shale

Coal sequences

Shale, siltstone, and sandstone

WELL YIELD (gallons per minute)

APPALACHIAN PLATEAUS PROVINCE

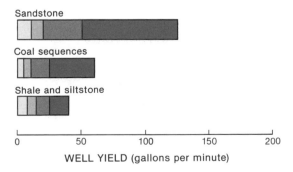

Sandstone

Coal sequences

Shale and siltstone

WELL YIELD (gallons per minute)

Figure 44–6. Cumulative-frequency distributions of yields from wells. "Percent > tip value" means that the indicated percentage of wells exceeds the maximum yield value shown by that pattern on the bar. For example, 25 percent of the wells in glacial and alluvial deposits have yields that exceed 500 gallons per minute.

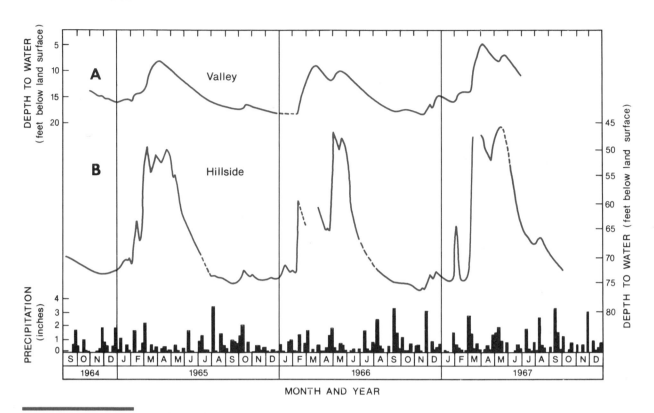

Figure 44–7. Groundwater levels for a hillside well and a valley well in Juniata County. The valley well (A) is in the Wills Creek Formation, and the hillside well (B) is in the Mifflintown and Rose Hill Formations, all of Silurian age. Precipitation data are for Newport, Perry County (slightly modified from Johnston, 1970, p. 34).

cording to latitude, depth, and land use. Water temperatures tend to decrease with increasing latitude. Water at depths of less than 100 feet can be affected by seasonal air temperature. Below about 100 feet, water temperature follows the average geothermal gradient of 1°F increase per 100 feet of depth, except where heat transfer by flowing water disrupts the gradient. Groundwater temperatures under urban areas commonly are elevated above those of adjacent areas because of insolation and anthropogenic heat production.

The specific conductance of natural groundwater varies with mineral solubility and aquifer residence time. Rocks that have low solubility in water and weak acid, such as quartzite, contain water having a specific conductance as low as 20 μmho/cm (micromhos per centimeter at 25° Celsius). The specific conductance of water from carbonate rocks commonly ranges from 400 to 600 μmho/cm and for shale from 200 to 400 μmho/cm. Water from some mined coal-bearing sequences has a specific conductance that exceeds 10,000 μmho/cm. Saline and brackish water beneath the freshwater flow systems of the Appalachian Plateaus province at depths of as little as 650 feet commonly have values greater than 10,000 μmho/cm (Poth, 1962).

Rocks composed of soluble minerals containing calcium and magnesium yield hard water. Most groundwater in Pennsylvania has a pH in the near-neutral range of 6.0 to 8.0. Water containing low concentrations of dissolved solids and water in rocks containing significant amounts of iron sulfide minerals commonly have a pH that is less than 6.0. Water from carbonate and evaporite rocks typically has a pH greater than 6.5.

The natural inorganic chemical composition of groundwater depends chiefly on the mineralogy of the containing rock. Median concentrations of major dissolved constituents in groundwater of rocks in Pennsylvania are summarized in Figure 44–9. These pattern diagrams are based on about 5,000 analyses of well and spring water that are stored in the U.S. Geological Survey Water Quality database (Barker, 1984). Each pattern characterizes the water chemistry of a major and distinctive group of rock formations having similar lithologies.

Trace elements and organic compounds at concentrations harmful to people, animals, or plants are not well documented in records of groundwater in Pennsylvania. Existing data in the U.S. Geological Survey database are meager and come mostly from areas

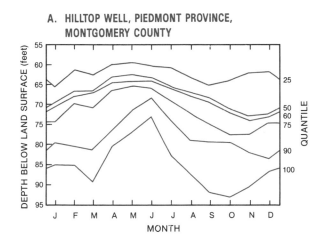

A. HILLTOP WELL, PIEDMONT PROVINCE, MONTGOMERY COUNTY

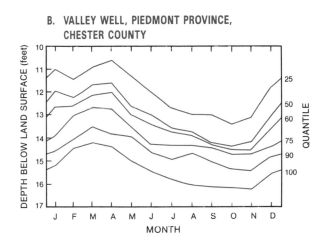

B. VALLEY WELL, PIEDMONT PROVINCE, CHESTER COUNTY

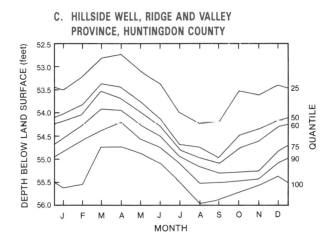

C. HILLSIDE WELL, RIDGE AND VALLEY PROVINCE, HUNTINGDON COUNTY

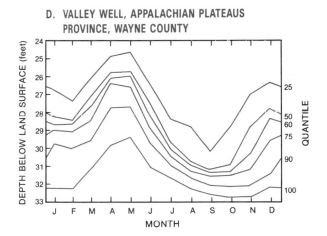

D. VALLEY WELL, APPALACHIAN PLATEAUS PROVINCE, WAYNE COUNTY

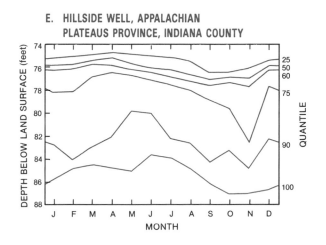

E. HILLSIDE WELL, APPALACHIAN PLATEAUS PROVINCE, INDIANA COUNTY

Figure 44-8. Trends of average monthly water levels of typical wells that represent different topographic and geologic settings. All wells are in fractured bedrock except D, which is in glacial outwash. The average depth to water for any month on any of the quantile curves is exceeded less often than the percentile shown. For example, the average water level for February in the Montgomery County well (A) exceeds a depth of 70 feet less than 75 percent of the time. The depths of the wells and periods of record are as follows: A, 600 feet, 1966–83; B, 34 feet, 1951–83; C, 105 feet, 1969–83; D, 52 feet, 1967–83; and E, 198 feet, 1944–83.

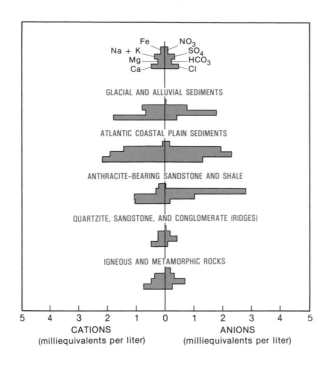

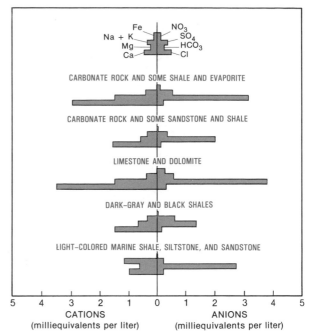

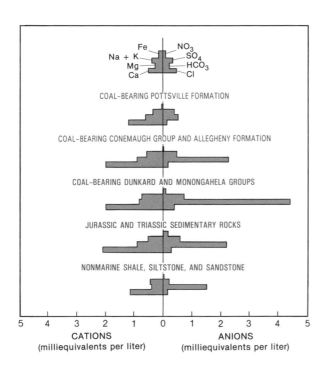

Figure 44–9. Inorganic chemical composition of groundwater in Pennsylvania, in aquifers grouped by lithology. Coal-bearing rock sequences have been further subdivided to show major differences in water quality.

that were sampled because a water-quality problem was suspected or discovered. Zinc, at concentrations harmful to fish, has been found in groundwater from coal-mining areas. Widespread natural occurrences of radon gas and other radioactive daughter products of uranium recently have been found in rocks and water of the Piedmont province and other areas of Pennsylvania (see Chapter 55B).

EFFECTS OF HUMAN ACTIVITIES

Mankind's use of the land and water affects both the quantity and quality of groundwater. In Pennsylvania, most adverse effects have been to groundwater quality. However, excessive withdrawals from the Triassic rocks in parts of Montgomery County (Rima, 1955) and in carbonate rocks at Friedensville, in the

Saucon Valley of Lehigh County, have resulted in water shortages (Wood and others, 1972). Since the statewide drought in the mid-1960s, periods of below-normal precipitation have had increasingly greater impacts on groundwater supplies in some areas of large withdrawal. Parts of the carbonate valleys in central and southern Pennsylvania and numerous places in the southern part of the Delaware River basin have undergone periods of water shortages and severe restrictions on use.

Shortages of water are aggravated if undesirable constituents have been added to the groundwater by human activities. Coal mining in the anthracite fields of eastern Pennsylvania (Growitz and others, 1985), and bituminous coal mining and oil and gas development in the Appalachian Plateaus province are examples of activities that have adversely affected groundwater quality. Groundwater in rock sequences extensively mined for coal commonly contains concentrations of iron, manganese, and sulfate that are several orders of magnitude greater than acceptable for most uses (Barker, 1984). Brine from natural seeps and abandoned oil and gas wells (Poth, 1962) has moved into freshwater zones and increased the dissolved-solids content of local groundwater.

Agricultural practices have had a serious effect on water quality, especially in the central and southeastern parts of the state. Barker (1984) has documented elevated nitrate concentrations in groundwater in several parts of the state. Meisler and Becher (1971) and Becher and Root (1981) have shown that increased nitrate concentrations in agricultural areas have had a major effect on the water quality in carbonate rocks. Toxic wastes from industrial chemical sources, petroleum spills, landfills, and dumps have contaminated groundwater locally throughout the state.

Groundwater quality in the Atlantic Coastal Plain province and crystalline rocks in Philadelphia has deteriorated significantly (Paulachok, 1991). Figure 44–10 shows the expansion through time of the area in which dissolved-solids concentration exceeds 500 mg/L (milligrams per liter) in Philadelphia. Zones of elevated concentrations of iron (greater than 0.3 mg/L) and manganese (greater than 0.05 mg/L) have expanded also. Elevated groundwater temperatures and widespread contamination by phenols and volatile organic compounds further characterize deterioration of the resource.

A mixture of refined petroleum products, mostly gasoline, was discovered in carbonate rocks near Me-

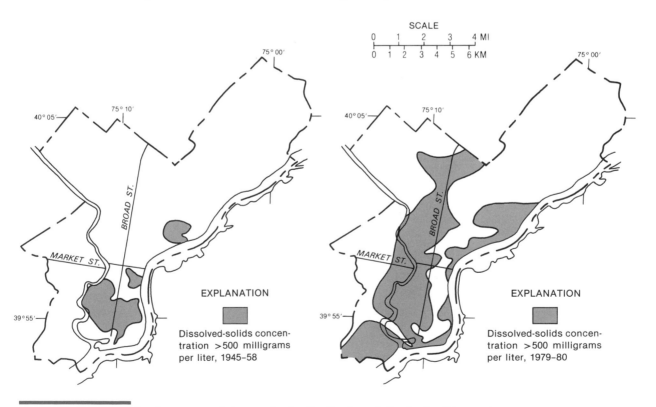

Figure 44–10. Maps showing temporal changes in the distribution of dissolved solids that indicate the increased contamination in groundwater in the urban environment of Philadelphia (from Paulachok, 1991, p. 52, 53).

chanicsburg, Cumberland County, in 1969 (Figure 44–11). High water-table conditions floated the mixture into basements and wells and onto the land surface. About 220,000 gallons of the mixture was removed, but the groundwater in the area remained contaminated. Infiltrating water will continue to recontaminate the aquifer until all of the mixture is removed from the soil and rock.

PROBLEMS AND FUTURE RESEARCH

The types of research needed to address groundwater problems in Pennsylvania are similar to those in other states of the eastern United States. Studies of the basic processes in the hydrologic cycle that in-

volve groundwater are needed. Studies need to be focused on (1) the quantity and chemistry of recharge; (2) the storage, movement, geochemistry, and biogeochemistry of water in the regolith; (3) the distribution and size of water-bearing zones and their relation to structure and lithology; and (4) equilibria and kinetic geochemistry in fractured rock. These processes need to be expressed mathematically and applied to the fractured-rock systems of Pennsylvania. Methods for efficiently estimating the variables that define the systems need to be developed.

Current (1996) directions of applied research are based on computer technology extensively. Statistical analysis of large amounts of data using computer software is improving the ability to define hydraulic factors.

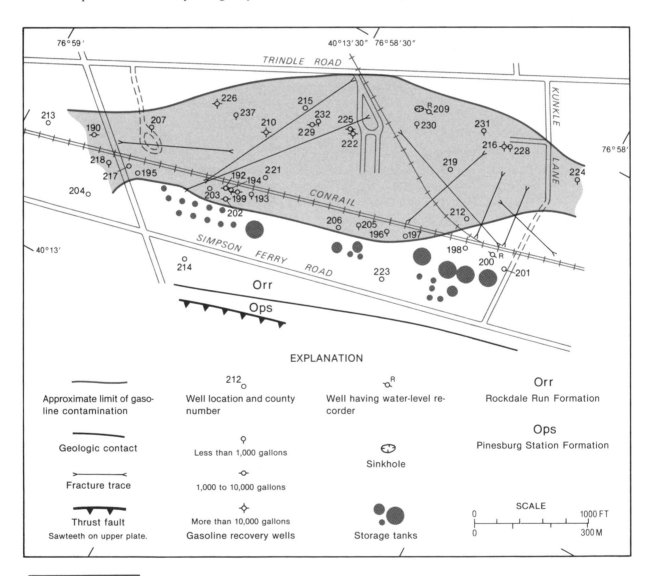

Figure 44–11. Hydrogeology at a petroleum product spill site near Mechanicsburg, Cumberland County (from Becher and Root, 1981, p. 51).

Simulations of groundwater-flow systems in fractured rock, using finite-difference and finite-element methods designed for intergranular flow systems, are proving useful. Verification of general groundwater movement, detemination of the water balance in the system, and refinement of hydraulic parameter estimates have been shown to be possible (Gerhart and Lazorchick, 1988). Model simulations have improved an understanding of groundwater-flow systems and aided water-resource managers in southeastern Pennsylvania (Mc-Greevy and Sloto, 1980; Sloto, 1988). The refinement and widespread application of flow models remains for future workers. Geographic information systems as pre- and post-processors of data will improve the accuracy and efficiency of model simulations.

Contamination problems from toxic chemicals produced by an increasingly technological society will continue to threaten groundwater resources. Studies of organic and inorganic geochemistry in groundwater systems and development of solute transport models applicable to water-quality problems in fractured-rock systems are important areas of research.

RECOMMENDED FOR FURTHER READING

Becher, A. E. (1971), *Ground water in Pennsylvania,* Pennsylvania Geological Survey, 4th ser., Educational Series 3, 42 p.

Parker, G. G., Hely, A. G., Keighton, W. B., and others (1964), *Water resources of the Delaware River basin,* U.S. Geological Survey Professional Paper 381, 200 p.

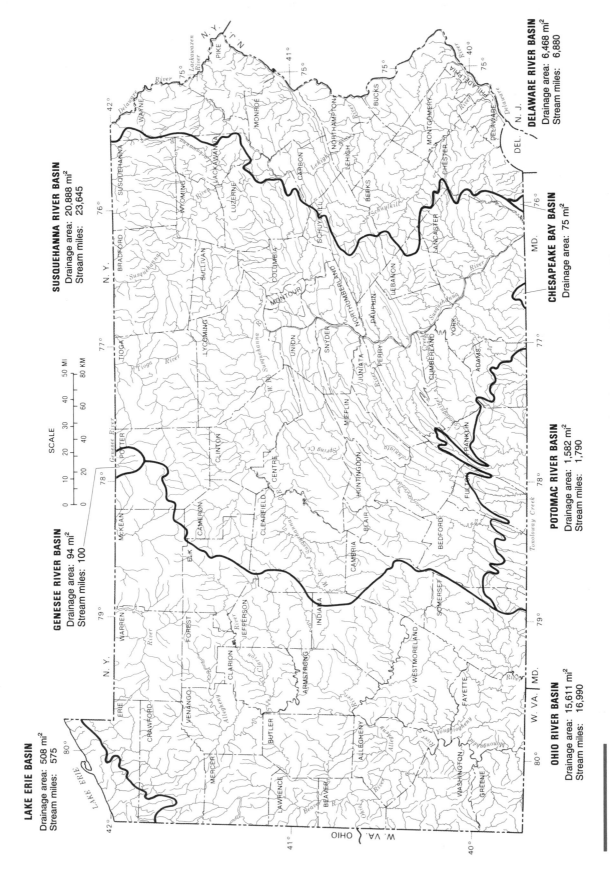

LAKE ERIE BASIN
Drainage area: 508 mi²
Stream miles: 575

GENESEE RIVER BASIN
Drainage area: 94 mi²
Stream miles: 100

SUSQUEHANNA RIVER BASIN
Drainage area: 20,888 mi²
Stream miles: 23,645

DELAWARE RIVER BASIN
Drainage area: 6,468 mi²
Stream miles: 6,880

CHESAPEAKE BAY BASIN
Drainage area: 75 mi²

POTOMAC RIVER BASIN
Drainage area: 1,582 mi²
Stream miles: 1,790

OHIO RIVER BASIN
Drainage area: 15,611 mi²
Stream miles: 16,990

Figure 45–1. Index map of Pennsylvania streams and major drainage basins (modified from Frey, 1988, Figure ES-1; data on drainage areas from Shaw and Busch, 1970, and subsequent errata corrections, March 1973). Stream miles for the Chesapeake Bay basin are included with the stream miles for the Susquehanna River basin.

678

CHAPTER 45   SURFACE WATER

DAVID E. CLICK*
  U.S. Geological Survey
  Water Resources Division
  840 Market Street
  Lemoyne, PA 17043

INTRODUCTION

Surface water is the water found on the surface of the earth in the form of natural or, in some places, man-made streams, lakes, swamps, and marshes. In Pennsylvania, streams commonly are called rivers, creeks, and runs. The source of surface water is precipitation, coming directly from rain or melting ice and snow and indirectly from groundwater discharging through springs and seeps into the streams. Relative to other areas of the country, Pennsylvania is known to be very rich in its surface-water resources, having approximately 45,000 miles of streams, more than 2,300 reservoirs, and 76 lakes with surface areas greater than 20 acres. Surface water is used extensively in Pennsylvania for transportation, power generation, recreation, and water supply.

Both the quantity and quality of water in Pennsylvania streams are cause for concern. Flooding commonly causes major damage to structures and crops on floodplains and causes general public disruptions (see Chapter 52). At other times, many streams have extremely low flows or even dry up during extended periods of deficient rainfall, thus causing major shortage problems for water purveyors. The quality of many streams has been adversely affected by degrading substances from point or nonpoint (diffuse) sources.

IMPORTANCE OF SURFACE WATER TO PENNSYLVANIA

The surface-water bodies of Pennsylvania have been of great importance throughout its history. Rivers or Indian paths were the only transportation routes available for Pennsylvania travelers before the French and Indian War. The population in the eighteenth century was concentrated in river valleys, where water provided the safest and most certain contact with trading posts or villages. Many of these have since become modern-day cities. Commerce was waterborne from the point of origin to the point of destination. As the industrial revolution took form, surface water continued to play a major role in the development of

*Retired.

the state. It provided mechanical power to the mills and factories, formed transportation routes, provided electricity through hydro- and thermal-power developments, and was a direct source of industrial and municipal water supplies. The abundant supply of water and topography favorable for the development of reservoir storage were major factors in the growth of steel and related industries in the Commonwealth.

MAJOR RIVERS

Portions of five major rivers in the United States flow through Pennsylvania. The Allegheny and the Monongahela Rivers join at Pittsburgh, in western Pennsylvania, to form the Ohio River. The Susquehanna River and its tributaries flow through central Pennsylvania, and the Delaware River and its tributaries are in eastern Pennsylvania. The headwater of the Genesee River is in the north-central part of the state and is tributary to the St. Lawrence River. Small tributaries to the Potomac River flow out of south-central Pennsylvania. The drainage basins for these rivers are shown in Figure 45–1.

The Susquehanna River, which flows southward through the east-central part of the state, drains 20,888 square miles in Pennsylvania and is the largest drainage system in the state. The origin of the Susquehanna River is Otsego Lake in east-central New York, and its mouth is at the head of the Chesapeake Bay; the total drainage area is 27,225 square miles. Major tributaries to the Susquehanna in Pennsylvania include the Tioga, Lackawanna, West Branch Susquehanna, and Juniata Rivers.

The Ohio River, formed by the confluence of the Allegheny and Monongahela Rivers, flows northwestward from Pittsburgh and is joined by the Beaver River before flowing westward out of the state. The total drainage area of the Ohio, Allegheny, and Monongahela Rivers in Pennsylvania is 15,611 square miles, covering the western third of the state.

The Delaware River forms the state boundary with New York and New Jersey. The Delaware's drainage area in Pennsylvania is 6,468 square miles, 62 percent of its total 10,360 square miles. The Delaware has three major tributaries wholly within Pennsylvania: the Lackawaxen, the Lehigh, and the Schuylkill Rivers, which have 597, 1,361, and 1,912 square miles of drainage area, respectively.

The Potomac River and the St. Lawrence River basins each have relatively small drainage areas in Pennsylvania; these are 1,582 and 602 square miles, respectively.

LAKES AND RESERVOIRS

Lakes and reservoirs are major surface-water resources in the state. The most recent inventory of lakes and reservoirs in Pennsylvania (Pennsylvania Department of Forests and Waters, 1970) included more than 2,300 dams and reservoirs and, in addition, 76 lakes with surface areas exceeding 20 acres. The total volume and surface area of reservoirs and lakes by major basin is shown in Table 45–1. Figure 45–2 shows the statewide distribution of 53 recreational lakes in Pennsylvania where reconnaissance limnological surveys have been conducted (Barker, 1978). These impoundments range in size from 4 to 14,500 acres of surface area and represent a cross section of the chemical and trophic types occurring in Pennsylvania.

WETLANDS

Nearly one-half million acres of wetlands are present in Pennsylvania, representing about 2 percent of the area of the state. The largest areas of wetlands occur in northwestern Pennsylvania and in the Pocono area of northeastern Pennsylvania, where glaciation has occurred.

Between 1956 and 1979, Pennsylvania experienced a net loss of nearly 28,000 acres (6 percent) of

Table 45–1. *Volumes and Surface Areas of Reservoirs and Lakes in Pennsylvania[1]*

Basin	Reservoirs			Natural lakes		
	Number	Total volume (millions of gallons)	Total surface area (acres)	Number	Total volume (millions of gallons)	Total surface area (acres)
Delaware River	880	244,890	33,751	40	11,885	2,375
Susquehanna River	938	332,180	39,658	30	5,948	1,422
Potomac River	38	8,589	1,097	0	0	0
Ohio River	461	1,039,823	69,212	6	8,605	1,469
St. Lawrence River	7	100	47	0	0	0

[1]From Pennsylvania Department of Forests and Waters (1970).

vegetated wetlands. Losses were greatest in the northern Pocono region, where 15 percent of the wetlands were lost. The greatest cause of wetland loss was pond construction, and pond acreage in Pennsylvania recently increased by about 130 percent (Tiner, 1987).

SURFACE-WATER QUANTITIES

Pennsylvania has abundant water resources. The mean annual precipitation ranges from about 34 to almost 51 inches per year across the state and averages about 42 inches (Figure 45-3). Pennsylvania has a high-density stream system (stream miles per square mile of land) to discharge the precipitation received. It has been estimated that Pennsylvania has more than 45,000 miles of streams, evidenced by the fact that one need not go very far in any direction before encountering some type of surface-water body.

Streams in Pennsylvania discharge the equivalent of approximately one half of the annual precipitation received. Average annual runoff ranges from about 16 to 28 inches (Figure 45-4). The rate of discharge at a specific point along a stream is mainly a function of the size of the drainage basin (Figure 45-5). The Delaware River at Trenton, N. J. (drainage area of 6,780 square miles), the Susquehanna River at Harrisburg (drainage area of 24,100 square miles), and the Ohio River at Sewickley, near Pittsburgh (drainage area of 19,500 square miles), have long-term average annual discharges of 11,667, 34,341, and 32,920 cubic feet per second, respectively, according to data obtained from 1975 through 1984 (U.S. Geological Survey, 1976–85).

Surface-water flows in Pennsylvania are measured by the U.S. Geological Survey in cooperation with state and local agencies as well as other federal agencies. These data are analyzed, compiled, and published annually as Water-Data Reports in three volumes, according to major river basin, by the U.S. Geological Survey. Historical records are stored in computer files and are available upon request.

VARIABILITY OF SURFACE-WATER FLOW

Regardless of drainage-basin size, all streams show the same general trend in streamflow. Maximum flows are during the period March through May, when snowmelt and heavy spring precipitation occur. Low flows occur during the summer months of June through September, when precipitation is low and streamflow is provided mainly by groundwater. The mean monthly discharges (reference period 1951–80) from three drainage areas of different sizes

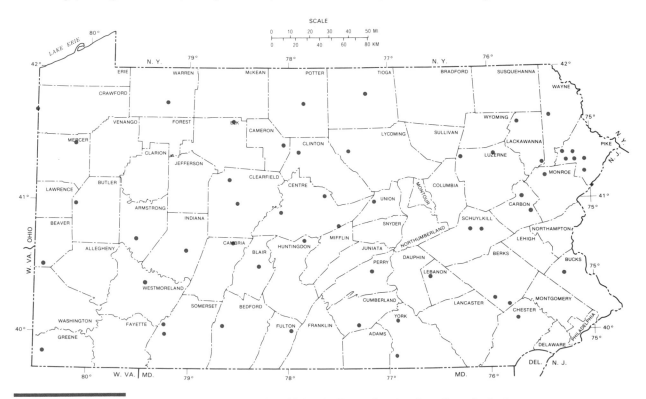

Figure 45–2. Locations of 53 significant recreational lakes in Pennsylvania where limnological surveys have been conducted (slightly modified from Barker, 1978, Figure 1).

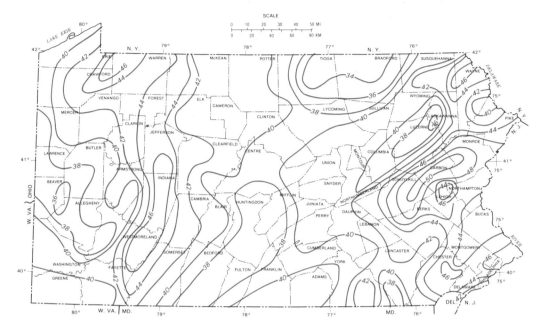

Figure 45-3. Average annual precipitation in Pennsylvania, 1951–80 (based on data from the U.S. National Oceanic and Atmospheric Administration, 1951–80). Contour interval is 2 inches.

are shown in Figure 45-6 to illustrate the seasonal variability of streamflow.

Evaluating the degree of variability of daily, monthly, and annual flow is important in appraising the water resources of an area. The magnitude and frequency of occurrence of extreme high-flow values are important to those concerned with flood protection and warning, hydraulic-structure design, and land use planning. Low-flow values and associated durations are important to those concerned with water supply, stream assimilation of waste, and in-stream flow requirements. Figure 45-7 compares the monthly median discharges for the Susquehanna River at Harrisburg with the monthly maximum and minimum discharges, illustrating the variability of flow over a long period of record (1891–1984).

Knowledge of flood potential (see Chapter 52) is a necessary factor in the design of floodway structures and the effective management of flood-prone lands. Magnitude and frequency of peak discharges can be computed by statistical regression analysis for streams having a sufficient length of streamflow record. This procedure is described by Flippo (1977) for unregulated and unurbanized streams that drain more than 2 square miles in Pennsylvania. Flippo's report also provides frequency-discharge profiles for regulated reaches on 11 major streams. His graphed analysis of peak discharges having recurrence intervals (T-years) of 2.33, 10, 25, 50, and 100 years for the Allegheny River, a regulated river, is reproduced here as Figure 45-8.

Flow-duration curves are magnitude-frequency summaries of daily mean streamflow values. The

flow-duration curve for the gaging station on Spring Creek near Axemann, Centre County, is shown in Figure 45-9. This curve shows that a discharge of 100 cubic feet per second is equaled or exceeded about 32 percent of the time. The duration curve is not a probability curve, but it is useful as a description of the distribution of daily mean discharges that have occurred and may be expected to recur over a period of years.

Frequency curves relate the magnitude of streamflow to frequency of occurrence. Flood-frequency curves are used widely for floodplain zoning, in studies of economics of flood-protection works, and in the design of bridge openings, channel capacities, and roadbed elevations. Data for 1966 to 1986 from Tonoloway Creek at Needmore, Fulton County, were used to create the flood-frequency curve in Figure 45-10. The curve in this figure indicates that the recurrence interval for a discharge of 400 cubic feet per second is 10 years. This means that the annual maximum discharge will exceed 400 cubic feet per second at intervals averaging 10 years in length, or that the probability of the annual maximum discharge exceeding 400 cubic feet per second in any one year is 0.10. Guidelines for determining flood-flow frequency have been issued in Bulletin 17B by the Hydrology Committee of the United States Water Resources Council. The latest revision of this bulletin is September 1981.

The adequacy of streamflow to meet requirements for disposal of liquid wastes, municipal or industrial supplies, supplemental irrigation, and maintenance of suitable conditions for fish is commonly evaluated in terms of low-flow characteristics. Statis-

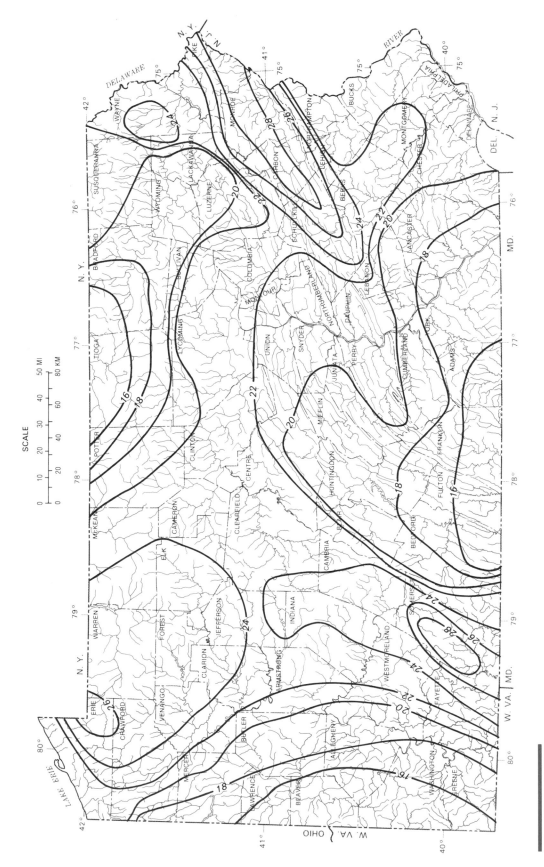

Figure 45-4. Average annual runoff in Pennsylvania, 1951–80 (modified from Wetzel, 1986, Figure 1). Contour interval is 2 inches.

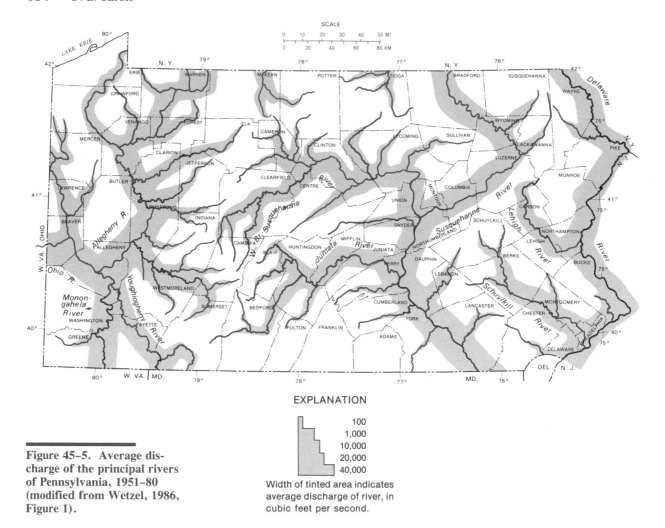

SCALE

Figure 45–5. Average discharge of the principal rivers of Pennsylvania, 1951–80 (modified from Wetzel, 1986, Figure 1).

EXPLANATION

	100
---	1,000
	10,000
	20,000
	40,000

Width of tinted area indicates average discharge of river, in cubic feet per second.

tical procedures are also used to estimate low-flow frequency characteristics. These characteristics are commonly expressed as a value of average daily flow having an average recurrence interval for a specified number of consecutive days. For example, the widely used "7 day, 10 year" term means that a designated average daily flow is estimated to occur for 7 consecutive days having an average recurrence interval of 10 years, or a probability of 0.1 in any one year. Typical low-flow frequency curves for 7-, 14-, 30-, and 60-day periods are shown in Figure 45–11 using 73 years of record (1913–85) for Conodoguinet Creek near Hogestown, Cumberland County.

Studies of low-flow discharges have been published by Busch and Shaw (1966), Page (1970), Page and Shaw (1977), and Flippo (1982). The Flippo report provides the most accurate information for estimating low flows at sites on unregulated streams for which little or no low-flow record is available. Computer files and programs of the U.S. Geological Survey provide the capability to compute low-flow char-

acteristics for durations from 1 to 365 days for stations having 10 or more years of record.

QUALITY OF SURFACE WATER

Pennsylvania's rivers and streams have been receiving contamination for more than 100 years (see Chapter 51). Pollution-control programs have been in effect since 1905; additional comprehensive legislation was enacted in 1937 and strengthened many times by amendments, the most recent of which was in 1980.

Contamination sources have been categorized as point or nonpoint. Point sources are those such as sewage discharges, industrial-waste discharges, and storm or combined sewer drainage being conveyed to a water body by a pipe or channel. Nonpoint sources include diffuse discharges such as drainage from active and abandoned coal mines, discharging contaminated groundwater, direct stormwater runoff, and runoff from agricultural areas. In addition, contamination can occur from dumping or spills, either accidental or deliberate.

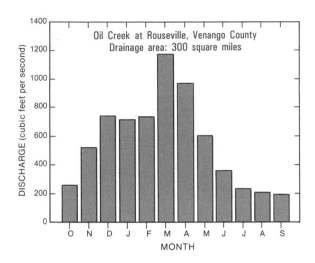

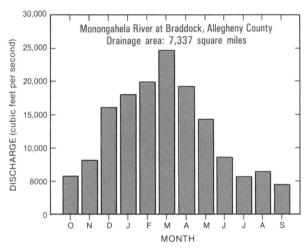

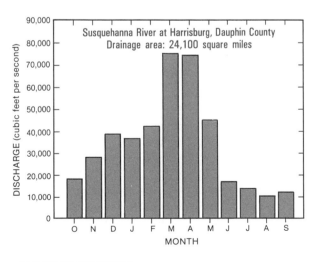

Figure 45-6. Variations in mean monthly discharges at selected sites, 1951–80 (based on water resources data from the U.S. Geological Survey).

An assessment and subsequent statement of water quality can be made only if a standard exists to which a comparison can be made. A water-quality standard is "the combination of water uses to be protected and the specific water quality criteria necessary to protect those uses" (Pennsylvania Department of Environmental Resources, Bureau of Water Quality Management, 1984, p. 3). Section 303(c) of the Clean Water Act requires a state at least once every three years to review and revise, if necessary, its water-quality standards. These standards are promulgated and published in the *Pennsylvania Bulletin*. A comprehensive revision of Pennsylvania's water-quality standards was published in 1979 and subsequently approved by the U.S. Environmental Protection Agency on January 26, 1981 (Pennsylvania Bulletin, v. 9, no. 36).

In 1988, 3,599 miles, or approximately 27 percent of major stream miles in Pennsylvania, failed to meet water-quality standards. Abandoned-mine drainage, either by itself or in combination with other contamination sources, was responsible for 1,701 of the total miles polluted (Frey, 1988).

For the purposes of illustration, pollution sources causing noncompliance have been grouped into three categories: (1) organic; (2) toxic/inorganic; and (3) a combination of these. The percentage and number of stream miles in each of the pollution categories are shown in Figure 45–12.

Water temperature is an important measure of stream quality, inasmuch as many physical, chemical, and biological processes are direct functions of temperature. Flippo (1975) provided a summary of water-temperature records for 72 stream sites in Pennsylvania. Figure 45–13 illustrates the statistical analysis of data for the Allegheny River at Warren in Warren County, showing the conventional seasonal variation and the range of water temperature for three key probabilities.

The quality of a lake or reservoir is usually expressed as the trophic (nutritional) condition of the lake, notwithstanding that all inorganic, organic, and bacterial factors may not have been appraised. Major studies relating to the trophic condition of Pennsylvania's recreational and publicly owned lakes have been done by Barker (1978) and by Ulanoski and others (1981). Barker (1978) reported on the results of limnological surveys of 53 multiple-use impoundments throughout the state (Figure 45–2), representing a cross section of the chemical and trophic types found in Pennsylvania. In order to provide a baseline and framework for further assessment and manage-

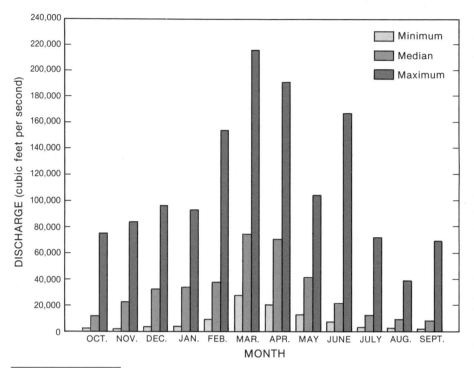

Figure 45–7. Monthly median and extreme discharges for the Susquehanna River at Harrisburg in Dauphin County, 1891–1984 (based on water resources data from the U.S. Geological Survey).

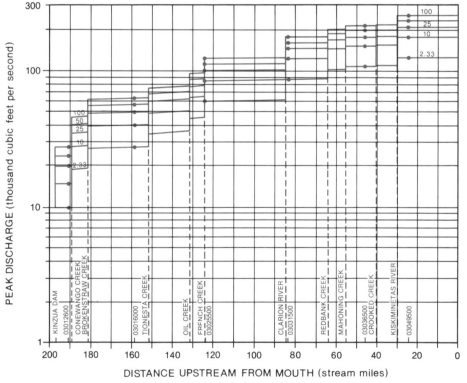

Figure 45–8. Relation of peak discharge for selected recurrence intervals (T-years) of 2.33, 10, 25, 50, and 100 years to stream distance, Allegheny River from Kinzua Dam in Warren County to Pittsburgh in Allegheny County (from Flippo, 1977, Figure 8). Solid circles show T-year peaks for gaging stations numbered along the horizontal axis.

ment programs, water samples for chemical analysis were collected, temperature and oxygen profiles were obtained, and plankton and submersed aquatic plants were collected.

In a follow-up to the 1978 study, Ulanoski and others (1981) provided detailed information on the trophic condition of 26 lakes within the state. The lake types have been categorized as mesotrophic (intermediate in nutrients), eutrophic (rich in nutrients), and hypereutrophic (very high in nutrients). The 26 lakes are ranked in Table 45–2 based on their trophic condition as defined by the U.S. Environmental Protection Agency (1974).

USE OF SURFACE WATER

Use of surface water is generally classified as in-stream use or withdrawal for off-stream use. In-stream uses are those in which water within lakes and streams is used without changing the quantity. These uses include transportation and navigation, swimming, boating, fish and wildlife habitat, water-quality maintenance, hydroelectric power generation, and the enhancement of general environmental and esthetic values. Withdrawal water uses are categorized as public supply, rural use, irrigation use, thermoelectric power generation, and self-supplied industrial use. Each of these includes total consumptive use and partial consumptive use (when

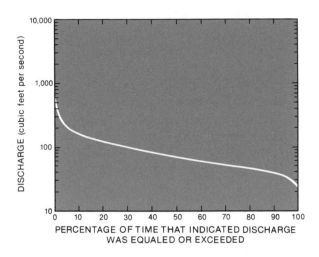

Figure 45-9. Duration curve of daily flow for Spring Creek near Axemann in Centre County, 1940-86 (based on water resources data from the U.S. Geological Survey). The drainage area is 87.2 square miles.

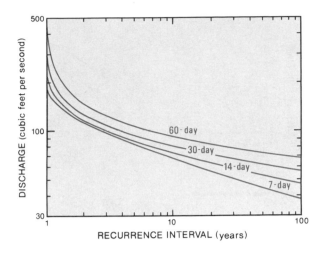

Figure 45-11. Low-flow frequency curves for Conodoguinet Creek near Hogestown in Cumberland County, 1913-85 (based on water resources data from the U.S. Geological Survey). The drainage area is 470 square miles.

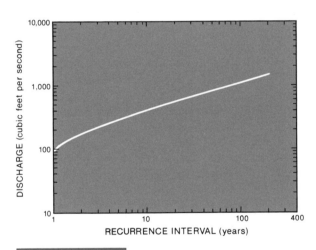

Figure 45-10. Frequency of floods on Tonoloway Creek at Needmore in Fulton County, 1966-86 (based on water resources data from the U.S. Geological Survey). The drainage area is 10.7 square miles.

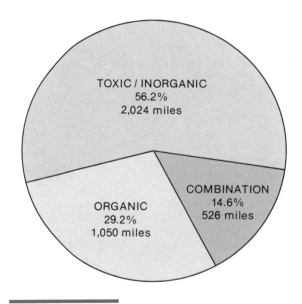

Figure 45-12. Number and percentage of miles of major streams not meeting water-quality standards in 1988 by types of pollution. Values were calculated from data given in Frey (1988, Table ES-1).

some of the water is returned to the source). Total consumptive use would include withdrawals for interbasin transfers, irrigation, no-return cooling systems, and so forth. Partial consumptive use would include once-through cooling water and industrial and municipal withdrawals having wastewater return flows.

Hydroelectric power generation, the largest single water-use category, accounted for 81 percent of the state's estimated total off-stream and in-stream water use in 1985. Excluding thermoelectric power generation uses, surface-water withdrawals represented 80 percent of the state's estimated total water use (Solley and others, 1987).

Several categories of water use in Pennsylvania in 1985 (Solley and others, 1987) are tabulated in Table 45-3. Hydroelectric power generation is the only in-stream use quantified for the summary. Additional categories and values for 1970, 1980, and estimated 1990 water use in Pennsylvania have been tabulated by watershed in the State Water Plan Bulletins (Pennsylvania Department of Environmental Resources, 1975-83).

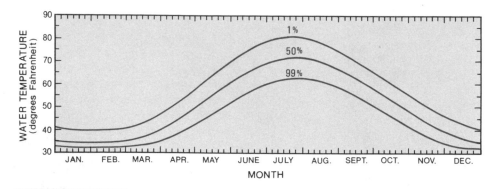

Figure 45–13. Temperature curves for 1-, 50-, and 99-percent probabilities of exceedance of daily means, based on daily records for the periods 1949–51 and 1962–70 for the Allegheny River at Warren in Warren County, northwestern Pennsylvania (water resources data from the U.S. Geological Survey). Temperatures are slightly affected by flow regulation at Kinzua Dam. The drainage area is 2,223 square miles.

Table 45–2. *Lake Ranking According to Trophic Condition[1]*

Rank	Lake	County	Trophic classification
1	Harveys Lake	Luzerne	Mesotrophic
2	Parker Dam	Clearfield	do.
3	Canoe Lake	Blair	do.
4	Lake Winola	Wyoming	Meso-eutrophic
5	Chapman Lake	Warren	do.
6	Tamarack Lake	Crawford	Eutrophic
7	Yellow Creek Lake	Indiana	do.
8	C. F. Walker Lake	Snyder	do.
9	Marsh Creek Lake	Chester	do.
10	Conneaut Lake	Crawford	do.
11	Shawnee Lake	Bedford	do.
12	Laurel Hill Lake	Somerset	do.
13	Canadohta Lake	Crawford	do.
14	Lake Arthur	Butler	do.
15	Keystone Lake	Westmoreland	do.
16	Lackawanna Lake	Lackawanna	do.
17	Raccoon Lake	Beaver	do.
18	Lake Carey	Wyoming	do.
19	Ford Lake	Lackawanna	do.
20	Lake Wilhelm	Mercer	do.
21	Hills Creek Lake	Tioga	do.
22	Ryerson Lake	Greene	do.
23	Nockamixon Lake	Bucks	do.
24	Lake Edinboro	Erie	do.
25	Pymatuning Reservoir	Crawford	do.
26	Speedwell Forge Lake	Lancaster	Hypereutrophic

[1]Information on the trophic condition of the lakes is from Ulanoski and others (1981). Ranking of the lakes is based on their trophic condition as defined by the U.S. Environmental Protection Agency (1974).

Quantities of water required for in-stream use are usually assigned for a specific reach of stream and on a temporal basis. For streams that are regulated, desired values for in-stream use usually express the minimum amount required to support a specified use; however, maximum values may also be of concern.

PROBLEMS AND FUTURE RESEARCH

Because surface water is an abundant renewable resource in Pennsylvania, it will continue to play a major role in providing water to a heavily populated state. Industries and institutions will continue to have large requirements, and decreased use by some industries will be offset by increased use by others. During periods of deficient rainfall, agricultural irrigation tends to increase, adding more stress to a highly committed surface-water system.

With the enactment of the clean-water laws, attention will continue to be focused on preventing contamination of the resource and cleaning up known problem areas. Acid mine drainage will continue to be a major problem, as will the effect of acid rain in areas where natural buffering of the surface water is low.

As more public and private facilities become available, the in-stream uses of surface water will increase, and recreational uses will expand. Transportation and navigation uses probably will be slow to change, because these uses generally are reflective of the vigor of basic commerce. In the more densely industrialized reaches of Pennsylvania rivers, de-

Table 45–3. *Facts on Surface-Water Use in Pennsylvania[1]*

(Figures may not add to totals because of independent rounding)

POPULATION SERVED FROM SURFACE-WATER SOURCES, 1985	
By public water-supply systems	
Number (thousands)	6,850
Percentage of total state population	58

OFF-STREAM USE, 1985	
Freshwater Withdrawals	
Surface water and groundwater, total (Mgal/d)[2]	14,300
Surface water only (Mgal/d)	13,500
Percentage of total freshwater withdrawals	94
Percentage of total excluding withdrawals for thermoelectric power	80
Category of Use	
Public-supply withdrawals	
Surface water (Mgal/d)	1,340
Percentage of total surface-water withdrawals	10
Percentage of total withdrawals for public supply	84
Per capita (gal/d)[3]	196
Rural-supply withdrawals	
Domestic	
Surface water (Mgal/d)	0
Percentage of total surface-water withdrawals	0
Percentage of total withdrawals for rural domestic	0
Per capita (gal/d)	0
Livestock	
Surface water (Mgal/d)	8
Percentage of total surface-water withdrawals	< 1
Percentage of total withdrawal for livestock	12
Industrial self-supplied withdrawals	
Surface water (Mgal/d)	12,140
Percentage of total surface-water withdrawals	90
Percentage of total industrial self-supplied	
Including withdrawals for thermoelectric power	98
Excluding withdrawals for thermoelectric power	88
Irrigation withdrawals	
Surface water (Mgal/d)	9
Percentage of total surface-water withdrawals	< 1
Percentage of total withdrawals for irrigation	84

IN-STREAM USE, 1985	
Hydroelectric power (Mgal/d)	60,700

[1]From Solley and others (1987).
[2]Mgal/d, millions of gallons per day; gal/d, gallons per day.
[3]gal/d, gallons per day.

mand for assimilation of waste to the rivers will increase to the point where more stringent effluent limitations and waste-load allocations will be needed to protect water quality.

Water use by diversion will also continue to increase as more thermoelectric-power-generating plants come into use. However, this type of use during periods of drought will be obtained from prearranged storage.

RECOMMENDED FOR FURTHER READING

Barker, J. L. (1978), *Characteristics of Pennsylvania recreational lakes,* Pennsylvania Department of Environmental Resources, Office of Resources Management, Water Resources Bulletin 14, 226 p.

Bartlett, R. A., ed. (1984), *Rolling rivers,* New York, McGraw-Hill, 398 p.

Flippo, H. N., Jr. (1975), *Temperatures of streams and selected reservoirs in Pennsylvania,* Pennsylvania Department of Environmental Resources, Office of Resources Management, Water Resources Bulletin 11, 95 p.

_____ (1977), *Floods in Pennsylvania,* Pennsylvania Department of Environmental Resources, Office of Resources Management, Water Resources Bulletin 13, 59 p.

_____ (1982), *Technical manual for estimating low-flow characteristics of Pennsylvania streams,* Pennsylvania Department of Environmental Resources, Office of Resources Management, Water Resources Bulletin 15, 86 p.

Moody, D. W., Chase, E. B., and Aronson, D. A., compilers (1986), *National water summary, 1985—hydrologic events and surface-water resources,* U.S. Geological Survey Water-Supply Paper 2300, 506 p.

Page, L. V., and Shaw, L. C. (1977), *Low-flow characteristics of Pennsylvania streams,* Pennsylvania Department of Environmental Resources, Office of Resources Management, Water Resources Bulletin 12, 441 p.

Riggs, H. C. (1968), *Frequency curves, Chapter A2,* U.S. Geological Survey Techniques of Water-Resources Investigations 4–A2, 15 p.

_____ (1972a), *Low-flow investigations,* U.S. Geological Survey Techniques of Water-Resources Investigations 4–B1, 18 p.

_____ (1972b), *Regional analyses of streamflow characteristics,* U.S. Geological Survey Techniques of Water-Resources Investigations 4–B3, 15 p.

Searcy, J. K. (1959), *Flow-duration curves,* U.S. Geological Survey Water-Supply Paper 1542–A, p. 1–33.

Tiner, R. W., Jr. (1987), *Mid-Atlantic wetlands: a disappearing natural treasure,* U.S. Fish and Wildlife Service and U.S. Environmental Protection Agency, 28 p.

Ulanoski, J. T., Shertzer, R. H., Barker, J. L., and Hartman, R. T. (1981), *Trophic classification and characteristics of twenty-six publicly-owned Pennsylvania lakes,* Pennsylvania Department of Environmental Resources, Bureau of Water Quality Management, Publication 61, 240 p.

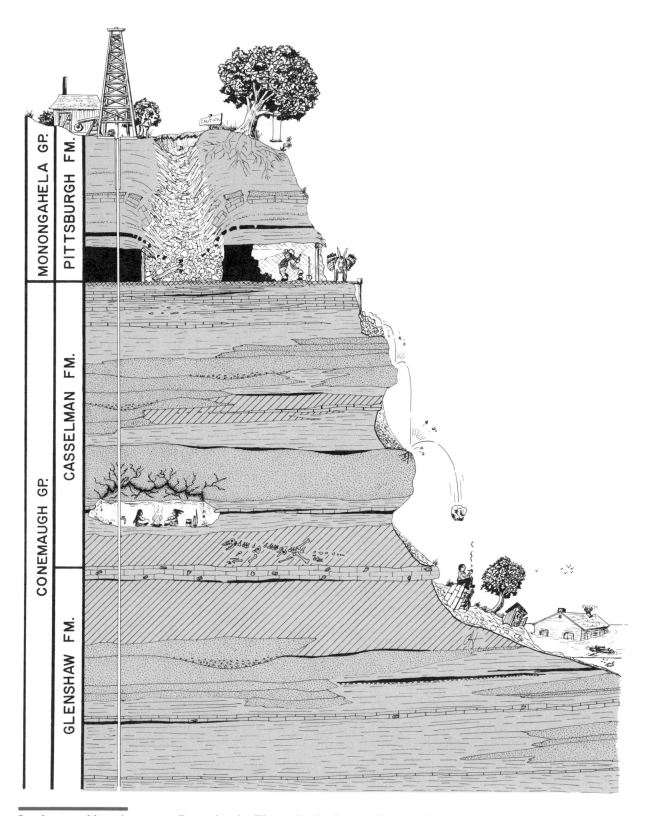

Land use problems in western Pennsylvania. Illustration by John A. Harper, from Adams and others (1980, cover).

690

Part IX

ENVIRONMENTAL AND ENGINEERING APPLICATIONS

The abundance of Pennsylvania's natural resources made the state a leader in the American industrial revolution. Failure to properly understand the impacts of the exploitation and utilization of these resources, however, resulted in environmental problems that plague us today. Mineralized mine drainage, surface subsidence over underground mines, and groundwater contamination are widespread relics of this industrial activity. Hand-in-hand with industrialization came intensified urbanization. With it came unrecognized, but almost inevitable, consequences, such as the need to manage ever greater masses of wastes of all kinds and to construct ever larger public works. Such problems of development remain acute today.

Widespread natural calamities, such as flooding during tropical storm Agnes in 1972, provide vivid scenes of wholesale destruction that overshadow less newsworthy, but more frequent, problems that are also related to the geological setting. In aggregate, these problems can be as damaging and costly as a major flood. They range from geologic hazards that are not influenced by prior human activity, such as an earthquake, to hazards directly traceable to human activity, such as excavation in an area known to be prone to landsliding.

In the last few decades, the subdisciplines of engineering geology and environmental geology have become established to deal with this multiplicity of problems. These problems can be ameliorated or, at least locally, be completely avoided by rational planning or good engineering design and practice.

—Reginald P. Briggs

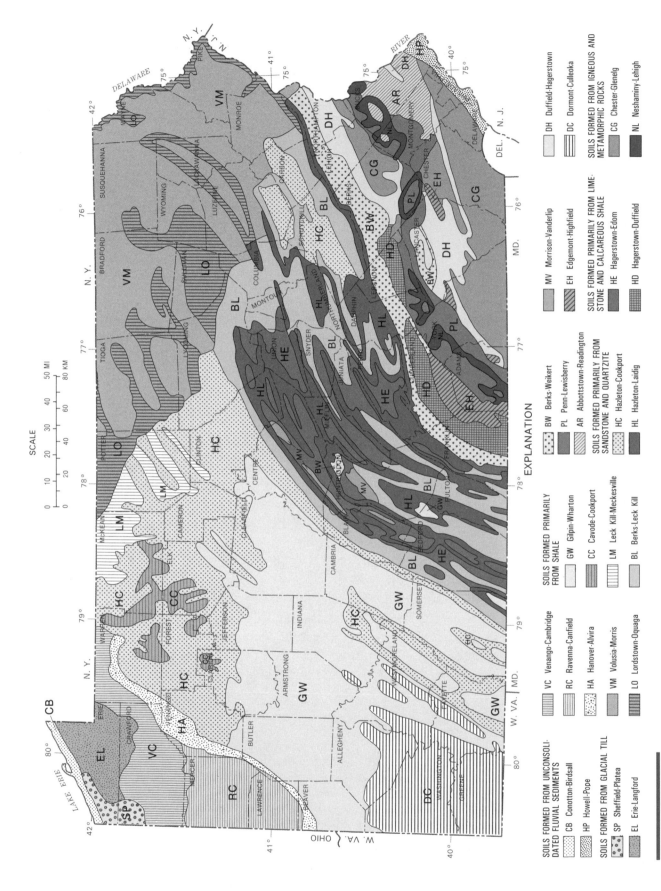

EXPLANATION

SOILS FORMED FROM UNCONSOLI-
DATED FLUVIAL SEDIMENTS

CB Conotton-Birdsall
HP Howell-Pope

SOILS FORMED FROM GLACIAL TILL

SP Sheffield-Platea
EL Erie-Langford

VC Venango-Cambridge
RC Ravenna-Canfield
HA Hanover-Alvira
VM Volusia-Morris
LO Lordstown-Oquaga

SOILS FORMED PRIMARILY
FROM SHALE

GW Gilpin-Wharton
CC Cavode-Cookport
LM Leck Kill-Meckesville
BL Berks-Leck Kill

BW Berks-Weikert
PL Penn-Lewisberry
AR Abbottstown-Readington

SOILS FORMED PRIMARILY FROM
SANDSTONE AND QUARTZITE

HC Hazleton-Cookport
HL Hazleton-Laidig

MV Morrison-Vanderlip
EH Edgemont-Highfield

SOILS FORMED PRIMARILY FROM LIME-
STONE AND CALCAREOUS SHALE

HE Hagerstown-Edom
HD Hagerstown-Duffield

DH Duffield-Hagerstown
DC Dormont-Culleoka

SOILS FORMED FROM IGNEOUS AND
METAMORPHIC ROCKS

CG Chester-Glenelg
NL Neshaminy-Lehigh

Figure 46–1. Soil associations of Pennsylvania (see Table 46–3 for characteristics and classification).

692

CHAPTER 46   SOILS (PEDOLOGY)

EDWARD J. CIOLKOSZ
116 ASI Building
Agronomy Department
The Pennsylvania State University
University Park, PA 16802

RICK L. DAY
116 ASI Building
Agronomy Department
The Pennsylvania State University
University Park, PA 16802

RICHARD C. CRONCE
R. E. Wright Associates
3240 Schoolhouse Road
Middletown, PA 17057

ROBERT R. DOBOS
U.S. Department of Agriculture
Natural Resources Conservation Service
P. O. Box 2678
Lebanon, VA 24266

INTRODUCTION

The soil is an unconsolidated, three-dimensional natural body that mantles the landscape. Its lateral boundaries are bedrock or water too deep to support the growth of rooted plants. Its upper boundary is the atmosphere, and its lower boundary is the rooting depth of the natural vegetation of the area or the depth to which the soil-forming reactions have significantly altered the underlying material. The characteristics and properties of soils are the result of a complex interaction of physical, chemical, and biological reactions. The rate and extent to which these reactions proceed are governed by the soil-forming factors (climate, organisms, parent material, topography, and time). Thus, the interaction between the soil-forming factors and the reactions determine the physical and chemical characteristics of a soil. Most soil-forming reactions are surface related; thus, soil characteristics vary from the surface downward from one zone or horizon to another. The major soil horizons are the A, topsoil; B, subsoil; and C, parent material. For a more complete discussion of the principles of soil genesis, the reader is referred to the excellent texts of U.S. Department of Agriculture, Soil Conservation Service (1975, 1994), Jenny (1980), Wilding and others (1983a, b), Birkeland (1984), Buol and others (1989), and Fanning and Fanning (1989).

CLASSIFICATION

Soil Taxonomy has been the official soil classification system of the United States since 1965 (U.S. Department of Agriculture, Soil Conservation Service, 1975). It has six hierarchical levels: order, suborder, great group, subgroup, family, and series. A soil or group of soils can be discussed or mapped at any of the levels. The examples given in Table 46–1 indicate that the soil orders have a specific formative element joined to the suffix -sol (solum is Latin for soil); examples are Inceptisol, Alfisol, and Ultisol. At the suborder through subgroup levels, other formative elements are added to the formative element of the order to give these categories distinctive names. Each of these formative elements provides a significant amount of information about a particular soil. For example, the Hagerstown soil series is an Alfisol (order), meaning it has a subsurface horizon of clay accumulation and a high base

Table 46–1. *Soil Taxonomy Classification of Three Common Soils of Pennsylvania*

ORDER:	Inceptisol	Alfisol	Ultisol
SUBORDER:	Aquept	Udalf	Udult
GREAT GROUP:	Fragiaquept	Hapludalf	Hapludult
SUBGROUP:	Aeric Fragiaquept	Typic Hapludalf	Typic Hapludult
FAMILY:	Fine-loamy, mixed, mesic	Clayey, mixed, mesic	Fine-loamy, mixed, mesic
SERIES:	Volusia	Hagerstown	Chester

Table 46–2. *Formative Elements, Percentage of the State Covered by the Various Soil Orders, and a Brief Description of the Meaning of the Formative Element of Common Pennsylvania Soils[1]*

Formative element	Percentage of state covered	Description
		ORDER
Ent (Entisol)	5.0	Weakly developed (young) soil without a B horizon or A/C profile, or, if sandy, a very weakly developed B.
Ept (Inceptisol)	43.1	Weak to moderately well developed (relatively young) soil having a color, structural, or fragipan B horizon.
Alf (Alfisol)	20.2	Moderately well developed soil having a B horizon of clay accumulation (argillic horizon) and relatively high subsoil base (Ca+Mg+Na+K) saturation status (>35 percent of the cation-exchange capacity).
Ult (Ultisol)	31.1	Moderately well developed soil having a B horizon of clay accumulation (argillic horizon) and low subsoil base saturation status (<35 percent of the cation-exchange capacity).
Od Spodosol)	.5	Weak to moderately well developed, sandy soil having a spodic B horizon (subsurface horizon of humus, Fe, and Al accumulation).
Ist (Histosol)	.1	Soil composed of organic materials (peats and mucks).
		SUBORDER
Aqu	—	Wet-aquic moisture regime (somewhat poorly and poorly drained).
Ochr	—	Thin, light-colored A horizon.
Psamm	—	Sand or loamy sand texture.
Ud	—	Humid climate.
		GREAT GROUP
Dystr	—	Low base saturation status soil.
Frag	—	Fragipan (dense, impermeable, subsurface B horizon).
Hapl	—	Moderate degree of soil horizon development
Hum	—	High organic matter content in A horizon.
Ochr	—	Thin, light-colored A horizon.
Quartz	—	Greater than 95 percent quartz mineralogy.
		SUBGROUP
Aeric	—	Better aerated (drained) than typical (Typic).
Aqueptic	—	Wetter than typical; some Inceptisol properties.
Aquic	—	Wetter than typical.
Fluventic	—	On a floodplain; some Entisol properties.
Lithic	—	Bedrock within 20 inches of surface.
Typic	—	Typical development of the great group.
Ultic	—	Lower base saturation status than typical (Typic).

[1]State coverage data are from Day and others (1988).

(Ca+Mg+Na+K) saturation (of the cation-exchange capacity) status. It is also an Udalf (suborder), which is an Alfisol in a humid climate. It is also classed as a Hapludalf (great group), which is an Udalf having only a moderate degree of development. Finally, it is a Typic Hapludalf (subgroup), meaning it has a typical set of horizons for a Hapludalf. Applicable connotative terms for the Hagerstown soil series at the family level are clayey, mixed, and mesic. Clayey means that the texture of the soil is clay with the possible exception of the surface horizon, and mixed implies that it has a mixture of various kinds of clay minerals. Mesic means that it belongs to the temperate soil-temperature regime. Additional formative-element information for common Pennsylvania soils is given in Table 46–2. More information on the Soil Taxonomy soil classification system can be found in the following references: U.S. Department of Agriculture, Soil Conservation Service (1975, 1994), Birkeland (1984), Buol and others (1989), and Fanning and Fanning (1989).

DISTRIBUTION AND GENESIS

The discussion of the genesis and distribution of Pennsylvania soils is presented on a general physiographic province basis and follows the soil associations shown in Figure 46–1 and described in Table 46–3. Some of the physiographic terms used do not correspond exactly to those on the map of the physiographic provinces of Pennsylvania (see map B, p. 342, and footnotes 2, 3, 4, and 5 in Table 46–4). Compare Figure 46–1 with the generalized geologic map of the state (Figure 2 in the color section).

The soils of northeastern and northwestern Pennsylvania are similar in that they have developed primarily in glacial till. The till in the northeast is derived from sandstone and shale bedrock, and the till in the northwest is derived from sandstone, shale, and a limited amount of limestone. The bulk of these tills were deposited during the late Wisconsinan glacial stage (Woodfordian substage, approximately 18,000 years B.P.) (White and others, 1969; Crowl and Sevon, 1980).

The soils developed in the acid loamy tills of the northeast are primarily Fragiaquepts (Volusia-Morris), which occur mainly on gently sloping uplands, and moderately deep Dystrochrepts (Lordstown-Oquaga), which occur on steep slopes. Both groups of soils exhibit weak to moderate development. They have cambic (color or structural) and/or fragipan (dense, firm, somewhat impermeable) B horizons (Ciolkosz and others, 1992). These horizons reflect both the youthful age of the soils and their parent materials, which are somewhat resistant to weathering. The wetness of the Fragiaquepts is a result of both their location on gen-

Table 46–3. *Soil Characteristics and Classification of the Soil Associations of Pennsylvania*

Map symbol[1]	Soil series	Depth class[2]	Drainage class	Surface texture	Subsoil texture	Color	Parent material	Classification (subgroup)
AR	Abbottstown	Deep[3]	Somewhat poorly	Silt loam	Silt loam[4]	Grayish red	Acid red shale	Aeric Fragiaqualf
	Readington	do.[3]	Mod. well[5]	do.	do.[4]	Reddish brown	do.	Typic Fragiudalf
BL	Berks	Mod. deep	Well	Loam[4]	Loam[6]	Yellowish brown	Acid brown shale	Typic Dystrochrept
	Leck Kill	Deep	do.	Silt loam	Silt loam[4]	Reddish brown	Acid red shale	Typic Hapludult
BW	Berks	Mod. deep	do.	Loam[4]	Loam[6]	Yellowish brown	Acid brown shale	Typic Dystrochrept
	Weikert	Shallow	do.	do.[4]	do.[6]	do.	do.	Lithic Dystrochrept
CB	Conotton	Deep	do.	Sandy loam[4]	Sandy loam[6]	Brown	Sand and gravel	Typic Hapludalf
	Birdsall	do.	Very poorly	Silt loam	Silt loam	Gray	Glacial silts	Typic Humaquept
CC	Cavode	do.	Somewhat poorly	do.	Silty clay	Grayish brown	Acid clay shale	Aeric Ochraquult
	Cookport	do.[3]	Mod. well	Loam	Clay loam[4]	Yellowish brown	Acid brown shale	Aquic Fragiudult
CG	Chester	do.	Well	Silt loam	Silty clay loam	Brown	Gneiss and schist	Typic Hapludalf
	Glenelg	do.	do.	Loam[4]	Silt loam[4]	do.	do.	do.
DC	Dormont	do.	Mod. well	Silt loam	Silty clay loam[4]	Yellowish brown	Limestone and shale	Ultic Hapludalf
	Culleoka	Mod. deep	Well	do.	Silt loam[4]	Brown	Shaly limestone	do.
DH	Duffield	Deep	do.	do.	Silty clay loam	Yellowish brown	Shaly limestone	Typic Hapludalf
	Hagerstown	do.	do.	do.	Clay	Red	Limestone	do.
EH	Edgemont	do.	do.	Sandy loam[4]	Loam[4]	Yellowish brown	Quartzite	Typic Hapludult
	Highfield	do.	do.	Silt loam[4]	Silt loam[4]	do.	Metarhyolite	Ultic Hapludalf
EL	Erie	do.[7]	Somewhat poorly	do.[4]	Loam[4]	Grayish brown	Calcareous till	Aeric Fragiaquept
	Langford	do.[3]	Mod. well	do.[4]	do.[4]	Yellowish brown	do.	Typic Fragiochrept
GW	Gilpin	Mod. deep	Well	do.[4]	Silt loam[4]	do.	Shale and sandstone	Typic Hapludult
	Wharton	Deep	Mod. well	do.	Silty clay loam[4]	Brown	Shale and siltstone	Aquic Hapludult
HA	Hanover	do.[3]	Well to mod. well	do.[4]	Silt loam[4]	Yellowish brown	Leached till	Typic Fragiudalf
	Alvira	do.[3]	Somewhat poorly	do.[4]	do.[4]	Grayish brown	do.	Aeric Fragiaquult
HC	Hazleton	do.	Well	Sandy loam[4]	Sandy loam[6]	Yellowish brown	Acid sandstone	Typic Dystrochrept
	Cookport	do.[3]	Mod. well	Loam	Clay loam[4]	do.	do.	Aquic Fragiudult
HD	Hagerstown	do.	Well	Silt loam	Clay	Red	Limestone	Typic Hapludalf
	Duffield	do.	do.	do.	Silty clay loam	Yellowish brown	Shaly limestone	Ultic Hapludalf
HE	Hagerstown	do.	do.	do.	Clay	Red	Limestone	Typic Hapludalf
	Edom	do.	do.	Silty clay loam	do.[4]	Yellowish brown	Shaly limestone	do.
HL	Hazleton	do.	do.	Sandy loam[4]	Sandy loam[6]	do.	Acid sandstone	Typic Dystrochrept
	Laidig	do.[3]	do.	Loam[4]	Loam[4]	Brown	Sandstone colluvium	Typic Fragiudult
HP	Howell	do.	do.	Sandy loam	Clay	do.	Sand, silt, and clay	Typic Hapludult
	Pope	do.	do.	Loam	Loam	Yellowish brown	Silty alluvium	Fluventic Dystrochrept
LM	Leck Kill	do.	do.	Silt loam	Silt loam[4]	Reddish brown	Acid red shale	Typic Hapludult
	Meckesville	do.[3]	do.	Loam	Clay loam	do.	Red-shale colluvium	Typic Fragiudult
LO	Lordstown	Mod. deep	do.	Silt loam[4]	Silt loam[4]	Yellowish brown	Acid brown till	Typic Dystrochrept
	Oquaga	do.	do.	Loam[4]	Loam[4]	Reddish brown	Acid red till	do.
MV	Morrison	Deep	do.	Sandy loam	Sandy clay loam[4]	Brown	Sandy limestone	Ultic Hapludalf
	Vanderlip	do.	do.	Loamy sand	Loamy sand[4]	Yellowish brown	do.	Typic Quartzipsamment
NL	Neshaminy	do.	do.	Silt loam	Clay loam[4]	Yellowish red	Diabase	Ultic Hapludalf
	Lehigh	do.	Mod. well to somewhat poorly	do.	Silt loam[4]	Gray	Metamorphosed shale	Aquic Hapludalf
PL	Penn	Mod. deep	Well	do.[4]	do.[4]	Reddish brown	Red shale	Ultic Hapludalf
	Lewisberry	Deep	do.	Sandy loam[4]	Sandy loam[4]	do.	Red sandstone	do.
RC	Ravenna	do.[3]	Somewhat poorly	Silt loam	Loam[4]	Grayish brown	Neutral till	Aeric Fragiaqualf
	Canfield	do.[3]	Mod. well	do.	do.[4]	Yellowish brown	do.	Aquic Fragiudalf
SP	Sheffield	do.[3]	Poorly	do.	Silty clay loam	Brownish gray	Fine-textured till	Typic Fragiaqualf
	Platea	do.[3]	Somewhat poorly	do.	Silt loam	Grayish brown	do.	Aeric Fragiaqualf
VC	Venango	do.[3]	do.	do.	Loam[4]	do.	Calcareous till	do.
	Cambridge	do.[3]	Mod. well	do.	do.[4]	Yellowish brown	do.	Ochreptic Fragiudalf
VM	Volusia	do.[7]	Somewhat poorly	do.[4]	Silt loam[4]	Grayish brown	Acid brown till	Aeric Fragiaquept
	Morris	do.[7]	do.	Loam[4]	Loam[4]	Grayish red	Acid red till	do.

[1] See Figure 46–1.
[2] Depth to bedrock: shallow, <20 inches; moderately deep, 20 to 40 inches; deep, >40 inches.
[3] Fragipan at 16 to 36 inches from the soil surface.
[4] Some (15 to 35 percent) rock fragments.
[5] Mod., moderately.
[6] Many (>35 percent) rock fragments.
[7] Fragipan at 10 to 16 inches from the soil surface.

tle slopes, which reduces runoff, and the presence of a fragipan, which causes water to be perched above it.

The soils of the northwestern Woodfordian till area are primarily Fragiaqualfs and Fragiudalfs (Erie-Langford, Venango-Cambridge, and Ravenna-Canfield). The landscapes in this area are not as steep as those in the northeast (Table 46–4); thus, moderately deep Dys-trochrepts are not extensive. The tills of the northwest are also more variable in texture (silty clay loam to loam, Table 46–3 and Figure 46–1) than those of the northeast, and they are weakly calcareous. The till soils of the northwest, like those of the northeast, have fragipans. The tills of both areas are ideal materials for fragipan formation because fragipans tend to form in medium-textured (not sandy or clayey), acid, transported parent material (Ciolkosz and others, 1992). In both till areas, soils with fragipans occupy most of the area (Table 46–4). In addition, many of the till soils of the northwest have weakly developed argillic horizons (textural B horizons) (Ciolkosz and others, 1994). In fact, there is a trend of increasing argillic horizon development from the northern to the southern part of this area. The reason for this trend is not totally clear, but it may be related to slightly older soils or higher carbonate content of the till in the southern part of this area. In addition, soils developed in finer textured till (Sheffield-Platea) and in till of early Wisconsinan age (Altonian substage, 40,000 years B.P.) (Hanover-Alvira) also have argillic horizons. The Altonian-age soils are also Ultisols, which means that they are more leached than those of Woodfordian age. Thus, fine-textured parent material, the presence of carbonates, and time have contributed to the development of argillic horizons and Ultisols in the till soils of the northwest.

The major soils occurring in the southwestern part of the Appalachian Plateaus province (Figure 46–1) are Hapludalfs (Dormont-Culleoka). The moderately deep Hapludalf (Culleoka) occurs on steep slopes and narrow ridge crests, whereas the deep Hapludalf (Dormont) occurs on more gently rolling uplands. These soils have derived silty textures and a relatively high base-saturation status from their interbedded shale and limestone parent material. The soils show only weak to moderate development, which is apparently a reflection of having developed on a landscape that was eroded by periglacial processes during the late Pleistocene. Although relatively young, the soils weather rapidly enough to provide clay material for the de-

velopment of argillic horizons. This area also has soils that are very prone to landslides. The instability of these soils seems to be related to their location on steep slopes and to a high clay content, which is dominantly expandable clay minerals (Table 46–4) (Ciolkosz, Petersen, and Cunningham, 1979).

The major soils of the central part of the Appalachian Plateaus are Hapludults (Gilpin-Wharton). The Gilpin occurs on steep slopes and narrow ridges similar to the Culleoka, and the Wharton occurs on more gently rolling uplands similar to the Dormont. These Hapludults have developed from acid shales and siltstones. They, like the Hapludalfs in the southwestern part of the Appalachian Plateau, show weak to moderate development, but they have low base status and are thus classified as Ultisols. Their weak development, like the Hapludalfs, is related to their location on youthful landscapes, and their low base-saturation status is due not to extreme weathering and leaching, but rather to having developed from base-poor (acid) shales and siltstones. These soils could well be called parent material Ultisols. Extensive coal mining in the central and southwestern areas of the Plateaus has created new parent materials (spoil piles and reclaimed areas) in which minesoils have developed. These very young soils have a high rock fragment content, show no or very weak B horizon development, and are classified as Entisols or Inceptisols (Ciolkosz and others, 1985).

The unglaciated northern part of the Plateaus (Figure 46–1) is dominated by a Dystrochrept (Hazleton) developed from acid sandstones, although there are large areas of an Ochraquult (Cavode), a Hapludult (Leck Kill), and Fragiudults (Cookport, Meckes-

Table 46–4. *Percentage of the Region of the State that Has Various Soil or Land Characteristics[1]*

Soil or land character	Glaciated northeast	Glaciated northwest	Southwestern Plateaus[2]	Central Plateaus[3]	Northern Plateaus[4]	Ridge and Valley	Triassic-Piedmont[5]	Pennsylvania
Fragipan	55	63	3	22	37	21	14	30
Argillic horizon	2	66	83	72	42	52	74	51
Aquic moisture regime[6]	29	51	6	11	9	8	12	16
Stoniness[7]	83	23	1	41	73	65	36	55
Slope (percent)								
0–3	8	28	7	7	7	10	24	11
3–8	37	43	12	29	29	32	42	33
8–15	17	15	17	21	12	16	20	17
15–25	24	8	30	25	20	22	10	21
>25	14	6	34	18	32	20	4	18

[1]Data from Day and others (1988).
[2]Southwestern part of the Pittsburgh Plateaus section of the Appalachian Plateaus province (Pennsylvania Geological Survey, 1962).
[3]Northern part of the Pittsburgh Plateaus section and all of the Allegheny Mountain section of the Appalachian Plateaus province (Pennsylvania Geological Survey, 1962).
[4]Allegheny High Plateaus section of the Appalachian Plateaus province (Pennsylvania Geological Survey, 1962).
[5]Includes the South Mountain section of the Blue Ridge province and the Reading Prong section of the New England province (Pennsylvania Geological Survey, 1962).
[6]Somewhat poorly and poorly drained. The remainder is well or moderately well drained.
[7]Greater than 15 percent of the soil surface is covered with rock fragments.

ville) that have developed from red and gray shales. Although this area has some relatively broad, rolling uplands, it is highly dissected and has some of the steepest topography in the state (Table 46–4). Because of the steepness of this area and its proximity to the glacial border, it was subjected to the greatest amount of periglacial erosion during the Pleistocene (Waltman and others, 1990). The Dystrochrept developed from sandstone (Hazleton) has a relatively high rock-fragment content and only a cambic (color) B horizon. These features attest to the very resistant nature of the sandstones to weathering and soil formation. This soil contrasts markedly with soils in the area that have developed from shales. The soils developed from shales have silty textures, few rock fragments, and weakly developed argillic B horizons (Cronce and Ciolkosz, 1983). Apparently, the shales have weathered enough (during an equivalent amount of time) to release clay for argillic-horizon development. Because of periglacial erosion and resistant parent materials, the soils in this area show only weak to moderate soil development (Aquilar and Arnold, 1985).

The major soil occurring on the ridges in the Appalachian Mountain section of the Ridge and Valley province is a deep Dystrochrept (Hazleton). This is the same soil that occurs in the northern part of the Plateaus. Although the geologic formations are different in these two areas, the sandstones weather to form the same kind of soil. The Dystrochrept is deep to bedrock even though its parent material is very resistant to weathering (Carter, 1983). Apparently, the high degree of fracturing in the bedrock has greatly encouraged deep soil development (Carter and Ciolkosz, 1986; Ciolkosz, Cronce, Cunningham, and Petersen, 1986; Carter and Ciolkosz, 1991). Downslope from the Dystrochrept, a Fragiudult (Laidig) has formed in thick colluvial side-slope deposits (Ciolkosz and others, 1990). These materials are believed to have formed in the late Pleistocene as periglacial deposits (Ciolkosz, Petersen, Cunningham, and Matelski, 1979; Hoover and Ciolkosz, 1988). Colluvium showing a similar degree of soil development also occurs in the other areas of the state, but it is less extensive than in the Ridge and Valley region (Ciolkosz, Cronce, Cunningham, and Petersen, 1986). In the valleys, Hapludalfs have developed from limestones (Hagerstown-Edom-Duffield), a moderately deep Dystrochrept (Berks) has developed from brown shales, and a deep Hapludult (Leck Kill) has developed from red shales. The Dystrochrept and Hapludult are present on similar landscapes, but the soils are different apparently because the red shales are less resistant to weathering and soil development than the brown shales.

The geology of the Piedmont area of southeastern Pennsylvania is complex. Hapludults (Chester-Glenelg)

are present on granites and gneisses, whereas Hapludalfs (Duffield-Hagerstown) occur on the limestones and calcareous schists. The Chester soil shows a more strongly developed profile than the Glenelg and occurs on the gently rolling uplands, whereas the Glenelg is present on steep side slopes. These soils also occur on rocks of the Reading Prong (New England province) in similar landscape positions. The solum (A and B horizons) of the Hapludults on the Piedmont is 20 to 50 inches thick, and depth to bedrock is from 5 to 20 feet (Pollack, 1992). Apparently, either the bedrock is weathering at a rate more rapid than solum formation or the soil is forming in saprolitic material that has been truncated by erosion. The Gettysburg-Newark Lowland section of the Piedmont has Hapludalfs (Penn-Lewisberry) and Fragiaqualfs (Abbottstown-Readington) on the low, rolling parts of the landscape, and Hapludalfs (Neshaminy) on diabase ridges. Hapludalfs (Lehigh) have formed from baked shale (hornfels) next to the diabase ridges. South Mountain (Blue Ridge province) has soils similar to those on the ridge tops of the Ridge and Valley and those of the crystalline Piedmont. These similarities are a direct influence of the parent material.

The soils of Pennsylvania show weak to moderate development. Strongly developed soils are not extensive and occur only on the most stable landscape positions. Apparently, during the late Pleistocene, significant erosion occurred on most sloping surfaces; the present-day soils are developed on these eroded surfaces as well as in deposits formed during the late Pleistocene. Because of the youthful age of Pennsylvania soils, many of their characteristics are closely related to the character of their parent materials.

INTERPRETATIONS AND LAND USE

Soil interpretations play a major role in decisions involving agriculture, town and country planning, wildlife habitat, recreational development, woodland management, and engineering uses of land areas. Soils can be rated slight, moderate, or severe for various types of land use based upon such properties as texture, rock-fragment content, depth to the water table, depth to bedrock or fragipan, stoniness, rockiness, slope, and susceptibility to flooding. The ratings for three common Pennsylvania soils are given in Table 46–5. The Volusia soil is characteristic of many of the soils in the glaciated areas, which have fragipans and saturated moisture conditions during much of the year. These conditions make the disposal of additional water in these kinds of soils impossible. The wet conditions also make these soils susceptible to frost action during the winter. Thus, special construction techniques should be employed

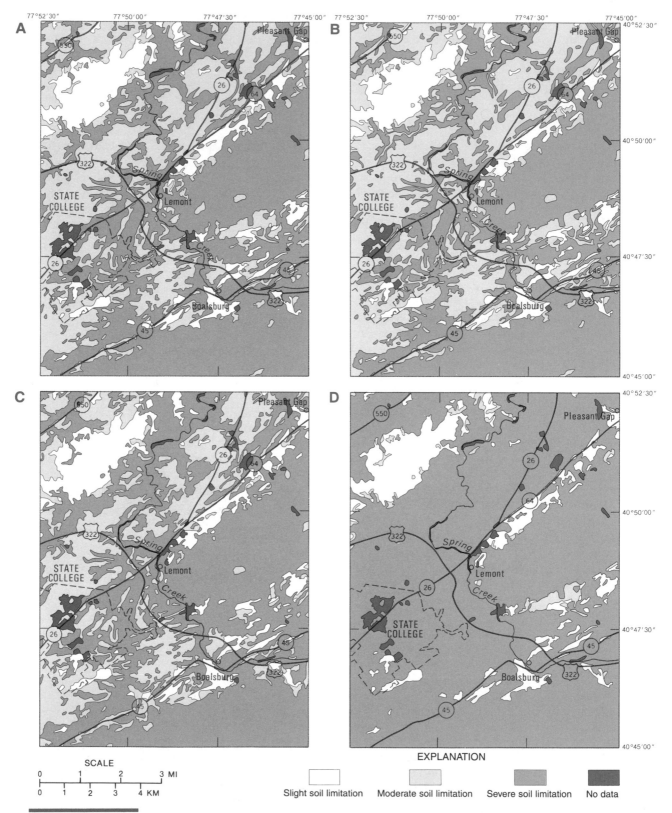

SCALE

| 0 | | 1 | | 2 | | 3 MI |

| 0 | 1 | 2 | 3 | | 4 KM |

Slight soil limitation   Moderate soil limitation   Severe soil limitation   No data

Figure 46–2. Maps showing suitability of soils in the State College 7.5-minute-quadrangle area, Centre County, for septic-tank absorption fields (A), buildings having no basements (B), local roads and streets plus buildings that have basements (C), and sanitary landfills (D) (based on data from Day and others, 1988).

to drain excess water so that freezing and thawing do not destroy the road surfaces. In addition, road-banks cut through fragipans tend to slump, causing maintenance problems. The wetness problem also limits these soils to only a fair rating for crop production.

The Hagerstown, like the Volusia, is a deep soil, but it has limestone ledges that commonly occur within 40 inches of the surface. These ledges can be difficult to excavate and add to construction costs. Without renovation, they may also provide solution channels that allow wastewater flow, thus limiting the usefulness of this soil for septic-tank absorption fields. The B horizon of the Hagerstown has a high clay content (40 to 70 percent) and thus has considerable potential to shrink and swell with changes in moisture content. The shrinking and swelling can cause structural cracking. Areas underlain by Hagerstown soils typically show karst topography and are susceptible to the formation of new sinkholes. Although Hagerstown soils are excellent for agriculture crops, some chert or quartz rock fragments may interfere with tillage. The Chester soil, unlike the Volusia or Hagerstown, is well suited to most uses (Table 46–5).

Soil limitation classes (slight, moderate, and severe) can also be applied to delineate units on soil maps. Figure 46–2 gives examples of four computer-generated interpretative maps of the State College 7.5-minute quadrangle in Centre County. Figure 46–2A shows that most of the soils in this area have a severe limitation for septic-tank absorption fields; however, a sizable area of soils in the upper left-hand quadrant has only a slight limitation. The limitations for dwellings that have basements and for local

roads (Figure 46–2C) are the same because the same soil properties impact these uses. If buildings are not designed to have basements, then more areas have only moderate limitations (Figure 46–2B). Some uses, such as sanitary landfills, have more restrictive soil requirements, and the interpretative map (Figure 46–2D) shows much less area with moderate limitations. These, as well as other computer-generated interpretative maps, can be produced at the same scale as other resource-information maps, thus further enhancing the use of soils data for land use decisions.

PROBLEMS AND FUTURE RESEARCH

The major problems in soil-genesis research in Pennsylvania center on obtaining a better understanding of the quantitative aspects of soil development. In particular, the rate at which soil structure and argillic horizons form is largely unknown. Also, a better understanding of the relationship between soils and geomorphology would aid greatly in explaining how our present-day soils have developed. More research needs to be pointed toward process pedology and modeling if breakthroughs are to be made in our understanding of soil genesis in Pennsylvania.

RECOMMENDED FOR FURTHER READING

Blumberg, B., and Cunningham, R. L. (1982), *An introduction to the soils of Pennsylvania,* Pennsylvania State University, Department of Agriculture and Extension Education, Teacher Education Series, v. 23, no. 4, 24 p.

Brady, N. C. (1990), *The nature and properties of soils,* 10th ed., New York, Macmillan Publishing Company, 621 p.

Ciolkosz, E. J., Cronce, R. C., and Sevon, W. D. (1986), *Periglacial features in Pennsylvania,* Pennsylvania State University Agronomy Series 92, 15 p.

Ciolkosz, E. J., Gardner, T. W., and Dobos, R. R. (1988), *Paleosols in Pennsylvania,* Pennsylvania State University Agronomy Series 100, 9 p.

Ciolkosz, E. J., Waltman, W. J., Simpson, T. W., and Dobos, R. R. (1989), *Distribution and genesis of soils of the northeastern United States,* Geomorphology, v. 2, p. 285–302.

Clark, G. M., Behling, R. E., Braun, D. D., and others (1992), *Central Appalachian periglacial geomorphology,* Pennsylvania State University Agronomy Series 120, 173 p.

Clark, G. M., and Ciolkosz, E. J. (1988), *Periglacial geomorphology of the Appalachian Highlands and Interior Highlands south of the glacial border—a review,* Geomorphology, v.1, p. 191–220.

Cunningham, R. C., and Ciolkosz, E. J. (1984), *Soil of the northeastern United States,* Pennsylvania State University Agricultural Experiment Station Bulletin 848, 47 p.

Foth, H. D., and Schafer, J. W. (1980), *Soil geography and land use,* New York, John Wiley and Sons, 467 p.

Levine, E. R., and Ciolkosz, E. J. (1983), *Soil development in till of various ages in northeastern Pennsylvania,* Quaternary Research, v. 19, p. 85–99.

Table 46–5. *Land-Use Limitations (Slight, Moderate, and Severe) of the U.S. Department of Agriculture, Soil Conservation Service, for Three Common Soils of Pennsylvania with 0 to 3 Percent Slope[1]*

Soil use	Volusia	Hagerstown	Chester
Septic-tank absorption fields	Severe (wetness)	Moderate (depth to rock)	Slight
Dwellings that have basements	Severe (wetness)	Moderate (depth to rock, low strength)	Slight
Local roads and streets	Moderate (frost action)	Moderate (shrink-swell potential, frost action, sinkhole hazard)	Moderate (frost action, low strength)
Sanitary landfills	Severe (wetness)	Severe (too clayey, depth to rock)	Slight

[1]Additional interpretations for these and other Pennsylvania soils were presented by Cunningham and others (1983) and in various county soil survey reports available from the U.S. Department of Agriculture, Soil Conservation Service.

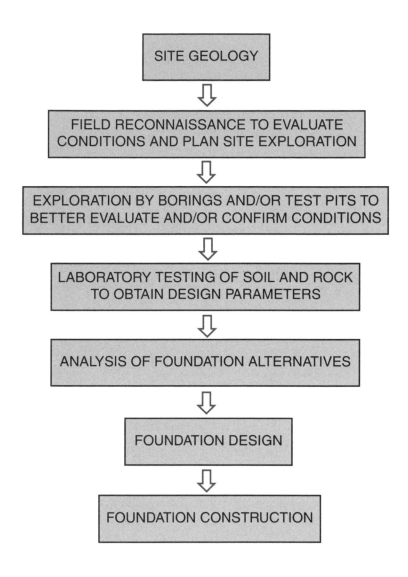

Figure 47–1. Steps required in foundation design and construction. Geology serves as a framework and starting point. Site exploration and the testing program are planned based on anticipated site geology. The field reconnaissance and data obtained during exploration and laboratory testing should confirm the anticipated site geology. If not, steps should be taken to establish the reason(s) for the unanticipated results prior to analysis and design. Foundation construction should be monitored to ensure that actual field conditions are consistent with the design assumptions.

CHAPTER 47   FOUNDATIONS

RICHARD E. GRAY
GAI Consultants, Inc.
570 Beatty Road
Monroeville, PA 15146

The diverse geology of Pennsylvania results in many foundation types being used to support structures. Of course, the type and size of structure, site-specific conditions, local practice, and the designer's preference may influence the type of foundation selected as much as geology. Downtown Pittsburgh serves as an example. In an area of approximately equal subsurface conditions (recent alluvium overlying dense glacial sand and gravel), large buildings are supported on spread footings, a mat, friction piles, and piles bearing on rock.

Some geological environments, such as the glaciated northeast and northwest corners of the state with peat-filled kettle holes, or karst areas in central Pennsylvania with extensive sinkhole development, pose obvious foundation difficulties, whereas areas of shallow rock or stiff residual soils, which cover large parts of the state, generally do not. However, because conditions immediately below a foundation are critical, the microenvironment within a geologic region that normally has no foundation problems may cause difficulties. Examples are backfilled ponds and wetlands; streams placed in culverts with the channel and floodplain filled; and site grading, which results in a structure bearing partly on rock and partly on fill. Thus, selection of an appropriate foundation is site specific and requires careful exploration, including borings and/or test pits.

In spite of the factors discussed above, regional geology sets the framework for foundation engineering (Figure 47–1). Knowledge of the local geology aids in planning the site-exploration program and alerts one on what to expect in site reconnaissance and exploration. Early in a project, evaluation of site conditions based on a literature search and field reconnaissance should result in consideration of the potential for special foundation problems such as subsidence due to mining (Gray and Bruhn, 1982; Chapter 49B in this volume), natural dissolution of limestone and other soluble rocks (Sowers, 1975; Chapter 49A in this volume), landsliding (Schuster and Krizek, 1978; Chapter 48 in this volume), and expansive soil or rock (Dougherty and Barsotti, 1972). If geologic conditions noted during field exploration are different than those indicated by regional geological data, the reason for the difference should be determined. It may indicate an anomalous condition that, if not understood, could result in selection of an improper foundation. Also, results of laboratory tests to establish foundation-design parameters and the analysis of foundation types should be consistent with the regional geology. If the site conditions encountered are different than anticipated, the design parameters selected should be consistent with the actual geologic conditions at the site.

In general, residual soils throughout Pennsylvania are adequate to support the foundations of homes and light-commercial buildings. For heavier foundation loads, rock normally provides adequate support, except where deeply weathered. However, all regions of Pennsylvania contain areas that may require special foundation considerations. Examples are floodplains, wetlands, land disturbed by resource recovery, and waste-disposal areas. Also, most regions contain some soil or rock that, either in its natural condition or when weathered or saturated, may cause problems in foundation construction or performance. Examples are schist of the lower Paleozoic Wissahickon Formation in southeastern Pennsylvania, where deep weathering may require foundations to extend far below the top of rock, and claystone and some shales of the Appalachian Plateaus province that slake (crumble) when exposed to the atmosphere. Pile driving also shatters these shales and claystones. Removal of

the softened rock from the excavation is required immediately prior to placement of foundation concrete, and piles may have to be redriven several times before rock is encountered that does not deteriorate.

Areas of Pennsylvania underlain by limestone (particularly in the Ridge and Valley province) commonly exhibit a highly irregular rock surface owing to solution weathering, which can result in high foundation costs. Subsidence caused by limestone dissolution is also a significant problem (see Chapter 49A in this volume).

A foundation designer must consider both mining (coal, claystone, and limestone) and expansive shales when building on the Pennsylvanian rocks of the Appalachian Plateaus province. Although no cases of foundation heave in Pennsylvania are known in shales of other than Pennsylvanian age, all pyritic shales should be considered a potential problem. Devonian shales have caused foundation heaving in Ohio (Engineering News Record, 1960).

The glaciated parts of Pennsylvania contain many soils, such as tills and granular outwash, that can safely support residential and light-commercial buildings. However, the potential presence of peat- or organic-soil-filled depressions requires careful site exploration in glaciated areas.

Stream valleys generally contain softer soils than the surrounding highlands, and the depth to rock is greater. However, the valleys of streams originating in the glaciated northern corners of the state contain sands and gravels, which generally provide good foundation support. Abandoned stream channels and high

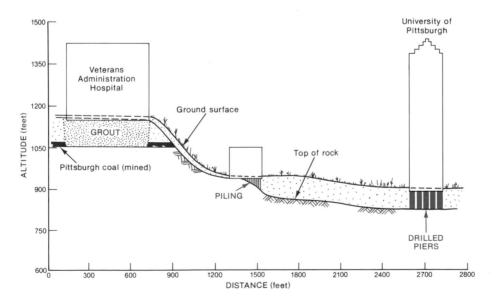

Figure 47–2. Schematic cross section of the Oakland area on the east side of Pittsburgh (from Philbrick, 1959, p. 195). This section cuts through a hill containing mined Pittsburgh coal and the abandoned high-level channel of the Monongahela River. The University of Pittsburgh high-rise building is supported on deep foundations bearing on rock, but grouting was required in the mined area.

terraces may result in alluvial deposits high above present stream levels. An example from the Pittsburgh area is shown in Figure 31–7 (p. 387). The high-level terraces and abandoned channels are about 200 feet above the present level of the rivers in Pittsburgh. Figure 47–2 shows diverse foundation conditions in the Oakland section of Pittsburgh. The University of Pittsburgh high-rise building (Cathedral of Learning) is supported on deep foundations to bypass alluvium in the abandoned high-level river channel. A building at the edge of the channel is supported both by shallow and deep foundations (pilings), and a nearby hospital required grouting to stabilize an abandoned mine.

PROBLEMS AND FUTURE RESEARCH

Foundation design and construction technology are well developed. The prime future research need,

although not unique to Pennsylvania, is the development of methods of identifying areas of potential sinkhole development in limestone regions.

RECOMMENDED FOR FURTHER READING

Gardner, G. D., and Salver, H. A. (1977), *Foundation performances of single family houses,* in Freedman, J. L., ed., *"Lots" of danger—Property buyer's guide to land hazards of southwestern Pennsylvania,* Pittsburgh Geological Society, p. 17–28.

Holzer, T., ed. (1984), *Man-induced land subsidence,* Geological Society of America Reviews in Engineering Geology, v. 6, 2,231 p.

Leonards, G. A., ed. (1962), *Foundation engineering,* New York, McGraw-Hill, 1,136 p.

National Research Council, Transportation Research Board (1958), *Landslides and engineering practice,* Washington, D. C., National Academy of Sciences, National Research Council Special Report 29, 231 p.

Sowers, G. B., and Sowers, G. F. (1979), *Introductory soil mechanics and foundations,* 4th ed., New York, Macmillan, 556 p.

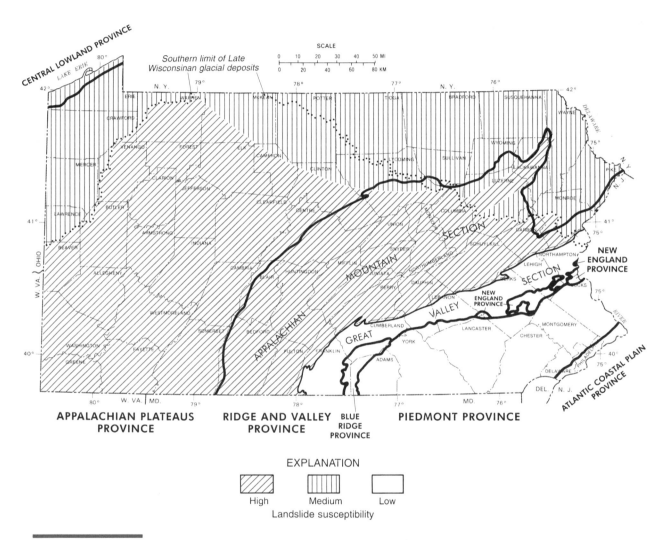

Figure 48–1. Map of Pennsylvania showing landslide susceptibility (modified from Baker and Chieruzzi, 1959, Figure 2 and Table 6, p. 10 and 11; and Radbruch-Hall and others, 1982, Plate 1) superimposed on physiographic provinces (from Berg and others, 1989).

704

CHAPTER 48   LANDSLIDING

JAMES V. HAMEL
Hamel Geotechnical Consultants
1992 Butler Drive
Monroeville, PA 15146

HARRY F. FERGUSON*
Harry F. Ferguson and Associates, Ltd.
370 Baird Court
North Huntington, PA 15642

INTRODUCTION

Landsliding is a general term for the perceptible downward and outward movement of slope-forming materials, including natural rocks, soils (regolith), artificial fills, and combinations of these materials. The term is generally understood to include slope movements involving falls, topples, spreads, flows, and avalanches, as well as slides where shear failure occurs along a specific surface or combination of surfaces (Schuster and Krizek, 1978).

Pennsylvania has a long history of significant landslide activity. This has resulted from a combination of humid temperate climate, locally steep and rugged topography, and great diversity in the erosion and weathering characteristics of relatively near surface sedimentary rocks. Superimposed on this and compounding the problem are the activities of man, which include commercial, industrial, and residential developments, transportation, and mining, particularly coal mining.

Landslides have occurred in many parts of Pennsylvania but are most abundant and most troublesome in much of the Appalachian Plateaus physiographic province of western and north-central Pennsylvania and adjacent states (Figure 48–1). This region is recognized as one of the major areas of landslide susceptibility and severity in the United States (Baker and Chieruzzi, 1959; Radbruch-Hall and others, 1982). The Monongahela River valley of northern West Virginia and southwestern Pennsylvania has a special place in landslide folklore. The name "Monongahela" is derived from an American Indian word that is translated as "river with the sliding banks" or "high banks which break off and fall down" (Espenshade, 1925). The part of southwestern Pennsylvania that includes the Monongahela Valley and Pittsburgh is the most slide-prone portion of the state.

Numerous papers and reports on landslides in Pennsylvania can be referred to for more detailed descriptions. These include Ackenheil (1954), Hamel (1972, 1980), Hamel and Flint (1972), Gray and others (1979), Pomeroy (1980, 1982a, 1984), Ferguson and Hamel (1981), Hamel and Adams (1981), Hamel and Ferguson (1983), Adams (1986), and Delano and Wilshusen (in press).

*Deceased.

LANDSLIDE TYPES AND PROCESSES

Slope movement types (Schuster and Krizek, 1978, Figure 2.1) in Pennsylvania include bedrock slides, falls, and topples; soil slides, avalanches, and flows; and many others caused by improperly constructed fills. In this chapter, "soil" is used in the engineering sense, synonymously with regolith, meaning any material that can be excavated without blasting.

Deep-seated rockslides (Figures 48–2A, 48–3, and 48–4) are uncommon at present in the Appalachian Plateaus province. However, during the Pleistocene Epoch, when climate was more rigorous and rivers were rapidly downcutting their valleys into the nearly horizontal beds of the Appalachian Plateaus, this type of slide is believed to have been much more common. The best documented recent bedrock slide

of this type occurred at the Brilliant cut in Pittsburgh in 1941 (Hamel, 1972; Figure 48–4). Farther east, in the Appalachian Mountain section of the Ridge and Valley province, shallow, slab-type bedrock slides are fairly common on dip slopes of steeply tilted strata (Wilshusen, 1979).

Rockfalls and topples (Figure 48–2D) are much more common than rock slides, particularly in the Appalachian Plateaus province and Appalachian Mountain section of the Ridge and Valley province (Wilshusen, 1979). This type of landsliding occurs on both natural and excavated slopes, where weathering and erosion have removed less competent rock from underneath thicker slabs of massive and jointed rock. The resulting detached blocks either slump or topple forward. The process is aided by water pressure in joints, and by ice or roots that act as wedges. Rockfall volumes are usually quite small, ranging between 0.1 and 100 cubic yards.

Soil slope movements in Pennsylvania include slides, avalanches, flows, falls, and topples (Schuster and Krizek, 1978). Slides occur in most soils and are especially common in colluvium on natural or undercut slopes (Figures 48–2B, 48–3, and 48–5) and in fill (Figure 48–6) often underlain by or adjacent to colluvium. Most soil slides in Pennsylvania have relatively slow rates of movement. These slides include slumps with

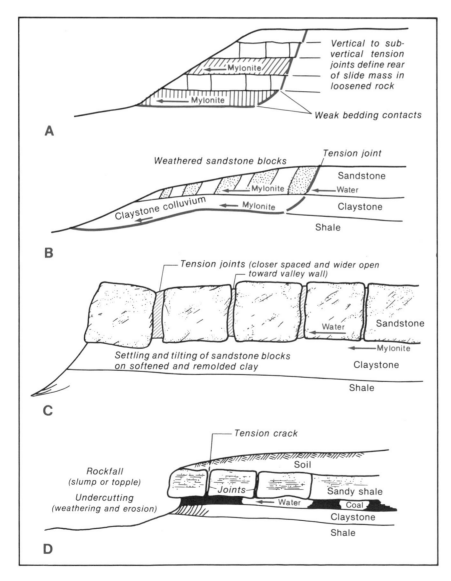

Figure 48–2. Diagrammatic cross sections of valley-wall features in the Appalachian Plateaus for various types of landslides: A, bedrock block slide; B, colluvial slide; C, block creep; and D, rockfall or topple. Note that "mylonite" is used in the engineering sense to refer to a clay-filled shear zone. Slightly modified from Ferguson, H. F., and Hamel, J. V. (1981), *Valley stress relief in flat-lying sedimentary rocks*, in Akai, Koichi, Hayashi, Masao, and Nishimatsu, Yuichi, eds., *Weak rock—Soft, fractured and weathered rock,* International Symposium on Weak Rock, Tokyo, 1981, Proceedings, Rotterdam, A. A. Balkema, v. 2, Figure 4, p. 1237, © A. A. Balkema, 1981.

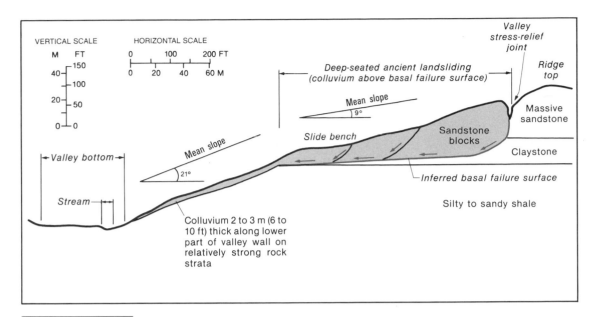

Figure 48–3. Cross section of a prehistoric slide caused by valley stress relief and a clay-filled bedding-plane shear zone (inferred basal failure surface) underlying massive sandstone (slightly modified from Hamel, 1980, Figure 5, p. 10). Note the thin colluvium on the lower steep part of the slope. The slide location is 10 miles northwest of downtown Pittsburgh; Interstate Route 79 was constructed in a side-hill excavation of the slide bench approximately halfway up the slope.

rotational movements, block slides with translational movements, and combinations of both. This type of slide is especially common in the Appalachian Plateaus province. Some slides of this type also occur in the residual soils of the Piedmont province and the Appalachian Mountain section of the Ridge and Valley province. They also occur in the glacial soils of northeastern and northwestern Pennsylvania and in alluvial soils along major rivers.

Colluvium is particularly thick in the Appalachian Plateau of western and north-central Pennsylvania. The boundary between colluvium and more stable material beneath is generally parallel or subparallel to the slope, thus creating sloping surfaces of greatly reduced strength (Figures 48–2B, 48–3, and 48–5). Talus deposits, common in north-central Pennsylvania, behave in a similar manner.

Debris avalanches and flows occur in most soils but are especially common in colluvium and fill. This type of mass wasting is frequently associated with heavy rainfall and/or a rapid rise in groundwater level. Movement rates range from slow for some earthflows to very rapid for other earthflows and debris avalanches. The lower portions of soil slide masses often disintegrate into debris avalanches or flows dur-

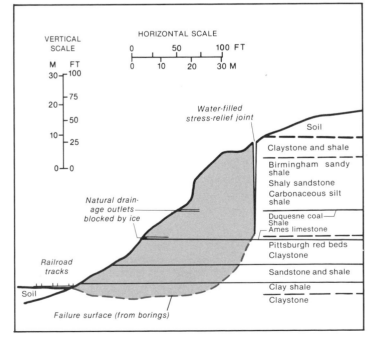

Figure 48–4. Cross section showing conditions before the 1941 rock slide at the Brilliant cut along the south side of the Allegheny River, 6 miles northeast of downtown Pittsburgh (modified from Gray and others, 1979, Figure 7, p. 459).

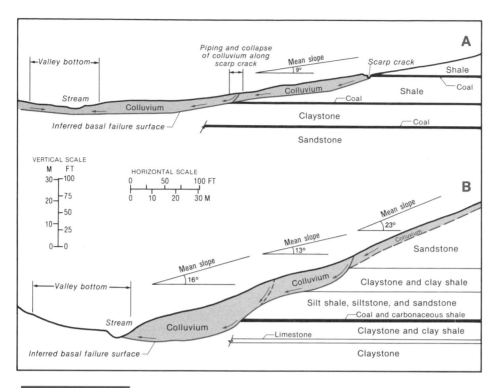

Figure 48–5. Cross sections of colluvial slopes overlying horizontal beds consisting of thick layers of weak rock (A) and interbedded layers of strong and weak rock (B) (slightly modified from Hamel, 1980, Figure 4, p. 9).

ing periods of heavy rainfall or rapid groundwater rise (Figure 48–6).

Soil falls and topples, which are similar to rockfalls and topples, occur rapidly on excavated slopes in all soil types and on oversteepened slopes, such as stream banks in glacial and alluvial soils.

Fill, composed of either soil or rock, varies widely in stability depending on its nature, the technique of placement, and surface and subsurface drainage. Engineered fills that are constructed of properly compacted soil and/or rock materials spread in horizontal layers of appropriate thickness are comparatively stable. The fill is typically placed on benches cut into residual soil or weathered rock and provided with appropriate subsurface drainage (Figure 48–7). Nonengineered or random fills are commonly dumped or pushed over hillsides. Fill slides are particularly common in the Appalachian Plateau as a result of steep slopes, weak rock strata, abundant colluvium, and a large number of springs. The problems are compounded by coal mining and related spoil piles and by refuse placement. The abundance of nonengineered fills in these areas apparently reflects an Appalachian heritage of throwing and pushing fill and other material over hillsides.

CAUSES AND EFFECTS

Landslides may be due to natural causes, man-made causes, or combinations of both. Natural processes related to landsliding in Pennsylvania include weathering, erosion, and creep (Figure 48–2). Also important are valley stress-relief features, such as near-vertical tension joints and clay-filled bedding-plane shear zones (clay mylonites of engineering terminology) (Figure 48–2A, B, C). Abnormally heavy precipitation is a common triggering mechanism for landslides. Examples of such precipitation events include tropical storm Agnes of June 1972, the Johnstown (Cambria County) storm of July 1977, and the East Brady (Armstrong County) storm of August 1980.

Site development and other construction activities of man may lead to landsliding. Surface excavations in rock may result in rockfalls. Such excavations in soil remove lateral support and sometimes trigger landslides, a problem that is particularly common in colluvial slopes of the Appalachian Plateau. Subsurface excavation can contribute to, or even trigger, landslides. Slope movements induced by coal-mine subsidence are not uncommon in the Appalachian Plateau. Strip mining of coal has produced extensive failures in spoil banks and regraded spoil areas. Slope movements of this type are especially common in Armstrong, Butler, and Washington Counties (Pomeroy, 1982b).

Overloading of a slope by adding fill can also cause landslides by increasing the stress on underlying materials. Any alteration of natural patterns of drainage, such as blocking of surface-water paths and/or subsurface drainage outlets, including spring discharge areas, can also trigger slides. Poor fill placement and compaction are responsible for many landslides, particularly in the Appalachian Plateau.

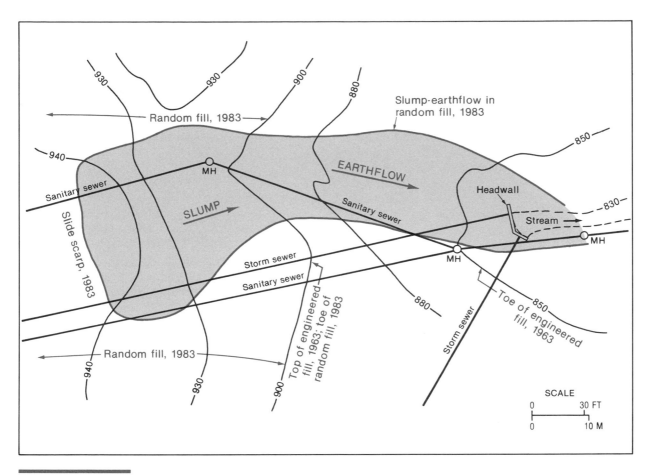

Figure 48–6. Map of a typical slide in a poorly constructed random fill. MH, manhole; contours are in feet.

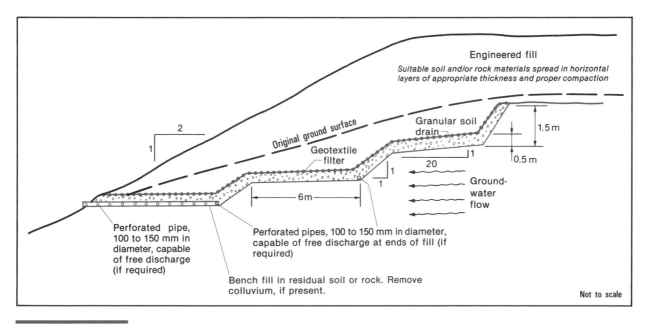

Figure 48–7. Diagrammatic cross section showing features of a typical well-engineered fill.

The effect of landsliding on the human population in Pennsylvania is substantial. Included here are distress and damage to property, structures (see Figure 54 in the color section), facilities, and utilities, plus traffic delays and detours (Figure 48–8), and continuing maintenance requirements along transportation routes. Some of this damage can lead to litigation. Cost data on landslide damage are sparse. Fleming and Taylor (1980) have published landslide damage estimates for Allegheny County (Pittsburgh and suburbs) from 1970 to 1976. Annual costs ranged from $1.3 to $4.0 million over this 7-year period and averaged $2.2 million per year. The maximum annual cost of $4 million was for 1972, the year of tropical storm Agnes. Data from the Pennsylvania Department of Transportation indicate that $6 million was spent to repair landslide damage along state roads in Allegheny County during the 6.5-year period from January 1971 through July 1977. To this must be added undeterminable costs to private citizens, which result from transportation delays and detours.

Injuries and fatalities due to landslides are fairly rare and result mainly from rockfalls on highway slopes and soil falls in trench excavations. In December 1942, a 150-cubic-yard rockfall from a highway cut along the Ohio River opposite Ambridge, Beaver County, crushed a bus. Twenty-two persons were killed and four were injured (Ackenheil, 1954;

Gray and others, 1979). A 300-cubic-yard rockfall occurred in Pittsburgh in February 1983 during remedial excavation of a highway slope having a long history of rockfalls. This rockfall crushed three vehicles (Figure 48–8). Two persons were killed and one was injured. Typically, every year one or more construction workers are killed or injured in cave-ins of trenches and other excavations in Pennsylvania.

INVESTIGATION AND TREATMENT

On natural slopes in remote areas, or in other areas where there will be no adverse effects, landslides are simply left alone. In critical areas, where the works of man are likely to be impacted, landslides on natural slopes are treated similarly to those on man-made slopes. Such slopes include those modified by excavation and/or fill placement. Proven technology is available for minimizing the adverse effects of landslides on man-made or man-altered slopes. This technology includes procedures and techniques for investigation, design, construction, and maintenance (Schuster and Krizek, 1978). The most critical item is a knowledge of both the geological features and the engineering characteristics of the slope. If these are understood and the economics can be justified, proper design and construction procedures can be implemented.

Bedrock slides are of two basic types: deep-seated and shallow. Deep-seated rockslides are treated on an individual basis because they are rare. Shallow rockslides, along with rockfalls and rock topples, can be avoided or planned for through proper design and construction on excavated slopes. Controlled blasting minimizes overbreak and rock loosening. Potentially unstable blocks can be removed during excavation, and benches or drop zones can be provided to catch other falling blocks. Support and stabilization measures, such as rock anchors, rock bolts, wire mesh, and retaining and drainage structures, can be

Figure 48–8. Photograph showing vehicles crushed by a rockfall on Pa. Route 51 in Pittsburgh, February 1983. Photograph by V. W. H. Campbell, Jr., *Pittsburgh Post-Gazette*.

installed or constructed (Schuster and Krizek, 1978). On natural rock slopes, the options are usually limited to removal of potentially unstable rock masses or to supporting or stabilizing such rock masses.

On colluvial slopes, recognition of old landslide masses is critical. Such masses can commonly be recognized by hummocky topography, displaced rock blocks, and isolated wet patches. Colluvial masses, especially the larger ones, should be avoided to the extent practicable. If they cannot be avoided, such masses can in some cases be stabilized with buttress fills or retaining structures (Schuster and Krizek, 1978). Stabilization of a colluvial mass by excavation alone generally requires removal of virtually the entire mass. This is seldom practical with the larger colluvial masses. Improvement of subsurface and surface drainage is an important component of stabilization measures for many colluvial masses, though drainage control by itself may not be sufficient for stabilization.

The stability of fill slopes begins with the foundation. All soil foundations must be carefully investigated by methods such as test pits, borings, and soil samples. Underlying rock foundations are typically investigated by core drilling. In the long run, fills placed on colluvium are seldom stable. Assuming a secure and solid foundation, however, good grading techniques are mandatory to ensure a stable fill slope. The necessary practices involve utilization of proper design and appropriate materials. Well-engineered fill techniques include keying or benching the fill into stable underlying soil or rock and adequate compaction of the fill materials (Figure 48-7). Surface and subsurface drainage must also be provided for a stable fill.

Some municipalities in Pennsylvania have grading codes and ordinances intended to ensure appropriate geological and engineering investigation, design, and construction of excavated slopes and fill slopes. In many cases, the objectives of these codes are not met because of limited or nonexistent capability for knowledgeable review and follow-up inspection and enforcement of their provisions. Rigorous review, inspection, and enforcement are essential for implementation of the state-of-the-art slope engineering and construction necessary to reduce landslide damage, particularly in the Appalachian Plateau of western and north-central Pennsylvania. The costs of proper investigation and execution are sometimes high, but the costs of repair of poorly planned projects are often much higher.

PROBLEMS AND FUTURE RESEARCH

Geological and geotechnical aspects of landsliding in Pennsylvania are well understood, and most landslide problems result from failure to apply existing knowledge. Funding for correction of landslide problems is often insignificant or nonexistent, particularly for individual homeowners. Future efforts are recommended in the following areas:

1. Increased education and awareness of landslide problems and their avoidance.
2. Stricter enforcement of building and grading codes in landslide-prone areas.
3. A statewide program of landslide insurance similar to the federal flood-insurance program or the state mine-subsidence insurance program. This will require data on landslide probability in order to quantitatively assess landslide risk and establish insurance rates.

RECOMMENDED FOR FURTHER READING

Briggs, R. P., Pomeroy, J. S., and Davies, W. E. (1975), *Landsliding in Allegheny County, Pennsylvania*, U.S. Geological Survey Circular 728, 18 p.

Ferguson, H. F., and Hamel, J. V. (1981), *Valley stress relief in flat-lying sedimentary rocks*, in Akai, K., and others, eds., *Weak rock; soft, fractured, and weathered rock*, International Symposium on Weak Rock, Tokyo, 1981, Proceedings, v. 2, p. 1235-1240.

Gray, R. E., Ferguson, H. F., and Hamel, J. V. (1979), *Slope stability in the Appalachian Plateau, Pennsylvania and West Virginia, U.S.A.*, in Voight, Barry, ed., *Rockslides and avalanches—Volume 2, Engineering sites*, Amsterdam, Elsevier, v. 2, p. 447-471.

Hamel, J. V. (1980), *Geology and slope stability in western Pennsylvania*, Association of Engineering Geologists Bulletin, v. 17, p. 1-26.

Hamel, J. V., and Adams, W. R., Jr. (1981), *Claystone slides, Interstate Route 79, Pittsburgh, Pennsylvania, USA*, in Akai, K., and others, eds., *Weak rock; soft, fractured, and weathered rock*, International Symposium on Weak Rock, Tokyo, 1981, Proceedings, v. 1, p. 549-553, and v. 3, p. 1389-1390.

Pomeroy, J. S. (1982), *Landslides in the Greater Pittsburgh region, Pennsylvania*, U.S. Geological Survey Professional Paper 1229, 48 p.

Schuster, R. L., and Krizek, R. J., eds. (1978), *Landslides: analysis and control*, National Research Council Special Report 176, Washington, D. C., Transportation Research Board, 234 p.

Wilshusen, J. P. (1979), *Geologic hazards in Pennsylvania*, Pennsylvania Geological Survey, 4th ser., Educational Series 9, 56 p.

Westward-looking view across a sinkhole in Vera Cruz Road, Upper Saucon Township, Lehigh
County, which developed in December 1983. A different view of the same feature is presented
in Figure 49A–8. Photograph courtesy of the Pennsylvania Geological Survey.

CHAPTER 49   LAND SUBSIDENCE

Land subsidence can result from natural causes or the activities of man. Allen (1969) discussed natural subsidence and identified six causes: (1) dissolution of soluble rocks, (2) underground erosion (piping), (3) plastic flow, (4) compaction of sediments, (5) tectonic movements, and (6) volcanic activity. Man-induced subsidence is usually caused by mining or fluid extraction. Holzer (1984) presented an excellent review of induced subsidence. This chapter focuses on the two most common types of subsidence in Pennsylvania: dissolution of limestone, and mining.

—Richard E. Gray

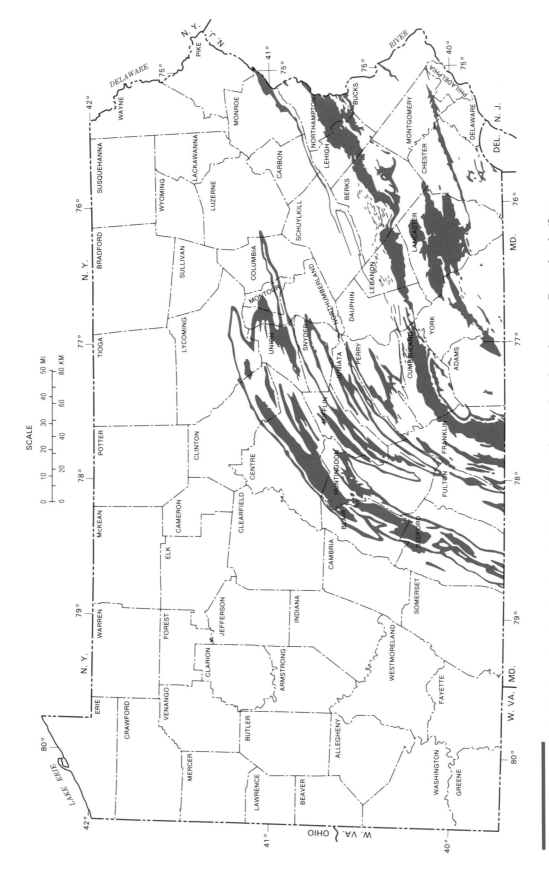

Figure 49A–1. Surface distribution of carbonate rocks (color) in central, south-central, and southeastern Pennsylvania (from Pennsylvania Geological Survey, 1984).

CHAPTER 49A   LAND SUBSIDENCE—CARBONATE TERRANE

J. PETER WILSHUSEN*
 Bureau of Topographic and Geologic Survey
 Department of Conservation and Natural
  Resources
 P. O. Box 8453
 Harrisburg, PA 17105

WILLIAM E. KOCHANOV
 Bureau of Topographic and Geologic Survey
 Department of Conservation and Natural
  Resources
 P. O. Box 8453
 Harrisburg, PA 17105

OCCURRENCE

Thick sequences of structurally deformed carbonates comprise the surface bedrock of a sizable area in central, south-central, and southeastern Pennsylvania (Figure 49A–1). The carbonate rock formations, which are Cambrian through Devonian in age, have developed karstic landforms, resulting in significant land-subsidence problems. Most carbonate rock terranes subject to subsidence in Pennsylvania are the structurally deformed lower Paleozoic carbonates. Folds, commonly overturned and attenuated, and numerous faults have resulted in extensively fractured bedrock. Weathering of the deformed carbonate units along the many lines of weakness for millions of years under temperate to arctic climatic conditions has produced a subdued, but deeply developed, karst.

RECOGNITION

In karstic terrane, subsidence features generally occur as individual or small groups of collapse, solution, and subsidence dolines. See Jennings (1985) and Sweeting (1973) for a discussion of doline morphology. The more commonly used American terms "sinkhole" and "closed depression" are synonymous with various types of dolines and will be used in referring to subsidence features in this chapter.

The contact between residual soil and well-indurated carbonate bedrock is sharp but extremely irregular (Figure 49A–2). Surface-water and groundwater movements have transported the soil, filling some voids and solution channels but leaving others partially filled or entirely empty. In general, the karst landscape functions as a well-established plumbing system. Sinkholes and closed depressions act as drains, first accepting meteoric waters and then providing a connection to the fractures within the bedrock to help convey the groundwater to the water table. In karst areas adjacent to mountain ridges, greater thicknesses of colluvium have been added to the carbonate residuum, such as along the north flank of South Mountain in Cumber-

*Deceased.

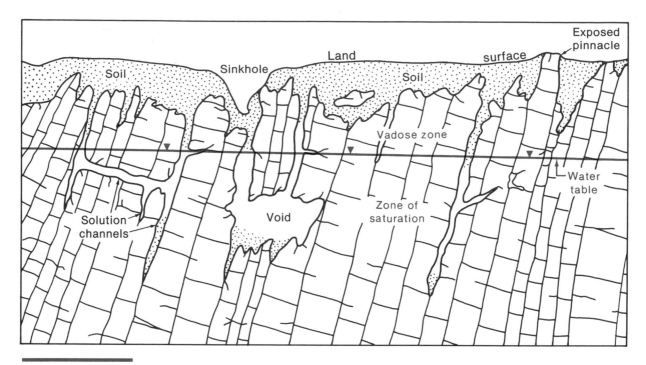

Figure 49A–2. Sketch profile of solution channels and sinkhole development in carbonate bedrock. The movement of surface water and groundwater is a key factor in the development of a karst landscape as well as in the shifting of residual soils that generates sinkholes.

land and Franklin Counties. Glacial till and outwash have also been deposited on top of the carbonate residuum in a few places, most importantly in the Lehigh Valley of Lehigh and Northampton Counties.

Closed depressions, which reflect the carbonate bedrock profile, are the most common karst surface feature. They are typically bowl shaped but can be linear and troughlike and can be of various sizes and depths. Closed depressions are commonly numerous and areally extensive (Figure 49A–3). During late winter and spring, meteoric water can collect in these surface depressions and make them easy to recognize on aerial photographs and in field surveys (Figure 49A–4).

Sinkholes are genetically similar to closed depressions. Both features are surface expressions of residual soil and colluvium being transported into voids within the carbonate bedrock or overlying regolith. Both are generally circular in outline and are internally drained. They differ in that sinkholes exhibit a distinct break in the ground surface.

Both features are temporal and change character over a period of time. Surface depressions can become sinkholes and sinkholes can be filled, resembling depressions. Historical records and aerial photographs that cover a number of years can be useful tools in differentiating the two surface features.

The most significant factors in sinkhole development are (1) lithologic composition of the carbonate bedrock, (2) structural geology, (3) the movement of meteoric water through the vadose zone, and (4) fluctuations in the water table. Sinkhole development usually involves a combination of these factors (see Jennings, 1985, and Sweeting, 1973, for a discussion of the factors). Classic sinkhole localities such as the Saucon Valley of Lehigh County, the greater Harrisburg metropolitan area in Dauphin and Cumberland Counties, and the Nittany Valley in Blair, Centre, and Clinton Counties, typify the complexity and variability of sinkhole development.

LAND USE AND SUBSIDENCE PROBLEMS

Areas of karst in Pennsylvania are found in large and small northeast-trending valleys (Figure 49A–1). These are more desirable than the adjacent ridges as sites for homes, farms, industry, and transportation routes. The residual soil in these valleys is excellent for agriculture, and, in many places, the carbonate rock is a valuable mineral resource and is a host rock for some metallic ore deposits.

As population increases in these regions, rural areas are targeted for urban expansion. Figure 49A–5

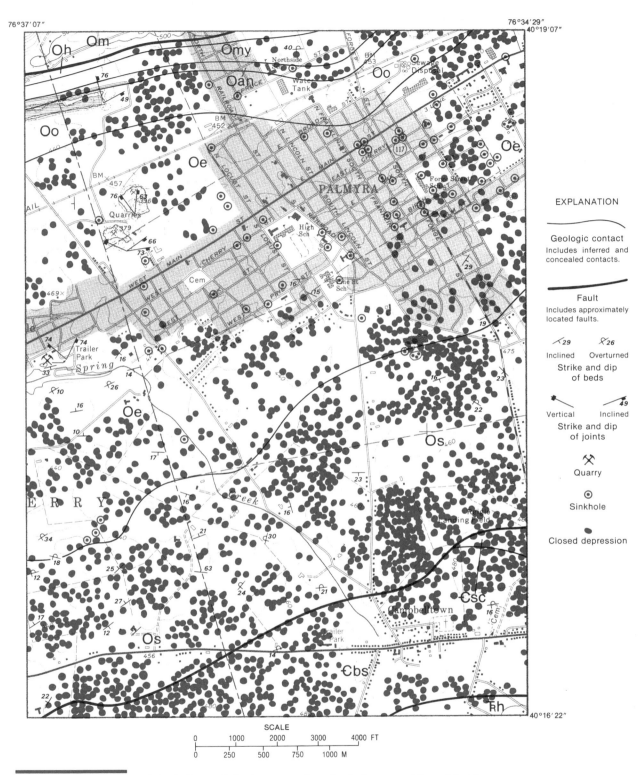

Figure 49A–3. Portion of the Palmyra 7.5-minute quadrangle, Lebanon and Dauphin Counties, showing the location of mapped sinkholes and closed-depression features (from Kochanov, 1988). Geologic units are as follows: Triassic—Ƭh, Hammer Creek Formation; Ordovician—Om, Martinsburg Formation; Oh, Hershey Formation; Omy, Myerstown Formation; Oan, Annville Formation; Oo, Ontelaunee Formation; Oe, Epler Formation; Os, Stonehenge Formation; and Cambrian—€sc, Snitz Creek Formation; €bs, Buffalo Springs Formation.

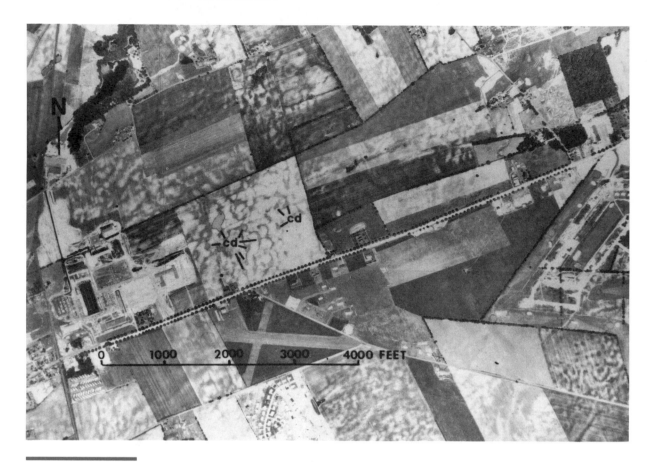

Figure 49A–4. Water-filled closed depressions (cd) in the northwest quarter of the Allentown West 7.5-minute quadrangle, Lehigh County (U.S. Department of Agriculture aerial photograph, 6–17–64, AQU–4EE–196).

shows the location of population centers within, or in close proximity to, the major carbonate regions of Pennsylvania. As these areas become increasingly developed, the potential for development in karstic areas and subsequent subsidence problems increases.

Intensive land use has led to many incidences of subsidence, principally in the form of sinkholes (Figure 49A–6). Subsidence processes may have developed slowly over months and years, but the final collapse generally takes place very rapidly.

Many carbonate units in Pennsylvania are prone to sinkhole development. In a study of sinkhole occurrences in the eastern half of the Great Valley section of the Ridge and Valley province, the Cambrian Allentown Formation and the Ordovician Epler Formation had the highest number of sinkholes (Kochanov, 1993). These two units accounted for approximately 85 percent of all recorded sinkholes in Northampton and Lehigh Counties. In the western half of the Great Valley section, stratigraphic equivalents of the Allentown and Epler Formations appear to follow the same

trends (e.g., Cambrian Richland and Zullinger Formations; Ordovician Rockdale Run Formation and St. Paul Group). Examples of carbonate units in the Piedmont province having a high incidence of sinkholes include the Cambrian Vintage and Ledger Formations, the Cambrian-Ordovician Conestoga Formation, and the Ordovician Stonehenge and Epler Formations. Some sinkholes have been recorded from the Upper Triassic limestone fanglomerates in the Piedmont. In the Appalachian Mountain section of the Ridge and Valley province, sinkhole-prone units include the Cambrian Gatesburg Formation, the Ordovician Stonehenge, Larke, Nittany, Benner, Nealmont, Salona, and Coburn Formations, the Silurian Tonoloway Formation, and the Silurian-Devonian Keyser Formation.

Subsidence in carbonate terranes is a natural process that is often disrupted by the activities of man. A number of man-induced factors can account for the majority of sinkhole occurrences. Examples vary from leaking water pipelines (Berry, 1986) to groundwater withdrawal from quarries (Foose, 1953). Many sink-

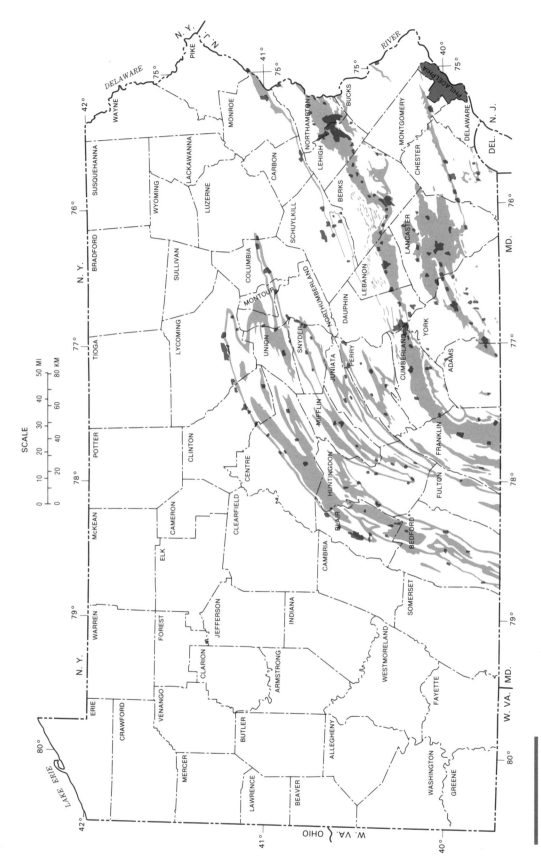

Figure 49A–5. Population centers (color) and carbonate bedrock (gray). Population centers are from Pennsylvania Department of Community Affairs (1969); carbonate areas are from Pennsylvania Geological Survey (1984).

Figure 49A–6. Sinkhole in the Ordovician Epler Formation on U.S. Route 322 in Hershey, Dauphin County, March 1983.

holes can be related to storm-water runoff and the facilities used to either convey, drain, or hold the water in storage (Kochanov, 1995; Figure 49A–7).

A primary cause for subsidence problems is the failure to be cognizant of karst processes and their impact, prior to land development. Most guidelines for construction are determined by the municipal governments. In some cases, the local zoning laws are ineffective or nonexistent in regulating land development in potential subsidence areas. There are special regulations, however, that have been established at the state level for construction of certain facilities, such as sanitary landfills.

Areas that have already undergone development have special problems in redesign and reconstruction. The after-the-fact methods of subsidence repair are often expensive and offer no guarantee that the problem will not recur. Sinkhole repair for Vera Cruz Road in Lehigh County cost nearly $800,000, and a new sinkhole opened, just outside the repair area, within six months (photograph on p. 712; Figure 49A–8).

CORRECTION AND PREVENTION

No two sinkholes are exactly alike. They may be narrow and deep with no apparent bedrock or

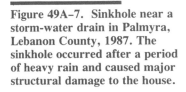

Figure 49A–7. Sinkhole near a storm-water drain in Palmyra, Lebanon County, 1987. The sinkhole occurred after a period of heavy rain and caused major structural damage to the house.

Figure 49A–8. Continued subsidence of an existing sinkhole caused a section of highway to collapse and severed a water line along Vera Cruz Road, Upper Saucon Township, Lehigh County.

wide and shallow with several pinnacles of bedrock appearing in the bottom and flanks (Figure 49A–9). Sinkholes are normally funnel shaped and have a well-defined tube or throat. The varied physical characteristics of sinkholes necessitate different design methods for repair. Methods vary from the use of concrete plugs and crushed rock to compacted clay and bentonite layers. Repair methods are often determined by public-safety factors, materials available, and economics. A sinkhole in the borough of Macungie, Lehigh County (Dougherty and Perlow, 1987), is an example of how a potentially hazardous situation was remedied by a thorough site investigation and cooperative efforts between local and state

governing officials, engineering consultants, and building contractors. These actions provided the necessary background information to determine an appropriate stabilization and repair plan. There is, however, a sequence of repair procedures that has proven to be successful in most cases. It can generally be followed with modifications dictated by special site conditions.

The procedure entails filling the sinkhole and controlling surface-water runoff to inhibit further subsidence. Efforts to bridge a sinkhole with elaborate structures are often frustrated by continued collapse (Figure 49A–8). It is important to stabilize the sinkhole by replacing the materials that erosion and weathering have removed. First, all loose, collapsed

Figure 49A–9. Naturally occurring sinkhole in the Cambrian Ledger Formation in Manchester Township, York County, showing pinnacles.

A

B

Figure 49A–10. Sinkhole repair in Whitehall Township, Lehigh County, winter 1981. A. Large rocks, 2 to 4 feet in diameter, are being placed at the bottom of the sinkhole prior to adding concrete. B. Concrete is vibrated to fill voids between the large rocks. C. After the rock and concrete plug is completed, layers of compacted soil are used to bring the collapsed area to grade.

C

material is removed from the sinkhole, and overhanging edges are cut back. Next, water is injected into the sinkhole to wash pinnacles, open throats, and test for further subsidence and drainage. In some cases, more than one throat is present. Then, several layers of large blocky rocks (Figure 49A–10A) are placed in the bottom. Concrete is then added to fill the voids between the rocks (Figure 49A–10B). This rock and concrete plug is allowed to cure, and the sinkhole is observed for evidence of further subsidence. In instances where bedrock is not visible, the concrete plug serves to surcharge the underlying materials to promote any minor subsidence before final backfilling commences. Finally, an impervious silty clay with the correct moisture content is compacted in layers (Figure 49A–10C), filling the sinkhole to grade. After the filling is complete, surface-water drainage is directed away from the area.

The different methods of sinkhole repair have evolved over the years for applications in urbanized areas. Sinkhole occurrences in rural areas usually do not have the same economic impact. Repair methods involve the use of available materials, typically soil and rocks. An alternative method is to treat the sinkhole as a natural point of recharge to local aquifers. The sinkhole is filled with aggregate of different sizes integrated with layers of filter fabric. The concept is to let surface water enter the sinkhole, which functions as a french drain and serves as a permanent recharge area. The use of sinkholes as recharge points has the drawback of increasing the potential for groundwater contamination.

Land development and building construction in carbonate bedrock terranes should be preceded by a subsurface investigation to clearly define subsidence-prone areas. Depending upon the nature of development that is planned, foundations can be designed to avert potential problems. Remedial backfilling or grouting can be undertaken, and storm-water runoff can be managed so that it is not locally directed into the ground.

PROBLEMS AND FUTURE RESEARCH

The distribution of sinkholes is not related solely to lithology, variations in solubility, or degree of structural deformation, but to a combination of these and other factors (Parizek and others, 1971). An accurate geological picture of subsurface site conditions must be determined to aid the engineer in effectively outlining the best methods for site preparation and construction in subsidence-prone areas (Knight, 1971). Remote-sensing techniques such as electrical resistivity and conductivity surveys (Smith and Riddle, 1984; Trojan, 1974), seismic methods (Belesky and others, 1987), and infrared and standard aerial photography have been used effectively as aids to site investigations. However, interpretation of the data is sometimes nebulous and is not always foolproof.

Statewide surveys of subsidence-prone areas (Kochanov, 1989) can help coordinate the efforts of planning groups so they can recognize problems during the planning stages of a project and minimize or eliminate subsidence problems in the future. Once base studies have been established, quantitative analyses of karst areas can be used to delineate carbonate units that have the greatest potential for sinkhole development (White and White, 1979; Myers and Perlow, 1984; Kochanov, 1993). This information would be invaluable to regional planners as a source of background information for more effective land use management. The information could also be used in developing or upgrading zoning laws within subsidence-prone areas.

Primarily, problems related to subsidence include the disruption of utility services and damages to private and public property. If a sinkhole occurs on private property, it is normally the responsibility of the property owner to initiate repairs. Home insurance often does not cover damages attributed to sinkholes. The problem becomes even more complicated if the cause of the sinkhole is questioned. Liability can become a major issue. Was the sinkhole an "act of God" or was it caused by a broken water line maintained by a municipality? Both points can be argued, and the homeowner is usually caught in the middle. Since 1987, however, sinkhole insurance has been available within Pennsylvania and may serve to eliminate the financial burdens placed on the homeowner.

Municipalities are responsible for maintaining public property within their jurisdiction. Yearly budgets are based on maintenance costs and are proportioned to handle specific activities. Catastrophic collapse, such as the sinkhole in the borough of Macungie (Dougherty and Perlow, 1987), can place undue strain on the economic stability of municipalities. With no state funds set aside for the repair of sinkholes, municipalities must be self sustaining with respect to sinkhole repair.

Several methods can be employed to offset the costs of sinkhole repair. Municipalities within a county could contribute money to a county loan pool. This would establish a financial base for handling the costs of repair due to subsidence and would be available for instances of catastrophic collapse. The state government could subsidize an insurance package providing assistance to those groups or individuals who currently reside within subsidence-prone areas. If new construction is proposed for an area, the banks or mortgage institutions could make sinkhole insurance mandatory as a part of the loan procedure.

The best method for dealing with karst subsidence problems is planning. Municipalities could minimize the potential for sinkhole development through proper maintenance and updating of existing utility lines. Zoning laws can also be enacted to regulate development within karst regions.

RECOMMENDED FOR FURTHER READING

Dougherty, P. H., and Perlow, Michael, Jr. (1987), *The Macungie sinkhole, Lehigh Valley, Pennsylvania: cause and repair,* in Beck, B. F., and Wilson, W. L., eds., *Karst hydrogeology: engineering and environmental applications,* Multidisciplinary Conference on Sinkholes and the Environmental Impacts of Karst, 2nd, Orlando, Fla., 1987, Proceedings, Rotterdam, A. A. Balkema, p. 425–435.

Jennings, J. N. (1985), *Karst geomorphology,* New York, Basil Blackwell, 293 p.

Knight, F. J. (1971), *Geologic problems of urban growth in limestone terrains of Pennsylvania,* Association of Engineering Geologists Bulletin, v. 8, p. 91–101.

Newton, J. G. (1987), *Development of sinkholes resulting from man's activities in the Eastern United States,* U.S. Geological Survey Circular 968, 54 p.

Sweeting, M. M. (1973), *Karst landforms,* New York, Columbia University Press, 362 p.

Trudgill, S. T. (1985), *Limestone geomorphology,* in Clayton, K. M., ed., *Geomorphology texts,* no. 8, New York, Longman, 196 p.

White, W. B., ed. (1976), *Geology and biology of Pennsylvania caves,* Pennsylvania Geological Survey, 4th ser., General Geology Report 66, 103 p.

Wilshusen, J. P. (1979), *Geologic hazards in Pennsylvania,* Pennsylvania Geological Survey, 4th ser., Educational Series 9, 56 p.

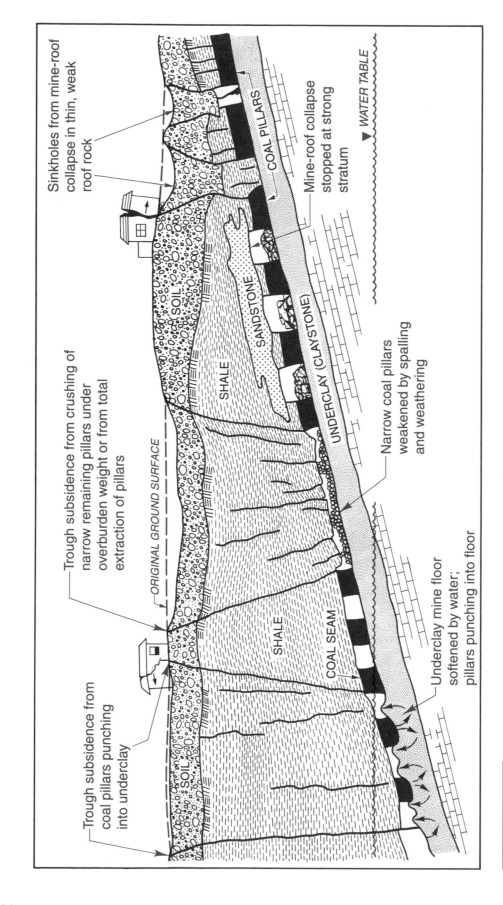

Figure 49B-1. Schematic drawing showing two modes of mine subsidence: sinkholes and troughs (modified from Bruhn and others, 1978, p. 48). Sinkholes are limited to areas of thin overburden. Trough subsidence can occur where the mining is at depths of several thousand feet.

Sinkholes from mine-roof collapse in thin, weak roof rock

Trough subsidence from crushing of narrow remaining pillars under overburden weight or from total extraction of pillars

ORIGINAL GROUND SURFACE

Trough subsidence from coal pillars punching into underclay

Mine-roof collapse stopped at strong stratum

COAL PILLARS

(SOIL)

SANDSTONE

SHALE

UNDERCLAY (CLAYSTONE)

▼ *WATER TABLE*

Narrow coal pillars weakened by spalling and weathering

SOIL

SHALE

COAL SEAM

Underclay mine floor softened by water; pillars punching into floor

CHAPTER 49B   LAND SUBSIDENCE—MINES

RICHARD E. GRAY
GAI Consultants, Inc.
570 Beatty Road
Monroeville, PA 15146

Underground mining has been used in Pennsylvania to extract metal ores (copper, iron, and zinc), clay and shale, limestone, and coal. Most of these deposits are of limited extent, so only small areas have been undermined. However, coal has been mined under large areas of the state. This mining poses a significant subsidence problem. Because of the widespread problem of coal-mine subsidence in Pennsylvania, the remainder of this chapter is limited to that topic.

Figure 37–1 shows the location of coal deposits in Pennsylvania. The anthracite fields have yielded 4.6 billion tons of coal and the bituminous fields over 9.3 billion tons, largely from underground mines (Gray and Bruhn, 1984). It has been estimated in a U.S. Bureau of Mines study that potential subsidence in urban areas resulting from coal mining threatens 54,400 acres in the anthracite fields and 97,000 acres in the bituminous fields (Johnson and Miller, 1979). Although the anthracite fields are more structurally complex than the bituminous fields, the most significant difference between the two areas from a subsidence standpoint is the large extent of multiple-seam mining in the anthracite fields.

SUBSIDENCE MODES

Subsidence features over mines are classified as sinkholes or troughs (Figure 49B–1). A sinkhole is a depression in the ground surface that occurs from collapse of the overburden into a mine opening (a room or an entry). A trough is a shallow, commonly broad, dish-shaped depression that develops when the overburden sags downward into a mine opening in response to coal extraction, crushing of mine pillars, or punching of pillars into the mine floor.

Sinkholes generally develop where the cover above a mine is thin (Figure 49B–2). Competent strata above the coal limit sinkhole development (Figure 49B–1). Piggott and Eynon (1978) indicated that sinkhole development normally occurs where the interval to the ground surface is less than three to five times the thickness of the extracted seam and

Figure 49B-2. Large sinkhole developed over a mine at shallow depth in the Pittsburgh coal.

the maximum interval is up to 10 times the thickness of the extracted seam. In western Pennsylvania, most sinkholes develop where the soil and rock above a mine are less than 50 feet thick (Bruhn and others, 1978). A study of subsidence in the Pittsburgh area revealed that the majority of sinkholes, which constituted about 95 percent of all reported subsidence incidents, occurred on sites located less than 60 feet above mine level (Bruhn and others, 1981).

Troughs develop over both active and abandoned mines. There appears to be no safe depth of mining that prevents trough development.

ABANDONED MINES

Underground mining has been practiced in Pennsylvania for over 200 years. Much of the early mining was not as efficient as that of today, and coal remains in many abandoned mines as pillars, commonly of variable size and spacing, which support the overlying strata. This is a potential subsidence problem, because heavily stressed pillars will eventually fail. The possibility of subsidence above an abandoned mine must be anticipated except where total extraction has been achieved, permitting subsidence concurrent with mining, or where large coal pillars adequate for long-term support remain in the mine. Figure 49B-3 shows subsidence damage in a building above an abandoned mine.

From the author's experience with subsidence over abandoned mines, it appears that (1) unless total extraction has occurred, there is no interval above an abandoned mine that is safe from subsidence, nor is there necessarily a reduction in severity of damage with increased intervals; (2) subsidence occurs at reduced frequency with increasing overburden thickness; (3) unless total extraction has been achieved, subsidence may occur long after mining and may not be limited to a single episode (Gray, 1988). Item (3) implies that the possibility of future subsidence at a site cannot be ruled out merely because subsidence has not occurred in the first 50 to 100 years after mining. If abandoned mine openings beneath a site have not been designed for long-term stability, the potential for subsidence remains until the openings collapse, or until they are stabilized by backfilling, grout columns, or some other means (Gray and others, 1974). Precisely when collapse might take place in the absence of stabilization is not predictable. Even after subsidence has taken place at a particular site, the possibility of future additional subsidence may remain. Multiple episodes of subsidence have been documented at many sites in the Pittsburgh region (Bruhn and others, 1978). Pillar failure can be delayed, progressive, or sporadic (Abel and Lee, 1983). Site surveillance programs of a few months' duration or, in fact, indefinite duration cannot provide definitive evidence that a site overlying a mine with open voids will experience no future subsidence (Bruhn and others, 1981).

Figure 49B–3. Building damaged by subsidence in western Pennsylvania. The abandoned mine is 175 feet below ground surface.

In some cases, activities by man, such as draining a mine, have hastened the onset of subsidence, if not initiated it. The latter concept was recognized in 1871 by the Belgian engineer G. Dumont, who noted that the draining of old workings or the flooding of a mine could reinitiate subsidence a long time after the initial movement had ceased (Young and Stoek, 1916).

Bruhn and others (1978), reporting on a study of the Pittsburgh coal, indicated annual costs for remedial measures and repairs of $438,000. Not included are costs of damage to commercial structures, utilities, or transportation rights-of-way, and the cost of engineering and construction measures undertaken to prevent or minimize subsidence damage.

ACTIVE MINES

With active mines, subsurface conditions are known; the time, amount, and areal extent of subsidence can be reasonably estimated; and surface developments can be designed to minimize the impact. Also, partial mining can be utilized so that coal pillars designed to support the ground surface are left in place, or construction of surface structures can be delayed until subsidence is complete.

Mining a small area underground initially results in small deformations of the mine roof and imperceptible movements at the ground surface. As the area of extraction increases, measurable movements occur at the ground surface. Although this subsidence involves primarily downward vertical movements, horizontal and small upward vertical movements may also occur. The surface expression of these movements is a large, shallow depression in the shape of a trough. In most cases, the surface area affected by subsidence exceeds the area of the seam extracted (Figure 49B–4). Where total extraction is practiced, subsidence is essentially contemporaneous with mining.

In a study of damage from active mining in western Pennsylvania, Bruhn and others (1982) reported home repair costs (1981 dollars) from a few hundred dollars to more than $100,000, the median repair cost being $6,000 to $10,000 per home.

PREVENTION AND CONTROL ALTERNATIVES

Consideration of surface owners' rights to protection from subsidence, a coal owner's right to mine, national energy needs, and potential impacts on land use and groundwater clearly indicates that subsidence prevention and control is a very complex socioeconomic problem. Alternative solutions include (1) land use controls, (2) insurance programs, (3) subsidence-resistant designs, and (4) selective support or mine filling.

Land use control such as zoning to limit mining or to limit construction in areas subject to subsi-

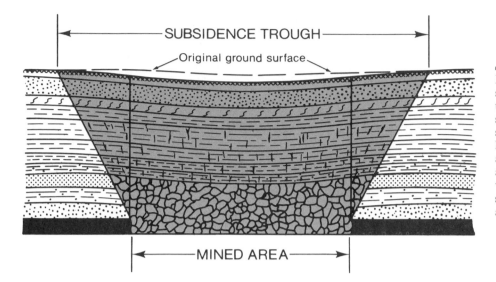

Figure 49B–4. Cross-sectional profile of a trough caused by mine subsidence. The affected surface area is normally larger than the mined area. Roof rock breaks and falls into the mine void, and the overlying strata sag into the mined area.

dence should be considered (U.S. Government Accounting Office, Report by Comptroller General, 1979). The potential magnitude of the subsidence problem in some areas is great enough to justify zoning controls in mining and surface development to protect the public from future subsidence costs. Landslide-prevention controls through site-grading requirements and floodplain zoning are examples of this approach in similar situations.

The Surface Mining Control and Reclamation Act of 1977 imposes land use controls on active mines. This law requires an evaluation of whether subsidence could occur and cause material damage or diminution of use of structures or renewable resource lands. If a potential for damage is present, a plan to prevent or mitigate the damage is required.

Insurance programs to provide assistance, if and when subsidence occurs, appear desirable (DuMontelle and others, 1981). Pennsylvania and seven other states have mine-subsidence insurance programs. Such an approach appears more desirable than large-scale urban stabilization programs for residential areas (Gray, 1983).

Subsidence-resistant designs appear to be a viable approach in areas of abandoned mines and may permit full extraction without serious structural damage in areas of active mining. The goal of subsidence-resistant designs is to minimize damage, because the complete prevention of damage is not cost effective. The difficulty the designer has is to select reasonable parameters of movement or force that will effectively minimize damage without a prohibitive cost. Chen and others (1974) summarized allowable ground de-

formations for active mining in Europe and Japan. However, a structure may not move in the same manner as the subsiding ground, because movements and strains in a structure depend on its design. Small structures are less likely to be damaged than large ones (Gray, 1988). Yokel and others (1981) and Michael Baker, Jr., Inc. (1974) suggested construction procedures for subsidence areas.

Site stabilization and special foundations for particular structures, based on detailed engineering evaluations, appear to be reasonable solutions. Large-scale urban stabilization programs for residential areas should be carefully considered. For example, a cost estimate of a coal-mine stabilization project in Wilkes-Barre, Pa., was over six times the value of the protected properties (A. W. Martin Associates, Inc., 1975). Measures commonly implemented to prevent or reduce subsidence may be grouped into two categories: (1) those providing general filling of mine voids to support the overburden, and (2) those providing only local support of the overburden or surface structures (Gray and others, 1974).

PROBLEMS AND FUTURE RESEARCH

Subsidence resulting from active mining can be reasonably predicted as to time and extent. However, for abandoned mines where coal pillars were not designed for long-term support or where total extraction was not achieved, the time and extent of subsidence are unpredictable and are likely to remain so.

Also, current knowledge does not permit accurate prediction of damage to buildings (Gray, 1988). The damage to structures in response to subsidence needs to be better documented if cost-effective designs to resist subsidence are to be utilized.

There is no zoning approach for the prevention or mitigation of subsidence damage. In active mine areas, restrictions on surface land use until full extraction and subsidence have occurred may be the best solution in some cases. In abandoned mine areas, surface developments could be restricted until studies to evaluate the subsidence potential have been completed, and preventive or control measures could then be implemented where necessary.

RECOMMENDED FOR FURTHER READING

Bell, F. G., ed. (1978), *Foundation engineering in difficult ground,* London, Newnes-Butterworths, 598 p.

_____ (1988), *The history and techniques of coal mining and the associatd effects and influence on construction,* Association of Engineering Geologists Bulletin, v. 25, p. 471–504.

Bruhn, R. W. (1980), *Mine subsidence in the Pittsburgh area,* in Adams, W. R., Jr., and others, *Land use and abuse—The Allegheny County problem,* Annual Field Conference of Pennsylvania Geologists, 45th, Pittsburgh, Pa., Guidebook, p. 25–35.

Bushnell, K. O. (1977), *Mine subsidence,* in Freedman, J. L., ed., *"Lots" of danger—Property buyer's guide to land hazards of southwestern Pennsylvania,* Pittsburgh Geological Society, p. 9–16.

Gray, R. E., and Meyers, J. F. (1970), *Mine subsidence and support methods in the Pittsburgh area,* American Society of Civil Engineers, Proceedings, Journal of the Soil Mechanics and Foundations Division, v. 96, p. 1267–1287.

Geddes, J. D., ed. (1978), *Large ground movements and structures* [Proceedings, 1st Conference on Large Ground Movements and Structures, Cardiff, Wales, 1977], New York, John Wiley and Sons, 1,064 p.

Holzer, T. L., ed. (1984), *Man-induced land subsidence,* Geological Society of America Reviews in Engineering Geology, v. 6, 221 p.

Institution of Civil Engineers (1977), *Ground subsidence,* London, Institution of Civil Engineers, 99 p.

Peng, S. S. (1978), *Coal mine ground control,* New York, Wiley Interscience, 450 p.

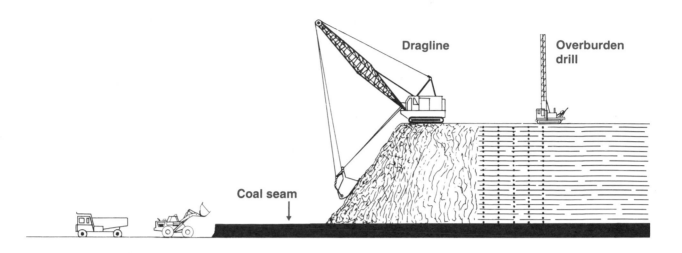

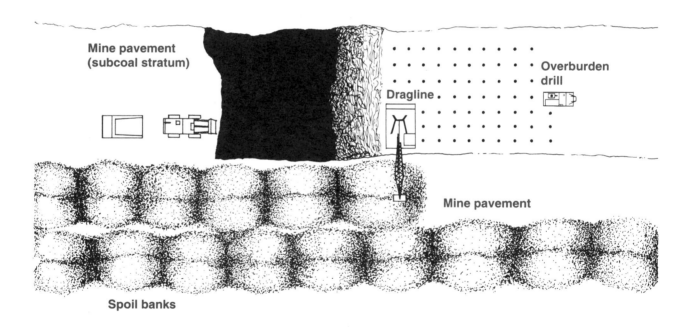

Figure 50–1. Major features of an area-type stripping operation. Blasted overburden is removed by a dragline and the coal is removed, exposing the mine pavement. Drawing by L. Rasmussen.

CHAPTER 50   MINING AND RECLAMATION

JAMES P. NAIRN
Civil and Environmental Consultants, Inc.
Foster Plaza 3
601 Holiday Drive
Pittsburgh, PA 15220

HAROLD L. LOVELL*
The Pennsylvania State University
120 West Mitchell Avenue
State College, PA 16803

JAMES M. KING
GAI Consultants, Inc.
1400 Airport North Office Park
Fort Wayne, IN 46825

INTRODUCTION

Mining, including surface, underground, and open-pit operations, was conducted in Pennsylvania before the 1680's and was instrumental in the development of the Commonwealth. Coal mining, bituminous in the west and anthracite in the northeast, was probably the most important of Pennsylvania's mining activities and continues to be a major industry. The mining of other nonmetallic substances remains viable, including limestone, dolostone, sandstone, slate, clay, micaceous filler, sand and gravel, and peat. Metal mining also played a vital role in the development of Pennsylvania, though the mining of metallic ores has not occurred since 1983 due to resource depletion, other competitive resources and sources, and economics. Production volumes and values for metallic ores of Pennsylvania can be obtained from Ridge (1968), Rose (1970), and Prosser and others (1985a).

Mine reclamation, a more recent development, has been required in some form since the mid-1960's. Although Pennsylvania was one of the first states to initiate, promulgate, and enforce environmental regulations related to mining, there remains a legacy of abandoned mines, waste piles, and degraded groundwater and surface water. Both coal and noncoal mining are regulated in order to minimize these impacts.

SURFACE MINING

Surface mining of bedded deposits is conducted primarily by contour and area methods in Pennsylvania. Geological conditions, economic constraints (e.g., overburden ratios, site reserves, and resource quality), and equipment selection usually dictate the mining method. Mining proceeds with bulldozers, front-end loaders, draglines, trucks, and material-handling equipment to recover and load the mineral. The beneficiation rejects are pumped to slurry or tailings dams for removal by sedimentation, and the supernatant liquid is recirculated.

In contour stripping, a coal seam is removed along and into a hillside until the overburden becomes uneconomical to remove in relation to the seam thickness (overburden-to-coal ratio). The storage of topsoil for later use, handling of the overburden material, and limiting pit-access time prior to backfilling have become critical environmental-planning considerations that are now required by law (Stefanko, 1978). Water- and sedimentation-control structures, such as diversion ditches and siltation basins, are fundamental to all surface-mining activities to minimize offsite environmental impacts. A mine is backfilled after coal removal to approximately replicate the original topography.

Area-type mining is a more recent development brought about by the availability of larger equipment (e.g., draglines, power shovels, front-end loaders, and off-road trucks) and is impractical for mines of less than 100 acres (Figures 50–1 and 50–2). The large area-mining operations tend to be concentrated near the fringes of the bituminous fields where the coal is continuous and the overburden is relatively thin.

Nonentry mining methods, such as auger mining, include techniques for mineral recovery from an available surface elevation. Augering is an extension of contour and area operations. Mechanical augers up to several feet in diameter extract coal under highwalls after the cost of removing additional overburden becomes prohibitive. It is possible to auger 200 feet into a seam.

Surface mining in Pennsylvania also includes open-pit mining. Pennsylvania's mineral commodities currently obtained via open-pit methods include clay, stone, sand, and gravel. These nonmetallic minerals have the most stable demand of all Pennsylvania minerals. Figure 50–3 shows an active open-pit quarry in Upper Ordovician carbonates at the Union Furnace Plant near Tyrone, Huntingdon County. In open-pit mining, as in any mining system, safe working conditions must be maintained while the production of quality ore is maximized. The operations must be economically competitive, but prevailing environmental regulations must be observed. The factors controlling open-pit mining include mineralization, geology, reserves, climate, capitalization, product market specificity, and pit-slope stability. The amount of waste material (overburden and development rock) handled is relatively small in contrast to surface coal production. Stone productivity typically exceeds 5 tons/manhour, whereas sand-gravel values are often double this amount. These products are seldom transported great distances owing to their wide distribution and low unit value (see Chapter 41C, Part 2).

Figure 50–4 shows a floating dredge and processing plant on the Allegheny River near Pittsburgh. The dredge mines sand and gravel deposits from the river bottom, processes the minerals, and returns waste rock and silt to the river in an environmentally acceptable manner.

UNDERGROUND MINING

Underground mining methods vary with the size, type, and configuration of the mineral deposit. The mining method is chosen to maximize safety, ore recovery, and competitiveness while minimizing undesirable environmental consequences.

Subsurface access to horizontal or gently dipping bedded deposits is gained by a drift entry or adit (a horizontal opening made directly into the outcrop of an orebody through a hillside), a slope entry (an inclined opening), or a shaft (a vertical entry affording access to the orebody). Nearly verti-

Figure 50–2. An area stripping operation in western Pennsylvania showing overburden drill, off-road truck, and dragline. Photograph courtesy of D. Spicuzza, Adobe Mining Company.

Figure 50–3. An active open-pit quarry at the Union Furnace Plant near Tyrone, Huntingdon County. Photograph courtesy of Atlas Powder Company.

Figure 50–4. Dredge Allegheny II, owned by Davison Sand and Gravel, on the Allegheny River near New Kensington, Westmoreland County. The floating dredge mines and processes sand and gravel and returns waste materials to the river. Photograph by J. Nairn.

cal, vein-type bodies are mined by sectioning the ore into blocks, which are recovered by one or more classical stoping methods, such as open-stope mining, shrinking stoping, stull stoping, or sublevel stoping. Cummins and Givens (1973) gave complete descriptions of these techniques. The underground parts of the Cornwall iron mines in Lebanon County and the Friedensville zinc orebody in Lehigh County were worked using a number of these techniques. Gray and Socolow (1959) discussed the geology, mineralogy, and mining methods employed at these and other eastern Pennsylvania mineral deposits. An excellent historical perspective of the mining history at Cornwall is also provided by Peets (1957).

Horizontal coal seams are mined underground by several methods employing distinctive types of equipment. Conventional room-and-pillar mining requires drills, cutting machines, blasting, and loading. A disadvantage of this method is the substantial volume of coal that must be left in place to support the mine roof. Although still practiced in the anthracite fields, conventional mining is only minimally practiced in Pennsylvania, having given way to more efficient techniques.

Continuous room-and-pillar mining systems (they are not continuous in operation) use a machine to extract coal from a seam and load it for conveyance to the surface. The machine cuts only a limited distance into the coal face so that the operator remains protected beneath roof-bolted strata. A variation of the room-and-pillar approach is retreat mining, in which coal-support pillars are systematically removed as the operation "backs out" of the mine (Figure 50–5). This technique is used in many of the older mines in Pennsylvania that have nearly depleted resources in order to enhance recovery prior to closure.

Longwall mining is a system for extracting large blocks of coal in a continuous operation. A moving, cylindrical cutter head undercuts the coal from a working face 600 to 1,000 feet wide. The coal falls onto a conveyor belt as the cutter alternately traverses the face in each direction, moving up the full height of the seam (Figure 50–6). Self-advancing hydraulic jacks or "chocks" support the roof at the working face to protect personnel and equipment. As the "chocks" advance toward the face, the roof behind is allowed to collapse in a controlled manner (Figure 50–7). The system is safe, results in high recov-

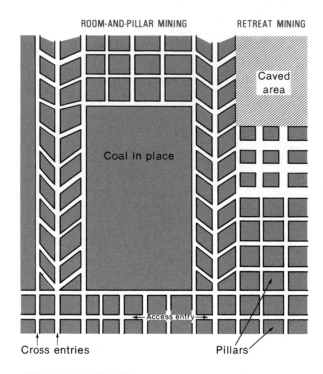

Figure 50-5. Major features of a room-and-pillar mining operation. Note the caving in the area where pillars were removed (retreat mining). Drawing by L. Rasmussen.

ery and productivity, and creates nearly immediate surface subsidence, if any. The equipment, however, is expensive, time-consuming to install, and must also be moved within the mine as each panel is completed. Longwall systems are currently used in sev-

eral areas of southwestern Pennsylvania, where continuous coal seams and substantial overburden thicknesses favor this mining method.

RECLAMATION AFTER MINING

Large areas of Pennsylvania have been negatively affected by mining activities. Major impacts from mining include surface-elevation changes and subsidence, modification of vegetation, the chemical degradation and flow redistribution of surface water and groundwater, the creation of mine voids and entry openings, adverse aesthetic impacts, and changes in land use. In 1988, the Pennsylvania Department of Environmental Resources (now the Department of Environmental Protection) estimated that more than 1,700 miles of streams, 166,000 acres of disturbed strip-mined lands, 600 acres of burning refuse, 1,400 dangerous highwalls, 1,200 vertical openings, and many other health and safety problems remained as legacies from past mining operations (A. E. Friedrich, personal communication, 1988). State and federal (U.S. Department of Labor, U.S. Environmental Protection Agency, and the Office of Surface Mining and Reclamation) laws now require occupational health, safety, and environmental protection in all mining activities. Environmental protection is accomplished through an application, permitting, inspection, and bonding system that includes surface restoration to approximate original contour; surface-water and water-quality controls; controls on the effects of dust, noise, and vibrations on nearby areas; and the use of mining-

Figure 50-6. The working face of a longwall mining unit at the Bailey mine in southwestern Pennsylvania. Workers are protected by movable "chocks," or shields. The cutting head moves along the face of the exposed coal seam. Coal drops onto a belt and is conveyed to the surface. Photograph courtesy of Consolidation Coal Company.

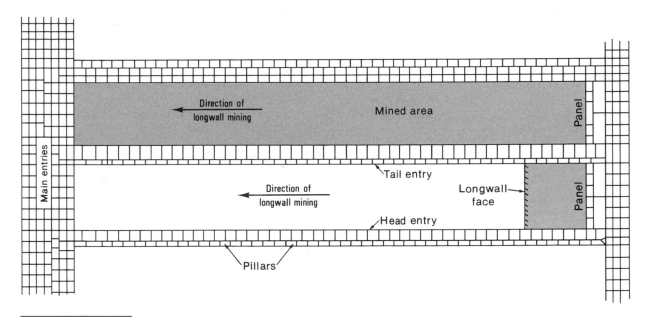

Figure 50–7. Major features of a typical longwall mining operation. Drawing by L. Rasmussen.

area haulage systems. Water-quality control is mandated by the National Pollution Discharge Elimination System (NPDES), and the treatment of degraded waters is commonly necessary (see Chapter 51). The Department of Environmental Protection also manages a program to mitigate environmental problems stemming from abandoned mined areas and encourages the remining of these areas as a means of reclamation.

Several Pennsylvania laws, including the Bituminous Mine Subsidence and Land Conservation Act (April 27, 1966), the Coal Refuse Disposal and Control Act (September 24, 1968), and the Surface Mining Conservation and Reclamation Act (May 31, 1945), served as foundations for the comprehensive, federally mandated Surface Mining Control and Reclamation Act (SMCRA). Passed on August 3, 1977, SMCRA provides minimum standards for mining and reclamation activities throughout the United States. It also regulates the surface activities and facilities of underground mines, such as shafts, buildings, roads, and refuse areas, and provides for the reclamation of abandoned mined lands. The programs resulting from the law are funded by a tax surcharge on every ton of coal mined in the country. The funds are distributed to the individual states to be used in ameliorating dangerous and unacceptable conditions resulting from past mining.

In the late 1960's, Pennsylvania launched its own environmental program to deal with the impacts of past mining activities. This ambitious program, known as "Operation Scarlift," encompassed the rec-

lamation of polluted streams, the extinguishment of mine and refuse fires, and the reclamation of orphaned lands. Operation Scarlift served as a forerunner for similar programs developed by other states and the federal government.

Pennsylvania's coal-mining regulations, which are administered by the Department of Environmental Protection, contain provisions aimed at minimizing the adverse impacts of surface and underground coal mining by establishing design and/or performance standards, bonds, civil penalties, and avenues for public participation in the mine-permitting process. The regulations also include provisions that specifically protect prime farmlands, single-source aquifers and water supplies, schools, public buildings, and items or areas of cultural and historical significance. Provisions have also been made to allow certain areas of the Commonwealth to be designated as unsuitable for mining because there is a high probability that environmental damage would ensue from mining in those areas. Examples of areas declared unsuitable for mining are the Cold Stream watershed in Centre County and the North Fork Tangascootack Creek area of Clinton County. The former was judged by the Bureau of Mining and Reclamation to be unsuitable for mining because of probable adverse impacts on a drinking-water supply. The latter was declared unsuitable because of potential impacts on a native trout fishery.

A parallel set of state regulations (25 Pennsylvania Code, Chapter 77, Non-Coal Mining) addresses surface mining of minerals other than coal. These regulations implement the Non-Coal Surface Mining Conservation and Reclamation Act of December 19, 1984 (P.L. 1093, No. 219).

Surface subsidence resulting from underground mining continues to be a major concern of those impacted by the mining industry (see Chapter 49B). Despite the use of deep-mine roof-support methods, some subsidence will eventually occur. Many older mines with support pillars have subsidence problems 30 to 80 years after closure due to pillar spalling and floor failure. For this reason, many within the industry favor complete mineral extraction, which results in nearly immediate subsidence. Some mitigation can then be accomplished as mining proceeds. Complete-extraction techniques (room-and-pillar retreat and longwall mining) tend to impact surface water and groundwater to a greater degree than conventional room-and-pillar mining, which leaves more surface support. Recent studies (Bruhn, 1985; Bruhn, personal communication, 1988) indicate that pillar extraction and longwall mining may improve groundwater productivity in areas of thick overburden. These studies have also indicated that groundwater levels in subsided areas may rapidly fall initially, but then gradually recover to near premining levels.

Another major environmental concern in Pennsylvania is mineral-waste disposal. Past disposal practices have dotted Pennsylvania's landscape with unsightly refuse piles and equally unaesthetic and potentially dangerous slurry or tailings dams (Figure 50-8). Many of the refuse piles contain combustible materials that cause long-term air-quality problems if ignited. Burning refuse piles have also been linked to major underground coal fires, such as those at Centralia and Shamokin in the Anthracite region of Pennsylvania.

Reject wastes containing sulfide minerals degrade groundwater and surface water coming into contact with them. Coal refuse piles have historically been prolific sources of acid drainage, although the mining of sulfide ores, such as those at Friedensville in Lehigh County, is also a source of acid pollution.

Pennsylvania law currently requires residuals from mining to be managed in ways that minimize environmental impacts. In the late 1980's, The Department of Environmental Resources required the mining industry to install low-permeability liners and leachate-collection systems beneath some refuse piles in Clearfield and Indiana Counties, to provide waste compaction to reduce combustion hazards, and to provide graded and vegetated soil covers on disposal areas to reduce water-quality problems and mitigate their aesthetically displeasing aspects (Figure 50-9).

It is likely that Pennsylvania will continue to modify its laws to reflect additional environmental awareness. Stricter controls on reclamation, perhaps specifically addressing the disposal of mining residuals, are likely. State and federal laws and programs have historically placed an emphasis on environmental preservation and reclamation. As in the past, it seems likely that Pennsylvania will be at the forefront of these programs.

PROBLEMS AND FUTURE TRENDS

A perennial problem facing the mining industry is the delicate balance between maintaining economic competitiveness while dealing with various safety, health, and environmental pressures. A case in point is the emergence of longwall mining systems

Figure 50–8. Typical slurry or tailings (coal-fines) impoundment in Pennsylvania's Anthracite region.

Figure 50-9. Aerial view of a coal-refuse disposal area at Warwick mine in Greene County. Vegetation has been established directly on the refuse. Photograph courtesy of Duquesne Light Company, August 1981.

in the last decade, particularly in the Pittsburgh coal seam in southwestern Pennsylvania. As many as 10 longwall units are currently in place in the region. The use of this efficient technique, however, has been seriously curtailed by political pressures stemming from concerns over subsidence and impacts on surface-water and groundwater resources. Additional research is needed to provide reliable techniques for predicting the impacts of this mining method.

In a related matter, mining permits are being evaluated and "lands unsuitable" petitions are being reviewed on the basis of overburden analyses that have limited predictive value. Additional research is therefore imperative to develop valid, practical, and cost-effective methods for predicting mining impacts on water quality.

Much of the current mining research conducted by the U.S. Bureau of Mines and various universities is centered on acid-mine-drainage abatement and/or reduction of treatment costs. Some relatively recent applications that show promise include the use of surfactants and "constructed wetlands" for mine-drainage treatment. Acid drainage is considered in more detail in Chapter 51.

If the past is any indication of future trends, the coal and noncoal mining industries should antici-

pate increasing levels of regulation. Hopefully, these new regulations will be focused to allow the controlled use of our natural resources and affirm their historical and economic significance in the Commonwealth.

RECOMMENDED FOR FURTHER READING

Behre, C. H., Jr. (1933), *Slate in Pennsylvania*, Pennsylvania Geological Survey, 4th ser., Mineral Resource Report 16, 400 p.

Cassidy, S. M., ed., (1973), *Elements of practical coal mining*, New York, Society of Mining, Metallurgical and Petroleum Engineers, 614 p.

O'Neill, B. J., Jr. (1964), *Limestones and dolomites of Pennsylvania*, Pennsylvania Geological Survey, 4th ser., Mineral Resource Report 50, Pt. 1, 40 p.

_____ (1974), *Greater Pittsburgh region construction aggregates*, Pennsylvania Geological Survey, 4th ser., Mineral Resource Report 67, 60 p.

Sholes, M. A., and Skema, V. W., compilers (1974), *Bituminous coal resources in western Pennsylvania*, Pennsylvania Geological Survey, 4th ser., Mineral Resource Report 68, scale 1:250,000, 7 sheets.

Thomas, L. J. (1973), *An introduction to mining*, Sydney, Hick, Smith and Sons.

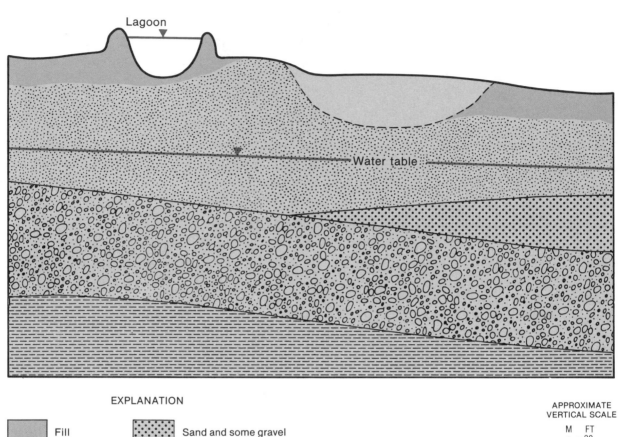

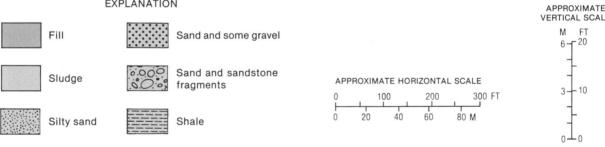

Figure 51–1. Geologic cross section of the deposits beneath a waste impoundment. The contaminated aquifer extends the range of the units shown. The flow rate of leachate varies from one unit to another.

CHAPTER 51 WASTE DISPOSAL AND WATER CONTAMINATION

DANIEL THRELFALL
Chemviron, Inc.
505 William Pitt Way
Pittsburgh, PA 15238

BURT A. WAITE
Moody and Associates, Inc.
R. D. 4, Cotton Road
Meadville, PA 16335

WILLIAM R. GOUGH
Moody and Associates, Inc.
R. D. 4, Cotton Road
Meadville, PA 16335

INTRODUCTION

Contamination from inadequate or uncontrolled waste disposal is a serious threat to the quality of surface water and groundwater in Pennsylvania. It presents a hazard to human health and the environment and can have significant economic impacts in the public or private sector. It also causes a general reduction in the quality of life where it occurs.

The release of harmful levels of pollutants into the surrounding environment will occur at any location where waste products are mishandled. Pennsylvania has its own particular set of factors that further influence the occurrence of water contamination. The state has long supported the nation as a center of industry and has been a leader in coal mining, oil and gas production, petrochemicals, steel, and general manufacturing. These industries were producing and disposing waste products long before the need for environmental protection was identified. Many of the contamination problems in Pennsylvania stem from waste-disposal activities that were initiated years before adequate environmental legislation existed to control them.

Pennsylvania's humid climate is also a factor. The abundance of precipitation, surface water, and groundwater provides a medium that can remove pollutants from waste products and form a leachate that carries these pollutants into the surrounding environment. Leachate has contaminated aquifers, surface water, household wells, and public water supplies at locations throughout the state.

The particular geologic conditions associated with a waste-disposal site control or have a high degree of influence over the generation and flow of leachate. In Pennsylvania, the diverse geology provides a wide range of conditions in which water contamination can occur.

TYPES OF INADEQUATE WASTE DISPOSAL

Landfills have been, and continue to be, the primary method of solid waste disposal in Pennsylvania.

Wastes going to landfills include household or municipal garbage, residues from industrial processes, ash from the burning of coal, and discarded materials from other sources. In Pennsylvania, as in other states, landfills were originally located for convenience. They were often located in abandoned mines, gravel pits, and unused ravines, or along hillsides close to centers of waste generation, regardless of the potential to contaminate water supplies. Few, if any, measures were provided to control leachate or protect water supplies at early landfills.

Unlined impoundments are another source of water contamination. These have been associated with a variety of industrial activities in which liquid or semi-solid waste was retained. In the oil and gas districts of Pennsylvania, for example, small impoundments or production pits were the accepted method of managing brine water for many oil wells (Waite, 1982). Until recently, many industrial-waste impoundments were unlined and located where leachate could easily transport contaminants into underlying aquifers or into nearby rivers.

Coal-refuse piles are another form of inadequate waste disposal. Many abandoned piles contain iron sulfides that react with oxygen and infiltrating water to form an acidic leachate containing high levels of dissolved iron, manganese, sulfate, and other pollutants. Although the chemical-producing acids are reduced through time, it is often a very slow process, and water degradation may continue for years.

Not all waste sources of water contamination are associated with industry. On-lot septic systems, the historically accepted method of domestic sewage disposal in rural Pennsylvania, also contribute to the contamination of groundwater, private water wells, and nearby surface water. Overcrowded and uncontrolled installation of septic systems has overloaded the natural capacity of soil to alleviate or break down pollutants.

Until the 1960's and 1970's, little consideration was given to environmental aspects of geologic parameters. As the dangers and hazards of inadequate waste-disposal practices became apparent, the importance of geology as a factor in the occurrence or prevention of contamination was realized.

GEOLOGY AND WATER DISPOSAL

The overall geologic framework at an inadequate waste-disposal site will determine if, and to what extent, water contamination will occur. Specific conditions at each site are different, but the common parameters to be considered are topography, unconsolidated deposits, and bedrock characteristics, and the relationship of these factors to groundwater and surface-water hydrology. The most important aspect of these parameters is how they influence the generation and movement of leachate.

Topography

Topography has some obvious influences on the formation and generation of leachate. Examples include sites where wastes were disposed in low-lying areas near, or even below, the water table, where pollutants can be constantly leached. Although this situation is not unique to Pennsylvania, the extensive industrial areas that developed along major river valleys have resulted in a large number of low-lying impoundments or landfills where pollutants are easily leached into both surface water and groundwater.

Topography can also concentrate the flow of surface water toward improperly disposed waste. In the coal fields of southwestern Pennsylvania, abandoned strip cuts accumulate water, which can provide an ongoing source of fluid to leach pollutants from nearby spoil piles.

Unconsolidated Deposits

There is an extremely wide range of unconsolidated deposits in Pennsylvania. With glacial deposits in portions of the northern part of the state, saprolite in portions of the southeast, and a variety of soils, colluvium, and alluvium throughout, the need for site-specific information where improper waste disposal has occurred cannot be overstated.

Permeability and textural characteristics will influence the rate, extent, and direction of leachate flow through porous unconsolidated deposits. Problems caused by waste disposal in low-lying areas have already been mentioned. Not only can such sites be close to the water table, but many are underlain by coarse sands and gravel that allow leachate to flow at a high rate into alluvial aquifers and river waters. Alluvium in major river valleys, such as the Susquehanna, Allegheny, and Ohio Valleys, is an important source of high-quality groundwater where not impacted by contamination.

In addition to permeability of unconsolidated deposits, vertical and horizontal textural variations are important. The highly variable nature of glacial deposits and the manner in which they can influence the flow of leachate is a good example of this. Dense, fine-grained till may slow the rate of leachate flow. Overlying, less compact till or adjacent sand and gravel deposits may allow rapid expansion of a contamination plume. The large number of contacts associated with drift can serve as flow paths for contamination. Contacts between till and outwash and between till and bedrock, as well as the contact between one till layer and another, can all serve as flow zones. These contacts can allow eventual discharge into other drift deposits that are productive sources of groundwater.

Bedrock

The flow of groundwater and leachate through bedrock presents different concerns than their flow through porous unconsolidated deposits. Folds, faults, bedding planes, and other geologic structures influence leachate and groundwater flow in bedrock. Open fractures, whether occurring in isolated zones or in large, complex systems, such as those found in the limestone areas of central Pennsylvania, normally allow a high rate of flow. Also, the direction and extent of leachate flow through fractures is much less predictable than in porous media.

In Pennsylvania, multiaquifer systems separated by lower permeability strata are common, and different water-bearing units underlying the same site can have a wide variation in chemical quality and flow characteristics. Natural barriers of shale may inhibit the flow of contamination between aquifers, but fractures may allow hydraulic communication between them.

Geologic Investigations

Geologic investigations at waste-disposal sites must be planned to take into account local geologic variations. Geologic reconnaissance, test borings, core drilling, test pits, and, where appropriate, geophysical techniques are common investigative tools at contamination sites. The installation of monitoring wells to allow sampling of groundwater to detect leachate is an essential part of most investigations. Pump tests are often done to determine the extent of hydraulic communication between various water-bearing units. All of these techniques may be used at a given site, but in some cases, there may be an emphasis on using a few particular techniques.

EXAMPLES OF GEOLOGIC FACTORS AT CONTAMINATED SITES IN PENNSYLVANIA

Alluvial Setting

An unlined waste-disposal site in north-central Pennsylvania was located on alluvial deposits consisting of an upper zone of silty sand and a lower zone of sand and sandstone fragments (Nazar and others, 1984). These sediments overlaid fractured shale bedrock (Figure 51–1). This combination of units formed a single aquifer that discharged into an adjacent river. Each of three units had a different permeability. Leachate flow toward the river was most rapid in the sand and gravel. The flow rate was significantly slower in the fractured shale and even slower in the upper silty sand horizon.

Multilevel groundwater samplers were installed in bore holes. Analysis showed that contaminants were not uniformly distributed in the leachate plume. Some contaminants were concentrated in the lower zones, whereas others were concentrated near the top of the plume. The chemical stratification caused certain contaminants to enter the river at varying rates, depending on whether the contaminants occurred within the silty sand, sand and gravel, or fractured shale. Without sampling of the vertical distribution of contamination in a single aquifer, the chemical nature and rate of leachate flow would not have been thoroughly understood, possibly inhibiting the effectiveness of remedial efforts.

Bedrock Setting in a Mined Area

An investigation was conducted to determine groundwater conditions, extent of contamination, and needed remedial action at a site located over coal-bearing bedrock in western Pennsylvania (Dowiak and others, 1982). Locally, the geologic structure consisted of subparallel anticlines and synclines having a northeast trend, gently dipping sedimentary strata, and multiaquifer conditions. Rocks of the Monongahela Group and underlying Conemaugh Group are exposed.

The Pittsburgh coal, which is at the base of the Monongahela Group, was mined in the 1920's and 1930's using the room-and-pillar method. Where it was economical, surface mining was used to extract pillars in the 1930's and 1950's. Surface mining resulted in an abandoned pit that was elongate and followed the contour of the land. A bedrock highwall formed one side of the pit, and piles of coarse mine spoil formed another (Figure 51–2). The beginning and end of the elongated pit consisted of bedrock or mine spoil.

The pit was later used as an unlined industrial-waste impoundment. The principal wastes were pickling acids (neutralized with lime) and heavy-metal sludges. At that time, no barriers were required to control leachate. As environmental legislation became more strict, this disposal operation could no longer meet regulatory compliance. The owner and the Pennsylvania Department of Environmental Resources (now Department of Environmental Protection) agreed to investigate site conditions and develop an effective plan to close the site.

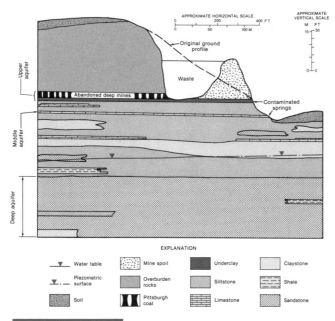

Figure 51–2. Cross section of a waste impoundment and its relationship to geology, deep mining, and aquifers.

The groundwater investigation was designed to determine the existence, lateral extent, and depth of groundwater contamination. The major investigative techniques utilized were test borings, monitoring wells, water-quality analyses, and in-situ aquifer tests. The geologic investigation revealed three aquifers. An upper aquifer occurred in bedrock, in an abandoned deep mine, and in mine spoil lying above the coal underclay. A middle aquifer occurred in a limestone unit approximately 5 to 15 feet below the base elevation of the waste and coal seam. A deep aquifer was found approximately 100 feet below the base elevation of the waste in a sandstone unit. Evidence of contamination was found in the upper and middle aquifers, but the deep aquifer was unaffected.

Investigation to determine the lateral extent of contamination showed that groundwater from the two affected aquifers discharged as springs. As a result, contaminated groundwater could be collected and treated after discharge to the surface. After the investigation, the solidified gypsiferous waste was covered with an impermeable barrier to minimize rainfall infiltration and reduce further development of leachate.

ENVIRONMENTAL LEGISLATION CONTROLLING WASTE DISPOSAL

Control over waste disposal and water quality is maintained by the Pennsylvania Department of Environmental Protection (formerly Department of Environmental Resources). Regulations have become more strict as environmental awareness has increased. Requirements for the closure of old sites, siting of new ones, and design and operating standards for waste disposal have been established.

Geologic factors have been given strong regulatory consideration in all phases of waste disposal. Waste-disposal sites will not be permitted in floodplains or other geologically high-risk areas. Standards have been established for groundwater conditions at new waste-disposal sites and must be met in order for a permit to be issued. Ongoing water-quality-monitoring programs must be in effect at landfills, and unlined hazardous-waste landfills are no longer allowed. Leachate controls, waste and leachate treatment, and long-term monitoring and care of landfills must be implemented. The Department of Environmental Protection is also developing a comprehensive groundwater protection strategy for the entire state.

At the federal level, two major regulatory actions have been initiated. The first is the Resource Conservation and Recovery Act of 1976 (RCRA), which was revised in 1980 and again in 1984 to respond to technological changes, population expansion, and economic growth that present new environmental challenges. The primary goals of RCRA are to protect human health and the environment from the possible hazards of waste disposal, to conserve energy and natural resources, to reduce the amount of waste generated, and finally, to ensure that waste is managed in an environmentally sound manner.

Problems associated with past mismanagement of hazardous waste are covered by RCRA's companion law, the Comprehensive Environmental Response, Compensation, and Liability Act of 1980 (CERCLA, or Superfund). This law provides broad federal authority and resources to respond directly to releases (or threatened releases) of hazardous substances. Costs for the first five years of the U.S. Superfund program were covered by a $1.6 billion Hazardous Substance Response Trust Fund, which was increased to $8.6 billion in 1986. This fund is used to pay for cleanup of abandoned or uncontrolled hazardous-waste sites. The law also authorizes enforcement action and cost recovery from those responsible for a release. As of June 30, 1994, 100 sites in Pennsylvania were on the federal Superfund list (Figure 51–3). Most sites are in the southeast part of the state; Montgomery and Chester Counties have the highest number. Since the list was issued, eight toxic-waste sites have been cleaned up (Pennsylvania Department of Environmental Resources, 1994, p. 19).

In October 1988, Pennsylvania adopted Act 108, entitled the Hazardous Sites Cleanup Act (HSCA,

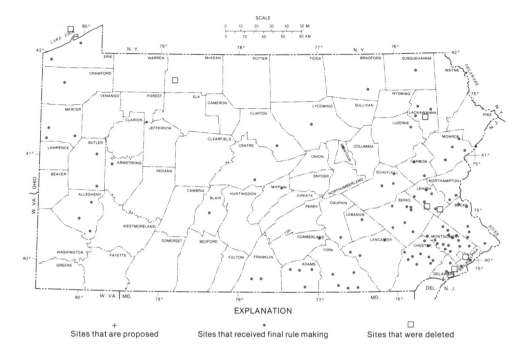

Figure 51–3. Location of sites on the National Priority List of the U.S. Environmental Protection Agency (U.S. Superfund sites) (from Pennsylvania Department of Environmental Resources, 1994, p. 24).

EXPLANATION

+   •   □
Sites that are proposed   Sites that received final rule making   Sites that were deleted

or Pennsylvania Superfund). This legislation enables the Department of Environmental Protection to contribute to the cleanup of U.S. Superfund sites and to clean up other sites not on the national priority list. It provides permanent sources of funding for the program and enhances the department's authority to respond to spills and environmental emergencies. By June 30, 1994, the Department of Environmental Resources had initiated cleanups at 45 hazardous-waste sites covered by the federal Superfund program. The Department anticipated that 100 sites covered by HSCA would be cleaned up by the year 2000 (Pennsylvania Department of Environmental Resources, 1994, p. 4).

PROBLEMS AND FUTURE RESEARCH

Abating and preventing contamination from improper waste disposal is a relatively new technology. Much research is needed, and many problems remain to be solved. Only a few are mentioned here.

1. Pennsylvania is one of the most industrialized states, yet few hazardous-waste-disposal facilities are presently available in the state for use by industry. The Pennsylvania Department of Environmental Protection, the industrial community, and the general public must face the realities of this problem. Practical solutions must be developed in order to retain industry and, at the same time, protect surface water and groundwater. In addition, new methods of waste treatment, reuse, or recycling are needed to minimize future land burial of waste materials and reduce the potential for water contamination.

2. A better understanding and improved investigative techniques are required for flow in fractured rock. Field investigative methods are needed that can provide useful results economically. Theoretical approaches to this problem do not usually provide solutions within a practical budget.

3. The concept of natural geologic barriers to contaminant flow should be further evaluated to determine the long-term effectiveness of groundwater protection. This could be an important factor in the siting of new waste-disposal facilities, the selection of remedial measures for contaminated sites, the development of groundwater-monitoring programs, and the designation of aquifer classifications.

RECOMMENDED FOR FURTHER READING

Barcelona, M. J., Gibb, J. P., Helfrich, J. A., and Garske, E. E. (1985), *Practical guide for ground water sampling,* Champaign, Ill., Illinois State Water Survey, Department of Energy and Natural Resources, Report 374, 94 p.

Driscoll, F. G. (1986), *Groundwater and wells,* 2nd ed., St. Paul, Minn., Johnson Division, 1,089 p.

U.S. Environmental Protection Agency (1985), *Handbook—remedial action at waste disposal sites,* revised, U.S. Environmental Protection Agency, Report EPA/615/6–85/006, 681 p.

An artist's portrayal of the fire at the Stone Bridge during the Great Johnstown Flood of 1889. Photograph courtesy of Louise Bem (Johnstown Flood Centennial Project) and the Johnstown Flood Museum.

CHAPTER 52   FLOODING

GERT ARON
  212 Sackett Building
  Department of Civil Engineering
  The Pennsylvania State University
  University Park, PA 16802

INTRODUCTION

Flooding is best defined as nature's way of claiming or reclaiming its natural rights-of-way for storm runoff. Occasional freak storms may be of a nature that could not have been reasonably foreseen, and some flooding may be caused by natural catastrophic events like earthquakes or landslides. Most flood events, however, are merely the logical and natural consequence of snow or rain precipitation events entirely within the realm of normal expectations, coupled occasionally with man's folly in believing that he has conquered the earth.

FLOODING CAUSES AND EFFECTS

Flooding in Pennsylvania is usually associated with abnormally high and intense rainfall amounts. In addition, however, flooding can be caused by sudden snowmelt, landslides, or dam failures.

If a flood is caused by rainfall, the duration, intensity, and total amount of precipitation may be important. In general, the critical duration of a storm is roughly equal to the longest time that it takes for rainwater to travel from the point of impact to the outflow point of a watershed. The runoff travel time through a small urban watershed (see Chapter 55C) may, by observations of runoff speeds and simple calculations, be estimated as 20 to 30 minutes. In this case, a 1-inch cloudburst of 30 minutes' duration is likely to produce much more serious flooding on such a small watershed than a broad-scale hurricane-type storm like "Agnes" in 1972 (see Appendix 52A), in which 8 to 12 inches of rain fell in many areas of Pennsylvania over a time span of about 60 hours. On the other hand, scattered intense thunderstorms are not likely to have any major effects on the Susquehanna River stage in Harrisburg, with a total drainage area of 22,400 square miles upstream from that city, and a corresponding travel time of roughly 3 days. For this reason, the persistent 1972 storm Agnes had its most dramatic flooding effects on locations with several thousand square miles of drainage area, such as Wilkes-Barre and Harrisburg (see Appendix 52A).

Although most of the major historic Pennsylvania floods have occurred in the summer, occasionally, as in March 1936, flooding has been caused by a moderate warm winter rain following a deep snow accumulation. Furthermore, and particularly in small drainage areas, frozen surfaces can more than double the normal runoff velocities, causing flash floods aggravated by ice and debris jams in channels and culverts.

Flood effects can be volume- or force-related. Major floods along larger streams having wide floodplains tend to result in large-scale inundations, which cause widespread damage through soaking and silt deposits in homes, businesses, and industrial plants, but which seldom result in a major loss of life. When they occur early in the year, such floods may sometimes be beneficial to agricultural soils because organic sediments are deposited on the land. In more hilly regions, on the other hand, where runoff paths are steep, flash floods may be prevalent. In these floods, the velocity rather than the volume of water is chiefly responsible for flood damages. Torrents of water roar down minor hillside gullies at 30 to 50 miles per hour, carrying trees, debris, and rocks and destroying everything in their paths. These floods are the least predictable and, particularly if they occur at night, often cause major panic and loss of life.

Landslides and avalanches can have disastrous flood effects because of the suddenness of their occurrence. Such slides may descend directly onto towns and villages, and may block a stream, forcing the water to back up. Moreover, there commonly are no economically feasible measures of prevention or protection against such occurrences, except for staying away from areas prone to slides. This action could, however, eliminate such large areas of land that it would become practically impossible to find a safe place to live. Flat lowlands may be floodplains, valleys may be subject to flash floods, and hillside developments can lead to landslides, which leaves only high plateaus as safe development ground.

Dam failures may or may not leave enough time for evacuation of people and property, depending on their abruptness. Seepages in earth dams usually develop gradually, and, if the embankment damage is detected early, downhill residents have at least a few hours or days to evacuate. Failures of concrete or masonry dams, on the other hand, tend to occur suddenly, sending a wall of water and debris down the valley at more than 100 miles per hour, and survival would be a matter of having the good fortune not to be in the flood path at the time of the break. Dam failures due to overtopping of a dam normally give sufficient lead time for evacuation, but in the late-night storm of the 1977 Johnstown flood, the filling of the lake and overtopping of the Laurel Run dam went unnoticed; hence, the dam break came as a complete surprise, even though it probably occurred over a time span of roughly one hour.

The locations of major cities, streams, and reservoirs cited in this chapter are shown in Figure 52-1.

FLOOD EXPERIENCES

Pennsylvania has a long and continuous history of floods. Rainfall in Pennsylvania is about average for the eastern United States, but the relatively steep topography in large parts of the state promotes quick and flashy runoff. Most storms track from west to east, but some storms originate in the Great Lakes or in the Atlantic Ocean. Rapidly changing weather patterns and temperatures may cause large-scale snowmelting events in which ice jams in the receiving streams may aggravate the already serious problem of large water volumes contributed by thousands of small tributaries.

Pennsylvania has the dubious honor of having recorded the largest storm event in the history of the United States. In August 1942, more than 30 inches fell within a span of 5 hours near Smethport, a small town near the New York state border in McKean County (Eisenlohr, 1952). Whereas Smethport received the largest rainfall, it was estimated that more than 20 inches fell over a 200-square-mile area between Emporium and Austin. A peak flow rate of 80,000 cubic feet per second was estimated in Sinnemahoning Creek from high-water marks, almost 10 times as large as any other flood recorded in that stream. The storm and resulting floods undoubtedly caused a large amount of destruction, but possibly owing to more pressing World War II problems, the event never received a great amount of publicity.

Probably the most disastrous flood experienced anywhere in the United States was the notorious Great Johnstown Flood of 1889 in Cambria County (Appendix 52C; Shank, 1972). An unusually large amount of rain fell over western Pennsylvania late in May of that year. An earth dam on South Fork, a tributary of the Little Conemaugh River, had been known to be leaking and gave way when it was overtopped by the floodwaters, which rushed through the city of Johnstown, killing over 2,200 people. The narrow valley and the dense buildup along the Conemaugh floodplain downstream from the dam aggravated the flood catastrophe.

The March 1936 flood was caused by a large accumulation of snow during a cold January, fol-

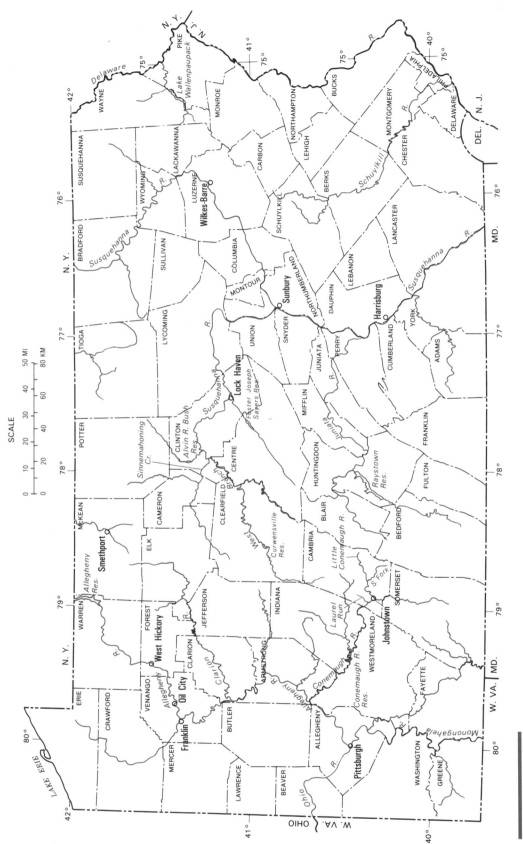

Figure 52-1. Locations of the major cities, streams, and reservoirs cited in this chapter.

lowed by a steady warming trend in February and rainfall. There was rapid snow and ice melting in almost all major watersheds in Pennsylvania. Ice jams caused enormous backup effects on bridges, and many cities experienced the highest flood levels ever recorded. Figures 52-2 and 52-3 show street flooding effects in Pittsburgh, one of the hardest hit cities.

In reaction to the severe damages suffered in the 1936 flood, major flood-control structures were built throughout much of Pennsylvania, including a concrete floodway channel through Johnstown. Thanks to these efforts, Johnstown escaped major damage in 1972, when tropical storm Agnes moved inland and dumped 4.6 inches of rain in 3 days on a soil saturated by 2 inches that had fallen during the previous 2 weeks. On July 19 and 20, 1977, however, a storm that originated at the Great Lakes stalled over Johnstown and dumped up to 12 inches of rain in less than 12 hours (Jenkins, 1977). The flooding was not confined to the main valley but was equally severe along the presumedly safe hillsides. Water in minor creeks and gullies on the hillsides swelled to torrential magnitudes, uprooting trees and other debris and ramming them through houses and streets. Several small dams were overtopped and washed out; the largest of these, Laurel Run, held about 300 acre-feet, or 100 million gallons, of water. The 40-foot-high earth dam, once topped, eroded within an estimated 30 to 40 minutes, resulting in a flood peak of more than 10,000 cubic feet per second, far in excess of the small channel capacity below the dam. Sixty-seven lives were lost.

The notorious June 1972 flood caused by tropical storm "Agnes" accounted for the largest total flood damage in Pennsylvania. The storm lasted between 2 and 3 days, during which the rainfall varied from 4 inches in the western part of the state up to 20 inches in some regions north of Harrisburg. Owing to the long duration of the storm, most major streams rose to record stages, causing hundreds of millions of dollars in damages in cities such as Wilkes-Barre, Lock Haven,

Figure 52-2. The effects of the March 1936 flood in downtown Pittsburgh. The picture was taken on Sixth Avenue in front of Trinity Episcopal Church. Photograph by V. Loczi.

and Harrisburg (see Appendix 52A). In Pittsburgh, the Allegheny and Monongahela Rivers rose to within a few inches of the top of their banks, and the

Figure 52-3. Street flooding in Pittsburgh during the March 1936 flood. The picture was taken on Liberty Avenue near Stanwix Street. Photograph by V. Loczi.

town escaped major flood damage because of the large capacities of several flood-control reservoirs, notably the Allegheny and Conemaugh, which held back a combined volume of over 1 million acre-feet. In the Susquehanna River watershed, the recently completed Curwensville (Clearfield County), Foster Joseph Sayers (Centre County), and Alvin R. Bush (Clinton County) Dams (Figure 52–1), together with some older dams, held back a total volume of roughly 250,000 acre-feet. This reduced the potential Susquehanna River stages by several feet, but storage volumes were not nearly large enough to prevent flooding in the downstream reaches of the river.

Another summer storm, of a somewhat smaller scale, devastated Franklin and Oil City in June 1981 (see Appendix 52B).

ESTIMATES OF FLOOD POTENTIAL

A major concern of people involved in almost any activity in the vicinity of a stream is the area's vulnerability to flooding. Maps of the flood hazard along most major and minor streams in the eastern United States have been drawn by local, state, and federal agencies (Figure 52–4). A question that is often asked is which areas in the state are the most flood-prone. The answer is that practically all floodplains are prone to flooding, whether or not they have had any recorded floods. The *Land Resource Map of Pennsylvania* (Higbee, 1967) shows about 40,000 miles of minor and major streams, and between 10,000 and 15,000 miles of these can be considered floodprone. The potential flooding depth above a streambed depends mostly on the upstream drainage area. In Figure 52–5, a plot of high-watermark elevations versus drainage area is presented, and a "reasonably safe" zone is defined. According to the graph, for example, a resident of Millerstown in Allegheny County (northeast of Pittsburgh), which occupies about 10 square miles of Bull Creek watershed, could feel relatively safe if located 10 feet above the streambed, whereas a resident of Chadds Ford in Chester County (south of West Chester), which occupies about 290 square miles of the Brandywine Creek watershed, should be located 25 feet above the streambed. The drainage area includes that portion of the watershed that is located upstream from a point of interest, excluding areas subject to the influence of major flood-control dams. A graph of this type provides only a rough approximation, and flood hazards are enhanced by low-permeability soils, steep slopes, and dense urbanization. With more reliance on hydraulic-hydrologic

principles, one of the many available flood-estimating methods may be used, such as the U.S. Geological Survey index-flood method (Tice, 1968), which was developed in separate regional studies for the entire nation. Other commonly used methods for estimating Pennsylvania flood peaks are described in Aron and others (1981) and Flippo (1977).

Most streams that have well-defined drainage channels have a channel capacity roughly equivalent to the 2-year flood event. The larger, less frequent floods will go over banks and onto the floodplain. Unfortunately, many overeager developers tend to consider the stream channel as the only legitimate flow path for the stream. Consequently, they build on the floodplain and are surprised when nature disagrees with their judgment.

FLOOD DAMAGE PREVENTION

The most effective solution to the problem of ever-increasing flood damages is to minimize development on the floodplains. Flood-protection walls or dikes can be effective in preventing flood damages locally, but they tend to pass the problem on to downstream regions. Besides, such flood protection may only be effective up to a certain point. During the 1972 flood, for example, the Wilkes-Barre dike was overtopped and partially washed out, which aggravated the problem on the floodplain behind the dike. In the same flood, the Sunbury flood wall, 65 miles downstream from Wilkes-Barre, barely held back the maximum flood wave (with the aid of sandbags placed on top of the wall). However, the wall may have been overtopped if the Wilkes-Barre dike had not breached just in time to open up an unintended but substantial volume of temporary flood storage.

Large flood-control reservoirs can be highly effective in storing storm runoff and thus reducing downstream flood magnitudes. A good example of efficient flood control provided by large dams is illustrated in Figure 52–6, which shows the effect of Kinzua Dam (with over 500,000 acre-feet of active flood-storage capacity) on expected Allegheny River flood peaks near West Hickory, Forest County. The flood-peak reduction varies between 40 percent for the 2-year flood and 60 percent for the 100-year flood. Unfortunately, in spite of the capability of large dams to reduce flood hazards, the opposite effect is often found. A common problem with most flood-control reservoirs is an almost immediate intensive development on the floodplains downstream from the dams. Thus, in many cases, flood damages have actually increased after construction of a flood-

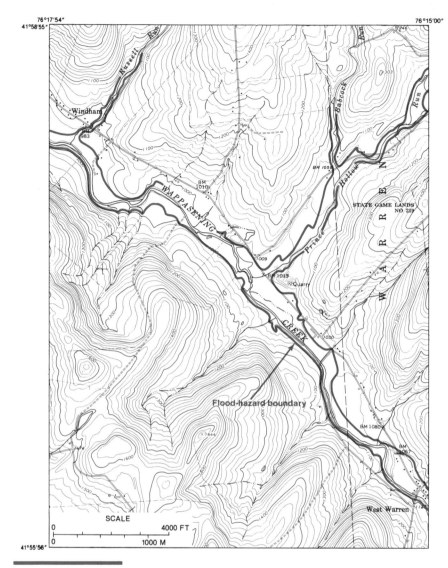

Figure 52–4. **Typical flood-hazard map prepared for the Federal Emergency Management Agency by the U.S. Geological Survey, 1970–75. The map shows a portion of Wappasening Creek, Windham 7.5-minute quadrangle, Bradford County.**

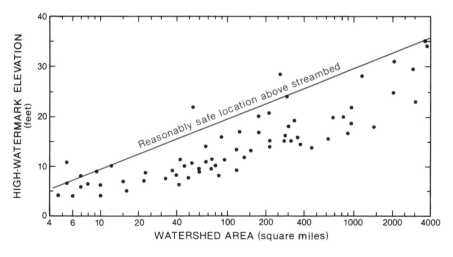

control dam, not because of the dam but rather because of the lack of communication between the agency operating the dam and local development planning authorities.

Programs of floodplain zoning and flood insurance have been only partially successful. Realistic flood insurance rates for developments inside a designated 100-year floodplain are high compared to the typical homeowner's insurance rates. Therefore, a large amount of political maneuvering usually takes place, and pressure is applied by landowners and developers to move the delineated 100-year-floodplain boundary closer to the stream in an effort to remove the requirements of flood insurance. In areas having broad and flat floodplains, the delineation of a 100-year-floodplain boundary is always subject to major uncertainties and is thus easily open to dispute.

Urban development on floodplains per se is not necessarily wrong or objectionable. As long as developments are far enough away from the natural flood paths of streams and their areal extent is small enough not to increase downstream or upstream flood magnitudes appreciably, they could be allowed provided that landowners accept the flood-damage risks. Flood proofing in the form of elevated building entrances (Figure 52–7) or readily erected sandbag barriers

Figure 52–5. **Plot of high watermarks for Pennsylvania floods as a function of watershed area. Graph produced from U.S. Geological Survey flood records by G. Aron.**

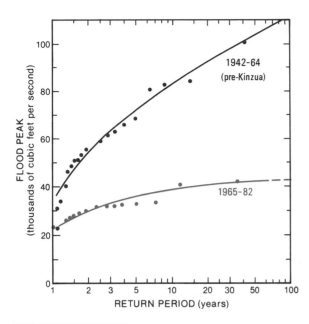

Figure 52–6. Plot showing the effect of a large flood-control dam (Kinzua Dam, Warren County) on flood frequency and magnitude on the Allegheny River near West Hickory, Forest County.

could be instituted by each building owner. Major floods may properly be called "acts of God," but in most cases they can be reasonably expected, and it is not necessarily justified to demand compensation for flood damages as a God-given right.

Figure 52–7. Flood-proofed building of the Susquehanna River Basin Commission on Front Street in Harrisburg. Photograph courtesy of the Susquehanna River Basin Commission.

PROBLEMS AND FUTURE RESEARCH

The fact that flood damages continue to increase in spite of considerable public investments in flood-control measures indicates that further research and improved communication are needed. The rigidity of flood-boundary maps as shown in Figure 52–4, combined with the uncertainties of flood-frequency estimates, invites landowners to obtain special variances by applying legal or political pressures. Research should be oriented toward specifying types of land uses on floodplains that minimize damages from flooding and have no detrimental effects on upstream or downstream communities. Subsequently, model ordinances could be written that would be acceptable to state and local regulating agencies and would buffer the present abrupt discontinuities in land values on flood fringes and floodplains.

Some progress has been made, but more research is needed, in the field of timely flood warning. The most promising approach to this problem is real-time hydrologic modeling, a process in which rainfall and runoff data are continuously entered into a computer program, which generates the most likely scenario for conditions a few hours ahead.

RECOMMENDED FOR FURTHER READING

Bailey, J. F., Patterson, J. L., and Paulhus, J. L. H. (1975), *Hurricane Agnes rainfall and floods, June-July 1972,* U.S. Geological Survey Professional Paper 924, 403 p.

Eisenlohr, W. S., Jr. (1952), *Floods of July 18, 1942 in north-central Pennsylvania,* U.S. Geological Survey Water-Supply Paper 1134-B, p. 59–158.

Grover, N. C. (1937), *The floods of March 1936—Part 2, Hudson River to Susquehanna River region,* U.S. Geological Survey Water-Supply Paper 799, 380 p.

————— (1937), *The floods of March 1936—Part 3, Potomac, James and upper Ohio River,* U.S. Geological Survey Water-Supply Paper 800, 351 p.

Hoxit, L. R., Maddox, R. A., Chappell, C. F., and Brua, S. A. (1982), *Johnstown-western Pennsylvania storm and floods of July 19-20, 1977,* U.S. Geological Survey Professional Paper 1211, 68 p.

McCullough, D. G. (1968), *The Johnstown Flood,* New York, Simon and Schuster, 302 p.

Morgan, J. W. (1936), *The floods of March 1936 in Pennsylvania,* Pennsylvania Department of Environmental Resources, 67 p.

Shank, W. H. (1972), *Great floods of Pennsylvania,* York, Pa., American Canal and Transportation Center, 90 p.

U.S. Geological Survey (1970–75), Unpublished flood-prone area maps, prepared on 7.5-minute topographic quadrangle base maps for Federal Emergency Management Agency.

Figure 52A–1. Agnes flood on Conodoguinet Creek northwest of Carlisle, Pa., at Pa. Route 74, June 23, 1972. The creek normally flows in the channel between two rows of trees to the right of the bridge. Ground views of this bridge in the same general view direction are shown in Figures 52A–2 and 52A–3.

APPENDIX 52A   THE AGNES FLOOD

NOEL POTTER, JR.
   Department of Geology
   Dickinson College
   Carlisle, PA 17013

In June 1972, the greatest flood of record struck central and eastern Pennsylvania. The greatest effects of tropical storm Agnes were concentrated in the Susquehanna River basin, where, within the period June 18–25, many stations received 10 inches of precipitation and some received as much as 18 inches. Harrisburg recorded 12.53 inches in one 24-hour period (DeAngelis and Hodge, 1972).

I began taking photographs of the flood in the Carlisle area in its early stages, mostly at local bridges, with little realization that it was to become a record flood. Eventually, I attempted to return to sites near the projected peak of the flood. On June 23, when the clouds had lifted sufficiently for flying, I arranged for a photographic flight with Kenneth Laws, a colleague at Dickinson College. Later, during the same summer, I returned to many of the bridges photographed at the peak of the flood and repeated the scenes at normal mid-summer flow conditions.

What follows is a small sample of some of the several hundred photographs that I took of the flood in both black and white and color.

Figure 52A–2. Agnes flood near its peak on Conodoguinet Creek northwest of Carlisle, Pa., at Pa. Route 74, looking north. Compare the post-Agnes view in Figure 52A–3.

Figure 52A–3. Post-Agnes flood view of Pa. Route 74 where it crosses Conodoguinet Creek northwest of Carlisle, Pa., August 5, 1972, for comparison with Figure 52A–2.

Figure 52A–4. Agnes flood on the Susquehanna River, June 24, 1972. The view is from the west shore, looking along Market Street Bridge toward City Island and Harrisburg. Half the total width of the river is out of view beyond tree-covered City Island. Discharge was approximately 1 million cubic feet per second near the flood crest. Compare the post-Agnes view in Figure 52A–5.

Figure 52A–5. Post-Agnes flood view of the Susquehanna River, August 5, 1972. The view is from the west shore, looking along Market Street Bridge toward City Island and Harrisburg. Compare with Figure 52A–4.

Figure 52A–6. Agnes flood on the Susquehanna River, June 24, 1972. The view is from the west shore opposite Harrisburg, looking upstream toward Walnut Street Bridge. The tree-covered area on the right is City Island, which is in the middle of the river. Compare the post-Agnes view in Figure 52A–7.

Figure 52A–7. Post-Agnes flood view of the Susquehanna River, August 5, 1972. The view is from the west shore, looking upstream toward Walnut Street Bridge. City Island is the tree-covered area on the right. Compare with Figure 52A–6.

APPENDIX 52B FRANKLIN AND OIL CITY FLOOD

HELEN L. DELANO
Bureau of Topographic and Geologic Survey
Department of Conservation and Natural
  Resources
P. O. Box 8453
Harrisburg, PA 17105

Flash floods affected a large area of northwestern Pennsylvania on June 9, 1981. A minimum of 4 inches of rain fell on a 70- by 10-mile area across parts of Crawford, Venango, Clarion, Jefferson, and Forest Counties (Pomeroy and Popp, 1982) (Figure 52B–1). Local rainfalls of 4.5 inches in Franklin and 6.4 inches in Cooperstown were recorded. Flash flooding occurred in many small streams, causing one death and at least $65 million in damages. Two small streams in Cranberry Township, Venango County, were especially hard hit. The lower part of Twomile Run, which joins the Allegheny just below Franklin, has a drainage basin area of 12.4 square miles, and Sage Run, near Oil City, drains 5.4 square miles (Shaw and Busch, 1970). These normally small streams swelled far beyond their banks and destroyed bridges, houses, and industrial facilities. The accompanying photographs (Figures 52B–2, 52B–3, 52B–4, and 52B–5) were taken on June 19, more than a week after the flood.

Although this was the largest flood event in memory for many local residents, floods of this type and magnitude are not uncommon across the Allegheny Plateau in western Pennsylvania. Similar floods, caused by intense rainfall over a limited area, have occurred in Johnstown in May 1889 and July 1977; in East Brady, Armstrong County, in August 1980; in Hyndman, Bedford County, in August 1984; and in the northern suburbs of Pittsburgh in May 1986 and 1987.

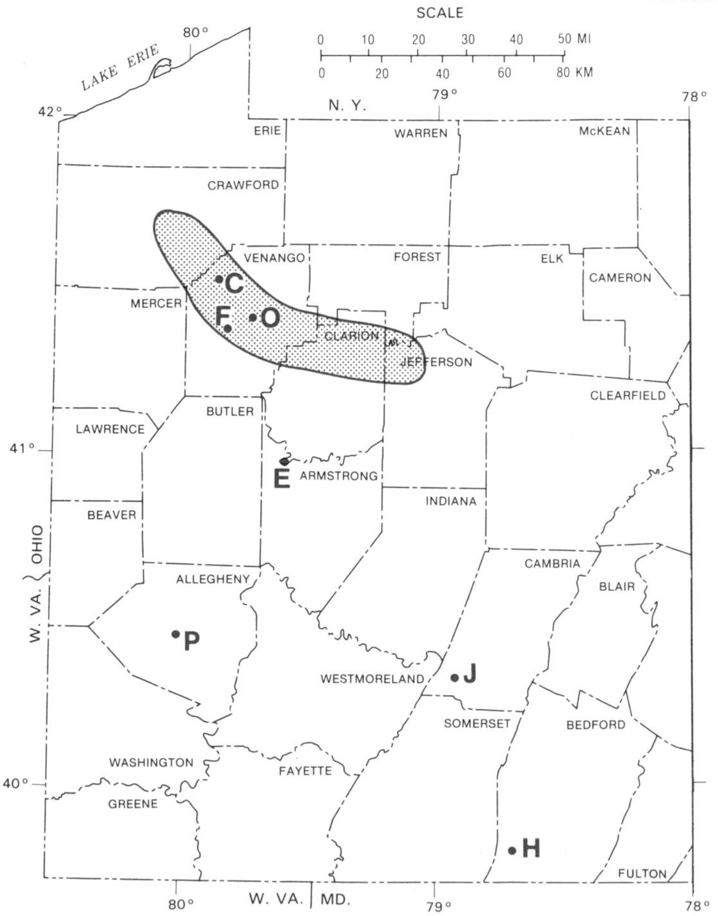

Figure 52B–1. Location map for flash-flood events. City locations are indicated by letters: C, Cooperstown; F, Franklin; O, Oil City; E, East Brady; P, Pittsburgh; J, Johnstown; and H, Hyndman. The stippled area (after Pomeroy and Popp, 1982, Figure 1, p. 13) received more than 4 inches of rain on June 9, 1981.

Figure 52B-2. U.S. Route 322 bridge across the lower part of Twomile Run just above its confluence with the Allegheny River near Franklin. The broken pavement slabs in the center and broken culvert are the remains of the "new" bridge, which was washed out when floodwaters in the creek overwhelmed the culvert opening. The railroad bridge in the background and the "old" highway bridge (out of the view of the photograph) were damaged but not destroyed.

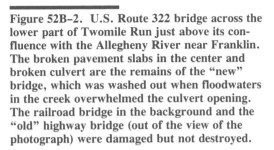

Figure 52B-3. Remains of two houses that were washed from their foundations along the lower part of Twomile Run just above the site of Figure 52B-2.

Figure 52B-4. These oil storage tanks were damaged when they floated off their bases in floodwaters along the lower part of Twomile Run.

Figure 52B-5. Flood-damaged house along Sage Run, near Oil City.

APPENDIX 52C   THE GREAT JOHNSTOWN FLOOD

LOUISE BEM
Johnstown Flood Centennial Project
319 Washington Street
Johnstown, PA 15901

The photographs in this collection are copies of originals from the archive of the Johnstown Flood Museum in Johnstown, Cambria County. The focus of the museum is the interpretation of the 1889 Johnstown Flood.

The flood, which occurred on May 31, 1889, is one of America's best-known disasters. The disaster was caused when the South Fork dam burst and released 20 million tons of water into the Conemaugh River valley. As the water rushed through the valley, it swept away part of the community of South Fork and the communities of Mineral Point, Woodvale, Franklin, East Conemaugh, and, finally, Johnstown.

When the flood was over, 16,000 people were homeless and 2,209 were dead.

For a detailed history of the disaster, read *The Johnstown Flood* by David G. McCullough (New York, Simon and Schuster, 1968, 302 p.).

Figure 52C–1. Lake Conemaugh as it was held back by the South Fork dam between 1881 and 1889. The lake was slightly more than 2 miles long and was 1 mile wide at its widest point.

Figure 52C–2. The lake bed after the dam burst on May 31, 1889. Water seemed to have eroded the earthen structure, and witnesses said that the dam did not break but simply moved away. The lake was emptied of 20 million tons of water in just 45 minutes.

Figure 52C–3. An artist's illustration of the dam after it broke and the lake drained. The view is from the upstream side of the dam.

Figure 52C–4. The Shultz house with a large tree protruding from the window is probably one of the most often photographed images of the Johnstown Flood. There are many different photographs of this house, mainly because the Brownie camera was invented shortly before the Johnstown Flood, and the many tourists who traveled to the community to survey its damage found this to be one of the most striking scenes.

Figure 52C–5. A part of Johnstown just before the famous flood. Compare with Figure 52C–6.

Figure 52C–6. The same section of Johnstown shown in Figure 52C–5, after the flood. Stony Creek River is in the foreground. The Little Conemaugh River separates the rows of white houses on the distant hillside and the remainder of the community on the floodplain. The 35-foot flood wave moved along the path of the Little Conemaugh River until it swept into Johnstown just above the area shown in this photograph.

Figure 52C–7. Destruction on Franklin Street, facing west. The church and the Tribune building remain in downtown Johnstown today. The church is the Franklin Street United Methodist Church, and the Tribune building is now used as a restaurant. Although many of the buildings in the downtown area were destroyed, these in the foreground were saved because the Franklin Street United Methodist Church disbursed the flood wave.

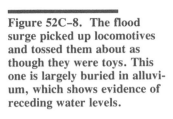
Figure 52C-8. The flood surge picked up locomotives and tossed them about as though they were toys. This one is largely buried in alluvium, which shows evidence of receding water levels.

Figure 52C-9. Debris and a sand wave (stream dune) built to a height of 21 feet on Main Street in Johnstown.

Figure 52C-10. View to the east-northeast of a partially reconstructed Johnstown in the 1890's. The flood surge followed the valley of the Little Conemaugh River and came toward the viewer through the gap in the upper center of the photograph. The Little Conemaugh joins the Conemaugh River (bottom center) just to the left of the picture.

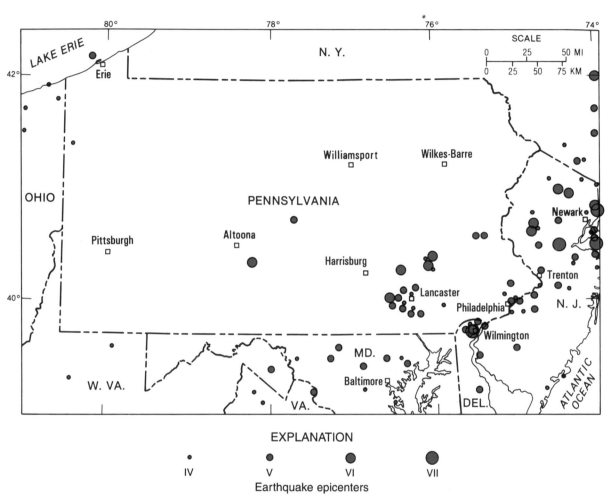

EXPLANATION

IV   V   VI   VII

Earthquake epicenters

Roman numerals indicate earthquake intensities represented by the size of the
circles shown on the map. Intensities are based on the Modified Mercalli scale.

Figure 53–1. Epicenters of historic earthquakes in Pennsylvania and adjacent areas having a maximum intensity of IV or more. Foreshocks and aftershocks have not been plotted. A few of the intensity IV events have also been deleted in places where epicenter density is high.

762

CHAPTER 53   EARTHQUAKES

DAVID W. GORDON*
  U.S. Geological Survey
  National Earthquake Information Center
  Denver Federal Center
  Box 25046, MS 966
  Denver, CO 80225

JAMES W. DEWEY
  U.S. Geological Survey
  National Earthquake Information Center
  Denver Federal Center
  Box 25046, MS 966
  Denver, CO 80225

Note: On September 25, 1998, a magnitude 5.2 earthquake occurred in northwestern Pennsylvania near the Ohio border (epicenter at 41.4°N latitude and 80.4°E longitude). This was the largest earthquake yet recorded that was centered in the state. Early damage reports suggested a maximum intensity of VI. The earthquake occurred after this book went to press and is not included in the text discussion.

*Retired.

INTRODUCTION

About 35 earthquakes have caused light damage in Pennsylvania since the beginning of the Colonial period. Occasional broken windows, cracked plaster, and glassware toppled from shelves have characterized this damage. Nearly one half of these damaging events had out-of-state epicenters. Foremost among the class of distant shocks that were felt strongly in Pennsylvania were a trio of major earthquakes near New Madrid, Mo., in 1811–12, and the Charleston, S. C., earthquake of 1886. Most earthquakes with epicenters inside the state have been located in southeastern Pennsylvania.

Figure 53–1 is an epicenter plot of earthquakes centered in Pennsylvania and adjacent areas that had a maximum intensity of IV or more on the Modified Mercalli scale (see Table 53–1). Table 53–2 is a catalog containing epicentral coordinates, magnitudes, and other data associated with the events plotted in the figure.

Table 53–2 was assembled from published and unpublished lists of historic earthquakes and from descriptions of earthquakes in professional journals and government reports. The rediscovery of 10 previously forgotten Pennsylvania earthquakes by Armbruster and Seeber (1987) made a significant contribution to the catalog. Winkler's (1979, 1982) reviews of East Coast seismicity and the compilation of original newspaper accounts of Pennsylvania earthquakes by Abdypoor and Bischke (1982) were also very helpful in preparing this paper. More than 100 additional historic events that had maximum intensities of III or less had epicenters in the area corresponding to Figure 53–1. The authors tabulated only those events having a maximum intensity of IV or more because the historic record is incomplete below this level, and because some of the shocks reported at level II or III are nontectonic events such as quarry blasts or rockbursts (Scharnberger, 1988). Table 53–2 does not include strong local shocks on February 21 and 24, 1954, which caused heavy damage in a five-block area of Wilkes-Barre, Pa. Most seismologists now attribute these events to mine subsidence.

Table 53–1. *Summary of the Modified Mercalli Intensity Scale[1]*

Intensity	Description
I	Not felt except by a very few under especially favorable circumstances.
II	Felt only by a few persons at rest, especially on upper floors of buildings.
III	Felt quite noticeably indoors, especially on upper floors. Many people do not recognize it as an earthquake.
IV	During the day, felt indoors by many and outdoors by few. At night some are awakened. Dishes, windows, and doors are disturbed; walls make creaking sound.
V	Felt by nearly everyone; many are awakened. Some dishes and windows are broken; a few instances of cracked plaster; unstable objects are overturned.
VI	Felt by all; many are frightened and run outdoors. Some heavy furniture is moved; a few instances of fallen plaster or damaged chimneys. Damage is slight.
VII	Everybody runs outdoors. Damage is negligible in buildings of good design and construction, slight to moderate in well-built ordinary structures, and considerable in poorly built or badly designed structures; some chimneys are broken.
VIII	Damage is slight in specially designed structures, considerable in ordinary substantial buildings, and great in poorly built structures. Fall of chimneys, factory stacks, columns, and walls. Heavy furniture is overturned.
IX	Damage is considerable in specially designed structures; well-designed frame structures are thrown out of plumb; damage is great in substantial buildings. Buildings are shifted off foundations.
X	Some well-built wooden structures are destroyed; most masonry and frame structures are destroyed along with foundations. Rails are bent.
XI	Few, if any, masonry structures remain standing. Bridges are destroyed. Underground pipelines are completely out of service. Rails are bent greatly.
XII	Damage is total. Lines of sight and level are distorted. Objects are thrown upward into the air.

[1]Abbreviated and slightly modified from Wood and Neumann (1931).

Table 53–2. *Catalog of Earthquakes in Pennsylvania and Adjacent Areas Having a Maximum Intensity of IV or More[1]*

Date (yr.mo.day)	Time (UTC)	N latitude (degrees)	W longitude (degrees)	[3]Magnitude	Maximum intensity	[2]Area (km^2)
1724.08.16	9:30:00	40.00	75.10	—	IV	—
1737.12.19	3:45:00	40.80	74.00	5.0	VII	200,000
1752.12.17	23:00:00	39.98	75.90	3.6	IV	—
1763.10.30	21:15:00	40.00	75.10	—	IV	—
[4]1783.11.24	—	41.00	74.50	—	IV	—
[4]1783.11.30	2:00:00	41.00	74.50	—	IV	—
1783.11.30	3:50:00	41.00	74.50	4.7	VI	200,000
[4]1783.11.30	7:00:00	41.00	74.50	—	IV	—
1798.01.11	7:00:00	40.02	76.32	—	IV	—
1800.11.20	10:00:00	40.12	76.39	4.1	V	—
1801.01.27	20:40:00	40.02	76.32	—	IV	—
1820.08.21	14:40:00	40.03	76.50	3.4	V	—
1820.08.27	7:30:00	39.54	76.35	—	V	—
1823.05.30	—	41.50	81.00	—	IV	—
1834.05.03	4:30:00	39.90	76.18	4.0	V	—
1840.11.11	—	40.00	75.10	—	V	—
1847.09.29	—	40.50	74.00	4.3	V	100,000
1848.09.09	4:00:00	40.40	74.00	4.3	V	100,000
1855.02.07	4:30:00	42.00	74.00	—	VI	—
1856.01.16	8:00:00	39.20	78.20	—	IV	—
1857.03.01	1:40:00	41.80	80.60	—	IV	—
1865.09.17	20:00:00	40.04	76.31	—	IV	—
1871.10.09	14:40:00	39.70	75.50	4.1	VII	5,700
[4]1871.10.10	5:08:00	39.70	75.50	—	IV	—
1877.01.04	4:30:00	39.50	77.30	—	V	—

Table 53–2. *(Continued)*

Date (yr.mo.day)	Time (UTC)	N latitude (degrees)	W longitude (degrees)	[3]Magnitude	Maximum intensity	[2]Area (km^2)
1877.09.10	14:59:00	40.10	74.80	3.2	IV	3,400
1878.10.04	7:30:00	41.50	74.00	3.2	V	1,000
1879.03.26	0:30:00	39.20	75.50	3.3	V	1,500
1883.03.11	23:57:00	39.50	76.40	—	IV	—
1884.05.31	—	40.60	75.50	—	V	—
1884.08.10	19:07:00	40.50	74.50	5.1	VII	300,000
[4]1884.08.11	17:30:00	40.50	74.50	—	V	—
1885.01.03	2:12:00	39.20	77.50	3.6	V	9,000
1885.03.09	1:00:00	40.02	76.32	—	IV	—
1887.01.03	4:30:00	39.60	77.20	3.4	V	3,000
1889.03.08	23:40:00	40.00	76.55	4.3	VI	—
1893.03.09	5:30:00	40.60	74.00	3.3	V	1,800
1895.09.01	11:09:00	40.70	74.80	4.5	VI	91,000
1895.11.20	8:00:00	39.80	75.60	—	IV	—
1897.06.08	0:53:00	40.10	74.40	—	IV	—
1900.04.29	0:07:00	39.90	75.10	—	IV	—
1909.04.02	7:25:00	39.40	78.00	3.5	V	6,000
1912.03.23	4:40:00	40.60	74.10	—	IV	—
1914.03.06	—	40.80	74.10	—	IV	—
1914.03.25	7:00:00	39.20	74.70	—	IV	—
1921.01.26	23:40:00	40.00	75.00	3.3	V	1,400
1923.10.30	18:00:00	39.30	74.50	—	IV	—
1924.01.01	5:00:00	39.10	78.10	—	IV	—
1927.06.01	12:20:00	40.50	74.05	4.3	VII	16,000
1930.11.01	6:34:00	39.10	76.50	—	IV	—
1933.01.25	2:00:00	40.20	74.70	3.3	V	1,500
1934.10.29	20:07:00	42.20	80.20	3.4	V	2,500
1936.08.26	8:55:00	41.40	80.40	—	IV	—
1938.07.15	22:46:12	40.37	78.23	—	VI	—
[4]1938.08.23	3:36:31	40.13	74.53	—	V	—
1938.08.23	5:04:53	40.13	74.53	3.8	V	18,000
[4]1938.08.23	7:03:29	40.13	74.53	—	IV	—
1939.11.15	2:53:48	39.58	75.05	3.8	V	15,000
[4]1939.11.18	2:33:00	39.50	76.60	3.1	IV	1,800
1939.11.26	5:20:00	39.50	76.60	—	V	—
1944.01.08	—	39.80	75.50	3.2	V	1,000
1951.09.03	21:26:24	41.25	74.25	3.7	V	14,000
1952.10.08	21:40:00	41.70	74.00	—	V	—
1953.08.17	4:22:50	41.00	74.00	3.1	IV	2,000
1954.01.07	7:25:00	40.42	76.02	—	VI	—
[4]1954.01.07	19:34:00	40.42	76.02	—	V	—
1954.03.31	21:25:00	40.28	74.03	3.1	IV	1,400
1954.08.11	3:40:00	40.33	76.02	—	IV	—
[4]1954.09.24	11:00:00	40.33	76.02	—	IV	—
[4]1955.01.20	3:00:00	40.33	76.02	—	IV	—
1957.03.23	19:02:00	40.63	74.83	3.5	VI	1,300
1961.09.15	2:16:56	40.60	75.40	—	V	—
1961.12.27	17:06:00	40.50	74.75	—	V	—
1962.09.04	23:40:00	39.50	77.70	—	IV	—
1964.05.12	6:45:10	40.30	76.41	3.2	VI	—
1965.09.29	20:57:39	41.40	74.40	—	IV	—
1966.09.28	20:59:06	39.30	80.40	—	IV	—
1968.12.10	9:12:48	39.92	74.82	3.0	V	1,500
1969.10.06	—	41.10	74.60	—	IV	—
[4]1971.07.14	—	39.75	75.55	—	IV	—

Table 53–2. *(Continued)*

Date (yr.mo.day)	Time (UTC)	N latitude (degrees)	W longitude (degrees)	[3]Magnitude	Maximum intensity	[2]Area (km^2)
[4]1971.12.29	—	39.75	75.55	—	IV	—
[4]1972.01.02	7:08:00	39.75	75.55	—	IV	—
[4]1972.01.03	0:00:00	39.75	75.55	—	IV	—
[4]1972.01.07	3:45:00	39.75	75.55	—	IV	—
[4]1972.01.22	6:40:00	39.75	75.55	—	IV	—
[4]1972.01.23	1:35:00	39.75	75.55	—	IV	—
[4]1972.01.23	7:22:00	39.75	75.55	—	IV	—
1972.02.11	0:16:30	39.75	75.55	3.2	V	1,000
[4]1972.08.14	1:09:00	39.75	75.55	—	IV	—
1972.12.08	3:00:33	40.14	76.24	3.5	V	2,400
1973.02.28	8:21:33	39.78	75.42	3.8	V	40,000
1973.07.10	4:38:02	39.75	75.50	—	IV	—
1974.04.28	14:19:20	39.70	75.60	—	IV	—
1976.03.11	21:07:20	40.96	74.37	3.5	VI	1,600
1976.04.13	15:39:13	40.84	74.05	3.1	VI	—
1976.05.06	18:46:08	39.60	79.90	—	IV	—
1977.02.10	19:14:25	39.76	75.54	—	VI	—
1978.06.30	20:13:43	41.08	74.20	2.9	IV	—
1978.07.16	6:39:39	39.91	76.31	3.1	V	2,300
1978.10.06	19:25:41	39.97	76.51	3.0	V	3,000
1979.01.30	16:30:52	40.38	74.31	3.3	V	2,800
1979.02.23	10:23:57	40.80	74.81	2.9	IV	—
1979.03.10	4:49:39	40.72	74.50	3.1	V	1,800
[4]1980.03.05	17:06:54	40.16	75.10	2.9	IV	—
1980.03.11	6:00:26	40.16	75.10	3.3	V	2,600
1982.04.12	22:14:31	40.05	74.82	3.3	V	1,600
1983.02.19	5:45:45	40.65	74.77	2.5	IV	—
1983.11.17	19:55:06	39.75	75.56	—	IV	—
[4]1983.12.12	5:15:09	39.75	75.56	—	IV	—
[4]1984.01.19	23:03:34	39.75	75.56	—	IV	—
[4]1984.04.19	4:54:58	39.92	76.36	3.0	V	2,100
1984.04.23	1:36:00	39.92	76.36	4.1	V	77,000
1986.05.02	13:53:52	39.92	76.36	—	IV	—
1987.07.13	5:49:17	41.90	80.77	3.8	IV	—
1990.01.13	20:47:55	39.42	76.88	2.5	V	—
1990.10.23	1:34:48	39.51	75.51	2.9	V	—
1991.08.15	7:16:07	40.79	77.66	3.0	V	—
1992.01.09	8:50:45	40.36	74.34	3.0	IV	—
1992.01.15	17:16:28	41.24	74.16	—	IV	—
1993.02.26	21:13:34	39.88	74.94	2.5	IV	—
1993.03.10	14:32:22	39.23	76.88	—	IV	—
1993.05.10	9:15:09	40.35	76.02	2.8	IV	—
[4]1993.05.11	2:41:48	40.35	76.02	2.3	V	—
[4]1993.05.18	9:45:24	40.35	76.02	2.1	IV	—
1993.10.16	6:30:05	41.70	81.01	3.4	IV	—
[4]1994.01.16	0:42:43	40.33	76.01	4.0	V	—
1994.01.16	1:49:16	40.33	76.04	4.6	VI	16,000

[1]Sources consulted to compile this catalog include Winkler (1979, 1982), Stover and others (1981), Abdypoor and Bischke (1982), Armbruster and Seeber (1987), Scharnberger (1988), and data on file at the U.S. Geological Survey, National Earthquake Information Center in Denver, Colo.

[2]Total area in which the earthquake was felt. Taken from published sources or estimated in this study.

[3]All magnitudes listed for earthquakes after 1957 are instrumental [m_b(Lg)] magnitudes. The m_b(Lg) magnitudes (Nuttli, 1973) are based on the amplitudes of 1-sec-period Lg waves recorded by seismographs at regional distances. All other listed magnitudes are comparable magnitudes based on felt area and epicentral intensity (Sibol and others, 1987).

[4]Foreshock or aftershock.

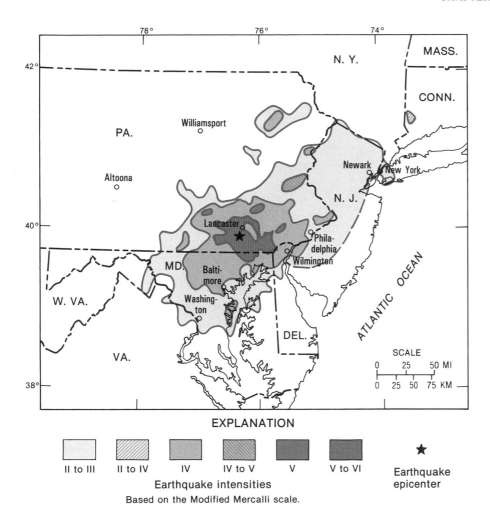

EXPLANATION

II to III   II to IV   IV   IV to V   V   V to VI   ★ Earthquake epicenter

Earthquake intensities
Based on the Modified Mercalli scale.

Figure 53–2. Isoseismal lines of the April 23, 1984, earthquake in Lancaster County (modified from Stover, 1988). The irregularity and complexity of these isoseismal lines is partly a consequence of dense sampling.

NOTABLE EARTHQUAKES

Remarkably few earthquakes having a maximum intensity of IV or higher have been centered in Pennsylvania outside the southeastern part of the state (Figure 53–1). Pennsylvania's strongest earthquakes with in-state epicenters have persistently occurred in an area near Lancaster (Armbruster and Scharnberger, 1986; Armbruster and Seeber, 1987). These shocks include the earthquake of March 8, 1889, which shook southeastern Pennsylvania, northern Maryland, and the northern tip of Delaware. Chimneys fell at Harrisburg and York, where the 1889 tremor was severe. The most widely felt earthquake known to be centered in Pennsylvania occurred in the Lancaster zone on April 23, 1984 (Armbruster and Seeber, 1987; Scharnberger and Howell, 1985). Figure 53–2 is an isoseismal map of this earthquake, which was felt from New York City to Washington, D. C. On January 16, 1994, a magnitude 4.6 earthquake caused damage exceeding 2 million dollars in the Reading area.

Another group of epicenters in southeastern Pennsylvania is spatially associated with a seismic trend along the lower Delaware River, which apparently continues northeasterly through New Jersey. One of the strongest shocks in this northeast-trending zone occurred on August 23, 1938 (Figure 53–3). This tremor, which was centered in New Jersey about 31 miles northeast of Philadelphia, was the principal shock of a swarm of about a dozen tremors in this area that were felt in Philadelphia. The main shock of the swarm alarmed many people and broke a few windows in the Philadelphia area.

Stover and others (1981) listed 10 historic earthquakes having maximum intensities of III or more and epicenters in the immediate vicinity of Philadelphia. The largest of these, a shock having a maximum intensity of about V, occurred on November 11, 1840. Small tremors in the Philadelphia area, such as the shocks on March 5 and March 11 in 1980 (Table 53–2), are often both felt and heard (Bischke, 1980). Witnesses usually describe the accompanying noise as a sonic boom or furnace explosion.

The strongest, most widely felt shock known to have originated in the region covered by Figure 53–1 was the earthquake of August 10, 1884, which was apparently centered in New Jersey about 50 miles northeast of Philadelphia. Contemporary newspapers contained reports that this earthquake caused a few chimneys to fall and glassware and other small objects to be upset in greater Philadelphia. Waves on the Delaware River were reported to have swamped

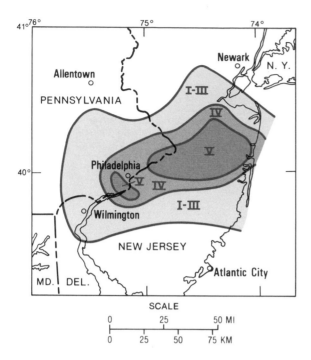

Figure 53-3. Isoseismal lines of the New Jersey earthquake of August 23, 1938 (modified from Neumann, 1940). Studies of earthquakes in the United States show that intensity falls off less rapidly with distance (seismic wave attenuation is less) in the eastern part of the country than in the western part.

sity associated with this shock, extended northeasterly along both sides of the Delaware River to the vicinity of Philadelphia, where the shock cracked plaster and toppled glassware.

EARTHQUAKE FREQUENCY AND SEISMIC HAZARD

Figure 53-5 is a plot of the cumulative number (N) of earthquakes versus epicentral intensity (I_o) for the period 1786–1986 in the study region. In the figure, the straight line (log $N = 4.87 - 0.63\ I_o$) has been fit to the observed frequencies at intensities V, VI, and VII. The calculated frequency derived from the linear expression shown in the figure is more than twice the observed frequency at the intensity IV level. This discrepancy, the fact that the observed frequency falls below the calculated frequency, is proba-

small boats. Figure 53-4 is an adaptation of Rockwood's (1885) isoseismal map of this shock. The original map is the oldest published isoseismal plot of a North American earthquake that has come to the attention of the authors. The isoseismal lines in the figure exhibit southwest-northeast elongation that is characteristic of shocks in this region.

On October 9, 1871, an earthquake having a maximum intensity of VII struck Wilmington, Del., located about 25 miles southwest of Philadelphia. This shock, Wilmington's most famous earthquake, was felt in a northeast-trending, elliptically shaped area about 40 miles wide and 68 miles long; chimneys were thrown down in Oxford, Pa., and doors and windows were rattled in Philadelphia. Another relatively strong earthquake centered near Wilmington occurred on February 28, 1973. The area characterized by intensity V, the highest inten-

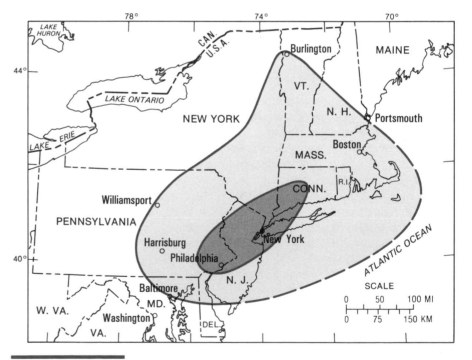

Figure 53-4. Isoseismal lines of the August 10, 1884, earthquake in New Jersey (modified from Rockwood, 1885). The outer isoseismal line surrounds the felt area. The inner isoseismal line encloses the area characterized by cracked plaster and bricks thrown from chimneys.

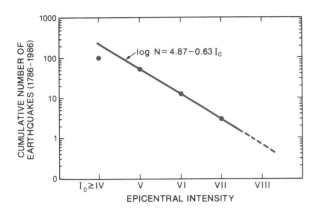

Figure 53–5. Cumulative number (N) of earthquakes versus epicentral intensity (I_o) for the period 1786–1986 in Pennsylvania and adjacent areas. The straight line (log N=4.87–0.63 I_o) has been fit to the observed frequencies at the V, VI, and VII intensity levels. In regions where earthquake records have been kept for a long time, log N versus I_o relationships are nearly linear over the range of higher intensities. In regions that have short-term histories, a linear log N relation is commonly assumed to extrapolate the frequencies of shocks larger than those that have actually been observed.

bly due to the incomplete cataloging of intensity IV events in the eighteenth and nineteenth centuries.

Pennsylvania has not experienced an earthquake of intensity VIII, the threshold of serious damage to ordinary structures, or greater in historic time. Assuming that the expression for log N (Figure 53–5) that has been derived may be extrapolated to higher intensities, it is estimated that, on average, three to four such events ($I_o \geq$VIII) will take place in 1,000 years. This result is similar to Algermissen's (1969) estimate of seismicity rates for the entire East Coast region (2.3 shocks per 100,000 km² [38,600 mi²] with $I_o \geq$VIII over a 1,000-year period). Using extreme-value theory and certain assumptions about the maximum size of earthquakes in the region, Howell (1979) estimated average return periods of between 100 and 300 years for earthquakes in Pennsylvania having a maximum intensity of VIII.

The first attempts to delineate seismic hazard in the United States were based on the historic records of the highest intensity earthquake ever experienced at individual localities. Using this concept, Algermissen (1969) placed Pennsylvania in a zone where relatively minor damage (intensity V to VI) is expected. Algermissen and others (1982) used probabilistic methods to map earthquake hazard in the United States. In southeastern Pennsylvania, the zone of highest seismic hazard in the state, they indicated that the probability is 90 percent that a maximum hori-

zontal acceleration in rock of 10 percent of gravity will not be exceeded in a 50-year period (an acceleration of 10 percent of gravity is commonly associated with structural damage to ordinary buildings not specifically designed to resist earthquakes). In comparison, for the same probability and exposure period, a maximum horizontal acceleration of about 60 percent of gravity characterizes high-risk areas along the San Andreas fault in California.

PROBLEMS AND FUTURE RESEARCH

Extrapolation from the several-century-long record of small and moderate Pennsylvania earthquakes to estimate the rate of occurrence of infrequent strong earthquakes will be improved by a better understanding of seismogenic faults in the state (see Chapter 27) and by a more complete cataloging of the historical shocks. Felt-area estimates, magnitudes, and approximate focal depths can probably be developed for more of the preinstrumental earthquakes. A thorough search of original sources for the eighteenth and nineteenth centuries would probably result in the discovery of many additional, previously unlisted earthquakes.

Few precise data exist with regard to the focal depths of Pennsylvania earthquakes. The only reliable instrumental data, which comes from close-in studies of aftershocks in Lancaster County, indicate an average focal depth of about 3 miles. In Table 53–2, some of the shocks that have relatively high epicentral intensities were felt over anomalously small areas, suggesting that these events were very shallow.

RECOMMENDED FOR FURTHER READING

Beavers, J. E., ed. (1981), *Earthquakes and earthquake engineering: the eastern United States,* Ann Arbor, Mich., Ann Arbor Science Publishers, 2 v., 1,189 p.

Nottis, G. N., ed. (1983), *Epicenters of northeastern United States and southeastern Canada, onshore and offshore; time period 1534–1980,* New York State Museum Map and Chart Series 38, 39 p.

Richter, C. F. (1958), *Elementary seismology,* San Francisco, W. H. Freeman and Company, 768 p.

Scharnberger, C. K. (1989), *Earthquake hazard in Pennsylvania,* Pennsylvania Geological Survey, 4th ser., Educational Series 10, 14 p.

Stover, C. W., and Coffman, J. L. (1993), *Seismicity of the United States, 1568–1989 (revised),* U.S. Geological Survey Professional Paper 1527, 418 p.

Thenhaus, P. C., Perkins, D. M., Algermissen, S. T., and Hanson, S. L. (1987), *Earthquake hazard in the eastern United States: consequences of alternative seismic source zones,* Earthquake Spectra, v. 3, p. 227–261.

PERIOD		CHARACTERISTICS
HISTORIC		
		─────── A.D. 1492 ───────
WOODLAND	Late Middle Early	Development of pottery, bow and arrow, horticulture, permanent villages, mortuary mounds, and more long-distance trade and exchange networks.
		─────── 1000 B.C. ───────
ARCHAIC	Late Middle Early	Migratory, hunting and gathering peoples having a more diverse lithic tool "kit" than in Paleo-Indian times.
		─────── 8000 B.C. ───────
PALEO-INDIAN		Small groups of migratory, hunting and gathering peoples having a simple lithic tool "kit" characterized by fluted projectile points. Entrance into the Western Hemisphere from Siberia probably occurred 20,000 to 30,000 years ago.

Figure 54–1. Cultural time scale for Pennsylvania.

CHAPTER 54 GEOARCHAEOLOGY

FRANK J. VENTO
Department of Geography-Earth Science
Clarion University
Clarion, PA 16214

JACK DONAHUE
Department of Geology and Planetary Science and
Department of Anthropology
University of Pittsburgh
Pittsburgh, PA 15260

JAMES M. ADOVASIO
Department of Geology
Mercyhurst College
Erie, PA 16546

INTRODUCTION

Geoarchaeology is the interface between geology and archaeology. It makes use of geological methods to expand archaeological interpretation and understanding. On the other side of the interface, archaeological data, especially the closely spaced and generally well documented time framework, is useful in geological studies because it promotes a better and more detailed understanding of the last 1 to 2 million years of geological history. The rapid growth of geoarchaeology over the last two decades as an interdisciplinary science has involved geologists, physical geographers, and archaeologists from almost every field of specialization. In Pennsylvania, geoarchaeology has helped to answer questions concerning (1) the effects of vegetation, climate, and physiography on site selection, site geomorphology, and paleogeography; (2) sediment sources and processes in site deposition; (3) provenance studies of raw materials for artifacts; and (4) geochemical analyses of archaeological sediments.

CULTURAL HISTORY

As is the case with geology, a time scale is used to define changes in prehistoric culture in Pennsylvania. The main subdivisions include the Paleo-Indian, Archaic, and Woodland periods (Figure 54–1).

Paleo-Indian

The earliest cultural period has an as yet undetermined beginning and terminated about 8000 B.C. with the development of an open white-pine/oak woodland and a cultural change to the Early Archaic (Griffin, 1967). There are only three described sites in Pennsylvania that have a significant Paleo-Indian component (Figure 54–2): Meadowcroft Rockshelter (Adovasio and Carlisle, 1982), Shoop (Witthoft, 1952), and Shawnee Minisink (McNett, 1985). Occupation of the sites occurred south of the late Wisconsinan glacial boundary. The glacial boundary illustrated in

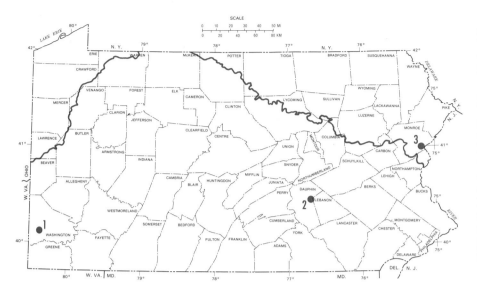

Figure 54–2. Location map of the three documented, in situ Paleo-Indian sites: 1, Meadowcroft; 2, Shoop; and 3, Shawnee Minisink. The glacial boundary shown on the map records the maximum advance of late Wisconsinan glaciers (modified from Berg and others, 1989). By the time of occupation of Shawnee Minisink, the glaciers had retreated to the north so that glacial ice was not present in the vicinity of the site.

Figure 54–2 represents the full extent of the late Wisconsinan Woodfordian advance. At the time of occupation of Shawnee Minisink, however, glacial ice had retreated northward.

Artifacts from the Paleo-Indian period are sparse and consist primarily of distinctive fluted and unfluted projectile points (Figure 54–3), and less diagnostic flaked stone tools or implements. The presence of projectile points such as the one illustrated in Figure 54–3 is used to identify Paleo-Indian sites. With the exception of the sites mentioned above, however, most Paleo-Indian finds consist of scattered or solitary lithic tools, both in upland and valley settings.

Archaic

The changing climate and vegetation patterns during warming after the terminal Pleistocene and early Holocene resulted in an increase in Indian populations that had adapted to expanding forest zones. The Archaic period lasted from circa 8000 B.C. to 1000 B.C. (Figure 54–1). In Pennsylvania, Archaic sites dramatically increase in number, and settings vary from upland to river terrace, as well as rockshelters.

The stone tool "kit" used to identify Archaic period sites shows an increasing diversity over that of the preceding Paleo-Indian period and is characterized by the appearance of local and regional projectile point styles. This includes the appearance of new types of projectile points and knives, as well as other flaked stone tools, by the Middle Archaic period (circa 6000 B.C.; Figure 54–4).

Woodland

The Woodland period ranges from circa 1000 B.C. up to the time of historic contact with Europeans (Figure 54–1). Sites that have a Woodland component are common throughout Pennsylvania in the same topographic settings as those of the Late Archaic period.

The use of ceramics for cooking and storage is the major technological innovation in the earlier part of this period. During the terminal Middle to initial Late Woodland (circa 550 to 200 B.C.), the introduction of the bow and arrow resulted in the use of smaller, standardized projectile points (Figure 54–5). By Middle to Late Woodland time, many of the archaeological sites were permanent villages surrounded by wooden stockades and agricultural fields.

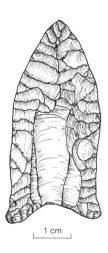

Figure 54–3. Temporally diagnostic Paleo-Indian projectile point from the upper Ohio River valley in Pennsylvania. This is an idealized drawing of a fluted Clovis point, which is considered to represent Paleo-Indian time.

1 cm

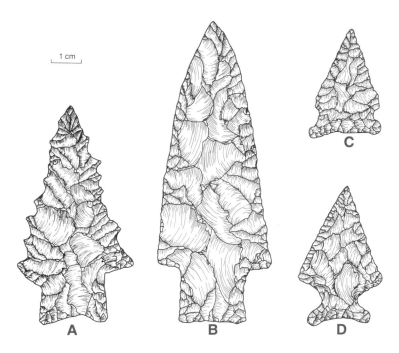

1 cm

Figure 54-4. Temporally diagnostic Archaic projectile point types in Pennsylvania: A, Kirk Serrated point, characteristic of the Early Archaic; B, Stanley Stemmed point, characteristic of the Middle Archaic; C, Brewerton Corner notched point, typical of the Late Archaic; and D, Susquehanna Broad spear point, characteristic of the terminal Archaic.

ARCHAEOLOGICAL SITES AND REGIONAL ANALYSIS

Archaeological sites vary greatly in the preservation of the artifacts they contain. This is usually a function of the rate of sedimentation, concurrent weathering, and subsequent erosion. The most rapid sedimentation rates generally occur in aggrading river valleys, such as the Susquehanna River valley, whereas the best protection from weathering and erosion tends to be in rockshelters and caves. In each topographic setting, the nature and extent of the archaeological record is often highly dependent on the human activity carried out at the site (e.g., quarry site, temporary camp, permanent settlement, and so forth). Moreover, Paleo-Indian and Archaic sites were relatively short duration, commonly seasonal camps, whereas by Late Woodland time, permanent settlements had become dominant. This variability is evident in the sites excavated in Pennsylvania.

The identification and, especially, excavation of ar-

chaeological sites are reported to the State Museum in Harrisburg. All reported sites are assigned a tripartite designation with the first part, the number 36, representing Pennsylvania. The second part consists of two letters, representing the county in which the site is located. The third part of the designation represents the number of the site for that particular county. Thus, one example of an archaeological site, Meadowcroft Rockshelter, is designated 36Wh297; it is the 297th site recorded for Washington County.

Figure 54-5. Temporally diagnostic Woodland projectile point types in Pennsylvania: A, Adena point, characteristic of the Early Woodland; B, Jack Reef point, typical of the Middle Woodland; and C, Levanna point, characteristic of the Late Woodland.

1 cm

Figure 54–6 shows the number of archaeological sites in each county in Pennsylvania as of 1985. Although some of the northern counties, close to the glacial boundary, show a lower number of sites, the main factor determining the present distribution of sites is how much archaeological survey work has been done in the area. Washington County, which has the greatest number of reported sites, is an area where extensive survey work was done in the 1970's. In contrast, Columbia County, which has only 10 recorded sites, has received little attention.

Rockshelters and Caves

Rockshelters, located under overhanging rock outcrops (Figure 54–7), and caves are commonly situated along valley slopes and can act as natural catchments for sediment (Figure 54–8), forming thick stratigraphic sequences. The stratigraphy at Meadowcroft Rockshelter (Figure 54–9) is an excellent example. The rockshelter developed in late Wisconsinan time after valley downcutting by Cross Creek (Beynon and Donahue, 1982). The first occupation of the shelter occurred at about 16,000 years B.P., and, because sedimentation took place simultaneously with occupation, a 5-m (16-ft) stratigraphic sequence developed,

which fully represents the cultural periods from Paleo-Indian through Historic. Because this site was used primarily as a hunting and gathering camp, human modification of the sediments was relatively slight. Thus, the primary evidence of its prehistoric occupation is scattered lithic artifacts, fire pits, trash pits, and burned remains of plants and animals that were brought into the rockshelter by its occupants.

Upland Settings

Flat or hilly upland areas are characterized by thin residual soils. Wind and mass wasting are the primary and relatively minor sources of sediment accumulation. Stratigraphic sequences tend to be relatively thin, increasing the potential for the mixing of artifacts from different cultural periods. This is particularly common in upland areas that have been plowed. Artifact mixing could also be caused by bioturbation or the reuse of older artifacts by more recent occupants of the site. An exception occurs at the base of slopes, where thicker deposits of colluvium can form during downslope movement of sediments.

Figure 54–10 is an idealized profile for an upland site in western Pennsylvania. Occupation of the site spanned the Archaic through Late Woodland cul-

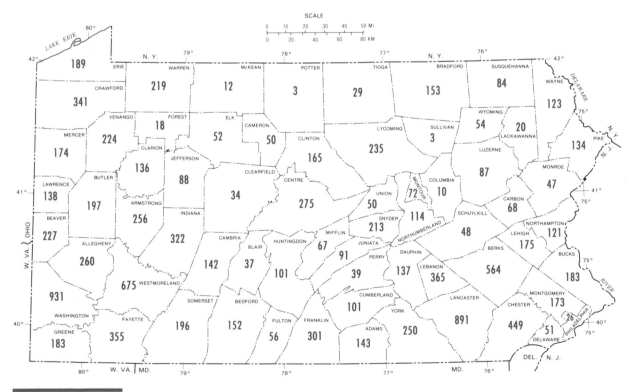

Figure 54–6. Number of recorded archaeological sites in each county in Pennsylvania as of 1985.

Figure 54–7. A view across Meadowcroft Rockshelter, Washington County, looking west and showing the sandstone overhang that forms the shelter. The photograph was taken in 1973 before excavation began. The pile of stones in the center of the photograph marks the location of a recent hearth used by campers and hikers. The presence of this feature testifies to the continuing importance of the site as a shelter for humans. The people who constructed this hearth, however, probably had no idea that their campfire was only the most recent archaeological deposit in a site that has been occupied for the last 16,000 years.

Figure 54–8. Beginning stage of excavation at Meadowcroft Rockshelter in 1973. A careful record is kept of the depth of excavation and the position of any artifacts that are found during excavation. All soil removed from the site is passed through screens like those in the upper left corner of the photograph so that even small artifacts are recovered.

Figure 54–9. Stratigraphy of the east wall of Meadowcroft Rockshelter in 1977 after the excavation was nearly complete. The large white tags mark the vertical and horizontal extent of the 11 major strata defined at the site. The smaller tags mark the locations of archaeological features, such as fire hearths, and geological, microfloral, and microfaunal samples. The rock fragments in the photograph are evidence for roof falls that occurred sporadically during the more than 16,000 year history of the rockshelter.

tural time periods. There has been little sediment added through mass wasting or eolian deposition, and nearly all aggradation is from the accumulation of cultural material. Reuse and/or disturbance by later occupants is likely. This is evident at many upland sites in Pennsylvania, as indicated by the mixing of artifacts from several cultural periods.

Valley Slopes

Artifacts found on slopes of greater than 7 degrees have in most cases been moved by mass wasting or erosion from an adjacent upland site or from the drip line of a rockshelter or cave. Smaller, in situ sites can, however, be located on slopes, especially in

the vicinity of springs, or seeps, and chert outcrops. At the base of slopes, especially adjacent to river terraces, thick colluvial deposits have the potential of containing in situ cultural material (Gardner and Donahue, 1985).

Fluvial Terraces

River terraces commonly contain archaeological sites because they are relatively level, well drained, near water and food, and relatively easy to exploit for primitive agriculture. They are excellent prospects for preservation by burial beneath recurrent flood deposits. Two good examples occur at the High Bank site (36Ly62) and Memorial Park site (36Cl56), which

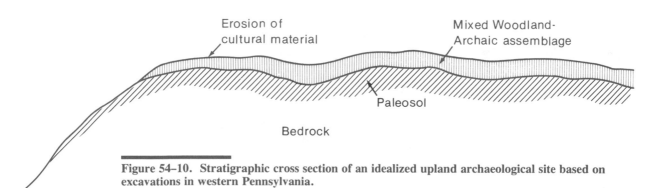

Figure 54–10. Stratigraphic cross section of an idealized upland archaeological site based on excavations in western Pennsylvania.

are situated along the West Branch of the Susquehanna River in the vicinity of Williamsport (Lycoming County) and Lock Haven (Clinton County), respectively. These sites occur on a low, late-Wisconsinan-age terrace of the Susquehanna River and contain Holocene-age vertical-accretion (overbank) deposits in excess of 4 m (13 ft). The vertical-accretion package at these sites consists of at least four stacked and buried solas (paleosols). These lower paleosols have been radiocarbon dated to the early Holocene (circa 7000 B.C. to 6000 B.C.) and reflect a change from a braided to a meandering channel habit. They contain artifacts that range in age from Early Archaic through Woodland. The occurrence of buried paleosols on low-terrace contexts indicates periods of relative fluvial stability, probably associated with a warmer and moister climate, that favored development of A horizons. During these times of stability, soil development occurred concomitantly with the occupation of the terrace surface by humans. In contrast, during periods of warmer/dryer or cooler/wetter climatic conditions, more frequent flood deposition and/or active channel erosion occurred. Thus, during these times, archaeological materials may have been removed by flood scouring and the subsequent emplacement of coarser grained lateral and vertical accretionary deposits (C horizons), or the archaeological materials may have accumulated in discrete occupation horizons contained within variably thick B horizons deposited through overbanking events.

PROBLEMS AND FUTURE RESEARCH

As the interaction between geologists and archaeologists continues to grow, we can expect the development of an increasingly detailed picture of earth history for Pennsylvania during the last 20,000 years. For example, systematic deep-testing investigations along the major river courses (i.e., Susquehanna, Monongahela, and Ohio Rivers), designed to locate deeply buried Paleo-Indian and Archaic sites, will increase our knowledge of Holocene changes in river drainages in Pennsylvania. As newly located archaeological sites are reported to the State Museum of Pennsylvania, the distribution of prehistoric occupants and landscape changes within the state will increase. In addition, analysis of faunal and floral remains found at archaeological sites will refine our understanding of climatic changes and perhaps help predict future changes.

RECOMMENDED FOR FURTHER READING

Adovasio, J. M., and Carlisle, R. C., eds. (1982), *Meadowcroft: collected papers on the archaeology of Meadowcroft Rockshelter and the Cross Creek drainage,* Pittsburgh, University of Pittsburgh Press, 274 p.

Butzer, K. W. (1984), *Archaeology as human ecology,* Cambridge, Mass., Cambridge University Press, 364 p.

Donahue, Jack, ed. (1986), *Geoarchaeology—An international journal,* New York, John Wiley and Sons.

Rapp, George, Jr., and Gifford, J. A. (1985), *Archaeological geology,* New Haven, Conn., Yale University Press, 435 p.

Stein, J. K., and Farrand, W. R., eds. (1985), *Archaeological sediments in context,* Orono, Maine, Center for the Study of Early Man, Institute for Quaternary Studies, University of Maine, Peopling of the Americas Series, v. 1, 147 p.

Thomas, D. H. (1989), *Archaeology,* 2nd ed., New York, Holt, Rinehart and Winston, 510 p.

Oblique aerial photograph of a residential development along the Lake Erie bluffs west of Erie. The bluff height is about 100 feet. Note the active debris flows on the bluff face and the accumulation of soil and vegetation at the toe of the bluff along the beach. Photograph by Helen L. Delano, April 1989.

CHAPTER 55   OTHER GEOLOGIC ENVIRONMENTAL PROBLEMS

The geologic hazards that are described in this chapter include those that bring about sudden, acute problems and others that are the cause of chronic problems that exist over long periods of time. A common thread is that they draw prominent media attention and, thus, are much in the public eye. Most geology-related hazards are largely self-inflicted by people who elect to build, live, and play in places that are geologically unsuitable.

The Lake Erie shoreline presents two chronic problems: continual bluff recession that threatens property, and erosion on the compound hooked spit called Presque Isle. The latter requires expensive annual maintenance to preserve recreational values and the commercial viability of Erie Harbor.

In the late 1980's, high levels of radioactive radon gas in dwellings became a newly recognized hazard and the subject of intense research. This emotion-charged issue generated much media attention, and the public need for information frequently exceeded the ability of government agencies to supply answers.

Urban flash flooding is a catastrophic, commonly life-threatening hazard that often recurs at the same localities. As impervious paved surfaces spread in urbanized areas, the incidence of flash flooding and resulting damage will probably worsen with time.

—*Charles H. Shultz*

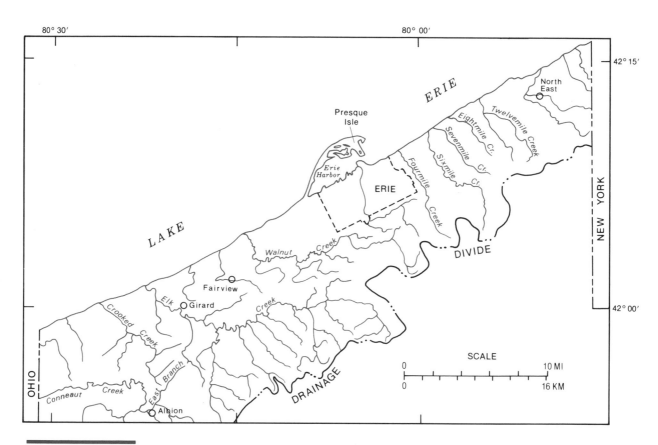

Figure 55A–1. Location map of major features of the Lake Erie shoreline of Pennsylvania. Streams and political boundaries are from U.S. Geological Survey Erie (1985), Ashtabula (1986), and Jamestown (1986) 30- by 60-minute topographic maps.

CHAPTER 55A   OTHER GEOLOGIC ENVIRONMENTAL PROBLEMS— LAKE ERIE SHORELINE

HELEN L. DELANO
    Bureau of Topographic and Geologic Survey
    Department of Conservation and Natural
        Resources
    P. O. Box 8453
    Harrisburg, PA 17105

The Lake Erie shoreline in Pennsylvania is a small, but geologically active, part of the state (Figure 55A-1). The 47-mile-long stretch across the northern border of Erie County includes the highest bluffs anywhere on the Lake Erie shore; it also includes Presque Isle, which is the only significant coastal depositional feature on the south shore of the lake.

Most of the Pennsylvania lake shore consists of narrow beaches in front of bluffs, 15 to 170 feet high, cut in Pleistocene and early Holocene glacial and lacustrine sediments and Devonian shale bedrock (Figure 55A-2). Only a small part of northwestern Pennsylvania drains into the lake (see Chapter 31), but

Figure 55A–2. A typical bluff section. The pictured section is located just east of Eightmile Creek, is about 60 feet high, and has shale exposed at lake level. The gravel beach in the foreground is part of a stream-mouth gravel bar associated with Eightmile Creek. The lighter material in the bluff face is in-place silt and sand; the darker shades indicate colluvium.

Figure 55A–3. Sevenmile Creek flowing on Devonian shale bedrock a few hundred feet upstream of its entry into Lake Erie.

small streams have cut down through the surficial deposits into shale bedrock (Figure 55A–3). Stream mouths provide the only breaks in the otherwise continuous bluff face.

GEOLOGY

The Quaternary stratigraphy of the bluffs is complex. A typical section includes 10 to 40 feet of massive to stratified silt and pebble diamict overlain by up to 130 feet of interbedded silt, clay, sand, and gravel. Depositional environments are not known in detail, but the diamicts are believed to be tills, flow tills, and debris-flow deposits related to late Wisconsinan glaciation. The better sorted and stratified deposits are believed to include deltaic and quiet-water deposits of proglacial lakes, and may include deposits of sandur and beach environments as well (Thomas and others, 1987).

The upper surface of the Devonian shale bedrock is near lake level along the shoreline but varies from a few feet below to up to about 10 feet above the lake. Where it is exposed above lake level, it is generally cut back in a nearly vertical bluff face. A wave-cut platform just below water level is commonly present where bedrock is exposed.

Narrow beaches of sand and gravel with cobbles are present at the toe of some bluffs. The presence or absence of a beach is a function of lake level, the amount of sediment available from eroded bluffs, and material brought to the lake by streams. Wide gravel

beaches commonly occur at the mouths of streams. Bluff sediments are predominantly fine grained (some samples are over 80 percent silt) and provide very little beach-forming material.

LAKE ERIE

The present shoreline configuration is the product of approximately 12,000 years of erosion acting on landforms created by Wisconsinan glaciers and modified by a series of proglacial lakes that occupied the Lake Erie basin as ice retreated from the area (Calkin and Feenstra, 1985). When Lake Erie became established in the basin, after the last Wisconsinan ice was gone, isostatic depression of the outlet near Niagara caused the lake level to be at least 120 feet lower than at present. Shoreline erosion and rising lake levels associated with the rebound of the outlet area have both led to the enlargement of the lake, although relative contributions of each process are unknown.

Glacial isostatic rebound may still be a small factor in changing lake levels, but most modern lake-level changes are attributable to climatic factors. Long-term changes are caused by variations in precipitation and evapotranspiration rates. Figure 55A–4 shows average annual lake levels for the period 1876–1987. The droughts of the 1930's and 1960's are clearly reflected in the lake levels. Between 1987 and 1989, the lake level dropped to near its long-term average. An annual cycle and short-term changes related to weather also affect the lake level.

BLUFFS

The bluffs along the lake shore in Pennsylvania vary considerably in height and composition. Most of the bluffs range from 50 to 100 feet in height, but the highest section reaches 170 feet. This increase is due largely to a deposit of sand and gravel believed to be related to proglacial Lakes Whittlesey and Warren (Thomas and others, 1987; Schooler, 1974). This deposit, which has been variously interpreted as beach and delta, is extensive on the upland but intersects the bluff line only between Twelvemile and Sixteenmile Creeks. Bedrock is rarely exposed above lake level along the shore west of Presque Isle and Erie, but in the eastern part of Erie County, the lower 6 to 10 feet of bluff is commonly shale.

Long-term average erosion rates along the Pennsylvania shore range up to about 3 feet per year, but erosion rates vary greatly over both time and space. A cycle of bluff erosion generally begins with high lake levels and direct wave erosion of the base of the bluff (Figure 55A–5). This steepens the total bluff profile, and a variety of mass-movement processes lead

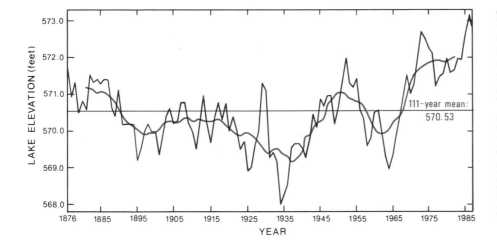

Figure 55A-4. The average annual water level for Lake Erie for the period 1876–1987 (slightly modified from Thomas and others, 1987, p. 21). The mean lake level is 570.53 feet above the International Great Lakes Datum (IGLD) of 1955. The smooth curve (color) is drawn from the 11-year moving mean of lake height calculated for each year from 1881 to 1982.

to progressive failure of the upper bluff face. These are basically landslide processes and include topple and fall of blocks of jointed diamict (Figure 55A-5), liquefaction and flow of well-sorted silts and sands, and slump of blocks of sediment held together by tree roots (Figure 55A-6). Groundwater seepage from the face of the bluff is an important factor in many of the bluff-face processes. Grain-by-grain erosion of sand and silt in some cases leads to development of large soil pipes (Figure 55A-7). These can be 20 feet in diameter and can extend into the bluff face for tens of feet. When the roof of a pipe collapses, large embayments in the top of the bluff result.

Figure 55A-6. Concrete cribbing wall built to protect the toe of the slope from lake erosion, east of Walnut Creek. The slopes behind and adjacent to the wall show evidence of debris flow and sliding of large blocks of soil held together by tree roots.

Accumulation of material at the toe of the bluff provides some protection from further retreat at the toe, but the colluvial sediment can be quickly removed by storm waves at times of high lake level. The most effective erosional waves typically occur during spring and fall storms. Winter storms may have more energy, but ice buildup protects the shore from erosion.

Bluff erosion is of more than just academic interest. The Pennsylvania shoreline has been moderately developed with vacation cottages and year-round residences (Figure 55A-8). Property owners are greatly affected by loss of bluff-top land, and

Figure 55A-5. A wave-cut notch forming in diamict near the Ohio-Pennsylvania state line. The large block of diamict in the water toppled from near the bluff top. Note the can in the left foreground for scale.

Figure 55A–7. Photograph of soil piping in a bluff. The pipes formed at an area of concentrated groundwater seepage at the contact between diamict (lighter shade) and overlying permeable sand and silt. The large pipe opening is approximately 5 feet wide. The debris cone below the pipe is composed of material that has slid down from the bluff above the piping zone. The small openings at the top of the photograph are cliff-swallow nests.

Figure 55A–8. A soil pipe formed in the bluff below a cottage in the western part of Erie County.

sometimes houses, to the lake. A variety of shore-protection structures have been built in attempts to slow or stop erosion (Figure 55A–7). These can be effective for protecting small areas, but the interruption of longshore sand movement generally leads to other problems elsewhere along the shore.

PRESQUE ISLE

Presque Isle is a compound recurved spit that protects Erie Harbor. Its wide variety of beach, dune, and interdune-pond environments provides habitats for many species of wildlife that are rare elsewhere in Pennsylvania. It also provides the only extensive sandy recreational beaches in the area and is a heavily used state park. This unique feature probably developed about 4,000 to 5,000 years ago as rising lake levels winnowed sand from the late Wisconsinan mo-

raine that extends across the lake from Long Point, Ontario, Canada, toward Erie (Figure 55A–9). Loose sand accumulated on the raised surface of the moraine platform, where it could be reworked and shaped by waves and currents. The predominant northeastward longshore transport of sand has controlled the shape and location of the spit. Past erosion of the west side and deposition at the east end has caused migration of the feature, possibly as much as 5 miles. At present, the spit is at the eastern edge of the moraine platform, and in order to grow much further eastward, will have to extend into deep water.

Presque Isle has a history of man's efforts to control erosion. Since the early 1800's, millions of federal and state dollars have been spent to protect Erie Harbor and, more recently, to maintain recreational beaches at Presque Isle (Pope and Gorecki, 1982; Thomas and others, 1987). The supply of new sediment from the west is limited because of shore-protection structures along the bluffs and long jetties built to protect the harbors at stream mouths. The jetties effectively stop all sand transport into Pennsylvania from the west because they extend into water too deep for wave transport of sand. The limited supply of new sand and continuing redistribution and erosion of the beaches has led to artificial nourishment of beaches as a shore-protection strategy. The high cost of this method of maintaining recreational beaches is justified on the grounds of the large contribution of tourism to the economic base of the Erie community. The

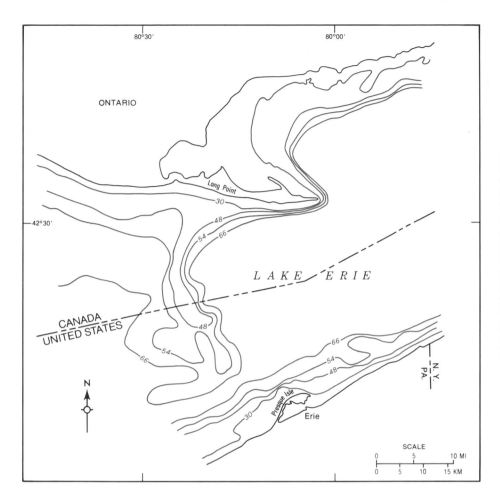

Figure 55A–9. Map of the central Lake Erie basin showing the transverse moraine that connects with Long Point, Ontario, Canada, and extends toward Presque Isle (slightly modified from Williams and Meisburger, 1982, p. 13). Contours are in feet below lake level.

construction of more than 50 detached breakwaters along the shore of the peninsula in the early 1990's was the latest in the long series of attempts to stabilize the shore of what is perhaps the most dynamic geological setting in Pennsylvania.

PROBLEMS AND FUTURE RESEARCH

There are many unanswered questions concerning the geology of the Lake Erie shoreline in Pennsylvania. The depositional history and distribution of the materials in the bluffs is poorly known. The history of former lake levels and shoreline erosion could help to predict future erosion rates. The dynamics of sediment transport in the nearshore zone is poorly understood. The relative contributions to longshore drift of bluff erosion and sediment carried to the lake by streams are unknown. Controlling factors for the mass-wasting processes on the bluffs are only beginning to be studied. Coastal engineering efforts to preserve one section of shoreline inevitably affect neighboring areas and can be extremely expensive. Cooperation between geologists, engineers, planners, and local governments is needed to resolve conflicting opinions on issues such as coastal land use, set-back regulations versus structural solutions, and expenditure of public money for erosion control.

RECOMMENDED FOR FURTHER READING

Carter, C. H., Neal, W. J., Haras, W. S., and Pilkey, O. H., Jr. (1987), *Living with the Lake Erie shore,* Durham, N. C., Duke University Press, 263 p.

Cobb, C. E., Jr. (1987), *The Great Lakes' troubled waters,* National Geographic, v. 172, no. 1, p. 2–31.

Schooler, E. E. (1974), *Pleistocene beach ridges of northwestern Pennsylvania,* Pennsylvania Geological Survey, 4th ser., General Geology Report 64, 38 p.

Thomas, D. J., Delano, H. L., Buyce, M. R., and Carter, C. H. (1987), *Pleistocene and Holocene geology on a dynamic coast,* Annual Field Conference of Pennsylvania Geologists, 52nd, Erie, Pa., Guidebook, 88 p.

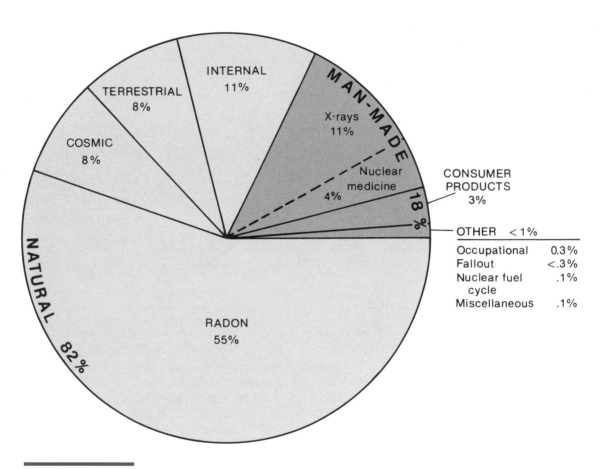

Figure 55B–1. Estimated sources of annual radioactivity exposure for humans (from National Council on Radiation Protection and Measurement, 1987).

786

CHAPTER 55B   OTHER GEOLOGIC ENVIRONMENTAL PROBLEMS— RADON

ARTHUR W. ROSE
Department of Geosciences
The Pennsylvania State University
University Park, PA 16802

Radioactivity caused by airborne radon has been recognized for many years as an important component in the natural background radioactivity exposure of humans (Figure 55B–1), but it was not until the 1980's that the wide geographic distribution of elevated values in houses and the possibility of extremely high radon values in houses were recognized. In 1984, routine monitoring of employees leaving the Limerick nuclear power plant near Reading, Pa., showed that readings on Stanley Watras frequently exceeded the expected radiation levels, yet only natural, nonfission-product radioactivity was detected on him. Radon levels in his home were found to be about 2,500 pCi/L (picocuries per liter), much higher than the 4 pCi/L guideline of the Environmental Protection Agency or even the 67 pCi/L limit for uranium miners (Figure 55B–10). As a result of this event, the Reading Prong section of the New England province where Watras lived became the focus of the first large-scale radon scare in the world.

Radon is a noble gas that originates by the natural radioactive decay of uranium and thorium. Like other noble gases (e.g., helium, neon, and argon), radon forms essentially no chemical compounds and tends to exist as a gas or as a dissolved atomic constituent in groundwater. Two isotopes of radon are significant in nature, ^{222}Rn and ^{220}Rn, formed in the radioactive decay series of ^{238}U and ^{232}Th, respectively (Figure 55B–2). The isotope ^{220}Rn (also called thoron) has a half-life (time for decay of half of a given group of atoms) of 55 seconds, barely long enough for it to migrate from its source to the air inside a house and pose a health risk. However, ^{222}Rn ("radon"), which has a half-life of 3.8 days, is a widespread hazard.

The distribution of radon is correlated with the distribution of radium (^{226}Ra), its immediate radioactive parent, and with uranium, its original ancestor. Because of the short half-life of ^{222}Rn, the distance that radon atoms can travel from their parent before decay is generally limited to distances of feet or tens of feet.

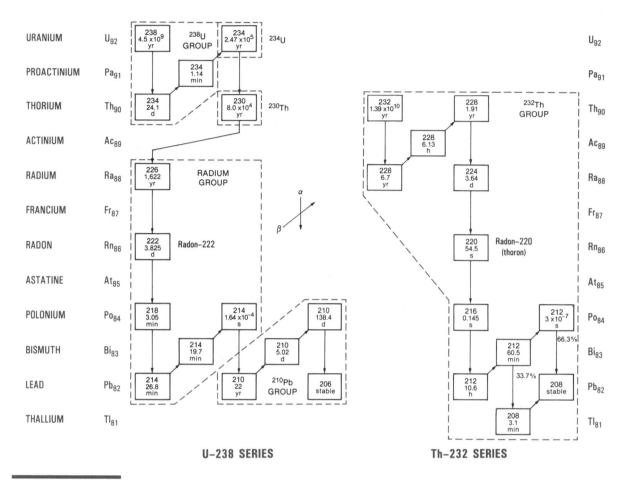

Figure 55B–2. Radioactive decay series of uranium-238 and thorium-232, showing atomic weights and half-lives (in boxes) and types of decays (modified from Rosholt, 1959, p. 3).

Three sources of radon in houses are now recognized:
1. Radon in soil air that flows into the house (Figure 55B–3).
2. Radon dissolved in water from private wells and exsolved during water usage; this is rarely a problem in Pennsylvania.
3. Radon emanating from uranium-rich building materials (e.g., concrete blocks or gypsum wallboard), which is not known to be a problem in Pennsylvania.

A high level of radon in houses was initially thought to be exacerbated in houses that are tightly sealed, but it is now recognized that rates of air flow into and out of houses, plus the location of air inflow and the radon content of air in the surrounding soil, are the keys. Outflows of air from a house, caused by a furnace, fan, thermal "chimney" effect, or wind effects, require that air be drawn into the house to compensate. If the upper part of the house is tight enough to impede influx of outdoor air (radon

concentration generally < 0.1 pCi/L), then an appreciable fraction of the air may be drawn in from the soil or fractured bedrock through the foundation and slab beneath the house, or through cracks and openings for pipes, sumps, and similar features (Figure 55B–3). Because soil gas typically contains from a few hundred to a few thousand pCi/L of radon, even a small rate of soil gas inflow can lead to elevated radon concentrations in a house.

The radon concentration of soil gas depends upon a number of soil properties, the importance of which is still being evaluated. In general, 10 to 50 percent of newly formed radon atoms escape the host mineral of their parent radium and gain access to the air-filled pore space (Figure 55B–4). The radon content of soil gas clearly tends to be higher in soils containing higher levels of radium and uranium, especially if the radium occupies a site on or near the surface of a grain from which the radon can easily escape. The amount of pore space in the soil and its permeability for air flow, including cracks and channels, are important

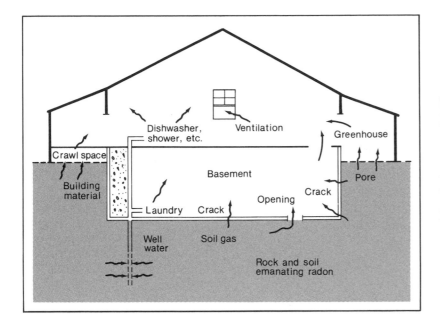

Figure 55B–3. Sketch showing entry points of radon into a house (slightly modified from Hileman, 1983, p. 471A, which was taken from Land and Water Resources Center, University of Maine at Orono, and Division of Health Engineering, Maine Department of Human Services, 1983, p. 8).

Figure 55B–4. Schematic sketch of the process of radon emanation from soil particles into pore spaces filled by air and water (modified from Tanner, 1986, p. 12). Radon atoms formed within about 0.04 μm of the particle surface (dashed line) may escape from the solid particle as a result of the energy released in radioactive decay of radium. Atom A does not reach the surface; atom B embeds itself in the adjacent grain; atom C stops within the water-saturated pore space and is available to migrate; and atom D escapes into the air-filled pore space but is little slowed in this medium and embeds itself in the opposite grain. R, recoil range; α, alpha particle for atom A.

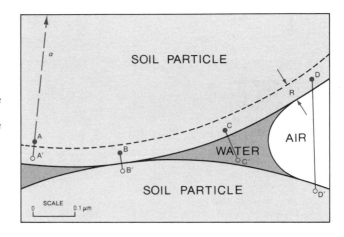

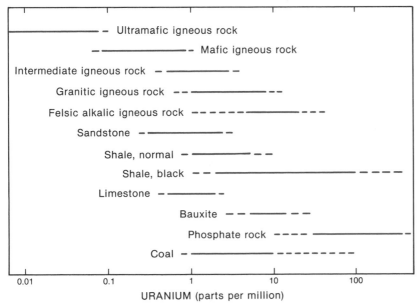

Figure 55B–5. Normal uranium content of rocks, showing types having elevated uranium (based on data in Rogers and Adams, 1970). Dashes indicate less common values.

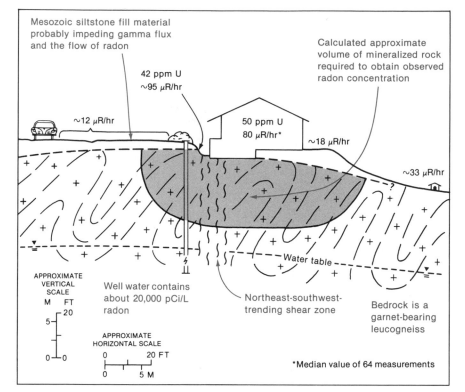

Figure 55B–6. Generalized cross section of the Watras house in Colebrookdale Township, Berks County, as viewed from the east, showing shear zone, uranium contents of rock from beneath the basement and from a trench outside the foundation, and radioactivity levels in microRoentgens per hour ($\mu R/hr$) (from Smith and others, 1987, p. 5).

Figure 55B–7. Radon levels in houses built on two rock groups in Centre County, showing higher levels over limestone-dolomite in Bald Eagle Valley in the Ridge and Valley province than over sandstone-shale in the Appalachian Plateaus province (unpublished data courtesy of Rodger Granlund, 1987).

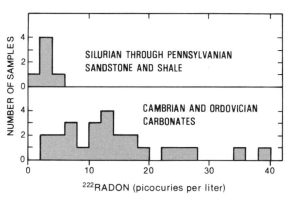

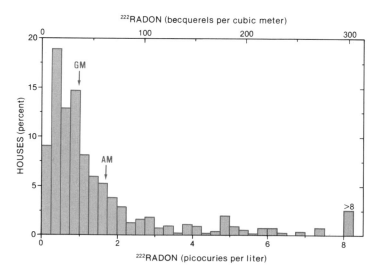

factors determining radon concentration in soil gas and its rate of flow into a house. Soil depth and moisture content, mineral host and form for radium, and other soil properties may also be important. For houses built on bedrock, fractured zones may supply air having radon concentrations similar to those in deep soil.

Areas where houses have high levels of radon can be divided into three groups in terms of uranium content in rock and soil:

1. Areas of very elevated uranium content (>50 ppm [parts per million]) around uranium deposits and prospects. Although very high levels of radon can occur in such areas, the hazard normally is restricted to within a few hundred feet of the deposit. In Pennsylvania, such localities occupy an insignificant area (see Figure 39–1, p. 548).

Figure 55B–8. Radon levels in homes in the United States. GM, geometric mean of data; AM, arithmetic mean. Modified with permission from Nero, A. V., Schwehr, M. B., Nazaroff, W. W., and Revzan, K. L. (1986), *Distribution of airborne radon-222 concentrations in U.S. homes*, Science, v. 234, Figure 2, p. 995. Copyright 1986 American Association for the Advancement of Science.

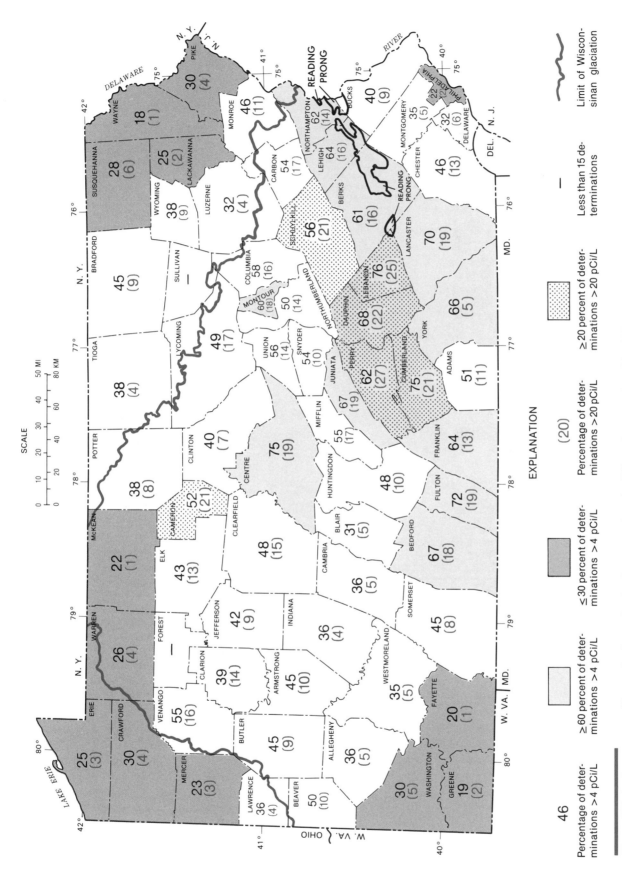

Figure 55B–9. Percentages of homes having radon levels greater than 4 pCi/L and greater than 20 pCi/L, as reported to the Pennsylvania Department of Environmental Resources (April 1989). State-sponsored samples in the Reading Prong are not included. Data for single counties may be misleading because of biased sampling, but general patterns are considered to be real. Wisconsinan glacial border is modified from Berg and others (1989).

Bq/m³	pCi/L	WL	EXPOSURE LEVEL	COMPARABLE RISK[1]		STANDARDS AND GUIDELINES[2]
7400	200	1	1,000 times average outdoor level	More than 75 times a nonsmoker's risk of dying from lung cancer		
				4 packs of cigarettes per day		
3700	100	.5	100 times average indoor level	10,000 chest X-rays per year		
					pCi/L 67	Limit for uranium miners (170 hours per month for 12 months)
1480	40	.2		30 times a nonsmoker's risk of dying from lung cancer		
					30	Prompt action required, Canada
740	20	.1	100 times average outdoor level	2 packs of cigarettes per day	20	U.S. Environmental Protection Agency guideline for remedial action within a few months
370	10	.05	10 times average indoor level	1 pack of cigarettes per day	11	Limit for existing buildings, Sweden
					5	Remedial action indicated, Union of Concerned Scientists
148	4	.02		3 times a nonsmoker's risk of dying from lung cancer	4	U.S. Environmental Protection Agency guideline for remedial action within a few years; remedial action required, Canada
74	2	.01	10 times average outdoor level	200 chest X-rays per year	2	Limit for new houses, Sweden; investigation recommended, Canada
				Nonsmoker's risk of dying from lung cancer		
37	1	.005	Average indoor level			
7.4	.2	.001	Average outdoor level			

Figure 55B–10. Estimated risk of lung cancer associated with radon exposure, and comparison of health limits and radioactivity units (modified from U.S. Environmental Protection Agency and U.S. Department of Health and Human Services, 1986). Bq/m³, becquerel per cubic meter; pCi/L, picocuries per liter; WL, working levels. Health limits and guidelines for radon exposure are from U.S. Environmental Protection Agency and U.S. Department of Health and Human Services (1986), U.S. Secretary of Labor (1968), and Hileman (1983).

[1]Based on lifetime exposure at corresponding radon level.
[2]All standards and guidelines refer to radon levels in buildings except the limit for uranium miners, which refers to radon levels in the mine.

2. Areas of common rocks having higher than average uranium content (5 to 50 ppm). In Pennsylvania, such rock types include granitic and felsic alkalic igneous rocks and black shales (Figure 55B–5). In the Reading Prong, high uranium values in rock or soil and high radon levels in houses are associated with Precambrian granitic gneisses commonly containing 10 to 20 ppm uranium, but locally containing more than 500 ppm uranium. The Watras house in this area (Figure 55B–6) was built on sheared gneiss (Gunderson and others, 1988) containing about 50 ppm uranium, and the basement was dug into bedrock (Smith and others, 1987). High uranium values in black shale are known to be associated with high radon levels in homes in New York State (Lilly and others, 1987). In Pennsylvania, elevated uranium occurs in black shales of the Devonian Marcellus Formation and possibly the Ordovician Martinsburg Formation. High radon values are locally present in areas underlain by these formations.

3. Areas of soil or bedrock that have normal uranium content but properties that promote high radon levels in houses. This group is incompletely understood at present. Relatively high soil permeability can lead to high

radon, the clearest example being houses built on glacial eskers. Limestone-dolomite soils also appear to be predisposed for high radon levels in houses, perhaps because of the deep clay-rich residuum in which radium is concentrated by weathering on iron oxide or clay surfaces, coupled with moderate porosity and permeability. The importance of carbonate soils is indicated by the fact that radon contents in 93 percent of a sample of houses built on limestone-dolomite soils near State College, Centre County, exceeded 4 pCi/L, and 21 percent exceeded 20 pCi/L, even though the uranium values in the underlying bedrock are all in the normal range of 0.5 to 5 ppm uranium, so far as is known (Figure 55B-7).

Current data on abundance and distribution of radon in Pennsylvania houses (Figures 55B-8 and 55B-9) are undoubtedly incomplete and biased, but some general patterns can be suggested. First of all, values exceeding the U.S. Environmental Protection Agency guideline of 4 pCi/L occur in all regions of the state. Glaciated areas in northern Pennsylvania tend to have relatively low frequencies of elevated radon, perhaps because of thin soils and incomplete weathering. The Appalachian Plateaus province in western Pennsylvania also appears to have lower than average radon, as does the Atlantic Coastal Plain near Philadelphia and other areas having a shallow water table. The highest proportion of elevated values is in a zone extending from central Pennsylvania to southeastern Pennsylvania, and in the Reading Prong. High values in the latter area are attributed to known uranium-rich granitic gneisses (R. C. Smith, II, personal communication, 1976; Gunderson and others, 1988), accentuated by local factors such as shear zones, and include a surprising number of extremely high radon values (>200 pCi/L). Elevated radon values in the larger, northwest-southeast-trending zone (Centre through York Counties) are not understood, but may represent some combination of black shale (Martinsburg Formation), limestone soil, and deep weathering. Some houses (0.6 percent in Cumberland and Dauphin Counties) exceed 200 pCi/L, a clearly hazardous level.

The estimated health hazard of radon is summarized in Figure 55B-10. The main hazard is actually from the radon daughter products (^{218}Po, ^{214}Pb, ^{214}Bi), which may become attached to lung tissue and induce lung cancer by their radioactive decay. Although the hazard is low compared with automobile accidents and cigarette smoking, the annual death rate is estimated at 5,000 to 20,000 people per year (Nero and others, 1986; U.S. Environmental Protection Agency and U.S. Department of Health and Human Services, 1986), which is very large compared to deaths from most chemical pollutants or from normal operation of nuclear power plants. Recent research indicates that smoking and radon interact to produce a greater hazard than either taken individually (U.S. Environmental Protection Agency, 1992). Various standards and guidelines ranging from 2 to 30 pCi/L have been recommended as limits or action levels for radon in homes (Figure 55B-10).

A number of methods for testing for and correcting high radon levels in homes have been suggested by the U.S. Environmental Protection Agency (1986, 1992).

PROBLEMS AND FUTURE RESEARCH

The distribution of high radon values shown on Figure 55B-9 is at best only partly understood and probably involves multiple factors. The wide observed range of variability between nearby homes presumably results at least partly from geologic factors, but these are generally location specific. Radon concentrations and transport in fractured bedrock are deserving of study, as is the correlation of radon with the multitude of soil, geologic, and geomorphic factors.

RECOMMENDED FOR FURTHER READING

Kerr, R. A. (1988), *Indoor radon: the deadliest pollutant*, Science, v. 240, p. 606-608.

Spencer, J. E. (1986), *Radon gas: a geologic hazard*, Arizona Bureau of Geology and Mineral Technology, Fieldnotes, v. 16, no. 4, p. 1-6.

Tanner, A. B. (1964), *Radon migration in the ground—A review*, in Adams, J. A. S., and Lowder, W. M., eds., *The natural radiation environment*, University of Chicago Press, p. 161-190.

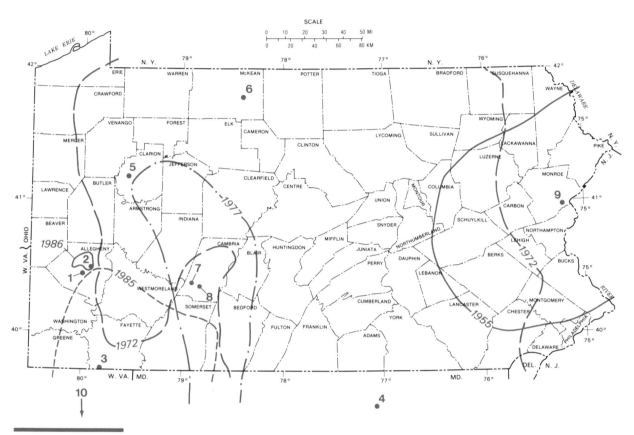

Figure 55C–1. Locations of high-precipitation stations and approximate boundaries of floods discussed in the text. The high-precipitation stations are as follows: 1, Pittsburgh; 2, Etna, North Hills; 3, Point Marion; 4, Unionville, Md.; 5, St. Petersburg; 6, Smethport; 7, Johnstown; 8, Ferndale; 9, Minisink Hills; and 10, Rockport, W. Va.

CHAPTER 55C   OTHER GEOLOGIC ENVIRONMENTAL PROBLEMS— URBAN FLASH FLOODING

ROBERT W. SCHMITT*
Hydrology and Hydraulics Branch
U.S. Army Engineer District, Pittsburgh
1000 Liberty Avenue
Pittsburgh, PA 15222

A shortened version of this paper was published as *Flash flooding in Pennsylvania*, in *Partnerships: effective flood hazard management—Proceedings of the 13th Annual Conference of the Association of State Floodplain Managers [Scottsdale, Ariz., May 22–27, 1989]*, Boulder, Colo., University of Colorado, Natural Hazards Research and Applications Information Center, Special Publication 22, p. 291–295.

*Retired.

INTRODUCTION

Everyone has some recollection of flash flooding, whether from personal experience, the news media, or the vivid tales of those who have endured its hardships. The flash flood, one of several of nature's unexpected "hit and run" marvels, is a high-intensity, relatively short duration event that occurs in a somewhat localized area. It results from unusual concentrations of rainfall and is often aggravated by "on-ground" conditions.

Urban flash flooding relates to losses in populated settings, but it often includes many suburban areas as well. Some flash floods with which this author has been involved are the 1955 eastern Pennsylvania flood, the 1972 central and western Pennsylvania flood, the 1977 Johnstown flood, the 1985 Monongahela River basin flood, the 1986 North Hills of Pittsburgh flood, and many smaller ones that were less notorious or totally unknown to those outside their limited confines. Although the above "name" floods covered varied expanses (Figure 55C–1), all or portions of these, as well as the lesser known ones, were characteristically flashy with unwelcome surprise and fury.

CAUSES

In this and adjacent states, past records (Table 55C–1) indicate a susceptibility to very high rainfall intensities. History has shown that flooding revisits some sites more often than others, but all low-lying areas become more vulnerable with the passage of time. Heavy rains, which some people seem to always regard as unprecedented, have produced flash flooding in certain instances that may have been aggravated by increased urbanization rather than by record-breaking intensity. Regardless, gross destruction and loss of life remain the worst casualties of such floods. Statistics of the above-mentioned "name" floods in

Table 55C-1. *High Precipitation Intensities in and Adjacent to Pennsylvania[1]*

Location	Date	Precipitation and time span
Rockport, W. Va.	July 1889	19.0 inches in 2 hours and 10 minutes[2]
Smethport, Pa.	July 1942	30.8 inches in 4.5 hours[2]
Unionville, Md.	July 1956	1.23 inches in 1 minute[2]
Johnstown, Pa.	July 1977	12.0 inches in 8.0 hours
Cheat and Monongahela Rivers, W. Va. and Pa.	Nov. 1985	10.0 inches in 12.0 hours
Pine Creek, North Hills, Pittsburgh, Pa.	May 1986	8.0 inches in 2.0 hours (max. spot[3])
Pine Creek, North Hills, Pittsburgh, Pa.	May 1987	4.5 inches in 2.0 hours

[1]Data from Jennings (1950).
[2]These values are among the world's greatest observed point rainfalls according to Jennings (1950).
[3]"Max. spot" refers to the greatest concentrated intensity of rainfall over a small area.

Pennsylvania, all or parts of which can be classified as flash floods, are presented in Table 55C–2. Flash floods can occur at any time of the year in Pennsylvania, but most strike during the summer. Winter or spring thaws, nevertheless, cannot be ignored. Heavy rains, frozen ground, ice jams, and snowmelt can quickly spawn a flood. Also, dam breaks have caused flash floods and severe loss of life. Forty-one people drowned following a dam break on Laurel Run, one of the many swollen tributaries involved in the 1977 Johnstown flood. The 1889 breach of the South Fork dam, which was located 12 miles upstream northeast of Johnstown, caused 2,209 deaths and is ranked among the nation's worst catastrophes (see Chapter 52, Appendix C).

Although flash floods are notably damaging in unprotected populated areas, flooding from excessive rainfall has even occasionally devastated urban sites that had a high degree of flood protection. Figure 55C–2 illustrates this for the Conemaugh River at Johnstown in 1977. Despite a sizable reduction of 11 feet provided by the in-place flood-reduction project, the 1977 runoff exceeded the economical 1936 design flood by

Table 55C–2. *Statistics of Selected Floods in Pennsylvania*

Date and location	No. of lives lost Pa.	No. of lives lost Elsewhere	Rainfall[1] (inches)	Total damage (millions of dollars)	Remarks
August 1955 (eastern Pa.)	101	200	11	500	At Minisink Hills, Pa., water rose 7 feet in 1 hour.
June 1972 (western Pa.)	Uncertain		12	91	At St. Petersburg, Pa., water rose 4 feet in 1 hour. *$850 million.[2]*
July 1977 (Johnstown, Pa., and vicinity)	78	0	12	142	At Ferndale, Pa., water rose 9.5 feet in 1 hour. *$335 million.[3]*
November 1985 (Monongahela River basin)	0	38	10	127	At Point Marion, Pa., water rose 3 feet in 1 hour. *$242 million.[2]*
May 1986 (North Hills, Pittsburgh, Pa.)	8	0	8	6	At Etna, Pa., water rose 5.2 feet in 1 hour.

[1]From isohyetal maps on file at the U.S. Army Corps of Engineers, Pittsburgh.
[2]Italic type indicates the amount of damages averted due to Corps of Engineers reservoir reductions and local flood-reduction projects.
[3]Italic type indicates the amount of total damages averted. Of the $335 million, $322 million is credited to the Johnstown flood-reduction project (see Figure 55C–2).

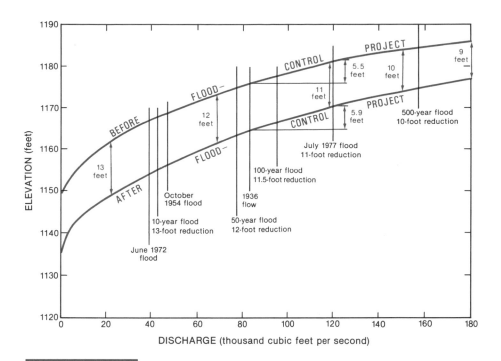

Figure 55C–2. Elevation versus discharge for the Conemaugh River at Johnstown, Pa. The graph shows that although flood protection does reduce flood peaks, it may not prevent flooding if precipitation is so intense that it exceeds the economical design limits of a project. The height of the July 1977 flood above the 1936 design flood without the project would have been 5.5 feet. The height of the 1977 flood above the 1936 design flood with the project was 5.9 feet. The total flood-height reduction of the July 1977 flood as a result of the project was 11 feet.

almost 6 feet. The term "design flood" refers to the flood on which a construction project is based, the object being to accommodate such a flood with little or no damage economically. Although a project could be constructed to provide total flood protection, there are limits beyond which the cost to build or the environmental impacts become prohibitive.

A number of "on-ground" conditions and activities help to create flash flooding. Some of these are listed below:

1. Steep terrain causing rapid and greater concentration of runoff.
2. Narrow channels and small floodplains providing little or no storage space to reduce and retard the passage of high flows.
3. Continuing development in a basin where ever-increasing quantities of impervious surfaces (e.g., roofs, drives, streets, and courts) prevent natural infiltration of runoff.
4. Vegetation removal resulting in loss of soil and water-holding materials.

5. Encroachments (construction on floodplains, bridges, and so forth) causing reduction of stream capacity, which is further worsened when debris is caught and subsequently accumulates.
6. Channel washouts causing erosion, sedimentation, and bank misalignment to propagate at successive downstream locations.
7. Geography and geology (e.g., unusual basin shape, poor channel orientation, and little subsurface storage capability) adversely affecting runoff.
8. Ill-advised siting by some enterprising builders and revenue-conscious local governments, creating problems that the author has repeatedly observed in one or more of the floods listed in Table 55C–2.

Elements of a typical flash flood are shown in Figures 55C–3, 55C–4, and 55C–5 for the North Hills of Pittsburgh flood of May 1986. These figures show, in order, the isohyetal precipitation map of the

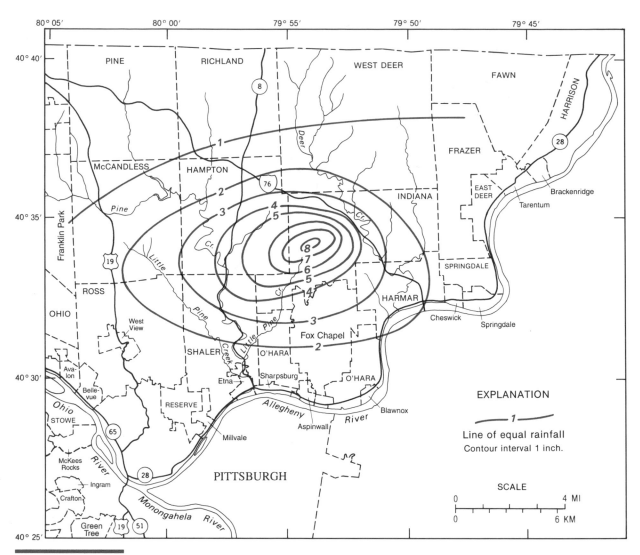

Figure 55C–3. Isohyetal map for a large thunderstorm that occurred 15 miles north of Pittsburgh, Allegheny County, on May 30, 1986 (data from National Weather Service).

storm, a hydrograph of rapidly developing discharge, and photographic evidence of destruction.

ESTIMATING THE DEPTH OF FLASH FLOODING IN PENNSYLVANIA

Figure 55C–6 shows a relationship between drainage areas and peak discharges for streams in the state. The author has constructed this curve by plotting flows that occurred during some of the more extreme flash floods in the state over a 72-year period. Drainage area is the greatest factor, after rainfall, affecting peak flows. This curve can be used to estimate flash-flood flows in urban and mixed-cover areas. For urban areas that have exceptional imperviousness, these values may be exceeded; that is, the plot of discharge for a given area could lie above the curve. The more urban the area, the more likely it is that the curve value will be reached or exceeded. If a reliable elevation-versus-discharge relationship is obtained for a site of concern (such as that shown in Figure 55C–2) and the drainage area is known or calculated, an approximation can be made of the expected depth of a flash flood. Where such an evaluation is made, it must be cautioned that this depth could be exceeded if a channel blockage occurs downstream from the site. This information may save a developer or a resident much grief and money if it is known in advance of flooding.

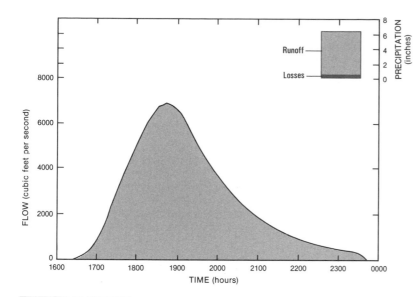

Figure 55C–4. Discharge hydrograph for Little Pine Creek (eastern tributary to Pine Creek), North Hills, Pittsburgh, for May 30, 1986. The graph shows the flow of a flood caused by an intense thunderstorm. The total precipitation upstream of this specific point was 6.25 inches over a period of 1 hour. The time from the onset of rain to the peak discharge was only 2.25 hours. The "flashy" stream returned to normal base flow in about 5 hours after the peak. Losses shown, which were due mostly to infiltration, amounted to about one-half inch, thereby allowing about 5.75 inches of rain to run off.

Figure 55C–5. Two photographs showing some of the destruction caused by the May 30, 1986, flash flood on Pine Creek in the North Hills of Pittsburgh. The upper photograph shows Spring Street in Etna Borough, and the lower photograph shows a view to the east along Saxonburg Boulevard, Shaler Township. Photographs courtesy of U.S. Army Corps of Engineers.

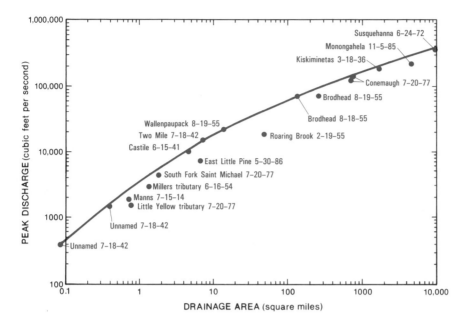

Figure 55C–6. Plot of peak discharge versus drainage area for estimating Pennsylvania flash floods. Flash floods between 1914 and 1986 are plotted on log-log scales for selected streams to define the relationship between a flow and drainage area. This can be used to estimate flows that might be reasonably expected from flash floods in this state. These values can be converted to depth when applied to an elevation-versus-discharge curve for a specific site, such as that shown in Figure 55C–2. Elevation-discharge curves can be observed and recorded over a period of time or computed by most hydraulic engineers for locations of interest.

PROBLEMS AND FUTURE RESEARCH

Short of controlling the weather, the recourse for combatting flash floods lies with "on-ground" modifications. Improvement of sensitive "on-ground" problem conditions should be pursued as follows:

1. Persuade owners of structures along streams to share crossings, thereby pooling resources to construct and maintain adequate facilities. This would eliminate multiple constrictions, which raise flood levels.

2. Provide bank stabilization, uniform channel widths, stable bottom grades, and good channel alignment to minimize scour and fill, maintain capacity, and discourage encroachments and blockages.

3. Relocate all movable materials deposited in or stored next to streams. This includes fallen trees, discarded appliances, fuel tanks, sheds, and automobile bodies.

4. Establish ponding areas on and off streams to store and delay floodwater passage, thereby reducing downstream flows and depths. Ponding areas should be constructed to compensate for urbanization, because streets and roofs increase the amount of runoff two or three times over that of green areas. Ponding can detain this excess runoff to approximate pre-urban rates.

5. Consider flood-control methods, such as channel-improvement projects (widening and deepening, or dikes) and dry-bed reservoirs, all of which can offer effective relief.

Practical research is under way utilizing various warning systems that employ remote-sensing techniques. Several pilot projects are now in place in the state and are under close scrutiny to assess their ability to provide an early warning of flash floods for evacuation purposes.

It is essential that remedial measures within a basin be "engineered" when modifying "on-ground" conditions. Corrections made independently at one location have been known to worsen already intolerable conditions elsewhere. Local governments and residents have proven, with few exceptions, that they are not up to the task of dealing with flooding. Therefore, it is incumbent that higher political bodies seize the initiative to zone all vulnerable areas and take remedial action. This can be done with local cooperation, using the abundant data that are available from floodplain and flood-insurance studies by the federal government, the state's Flood Plain and Storm Water Management Acts, and county storm-water studies. The state's two acts seek to regulate new construction in flood-prone areas and to control storm-water discharges. Subsequent implementation of the prevention and relief alternatives mentioned above, including outright property acquisition as necessary, could then be made on a population-density priority basis.

Flash floods can be dealt with effectively, given the cooperation of responsible governments and the application of the above solutions.

RECOMMENDED FOR FURTHER READING

Bogart, D. B. (1960), *Floods of August-October 1955, New England to North Carolina*, U.S. Geological Survey Water-Supply Paper 1420, 854 p.

Crippen, J. R., and Bue, C. D. (1977), *Maximum floodflows in the conterminous United States*, U.S. Geological Survey Water-Supply Paper 1887, 52 p.

Lane, F. W. (1986), *The violent earth*, Topsfield, Mass., Salem House, p. 118–139.

Schmitt, R. W. (1981), *The upper Ohio River water resources system*, International Association for Hydraulic Research, 19th, New Delhi, India, 5 p.

U.S. Army Engineer District, Pittsburgh, Hydrology and Hydraulics Branch (1974), *Post-flood report, June 1972*, in-house report, 40 p.

———— (1986), *The storm and flood of 3-6 November 1985, Monongahela River basin*, in-house report, 17 p.

U.S. Army Engineer District, Pittsburgh, Public Affairs Office (1978), *The 1977 southwestern Pennsylvania flood*, in-house report, 75 p.

Typical view in the Appalachian Mountain section of the Ridge and Valley province, characterized by long, linear ridges and intervening valleys. Pictured here is Tuscarora Mountain, viewed from the west near the junction of Pa. Routes 74 and 75 in Juniata County. The ridge, topped by resistant quartzites of the Lower Silurian Tuscarora Formation, rises more than 1,600 feet above the valley, which is underlain largely by shales of the Upper Silurian Wills Creek Formation.

Part X

THE GEOLOGIC TOURIST

Perhaps the best has been saved for last. What geologist has not marveled at the beauty of the natural world and contemplated the geological processes involved in its creation? Whereas anyone can enjoy a grand vista, a cluster of glistening stalactites, a tree-mantled chasm, or a pounding waterfall, many geologists achieve greater exhilaration and appreciation because they sense the geology behind the beauty.

We hope that you will have an opportunity to explore and to travel through Pennsylvania. Enjoy its diverse and magnificent scenery, and absorb its cultural history, which is so intertwined with its geology. Make an extra effort to see some of those very special places described herein. Your journey will be very rewarding.

—Charles H. Shultz

Figure 56–1. The Ice Cave, a talus cave in sandstone of the Pocono Formation, Trough Creek State Park, Huntingdon County. Foreground blocks are 1 to 2 feet across.

CHAPTER 56   CAVES

WILLIAM B. WHITE
  Materials Research Laboratory
  Department of Geosciences
  The Pennsylvania State University
  University Park, PA 16802

ELIZABETH L. WHITE
  Department of Civil and Environmental
    Engineering
  Environmental Resources Research Institute
  The Pennsylvania State University
  University Park, PA 16802

INTRODUCTION

Caves are natural openings large enough to admit human explorers. The Survey of Pennsylvania Caves (Mid-Appalachian Region, National Speleological Society) has recorded more than 1,220 caves of various geologic types in the Commonwealth, including solution caves, tectonic caves, talus caves, and rockshelters. Tectonic caves are openings formed by the mechanical slippage of rock masses. Many small tectonic caves occur in massive sandstones but have not been cataloged. Talus caves are openings formed within loose piles of scree and boulders on mountainsides. Although small, some, such as the Ice Cave in Trough Creek State Park, are of interest because they act as cold-air traps (Figure 56–1). Resistant sandstones commonly develop rock overhangs, forming rockshelters, which are marked on some maps and in some reports as "caves." Rockshelters, such as Sheep Rock in Huntingdon County or Christopher Gist Cave in Fayette County, are commonly of archeological or historic interest (see Chapter 54).

By far the greatest number of caves, and also the largest caves, are solution caves formed in limestone or dolomite by the dissolving action of groundwater. Cave development tends to take place near or just below the water table. Solution caves commonly carry underground streams that are integrated with surface drainage in the form of sinking creeks or large karst springs.

Most of the caves of the state have been explored, described, and surveyed by cave enthusiasts over the past 50 years. Maps and written descriptions may be found in Stone and others (1932), Stone (1953), Reich (1974), and White (1976), and in the county-by-county cave-survey bulletins published by the Mid-Appalachian Region of the National Speleological Society.

GEOLOGIC AND PHYSIOGRAPHIC DISTRIBUTION

Caves occur in all of the principal physiographic provinces of Pennsylvania but are concentrated in the limestone valleys of the Appalachian Mountain

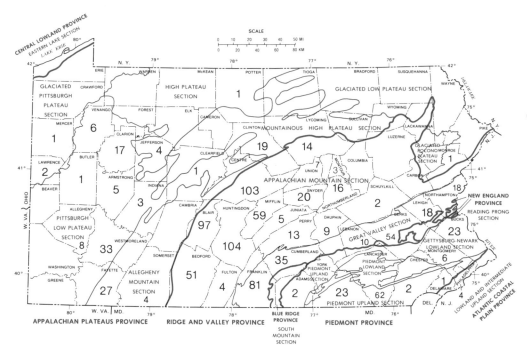

Figure 56–2. Map of the physiographic provinces of Pennsylvania (from Berg and others, 1989) showing the number of caves in each county.

section of the Ridge and Valley province (Figure 56–2). The few caves that are present in the northern plateaus and in the glaciated low plateaus are mainly talus and tectonic caves.

In the Pittsburgh Low Plateau, Glaciated Pittsburgh Plateau, and Allegheny Mountain sections of the Appalachian Plateaus province, caves occur in the Mississippian Loyalhanna and Pennsylvanian Vanport limestones. The Loyalhanna caves occur mainly along the crest of the Chestnut Ridge anticline in Westmoreland and Fayette Counties. Some, such as Bear and Coon Caves, are laid out in the "city block" pattern known as a network maze; others, such as Laurel Caverns and Copperhead Cave, are long passages parallel to the dip. The Vanport caves occur in the valley of the Allegheny River and its tributaries. They are complex network mazes that result from a combination of slow seepage of groundwater through the jointed limestone and base-level backflooding from the river.

About 6,000 feet of Cambrian and Ordovician carbonate rocks underlies the eroded anticlinal valleys in the Appalachian Mountain section in central Pennsylvania. In addition, limestones of the Silurian-Devonian Keyser Formation and the Lower Devonian Helderberg Group crop out in long, parallel bands along secondary ridges. Caves form in both stratigraphic sequences. However, few caves form in dolomite, and most of the caves in Ordovician limestones are concentrated in about 400 to 500 feet of the uppermost carbonate units (Rauch and White, 1970). The Upper Ordovician Salona and Coburn Formations are too shaly to be good cave formers, and the Milroy

Member of the Upper Ordovician Loysburg Formation is too dolomitic. Because of the physiographic placement of the most cavernous units at the base of the mountain ridges, caves in the Appalachian Mountain section of the Ridge and Valley province tend to be concentrated in long, parallel bands along the flanks of the mountains. Here, they receive sinking streams draining from the clastic rocks of the ridges. The best developed surface karst is also concentrated in bands marking the outcrop line of the Upper Ordovician limestones. Caves in the Keyser and Helderberg limestones occur in the secondary ridges, which are commonly capped with resistant sandstone of the Lower Devonian Ridgeley ("Oriskany") Formation. Because of their locations on the ridge flanks, the Keyser/Helderberg caves are less commonly the routes of active underground drainage. These caves also tend to have small and obscure entrances unrelated to other aspects of the surface landscape.

Caves in the carbonate rocks that underlie the Great Valley section of the Ridge and Valley province are most numerous in Cumberland and Franklin Counties. In contrast to those of the Appalachian Mountain section, the caves of the Great Valley form in many of the rock units present there, but, as is true elsewhere, the largest and best developed caves are in limestones rather than dolomites. Because of the modest relief in the Great Valley, caves tend to occur at shallow depths below the land surface, and many are related to underground drainage systems.

Caves occur in the Cambrian and Ordovician rocks of the Piedmont province in southeastern Pennsylvania. These are mainly small caves that are not integrated with present underground drainage systems. The largest number of caves occurs in Lancaster and York Counties (Figure 56–2). In York County, many of the carbonate rocks have been metamorphosed into marble; these caves have walls of marble commonly punctuated by bands of schist.

CAVE PATTERNS

Caves are initiated along joints, fractures, and bedding-plane partings. Evidence from Pennsylvania is that most of the caves are guided by joints; however, not all joints enlarge into cave passages. If groundwater flow is concentrated along a single joint or set of joints, a linear or angulate cave results (Figure 56–3). Deike's (1969) study in central Pennsylvania shows that tension joints parallel to the strike are most effective and, as a result, many caves are strike oriented. When all joint sets in a system are enlarged to form cave passages, the result is a network maze

(Figure 56–3). Caves in steeply dipping rocks tend to take on linear or angulate patterns, whereas caves in rocks of low dip commonly have maze patterns.

Caves are fragments of conduits that were, at one time, part of a groundwater-flow system (Figure 56–4). Breakdown, sediment infilling, and deposition of speleothems modifies the shape and accessibility of cave passages as seen by present-day explorers. As joints and fractures are enlarged by solution, several thresholds are crossed when the width of the fracture reaches roughly 0.25 to 0.5 inch. The rate at which the carbonate rock dissolves begins to increase, the flow may become turbulent, and the water moving through the proto-cave gains the ability to transport clastic sediment. These processes allow the selection of an optimum hydraulic path through the carbonate rock that then evolves into a single-conduit type of cave passage. If the rate of flow through the joint system is regulated, either by diffuse infiltration of water from overlying clastic rocks, as occurs in Vanport caves, or by other hydrologic or geologic barriers, the runaway process of solution does not take place. All

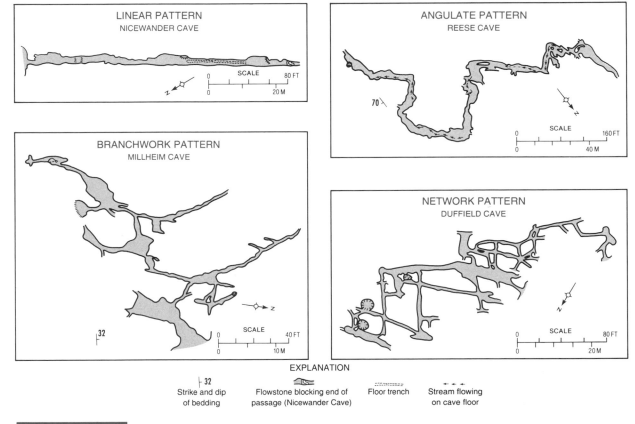

Figure 56–3. Sketch maps of some Pennsylvania caves illustrating types of cave patterns (adapted from White, 1960, Figure 1, p. 49). Nicewander, Reese, and Duffield Caves are in Franklin County in the Great Valley section of the Ridge and Valley province; Millheim Cave is in Centre County in the Appalachian Mountain section of the Ridge and Valley province.

Figure 56–4. Tytoona Cave, Blair County, an example of an active groundwater conduit. Tytoona Cave is in the Ordovician Hatter Formation. Note the alluvial bed of the underground stream.

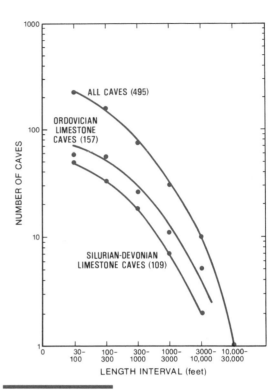

Figure 56–5. Length distribution for caves in Pennsylvania. Numbers of caves in each population are given in parentheses.

joints enlarge at approximately equal rates, and a maze cave develops.

Although regional-scale underground drainage systems occur in Penns Valley, Nittany Valley, Kishacoquillas Valley, and Nippenose Valley in the Appalachian Mountain section of central Pennsylvania, and to a more limited extent in the Great Valley section, most Pennsylvania caves are rather small (Figure 56–5). Explorable caves tend to occur only at the inlet points of sinking streams and at some outlet points where the underground drainage returns to the surface through karst springs, for example at Penns Cave in Centre County. Commonly, as in Brush Valley, Centre County, the anticlinal structure of the valley requires that surface water sinking into Upper Ordovician limestones on one limb of the anticline must cross the dolomite core of the anticline to reach the spring on the opposite limb. The combination of geologic setting, ceiling collapse, clastic sediment plugs, and sumps where caves intersect the water table all act to break the conduit systems into fragments that become the individual caves.

SPELEOTHEMS

The cave environment is generally wet, oxidizing, in the pH range 6 to 8, and at a constant temperature near 50°F . Caves are depositional sites for minerals, the three most common of which are calcite, gypsum,

and aragonite. Some 178 minerals have been identified from caves (Hill and Forti, 1986), but of these, only a few have been found in Pennsylvania caves.

Infiltrating groundwater absorbs carbon dioxide in the upper soil layers, converting it to carbonic acid. The acidified water reacts with carbonate rock at the base of the soil, producing a solution of Ca^{++} and HCO_3^-. This solution then percolates downward through tight joints and fractures in the bedrock, commonly with little further reaction. When the supersaturated solutions emerge from the roof of a cave, they lose CO_2, and consequently calcite ($CaCO_3$) is deposited. The principal forms are stalactites, stalagmites, and flowstone (Figure 56–6). Many other complex depositional forms also occur. Calcite crystallization requires constant and undisturbed conditions for long periods of time. Therefore, the largest crystals and the most aesthetically attractive deposits occur in caves where there is little circulation of outside air and little evaporation.

Gypsum ($CaSO_4 \cdot 2H_2O$) occurs sparsely in Pennsylvania caves because it is a moderately soluble mineral and most Pennsylvania caves are wet. Aragonite, the metastable form of $CaCO_3$, occurs rather widely but in minor amounts. It commonly appears as radiating clusters of acicular crystals known as anthodites.

Figure 56–6. Stalactite, stalagmite, and flowstone speleothems in Lincoln Caverns, Huntingdon County. The height of the stalagmite is approximately 8 feet.

Uranium is easily complexed by carbonate ions and, so, is mobile in carbonate groundwaters, whereas thorium occurs only in highly insoluble minerals. Most calcite deposits in caves contain uranium at the part per million level, and any thorium present can be assumed to be a daughter of uranium decay. Thus, $^{230}Th/^{234}U$ ratios provide an age-dating method for speleothems that is effective to 300,000 years B.P. (Thompson and others, 1976). It appears, from the measurements that have been made in central Appalachian caves, that there are at least two populations of speleothems: those deposited during the Sangamon interglacial between Illinoian and Wisconsinan glaciations, and those deposited in recent time. Deposition during the Wisconsinan ice advance was meager.

GEO-AESTHETICS

Caves are considered by cave explorers to be valuable both as aesthetic objects and as fragments of untrammeled wilderness. The sculpturing of cave walls and the dripstone and flowstone speleothems are bits of landscape that have a beauty comparable to wild rivers or to hills with unbroken forest. Although caves are small, there is a sense of remoteness which, combined with the dark and raw bedrock environment, produces a sense of wilderness that might require many miles of hiking to achieve in open country aboveground. For these reasons, there has been a considerable effort in Pennsylvania and elsewhere to preserve caves in their natural state and to educate those who would explore them, both for safety and for preservation of what is, in fact, a very fragile environment. To an encouraging extent, these efforts have been successful, and there is a strong conservation ethic among Pennsylvania's cavers.

Many active cavers are organized in local clubs (known as "grottos") that are chapters of the National Speleological Society (1 Cave Avenue, Huntsville, AL 35810). The organized caving groups maintain a cave rescue organization, and many offer training in techniques and safety.

COMMERCIAL CAVES

At the time of this writing (1994), 10 Pennsylvania caves are open to the public: Laurel Caverns in the Loyalhanna Limestone in western Pennsylvania; Coral Caverns and Lincoln Caverns in the Keyser/Helderberg limestones in central Pennsylvania; Historic Indian Caverns, Penns Cave, and Woodward Cave in the Upper Ordovician limestones in central Pennsylvania; and Crystal Cave, Indian Echo Caverns, Lost River Caverns, and Onyx Cave in the Ordovician limestones of the Great Valley. These caves have been adapted for easy visitation by the installation of smooth trails, stairs, and electric lighting. Together, they form a moderately representative cross section of the hydrologic and geologic settings of Pennsylvania caves.

PROBLEMS AND FUTURE RESEARCH

In spite of the large number of explored caves, knowledge of their relationship to the karst drainage systems remains fragmentary. Improved understanding of Pennsylvania's carbonate aquifers is needed for the preservation of present water supplies and the development of future ones. Caves and their contents are important records of drainage-basin evolution and Pleistocene history in the Appalachian Highlands.

RECOMMENDED FOR FURTHER READING

Jackson, D. D. (1982), *Underground worlds,* Alexandria, Va., Time-Life Books, 176 p.

Stone, R. W., Barnsley, E. R., and Hickok, W. O., IV (1932), *Pennsylvania caves,* 2nd ed., Pennsylvania Geological Survey, 4th ser., General Geology Report 3, 143 p.

White, W. B., ed. (1976), *Geology and biology of Pennsylvania caves,* Pennsylvania Geological Survey, 4th ser., General Geology Report 66, 103 p.

_____ (1988), *Geomorphology and hydrology of karst terrain,* New York, Oxford University Press, 464 p.

Figure 57–1. Looking east toward The Point of Pittsburgh, formed where the Allegheny (left) and Monongahela Rivers join to form the Ohio River, in the foreground. At The Point State Park, in the middle background, approximately 70 feet of alluvium overlies gently dipping bedrock of the Pennsylvanian Glenshaw Formation of the Conemaugh Group. The north-facing slope of Mount Washington, capped by the Pennsylvanian Monongahela Group, is at the right. Photograph courtesy of the Pennsylvania Department of Transportation, Photogrammetry and Surveys Division.

CHAPTER 57 GEOLOGICAL INFLUENCES ON PENNSYLVANIA'S HISTORY AND SCENERY

GLENN H. THOMPSON, JR.*
Department of Physics/Earth Science
Elizabethtown College
Elizabethtown, PA 17022

J. PETER WILSHUSEN**
Bureau of Topographic and Geologic Survey
Department of Conservation and Natural
  Resources
P. O. Box 8453
Harrisburg, PA 17105

INTRODUCTION

Pennsylvania's complex geological framework, described by authors in the preceding chapters, when coupled with climatic factors past and present, has produced a varied landscape of mountains, valleys, plateaus, and an attendant hydrologic system. Taken collectively, these physiographic features have given rise to a diverse and often beautiful landscape, which, in turn, has had a strong influence on the historical development of the state's culture and economy and the society that thus arose. The landscape has been modified in some places by the activities of that society.

In this chapter, examples are given of notable geologic factors that have influenced the course of human history and some effects that people have had on the landscape. Three significant geologic features representative of Pennsylvania's statewide outdoor museum are discussed in detail.

GEOLOGIC INFLUENCES ON PENNSYLVANIA'S HISTORY

If maps of Pennsylvania's highways and Pennsylvania's geology are placed side by side, even the most casual observer will immediately notice pattern correspondence, which is particularly well developed in the central region. There, bright colors seem swirled, then elongated into a broadly recurved system of artistic form and intrinsic beauty, the patterns of which are mimicked by marked parallelism of its superimposed roadways. To the west and north, the geologic artist has used a broader paintbrush. Accordingly, transportation routes clearly display their purpose of connecting cities and towns directly with each other. On both maps, the southeast displays a curious mix of organized patterns and near chaos.

The positions of cities, like the patterns of roadways, are related to the Commonwealth's physical characteristics. The two largest urban areas, Philadelphia and Pittsburgh (Figure 57-1), are located on navigable waterways. The cities of Allentown, Bethlehem, Wilkes-Barre, Johnstown, and Reading are also sited on rivers, though less navigable. Harrisburg (Figure 57-2) is located at the intersection of the Great Valley and the Susquehanna River. Erie (Figure 57-3) rests where Pennsylvania juxtaposes the Great Lakes.

These patterns and similarities are not accidental. Pennsylvania's human history dates back to the waning stages of the Wisconsinan glaciation, when Native

Figure 57-2. Looking north, upstream along the Susquehanna River. The city of Harrisburg is on the right. It is built on 5 to approximately 25 feet of alluvium on the steeply dipping Ordovician Martinsburg Formation. In the right background, the southernmost water gap of the Susquehanna River is cut in steeply dipping, commonly overturned, folded and faulted Silurian and Devonian bedrock.

Americans first lived here. Like later people, they created pathways following natural corridors that provided relative ease of passage from one place to another. Beginning in 1681, when King Charles II of England settled a debt by granting a charter that allowed William Penn to proceed with his "holy experiment," migrating Europeans proliferated in lands west of the Delaware River. The Pennsylvania highway map depicts the current status of 300 years of cultural evolution. This period embraces major dramas involving the rise, and sometimes fall, of entire transportation systems, natural-resource exploitation, population centers, ethnic concentrations, and wars and political events

that shaped a nation. All were variously influenced by Pennsylvania's geological underpinnings.

Economic growth and development moved generally from east to west across Pennsylvania, a trend common in eastern seaboard locations. There were exceptions, however, as settlers also entered Pennsylvania via waterways from the north and the southwest. Westward expansion of commerce and the development of economic resources required dealing with the transportation barrier of the Appalachian Mountains (Figure 57-4), which in Pennsylvania includes the Ridge and Valley and Appalachian Plateaus physiographic provinces, divided from each other by the topographically imposing Allegheny Front. To surmount these obstacles, several innovative engineering works were developed (Figure 57-5). Notwithstanding these heroic efforts, modern transportation routes yet follow many of those created by Native Americans and pioneers who established footpaths, canoeways, and wagon roads, taking advantage of natural breaks in the "endless" mountains wherever they could. Thus, rivers, water gaps, and stream incursions into the Allegheny Front itself became of prime importance in east-west travel. Ultimately, the intersections of these natural breaks with major valleys became transportation junction points, many of which grew to become Pennsylvania cities.

When explaining the location of cities, geographers commonly refer to "break-in-bulk" points. Those are places where bulk goods are removed from one form of conveyance and transferred to another. Philadelphia, a fall-line city, is naturally situated at the boundary between the Coastal Plain and Piedmont provinces where the Schuylkill River cascades down before joining the tidewater Delaware. Here, a community developed where the geologic setting provided the optimum point on the Delaware River for trading ships to reach prior to unloading their cargoes. It was from there that other transportation forms, some quite innovative, branched out. These included the Lancaster-Philadelphia Road, the Schuylkill Canal, and, by 1830, a railroad that pressed westward toward the Susquehanna River (Shank, 1988).

Regardless of transportation mode, be it floating or rolling, east-west travel across Pennsylvania was seriously hindered by the Allegheny Front, where ele-

Figure 57-3. The City of Erie, in northwestern Pennsylvania, is near the center of the 62-mile part of the shoreline of Lake Erie that lies in this state. Erie was built on 0 to 100 feet of unconsolidated Pleistocene deposits that form bluffs on the lakeshore and overlie gently dipping bedrock of the Devonian Northeast Shale. Erie's natural harbor exists because of Presque Isle, in the middle background, a migrating sand spit on a sublacustrine platform of glacial sediments.

Figure 57-4. View to the north of Everett on the north side of the Pennsylvania Turnpike and Earlston on the south, Bedford County. The builders of the Pennsylvania Turnpike took advantage of a water gap in Tussey Mountain, on the left, to ease the route through this part of the Appalachian Mountain section of the Ridge and Valley physiographic province. Tussey Mountain and Warrior Ridge, in the center of the photograph, are offset by faulting at this location. Photograph courtesy of the Pennsylvania Department of Transportation, Photogrammetry and Surveys Division.

vations to be overcome in many places approached 1,500 feet. This problem induced at least two innovative engineering works as solutions—the Allegheny Portage Railroad and the Horseshoe Curve on the Pennsylvania Railroad.

Begun on July 4, 1826 (Ward, 1980), the Pennsylvania Main Line Canal was conceived as the western component of the Main Line Public Works rail/canal system connecting Philadelphia with Pittsburgh and was to include Harrisburg, Altoona, and Johns-

town. Begun in 1826, the eastern section from Philadelphia to Columbia, a few miles south of Harrisburg, was constructed as a rail line. From there to Hollidaysburg (Altoona area) and from Johnstown to Pittsburgh, travel was by canal. Its completion in 1834 depended on an engineering feat, the construction of the Allegheny Portage Railroad, not even imagined at the outset when a 4-mile tunnel was proposed as a solution to negotiate the Allegheny Front. Difficulties regarding construction of a tunnel of unprecedented length

Figure 57–5. View of the Horseshoe Curve, Blair County, from the southeast side of the Burgoon Run valley. Kittanning Point, at the head of the curve, is capped by Mississippian Burgoon Sandstone. Exposed on the railroad below Kittanning Point are sandstone and shale of the Rockwell Formation, which is transitional in age between Devonian and Mississippian. The first train traveled this route in 1854, beginning regular service on one of the innovative transportation routes surmounting the Allegheny Front. Photograph courtesy of the Altoona Public Library and the Railroaders Memorial Museum.

forced other options to be weighed. As inclined planes were already successfully operating in the anthracite district (Figure 57–6) and at mountainside gannister quarries, the Canal Commissioners decided on this model as a means of crossing the mountain. Canals were constructed to follow the Juniata River from the east and the Conemaugh River from the west. Canal boats were fashioned to be broken into two sections and loaded onto inclined-plane cars. Five planes and intervening conventional grades were used to lift cars and loads up one side to the summit, and five more planes lowered the cars down the other side between Hollidaysburg, Blair County, and Johnstown, Cambria County (Welch, 1833). From Hollidaysburg, the total lift was about 1,400 feet, whereas from Johnstown it was only 1,170 feet. The planes varied in length from 0.28 to 0.58 mile. The cars, pulled by gigantic 7-inch-circumference hemp ropes, traveled at

Figure 57–6. Reproduction of a painting by George Storm of the inclined plane on the Allegheny Portage Railroad. Part of the Pennsylvania Main Line system, which comprised railroads to the east of the Susquehanna and mostly canals to the west, the Allegheny Portage Railroad was constructed to transport canal boats across the Allegheny Front. A system of 10 inclined planes in a distance of 36.7 miles carried canal boats over an elevation change of about 1,380 feet in order to transport passengers and goods from the Susquehanna to the Ohio River basin.

4 miles per hour on the planes. The system was abandoned in 1857, when a new engineering triumph allowed a conventional railroad to cross the mountain.

Early in 1852, J. Edgar Thomson was made president of the Pennsylvania Railroad, a line he had been building west toward the Allegheny Front at the Hollidaysburg canal termination (Ward, 1980). Realizing that travel time was the critical element in transportation economics, he immediately sought to engineer continuous trackage across the mountain barrier, thus dramatically reducing this key factor for goods in transport. To accomplish this, he surveyed and resurveyed until a route was selected that, with massive cuts and fills, could allow large railroad trains to traverse the central obstacle. This route, including several tunnels, featured the famous Horseshoe Curve (Figure 57–5), where 2 miles of patterned convolution reduced the grade to acceptable standards. Thomson's economic prowess and engineering genius had combined to produce a railroad transportation monument that, today, continues to serve the needs of the nation.

One final case history illustrating the influence of Pennsylvania geology upon its development ironically involves a precursor to the Philadelphia-to-Pittsburgh routes outlined above. The story of the Pennsylvania Turnpike, America's "dream highway," began in 1759 when General John Forbes completed a major southern road from Shippensburg through Bedford to Pittsburgh. More than 100 years later, in 1883, Andrew Carnegie teamed up with William Vanderbilt to build the South Penn Railroad (Cleaves and Stephenson, 1949). Following, somewhat, the Forbes road, construction began, and by 1885, about 60 percent of the grade was completed, including 4.5 miles of tunnel. In the fall of that year, financial pressures led to the sale of the South Penn to the Pennsylvania Railroad, and the unfinished project was immediately abandoned.

Following the year of its demise, scattered attempts to revive the railroad met with failure. However, in the late 1930's, its fate began to change. Suspicions were strong that America might be drawn into a second world war, and in that event, Pennsylvania's steel-making and manufacturing capacity would be taxed to the utmost. This implied that transportation eastward from Pittsburgh would also be heavily affected. Modern trucks of the day would be needed to supplement rail travel, thereby necessitating roadways capable of handling such traffic. The challenge was met in 1937 when the Pennsylvania Turnpike Commission was created by the General Assembly for the purpose of constructing and maintaining an east-west superhighway across southern Pennsylvania. Largely utilizing the partly completed South Penn

right-of-way, the Turnpike was opened in 1941 after only 20 months of construction time. Its initial length stretched from Irwin, near Pittsburgh, to Middlesex, close to Harrisburg. After serving well during World War II, it was extended across the entire Commonwealth and was given a branch north to Scranton. The geology of Pennsylvania had again induced a transportation innovation, the prototype of the nation's four-lane interstate highway system.

The relationship of development in Pennsylvania to geology has not been one sided. Human activity has also affected the landscape. Perhaps the most obvious examples of this alteration are mining and quarrying. The former has left mountainous culm banks, stripping scars, openings into subsurface workings, acidic water, and streambeds stained by "yellow boy," a mixture of iron anhydride and other materials. Anthracite-coal washings from the northeast sent good-quality fines down the Susquehanna River, where they were dredged and used to fuel the unique combination hydro- and steam-electric generating plant at the Holtwood Dam, more than 100 miles to the south in Lancaster County (Figure 57–7). The stone industry has removed vast quantities of limestone, slate, and, to a lesser extent, other materials, leaving a legacy of huge open pits in the landscape. The petroleum industry began at Titusville, Pa., in 1859 when Colonel Edwin L. Drake drilled the world's first commercial oil well. From abandoned drill holes to pipelines, the changed complexion of northwestern Pennsylvania expanded to characterize a petroleum-dependent world.

Some areas of the state have been affected by other activities. In the Pittsburgh area, for instance, construction of highways and leveling for building sites have oversteepened the slopes of an area already susceptible to landsliding, thereby accelerating this form of mass wasting. In several places, leaking underground water mains have contributed to the formation of sinkholes that have caused considerable property damage (Figure 57–8). Urbanization has increased flash flooding. Mining has lowered local water tables. Perhaps the most bizarre and insidious of all changes are wrought by underground fires, such as at Centralia, where an entire town was condemned because of a coal-mine fire that has been burning since about 1962.

GEOLOGIC INFLUENCES ON PENNSYLVANIA SCENERY

In sharp contrast to these early engineering works and mining activities that left a signature of human activities on Pennsylvania's landscape, there are natural

Figure 57–7. Coal dredging at the Holtwood Power Station on the lower Susquehanna River, Lancaster County. The dredge is recovering coal fines trapped behind the Holtwood Dam, built in 1910. The impoundment has trapped sufficient coal, which came from breakers and coal operations more than 100 miles upstream, to contribute to the operation of the power plant. Coal dredging started in 1925 and continued until 1953, the influx of fresh coal having stopped in 1931 after construction of the Safe Harbor Dam upstream.

Figure 57–8. Broken pavement and foundation damage caused by a sinkhole in the Cambrian Allentown Formation. This sinkhole was caused by a leaking water main that triggered movement of insoluble residue in partially filled solution openings in this carbonate bedrock. The development of sinkholes does not require measurable dissolution of carbonate rock in modern time, but can be brought about by the subsidence of insoluble residue, frequently caused by works of man that change drainage patterns.

features, such as overlooks, waterfalls, springs, and gorges, that contribute to the overall beauty of the state. Five hundred fourteen such features have been documented in two Pennsylvania Geological Survey publications (Geyer and Bolles, 1979, 1987). Three of those that are representative of the state are described here. Visiting and examining them gives geologists and students of geology an added appreciation of a varied and, in many places, spectacular geologic framework.

The Delaware Water Gap

The Delaware Water Gap (Figure 57–9) is a splendid example of a dominant physiographic feature in the folded Appalachians. It is in Monroe County, eastern Pennsylvania, and adjacent New Jersey (Figure 57–10). On first seeing it, the geologist will ask the question, "Why?" By what mechanism has a river cut laterally through steeply dipping, erosion-resistant beds to form a deep, V-shaped notch in a narrow, linear mountain? Furthermore, does the feature we see today give reasonable clues as to its origin?

Epstein (1966) studied the Delaware Water Gap, producing and interpreting data that help us decipher the origin and formation of water gaps in general. Although water gaps, along with wind gaps, are not completely understood, certain characteristics are common to many of them. These characteristics show that

Figure 57–9. Looking northeast across the Delaware Water Gap from the Appalachian Trail on Mount Minsi in Pennsylvania to Mount Tammany in New Jersey. North-dipping sandstone and conglomerate of the Silurian Shawangunk Formation, shown in outcrop on the east side of the Delaware River, has a different dip from that on the west side, from where the photograph was taken. Beds, however, are continuous, indicating a flexure in the bedrock at this locality.

a major river system, as we see it today, did not come about solely by the downcutting and removal of soft, flat-lying sediments followed by epeirogenic uplift and the subsequent cutting into steeply dipping rock units below, as was once believed.

Water gaps appear as breaks or interruptions in the otherwise continuous, linear pattern of a folded Appalachian mountain ridge. They extend from the ridge crest down to the elevation of the adjacent valley floor, bisecting the entire ridge. Those that have been studied in detail prove to be at places in the ridges where there are inherent weaknesses such as faults, changes in lithology, or, as at the Delaware Water Gap, a flexure with a differing dip of bedrock units on either side.

Precipitation runoff down mountain slopes starts to cut ravines on both slopes of a linear ridge, opposite one another. As headward erosion progresses, a notch forms at the ridge crest. As this process continues, the notch becomes deeper until the gap is almost complete. At this point, the dominant stream captures the other, and a through-flowing water gap is formed. If the part of the stream system that is captured is in the process of developing the beginning of another water gap farther along the ridge, that gap will be abandoned and left as a wind gap.

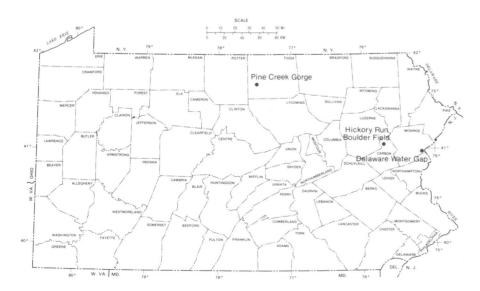

Figure 57–10. Locations of three significant features that are representative of Pennsylvania's many scenic geologic features.

Pine Creek Gorge

Pine Creek Gorge (Figure 57–11) is an interesting periglacial feature, the origin of which involves stream reversal and downcutting at a time of withdrawal of continental glaciers from northern Pennsylvania and New York. It is of considerable geological significance, representative of Pennsylvania's scenic features, and is a noted recreational locality for canoeing, bicycling, and hiking, as well as hunting and fishing. The gorge is in southwestern Tioga County, north-central Pennsylvania (Figure 57–10).

Pine Creek Gorge is similar to the Delaware Water Gap in that a substantial stream has changed its course and taken a seemingly difficult path, cutting through a mountain rather than flowing in an adjacent valley. It is, however, different in that there is direct evidence of glacial activity here relating to the last ice age.

The geological history of the gorge was well described by Crowl (1981). Pine Creek Gorge is just inside the late Wisconsinan (Woodfordian) glacial border. It is an example of a normal stream modified by stream piracy and glacial ponding of streams during the Pleistocene, and the resulting diversion of a stream across a glacial divide. Pine Creek first flows in an eastward direction in a broad, open valley and then is diverted southward by glacial drainage diversion through an approximately 15 mile long gorge before emptying into the Susquehanna River at Jersey Shore from a narrow valley below the gorge. The eastern part of the valley from which Pine Creek was diverted now contains a small, underfit, westward-flowing stream that enters Pine Creek at Ansonia.

During the Mesozoic and early Cenozoic Eras, the Pine Creek Gorge prototype was developed through successive periods of stream piracy and headward erosion of north- and south-flowing streams. The gorge was modified during the Quaternary Period to its present configuration by mechanisms of glaciation, stream diversion, and periglacial weathering.

Hickory Run Boulder Field

A great deal has been written about boulder fields in Pennsylvania. A few notable references are Potter and Moss (1968), Sevon and others (1975), Sevon (1987a), Wilshusen (1983), and Smith (1953).

A boulder field is a flat or gently sloping area having gradients of 1 to 5 degrees, covered with a continuous veneer of large, angular and subangular blocks of rock that were derived from well-jointed bedrock by intensive frost action. They differ from the similarly defined felsenmeer in that the blocks are not necessarily derived from underlying, well-jointed bedrock, but typically from fractured bedrock forming adjacent ridges that provided a source away from and above the boulder field. The boulder field, therefore, may overlie a lithology different from its own lithology.

Most of the boulder fields in Pennsylvania have resulted from periglacial activity near the margins of continental glacial advances (Sevon, 1969a). They generally occur in valleys adjacent to ridges that are composed of hard, fractured sandstone, conglomerate, and sedimentary quartzite, providing a source rock from which the boulder field is comprised.

A boulder field typically occupies a rough, wooded area covered by boulder colluvium within which a smaller boulder-strewn area devoid of vegetation has developed. Large, blocky to subrounded boulders, having no matrix of finer material in the upper 6 to 8 feet, can occupy an area of several acres, accumulating on a gently sloping surface. Standing in the middle of a boulder field, an observer can commonly hear a stream flowing at depth beneath the boulders.

Figure 57–11. Looking south through Pine Creek Gorge. Called the Grand Canyon of Pennsylvania, this gorge was cut during successive stages of stream piracy and headward erosion during continental glacial withdrawal from northern Pennsylvania. The stream is cut through the Devonian Catskill Formation into the Lock Haven Formation.

Figure 57–12. The gently sloping surface of the Hickory Run Boulder Field, which has resulted from periglacial weathering of the Duncannon Member of the Devonian Catskill Formation. In this area, the Duncannon Member is composed of hard sandstone and conglomerate, the latter being well displayed in boulders in the foreground. This is one of Pennsylvania's most impressive and accessible scenic geologic features.

It is considered that the boulders have accumulated by solifluction (Sevon, 1969a), through which mechanism ice-packed boulders move downslope from adjacent ridges. This is supported by the characteristics of the internal fabric of a boulder field that generally reveal stone rings, elongate flow mounds, imbrication, and other features. As interstitial ice melted, small amounts of fine-grained material were removed from the upper part of the boulder accumulation and boulders within the field set up in a well-stabilized mass, illustrating the array of patterns resulting from a freeze-thaw sequence in a periglacial environment (Sevon, 1969a).

Although very stable in today's climate, boulder fields are decreasing in size due to encroaching vegetation from the surrounding colluviated terrain. First, moss grows in the shade adjacent to the forest, then humic material from trees fills in nearby voids, and, finally, vegetation grows slowly and progressively into the boulder field, advancing on its own infilling of seasonal woody debris.

Hickory Run Boulder Field (Figure 57–12) illustrates all of these features. It is in northern Carbon County, in the Appalachian Mountain section of the Ridge and Valley physiographic province (Figure 57–10). Its source rock is hard sandstone and conglomerate from the Duncannon Member of the Devonian Catskill Formation (Sevon, 1969a). The boulder size ranges from a few inches to more than 30 feet long. Individual boulders are angular to rounded. The size of the boulders decreases and roundness increases from the upper to the lower part of the field, that is, from east to west.

This boulder field is reported to be the largest of its kind in Pennsylvania (Smith, 1953). The part that is unvegetated is approximately 1,600 feet long and 400 feet wide, comprising about 15 acres, with a small vegetated, but treeless, area to one side. Although only gently sloping when looked at in its entirety, the boulder field has a complex microrelief consisting of stone rings, boulder mounds, elongate mounds, channels, pits, lobe fronts, and boulder imbrication (Sevon, 1969a). All of these features lead to the conclusion that this, as well as other boulder fields near continental glacial margins, is the result of solifluction in a periglacial environment. The Hickory Run Boulder Field is, therefore, worthy of careful geologic scrutiny on aerial photographs and in the field.

RECOMMENDED FOR FURTHER READING

Geyer, A. R., and Bolles, W. H. (1979), *Outstanding scenic geological features of Pennsylvania,* Pennsylvania Geological Survey, 4th ser., Environmental Geology Report 7, pt. 1, 508 p.

_____ (1987), *Outstanding scenic geological features of Pennsylvania, Part 2,* Pennsylvania Geological Survey, 4th ser., Environmental Geology Report 7, pt. 2, 270 p.

REFERENCES CITED

Aaron, J. M. (1969), *Petrology and origin of the Hardyston Quartzite (Lower Cambrian) in eastern Pennsylvania and western New Jersey,* in Subitzky, Seymour, ed., *Geology of selected areas in New Jersey and eastern Pennsylvania and guidebook of excursions,* New Brunswick, N. J., Rutgers University Press, p. 21–34.

Abdypoor, Gladees, and Bischke, R. E. (1982), *Earthquakes felt in the state of Pennsylvania; with emphasis on earthquakes felt in Philadelphia, Pa. and surrounding areas,* Philadelphia, Temple University Department of Geology, 354 p.

Abel, J. F., Jr., and Lee, F. T. (1983), *Lithologic controls on subsidence,* Transactions of the Society of Mining Engineers of AIME, v. 274, p. 2028–2034.

Abel, K. D., and Heyman, Louis (1981), *The Oriskany Sandstone in the subsurface of Pennsylvania,* Pennsylvania Geological Survey, 4th ser., Mineral Resource Report 81, 9 p.

Ackenheil, A. C. (1954), *A soil mechanics and engineering geology analysis of landslides in the area of Pittsburgh, Pennsylvania,* University of Pittsburgh, Ph.D. thesis, 121 p.

Adams, R. W. (1970), *Loyalhanna Limestone—cross-bedding and provenance,* in Fisher, G. W., and others, eds., *Studies of Appalachian geology: central and southern,* New York, Interscience Publishers, p. 83–100.

Adams, W. R., Jr. (1986), *Landsliding in Allegheny County, Pennsylvania—Characteristics, causes, and cures,* University of Pittsburgh, Ph.D. thesis, 306 p.

Adams, W. R., Jr., Briggs, R. P., Ferguson, H. F., and others (1980), *Land use and abuse—The Allegheny County problem,* Annual Field Conference of Pennsylvania Geologists, 45th, Pittsburgh, Pa., Guidebook, 116 p.

Adovasio, J. M., and Carlisle, R. C., eds. (1982), *Meadowcroft: collected papers on the archaeology of Meadowcroft Rockshelter and the Cross Creek drainage,* Pittsburgh, University of Pittsburgh Press, 274 p.

Agron, S. L. (1950), *Structure and petrology of the Peach Bottom Slate, Pennsylvania and Maryland, and its environment,* Geological Society of America Bulletin, v. 61, p. 1265–1306.

Alcock, J. (1994), *The discordant Doe Run thrust: implications for stratigraphy and structure in the Glenarm Supergroup, southeastern Pennsylvania Piedmont,* Geological Society of America Bulletin, v. 106, p. 932–941.

Alexander, S. S., and Lavin, P. M. (1983), *Tectonic elements and earthquake associations in the Northeast* [abs.], Geological Society of America Abstracts with Programs, v. 15, no. 3, p. 138.

Alexander, S. S., and Stockar, D. X. (1984), *The earthquake of April 23, 1984 near Lancaster, Pennsylvania and its associated seismotectonic setting* [abs.], Earthquake Notes, v. 55, no. 3, p. 12.

Algermissen, S. T. (1969), *Seismic risk studies in the United States,* Proceedings of the Fourth World Conference on Earthquake Engineering, v. 1, p. 14–27.

Algermissen, S. T., Perkins, D. M., Thenhaus, P. C., and others (1982), *Probabilistic estimates of maximum acceleration and velocity in rock in the contiguous United States,* U.S. Geological Survey Open-File Report 82-1033, 99 p.

Allen, A. S. (1969), *Geologic settings of subsidence,* in Varnes, D. J., and Kiersch, George, eds., *Reviews in engineering geology, Volume II,* Geological Society of America Reviews in Engineering Geology, v. 2, p. 305–342.

Alling, H. L., and Briggs, L. I. (1961), *Stratigraphy of Upper Silurian Cayugan evaporites,* AAPG Bulletin, v. 45, p. 515–547.

Al-Qayim, B. A. (1983), *Facies analysis and depositional environment of the Ames marine member (Virgilian) of the Conemaugh Group (Pennsylvanian) in the Appalachian basin,* University of Pittsburgh, Ph.D. thesis, 344 p.

Amenta, R. V. (1974), *Multiple deformation and metamorphism from structural analysis in the eastern Pennsylvania Piedmont,* Geological Society of America Bulletin, v. 85, p. 1647–1660.

American Association of State Highway and Transportation Officials (AASHTO) (1986), *Standard specifications for transportation materials and methods of sampling and testing,* 14th ed., 2 v., 2,494 p.

American Society for Testing and Materials (1988a), *Standard definitions of terms relating to materials for roads and pavements, ASTM Designation D8,* in *Concrete and aggregates,* 1988 Annual Book of ASTM Standards, Philadelphia, American Society for Testing and Materials, v. 04.02, p. 553.

———— (1988b), *Standard practice for sampling aggregates, ASTM Designation D75,* in *Concrete and aggregates,* 1988 Annual Book of ASTM Standards, Philadelphia, American Society for Testing and Materials, v. 04.02, p. 555.

Ames, J. A., and Cutcliffe, W. E. (1983), *Construction materials—Cement and cement raw materials,* in Lefond, S. J., and others, eds., *Industrial minerals and rocks,* 5th ed., New York, American Institute of Mining, Metallurgical, and Petroleum Engineers, v. 1, p. 133–159.

Ames, M. L. (1909), *Life and letters of Peter and Susan Lesley,* New York, G. P. Putnam's Sons, v. 1, 526 p., v. 2, 562 p.

Ampian, S. G. (1984), *Clays,* preprint from U.S. Bureau of Mines Minerals Yearbook 1982, 32 p.

Anderson, E. J., and Goodwin, P. W. (1980), *Helderberg PAC's,* Society of Economic Paleontologists and Mineralogists, Eastern Section, 1980, Guidebook, 32 p.

Ando, C. J., Cook, F. A., Oliver, J. E., and others (1983), *Crustal geometry of the Appalachian orogen from seismic reflection studies,* in Hatcher, R. D., Jr., and others, eds., *Contributions to the tectonics and geophysics of mountain chains,* Geological Society of America Memoir 158, p. 83–101.

Anonymous [probably Beck, L. C.] (1840), *Association of American Geologists,* American Journal of Science, 1st ser., v. 39, p. 189–191.

Anonymous [probably Rogers, R. E., and/or Rogers, W. B., Jr.] (1859), *A few facts regarding the geological survey of Pennsylvania, exposing the erroneous statements and claims of J. P. Lesley, Secretary of the American Iron Association,* Philadelphia, Collins, 22 p.

Aquilar, R., and Arnold, R. W. (1985), *Soil-landscape relationships of a climax forest in the Allegheny High Plateau, Pennsylvania,* Soil Science Society of America Journal, v. 49, p. 695–701.

Arguden, A. T., and Rodolfo, K. S. (1986), *Sedimentary facies and tectonic implications of lower Mesozoic alluvial-fan conglomerates of the Newark basin, northeastern United States,* Sedimentary Geology, v. 51, no. 1–2, p. 97–118.

Armbruster, J. G., and Scharnberger, C. K. (1986), *Lancaster earthquakes,* Journal of the Lancaster County Historical Society, v. 90, p. 79–87.

Armbruster, J. G., and Seeber, Leonardo (1987), *The 23 April 1984 Martic earthquake and the Lancaster seismic zone in eastern Pennsylvania,* Bulletin of the Seismological Society of America, v. 77, p. 877–890.

Armstrong, Elizabeth (1941), *Mylonization of hybrid rocks near Philadelphia, Pennsylvania,* Geological Society of America Bulletin, v. 52, p. 667–694.

Arndt, H. H. (1963), *Carboniferous rocks,* in Wood, G. H., Jr., and others, *Geology of the southern part of the Pennsylvania Anthracite region,* Annual Meeting of the Geological Society of America and Associated Societies, 1963, Guidebook, Field Trip 4, p. 3–10.

Arndt, H. H., Averitt, Paul, Dowd, James, and others (1968), *Coal,* in U.S. Geological Survey and U.S. Bureau of Mines, *Mineral resources of the Appalachian region,* U.S. Geological Survey Professional Paper 580, p. 102–133.

Aron, Gert, Kibler, D. F., and White, E. L. (1981), *Field manual of procedure PSU-IV for estimating design flood peaks on ungaged Pennsylvania watersheds,* University Park, Pennsylvania State University Department of Civil Engineering and Environmental Resources Research Institute.

Ashburner, C. A. (1886), *Report on the Wyoming Valley limestone-beds,* in Lesley, J. P., *Annual report of the Geological Survey of Pennsylvania for 1885,* Pennsylvania Geological Survey, 2nd ser., Annual Report 1885, p. 437–450.

Ashley, G. H. (1920), *The story of the Pennsylvania Survey,* Pennsylvania Geological Survey, 4th ser., Miscellaneous Paper 1, 20 p.

_____ (1923), *The work of the Survey, 1919–1922,* Pennsylvania Geological Survey, 4th ser., Miscellaneous Paper 2, 18 p.

_____ (1931a), *A syllabus of Pennsylvania geology and mineral resources,* Pennsylvania Geological Survey, 4th ser., General Geology Report 1, 160 p.

_____ (1931b), *The Pennsylvania Geological Survey—Administrative report,* Pennsylvania Geological Survey, 4th ser., Miscellaneous Paper 3, 38 p.

_____ (1934), *Fifteen years, September 1, 1919 to September 1, 1934,* Pennsylvania Geological Survey, 4th ser., Miscellaneous Paper 5, 8 p.

_____ (1944), *A quarter century of progress,* Pennsylvania Geological Survey, 4th ser., Miscellaneous Paper 6, 10 p.

_____ (1945), *Anthracite reserves,* Pennsylvania Geological Survey, 4th ser., Progress Report 130, 13 p.

Ashmead, D. C. (1926), *Anthracite losses and reserves in Pennsylvania,* Pennsylvania Geological Survey, 4th ser., Mineral Resource Report 8, 71 p.

A. W. Martin Associates, Inc. (1975), *Relationship between underground mine water pools and subsidence in the northeastern Pennsylvania anthracite fields,* Appalachian Regional Commission Report ARC–73–111–2553, 130 p., variously paged appendices.

Badger, R. L., and Sinha, A. K. (1988), *Age and Sr isotopic signature of the Catoctin volcanic province: implications for subcrustal mantle evolution,* Geology, v. 16, p. 692–695.

Baer, A. J. (1981), *A Grenvillian model of Proterozoic plate tectonics,* in Kroener, A., *Precambrian plate tectonics,* in the collection *Developments in Precambrian geology,* Amsterdam, Elsevier, p. 353–385.

Bailey, E. B., and Mackin, J. H. (1937), *Recumbent folding in the Pennsylvania Piedmont—preliminary statement,* American Journal of Science, 5th ser., v. 33, p. 187–190.

Baker, R. F., and Chieruzzi, R. (1959), *Regional concept of landslide occurrence,* Highway Research Board Bulletin 216, p. 1–16.

Ballieul, T. A., Indelicato, G. J., and Penley, H. M. (1980), *National uranium resource evaluation, Scranton quadrangle, Pennsylvania, New York, and New Jersey,* U.S. Department of Energy Report GJQ–003(80), 30 p.

Barker, J. L. (1978), *Characteristics of Pennsylvania recreational lakes,* Pennsylvania Department of Environmental Resources, Office of Resources Management, Water Resources Bulletin 14, 226 p.

_____ (1984), *Compilation of ground-water-quality data in Pennsylvania,* U.S. Geological Survey Open-File Report 84–706, 102 p.

Barlow, J. A., and Burkhammer, Susan, eds. (1975), *Proceedings of the First I. C. White Memorial Symposium [Morgantown, W. Va., 1972]—"The age of the Dunkard,"* West Virginia Geological and Economic Survey, 352 p.

Barrell, Joseph (1913), *The Upper Devonian delta of the Appalachian geosyncline—Part 1, The delta and its relations to the interior sea,* American Journal of Science, 4th ser., v. 36, p. 429–472.

Barron, E. J. (1989), *Climate variations and the Appalachians from the late Paleozoic to the present: results from model simulations,* in Gardner, T. W., and Sevon, W. D., eds., *Appalachian geomorphology,* Amsterdam, Elsevier, p. 99–118 [reprinted from Geomorphology, v. 2, no. 1–3].

Barron, E. J., Harrison, C. G. A., Sloan, J. L., II, and Hay, W. W. (1981), *Paleogeography, 180 million years ago to the present,* Eclogae Geologicae Helvetiae, v. 74, p. 443–470.

Barton, C. C., Larsen, Eric, and Baechle, P. E. (1985), *Fractal geometry of two-dimensional planar sections through fracture networks at Yucca Mountain, southwestern Nevada* [abs.], Eos (American Geophysical Union Transactions), v. 66, p. 1089.

Bascom, F. (1925), *The resuscitation of the term Bryn Mawr gravel,* U.S. Geological Survey Professional Paper 132, p. 117–119.

Bascom, F., Clark, W. B., Darton, N. H., and others (1909), *Philadelphia folio, Pennsylvania-New Jersey-Delaware,* U.S. Geological Survey Geologic Atlas of the U.S., Folio 162, 23 p.

Bascom, F., and Stose, G. W. (1932), *Coatesville-West Chester folio, Pennsylvania-Delaware,* U.S. Geological Survey Geologic Atlas of the U.S., Folio 223, 15 p.

_____ (1938), *Geology and mineral resources of the Honeybrook and Phoenixville quadrangles, Pennsylvania,* U.S. Geological Survey Bulletin 891, 145 p.

Bass, M. N. (1959), *Basement rocks from the Sandhill well, Wood County, West Virginia,* in Woodward, H. P., ed., *A Symposium on the Sandhill Deep Well, Wood County, West Virginia [Tucker County, W. Va., 1957],* West Virginia Geological and Economic Survey Report of Investigations 18, p. 145–158.

_____ (1960), *Grenville boundary in Ohio,* Journal of Geology, v. 68, p. 673–677.

Bates, R. G. (1964), *Aeroradioactivity survey and areal geology of the Pittsburgh area, Pennsylvania, Ohio, West Virginia, and Maryland (ARMS–I),* U.S. Atomic Energy Commission Report CEX–59.4.12, 19 p.

_____ (1966), *Natural gamma aeroradioactivity map of the Pittsburgh area, Pennsylvania, Ohio, West Virginia, and Maryland,* U.S. Geological Survey Geophysical Investigations Map GP–555, scale 1:250,000.

Bates, R. L., and Jackson, J. A., eds. (1987), *Glossary of geology,* 3rd ed., Alexandria, Va., American Geological Institute, 788 p.

Bayles, R. E. (1949), *Subsurface Upper Devonian sections in southwestern Pennsylvania,* AAPG Bulletin, v. 33, p. 1682–1703.

Bayley, W. S. (1910), *Iron mines and mining in New Jersey,* New Jersey Geological Survey, v. 7, 512 p.

_____ (1941), *Pre-Cambrian geology and mineral resources of the Delaware Water Gap and Easton quadrangles, New Jersey and Pennsylvania,* U.S. Geological Survey Bulletin 920, 98 p.

Beard, J. H., Sangree, J. B., and Smith, L. A. (1982), *Quaternary chronology, paleoclimate, depositional sequences, and eustatic cycles,* AAPG Bulletin, v. 66, p. 158–169.

Becher, A. E., and Root, S. I. (1981), *Groundwater and geology of the Cumberland Valley, Cumberland County, Pennsylvania,* Pennsylvania Geological Survey, 4th ser., Water Resource Report 50, 95 p.

Beck, A. (1957), *A steady-state method for the rapid measurement of the thermal conductivity of rocks,* Journal of Scientific Instruments, v. 34, p. 186–189.

Beck, A. E. (1965), *Techniques of measuring heat flow on land,* in Lee, E. H. K., ed., *Terrestrial heat flow,* American Geophysical Union Monograph 8, p. 24–50.

_____ (1988), *Methods for determining thermal conductivity and thermal diffusivity,* in Haenel, R., and others, eds., *Handbook of heat-flow density determination,* Dordrecht, Netherlands, Kluwer Academic Publishers, p. 87–124.

Beck, A. E., and Balling, N. (1988), *Determination of virgin rock temperatures,* in Haenel, R., and others, eds., *Handbook of heat-flow density determination,* Dordrecht, Netherlands, Kluwer Academic Publishers, p. 59–85.

Beck, M. E., Jr. (1965), *Paleomagnetic and geological implications of magnetic properties of the Triassic diabase of southeastern Pennsylvania,* Journal of Geophysical Research, v. 70, p. 2845–2856.

Beck, M. E., Jr., and Mattick, R. E. (1964), *Interpretation of an aeromagnetic survey in western Pennsylvania and parts of eastern Ohio, northern West Virginia, and western Maryland,* Pennsylvania Geological Survey, 4th ser., Information Circular 52, 10 p.

Beerbower, J. R. (1961), *Origin of cyclothems of the Dunkard Group (Upper Pennsylvanian-Lower Permian) in Pennsylvania, West Virginia, and Ohio,* Geological Society of America Bulletin, v. 72, p. 1029–1050.

Behre, C. H., Jr. (1927), *Slate in Northampton County, Pennsylvania,* Pennsylvania Geological Survey, 4th ser., Mineral Resource Report 9, 308 p.

Behre, C. H., Jr. (1933), *Slate in Pennsylvania,* Pennsylvania Geological Survey, 4th ser., Mineral Resource Report 16, 400 p.

Belesky, R. M., Hardy, H. R., Jr., and Strouse, F. F. (1987), *Sinkholes in airport pavements: engineering implications,* in Beck, B. F., and Wilson, W. L., eds., *Karst hydrogeology: engineering and environmental applications,* Multidisciplinary Conference on Sinkholes and the Environmental Impacts of Karst, 2nd, Orlando, Fla., 1987, Proceedings, Rotterdam, A. A. Balkema, p. 411–417.

Benfield, A. E. (1939), *Terrestrial heat flow in Great Britain,* Royal Society of London Proceedings, v. 173–A, p. 428–450.

Berdan, J. M. (1964), *The Helderberg Group and the position of the Silurian-Devonian boundary in North America,* U.S. Geological Survey Bulletin 1180-B, 19 p.

Berg, T. M., Barnes, J. H., Sevon, W. D., and others, compilers (1989), *Physiographic provinces of Pennsylvania,* Pennsylvania Geological Survey, 4th ser., Map 13, scale 1:2,000,000.

Berg, T. M., and Dodge, C. M., compilers and eds. (1981), *Atlas of preliminary geologic quadrangle maps of Pennsylvania,* Pennsylvania Geological Survey, 4th ser., Map 61, 636 p.

Berg, T. M., Dodge, C. H., and Lentz, L. J. (1986), *Upper Devonian and Mississippian stratigraphy of the Broad Top region,* in Sevon, W. D., ed., *Selected geology of Bedford and Huntingdon Counties,* Annual Field Conference of Pennsylvania Geologists, 51st, Huntingdon, Pa., Guidebook, p. 81–92.

Berg, T. M., and Edmunds, W. E. (1979), *The Huntley Mountain Formation: Catskill-to-Burgoon transition in north-central Pennsylvania,* Pennsylvania Geological Survey, 4th ser., Information Circular 83, 80 p.

Berg, T. M., Edmunds, W. E., Geyer, A. R., and others, compilers (1980), *Geologic map of Pennsylvania,* Pennsylvania Geological Survey, 4th ser., Map 1, scale 1:250,000, 3 sheets.

Berg, T. M., and Glover, A. D. (1976), *Geology and mineral resources of the Sabula and Penfield quadrangles, Clearfield, Elk, and Jefferson Counties, Pennsylvania,* Pennsylvania Geological Survey, 4th ser., Atlas 74ab, 98 p.

Berg, T. M., McInerney, M. K., Way, J. H., and MacLachlan, D. B. (1983), *Stratigraphic correlation chart of Pennsylvania,* Pennsylvania Geological Survey, 4th ser., General Geology Report 75.

———— (1986), *Stratigraphic correlation chart of Pennsylvania,* 2nd printing, revised, Pennsylvania Geological Survey, 4th ser., General Geology Report 75.

Berg, T. M., Sevon, W. D., and Abel, Robin, compilers (1984), *Rock types of Pennsylvania,* Pennsylvania Geological Survey, 4th ser., Map 63, scale 1:500,000.

Berg, T. M., Sevon, W. D., and Bucek, M. F. (1977), *Geology and mineral resources of the Pocono Pines and Mount Pocono quadrangles, Monroe County, Pennsylvania,* Pennsylvania Geological Survey, 4th ser., Atlas 204cd, 66 p.

Berkheiser, S. W., Jr. (1983), *Reconnaissance survey of potential carbonate whiting sources in Pennsylvania,* Pennsylvania Geological Survey, 4th ser., Mineral Resource Report 83, 53 p.

———— (1984), *Fetid barite occurrences, western Berks County, Pennsylvania,* Pennsylvania Geological Survey, 4th ser., Mineral Resource Report 84, 43 p.

———— (1985a), *High-purity silica occurrences in Pennsylvania,* Pennsylvania Geological Survey, 4th ser., Mineral Resource Report 88, 67 p.

———— (1985b), *Pennsylvania's slate industry: alive and well,* in Glaser, J. D., and Edwards, J., eds., *Twentieth Forum on the Geology of Industrial Minerals [Baltimore, Md., 1984],* Maryland Geological Survey Special Publication 2, p. 23–33.

———— (1985c), *Warner Company's Bellefonte operation,* Pennsylvania Geology, v. 16, no. 2, p. 6–10.

———— (1987), *Erie Sand and Gravel Company—Suction hopper dredging on Lake Erie,* Pennsylvania Geology, v. 18, no. 3, p. 2–6.

Berkheiser, S. W., Jr., Barnes, J. H., and Smith, R. C., II (1985), *Directory of the nonfuel-mineral producers in Pennsylvania,* 4th ed., Pennsylvania Geological Survey, 4th ser., Information Circular 54, 165 p.

Berkheiser, S. W., Jr., and Hoff, D. T. (1983), *The Arthur L. Long lime kiln, an active record of yesteryear,* Pennsylvania Geology, v. 14, no. 5, p. 9–15.

Berkheiser, S. W., Jr., and Inners, J. D. (1984), *What does it take to make a brick? The Watsontown story,* Pennsylvania Geology, v. 15, no. 2, p. 2–6.

Berkheiser, S. W., Jr., and Smith, R. C., II (1984), *High-alumina clay discovered in Berks County,* Pennsylvania Geology, v. 15, no. 1, p. 2–6.

Berry, M. H. (1986), *Sinkhole investigation: south-central Pennsylvania,* in Dilamarter, R. R., and others, eds., *Proceedings of the Environmental Problems in Karst Terranes and Their Solutions Conference [Bowling Green, Ky., 1986],* Dublin, Ohio, National Water Well Association, p. 325–344.

Berry, W. B. N., and Boucot, A. J., eds. (1970), *Correlation of the North American Silurian rocks,* Geological Society of America Special Paper 102, 289 p.

Berryhill, H. L., Jr. (1967), *Chapter A, Allegheny region,* in McKee, E. D., and others, *Paleotectonic investigations of the Permian System in the United States,* U.S. Geological Survey Professional Paper 515, p. 1–7.

Berryhill, H. L., Jr., Schweinfurth, S. P., and Kent, B. H. (1971), *Coal-bearing Upper Pennsylvanian and Lower Permian rocks, Washington area, Pennsylvania,* U.S. Geological Survey Professional Paper 621, 47 p.

Berryhill, H. L., Jr., and Swanson, V. E. (1962), *Revised stratigraphic nomenclature for Upper Pennsylvanian and Lower Permian rocks, Washington County, Pennsylvania,* in *Short papers in geology and hydrology, articles 60–119—Geological Survey research 1962,* U.S. Geological Survey Professional Paper 450-C, p. C43–C46.

Beynon, D., and Donahue, J. (1982), *The geology and geomorphology of Meadowcroft Rockshelter and the Cross Creek drainage,* in Adovasio, J. M., and Carlisle, R. C., eds., *Meadowcroft: collected papers on the archaeology of Meadowcroft Rockshelter and the Cross Creek drainage,* Pittsburgh, University of Pittsburgh Press, p. 31–52.

Bining, A. C. (1979), *Pennsylvania iron manufacture in the eighteenth century,* 2nd ed., Pennsylvania Historical and Museum Commission, 215 p.

Birch, Francis (1948), *The effects of Pleistocene climatic variations upon geothermal gradients,* American Journal of Science, v. 246, p. 729–760.

———— (1950), *Flow of heat in the Front Range, Colorado,* Geological Society of America Bulletin, v. 61, p. 567–630.

Birkeland, P. W. (1984), *Soils and geomorphology,* New York, Oxford University Press, 372 p.

Bischke, R. E. (1980), *The Abington-Cheltenham, Pa. earthquake sequence of March–May, 1980,* Pennsylvania Geology, v. 11, no. 5, p. 10–13.

———— (1982), *1982 Earthquakes: Cornwall Heights and Penndel,* Pennsylvania Geology, v. 13, no. 5, p. 8–12.

Bishop, J. B. (1861), *A history of American manufactures from 1608–1860,* Philadelphia, p. 227–228.

Bjerstedt, T. W. (1986), *Regional stratigraphy and sedimentology of the Lower Mississippian Rockwell Formation and Purslane Sandstone based on the new Sideling Hill road cut, Maryland,* Southeastern Geology, v. 27, p. 69–94.

Bjerstedt, T. W., and Kammer, T. W. (1988), *Genetic stratigraphy and depositional systems of the Upper Devonian-Lower Mississippian Price-Rockwell deltaic complex in the central Appalachians, U.S.A.,* Sedimentary Geology, v. 54, p. 265–301.

Blackmer, G. C. (1987), *Engineering geologic parameters and their relationship to roof falls in a coal mine on the Appalachian Plateau, Pennsylvania,* University Park, Pennsylvania State University, M.S. thesis, 87 p.

Blackwell, D. D., Steele, J. L., and Brott, C. A. (1980), *The terrain effect on terrestrial heat flow,* Journal of Geophysical Research, v. 85, no. B9, p. 4757–4772.

Boswell, R. N. (1988), *Upper Devonian-Lower Mississippian Acadian clastic wedge basin analysis: northern West Virginia and adjacent areas,* Morgantown, West Virginia University, Ph.D. thesis, 351 p.

Bouma, A. H. (1962), *Sedimentology of some flysch deposits, a graphic approach to facies interpretation,* Amsterdam, Elsevier, 168 p.

Bowen, N. L. (1928), *The evolution of the igneous rocks,* Princeton, N. J., Princeton University Press, 332 p.

Bowen, Z. P. (1967), *Brachiopoda of the Keyser Limestone (Silurian-Devonian) of Maryland and adjacent areas,* Geological Society of America Memoir 102, 103 p.

Boyer, S. E., and Elliott, David (1982), *Thrust systems,* AAPG Bulletin, v. 66, p. 1196–1230.

Boynton, G. R., Pittillo, D. R., and Zandle, G. L. (1966a), *Natural gamma aeroradioactivity map of the Bangor quadrangle, New Jersey and Pennsylvania,* U.S. Geological Survey Geophysical Investigations Map GP-568, scale 1:24,000.

_____ (1966b), *Natural gamma aeroradioactivity map of the Belvidere quadrangle, New Jersey and Pennsylvania,* U.S. Geological Survey Geophysical Investigations Map GP-569, scale 1:24,000.

Boynton, R. S. (1980), *Chemistry and technology of lime and limestone,* 2nd ed., New York, Interscience Publishers, 563 p.

Bragonier, W. A. (1970), *Genesis and geologic relations of the high-alumina Mercer fireclay, western Pennsylvania,* University Park, Pennsylvania State University, M.S. thesis, 212 p.

Branson, C. C. (1962), *Pennsylvanian System of central Appalachians,* in Branson, C. C., ed., *Pennsylvanian System in the United States—A symposium,* American Association of Petroleum Geologists, p. 97–116.

Brant, L. A. (1971), *A study of the faunal succession in the Brush Creek shale (Pennsylvanian), near Shelocta, Pennsylvania,* University Park, Pennsylvania State University, M.S. thesis, 86 p.

Braun, D. D. (1988), *Glacial geology of the Anthracite and North Branch Susquehanna lowland regions,* in Inners, J. D., ed., *Bedrock and glacial geology of the North Branch Susquehanna lowland and the Eastern Middle Anthracite field, northeastern Pennsylvania,* Annual Field Conference of Pennsylvania Geologists, 53rd, Hazleton, Pa., Guidebook, p. 3–25.

_____ (1989), *The depth of post middle Miocene erosion and the age of the present landscape,* in Sevon, W. D., *The rivers and valleys of Pennsylvania—Then and now,* Annual Geomorphology Symposium, 20th, Carlisle, Pa., 1989, Guidebook, Harrisburg Area Geological Society, p. 16–20.

Brett, C. E. (1983), *Sedimentology, facies and depositional environments of the Rochester Shale (Silurian; Wenlockian) in western New York and Ontario,* Journal of Sedimentary Petrology, v. 53, p. 947–971.

Brewer, Charles, Jr. (1928), *Genetic relationship of oil reservoirs to shoreline deposits,* AAPG Bulletin, v. 12, p. 597–615.

Brezinski, D. K. (1984), *Dynamic lithostratigraphy and paleoecology of Upper Mississippian (Chesterian) strata of the northcentral Appalachian basin,* University of Pittsburgh, Ph.D. thesis, 132 p.

_____ (1989a), *Facies relationships and correlations between the Greenbrier of West Virginia and the Mauch Chunk of Pennsylvania,* in Harper, J. A., ed., *Geology in the Laurel Highlands of southwestern Pennsylvania,* Annual Field Conference of Pennsylvania Geologists, 54th, Johnstown, Pa., Guidebook, p. 63–68.

_____ (1989b), *Late Mississippian depositional patterns in the north-central Appalachian basin, and their implications to Chesterian hierarchal stratigraphy,* Southeastern Geology, v. 30, p. 1–23.

_____ (1989c), *The Mississippian System in Maryland,* Maryland Geological Survey, Report of Investigations 52, 75 p.

Brezinski, D. K., and Kertis, C. A. (1987), *Depositional environment of some Late Devonian and Early Mississippian coals of the north-central Appalachian basin* [abs.], Geological Society of America Abstracts with Programs, v. 19, no. 1, p. 6.

Bricker, O. P., and others (1968), *Mineral-water interaction during the chemical weathering of silicates,* American Chemical Society, Advances in Chemistry Series 73, p. 128–142.

Bridge, J. (1950), *Bauxite deposits of the southeastern United States,* in Snyder, F. G., ed., *Symposium on mineral resources of the southeastern United States,* Knoxville, Tenn., Tennessee University Press, p. 170–201.

Briggs, R. P., and Tatlock, D. B. (1983), *Estimates of undiscovered recoverable natural gas resources in Pennsylvania,* unpublished report prepared for the Pennsylvania Oil and Gas Association and the Pennsylvania Natural Gas Associates, 35 p.

Bristow, Q. (1979), *Gamma ray spectrometric methods in uranium exploration—airborne instrumentation,* in Hood, P. J., ed., *Geophysics and geochemistry in the search for metallic ores,* Geological Survey of Canada Economic Geology Report 31, p. 135–146.

Bromery, R. W. (1960), *Preliminary interpretation of aeromagnetic data in the Allentown quadrangle, Pennsylvania,* in *Short papers in the geological sciences—Geological Survey research 1960,* U.S. Geological Survey Professional Paper 400-B, p. B178–B180.

_____ (1968), *Geological interpretation of aeromagnetic and gravity surveys of the northeastern end of the Baltimore-Washington anticlinorium, Harford, Baltimore, and part of Carroll County, Maryland,* Baltimore, Johns Hopkins University, Ph.D. thesis, 124 p.

Bromery, R. W., and Griscom, Andrew (1967), *Aeromagnetic and generalized geologic map of southeastern Pennsylvania,* U.S. Geological Survey Geophysical Investigations Map GP-577, scale 1:125,000, 2 sheets.

Brown, A. P., and Ehrenfeld, Frederick (1913), *Minerals of Pennsylvania,* Pennsylvania Geological Survey, 3rd ser., Report 9, 160 p.

Brown, L. D., and Oliver, J. P. (1976), *Vertical crustal movements from leveling data and their relation to geologic structure in the eastern United States,* Reviews of Geophysics and Space Physics, v. 14, p. 13–35.

Bruhn, R. W. (1985), *A note on the movements and associated groundwater responses at an underground Appalachian mine,* SME-AIME Annual Meeting, New York, Reprint 85-63.

Bruhn, R. W., Magnuson, M. O., and Gray, R. E. (1978), *Subsidence over the mined-out Pittsburgh coal,* in *Coal Mine Subsidence Proceedings,* Session 71, American Society of Civil Engineers Spring Convention, Pittsburgh (ASCE Preprint 3293), p. 26–55.

_____ (1981), *Subsidence over abandoned mines in the Pittsburgh coalbed,* in Geddes, J. D., ed., *Ground movements and structures,* New York, John Wiley and Sons, p. 142–156.

Bruhn, R. W., McCann, W. S., Speck, R. C., and Gray, R. E. (1982), *Damage to structures above active underground coal mines in the northern Appalachian coal field,* in *Proceedings of First International Conference on Stability in Underground Mining,* West Vancouver, British Columbia, Canada.

Buckwalter, T. V. (1959), *Geology of the Precambrian rocks and Hardyston Formation of the Boyertown quadrangle,* Pennsylvania Geological Survey, 4th ser., Atlas 197, [15 p.].

_____ (1962), *The Precambrian geology of the Reading 15' quadrangle,* Pennsylvania Geological Survey, 4th ser., Progress Report 161, 49 p.

Budel, Julius (1982), *Climatic geomorphology,* Princeton, N. J., Princeton University Press, 433 p.

Buol, S. W., Hole, F. D., and McCracken, R. J. (1989), *Soil genesis and classification,* 3rd ed., Ames, Iowa, Iowa State University Press, 446 p.

Burke, J. J. (1967), *A new Endelocrinus from the Brush Creek Limestone (Pennsylvanian) of Pennsylvania,* Carnegie Museum Annals, v. 39, art. 4, p. 75–83.

_____ (1968), *Pachylocrinids from the Conemaugh Group, Pennsylvanian,* Kirtlandia, no. 3, 18 p.

_____ (1970), *Some ornamented erisocrinids from the Ames Limestone,* Kirtlandia, no. 9, 17 p.

Busch, R. M., and Rollins, H. B. (1984), *Correlation of Carboniferous strata using a hierarchy of transgressive-regressive units,* Geology, v. 12, p. 471–474.

Busch, W. F., and Shaw, L. C. (1960), *Floods in Pennsylvania, frequency and magnitude,* U.S. Geological Survey, 230 p.

Busch, W. F., and Shaw, L. C. (1966), *Pennsylvania streamflow characteristics—Low-flow frequency and flow duration*, Pennsylvania Department of Forests and Waters Water Resources Bulletin 1, 289 p.

Butler, R. W. H. (1987), *Thrust sequences*, Journal of the Geological Society, v. 144, p. 619-634.

Butts, Charles (1904), *Kittanning folio, Pennsylvania*, U.S. Geological Survey Atlas of the U.S., Folio 115, 15 p.

_____ (1945), *Hollidaysburg-Huntingdon folio, Pennsylvania*, U.S. Geological Survey Geologic Atlas of the U.S., Folio 227, 20 p.

Byrer, C. W., Mroz, T. H., and Covatch, G. L. (1984), *Production potential for coalbed methane in U.S. basins*, in Proceedings— Unconventional Gas Recovery Symposium [Pittsburgh, Pa., 1984], Society of Petroleum Engineers of AIME, p. 15-28.

Cadisch, Joos (1946), *On some problems of Alpine tectonics*, Experientia, v. 2, no. 1, p. 18-23.

Calkin, P. E., and Feenstra, B. H. (1985), *Evolution of the Erie-basin Great Lakes*, in Karrow, P. F., and Calkin, P. E., eds., Quaternary evolution of the Great Lakes, Geological Association of Canada Special Paper 30, p. 149-170.

Callahan, W. H. (1968), *Geology of the Friedensville zinc mine, Lehigh County, Pennsylvania*, in Ridge, J. D., ed., Ore deposits of the U.S., 1933-1967, New York, American Institute of Mining Engineers, p. 95-107.

Cameron, C. C. (1970), *Peat deposits of northeastern Pennsylvania*, U.S. Geological Survey Bulletin 1317-A, 90 p.

Cameron, E. N. (1980), *Evolution of the lower critical zone, central sector, eastern Bushveld Complex, and its chromite deposits*, Economic Geology, v. 75, p. 845-871.

Cameron, E. N., and Weis, P. L. (1960), *Strategic graphite—A survey*, U.S. Geological Survey Bulletin 1082-E, p. 201-322.

Camp, W. H. (1956), *The forests of past and present*, in Hayden-Guest, S., and others, eds., A world geography of forest resources, American Geographical Society Special Publication 33, p. 13-47.

Campbell, L. D. (1971), *Occurrence of "Ogygopsis shale" fauna in southeastern Pennsylvania*, Journal of Paleontology, v. 45, p. 437-440.

Campbell, M. R. (1902), *Masontown-Uniontown folio, Pennsylvania*, U.S. Geological Survey Geologic Atlas of the U.S., Folio 82, 21 p.

_____ (1903a), *Brownsville-Connellsville folio, Pennsylvania*, U.S. Geological Survey Geologic Atlas of the U.S., Folio 94, 19 p.

_____ (1903b), *Geographic development of northern Pennsylvania and southern New York*, Geological Society of America Bulletin, v. 14, p. 277-296.

_____ (1933), *Chambersburg (Harrisburg) peneplain in the Piedmont of Maryland and Pennsylvania*, Geological Society of America Bulletin, v. 44, p. 553-573.

Canich, M. R. (1976), *A study of the Tyrone-Mount Union lineament by remote sensing techniques and field methods*, ORSER Technical Report 12-77, NASA, Greenbelt, Md.

Canich, M. R., and Gold, D. P. (1985), *Structural features in the Tyrone-Mt. Union lineament, across the Nittany anticlinorium in central Pennsylvania*, in Gold, D. P., and others, Central Pennsylvania geology revisited, Annual Field Conference of Pennsylvania Geologists, 50th, State College, Pa., Guidebook, p. 120-137, 199-203.

Carll, J. F. (1880), *The geology of the oil regions of Warren, Venango, Clarion, and Butler Counties*, Pennsylvania Geological Survey, 2nd ser., Report III, 482 p.

Carlston, C. W. (1946), *Appalachian drainage and the highland border sediments of the Newark Series*, Geological Society of America Bulletin, v. 57, p. 997-1032.

_____ (1962), *Character and history of the upper Ohio River valley*, U.S. Geological Survey Bulletin 1141-I, 10 p.

Carpenter, F. M. (1960), *Studies on North American Carboniferous insects—the Protodonta*, Psyche, v. 67, p. 98-110.

_____ (1967), *Studies of North American insects—the genera Metropator, Eubleptus, Hapoloptera, and Hadentomum*, Psyche, v. 72, p. 175-190.

Carslaw, H. S., and Jaeger, J. C. (1959), *Conduction of heat in solids*, 2nd ed., Oxford Claredon Press, 510 p.

Carson Helicopters and Texas Instruments (1980), *Aerial radiometric and magnetic reconnaissance survey of portions of Alabama, Georgia, Kentucky, Maryland, North Carolina, Ohio, Pennsylvania, Virginia, and West Virginia—Final report*, U.S. Department of Energy, GJBX-92(80), variously paged.

Carswell, L. D., and Bennett, G. D. (1963), *Geology and hydrology of the Neshannock quadrangle, Mercer and Lawrence Counties, Pennsylvania*, Pennsylvania Geological Survey, 4th ser., Water Resource Report 15, 90 p.

Carswell, L. D., and Lloyd, O. B., Jr. (1979), *Geology and groundwater resources of Monroe County, Pennsylvania*, Pennsylvania Geological Survey, 4th ser., Water Resource Report 47, 61 p.

Carter, B. J. (1983), *The effect of slope gradient and aspect on the genesis of soils formed on a sandstone ridge in central Pennsylvania*, University Park, Pennsylvania State University, Ph.D. thesis, 245 p.

Carter, B. J., and Ciolkosz, E. J. (1986), *Sorting and thickness of waste mantle material on a sandstone spur in central Pennsylvania*, Catena, v. 13, p. 245-256.

_____ (1991), *Slope gradient and aspect effects on soils developed from sandstone in Pennsylvania*, Geoderma, v. 49, p. 199-213.

Carter, W. D. (1969), *The W. L. Newman phosphate mine, Juniata County, Pennsylvania*, Pennsylvania Geological Survey, 4th ser., Information Circular 64, 16 p.

Caster, K. E. (1934), *The stratigraphy and paleontology of northwestern Pennsylvania—Part 1, Stratigraphy*, Bulletins of American Paleontology, v. 21, no. 71, 185 p.

Cate, A. S. (1962), *Subsurface structure of the Plateau region of north-central and western Pennsylvania on top of the Oriskany Formation*, Pennsylvania Geological Survey, 4th ser., Map 9, scale 1:250,000.

Cathcart, S. H. (1934), *Geologic structure in the Plateaus region of northern Pennsylvania and its relation to the occurrence of gas in the Oriskany sand*, Pennsylvania Geological Survey, 4th ser., Progress Report 108, 24 p.

Cavaroc, V. V., Jr., and Saxena, R. S. (1979), *Crevasse splay deposits in the state line area of northwestern Pennsylvania and northeastern Ohio*, in Ferm, J. C., and others, eds., Carboniferous depositional environments in the Appalachian region, Columbia, S. C., Carolina Coal Group, University of South Carolina Department of Geology, p. 160-172.

Cecil, C. B. (1990), *Paleoclimate controls on stratigraphic repetition of chemical and siliciclastic rocks*, Geology, v. 18, p. 533-536.

Cecil, C. B., Stanton, R. W., Neuzil, S. G., and others (1985), *Paleoclimate controls on late Paleozoic sedimentation and peat formation in the central Appalachian basin (U.S.A.)*, in Phillips, T. L., and others, eds., Paleoclimatic controls on coal resources of the Pennsylvanian System of North America, International Journal of Coal Geology, v. 5, p. 195-230.

Cermak, V. (1976), *Paleoclimatic effect on the underground temperature and some problems of correcting heat flow*, in Adam, A., ed., Geoelectric and geothermal studies (east-central Europe, Soviet Asia), Budapest, Hungary, Akademiya Kiado, p. 59-66.

Chafetz, H. S. (1969), *Carbonates of the Lower and Middle Ordovician in central Pennsylvania*, Pennsylvania Geological Survey, 4th ser., General Geology Report 58, 39 p.

Chaffin, D. L. (1981), *Implications of regional gravity and magnetic data for structure beneath western Pennsylvania*, University Park, Pennsylvania State University, M.S. thesis, 72 p.

Chamberlin, T. C., and Salisbury, R. D. (1905), *Geology—Volume 2, Earth history*, 2nd ed., revised, New York, Henry Holt and Company, 692 p.

Chance, H. M. (1880), *The geology of Clarion County*, Pennsylvania Geological Survey, 2nd ser., Report VV, 232 p.

Chapman, D. S., and Pollack, H. N. (1975), *Global heat flow—a new look*, Earth and Planetary Science Letters, v. 28, p. 23-32.

Chase, C. M. (1977), *Central Pennsylvania sand dunes*, Pennsylvania Geology, v. 8, no. 3, p. 9-12.

Chen, C. Y., Chen, Y. N., and Gaffney, D. V. (1974), *Engineering and architectural measures to minimize subsidence damage*, Canadian Geotechnical Conference, 27th, Edmonton, Alberta, Canada, 49 p.

Chow, M. M. (1951), *The Pennsylvanian Mill Creek limestone in Pennsylvania,* Pennsylvania Geological Survey, 4th ser., General Geology Report 26, 36 p.

Ciolkosz, E. J., Carter, B. J., Hoover, M. T., and others (1990), *Genesis of soils and landscapes in the Ridge and Valley province of central Pennsylvania,* Geomorphology, v. 3, p. 245–261.

Ciolkosz, E. J., Cronce, R. C., Cunningham, R. L., and Petersen, G. W. (1985), *Characteristics, genesis, and classification of Pennsylvania minesoils,* Soil Science, v. 139, p. 232–238.

———— (1986), *Geology and soils of Nittany Valley,* Pennsylvania State University Agronomy Series 88, 55 p.

Ciolkosz, E. J., Cronce, R. C., and Sevon, W. D. (1986), *Periglacial features in Pennsylvania,* Pennsylvania State University Agronomy Series 92, 15 p.

Ciolkosz, E. J., Petersen, G. W., and Cunningham, R. L. (1979), *Landscape-prone soils of southwestern Pennsylvania,* Soil Science, v. 128, p. 348–352.

———— (1980), *Soils of Nittany Valley,* in Ciolkosz, E. J., and others, eds., *Soils and geology of Nittany Valley,* Pennsylvania State University Agronomy Series 64, p. 24–51.

Ciolkosz, E. J., Petersen, G. W., Cunningham, R. L., and Matelski, R. P. (1979), *Soils developed from colluvium in the Ridge and Valley area of Pennsylvania,* Soil Science, v. 128, p. 153–162.

Ciolkosz, E. J., Thurman, N. C., Waltman, W. J., and others (1994), *Argillic horizons in Pennsylvania soils,* Pennsylvania State University Agronomy Series 131, 35 p.

Ciolkosz, E. J., Waltman, W. J., and Thurman, N. C. (1992), *Fragipans in Pennsylvania soils,* Pennsylvania State University Agronomy Series 119, 18 p.

Clark, G. M. (1991), *South Mountain geomorphology,* in Sevon, W. D., and Potter, Noel, Jr., eds., *Geology in the South Mountain area, Pennsylvania,* Annual Field Conference of Pennsylvania Geologists, 56th, Carlisle, Pa., Guidebook, p. 55–94.

Clark, J. H. (1970), *Geology of the carbonate rocks in western Franklin County, Pennsylvania,* Pennsylvania Geological Survey, 4th ser., Progress Report 180, scale 1:24,000.

Clarke, J. W. (1984), *The core of the Blue Ridge anticlinorium in northern Virginia,* in Bartholomew, M. J., ed., *The Grenville event in the Appalachians and related topics,* Geological Society of America Special Paper 194, p. 155–160.

Claypole, E. W. (1885), *A preliminary report on the palaeontology of Perry County,* Pennsylvania Geological Survey, 2nd ser., Report F2, 437 p.

Cleaves, A. B., and Stephenson, R. C. (1949), *Guidebook to the geology of the Pennsylvania Turnpike, Carlisle to Irwin,* Pennsylvania Geological Survey, 4th ser., General Geology Report 24, 72 p.

Cleaves, E. T. (1989), *Appalachian Piedmont landscapes from the Permian to the Holocene,* in Gardner, T. W., and Sevon, W. D., eds., *Appalachian Geomorphology,* Amsterdam, Elsevier, p. 159–179 [reprinted from Geomorphology, v. 2, no. 1–3].

Cleaves, E. T., and Costa, J. E. (1979), *Equilibrium, cyclicity, and problems of scale—Maryland's Piedmont landscape,* Maryland Geological Survey Information Circular 29, 32 p.

Cleaves, E. T., Edwards, Jonathan, Jr., and Glaser, J. D., compilers and eds. (1968), *Geologic map of Maryland,* Maryland Geological Survey, scale 1:250,000.

Cleaves, E. T., Godfrey, A. E., and Bricker, O. P. (1970), *Geochemical balance of a small watershed and its geomorphic implications,* Geological Society of America Bulletin, v. 81, p. 3015–3032.

Clendening, J. A. (1975), *Palynological evidence for a Pennsylvanian age assignment of the Dunkard Group in the Appalachian basin: Part I,* in Barlow, J. A., and Burkhammer, Susan, eds., *Proceedings of the First I. C. White Memorial Symposium [Morgantown, W. Va., 1972]—"The age of the Dunkard,"* West Virginia Geological and Economic Survey, p. 195–216.

Clendening, J. A., and Gillespie, W. H. (1964), *Characteristic small spores of the Pittsburgh coal in West Virginia and Pennsylvania,* West Virginia Academy of Science Proceedings, v. 35, p. 141–150.

———— (1972), *Stratigraphic placement of the Dunkard—a review of paleobotanical and other evidence,* Castanea, v. 37, 26 p.

Cloos, Ernst (1947), *Oölite deformation in the South Mountain fold, Maryland,* Geological Society of America Bulletin, v. 58, p. 843–918.

———— (1968), *Thomasville Stone and Lime Company, Thomasville, Pennsylvania,* in Cloos, Ernst, and others, *The geology of mineral deposits in south-central Pennsylvania,* Annual Field Conference of Pennsylvania Geologists, 33rd, Harrisburg, Pa., Guidebook, p. 16–24.

———— (1971), *Microtectonics along the western edge of the Blue Ridge, Maryland and Virginia,* John Hopkins University Studies in Geology No. 20, Baltimore, Md., Johns Hopkins Press, 234 p.

Cloos, Ernst, and Hietanen, A. M. (1941), *Geology of the "Martic overthrust" and the Glenarm Series in Pennsylvania and Maryland,* Geological Society of America Special Paper 35, 207 p.

Cloos, Ernst, and Pettijohn, F. J. (1973), *Southern border of the Triassic basin, west of York, Pennsylvania: fault or overlap?,* Geological Society of America Bulletin, v. 84, p. 523–536.

Coakley, J. P., and Lewis, C. F. M. (1985), *Postglacial lake levels in the Erie basin,* in Karrow, P. F., and Calkin, P. E., eds., *Quaternary evolution of the Great Lakes,* Geological Association of Canada Special Paper 30, p. 195–213.

Coffman, J. L., and von Hake, C. A., eds. (1973), *Earthquake history of the United States,* U.S. Department of Commerce, National Oceanic and Atmospheric Administration, Publication 41–1, 208 p.

Collins, H. R. (1979), *The Mississippian and Pennsylvanian (Carboniferous) Systems in the United States—Ohio,* U.S. Geological Survey Professional Paper 1110-E, 26 p.

Colton, G. W. (1963), *Devonian and Mississippian correlations in part of north-central Pennsylvania—a report of progress,* in Shepps, V. C., ed., *Symposium on Middle and Upper Devonian stratigraphy of Pennsylvania and adjacent states,* Pennsylvania Geological Survey, 4th ser., General Geology Report 39, p. 115–125.

———— (1970), *The Appalachian basin—its depositional sequences and their geologic relationships,* in Fisher, G. W., and others, eds., *Studies of Appalachian geology: central and southern,* New York, Interscience Publishers, p. 5–47.

Conlin, R. R., and Hoskins, D. M. (1962), *Geology and mineral resources of the Mifflintown quadrangle, Pennsylvania,* Pennsylvania Geological Survey, 4th ser., Atlas 126, 46 p.

Conrad, J. A. (1985), *Shelf sedimentation above storm wave base in the Upper Ordovician Reedsville Formation in central Pennsylvania,* Newark, University of Delaware, M.S. thesis, 170 p.

Cook, T. D., and Bally, A. W., eds. (1975), *Stratigraphic atlas of North and Central America,* Princeton, N. J., Princeton University Press, 272 p.

Cooper, B. N. (1944), *Geology and mineral resources of the Burkes Garden quadrangle, Virginia,* Virginia Geological Survey Bulletin 60, 299 p.

Cooper, F. D. (1972), *The mineral industry of Pennsylvania,* in *Area reports: domestic,* U.S. Bureau of Mines Minerals Yearbook 1970, v. 2, p. 597–631.

Corbin, J. R. (1922), *Bog-iron ore,* Pennsylvania Geological Survey, 4th ser., Progress Report 59, 5 p.

Cornet, B. (1977), *The palynostratigraphy and age of the Newark Supergroup,* University Park, Pennsylvania State University, Ph.D. thesis, 527 p.

Cornet, B., and Olsen, P. E. (1985), *A summary of the biostratigraphy of the Newark Supergroup of eastern North America with comments on early Mesozoic provinciality,* III Congreso Latino-Americano de Paleontologia, Mexico, Simposia Sobre Floras del Triassico Tardio, su Fitgeografia y Paleoecologia, Memoria, p. 67–81.

———— (1989), *Jurassic rift basin floras and their climatic implications* [abs.], International Geological Congress, 28th, Washington, D. C., Abstracts, v. 1, p. 1–328.

Cornet, B., Traverse, A., and McDonald, N. G. (1973), *Fossil spores, pollen, and fishes from Connecticut indicate Early Jurassic age for part of the Newark Group*, Science, v. 182, p. 1243–1247.

Costa, J. E., and Cleaves, E. T. (1984), *The Piedmont landscape of Maryland: a new look at an old problem*, Earth Surfaces Processes and Landforms, v. 9, p. 59–74.

Cotter, Edward (1978), *The evolution of fluvial style, with special reference to the central Appalachian Paleozoic*, in Miall, A. D., ed., *Fluvial sedimentology*, Canadian Society of Petroleum Geologists Memoir 5, p. 361–383.

———— (1982), *Tuscarora Formation of Pennsylvania*, Society of Economic Paleontologists and Mineralogists, Eastern Section, 1982 Field Trip, Lewistown, Pa., Guidebook, 105 p.

———— (1983a), *Shelf, paralic, and fluvial environments and eustatic sea-level fluctuations in the origin of the Tuscarora Formation (Lower Silurian) of central Pennsylvania*, Journal of Sedimentary Petrology, v. 53, p. 25–49.

———— (1983b), *Silurian depositional history*, in Nickelsen, R. P., and Cotter, Edward, eds., *Silurian depositional history and Alleghanian deformation in the Pennsylvania Valley and Ridge*, Annual Field Conference of Pennsylvania Geologists, 48th, Danville, Pa., Guidebook, p. 3–28.

———— (1988), *Hierarchy of sea-level cycles in the medial Silurian siliciclastic succession of Pennsylvania*, Geology, v. 16, p. 242–245.

Cotter, Edward, and Inners, J. D. (1986), *Silurian stratigraphy and sedimentology in the Huntingdon County area*, in Sevon, W. D., ed., *Selected geology of Bedford and Huntingdon Counties*, Annual Field Conference of Pennsylvania Geologists, 51st, Huntingdon, Pa., Guidebook, p. 27–39.

Cotter, J. F. P. (1983), *The minimum age of the Woodfordian deglaciation of northeastern Pennsylvania and northwestern New Jersey*, Bethlehem, Pa., Lehigh University, Ph.D. thesis, 152 p.

———— (1985), *Late-glacial and postglacial vegetation changes in northeastern Pennsylvania and northwestern New Jersey and inferred climatic conditions* [abs.], Geological Society of America Abstracts with Programs, v. 17, no. 1, p. 13.

Crawford, M. L., and Crawford, W. A. (1980), *Metamorphic and tectonic history of the Pennsylvania Piedmont*, Journal of the Geological Society of London, v. 137, p. 311–320.

Crawford, M. L., and Mark, L. E. (1982), *Evidence from metamorphic rocks for overthrusting, Pennsylvania Piedmont, U.S.A.*, Canadian Mineralogist, v. 20, p. 333–347.

Crawford, W. A., and Hoersch, A. L. (1984), *The geology of the Honey Brook Upland, southeastern Pennsylvania*, in Bartholomew, M. J., ed., *The Grenville event in the Appalachians and related topics*, Geological Society of America Special Paper 194, p. 111–125.

Crawford, W. A., and Valley, J. W. (1990), *Origin of graphite in the Pickering Gneiss and the Franklin Marble, Honey Brook Upland, Pennsylvania Piedmont*, Geological Society of America Bulletin, v. 102, p. 807–811.

Creutzburg, H. (1964), *Untersuchungen uber den warmestrom der Erde in Westdeutschland*, Kali u. Steinsalz, v. 4, p. 73–108.

Cronce, R. C., and Ciolkosz, E. J. (1983), *Soils of the Allegheny National Forest*, in Auchmody, R. L., and others, eds., *Northeast Forest Soil Conference 1983*, U.S. Forest Service, Warren, Pa., p. 8–19.

Cross, A. T. (1975), *The Dunkard in perspective: geology, sedimentation, and life*, in Barlow, J. A., and Burkhammer, Susan, eds., *Proceedings of the First I. C. White Memorial Symposium [Morgantown, W. Va., 1972]—"The age of the Dunkard,"* West Virginia Geological and Economic Survey, p. 297–299.

Cross, A. T., and Arkle, Thomas, Jr. (1952), *The stratigraphy, sedimentation and nomenclature of the Upper Pennsylvanian-Lower Permian (Dunkard) strata of the Appalachian area*, International Congress on Carboniferous Stratigraphy and Geology, 3rd, Heerlen, 1951, Compte Rendu, v. 1, p. 101–111.

Cross, A. T., and Schemel, M. P. (1952), *Representative microfossil floras of some Appalachian coals*, International Congress on Carboniferous Stratigraphy and Geology, 3rd, Heerlen, 1951, Compte Rendu, v. 1, p. 123–130.

Crowl, G. H. (1981), *Glaciation in north-central Pennsylvania and the Pine Creek Gorge*, in Berg, T. M., and others, *Geology of Tioga and Bradford Counties, Pennsylvania*, Annual Field Conference of Pennsylvania Geologists, 46th, Wellsboro, Pa., Guidebook, p. 39–44.

Crowl, G. H., and Sevon, W. D. (1980), *Glacial border deposits of late Wisconsinan age in northeastern Pennsylvania*, Pennsylvania Geological Survey, 4th ser., General Geology Report 71, 68 p.

Crowley, D. J. (1973), *Middle Silurian patch reefs in Gasport Member (Lockport Formation), New York*, AAPG Bulletin, v. 57, p. 283–300.

Crowley, W. P. (1976), *The geology of the crystalline rocks near Baltimore and its bearing on the evolution of the eastern Maryland Piedmont*, Maryland Geological Survey Report of Investigations 27, 40 p.

Cuffey, R. J., Davidheiser, C. E., Fonda, S. S., and others (1985), *A mid-Silurian coral-bryozoan reef in central Pennsylvania*, in Gold, D. P., and others, *Central Pennsylvania geology revisited*, Annual Field Conference of Pennsylvania Geologists, 50th, State College, Pa., Guidebook, p. 1–19.

Cummins, A. B., and Givens, I. A. (1973), *Society of Mining Engineers, mining engineers handbook*, American Institute of Mining, Metallurgical, and Petroleum Engineers, v. 1, 2.

Cunningham, R. L., Lipscomb, G. H., Petersen, G. W., and others (1983), *Soils of Pennsylvania: characteristics, interpretations and extent*, Pennsylvania State University Agricultural Experiment Station Progress Report 380, 135 p.

Currie, J. B., Patnode, H. W., and Trump, R. P. (1962), *Development of folds in sedimentary strata*, Geological Society of America Bulletin, v. 73, p. 655–674.

Daily, P. W. (1971), *Climate of Pennsylvania*, in *Climates of the states*, National Oceanic and Atmospheric Administration, Silver Spring, Md., no. 60–36, p. 1–24.

Dana, J. D. (1873), *On some results of the earth's contraction from cooling, Pt. IV, Igneous injections, volcanoes*, American Journal of Science, 3rd ser., v. 6, p. 104–115.

Daniels, D. L. (1985), *Gravimetric character and anomalies in the Gettysburg basin, Pennsylvania—a preliminary appraisal* [abs.], in Robinson, G. R., Jr., and Froelich, A. J., eds., *Proceedings of the Second U.S. Geological Survey Workshop on the Early Mesozoic Basins of the Eastern United States*, U.S. Geological Survey Circular 946, p. 128–132.

Darby, William (1824), *Geographical, historical, and statistical repository*, Philadelphia, published by author, v. 1, no. 1 [Sept.], no. 2 [Oct.], 136 p.

Darrah, W. C. (1937), *Sur la présence d'équivalents des terrains Stéphanians dans l'Amerique du Nord*, Société Géologique du Nord Annales, v. 61, p. 187–197.

———— (1969), *A critical review of the Upper Pennsylvanian floras of eastern United States with notes on the Mazon Creek flora of Illinois*, published by author, 220 p.

———— (1975), *Historical aspects of the Permian flora of Fontaine and White*, in Barlow, J. A., and Burkhammer, Susan, eds., *Proceedings of the First I. C. White Memorial Symposium [Morgantown, W. Va., 1972]—"The age of the Dunkard,"* West Virginia Geological and Economic Survey, p. 81–102.

Davis, W. M. (1889), *The rivers and valleys of Pennsylvania*, National Geographic Magazine, v. 1, no. 3, p. 183–253.

Dawson, J. B. (1980), *Kimberlites and their xenoliths*, New York, Springer-Verlag, 252 p.

Day, D. T. (1885), *Cobalt*, in Williams, Albert, Jr., ed., *Mineral resources of the United States—Calendar years 1883 and 1884*, U.S. Geological Survey, p. 544–549.

———— (1894), *Mineral resources of the United States—Calendar year 1893*, U.S. Geological Survey, 810 p.

Day, R. L., Cunningham, R. C., and Ciolkosz, E. J. (1988), *Pennsylvania soils information system; a computer data base*, Pennsylvania State University Agronomy Department.

DeAngelis, R. M., and Hodge, W. T. (1972), *Preliminary climatic data report, Hurricane Agnes, June 14–23, 1972,* U.S. National Oceanic and Atmospheric Administration Technical Memorandum EDS NCC-1, 62 p.

De Boer, Jelle (1967), *Paleomagnetic-tectonic study of Mesozoic dike swarms in the Appalachians,* Journal of Geophysical Research, v. 72, p. 2237–2250.

_____ (1968), *Paleomagnetic differentiation and correlation of the Late Triassic volcanic rocks in the central Appalachians (with special reference to the Connecticut Valley),* Geological Society of America Bulletin, v. 79, p. 609–626.

Deike, R. G. (1969), *Relations of jointing to orientation of solution cavities in limestones of central Pennsylvania,* American Journal of Science, v. 267, p. 1230–1248.

Deines, P. (1968), *The carbon and oxygen isotopic composition of carbonates from a mica peridotite dike near Dixonville, Pennsylvania,* Geochimica et Cosmochimica Acta, v. 32, p. 613–625.

Delano, H. L., and Wilshusen, J. P. (in press), *Landslide susceptibility in the Williamsport 1- by 2-degree quadrangle, Pennsylvania,* Pennsylvania Geological Survey, 4th ser., Environmental Geology Report 9.

Denkler, K. E. (1984), *Upper Silurian biostratigraphy of the Andreas quarry, Pennsylvania,* in Lash, G. G., and others, eds., *Geology of an accreted terrane: the eastern Hamburg klippe and surrounding rocks, eastern Pennsylvania,* Annual Field Conference of Pennsylvania Geologists, 49th, Reading, Pa., Guidebook, p. 102–104.

Dennison, J. M. (1982), *Geologic history of the 40th parallel lineament in Pennsylvania,* Appalachian Basin Industrial Associates, Spring 1982 meeting, Knoxville, Tenn., Morgantown, W. Va., Department of Geology and Geography, West Virginia University, 19 p.

Dennison, J. M., and Head, J. W. (1975), *Sealevel variations interpreted from the Appalachian basin Silurian and Devonian,* American Journal of Science, v. 275, p. 1089–1120.

Deul, Maurice (1975), *Gas production from coal-beds—accomplishments and prospects,* American Gas Association, Transmission Conference, Bal Harbour, Fla., 1975, Proceedings, p. T227–T229.

Dewees, J. H. (1878), *Report of progress in the Juniata district on the fossil iron ore beds of middle Pennsylvania,* in Dewees, J. H., and Ashburner, C. A., *Report of progress in the Juniata district on the fossil iron ore beds of middle Pennsylvania, with a report of the Aughwick Valley and East Broad Top district,* Pennsylvania Geological Survey, 2nd ser., Report F, p. 1–139.

Dewey, J. F., and Burke, K. C. A. (1973), *Tibetan, Variscan, and Precambrian basement reactivation: products of continental collision,* Journal of Geology, v. 81, p. 683–692.

de Witt, Wallace, Jr. (1969), *Correlation of the Lower Mississippian rock in western Maryland and adjacent states* [abs.], Geological Society of America Special Paper 121, p. 431.

_____ (1970), *Age of the Bedford Shale, Berea Sandstone, and Sunbury Shale in the Appalachian and Michigan basins, Pennsylvania, Ohio, and Michigan,* U.S. Geological Survey Bulletin 1294-G, 11 p.

de Witt, Wallace, Jr., and Colton, G. W. (1964), *Bedrock geology of the Evitts Creek and Pattersons Creek quadrangles, Maryland, Pennsylvania, and West Virginia,* U.S. Geological Survey Bulletin 1173, 90 p.

Diamond, S. (1978), *Chemical reactions other than carbonate reactions,* in *Significance of tests and properties of concrete and concrete-making materials,* American Society for Testing and Materials Special Technical Publication 169B, p. 708–721.

Dickeson, M. W. (1860), *Report of the geological survey and condition of the Gap Mining Company's property: Lancaster County,* Philadelphia, J. B. Chandler, 26 p.

Dickey, P. A., Sherrill, R. E., and Matteson, L. S. (1943), *Oil and gas geology of the Oil City quadrangle, Pennsylvania,* Pennsylvania Geological Survey, 4th ser., Mineral Resource Report 25, 201 p.

Diment, W. H., Muller, O. H., and Lavin, P. M. (1980), *Basement tectonics of New York and Pennsylvania as revealed by gravity and magnetic studies,* in Wones, D. R., ed., *Proceedings of "The Cale-*

donides in the USA," Blacksburg, Virginia Polytechnic Institute, Department of Geological Sciences, Memoir 2, p. 221–227.

Diment, W. H., Urban, T. C., and Revetta, F. A. (1972), *Some geophysical anomalies in the eastern United States,* in Robertson, E. C., and others, eds., *The nature of the solid earth,* New York, McGraw-Hill, p. 544–572.

d'Invilliers, E. V. (1883), *The geology of the South Mountain belt of Berks County,* Pennsylvania Geological Survey, 2nd ser., Report D3, v. 2, pt. 1, 441 p.

_____ (1887), *Report on the iron mines and limestone quarries of the Cumberland-Lebanon Valley, 1886,* in Lesley, J. P., *Annual report of the Geological Survey of Pennsylvania for 1886—Part IV, Miscellaneous reports,* Pennsylvania Geological Survey, 2nd ser., Annual Report 1886, pt. 4, p. 1409–1567.

_____ (1891), *Report on the geology of the four counties—Union, Snyder, Mifflin and Juniata,* Pennsylvania Geological Survey, 2nd ser., Report F3, 420 p.

Dixon, W. H. (1974), *Reservoir geology of the Sage farm, Bradford oil field,* American Association of Petroleum Geologists, Eastern Section, Field Trip Guidebook, sec. 3, 22 p.

Dobrin, M. B. (1976), *Introduction to geophysical prospecting,* 3rd ed., New York, McGraw-Hill, 630 p.

Dodge, C. H. (1981), *The geologic genius of Charles Albert Ashburner,* Northeastern Geology, v. 3, p. 86–93.

_____ (1987), *The Second Geological Survey of Pennsylvania— The golden years,* Pennsylvania Geology, v. 18, no. 1, p. 9–15.

_____ (1992), *Bedrock lithostratigraphy of Warren County, Pennsylvania,* in Sevon, W. D., ed., *Geology of the upper Allegheny River region in Warren County, northwestern Pennsylvania,* Annual Field Conference of Pennsylvania Geologists, 57th, Warren, Pa., Guidebook, p. 1–20.

Dodge, C. H., and Berg, T. M. (1986), *Warrior Path section,* in Sevon, W. D., ed., *Selected geology of Bedford and Huntingdon Counties,* Annual Field Conference of Pennsylvania Geologists, 51st, Huntingdon, Pa., Guidebook, p. 200–221.

Dolar-Mantuani, Ludmila (1983), *Handbook of concrete aggregates: a petrographic and technological evaluation,* Park Ridge, N. J., Noyes Publications, 345 p.

Dolton, G. L., Carlson, K. H., Charpentier, R. R., and others (1981), *Estimates of undiscovered recoverable conventional resources of oil and gas in the United States,* U.S. Geological Survey Circular 860, 87 p.

Donahue, J., and Rollins, H. B. (1974), *Conemaugh (Glenshaw) marine events,* American Association of Petroleum Geologists, Eastern Section, Annual Meeting, 3rd, and Society of Economic Paleontologists and Mineralogists, Eastern Section, Spring Field Trip, Pittsburgh, Pa., Guidebook, p. 1–47.

Donahue, J. D., Rollins, H. B., and Shaak, G. D. (1972), *Asymmetrical community succession in a transgressive-regressive sequence,* in *Paleontology,* International Geological Congress, 24th, Montreal, Quebec, Canada, 1972, Proceedings, Sec. 7, p. 74–81.

Donaldson, A. C. (1969), *Ancient deltaic sedimentation (Pennsylvanian) and its control on the distribution, thickness and quality of coals,* in *Some Appalachian coals and carbonates: models of ancient shallow-water deposition,* Geological Society of America, Coal Division, Preconvention Field Trip, 1969, Guidebook, West Virginia Geological and Economic Survey, p. 93–121.

_____ (1974), *Pennsylvanian sedimentation of central Appalachians,* in Briggs, Garrett, ed., *Carboniferous of the southeastern United States,* Geological Society of America Special Paper 148, p. 47–78.

_____ (1979), *Depositional environments of the Upper Pennsylvanian Series,* in Englund, K. J., and others, eds., *Proposed Pennsylvanian System stratotype—Virginia and West Virginia,* International Congress of Carboniferous Stratigraphy and Geology, 9th, Field Trip 1, American Geological Institute Selected Guidebook Series 1, p. 123–131.

Donaldson, A. C., Renton, J. J., and Presley, M. W. (1985), *Pennsylvanian deposystems and paleoclimates of the Appalachians,* in

Phillips, T. L., and others, eds., *Paleoclimatic controls on coal resources of the Pennsylvanian System of North America*, International Journal of Coal Geology, v. 5, p. 167–193.

Dott, R. H., Jr., and Batten, R. L. (1976), *Evolution of the earth*, 2nd ed., New York, McGraw-Hill, 504 p.

Dougherty, M. T., and Barsotti, N. J. (1972), *Structural damage and potentially expansive sulfide minerals*, Bulletin of the Association of Engineering Geologists, v. 9, p. 105–125.

Dougherty, P. H., and Perlow, Michael, Jr. (1987), *The Macungie sinkhole, Lehigh Valley, Pennsylvania: cause and repair*, in Beck, B. F., and Wilson, W. L., eds., *Karst hydrogeology: engineering and environmental applications*, Multidisciplinary Conference on Sinkholes and the Environmental Impacts of Karst, 2nd, Orlando, Fla., 1987, Proceedings, Rotterdam, A. A. Balkema, p. 425–435.

Dowiak, M. J., Lucas, R. A., Nazar, A., and Threlfall, D. (1982), *Selection, installation and post-closure monitoring of a low permeability cover over a hazardous waste disposal facility*, HMCRI and U.S. Environmental Protection Agency Conference on the Management of Uncontrolled Hazardous Waste Sites, Proceedings, p. 187–190.

Drake, A. A., Jr. (1967), *Geologic map of the Easton quadrangle, New Jersey-Pennsylvania*, U.S. Geological Survey Geologic Quadrangle Map GQ-594, scale 1:24,000.

_____ (1969), *Precambrian and lower Paleozoic geology of the Delaware Valley, New Jersey-Pennsylvania*, in Subitzky, Seymour, ed., *Geology of selected areas in New Jersey and eastern Pennsylvania and guidebook of excursions*, New Brunswick, N. J., Rutgers University Press, p. 51–131.

_____ (1970), *Structural geology of the Reading Prong*, in Fisher, G. W., and others, eds., *Studies of Appalachian geology: central and southern*, New York, Interscience Publishers, p. 271–291.

_____ (1978), *The Lyon Station-Paulins Kill nappe—the frontal structure of the Musconetcong nappe system in eastern Pennsylvania and New Jersey*, U.S. Geological Survey Professional Paper 1023, 20 p.

_____ (1980), *The Taconides, Acadides, and Alleghenides in the central Appalachians*, in Wones, D. R., ed., *Proceedings of "The Caledonides in the USA,"* Blacksburg, Virginia Polytechnic Institute, Department of Geological Sciences, Memoir 2, p. 179–187.

_____ (1984), *The Reading Prong of New Jersey and eastern Pennsylvania—an appraisal of rock relations and chemistry of a major Proterozoic terrane in the Appalachians*, in Bartholomew, M. J., ed., *The Grenville event in the Appalachians and related topics*, Geological Society of America Special Paper 194, p. 75–109.

_____ (1987), *Geologic map of the Topton quadrangle, Lehigh and Berks Counties, Pennsylvania*, U.S. Geological Survey Geologic Quadrangle Map GQ-1609, scale 1:24,000.

Drake, A. A., Jr., Aleinikoff, J. N., and Volkert, R. A. (1991), *The Byram Intrusive Suite of the Reading Prong—age and tectonic environment*, in Drake, A. A., Jr., ed., *Contributions to New Jersey Geology*, U.S. Geological Survey Bulletin 1952, Chapter D, p. D1–D14.

Drake, A. A., Jr., and Epstein, J. B. (1967), *The Martinsburg Formation (Middle and Upper Ordovician) in the Delaware Valley, Pennsylvania-New Jersey*, U.S. Geological Survey Bulletin 1244-H, 16 p.

Drake, A. A., Jr., Hall, L. M., and Nelson, A. E. (1988), *Basement and basement-cover relation map of the Appalachian orogen in the United States*, U.S. Geological Survey Miscellaneous Investigations Series Map I-1655, scale 1:1,000,000, 2 sheets.

Drake, A. A., Jr., McLaughlin, D. B., and Davis, R. E. (1967), *Geologic map of the Riegelsville quadrangle, Pennsylvania-New Jersey*, U.S. Geological Survey Geologic Quadrangle Map GQ-593, scale 1:24,000.

Drake, A. A., Jr., Volkert, R. A., Lyttle, P. T., and Germine, Mark (1993), *Bedrock geologic map of the Tranquility quadrangle, Warren, Sussex, and Morris Counties, New Jersey*, U.S. Geological Survey Geologic Quadrangle Map GQ-1717, scale 1:24,000.

Drake, A. A., Jr., Volkert, R. A., Monteverde, D. H., and Kastelic, R. L., Jr. (1994), *Bedrock geologic map of the Washington quadran-*

gle, *Warren, Hunterdon, and Morris Counties, New Jersey*, U.S. Geological Survey Geologic Quadrangle Map GQ-1741, scale 1:24,000.

Duffy, L. J., and Myer, G. H. (1984), *Additional evidence for an overthrust in southeastern Pennsylvania* [abs.], Geological Society of America Abstracts with Programs, v. 16, no. 1, p. 13.

Duke, W. L. (1987a), *Revised internal stratigraphy of the Medina Formation in outcrop: an illustration of the inadequacy of color variation as a criterion for lithostratigraphic correlation*, in Duke, W. L., ed., *Sedimentology, stratigraphy, and ichnology of the Lower Silurian Medina Formation in New York and Ontario*, Society of Economic Paleontologists and Mineralogists, Eastern Section, Niagara Falls, Ontario, Canada, 1987 Field Trip, Guidebook, p. 16–30.

_____ ed. (1987b), *Sedimentology, stratigraphy, and ichnology of the Lower Silurian Medina Formation in New York and Ontario*, Society of Economic Paleontologists and Mineralogists, Eastern Section, Niagara Falls, Ontario, Canada, 1987 Field Trip, Guidebook, 185 p.

Duke, W. L., and Brusse, W. C. (1987), *Cyclicity and channels in the upper members of the Medina Formation in the Niagara Gorge*, in Duke, W. L., ed., *Sedimentology, stratigraphy, and ichnology of the Lower Silurian Medina Formation in New York and Ontario*, Society of Economic Paleontologists and Mineralogists, Eastern Section, Niagara Falls, Ontario, Canada, 1987 Field Trip, Guidebook, p. 46–65.

Duke, W. L., and Fawcett, P. J. (1987), *Depositional environments and regional sedimentation patterns in the upper members of the Medina Formation*, in Duke, W. L., ed., *Sedimentology, stratigraphy, and ichnology of the Lower Silurian Medina Formation in New York and Ontario*, Society of Economic Paleontologists and Mineralogists, Eastern Section, Niagara Falls, Ontario, Canada, 1987 Field Trip, Guidebook, p. 81–95.

DuMontelle, P. B., Bradford, S. C., Bauer, R. A., and Killey, M. M. (1981), *Mine subsidence in Illinois; facts for the homeowner considering insurance*, Environmental Geology Notes, v. 99, 24 p.

Durden, C. J. (1975), *Age of the Dunkard: evidence of the insect fauna* [abs.], in Barlow, J. A., and Burkhammer, Susan, eds., *Proceedings of the First I. C. White Memorial Symposium [Morgantown, W. Va., 1972]—"The age of the Dunkard,"* West Virginia Geological and Economic Survey, p. 295.

Duval, J. S. (1983), *Composite color images of aerial gamma-ray spectrometric data*, Geophysics, v. 48, p. 722–735.

Eagar, R. M. C. (1975), *Some nonmarine bivalve faunas from the Dunkard Group and underlying measures*, in Barlow, J. A., and Burkhammer, Susan, eds., *Proceedings of the First I. C. White Memorial Symposium [Morgantown, W. Va., 1972]—"The age of the Dunkard,"* West Virginia Geological and Economic Survey, p. 23–67.

Ebright, J. R., Fettke, C. R., and Ingham, A. I. (1949), *East Fork-Wharton gas field, Potter County, Pennsylvania*, Pennsylvania Geological Survey, 4th ser., Mineral Resource Report 30, 43 p.

Eckstein, Y., Heimlich, R. A., Palmer, D. F., and Shannon, S. S., Jr. (1982), *Geothermal investigations in Ohio and Pennsylvania*, Los Alamos National Laboratory, LA-9223-HDR, UC-66b, 89 p.

Edgerton, C. D. (1969), *Peat bog investigations in northeastern Pennsylvania*, Pennsylvania Geological Survey, 4th ser., Information Circular 65, 53 p.

Edmunds, W. E. (1968), *Geology and mineral resources of the northern half of the Houtzdale 15-minute quadrangle, Pennsylvania*, Pennsylvania Geological Survey, 4th ser., Atlas 85ab, 150 p.

_____ (1972), *Coal reserves of Pennsylvania: total, recoverable, and strippable (January 1, 1970)*, Pennsylvania Geological Survey, 4th ser., Information Circular 72, 40 p.

_____ (1988), *The Pottsville Formation of the Anthracite region*, in Inners, J. D., ed., *Bedrock and glacial geology of the North Branch Susquehanna lowland and the Eastern Middle Anthracite field, northeastern Pennsylvania*, Annual Field Conference of Pennsylvania Geologists, 53rd, Hazleton, Pa., Guidebook, p. 40–50.

_____ (1992), *Early Pennsylvanian (middle Morrowan) marine transgression in south-central Pennsylvania*, Northeastern Geology, v. 14, no. 2, p. 225–231.

Edmunds, W. E. (1993), *Pottsville Formation,* in Eggleston, J. R., and others, field trip leaders, *Carboniferous geology of the anthracite fields of eastern Pennsylvania and New England,* Geological Society of America, Coal Geology Division, Field Trip 11, 1993, Guidebook, p. 10–19.

Edmunds, W. E., and Berg, T. M. (1971), *Geology and mineral resources of the southern half of the Penfield 15-minute quadrangle, Pennsylvania,* Pennsylvania Geological Survey, 4th ser., Atlas 74cd, 184 p.

Edmunds, W. E., Berg, T. M., Sevon, W. D., and others (1979), *The Mississippian and Pennsylvanian (Carboniferous) Systems in the United States—Pennsylvania and New York,* U.S. Geological Survey Professional Paper 1110-B, p. B1–B33.

Edmunds, W. E., and Glover, A. D. (1986), *Broad Top coal field,* in Sevon, W. D., ed., *Selected geology of Bedford and Huntingdon Counties,* Annual Field Conference of Pennsylvania Geologists, 51st, Huntingdon, Pa., Guidebook, p. 93–102.

Eggleston, J. R., Wnuk, Christopher, and Edmunds, W. E. (1988), *The age of the upper part of the Llewellyn Formation in the Pennsylvania Anthracite region* [abs.], Journal of the Pennsylvania Academy of Science, v. 62, p. 45.

Eisenlohr, W. S., Jr. (1952), *Floods of July 18, 1942 in north-central Pennsylvania,* U.S. Geological Survey Water-Supply Paper 1134-B, p. 59–158.

Elliott, D., Fisher, G. W., and Snelson, S. (1982), *A restorable cross section through the central Appalachians* [abs.], Geological Society of America Abstracts with Programs, v. 14, no. 7, p. 482.

Engelder, Terry, and Engelder, Richard (1977), *Fossil distortion and décollement tectonics of the Appalachian Plateau,* Geology, v. 5, p. 457–460.

Engelder, Terry, and Geiser, Peter (1980), *On the use of regional joint sets as trajectories of paleostress fields during the development of the Appalachian Plateau, New York,* Journal of Geophysical Research, v. 85, p. 6319–6341.

Engineering News Record (1960), *Structures don't settle in this shale; but watch out for heave,* Engineering News Record, v. 164, no. 5, p. 46–48.

——— (1989), *ENR materials prices,* Engineering News Record, v. 222, no. 18, p. 51.

Englund, K. J. (1979), *The Mississippian and Pennsylvanian (Carboniferous) Systems in the United States—Virginia,* U.S. Geological Survey Professional Paper 1110-C, 21 p.

Epstein, A. G., Epstein, J. B., and Harris, L. D. (1977), *Conodont color alteration—an index to organic metamorphism,* U.S. Geological Survey Professional Paper 995, 27 p.

Epstein, A. G., Epstein, J. B., Spink, W. J., and Jennings, D. S. (1967), *Upper Silurian and Lower Devonian stratigraphy of northeastern Pennsylvania, New Jersey, and southeasternmost New York,* U.S. Geological Survey Bulletin 1243, 74 p.

Epstein, J. B. (1966), *Structural control of wind gaps and water gaps and of stream capture in the Stroudsburg area, Pennsylvania and New Jersey,* in *Geological Survey research 1966, Chapter B,* U.S. Geological Survey Professional Paper 550-B, p. B80–B86.

——— (1969), *Surficial geology of the Stroudsburg quadrangle, Pennsylvania-New Jersey,* Pennsylvania Geological Survey, 4th ser., General Geology Report 57, 67 p.

——— (1974), *Metamorphic origin of slaty cleavage in eastern Pennsylvania* [abs.], Geological Society of America Abstracts with Programs, v. 6, no. 7, p. 724.

Epstein, J. B., and Epstein, A. G. (1967), *Geology in the region of the Delaware to Lehigh water gaps,* Annual Field Conference of Pennsylvania Geologists, 32nd, East Stroudsburg, Pa., Guidebook, 89 p.

——— (1972), *The Shawangunk Formation (Upper Ordovician(?) to Middle Silurian) in eastern Pennsylvania,* U.S. Geological Survey Professional Paper 744, 45 p.

Epstein, J. B., and Hosterman, J. W. (1969), *Residual clay deposits in rocks of Early and Middle Devonian age near Kunkletown, Pennsylvania,* in *Geological Survey research 1969, Chapter D,* U.S. Geological Survey Professional Paper 650-D, p. D94–D105.

Epstein, J. B., Sevon, W. D., and Glaeser, J. D. (1974), *Geology and mineral resources of the Lehighton and Palmerton quadrangles, Carbon and Northampton Counties, Pennsylvania,* Pennsylvania Geological Survey, 4th ser., Atlas 195cd, 460 p.

Espenshade, A. H. (1925), *Pennsylvania place names,* State College, Pennsylvania State College, p. 190.

Espenshade, G. H. (1970), *Geology of the northern part of the Blue Ridge anticlinorium,* in Fisher, G. W., and others, eds., *Studies of Appalachian geology: central and southern,* New York, Interscience Publishers, p. 199–211.

Ettensohn, F. R. (1985), *Controls on development of Catskill delta complex basin-facies,* in Woodrow, D. L., and Sevon, W. D., eds., *The Catskill delta,* Geological Society of America Special Paper 201, p. 65–78.

Ettensohn, F. R., and Barron, L. S. (1981), *Depositional model for the Devonian-Mississippian black shale sequence in North America: a tectonoclimatic approach,* U.S. Department of Energy, DOE/METC/12040-2, Morgantown, W. Va., 80 p.

Ettensohn, F. R., and Chesnut, D. R., Jr. (1989), *Nature and probable origin of the Mississippian-Pennsylvanian unconformity in the eastern United States,* Beijing, XI Congrès International de Stratigraphie et de Géologie du Carbonifère, Compte Rendu 4, p. 145–159.

Eugster, H. P., and Chou, I-Ming (1979), *A model for the deposition of Cornwall-type magnetite deposits,* Economic Geology, v. 74, p. 763–774.

Evans, Louis (1749), *A map of Pensilvania, New-Jersey, New-York, and the three Delaware counties,* New York, James Parker (printer).

——— (1755), *Geographical, historical, political, philosophical, and mechanical essays—The first, containing an analysis of a general map of the middle British colonies in America; and of the country of the confederate Indians: a description of the face of the country; the boundaries of the confederates; and the maritime and inland navigations of the several rivers and lakes contained therein,* Philadelphia, B. Franklin and D. Hall, 32 p. and map.

Evenson, E. B., Myers, P. B., and Sevon, W. D. (1975), *Vadose-zone gypsum cementation of Wisconsinan kame delta gravels in eastern Pennsylvania* [abs.], Geological Society of America Abstracts with Programs, v. 7, no. 1, p. 55.

Eyles, Nicholas, and Westgate, J. A. (1987), *Restricted regional extent of the Laurentide Ice Sheet in the Great Lakes basins during early Wisconsin glaciation,* Geology, v. 15, p. 537–540.

Faill, R. T. (1969), *Kink band structures in the Valley and Ridge province, central Pennsylvania,* Geological Society of America Bulletin, v. 80, p. 2539–2550.

——— (1973a), *Kink-band folding, Valley and Ridge province, Pennsylvania,* Geological Society of America Bulletin, v. 84, p. 1289–1313.

——— (1973b), *Tectonic development of the Triassic Newark-Gettysburg basin in Pennsylvania,* Geological Society of America Bulletin, v. 84, p. 725–740.

——— (1976), *High calcium limestone discovered in the Williamsport-Bloomsburg area,* Pennsylvania Geology, v. 7, no. 6, p. 13–16.

——— (1977), *Fossil distortion, Valley and Ridge province, Pennsylvania* [abs.], Geological Society of America Abstracts with Programs, v. 9, no. 3, p. 262–263.

——— (1978), *Geology of Laurel Creek reservoir and filtration plant, Lewistown water supply system,* in Branthoover, G. L., chairman, *Field trip guidebook—1978 Annual Meeting, Hershey, Penna.,* Association of Engineering Geologists, p. 212–221.

——— (1979), *Geology and mineral resources of the Montoursville South and Muncy quadrangles and part of the Hughesville quadrangle, Lycoming, Northumberland, and Montour Counties, Pennsylvania,* Pennsylvania Geological Survey, 4th ser., Atlas 144ab, 114 p.

——— (1981), *The Tipton block—an unusual structure in the Appalachians,* Pennsylvania Geology, v. 12, no. 2, p. 5–9.

——— (1985a), *The Acadian orogeny and the Catskill delta,* in Woodrow, D. L., and Sevon, W. D., eds., *The Catskill delta,* Geological Society of America Special Paper 201, p. 15–37.

Faill, R. T. (1985b), *The Anthracite region in eastern Pennsylvania* [abs.], Geological Society of America Abstracts with Programs, v. 17, no. 1, p. 18.

———— (1986a), *Introduction,* in Sevon, W. D., ed., *Selected geology of Bedford and Huntingdon Counties,* Annual Field Conference of Pennsylvania Geologists, 51st, Huntingdon, Pa., Guidebook, p. 131–144.

———— (1986b), *Structure,* in Sevon, W. D., ed., *Selected geology of Bedford and Huntingdon Counties,* Annual Field Conference of Pennsylvania Geologists, 51st, Huntingdon, Pa., Guidebook, p. 119–126.

———— (1987), *The Fourth Geological Survey of Pennsylvania: the resource years,* Pennsylvania Geology, v. 18, no. 1, p. 23–32.

———— (1991), *Out-of-sequence (west-to-east) deformation in the central Appalachian foreland* [abs.], Geological Society of America Abstracts with Programs, v. 23, no. 1, p. 28.

———— (in preparation), *Tectonic map of Pennsylvania,* Pennsylvania Geological Survey, 4th ser., Map 65, scale 1:250,000, 4 sheets.

Faill, R. T., Glover, A. D., and Way, J. H. (1989), *Geology and mineral resources of the Blandburg, Tipton, Altoona, and Bellwood quadrangles, Blair, Cambria, Clearfield, and Centre Counties, Pennsylvania,* Pennsylvania Geological Survey, 4th ser., Atlas 86, 209 p.

Faill, R. T., Hoskins, D. M., and Wells, R. B. (1978), *Middle Devonian stratigraphy in central Pennsylvania—a revision,* Pennsylvania Geological Survey, 4th ser., General Geology Report 70, 28 p.

Faill, R. T., and MacLachlan, D. B. (1989), *Tectonic terranes of southeastern Pennsylvania* [abs.], Geological Society of America Abstracts with Programs, v. 21, no. 2, p. 13.

Faill, R. T., and Nickelsen, R. P. (1973), *Structural geology,* in Faill, R. T., ed., *Structure and Silurian-Devonian stratigraphy of the Valley and Ridge province, central Pennsylvania,* Annual Field Conference of Pennsylvania Geologists, 38th, Camp Hill, Pa., Guidebook, p. 9–38.

Faill, R. T., and Valentino, D. W. (1989), *Metamorphic isograds and regional structures in the Pennsylvania Piedmont* [abs.], Geological Society of America Abstracts with Programs, v. 21, no. 2, p. 13.

Faill, R. T., and Wells, R. B. (1974), *Geology and mineral resources of the Millerstown quadrangle, Perry, Juniata, and Snyder Counties, Pennsylvania,* Pennsylvania Geological Survey, 4th ser., Atlas 136, 276 p.

Faill, R. T., Wells, R. B., and Sevon, W. D. (1977a), *Geology and mineral resources of the Linden and Williamsport quadrangles, Lycoming County, Pennsylvania,* Pennsylvania Geological Survey, 4th ser., Atlas 134ab, 66 p.

———— (1977b), *Geology and mineral resources of the Salladasburg and Cogan Station quadrangles, Lycoming County, Pennsylvania,* Pennsylvania Geological Survey, 4th ser., Atlas 133cd, 44 p.

Fanning, D. S., and Fanning, M. C. B. (1989), *Soil morphology, genesis, and classification,* New York, John Wiley and Sons, 395 p.

Fauth, J. L. (1968), *Geology of the Caledonia Park quadrangle area, South Mountain, Pennsylvania,* Pennsylvania Geological Survey, 4th ser., Atlas 129a, 133 p.

———— (1978), *Geology and mineral resources of the Iron Springs area, Adams and Franklin Counties, Pennsylvania,* Pennsylvania Geological Survey, 4th ser., Atlas 129c, 72 p.

Feakes, C. R., and Retallack, G. J. (1988), *Recognition and characterization of fossil soils developed on alluvium; a Late Ordovician example,* in Reinhardt, J., and Sigleo, W. R., eds., *Paleosols and weathering through geologic time: principles and applications,* Geological Society of America Special Paper 216, p. 35–47.

Fenneman, N. M. (1938), *Physiography of eastern United States,* New York, McGraw-Hill, 714 p.

Ferguson, H. F. (1967), *Valley stress relief in the Allegheny Plateau,* Bulletin of the Association of Engineering Geologists, v. 4, p. 63–68.

Ferguson, H. F., and Hamel, J. V. (1981), *Valley stress relief in flat-lying sedimentary rocks,* in Akai, Koichi, and others, eds., *Weak rock—Soft, fractured and weathered rock,* International Symposium on Weak Rock, Tokyo, 1981, Proceedings, Rotterdam, A. A. Balkema, v. 2, p. 1235–1240. [The following information is provided at the request of the publisher as a condition of copyright release: Please order from A. A. Balkema, Old Post Road, Brookfield, Vt., 05036; telephone, 802-276-3162; telefax, 802-276-3837; e-mail, info@ashgate.com; 3 volume set, Hfl. 875/US $490.00.]

Fergusson, W. B. (1981), *Eighteenth century geologic studies in eastern Pennsylvania,* Northeastern Geology, v. 3, p. 62–70.

Fergusson, W. B., and Prather, B. A. (1968), *Salt deposits in the Salina Group in Pennsylvania,* Pennsylvania Geological Survey, 4th ser., Mineral Resource Report 58, 41 p.

Ferm, J. C. (1962), *Petrology of some Pennsylvanian sedimentary rocks,* Journal of Sedimentary Petrology, v. 32, p. 104–123.

———— (1970), *Allegheny deltaic deposits,* in Morgan, J. P., and Shaver, R. H., eds., *Deltaic sedimentation—Modern and ancient,* Society of Economic Paleontologists and Mineralogists Special Publication 15, p. 246–255.

———— (1974), *Carboniferous environmental models in eastern United States and their significance,* in Briggs, Garrett, ed., *Carboniferous of the southeastern United States,* Geological Society of America Special Paper 148, p. 79–95.

———— (1975), *Pennsylvanian cyclothems of the Appalachian Plateau, a retrospective view,* in McKee, E. D., and others, *Paleotectonic investigations of the Pennsylvanian System in the United States—Part II, Interpretive summary and special features of the Pennsylvanian System,* U.S. Geological Survey Professional Paper 853, pt. 2, p. 57–64.

———— (1979a), *Pennsylvanian cyclothems of the Appalachian region, a retrospective view,* in Ferm, J. C., and others, eds., *Carboniferous depositional environments in the Appalachian region,* Columbia, S. C., Carolina Coal Group, University of South Carolina Department of Geology, p. 284–290.

———— (1979b), *Allegheny deltaic deposits: a model for the coal bearing strata,* in Ferm, J. C., and others, eds., *Carboniferous depositional environments in the Appalachian region,* Columbia, S. C., Carolina Coal Group, University of South Carolina Department of Geology, p. 291–294.

Ferm, J. C., and Cavaroc, V. V., Jr. (1969), *A field guide to Allegheny deltaic deposits in the upper Ohio Valley,* Ohio Geological Society and Pittsburgh Geological Society, 21 p.

Ferm, J. C., and Williams, E. G. (1965), *Characteristics of a Carboniferous marine invasion in western Pennsylvania,* Journal of Sedimentary Petrology, v. 35, p. 319–330.

Fettke, C. R. (1919), *Glass manufacture and the glass sand industry of Pennsylvania,* Pennsylvania Geological Survey, 3rd ser., Economic Report 12, 278 p.

———— (1938), *The Bradford oil field, Pennsylvania and New York,* Pennsylvania Geological Survey, 4th ser., Mineral Resource Report 21, 454 p.

———— (1941), *Music Mountain oil pool, McKean County, Pennsylvania,* in Levorsen, A. I., ed., *Stratigraphic type oil fields,* Tulsa, Okla., American Association of Petroleum Geologists, p. 492–506.

———— (1950), *Summarized record of deep wells in Pennsylvania,* Pennsylvania Geological Survey, 4th ser., Mineral Resource Report 31, 148 p.

———— (1954), *Structure-contour maps of the Plateau region of north-central and western Pennsylvania,* Pennsylvania Geological Survey, 4th ser., General Geology Report 27, 23 p. plus unpaged appendix.

———— (1961), *Well-sample descriptions in northwestern Pennsylvania and adjacent states,* Pennsylvania Geological Survey, 4th ser., Mineral Resource Report 40, 691 p.

Fettke, C. R., and Bayles, R. E. (1945), *Conemaugh Gorge section of the Mississippian System southeast of Cramer, Pennsylvania,* Pennsylvania Academy of Science Proceedings, v. 19, p. 86–95.

Field Conference of Pennsylvania Geologists [Hoskins, D. M.] (1985), *Part 5, A short history and a synopsis of the Field Conferences,* in *Commemorative guidebook to the First Field Conference—May 29, 30, and 31, 1931—State College, Pennsylvania,* Field Conference of Pennsylvania Geologists, unpaged.

Finn, F. H. (1949), *Geology and occurrence of natural gas in Oriskany sandstone in Pennsylvania and New York,* AAPG Bulletin, v. 33, p. 303–335.

Fischer, R. P. (1970), *Similarities, differences, and some genetic problems of the Wyoming and Colorado Plateau types of uranium deposits in sandstone,* Economic Geology, v. 65, p. 778–784.

Fisher, D. W. (1954), *Stratigraphy of Medinan Group, New York and Ontario,* AAPG Bulletin, v. 38, p. 1979–1996.

Fisher, G. W., Higgins, M. W., and Zietz, Isidore (1979), *Geological interpretations of aeromagnetic maps of the crystalline rocks in the Appalachians, northern Virginia to New Jersey,* Maryland Geological Survey Report of Investigations 32, 43 p.

Fleming, R. S. (1975), *A geophysical study of the southwestern end of the Scranton gravity high,* Bethlehem, Pa., Lehigh University, M.S. thesis, 44 p.

Fleming, R. S., and Sumner, J. R. (1975), *Interpretation of geophysical anomalies over the arcuate Appalachians* [abs.], Geological Society of America Abstracts with Programs, v. 7, no. 1, p. 58.

Fleming, R. W., and Taylor, F. A. (1980), *Estimating the cost of landslide damage in the United States,* U.S. Geological Survey Circular 832, p. 14–17.

Flint, N. K. (1965), *Geology and mineral resources of southern Somerset County, Pennsylvania,* Pennsylvania Geological Survey, 4th ser., County Report 56A, 267 p.

Flippo, H. N., Jr. (1975), *Temperatures of streams and selected reservoirs in Pennsylvania,* Pennsylvania Department of Environmental Resources, Office of Resources Management, Water Resources Bulletin 11, 95 p.

———— (1977), *Floods in Pennsylvania,* Pennsylvania Department of Environmental Resources, Office of Resources Management, Water Resources Bulletin 13, 59 p.

———— (1982), *Technical manual for estimating low-flow characteristics of Pennsylvania streams,* Pennsylvania Department of Environmental Resources, Office of Resources Management, Water Resources Bulletin 15, 86 p.

Foland, K. A., and Muessig, K. W. (1978), *A Paleozoic age for some charnockitic-anorthositic rocks,* Geology, v. 6, p. 143–146.

Folk, R. L. (1960), *Petrography and origin of the Tuscarora, Rose Hill, and Keefer Formations, Lower and Middle Silurian of eastern West Virginia,* Journal of Sedimentary Petrology, v. 30, p. 1–58.

Fontaine, W. M., and White, I. C. (1880), *The Permian or Upper Carboniferous flora of West Virginia and S. W. Pennsylvania,* Pennsylvania Geological Survey, 2nd ser., Report PP, 143 p., 38 pls.

Foose, R. M. (1944), *High-alumina clays of Pennsylvania,* Economic Geology, v. 39, p. 557–577.

———— (1945a), *Iron-manganese ore deposit at White Rocks, Cumberland County, Pennsylvania,* Pennsylvania Geological Survey, 4th ser., Mineral Resource Report 26, 35 p.

———— (1945b), *Manganese minerals of Pennsylvania,* Pennsylvania Geological Survey, 4th ser., Mineral Resource Report 27, 130 p.

———— (1953), *Ground-water behavior in the Hershey Valley, Pennsylvania,* Geological Society of America Bulletin, v. 64, p. 623–646.

Forgotson, J. M., Jr. (1957), *Nature, usage, and definition of marker-defined vertically segregated rock units,* AAPG Bulletin, v. 41, p. 2108–2113.

Frakes, L. A. (1967), *Stratigraphy of the Devonian Trimmers Rock in eastern Pennsylvania,* Pennsylvania Geological Survey, 4th ser., General Geology Report 51, 208 p.

Frazer, Persifor, Jr. (1876), *Report of progress in the district of York and Adams Counties,* Pennsylvania Geological Survey, 2nd ser., Report C, 198 p.

———— (1880), *The geology of Lancaster County,* Pennsylvania Geological Survey, 2nd ser., Report CCC, 350 p.

Frederiksen, N. O. (1984), *Stratigraphic, paleoclimatic, and paleobiogeographic significance of Tertiary sporomorphs from Massachusetts,* U.S. Geological Survey Professional Paper 1308, 25 p.

Freedman, Jacob (1967), *Geology of a portion of the Mount Holly Springs quadrangle, Adams and Cumberland Counties, Pennsylvania,* Pennsylvania Geological Survey, 4th ser., Progress Report 169, 66 p.

Freedman, J., Wise, D. U., and Bentley, R. D. (1964), *Pattern of folded folds in the Appalachian Piedmont along Susquehanna River,* Geological Society of America Bulletin, v. 75, p. 621–638.

Freeze, R. A., and Cherry, J. A. (1979), *Groundwater,* New York, Prentice-Hall, 604 p.

Frey, R. F., ed. (1988), *Commonwealth of Pennsylvania—1988 water quality assessment—Volume I, Executive summary,* Pennsylvania Department of Environmental Resources, Bureau of Water Quality Management, 40 p.

Frey, M. G. (1973), *Influence of Salina salt on structure in New York-Pennsylvania part of Appalachian Plateau,* AAPG Bulletin, v. 57, p. 1027–1037.

Fridley, H. M., and Eddy, G. E. (1964), *Divide shifting between the Ohio and Monongahela Rivers,* West Virginia Academy of Science Proceedings, v. 36, p. 152–153.

Friedman, G. M. (1987), *Vertical movements of the crust: case histories from the northern Appalachian basin,* Geology, v. 15, p. 1130–1133.

Friedman, G. M., and Johnson, K. G. (1966), *The Devonian Catskill delta complex of New York, type example of a "tectonic delta complex,"* in Shirley, M. L., and Ragsdale, J. A., eds., *Deltas in their geologic framework,* Houston Geological Society, p. 177–188.

Froelich, A. J., and Gottfried, D. (1985), *Early Jurassic diabase sheets of the Eastern United States—a preliminary overview,* in Robinson, G. R., Jr., and Froelich, A. J., eds., *Proceedings of the Second U.S. Geological Survey Workshop on the Early Mesozoic Basins of the Eastern United States,* U.S. Geological Survey Circular 946, p. 79–86.

Froelich, A. J., and Olsen, P. E. (1985), *Newark Supergroup, a revision of the Newark Group in eastern North America,* in Robinson, G. R., Jr., and Froelich, A. J., eds., *Proceedings of the Second U.S. Geological Survey Workshop on the Early Mesozoic Basins of the Eastern United States,* U.S. Geological Survey Circular 946, p. 1–3.

Fuller, J. O. (1955), *Source of Sharon Conglomerate of northeastern Ohio,* Geological Society of America Bulletin, v. 66, p. 159–175.

Gallagher, R. A., and Parks, J. M. (1983), *Depositional environments of the Loyalhanna Member of the Mauch Chunk Formation, north-central Pennsylvania* [abs.], Geological Society of America Abstracts with Programs, v. 15, no. 3, p. 127.

Ganis, G. R. (1983), *Carbonate mining in the folded Appalachians of Pennsylvania,* SME–AIME Annual Meeting, 1983, Preprint 83–23.

Gannett, Henry (1901), *Profiles of rivers in the United States,* U.S. Geological Survey Water-Supply Paper 44, 100 p.

Gardner, G. D., and Donahue, J. (1985), *The Little Platte drainage, Missouri: a model for locating temporal surfaces in a fluvial environment,* in Stein, J. K., and Farrand, W. R., eds., *Archaeological sediments in context,* Orono, Maine, Center for the Study of Early Man, Institute for Quaternary Studies, University of Maine, Peopling of the Americas Series, v. 1, p. 69–89.

Gardner, J. H. (1913), *The Broad-Top coal field of Huntingdon, Bedford and Fulton Counties,* Pennsylvania Geological Survey, 3rd ser., Report 10, 81 p.

Gardner, T. W., Sasowsky, I. D., and Schmidt, V. A. (1994), *Reversed-polarity glacial sediments and revised glacial chronology, West Branch Susquehanna River valley, central Pennsylvania,* Quaternary Research, v. 42, p. 131–135.

Gardner, T. W., and Sevon, W. D., eds. (1989), *Appalachian geomorphology,* Amsterdam, Elsevier, 318 p. [reprinted from Geomorphology, v. 2, no. 1–3].

Gault, H. R., Goth, J. H., Jr., and Tooker, E. W. (1959), *Mineral resources,* in Willard, Bradford, and others, *Geology and mineral resources of Bucks County, Pennsylvania,* Pennsylvania Geological Survey, 4th ser., County Report 9, p. 185–218.

Gedde, R. W. (1965), *Geophysical investigation of a magnetite deposit, Chester County,* University Park, Pennsylvania State University, M.S. thesis, 59 p.

Geiser, P. A. (1988), *The role of kinematics in the construction and analysis of geological cross sections in deformed terranes,* in Mitra,

Gautam, and Wojtal, Steven, eds., *Geometries and mechanisms of thrusting*, Geological Society of America Special Paper 222, p. 47–76.

Geiser, Peter, and Engelder, Terry (1983), *The distribution of layer parallel shortening fabrics in the Appalachian foreland of New York and Pennsylvania: evidence for two non-coaxial phases of the Alleghanian orogeny*, in Hatcher, R. D., Jr., and others, eds., *Contributions to the tectonics and geophysics of mountain chains*, Geological Society of America Memoir 158, p. 161–175.

Genth, F. A. (1875), *Preliminary report on the mineralogy of Pennsylvania*, Pennsylvania Geological Survey, 2nd ser., Report B, 206 p.

_____ (1876), *Second preliminary report on the mineralogy of Pennsylvania*, Pennsylvania Geological Survey, 2nd ser., Report B2, p. 207–238.

Geological Society of Pennsylvania (1834–35), *Transactions*, Philadelphia, published by the Society, v. 1, pt. 1, 1834; v. 1, pt. 2, 1835, 428 p.

Geodata International (1980), *Aerial radiometric and magnetic survey, Wilmington national topographic map, Delaware/Maryland/New Jersey/Pennsylvania, southeast U.S. project*, U.S. Department of Energy, GJBX–68(80), variously paged.

Geomega, Inc. [Briggs, R. P., and Tatlock, D. B.] (1983), *Estimates of undiscovered recoverable natural gas resources in Pennsylvania*, Bradford, Pa., Pennsylvania Oil and Gas Association, 33 p.

Gerhart, J. M., and Lazorchick, G. J. (1988), *Evaluation of the ground-water resources of the Lower Susquehanna River basin, Pennsylvania and Maryland*, U.S. Geological Survey Water-Supply Paper 2284, 128 p.

Gertsner, P. A. (1979), *Henry Darwin Rogers and William Barton Rogers on the nomenclature of the American Paleozoic rocks*, in Schneer, C. J., ed., *Two hundred years of geology in America*, Hanover, N. H., University Press of New England, p. 178–186.

Geyer, A. R. (1970), *Geology, mineral resources and environmental geology of the Palmyra quadrangle, Lebanon and Dauphin Counties*, Pennsylvania Geological Survey, 4th ser., Atlas 157d, 46 p.

Geyer, A. R., and Bolles, W. H. (1979), *Outstanding scenic geological features of Pennsylvania*, Pennsylvania Geological Survey, 4th ser., Environmental Geology Report 7, pt. 1, 508 p.

_____ (1987), *Outstanding scenic geological features of Pennsylvania, Part 2*, Pennsylvania Geological Survey, 4th ser., Environmental Geology Report 7, pt. 2, 270 p.

Geyer, A. R., Buckwalter, T. V., McLaughlin, D. B., and Gray, Carlyle (1963), *Geology and mineral resources of the Womelsdorf quadrangle*, Pennsylvania Geological Survey, 4th ser., Atlas 177c, 96 p.

Geyer, A. R., Gray, Carlyle, McLaughlin, D. B., and Moseley, J. R. (1958), *Geology of the Lebanon quadrangle*, Pennsylvania Geological Survey, 4th ser., Atlas 167c, scale 1:24,000.

Geyer, A. R., Smith, R. C., II, and Barnes, J. H. (1976), *Mineral collecting in Pennsylvania*, 4th ed., Pennsylvania Geological Survey, 4th ser., General Geology Report 33, 260 p.

Gillespie, W. H., Hennen, G. J., and Balasco, Charles (1975), *Plant megafossils from Dunkard strata in northwestern West Virginia and southwestern Pennsylvania*, in Barlow, J. A., and Burkhammer, Susan, eds., *Proceedings of the First I. C. White Memorial Symposium [Morgantown, W. Va., 1972]—"The age of the Dunkard,"* West Virginia Geological and Economic Survey, p. 223–248.

Gillespie, W. H., and Pfefferkorn, H. W. (1979), *Distribution of commonly occurring plant megafossils in the proposed Pennsylvanian System stratotype*, in Englund, K. J., and others, *Proposed Pennsylvanian System stratotype—Virginia and West Virginia*, International Congress of Carboniferous Stratigraphy and Geology, 9th, Field Trip 1, American Geological Institute Selected Guidebook Series 1, p. 87–96.

Girty, G. H. (1928), *The Pocono fauna of the Broad Top coal field, Pennsylvania*, U.S. Geological Survey Professional Paper 150-E, p. 111–127.

Glaeser, J. D. (1963), *Lithostratigraphic nomenclature of the Triassic Newark-Gettysburg basin*, Pennsylvania Academy of Science Proceedings, v. 37, p. 179–188.

_____ (1966), *Provenance, dispersal, and depositional environments of Triassic sediments in the Newark-Gettysburg basin*, Pennsylvania Geological Survey, 4th ser., General Geology Report 43, 168 p.

_____ (1969), *Geology of flagstones in the Endless Mountains region, northern Pennsylvania*, Pennsylvania Geological Survey, 4th ser., Information Circular 66, 14 p.

Glass, G. B. (1971), *Wrench faulting in the Appalachian Plateaus of Pennsylvania*, Pennsylvania Geology, v. 2, no. 3, p. 7–11.

Glass, G. B., Edmunds, W. E., Shepps, V. C., and others (1977), *Geology and mineral resources of the Ramey and Houtzdale quadrangles, Clearfield and Centre Counties, Pennsylvania*, Pennsylvania Geological Survey, 4th ser., Atlas 85cd, 94 p.

Glover, A. D. (1970), *Geology and mineral resources of the southern half of the Clearfield 15-minute quadrangle, Pennsylvania*, Pennsylvania Geological Survey, 4th ser., Atlas 84cd, 139 p.

Gohn, G. S. (1976), *Sedimentology, stratigraphy, and paleogeography of lower Paleozoic carbonate rocks, Conestoga Valley, southeastern Pennsylvania*, Newark, University of Delaware, Ph.D. thesis, 298 p.

_____ (1978), *Revised ages of Cambrian and Ordovician formations of the Conestoga Valley near York and Lancaster, southeastern Pennsylvania*, in Sohl, N. F., and Wright, W. B., *Changes in stratigraphic nomenclature by the U.S. Geological Survey, 1977*, U.S. Geological Survey Bulletin 1457-A, p. A94–A97.

Gold, D. P. (1980), *Structural geology*, in Siegal, B. S., and Gillespie, A. R., eds., *Remote sensing in geology*, New York, John Wiley and Sons, p. 419–483.

Gold, D. P., Alexander, S. S., and Parizek, R. R. (1974), *Application of remote sensing to natural resources and environmental problems in Pennsylvania*, Earth and Mineral Sciences, v. 43, no. 7, p. 49–53.

Gold, D. P., and Kowalik, W. S. (1976), *Lineaments and mineral occurrences*, in *Interdisciplinary applications and interpretations of EREP data within the Susquehanna River basin*, ORSER-SSEL Technical Report 2–76, NASA, Houston, Tex., p. 4–49—4–58.

Gold, D. P., and Parizek, R. R. (1976), *Field guide to lineaments and fractures in central Pennsylvania*, International Conference on Basement Tectonics, 2nd, Newark, Del., 1976, Guidebook, 75 p.

Good, R. S. (1955), *A chromographic study of nickel in soils and plants at the Lancaster Gap mine, Pennsylvania*, University Park, Pennsylvania State University, M.S. thesis, 53 p.

Goodwin, P. W., and Anderson, E. J. (1974), *Associated physical and biogenic structures in environmental subdivision of a Cambrian tidal sand body*, Journal of Geology, v. 82, p. 779–794.

Gordon, S. G. (1921), *Desilicated granitic pegmatites*, Academy of Natural Sciences of Philadelphia Proceedings, v. 73, pt. 1, p. 169–192.

_____ (1922), *The mineralogy of Pennsylvania*, Academy of Natural Sciences of Philadelphia Special Publication 1, 255 p.

Gottfried, David, and Froelich, A. J. (1988), *Variations of palladium and platinum contents and ratios in selected early Mesozoic tholeiitic rock associations in the Eastern United States*, in Froelich, A. J., and Robinson, G. R., Jr., eds., *Studies of the early Mesozoic basins of the Eastern United States*, U.S. Geological Survey Bulletin 1776, p. 332–341.

Gottfried, David, Froelich, A. J., Rait, Norma, and Aruscavage, P. J. (1990), *Fractionation of palladium and platinum in a Mesozoic diabase sheet, Gettysburg basin, Pennsylvania: implications for mineral exploration*, in Dunn, C. E., and others, eds., *Geochemistry of platinum-group elements*, Journal of Geochemical Exploration, v. 37, p. 75–89.

Graham, R. H. (1978), *Quantitative deformation studies in the Permian rocks of Alpes-Maritimes*, Proceedings of Goguel Symposium, Mémoire du Bureau de recherches géologiques et minières de francalis, v. 91, p. 219–238.

Grasty, R. L. (1979), *Gamma-ray spectrometric methods in uranium exploration—theory and operational procedures*, in Hood, P. J., ed., *Geophysics and geochemistry in the search for metallic ores*, Geological Survey of Canada Economic Geology Report 31, p. 147–161.

Grauch, R. I., and Ludwig, K. R. (1979), *Uranium mineralization at Easton, Pennsylvania,* Pennsylvania Geology, v. 10, no. 5, p. 14–16.

Grauert, B., and Wagner, M. E. (1975), *Age of the granulite-facies metamorphism of the Wilmington Complex, Delaware-Pennsylvania Piedmont,* American Journal of Science, v. 275, p. 683–691.

Gray, Carlyle (1954), *Recumbent folding in the Great Valley,* Pennsylvania Academy of Science Proceedings, v. 28, p. 96–101.

———— (1959), *Nappe structures in Pennsylvania* [abs.], Geological Society of America Bulletin, v. 70, p. 1611.

Gray, Carlyle, Geyer, A. R., and McLaughlin, D. B. (1958), *Geology of the Richland quadrangle,* Pennsylvania Geological Survey, 4th ser., Atlas 167d, scale 1:24,000.

Gray, Carlyle, and Lapham, D. M. (1961), *Guide to the geology of Cornwall, Pennsylvania,* Pennsylvania Geological Survey, 4th ser., General Geology Report 35, 18 p.

Gray, Carlyle, Shepps, V. C., Conlin, R. R., and others, compilers and eds. (1960), *Geologic map of Pennsylvania,* Pennsylvania Geological Survey, 4th ser., scale 1:250,000, 2 sheets.

Gray, Carlyle, and Socolow, A. A. (1959), *Field Trip 4—Mineral deposits of eastern Pennsylvania,* in *Guidebook for field trips—Pittsburgh Meeting, 1959,* Geological Society of America, p. 143–166.

———— (1961), *A metasedimentary specularite deposit in the Harpers Formation of Pennsylvania* [abs.], Economic Geology, v. 56, p. 1339.

Gray, L. R. (1965a), *Palynology of four Allegheny coals, northern Appalachian coal field,* Urbana, University of Illinois, Ph.D. thesis, 128 p.

———— (1965b), *Palynology of four Allegheny coals, northern Appalachian coal field,* Paleontographica, ser. B, v. 121, p. 65–86.

Gray, M. B. (1991), *Progressive deformation and structural evolution of the Southern Anthracite region, Pennsylvania,* Rochester, N. Y., University of Rochester, Ph.D. thesis, 277 p.

Gray, M. B., and Mitra, Gautam (1993), *Migration of deformation fronts during progressive deformation: evidence from detailed structural studies in the Pennsylvania Anthracite region, U.S.A.,* Journal of Structural Geology, v. 15, p. 435–449.

Gray, M. B., and Nickelsen, R. P. (1989), *Pedogenic slickensides, indicators of strain and deformation processes in redbed sequences of the Appalachian foreland,* Geology, v. 17, p. 72–75.

Gray, R. E. (1983), *Alternative measures in undermined areas,* Northeastern Environmental Science, v. 2, p. 79–89.

———— (1988), *Coal mine subsidence and structures,* in *Mine induced subsidence,* American Society of Civil Engineers Convention, Nashville, Tenn., Proceedings, p. 69–86.

Gray, R. E., and Bruhn, R. W. (1982), *Subsidence above abandoned coal mines,* Symposium on State-of-the-Art of Ground Control in Longwall Mining and Mining Subsidence, Hawaii, Society of Mining Engineers of the American Institute of Mining, Metallurgical, and Petroleum Engineers, Proceedings, 19 p.

———— (1984), *Coal mine subsidence—eastern United States,* in Holzer, T. L., ed., *Man-induced land subsidence,* Geological Society of America Reviews in Engineering Geology, v. 6, p. 123–149.

Gray, R. E., Ferguson, H. F., and Hamel, J. V. (1979), *Slope stability in the Appalachian Plateau, Pennsylvania and West Virginia, U.S.A.,* in Voight, Barry, ed., *Rockslides and avalanches, 2—Engineering sites,* Amsterdam, Elsevier, v. 2, p. 447–471.

Gray, R. E., Gamble, J. C., McLaren, R. J., and Rogers, D. J. (1974), *State of the art of subsidence control,* Appalachian Regional Commission Report ARC-73-111-2550, p. I-1—I-109, p. II-1—II-156.

Greenman, D. W., Rima, D. R., Lockwood, W. N., and Meisler, Harold (1961), *Ground-water resources of the Coastal Plain area of southeastern Pennsylvania,* Pennsylvania Geological Survey, 4th ser., Water Resource Report 13, 375 p.

Griffin, J. B. (1967), *Eastern North American archaeology,* Science, v. 156, p. 174–191.

Grim, R. E. (1962), *Applied clay mineralogy,* New York, McGraw-Hill, 422 p.

Groot, J. J. (1955), *Sedimentary petrology of the Cretaceous sediments of northern Delaware in relation to paleogeographic problems,* Delaware Geological Survey Bulletin 5, 157 p.

Groth, P. K. H. (1966), *Palynological delineation of environments in the Columbiana shale of western Pennsylvania,* University Park, Pennsylvania State University, M.S. thesis, 192 p.

Growitz, D. J., Reed, L. A., and Beard, M. M. (1985), *Reconnaissance of mine drainage in the coal fields of eastern Pennsylvania,* U.S. Geological Survey Water-Resources Investigations 83-4274, 54 p.

Guber, A. L. (1972), *Pyritic sulfur as a paleoecologic indicator in Carboniferous cycles,* in McLaren, D. J., and Middleton, G. V., conveners, *Section 6, Stratigraphy and sedimentology,* International Geological Congress, 24th, Montreal, Quebec, Canada, p. 389–396.

Guillou, R. D. (1961), *Camden-Delaware Valley area (ARMS-II),* U.S. Atomic Energy Commission Report CEX-61.6.3, 20 p.

———— (1964), *The aerial radiological measuring surveys (ARMS) program,* in Adams, J. A. S., and Lowder, W. M., eds., *The natural radiation environment,* Chicago, University of Chicago Press, p. 705–721.

Gundersen, L. C. S., Reimer, G. M., and Agard, S. S. (1988), *Correlation between geology, radon in soil gas, and indoor radon in the Reading Prong,* in Marikos, M. A., and Hansman, R. H., eds., *Geologic causes of natural radionuclide anomalies,* Missouri Department of Natural Resources Special Publication 4, p. 91–102.

Gunsallus, B. L., and Ritenour, V. E. (1953), *Clays,* U.S. Bureau of Mines Minerals Yearbook 1950, p. 245–262.

Gutschick, R. C., and Moreman, W. L. (1967), *Devonian-Mississippian boundary relations along the cratonic margin of the United States,* in Oswald, D. H., ed., *International Symposium on the Devonian System,* Calgary, Alberta, Canada, Alberta Society of Petroleum Geologists, v. 2, p. 1009–1023.

Gwinn, V. E. (1964), *Thin-skinned tectonics in the Plateau and northwestern Valley and Ridge provinces of the central Appalachians,* Geological Society of America Bulletin, v. 75, p. 863–900.

———— (1970), *Kinematic patterns and estimates of lateral shortening, Valley and Ridge and Great Valley provinces, central Appalachians, south-central Pennsylvania,* in Fisher, G. W., and others, eds., *Studies of Appalachian geology: central and southern,* New York, Interscience Publishers, p. 127–146.

Habib, D. (1965), *Distribution of spore and pollen assemblages in the Lower Kittanning coal of western Pennsylvania,* University Park, Pennsylvania State University, Ph.D. thesis, 310 p.

———— (1966), *Distribution of spore and pollen assemblages in the Lower Kittanning coal of western Pennsylvania,* Paleontology, v. 9, p. 629–666.

Hack, J. T. (1960), *Interpretation of erosional topography in humid temperate regions,* American Journal of Science, v. 258-A, p. 80–97.

———— (1965), *Geomorphology of the Shenandoah Valley, Virginia and West Virginia, and origin of the residual ore deposits,* U.S. Geological Survey Professional Paper 484, 84 p.

———— (1973), *Stream-profile analysis and stream-gradient index,* Journal of Research of the U.S. Geological Survey, v. 1, no. 4, p. 421–429.

———— (1975), *Dynamic equilibrium and landscape evolution,* in Melhorn, W. N., and Flemal, R. C., eds., *Theories of landform development,* Binghamton, N. Y., State University of New York, Annual Geomorphology Symposia Series, 6th, Proceedings, Publications in Geomorphology, p. 87–102.

———— (1980), *Rock control and tectonism—their importance in shaping the Appalachian Highlands,* in *Shorter contributions to stratigraphy and structural geology, 1979,* U.S. Geological Survey Professional Paper 1126-B, p. B1–B17.

———— (1982), *Physiographic divisions and differential uplift in the Piedmont and Blue Ridge,* U.S. Geological Survey Professional Paper 1265, 49 p.

Hall, C. E. (1883), *Itinerary survey of the mountains,* in Lesley, J. P., and others, *The geology of Lehigh and Northampton Counties,* Pennsylvania Geological Survey, 2nd ser., Report D3, v. 1, p. 215–259.

Hamel, J. V. (1972), *The slide at Brilliant cut,* in Cording, E. J., ed., *Stability of rock slopes,* Symposium on Rock Mechanics, 13th, Urbana, Ill., 1971, Proceedings, American Society of Civil Engineers, p. 487-510.

_____ (1980), *Geology and slope stability in western Pennsylvania,* Bulletin of the Association of Engineering Geologists, v. 17, p. 1-26.

Hamel, J. V., and Adams, W. R., Jr. (1981), *Claystone slides, Interstate Route 79, Pittsburgh, Pennsylvania, USA,* in Akai, Koichi, and others, eds., *Weak rock—Soft, fractured and weathered rock,* International Symposium on Weak Rock, Tokyo, 1981, Proceedings, Rotterdam, A. A. Balkema, v. 1, p. 549-553, v. 3, p. 1389-1390.

Hamel, J. V., and Ferguson, H. F. (1983), *Discussion on "An analysis of secondary toppling rock failures; the stress distribution method," by R. S. Evans* [Quarterly Journal of Engineering Geology, v. 14, p. 77-86], Quarterly Journal of Engineering Geology, v. 16, p. 244-245.

Hamel, J. V., and Flint, N. K. (1972), *Failure of colluvial slope,* Journal of Soil Mechanics and Foundations Division, American Society of Civil Engineers, v. 98, no. SM2, p. 167-180.

Haq, B. U., and Van Eysinga, F. W. B. (1987), *Geological time table,* 4th ed., Amsterdam, Elsevier.

Harper, J. A., compiler (1981), *Oil and gas developments in Pennsylvania in 1980 with ten year review and forecast,* Pennsylvania Geological Survey, 4th ser., Progress Report 194, 97 p.

_____ (1982), *"Oriskany" Sandstone oil potential, northwestern Pennsylvania,* Pennsylvania Geology, v. 13, no. 2, p. 2-7.

_____ (1987), *Oil and gas developments in Pennsylvania in 1986,* Pennsylvania Geological Survey, 4th ser., Progress Report 200, 93 p.

_____ (1990), *Leidy gas field, Clinton and Potter Counties, Pennsylvania,* in Beaumont, E. A., and Foster, N. H., compilers, *Structural traps I—Tectonic fold traps,* Tulsa, Okla., American Association of Petroleum Geologists, Treatise of Petroleum Geology, Atlas of Oil and Gas Fields, p. 157-190.

_____ (1993), *Giving the Mississippian/Devonian boundary a facelift,* Pennsylvania Geology, v. 24, no. 3, p. 9-14.

Harper, J. A., and Cozart, C. L. (1992), *Oil and gas developments in Pennsylvania in 1990 with ten-year review and forecast,* Pennsylvania Geological Survey, 4th ser., Progress Report 204, 85 p.

Harper, J. A., and Laughrey, C. D. (1982), *The "Eastern Overthrust Belt": an explanation of oil and gas activities in central and eastern Pennsylvania,* Pennsylvania Geology, v. 13, no. 5, p. 2-7.

_____ (1987), *Geology of the oil and gas fields of southwestern Pennsylvania,* Pennsylvania Geological Survey, 4th ser., Mineral Resource Report 87, 166 p.

Harper, J. A., Laughrey, C. D., and Lytle, W. S., compilers (1982), *Oil and gas fields of Pennsylvania,* Pennsylvania Geological Survey, 4th ser., Map 3, scale 1:250,000, 2 sheets.

Harper, J. A., and Piotrowski, R. G. (1979), *Stratigraphic correlation of surface and subsurface Middle and Upper Devonian, southwestern Pennsylvania,* in Dennison, J. M., and others, *Devonian shales in south-central Pennsylvania and Maryland,* Annual Field Conference of Pennsylvania Geologists, 44th, Bedford, Pa., Guidebook, p. 18-37.

Harper, R. M. (1985), *Bass Islands production in northwestern Pennsylvania,* Pennsylvania Geology, v. 16, no. 1, p. 7-13.

Harper, R. M., and Laughrey, C. D. (1986), *Geology and reservoir characteristics of the Bald Eagle Formation in the Texaco-Marathon #1 Pennsylvania State Forest Tract 285 well, Clinton County, Pennsylvania* [abs.], in *The Seventeenth Annual Appalachian Petroleum Geology Symposium—"Appalachian basin architecture,"* West Virginia Geological and Economic Survey Circular C-38, p. 27-29.

Harris, A. G., Harris, L. D., and Epstein, J. B. (1978), *Oil and gas data from Paleozoic rocks in the Appalachian basin: maps for assessing hydrocarbon potential and thermal maturity (conodont color alteration isograds and overburden isopachs),* U.S. Geological Survey Miscellaneous Investigations Series Map I-917-E, scale 1:2,500,000, 4 sheets.

Harris, L. D. (1970), *Details of thin-skinned tectonics in parts of Valley and Ridge and Cumberland Plateau provinces of the southern Appalachians,* in Fisher, G. W., and others, eds., *Studies of Appalachian geology: central and southern,* New York, Interscience Publishers, p. 161-173.

_____ (1979), *Similarities between the thick-skinned Blue Ridge anticlinorium and the thin-skinned Powell Valley anticline,* Geological Society of America Bulletin, v. 90, p. 1525-1539.

Harris, L. D., de Witt, Wallace, Jr., and Bayer, K. C. (1982), *Interpretive seismic profile along Interstate I-64 from the Valley and Ridge to the Coastal Plain in central Virginia,* U.S. Geological Survey Oil and Gas Investigations Chart OC-123.

Harrison, W., Malloy, R. J., Rusnak, G. A., and Terasmae, J. (1965), *Possible late Pleistocene uplift, Chesapeake Bay entrance,* Journal of Geology, v. 73, p. 201-229.

Harshman, E. N. (1972), *Geology and uranium deposits, Shirley basin area, Wyoming,* U.S. Geological Survey Professional Paper 745, 82 p.

Hartford, W. H. (1980), *Chromium deposits of Maryland and eastern Pennsylvania,* Rocks and Minerals, v. 55, no. 2, p. 52-59.

Hatcher, P. G., and Romankiw, L. A. (1985), *Nuclear magnetic resonance studies of organic-matter-rich sedimentary rocks of some early Mesozoic basins of the Eastern United States,* in Robinson, G. R., Jr., and Froelich, A. J., eds., *Proceedings of the Second U.S. Geological Survey Workshop on the Early Mesozoic Basins of the Eastern United States,* U.S. Geological Survey Circular 946, p. 65-70.

Hawkes, H. E., Wedow, Helmuth, and Balsley, J. R. (1953), *Geologic investigation of the Boyertown magnetite deposits in Pennsylvania,* U.S. Geological Survey Bulletin 995-D, p. 135-149.

Hawman, R. B. (1980), *Crustal models for the Scranton and Kentucky gravity highs: regional bending of the crust in response to emplacement of failed rift structures,* University Park, Pennsylvania State University, M.S. thesis, 107 p.

Hayes, C. W., chief compiler (1911), *Pennsylvania,* in *The State Geological Surveys of the United States,* U.S. Geological Survey Bulletin 465, p. 122-130.

Head, J. W. (1972), *Upper Silurian-Lower Devonian stratigraphy and nomenclature in the central Appalachians,* in Dennison, J. M., ed., *Stratigraphy, sedimentology, and structure of Silurian and Devonian rocks along the Allegheny Front in Bedford County, Pennsylvania, Allegany County, Maryland, and Mineral and Grant Counties, West Virginia,* Annual Field Conference of Pennsylvania Geologists, 37th, Bedford, Pa., Guidebook, p. 96-103.

Head, J. W., III (1969), *An integrated model of carbonate depositional basin evolution: Late Cayugan (Upper Silurian) and Helderbergian (Lower Devonian) of the central Appalachians,* Providence, R. I., Brown University, Ph.D. thesis, 390 p.

_____ (1974), *Correlation and paleogeography of upper part of Helderberg Group (Lower Devonian) of central Appalachians,* AAPG Bulletin, v. 58, p. 247-259.

Hearn, P. P., Jr., Sutter, J. F., and Belkin, H. E. (1987), *Evidence for late-Paleozoic brine migration in Cambrian carbonate rocks of the central and southern Appalachians: implications for Mississippi Valley-type sulfide mineralization,* Geochimica et Cosmochimica Acta, v. 51, p. 1323-1334.

Heckel, P. H. (1973), *Nature, origin, and significance of the Tully Limestone,* Geological Society of America Special Paper 138, 244 p.

_____ (1986), *Sea-level curve for Pennsylvanian eustatic marine transgressive-regressive depositional cycles along midcontinent outcrop belt, North America,* Geology, v. 14, p. 330-334.

Heller, P. L., and Dickinson, W. R. (1985), *Submarine ramp facies model for delta-fed, sand-rich turbidite systems,* AAPG Bulletin, v. 69, p. 960-976.

Henderson, G. J., and Timm, C. M. (1985), *Ordovician stratigraphic hydrocarbon entrapment potential of Appalachia,* Oil and Gas Journal, v. 83, no. 17, p. 118-125.

Henderson, J. R., Johnson, R. W., and Gilbert, F. P. (1963), *Aeromagnetic map of the Wilmington, Delaware area and adjacent parts of Pennsylvania and Maryland,* U.S. Geological Survey Geophysical Investigations Map GP-363, scale 1:62,500.

Henfrey, Benjamin (1797), *A plan with proposals for forming a company to work mines in the United States; and to smelt and refine the ores, whether of copper, lead, tin, silver, or gold,* Philadelphia, Snowden and McCorkle, 34 p.

Herman, G. C., and Geiser, P. A. (1985), *A "passive roof duplex" solution for the Juniata culmination; central Pennsylvania* [abs.], Geological Society of America Abstracts with Programs, v. 17, no. 1, p. 24.

Hersey, J. B. (1944), *Gravity investigation of central-eastern Pennsylvania,* Geological Society of America Bulletin, v. 55, p. 417–444.

Hewett, D. F. (1916), *Some manganese mines in Virginia and Maryland,* U.S. Geological Survey Bulletin 640–C, p. 37–71.

Heyman, Louis (1969), *Geology of the Elk Run gas pool, Jefferson County, Pennsylvania,* Pennsylvania Geological Survey, 4th ser., Mineral Resource Report 59, 18 p.

――――― (1970), *History of Pittsburgh's rivers,* in Wagner, W. R., and others, *Geology of the Pittsburgh area,* Pennsylvania Geological Survey, 4th ser., General Geology Report 59, p. 84–92.

――――― (1977), *Tully (Middle Devonian) to Queenston (Upper Ordovician) correlations in the subsurface of western Pennsylvania,* Pennsylvania Geological Survey, 4th ser., Mineral Resource Report 73, 16 p.

Hice, R. R. (1911), *Clay and clay products,* Pennsylvania Geological Survey, 3rd ser., Report 8C, 51 p.

Hickok, W. O., IV, and Moyer, F. T. (1940), *Geology and mineral resources of Fayette County, Pennsylvania,* Pennsylvania Geological Survey, 4th ser., County Report 26, 530 p.

Higbee, H. W. (1967), *Land resource map of Pennsylvania,* Agricultural Extension Service, Pennsylvania State University, scale 1:380,160.

Higgins, M. W. (1972), *Age, origin, regional relations, and nomenclature of the Glenarm Series, central Appalachian Piedmont: a reinterpretation,* Geological Society of America Bulletin, v. 83, p. 989–1026.

Higgins, M. W., Fisher, G. W., and Zietz, Isidore (1973), *Aeromagnetic discovery of a Baltimore Gneiss dome in the Piedmont of northwestern Delaware and southeastern Pennsylvania,* Geology, v. 1, p. 41–43.

High Life Helicopters and QEB (1982), *Airborne gamma-ray spectrometer and magnetometer survey, Cleveland quadrangle (Pa., Ohio), Erie quadrangle (Pa.), Warren quadrangle (Pa.), Pittsburgh quadrangle (Pa.)—Final report,* U.S. Department of Energy, GJBX–42(82), variously paged.

Hileman, Bette (1983), *Indoor air pollution,* Environmental Science and Technology, v. 17, p. 469A–472A.

Hill, C. A., and Forti, Paolo (1986), *Cave minerals of the world,* Huntsville, Ala., National Speleological Society, 238 p.

Hill, M. L. (1989), *Structure of the Martic zone, southeastern Pennsylvania* [abs.], Geological Society of America Abstracts with Programs, v. 21, no. 2, p. 22.

Hoagland, A. D. (1971), *Appalachian strata-bound deposits: their essential features, genesis and the exploration problem,* Economic Geology, v. 66, p. 805–810.

Hobbs, W. H. (1904), *Lineaments of the Atlantic border region,* Geological Society of America Bulletin, v. 15, p. 483–506.

Hoersch, A. L., and Crawford, W. A. (1988), *The Mine Ridge of the SE Pennsylvania Piedmont,* Northeastern Geology, v. 10, p. 181–194.

Holland, F. D., Jr. (1958), *The Brachiopoda of the Oswayo and Knapp Formations of the Penn-York embayment,* University of Cincinnati, Ph.D. thesis, 524 p.

Holzer, T. L., ed. (1984), *Man-induced land subsidence,* Geological Society of America Reviews in Engineering Geology, v. 6, 221 p.

Honess, A. P., and Graeber, C. K. (1924), *A new occurrence of an igneous dike in southwestern Pennsylvania,* American Journal of Science, 5th ser., v. 7, p. 313–315.

――――― (1926), *Petrography of the mica peridotite dike at Dixonville, Pennsylvania,* American Journal of Science, 5th ser., v. 12, p. 484–494.

Hoover, K. V., Saylor, T. E., Lapham, D. M., and Tyrell, M. E. (1971), *Properties and uses of Pennsylvania shales and clays, southeastern Pennsylvania,* Pennsylvania Geological Survey, 4th ser., Mineral Resource Report 63, 329 p.

Hoover, M. T. (1983), *Soil development in colluvium in footslope positions in the Ridge and Valley physiographic province of Pennsylvania,* University Park, Pennsylvania State University, Ph.D. thesis, 286 p.

Hoover, M. T., and Ciolkosz, E. J. (1988), *Colluvial soil parent material relationships in the Ridge and Valley physiographic province of Pennsylvania,* Soil Science, v. 145, p. 163–172.

Hopkins, D. A. (1985), *Refractory dolomite production in southeastern Pennsylvania—The J. E. Baker Co.,* Pennsylvania Geology, v. 16, no. 3, p. 2–4.

Hopkins, T. C. [1898], *Clays and clay industries of Pennsylvania—I, Clays of western Pennsylvania (in part),* Appendix to *Annual Report of Pennsylvania State College for 1897,* Official Document 21, 184 p.

――――― (1899), *Conshohocken plastic clays,* Geological Society of America Bulletin, v. 10, p. 480–484.

――――― [1900], *Clays and clay industries of Pennsylvania—II, Clays of southeastern Pennsylvania (in part),* Appendix to *Annual Report of Pennsylvania State College for 1898–99,* Official Document 22, 76 p.

Hopson, C. A. (1964), *The crystalline rocks of Howard and Montgomery Counties,* in *The geology of Howard and Montgomery Counties,* Maryland Geological Survey, p. 27–215.

Hoque, M. U. (1968), *Sedimentologic and paleocurrent study of Mauch Chunk sandstones (Mississippian), south-central and western Pennsylvania,* AAPG Bulletin, v. 52, p. 246–263.

――――― (1975), *Paleocurrent and paleoslope—a case study,* Palaeogeography, Palaeoclimatology, Palaeoecology, v. 17, p. 77–85.

Horne, J. C., Ferm, J. C., Carruccio, F. T., and Baganz, B. P. (1978), *Depositional models in coal exploration and mine planning in Appalachian region,* AAPG Bulletin, v. 62, p. 2379–2411.

Horowitz, D. H. (1966), *Evidence for deltaic origin of an Upper Ordovician sequence in the central Appalachians,* in Shirley, M. L., and Ragsdale, J. A., eds., *Deltas in their geologic framework,* Houston Geological Society, p. 159–169.

Hoskins, D. M. (1961), *Stratigraphy and paleontology of the Bloomsburg Formation of Pennsylvania and adjacent states,* Pennsylvania Geological Survey, 4th ser., General Geology Report 36, 125 p.

――――― (1981), *George Hall Ashley—First State Geologist of the Fourth Geological Survey of Pennsylvania,* Northeastern Geology, v. 3, p. 94–99.

――――― (1986), *William Darby's 1824 Geologic Map of Pennsylvania—unseen for 162 years* [abs.], Geological Society of America Abstracts with Programs, v. 18, no. 6, p. 640–641.

――――― (1987a), *The First Geological Survey of Pennsylvania: the discovery years,* Pennsylvania Geology, v. 18, no. 1, p. 1–8.

――――― (1987b), *The Susquehanna River water gaps near Harrisburg, Pennsylvania,* in Roy, D. C., ed., *Northeastern Section of the Geological Society of America,* Geological Society of America Centennial Field Guide, v. 5, p. 47–50.

Hoskins, D. M., Inners, J. D., and Harper, J. A. (1983), *Fossil collecting in Pennsylvania,* 3rd ed., Pennsylvania Geological Survey, 4th ser., General Geology Report 40, 215 p.

Hosterman, J. W. (1969), *White-clay deposits near Mount Holly Springs, Cumberland County, Pennsylvania,* in *Geological Survey research 1969, Chapter B,* U.S. Geological Survey Professional Paper 650–B, p. B66–B72.

――――― (1972), *White clay deposits of Centre, Blair, Huntingdon, and Bedford Counties, Pennsylvania,* in *Geological Survey research 1972, Chapter B,* U.S. Geological Survey Professional Paper 800–B, p. B57–B65.

――――― (1984), *White clays of Pennsylvania,* U.S. Geological Survey Bulletin 1558–D, 38 p.

Hosterman, J. W., Wood, G. H., Jr., and Bergin, M. J. (1970), *Mineralogy of underclays in the Pennsylvania Anthracite region,* in

Geological Survey research 1970, Chapter C, U.S. Geological Survey Professional Paper 700-C, p. C89–C97.

Hotz, P. E. (1950), Diamond-drill exploration of the Dillsburg magnetite deposits, York County, Pennsylvania, U.S. Geological Survey Bulletin 969–A, 27 p.

———— (1952), Form of diabase sheets in southeastern Pennsylvania, American Journal of Science, v. 250, p. 375–388.

Hovey, E. O. (1904), Phosphate rock, in Mineral resources of the United States, calendar year 1903, U.S. Geological Survey, p. 1047–1058.

Howell, B. F., Jr. (1979), Earthquake expectancy in Pennsylvania, Pennsylvania Academy of Science Proceedings, v. 53, p. 205–208.

Howell, B. F., Jr., and Vozoff, Keeva (1953), Gravity investigation in north-central Pennsylvania, American Geophysical Union Transactions, v. 34, p. 357–359.

Hower, J. C., and Davis, Alan (1981), Application of vitrinite reflectance anisotropy in the evaluation of coal metamorphism, Geological Society of America Bulletin, v. 92, p. 350–366.

Hoyt, J. C., and Anderson, R. H. (1905), Hydrography of the Susquehanna River drainage basin, U.S. Geological Survey Water-Supply Paper 109, 215 p.

Hubert, J. F., Reed, A. A., Dowdall, W. L., and Gilchrist, J. M. (1978), Guide to the redbeds of central Connecticut: 1978 field trip, Eastern Section of the Society of Economic Paleontologists and Mineralogists, Amherst, University of Massachusetts, Department of Geology and Geography, Contribution 21, 129 p.

Hunt, J. M. (1979), Petroleum geochemistry and geology, San Francisco, W. H. Freeman, 615 p.

Hunter, P. M. (1977), The environmental geology of the Pine Grove Mills-Stormstown area, central Pa., with emphasis on the bedrock geology and ground water resources, University Park, Pennsylvania State University, M.S. thesis, 319 p.

Hunter, R. H., Kissling, R. D., and Taylor, L. A. (1984), Mid- to late-stage kimberlitic melt evolution: phlogopites and oxides from the Fayette County kimberlite, Pennsylvania, American Mineralogist, v. 69, p. 30–40.

Hunter, R. H., and Taylor, L. A. (1984), Magma-mixing in the low velocity zone: kimberlitic megacrysts from Fayette County, Pennsylvania, American Mineralogist, v. 69, p. 16–29.

Hurtig, Eckart, and Brugger, Hartmut (1970), Waermeleitfaehigkeitsmessungen unter einaxialem druck [Heat conductivity measurements under uniaxial pressure], Tectonophysics, v. 10, p. 67–77.

Husch, J. M. (1988), Significance of major- and trace-element variation trends in Mesozoic diabase, west-central New Jersey and eastern Pennsylvania, in Froelich, A. J., and Robinson, G. R., Jr., eds., Studies of the early Mesozoic basins of the Eastern United States, U.S. Geological Survey Bulletin 1776, p. 141–150.

Hutchins, Thomas (1786), Description of a remarkable rock and cascade, near the western side of the Youghiogeny River, a quarter of a mile from Crawford's ferry, and about twelve miles from Uniontown in Fayette County, in the state of Pennsylvania, American Philosophical Society Transactions, old ser., v. 2, p. 50–51.

Iannacchione, A. T., and Puglio, D. G. (1979), Geology of the Lower Kittanning coalbed and related mining and methane emission problems in Cambria County, Pa., U.S. Bureau of Mines Report of Investigations 8354, 31 p.

Ihlseng, M. C. (1896), A phosphate prospect in Pennsylvania, in Seventeenth annual report of the United States Geological Survey—Part III, Mineral resources of the United States, 1895, metallic products and coal, U.S. Geological Survey Annual Report 17, pt. 3, p. 955–957.

Inners, J. D. (1978), Geology and mineral resources of the Berwick quadrangle, Luzerne and Columbia Counties, Pennsylvania, Pennsylvania Geological Survey, 4th ser., Atlas 174c, 34 p.

———— (1979), The Onesquethaw Stage in south-central Pennsylvania and nearby areas, in Dennison, J. M., and others, Devonian shales in south-central Pennsylvania and Maryland, Annual Field Conference of Pennsylvania Geologists, 44th, Bedford, Pa., Guidebook, p. 38–55.

———— (1981), Geology and mineral resources of the Bloomsburg and Mifflinville quadrangles and part of the Catawissa quadrangle, Columbia County, Pennsylvania, Pennsylvania Geological Survey, 4th ser., Atlas 164cd, 152 p.

———— (1984), A Niagaran (mid-Silurian) patch reef near Allenwood, Union County, Pennsylvania Geology, v. 15, no. 5, p. 12–16.

———— (1988), The Eastern Middle Anthracite field, in Inners, J. D., ed., Bedrock and glacial geology of the North Branch Susquehanna lowland and the Eastern Middle Anthracite field, northeastern Pennsylvania, Annual Field Conference of Pennsylvania Geologists, 53rd, Hazleton, Pa., Guidebook, p. 32–39.

Inners, J. D., and Williams, J. H. (1983), Clinton iron-ore mines of the Danville-Bloomsburg area, Pennsylvania: their geology, history, and present-day environmental effects, in Nickelsen, R. P., and Cotter, Edward, Silurian depositional history and Alleghanian deformation in the Pennsylvania Valley and Ridge, Annual Field Conference of Pennsylvania Geologists, 48th, Danville, Pa., Guidebook, p. 53–63.

Inners, J. D., Williams, J. H., and Sternagle, A. M. (1984), Environmental effects of abandoned Clinton iron-ore mines in central Pennsylvania [abs.], in Sherman, R. G., chairperson, Abstracts and program, Association of Engineering Geologists, 27th Annual Meeting, Boston, Mass., 1984, p. 60–61.

Jachens, R. C., Simpson, R. W., Blakely, R. J., and Saltus, R. W. (1985), Isostatic residual gravity map of the United States, National Geophysical Data Center, National Oceanic and Atmospheric Administration.

Jacobeen, F., Jr., and Kanes, W. H. (1975), Structure of Broadtop synclinorium, Wills Mountain anticlinorium, and Allegheny frontal zone, AAPG Bulletin, v. 59, p. 1136–1150.

Jacobson, R. B., Elston, D. P., and Heaton, J. W. (1988), Stratigraphy and magnetic polarity of the high terrace remnants in the upper Ohio and Monongahela Rivers in West Virginia, Pennsylvania, and Ohio, Quaternary Research, v. 29, p. 216–232.

James, N. P. (1979), Shallowing-upward sequences in carbonates, in Walker, R. G., ed., Facies models, Geological Association of Canada, Geoscience Canada, Reprint Series 1, p. 109–119.

Jenkins, K. (1977), The great flood of 1977, a story of catastrophy in the Conemaugh Valley, Altoona, Pa., Mirror Printing Co., 63 p.

Jennings, A. H. (1950), World's greatest observed rainfalls, Monthly Weather Review, U.S. Department of Commerce, Weather Bureau, v. 78, p. 4–5.

Jennings, J. N. (1985), Karst geomorphology, 2nd ed., New York, Basil Blackwell, 293 p.

Jenny, H. (1980), The soil resource: origin and behavior, New York, Springer-Verlag, 368 p.

Jenson, Homer (1951), Aeromagnetic survey helps find new Pennsylvania iron orebody, Engineering and Mining Journal, v. 152, p. 57–59.

Jessop, A. M. (1990), Thermal geophysics, Amsterdam, Elsevier, 306 p.

Joesting, H. R., Keller, Fred, Jr., and King, Elizabeth (1949), Geologic implications of aeromagnetic survey of Clearfield-Philipsburg area, Pennsylvania, AAPG Bulletin, v. 33, p. 1747–1766.

Johnson, D. W. (1931), Stream sculpture on the Atlantic slope, New York, Columbia University Press, 142 p.

Johnson, J. G., Klapper, Gilbert, and Sandberg, C. A. (1985), Devonian eustatic fluctuations in Euramerica, Geological Society of America Bulletin, v. 96, p. 567–587.

Johnson, M. J. (1984), The thermal and burial history of south central New York: evidence from vitrinite reflectance, clay mineral diagenesis, and fission track dating of apatite and zircon, Hanover, N. H., Dartmouth College, Ph.D. thesis, 154 p.

Johnson, S. S. (1984), Depositional environment and reservoir characteristics of Upper Devonian Kane sandstone in central western Pennsylvania [abs.], AAPG Bulletin, v. 68, p. 1921.

Johnson, Wilton, and Miller, G. C. (1979), Abandoned coal-mined lands; nature, extent, and cost of reclamation, U.S. Bureau of Mines Special Publication 6–79, 29 p.

Johnston, H. E. (1970), *Ground-water resources of the Loysville and Mifflintown quadrangles in south-central Pennsylvania,* Pennsylvania Geological Survey, 4th ser., Water Resource Report 27, 96 p.

Jonas, A. I., and Stose, G. W. (1930), *Lancaster quadrangle—Geology and mineral resources,* Pennsylvania Geological Survey, 4th ser., Atlas 168, 106 p.

Jones, T. H., and Cate, A. S. (1957), *Preliminary report on a regional stratigraphic study of Devonian rocks of Pennsylvania,* Pennsylvania Geological Survey, 4th ser., Special Bulletin 8, 5 p.

Jordan, R. R., and Smith, R. V., compilers (1983), *Atlantic Coastal Plain region correlation chart,* in *Correlation chart series; correlation of stratigraphic units in North America,* American Association of Petroleum Geologists, 1 sheet.

Jordan, W. M., and Pierce, N. A. (1981), *J. Peter Lesley and the Second Geological Survey of Pennsylvania,* Northeastern Geology, v. 3, p. 75–85.

Joyner, W. B. (1960), *Heat flow in Pennsylvania and West Virginia,* Geophysics, v. 25, p. 1229–1241.

Judson, Sheldon (1975), *Evolution of Appalachian topography,* in Melhorn, W. N., and Flemel, R. C., eds., *Theories of landform development,* Binghamton, N. Y., State University of New York, Annual Geomorphology Symposia Series, 6th, Proceedings, Publications in Geomorphology, p. 29–44.

Kaiser, W. R. (1972), *Delta cycles in the Middle Devonian of central Pennsylvania,* Baltimore, Md., Johns Hopkins University, Ph.D. thesis, 183 p.

Kaktins, T. L. (1986), *Fluvial terraces of the Juniata River valley in central Pennsylvania,* University Park, Pennsylvania State University, M.S. thesis, 283 p.

Kaktins, Uldis (1986), *Conemaugh Gorge near Johnstown, PA* [abs.], Geological Society of America Abstracts with Programs, v. 18, no. 1, p. 25.

Kalm, Peter (1771), *Travels into North America* [translated by J. R. Forster], London, Warrington, 3 v.

Kane, M. F. (1983), *Gravity evidence of crustal structure in the United States Appalachians,* in Schenk, P. E., and others, eds., *Regional trends in the geology of the Appalachian-Caledonian-Hercynian-Mauritanide orogen,* Boston, D. Reidel, p. 45–54.

Kappelmeyer, O., and Haenel, R. (1974), *Geothermics—with special reference to application,* Geoexploration Monograph Series 1, no. 4, 238 p.

Kauffman, M. E., and Campbell, Lyle (1969), *Revised interpretation of the Cambrian Kinzers Formation in southeastern Pennsylvania* [abs.], Geological Society of America Abstracts with Programs, v. 1, no. 1, p. 32–33.

Kauffman, M. E., and Frey, E. P. (1979), *Antietam sandstone ridges—exhumed barrier islands or fault-bounded blocks?* [abs.], Geological Society of America Abstracts with Programs, v. 11, no. 1, p. 18.

Kay, Marshall (1951), *North American geosynclines,* Geological Society of America Memoir 48, 143 p.

Kebblish, William (1979), *The mineral industry of Pennsylvania,* in *Area reports: domestic,* U.S. Bureau of Mines Minerals Yearbook 1976, v. 2, p. 627–658.

———— (1981a), *The mineral industry of Pennsylvania,* in *Area reports: domestic,* U.S. Bureau of Mines Minerals Yearbook 1977, v. 2, p. 501–517.

———— (1981b), *The mineral industry of Pennsylvania,* in *Area reports: domestic,* U.S. Bureau of Mines Minerals Yearbook 1978–79, v. 2, p. 449–460.

———— (1984a), *The mineral industry of Pennsylvania,* in *Area reports: domestic,* U.S. Bureau of Mines Minerals Yearbook 1982, v. 2, p. 453–468.

———— (1984b), *The mineral industry of Pennsylvania,* preprint from U.S. Bureau of Mines Minerals Yearbook 1982, 16 p.

Kebblish, William, and Tuchman, R. J. (1982), *The mineral industry of Pennsylvania,* in *Area reports: domestic,* U.S. Bureau of Mines Minerals Yearbook 1980, v. 2, p. 447–459.

———— (1983), *The mineral industry of Pennsylvania,* in *Area reports: domestic,* U.S. Bureau of Mines Minerals Yearbook 1981, v. 2, p. 413–428.

Keller, Gerta, and Barron, J. A. (1983), *Paleoceanographic implications of Miocene deep-sea hiatuses,* Geological Society of America Bulletin, v. 94, p. 590–613.

Kelley, D. R. (1966), *The Kastle Medina gas field, Crawford County,* in Lytle, W. S., and others, *Oil and gas developments in Pennsylvania in 1965,* Pennsylvania Geological Survey, 4th ser., Progress Report 172, p. 30–44.

Kelley, D. R., Lytle, W. S., Wagner, W. R., and Heyman, Louis (1970), *The petroleum industry and the future petroleum province in Pennsylvania, 1970,* Pennsylvania Geological Survey, 4th ser., Mineral Resource Report 65, 39 p.

Kelley, D. R., and McGlade, W. G. (1969), *Medina and Oriskany production along the shore of Lake Erie, Pierce field, Erie County, Pennsylvania,* Pennsylvania Geological Survey, 4th ser., Mineral Resource Report 60, 38 p.

Kemp, J. F. (1895a), *The nickel mine at Lancaster Gap, Pennsylvania, and the pyrrhotite deposits at Anthony's Nose, on the Hudson,* American Institute of Mining Engineers Transactions, v. 24, p. 620–633.

———— (1895b), *The ore deposits of the United States,* revised ed., New York, Scientific Publishing Company, 343 p.

Kemp, J. F., and Ross, J. G. (1907), *A peridotite dike in the coal measures of southwestern Pennsylvania,* New York Academy of Science Annals, v. 17, p. 509–518.

Kent, B. H. (1969), *Geologic map of part of the Carmichaels quadrangle, southwestern Pennsylvania,* U.S. Geological Survey Miscellaneous Investigations Series Map I-588, scale 1:24,000.

———— (1972), *Geologic map of the Prosperity quadrangle, southwestern Pennsylvania,* U.S. Geological Survey Geologic Quadrangle Map GQ-1003, scale 1:24,000.

———— (1974), *Geologic causes and possible preventions of roof fall in room-and-pillar coal mines,* Pennsylvania Geological Survey, 4th ser., Information Circular 75, 17 p.

Keppie, J. D. (1977), *Plate tectonic interpretation of Paleozoic world maps,* Nova Scotia Department of Mines Paper 77-3, 45 p.

Killeen, P. G. (1979), *Gamma-ray spectrometric methods in uranium exploration—application and interpretation,* in Hood, P. J., ed., *Geophysics and geochemistry in the search for metallic ores,* Geological Survey of Canada Economic Geology Report 31, p. 163–229.

Kim, A. G. (1975), *Methane in the Pittsburgh coalbed, Greene County, Pa.,* U.S. Bureau of Mines Report of Investigations 8026, 10 p.

———— (1977), *Estimating methane content of bituminous coalbeds from adsorption data,* U.S. Bureau of Mines Report of Investigations 8245, 22 p.

Kimmel, S. L., and Fulton, P. F. (1983), *Results of pressure transient well testing in Appalachian gas reservoirs,* Society of Petroleum Engineers, SPE 12303, p. 59–65.

King, E. R., and Zietz, Isidore (1978), *The New York-Alabama lineament: geophysical evidence for a major crustal break in the basement beneath the Appalachian basin,* Geology, v. 6, p. 312–318.

King, P. B. (1971), *Systematic pattern of Triassic dikes in the Appalachian region—second report,* in *Geological Survey research 1971, Chapter D,* U.S. Geological Survey Professional Paper 750-D, p. D84–D88.

Klemic, Harry (1962), *Uranium occurrences in sedimentary rocks of Pennsylvania,* U.S. Geological Survey Bulletin 1107-D, 46 p.

Klemic, Harry, Warman, J. C., and Taylor, A. R. (1963), *Geology and uranium occurrences of the northern half of the Lehighton Pennsylvania, quadrangle and adjoining areas,* U.S. Geological Survey Bulletin 1138, 97 p.

Klitgord, K. D., and Hutchinson, D. R. (1985), *Distribution and geophysical signatures of early Mesozoic rift basins beneath the U.S. Atlantic continental margin,* in Robinson, G. R., Jr., and Froelich, A. J., eds., *Proceedings of the Second U.S. Geological Survey Workshop on the Early Mesozoic Basins of the Eastern United States,* U.S. Geological Survey Circular 946, p. 45–61.

Knight, F. J. (1971), *Geologic problems of urban growth in limestone terrains of Pennsylvania,* Bulletin of the Association of Engineering Geologists, v. 8, p. 91–101.

Knight, J. B. (1941), *Paleozoic gastropod genotypes,* Geological Society of America Special Paper 32, 510 p.

Knight, W. V. (1969), *Historical and economic geology of Lower Silurian Clinton sandstone of northeastern Ohio,* AAPG Bulletin, v. 53, p. 1421–1452.

Knopf, E. B. (1931), *Retrogressive metamorphism and phyllonitization,* American Journal of Science, 5th ser., v. 21, p. 1–27.

Knopf, E. B., and Jonas, A. I. (1929), *Geology of the McCalls Ferry-Quarryville district, Pennsylvania,* U.S. Geological Survey Bulletin 799, 156 p.

Kochanov, W. E. (1988), *Sinkholes and karst-related features of Lebanon County, Pennsylvania,* Pennsylvania Geological Survey, 4th ser., Open-File Report 88–02, scale 1:24,000, 5 maps plus 8-page text.

_____ (1989), *Karst mapping and applications to regional land management practices in the Commonwealth of Pennsylvania,* in Beck, B. F., ed., *Engineering and environmental impacts of sinkholes and karst,* Multidisciplinary Conference on Sinkholes and the Engineering and Environmental Impacts of Karst, 3rd, St. Petersburg Beach, Fla., 1989, Proceedings, Rotterdam, A. A. Balkema, p. 363–368.

_____ (1993), *Areal analysis of karst data from the Great Valley of Pennsylvania,* in Beck, B. F., ed., *Applied karst geology,* Multidisciplinary Conference on Sinkholes and the Engineering and Environmental Impacts of Karst, 4th, Panama City, Fla., 1993, Proceedings, Rotterdam, A. A. Balkema, p. 37–41.

_____ (1995), *Storm-water management and sinkhole occurrence in the Palmyra area, Lebanon County, Pennsylvania,* in Beck, B. F., ed., *Karst geohazards: engineering and environmental problems in karst terrane,* Multidisciplinary Conference on Sinkholes and the Engineering and Environmental Impacts of Karst, 5th, Gatlinburg, Tenn., 1995, Proceedings, Rotterdam, A. A. Balkema, p. 285–290.

Köppen, W. P., and Wegener, A. L. (1925), *Die Klimate der geoligischen Vorzeit,* Berlin, Gebrüder Borntraeger, 255 p.

Kowalik, W. S., and Gold, D. P. (1976), *The use of Landsat-1 imagery in mapping lineaments in Pennsylvania,* in Hodgson, R. A., and others, eds., *Proceedings of the First International Conference on the New Basement Tectonics [Salt Lake City, Utah, 1974],* Salt Lake City, Utah Geological Association, Publication 5, p. 236–249.

Krajewski, S. A., and Williams, E. G. (1971), *Upper Devonian flagstones from northeastern Pennsylvania,* Pennsylvania State University, College of Earth and Mineral Sciences, Special Publication 3–71, 185 p.

Kulander, B. R., and Dean, S. L. (1986), *Structure and tectonics of central and southern Appalachian Valley and Ridge and Plateau provinces, West Virginia and Virginia,* AAPG Bulletin, v. 70, p. 1674–1684.

_____ (1988), *The North Mountain-Pulaski fault system and related thrust sheet structure,* in Mitra, Gautam, and Wojtal, Steven, eds., *Geometries and mechanisms of thrusting, with special reference to the Appalachians,* Geological Society of America Special Paper 222, p. 107–118.

Kunk, M. J., Simonson, B. M., and Smoot, J. P. (1995), $^{40}Ar/^{39}Ar$ constraints on the age of K-feldspar cementation in non-marine sediments of the Newark, Gettysburg, and Culpeper basins [abs.], Geological Society of America Abstracts with Programs, v. 27, no. 1, p. 62.

Lacey, J. E. (1960), *Cyclic sedimentation in the Silurian Wills Creek and Tonoloway Formations at Mt. Union, Pennsylvania,* University of Pittsburgh, M.S. thesis, 63 p.

Laird, W. M. (1941), *The Upper Devonian and Lower Mississippian of southwestern Pennsylvania,* Pennsylvania Geological Survey, 4th ser., Progress Report 126, 23 p.

Land and Water Resources Center, University of Maine at Orono, and Division of Health Engineering, Maine Department of Human Services (1983), *Radon in water and air—Health risks and control measures,* Land and Water Resources Center, University of Maine at Orono, and Division of Health Engineering, Maine Department of Human Services, 12 p.

Landsberg, Helmut (1938), *The Clover Creek earthquake of July 15, 1938,* Bulletin of the Seismological Society of America, v. 28, p. 237–241.

Lane, E. C., and Garton, E. L. (1938), *Analyses of crude oils from some fields of Pennsylvania and New York,* U.S. Bureau of Mines Report of Investigations 3385, 68 p.

Lanning, R. M. (1972), *An olivine tholeiite dike swarm in Lancaster County, Pennsylvania,* University Park, Pennsylvania State University, M.S. thesis, 80 p.

Lapham, D. M. (1975), *Interpretation of K-Ar and Rb-Sr isotopic dates from a Precambrian basement core, Erie County, Pennsylvania,* Pennsylvania Geological Survey, 4th ser., Information Circular 79, 26 p.

Lapham, D. M., and Gray, Carlyle (1973), *Geology and origin of the Triassic magnetite deposit and diabase at Cornwall, Pennsylvania,* Pennsylvania Geological Survey, 4th ser., Mineral Resource Report 56, 343 p.

Lapham, D. M., and McKague, H. L. (1964), *Structural patterns associated with the serpentinites of southeastern Pennsylvania,* Geological Society of America Bulletin, v. 75, p. 639–660.

Lapham, D. M., and Root, S. I. (1971), *Summary of isotopic age determinations in Pennsylvania,* Pennsylvania Geological Survey, 4th ser., Information Circular 70, 29 p.

Larrabee, D. M. (1966), *Map showing distribution of ultramafic and intrusive mafic rocks from northern New Jersey to eastern Alabama,* U.S. Geological Survey Miscellaneous Geologic Investigations Map I-476, scale 1:500,000, 3 sheets.

Lash, G. G. (1985), *Geologic map of the Kutztown quadrangle, Berks and Lehigh Counties, Pennsylvania,* U.S. Geological Survey Geologic Quadrangle Map GQ–1577, scale 1:24,000.

Lash, G. G., and Drake, A. A., Jr. (1984), *The Richmond and Greenwich slices of the Hamburg klippe in eastern Pennsylvania—Stratigraphy, sedimentology, structure, and plate tectonic implications,* U.S. Geological Survey Professional Paper 1312, 40 p.

Lash, G. G., Lyttle, P. T., and Epstein, J. B., eds. (1984), *Geology of an accreted terrane: the eastern Hamburg klippe and surrounding rocks, eastern Pennsylvania,* Annual Field Conference of Pennsylvania Geologists, 49th, Reading, Pa., Guidebook, 151 p.

Lattman, L. H. (1958), *Techniques of mapping geologic fracture traces and lineaments on aerial photographs,* Photogrammetric Engineering, v. 19, p. 568–576.

Laughrey, C. D. (1982), *High-potential gas production and fracture-controlled porosity in Upper Devonian Kane "sand," central-western Pennsylvania,* AAPG Bulletin, v. 66, p. 477–482.

_____ (1984), *Petrology and reservoir characteristics of the Lower Silurian Medina Group sandstones, Athens and Geneva fields, Crawford County, Pennsylvania,* Pennsylvania Geological Survey, 4th ser., Mineral Resource Report 85, 126 p.

_____ (1987), *Evaluating the Lockport Dolomite—problems, pores and possibilities* [abs.], in *The Eighteenth Annual Appalachian Petroleum Geology Symposium—"Rifts, ramps, reefs, and royalties,"* West Virginia Geological and Economic Survey Circular C–40, p. 56–58.

Laughrey, C. D., and Harper, J. A. (1986), *Comparisons of Upper Devonian and Lower Silurian tight formations in Pennsylvania—geological and engineering characteristics,* in Spencer, C. W., and Mast, R. F., eds., *Geology of tight gas reservoirs,* AAPG Studies in Geology 24, p. 9–43.

Lavin, P. M., Chaffin, D. L., and Davis, W. F. (1982), *Major lineaments and the Lake Erie-Maryland crustal block,* Tectonics, v. 1, p. 431–440.

Leggette, R. M. (1936), *Ground water in northwestern Pennsylvania,* Pennsylvania Geological Survey, 4th ser., Water Resource Report 3, 215 p.

Leighton, Henry (1932), *Clay and shale resources in southwestern Pennsylvania,* Pennsylvania Geological Survey, 4th ser., Mineral Resource Report 17, 190 p.

Leighton, Henry (1934), *The white clays of Pennsylvania,* Pennsylvania Geological Survey, 4th ser., Progress Report 112, 19 p.

_____ (1941), *Clay and shale resources in Pennsylvania,* Pennsylvania Geological Survey, 4th ser., Mineral Resource Report 23, 245 p.

Leon, R. R. (1985), *Provenance of sandstone in the Upper Ordovician Bald Eagle and Juniata Formations, central Pennsylvania: implications for tectonic setting,* Newark, University of Delaware, M.S. thesis, 137 p.

Lesley, J. P. (1856), *Manual of coal and its topography,* Philadelphia, J. P. Lippincott, 222 p.

_____ (1859), *The iron manufacturer's guide to the furnaces, forges and rolling mills of the United States,* New York, John Wiley, 772 p.

_____ (1876a), *Historical sketch of geological explorations in Pennsylvania and other states,* Pennsylvania Geological Survey, 2nd ser., Report A, 200 p., appendix, 206 p. (reprinted in 1878 with an author's preface).

_____ (1876b), *The Boyd's Hill gas well at Pittsburg,* in Platt, Franklin, *Special report on the coke manufacture of the Youghiogheny River valley in Fayette and Westmoreland Counties,* Pennsylvania Geological Survey, 2nd ser., Report L, p. 217–237.

_____ (1879), *Preface,* in White, I. C., *The geology of Lawrence County,* Pennsylvania Geological Survey, 2nd ser., Report QQ, p. ix–xxxvi.

_____ ed. (1883), *The geology of Chester County,* Pennsylvania Geological Survey, 2nd ser., Report C4, 394 p.

_____ (1885), *A geological hand atlas of the sixty-seven counties of Pennsylvania, embodying the results of the field work of the Survey, from 1874 to 1884,* Pennsylvania Geological Survey, 2nd ser., Report X, 112 p., 61 maps.

_____ (1892), *A summary description of the geology of Pennsylvania,* Pennsylvania Geological Survey, 2nd ser., Final Report 1892, v. 1, 719 p.

Lesley, J. P., Sanders, R. N., Chance, H. M., and others (1883), *The geology of Lehigh and Northampton Counties,* Pennsylvania Geological Survey, 2nd ser., Report D3, v. 1, 283 p.

Lesquereux, Leo (1879), *Atlas to the coal flora of Pennsylvania and of the Carboniferous formation throughout the United States,* Pennsylvania Geological Survey, 2nd ser., Report P, 18 p., pls. 1–85.

_____ (1880), *Description of the coal flora of the Carboniferous formation in Pennsylvania and throughout the United States,* Pennsylvania Geological Survey, 2nd ser., Report P, v. 1–2, 694 p., pls. 86–87.

_____ (1884), *Description of the coal flora of the Carboniferous formation in Pennsylvania and throughout the United States,* Pennsylvania Geological Survey, 2nd ser., Report P, v. 3, p. 695–977, pls. 88–111.

Lessig, H. D. (1963), *Calcutta Silt, a very early Pleistocene deposit, upper Ohio Valley,* Geological Society of America Bulletin, v. 74, p. 129–140.

Leverett, Frank (1902), *Glacial formations and drainage features of the Erie and Ohio basins,* U.S. Geological Survey Monograph 41, 802 p.

_____ (1934), *Glacial deposits outside the Wisconsin terminal moraine in Pennsylvania,* Pennsylvania Geological Survey, 4th ser., General Geology Report 7, 123 p.

Levine, J. R. (1983), *Tectonic history of coal-bearing sediments in eastern Pennsylvania using coal reflectance anisotropy,* University Park, Pennsylvania State University, Ph.D. thesis, 314 p.

_____ (1985), *Interpretation of Alleghanian tectonic events in the Anthracite region, Pennsylvania using aspects of coal metamorphism* [abs.], Geological Society of America Abstracts with Programs, v. 17, no. 1, p. 31.

_____ (1986), *Deep burial of coal-bearing strata, Anthracite region, Pennsylvania: sedimentation or tectonics?,* Geology, v. 14, p. 577–580.

Levine, J. R., and Davis, Alan (1983), *Tectonic history of coal-bearing sediments in eastern Pennsylvania using coal reflectance aniso-*

tropy, Pennsylvania State University, College of Earth and Mineral Sciences Experiment Station Special Research Report SR–118, 314 p.

Lewis, H. C. (1881), *The iron ores and lignite of the Montgomery County valley,* Academy of Natural Sciences of Philadelphia Proceedings, v. 32, p. 282–291.

_____ (1887), *On a diamantiferous peridotite and the genesis of the diamond* [abs.], Geological Magazine, v. 4, p. 22–24.

Lewis, P. F. (1977), *United States of America—I, The natural landscape,* in *The New Encyclopædia Britannica—Macropædia,* 15th ed., Chicago, Encyclopædia Britannica, Inc., v. 18, p. 905–946.

Libby-French, Jan (1984), *Stratigraphic framework and petroleum potential of northeastern Baltimore Canyon trough, mid-Atlantic outer continental shelf,* AAPG Bulletin, v. 68, p. 50–73.

Liebling, R. S., and Scherp, H. S. (1984), *Development of the Susquehanna River drainage across the folded Appalachians,* Northeastern Geology, v. 6, p. 1–3.

Lilly, W. D., Kunz, Charles, and Kothari, B. (1987), *Evaluating geologic factors in predicting radon levels* [abs.], Geological Society of America Abstracts with Programs, v. 19, no. 2, p. 95.

LKB Resources (1977), *NURE aerial gamma ray and magnetic reconnaissance survey, Thorpe area, Newark NK18–11 quadrangle—Volume I, Narrative report,* and *Volume II [Data],* U.S. Department of Energy, GJBX–16(78), v. 1, variously paged, v. 2, unpaged.

_____ (1978a), *NURE aerial gamma ray and magnetic reconnaissance survey, Thorpe area, Harrisburg NK18–10 quadrangle—Volume I, Narrative report,* and *Volume II [Data],* U.S. Department of Energy, GJBX–33(78), v. 1, variously paged, v. 2, unpaged.

_____ (1978b), *NURE aerial gamma ray and magnetic reconnaissance survey, Thorpe area, Scranton NK18–8 quadrangle—Volume I, Narrative report,* and *Volume II [Data],* U.S. Department of Energy, GJBX–32(78), v. 1, variously paged, v. 2, unpaged.

_____ (1978c), *NURE aerial gamma ray and magnetic reconnaissance survey, Thorpe area, Williamsport NK18–7 quadrangle—Volume I, Narrative report,* and *Volume II [Data],* U.S. Department of Energy, GJBX–34(78), v. 1, variously paged, v. 2, unpaged.

Lobeck, A. K. (1939), *Geomorphology—An introduction to the study of landscapes,* New York, McGraw-Hill, 731 p.

_____ (1951), *Physiographic diagram of Pennsylvania,* preliminary sketch edition, New York, Columbia University, Geographical Press, scale 1:1,000,000, in Pittsburgh Geological Society (1955), *Field guidebook of Appalachian geology—Pittsburgh to New York,* Pittsburgh Geological Society, p. 69.

Lockwood, W. N., and Meisler, Harold (1960), *Illinoian outwash in southeastern Pennsylvania,* U.S. Geological Survey Bulletin 1121-B, 9 p.

Lohman, S. W. (1941), *Ground-water resources of Pennsylvania,* Pennsylvania Geological Survey, 4th ser., Water Resource Report 7, 32 p.

Loper, C. A., Lent, S. D., and Wetzel, K. L. (1989), *Withdrawals and consumptive use of water in Pennsylvania,* U.S. Geological Survey Water-Resources Investigations 88-4095, 50 p.

Lovell, H. L., and Leonard, J. W. (1958), *An investigation of beneficiation of iron-bearing sandstone,* Pennsylvania State University, College of Earth and Mineral Sciences Experiment Station Bulletin 71, p. 29–35.

Lucas, M., Hull, J., and Manspeizer, W. (1988), *A foreland-type fold and related structures,* in Manspeizer, Warren, ed., *Triassic-Jurassic rifting; continental breakup and the origin of the Atlantic ocean and passive margins,* Amsterdam, Elsevier, p. 307–332.

Luce, P. B. (1981), *Stop 9, Mansfield ore bed,* in Berg, T. M., and others, *Geology of Tioga and Bradford Counties, Pennsylvania,* Annual Field Conference of Pennsylvania Geologists, 46th, Wellsboro, Pa., Guidebook, p. 146–148.

Lund, Richard (1975), *Vertebrate-fossil zonation and correlation of the Dunkard basin,* in Barlow, J. A., and Burkhammer, Susan, eds., *Proceedings of the First I. C. White Memorial Symposium [Morgantown, W. Va., 1972]—"The age of the Dunkard,"* West Virginia Geological and Economic Survey, p. 171–182.

Lundegard, P. D., Samuels, N. D., and Pryor, W. A. (1980), *Sedimentology, petrology, and gas potential of the Brallier Formation—*

Upper Devonian turbidite facies of the central and southern Appalachians, U.S. Department of Energy, USDOE/METC/5201-5, Morgantown, W. Va., 220 p.

Luttrell, G. W. (1989), *Stratigraphic nomenclature of the Newark Supergroup of eastern North America,* U.S. Geological Survey Bulletin 1572, 136 p.

Lyman, B. S. (1895), *Report on the New Red of Bucks and Montgomery Counties,* in Lesley, J. P., *A summary description of the geology of Pennsylvania,* Pennsylvania Geological Survey, 2nd ser., Final Report 1895, v. 3, pt. 2, p. 2589–2638.

Lyons, P. L., and O'Hara, N. W., chairmen (1982), *Gravity anomaly map of the United States,* Society of Exploration Geophysicists, Tulsa, Okla.

Lytle, W. S. (1963), *Underground gas storage in Pennsylvania,* Pennsylvania Geological Survey, 4th ser., Mineral Resource Report 46, 31 p.

_____ (1965), *Oil and gas geology of the Warren quadrangle, Pennsylvania,* Pennsylvania Geological Survey, 4th ser., Mineral Resource Report 52, 84 p.

Lytle, W. S., Bergsten, J. M., Cate, A. S., and Wagner, W. R. (1961), *Oil and gas developments in Pennsylvania in 1960,* Pennsylvania Geological Survey, 4th ser., Progress Report 158, 50 p.

Lytle, W. S., Cate, A. S., McGlade, W. G., and Wagner, W. R. (1964), *Oil and gas developments in Pennsylvania in 1963,* Pennsylvania Geological Survey, 4th ser., Progress Report 166, 47 p.

Lytle, W. S., McGlade, W. G., and Wagner, W. R. (1965), *Oil and gas developments in Pennsylvania in 1964,* Pennsylvania Geological Survey, 4th ser., Progress Report 168, 55 p.

Lyttle, P. T. (1982), *The South Valley Hills phyllites—a high Taconic slice in the Pennsylvania Piedmont* [abs.], Geological Society of America Abstracts with Programs, v. 14, no. 1-2, p. 37.

Lyttle, P. T., and Drake, A. A., Jr. (1979), *Discussion—Regional implications of the stratigraphy and structure of Shochary Ridge, Berks and Lehigh Counties, Pennsylvania,* American Journal of Science, v. 279, p. 721–728.

Lyttle, P. T., and Epstein, J. B. (1987), *Geologic map of the Newark 1° x 2° quadrangle, New Jersey, Pennsylvania, and New York,* U.S. Geological Survey Miscellaneous Investigations Series Map I-1715, scale 1:250,000, 2 sheets.

Lyttle, P. T., Lash, G. G., and Epstein, J. B. (1986), *Geologic map of the Slatedale quadrangle, Lehigh and Carbon Counties, Pennsylvania,* U.S. Geological Survey Geologic Quadrangle Map GQ-1598, scale 1:24,000.

Macfarlane, James (1873), *The coal regions of America, their topography, geology, and development,* New York, D. Appleton, 679 p.

MacKichan, K. A. (1951), *Estimated use of water in the United States, 1950,* U.S. Geological Survey Circular 115, 13 p.

_____ (1957), *Estimated use of water in the United States, 1955,* U.S. Geological Survey Circular 398, 18 p.

MacKichan, K. A., and Kammerer, J. C. (1961), *Estimated use of water in the United States, 1960,* U.S. Geological Survey Circular 456, 26 p.

Mackin, J. H. (1938), *The origin of Appalachian drainage—a reply,* American Journal of Science, 5th ser., v. 36, p. 27–53.

_____ (1962), *Structure of the Glenarm Series in Chester County, Pennsylvania,* Geological Society of America Bulletin, v. 73, p. 403–410.

MacLachlan, D. B. (1967), *Structure and stratigraphy of the limestones and dolomites of Dauphin County, Pennsylvania,* Pennsylvania Geological Survey, 4th ser., General Geology Report 44, 168 p.

_____ (1979), *Geology and mineral resources of the Temple and Fleetwood quadrangles, Berks County, Pennsylvania,* Pennsylvania Geological Survey, 4th ser., Atlas 187ab, 71 p.

_____ (1983), *Geology and mineral resources of the Reading and Birdsboro quadrangles, Berks County, Pennsylvania,* Pennsylvania Geological Survey, 4th ser., Atlas 187cd, scale 1:24,000.

_____ (1985), *Pennsylvania anthracite as foreland effect of Alleghenian thrusting* [abs.], Geological Society of America Abstracts with Programs, v. 17, no. 1, p. 53.

_____ (1994), *Some aspects of the lower Paleozoic Laurentian margin and slope in southeastern Pennsylvania,* in Faill, R. T., and Sevon, W. D., eds., *Various aspects of Piedmont geology in Lancaster and Chester Counties, Pennsylvania,* Annual Field Conference of Pennsylvania Geologists, 59th, Lancaster, Pa., Guidebook, p. 9–38.

MacLachlan, D. B., Buckwalter, T. V., and McLaughlin, D. B. (1975), *Geology and mineral resources of the Sinking Spring quadrangle, Berks and Lancaster Counties, Pennsylvania,* Pennsylvania Geological Survey, 4th ser., Atlas 177d, 228 p.

MacLachlan, D. B., and Root, S. I. (1966), *Comparative tectonics and stratigraphy of the Cumberland and Lebanon Valleys,* Annual Field Conference of Pennsylvania Geologists, 31st, Harrisburg, Pa., Guidebook, 90 p.

Maclure, William (1809), *Observations on the geology of the United States, explanatory of a geological map,* American Philosophical Society Transactions, v. 6, p. 411–428, map.

_____ (1817), *Observations on the geology of the United States,* Philadelphia, Abraham Small, 127 p., map.

Main, L. D. (1978), *A structural interpretation of the Cove fault and petrofabric study of the Tuscarora Sandstone, Fulton County, Pennsylvania,* Norman, University of Oklahoma, M.S. thesis, 87 p.

Maloney, F. J. T. (1974), *Glass products and production,* in *The New Encyclopædia Britannica—Macropædia,* 15th ed., Chicago, Encyclopædia Britannica, Inc., v. 8, p. 196–207.

Manspeizer, W. (1981), *Early Mesozoic basins of the central Atlantic passive margins,* AAPG Continuing Education Course Notes Series 19, pt. 4, 60 p.

Manspeizer, W., and Cousminer, H. L. (1988), *Late Triassic-Early Jurassic synrift basins of the U.S. Atlantic margin,* in Sheridan, R. E., and Grow, J. A., eds., *The Atlantic continental margin: U.S.,* Geological Society of America, The Geology of North America, v. I-2, p. 217–241.

Marchand, D. E. (1978), *Quaternary deposits and Quaternary history,* in Marchand, D. E., and others, *Quaternary deposits and soils of the central Susquehanna Valley of Pennsylvania,* Reunion of Friends of the Pleistocene, 41st, Lewisburg, Pa., Guidebook, Pennsylvania State University Agronomy Series 52, p. 1–19.

Marrs, T. O. (1981), *Lithologic characteristics and depositional environments of the non-marine Benwood limestone (Upper Pennsylvanian) in the Dunkard basin, Ohio, Pennsylvania, and West Virginia,* University of Pittsburgh, M.S. thesis, 107 p.

Martin, R. A. (1971), *Geology of Devil's Racecourse boulderfield, Dauphin County, Pennsylvania,* Millersville, Pa., Millersville State College, M.Ed. thesis, 27 p.

Martini, I. P. (1971), *Regional analysis of sedimentology of Medina Formation (Silurian), Ontario and New York,* AAPG Bulletin, v. 55, p. 1249–1261.

Mathews, W. H. (1975), *Cenozoic erosion and erosion surfaces of eastern North America,* American Journal of Science, v. 275, p. 818–824.

Matthews, L. G. (1982), *Evidence for an offset crustal block in the southern Appalachians,* University Park, Pennsylvania State University, M.S. thesis, 86 p.

Maurath, G. C. (1980), *Heat generation and terrestrial heat flow in northwestern Pennsylvania,* Kent, Ohio, Kent State University, M.S. thesis, 156 p.

McBride, E. F. (1962), *Flysch and associated beds of the Martinsburg Formation (Ordovician), central Appalachians,* Journal of Sedimentary Petrology, v. 32, p. 39–91.

McCarl, H. N. (1983), *Construction materials—Aggregates—lightweight aggregates,* in Lefond, S. J., and others, eds., *Industrial minerals and rocks—(Nonmetallics other than fuels),* 5th ed., New York, American Institute of Mining, Metallurgical, and Petroleum Engineers, v. 1, p. 81–95.

McCauley, J. F. (1961), *Uranium in Pennsylvania,* Pennsylvania Geological Survey, 4th ser., Mineral Resource Report 43, 71 p.

McCormick, G. R. (1961), *Petrology of Precambrian rocks in Ohio,* Ohio Division of Geological Survey Report of Investigations 41, 60 p.

McCulloch, C. M., Diamond, W. P., Bench, B. M., and Deul, Maurice (1975), *Selected geologic factors affecting mining of the Pittsburgh coalbed,* U.S. Bureau of Mines Report of Investigations 8093, 72 p.

McCullough, D. G. (1968), *The Johnstown flood,* New York, Simon and Schuster, 302 p.

McGlade, W. G. (1964), *Oil and gas geology of the Youngsville quadrangle, Pennsylvania,* Pennsylvania Geological Survey, 4th ser., Mineral Resource Report 53, 56 p.

McGreevy, L. J., and Sloto, R. A. (1980), *Development of a digital model of ground-water flow in deeply weathered crystalline rock, Chester County, Pennsylvania,* U.S. Geological Survey Water-Resources Investigations 80–2, 42 p.

McKague, H. L. (1964), *The geology, mineralogy, petrology, and geochemistry of the State Line serpentinite and associated chromite deposits,* University Park, Pennsylvania State University, Ph.D. thesis, 166 p.

McKinstry, H. E. (1953), *Shears of the second order,* American Journal of Science, v. 251, p. 401–414.

McKinstry, Hugh (1961), *Structure of the Glenarm Series in Chester County, Pennsylvania,* Geological Society of America Bulletin, v. 72, p. 557–578.

McLaughlin, D. B. (1932), *The thickness of the Newark Series in Pennsylvania and the age of the border conglomerate,* Papers of the Michigan Academy of Science, Arts and Letters, v. 16, p. 421–427.

_____ (1945), *Type sections of the Stockton and Lockatong Formations,* Pennsylvania Academy of Science Proceedings, v. 19, p. 102–113.

_____ (1957), *Triassic alluvial fans in Pennsylvania* [abs.], Geological Society of America Bulletin, v. 68, p. 1765–1766.

_____ (1960), *Notes on the New Oxford Formation and the limestone conglomerate at Conoy Creek,* in Wise, D. U., and Kauffman, M. E., *Some tectonic and structural problems of the Appalachian Piedmont along the Susquehanna River,* Annual Field Conference of Pennsylvania Geologists, 25th, Lancaster, Pa., Guidebook, p. 84–88.

McLaughlin, D. B., and Gerhard, R. C. (1953), *Stratigraphy and origin of Triassic fluviatile sediments, Lebanon and Lancaster Counties,* Pennsylvania Academy of Science Proceedings, v. 27, p. 136–142.

McLelland, J., and Isachsen, Y. W. (1980), *Structural synthesis of the southern and central Adirondacks: a model for the Adirondacks as a whole and plate-tectonics interpretations,* Geological Society of America Bulletin, v. 91, pt. 2, p. II208–II292.

McNeal, J. M. (1985), *The use of sulfur isotopes as a geochemical exploration technique in the early Mesozoic basins of Pennsylvania,* in Robinson, G. R., Jr., and Froelich, A. J., eds., *Proceedings of the Second U.S. Geological Survey Workshop on the Early Mesozoic Basins of the Eastern United States,* U.S. Geological Survey Circular 946, p. 136–139.

McNett, C. W., Jr. (1985), *Shawnee Minisink: a stratified paleoindian-Archaic site in the upper Delaware Valley of Pennsylvania,* Orlando, Fla., Academic Press, 329 p.

Meckel, L. D. (1964), *Pottsville sedimentology, central Appalachians,* Baltimore, Md., Johns Hopkins University, Ph.D. thesis, 412 p.

_____ (1967), *Origin of Pottsville conglomerates (Pennsylvanian) in the central Appalachians,* Geological Society of America Bulletin, v. 78, p. 223–258.

_____ (1970), *Paleozoic alluvial deposition in the central Appalachians: a summary,* in Fisher, G. W., and others, eds., *Studies of Appalachian geology: central and southern,* New York, Interscience Publishers, p. 49–67.

Meinzer, O. E., ed. (1942), *Hydrology,* New York, McGraw-Hill, 712 p.

Meisler, Harold, and Becher, A. E. (1968), *Carbonate rocks of Cambrian and Ordovician age in the Lancaster quadrangle, Pennsylvania,* U.S. Geological Survey Bulletin 1254-G, 14 p.

_____ (1971), *Hydrogeology of the carbonate rocks of the Lancaster 15-minute quadrangle, southeastern Pennsylvania,* Pennsylvania Geological Survey, 4th ser., Water Resource Report 26, 149 p.

Merrill, G. K. (1970–71), *The central Appalachians,* in Sweet, W. C., and Bergström, S. M., eds., *Symposium on conodont biostratigraphy,* Geological Society of America Memoir 127, p. 407–414.

Merrill, G. P. (1924), *The first one hundred years of American geology,* New Haven, Conn., Yale University Press, 773 p.

Metsger, R. W. (1979), *Mining problems in a karst valley—technical and social,* Bulletin of the Association of Engineering Geologists, v. 16, p. 427–447.

Meyer, H. O. A. (1976), *Kimberlites of the continental United States: a review,* Journal of Geology, v. 84, p. 377–403.

Meyerhoff, H. A. (1972), *Postorogenic development of the Appalachians,* Geological Society of America Bulletin, v. 83, p. 1709–1728.

Meyerhoff, H. A., and Olmsted, E. W. (1936), *The origins of Appalachian drainage,* American Journal of Science, 5th ser., v. 32, p. 21–42.

Michael Baker, Jr., Inc. (1974), *Architectural measures to minimize subsidence damage,* Appalachian Regional Commission Report ARC–73–111–2551, 105 p.

Mickelson, D. M., Clayton, Lee, Fullerton, D. S., and Borns, H. W., Jr. (1983), *The late Wisconsin glacial record of the Laurentide ice sheet in the United States,* in Porter, S. C., ed., *The late Pleistocene,* Volume 1 of Wright, H. E., Jr., ed., *Late-Quaternary environments of the United States,* Minneapolis, University of Minnesota Press, p. 3–37.

Middleton, G. V., Rutka, M. A., and Salas, C. J. (1987), *Depositional environments in the Whirlpool Sandstone Member of the Medina Formation,* in Duke, W. L., ed., *Sedimentology, stratigraphy, and ichnology of the Lower Silurian Medina Formation in New York and Ontario,* Society of Economic Paleontologists and Mineralogists, Eastern Section, Niagara Falls, Ontario, Canada, 1987 Field Trip, Guidebook, p. 31–45.

Middleton, Jefferson (1901), *Clay products,* in *Mineral resources of the United States, calendar year 1900,* U.S. Geological Survey, p. 693–736.

_____ (1911), *Clay-working industries,* in *Mineral resources of the United States, calendar year 1910—Part II, Nonmetals,* U.S. Geological Survey, p. 537–600.

_____ (1923), *Clay-working industries, clay and silica brick,* in *Mineral resources of the United States, 1920—Part II, Nonmetals,* U.S. Geological Survey, p. 323–359.

Millbrooke, Anne (1976), *The Geological Society of Pennsylvania 1832–1836 [Part 1],* Pennsylvania Geology, v. 7, no. 6, p. 7–11.

_____ (1977), *The Geological Society of Pennsylvania 1832–1836 [Part 2],* Pennsylvania Geology, v. 8, no. 2, p. 12–16.

Miller, B. L. (1912a), *Graphite deposits of Pennsylvania,* Pennsylvania Geological Survey, 3rd ser., Report 6, 147 p.

_____ (1912b), *The geology of the graphite deposits of Pennsylvania,* Economic Geology, v. 7, p. 762–777.

_____ (1924), *Lead and zinc ores of Pennsylvania,* Pennsylvania Geological Survey, 4th ser., Mineral Resource Report 5, 91 p.

_____ (1934), *Limestones of Pennsylvania,* Pennsylvania Geological Survey, 4th ser., Mineral Resource Report 20, 729 p.

_____ (1942), *Exploration for iron ore in Huntingdon and Bedford Counties, Pennsylvania,* unpublished report for Huntingdon and Broad Top Mountain Railroad and Coal Company and Riddlesburg Coal and Iron Company, 12 p.

Miller, B. L., Fraser, D. M., and Miller, R. L. (1939), *Northampton County, Pennsylvania,* Pennsylvania Geological Survey, 4th ser., County Report 48, 496 p.

Miller, B. L., Fraser, D. M., Miller, R. L., and others (1941), *Lehigh County, Pennsylvania,* Pennsylvania Geological Survey, 4th ser., County Report 39, 492 p.

Miller, J. T. (1961), *Geology and mineral resources of the Loysville quadrangle, Pennsylvania,* Pennsylvania Geological Survey, 4th ser., Atlas 127, 47 p.

Miller, K. G., Fairbanks, R. G., and Mountain, G. S. (1987), *Tertiary oxygen isotope synthesis, sea level history, and continental margin erosion,* Paleoceanography, v. 2, p. 1–19.

Mitra, Shankar, and Namson, J. S. (1989), *Equal-area balancing*, American Journal of Science, v. 289, p. 563–599.

Mixon, R. B., and Newell, W. L. (1977), *Stafford fault system: structures documenting Cretaceous and Tertiary deformation along the Fall Line in northeastern Virginia*, Geology, v. 5, p. 437–440.

Moebs, N. N., and Hoy, R. B. (1959), *Thrust faulting in Sinking Valley, Blair and Huntingdon Counties, Pennsylvania*, Geological Society of America Bulletin, v. 70, p. 1079–1088.

Montgomery, Arthur (1955), *Paragenesis of the serpentine-talc deposits near Easton, Pa.*, Pennsylvania Academy of Science Proceedings, v. 29, p. 203–215.

_____ (1957), *Three occurrences of high-thorian uraninite near Easton, Pennsylvania*, American Mineralogist, v. 42, p. 804–820.

_____ (1969), *The mineralogy of Pennsylvania, 1922–1965*, Academy of Natural Sciences of Philadelphia Special Publication 9, 104 p.

Moore, E. S. (1922), *White clay deposits in central Pennsylvania*, Pennsylvania Geological Survey, 4th ser., Progress Report 45, 7 p.

Moore, J. M. (1986), *The "Grenville problem" then and now*, in Moore, J. M., and others, *The Grenville province*, Geological Association of Canada Special Paper 31, p. 1–11.

Moore, R. C., Wanless, H. R., Weller, J. M., and others (1944), *Correlation of Pennsylvanian formations of North America*, Geological Society of America Bulletin, v. 55, p. 657–706.

Morgan, B. A. (1977), *The Baltimore Complex, Maryland, Pennsylvania, and Virginia*, in Coleman, R. G., and Irwin, W. P., eds., *North American ophiolites*, Oregon Department of Geology and Mineral Industries Bulletin 95, p. 41–49.

Morris, D. A. (1967), *Lower Conemaugh (Pennsylvanian) depositional environments and paleogeography in the Appalachian coal basin*, Lawrence, University of Kansas, Ph.D. thesis, 800 p.

Moyd, Louis (1942), *Evidence of sulphide-silicate immiscibility at Gap nickel mine, Pennsylvania*, American Mineralogist, v. 27, p. 389–393.

Muller, E. H., and Prest, V. K. (1985), *Glacial lakes in the Ontario basin*, in Karrow, P. F., and Calkin, P. E., eds., *Quaternary evolution of the Great Lakes*, Geological Association of Canada Special Paper 30, p. 213–229.

Muller, O. H., Ackermann, H. D., Diment, W. H., and others (1979), *A preliminary gravity map of Pennsylvania* [abs.], Geological Society of America Abstracts with Programs, v. 11, no. 1, p. 46.

Muller, P. D., and Chapin, D. A. (1984), *Tectonic evolution of the Baltimore Gneiss anticlines, Maryland*, in Bartholomew, M. J., and others, eds., *The Grenville event in the Appalachians and related topics*, Geological Society of America Special Paper 194, p. 127–148.

Murphy, J. L. (1966), *The Pennsylvanian nautiloid Kionoceras ungeri (Sturgeon and Miller)*, Journal of Paleontology, v. 40, p. 1388–1390.

_____ (1970), *Coiled nautiloid cephalopods from the Brush Creek limestone (Conemaugh) of eastern Ohio and western Pennsylvania*, Journal of Paleontology, v. 44, p. 195–205.

Murray, C. R. (1968), *Estimated use of water in the United States, 1965*, U.S. Geological Survey Circular 556, 53 p.

Murray, C. R., and Reeves, E. B. (1972), *Estimated use of water in the United States in 1970*, U.S. Geological Survey Circular 676, 37 p.

_____ (1977), *Estimated use of water in the United States in 1975*, U.S. Geological Survey Circular 765, 39 p.

Myers, P. B., Jr., and Perlow, Michael, Jr. (1984), *Development, occurrence, and triggering mechanisms of sinkholes in the carbonate rocks of the Lehigh Valley, eastern Pennsylvania*, in Beck, B. F., ed., *Sinkholes: their geology, engineering and environmental impact*, Multidisciplinary Conference on Sinkholes, 1st, Orlando, Fla., 1984, Proceedings, Rotterdam, A. A. Balkema, p. 111–115.

Naldrett, A. J. (1981), *Nickel sulfide deposits: classification, composition, and genesis*, in Skinner, B. J., ed., *Seventy-fifth anniversary volume, 1905–1980*, Economic Geology, p. 628–685.

National Council on Radiation Protection and Measurement (1987), *Ionizing radiation exposure of the population of the United States*, National Council on Radiation Protection and Measurements, Bethesda, Md., NCRP Report 93, p. 55.

Nazar, Andrzej, Prieur, James, and Threlfall, Daniel (1984), *An integrated ground water monitoring program using multilevel gas-driven samplers and conventional monitoring wells*, Ground Water Monitoring Review, v. 4, no. 4, p. 43–47.

Nelson, B. E., and Coogan, A. H. (1984), *The Silurian Brassfield-Rochester Shale sequence in the subsurface of eastern Ohio*, Northeastern Geology, v. 6, p. 4–11.

Nero, A. V., Schwehr, M. B., Nazaroff, W. W., and Revzan, K. L. (1986), *Distribution of airborne radon-222 concentrations in U.S. homes*, Science, v. 234, p. 992–997.

Nettleton, L. L. (1941), *Relation of gravity to structure in the northern Appalachian area*, Geophysics, v. 6, p. 270–286.

Neumann, Frank (1940), *United States earthquakes, 1938*, U.S. Department of Commerce, Coast and Geodetic Survey, ser. 629, 59 p.

Newsom, S. W. (1983), *Middle Ordovician paleogeography of the Appalachian Valley and Ridge province, central Pennsylvania*, University of Delaware, M.S. thesis, 235 p.

New York State Department of Health, Water Pollution Control Board (1960), *The Delaware River drainage basin*, New York State Department of Health, Report, 305 p.

Nickelsen, R. P. (1963), *Fold patterns and continuous deformation mechanisms of the central Pennsylvania folded Appalachians*, in *Tectonics and Cambrian-Ordovician stratigraphy, central Appalachians of Pennsylvania*, Pittsburgh Geological Society and Appalachian Geological Society, Guidebook, p. 13–29.

_____ (1966), *Fossil distortion and penetrative rock deformation in the Appalachian Plateau, Pennsylvania*, Journal of Geology, v. 74, p. 924–931.

_____ (1972), *Attributes of rock cleavage in some mudstones and limestones of the Valley and Ridge province, Pennsylvania*, Pennsylvania Academy of Science Proceedings, v. 46, p. 107–112.

_____ (1974), *Origin of cleavage and distorted mudcrack polygons* [abs.], Geological Society of America Abstracts with Programs, v. 6, no. 1, p. 59.

_____ (1979), *Sequence of structural stages of the Alleghany orogeny, at the Bear Valley strip mine, Shamokin, Pennsylvania*, American Journal of Science, v. 279, p. 225–271.

_____ (1980), *Sequential and spatial development of the Alleghany orogeny in the middle Appalachians* [abs.], Geological Society of America Abstracts with Programs, v. 12, no. 2, p. 75.

_____ (1983a), *Ambient temperatures during the Alleghany orogeny*, in Nickelsen, R. P., and Cotter, Edward, eds., *Silurian depositional history and Alleghanian deformation in the Pennsylvania Valley and Ridge*, Annual Field Conference of Pennsylvania Geologists, 48th, Danville, Pa., Guidebook, p. 64–66.

_____ (1983b), *Aspects of Alleghanian deformation*, in Nickelsen, R. P., and Cotter, Edward, eds., *Silurian depositional history and Alleghanian deformation in the Pennsylvania Valley and Ridge*, Annual Field Conference of Pennsylvania Geologists, 48th, Danville, Pa., Guidebook, p. 29–39.

_____ (1986), *Cleavage duplexes in the Marcellus Shale of the Appalachian foreland*, Journal of Structural Geology, v. 8, p. 361–371.

_____ (1988), *Structural evolution of folded thrusts and duplexes on a first-order anticlinorium in the Valley and Ridge province of Pennsylvania*, in Mitra, Gautam, and Wojtal, Steven, eds., *Geometries and mechanisms of thrusting, with special reference to the Appalachians*, Geological Society of America Special Paper 222, p. 89–106.

Nickelsen, R. P., and Cotter, Edward, eds. (1983), *Silurian depositional history and Alleghanian deformation in the Pennsylvania Valley and Ridge*, Annual Field Conference of Pennsylvania Geologists, 48th, Danville, Pa., Guidebook, 192 p.

Nickelsen, R. [P.], and Engelder, T. (1989), *Fold-thrust geometries of the Juniata Culmination, central Appalachians of Pennsylvania*, in Engelder, Terry, ed., *Structures of the Appalachian foreland fold-thrust belt*, International Geological Congress, 28th, Washington, D. C., Guidebook T166, p. 38–43, Figures 10, 14.

Nickelsen, R. P., and Hough, V. D. (1967), *Jointing in the Appalachian Plateau of Pennsylvania*, Geological Society of America Bulletin, v. 78, p. 609–629.

Norton, C. W. (1975), *Foraminiferal distribution and paleogeography of the Brush Creek marine event (Missourian: Pennsylvanian) Appalachian basin,* University of Pittsburgh, Ph.D. thesis.

Nummedal, Dag (1987), *Preface,* in Nummedal, Dag, and others, eds., *Sea-level fluctuation and coastal evolution,* Society of Economic Paleontologists and Mineralogists Special Publication 41, p. iii–iv.

Nuttli, O. W. (1973), *Seismic wave attenuation and magnitude relations for eastern North America,* Journal of Geophysical Research, v. 78, p. 876–885.

Oberlander, Theodore (1965), *The Zagros streams: a new interpretation of transverse drainage in an orogenic zone,* Syracuse University, Department of Geology, Syracuse Geographical Series 1, 168 p.

Oberlander, T. M. (1985), *Origin of drainage transverse to structures in orogens,* in Morisawa, M., and Hack, J. T., eds., *Tectonic geomorphology,* Boston, Allen and Unwin, p. 155–182.

Oleksyshyn, John (1982), *Fossil plants from the anthracite coal fields of eastern Pennsylvania,* Pennsylvania Geological Survey, 4th ser., General Geology Report 72, 157 p.

Oliver, W. A., Jr., de Witt, Wallace, Jr., Dennison, J. M., and others (1971), *Isopach and lithofacies maps of the Devonian in the Appalachian basin,* Pennsylvania Geological Survey, 4th ser., Progress Report 182, 7 sheets.

Olsen, P. E. (1980a), *Fossil great lakes of the Newark Supergroup in New Jersey,* in Manspeizer, Warren, ed., *Field studies of New Jersey geology and guide to field trips,* New York State Geological Association Annual Meeting, 52nd, Newark, N. J., Rutgers University Geology Department, p. 352–398.

——— (1980b), *Triassic and Jurassic formations of the Newark basin,* in Manspeizer, Warren, ed., *Field studies of New Jersey geology and guide to field trips,* New York State Geological Association Annual Meeting, 52nd, Newark, N. J., Rutgers University Geology Department, p. 2–39.

——— (1984), *Comparative paleolimnology of the Newark Supergroup: a study of ecosystem evolution,* New Haven, Conn., Yale University, Ph.D. thesis, 756 p.

——— (1985a), *Distribution of organic-matter-rich lacustrine rocks in the early Mesozoic Newark Supergroup,* in Robinson, G. R., Jr., and Froelich, A. J., eds., *Proceedings of the Second U.S. Geological Survey Workshop on the Early Mesozoic Basins of the Eastern United States,* U.S. Geological Survey Circular 946, p. 61–64.

——— (1985b), *Significance of great lateral extent of thin units in Newark Supergroup (lower Mesozoic, eastern North America)* [abs.], AAPG Bulletin, v. 69, p. 1444.

——— (1986), *A 40-million-year lake record of early Mesozoic orbital climatic forcing,* Science, v. 234, p. 842–848.

——— (1988), *Paleontology and paleoecology of the Newark Supergroup (early Mesozoic, eastern North America),* in Manspeizer, Warren, ed., *Triassic-Jurassic rifting; continental breakup and the origin of the Atlantic Ocean and passive margins,* Amsterdam, Elsevier, p. 185–230.

Olsen, P. E., Kent, D. V., Cornet, Bruce, and others (1996), *High-resolution stratigraphy of the Newark rift basin (early Mesozoic, eastern North America),* Geological Society of America Bulletin, v. 108, p. 40–77.

Olsen, P. E., McCune, A. R., and Thomson, K. S. (1982), *Correlation of the early Mesozoic Newark Supergroup by vertebrates, principally fishes,* American Journal of Science, v. 282, p. 1–44.

Olsen, P. E., and Schlische, R. W. (1988), *Quantitative rift basin evolution: application of extensional basin filling model to early Mesozoic rifts e. North America* [abs.], Geological Society of America Abstracts with Programs, v. 20, no. 1, p. 59.

Olson, E. C. (1975), *Vertebrates and the biostratigraphic position of the Dunkard,* in Barlow, J. A., and Burkhammer, Susan, eds., *Proceedings of the First I. C. White Memorial Symposium, [Morgantown, W. Va., 1972]—"The age of the Dunkard,"* West Virginia Geological and Economic Survey, p. 155–165.

O'Neill, B. J., Jr. (1975), *Potential high-calcium limestone resources in the Mount Joy area, Lancaster County, Pennsylvania,* Pennsylvania Geological Survey, 4th ser., Information Circular 76, 18 p.

——— (1976), *Atlas of Pennsylvania's mineral resources—Part 4, The distribution of limestones containing at least 90 percent $CaCO_3$ in Pennsylvania,* Pennsylvania Geological Survey, 4th ser., Mineral Resource Report 50, pt. 4, 2 p.

——— (1977), *Directory of the mineral industry in Pennsylvania,* 3rd ed., Pennsylvania Geological Survey, 4th ser., Information Circular 54, 140 p.

O'Neill, B. J., Jr., and Barnes, J. H. (1979), *Properties and uses of shales and clays, southwestern Pennsylvania,* Pennsylvania Geological Survey, 4th ser., Mineral Resource Report 77, 689 p.

——— (1981), *Properties and uses of shales and clays, south-central Pennsylvania,* Pennsylvania Geological Survey, 4th ser., Mineral Resource Report 79, 201 p.

O'Neill, B. J., Jr., Lapham, D. M., Jaron, M. G., and others (1965), *Properties and uses of Pennsylvania shales and clays,* Pennsylvania Geological Survey, 4th ser., Mineral Resource Report 51, 448 p.

Oshchudlak, M. E., and Hubert, J. F. (1988), *Petrology of Mesozoic sandstones in the Newark basin, central New Jersey and adjacent New York,* in Manspeizer, Warren, ed., *Triassic-Jurassic rifting; continental breakup and the origin of the Atlantic Ocean and passive margins,* Amsterdam, Elsevier, p. 333–352.

Owen, E. W. (1975), *Trek of the oil finders: a history of exploration for petroleum,* AAPG Memoir 6, 1,647 p.

Owens, J. P., and Denny, C. S. (1979), *Upper Cenozoic deposits of the central Delmarva Peninsula, Maryland and Delaware,* U.S. Geological Survey Professional Paper 1067–A, 28 p.

Owens, J. P., and Glaser, J. D. (1989), *Cretaceous and Tertiary stratigraphy of the Elk Neck area, northeastern Maryland,* International Geological Congress, 28th, Washington, D. C., Guidebook, Field Trip T211, 26 p.

Owens, J. P., and Gohn, G. S. (1985), *Depositional history of the Cretaceous Series in the U.S. Atlantic Coastal Plain: stratigraphy, paleoenvironments, and tectonic controls of sedimentation,* in Poag, C. W., ed., *Geologic evolution of the United States Atlantic margin,* New York, Van Nostrand Reinhold, p. 25–86.

Owens, J. P., and Minard, J. P. (1964), *Pre-Quaternary geology of the Bristol quadrangle, New Jersey-Pennsylvania,* U.S. Geological Survey Geologic Quadrangle Map GQ–342, scale 1:24,000.

——— (1975), *Geologic map of the surficial deposits in the Trenton area, New Jersey and Pennsylvania,* U.S. Geological Survey Miscellaneous Investigations Series Map I–884, scale 1:48,000.

——— (1979), *Upper Cenozoic sediments of the lower Delaware Valley and the northern Delmarva Peninsula, New Jersey, Pennsylvania, Delaware, and Maryland,* U.S. Geological Survey Professional Paper 1067–D, 47 p.

Owens, J. P., and Sohl, N. F. (1969), *Shelf and deltaic paleoenvironments in the Cretaceous-Tertiary formations of the New Jersey Coastal Plain,* in Subitzky, Seymour, ed., *Geology of selected areas in New Jersey and eastern Pennsylvania and guidebook of excursions,* New Brunswick, N. J., Rutgers University Press, p. 235–278.

Page, L. V. (1970), *A proposed streamflow data program for Pennsylvania,* Pennsylvania Department of Forests and Waters Technical Bulletin 3, 66 p.

Page, L. V., and Shaw, L. C. (1977), *Low-flow characteristics of Pennsylvania streams,* Pennsylvania Department of Environmental Resources, Office of Resources Management, Water Resources Bulletin 12, 441 p.

Pakiser, L. C., and Steinhart, J. S. (1964), *Explosion seismology in the western hemisphere,* in Odishaw, H., ed., *Research in geophysics,* Cambridge, Mass., MIT Press, p. 123–147.

Palmer, A. R. (1962), *Glyptagnostus and associated trilobites in the United States,* U.S. Geological Survey Professional Paper 374–F, 49 p.

——— (1971), *The Cambrian of the Appalachian and eastern New England regions, eastern United States,* in Holland, C. H., ed., *Lower Paleozoic rocks of the world—Volume I, Cambrian of the New World,* New York, Wiley-Interscience, p. 169–217.

——— compiler (1983), *The Decade of North American Geology, 1983 geologic time scale,* Geology, v. 11, p. 503–504.

Parizek, R. R. (1975), *On the nature and significance of fracture traces and lineaments in carbonate and other terranes,* in *Karst hydrology and water resources,* Proceedings of the U.S.-Yugoslavian Symposium, Dubrovnik, v. 1, p. 3–1—3–62.

Parizek, R. R., and White, W. B. (1985), *Application of Quaternary and Tertiary geological factors to environmental problems in central Pennsylvania,* in Gold, D. P., and others, *Central Pennsylvania geology revisited,* Annual Field Conference of Pennsylvania Geologists, 50th, State College, Pa., Guidebook, p. 63–119.

Parizek, R. R., White, W. B., and Langmuir, Donald, eds. (1971), *Hydrogeology and geochemistry of folded and faulted carbonate rocks of the central Appalachian type and related land use problems,* Pennsylvania State University, College of Earth and Mineral Sciences Experiment Station Circular 82, 183 p.

Parker, R. A., Houghton, H. F., and McDowell, R. C. (1988), *Stratigraphic framework and distribution of early Mesozoic rocks of the northern Newark basin, New Jersey and New York,* in Froelich, A. J., and Robinson, G. R., Jr., eds., *Studies of the early Mesozoic basins of the Eastern United States,* U.S. Geological Survey Bulletin 1776, p. 31–39.

Parrish, J. B. (1978), *The relationship of geophysical and remote sensing lineaments to regional structure and kimberlite intrusions in the Appalachian Plateau of Pennsylvania,* University Park, Pennsylvania State University, M.S. thesis, 65 p.

Parrish, J. B., and Lavin, P. M. (1982), *Tectonic model for kimberlite emplacement in the Appalachian Plateau of Pennsylvania,* Geology, v. 10, p. 344–347.

Patchen, D. G., and Smosna, R. A. (1975), *Stratigraphy and petrology of Middle Silurian McKenzie Formation in West Virginia,* AAPG Bulletin, v. 59, p. 2266–2287.

Paulachok, G. N. (1991), *Geohydrology and ground-water resources of Philadelphia, Pennsylvania,* U.S. Geological Survey Water-Supply Paper 2346, 79 p.

Pavich, M. J. (1986), *Processes and rates of saprolite production and erosion on a foliated granitic rock of the Virginia Piedmont,* in Colman, S. M., and Dethier, D. P., eds., *Rates of chemical weathering of rocks and minerals,* Orlando, Fla., Academic Press, p. 551–590.

_____ (1989), *Regolith residence time and the concept of surface age of the Piedmont "peneplain,"* in Gardner, T. W., and Sevon, W. D., eds., *Appalachian geomorphology,* Amsterdam, Elsevier, p. 181–196 [reprinted from Geomorphology, v. 2, no. 1–3].

Paxton, S. T. (1983), *Relationships between Pennsylvanian-age lithic sandstone and mudrock diagenesis and coal rank in the central Appalachians,* University Park, Pennsylvania State University, Ph.D. thesis, 526 p.

Paxton, S. T., and Williams, E. G. (1985), *Porosity of coal-bearing Allegheny Group rocks, Pennsylvania, U.S.A., and inference of former burial depths* [abs.], Geological Society of America Abstracts with Programs, v. 17, no. 1, p. 57–58.

Pazzaglia, F. J. (1993), *Stratigraphy, petrography, and correlation of late Cenozoic middle Atlantic Coastal Plain deposits: Implications for late-stage passive-margin geologic evolution,* Geological Society of America Bulletin, v. 105, p. 1617–1634.

Pazzaglia, F. J., and Gardner, T. W. (1993), *Fluvial terraces of the lower Susquehanna River,* Geomorphology, v. 8, p. 83–113.

Pearre, N. C. (1958), *Corundum mining in the Piedmont province of Pennsylvania,* Pennsylvania Geological Survey, 4th ser., Information Circular 13, 9 p.

Pearre, N. C., and Heyl, A. V., Jr. (1960), *Chromite and other mineral deposits in serpentine rocks of the Piedmont Upland, Maryland, Pennsylvania, and Delaware,* U.S. Geological Survey Bulletin 1082–K, p. 707–833.

Peck, F. B. (1908), *Geology of the cement belt, in Lehigh and Northampton Counties, Pa., with brief history of the origin and growth of the industry and a description of the methods of manufacture,* Economic Geology, v. 3, p. 37–76.

_____ (1911), *Preliminary report on the talc and serpentine of Northampton County and the portland cement materials of the Lehigh district,* Pennsylvania Geological Survey, 3rd ser., Report 5, 65 p.

_____ (1922a), *Pennsylvania—Saylorsburg district,* in Ries, H., and others, *High-grade clays of the eastern United States,* U.S. Geological Survey Bulletin 708, p. 109–116.

_____ (1922b), *White clay deposits at Saylorsburg, Monroe County, Pennsylvania,* Pennsylvania Geological Survey, 4th ser., Progress Report 40, 8 p.

Pedlow, G. W. (1977), *A peat island hypothesis for the formation of thick coal,* Columbia, University of South Carolina, Ph.D. thesis, 181 p.

Pees, S. T. (1983a), *Model area describes NW Pennsylvania's Medina play,* Oil and Gas Journal, v. 81, no. 21, p. 55–60.

_____ (1983b), *Remote sensing can aid finding efforts,* Northeast Oil Reporter, v. 3, no. 6, p. 33–36.

Peets, R. G. (1957), *Mining history at Cornwall, Pennsylvania,* Mining Engineering, July, p. 741–744.

Pelletier, B. R. (1958), *Pocono paleocurrents in Pennsylvania and Maryland,* Geological Society of America Bulletin, v. 69, p. 1033–1064.

Peltier, L. C. (1949), *Pleistocene terraces of the Susquehanna River, Pennsylvania,* Pennsylvania Geological Survey, 4th ser., General Geology Report 23, 158 p.

Pemberton, S. G. (1987), *Ichnology of the Thorold Sandstone in the vicinity of Hamilton, Ontario: a Silurian storm-influenced deposit,* in Duke, W. L., ed., *Sedimentology, stratigraphy, and ichnology of the Lower Silurian Medina Formation in New York and Ontario,* Society of Economic Paleontologists and Mineralogists, Eastern Section, Niagara Falls, Ontario, Canada, 1987 Field Trip, Guidebook, p. 66–80.

Pemberton, S. G., and Frey, R. W. (1984), *Ichnology of a storm-influenced shallow marine sequence: Cardium Formation (Upper Cretaceous) at Seebe, Alberta,* in Stott, D. F., and Glass, D. J., eds., *The Mesozoic of middle North America,* Canadian Society of Petroleum Geologists Memoir 9, p. 281–304.

Penn, W. (1685), *A further account of the province of Pennsylvania and its improvements,* London.

Pennsylvania Department of Community Affairs (1969), *Pennsylvania political subdivisions,* Pennsylvania Department of Community Affairs, scale approximately 1:70,000.

Pennsylvania Department of Environmental Protection (1995), *1995—Annual report on mining activities,* Pennsylvania Department of Environmental Protection, 391 p.

Pennsylvania Department of Environmental Resources (1987), *Annual report on mining, oil and gas, and land reclamation and conservation activities,* Pennsylvania Department of Environmental Resources, 450 p.

_____ (1994), *Annual report to the General Assembly pursuant to the Hazardous Sites Cleanup Act—Fiscal year July 1, 1993 to June 30, 1994,* Pennsylvania Department of Environmental Resources, 35 p.

Pennsylvania Department of Environmental Resources, Bureau of Water Quality Management (1984), *Water quality inventory,* Pennsylvania Department of Environmental Resources, 181 p.

Pennsylvania Department of Environmental Resources, Bureau of Water Resources Management (1975–83), *The State Water Plan,* Pennsylvania Department of Environmental Resources Bulletins SWP-1–20, contain information on planning principles and 20 subbasins.

Pennsylvania Department of Forests and Waters, Bureau of Engineering (1970), *Dams, reservoirs and natural lakes—Water Resources Planning Inventory No. 1,* Pennsylvania Department of Environmental Resources Water Resources Bulletin 5, 101 p.

Pennsylvania Department of Internal Affairs, Bureau of Statistics and Bureau of Topographic and Geologic Survey, and Pennsylvania State College, School of Mineral Industries (1944a), *Pennsylvania's mineral heritage,* Pennsylvania Department of Internal Affairs, 248 p.

_____ (1944b), *The mineral industries in Pennsylvania,* in *Pennsylvania's mineral heritage,* Pennsylvania Department of Internal Affairs, p. 5.

Pennsylvania Department of Transportation (1986), *Field test manual,* Pennsylvania Department of Transportation Publication 19, unpaged.

_____ (1987), *Specifications,* Pennsylvania Department of Transportation Publication 408, 684 p.

Pennsylvania Department of Transportation, Bureau of Construction and Materials (1988), *Bulletin 14—Aggregate producers,* Pennsylvania Department of Transportation Publication 34, 59 p.

Pennsylvania Geological Survey (1962), *Physiographic provinces of Pennsylvania,* Pennsylvania Geological Survey, 4th ser., Map 13, scale approximately 1:2,000,000.

_____ (1978), *Uranium near Oley, Berks County,* Pennsylvania Geology, v. 9, no. 4, p. 29–31.

_____ (1981), *Glacial deposits of Pennsylvania,* Pennsylvania Geological Survey, 4th ser., Map 59, scale approximately 1:2,000,000.

_____ (1982), *Geologic map of Pennsylvania,* Pennsylvania Geological Survey, 4th ser., Map 7, scale 1:2,000,000.

_____ (1984), *Limestone and dolomite distribution in Pennsylvania,* Pennsylvania Geological Survey, 4th ser., Map 15, scale approximately 1:2,000,000.

_____ (1985), *Gross Minerals—A force in the fine phyllite fillers field,* Pennsylvania Geology, v. 16, no. 6, p. 2–5.

_____ (1986), *Building stones from Cumberland County,* Pennsylvania Geology, v. 17, no. 1, p. 10–12.

_____ (1990), *Geologic map of Pennsylvania,* Pennsylvania Geological Survey, 4th ser., Map 7, scale 1:2,000,000.

_____ (1992), *Distribution of Pennsylvania coals,* Pennsylvania Geological Survey, 4th ser., Map 11, scale 1:2,000,000.

_____ (1993), *Oil and gas fields of Pennsylvania,* Pennsylvania Geological Survey, 4th ser., Map 10, scale 1:2,000,000.

Pennsylvania Legislative Reference Bureau (published weekly), *Pennsylvania Bulletin.*

Perry, W. J., Jr. (1978), *Sequential deformation in the central Appalachians,* American Journal of Science, v. 278, p. 518–542.

Pettijohn, F. J. (1957), *Sedimentary rocks,* 2nd ed., New York, Harper and Row, 718 p.

Phemister, T. C. (1924), *A note on the Lancaster Gap mine, Pennsylvania,* Journal of Geology, 5th ser., v. 32, p. 498–510.

Philbrick, S. S. (1959), *Field Trip 6—Engineering geology of the Pittsburgh area,* in *Guidebook for field trips, Pittsburgh Meeting, 1959,* Geological Society of America Guidebook Series, p. 189–203.

_____ (1976), *Kinzua Dam and the glacial foreland,* in Coates, D. R., ed., *Geomorphology and engineering,* Stroudsburg, Pa., Dowden, Hutchinson and Ross, p. 175–197.

Phillips, J. D. (1985), *Aeromagnetic character and anomalies of the Gettysburg basin vicinity, Pennsylvania—a preliminary appraisal,* in Robinson, G. R., Jr., and Froelich, A. J., eds., *Proceedings of the Second U.S. Geological Survey Workshop on the Early Mesozoic Basins of the Eastern United States,* U.S. Geological Survey Circular 946, p. 133–135.

Phillips, T. L., and Peppers, R. A. (1984), *Changing patterns of Pennsylvanian coal-swamp vegetation and implications of climatic control on coal occurrence,* International Journal of Coal Geology, v. 3, p. 205–255.

Pierce, K. L. (1965), *Geomorphic significance of a Cretaceous deposit in the Great Valley of southern Pennsylvania,* in *Geological Survey Research 1965, Chapter C,* U.S. Geological Survey Professional Paper 525-C, p. C152–C156.

_____ (1966), *Bedrock and surficial geology of the McConnellsburg quadrangle, Pennsylvania,* Pennsylvania Geological Survey, 4th ser., Atlas 109a, 111 p.

Pierce, N. A., and Jordan, W. M. (1982), *Economics, science, and politics: establishment of the Second Geological Survey of Pennsylvania* [abs.], Geological Society of America Abstracts with Programs, v. 14, no. 1–2, p. 73.

Piggott, R. J., and Eynon, P. (1978), *Ground movements arising from the presence of shallow abandoned mine workings,* in Geddes, J. D., ed., *Large ground movements and structures [1977, Cardiff, Wales],* New York, John Wiley and Sons, p. 749–780.

Pimentel, N. R., Bikerman, Michael, and Flint, N. K. (1975), *A new K-Ar date on the Masontown dike, southwestern Pennsylvania,* Pennsylvania Geology, v. 6, no. 3, p. 5–7.

Piotrowski, R. G. (1976), *Onondaga "reefs"—McKean County, Pennsylvania,* in Lytle, W. S., and others, *Oil and gas developments in Pennsylvania in 1975,* Pennsylvania Geological Survey, 4th ser., Progress Report 189, p. 29–35.

_____ (1978), *Devonian shale gas—new interest in old resource,* Pennsylvania Geology, v. 9, no. 1, p. 2–5.

_____ (1981), *Geology and natural gas production of the Lower Silurian Medina Group and equivalent rock units in Pennsylvania,* Pennsylvania Geological Survey, 4th ser., Mineral Resource Report 82, 21 p.

Piotrowski, R. G., and Harper, J. A. (1979), *Black shale and sandstone facies of the Devonian "Catskill" clastic wedge in the subsurface of western Pennsylvania,* U.S. Department of Energy, Eastern Gas Shales Project, EGSP Series 13, 40 p.

Pitkin, J. A., and Duval, J. S. (1980), *Design parameters for aerial gamma-ray surveys,* Geophysics, v. 45, p. 1427–1439.

Pitkin, J. A., Neuschel, S. K., and Bates, R. G. (1964), *Aeroradioactivity surveys and geologic mapping,* in Adams, J. A. S., and Lowder, W. M., eds., *The natural radiation environment,* Chicago, University of Chicago Press, p. 723–736.

Platt, Franklin (1881), *The geology of Blair County,* Pennsylvania Geological Survey, 2nd ser., Report T, 311 p.

Platt, Franklin, and Platt, W. G. (1877), *Report of progress in the Cambria and Somerset district of the bituminous coal-fields of western Pennsylvania—Part I, Cambria,* Pennsylvania Geological Survey, 2nd ser., Report HH, 194 p.

Platt, L. B., Loring, R. B., Papaspyros, Athanasios, and Stephens, G. C. (1972), *The Hamburg klippe reconsidered,* American Journal of Science, v. 272, p. 305–318.

Poag, C. W., and Sevon, W. D. (1989), *A record of Appalachian denudation in postrift Mesozoic and Cenozoic sedimentary deposits of the U.S. Middle Atlantic continental margin,* in Gardner, T. W., and Sevon, W. D., eds., *Appalachian geomorphology,* Amsterdam, Elsevier, p. 119–157 [reprinted from Geomorphology, v. 2, no. 1–3].

Pohn, H. A., and Purdy, T. L. (1982), *Disturbed zones: indicators of deep-seated subsurface faults in the Valley and Ridge and Appalachian structural front of Pennsylvania,* U.S. Geological Survey Open-File Report 82-967, 42 p.

Polak, A. B. (1975), *Glass: its traditions and its makers,* New York, Putnam, 224 p.

Pollack, J. B. (1982), *Solar, astronomical, and atmospheric effects on climate,* in Geophysics Study Committee and others, *Climate in earth history,* Washington, D. C., National Academy Press, p. 68–76.

Pollack, Jonathan (1992), *Pedo-geomorphology of the Pennsylvania Piedmont,* University Park, Pennsylvania State University, M.S. thesis, 294 p.

Pomeroy, J. S. (1980), *Storm-induced debris avalanching and related phenomena in the Johnstown area, Pennsylvania, with references to other studies in the Appalachians,* U.S. Geological Survey Professional Paper 1191, 24 p.

_____ (1982a), *Landslides in the Greater Pittsburgh region, Pennsylvania,* U.S. Geological Survey Professional Paper 1229, 48 p.

_____ (1982b), *Mass movement in two selected areas of western Washington County, Pennsylvania,* U.S. Geological Survey Professional Paper 1170-B, 17 p.

_____ (1984), *Storm-induced slope movements at East Brady, northwestern Pennsylvania,* U.S. Geological Survey Bulletin 1618, 16 p.

Pomeroy, J. S., and Popp, J. W. (1982), *Storm-induced landsliding, June 1981, in northwestern Pennsylvania,* Pennsylvania Geology, v. 13, no. 2, p. 12–15.

Pope, Joan, and Gorecki, R. J. (1982), *Geologic and engineering history of Presque Isle Peninsula, PA,* in Buehler, E. J., and Calkin, P. E., eds., *Guidebook for field trips in western New York, northern Pennsylvania, and adjacent southern Ontario—Geology of the north-*

ern Appalachian basin, western New York, New York State Geological Association Annual Meeting, 54th, Amherst, N. Y., p. 183–216.

Popenoe, Peter, Petty, A. J., and Tyson, N. S. (1964), *Aeromagnetic map of western Pennsylvania and parts of eastern Ohio, northern West Virginia, and western Maryland*, U.S. Geological Survey Geophysical Investigations Map GP–445, scale 1:250,000.

Popper, G. H. (1982), *National uranium resource evaluation, Harrisburg quadrangle, Pennsylvania*, U.S. Department of Energy Open-File Report PGJ/F–086(82), 39 p.

Popper, G. H., and Martin, T. S. (1981), *Uranium resource evaluation, Newark quadrangle, Pennsylvania and New Jersey*, U.S. Department of Energy Open-File Report PGJ–123(81), 97 p.

Postel, A. W. (1940), *Hydrothermal emplacement of granodiorite near Philadelphia*, Philadelphia Academy of Natural Science Proceedings, v. 92, p. 123–152.

Potential Gas Agency (1983), *Potential supply of natural gas in the United States (as of December 31, 1982)—Report of the Potential Gas Committee*, Golden, Colorado School of Mines, 74 p.

Poth, C. W. (1962), *The occurrence of brine in western Pennsylvania*, Pennsylvania Geological Survey, 4th ser., Mineral Resource Report 47, 53 p.

———— (1963), *Geology and hydrology of the Mercer quadrangle, Mercer, Lawrence, and Butler Counties, Pennsylvania*, Pennsylvania Geological Survey, 4th ser., Water Resource Report 16, 149 p.

Potter, Noel, Jr. (1985), *Colluvial and alluvial gravels, carbonate weathering, and the preservation of a Cenozoic erosional history in the Great Valley, southcentral Pennsylvania* [abs.], Geological Society of America Abstracts with Programs, v. 17, no. 1, p. 59.

Potter, Noel, Jr., and Moss, J. H. (1968), *Origin of the Blue Rocks block field and adjacent deposits, Berks County, Pennsylvania*, Geological Society of America Bulletin, v. 79, p. 255–262.

Potter, P. E., Maynard, J. B., and Pryor, W. A. (1981), *Sedimentology of gas-bearing Devonian shales of the Appalachian basin*, U.S. Department of Energy, USDOE/METC–114, Morgantown, W. Va., 43 p.

Power, W. R. (1975), *Dimension and cut stone*, in Lefond, S. J., ed., *Industrial minerals and rocks*, 4th ed., New York, American Institute of Mining, Metallurgical, and Petroleum Engineers, p. 157–174.

Preston, F. W. (1977), *Drainage changes in the late Pleistocene in central western Pennsylvania*, Pittsburgh, Carnegie Museum of Natural History, 56 p.

Price, J. W. (1953), *A history of the magnetite mines of Conestoga and Martic Townships*, Papers of Lancaster County Historical Society, v. 56.

Price, P. H., and Headlee, A. J. W. (1937), *Physical and chemical properties of natural gas of West Virginia*, West Virginia Geological Survey, v. 9, 223 p.

Prosser, L. J., Jr., and Berkheiser, S. W., Jr. (1987), *The mineral industry of Pennsylvania*, preprint from U.S. Bureau of Mines Minerals Yearbook 1986, 11 p.

———— (1988), *The mineral industry of Pennsylvania*, in *Area reports: domestic*, U.S. Bureau of Mines Minerals Yearbook 1986, v. 2, p. 407–417.

Prosser, L. J., Jr., and Smith, R. C. (1987a), *The mineral industry of Pennsylvania*, in *Area reports: domestic*, U.S. Bureau of Mines Minerals Yearbook 1985, v. 2, p. 475–485.

———— (1987b), *The mineral industry of Pennsylvania in 1985*, Pennsylvania Geological Survey, 4th ser., Information Circular 96, 11 p.

———— (1989), *The mineral industry of Pennsylvania*, in *Area reports: domestic*, U.S. Bureau of Mines Minerals Yearbook 1987, v. 2, p. 331–338.

Prosser, L. J., Jr., Socolow, A. A., and Berkheiser, S. W., Jr. (1986), *The mineral industry of Pennsylvania*, in *Area reports: domestic*, U.S. Bureau of Mines Minerals Yearbook 1984, v. 2, p. 501–513.

Prosser, L. J., Socolow, A. A., and Smith, R. C. (1984), *The mineral industry of Pennsylvania*, preprint from U.S. Bureau of Mines Minerals Yearbook 1983, 14 p.

———— (1985a), *The mineral industry of Pennsylvania*, in *Area reports: domestic*, U.S. Bureau of Mines Minerals Yearbook 1983, v. 2, p. 467–480.

———— (1985b), *The mineral industry of Pennsylvania in 1983*, Pennsylvania Geological Survey, 4th ser., Information Circular 94, 14 p.

Prucha, J. J. (1968), *Salt deformation and décollement in the Fir Tree Point anticline of central New York*, Tectonophysics, v. 6, p. 273–299.

Quinlan, G. M., and Beaumont, C. (1984), *Appalachian thrusting, lithospheric flexure, and the Paleozoic stratigraphy of the eastern interior of North America*, Canadian Journal of the Earth Sciences, v. 21, p. 973–996.

Radbruch-Hall, D. H., Colton, R. B., Davies, W. E., and others (1982), *Landslide overview map of the conterminous United States*, U.S. Geological Survey Professional Paper 1183, 25 p.

Rankin, D. W. (1975), *The continental margin of eastern North America in the southern Appalachians: the opening and closing of the proto-Atlantic ocean*, American Journal of Science, v. 275–A, p. 298–336.

———— (1976), *Appalachian salients and recesses: late Precambrian continental breakup and the opening of the Iapetus Ocean*, Journal of Geophysical Research, v. 81, p. 5605–5619.

Rankin, D. W., Drake, A. A., Jr., Glover, L., III, and others (1989), *Pre-orogenic terranes*, in Hatcher, R. D., Jr., Thomas, W. A., and Viele, G. W., eds., *The Appalachian-Ouachita orogen in the United States*, Geological Society of America, The Geology of North America, v. F–2, p. 7–100.

Rankin, D. W., Stern, T. W., McLelland, James, and others (1983), *Correlation chart for Precambrian rocks of the eastern United States*, U.S. Geological Survey Professional Paper 1241–E, 18 p.

Rankin, D. W., Stern, T. W., Reed, J. C., Jr., and Newell, M. F. (1969), *Zircon ages of felsic volcanic rocks in the upper Precambrian of the Blue Ridge, central and southern Appalachian Mountains*, Science, v. 166, p. 741–744.

Ratcliffe, N. M. (1988), *Reinterpretation of the relationship of the western extension of the Palisades sill to the lava flows at Ladentown, New York, based on new core data*, in Froelich, A. J., and Robinson, G. R., Jr., eds., *Studies of the early Mesozoic basins of the Eastern United States*, U.S. Geological Survey Bulletin 1776, p. 113–135.

Ratcliffe, N. M., and Burton, W. C. (1985), *Fault reactivation models for origin of the Newark basin and studies related to Eastern U.S. seismicity*, in Robinson, G. R., Jr., and Froelich, A. J., eds., *Proceedings of the Second U.S. Geological Survey Workshop on the Early Mesozoic Basins of the Eastern United States*, U.S. Geological Survey Circular 946, p. 36–45.

———— (1988), *Structural analysis of the Furlong fault and the relation of mineralization to faulting and diabase intrusion, Newark basin, Pennsylvania*, in Froelich, A. J., and Robinson, G. R., Jr., eds., *Studies of the early Mesozoic basins of the Eastern United States*, U.S. Geological Survey Bulletin 1776, p. 176–193.

Ratcliffe, N. M., Burton, W. C., D'Angelo, R. M., and Costain, J. K. (1986), *Low-angle extensional faulting, reactivated mylonites, and seismic reflection geometry of the Newark basin margin in eastern Pennsylvania*, Geology, v. 14, p. 766–770.

Rauch, H. W., and White, W. B. (1970), *Lithologic controls on the development of solution porosity in carbonate aquifers*, Water Resources Research, v. 6, p. 1175–1192.

Rautman, C. A., compiler (1980), *Geology and mineral technology of the Grants uranium region 1979*, New Mexico Bureau of Mines and Mineral Resources Memoir 38, 400 p.

Raymond, P. E. (1911), *A preliminary list of the fauna of the Allegheny and Conemaugh Series in western Pennsylvania*, Pennsylvania Geological Survey, 3rd ser., Biennial Report 1908–1910, p. 81–98.

Read, C. B. (1946), *A Pennsylvanian florule from the Forkton coal in the Dutch Mountain outlier, northeastern Pennsylvania*, U.S. Geological Survey Professional Paper 210–B, p. 17–28.

Read, C. B. (1955), *Floras of the Pocono Formation and Price Sandstone in parts of Pennsylvania, Maryland, West Virginia, and Virginia,* U.S. Geological Survey Professional Paper 263, 32 p.

Read, C. B., and Mamay, S. H. (1964), *Upper Paleozoic floral zones and floral provinces of the United States,* U.S. Geological Survey Professional Paper 454–K, 35 p.

Read, J. F. (1980), *Carbonate ramp-to-basin transitions and foreland basin evolution, Middle Ordovician, Virginia Appalachians,* AAPG Bulletin, v. 64, p. 1575–1612.

Reed, J. C., Jr. (1955), *Catoctin Formation near Luray, Virginia,* Geological Society of America Bulletin, v. 66, p. 871–896.

Reed, J. C., Jr., and Morgan, B. A. (1971), *Chemical alteration and spilitization of the Catoctin greenstones, Shenandoah National Park, Virginia,* Journal of Geology, v. 79, p. 526–548.

Reger, D. B. (1927), *Pocono stratigraphy in the Broadtop basin of Pennsylvania,* Geological Society of America Bulletin, v. 38, p. 397–410.

———— (1931), *Pennsylvanian cycles in West Virginia,* Illinois State Geological Survey Bulletin 60, p. 217–239.

Reich, J. R., Jr., compiler (1974), *Caves of southeastern Pennsylvania,* Pennsylvania Geological Survey, 4th ser., General Geology Report 65, 120 p.

Repetski, J. E. (1984a), *Conodonts from Spitzenberg,* in Lash, G. G., and others, eds., *Geology of an accreted terrane: the eastern Hamburg klippe and surrounding rocks, eastern Pennsylvania,* Annual Field Conference of Pennsylvania Geologists, 49th, Reading, Pa., Guidebook, p. 94–101.

———— (1984b), *Conodonts from the Greenwich slice of the Hamburg klippe near Greenawald, Pennsylvania,* in Lash, G. G., and others, eds., *Geology of an accreted terrane: the eastern Hamburg klippe and surrounding rocks, eastern Pennsylvania,* Annual Field Conference of Pennsylvania Geologists, 49th, Reading, Pa., Guidebook, p. 92–93.

Resource Technologies Corporation (1984), *Defining the anthracite resources of north-eastern Pennsylvania,* U.S. Bureau of Mines Contract J0333932, 228 p.

Revetta, F. A. (1970), *A regional gravity survey of New York and eastern Pennsylvania,* Rochester, N.Y., University of Rochester, Ph.D. thesis, 230 p.

Reynolds, J. H. (1979), *LANDSAT linear features of West Virginia,* West Virginia Geological and Economic Survey Map WV–7.

Rhinehart, J. (1979), *Lithofacies and paleoenvironments of Guelph-Lockport Group (Middle Silurian), subsurface of western Pennsylvania,* State University of New York, College at Fredonia, M.S. thesis, 109 p.

Rice, B. J. (1983), *Major crustal lineaments and the Rome trough in West Virginia,* University Park, Pennsylvania State University, M.S. thesis, 58 p.

Rice, C. L., and Schwietering, J. F. (1988), *Fluvial deposition in the central Appalachians during the Early Pennsylvanian,* U.S. Geological Survey Bulletin 1839, p. B1–B10.

Richardson, G. B. (1904), *Indiana folio, Pennsylvania,* U.S. Geological Survey Geologic Atlas of the U.S., Folio 102, 7 p.

Rickard, L. V. (1969), *Stratigraphy of the Upper Silurian Salina Group, New York, Pennsylvania, Ohio, Ontario,* New York State Museum and Science Service Map and Chart Series 12, 57 p.

———— (1975), *Correlation of the Silurian and Devonian rocks in New York State,* New York State Museum and Science Service Map and Chart Series 24, 16 p.

Ridge, J. D., ed. (1968), *Ore deposits of the United States, 1933–1967,* New York, American Institute of Mining, Metallurgical, and Petroleum Engineers, 2 v., 1,880 p.

Rima, D. R. (1955), *Ground water resources of the Lansdale area, Pennsylvania,* Pennsylvania Geological Survey, 4th ser., Progress Report 146, 24 p.

Rivers, T., Martignole, J., Gower, C. F., and Davidson, A. (1989), *New tectonic divisions of the Grenville province, southeast Canadian Shield,* Tectonics, v. 8, p. 63–84.

Roberts, F. R. (1969), *Ultramafic rocks along the Precambrian axis of southeastern Pennsylvania,* Bryn Mawr, Pa., Bryn Mawr College, Ph.D. thesis, 50 p.

Robinson, G. R., Jr. (1985), *Magnetite skarn deposits of the Cornwall (Pennsylvania) type—a potential cobalt, gold, and silver resource,* in Robinson, G. R., Jr., and Froelich, A. J., eds., *Proceedings of the Second U.S. Geological Survey Workshop on the Early Mesozoic Basins of the Eastern United States,* U.S. Geological Survey Circular 946, p. 126–128.

———— (1988), *Base and precious metals associated with diabase in the Newark, Gettysburg, and Culpeper basins of the Eastern United States,* in Froelich, A. J., and Robinson, G. R., Jr., eds., *Studies of the early Mesozoic basins of the Eastern United States,* U.S. Geological Survey Bulletin 1776, p. 303–320.

Robinson, P. L. (1973), *Palaeoclimatology and continental drift,* in Tarling, D. H., and Runcorn, S. K., eds., *Implications of continental drift to the earth sciences, Volume 1,* London, Academic Press, p. 451–476.

Rockwood, C. G. (1885), *Notes on American earthquakes,* American Journal of Science, 3rd ser., v. 29, p. 425–437.

Roden, M. K., and Miller, D. S. (1989), *Apatite fission-track thermochronology of the Pennsylvania Appalachian basin,* in Gardner, T. W., and Sevon, W. D., eds., *Appalachian geomorphology,* Amsterdam, Elsevier, p. 39–51 [reprinted from Geomorphology, v. 2, no. 1–3].

Rodgers, John (1949), *Evolution of thought on structure of middle and southern Appalachians,* AAPG Bulletin, v. 33, p. 1643–1654.

———— (1963), *Mechanics of Appalachian foreland folding in Pennsylvania and West Virginia,* AAPG Bulletin, v. 47, p. 1527–1536.

———— (1968), *The eastern edge of the North American continent during the Cambrian and Early Ordovician,* in Zen, E-an, and others, eds., *Studies of Appalachian geology: northern and maritime,* New York, Interscience Publishers, p. 141–149.

———— (1970), *The tectonics of the Appalachians,* New York, Wiley-Interscience, 271 p.

Rodgers, M. R., and Anderson, T. H. (1984), *Tyrone-Mt. Union cross-strike lineament of Pennsylvania: a major Paleozoic basement fracture and uplift boundary,* AAPG Bulletin, v. 68, p. 92–105.

Roe, L. M., II, and Martin, T. S. (1982), *Williamsport quadrangle, Pennsylvania and New York,* U.S. Department of Energy, National Uranium Resource Evaluation Program, PGJ/F–085(82), 24 p.

Roen, J. B. (1968), *A transcurrent structure in Fayette and Greene Counties, Pennsylvania,* in *Geological Survey research 1968, Chapter C,* U.S. Geological Survey Professional Paper 600–C, p. C149–C152.

Roen, J. B., and Hosterman, J. W. (1982), *Misuse of the term "bentonite" for ash beds of Devonian age in the Appalachian basin,* Geological Society of America Bulletin, v. 93, p. 921–925.

Roen, J. B., and Kreimeyer, D. F. (1973), *Preliminary map showing the distribution and thickness of sandstone in the lower member of the Pittsburgh Formation, southwestern Pennsylvania and northern West Virginia,* U.S. Geological Survey Miscellaneous Field Studies Map MF–529, scale 1:250,000.

Rogers, H. D. (1858a), *On the laws of structure of the more disturbed zones of the earth's crust,* in *The geology of Pennsylvania—A government survey,* Philadelphia, J. B. Lippincott, v. 2, p. 885–916.

———— (1858b), *The geology of Pennsylvania—A government survey,* Edinburgh, William Blackwood and Sons [Philadelphia, J. B. Lippincott], v. 1, 586 p., v. 2, 1,045 p.

Rogers, J. J. W., and Adams, J. A. S. (1970), *Uranium,* in Wedepohl, K. H., ed., *Handbook of geochemistry,* Berlin, Springer-Verlag, p. 92E1—92G–3.

Rollins, H. B., Carothers, Marshall, and Donahue, Jack (1979), *Transgression, regression and fossil community succession,* Lethaia, v. 12, p. 89–104.

Rollins, H. B., and Donahue, Jack (1975), *Towards a theoretical basis of paleoecology: concepts of community dynamics,* Lethaia, v. 8, p. 255–270.

Rones, Morris (1969), *A lithostratigraphic, petrographic and chemical investigation of the lower Middle Ordovician carbonate rocks in central Pennsylvania,* Pennsylvania Geological Survey, 4th ser., General Geology Report 53, 224 p.

Root, S. I. (1968), *Geology and mineral resources of southeastern Franklin County, Pennsylvania,* Pennsylvania Geological Survey, 4th ser., Atlas 119cd, 118 p.

_____ (1970), *Structure of the northern terminus of the Blue Ridge in Pennsylvania,* Geological Society of America Bulletin, v. 81, p. 815–830.

_____ (1971), *Geology and mineral resources of northeastern Franklin County, Pennsylvania,* Pennsylvania Geological Survey, 4th ser., Atlas 119ab, 104 p.

_____ (1973a), *Sequence of faulting, southern Great Valley of Pennsylvania,* American Journal of Science, v. 273, p. 97–112.

_____ (1973b), *Structure, basin development, and tectogenesis in the Pennsylvania portion of the folded Appalachians,* in De Jong, K. A., and Scholten, Robert, eds., *Gravity and tectonics,* New York, John Wiley and Sons, p. 343–360.

_____ (1977), *Geology and mineral resources of the Harrisburg West area, Cumberland and York Counties, Pennsylvania,* Pennsylvania Geological Survey, 4th ser., Atlas 148ab, 106 p.

_____ (1978), *Possible recurrent basement faulting, Pennsylvania: Part 1, Geologic framework,* Pennsylvania Geological Survey, 4th ser., Open-File Report, 23 p.

_____ (1988), *Structure and hydrocarbon potential of the Gettysburg basin, Pennsylvania and Maryland,* in Manspeizer, W., ed., *Triassic-Jurassic rifting—Continental breakup and the origin of the Atlantic Ocean and passive margins,* Amsterdam, Elsevier, p. 353–367.

_____ (1989), *Basement control of structure in the Gettysburg rift basin, Pennsylvania and Maryland,* Tectonophysics, v. 166, p. 281–292.

Root, S. I., and Hoskins, D. M. (1977), *Lat 40°N fault zone, Pennsylvania: a new interpretation,* Geology, v. 5, p. 719–723.

Root, S. I., and MacLachlan, D. B. (1978), *Western limit of the Taconic allochthons in Pennsylvania,* Geological Society of America Bulletin, v. 89, p. 1515–1528.

Rose, A. W. (1970), *Atlas of Pennsylvania's mineral resources—Part 3, Metal mines and occurrences in Pennsylvania,* Pennsylvania Geological Survey, 4th ser., Mineral Resource Report 50, pt. 3, 14 p.

Rose, A. W., Herrick, D. C., and Deines, Peter (1985), *An oxygen and sulfur isotope study of skarn-type magnetite deposits of the Cornwall type, southeastern Pennsylvania,* Economic Geology, v. 80, p. 418–443.

Rose, A. W., Smith, A. T., Lustwerk, R. L., and others (1986), *Geochemical aspects of stratiform and red-bed copper deposits in the Catskill Formation (Pennsylvania, USA) and Redstone area (Canada)—Sequence of mineralization in sediment-hosted copper deposits (Part 3),* in Friedrich, G. H., and others, eds., *Geology and metallogeny of copper deposits,* Berlin, Springer-Verlag, p. 412–421.

Rosholt, J. N., Jr. (1959), *Natural radioactive disequilibrium of the uranium series,* U.S. Geological Survey Bulletin 1084–A, p. 1–30.

Ross, C. A., and Ross, J. R. P. (1985), *Carboniferous and Early Permian biogeography,* Geology, v. 13, p. 27–30.

Rowlands, David, and Kanes, W. H. (1972), *The structural geology of a portion of the Broadtop synclinorium, Maryland and south-central Pennsylvania,* in Lessing, Peter, and others, eds., *Appalachian structures—origin, evolution, and possible potential for new exploration frontiers,* West Virginia University and West Virginia Geological and Economic Survey, p. 195–225.

Roy, R. F., Blackwell, D. D., and Birch, Francis (1968), *Heat generation of plutonic rocks and continental heat flow provinces,* Earth and Planetary Science Letters, v. 5, p. 1–12.

Rubey, W. W., and Hubbert, M. K. (1959), *Role of fluid pressure in mechanics of overthrust faulting—II, Overthrust belt in geosynclinal area of western Wyoming in light of fluid-pressure hypothesis,* Geological Society of America Bulletin, v. 70, p. 167–206.

Ruder, M. E., and Alexander, S. S. (1986), *Magsat equivalent source anomalies over the southeastern United States: implications*

for crustal magnetization, Earth and Planetary Science Letters, v. 78, p. 33–43.

Salisbury, R. D., and Knapp, G. N. (1917), *The Quaternary formations of southern New Jersey,* New Jersey Geological Survey, Final Report Series of the State Geologist, v. 8, 218 p.

Saltsman, A. L. (1986), *Paleoenvironments of the Upper Pennsylvanian Ames Limestone and associated rocks near Pittsburgh, Pennsylvania,* Geological Society of America Bulletin, v. 97, p. 222–231.

Sanford, R. S., and Lamb, F. D. (1949), *Investigation of the Benjamin Franklin graphite mine (government owned) and the Just graphite mine, Chester County, Pa.,* U.S. Bureau of Mines Report of Investigations 4530, 17 p.

Sarwar, G. (1984), *Depositional model for the Middle Devonian Mahantango Formation of south-central Pennsylvania,* Stony Brook, State University of New York, M.S. thesis, 251 p.

Sass, D. B. (1960), *Some aspects of the paleontology, stratigraphy, and sedimentation of the Corry Sandstone of northwestern Pennsylvania,* Bulletins of American Paleontology, v. 41, no. 192, p. 251–381.

Saunders, D. F., Terry, S. A., and Thompson, C. K. (1987), *Test of National Uranium Resource Evaluation gamma-ray spectral data in petroleum reconnaissance,* Geophysics, v. 52, p. 1547–1556.

Saunders, W. B., and Ramsbottom, W. H. C. (1986), *The mid-Carboniferous eustatic event,* Geology, v. 14, p. 208–212.

Savin, S. M. (1977), *The history of the earth's surface temperature during the past 100 million years,* Annual Review of Earth and Planetary Sciences, v. 5, p. 319–355.

Saylor, T. E. (1968), *The Precambrian in the subsurface of northwestern Pennsylvania and adjoining areas,* Pennsylvania Geological Survey, 4th ser., Information Circular 62, 25 p.

Sbar, M. L., and Sykes, L. R. (1973), *Contemporary compressive stress and seismicity in eastern North America: an example of intra-plate tectonics,* Geological Society of America Bulletin, v. 84, p. 1861–1882.

Scharnberger, C. K. (1988), *Pennsylvania seismicity reexamined* [abs.], Seismological Research Letters, v. 59, p. 14.

Scharnberger, C. K., and Howell, B. F., Jr. (1985), *Intensities and structural setting of the earthquakes of 19 April and 23 April, 1984, Lancaster County, Pennsylvania,* Earthquake Notes, v. 56, p. 43–46.

Scheckler, S. E. (1986), *Old Red continent facies in the Late Devonian and Early Carboniferous of Appalachian North America,* Annales de la Société Géologique de Belgique, v. 109, p. 223–236.

Schiner, G. R., and Kimmel, G. E. (1972), *Mississippian stratigraphy of northwestern Pennsylvania,* U.S. Geological Survey Bulletin 1331–A, 27 p.

Schlee, J. S. (1981), *Seismic stratigraphy of Baltimore Canyon trough,* AAPG Bulletin, v. 65, p. 26–53.

Schlische, R. W., and Olsen, P. E. (1990), *Quantitative filling model for continental extensional basins with applications to early Mesozoic rifts of eastern North America,* Journal of Geology, v. 98, p. 135–155.

Schmiermund, R. L. (1977), *Geology and geochemistry of uranium deposits near Penn Haven Junction, Carbon County, Pennsylvania,* Pennsylvania State University, M.S. thesis, 152 p.

Schooler, E. E. (1974), *Pleistocene beach ridges of northwestern Pennsylvania,* Pennsylvania Geological Survey, 4th ser., General Geology Report 64, 38 p.

Schopf, D. Johann David (1787), *Beitraege zur mineralogischen Kenntniss des östlichen Teils von Nordamerika und seiner Gebürge,* Erlangen, Joh. Jacob Palm, 195 p.

_____ (1788), *Reise durch einige der mittlern und südlichen vereinigten nordamerikanischen staaten nach Ost-Florida und den Bahama-Inseln, unternommen in den Jahren 1783 und 1784—Mit einem hand chärtchen,* Erlangen, Joh. Jacob Palm, 2 v.

Schroder, J. (1963), *Apparatus for determining the thermal conductivity of solids in the temperature range from 20 deg to 200 deg,* Review of Scientific Instruments, v. 34, p. 615–621.

Schuster, R. L., and Krizek, R. J., eds. (1978), *Landslides: analysis and control,* National Research Council Special Report 176, Washington, D. C., Transportation Research Board, 234 p.

Schwab, F. L. (1972), *The Chilhowee Group and the late Precambrian-early Paleozoic sedimentary framework in the central and southern Appalachians,* in Lessing, P., and others, eds., *Appalachian structures—origin, elevation, and possible potential for new exploration frontiers,* West Virginia University and West Virginia Geological and Economic Survey, p. 59–101.

Scotese, C. R., Bambach, R. K., Barton, Colleen, and others (1979), *Paleozoic base maps,* Journal of Geology, v. 87, p. 217–277.

Scott, D. F., and Aiken, J. D. (1982), *Continental platforms and basins of Canada,* in Palmer, A. R., ed., *Perspectives in regional geological synthesis: planning for the Geology of North America,* Geological Society of America, DNAG Special Publication 1, p. 15–26.

Seaman, D. M. (1940), *The Ames Limestone of western Pennsylvania,* Pennsylvania Academy of Science Proceedings, v. 14, p. 77–80.

———— (1941), *The Cambridge (Pine Creek) limestone of western Pennsylvania,* Pennsylvania Academy of Science Proceedings, v. 15, p. 60–65.

———— (1942), *The Brush Creek limestone of western Pennsylvania,* Pennsylvania Academy of Science Proceedings, v. 16, p. 72–76.

Sears, C. E. (1964), *Geophysics and Appalachian structure* [abs.], Geological Society of America Special Paper 76, p. 257.

Sedgwick, Adam, and Murchison, R. I. (1839), *On the physical structure of Devonshire, and on its subdivision and geological relation of its older stratified deposits, &c.,* Geological Society of London Transactions, 2nd ser., v. 5, pt. 3, p. 633–704.

Sevon, W. D. (1969a), *Sedimentology of some Mississippian and Pleistocene deposits of northeastern Pennsylvania,* in Subitzky, Seymour, ed., *Geology of selected areas in New Jersey and eastern Pennsylvania and guidebook of excursions,* New Brunswick, N. J., Rutgers University Press, p. 214–234.

———— (1969b), *The Pocono Formation in northeastern Pennsylvania,* Annual Field Conference of Pennsylvania Geologists, 34th, Hazleton, Pa., Guidebook, 129 p.

———— (1974), *Relative age and sequence of glacial deposits in Carbon and Monroe Counties, Pennsylvania* [abs.], Geological Society of America Abstracts with Programs, v. 6, no. 1, p. 71.

———— (1975), *Sandstone saprolite, roundstone diamicton and the Harrisburg peneplain in eastern Pennsylvania* [abs.], Geological Society of America Abstracts with Programs, v. 7, no. 1, p. 118.

———— (1979a), *Polymictic diamictites in the Spechty Kopf and Rockwell Formations,* in Dennison, J. M., and others, *Devonian shales in south-central Pennsylvania and Maryland,* Annual Field Conference of Pennsylvania Geologists, 44th, Bedford, Pa., Guidebook, p. 61–66.

———— (1979b), *Stop 12, Crystal Spring,* in Dennison, J. M., and others, *Devonian shales in south-central Pennsylvania and Maryland,* Annual Field Conference of Pennsylvania Geologists, 44th, Bedford, Pa., Guidebook, p. 107–110.

———— (1981), *Evidence for the reality and age of the Chambersburg peneplane in southeastern Pennsylvania* [abs.], Geological Society of America Abstracts with Programs, v. 13, no. 3, p. 176.

———— (1985a), *Nonmarine facies of the Middle and Late Devonian Catskill coastal alluvial plain,* in Woodrow, D. L., and Sevon, W. D., eds., *The Catskill delta,* Geological Society of America Special Paper 201, p. 79–90.

———— (1985b), *Pennsylvania landscape development* [abs.], Geological Society of America Abstracts with Programs, v. 17, no. 7, p. 713.

———— (1985c), *Pennsylvania's polygenetic landscape,* Harrisburg Area Geological Society Annual Field Trip, 4th, Guidebook, 55 p.

———— (1987a), *The Hickory Run boulder field, a periglacial relict, Carbon County, Pennsylvania,* in Roy, D. C., ed., *Northeastern Section of the Geological Society of America,* Geological Society of America Centennial Field Guide, v. 5, p. 75–76.

———— (1987b), *The Third Geological Survey of Pennsylvania: the topographic years,* Pennsylvania Geology, v. 18, no. 1, p. 16–22.

———— (1988), *Saprolite,* in Thompson, G. H., Jr., coordinator, *The geology of the lower Susquehanna River area: a new look at some old answers,* Harrisburg Area Geological Society Annual Field Trip, 7th, Guidebook, p. 7–17.

———— (1989a), *Erosion in the Juniata River drainage basin, Pennsylvania,* in Gardner, T. W., and Sevon, W. D., eds., *Appalachian geomorphology,* Amsterdam, Elsevier, p. 303–318 [reprinted from Geomorphology, v. 2, no. 1–3].

———— compiler (1989b), *Surficial materials of Pennsylvania,* Pennsylvania Geological Survey, 4th ser., Map 64, scale 1:2,000,000.

———— (1989c), *The rivers and valleys of Pennsylvania—Then and now,* Annual Geomorphology Symposium, 20th, Carlisle, Pa., 1989, Guidebook, Harrisburg Area Geological Society, 59 p.

———— (1990), *The Hickory Run boulder field, Hickory Run State Park, Carbon County, Pennsylvania,* Northeastern Geology, v. 12, p. 42–45.

———— (1992), *Surficial geology and geomorphology of Warren County, Pa.,* in Sevon, W. D., ed., *Geology of the upper Allegheny River region in Warren County, northwestern Pennsylvania,* Annual Field Conference of Pennsylvania Geologists, 57th, Warren, Pa., Guidebook, p. 67–92.

———— (1994), *Solution below, injection within, and subsidence throughout alluvial-fan deposits, South Mountain, Pennsylvania* [abs.], Geological Society of America Abstracts with Programs, v. 26, no. 3, p. 72.

Sevon, W. D., and Berg, T. M. (1979), *Pennsylvania shale-chip rubble,* Pennsylvania Geology, v. 10, no. 6, p. 2–7.

———— (1986), *Polymictic diamictites and associated lacustrine deposits at the Mississippian-Devonian boundary in Pennsylvania* [abs.], Geological Society of America Abstracts with Programs, v. 18, no. 1, p. 65.

Sevon, W. D., Berg, T. M., Schultz, L. D., and Crowl, G. H. (1989), *Geology and mineral resources of Pike County, Pennsylvania,* Pennsylvania Geological Survey, 4th ser., County Report 52, 141 p.

Sevon, W. D., and Braun, D. D. (1997), *Glacial deposits of Pennsylvania,* 2nd ed., Pennsylvania Geological Survey, 4th ser., Map 59, scale 1:2,000,000.

Sevon, W. D., Crowl, G. H., and Berg, T. M. (1975), *The late Wisconsinan drift border in northeastern Pennsylvania,* Annual Field Conference of Pennsylvania Geologists, 40th, Bartonsville, Pa., Guidebook, 108 p.

Sevon, W. D., Potter, Noel, Jr., and Crowl, G. H. (1983), *Appalachian peneplains: an historical review,* in Jordan, W. M., ed., *History of geology and geological concepts in the northeastern United States,* Earth Sciences History, v. 2, p. 156–164.

Sevon, W. D., Rose, A. W., Smith, R. C., II, and Hoff, D. T. (1978), *Uranium in Carbon, Lycoming, Sullivan, and Columbia Counties, Pennsylvania,* Annual Field Conference of Pennsylvania Geologists, 43rd, Hazleton, Pa., Guidebook, 99 p.

Sevon, W. D., Van Scyoc, R. L., and Chichester, D. C. (1991), *Stop 6, Mainsville quarry, Valley Quarries, Inc.,* in Sevon, W. D., and Potter, Noel, Jr., eds., *Geology in the South Mountain area, Pennsylvania,* Annual Field Conference of Pennsylvania Geologists, 56th, Carlisle, Pa., Guidebook, p. 176–188.

Sevon, W. D., and Woodrow, D. L. (1981), *Upper Devonian sedimentology and stratigraphy,* in Berg, T. M., and others, *Geology of Tioga and Bradford Counties, Pennsylvania,* Annual Field Conference of Pennsylvania Geologists, 46th, Wellsboro, Pa., Guidebook, p. 11–26.

Shaak, G. D. (1972), *Species diversity and community structure of the Brush Creek marine interval (Conemaugh Group, Upper Pennsylvanian) in the Appalachian basin of western Pennsylvania,* University of Pittsburgh, Ph.D. thesis, 105 p.

Shaffner, M. N. (1958), *Geology and mineral resources of the New Florence quadrangle, Pennsylvania,* Pennsylvania Geological Survey, 4th ser., Atlas 57, 165 p.

Shank, W. H. (1972), *Great floods of Pennsylvania,* York, Pa., American Canal and Transportation Center, 90 p.

———— (1988), *Indian trails to super highways,* York, Pa., American Canal and Transportation Center, 71 p.

Sharp, M. B., and Thomas, W. H. (1966), *A guide to the old stone blast furnaces in western Pennsylvania,* Pittsburgh, Historical Society of western Pennsylvania, 90 p.

Shaub, F. J. (1975), *Interpretation of a gravity profile across the Gettysburg Triassic basin,* University Park, Pennsylvania State University, M.S. thesis, 65 p.

Shaw, H. F., and Wasserburg, G. J. (1984), *Isotopic constraints on the origin of Appalachian mafic complexes,* American Journal of Science, v. 284, p. 319–349.

Shaw, J. B. (1928), *Fire clays of Pennsylvania,* Pennsylvania Geological Survey, 4th ser., Mineral Resource Report 10, 69 p.

Shaw, L. C., and Busch, W. F. (1970), *Pennsylvania gazetteer of streams, Part I,* Pennsylvania Department of Forests and Waters Water Resources Bulletin 6, 280 p.

Shepard, F. P. (1937), *Origin of the Great Lakes basins,* Journal of Geology, v. 45, p. 76–88.

Shepps, V. C., White, G. W., Droste, J. B., and Sitler, R. F. (1959), *Glacial geology of northwestern Pennsylvania,* Pennsylvania Geological Survey, 4th ser., General Geology Report 32, 59 p.

Sherrill, R. E. (1934), *Symmetry of northern Appalachian foreland folds,* Journal of Geology, v. 42, p. 225–247.

Sherrill, R. E., and Matteson, L. S. (1941), *Oil and gas geology of the Franklin quadrangle, Pennsylvania,* Pennsylvania Geological Survey, 4th ser., Mineral Resource Report 24, 71 p.

Shervais, J. W., Taylor, L. A., and Laul, J. C. (1987), *Magma mixing and kimberlite genesis; mineralogic, petrologic, and trace element evidence from eastern U.S.A. kimberlites,* in Morris, E. M., and Pasteris, J. D., eds., *Mantle metasomatism and alkaline magmatism,* Geological Society of America Special Paper 215, p. 101–114.

Sherwood, Andrew (1878), *Limits of the Catskill and Chemung Formations,* in Sherwood, Andrew, and others, *Report of progress in Bradford and Tioga Counties,* Pennsylvania Geological Survey, 2nd ser., Report G, p. 1–96.

Sherwood, W. C. (1964), *Structure of the Jacksonburg Formation in Northampton and Lehigh Counties, Pennsylvania,* Pennsylvania Geological Survey, 4th ser., General Geology Report 45, 64 p.

Shideler, G. L., Ludwick, J. C., Oertel, G. F., and Finkelstein, Kenneth (1984), *Quaternary stratigraphic evolution of the southern Delmarva Peninsula coastal zone, Cape Charles, Virginia,* Geological Society of America Bulletin, v. 95, p. 489–502.

Sholes, M. A., Edmunds, W. E., and Skema, V. W. (1979), *The economic geology of the Upper Freeport coal in the New Stanton area of Westmoreland County, Pennsylvania: a model for coal exploration,* Pennsylvania Geological Survey, 4th ser., Mineral Resource Report 75, 51 p.

Sholes, M. A., and Skema, V. W., compilers (1974), *Bituminous coal resources in western Pennsylvania,* Pennsylvania Geological Survey, 4th ser., Mineral Resource Report 68, scale 1:250,000, 7 sheets.

Shukla, Vijai, and Friedman, G. M. (1983), *Dolomitization and diagenesis in a shallowing-upward sequence: the Lockport Formation (Middle Silurian), New York State,* Journal of Sedimentary Petrology, v. 53, p. 703–717.

Shumaker, R. C. (1976), *A digest of Appalachian structural geology,* in *Proceedings of the Seventh Annual Appalachian Petroleum Geology Symposium—Devonian shale—production and potential,* West Virginia Geological and Economic Survey, West Virginia University Department of Geology and Geography, and U.S. Energy Research and Development Administration, p. 75–78.

Sibol, M. S., Bollinger, G. A., and Birch, J. B. (1987), *Estimation of magnitudes in central and eastern North America using intensity and felt area,* Seismological Society of America Bulletin, v. 77, p. 1635–1654.

Simpson, E. L., and Eriksson, K. A. (1989), *Sedimentology of the Unicoi Formation in southern and central Virginia: evidence for late Proterozoic to Early Cambrian rift-to-passive margin transition,* Geological Society of America Bulletin, v. 101, p. 42–54.

Simpson, E. L., and Sundberg, F. A. (1987), *Early Cambrian age for synrift deposits of the Chilhowee Group of southwestern Virginia,* Geology, v. 15, p. 123–126.

Sims, S. J. (1968), *The Grace mine magnetite deposit, Berks County, Pennsylvania,* in Ridge, J. D., ed., *Ore deposits of the United States, 1933–1967,* New York, American Institute of Mining, Metallurgical, and Petroleum Engineers, v. 1, p. 109–124.

Singer, J. C. (1981), *Combustion fossil power systems,* Windsor, Conn., Combustion Engineering, Inc.

Sinha, A. K., and Hanan, B. B. (1987), *Age, origin and tectonic affinity of the Baltimore mafic complex, Maryland* [abs.], Geological Society of America Abstracts with Programs, v. 19, no. 2, p. 129.

Sinkankas, John (1959), *Gemstones of North America,* Princeton, N. J., D. Van Nostrand Company, v. 1, 675 p.

Sites, R. S. (1978), *Structural analysis of the Petersburg lineament, central Appalachians,* Morgantown, West Virginia University, Ph.D. thesis, 434 p.

Skema, V. W., Sholes, M. A., and Edmunds, W. E. (1982), *The economic geology of the Upper Freeport coal in northeastern Greene County, Pennsylvania,* Pennsylvania Geological Survey, 4th ser., Mineral Resource Report 76, 51 p.

Slingerland, Rudy, and Furlong, K. P. (1989), *Geodynamic and geomorphic evolution of the Permo-Triassic Appalachian Mountains,* in Gardner, T. W., and Sevon, W. D., eds., *Appalachian geomorphology,* Amsterdam, Elsevier, p. 23–37 [reprinted from Geomorphology, v. 2, no. 1–3].

Sloss, L. L. (1963), *Sequences in the cratonic interior of North America,* Geological Society of America Bulletin, v. 74, p. 93–114.

Sloto, R. A. (1988), *Simulation of ground-water flow in the lower sand unit of the Potomac-Raritan-Magothy aquifer system, Philadelphia, Pennsylvania,* U.S. Geological Survey Water-Resources Investigations 86–4055, 51 p.

Smith, A. DW. (1893), *Geological map of Pennsylvania,* Pennsylvania Geological Survey, 2nd ser., Atlas to accompany the final report, Atlas sheets 1–4.

_____ (1895), *Report on the Anthracite region,* in Lesley, J. P., and others, *A summary description of the geology of Pennsylvania,* Pennsylvania Geological Survey, 2nd ser., Final Report 1895, v. 3, pt. 1, p. 1916–2152.

Smith, A. G., Briden, J. C., and Drewry, G. E. (1973), *Phanerozoic world maps,* Special Papers in Palaeontology, v. 12, p. 1–42.

Smith, A. T., and Rose, A. W. (1985), *Relation of red-bed copper-uranium occurrences to the regional sedimentology of the Catskill Formation in Pennsylvania,* in Woodrow, D. L., and Sevon, W. D., eds., *The Catskill delta,* Geological Society of America Special Paper 201, p. 183–197.

Smith, H. M. (1940), *Correlation index to aid in interpreting crude-oil analyses,* U.S. Bureau of Mines Technical Paper 610, 34 p.

Smith, H. T. U. (1953), *The Hickory Run boulder field, Carbon County, Pennsylvania,* American Journal of Science, v. 251, p. 625–642.

Smith, L. B. (1912), *Appendix F—A peridotite dike in Fayette and Greene Counties,* Pennsylvania Geological Survey, 3rd ser., Biennial Report 1910–12, p. 150–155.

Smith, L. L. (1931), *Magnetite deposits of French Creek, Pennsylvania,* Pennsylvania Geological Survey, 4th ser., Mineral Resource Report 14, 52 p.

Smith, R. C., II (1973), *Geochemistry of Triassic diabase from southeastern Pennsylvania,* University Park, Pennsylvania State University, Ph.D. thesis, 262 p.

_____ (1977), *Zinc and lead occurrences in Pennsylvania,* Pennsylvania Geological Survey, 4th ser., Mineral Resource Report 72, 318 p.

_____ (1978), *The mineralogy of Pennsylvania, 1966–1975,* Friends of Mineralogy, Pennsylvania Chapter, Special Publication 1, 304 p.

Smith, R. C., II, Berkheiser, S. W., Jr., and Hoff, D. T. (1988), *Locations and analyses of selected early Mesozoic copper occurrences in Pennsylvania,* in Froelich, A. J., and Robinson, G. R., Jr., eds., *Studies of the early Mesozoic basins of the Eastern United States,* U.S. Geological Survey Bulletin 1776, p. 320–332.

Smith, R. C., II, and Hoff, D. T. (1984), *Geology and mineralogy of copper-uranium occurrences in the Picture Rocks and Sonestown quadrangles, Lycoming and Sullivan Counties, Pennsylvania,* Pennsylvania Geological Survey, 4th ser., Mineral Resource Report 80, 271 p.

Smith, R. C., II, Reilly, M. A., Rose, A. W., and others (1987), *Radon: a profound case,* Pennsylvania Geology, v. 18, no. 2, p. 3–7.

Smith, R. C., II, Rose, A. W., and Lanning, R. M. (1975), *Geology and geochemistry of Triassic diabase in Pennsylvania,* Geological Society of America Bulletin, v. 86, p. 943–955.

Smith, R. C., and Speer, J. A. (1980), *Maucherite, $Ni_{11}As_8$, from the State Line district, Lancaster County, Pennsylvania,* Friends of Mineralogy, Pennsylvania Chapter, Newsletter, v. 8, p. 7–11.

Smith, R. D. (1968), *Paleontology of the Columbiana shale near Corsica, Pennsylvania,* Pennsylvania State University, M.S. thesis.

Smith, R. E., and Riddle, D. J. (1984), *Terrain conductivity and its application in site assessment of karstic terrain in central Pennsylvania and Maryland,* in Proceedings—Geologic and geotechnical problems in karstic limestones, Engineering Geologists/American Society of Civil Engineers Meeting, Frederick, Md., 21 p.

Smoot, J. P. (1985), *The closed-basin hypothesis and its use in facies analysis of the Newark Supergroup,* in Robinson, G. R., Jr., and Froelich, A. J., eds., Proceedings of the Second U.S. Geological Survey Workshop on the Early Mesozoic Basins of the Eastern United States, U.S. Geological Survey Circular 946, p. 4–10.

——— (1991), *Sedimentary facies and depositional environments of early Mesozoic Newark Supergroup basins, eastern North America,* Palaeogeography, Palaeoclimatology, Palaeoecology, v. 84, p. 369–423.

Smoot, J. P., and Froelich, A. J. (in review), *Map 5A: Bedrock lithology map of the early Mesozoic Gettysburg basin, Pennsylvania and Maryland,* U.S. Geological Survey Miscellaneous Field Investigation Series (?), scale 1:125,000.

Smoot, J. P., Froelich, A. J., and Parker, R. A. (in review), *Map 4A: Bedrock lithology map of the early Mesozoic western Newark basin and vicinity, New Jersey and Pennsylvania,* U.S. Geological Survey Miscellaneous Field Investigation Series (?), scale 1:125,000.

Smoot, J. P., and Horowitz, M. R. (1988), *Vug-filling diagenetic minerals in early Mesozoic lacustrine mudstones of the Newark Supergroup* [abs.], Geological Society of America Abstracts with Programs, v. 20, no. 7, p. A52.

Smoot, J. P., and Olsen, P. E. (1988), *Massive mudstones in basin analysis and paleoclimatic interpretation of the Newark Supergroup,* in Manspeizer, Warren, ed., Triassic-Jurassic rifting—continental breakup and the origin of the Atlantic Ocean and passive margins, Developments in Geotectonics, v. 22, p. 249–274.

——— (1994), *Climatic cycles as sedimentary controls of rift-basin lacustrine deposits in the early Mesozoic Newark basin based on continuous core,* in Lomando, A. J., Schreiber, B. C., and Harris, P. M., eds., Lacustrine reservoirs and depositional systems, SEPM Core Workshop 19, p. 201–237.

Smoot, J. P., and Simonson, B. M. (1994), *Alkaline authigenic minerals in the early Mesozoic Newark basin, NY, NJ, PA: Evidence for late fluid movement through mudstones* [abs.], American Association of Petroleum Geologists Annual Meeting, 1994, Denver, Colo., Abstracts, p. 261–262.

Smosna, Richard, and Patchen, Douglas (1978), *Silurian evolution of central Appalachian basin,* AAPG Bulletin, v. 62, p. 2308–2328.

Smyth, Pauline (1974), *Fusulinids in the Appalachian basin,* Journal of Paleontology, v. 48, p. 856–858.

Socolow, A. A. (1959a), *Geologic interpretation of aeromagnetic map, Elverson quadrangle,* Pennsylvania Geological Survey, 4th ser., Information Circular 35, 5 p.

——— (1959b), *Geology of a barite occurrence, Fulton County, Pennsylvania,* Pennsylvania Geological Survey, 4th ser., Information Circular 17 [reprinted from Pennsylvania Academy of Science Proceedings, v. 33, 1959, p. 204–208].

——— (1974), *Geologic interpretation of aeromagnetic maps of southeastern Pennsylvania,* Pennsylvania Geological Survey, 4th ser., Information Circular 77, 85 p.

Socolow, A. A., Berg, T. M., Glover, A. D., and others (1980), *Coal resources of Pennsylvania,* Pennsylvania Geological Survey, 4th ser., Information Circular 88, 49 p.

Solley, W. B., Chase, E. B., and Mann, W. B., IV (1980), *Estimated use of water in the United States in 1980,* U.S. Geological Survey Circular 1001, 56 p.

Solley, W. B., Merk, C. F., and Pierce, R. R. (1988), *Estimated use of water in the United States in 1985,* U.S. Geological Survey Circular 1004, 82 p.

Solley, W. B., Pierce, R. R., and Merk, C. F. (1987), *Preliminary water-use estimates in the United States in 1985,* U.S. Geological Survey Open-File Report 87–692, 5 p.

Solley, W. B., Pierre, R. R., and Perlman, H. A. (1993), *Estimated use of water in the United States in 1990,* U.S. Geological Survey Circular 1081, 76 p.

Sosman, R. B. (1938), *Evidence on the intrusion-temperature of peridotites,* American Journal of Science, 5th ser., v. 35–A, p. 353–359.

Southwick, D. L. (1969), *Crystalline rocks of Harford County,* in The geology of Harford County, Maryland, Maryland Geological Survey, p. 1–76, 113–122.

——— (1970), *Structure and petrology of the Harford County part of the Baltimore-State Line gabbro-peridotite complex,* in Fisher, G. W., and others, eds., Studies of Appalachian geology: central and southern, New York, Interscience Publishers, p. 397–415.

Sowers, G. F. (1975), *Failures in limestones in humid subtropics,* Journal of the Soil Mechanics and Foundation Division, American Society of Civil Engineers, Proceedings, v. 101, p. 771–787.

Spencer, A. C. (1908), *Magnetite deposits of the Cornwall type in Pennsylvania,* U.S. Geological Survey Bulletin 359, 102 p.

Spencer, J. W. (1891), *Origin of the basins of the Great Lakes of America,* American Geologist, v. 7, p. 86–97.

Spoljaric, Nenad, and Jordan, R. R. (1966), *Generalized geologic map of Delaware,* Delaware Geological Survey, scale approx. 1:300,000.

Srogi, LeeAnn (1982), *A new interpretation of contact relationships and early Paleozoic tectonic history of the Delaware Piedmont* [abs.], Geological Society of America Abstracts with Programs, v. 14, no. 1, p. 85.

Stach, E., Mackowsky, M.-Th., Teichmüller, M., and others (1982), *Stach's textbook of coal petrography* [English translation], Berlin, Gebrüder Borntraeger, 535 p.

Stanley, R. S., and Ratcliffe, N. M. (1985), *Tectonic synthesis of the Taconian orogeny in western New England,* Geological Society of America Bulletin, v. 96, p. 1227–1250.

Stauffer, C. R., and Schroyer, C. R. (1920), *The Dunkard Series in Ohio,* Ohio Geological Survey, 4th ser., Bulletin 22, 167 p.

Steckler, M. S., Watts, A. B., and Thorne, J. A. (1988), *Subsidence and basin modeling at the U.S. Atlantic passive margin,* in Sheridan, R. E., and Grow, J. A., eds., The Atlantic continental margin: U.S., Geological Society of America, The Geology of North America, v. I–2, p. 399–416.

Stefanko, R. (1978), *Coal mining technology—theory and practice,* Mining Enforcement and Safety Administration, U.S. Department of the Interior.

Stephens, G. C., and Colman, C. S. (1979), *Geophysical and geochemical exploration of the Gap nickel mine, Lancaster County, Pennsylvania,* Pennsylvania Academy of Science Proceedings, v. 53, p. 209–211.

Stephens, G. C., Wright, T. O., and Platt, L. B. (1982), *Geology of the Middle Ordovician Martinsburg Formation and related rocks in Pennsylvania,* Annual Field Conference of Pennsylvania Geologists, 47th, New Cumberland, Pa., Guidebook, 87 p.

Stevenson, J. J. (1882), *The geology of Bedford and Fulton Counties,* Pennsylvania Geological Survey, 2nd ser., Report T2, 382 p.

Stockar, D. V. (1986), *Contemporary tectonics of the Lancaster, Pennsylvania, seismic zone,* University Park, Pennsylvania State University, M.S. thesis, 226 p.

Stoek, H. H. (1902), *The Pennsylvania anthracite coal field,* in Twenty-second annual report of the United States Geological Survey, 1900–

1901—Part III, Coal, oil, cement, U.S. Geological Survey Annual Report 1901, pt. 3, p. 55–117.

Stone, R. W. (1922), *Magnesite in Pennsylvania,* Pennsylvania Geological Survey, 4th ser., Progress Report 28, 3 p.

———— (1923), *Roofing granules industry in southeastern Pennsylvania,* Pennsylvania Geological Survey, 4th ser., Progress Report 82, 4 p.

———— (1932a), *Building stones of Pennsylvania,* Pennsylvania Geological Survey, 4th ser., Mineral Resource Report 15, 316 p.

———— (1932b), *Geology and mineral resources of Greene County, Pennsylvania,* Pennsylvania Geological Survey, 4th ser., County Report 30, 175 p.

———— (1939), *The minerals of Pennsylvania—Non-metallic minerals,* Pennsylvania Geological Survey, 4th ser., Mineral Resource Report 18-C, 46 p.

———— (1953), *Descriptions of Pennsylvania's undeveloped caves,* National Speleological Society Bulletin, v. 15, p. 51–137.

Stone, R. W., Barnsley, E. R., and Hickok, W. O., IV (1932), *Pennsylvania caves,* 2nd ed., Pennsylvania Geological Survey, 4th ser., General Geology Report 3, 143 p.

Stone, R. W., and Hughes, H. H. (1931), *Feldspar in Pennsylvania,* Pennsylvania Geological Survey, 4th ser., Mineral Resource Report 13, 63 p.

Stose, A. J., and Stose, G. W. (1944), *Geology of the Hanover-York district, Pennsylvania,* U.S. Geological Survey Professional Paper 204, 84 p.

———— (1946), *Geology of Carroll and Frederick Counties,* in *The physical features of Carroll County and Frederick County,* Maryland Geological Survey, p. 11–131.

Stose, G. W. (1904), *Barite in southern Pennsylvania and pure limestone in Berkeley County, W. Va.,* in Emmons, S. F., and Hayes, C. W., geologists in charge, *Contributions to economic geology, 1903,* U.S. Geological Survey Bulletin 225, p. 515–517.

———— (1907a), *Phosphorus ore at Mount Holly Springs, PA,* in Emmons, S. F., and Eckel, E. C., geologists in charge, *Contributions to economic geology, 1906—Part I, Metals and nonmetals, except fuels,* U.S. Geological Survey Bulletin 315, p. 474–483.

———— (1907b), *White clays of South Mountain, Pennsylvania,* in Emmons, S. F., and Eckel, E. C., geologists in charge, *Contributions to economic geology, 1906—Part I, Metals and nonmetals, except fuels,* U.S. Geological Survey Bulletin 315, p. 322–334.

———— (1909), *Mercersburg-Chambersburg folio, Pennsylvania,* U.S. Geological Survey Geologic Atlas of the U.S., Folio 170, 19 p.

———— (1919), *Glauberite crystal cavities in the Triassic rocks in the vicinity of Gettysburg, Pa.,* American Mineralogist, v. 4, p. 1–4.

———— (1925), *Mineral resources of Adams County, Pennsylvania,* Pennsylvania Geological Survey, 4th ser., County Report 1, pt. 2, p. 17–22.

———— (1930), *Unconformity at the base of the Silurian in southeastern Pennsylvania,* Geological Society of America Bulletin, v. 41, p. 629–658.

———— (1932), *Geology and mineral resources of Adams County, Pennsylvania,* Pennsylvania Geological Survey, 4th ser., County Report 1, pt. 1, 153 p.

———— (1946), *The Taconic sequence in Pennsylvania,* American Journal of Science, v. 244, p. 665–696.

Stose, G. W., and Bascom, F. (1929), *Fairfield-Gettysburg folio, Pennsylvania,* U.S. Geological Survey Geologic Atlas of the U.S., Folio 225, 22 p.

Stose, G. W., and Glass, J. J. (1938), *Garnet crystals in cavities in metamorphosed Triassic conglomerate in York County, Pennsylvania,* American Mineralogist, v. 23, p. 430–435.

Stose, G. W., and Jonas, A. I. (1935), *Highlands near Reading, Pennsylvania; an erosional remnant of a great overthrust sheet,* Geological Society of America Bulletin, v. 46, p. 757–779.

———— (1939), *Geology and mineral resources of York County, Pennsylvania,* Pennsylvania Geological Survey, 4th ser., County Report 67, 199 p.

Stose, G. W., and Swartz, C. K. (1912), *Pawpaw-Hancock folio, Maryland-West Virginia-Pennsylvania,* U.S. Geological Survey Geologic Atlas of the U.S., Folio 179, 24 p.

Stout, W. E. (1931), *Pennsylvanian cycles in Ohio,* Illinois State Geological Survey Bulletin 60, p. 195–216.

Stover, C. W. (1988), *United States earthquakes, 1984,* U.S. Geological Survey Bulletin 1862, 179 p.

Stover, C. W., Reagor, B. G., and Algermissen, S. T. (1981), *Seismicity map of the state of Pennsylvania,* U.S. Geological Survey Miscellaneous Field Studies Map MF-1280, scale 1:1,000,000.

Stow, M. H. (1938), *Conditions of sedimentation and sources of the Oriskany Sandstone as indicated by petrology,* AAPG Bulletin, v. 22, p. 541–564.

Sturgeon, M. T. (1958), *The geology and mineral resources of Athens County, Ohio,* Ohio Division of Geological Survey Bulletin 57, 600 p.

———— (1964), *New descriptions of hitherto inadequately known Pennsylvanian gastropods,* Journal of Paleontology, v. 38, p. 740–748.

Sturgeon, M. T., and Hoare, R. D. (1968), *Pennsylvanian brachiopods of Ohio,* Ohio Division of Geological Survey Bulletin 63, 95 p.

Sumner, J. R. (1977), *Geophysical investigation of the structural framework of the Newark-Gettysburg Triassic basin, Pennsylvania,* Geological Society of America Bulletin, v. 88, p. 935–942.

Sutter, J. F. (1985), *Progress on geochronology of Mesozoic diabases and basalts,* in Robinson, G. R., Jr., and Froelich, A. J., eds., *Proceedings of the Second U.S. Geological Survey Workshop on the Early Mesozoic Basins of the Eastern United States,* U.S. Geological Survey Circular 946, p. 110–114.

———— (1988), *Innovative approaches to the dating of igneous events in the early Mesozoic basins of the Eastern United States,* in Froelich, A. J., and Robinson, G. R., Jr., eds., *Studies of the early Mesozoic basins of the Eastern United States,* U.S. Geological Survey Bulletin 1776, p. 194–200.

Sutter, J. F., Crawford, M. L., and Crawford, W. A. (1980), *40Ar/ 39Ar age spectra of coexisting hornblende and biotite from the Piedmont of SE Pennsylvania: their bearing on the metamorphic and tectonic history* [abs.], Geological Society of America Abstracts with Programs, v. 12, no. 1, p. 85.

Sutter, J. F., and Smith, T. E. (1979), *40Ar/39Ar ages of diabase intrusions from Newark trend basins in Connecticut and Maryland: initiation of central Atlantic rifting,* American Journal of Science, v. 279, p. 808–831.

Swann, P. H. (1964), *Late Mississippian rhythmic sediments of Mississippi Valley,* AAPG Bulletin, v. 48, no. 5, p. 637–658.

Swanson, M. T. (1982), *Preliminary model for an early transform history in central Atlantic rifting,* Geology, v. 10, p. 317–320.

———— (1986), *Preexisting fault control for Mesozoic basin formation in eastern North America,* Geology, v. 14, p. 419–422.

Swartz, F. M. (1955), *Stratigraphy and structure in the Ridge and Valley area from University Park to Tyrone, Mount Union and Lewistown,* Annual Field Conference of Pennsylvania Geologists, 21st, University Park, Pa., Guidebook, p. S-1—S-11.

———— (1965), *Guide to the Horse Shoe Curve section between Altoona and Gallitzin, central Pennsylvania,* Pennsylvania Geological Survey, 4th ser., General Geology Report 50, 58 p.

Swartz, F. M., and Hambleton, H. J. (1958), *Potential tonnages of the Center iron sandstone in Perry County, Pennsylvania,* Pennsylvania State University, College of Earth and Mineral Sciences Experiment Station Bulletin 71, p. 19–27.

Sweeting, M. M. (1973), *Karst landforms,* New York, Columbia University Press, 362 p.

Tanner, A. B. (1986), *Geological factors that influence radon availability,* in *Indoor radon,* Pittsburgh, Air Pollution Control Association, Publication SP-54, p. 1–12.

Tasch, Paul (1975), *Dunkard estheriids as environmental and age indicators,* in Barlow, J. A., and Burkhammer, Susan, eds., *Proceedings of the First I. C. White Memorial Symposium [Morgantown, W. Va., 1972]—"The age of the Dunkard,"* West Virginia Geological and Economic Survey, p. 281–292.

Taylor, L. E., Werkheiser, W. H., and Kriz, M. L. (1983), *Ground-water resources of the West Branch Susquehanna River basin, Pennsylvania,* Pennsylvania Geological Survey, 4th ser., Water Resource Report 56, 143 p.

Tearpock, D. J., and Bischke, Richard (1980), *The structural analysis of the Wissahickon schist near Philadelphia, Pennsylvania,* Geological Society of America Bulletin, v. 91, pt. 2, p. 2432–2456.

Terriere, R. T. (1951), *The Mississippian sediments of the Bedford quadrangle region,* Pennsylvania State College, M.S. thesis, 103 p.

Tetra Tech, Inc. (1981a), *Evaluation of Devonian shale potential in New York,* U.S. Department of Energy, DOE/METC–118, 20 p.

———— (1981b), *Evaluation of Devonian shale potential in Ohio,* U.S. Department of Energy, DOE/METC–122, 33 p.

———— (1981c), *Evaluation of Devonian shale potential in Pennsylvania,* U.S. Department of Energy, DOE/METC–119, 56 p.

———— (1981d), *Evaluation of Devonian shale potential in West Virginia,* U.S. Department of Energy, DOE/METC–120, 51 p.

Texas Instruments (1978), *Aerial radiometric and magnetic reconnaissance survey of Baltimore, Washington, and Richmond quadrangles,* U.S. Department of Energy, GJBX–133(78), 2 v., unpaged.

Thayer, T. P. (1967), *Chemical and structural relations of ultramafic and feldspathic rocks in alpine intrusive complexes,* in Wyllie, P. J., ed., *Ultramafic and related rocks,* New York, John Wiley and Sons, p. 222–239.

Theisen, J. P. (1983), *Is there a fault in our gap?,* Pennsylvania Geology, v. 14, no. 3, p. 5–11.

Thomas, D. J., Delano, H. L., Buyce, M. R., and Carter, C. H. (1987), *Pleistocene and Holocene geology on a dynamic coast,* Annual Field Conference of Pennsylvania Geologists, 52nd, Erie, Pa., Guidebook, 88 p.

Thomas, W. A. (1977), *Evolution of Appalachian-Ouachita salients and recesses from reentrants and promontories in the continental margin,* American Journal of Science, v. 277, p. 1233–1278.

Thompson, A. M. (1970a), *Geochemistry of color genesis in red-bed sequence, Juniata and Bald Eagle Formations, Pennsylvania,* Journal of Sedimentary Petrology, v. 40, p. 599–615.

———— (1970b), *Sedimentology and origin of Upper Ordovician clastic rocks, central Pennsylvania,* Society of Economic Paleontologists and Mineralogists, Eastern Section, Guidebook, 88 p.

Thompson, A. M., and Sevon, W. D. (1982), *Excursion 19B: comparative sedimentology of Paleozoic clastic wedges in the central Appalachians, U.S.A.,* International Association of Sedimentologists, International Congress on Sedimentology, 11th, Guidebook, 136 p.

Thompson, Glenn (1983), *Triassic breccias and conglomerates,* in Mowery, J. R., ed., *Geology along the Susquehanna River, south central Pennsylvania,* Harrisburg Area Geological Society Annual Field Trip, 2nd, Guidebook, p. 45–46.

Thompson, H. D. (1949), *Drainage evolution in the Appalachians of Pennsylvania,* Annals of the New York Academy of Science, v. 52, p. 31–62.

Thompson, P., Schwarcz, H. P., and Ford, D. C. (1976), *Stable isotope geochemistry, geothermometry, and geochronology of speleothems from West Virginia,* Geological Society of America Bulletin, v. 87, p. 1730–1738.

Thomson, R. D., Otte, M. E., and Ela, R. E. (1961), *The mineral industry of Pennsylvania,* in *Area reports,* U.S. Bureau of Mines Minerals Yearbook 1960, v. 3, p. 845–889.

Thornbury, W. D. (1965), *Regional geomorphology of the United States,* New York, John Wiley and Sons, 609 p.

Tice, R. H. (1968), *Magnitude and frequency of floods in the United States—Part 1-B, North Atlantic slope basins, New York to York River,* U.S. Geological Survey Water-Supply Paper 1672, 585 p.

Tight, W. G. (1903), *Drainage modifications in southeastern Ohio and adjacent parts of West Virginia and Kentucky,* U.S. Geological Survey Professional Paper 13, 111 p.

Tilton, G. R., Wetherill, G. W., Davis, G. L., and Bass, M. N. (1960), *1000-million-year-old minerals from the eastern United States and Canada,* Journal of Geophysical Research, v. 65, p. 4173–4179.

Tiner, R. W., Jr. (1987), *Mid-Atlantic wetlands: a disappearing natural treasure,* U.S. Fish and Wildlife Service and U.S. Environmental Protection Agency, 28 p.

Ting, F. T. (1967), *The petrology of the Lower Kittanning coal in western Pennsylvania,* University Park, Pennsylvania State University, Ph.D. thesis, 138 p.

Tomikel, J. C., and Shepps, V. C. (1967), *The geography and geology of Erie County, Pennsylvania,* Pennsylvania Geological Survey, 4th ser., Information Circular 56, 64 p.

Tooker, E. W. (1949), *Barite deposit near Buckmanville, Pennsylvania,* Bethlehem, Pa., Lehigh University, M.S. thesis, 62 p.

Tourek, T. J. (1971), *Depositional environments and sediment accumulation models for the Upper Silurian Wills Creek Shale and Tonoloway Limestone, central Appalachians,* Baltimore, Md., Johns Hopkins University, Ph.D. thesis, 270 p.

Trainer, D. W., Jr. (1932), *The Tully Limestone of central New York,* New York State Museum Bulletin 291, 43 p.

Trexler, J. P., Wood, G. H., Jr., and Arndt, H. H. (1962), *Uppermost Devonian and Lower Mississippian rocks of the western part of the Anthracite region of eastern Pennsylvania,* in *Short papers in geology and hydrology, Articles 60–119—Geological Survey research 1962,* U.S. Geological Survey Professional Paper 450-C, p. C36–C39.

Trimble, S. W. (1974), *Man-induced soil erosion on the southern Piedmont, 1700–1970,* Ankeny, Iowa, Soil Conservation Society of America, 180 p.

Trojan, E. J. (1974), *The Route 202 sinkhole—A case history,* in Amenta, R. V., and others, *Geology of the Piedmont of southeastern Pennsylvania,* Annual Field Conference of Pennsylvania Geologists, 39th, King of Prussia, Pa., Guidebook, p. 33–40.

Tschudy, R. H. (1965), *An Upper Cretaceous deposit in the Appalachian Mountains,* in *Geological Survey research 1965, Chapter B,* U.S. Geological Survey Professional Paper 525-B, p. B64–B68.

Tsusue, Akio (1964), *Mineral aspects of the Grace mine magnetite deposit,* Pennsylvania Geological Survey, 4th ser., Mineral Resource Report 49, 10 p.

Turner-Peterson, C. E. (1977), *Uranium mineralization during early burial, Newark basin, Pennsylvania-New Jersey,* in Campbell, J. A., ed., *Short papers of the U.S. Geological Survey uranium-thorium symposium, 1977 [1977 Uranium and Thorium Research and Resources Conference, Golden, Colo.],* U.S. Geological Survey Circular 753, p. 3–4.

———— (1980), *Sedimentology and uranium mineralization in the Triassic-Jurassic Newark basin, Pennsylvania and New Jersey,* in Turner-Peterson, C. E., ed., *Uranium in sedimentary rocks—Application of the facies concept to exploration,* Society of Economic Paleontologists and Mineralogists, Rocky Mountain Section, Short Course Notes, p. 149–171.

Turner-Peterson, C. E., and Smoot, J. P. (1985), *New thoughts on facies relationships in the Triassic Stockton and Lockatong Formations, Pennsylvania and New Jersey,* in Robinson, G. R., Jr., and Froelich, A. J., eds., *Proceedings of the Second U.S. Geological Survey Workshop on the Early Mesozoic Basins of the Eastern United States,* U.S. Geological Survey Circular 946, p. 10–17.

Tyler, P. M., and Linn, A. (1943), *Clays,* U.S. Bureau of Mines Minerals Yearbook 1941, p. 1321–1337.

Ulanoski, J. T., Shertzer, R. H., Barker, J. L., and Hartman, R. T. (1981), *Trophic classification and characteristics of twenty-six publicly-owned Pennsylvania lakes,* Pennsylvania Department of Environmental Resources, Bureau of Water Quality Management, Publication 61, 240 p.

Umbgrove, J. H. F. (1950), *Symphony of the earth,* The Hague, Netherlands, Martinus Nijhoff, 220 p.

United States Water Resources Council (1981), *Guidelines for determining flood flow frequency,* revised September 1981, Hydrology Committee, Bulletin 17B, 183 p.

Urban, T. C. (1971), *Terrestrial heat flow in Middle Atlantic States,* Rochester, N. Y., University of Rochester, Ph.D. thesis, 398 p.

U.S. Bureau of Mines (1927-34), *Mineral resources of the United States [calendar years 1924-1931]*, U.S. Bureau of Mines Mineral Resources, each published in 2 pts.

———— (1933-90), *Minerals yearbook [calendar years 1932-1988]*, U.S. Bureau of Mines Minerals Yearbooks, each published in 1 to 3 v.

———— (1971), *Strippable reserves of bituminous coal and lignite in the United States*, Information Circular 8531, 148 p.

U.S. Department of Agriculture, Soil Conservation Service (1975), *Soil taxonomy—A basic system of soil classification for making and interpreting soil surveys*, Agriculture Handbook 436, 754 p.

———— (1994), *Keys to soil taxonomy*, 6th ed., 306 p.

U.S. Environmental Protection Agency (1974), *An approach to a relative trophic index system for classifying lakes and reservoirs (A preliminary analysis of national eutrophication survey data collected during the 1972 sampling period)*, Working Paper 24, Pacific Northwest Environmental Research Laboratory, Corvallis, Oreg.

———— (1986), *Radon reduction methods—A homeowner's guide*, U.S. Environmental Protection Agency, OPA-86-005, 24 p.

U.S. Environmental Protection Agency, Office of Air and Radiation, and U.S. Department of Health and Human Services, Centers for Disease Control (1986), *A citizen's guide to radon—What it is and what to do about it*, U.S. Environmental Protection Agency and U.S. Department of Health and Human Services, OPA-86-004, 14 p.

U.S. Environmental Protection Agency, U.S. Department of Health and Human Services, and U.S. Public Health Service (1992), *A citizen's guide to radon*, 2nd ed., 16 p.

U.S. Geological Survey (1911-27), *Mineral resources of the United States [calendar years 1910-1923]*, U.S. Geological Survey Mineral Resources, each published in 2 pts.

———— (1967), *Engineering geology of the Northeast Corridor, Washington, D. C., to Boston, Massachusetts: Coastal Plain and surficial deposits*, U.S. Geological Survey Miscellaneous Investigations Series Map I-514-B, 9 p., scale 1:250,000, 8 sheets.

———— (1969), *Aeromagnetic map of the Harrisburg-Scranton area, northeastern Pennsylvania*, U.S. Geological Survey Geophysical Investigations Map GP-669, scale 1:250,000.

———— (1973), *Nappes in the Allentown area, Pennsylvania*, in *Geological Survey research 1973*, U.S. Geological Survey Professional Paper 850, p. 36-37.

———— (1974a), *Aeromagnetic map of part of the Williamsport 1° by 2° quadrangle, Pennsylvania*, U.S. Geological Survey Open-File Report 74-17, scale 1:250,000.

———— (1974b), *Aeromagnetic map of parts of the Cleveland and Erie 1° by 2° quadrangles, Pennsylvania*, U.S. Geological Survey Open-File Report 74-12, scale 1:250,000.

———— (1974c), *Aeromagnetic map of parts of the Harrisburg and Baltimore 1° by 2° quadrangles, Pennsylvania*, U.S. Geological Survey Open-File Report 74-13, scale 1:250,000.

———— (1974d), *Aeromagnetic map of parts of the Pittsburgh and Cumberland 1° by 2° quadrangles, Pennsylvania*, U.S. Geological Survey Open-File Report 74-14, scale 1:250,000.

———— (1974e), *Aeromagnetic map of parts of the Scranton and Newark 1° by 2° quadrangles, Pennsylvania*, U.S. Geological Survey Open-File Report 74-15, scale 1:250,000.

———— (1974f), *Aeromagnetic map of parts of the Warren and Buffalo 1° by 2° quadrangles, Pennsylvania*, U.S. Geological Survey Open-File Report 74-16, scale 1:250,000.

———— (1974g), *Aeromagnetic map of Philadelphia and vicinity, Pennsylvania*, U.S. Geological Survey Open-File Report 74-370, scale 1:62,500.

———— (published annually, 1976-85), *Water resources data, Pennsylvania*, U.S. Geological Survey Water-Data Reports, Water Years 1975-84, each year in 3 v.

———— (1978), *Aeromagnetic map of Pennsylvania, 1978*, U.S. Geological Survey Geophysical Investigations Map GP-924, scale 1:250,000, 2 sheets.

U.S. Government Accounting Office, Report by Comptroller General (1979), *Alternatives to protect property owners from damages caused by mine subsidence*, U.S. Government Accounting Office, Report CED-79-25, 41 p.

U.S. National Oceanic and Atmospheric Administration (1951-80), *Climatological data, annual summary, Pennsylvania*, Environmental Data and Information Service, National Climatic Center, Asheville, N.C.

———— (1972), *Storm data*, Environmental Data and Information Service, National Climatic Center, Asheville, N. C., v. 14, no. 6, p. 91-92.

———— (1977a), *Climate of Pennsylvania*, Environmental Data and Information Service, National Climatic Center, Asheville, N. C., p. 1-7.

———— (1977b), *Storm data*, Environmental Data and Information Service, National Climatic Center, Asheville, N. C., v. 19, no. 7, p. 16.

———— (1982a), *Pennsylvania*, in *Climatography of the U.S.*, Environmental Data and Information Service, National Climatic Center, Asheville, N. C., no. 81, p. 1-9.

———— (1982b), *Tornado safety*, Rockville, Md., p. 1-8.

———— (1984a), *Pennsylvania stations*, in *Climatography of the U.S.*, Environmental Data and Information Service, National Climatic Center, Asheville, N. C., no. 20.

———— (1984b), *Thunderstorms and lightning*, Washington, D. C., p. 1-6.

———— (1985), *Natural disaster survey report to the Administrator of the National Oceanic and Atmospheric Administration*, Silver Spring, Md., p. 1-5.

U.S. Secretary of Labor (1968), *Walsh Healy Act*, Federal Register, v. 33, no. 11.

Vacquier, V., Steenland, N. C., Henderson, R. G., and Zietz, Isidore (1951), *Interpretation of aeromagnetic maps*, Geological Society of America Memoir 47, 151 p.

Van der Voo, Rob (1979), *Age of the Alleghenian folding in the central Appalachians*, Geology, v. 7, p. 297-298.

Van Houten, F. B. (1964), *Cyclic lacustrine sedimentation, Upper Triassic Lockatong Formation, central New Jersey and adjacent Pennsylvania*, in Merriam, D. F., ed., *Symposium on cyclic sedimentation*, Kansas Geological Survey Bulletin 169, v. 2, p. 497-531.

———— (1965a), *Composition of Triassic Lockatong and associated formations of the Newark Group, central New Jersey and adjacent Pennsylvania*, American Journal of Science, v. 263, p. 825-863.

———— (1965b), *Crystal casts in Upper Triassic Lockatong and Brunswick Formations*, Sedimentology, v. 4, p. 301-313.

———— (1969), *Late Triassic Newark Group, north central New Jersey and adjacent Pennsylvania and New York*, in Subitzky, Seymour, ed., *Geology of selected areas in New Jersey and eastern Pennsylvania and guidebook of excursions*, New Brunswick, N. J., Rutgers University Press, p. 314-347.

———— (1971), *Contact metamorphic mineral assemblages, Late Triassic Newark Group, New Jersey*, Contributions to Mineralogy and Petrology, v. 30, p. 1-14.

Ver Steeg, Karl (1930), *Wind gaps and water gaps of the northern Appalachians, their characteristics and significance*, Annals of the New York Academy of Science, v. 32, p. 87-220.

Villaume, J. F. (1969), *A reconnaissance study of the rocks of the Precambrian core of the Mine Ridge anticline, Gap, Pennsylvania, 7.5' quadrangle, Lancaster County, Pennsylvania*, Lancaster, Pa., Franklin and Marshall College, B.A. thesis, 33 p.

Villaume, J. F., Freedman, J., and Al-Mishwt, Ali (1969), *Geochemical and geophysical study of mafic and ultramafic rocks in Mine Ridge, southeastern Pennsylvania*, Pennsylvania Academy of Science Proceedings, v. 43, p. 169-171.

Vink, G. E., Morgan, W. J., and Zhao, Wu-Ling (1984), *Preferential rifting of continents: a source of displaced terranes*, Journal of Geophysical Research, v. 89, p. 10,072-10,076.

Volk, K. W. (1977), *The paleomagnetism of Mesozoic diabase and the deformational history of southeastern Pennsylvania*, University Park, Pennsylvania State University, Ph.D. thesis, 153 p.

Volney, C. F. (1804), *A view of the soil and climate of the United States of America* [translated with occasional remarks by C. B. Brown], Philadelphia, J. Conrad and Company, 446 p.

Wagner, M. E., and Crawford, M. L. (1975), *Polymetamorphism of the Precambrian Baltimore Gneiss in southeastern Pennsylvania,* American Journal of Science, v. 275, p. 653-682.

Wagner, M. E., and Srogi, LeeAnn (1987), *Early Paleozoic metamorphism at two crustal levels and a tectonic model for the Pennsylvania-Delaware Piedmont,* Geological Society of America Bulletin, v. 99, p. 113-126.

Wagner, W. R. (1966a), *Pennsylvanians must delve into rocks of ancient age,* Oil and Gas Journal, v. 64, no. 50, p. 152-158.

_____ (1966b), *Stratigraphy of the Cambrian to Middle Ordovician rocks of central and western Pennsylvania,* Pennsylvania Geological Survey, 4th ser., General Geology Report 49, 156 p.

_____ (1976), *Growth faults in Cambrian and Lower Ordovician rocks of western Pennsylvania,* AAPG Bulletin, v. 60, p. 414-427.

Wagner, W. R., Heyman, Louis, Gray, R. E., and others (1970), *Geology of the Pittsburgh area,* Pennsylvania Geological Survey, 4th ser., General Geology Report 59, 145 p.

Waite, B. A. (1982), *Oil and gas well pollution abatement project,* Pennsylvania Department of Environmental Resources, Bureau of Oil and Gas Management, ME 81495, pt. B, 74 p.

Walker, H. N. (1978), *Chemical reactions of carbonate aggregates in cement paste,* in *Significance of tests and properties of concrete and concrete-making materials,* American Society for Testing and Materials Special Technical Publication 169B, p. 722-743.

Walling, A. F., and Gray, O. W. (1872), *New topographical atlas of the state of Pennsylvania,* Philadelphia, Stedman, Brown, and Lyon, 110 p.

Waltman, W. J., Cunningham, R. L., and Ciolkosz, E. J. (1990), *Stratigraphy and parent material relationships of red substratum soils on the Allegheny Plateau,* Soil Science Society of America Journal, v. 54, p. 1049-1057.

Wanless, H. R. (1975), *Appalachian region,* Chapter C in McKee, E. D., and Crosby, E. J., coordinators, *Paleotectonic investigations of the Pennsylvanian System in the United States—Part I, Introduction and regional analyses of the Pennsylvanian System,* U.S. Geological Survey Professional Paper 853, pt. 1, p. 17-62.

Ward, J. A. (1980), *J. Edgar Thomson, master of the Pennsylvania,* Contributions in Economics and Economic History, no. 33, Westport, Conn., Greenwood Press, 265 p.

Ward, R. F. (1959), *Petrology and metamorphism of the Wilmington Complex, Delaware, Pennsylvania, and Maryland,* Geological Society of America Bulletin, v. 70, p. 1425-1458.

Watson, D. W. (1989), *Slippery Rock Creek gorge in western Pennsylvania, a proposed glacial origin,* Northeastern Geology, v. 11, p. 50-55.

Watson, E. H. (1958), *Triassic faulting near Gwynedd, Pennsylvania,* Pennsylvania Academy of Science Proceedings, v. 32, p. 122-127.

Watts, W. A. (1979), *Late Quaternary vegetation of central Appalachia and the New Jersey Coastal Plain,* Ecological Monographs, v. 49, p. 427-469.

Way, J. H., and Smith, R. C. (1983), *Barite in the Devonian Marcellus Formation, Montour County,* Pennsylvania Geology, v. 14, no. 1, p. 4-9.

_____ (1985), *Tioga ash zone: 6 or more ash beds in the Valley and Ridge of Pennsylvania* [abs.], Geological Society of America Abstracts with Programs, v. 17, no. 1, p. 68.

Weber, J. N., Bergenback, R. E., Williams, E. G., and Keith, M. L. (1965), *Reconstruction of depositional environments in the Pennsylvanian Vanport basin by carbon isotope ratios,* Journal of Sedimentary Petrology, v. 35, p. 36-48.

Wehr, Frederick, and Glover, Lynn, III (1985), *Stratigraphy and tectonics of the Virginia-North Carolina Blue Ridge: evolution of a Late Proterozoic-early Paleozoic hinge zone,* Geological Society of America Bulletin, v. 96, p. 285-295.

Weigand, P. W., and Ragland, P. C. (1970), *Geochemistry of Mesozoic dolerite dikes from eastern North America,* Contributions to Mineralogy and Petrology, v. 29, p. 195-214.

Weiss, Judith (1949), *Wissahickon schist at Philadelphia, Pennsylvania,* Geological Society of America Bulletin, v. 60, p. 1689-1726.

Weitz, J. H., and Bolger, R. C. (1964), *Map of the Mercer clay and adjacent units in Clearfield, Centre, and Clinton Counties, Pennsylvania,* Pennsylvania Geological Survey, 4th ser., Map 12, scale 1:95,040.

Welch, Sylvester (1833), report on the Allegheny Portage Railroad [reprinted as *Sylvester Welch's report on the Allegheny Portage Railroad* by American Canal and Transportation Center, York, Pa., 1983, p. 5, 7-9, 11-14, 16-18, 20, 22].

Wells, R. B. (1974), *Loyalhanna sandstone extended into north-central Pennsylvania* [abs.], Geological Society of America Abstracts with Programs, v. 6, no. 1, p. 84-85.

Wells, R. B., and Bucek, M. F. (1980), *Geology and mineral resources of the Montoursville North and Huntersville quadrangles, Lycoming County, Pennsylvania,* Pennsylvania Geological Survey, 4th ser., Atlas 143cd, 68 p.

Wescott, W. A. (1982), *Nature of porosity in Tuscarora Sandstone (Lower Silurian) in the Appalachian basin,* Oil and Gas Journal, v. 80, no. 34, p. 159-173.

West, T. R., Smith, N. M., and Johnson, R. B. (1969), *The use of statistical analysis in quarry evaluation,* in *A symposium on industrial mineral exploration and development,* Forum on the Geology of Industrial Minerals, Lawrence, Kan., University of Kansas, 1967, Proceedings, Kansas Geological Survey Special Distribution Publication 34, p. 10-25.

Wetzel, K. L. (1986), *Pennsylvania—Surface-water resources,* in Moody, D. W., and others, compilers, *National water summary 1985—hydrologic events and surface-water resources,* U.S. Geological Survey Water-Supply Paper 2300, p. 391-398.

Wherry, E. T. (1913), *North border relations of the Triassic in Pennsylvania,* Philadelphia Academy of Natural Sciences Proceedings, v. 65, p. 114-125.

_____ (1916), *Glauberite crystal-cavities in the Triassic rocks of eastern Pennsylvania,* American Mineralogist, v. 1, p. 37-43.

Whitcomb, Lawrence (1961), *Chesleigh Arthur Bonine, E.M., Lehigh University, 1912, Professor Emeritus, Pennsylvania State University* [dedication], in Ryan, J. D., ed., *Structure and stratigraphy of the Reading Hills and Lehigh Valley in Northampton and Lehigh Counties, Pennsylvania,* Annual Field Conference of Pennsylvania Geologists, 26th, Bethlehem, Pa., Guidebook, p. ii-iii.

White, David (1900), *The stratigraphic succession of the fossil floras of the Pottsville Formation in the Southern Anthracite coal field, Pa.,* in *Twentieth annual report of the United States Geological Survey, 1898-99—Part II, General geology and paleontology,* U.S. Geological Survey Annual Report 1899, pt. 2, p. 749-930.

_____ (1904), *Deposition of the Appalachian Pottsville,* Geological Society of America Bulletin, v. 15, p. 267-282.

_____ (1913), *Physiographic conditions attending the formation of coal,* in White, David, and Theissen, Reinhardt, *The origin of coal,* U.S. Bureau of Mines Bulletin 38, p. 52-84.

White, E. L., and White, W. B. (1979), *Quantitative morphology of landforms in carbonate rock basins in the Appalachian Highlands,* Geological Society of America Bulletin, v. 90, p. 385-396.

White, G. W., Totten, S. M., and Gross, D. L. (1969), *Pleistocene stratigraphy of northwestern Pennsylvania,* Pennsylvania Geological Survey, 4th ser., General Geology Report 55, 88 p.

White, I. C. (1877), *The geology of Lawrence County,* Pennsylvania Geological Survey, 2nd ser., Report QQ, p. 1-213, 305-336.

_____ (1896), *Origin of the high terrace deposits of the Monongahela River,* American Geologist, v. 18, p. 368-379.

White, W. B. (1960), *Terminations of passages in Appalachian caves as evidence for a shallow phreatic origin,* in Moore, G. W., ed., *Origin of limestone caves—A symposium with discussion,* National Speleological Society Bulletin, v. 22, pt. 1, p. 43-53.

White, W. B., compiler (1976), *Caves of western Pennsylvania,* Pennsylvania Geological Survey, 4th ser., General Geology Report 67, 97 p.

Whitehead, D. R. (1973), *Late-Wisconsin vegetational changes in unglaciated eastern North America,* Quaternary Research, v. 3, p. 621–631.

Wickstrom, L. H., Botoman, George, and Stith, D. A. (1985), *Report on a continuously cored hole drilled into the Precambrian in Seneca County, northwestern Ohio,* Ohio Division of Geological Survey Information Circular 51, 1 sheet.

Wilding, L. P., Smeck, N. E., and Hall, G. F., eds. (1983a), *Pedogenesis and soil taxonomy—I, Concepts and interactions,* Amsterdam, Elsevier, 303 p.

———— (1983b), *Pedogenesis and soil taxonomy—II, The soil orders,* Amsterdam, Elsevier, 410 p.

Willard, Bradford (1934), *Early Chemung shore line in Pennsylvania,* Geological Society of America Bulletin, v. 45, p. 897–908.

Willard, Bradford, Swartz, F. M., and Cleaves, A. B. (1939), *The Devonian of Pennsylvania,* Pennsylvania Geological Survey, 4th ser., General Geology Report 19, 481 p.

Williams, E. G. (1960), *Marine and fresh water fossiliferous beds in the Pottsville and Allegheny Groups of western Pennsylvania,* Journal of Paleontology, v. 34, p. 908–922.

———— (1972), *Structural control of high-alumina refractory clays in western Pennsylvania,* Earth and Mineral Sciences, v. 41, no. 7, p. 53–54.

Williams, E. G., and Bragonier, W. A. (1974), *Controls of Early Pennsylvanian sedimentation in western Pennsylvania,* in Briggs, Garrett, ed., *Carboniferous of southeastern United States,* Geological Society of America Special Paper 148, p. 135–152.

Williams, E. G., and Bragonier, William (1985), *Origin of the Mercer high-alumina clay,* in Gold, D. P., and others, *Central Pennsylvania geology revisited,* Annual Field Conference of Pennsylvania Geologists, 50th, State College, Pa., Guidebook, p. 204–211.

Williams, E. G., and Ferm, J. C. (1964), *Sedimentary facies in the lower Allegheny rocks of western Pennsylvania,* Journal of Sedimentary Petrology, v. 34, p. 610–614.

Williams, E. G., Guber, A. L., and Johnson, A. M. (1965), *Rotational slumping and the recognition of disconformities,* Journal of Geology, v. 73, p. 534–547.

Williams, E. G., and Holbrook, Philip (1985), *Origin of plastic underclays,* in Gold, D. P., and others, *Central Pennsylvania geology revisited,* Annual Field Conference of Pennsylvania Geologists, 50th, State College, Pa., Guidebook, p. 212–225.

Williams, E. G., Holbrook, R., and Lithgow, E. (1985), *Properties and occurrence of bloating shales and clays in the Pennsylvanian of western Pennsylvania,* in Gold, D. P., and others, *Central Pennsylvania geology revisited,* Annual Field Conference of Pennsylvania Geologists, 50th, State College, Pa., Guidebook, p. 255–259.

Williams, E. G., Holbrook, R. R., Lithgow, E. W., and Wilson, B. R. (1974), *Properties and occurrence of bloating shales and clays in the Pennsylvanian of western Pennsylvania,* Transactions of the American Institute of Mining, Metallurgical, and Petroleum Engineers, v. 256, p. 237–240.

Williams, E. G., and Keith, M. L. (1963), *Relationship between sulfur in coals and the occurrence of marine roof beds,* Economic Geology, v. 58, p. 720–729.

Williams, H. S. (1891), *Correlation papers, Devonian and Carboniferous,* U.S. Geological Survey Bulletin 80, p. 1–279.

Williams, Harold, and Hatcher, R. D., Jr. (1983), *Appalachian suspect terranes,* in Hatcher, R. D., Jr., and others, eds., *Contributions to the tectonics and geophysics of mountain chains,* Geological Society of America Memoir 158, p. 33–53.

Williams, S. J., and Meisburger, E. P. (1982), *Geological character and mineral resources of south central Lake Erie,* U.S. Army Corps of Engineers, CERC Miscellaneous Report 82–9, 62 p.

Wilshusen, J. P. (1979), *Geologic hazards in Pennsylvania,* Pennsylvania Geological Survey, 4th ser., Educational Series 9, 56 p.

———— (1983), *Geology of the Appalachian Trail in Pennsylvania,* Pennsylvania Geological Survey, 4th ser., General Geology Report 74, 121 p.

Wilson, J. L. (1952), *Upper Cambrian stratigraphy in the central Appalachians,* Geological Society of America Bulletin, v. 63, p. 275–322.

———— (1975), *Carbonate facies in geologic history,* New York, Springer-Verlag, 471 p.

Wiltschko, D. V., and Chapple, W. M. (1977), *Flow of weak rocks in Appalachian Plateau folds,* AAPG Bulletin, v. 61, p. 653–670.

Winkler, Louis (1979), *Catalog of U.S. earthquakes before the year 1850,* Seismological Society of America Bulletin, v. 69, p. 569–602.

———— (1982), *Catalog of earthquakes felt in the eastern United States megalopolis 1850–1930,* Seismological Society of America Bulletin, v. 72, pt. A, p. 2285–2306.

Winston, R. B. (1990), *Implications of paleobotany of Pennsylvanian-age coal of the central Appalachian basin for climate and coalbed development,* Geological Society of America Bulletin, v. 102, p. 1720–1726.

Wise, D. U. (1970), *Multiple deformation, geosynclinal transitions and the Martic problem in Pennsylvania,* in Fisher, G. W., and others, eds., *Studies of Appalachian geology: central and southern,* New York, Interscience Publishers, p. 317–333.

Witte, W. K., Kent, D. V., and Olsen, P. E. (1991), *Magnetostratigraphy and paleomagnetic poles from Late Triassic-earliest Jurassic strata of the Newark basin,* Geological Society of America Bulletin, v. 103, p. 1648–1662.

Witthoft, J. (1952), *A Paleo-Indian site in eastern Pennsylvania: an early hunting culture,* American Philosophical Society Proceedings, v. 96, p. 464–495.

Wolfe, J. A. (1978), *A paleobotanical interpretation of Tertiary climates in the northern hemisphere,* American Scientist, v. 66, p. 694–703.

Wolfe, J. A., and Upchurch, G. R., Jr. (1987), *North American nonmarine climates and vegetation during the Late Cretaceous,* Palaeogeography, Palaeoclimatology, Palaeoecology, v. 61, p. 33–77.

Wolfe, R. T., Jr. (1963), *The correlation of Upper Devonian Chemung sands in west central Pennsylvania, north of Pittsburgh,* in Shepps, V. C., ed., *Symposium on Middle and Upper Devonian stratigraphy of Pennsylvania and adjacent states,* Pennsylvania Geological Survey, 4th ser., General Geology Report 39, p. 241–257.

Wood, C. R. (1980), *Groundwater resources of the Gettysburg and Hammer Creek Formations, southeastern Pennsylvania,* Pennsylvania Geological Survey, 4th ser., Water Resource Report 49, 87 p.

Wood, C. R., Flippo, H. N., Jr., Lescinsky, J. B., and Barker, J. L. (1972), *Water resources of Lehigh County, Pennsylvania,* Pennsylvania Geological Survey, 4th ser., Water Resource Report 31, 263 p.

Wood, G. H., Jr. (1974a), *Geologic map of anthracite-bearing rocks in the southern half of the Delano quadrangle, Schuylkill County, Pennsylvania,* U.S. Geological Survey Miscellaneous Investigations Series Map I–737, scale 1:12,000.

———— (1974b), *Geologic map of the Tamaqua quadrangle, Carbon and Schuylkill Counties, Pennsylvania,* U.S. Geological Survey Geologic Quadrangle Map GQ-1133, scale 1:24,000.

Wood, G. H., Jr., and Bergin, M. J. (1970), *Structural controls of the Anthracite region, Pennsylvania,* in Fisher, G. W., and others, eds., *Studies of Appalachian geology: central and southern,* New York, Interscience Publishers, p. 147–160.

Wood, G. H., Jr., and Trexler, J. P. (1968), *Geologic maps of anthracite-bearing rocks in the west-central part of the Southern Anthracite field, Pennsylvania: western area,* U.S. Geological Survey Miscellaneous Investigations Series Map I–529, scale 1:12,000, 4 sheets.

Wood, G. H., Jr., Trexler, J. P., Arndt, H. H., and others (1956), *Subdivision of Pottsville Formation in Southern Anthracite field, Pennsylvania,* AAPG Bulletin, v. 40, p. 2669–2688.

Wood, G. H., Jr., Trexler, J. P., and Kehn, T. M. (1968), *Geologic maps of anthracite-bearing rocks in the west-central part of the Southern Anthracite field, Pennsylvania, eastern area,* U.S. Geological Survey Miscellaneous Investigations Series Map I-528, scale 1:12,000, 6 sheets.

Wood, G. H., Jr., Trexler, J. P., and Kehn, T. M. (1969), *Geology of the west-central part of the Southern Anthracite field and adjoining areas, Pennsylvania,* U.S. Geological Survey Professional Paper 602, 150 p.

Wood, H. O., and Neumann, Frank (1931), *Modified Mercalli intensity scale of 1931,* Seismological Society of America Bulletin, v. 21, p. 277-283.

Woodrow, D. L. (1968), *Stratigraphy, structure, and sedimentary patterns in the Upper Devonian of Bradford County, Pennsylvania,* Pennsylvania Geological Survey, 4th ser., General Geology Report 54, 78 p.

Woodrow, D. L., Fletcher, F. W., and Ahrnsbrak, W. F. (1973), *Paleogeography and paleoclimate at the deposition sites of the Devonian Catskill and Old Red facies,* Geological Society of America Bulletin, v. 84, p. 3051-3063.

Woodrow, D. L., and Isley, A. M. (1983), *Facies, topography, and sedimentary processes in the Catskill Sea (Devonian), New York and Pennsylvania,* Geological Society of America Bulletin, v. 94, p. 459-470.

Woodward, H. P. (1959), *Structural interpretations of the Burning Springs anticline,* in Woodward, H. P., compiler, *A Symposium on the Sandhill Deep Well, Wood County, West Virginia [Tucker County, W. Va., 1957],* West Virginia Geological and Economic Survey Report of Investigations 18, p. 159-168.

Woollard, G. P. (1943), *Transcontinental gravitational and magnetic profile of North America and its relation to geologic structure,* Geological Society of America Bulletin, v. 54, p. 747-790.

_____ (1979), *The new gravity system—changes in international gravity base values and anomaly values,* Geophysics, v. 44, p. 1352-1366.

Wright, G. F. (1914), *Evidence of a glacial dam in the Allegheny River between Warren, Pennsylvania, and Tionesta,* Geological Society of America Bulletin, v. 25, p. 215-218.

Wright, T. O., and Stephens, G. C. (1978), *Regional implications of the stratigraphy and structure of Shochary Ridge, Berks and Lehigh Counties, Pennsylvania,* American Journal of Science, v. 278, p. 1000-1017.

Wyckoff, Dorothy (1952), *Metamorphic facies in the Wissahickon schist near Philadelphia, Pennsylvania,* Geological Society of America Bulletin, v. 63, p. 25-58.

Yates, A. B. (1942), *The Gap nickel deposit, drill coring and magnetometer surveying during 1942,* unpublished report for the International Nickel Company Ltd., Copper Cliff, Ontario, Canada, 14 p.

Yeakel, L. S., Jr. (1962), *Tuscarora, Juniata, and Bald Eagle paleocurrents and paleogeography in the central Appalachians,* Geological Society of America Bulletin, v. 73, p. 1515-1540.

Yokel, F. Y., Salomone, L. A., and Chung, R. M. (1981), *Construction of housing in mine subsidence areas,* U.S. Department of Commerce, National Bureau of Standards Report 81-2215, 45 p.

Young, L. E., and Stoek, H. H. (1916), *Subsidence resulting from mining,* University of Illinois Engineering Experiment Station Bulletin 91, 205 p.

Zartman, R. E., Brock, M. R., Heyl, A. V., and Thomas, H. H. (1967), *K-Ar and Rb-Sr ages of some alkalic intrusive rocks from central and eastern United States,* American Journal of Science, v. 265, p. 848-870.

Zenger, D. H. (1965), *Stratigraphy of the Lockport Formation (Middle Silurian) in New York State,* New York State Museum and Science Service Bulletin 404, 210 p.

Zerrahn, G. J. (1978), *Ordovician (Trenton to Richmond) depositional patterns of New York State, and their relation to the Taconic orogeny,* Geological Society of America Bulletin, v. 89, p. 1751-1760.

Ziegler, A. M., Rowley, D. B., Lottes, A. L., and others (1985), *Paleogeographic interpretation: with an example from the mid-Cretaceous,* Annual Review of Earth and Planetary Sciences, v. 13, p. 385-425.

Zietz, Isidore, Gilbert, F. P., and Kirby, J. R., Jr. (1980), *Aeromagnetic map of Delaware, Maryland, Pennsylvania, West Virginia, and parts of New Jersey and New York,* U.S. Geological Survey Geophysical Investigations Map GP-927, scale 1:1,000,000.

Zietz, Isidore, and Gray, Carlyle (1960), *Geophysical and geological interpretation of a Triassic structure in eastern Pennsylvania,* in *Short papers in the geological sciences—Geological Survey research 1960,* U.S. Geological Survey Professional Paper 400-B, p. B174-B178.

Zietz, Isidore, King, E. R., Geddes, Wilburt, and Lidiak, E. G. (1966), *Crustal study of a continental strip from the Atlantic Ocean to the Rocky Mountains,* Geological Society of America Bulletin, v. 77, p. 1427-1448.

Zoback, M. D., and Zoback, M. L. (1981), *State of stress and intraplate earthquakes in the United States,* Science, v. 213, p 96-104.

Zoback, M. L., and Zoback, Mark (1980), *State of stress in the conterminous United States,* Journal of Geophysical Research, v. 85, p. 6113-6156.

INDEX

[Page numbers printed in italics refer to illustrations and their captions. Page numbers followed by *t* indicate tables.]

AAAS (American Association for the Advancement of Science), 5
Abandoned mines
  contamination from drainage, 685, 688
  environmental hazards from, 565
  mine subsidence, 726–27, *727*
Abrasion test for construction aggregates, 617, *618*
Absorption tests for construction aggregates, 617, 619*t*
Academy of Natural Sciences of Philadelphia, 6
Acadian orogeny, 17, 122, 125, 419, 428–30
Adams County, 13
  Devils Den, *410, 411*
  geologic history, 441
  Gettysburg National Military Park, 20, *410, 411*
  mineral resources (minor)
    copper, *654*
    corundum, 648, *649*
    gemstones, 654, *655*
    metabasalt, *649, 652, 653, 654*
    phyllite, 649
  mineral resources (nonmetallic)
    dimension stone, *598,* 600
    industrial clay and shale, 606–7
    quartz, 641, 643
  physiography, 347
  stratigraphy, *44*
  structural geology, 17, *298,* 303
Aerial Radiological Measuring Surveys (ARMS), 329–30
Aeromagnetics, 323–27
  Appalachian basin, *322, 324,* 326–27
  composite magnetic map, *322*
  generally, *322,* 323, *324,* 324*t*
  southeastern Pennsylvania, 323–24, *325,* 326
  See also Magnetic anomalies
Aeroradioactivity, 329–33
  generally, 329
  maps, *328, 330–31,* 332
  surveys, *328,* 329–30, 332
  uranium deposits. *See* Uranium
  See also Radioactivity anomalies
Aesthetics, 20
Agate, 654, *655*
Aggregate. *See* Construction aggregates
Agnes flood, 748–49, *752–55, 753*
Agriculture
  effects on water quality, 675
  use of lime in, 636–37
Akron Dolomite, 107
Albite, 653
Alleghanian orogeny, 17, 233, 263, 419, 430–31, *432,* 433
  temperature gradient in, 278
  Valley and Ridge structural province, 269–85
Allegheny anticline, *268,* 271
Allegheny County
  bituminous coal, 478
  flash flooding, *794,* 797–98, *798, 799*
  flood potential estimates, 749
  groundwater withdrawal, 668, *668*
  landslides, *409, 411,* 710
  mineral resources (nonmetallic), 641, *642*
  oil and natural gas resources
    natural gas, *534,* 538
    shallow reservoirs, 488*t,* 489*t*
  physiography, *371*
  stratigraphy, *155, 392, 402*
  water resources, *686*

Allegheny County *(Continued)*
  See also Pittsburgh
Allegheny Formation, 16
  bituminous coal, 153–54, *393, 394, 406,* 472, *472,* 473, 477
  chronostratigraphy, 162
  fossils, *153,* 160
  kimberlite dikes, 212
  mineral resources (nonmetallic), 616
  oil and natural gas resources, *493,* 495, *504,* 542
  physiography, *354*
  stratigraphy, *152,* 153–54, *154*
Allegheny Front, 14, 17, *86, 391, 401*
  coal in, 363
  engineering geology, 812–13, *813, 814*
  geologic history, 438–39, 444, *446–47*
  Mississippian stratigraphy, *138,* 139
  physiography, *354, 355, 366, 374,* 375
  structural geology, *290*
  See also "Eastern Overthrust Belt"
Allegheny Mountain section, 143
  caves, 806
  climate, 663, *663*
  Loyalhanna Limestone. *See* Loyalhanna Formation
  mineral resources (nonmetallic), *598,* 602
  physiography, 365, *366, 367,* 368*t, 369, 371, 372, 374,* 374–75
Allegheny Plateau, floods and flooding, 756, *756, 757*
Allegheny Portage Railroad, 813, *814*
Allegheny Reservoir, 749
Allegheny River, 365, *371, 376, 678, 680, 686, 810*
  alluvium, *387*
  drainage by, 379, *380–82,* 385, *386,* 387, *387*
  floods and flooding, 749, *751,* 756, *757*
  geologic history, *434,* 444, 455
  landslides, *707*
  mineral resources (nonmetallic), *625*
  source of, 379, 380, *381*
  Vanport caves, 806, 808
  water-temperature records, 685, 688, 688*t*
Allegheny structural front, 273, *275,* 427, 431, *432*
Allentown, magnetic anomalies, 324, *325*
Allentown Formation
  dolomite, 70
  sinkholes, 718, *816*
Allocyclic depositional controls, 167, 168
Alluvium
  at contaminated sites, *738,* 741
  flash flooding, *409, 410*
  geomorphology, 350
  Mesozoic Era, *178, 182,* 184–85, 192, *192, 193*
  Pennsylvanian Period, 157, 164, *165, 166,* 166–67
  Pittsburgh area, *387, 702,* 703, *810*
  Pocono Formation, 140, *142*
  Pottsville Formation, 157, 164, *165, 166*
  soil movements, 707
Almandine, 653
Almedia mine, *582*
Alvin R. Bush Dam, 749
Amazonite, 653
Amboy-Salem trench, 222, *222, 223*
American Association for the Advancement of Science (AAAS), 5
American Philosophical Society (APS), 6
Ames limestone, *154,* 155, *155*
Amethyst, 654
Amphibolite, *39,* 40, *41*
Amphibolite facies, 27, 29, 29*t, 30*

859

Recycled Paper

CRETACEOUS TO UPPER DEVONIAN

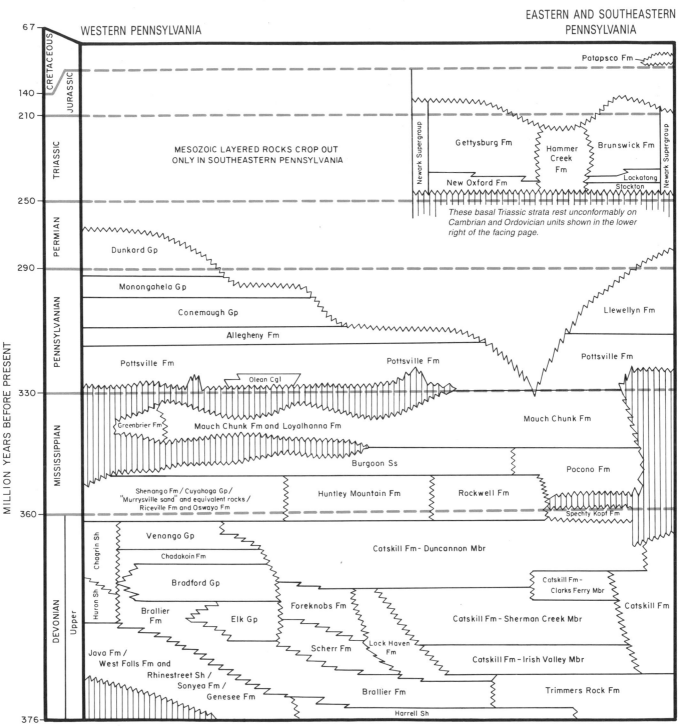

WESTERN PENNSYLVANIA

EASTERN AND SOUTHEASTERN
PENNSYLVANIA

MESOZOIC LAYERED ROCKS CROP OUT
ONLY IN SOUTHEASTERN PENNSYLVANIA

*These basal Triassic strata rest unconformably on
Cambrian and Ordovician units shown in the lower
right of the facing page.*

MILLION YEARS BEFORE PRESENT

Generalized from Berg and others (1983), with some updating. Absolute ages chiefly from Haq and Van Eysinga (1987). Vertical scale varies, but chiefly reflects relative thickness of rock units, not geologic time. No horizontal scale is implied. Slash (/) indicates superposition.

EXPLANATION

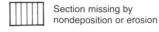

〰〰〰〰 Unconformity   Lateral facies or nomenclature boundary   Section missing by nondeposition or erosion